MW01680549

Legal Requirements for Information Technology Systems

LEGAL REQUIREMENTS FOR INFORMATION TECHNOLOGY SYSTEMS

Evidence, Regulation, Government and International Requirements

Donald S. Skupsky, JD, CRM, FAI

Information Requirements Clearinghouse
Denver, Colorado

Information Requirements Clearinghouse
5600 South Quebec Street, Suite 250C
Englewood, Colorado 80111
(303) 721-7500

Third Edition

Printed in the United States of America
99 98 97 5 4 3 2 1

Library of Congress Catalog Card Number: 90-086344

ISBN 0-929316-04-5

Contents

Preface

Records traditionally have been maintained in paper form. With the advent of improved records technologies, organizations now commonly maintain records on microfilm, computers, or optical disk systems. Realistically, most records are either originally created in paper for electronic form. They are then produced in a visible format such as paper or computer output microfilm. Once the originals have been created, they can then be duplicated using various technologies such as electronic imaging systems, photocopiers, facsimile, or other methods.

Previous Publications and Editions

See Chapter 5 and Appendix E for details regarding AIIM TR-31.

This edition has been renamed from *Legal Requirements for Microfilm, Computer and Optical Disk Records* (used 1991 to 1996) to *Legal Requirements for Information Technology Systems*. The new name was taken from the definition for records and information system technologies developed in the AIIM standard TR-31: *Performance Guideline for the Legal Acceptance of Records Produced From Information Technology Systems*.

The name change recognizes that the book also includes materials on electronic mail, electronic signatures, photocopies, fax, and other information technology systems, and is not restricted to the three technologies mentioned in the previous title. The change also correctly eliminates the use of the phrase "optical disk" in the title since "electronic imaging technology" or "electronic imaging system" is a more correct name for the overall technology and "optical disk" is only one of several possible storage media for scanned images.

The 1997 edition updates the 1994 edition and 1996 supplement with new, revised and deleted laws. Chapters 1 through 5 have been updated to reflect changes in the law, including revised information from the Internal Revenue Service, Securities and Exchange Commission, and the National Archives and Records Administration.

Audience

Whenever an organization develops an advanced records system utilizing technologies such as microfilm, computer and electronic imaging, legal questions can be expected. Will courts permit the use of alternate media in place of the original records? Can the original records be destroyed after they have been reproduced on microfilm or electronic media? When a regulation specifies the creation of particular records, must a particular form of the record be used?

Many organizations, both large and small, government or private, face these problems. This book was written primarily to end the guesswork regarding the legality of records media. Organizations can now refer to the text as well as the extensive appendix in this book to review the laws that affect the organization. Systems can then be designed with appropriate features to ensure that they comply with the law.

Scope

The book covers legal issues affecting technology and media used to manage records and information. Appendix A contains the uniform laws and lists the jurisdictions that have adopted each one. Appendix B and C contain a comprehensive compilation of United States federal and state laws. Appendix D contains a partial compilation of international laws affecting records that could be identified from available English translations of applicable laws. Specific provisions affecting records as evidence and record media were included. Other recordkeeping provisions have been included when the law contained no mention of microfilm, computers or other records media. Laws for many countries could not be located. Appendix E contains standards, guidelines and proposed model rules and laws.

Research Methodology

This book is based upon the research findings of Information Requirements Clearinghouse as published in its four-volume looseleaf service *Legal Requirements for Business Records* and supplemented by additional legal research for government and international requirements. *Legal Requirements for Business Records* provides the full text of federal and state recordkeeping requirements plus extensive research indexes. Over 8500 sections of federal and state law are addressed in this 2,800-page service which is updated annually. This looseleaf service served as the primary source for information related to federal and state requirements for evidence and regulatory requirements.

Additional legal research was undertaken to compile legal requirements affecting government and international requirements. In addition, letters were sent to all state archivists and records managers requesting government information for this publication.

Organization

This book has five chapters plus an extensive appendix.

Chapter 1 reviews the legal issues affecting records in general and original records in particular. The section reviews the legal requirements affecting evidence, regulation, government and international requirements. Chapter 2 reviews similar issues in the context of microfilm and other duplicate records. (For purposes of organization, electronic imaging is covered in Chapter 4 since the technology possesses properties found in both microfilm and duplicate records as well as computer records.) Chapter 3 addresses similar issues in the context of computer records plus special issues related to electronic data interchange (EDI), electronic mail and retention of electronic records. Chapter 4 addresses similar issues in the unique context of electronic imaging systems. Chapter 5 address new legal trends including standards, guidelines and proposed laws.

The appendices reproduce many of the relevant laws that affect microfilm, computer, electronic imaging and other information technology system issues. Appendix A provides several uniform laws found in the United States and indicates the jurisdictions where they have been adopted. Appendix B provides the various laws either prepared by the United States federal government or must be followed by the United States federal government agencies. Appendix C provides the basic laws prepared by United States state agencies that apply to general organizations and the laws that apply to government agencies. Appendix D provides the recordkeeping laws that could be identified that relate to countries outside of the United States. Appendix E provides standards, guidelines and proposed model laws and rules generally prepared by associations. Laws in the Appendix have been assigned codes to indicate the type of laws — evidence, regulation, or government requirements.

Registration

Since the laws change periodically, we expect that this book will be revised over the years. If you did not purchase the book directly from us, please complete the registration form in the back so that we can inform you of future revisions. Registered purchasers will be given the opportunity to purchase new editions at a substantial discount.

Request for Assistance

We have attempted to compile the most complete research tool on the subject of legal requirements for information technology systems. We realize that some laws were inadvertently omitted. Help us make future editions more complete! If you are aware of any additional relevant laws please send copies to our office. We are particularly interested in receiving copies of laws from countries outside the United States. We may elect to send a complementary copy of a future edition of the book to those who provide us with substantial new information.

Caution

This book contains information related to sensitive and important legal issues. No section of this book should be construed as providing legal advice. All legal decisions related to records and information management should be reviewed by competent legal counsel.

Although we have attempted to ensure the accuracy and completeness of this book, the reader should also be aware that not all laws have been included — some could not be found even after extraordinary research efforts, others were not deemed relevant and changes in the laws may have occurred since the book was printed.

Acknowledgments

I wish to thank Toni P. Mote, Administrative Associate, for typing and editing the materials found in this book and John C. Montaña, Director, Legal Research for coordinating the legal research for this book. I also wish to thank Tupper Cullum, paralegal and aspiring actor, for his expert legal research and attention to detail that has significantly improved the accuracy and completeness of this book.

In 1990, the first addition of this book was dedicated to my wife, Lorraine, and our newborn, beautiful triplet children — Irene Deborah, Benjamin Michael, and Katharine Rachel. Today the kids are 7 years old and Lorraine and the kids are doing fine.

Chapter 1 Legal Requirements for Original Records

Private and government organizations throughout the world use records. Records serve to record transactions within the organization, serve as the primary form of evidence in many court cases, show compliance with various statutes and regulations, and provide the recorded history of an organization.

Records traditionally start in paper form and then may be converted to other media such as microfilm. With the widespread use of computers, however, records are often originally created in electronic form and then may subsequently be converted to computer printouts.

This chapter reviews the general evidence, regulatory, government and international legal issues that affect records, especially original records. Subsequent chapters review specific legal issues related to microfilm, computer and optical disk records.

Legal and Operational Definitions of a Record

With the widespread use of information management technology — electronic mail, electronic data interchange, electronic imaging systems, computer output laser disk, object linking and embedding, and compound documents — it has become more difficult to determine exactly what is a "record". Traditional definitions of records have emerged from paper-based concepts and have merely been applied to these new technologies.

The ultimate definition of a record may have profound influence on the welfare of an organization. While certain types of records can be introduced into evidence, many others can be subpoenaed by an adverse party in litigation. In an organization's records retention program, records will normally be included in the program to ensure systematic implementation and preclude a judicial finding of improper destruction of records. Finally, from a practical organization perspective, specific forms, versions or information compilations must be recorded at some time to document the decisions and business of the organization.

This section reviews various issues affecting the definition of a record from both legal and operational perspectives. A new concept for a definition of a "record" is also included.

THE COURT DEFINITION OF A RECORD

Court rules of evidence have traditionally provided definitions of records for use in judicial proceedings.

The Uniform Rules of Evidence, adopted by the United States federal government as the Federal Rules of Evidence, have been accepted by the federal courts and most states.

The Uniform Rules of Evidence does not use the term "records", preferring instead to use the more traditional legal verbiage "writings and recordings":

> **Article X. Contents of writings, recordings, and photographs.**
>
> **Rule 1001. Definitions.**
>
> For purposes of this Article the following definitions are applicable:
>
> (1) *Writings and recordings*. "Writings" and "recordings" consist of letters, words, sounds, or numbers, or their equivalent, set down by handwriting, typewriting, printing, Photostating, photographing, magnetic impulse, mechanical or electronic recording, or other form of data compilation.

This definition would indeed include almost all forms of recorded information used by organizations today.

***See, Law Records and Information Management: The Court Cases,* Information Requirements Clearinghouse, Denver, CO, p. 16-28.**

However, while a record of an organization may meet the definition stated above, it may still not be admissible in evidence. Only a record that qualifies as "business record" is generally viewed by the courts as presumptively trustworthy in determining its admissibility into evidence to prove the truth of its contents.

"Hearsay" is a statement other than the one made by the declarant while testifying at the trial or hearing, offered in evidence to prove the truth of the matter asserted. Uniform Rules of Evidence, Rule 801.

Records are generally considered "hearsay". While hearsay is normally inadmissible in evidence, records which meet the definition of business records are admissible notwithstanding that they are hearsay.

The Business Records Exception to the Hearsay Rule and the Uniform Rules of Evidence, Rule 803(6) set forth the definition for business records which serves as the starting point for any judicial inquiry into the status of a business record.

From a judicial standpoint, a record or data compilation must have four qualities in order to qualify as a business record:

- It must be made at or near the time of the event that it records.
- It must be made by or from information transmitted by a person with knowledge of the event.
- It must be made in the course of a regularly conducted business activity.
- It must have been the regular practice of that business activity to make the document or data compilation.

The courts insist on this formula to ensure that records have achieved a sufficient level of quality and reliability to justify their introduction into evidence:

Monarch Federal Savings and Loans Assn. v. Genser*, 383 A.2d 475, 480 (N.J.Super. 1977) (quoting *Mahoney v. Minsky*, 188 A.2d 166, 218 (1963)) as quoted in *Law, Records and Information Management, id.

> [Business] records must be kept pursuant to some routine procedure designed to assure their accuracy, . . . they must be created for motives that would tend to assure accuracy . . . and they must not themselves be mere accumulations of hearsay or uninformed opinion.
>
> A business record is recognized as an exception to the hearsay rule because it is made in the regular course of business and therefore possesses certain "hallmarks of authenticity."
>
> The basic theory is that records which are properly shown to have been kept as required normally possess a circumstantial probability of trustworthiness, and therefore ought to be received in evidence unless the trial court, after examining them and hearing the manner of their preparation explained, entertains serious doubt as to whether they are dependable or worthy of confidence.

The courts also recognize that certain records such as public documents, treatises, historical documents, statements for purposes of medical diagnosis or treatment, recorded recollection or statements against interest also have such high probability of accuracy that they will also be admitted as exceptions to the hearsay rule.

Finally, the courts recognize the trustworthiness of records when the records of one party in litigation are admitted into evidence by the other party. This normally occurs when the records have been subpoenaed by the other party and admitted as an "admission by a party opponent". Due to the high weight that a court places on the trustworthiness of statements in one party's records that are favorable to an opponent, the courts will not even view such an admission as hearsay:

Federal Rules of Evidence, Rule 801(d)(2).

A statement is not hearsay if—

* * * * *

Admission by party opponent. The statement is offered against a party and is (A) his own statement, in either his individual or a representative capacity or (B) a statement of which he has manifested his adoption or belief in its truth, or (C) a statement by a person authorized him to make a statement concerning the subject or (D) a statement by his agent or servant concerning the matter within the scope of his agency or employment, made during the existence of the relationship or (E) a statement made by a co-conspirator of a party during the course and in furtherance of the conspiracy.

Courts will define any type of recorded information to be a record. A party may introduce certain records into evidence if they are business records and can be shown to be trustworthy. However, one party can always introduce records of the other party, regardless of form or technology, without having to prove trustworthiness.

OPERATIONAL DEFINITION OF A RECORD

Record

44 U.S.C. 3301.

The Federal Records Act defines government records as follows:

> [A]ll books, papers, maps, photographs, machine readable [i.e., electronic] materials, or other documentary materials, regardless of physical form or characteristics, made or received by an agency of the United States Government under Federal law or in connection with the transaction of public business and preserved or appropriate for preservation by that agency . . . as evidence of the organization, functions, policies, decisions, procedures, operations, or other activities of the Government or because of the informational value of data in them . . .

Federal records may be in any physical form or exhibit any characteristics if they were created or received "under federal law or in connection with the transaction of public business". The records must therefore be preserved if they incorporate "evidence of the organization, functions, policies, decisions, procedures, operations, or other activities . . .". Under federal law, records that fall under this definition can only be destroyed under guidelines approved by the National Archives and Records Administration.

Armstrong v. Executive Office of the President, 1 F.3d 127 (D.C.C. 1993) as quoted in *Law, Records and Information Management, p. 25.*

Recent regulations published by the National Archives indicate that electronic mail may constitute records under the Federal Records Act. See 36 CFR Part 1234.

In a recent court decision, *Armstrong v. The Executive Office of the President*, the court indicated that in the absence of a rational policy otherwise classifying electronic mail in the Executive Office of the President, records of all the electronic mail records fell under the Federal Records Act. The mere assertion by the government that E-mail was a non-record did not prevail without a specific policy defining the status of E-mail. The key point derived from this case is that the courts will view electronic mail records as records under the Federal Records Act and expect that the same standards of preservation, including a records retention policy approved by the National Archives and Records Administration, be established.

"Record" can also be defined by practical definitions developed by the records and information management industry. ARMA International defines a record as:

Glossary of Records Management Terms, ARMA International.

> Recorded information, regardless of medium or characteristics.

The Association for Information and Image Management (AIIM) defines a record as:

Performance Guideline for the Legal Acceptance of Records Produced by Information Technology Systems, **ANSI/AIIM TR31, Part I, 1993.**

> Information preserved by any technique in any medium, now known, or later developed, that can be recognized by ordinary human sensory capabilities either directly or with the aid of technology.

ARMA and AIIM definitions include all forms of recorded information, regardless of the technology used to produce the record. The issue becomes more complicated, however, when one considers the issues of "official records", "unofficial records", and "non-records".

Official Record

Glossary of Records Management Terms.

"Official record" reflects the final, official recorded position of an organization related to the specific content of the record. ARMA International defines an official record as: "A record which is legally recognized as establishing some fact." Official records reflects the intent of the organization. These records reflect the information or position the organization believes is true and complete, relies upon to conduct its affairs and expects others will also rely upon.

Law, Records and Information Management, **page 18.**

From a court perspective, organizations will likely attempt to introduce official records as "business records" under the Rules of Evidence. Official records must therefore be subject to rigorous procedures for creation, modification and destruction under a records management or records retention program.

Unofficial Record

Official records can be distinguished from drafts, works-in-progress, handwritten notes, copies of records, word processing, electronic records used to create official signed documents, unsigned letters and other material that is either in a preliminary state of development or has not yet been authorized or approved by an appropriate person. These unofficial records do not yet reflect the official position of the organization or remain subject to change before completion.

***S. C. Johnson & Son, Inc. v. Louisville & Nashville Railroad Co.*, 695 F.2d 253 (7th.Cir. 1982) as quoted in *Law, Records and Information Management*, page 18.**

In one court case, *S.C. Johnson & Son, Inc. v. Louisville & Nashville Railroad Co.*, the court in essence recognized handwritten notes as unofficial records when the information was later incorporated into a typed memorandum (the official record). The court did not feel that the destruction of these notes, even though not done under a records retention policy, represented bad faith, due to the lack of importance of the notes versus the importance of the final, typed document.

Even though unofficial records need not be subject to the same rigorous procedures as official records, they should still be covered by a general records retention policy. A policy could merely state that unofficial records may be destroyed when superseded, when the information has been transcribed to another record or when no longer useful. In any event, the unofficial record should not be retained longer than the official version.

Non-Record Material

"Non-record material" consists of library materials, printed publications, commercially-available computer software, blank forms and other material generally available to the public that does not reflect the recorded position of an organization.

The Federal Records Act also defines non-record material to include:

44 U.S.C. 3301.

> . . . Library and museum material made or acquired and preserved solely for reference or exhibition purposes, extra copies of documents preserved only for convenience of reference, and stocks of publications and processed documents . . .

ARMA International defines non-record material as:

Glossary of Records Management Terms.

> . . . Records not usually included within the scope of official records, e. g. administrative record, convenience file, day file, reference material, publications, etc.

Both definitions unfortunately define copies of records as non-record material rather than unofficial records. Because of litigation, these copies should be treated like unofficial records.

Since other forms of non-record materials are not records, they will not be subject to the same scrutiny as official or even unofficial records. Typically, non-record material will be created, modified and destroyed without formal procedures and will not be included in a records retention program.

THE INTENT TO MAKE A RECORD

The difference between the definition of record, official record and unofficial record relates primarily to the intent of the party. The judicial and industry definitions of "record" focus on the mere fact that the information has been recorded. For this reason, any recorded information including electronic mail, voice mail, notes, etc., will fall under the definition.

This result creates a serious problem when applied to modern information technology systems. Organizations now utilize electronic mail to facilitate communication between employees and between employees and the outside world. Electronic mail is often used as a replacement for face-to-face conversations, meetings and telephone calls. For the most part, it is merely a tool to facilitate communication rather "an official record of the organization". However, because electronic mail operates within a computer system, the communications will be recorded and, thus, will be deemed to be a "record" under traditional definitions.

Many parties do not intend E-mail communications to be a record of official organization business. In fact, they may not even consider that the communications are recorded.

While the judicial and industry definitions would treat electronic mail as a record, e-mail users generally treat electronic mail as a non-record, like verbal conversations. The E-mail users understanding of e-mail reflects their intent and belief: verbal communications or their equivalents — e.g., e-mail — are not official records of the organization, even when the communications are recorded. Otherwise, organizations would need to place recording devices into all offices, conference rooms and telephone systems to make records of all conversations addressing organization business.

But, most organizations recognize that the quality of telephone and other live conversations does not completely or accurately reflect organization business. Further, most organizations do not want to intrude on the privacy of their employees. Intrusions on employee privacy would also reduce or eliminate the use of electronic mail and reduce the efficiency potentially gained by the use of the technology.

Similarly, drafts of documents produced on word processing systems would meet the court and industry definition of a record and, yet, would be viewed as a non-record by the author. Word processing drafts are subject to multiple revisions before they are finally printed, signed and distributed.

To demonstrate the intent of the author, we have traditionally signed paper documents and distributed them in original form. With computer technology, we are currently developing signature encryption technology to similarly validate an electronic transmission with the unique mark or identification of an individual. Other electronic records can be given this stamp of "intent" through the assignment of record codes, retention codes, or other designators to indicate that they are to be construed as official records and not mere E-mail communications.

A NEW DEFINITION OF A RECORD

Due to the special issues of records in litigation and the diversity of information technology systems, it may never be possible to develop a universal definition that will meet the needs of both courts and the records and information management industry. In fact, it might even be best that the records and information management industry stopped using the term "record" altogether.

From a judicial perspective, records will continue to include any recorded information. However, even the courts will give greater credibility to official records as opposed to unofficial records. Official records reflect the intent of the party to establish the official position of the organization and to record organization business. Unofficial records merely represent recorded information without any particular intent on the part of the author. It may even be possible to conclude that when court decisions address "records" and "business records", they are really referring to "official records" as defined, in particular, by ARMA.

From a records and information management industry perspective, the use of the term "official record" instead of the word "record" may also be more meaningful. Official records must be included under a records retention program. For operational reasons, official records may be microfilmed or scanned into electronic imaging systems and maintained for long periods of time due to their enduring value. Organizations will only maintain unofficial records for short periods of time and normally should not incur the costs of maintaining them using expensive technology.

Both the courts and industry could therefore benefit by adopting definitions precisely referring to "official record" or "unofficial record," rather than using the term "record" alone. This would indicate the intent of the parties and the quality of the information. But this would require changes in many national definitions and reorientation of much of the population.

If the term "record" continues to be used, the following definition might be considered:

> *Record.* The result of recording or preserving information on any media with the intent to preserve information that reflects the position or business of an organization.

This definition reflects the essence of the court and industry definitions that records include any media. It adds the concept of "official record" by indicating that it was the intent of the party "to preserve information that reflects the position or business of an organization."

From a court prospective, recorded information (regardless of intent) found in one party's office may still be offered into evidence by the other party. The importance the court may place on that information, however, may be affected by whether the creating party can show that the recorded information was official or unofficial — whether or not it reflects the official position and business of the organization. The systematic implementation of the suggested definition may support the credibility of official records and discredit the importance of unofficial records.

This definition would remain effective even as we evolve into information technology systems in the future. With pieces of information located within networks and different computers, the record becomes that information which the author intended to preserve to reflect the position or business of the organization as evidenced by some formal procedures.

Evidence

Records are a principal form of evidence used in judicial and administrative proceedings. The proper creation and maintenance of records ensures that your organization can prove compliance with the law, show regular patterns of activities, and support your case in litigation. Without appropriate records, your organization can be fined or penalized, lose rights, or experience adverse consequences.

An "admission" is a confession or acknowledgment of facts relevant to the case of an adversary.

Records are generally introduced in evidence under one of two circumstances. First, the records may be introduced in support of your case or point of view. The records must be created and maintained according to certain requirements to be admissible. Second, records may be subpoenaed from you by an adverse party and used against you. Usually, all records created by the opposing party are admissible because, in the eyes of the law, they are "admissions" or "information against interest" of the creating party.

See Chapter 2 through 4, respectively, for the requirements for microfilm and duplicate records, computer records, and optical disk or electronic images.

This section reviews the general principles of law found in the United States as they apply to the admissibility of original records in evidence.

HISTORICAL BACKGROUND

Some people incorrectly think that records have always been admissible as evidence. In fact, the courts have traditionally *excluded* records from evidence. In modern times, courts have admitted records that qualify for admissibility under a recognized exception.

The law in the United States is based upon British Common Law, except that Louisiana state law is based upon Civil or Roman Law.

The United States legal system is based primarily on British Common Law. Through the Middle Ages, live testimony from witnesses or tangible evidence (for example, the stolen object) served as the principal evidence in British courts. At that time, records in any form were generally not admissible. Courts viewed live testimony as the most dependable evidence because the witnesses swore under oath to tell the truth and felt compelled to tell the truth when confronted with the solemnity of the court proceedings. The other party also had a fair opportunity to question or "cross examine" the witness to uncover the truth in the matter.

Until the fifteenth or sixteenth century, the exclusion of records as evidence in courts did not pose a major problem because few people could write and records rarely served as a vehicle for documenting transactions. As more people became literate and the industrial revolution opened new commercial markets, records quickly became a primary method for preserving information. It was no longer possible nor desirable to deal solely in cash transactions or to keep accounts by memory.

Records such as contracts and land deeds proved to be an effective method for preserving information and establishing relationships. Records also served a mobile population as a long-lasting "memory" of transactions, especially when some of the parties moved (perhaps to the colonies), died, or simply could not be found. This changing environment caused the courts to revise their attitudes toward records as evidence.

HEARSAY

Courts were initially reluctant to accept records because the judges felt that live testimony made under oath in court was trustworthy and both parties could effectively cross examine or challenge the other's witnesses. Records, on the other hand, were not prepared under oath and could not be cross examined in order to challenge their content—paper cannot answer questions. Of course, the people preparing the records could be cross examined, but often they were unavailable or could not remember the details of the transactions.

Some argued, on behalf of allowing records as evidence, that records were often more reliable than live testimony because they documented transactions close to the time the event occurred. Live testimony, on the other hand, was often given several months or years after the event and was subject to distortion or fabrication. Since records were often produced every day in order to document business transactions, they had to be accurate.

The primary reason for excluding records as evidence was that courts viewed records as "hearsay." "Hearsay" may be defined as follows:

Uniform Rules of Evidence, 28 United States Code Appendix. See Appendix A for other applicable sections plus a listing of states which have adopted this law. The law has been adopted by the United States federal government and 30 states.

ARTICLE VIII. HEARSAY

Rule 801. Definitions . . .

* * * * *

(c) Hearsay. "Hearsay" is a statement other than one made by the declarant while testifying at the trial or hearing, offered in evidence to prove the truth of the matter asserted.

Rule 802. Hearsay Rule

Hearsay is not admissible except as provided by law or by these rules.

In essence, records are considered "statements" from a source other than a "live" witness, offered to prove that the matter described in the record actually occurred. Records would normally be excluded under the Common Law "Hearsay Rule" unless the courts provided an exception. As the use of records to preserve information increased, the courts were forced to develop exceptions so that society could continue to function in an orderly manner.

Public Records Exception to the Hearsay Rule

The first exception to the Hearsay Rule permitted the introduction of public records in place of direct testimony by public officials. Public records were generally maintained to show land ownership and other property rights. Public policy and common sense dictated that the courts recognize these records because they established land ownership far better than live testimony and preserved information for long periods of time. The original parties or public recorder were often unavailable to testify or deceased.

Under the "Public Records Exception to the Hearsay Rule," a public official introduced the original recorded document. Modern law permits the public official to produce a duplicate, instead of bringing the original record to court.

Business Records Exception to the Hearsay Rule

Courts soon recognized the importance of admitting business records in evidence because the records often accurately documented business transactions. Although the safeguards provided by oaths and cross examination of witnesses are not available with records, the courts added safeguards to ensure their "trustworthiness." Parties desiring to admit records in evidence must generally show compliance with these requirements, and can exclude records from evidence which do not prove to be trustworthy. These requirements are designed to exclude self-serving, inaccurate, or fraudulent records from evidence and to enhance the trustworthiness of the "testimony" provided by the records.

THE UNIFORM RULES AND LAWS OF EVIDENCE

See Appendix A for the full text of the Uniform Rules of Evidence and a list of those states which have adopted the rules.

All states and the federal government have some version of the common law "Business Records Exception to the Hearsay Rule." Most states have adopted either the Uniform Business Records as Evidence Act or the Uniform Rules of Evidence based upon the 1974 version of the Federal Rules of Evidence.

Uniform laws are developed by the National Conference of Commissioners on Uniform State Laws in response to the need for consistency and uniformity. When the wording of a uniform law is approved by the Commissioners, it is offered to the federal government and state legislatures for consideration. The law becomes effective and controls activities only in the states approving it. If a law is approved by Congress, it controls only the activities of the federal government and those individuals subject to federal jurisdiction (e.g., working on a federal contract).

The Uniform Business Records as Evidence Act

The Uniform Business Records as Evidence Act was initially enacted in the federal government and most states. It states the business records exception to the hearsay rule as follows:

> **§ 1. "Business" defined.**
>
> The term "business" shall include every kind of business, profession, occupation, calling or operation of institutions, whether carried on for profit or not.
>
> **§ 2. Business records as evidence.**
>
> A record of an act, condition or event, shall in so far as relevant, be competent evidence if the custodian or other qualified witness testifies to its identity and the mode of its preparation, and if it was made in the regular course of business, at or near the time of the act, condition or event, and if, in the opinion of the court, the sources of information, method and time of preparation were such as to justify its admission.

The federal government and several states have repealed the Uniform Business Records as Evidence Act in favor of the more modern Uniform Rules of Evidence.

The Uniform Rules of Evidence

Over time, the Uniform Rules of Evidence replaced the Uniform Business Records as Evidence Act in the majority of United States jurisdictions. The Uniform Rules of Evidence states the business records exception as follows:

Rule 803. Hearsay Exceptions: Availability of Declarant Immaterial.

The following are not excluded by the hearsay rule, even though the declarant is available as a witness:

* * * * *

(6) *Records of Regularly Conducted Business Activity.* A memorandum, report, record, or data compilation, in any form, of acts, events, conditions, opinions, or diagnosis, made at or near the time by, or from information transmitted by, a person with knowledge, if kept in the course of a regularly conducted business activity, and if it was the regular practice of that business activity to make the memorandum, report, record, or data compilation, all as shown by the testimony of the custodian or other qualified witness, unless the source of information or the method or circumstances of preparation indicate lack of trustworthiness. The term "business" as used in this paragraph includes business, institution, association, profession, occupation, and calling of every kind, whether or not conducted for profit.

Records will be admitted in evidence under the Uniform Rules of Evidence (and other state laws containing the Business Records Exception to the Hearsay Rule) only if the requirements of the exceptions have been met. Otherwise, the judge may exclude the records from evidence or, in some cases, admit the records but diminish the weight of evidence attributed to them.

Rule 803(6) addresses the conditions under which original records will be admitted in evidence. In some cases, the absence or lack of certain information can show that an event did not occur. Rule 803(7) permits your organization to submit proof that certain information did not exist in your records system.

Uniform Rules of Evidence § 803(7). See Appendix A for the full text of the Uniform Rules of Evidence related to records.

Rule 803. Hearsay Exceptions: Availability of Declarant Immaterial.

The following are not excluded by the hearsay rule, even though the declarant is available as a witness:

* * * * *

(7) *Absence of entry in records kept in accordance with the provisions of paragraph* (6). Evidence that a matter is not included in the memoranda, reports, records, or other data compilations, in any form, kept in accordance with the provisions of paragraph (6), to prove the nonoccurrence or nonexistence of the matter, if the matter was of a kind of which a memorandum, report, record, or data compilation was regularly made and preserved, unless the sources of information or other circumstances indicate lack of trustworthiness.

You must demonstrate that you met the requirements of paragraph (6), you searched your databases and you did not find the records or information related to a particular matter. You can then introduce information that the event or transaction did not take place because if it had, you would have maintained a record.

The ability to show that a transaction did not take place can be critical to your case. For example, you may be involved in litigation where a vendor claims that because you failed to deliver a part by his company, he incurred substantial losses. If a search of your sales records shows you never received the sales order (as evidenced by the lack of an entry indicating the order), you may not be held liable for your opponent's losses.

The courts fully recognize that the absence of a record in your system could indicate either that the event or transaction did not occur or that you could not find the record because of poor recordkeeping practices. You will probably be closely scrutinized under paragraph (6) to ensure that your recordkeeping system is trustworthy and that the information never existed in the first place.

GUIDELINES FOR CREATING ORIGINAL RECORDS

Rule 803(6) states the requirements that must be met for records to be admissible. The requirements form the basis for good records creation practices and should be followed in all records management programs:

- *Records must be made at or near the time of the event.* Records made at or near the time of the event to which they relate are considered more reliable because the details are fresh in the mind of the person creating them and there is generally no reason to fabricate the information. After a period of time, people tend to forget, confuse, or fabricate details of the event.

- *Records must be made by or from a person with knowledge of the event.* Records are made "by a person with knowledge" if that person actually participated in the event or transaction. Records are made "from a person with knowledge" if the person creating the record received the information from someone who participated in the event or transaction. Obviously, records made by people with no knowledge of what transpired or based upon rumors are not reliable.

- *Records must be kept in the regular course of business.* This requirement reflects the courts' belief that records kept in the regular course of business will generally be accurate because the business requires accurate records to function properly. Records created on a one-time or haphazard basis do not achieve the same level of confidence.

- *Records are regularly created by that type of business activity.* This provision is usually not included in the Common Law version of the Business Records Exception to the Hearsay Rule. It would exclude certain records such as self-serving records or records created in anticipation of litigation. Records regularly created by a particular type of business or industry will be admitted in evidence if the other requirements are met.

- *The custodian of the records or other qualified witness must testify that the records submitted to the court meet the requirements for admissibility.* All evidence, even live testimony, must be properly introduced and authenticated to be admissible in court. To admit records, the custodian of the records or some other knowledgeable person must testify in court as to how the records were created. Often, the custodian does not have personal knowledge as to how the records were created. A written procedures manual, plus evidence that these procedures have been followed, may, therefore, be critical to authenticating and identifying records.

Even when the above criteria have been met, the court may elect to exclude certain records or diminish their weight if it finds the information or the method of creation for these records lacking in trustworthiness.

GUIDELINES FOR CREATING TRUSTWORTHY RECORDS

The purpose of the Business Records Exception to the Hearsay Rule is to ensure that records introduced in evidence are trustworthy since, in many instances, no sworn testimony is available to corroborate the details of the event or transaction. Because the outcome of cases may often be based upon the admissibility of certain records, these exceptions have been closely reviewed by courts.

Records created under the following scenarios are usually presumed to be trustworthy:

- *Records prepared in the regular course of business.* The ongoing, continuous preparation of records to meet legitimate business needs or legal requirements, generates records considered to be very trustworthy.

- *Records having an independent business purpose.* If the records are prepared in the regular course of business to meet legitimate business needs, the courts will view the records as trustworthy.

- *Records required by law.* Records prepared to meet specific legal requirements are considered trustworthy, especially since the courts and regulatory agencies levy severe fines and penalties for fraud.

- *Records prepared with no motive to misrepresent or commit fraud.* When records are prepared to meet legitimate business needs, rather than to protect an individual or the organization, there is generally no motive to prepare fraudulent records. On the other hand, when you prepare records to document certain activities in anticipation of litigation or other concerns, these may be viewed as self-serving and unreliable.

- *Records prepared before litigation is foreseen.* Records made specifically for litigation are viewed as self-serving and may not be admissible.

- *Records prepared by an independent third party.* Records prepared by public officials, religious organizations, and private attorneys or accountants on behalf of others are considered more reliable than records created by parties to the litigation. This particular view of trustworthiness, however, has led to certain undesirable results. Some groups, for example, have submitted fraudulent or inaccurate documents to public agencies, subpoenaed those records in later litigation, and attempted to have them admitted as trustworthy records because they were obtained from a public agency. Courts are now more sensitive to this ploy.

- *Records prepared by an experienced person.* Records prepared by an experienced person should generally be more accurate than those prepared by trainees or inexperienced persons.

- *Records containing factual information rather than opinions.* Records such as general ledgers, customer orders, and canceled checks represent factual information prepared in the regular course of business. On the other hand, internal memos or general correspondence often contain opinions and self-serving information.

- *Records corroborated by independent evidence.* The trustworthiness of records is enhanced if live testimony corroborates the information contained in the records. Most jurisdictions, however, have special rules about such live testimony or "parole evidence" in support of written contracts. The sanctity of written contracts is so well protected in our legal system that additional evidence about their content is often excluded under the "Parole Evidence Rule." Under a Parol Evidence Rule, the written contract constitutes the complete agreement between the parties and can not be interpreted through external evidence. This view reflects society's reliance on written contracts and ensures that the interpretation is based upon the words as written and approved by both parties.

AUTHENTICATION AND IDENTIFICATION

All records must be identified and authenticated prior to admissibility in court. The Uniform Rules of Evidence states this requirement as follows:

Uniform Rules of Evidence §901. See Appendix A for the full text of the Uniform Rules of Evidence related to records.

ARTICLE IX. AUTHENTICATION AND IDENTIFICATION

Rule 901. Requirements of Authentication or Identification

(a) *General provision.* The requirement of authentication or identification as a condition precedent to admissibility is satisfied by evidence sufficient to support a finding that the matter in question is what its proponent claims.

(b) *Illustrations.* By way of illustration only, and not by way of limitation, the following are examples of authentication or identification conforming with the requirements of this rule: . . .

* * * * *

(9) *Process or system.* Evidence describing a process or system used to produce a result and showing that the process or system produces an accurate result.

When witnesses are called to testify, the attorney first asks their name, address and, perhaps, occupation to establish they are who they claim to be. This established, the witnesses are then asked questions about their knowledge of the subject; for example, "Were you at the corner of 12th Street and Vine on Monday at 12:00 noon, and what did you see?"

Because records cannot provide this identification or authentication themselves, the court will expect you, your records custodian, or the authors of the records to supply it.

Assuming, however, that you or the records custodian do not know how the records were created, how can you identify and authenticate them for purposes of evidence? This issue is extremely important, especially in large organizations, because records may be produced by hundreds of individuals over many years, some of whom will no longer be available to testify. In other cases, you may not know who prepared the original records.

The key to successful identification and authentication of records is an established records management program. Rule 901(b)(9) identifies a method by which an individual with no knowledge as to how the records were created can introduce them in evidence. The rule permits you or your records custodian to present evidence describing the process or system used to create records and that the process or system produced an accurate result.

A records management program is certainly a process or system capable of producing an accurate result. You will be asked to show that your records management program did in fact provide the procedures for creating and maintaining records and that the records in question are in fact accurate because they were created and maintained under this program.

Generally, three components are required to show that the records management program produced trustworthy records:

- Written procedures and system documentation,
- Training, and
- Audits.

Written procedures and system documentation demonstrate to the court that your organization carefully developed its records management program and specified the practices to be followed. For purposes of evidence, you must maintain a copy of the actual procedures in effect at the time the records were created, not just the current procedures.

The training component shows the court that your staff was fully aware of the recordkeeping requirements and thus were likely to follow them.

Finally, the audit component verifies that the records management procedures were actually followed by your staff. Audits are particularly trustworthy when performed by a group other than the one responsible for preparing the records.

The three components — written procedures and system documentation, training, and audit — are important not only for written records, but become critical in the case of microfilm or duplicate records, computer records, and digitized records. By demonstrating that your organization has established procedures for creating, maintaining, and destroying records, you can overcome your inability to produce the authors of the records as witnesses. Without a records management program, the courts may bar the introduction of important records as evidence supporting your claims.

SCOPE OF ORIGINAL RECORDS

Rules 803(6) and 803(7) apply to any "memorandum, report, record or data compilation, in any form" which meets the stated requirements. The definition, then, encompasses computer output, microfilm, computer records, audio or video recordings, photographs, and digitized records.

Uniform Rules of Evidence § 1001. See also Appendix A for the full text of the Uniform Rules of Evidence provisions related to records.

ARTICLE X—CONTENTS OF WRITINGS, RECORDINGS, AND PHOTOGRAPHS

Rule 1001. Definitions.

For purposes of this article the following definitions are applicable:

(1) *Writings and recordings.* "Writings" and "recordings" consist of letters, words, sounds or numbers, or their equivalent, set down by handwriting, typewriting, printing, photostating, photographing, magnetic impulse, mechanical or electronic recording, or other form of data compilation.

(2) *Photographs.* "Photographs" include still photographs, X-ray films, video tapes, and motion pictures.

(3) *Original.* An "original" of a writing or recording is the writing or recording itself or any counterpart intended to have the same effect by a person executing or issuing it. An "original" of a photograph includes the negative or any print therefrom. If data are stored in a computer or similar device, any printout or other output readable by sight, shown to reflect the data accurately, is an "original."

Finally, the law recognizes that summaries of certain voluminous records are easier to review than original records:

Uniform Rules of Evidence § 1006. See also Appendix A for the full text of the Uniform Rules of Evidence provisions related to records.

Rule 1006. Summaries.

The contents of voluminous writings, recordings, or photographs which cannot conveniently be examined in court may be presented in the form of a chart, summary, or calculation. The originals or duplicates, shall be made available for examination or copying, or both, by other parties at a reasonable time and place. The court may order that they be produced in court.

Even though summary records may have been prepared specifically for a judicial proceeding and would otherwise not be viewed as trustworthy, they will often be admitted provided that the records from which the summaries were derived are available for review by the court or other parties.

Regulation

Regulatory agencies prefer records to live testimony because records can be reviewed at any convenient time and are generally more trustworthy. Agencies also prefer the information to be standardized on forms which present the facts in convenient formats.

Records created for submission to or inspection by a regulatory may not be subject to the same degree of scrutiny as records submitted to courts. They must still be accurate and reliable, but the methods of preparation are rarely specified.

Some regulatory agencies also have quasi-judicial authority. In this capacity, they can conduct hearings or administrative proceedings to determine whether you complied with the agency's regulations. The rules of evidence used in these hearings will generally be less strict than those used in court.

You are generally permitted to appeal any decision of a regulatory agency or administrative tribunal to the court system. Once there, the court rules of evidence will apply. By following the court requirements for records, you can safely submit your records to regulatory agencies, introduce them in administrative hearings, and ensure their admissibility in court.

Government

Government agencies follow various legal requirements related to the creation, form and destruction of records. Statutes sometimes specify which records must be created and maintained by the agency.

Statutes also may empower an agency to regulate a particular domain, but defer to the agency's discretion regarding the type of records to be created or maintained.

The appropriate state or federal archives must generally approve the outright destruction of government records or the destruction of original records after reproduction.

The laws addressing evidence discussed above also apply to government records. To simplify the production of government records into evidence, however, each jurisdiction also provides special exceptions for public records. Rule 803(8) of the Uniform Rules of Evidence states the public records exception to the hearsay rule. Rule 902(2) states that public records will also be admitted into evidence without the need for authentication.

International

Two major legal systems prevail in the world: the common law and the civil law systems. The United States, England and the British Commonwealth countries — predominantly the English speaking countries — follow the common law system. Even modern statutes, regulations, and rules of evidence adopted independently by these countries exhibit remarkable similarities regarding records media.

The remainder of the world predominately follows the civil law system. The civil law system is based upon ancient Roman law. Rome imposed this legal system on countries in its empire. Afterward, France and Spain in particular transferred this philosophy to other parts of the world. Historically, French served as the international language, especially the language of aristocrats and diplomats. Through conquest and diplomatic exchanges, France expanded this legal system, now know as the Napoleonic Code, to other countries. Spain also transferred the civil law system through exploration and conquest to countries under its domain — namely Latin and South America.

Most established and newly-formed countries fall into one of these two schools of legal philosophy. Recordkeeping laws generally conform to the type of legal system followed. You can often determine the legal philosophy of a country by reading its laws related to records.

INTERNATIONAL LEGAL PRINCIPLES

The two prevailing international legal systems exhibit distinctions that affect their attitudes toward records. Under the traditional common law philosophy, the courts exercised great discretion to establish new laws. England initially did not have many written laws specifying legal conduct of its citizens. Courts applied principles of fairness and equity to real-life fact situations. As more courts reached the same conclusion in law, consistent principles evolved. Judges faced with similar fact situations applied these standard principles rather than reviewing each matter from scratch.

Today, specific statutes, regulations and rules of evidence have replaced the common law process for evolving the law. Still, the basic principles of fairness, equity, and application of the law to modern day situations prevail. In common law countries we generally find an open attitude toward innovation and technology and a reluctance to restrict personal freedoms without precise restrictions in the law.

Common law countries generally follow the same major principle of law: you may perform any activity unless it is specifically prohibited or restricted. In a records context, you may use any system of recordkeeping unless the form of recordkeeping has been restricted in some way or prohibited. Legislatures and regulators alike may enact and enforce only clear, unambiguous laws that control conduct.

The civil law system is rooted in Roman law. Since the Romans conquered other countries and imposed their legal system, their laws tended to foster Rome's best interests. As a conqueror, they wanted to repress the local populace to prevent uprisings and simultaneously establish strict accounting and recordkeeping procedures to ensure prompt and complete payment of taxes and duties.

Modern civil law countries generally follow a major principle of law: you may not perform an activity unless it is specifically permitted. Although the needs of modern society has tempered the harsh roots of Roman law, countries following civil law philosophies often prescribe a specific method of recordkeeping and restrict the systems of records that an organization may use. Unless the law specifically permits a particular technology or system, you may be precluded from utilizing some systems in these countries. Courts will rarely intervene to reinterpret these laws to meet the needs of modern society.

Trials in civil law countries proceed before judges, rather than juries. Since judges have experience and knowledge with evidence, rules of evidence will generally be more relaxed than trials in common law countries. Most of the evidence will initially be considered by the judges, and untrustworthy evidence excluded. Judges may view "business records" and records technologies approved by legislation as trustworthy and other forms of recordkeeping as inherently suspect.

REQUIREMENTS IN COMMON LAW COUNTRIES

The following laws exemplify the prevailing principles in common law countries:

Australia

EVIDENCE AMENDMENT ACT OF 1978

PART 3A. — ADMISSIBILITY OF BUSINESS RECORDS

7B. (1) Subject to this Part, where, in any proceeding, evidence of a fact is admissible, a statement of the fact in a document is admissible as evidence . . .

"document" includes —

(a) a book, plan, paper, parchment, film or other material on which there is writing or printing, or on which there are marks, symbols or perforations having a meaning for persons qualified to interpret them;

(b) a disk, tape, paper, film or other device from which sounds or images are capable of being reproduced; and

(c) any other record of information.

Canada (Federal)

CHAPTER C-5. — CANADA EVIDENCE.

Documentary Evidence

30. (1) Where oral evidence in respect of a matter would be admissible in a legal proceeding, a record made in the usual and ordinary course of business that contains information in respect of that matter is admissible in evidence under this section in the legal proceeding on production of the record.

* * * * *

United Kingdom

VOLUME 7(1). — COMPANIES REGULATED BY THE COMPANIES ACT 1985.

(iv) Commencement of Business and Company Records

682. Form of company records.

Any register, index, minute book or accounting records required by the Companies Act to be kept by a company may be kept either by making entries in bound books or by recording the matters in question in any other manner. Where any such register, index, minute book or accounting record is not kept by making entries in a bound book, but by some other means, adequate precautions must be taken for guarding against falsification and facilitating its discovery. If default is made in complying with this last requirement, the company and every officer of it who is in default is liable on summary conviction after continued contravention, to a daily default fine not exceeding one-fiftieth of the statutory maximum.

REQUIREMENTS FOR CIVIL LAW COUNTRIES

Civil law countries tend to establish more stringent requirements related to records. In some cases, the country will require bound books with sequentially numbered pages. Original records are generally required in evidence.

Spain

Title 3. — Bookkeeping and Accounts in Commerce.

36. (1) Merchants shall present the books which they are compelled to keep, stamped and page-numbered, to the organs of the Municipal Justice Department of the place where their mercantile establishment is located in order that, before they use the first page of each of them, a formality shall be signed by those who had taken the book. The stamp of the Judge who authorizes them shall also be stamped on all the pages of each book.

Nevertheless, the writing of entries and annotations by any qualified procedure on pages which shall have been stamped afterwards correlatively in order to form the obligatory books, shall be validated before the end of the four months following the date of the close of the fiscal year, except the book of inventories and balances which shall be validated within the month following each one of the transcriptions ordered by article 37.

A merchant may demand that those validations performed by the organs of the Municipal Justice should take place in his own establishment.

The formation of books and the validation to which the preceding paragraphs refer shall be effected in the manner and with the guarantees which shall be determined by regulations, the successive numbering of the books being mandatory in any case.

Syria

PART ONE. — COMMERCIAL CODE.

Article 16. Every trader shall keep the following three books at least:

(a) The journal in which shall be entered, day by day, all the transactions relating to the business, and, month by month, the expenses which the trader spends on himself and his family.

(b) The correspondence book, in which shall be copied the correspondence and cables sent by the trader.

(c) The stocktaking and balance sheet book, which shall be drawn once at least in every year.

The trader is also required to keep and arrange all the correspondence and cables he receives.

These are the obligatory books which every trader is supposed to keep. He may keep any other books which he considers necessary for his trade or business. If these books are regularly kept they may be received in evidence.

The above books must have their folio numbered, marked and signed by the Civil Court of First Instance or by the magistrate in towns where there is no Court of First Instance. The above books must be written in the Arabic language, with power given to the Minister of National Economy to fix transitory periods for compliance with the new provisions.

Venezuela

TITLE 1. — CAPACITY TO DEAL IN COMMERCE.

MERCANTILE BOOKS

Article 33. The Journal and Inventory Book — These books cannot be used, until they have been previously presented to the Tribunal or Mercantile Registrar, if there is such a Registrar in the community in which a merchant is located. If there is not such Registrar in the community where the merchant is located, the books must be presented to the Judge of the highest category in the locality.

Article 38. Books kept pursuant to the foregoing Articles may serve as proof among merchants for acts of commerce. With respect to another person who is not a merchant, the entries in the books shall serve as proof only against their owner; but the other party cannot accept it as proof without also admitting any adverse proof which the books may contain.

In the above examples and in many other civil law countries, laws do not permit the use of microfilm, computers or other technologies — records must be kept in original paper form following manual procedures.

MULTI-NATIONAL RECORDS SYSTEMS

Some organizations have contemplated records systems that encompass operations in all countries worldwide. Based upon the above analysis, common law countries and a few civil law countries would recognize records maintained on various media including microfilm, computer and optical disk. Most other civil law countries — including the vast majority of countries in the world — appear reluctant to accept records technologies other than originals. They often establish severe restrictions to recordkeeping practices that would prohibit the use of even technologies such as microfilm and computers. They clearly do not permit (and therefore forbid) the use of sophisticated ones such as optical disk technology.

Organizations establishing record programs worldwide, should be aware of the differences in the countries in which they are doing business. They may still establish sophisticated microfilm, computer and optical disk systems to exchange information within the worldwide organizations. On the other hand, a separate set of paper records may be required in certain civil law countries to comply with their unique requirements. Multi-national organizations may be forced to either adopt a duplicate record system or exclude records in certain countries from a worldwide records system.

Chapter 2 Legal Requirements for Microfilm and Duplicates

The term "microfilm" includes all forms of microfilm (roll film, microfiche, film jackets, etc.) used to reproduce original documents, as well as duplicate copies of microfilm. Computer output microfilm (COM) is an original computer record and is controlled by the laws related to computer records; but it is often treated like microfilm in some laws.

Although attention has focused on the legality of microfilm in the last few years, microfilm represents only a specialized form of duplicate records. In fact, paper duplicates often create more cost and space problems. Large quantities of these duplicates are produced every day. Since these paper duplicates are sometimes indistinguishable from originals, organizations now use these duplicates interchangeably with originals.

The law concerning duplicate records is much different than for original records. Most government agencies accept microfilm in place of the original but impose additional standards on its production. Some businesses require copies of contracts to contain original signatures, instead of producing copies from one properly signed original. In addition, organizations place emphasis on the "record" copy (generally, the original) for records retention purposes and often ignore the problems resulting from the failure to destroy duplicates.

***See* Appendix C for the microfilm laws applicable to the states not adopting the uniform laws affecting microfilm and Appendix B for the specific requirement of the Internal Revenue Service.**

This chapter reviews the major laws which apply to microfilm and duplicate records. The law is fairly uniform on the federal level and among most states. In other states, the wording of the laws differ dramatically, but the legal principles are basically the same. You should research the particular laws concerning microfilm and duplicates for those states and countries in which you do business.

THE PROBLEM WITH DUPLICATES

The law of microfilm and duplicates has evolved slowly from the British Common Law. Some factors that have affected the acceptance of duplicates include the following:

- The law in most areas has traditionally been conservative and slow to evolve. While this ensures the stability of the legal process, it also slows the process of accepting new approaches. While the rate of change in the law is much faster today, it still evolves slower than some would like.

- Records in general (including originals) were initially considered less trustworthy than live testimony at trial. Today, business records are generally considered very reliable and save substantial time in proving business transactions.

See Chapter 1 for the business records exception to the hearsay rule which allows records, in general, to be admitted in evidence.

- Records traditionally were considered to be "hearsay." Today records are still classified as "hearsay" but are admissible in court under exceptions and safeguards provided under the rules of evidence.

- Original records have traditionally been considered more reliable than duplicates because duplicates were first made by copying the original by hand. Today, microfilm and office copiers reproduce images very reliably—dot for dot. A duplicate copy, however, can still be modified from the original.

- The law evolved for hundreds of years based upon a familiarity with paper only. Microfilm was a new and different technology. Today, microfilm and office copiers are widely used, even by judges.

- The authenticity of duplicates (whether the record is in fact what it seems to be) traditionally has been questioned. It is still true today that handwriting analysis from duplicates, for example, is much more difficult and imprecise, although most aspects of handwriting analysis can still be accomplished from duplicates.

- As a result of these concerns, the requirements developed to accommodate microfilm and duplicates over the years have often been strict and burdensome. Higher standards have been required for microfilm and duplicates than for paper originals.

Evidence

BEST EVIDENCE RULE

As the British Common Law developed in the United States and business records became an accepted form of evidence in court, the "Best Evidence Rule" evolved to provide alternatives when original records were not available. Simply stated, the Best Evidence Rule permits the introduction of a duplicate as evidence only if the absence of the original is satisfactorily explained. Some of the satisfactory explanations include:

- The original has been lost or destroyed without fraud (i.e. the original was not destroyed to conceal harmful information in anticipation of trial),
- The original is in the possession of a third party and could not be obtained,
- The original is in the possession of an adversary who failed to produce the records upon request, or
- The record is a public record and the original record cannot reasonably be brought to court.

In any of these circumstances, a duplicate record, if satisfactorily identified, can be introduced in place of the original.

STATUTES AND RULES OF EVIDENCE

***See* Appendix A for uniform laws that affect records. The United States federal government has adopted both laws; 30 states have adopted the UPA and the Uniform Rules of Evidence. As a practical matter, therefore, these two laws represent the major principles which govern the treatment of microfilm and duplicate records in the United States.**

The basic concepts of the Best Evidence Rule have been expanded by Congress and state legislatures through the enactment of statutes. The two most significant statutes related to microfilm and duplicate records are the "Uniform Photographic Copies of Business and Public Records as Evidence Act (UPA)," developed in 1949, and the "Uniform Rules of Evidence," developed in 1974.

The federal government and those states which adopted the UPA or the Uniform Rules of Evidence have generally maintained their original language with only minor variations. Those states which have not enacted the UPA or Uniform Rules of Evidence have adopted either their own statutes or some form of the Best Evidence Rule. Generally, these other laws impose similar requirements on the preparation and use of duplicates and rarely permit original records to be destroyed after microfilming as permitted by the UPA. Applicable state laws should be researched to determine their specific requirements.

Uniform Photographic Copies of Business and Public Records as Evidence Act (UPA)

The following is the UPA as adopted by the federal government:

United States Code, 28 USC 1732. *See also* Appendix A for the Uniform Photographic Copies of Business and Public Records as Evidence Act and a listing of the states that have adopted this law.

Section 1732. Record made in regular course of business; photographic copies.

If any business, institution, member of a profession or calling, or any department or agency of government, in the regular course of business or activity has kept or recorded any memorandum, writing, entry, print, representation or combination thereof, of any act, transaction, occurrence, or event, and in the regular course of business has caused any or all of the same to be recorded, copied, or reproduced by any photographic, photostatic, microfilm, micro-card, miniature photographic, or other process which accurately reproduces or forms a durable medium for so reproducing the original, the original may be destroyed in the regular course of business unless its preservation is required by law. Such reproduction, when satisfactorily identified, is as admissible in evidence as the original itself in any judicial or administrative proceeding whether the original is in existence or not and an enlargement or facsimile of such reproduction is likewise admissible in evidence if the original reproduction is in existence and available for inspection under direction of court. The introduction of a reproduced record, enlargement, or facsimile does not preclude admission of the original. This subsection shall not be construed to exclude from evidence any document or copy thereof which is otherwise admissible under the rules of evidence.

This is the principal statute permitting the use of microfilm and duplicates in the regular course of business and in judicial or administrative proceedings. Some key points of this statute are:

- The UPA only applies to microfilm or other duplicates prepared in the regular course of business. If the reproduction program is challenged, the organization must prove that microfilming or duplication took place on a regular, consistent basis over a period of time. This requirement might therefore preclude microfilming of records just before a trial. One-time microfilm projects—for example, a project to film records dated before 1980—are conducted in the regular course of business if properly planned and documented.

- Only one of two requirements must be met for microfilm or duplicate records: (1) the duplicates must accurately reproduce the original, or (2) the duplicates must form a durable medium for reproducing the original. This is a particularly important section of the UPA and one that is frequently misinterpreted and misunderstood, especially by government agencies.

- The rules of logic applied to the word "or" require us to interpret it to mean that only one of the two requirements stated must be fulfilled. As a result, the reproduction process must either accurately reproduce the original or the reproduction process must form a durable medium for reproducing the original. There is no requirement that the reproduction process perform both functions. If the reproduction process, therefore, accurately reproduces the original on a medium which is not permanent or archival, the requirement of the UPA has been met. It might reasonably be assumed, however, that the medium must last as long as the information is needed.

- The UPA permits the original record to be destroyed in the regular course of business ("unless its preservation is required by law"). According to the UPA, therefore, no government agency subject to the UPA can prevent an organization from microfilming records and destroying the originals, unless the law (statute or regulation) specifically requires the original records to be kept. A government agency has no authority to act contrary to a statute like the UPA. Verbal or unpublished interpretations which conflict with the UPA may not be binding on those affected.

***See Recordkeeping Requirements,* Chapter 2, for details regarding your responsibility when maintaining records in a custodial or fiduciary capacity.**

Some states have added a second clause prohibiting the destruction of originals even after microfilming if they are held in a custodial or fiduciary capacity. The same requirement would still hold even for those states that have not adopted this phrase based upon general principles of law. In short, you may not destroy records that do not belong to you, without the owner's permission, even though the records have been microfilmed.

- Under the UPA, duplicates can be used in place of originals as evidence in administrative and judicial proceedings.

- The UPA also permits the introduction of duplicates of duplicates (second generation microfilm) in evidence.

The UPA establishes the guidelines for the use of microfilm and the destruction of the original records. As a practical matter, the procedures for preparing reasonably good quality microfilm also meet the requirements of the UPA.

Uniform Rules of Evidence

The definitions and requirements in the Uniform Rules of Evidence apply to duplicates as follows:

Uniform Rules of Evidence § 1001, § 1002, and § 1003. ***See also*** **Appendix A for the full text of the law related to records and a listing of states that have adopted the law.**

ARTICLE X—CONTENTS OF WRITINGS, RECORDINGS, AND PHOTOGRAPHS

Rule 1001. Definitions.

For purposes of this article the following definitions are applicable:

* * * * *

(4) *Duplicate.* A "duplicate" is a counterpart produced by the same impression as the original, or from the same matrix, or by means of photography, including enlargements and miniatures, or by mechanical or electronic re-recording, or by chemical reproduction, or by other equivalent techniques which accurately reproduces the original.

Rule 1002. Requirement of Original

To prove the content of a writing, recording, or photograph, the original writing, recording, or photograph is required, except as otherwise provided in these rules or by [rules adopted by the Supreme Court of this State or by] statute.

Rule 1003. Admissibility of Duplicates

A duplicate is admissible to the same extent as an original unless (1) a genuine question is raised as to the authenticity or the continuing effectiveness of the original or (2) in the circumstances it would be unfair to admit the duplicate in lieu of the original.

Under the Uniform Rules of Evidence microfilm will be admitted in evidence under most circumstances. A duplicate can be admitted in evidence under the rules unless there is a problem with the duplicate or original. The language of the rules indicate that the nature of the problem would have to be substantial to prevent the introduction of duplicates in evidence. Rule 1003 does not require that the duplicate be made in the regular course of business or that the duplicate meet any standards other than accurately reproducing the original. This may therefore be the principal method for introducing those records in evidence which were produced as a result of a one-time microfilming project or were produced specifically for trial—but not in the regular course of business.

The Uniform Rules of Evidence does not grant explicit permission to destroy original records after microfilming. The rules were designed primarily to control the admission of records as evidence in court, rather than the use of microfilm or duplicate record technologies in daily activities. The authors of the URE, therefore, did not need to include specific permission to destroy records after they were reproduced.

Even though specific permission to destroy original records is not granted in the Uniform Rules of Evidence, the original records can in fact be destroyed, provided that the reproduction accurately reproduces the originals. Rule 1003 specifically indicates that duplicate records can be admitted in place of originals. Since you will have two sets of records (the originals and the duplicates) containing the same information and equally acceptable as evidence in court, you do not need to maintain both. As a practical matter, after inspecting the microfilm or duplicate records, you can destroy the originals unless another law specifically requires you to retain them.

Finally, Rule 1003 identifies two circumstances when duplicate records may not be admissible in place of originals. If a genuine question is raised as to the authenticity of an original, you would certainly expect the same question to be raised about the duplicate. Creation of a duplicate record does not eliminate the requirement that all records (in fact, all evidence) be authenticated and identified prior to submission to the court.

Duplicates cannot be admitted in place of originals under Rule 1003 if it would be unfair to admit them in place of originals. One can only surmise the circumstances when it would be unfair to admit duplicates. No known cases have interpreted this second condition (or the first one, for that matter). Handwriting analysis, for example, can still be performed from a duplicate copy although not to the degree of certainty that one can expect from the original. If original records have been destroyed in the regular course of business with good intent, it would never be unfair to introduce duplicates because the originals no longer exist.

Comparison of the Uniform Laws

The UPA clearly provides the strongest support for the use of duplicates and the destruction of originals, while the Uniform Rules of Evidence serves to expand the admissibility of microfilm and duplicate records in evidence. The following comparison is made between the UPA and the Uniform Rules of Evidence:

- The UPA permits destruction of the original records after reproduction according to the stated requirements. The Uniform Rules of Evidence does not address the destruction of originals.

- The UPA applies to both judicial and administrative proceedings. The Uniform Rules of Evidence was designed for judicial proceedings and applies to administrative proceedings only when specifically adopted by the agency.

- The UPA requires that microfilm or duplicates be produced in the regular course of business. The Uniform Rules of Evidence permits microfilm or duplicates to be produced at any time.

- The UPA specifies that the duplicates must adequately reproduce the originals or form a durable medium for reproducing originals. The Uniform Rules of Evidence also requires duplicates to accurately reproduce the originals.

The UPA and the Uniform Rules of Evidence, together, provide comprehensive support for an organization that microfilms or duplicates records. Some gaps in protection exist in those states that have not adopted both laws.

AUTHENTICATION AND IDENTIFICATION

***See* Chapter 1 for details regarding authentication and identification.**

The requirements for identification and authentication also apply to microfilm (and all other records in evidence, for that matter). Many people film a "Certificate of Authenticity" at the beginning and end of a role of microfilm to indicate the content of the roll, the date the film was prepared, the name of the preparer, and a statement that the microfilm accurately reproduces the original records. This certificate describes the contents of the microfilm and states that the microfilm was produced in the regular course of business and accurately reproduces the original. Government entities film the Certificate of Authenticity under legal requirements of statutes or archives. Private sector organizations film the certificate according to currently accepted microfilm practices and to facilitate the introduction of microfilm records into evidence.

Upon further examination, laws requiring this certificate should immediately be modified. Organizations currently filming this certificate should eliminate this practice. While the intent of this certificate is to enhance the admissibility of microfilm records in evidence, in reality, the certificate on the roll of microfilm could reduce the trustworthiness of the microfilm and actually preclude its admission into evidence.

What Is the Certificate of Authenticity?

The Certificate of Authenticity is one of several images, known as "targets", that are filmed at the beginning and the end of a roll of microfilm. Other targets may include roll number, description of the content, resolution test chart and density test chart.

While the content of the Certificate of Authenticity may vary, most certificates contain the following information:

- An identification of the target as a certificate or certifying document
- A statement of the range of records on the roll of film such as numbers, dates, etc.
- The name of the organization or department from which the records were taken
- A statement indicating that the records were filmed in the regular course of business
- A statement indicating that the records accurately reproduce the original
- The signature of the camera operator and the date the certificate was signed

Purpose of the Certificate of Authenticity

We do not know exactly when organizations started to film the Certificate of Authenticity on their rolls of microfilm. We can guess, however, that the certificate was probably developed in response to laws of evidence that required both original records and duplicates to be "adequately identified" before admission into evidence.

When legislative bodies began to adopt the Uniform Photographic Copies of Business and Public Records As Evidence Act. That law contained the following specific provision that may have influenced the use of the certificate on microfilm:

> Such reproduction, when satisfactorily identified, is as admissible in evidence as the original itself in any judicial or administrative proceeding whether the original is in existence or not and an enlargement or facsimile of such reproduction is likewise admissible in evidence if the original reproduction is in existence and available for inspection under direction of the court.

Those reading this provision, may have concluded that the best way to adequately identify a roll of microfilm was to film the Certificate of Authenticity at the beginning and the end of the roll. In that way, the certification always stayed with the microfilmed images.

In addition, all courts require that records be identified and authenticated prior to their introduction into evidence:

Uniform Rules of Evidence, Rule 901:

Rule 901. Requirement of Authentication or Identification

(a) *General provision.* The requirement of authentication or identification as a condition precedent to admissibility is satisfied by evidence sufficient to support a finding that the matter in question is what its proponents claim.

Many believe that the microfilm will only be admitted into evidence when the Certificate of Authenticity is filmed contiguously on the roll with the actual microfilm records. When the microfilm is introduced in evidence, the attorney refers to the certificate as a document prepared at the time of microfilm to indicate its authenticity and trustworthiness.

In the government sector, archivists and legislators adopted laws requiring that the Certificate of Authenticity appear on every roll of microfilm created by government entities. Under statutes and regulations of the archives (having the power of law), the government microfilm must contain these certificates before the government agency can legally destroy the paper records.

Legal Status

In reality, the Certificate of Authenticity is not legally required to admit a record into evidence. Microfilm records have often been introduced into evidence with or without the certificate. The key element regarding admissibility is convincing the judge that the original records and the duplicates are trustworthy. The judge must feel confident that the information contained is authentic, accurate, and trustworthy.

On the other hand, the laws affecting government microfilm often require the Certificate of Authenticity. An agency that microfilms without the certificate will violate the law. (However, the microfilm would still be admissible into evidence.)

The Certificate of Authenticity is Often Incorrect

Why then eliminate of the Certificate of Authenticity, especially since it commonly appears on most rolls of microfilm? Even if the certificate is not required by the laws of evidence, is it not helpful in permitting microfilm to be admitted into evidence?

Under closer scrutiny, the Certificate of Authenticity is actually dangerous from a legal perspective for three reasons:

- The person signing the Certificate of Authenticity does not know that the statements made in the Certificate are true at the time of signing.
- The content of the certificate often proves to not be true.
- The truthfulness of the certificate can only be confirmed at a later time, after the microfilm has been processed and inspected.

Since the Certificate of Authenticity is filmed at the beginning and the end of the roll of microfilm, the camera operator must sign the certificate before actually starting the microfilm process. How does the operator know that the film will accurately reproduce the original, until the actual roll of film becomes visible through processing? In reality, the camera operator is only guessing or anticipating that the film accurately reproduces the original, was prepared in the regular course of business, or includes even these records indicated in the certificate.

Only after the microfilm is processed and inspected does the camera operator really know whether the statements made in the certificate are true or not. In many cases, inspection actually confirms that the statements are not true. When defects in the microfilm are determined after inspection, corrective action is necessary. Either "retakes" are prepared for images that did not adequately reproduce on the film or, in case of major problems, the entire roll may be refilmed. Making retakes or refilming confirms that the statement originally made in the Certificate of Authenticity was in fact false.

The camera operator does not and cannot know whether the statements made in the certificate are true or not until after the film has been processed and inspected. The procedure of making the statements at a time when their accuracy cannot be confirmed merely discredits the perceived reliability of the operator and the microfilming process.

Attacking the Credibility of Microfilm

Since the statements contained in the Certificate of Authenticity are either false (as confirmed by retakes or refilming) or made at a time when its truthfulness could not be determined, the existence of a Certificate of Authenticity on a roll of microfilm will compromise or prevent its admissibility into evidence if properly attacked. Up to this point, lawyers have rarely challenged the admissibility of a roll of microfilm, especially when a certificate is included on the roll. Most judges and attorneys have merely acquiesced to this procedure and prefer instead to proceed with other matters related to the case.

A skilled attorney can now successfully challenge or even prevent the admissibility of any records contained on a roll of microfilm by asking the right questions.

Most organizations have not yet been confronted with this problem. We can expect that there will be more challenges in the future. How can an organization expect to introduce a microfilm record into evidence when the first information contained in the roll is either false or made without regard to its truthfulness? Since many judges are skeptical of microfilm or other duplicate records in the first place (although microfilm is admissible in evidence in all 50 states and the federal courts), the suspicions of many judges will be confirmed once a challenge to the microfilm is raised.

How to Identify and Authenticate Microfilm

Microfilm can successfully be introduced into evidence in spite of the problems discussed above. Of course, if the law requires specific procedures related to the Certificate of Authenticity you should follow the law, but also actively work to change the law. The following procedures should then be followed to ensure the admissibility of microfilm records into evidence.

- Do not microfilm a Certificate of Authenticity at the beginning of the roll of microfilm. Instead, you may elect to microfilm a Certificate of Identification to indicate the content of the roll for identification purposes only.

- Once the microfilm has been prepared, processed and inspected, the inspector can then prepare a Certificate of Authenticity. The certificate will confirm that the microfilm was prepared in the regular course of business and accurately reproduces the original. The certificate can also identify problems found in the microfilm and corrective actions that were taken. The certificate should be filed separately from the microfilm and kept along with other records that document the microfilming procedures to confirm the trustworthiness of your microfilm.

- You should maintain documentation of your microfilm system including procedures, standards, logs and other documentation indicating the steps followed in preparing microfilm within your organization. The documentation would also include the Certificate of Authenticity as described above.

- Your microfilm staff should be properly trained. You should maintain a set of training documentation to indicate to the court that the staff has been adequately trained. If your staff is trained there is a high likelihood that they will produce accurate microfilm.

- Besides your normal inspection and quality control procedures, you should undertake audits of the microfilm program. The audits can be conducted by your Auditing Department, disinterested third parties, or outside consultants. The audits should include a fair sampling of the microfilm images to confirm that the microfilm does in fact accurately reproduce the original. This audit should be conducted prior to destruction of the originals so that the microfilm images (or paper prints produced from the microfilm) can be compared with the original documents to confirm their accuracy. The documentation of the audits should be retained to support the introduction of the microfilm into evidence in the future.

Identifying and Authenticating Photocopies

Photocopies must also be identified and authenticated. Many courts seem to waive that requirement for photocopies because they "look like original records." When challenged, however, you must provide the same identification and authentication for photocopies as you would for microfilm or any other record.

THE MYTH ABOUT MICROFILM AND DUPLICATES

The law related to the acceptance of microfilm by courts and regulatory agencies has evolved slowly over the last 50 years. The legal acceptance has been hampered by poor equipment, procedures and image quality. The law often specifies quality standards in order to force users to produce readable and legible duplicate records.

When microfilm or other duplicate records are produced on good equipment following appropriate procedures, the output is generally readable and legible. Even without specific knowledge of the microfilm laws and regulations, you should be able to produce microfilm meeting the requirements of courts and government agencies.

The acceptance of these technologies has also been slowed because of the mistaken belief that original records are more reliable than duplicates. Realistically, original records can be forged or modified. A three-page contract, for example, held together by a flimsy staple, can be altered by removing the staple, replacing page two, and restapling it through the original holes. Original documents are not trustworthy just because they are originals.

But, you can also alter microfilm and duplicate copies. Information from the original document can be erased and replaced with new information and the change is not detectable on the photocopy. The microfilm itself, however, cannot be altered without a trace because of the nature of the technology.

The trustworthiness of the information really depends upon following trustworthy procedures, and does not depend upon the medium.

A system is made trustworthy by following written procedures, providing adequate training, and following up with audits. These components of a program should exist for microfilm, computer, and paper record systems. By identifying the proper procedures, ensuring that your staff knows them, and verifying that the procedures are followed, you can be certain that the information created and maintained is trustworthy, admissible in evidence, and acceptable to government agencies.

Microfilm and duplicate records have the same legal status as original records for most purposes of the federal government and those states where the Uniform Photographic Copies of Business and Public Records as Evidence Act (UPA) and the Uniform Rules of Evidence have both been adopted. The legal status of microfilm and duplicates is weaker, however, in jurisdictions where only one or neither of these laws have been adopted.

SPECIAL PROBLEMS

One-Time Microfilm Projects

An organization may consider microfilming older, but still valuable records on a one-time basis. Some older records occupy a great deal of space, yet must be kept for long periods due for legal, operational or historical purposes. Under the Uniform Photographic Copies of Business and Public Records as Evidence Act, microfilming must be done in the regular course of business if the original records are to be destroyed. The Uniform Rules of Evidence do not require microfilming to be done in the regular course of business.

A one-time microfilm project can be viewed as being in the regular course of business if it is properly planned and documented. Those records appropriate for a one-time microfilm project should be clearly identified, randomly reviewed, and specifically approved for microfilming. The microfilm plan should be documented along with the procedures followed. If these conditions are met, a one-time microfilming project can be viewed as being conducted in the regular course of business.

When Microfilm or Other Duplicates are not Sufficient

Although the law permits the use of microfilm and duplicates in place of originals, an original record may still be required or preferred in some of the following cases:

- The duplicates are poor quality reproductions. Poor quality reproductions can be difficult if not impossible to read and most judges and regulatory agencies will request the original records.

  To protect your organization, duplicates, especially microfilm, should be carefully inspected to ensure readability and completeness. If the original records are of a poor quality, you can either attempt to enhance their quality or microfilm targets before the poor quality originals to indicate "best copy available."

  If your microfilm or other duplicate cannot be read, however, the court or regulatory agency may treat you as though the records did not exist in the first place. Some tax deductions may be disallowed because you were unable to substantiate them through readable records. In a judicial proceeding, you may not be able to support your claims without readable records. The importance of good quality control, therefore, cannot be stressed enough.

- Duplicate records cannot be analyzed for handwriting as readily as the originals. Handwriting experts have indicated that they can analyze duplicate copies, but can only achieve a 70 percent degree of certainty. An analyst working from a duplicate cannot determine the weight of the impression made by the writer—often a critical factor in deciding the authenticity of the handwriting.

In a criminal case, the standard of proof for conviction is "beyond a reasonable doubt"—a 90 percent certainty of guilt. If handwriting analysis of a forged check is a critical piece of evidence for conviction, for example, the handwriting analysis cannot achieve a 90 percent certainty of guilt. Analysis of handwriting from a microfilm copy can only determine authenticity to a 70 percent degree of confidence. Banks and other organizations that regularly microfilm and destroy records may therefore be unable to convict forgers.

On the other hand, in a civil case, a party will win if they are right by a "preponderance of the evidence"—a 51 percent certainty that they are right. In the case of handwriting analysis, the 51 percent certainty that a party is right can be achieved with a microfilm of a record because handwriting analysis can reach a 70 percent certainty. Banks and other organizations who rely on microfilm should be able to recover amounts proven in civil suits.

- Microfilm and other reproduction techniques do not adequately reproduce photographs, pictures, and other information having a tonal quality. Microfilm, in particular, uses a high-contrast film which records material as either black or white, without any gray tones. Valuable information in the original may, therefore, be lost in the duplicates.

- The physical character of original records generally cannot be transmitted to the duplicates. Physical character includes paper texture, age of paper, paper color, and paper size. This information can be valuable for criminal investigations and historical preservation. While microfilm and other duplicate technologies preserve the information, they cannot preserve the original character of the documents.

Regulation

FEDERAL REQUIREMENTS

Microfilm Requirements for Tax Records

Internal Revenue Service, Revenue Procedure 81-46. ***See*** **Appendix B for the full text of the IRS microfilm requirements.**

The Internal Revenue Service has issued regulations governing the preparation of microfilm for tax purposes. Prior approval for microfilm is not required, but taxpayers will be held responsible for meeting the standards specified. If records are microfilmed and the originals destroyed, the IRS may disallow deductions or other tax benefits if the microfilm records are not adequate.

The basic provisions of Revenue Ruling 81-46 are as follows:

- Taxpayers must follow these requirements if they microfilm from source documents or produce computer output microfilm (COM) from computers.
- Taxpayers must obtain written approval for the microfilm program from the board of directors (corporations), general partners (partnership), or owner (sole proprietorship).
- The microfilm system must be complete and used regularly within the business.
- Taxpayers must establish procedures and document them so that the microfilm procedures can be audited.
- Taxpayers must provide internal procedures for inspection and quality control.
- Taxpayers must identify and preserve the microfilm for the period of time necessary for tax purposes.
- Taxpayers must document the production of the microfilm.
- Taxpayers must produce microfilm that is legible (individual characters can be read) and readable (groups of characters can be read).
- Taxpayers must produce an index to the microfilm to enable the retrieval of particular information.
- Taxpayers must produce microfilm which meets industry standards.
- Taxpayers must make available a reader printer for use by the Internal Revenue Service when it examines microfilm on site.

While industry standards do exist for manufacturers of microfilm equipment and supplies, no mandatory standards exist for users. You should produce legible and readable microfilm using recognized procedures.

Microfilm Requirements for Federal Contracts

***See* Title 48, Part 4, Appendix B, for the full text of the records retention and microfilm requirements for federal contracts.**

The federal government has specific requirements for the use of microfilm in place of original contracts and the subsequent destruction of records after microfilming. If you have a contract, grant, lease or other agreement with the federal government, review these requirements carefully before microfilming these records.

- Contractors may use any microfilm format.
- Contractors must microfilm all relevant notes, worksheets, and other papers necessary to reconstruct and understand the original records.
- Contractor must review all microfilm before destroying the original records to ensure legibility and reproducibility.

This very restrictive provision may effectively prohibit the use of microfilm for federal contracts in some cases.

- Contractors may not destroy the original documents after microfilming unless the retention period has expired, the contracting officer agrees to a lesser retention period, all claims under the contract are settled, or 18 months has passed since final payment.
- Contractors must maintain an effective indexing system.
- Contractor must provide strict security measures to prevent the loss of the microfilm and to safeguard classified information,.
- Contractors must store the microfilm in a fireproof vault and protect the microfilm during the records retention period.
- Contractors must provide adequate microfilm readers and produce paper prints close to the original size.
- Contractors must produce legible and readable microfilm and paper prints.

STATE REQUIREMENTS FOR TAX RECORDS

The states generally defer to the Internal Revenue Service for microfilm requirements for their tax records. The states often develop their own requirements, however, for sales tax records, because sales taxes are totally within the control of the individual states. A typical microfilm regulation for sales tax records is as follows:

California State Board of Equalization, California Administrative Code, § 1698.

Sales and Use Tax Regulations

§ 1698. Records

* * * * *

(b) *Microfilm Records*. Microfilm reproductions of general books of account, such as cash books, journals, voucher registers, ledgers, etc., are not acceptable in lieu of original records. However, microfilm reproductions of supporting records of details, such as sales invoices, purchase invoices, credit memoranda, etc., may be maintained providing the following conditions are met:

(1) Appropriate facilities are provided for preservation of the films for periods required.

(2) Microfilm rolls are indexed, cross referenced, labeled to show beginning and ending numbers or beginning and ending alphabetical listing of documents included, and are systematically filed.

(3) The taxpayer agrees to provide transcriptions of any information contained on microfilm which may be required for purposes of verification of tax liability.

(4) Proper facilities are provided for the ready inspection and location of the particular records, including modern projectors for viewing and copying the records.

A posting reference must be on each invoice. Credit memoranda must carry a reference to the document evidencing the original transaction. Documents necessary to support claimed exemptions from tax liability, such as bills of lading and purchase orders, must be maintained in an order by which they readily can be related to the transactions for which exemption is sought . . . .

State requirements for microfilming tax records generally promote good microfilm practices. You should review the specific requirements for the states in which you do business.

Government

***See* Appendix B, Code of Federal Regulations, Title 36, Part 1230 for the microfilm standards of the National Archives and Records Administration. Appendix C contains the laws affecting state government microfilming programs. Contact the state archives for published microfilm standards.**

The United States federal government has published extensive standards for microfilming federal government records. Many state archives have published similar provisions.

Government agencies may microfilm or reproduce their records. Normally, they may not destroy their records, however, unless the microfilm or reproductions are approved by the archives. This process ensures that reproductions adequately replicate the originals and ensures that the reproductions will last for the requisite period of time.

Laws that also permit government agencies to reproduce records may also state that the reproductions are admissible in evidence. What if the government microfilm program does not meet the standards stated in the government law but meets the criteria stated in the state's general evidence law? The government records will probably still be admissible in evidence under the evidence law. The agency, however, may be responsible for violating the government microfilm law.

The following state laws apply to microfilming government records and the destruction of the original records after microfilming:

Arizona Revised Statutes

TITLE 41. — STATE GOVERNMENT.

CHAPTER 8. — AGENCIES OF THE LEGISLATIVE DEPARTMENT.

§ 41-1348. Production and reproduction of records by agencies of the state and political subdivisions; admissibility; violation; classification.

A. Each agency of the state or any of its political subdivisions may implement a program for the production or reproduction by photography or other method of reproduction on film or electronic media of records in its custody, whether obsolete or current, and classify, catalog and index such records for convenient reference. Such agency, prior to the institution of any such program of production or reproduction, shall obtain approval from the director of the department of library, archives and pubic records of the types of records to be produced or reproduced and of the methods of production, reproduction and storage and the equipment which the agency proposes to use in connection with the production, reproduction and storage.

B. Except as otherwise provided by law, records reproduced as provided in subsection A of this section are admissible in evidence as provided in § 12-2262, subsection D.

New Mexico Statutes

CHAPTER 14. — RECORDS, LEGAL NOTICES AND OATHS.

Article 3. — Public Records.

§ 14-3-15. Reproduction on film; evidence; review, inventory and approval of systems.

A. Any public officer of the state or of any district or political subdivision may cause any public records, papers or documents kept by him to be photographed, microphotographed, or reproduced on film.

B. The state records administrator shall review any proposed state agency microphotography system and shall advise and consult with the agency. The administrator has the authority to approve or disapprove the system of any state agency.

C. The microphotography system used pursuant to this section shall comply with the minimum standards approved by the New Mexico commission of public records. The microphotography system used to reproduce such records shall be one which accurately reproduces the original in all details.

D. The administrator shall establish and maintain an inventory of all microfilm equipment owned or leased by state agencies. The administrator is authorized to arrange the transfer of microphotography equipment from a state agency which does not use it, and which has released it, to a state agency needing such equipment for a current microphotography system.

E. Photographs, microphotographs or photographic film made pursuant to this section shall be deemed to be original records for all purposes, including introduction in evidence in all courts and administrative agencies. A transcript, exemplification or certified copy, for all purposes, shall be deemed to be a transcript, exemplification or certified copy of the original.

F. Whenever such photographs, microphotographs or reproductions on film are properly certified and are placed in conveniently accessible files, and provisions are made for preserving, examining and using them, any public officer may cause the original records from which the photographs or microphotographs have been made, or any part thereof, to be disposed of according to methods prescribed by Sections 14-3-9 through 14-3-11 NMSA 1978. Copies shall be certified by their custodian as true copies of the originals before the originals are destroyed or lost, and the certified copies shall have the same effect as the originals. Copies of public records transferred from the office of origin to the administrator, when certified by the administrator or his deputy, shall have the same legal effect as if certified by the original custodian of the records.

G. For the purposes of this section, "state agency" shall include the district courts.

International

Most common law countries permit microfilm or other reproductions to be admitted in evidence in place of the original records.

Australia

EVIDENCE AMENDMENT ACT OF 1978

PART 3A. — ADMISSIBILITY OF BUSINESS RECORDS

7B. (1) Subject to this Part, where, in any proceeding, evidence of a fact is admissible, a statement of the fact in a document is admissible as evidence . . .

"document" includes —

(a) a book, plan, paper, parchment, film or other material on which there is writing or printing, or on which there are marks, symbols or perforations having a meaning for persons qualified to interpret them;

(b) a disk, tape, paper, film or other device from which sounds or images are capable of being reproduced; and

(c) any other record of information;

7K.(1) For the purposes of section 7B —

(a) a statement in the document may, as prescribed or by leave of the court, be proved by the production of a copy of the document, or of the material part of the document;

(b) a statement in a document that is designed to be used to reproduce the statement in the form of a visible display or of sound may be proved by reproducing the statement in that form in the presence of the court; and

(c) a statement in the record of information made by the use of a computer may be proved by the production of a document produced by the use of a computer containing the statement in a form that can be understood by sight.

See **Canada in Appendix D.**
Also see **Chapter 5 for Canadian Standards for Documentary Evidence.**

CHAPTER C-5. — CANADA EVIDENCE.

Documentary Evidence

30. (1) Where oral evidence in respect of a matter would be admissible in a legal proceeding, a record made in the usual and ordinary course of business that contains information in respect of that matter is admissible in evidence under this section in the legal proceeding on production of the record.

* * * * *

(3) Where it is not possible or reasonably practicable to produce any record described in subsection (1) or (2), a copy of the record accompanied by an affidavit setting out the reasons why it is not possible or reasonably practicable to produce the record and an affidavit of the person who made the copy setting out the source from which the copy was made and attesting to its authenticity, each affidavit having been sworn before a commissioner or other person authorized to take affidavits, is admissible in evidence under this section in the same manner as if it were the original of the record.

Canada (Ontario)

CHAPTER 39. — EVIDENCE ACT.

(2) Where a bill of exchange, promissory note, cheque, receipt, instrument, agreement, document, plan or a record of book or entry therein kept or held by a person,

(a) is photographed in the course of an established practice of such person of photographing objects of the same or a similar class in order to keep a permanent record thereof; and

(b) is destroyed or in the presence of such person or of one or more of his employees or delivered to another person in the ordinary course of business or lost, a print from the photographic film is admissible in evidence in all cases and for all purposes for which the object photographed would have been admissible.

United Kingdom

CIVIL EVIDENCE ACT 1968

CROSS-HEADING: PART 1. — HEARSAY EVIDENCE.

Section 6. Provisions supplementary to sections 2 to 5.

(1) Where in any civil proceeding a statement contained in a document is proposed to be given in evidence by virtue of section 2, 4 or 5 of this Act it may, subject to any rules of court, be proved by the production of that document or (whether or not that document is still in existence) by the production of a copy of that document, or of the material part thereof, authenticated in such manner as the court may approve.

Some civil law countries also permit microfilm or other reproductions to be admitted in place of the original records. However, many civil law countries permit only the original records to be admitted in evidence.

Italy

THE ITALIAN CIVIL CODE

TITLE 2. — EVIDENCE.

CHAPTER 2. — DOCUMENTARY EVIDENCE.

Section 4. — Mechanical Reproductions.

2712. Mechanical reproductions. Photographic or cinematographic reproductions, phonographic recordings and, in general, all other mechanical representations of facts or things, constitute full evidence of the facts or things represented, if the persons against whom they are offered do not deny their correspondence to the actual facts or things concerned.

Germany

COMMERCIAL CODE

44. Document storage; storage period.

(1) Every merchant is obligated to store the following documents in order:

* * * * *

(3) With the exception of the balance sheet, the documents listed in subsection (1) can also be stored on film or on other data storage records, if this complies with generally accepted accounting principles and it is assured that the reproductions or data

(1) facsimilate the incoming business correspondence and original records and concur with the other documents with regard to content when they are made legible

(2) are available during the period of storage and can be made legible at any time within a reasonable period of time.

* * * * *

Chapter 3 Legal Requirements for Computer Records

Organizations use the speed and accuracy of computers to manage great quantities of information. Although accounting functions represented the primary application of the computer in the 1970's, additional applications such as word processing, project management, data base management, electronic mail, and telecommunications have become significant.

The widespread use and availability of computers in the last twenty years have forced the legal system to develop new principles of law to handle this technology. Laws affecting paper records and microfilm provide the cornerstone for the legal attitudes toward computer records. Computers, however, present some unique problems which have influenced the associated body of law:

- Information stored in memory, magnetic media, or optical media cannot be read directly. The information must first be displayed on a terminal or printed on paper or microfilm.

- Computer information is often entered directly into the computer without the creation of an original paper document or data entry worksheet.

- While the content of the information may remain the same, the form of storage, display, and output requires a transformation of the information into a different form.

- Questions remain as to which records are originals and which are duplicates for legal purposes.

- Special procedures are necessary to ensure that data entry, processing, and production function properly and yield accurate information.

Evidence

Current legal attitudes toward computer records as evidence are reflected in both statutes and rules of evidence. This section summarizes the requirements for computer records found in both the Uniform Rules of Evidence and selected state laws.

UNIFORM RULES OF EVIDENCE

***See* Chapter 1 for a detailed discussion of the general requirements for the admissibility of records in evidence under the Uniform Rules of Evidence.**

The Uniform Rules of Evidence provides the basis for admitting all types of records, including computer records, into evidence. The rules specifically refer to computer records in Rule 803(6) by using the term "data compilation." The definitions in Rule 1001(1) for "writing and recordings" also address computer records by using the terms "magnetic impulse, mechanical or electronic recording, or other form of data compilation."

Visible Records

The Uniform Rules of Evidence contains only one specific requirement for computer records. This requirement identifies the form in which the computer record will be admitted in evidence:

Uniform Rules of Evidence, Rule 1001(3). *See also* Appendix A for the full text of the law related to records and a listing of the states that have adopted the law.

> **ARTICLE X. CONTENTS OF WRITINGS, RECORDINGS AND PHOTOGRAPHS.**
>
> **Rule 1001. Definitions.**
>
> For purposes of this article the following definitions are applicable:
>
> * * * * *
>
> (3) Original. . . . If data are stored in a computer or similar device, any printout or other output readable by sight, shown to reflect the data accurately, is an "original."

Prior to the widespread acceptance of the Uniform Rules of Evidence, some courts found that printouts made explicitly for litigation was inadmissible.

Jurisdictions adopting the Uniform Rules of Evidence have taken the position that only the visible form of the computer record can be admitted into evidence. Clearly, magnetic media including disk, tape, and memory cannot be read directly and do not possess the enduring qualities of a paper printout or other visible record. The law does not place any time limit on when the visible record is produced and does not specifically establish the status of the magnetic media.

Computer output microfilm (COM), although technically microfilm, is considered an original computer record under this definition. While some may claim that COM is not visible because the image must be enlarged, this technicality can be overcome by characterizing COM as a visible image which is enlarged for easier reading.

Authentication and Identification

See **Chapter 1 for an analysis of the requirements in the Uniform Rules of Evidence for authentication and identification of records and Chapter 2 for an analysis of certificates of authenticity for microfilm.**

The authentication and identification of computer systems is critical to determining the trustworthiness of the computerized information. Only through a process of written procedures, training, and audit can your organization be certain that records produced by computers will be admitted in evidence.

Computer information can be added to, deleted, or modified, generally, without a trace. Certain questions can be expected about the integrity of this information. You will then be responsible for clearly demonstrating that the computer information is trustworthy and can be relied upon as evidence.

As part of your documentation of the computer system, you need to maintain information about the operation of the computer hardware, the versions of computer software used, the dates each version of the computer software was used, auditing performed to verify the validity of data, and other records to indicate that your computer system operated properly and no deceptive practices are followed.

Summary Computer Records

See **Chapter 1 for additional discussion about summary records.**

Rule 1006 enables an organization to enter summary computer records into evidence rather than presenting all the detailed raw data. This rule is provided for the convenience of both the litigants and the court to reduce the quantity of information considered during the judicial proceedings. If questions arise about the accuracy or the propriety of the summary information, the judge or opposing party may require the production of the original detailed records.

STATE RULES OF EVIDENCE

Most states, other than those which have adopted the Uniform Rules of Evidence, do not have specific rules of evidence or other laws admitting computer records into evidence. These states depend upon the principles of the Best Evidence Rule which allow computer records to be admitted in evidence in those situations where they constitute the best evidence for the matter to be proven.

California adopted one of the few specific statutes establishing criteria for admitting computer records into evidence:

California Evidence Code, § 1500.5.

§ 1500.5. Printed representation of computer information or computer program used by or stored on computer or computer readable storage media; admissibility of evidence; presumption; burden of proof.

Notwithstanding the provisions of Section 1500, a printed representation of computer information or a computer program which is being used by or stored on a computer or computer readable storage media shall be admissible to prove the existence and content of the computer information or computer program.

Computer recorded information or computer programs, or copies of computer recorded information or computer programs shall not be rendered inadmissible by the best evidence rule. Printed representations of computer information and computer programs will be presumed to be accurate representations of the computer information or computer programs that they purport to represent. This presumption, however, will be a presumption affecting the burden of producing evidence only. If any party to a judicial proceeding introduces evidence that such a printed representation is inaccurate or unreliable, the party introducing it into evidence will have the burden of proving, by a preponderance of evidence, that the printed representation is the best available evidence of the existence and content of the computer information or computer programs that it purports to represent.

THE TRUSTWORTHINESS OF COMPUTER RECORDS

Computer records must meet a higher standard of trustworthiness than ordinary paper records, especially since data can be altered:

- *Reliability of Equipment.* Because equipment which is not functioning properly can alter the content of computerized information, the organization may be required to present evidence that the equipment operated reliably the day the computer record was prepared. A log of computer operations indicating the absence of any malfunction is generally adequate.

- *Integrity of Data Entry.* Computer errors often result from mistakes made during the entry of data. Trustworthiness is enhanced by verifying or proofreading the data after entry.

- *Methods Used to Prevent Loss of Data.* The reliability of computer records is enhanced if an accurate audit trail traces the steps followed in processing the data and the methods used to prevent loss of data.

- *Reliability of Computer Programs.* Errors in computer records can result from errors in the computer programs. You may be required to present evidence about the development and testing of the programs. Programs are often examined by an expert witness to determine their accuracy or reliability.

  You may also be required to present the specific version of the computer program used to process the data on the date the information entered into evidence was created. A different version of the program may be considered, if it is the only one available, but the absence of the exact version of the program may raise some serious questions about the trustworthiness of the computer records.

- *Time and Method for Preparing Printouts.* Computer printouts prepared in the regular course of business are considered more trustworthy than similar computer printouts prepared for trial. As a practical matter, however, if the organization can show an adequate audit trail leading to the creation of the data and merely a time lag before printing, no adverse consequences should result.

Regulation

Internal Revenue Service, Revenue Procedure 91-59. ***See*** **Appendix B for the full text of this revenue procedure.**

REQUIREMENTS OF THE INTERNAL REVENUE SERVICE

Internal Revenue Service Revenue Procedure 91-59 establishes requirements related to computer records maintained for tax purposes.

- All computer records must be retained by the taxpayer in a retrievable, machine-sensible form. The Internal Revenue Service can request your computer tapes or disks for analysis and review. The computer-readable information must therefore be fully documented and maintained in a retrievable and usable form. Even when a service bureau or time-sharing service is used, the taxpayer is still responsible for maintaining the information as indicated.

- Documentation must be provided describing the computerized accounting system including record formats, flowcharts, label descriptions, software program listings, software program changes maintained in chronological order, and detailed charts of accounts. Audit trails should be provided to ensure that the steps leading from detailed to summary information can be examined by the IRS.

The IRS specifically requires that major changes in the computer system be documented and preserved in chronological order. This means that each major version of the software programs must be retained for review by the IRS. The law does not state, however, what is a major software change.

See Recordkeeping Requirements, **Chapter 9, for detailed analysis of records retention requirements for tax records.**

- The computer records should be retained "so long as the contents may become material in the administration of any Internal Revenue law." The Internal Revenue Service suggests that the retention period should match the limitation of assessment for federal tax purposes (generally three to six years except for special circumstances such as fixed assets, insurance loss reserve, and voluntary extension of the audit period).

- Accounting records should also be retained in visible form, either on paper or microfilm. Although the requirement for creating a visible or hardcopy record in the original regulation has been preserved, the Internal Revenue Service stresses that the maintenance of a visible record does not replace the requirement for the retention of machine-sensible records. Microfilm may be retained in place of paper records.

- All computer records maintained for tax purposes should be clearly labeled and maintained in a secure environment, with backup files stored off-site. This requirement actually conforms to good computer practices for records protection.

- Computer records must be maintained in a retrievable form for the entire time they are needed for tax purposes. Even if the taxpayer converts to a new computer system, the computer records must be converted to that new format or maintained in a format that can be readily retrieved.

  This requirement is probably the most difficult and costly one to implement. Whenever an organization converts to a new computer system, the old computer tapes and disks may have to be converted to the new format. Under the previous regulation, taxpayers could simply produce visible output from the records and not worry about the various computer tapes or disks maintained in the storage area. Under the new regulation, all computer-readable material relevant for tax purposes must be maintained in a readily retrievable format. This creates a tremendous burden since audits are frequently extended for many years while computerized accounting systems change almost every three years.

The problem becomes more complicated in the case of acquisitions and mergers. Until the audit period expires, the surviving organization may be responsible for the computer records maintained by the former organizations. Since these computer records are often incompatible with the system used by the surviving organization and rarely are adequately documented, the survivor probably has no choice but to convert the tax records to one standard format.

- Computer records should be inspected periodically to ensure the integrity of the information. If information is lost or damaged, the taxpayer is responsible for notifying the Internal Revenue Service immediately.

  The computer records must be carefully protected by the taxpayer. Under previous regulations, the taxpayer was only responsible for producing a record in visible form and could ignore aging computer tapes. The new regulation requires the taxpayer to ensure that all computer records are protected and available. Standard computer practices should, therefore, include periodic inspection, rewinding of tapes, and storage in environmentally-protected areas.

- Database management systems may be used for maintaining tax records, but additional documentation is needed. In particular, the taxpayer must maintain a sequential file of all transactions entered into the database along with the appropriate documentation for the sequential file and the database management system.

  While many organizations maintain a dynamic database for tax purposes, the Internal Revenue Service requires an audit trail for all transactions and modifications made to the database. For some organizations, however, this is not a burden because the required sequential file and audit trails are a part of a good database management system.

- Taxpayers may use purely electronic information systems for tax purposes such as electronic data interchange (EDI). Paper records do not have to be maintained if the information from those records has been recorded and maintained in the computer system, or if the paper records are not normally prepared or received in the ordinary course of business. Taxpayers must prepare paper or other visible output from the computer records when requested by the IRS.

The following suggestions should be implemented to ensure that your organization will not be assessed additional taxes or be subject to criminal penalties for failing to properly maintain computer records.

- Conduct a tax audit of your existing computer system based upon the new Internal Revenue Service regulation. While computer systems containing tax information should be audited regularly to ensure their compliance with tax laws, the new regulation highlights the importance of such an audit. During the review, an auditor should focus on system documentation, storage procedures for computer records, and the compatibility of older computer records with the current computer system.

- Inventory existing magnetic tapes and disk files to determine their readability by the current computer system. Many older computer files were created with old versions of a computer system. Some of these records may have been prepared by outside service bureaus, time-sharing companies, or companies which have since been acquired by or merged into your organization.

  Revenue Procedure 91-59 requires that all computer records still subject to review by the Internal Revenue Service must be available and readable in machine-sensible format. Computer tapes and disks produced by other computer systems may now be totally incompatible and unreadable by your current system.

  According to this regulation, these computer tapes and disks must be converted into a retrievable format at the request of the Internal Revenue Service. This new format can conform to your existing computer system or it may conform to some other computer system. If the latter option is selected, the user is responsible for ensuring that the other computer system or service bureau is capable of converting the information to a format usable on request by the Internal Revenue Service.

- When developing new computer systems, include the Internal Revenue Service requirements in the design. For the most part, the requirements of the Internal Revenue Service conform to good computer practices. Documentation should be provided for all computer systems, not just because the IRS says so, but because you need this information to run the business.

REQUIREMENTS OF STATE REVENUE DEPARTMENTS

The departments of revenue in most states follow the requirements of the Internal Revenue Service regulations for income tax purposes because state income tax returns are generally based on the federal income tax returns with some adjustments. As a result, they have little choice but to follow the federal requirements for recordkeeping in the area of computer records.

The state departments of revenue, however, often develop additional recordkeeping regulations applicable to sales tax records, since sales tax falls totally within the control of the state. While many of these sales tax requirements parallel those of the IRS, most states have not revised their computer record requirements to correspond with IRS Revenue Procedure 91-59 or even its predecessor 86-19.. The typical state tax requirements for computer records, therefore, often remain similar to the previous IRS regulation:

Colorado Department of Revenue, Regulation 26-116(c). This regulation contains the major recordkeeping provisions previously found in IRS Revenue Procedure 64-12, previously adopted in 1964 and completely replaced by Revenue Procedure 91-59.

Regulation 26-116. Records

* * * * *

(c) Records prepared by automated data processing systems. An ADP tax accounting system must be capable of producing visible and legible records for verification of taxpayers' tax liability.
(1) Recorded or reconstructible data. ADP records must provide an opportunity to trace any transaction back to the original source or forward to a final point total. If detail printouts are not made of transactions at the time they are processed, the systems must have the ability to reconstruct these transactions.
(2) General and Subsidiary Books of Account. A general ledger, with source references, will be written out to coincide with financial reports for tax reporting periods. In cases where subsidiary ledgers are used to support the general ledger accounts, the subsidiary ledgers should also be written out periodically.
(3) Supporting Documents and Audit Trail. The audit trail should be designed so that the details underlying the summary accounting data may be identified and made available to the Department upon request. The system should be so designed that supporting documents, such as sales invoices, purchase invoices, credit memoranda, etc., are readily available.
(4) Program Documentation. A description of the ADP portion of the accounting system should be available. The statements and illustrations as to the scope of operations should be sufficiently detailed to indicate, (A) the application being performed, (B) the procedures employed in each application (which, for example, might be supported by flow charts, block diagrams, or other satisfactory description of the input or output procedures), and (C) the controls used to insure accurate and reliable processing. Important changes, together with their effective dates, should be noted in order to preserve an accurate chronological record.

The typical state tax law specifies audit trails, maintenance of detailed records, program documentation, and other features commonly found in a good computer accounting system.

Government

See Appendix B, Code of Federal Regulations, Title 36, Part 1234 for the computer records standards for federal programs. *See* Appendix C for additional laws that apply to state and local government.

Arizona Revised Statutes

The National Archives and Records Administration (NARA) established standards for the creation, preservation and disposition of computer records for the federal government. Some state archives have similar programs. The following laws are typical of those that apply to state and local government agencies.

TITLE 28. — TRANSPORTATION.

CHAPTER 2. — STATE AGENCIES AND OFFICERS.

Article 1. — Motor Vehicle Division.

§ 28-110. Reproduction of records; notification of reproduction; admissibility of reproductions as originals; destruction of nonessential or obsolete records; computer storage of information.

* * * * *

E. The director may cause the information contained on any original records or reproductions thereof made pursuant to this section to be placed on computer storage devices, but the original records or the copies shall be maintained by the department so long as required by law or the director deems necessary after which time the records may be disposed of as provided in this section. Signatures on records need not be placed in the computer storage devices.

F. A reproduction of the information placed on computer storage devices shall be deemed to be an original of the record for all purposes and shall be admissible in evidence without further foundation in all courts or administrative agencies when the following certification by a custodian of the record appears on each page:

The below named individual, being a duly designated custodian of the motor vehicle division's public records, certifies this document as a true reproduction of the information contained in the computer storage devices of the department of transportation, motor vehicle division, in accordance with Arizona Revised Statutes § 28-110, subsection F.

By: /s/__(Print full name)____________________

Kansas, Kansas Statutes Annotated

CHAPTER 45. — LAWS, JOURNALS AND PUBLIC INFORMATION.

§ 45-501. Records made on electronically accessed media; authorization, conditions and procedures; application; notice to state records board.

(a) Whenever any state agency or local agency is required by law to make a record or to record any transaction or any instrument, paper or document, the making of such record on computer disk, tape or other electronically accessed media, in accordance with this section, shall be deemed to be recording or the making of the record as required by law.

(b) When any such records are made on computer disks, tapes or other electronically accessed media under this section, such records shall be maintained and adequate provisions shall be made for their preservation, examination and availability for ready use by those persons lawfully entitled to view them through the use of computer terminal displays, computer printouts, other computer-generated displays or other suitable facilities which may be made available at one or more locations designated by the state agency or local agency therefore. The capability to produce a computer printout or other printed version of such records stored on computer disks, tapes or other electronically accessed media shall be maintained by the state agency or local agency at all times so that such a printed copy of such records may be made available to persons lawfully entitled to view the records, subject to any applicable fees for such printed copies, from one or more locations designated by the state agency or local agency therefore. Each computer or other electronically accessed media system used to make records under this section shall include adequate security procedures and other provisions for permanent record of all persons who have access to and make, amend or delete any records or other data in such system.

(c) No state agency or local agency which records or stores information on computer disks, tapes or other electronically accessed media shall be required to satisfy the standards and procedures imposed under this section, unless such records and information are records required by law and such records are not also made or maintained in another manner required or permitted by law. Each state agency or local agency which makes records or stores information on computer tapes, disks or other electronically accessed media in accordance with this section and which does not keep such records or information in another manner shall give written notice to the state records board thereof and shall identify all such records and information in such notice.

* * * * *

International

Several common law countries recognize the use of computer records both for purposes of evidence and regulatory requirements.

Australia

EVIDENCE AMENDMENT ACT OF 1978

PART 3A. — ADMISSIBILITY OF BUSINESS RECORDS.

7A. * * *

"document" includes —

* * * * *

(b) a disc, tape, paper, film or other device from which sounds or images are capable of being reproduced; and

* * * * *

7K. (1) For the purposes of section 7B —

* * * * *

(b) a statement in a document that is designed to be used to reproduce the statement in the form of a visible display or of sound may be proved by reproducing the statement in that form in the presence of the court; and

(c) a statement in the record of information made by the use of a computer may be proved by the production of a document produced by the use of a computer containing the statement in a form that can be understood by sight.

(2) For the purposes of section 7E, the absence of a record of the happening of an event in the record of information made by the use of a computer may be proved by the production of a document produced by the use of a computer containing a statement based on the absence of such a record.

* * * * *

(4) Where a person proposes to prove, or proves, a statement by reproducing the statement in the form of a visible display or of sound, the court may direct a record of the statement to be produced and, if the record is not produced, may reject the statement or, if it is in evidence, exclude it.

(5) For the purposes of this section, "computer" means any device for storing or processing information.

United Kingdom

VOLUME 7(1). — COMPANIES REGULATED BY THE COMPANIES ACT 1985.

683. Use of computers for company records.

The power conferred on a company to keep a register or other record by recording the matters in question otherwise than by making entries in bound books includes power to keep the register or other record by recording those matters otherwise than in a legible form, so long as the recording is capable of being reproduced in legible form. Any provision of an instrument made by a company before 12 February 1979 which requires a register of holders of the company's debentures to be kept in a legible form is to be read as requiring the register to be kept in a legible or nonlegible form.

If any such register or other record of a company, or a register of holders of a company's debentures, is kept by the company by recording the matters in question otherwise than in a legible form, any duty imposed on the company by the Companies Act of 1985 to allow inspection of, or to furnish a copy of, the register or other record or any part of it is to be treated as a duty to allow inspection of, or to furnish, a reproduction of the recording or of the relevant part of it in a legible form. The Secretary of State may by regulation in a statutory instrument make such additional provision as he considers appropriate in connection with such registers or other records as are mentioned above, and are kept as so mentioned; and the regulations may make modifications of provisions of the Companies Act of 1985 relating to such registers or other records.

CIVIL EVIDENCE ACT 1968

CROSS-HEADING: PART 1. — HEARSAY EVIDENCE.

Section 6. Provisions supplementary to §§ 2 to 5.

(3) In estimating the weight, if any, to be attached to a statement admissible in evidence by virtue of section 2, 3, 4, or 5 of this Act regard shall be had to all the circumstances from which any inference can reasonably be drawn as to the accuracy or otherwise of the statement and, in particular —

* * * * *

(c) in the case of a statement falling within section 5(1) of this Act, to the question whether or not the information which the information contained in the statement reproduces or is derived from was supplied to the relevant computer, or recorded for the purpose of being supplied thereto, contemporaneously with the occurrence or existence of the facts dealt with in that information, and to the question whether or not any person concerned with the supply of information to that computer, or with the operation of that computer or any equipment by means of which the document containing the statement was produced by it, had any incentive to conceal or misrepresent the facts.

China has adopted legal requirements for computer records.

China, Peoples Republic of

THE ACCOUNTING REGULATIONS OF THE PEOPLE'S REPUBLIC OF CHINA FOR JOINT VENTURES USING CHINESE AND FOREIGN INVESTMENT

CHAPTER 13. — ACCOUNTING DOCUMENTS AND ACCOUNTING BOOKS.

Article 72. A joint venture keeping its accounts by electronic computer shall maintain properly its accounting records stored in or printed out by the computer and shall regard such records as accounting books. The tapes, discs, etc. shall be kept and no deletion shall be allowed unless the records in them are printed out in visible form.

Electronic Data Interchange (EDI)

Electronic data interchange represents a logical extension from our traditional recordkeeping practices. Although these systems generally correspond to traditional accounting and purchasing functions, EDI systems are also being used to create legally binding contracts between organizations.

EDI records differ from traditional computer records in that the information is rarely printed or disseminated in printed form. Some of the information is actually transferred to the host computer by outside organizations.

Some of the records management issues related to this technology include the following:

- What is the relationship of EDI records to the traditional paper records that relate to the same function?
- What records must be maintained in an EDI system to meet legal requirements?
- Who is responsible for maintaining EDI records in an organization (i.e., who is the office of record)?

WHAT IS ELECTRONIC DATA INTERCHANGE?

Electronic data interchange is a method by which two different organizations can initiate and conduct business through computer communications. An EDI system eliminates several of the steps found in a paper-based system and eliminates paper records. A typical EDI system would function as follows:

- Company A would enter the purchase order information into their computer.
- Company A would then transmits this data in standard codes via communication link to Company B's computer.
- Company B's computer would analyze the codes and translate the information into the format used by its order entry system.
- Company B would then review the order for accuracy and for the availability of the items ordered.
- Company B would enter in its computer only changes or additions to the information transmitted by Company A.
- Company B would transmit an acknowledgment to Company A utilizing the data already communicated by Company A.
- Company B would ship the goods.
- Company B would communicate invoice information to Company A by communication link.
- Company A would review the invoice information and either print a check or instruct its bank to electronically transfer funds to Company B.

An EDI system promotes efficiency, accuracy, and speed in the purchasing process. Information is keyed into a computer only once and used by both organizations. The procedure is also much faster. For these reasons, many organizations, especially larger ones, have either implemented an EDI system or are seriously considering the implementation of this technology.

SPECIAL EDI LEGAL REQUIREMENTS

Those laws dealing with EDI primarily deal with regulatory reporting requirements met by submitting information using EDI. Some United States federal government agencies permit or require use of EDI for submitting contract and other related information. Several factors are driving this trend:

- EDI submission of this information significantly decreases the paperwork burden on the regulated parties;

- Receiving the information in electronic format enhances the agency's ability to manage and utilize the information; and

- For information available to the public, access is significantly enhanced through submission of electronic information that can rapidly be made available via electronic bulletin boards or the internet.

As of this writing, there are no laws regulating commercial use of EDI. However, we still need to consider certain laws that affect records in general that could affect EDI records. For example, the Internal Revenue Service requires that taxpayers maintain tax records systems that can be audited. This requirement would also apply to an EDI system.

Relationship to Paper Records System

As a general rule, the same legal requirements that affect paper records systems would affect EDI systems. These requirements could include the type of records maintained, the form of the records, and the records retention period.

The retention period for EDI records in particular would be the same as the retention period for the comparable paper records. For example, if tax records are maintained for six years under an organization's records retention schedule, the corresponding EDI records would be maintained for six years. Since EDI records may consist of files on magnetic disk and magnetic tape, this information must be erased after the retention period.

Scope of EDI Records

Many organizations are concerned with the type of EDI records that should be maintained to document the various transactions. In a paper-based purchasing and accounting system, an organization would typically maintain the purchasing records, shipment records, accounts receivable and accounts payable records.

Comparable records would be maintained in an EDI system. In some cases, the various records would consist of fields of data in a database management system. In other cases, records related to purchasing, shipping, and accounting may be maintained in separate files. Regardless of the method, appropriate, auditable records of the EDI transactions must be maintained .

The more difficult question is which form of the EDI record should be maintained? In the case of EDI, there are generally at least two versions of the EDI records. The first version corresponds to the computer information system used by the organization. The data fields, programs, and organization of information may conceivably be unique to the organization. Their purpose is to meet the unique purchasing, shipping, and accounting needs of the organization using them and generally do not conform to systems maintained by other organizations involved in the EDI transmission.

The second form of the EDI record consists of the standard data fields communicated between organizations participating in an EDI system. For example, after a purchase order is prepared and data entered into the unique purchasing information system of Company A, the data is then converted to the standard data format and communicated to Company B's computer. Company B will receive the standard codes and then translate them into the unique form used by its own order entry system. As such, the same data will be entered into one format, converted to a standard code, and then reconverted into another unique format. Both Company A and Company B will create or maintain comparable data in both its unique format and the standard format used for communication.

The American National Standards Institute's X12 Committee and the International Standards Organization are working energetically to establish international standards for EDI communications. At this time, some standards exist, others have been agreed to by participating companies, and others are in the developmental stage. At some point in the future we expect that the standards for interchanging data will be internationally accepted. This will simplify recordkeeping requirements for EDI records because only one standard format will exist and deviations will be prohibited.

The standard formats being developed are generally referred to as the "untranslated" form of the EDI records. The unique format used by each organization as part of their purchasing, shipping and accounting systems, is generally referred to as the "translated" records. Both types of records are currently required to allow an auditor to follow a transaction from start to finish — from one format to the other. Organizations should therefore maintain both sets of records until an accepted international standard format for communications of

EDI records is adopted. At that time, we may be able to relax this requirement and primarily maintain the translated records.

OFFICE OF RECORD

The Office of Record for EDI records will be the same as the Office of Record for other purchasing, shipping and accounting records. For example, even though the Data Processing Department manages the computerized accounting system for the Accounting Department, the Accounting Department still remains the Office of Record for all accounting records. The Data Processing Department merely operates the computers, manages the software, and handles the media affecting the records. The department has no interest in the content of the records other than ensuring that the programs work properly to produce an accurate result.

For this reason, the Data Processing Department can be viewed as an "independent records keeper" for ensuring the integrity of EDI records. This concept has arisen in the EDI field due to concerns that data can be modified and manipulated in a pure electronic system. Some authors have advocated the establishment of even a third party records keeper who would receive, log, and retransmit all EDI communications between organizations. This would establish an independent and auditable log of transactions to bolster the integrity of the EDI system.

Where a third party record keeper may not be available, an independent group within an organization might perform a similar function. Since the Data Processing Department has little or no interest in the information content of the EDI data, the department is ideally suited to perform this role.

This is similar to the role of an organization's Audit Department for auditing records prepared by the Accounting Department. While the audit group must be knowledgeable of the accounting functions, it does not perform accounting activities on a daily basis. It merely ensures that the accounting information is correct. By splitting the accounting function from the audit function, we establish the integrity of the accounting system. Similarly, by separating the accounting function from the data processing function, we ensure the integrity of the EDI system.

REQUIREMENT FOR PAPER RECORDS

Only a few laws require that paper records be maintained. Most other laws will permit any form of a record to be maintained as long as the appropriate information is maintained for the requisite period of time.

See **Appendix A for the Uniform Rules of Evidence, Rule 1001.**

For purposes of evidence, EDI records should be treated like traditional paper or computer records that document similar transactions. Rule 1001(1) of the Uniform Rules of Evidence (adopted by the United States federal courts and approximately 32 states) defines a record as follows:

> . . . Letters, words, sounds, or numbers, or their equivalent, set down by handwriting, typewriting, printing, photostating, photographing, magnetic impulse, mechanical or electronic recording, or other form of data compilation.

The terms "magnetic impulse," electronic recording," and "data compilation" relate to computer records as records under the rule. Rule 1001(3) permits data stored in a computer to be introduced into evidence when converted into a printout or other form "readable by sight, shown to reflect the data accurately."

Internal Revenue Service, Revenue Procedure 91-59.

The Internal Revenue Service accepted the use of EDI system by taxpayers in Rev. Proc. 91-59:

> **§ 5. Machine-Sensible Recordkeeping Requirements.**
>
> * * * * *
>
> .15 In order to be in compliance with this revenue procedure, a taxpayer that uses EDI technology must retain machine-sensible records that, in combination with any other records (e.g., the underlying contracts, price lists, and price changes), contain all of the detailed information required by section 6001 of the Code. The extent of the detail in the retained electronic and other records, if any, must be equivalent to the level of detail contained in an acceptable paper record. For example, the retained records for an electronic invoice must contain identification of the vendor by name, invoice date, product description, quantity purchased, price, etc. The taxpayer may capture this information at any level within the accounting system provided that the audit trail, authenticity, and integrity of the retained records can be established.
>
> **§ 6. Impact on Hardcopy Recordkeeping Requirements.**
>
> .01 Except as otherwise provided in this section, the provisions of this revenue procedure do not relieve taxpayers of the responsibility to rctain hardcopy records that are created or received in the ordinary

> course of business as required by existing law and regulations. Hard-copy records may be retained in microfiche or microfilm format in accordance with the requirements outlined in Rev. Proc. 81-46, 1981-2 C.B. 621. These records are not a substitute for the machine-sensible records required to be retained by this revenue procedure.
>
> .02 Hardcopy records generated at the time of a transaction (e.g., credit card receipts) need not be retained if all the details relating to the transaction are subsequently received by the taxpayer in an EDI transaction and are retained by the taxpayer in accordance with this revenue procedure.
>
> .03 If hardcopy records are not produced or received in the ordinary course of transacting business (as may be the case when utilizing EDI technology), or are not retained pursuant to section 6.02, hardcopy printouts of computerized records need not be created unless requested by the Service. These requests may be made either at the time of an examination or in conjunction with the testing described in section 4.04.
>
> .04 Computer printouts that are created for validation, control, or other temporary purposes need not be retained.

Paper records not otherwise received or creating in the ordinary course of business do not have to be maintained for tax purposes provided that the information had be recorded and preserved in the computer system.

EDI CONTRACTS

Currently, two parties wishing to participate in EDI transactions must initially approve a signed "trading partner agreement." This is necessary because some provisions of the Uniform Commercial Code and some statutes of fraud require a "writing" before an agreement for the sale of certain types of goods or property can be legally binding.

As stated above, the Uniform Rules of Evidence might accept an electronic record as a "writing" under its definition. Conservative lawyers prefer the writing to be a traditional signed contract.

Attorneys, working through the American Bar Association, are attempting to review the existing law in this area and propose modifications that would eliminate the need for a separate written agreement prior to the establishment of EDI communications between organizations. If the change occurs, a legally binding contract would result when Company A transmitted certain codes to Company B and Company B acknowledged the information by transmitting certain codes back to Company A.

This procedure is similar to the one followed with existing teller machines. A customer inserts the card into the teller machine and types their secret personal identification number (PIN). The teller machine checks the number and performs the transaction if the number is correct.

With a teller card system, however, a prior agreement between the bank and the customer is required. The approach proposed for EDI systems would preclude the need for a prior written agreement and establish a legally binding contract merely by the transfer of particular fields of information between organizations, perhaps including the use of secret passwords.

Once the legal complications are resolved, one organization could order products from another merely by transmitting the appropriate information to the other's computer. This transaction could take place even if the two parties have had no prior interactions and have not signed a prior agreement.

Electronic Mail

Many organization have established electronic mail systems to facilitate communications within the organization.

THE WHITE HOUSE CASE

See Appendix B for *Armstrong v. Executive Office of the President*, 62 USLW 2109, 1993 WL 304567, decided August 13, 1993.

The United States Court of Appeals, District of Columbia Circuit rendered the most extensive judicial decision ever recorded related to electronic mail.

Facts

Since the mid-1980's, the Executive Office of the President and the National Security Council participated in an electronic mail system to exchange information and improve efficiency. Over 1300 federal employees used this system to "relay lengthy substantive — even classified — 'notes' that, in content, are often indistinguishable from letters or memoranda." The system operates similar to other electronic mail systems in government and the private sector. Besides the actual text being communicated, the system tracked other information related to the communication, including the originating party name, receiving party name, date of transmission, and acknowledgment.

The sending or receiving parties could instruct the computer to delete, store, or print the message. Employees were instructed that "when any electronic document meets the definition of a federal record, the employee should either print out the information that appears on the computer screen or incorporate the material into a written memorandum." This procedure did not require that all information (such as transmission date, recipient's acknowledgment, etc.) related to the electronic message be preserved. Although backup tapes were maintained of the electronic mail, the Office of the President intended to destroy these tapes in the future.

On January 19, 1989, the day before President Ronald Reagan relinquished the presidency to George Bush, the National Security Archive filed a Freedom of Information Act request for the materials stored in the electronic mail system from the time of inception to the date of the request. Simultaneously, other plaintiffs filed suit requesting a declaratory judgment specifying that the records contained in the electronic communications system and the backup tapes were federal and presidential records, and requesting an injunction to prohibit destroying these records. On appeal, the District of Columbia Circuit Court of Appeals affirmed the injunction prohibiting the destruction of the tapes until the merits of the case could be heard.

On January 3, 1993, the District of Columbia District Court issued a ruling specifying that the electronic mail records were, in fact, federal records under the Federal Records Act. The court also determined that the procedure to selectively print electronic mail records followed by the Office of the President and the National Security Council was seriously flawed. These actions violated federal law as well as prevailing procedures of the National Archives and Records Administration for the retention of records. The defendants appealed this decision.

***Armstrong v. Executive Office of the President*, 810 F.Supp. 335 (D.D.C. 1993). Trial court decision not included in Appendix B.**

In the August 1993 Court of Appeals decision, the District Court conclusions were upheld. In addition, the Court of Appeals established guidelines for reviewing presidential procedures under the Presidential Records Act to determine whether federal records were properly categorized as also presidential records. This issue will be decided at a later date.

Background

44 USC Chapter 21, 29, 31 and 33

The Federal Records Act was approved by Congress to assure "accurate and complete documentation of policies and transactions of the federal government, control of the quantity and the quality of records produced by the federal government, and judicious preservation and disposal of records." Congress intended for the Act to guarantee that the records management programs of federal agencies strike a balance between developing an efficient and effective records management program and the substantive public need for federal records.

Under the Act, the heads of each federal agency must "make and preserve records containing adequate and proper documentation of the organization, functions, policies, decisions, procedures and essential transactions of the agency and designed to furnish the information necessary to protect the legal and financial rights of the government and of persons directly affected by the agency's activities" [44 USC §3101]. As a result, each agency must have an economical and efficient records management program, safeguard records against their removal or loss, and comply with the requirements of the National Archives.

The Federal Records Act indicates the mechanism for disposing of federal records and specifically prohibits the destruction of records by procedures other than those provided in the Act. For purposes of the Act, "records" was defined as follows:

44 USC §3314.

> All books, papers, maps, photographs, machine-readable materials (emphasis added), or other documents or materials, regardless of physical form or characteristics, made or received by an agency of the United States government under federal law or in connection with the transaction of public business and preserved or appropriate for preservation by that agency . . . as evidence of the organization, functions, policies, decisions, procedures, operations or other activities of the government or because of the information value of the data in them.

Once a record qualifies as a federal record, it may only be destroyed under retention procedures approved by the National Archives. The agency may either submit a listing of records slated for destruction and may then only destroy them with specific approval from the Archivist. Alternatively, the agency may regularly destroy records according to a records retention and disposal schedule approved in advance by the National Archives.

The Decision

The Court of Appeals concluded that the Executive Office of the President and the National Security Council did not prepare a written procedure related to the destruction of records in the electronic mail system. Individual employees were empowered to decide whether the Act addressed the e-mail records. In principle, when federal records were detected, they were to be printed and maintained. No written guidelines even existed to assist federal employees in making this decision. Employees could exercise their own discretion when destroying records. And, certainly, no records retention procedures had been approved by the National Archives.

The court decided that all the electronic mail records must initially be considered federal records since they were prepared in the conduct of federal business. Since no approved procedure existed to distinguish which records were not federal records, none of the electronic mail records could be destroyed under prevailing practices. Thus, the court concluded that the electronic version of the electronic mail must be maintained until proper disposition can be determined.

In addition, the court determined that electronic mail records could not be preserved simply by printing out the text that appeared on the screen. The Court also concluded that the electronic version contained a great deal of additional information, such as the date of transmission, date of receipt, detailed listing of recipients, linkages between messages sent and replies received, etc., not contained in the screen print. For this reason, the printed version could not be considered even a copy of the original version under the Federal Records Act.

The court also expressed concern over the possibility that the Office of the President could indiscriminately declare that all records in the Executive Branch were protected from court review under the Presidential Records Act. The court indicated a need for a specific procedure and methodology to determine which records would be "presidential" and which were not. This matter is now being reviewed further by the trial court.

Implications for Federal Agencies

This court decision impacts the electronic mail system of all federal agencies. In essence, all electronic records produced by the federal government will be considered "records" under the Federal Records Act unless appropriate procedures have been properly approved and implemented to exclude those records. For example, the electronic version of a word processing file could technically be excluded from the definition of the Federal Records Act if the text is printed in full onto a paper document. The electronic version would then become a copy of the record and could be discarded.

This procedure, however, may not be true with electronic mail records. The Court clearly indicated that merely printing of the screen text does not constitute printing of the entire electronic record. The

Court seems to require that a paper print produced from an electronic mail system include other "informational content" contained in the electronic version such as date of transmission, date of receipt, and distribution.

In order to overcome this objection, federal agencies should establish formal procedures to determine which electronic mail records are federal records and assign authorized records retention periods. Some affirmative action be required to convert an electronic mail record into a formal record of an organization. This procedure could be adopted by federal agencies to comply with the court decision.

A federal agency should first define which classes of communication within the electronic mail system constitutes a federal record and which communications do not. For example, communications regarding pure administrative procedures, such as scheduling a meeting, may not achieve record status — because it can be define as a "tool" to accomplish federal government business, not government business itself. Records creators could be required to complete an initial screen before transmitting information that would establish the identity, classification, retention, status and other information related to the record. When appropriate, this status information could be attributed to copies of the record by default that are subsequently transferred to a recipient's database or remote computer. Recipients could also utilize a pop-up screen to reclassify the record, or, alternatively, accept the default classification of this record as a duplicate.

Regardless, the court clearly indicated that electronic records within the federal domain may not be destroyed without formal procedures. It appears that the court was particularly disturbed by the informality of the procedures followed by the Executive Office of the President and the unlimited discretion given to federal employees.

It seems probable that the Court would not have overturned appropriate procedures established for the electronic mail system that included records retention provisions approved by the National Archives and Records Administration. For that reason, federal agencies should review existing procedures or develop new ones that establish guidelines for creating, managing, and destroying electronic mail records.

The court carefully indicated that its decision was not designed to impose significant new burden on the federal government nor to preclude the use of a cost-effective technology. In reality, this decision could have a detrimental effect on federal government E-mail systems.

E-mail is often used as a convenient tool to communicate information. As with telephone calls, the parties may not intend the communication to be private and not subject to scrutiny by others. Many certainly do not intend to create federal records though E-mail communications.

As a result of this court decision, some federal employees may elect to limit their use of the E-mail system or revert back to live, unrecorded conversations. Both outcomes would decrease their efficiency, reduce their response time to resolving problems and increase the cost of government. This would be an unfortunate consequence.

Impact on State Government

The Federal Records Act does not apply to state government. However, most states have enacted comparable state laws that would include electronic records within the definition of state government records. For this reason, the recommendations provided above for federal agencies should also be considered by state governments. Formal procedures should be established for electronic mail records and, when necessary, records retention procedures approved by the State Archives.

Impact on the Private Sector

This decision may have no impact upon the private sector. Clearly, the Federal Business Records Act does not apply to private organizations. For purposes of evidence, the definition of records will include computer records since you may introduce computer records into evidence. In addition, computer records can also be subpoenaed by adverse parties during litigation. On the other hand, the doctrine set forth in this case could also be extended to private parties by analogy. It will be necessary to monitor future cases to predict how far this holding will be extended.

At this time, no laws specifically address electronic mail records for the private sector. A large body of case law, however, suggests that records, once created, should be destroyed only under a records retention program. For this reason, indiscriminate destruction of even electronic mail records (or other records that the law does not require you to create) might cause legal problems.

Although the *Armstrong* case does not immediately impact the private sector, it does serve as an additional reminder — establish and document procedures related to the creation, management, and destruction of electronic mail records and all other electronic records in the system. Records managers know the importance of a records retention schedule and detailed procedures. This case merely reminds us that the time has come to include electronic records in our overall retention program.

Other Court Cases

See 96 CV 02840, filed in the United States Court for the District of Columbia.

Another case, *Public Citizen v. Carlin*, holds the possibility of expanding the doctrine of *Armstrong v. Executive Office of the President* considerably. Pursuant to the court's opinion in *Armstrong*, N.A.R.A. implemented its general records schedule 20. The plaintiffs' basic contention in this lawsuit is that public records are still being improperly destroyed, because schedule 20 only provides for preservation of a paper printout of the public records in question. According to the plaintiffs, electronic records so preserved lose a substantial part of the information integral to them – date and time stamps, routing information, etc. This, they contend, is a vital part of the public record, and so must be preserved along with the actual text.

Although the *Armstrong* court seemed to imply that this information might be part of the record, it did not explicitly require that it be preserved. In *Public Citizen,* however, this precise issue is being litigated, so if the plaintiffs are successful, federal agencies will face a substantial new information management obligation.

Public Citizen is also a debate over the definition of what information constitutes an integral part of an "electronic record." If the court decides that an electronic record must necessarily include the additional information sought by the plaintiffs, then by analogy, similar records held by other parties perhaps should contain similar information. If the plaintiffs prevail, it may therefore be reasonable to expect similar suits on the state level, or even against private parties and organizations, as litigants seek to expand the doctrine.

NATIONAL ARCHIVES AND RECORDS ADMINISTRATION PROCEDURES FOR ELECTRONIC MAIL

As a result of *Armstrong v. Executive Office of the President*, the National Archives and Records Administration prepared regulations affecting electronic mail to be followed by federal agencies. These regulations only affect federal government records. Even though they do not apply directly to the private sector and state government, they may be instructive by example.

See National Archives and Records Administration in Title 36, Code of Federal Regulations for requirements for federal government records. Specific requirements for electronic mail and electronic records appear primarily in 36 CFR Part 1234.
Since these requirements have no effect on the private sector or state government, electronic mail should be managed using the procedure outline presented above.

The National Archives has taken the position that all electronic records may be federal records under the Federal Records Act and must be treated as records. Under this philosophy, federal agencies must establish electronic recordkeeping systems that incorporate their approved records retention schedules. After preparation or receipt, all e-mail records will be transferred to the electronic recordkeeping system until the records can be destroyed according to the retention requirements of each recordkeeping category. In order to keep records only in the e-mail system, the e-mail system must have all the features of a full electronic recordkeeping system.

PART 1228 — DISPOSITION OF FEDERAL RECORDS

36 CFR 1228.1.

§ 1228.1 Scope of part.

This part sets policies and establishes standards, procedures, and techniques for the disposition of all Federal records in accordance with 44 U.S.C. chapters 21, 29, 31, and 33. The disposition of documentary materials created or acquired by a Federal agency, regardless of physical form or characteristics, is controlled by this part if any of the following conditions are met:

* * * * *

(e) The material was created or received on an electronic mail system and it meets the definition of record. For specific instructions on the disposition of records created or received on electronic mail systems, see 36 CFR 1234.32.

PART 1234 — ELECTRONIC RECORDS MANAGEMENT

36 CFR 1234.1.

§ 1234.1 Scope of part.

This part establishes the basic requirements related to the creation, maintenance, use, and disposition of electronic records. Electronic records include numeric, graphic, and text information, which may be recorded on any medium capable of being read by a computer and which satisfies the definition of a record. This includes, but is not limited to, magnetic media, such as tapes and disks, and optical disks. Unless otherwise noted, these requirements apply to all electronic information systems, whether on microcomputers, minicomputers, or main-frame computers, regardless of storage media, in network or stand-alone configurations. This part also covers creation, maintenance and use, and disposition of Federal records created by individuals using electronic mail applications.

36 CFR 1234.2.

§ 1234.2 Definitions.

Basic records management terms are defined in 36 CFR 1220.14. As used in part 1234 —

* * * * *

Electronic mail message. A document created or received on an electronic mail system including brief notes, more formal or substantive narrative documents, and any attachments, such as word processing and other electronic documents, which may be transmitted with the message.

Electronic mail system. A computer application used to create, receive, and transmit messages and other documents. Excluded from this definition are file transfer utilities (software that transmits files between users but does not retain any transmission data), data systems used to collect and process data that have been organized into data files or data bases on either personal computers or mainframe computers, and word processing documents not transmitted on an e-mail system.

* * * * *

Transmission and receipt data. (1) *Transmission data*. Information in electronic mail systems regarding the identities of sender and addressee(s), and the date and time messages were sent. (2) *Receipt data*. Information in electronic mail systems regarding date and time of receipt of a message, and/or acknowledgment of receipt or access by addressee(s).

* * * * *

36 CFR 1234.20.

§ 1234.20. Creation and use of data files.

(a) For electronic information systems that produce, use, or store data files, disposition instructions for the data shall be incorporated into the system's design.

(b) Agencies shall maintain adequate an up-to-date technical documentation for each electronic information system that produces, uses, or stores data files. Minimum documentation required is a narrative description of the system; physical and technical characteristics of the records, including a record layout that describes each field including its name, size, starting or relative position, and a description of the form of the data (such as alphabetic, zoned decimal, packed decimal, or numeric), or a data dictionary or the equivalent information associated with a data base management system including a description of the relationship between data elements in data bases; and any other technical information needed to read or process the records.

36 CFR 1234.22.

§ 1234.22. Creation and use of text documents.

(a) Electronic recordkeeping systems that maintain the official file copy of text documents on electronic media shall met the following minimum requirements:

(1) Provide a method for all authorized users of the system to retrieve desired documents, such as an indexing or text search system;

(2) Provide an appropriate level of security to ensure integrity of the documents;

(3) Provide a standard interchange format when necessary to permit the exchange of documents on electronic media between agency computers using different software/operating systems and the conversion or migration of documents on electronic media from one system to another, and

(4) Provide for the disposition of the documents including, when necessary, the requirements for transferring permanent records to NARA (see § 1228.188 of this chapter).

(b) Before a document is created electronically on electronic recordkeeping systems that will maintain the official file copy on electronic media, each document shall be identified sufficiently to enable authorized personnel to retrieve, protect, and carry out the disposition of documents in the system. Appropriate identifying information for each document maintained on the electronic media may include: office of origin, file code, key words for retrieval, addressee (if any), signature, author, date, authorized disposition (coded or otherwise), and security classification (if applicable). Agencies shall ensure that records maintained in such systems can be correlated with related records on paper, microform, or other media.

36 CFR 1234.24.

§ 1234.24 Standards for managing electronic mail records.

Agencies shall manage records created or received on electronic mail systems in accordance with the provisions of this chapter pertaining to adequacy of documentation, recordkeeping requirements, agency records management responsibilities, and records disposition (36 CFR parts 1220, 1222, and 1228).

(a) Agency instructions on identifying and preserving electronic mail messages will address the following unique aspects of electronic mail:

(1) Some transmission data (names of sender and addressee(s) and date the message was sent) must be preserved for each electronic mail record in order for the context of the message to be understood. Agencies shall determine if any other transmission data is needed for purposes of context.

(2) Agencies that use an electronic mail system that identifies users by codes or nicknames or identifies addressees only by the name of a distribution list shall instruct staff on how to retain names on directories or distributions lists to ensure identification of the sender and addressee(s) of messages that are records.

(3) Agencies that use an electronic mail system that allows users to request acknowledgments or receipts showing that a message reached the mailbox or inbox of each addressee, or that an addressee opened the message, shall issue instructions to e-mail users specifying when

to request such receipts or acknowledgments for recordkeeping purposes and how to preserve them.

(4) Agencies with access to external electronic mail systems shall ensure that Federal records sent or received on these systems are preserved in the appropriate recordkeeping system and that reasonable steps are taken to capture available transmission and receipt data needed by the agency for recordkeeping purposes.

(5) Some e-mail systems provide calendars and task lists for users. These may meet the definition of Federal record. Calendars that meet the definition of Federal records are to be managed in accordance with the provisions of General Records Schedule 23, Item 5.

(6) Draft documents that are circulated on electronic mail systems may be records if they meet the criteria specified in 36 CFR 1222.34.

(b) Agencies shall consider the following criteria when developing procedures for the maintenance of electronic mail records in appropriate recordkeeping systems, regardless of format.

(1) Recordkeeping systems that include electronic mail messages must:

(i) Provide for the grouping of related records into classifications according to the nature of the business purposes the records serve;

(ii) Permit easy and timely retrieval of both individual records and files or other groupings of related records;

(iii) Retain the records in a usable format for their required retention period as specified by a NARA-approved records schedule;

(iv) Be accessible by individuals who have a business need for information in the system;

(v) Preserve the transmission and receipt data specified in agency instructions; and

(vi) Permit transfer of permanent records to the National Archives and Records Administration (see 36 CFR 1228.188 and 36 CFR 1234.32(a)).

(2) Agencies shall not store the recordkeeping copy of electronic mail messages that are Federal records only on the electronic mail system, unless the system has all of the features specified in paragraph (b)(1) of this section. If the electronic mail system is not designed to be a recordkeeping system, agencies shall instruct staff on how to copy Federal records from the electronic mail system to a recordkeeping system.

(c) Agencies that maintain their electronic mail records electronically shall move or copy them to a separate electronic recordkeeping system unless their system has the features specified in paragraph (b)(1) of this section. Because they do not have the features specified in paragraph (b)(1) of this section, backup tapes should not be used for recordkeeping purposes. Agencies may retain records from electronic mail systems in an off-line electronic storage format (such as optical disk or magnetic tape) that meets the requirements described at 36 CFR 1234.30(a). Agencies that retain permanent electronic mail records scheduled for transfer to the National Archives shall either store them in a format and on a medium that conforms to the requirements concerning transfer at 36 CFR 1228.188 or shall maintain the ability to convert the records to the required format and medium at the time transfer is scheduled.

(d) Agencies that maintain paper files as their recordkeeping systems shall print their electronic mail records and the related transmission and receipt data specified by the agency.

* * * * *

This section was formerly designated as 36 CFR 1234.30.

§ 1234.32. Retention and disposition of electronic records.

Agencies shall establish policies and procedures to ensure that electronic records and their documentation are retained as long as needed by the Government. These retention procedures shall include provisions for:

(a) Scheduling the disposition of all electronic records, as well as related documentation and indexes, by applying General Records Schedules (particularly GRS 20 or GRS 23) as appropriate for Records Disposition Authority, to NARA (see part 1228 of this chapter). The information in electronic information systems, including those operated for the Government by a contractor, shall be scheduled as soon as possible but no later than one year after implementation of the system.

(b) Transferring a copy of the electronic records and any related documentation and indexes to the National Archives at the time specified in the records disposition schedule in accordance with instructions found in § 1228.188 of this chapter. Transfer may take place at an earlier date if convenient for both the agency and the National Archives and Records Administration.

(c) Establishing procedures for regular recopying, reformatting, and other necessary maintenance to ensure the retention and usability of electronic records throughout their authorized life cycle (see § 123.428).

(d) Electronic mail records may not be deleted or otherwise disposed of without prior disposition authority from NARA (44 U.S.C. 3303a). This applies to the original version of the record that is sent or received on the electronic mail system and any copies that have been transferred to a recordkeeping system. See 36 CFR part 1228 for records disposition requirements.

(1) Disposition of records on the electronic mail system. When an agency has taken the necessary steps to retain the record in a recordkeeping system, the identical version that remains on the user's screen or in the user's mailbox has no continuing value. Therefore, NARA has authorized deletion of the version of the record on the electronic mail system under General Records Schedule 20, Item 14, after the record has been preserved in a recordkeeping system along with all appropriate transmission data.

(2) Records in recordkeeping systems. The disposition of electronic mail records that have been transferred to an appropriate recordkeeping system is governed by the records schedule or schedules that control the records in that system. If the records in the system are not scheduled, the agency shall follow the procedures at 36 CFR part 1228.

36 CFR 1234.34.

§ 1234.34. Destruction of electronic records.

Electronic records may be destroyed only in accordance with a records disposition schedule approved by the Archivist of the United States, including General Records Schedules. At a minimum each agency shall ensure that:

(a) Electronic records scheduled for destruction are disposed of in a manner that ensures protection of any sensitive proprietary, or national security information.

(b) Magnetic recording media previously used for electronic records containing sensitive, proprietary, or national security information are not reused if the previously recorded information can be compromised by reuse in any way.

(c) Agencies shall establish and implement procedures that specifically address the destruction of electronic records generated by individuals employing electronic mail.

***See Retention of Other Electronic Records* below.**

RETENTION OF ELECTRONIC MAIL

Most larger organizations have established electronic mail systems. Electronic messages can be sent within the electronic mail network, or between the network and other computers through modems. Once created and sent, these electronic messages will often remain available on the system for many years, until the sender or recipient exercises the option to destroy the electronic records. Electronic mail messages may be printed onto paper at the user's option.

Information system managers generally develop elaborate procedures to backup and preserve the electronic mail records for many years. The backups can be used to reconstruct the electronic records in case of system failure or inadvertent destruction of records. Even after the original electronic records have been removed from the primary on-line storage media, many years of electronic mail history remain available on magnetic tapes.

Unfortunately, organizations rarely determine the records retention period for electronic mail. Most believe that "longer is better."

When individuals communicate via electronic mail, they often utilize "loose" language that may be appropriate for internal conversations but would be totally inappropriate for formal written documents. Some people use verbiage that reflects personal opinions or biases, believing that electronic mail is personal or private.

Court cases have now confirmed that electronic mail is neither personal nor private. Electronic mail messages can legitimately be reviewed and used by supervisors without infringing on the rights of employees.

During litigation or government investigation, all electronic files of an organization are subject to subpoena and review by the other party. Electronic mail messages will be treated like records of the organization — reflecting the position and actions taken by the organization! It is possible for the other party to require an organization to examine the entire electronic mail history to identify all communications between certain individuals or related to certain subjects. If electronic mail records have been backed-up over several years, this would represent a significant burden, and a significant legal risk.

The informal nature of the electronic mail messages could also be harmful to the organization. Messages and "loose" language could easily be taken out of context by judges or regulators, leading to inappropriate conclusions and potentially damaging conclusions.

Electronic mail rarely represents the "official" position of the organization. These communications reflect preliminary thought or ideas, have not been reviewed by the organization and typically only reflect the personal opinion of the parties involved. Yet, since employees of the organization created these communications, courts and regulatory agencies can construe these records to reflect the organizational view.

Electronic mail messages should automatically be erased from the system after a short period of time — 15 to 30 days. Backup tapes of the electronic mail should also be destroyed within this period.

Some individuals may need to preserve electronic messages for a longer period of time. The system can allow users to select an option to preserve selected messages for an additional 15 to 30 days.

Alternatively, selected messages can be "formalized" and converted into an official company record by either moving the records to a special electronic storage area on the computer or producing paper prints. The electronic method would require some formal activity such as assigning a record series or records retention code to the records or otherwise identifying the records as official organization records.

Electronic mail systems generally allow the transmission of messages to multiple locations. Rather than reproducing the electronic file at each location, the electronic record is typically maintained at one location on disk but made accessible to multiple users. Other systems may replicate the electronic message in the other locations. The rules established above for electronic mail messages must apply to all locations containing the message.

The discipline of managing electronic mail can readily be accomplished within a network. The problem occurs when stand-alone or multiple networks communicate messages. In these cases, actual copies of the electronic mail message could exist in multiple locations.

Within an organization, procedures can be established to control the retention of each electronic mail message at the source. Even company-operated stand-alone microcomputers could contain an "executive program" or other software product that imposes records retention discipline similar to that discussed for the electronic mail networks. For example, all company-purchased microcomputers could contain identical electronic mail software that would automatically erase electronic mail messages (even those transmitted to or received from an outside source) after the requisite period of time. Additionally, the procedures for formalizing records or converting electronic mail records to official company records could also be incorporated.

An organization, however, has no control over electronic mail messages created by or sent to computer systems outside the organization. This case is similar to when an outside organization creates a document and then submits it to your organization. Both your organization and the outside one would maintain a set of records according to their respective records retention programs.

Due to the potential legal risks associated with electronic mail messages, special care should be taken for messages sent outside the organization. Perhaps, only official company records should be sent outside your organization — regardless of whether the records are in paper or electronic form.

Retention of Other Electronic Records

***See also Retention of Electronic Mail* above**

Information is created and maintained in many forms: paper, microfilm, computer, and optical disk. When establishing a legally valid records management program, most organizations realize that all records, not just paper and microfilm records, must be included. A records retention schedule establishes the retention period for all records, regardless of form. Records Management principles such as records retention and official version designation (Office of Record) also apply to electronic records.

The discussion below applies traditional records management concepts of "record" and "non-record" (work-in-progress) status to help determine the retention of computer records.

The computer industry and the courts refer to all computer information as "records." For purposes of evidence, all computer records would be subject to subpoena by the adverse party under rules of discovery. This could include computer records related to the general ledger, communications in the electronic mail system, or even the word processing files used to create documents.

From an organization's perspective, however, some of these so-called "records" are really tools used to create official company records, not the official records themselves. Computer information may be just "work-in-progress" to facilitate the preparation or revision of the final printed paper documents. For example, computer information such as word processing files are merely tools or work-in-progress used to prepare drafts and the final official paper records. The author does not intend for the work-in-progress to be reviewed by others, to be treated as official records, nor to reflect the official position of the organization. Similarly, electronic mail records and voice mail records provide a convenient substitute for non-documented verbal communication. In short, some of these "computer records" only represent a step in the process of creating official company records.

In order to apply records management principles to computer information, you first determine which computer information is a "record" and which is a "non-record." You may elect to establish some of the following principles:

- Electronic mail is a non-record unless converted to records by some formal process.
- Voice mail is always a non-record.
- Word processing files and superseded printed drafts are non-records. The final printed outputs are records.
- One set of computer data containing accounting and tax information plus one copy of the visible output (e.g., printed report or computer output microfilm) are records under the Internal Revenue Service's Revenue Procedure 91-59.
- Computer backups and other duplicate files are non-records.
- Databases and other data compilations that are used for multiple purposes are records.

The exact implementation will vary for each organization.

When computer information is characterized as "record" material, it must be retained according to your organization's records retention schedule. When computer information is characterized as "non-record" material, it can be destroyed at the discretion of the user — generally, after a relatively short period of time or after the official record is produced.

Some common types of computer records are discussed below.

VOICE MAIL

Voice mail is similar to electronic mail except that the messages consist of voice communication rather than typewritten communication. Voice mail consists of even more informal messages than electronic mail. The potential for misinterpretation or use of loose language is even greater.

Voice mail is typically used to communicate short messages within an organization when the individual is not available to receive a telephone call. Procedures should generally be established to redirect or transcribe voice mail messages when an individual is unavailable for an extended period of time.

Voice mail, including all backups, should automatically be erased within the same 15 to 30 day period. Due to the short-term nature of voice mail, no procedures should be established to allow voice mail records to be formalized nor preserved like electronic mail records for a longer period of time.

ELECTRONIC TAX RECORDS

See also Requirements of the Internal Revenue Service earlier in this chapter.

Most organizations now utilize computers as part of their accounting system. Accounting transactions are recorded in the regular course of business and incorporated into the general ledger and other reports that reflect the status of the accounting system.

In Revenue Ruling 71-20, the Internal Revenue Service recognized that computer records meet the requirements for recordkeeping under the Internal Revenue Code. Revenue Procedure 91-59 specifies that taxpayers utilizing computer records must maintain the computer records in both electronic ("machine sensible") and visible format (paper or microfilm) for the period of time they are subject to a tax audit. A taxpayer may be asked to produce the electronic records in a form that is readable on a current computer system and make that data available to the IRS auditor. For this legal reason, computer records related to accounting and tax matters should be treated as official company records.

Taxpayers should then maintain the electronic records related to tax matters for the period of time they are subject to tax audit. According to Title 26, United States Code, Section 6501, the Internal Revenue Service may audit you for the following periods:

- within three years after you file a tax return for normal circumstances,
- within six years after you file a tax return if you understate your gross income by 25% or more, and
- indefinitely, in case of false return, willful attempt to evade tax, no return or extension by agreement.

Most organizations have established a records retention period of six years (and sometimes even the traditional seven years) to protect themselves during the most likely time period during which an audit could occur. This time period must be extended if the taxpayer signs an agreement to extend the audit with the Internal Revenue Service. The electronic version of records subject to tax review will normally be maintained for the full records retention period.

Revenue Procedure 91-59 places a burden on taxpayers related to the preservation of electronic records. Taxpayers must maintain the electronic records for the requisite period but also must make the records available on a current computer system. This burden is exceedingly difficult because as taxpayers will usually convert to newer, perhaps incompatible technologies over time. After a period of just a few years, the organization may not have equipment or software that can read the old tapes. Even if the equipment and software exist, magnetic tapes start to deteriorate and may become unreadable after a few years, even if the tapes are properly stored and periodically rewound.

With the increased use of electronic data interchange, attention to the retention requirements for electronic records becomes even more important. Revenue Procedure 91-59 recognizes electronic data interchange records and specifies that these records may be retained in electronic form unless a visible record is requested by a tax auditor. The taxpayer will be responsible for ensuring the continued preservation and retention of these electronic records for the full period they are subject to the administration of any tax law.

Other than this revenue procedure, no other legal provision known to this author requires an organization to maintain both the electronic and visible form of the same information. You may, therefore, maintain records in any form unless the law either specifies the form or restricts the forms that can be used. In the case of tax records, however, you must maintain both the electronic and visible version of the same information.

DATABASES

Databases may consist of a number of files and fields of data that provide useful information to the organization. Typically, databases are modified over time through the addition, deletion, or modification of records. Reports are periodically prepared to reflect information from the databases that may be useful for specific purposes. Due to the large volume of information typically maintained in databases, reports rarely reflect "all" the information found on the database. Well-operated systems will provide periodic backups to restore databases in case of accidental erasure or disaster.

Many databases contain tax-related information. Their records retention period will be established based upon the tax issues raised above.

Organizations maintain some databases for reasons other than tax. The information could include mailing lists, customer information, marketing information, parts inventory, etc. Since reports typically do not reflect the entire content of the database, the electronic form of the database contains different information than the visible reports. Regardless, the electronic databases are often more useful than the paper reports. For this reason, visible reports are not equivalent to electronic databases.

For records retention purposes, most organizations will want to uniquely define a database as an official record of the organization, even though it is a computer record. The retention period might appropriately be established as "until superseded (SUP)" to reflect that only the current version needs to be maintained. Backups can then be destroyed after a relatively short period of time such as one month. Other organizations may elect to maintain a "snapshot" of the database in electronic form on an annual basis and retain the snapshot for a designated retention period to reflect user or operational needs. For example, the annual snapshot of the database may be appropriate to determine the state of certain activity at the close of previous years.

WORD PROCESSING

Many organizational documents are prepared using word processing. A draft of the document is generally typed into the word processing system from hand-written notes or other materials, or transcribed from automated dictation devices. The word processing document is then printed and revised until the final printed version is accepted by the author.

For records retention purposes, the original notes and recorded media from dictation should be considered non-record material or work-in-progress. This version should be destroyed in a relatively short period of time after the final draft has been accepted. Similarly, successive drafts of a document and the successive revisions of the electronic word processing file should be considered non-record or work-in-progress. Only the final approved, paper record should be considered an official organization document.

If the final product of the word processing process is a communication in an electronic mail system, the communication will only become an official record of the organization if formalized as discussed.

For operational reasons, you may want to maintain some of the electronic-word processing files for extended periods of time to facilitate the revision of drafts. These decisions should be made based upon the importance of the final document produced and the likelihood of revision or use of the material for other purposes. The word processing operator would then destroy the computer version when it is no longer needed.

Lawyers often argue for the preservation of multiple drafts of contracts. They argue that problems with a final contract can often be resolved by determining the party's intent through the use of previous drafts. In some cases, the final agreement fails to include provisions that had been included and approved in previous drafts. Other attorneys argue that the "Parole Evidence Rule" prohibits the consideration of any evidence in court outside of the final written document of the parties. In fact, most contracts contain a clause that prohibits the consideration of previous drafts or other information that has not been incorporated into this final written document.

To meet the needs of attorneys, it may be appropriate for the Legal Department to maintain multiple, printed drafts of contracts as part of the final contract file. This decision must be made based upon the needs of the attorneys and experience in this area. But versions of the computer files related to each draft should not be kept — only the most current version.

Word processing computer information should be treated differently than databases. The computer information from a word processing file is generally printed letter-for-letter onto a final paper document. In essence, the paper document "mirrors" the information in the word processing systems so only the most useful version — the printed, paper version — should be kept.

ELECTRONIC SIGNATURES

As organizations develop electronic recordkeeping systems, they will need to rely more on electronic signatures. A few regulations now address specific requirements for electronic signatures.

The Federal Acquisition Regulations permit contractors to maintain electronic reproductions of signatures in place of the originals:

CHAPTER 1 — FEDERAL ACQUISITION REGULATION

PART 4 — ADMINISTRATIVE MATTERS

SUBPART 4.7 — CONTRACTOR RECORDS RETENTION

48 CFR 4.703

§ 4.703 Policy.

* * * * *

(c) Nothing in this section shall be construed to preclude a contractor from duplicating or storing original records in electronic form unless they contain significant information not shown on the record copy. Original records need not be maintained or produced in an audit if the contractor or subcontractor provides photographic or electronic images of the original records and meets the following requirements:

(1) The contractor or subcontractor has established procedures to ensure that the imaging process preserves accurate images of the original records, including signatures and other written or graphic images, and that the imaging process is reliable and secure so as to maintain the integrity of the records.

The Securities and Exchange Commission requires electronic submission of certain documents and has established specific procedures for electronic signatures.

TITLE 17 — COMMODITY AND SECURITY EXCHANGES

PART 232 — REGULATION S-T — GENERAL RULES AND REGULATIONS FOR ELECTRONIC FILINGS

PREPARATION OF ELECTRONIC SUBMISSIONS

17 CFR 232.302.

§ 232.302 Signatures.

(a) Signatures to or within an electronic submission shall be in typed form rather than manual format. When used in connection with an electronic filing, the term "signature" means an electronic entry in the form of a magnetic impulse or other form of computer data compilation of any letter or series of letters comprising a name, executed, adopted or authorized as a signature.

(b) Each signatory to an electronic filing shall manually sign a signature page or other document authenticating, acknowledging or otherwise adopting his or her signature that appears in typed form within the electronic filing. Such document shall be executed before or at the time the electronic filing is made and shall be retained by the filer for a period of five years. Upon request, an electronic filer shall furnish to the Commission or its staff a copy of any or all documents retained pursuant to this section.

(c) Where the Commission's rules require a registrant to furnish to a national securities exchange or national securities association paper copies of a document filed with the Commission in electronic format, signatures to such paper copies may be in typed form.

The Federal Communications Commission has established procedures for filing electronic applications that recognizes electronic signatures.

TITLE 47 — TELECOMMUNICATIONS

PART 1 — PRACTICE AND PROCEDURE

47 CFR 1.743.

§ 1.743 Who may sign applications.

(a) Except as provided in paragraph (b) of this section, applications, amendments thereto, and related statements of fact required by the Commission must be signed by the applicant, if the applicant is an individual; by one of the partners, if the applicant is a partnership; by an officer or duly authorized employee, if the applicant is a corporation; or by a member who is an officer, if the applicant is an unincorporated association. Applications, amendments, and related statements of fact filed on behalf of eligible government entities such as states and territories of the United States, their political subdivisions, the District of Columbia, and units of local government, including incorporated municipalities, must be signed by a duly elected or appointed official who is authorized to do so under the laws of the applicable jurisdiction.

* * * * *

(e) "Signed," as used in this section, means an original hand-written signature, except that by public notice in the Federal Register the Common Carrier Bureau may allow signature by any symbol executed or adopted by the applicant with the intent that such symbol be a signature, including symbols formed by computer-generated electronic impulses.

Other agencies have developed schemes which require specific procedures. The Environmental Protection Agency has schemes in place which utilize personal identification numbers (PINs) as authentication for a variety of required information submissions. Under these schemes, parties desiring to utilize EDI for regulatory filings sign a contract agreeing that the PIN is their signature and agreeing to safeguard the PINs issued to the organization. Unlike the Securities and Exchange Commission, no paper signature need be created or retained under these schemes. The full text of the terms and conditions memorandum which constitutes the agreement to enter into the PIN scheme is reproduced in Appendix B of this volume at 40 CFR Part 80

The Food and Drug Administration, at 21 CFR part 11, has set forth protocols for use of electronic signatures. While precautions to ensure security and authenticity are naturally deemed to be important, FDA has not specified the technology or procedures needed for compliance. Rather, criteria for acceptable compliance are listed and details left open, presumably to the discretion of the user or subject to negotiation between the user and FDA.

Chapter 4 Legal Requirements for Electronic Imaging Systems

This chapter considers technologies used to store *image* information. When the same technologies are used to store computer *data*, the requirements of Chapter 3 apply.

A number of organizations have implemented or will be implementing "electronic imaging systems (EIS)" to store images of documents on optical disks and other high density storage devices. These systems are capable of scanning documents, converting the images into electronic form, storing the images, and rapidly retrieving them. Experienced observers expect this technology to gain wide acceptance in the marketplace as an alternative to traditional microfilm or paper-based systems.

Electronic imaging systems may offer effective solutions to pressing information management problems. Organizations in both the public and private sector continue to explore the feasibility of adopting this technology to meet their own needs.

Some believe that the legal questions regarding this technology may present obstacles to its widespread acceptance. Will records maintained by this technology be admissible in evidence? Can records required by state and federal regulatory agencies be maintained using this technology? Can government agencies use this technology for their own purposes? What legal principles will apply to this technology in countries outside the United States?

Some jurisdictions have enacted laws addressing electronic imaging and optical disk records as evidence. Several other states have addressed the use of this technology by state government agencies.

Evidence

Concerns have been expressed about the legality of electronic images, including specifically the admissibility of these reproductions in evidence and their acceptance by government agencies. The courts have not yet reviewed the legal questions of records produced from electronic imaging systems. But numerous court decisions support the admissibility of computer records and reproductions using other technologies.

Until the courts specifically address this issue, what should you do in the interim? Should you wait until a body of law evolves for electronic imaging like it did for microfilm and computer records? Should you postpone buying a system until new legislation is enacted, or the technology has passed judicial review in a number of test cases? Should you wait several years to take advantage of the improved speed of retrieval and information sharing offered by this new technology?

The acceptance of this new technology depends upon the comfort level of the judges and administrators. It took several hundreds of years for the courts to accept paper records in evidence, approximately 40 years to accept microfilm, approximately 10 years to accept computer records. It will take a few more years for courts to feel comfortable with electronic imaging systems and digitized records — based on comfort level, alone. The *law* accepts the technology now!

Those using electronic imaging systems should carefully establish and follow procedures designed to ensure the trustworthiness of the image information and provide a detailed audit trail. You can capitalize on the benefits of this new technology if the system is properly designed and implemented to meet the anticipated legal requirements of tomorrow.

Electronic imaging technology is a reproduction technology that produces copies of records similar to photocopies, microfilm and facsimile. All mechanical or electronic reproduction techniques exhibit the same three characteristics.

- *Image Capture.* A photographic, electronic or other process to identify and capture the image of the original document.

- *Image Manipulation.* A photographic, electronic or other process that transforms the captured image into a format for storing and reproducing the image.

- *Visible Reproduction.* A photographic, printing or other process that converts the manipulated image into visible form.

An electronic imaging system, for example, utilizes an electronic scanner for image recognition, computer software, memory and disk storage for image manipulation and graphic terminals and laser printers to make the image visible. An electronic imaging system is therefore similar to other reproduction technologies. Like all other reproduction technologies, the image will be manipulated and converted from one form to another. As long as the final reproduced image "accurately reproduces the original," the law of evidence in the United States would allow the visible records produced by any technology to be admissible in evidence.

Most organizations recognize that courts will require paper prints of duplicate records. Even though microfilm would be admissible in evidence in court, few judges will be willing to accept the film itself, even when they are provided with a reader/printer. Instead, they will insist that paper prints be prepared because they feel more comfortable with paper records.

***See* Appendix A for the text of these Uniform Laws.**

UNIFORM LAWS

While traditional microfilm and computer laws do not specifically mention optical disk storage, these laws can serve as the basis for the admissibility of records maintained with this technology because it has characteristics of duplicate records such as microfilm and yet utilizes computers.

In the United States, two uniform laws clearly establish the basis for admitting records produced from electronic imaging systems into evidence: The Uniform Rules of Evidence and The Uniform Photographic Copies of Business and Public Records as Evidence Act (UPA). Both laws would admit duplicate records into evidence if they accurately reproduce the original.

Forty four states have either adopted the UPA or the Uniform Rules of Evidence. Either law would be available to permit the admissibility of records produced by electronic imaging systems.

Uniform Photographic Copies of Business and Public Records as Evidence Act (UPA)

***See* Chapter 2 for details regarding the Uniform Photographic Copies of Business and Public Records as Evidence Act.**

While the UPA deals primarily with the problems of microfilm or copier reproduction, it can be applied without change to the electronic imaging technology and storage of digitized records.

To qualify as a reproduction under this law, it must be produced:

> . . . by any photographic, photostatic, microfilm, micro-card, miniature photographic, or any other process which accurately reproduces or forms a durable medium for so reproducing the original . . . ."

The law recognizes the use of any process which "accurately reproduces . . . the original."

Electronic imaging systems basically convert the original document into a series of electronic "dots" (comparable to "bits" in a computer). These electronic "dots" are compressed and then stored on an optical disk or other high density storage media. The image information can be read from the storage media and either displayed on a high resolution terminal or printed on paper. This paper image "accurately reproduces . . . the original" and would be considered a duplicate copy under the UPA. The optical disks, themselves, or other high-density storage devices, and the associated technology merely serve as the vehicle for storing the image until it is requested, and would not have any status in the law.

The UPA explicitly permits you to destroy the original documents, provided that the duplicates are produced in the regular course of business. This is particularly important with an electronic imaging system because one of the reasons for employing the technology is to reduce the costs of storing paper.

Uniform Rules of Evidence

***See* Chapter 2 for the analysis of the Uniform Rules of Evidence as it applies to microfilm and duplicate copies.**

The Uniform Rules of Evidence also addresses duplicate records, such as microfilm and computer records. Rule 1001(4) specifies that a duplicate is any record produced "from the same matrix" as the original (i.e., dot-for-dot transformation from the original to the duplicate) or by "other equivalent techniques which accurately reproduce the original." Since electronic imaging systems meet the stated criteria, these duplicate records would be admissible in evidence, under Rule 1003, just like microfilm records. The printed output from the electronic imaging system would clearly be acceptable as a duplicate record under the Uniform Rules of Evidence. The optical disks or other storage devices might academically be considered duplicate records, but could not themselves be introduced in evidence.

The Uniform Rules of Evidence would also accept the records prepared by an electronic imaging system as computer records. Rule 1001(1) states that a "writing or recording" consists of information produced by "electronic recording, or other form of data compilation."

Under the definition of original records in Rule 1001(3), the original record of "data stored in the computer" (such as the image stored in an electronic imaging system) would be defined as "any printout or other output readable by sight, shown to reflect the data accurately."

A paper printout or microfiche produced by a computer output microfilm device, or a display of the image on a screen, would meet the requirements of the rule. Again, the actual storage media would not be admissible.

Because of the unique and dual nature of visible records produced by this technology, the Uniform Rules of Evidence leads to a bizarre and contradictory conclusion. Under Rule 1001(4) related to duplicates, the electronic image is considered a duplicate copy. Under Rule 1001(3) as it applies to computer records, the visible output is an original, even though it was produced from the "duplicate," electronic image.

Although some courts may find it unpalatable to conclude that an "original" can be produced from a "duplicate" under the law, they would be required to accept visible records produced from the system which accurately reflects those images. Perhaps the Uniform Rules of Evidence could be revised to read: "if data are stored in the computer or similar device, any printout or other output readable by sight, shown to reflect the data accurately, will be treated as an original."

Authentication and Identification

***See* Chapter 1 for details related to authentication and identification of all records admitted in evidence. *See also* Chapter 2 for discussion of certificates of authenticity.**

Under the Uniform Rules of Evidence and the UPA, duplicate or computer records must be satisfactorily identified and authenticated before they are admissible in evidence. In the case of electronic imaging systems, the identification and authentication information could be stored with each individual image. It is possible to scan and digitize a certificate of authenticity, similar to microfilm, and store that information in sequence with the scanned images. When the images are viewed in sequential order, the certification would appear in its proper place.

The records could also be identified and authenticated by showing that the process or system produces an accurate result. Strict procedures must be followed with this technology to alleviate concerns presented in the next section. There is, in particular, the potential for forging or altering signatures. By providing written procedures, training, and audits, you can ensure that proper procedures are followed and that the integrity of the information is preserved.

OTHER STATE LAWS RELATED TO ELECTRONIC IMAGING SYSTEMS

***See* "Government" is this chapter for additional state laws that affect admissibility of government records in evidence.**

Some states have modified their laws of evidence to specifically address optical disk or electronic image management systems. Missouri, Louisiana, Georgia and Virginia modified existing laws affecting microfilm and duplicate copies as evidence to include phrases such as "optical image", "electronic transfer to other material using . . . electronic processes," "electronic digitizing process" and "copies from optical disks."

Georgia Code Annotated.

TITLE 24. EVIDENCE.

CHAPTER 5. BEST EVIDENCE RULE.

§ 24-5-26. Reproductions made in regular course of business admissible; when enlargements or facsimiles admitted.

Any photostatic, microphotographic, photographic, or optical image reproduction of any original writing or record made in the regular course of business to preserve the writing or record shall be admissible in evidence in any proceeding in any court of this state and in any proceeding before any board, bureau, department, commission, or agency of the state, in lieu of and without accounting for the original of such writing or record. Any enlargement or facsimile of such reproduction shall likewise be admissible if the original of the reproduction is in existence and available for inspection under direction of the court or the agency conducting the proceeding.

Louisiana Revised Statutes.

TITLE 44. PUBLIC RECORDS AND RECORDERS

§ 139. Microfilm and electronic digitized records; use as evidence.

A. All persons and public bodies having custody or control of any public records of the state of Louisiana or any of its subdivisions may utilize any appropriate form of the microphotographic process, or an electronic digitizing process capable of reproducing an unalterable image of the original source document, for the recordation, filing, and preservation of all existing public records, forms, and documents or records, forms, and documents hereafter accumulated which pertain to the their functions and operations in order to maintain efficient and economical records management programs and to conserve storage space, provided that the use of such microphotographic or electronic digitizing processes are not otherwise prohibited by law and that all microforms produced comply with standards established by the division of archives, records management, and history of the Department of State in accordance with the provisions of R.S. 44:415.

B. Any microfilm or electronically digitized copy, when satisfactorily identified, shall be deemed to be an original itself, and shall be admissible in evidence in all courts or administrative proceedings in any agency, whether the original document is in existence or not, and an enlargement or facsimile of a reproduction is likewise admissible in evidence, if the original reproduction is in existence and available for inspection under direction of the court or the administrative agency. Original records shall remain subject to subpoena.

Missouri Revised Statutes.

TITLE 8. PUBLIC RECORDS.

CHAPTER 109. TRANSCRIBING AND REBINDING.

§ 109.120. Records reproduced by photostatic process — costs — marginal releases prohibited.

1. The head of any business, industry, profession, occupation or calling, or the head of any state, county or municipal department, commission, bureau or board may cause any and all records kept by such official, department, commission, bureau, board or business to be photographed, microphotographed, photostated or transferred to other material using photographic, video, or electronic processes and the judges and justices of the several courts of record within this state may cause all closed case files more than five years old to be photographed, microphotographed, photostated or transferred to other material using photographic, video, or electronic processes. Such reproducing material shall be of durable material and the device used to reproduce the records shall be such as to accurately reproduce and perpetuate the original records in all details.

*****

§ 109.130. Reproduced records deemed original, when.

Such reproduction of the original records shall be deemed to be an original record for all purposes provided that the reproduction is equal in resolution to microfilm produced under those standards set forth in subsection 4 of section 109.241 and shall be admissible in evidence in all courts or administrative agencies. A facsimile, exemplification, or certified copy thereof shall, for all purposes recited in sections 109.120 and 109.140, be deemed to be a transcript, exemplification or certified copy of the original.

Virginia Code Annotated.

TITLE 8.01. — CIVIL REMEDIES AND PROCEDURE.

CHAPTER 14. EVIDENCE.

Article 2. Laws, Public Records, and Copies of Original Records as Evidence.

8.01-391. Copies of originals as evidence.

* * * * *

C. If any business or member of a profession or calling in the regular course of business or activity has made any record, and again in the regular course of business has caused any or all of such record to be copied, the copy shall be as admissible in evidence as the original, whether the original exists or not, provided that such copy is satisfactorily identified and authenticated as a true copy both by the custodian of such record and by the person to whom said custodian reports, if they be different, and is accompanied by a certificate that said person does in fact have the custody. Copies in the regular course of business shall be deemed to include reproduction at a later time, if done in good faith and without intent to defraud. The original of which a copy has been made may be destroyed in the regular course of business unless its preservation is required by law, or its validity has been questioned.

D. The introduction in an action of a copy under this section neither precludes the introduction or admission of the original nor the introduction of a copy or the original in another action.

E. Copy, as used in this section, shall be deemed to include photographs, microphotographs, photostats, microfilm, microcard, printouts or other reproductions of electronically stored data, or copies from optical disks or any other reproduction of an original from a process which forms a durable medium for its recording, storing, and reproducing.

The laws in Missouri and Louisiana are unique for those states. The Georgia and Virginia laws are based on the Uniform Photographic Copies of Business and Public Records as Evidence Act, although the exact language of both statutes is substantially different than the uniform wording.

Three of these laws require that the image be on a "durable medium" or "unalterable." These laws are stricter than the standards found in Georgia, the other states and the federal government, where the duplicate must only accurately reproduce the original. These three states however have stricter standards for all duplicate records, not just for electronic images or optical disk records.

CONCERNS ABOUT ELECTRONIC IMAGING TECHNOLOGY

To determine the impact of existing laws on this new technology, you should anticipate the problems which might create legal obstacles to its use. These are the same issues which must be dealt with in designing an electronic imaging system, even after the legality of the technology has been established.

- *The electronic image may not be an exact reproduction of the original.* Most scanners detect a maximum of 200 to 300 dots per inch (DPI) across a page. While the resolution is adequate to fully reproduce the image, it means that some dots from the original do not appear in the duplicate. While this may seem to be a major obstacle, other technologies such as microfilm or other duplication methods also fail to reproduce every dot contained in the original, but generally reproduce enough so that the image appears complete and readable. In fact, the quality of a digitized image may sometimes exceed the quality of a microfilm image.

  Although the dot-for-dot transformation from the original document to an electronic image may suffice for legal acceptance, most systems do not store the image in terms of a series of "electronic dots." Instead, after scanning, the image is compressed ten or more times using a technique called "run length encoding (RLE)." Besides reducing storage requirements, RLE also enables the image to be transmitted to terminals or remote locations much faster. The RLE version of the image can, however, be reconverted back into the dot version by applying the appropriate decompression algorithm.

  Although the stored version of the image will have been electronically compressed and cease to have the same attributes as the original image, the information and visual qualities of the displayed image are not altered. Because the law looks to the visual image, rather than the stored image, this concern may not be relevant.

- *Information contained in an image (such as a signature or text) can be removed or modified without a trace.* Once the image is stored in computer memory (either after scanning or retrieval from the storage media), sections of the image may be electronically modified by deleting information, inserting new information, or transferring information from other documents. The resulting final image can then be stored and the index pointers directed to the new image. While the original image might still exist on a non-erasable media, the index would reference only the revised image. With erasable media, the previous image can be removed without a trace.

While some believe the ability to alter the image may be the "kiss of death" for this technology, you should consider the analogy with computer records. Computer information can be added to, deleted, or modified on magnetic disk and the new version stored without any trace that changes have taken place. Yet, courts and regulatory agencies have already established the legal acceptance of computer records in judicial or administrative proceedings.

The pivotal issue is not the erasability of the media or potential for modification of the image, but the trustworthiness of the procedures which created the records. Courts and regulatory agencies will require written procedures, training, and audits confirming what has occurred to the information in the system.

See Chapter 2 for discussion of certificates of authenticity.

- *Electronic images cannot be certified in terms of authenticity like microfilm records*. Actually, certifications can be scanned and stored before and after each batch of scanned images. This procedure, however, might waste a substantial amount of storage space on the storage media.

  The certificate of authenticity, however, is not generally a requirement of the law. Computer records, for example, cannot readily be certified, and, yet, they are admissible in court and before regulatory agencies, if properly identified and authenticated. Records produced using electronic imaging systems can be introduced to the courts or regulatory agencies by showing that the process or system produces an accurate result.

- *Electronic images can be enhanced after scanning and before storage on the storage media*. Image enhancement creates the biggest concern in terms of the legal acceptance of this technology. Image enhancement enables the system to actually improve the image by sharpening line edges, removing stains or colored background, removing specks from the background, and filling in broken letters. The purpose of image enhancement is to make the information found in the original records more readable.

  The concerns related to image enhancement have prompted some systems designers to suggest that the original images be microfilmed. Alternatively, an unaltered version of the original image can be scanned and stored on optical disk prior to image enhancement. While both procedures may facilitate the acceptance of electronic images, they require substantial additional time and expense on the part of the user to create duplicates for legal purposes. These procedures may not be necessary in the first place.

The argument can be made that the image enhancement algorithms merely improve the image rather than change the information. Since the information contained in a record ultimately is more important than its appearance, the courts or regulatory agencies may not object too strenuously. An audit trail must be maintained indicating the types of image enhancement algorithms used and, perhaps, the percentage of change that resulted when the algorithm was applied. The key, again, will be the "trustworthiness" of the procedures employed to generate the electronic image.

- *Optical disk is not considered an archival storage medium.* Some have expressed concern that the law requires information to be maintained on an archival media such as microfilm. In reality, the issue related to archival quality or longevity of the information has no relationship to its legal acceptance. The information must merely last as long as required by law or just long enough to be admitted in evidence. If a visible record can be made, no one really cares that the media will last for a hundred years.

  The Uniform Photographic Copies of Business and Public Records As Evidence Act and the Uniform Rules of Evidence do not require microfilm to be archival but merely require that the technology "accurately reproduces . . . the original." Magnetic media are not archival, and visible records produced from computer data are accepted in both courts and administrative proceedings. Even if the optical disk begins to deteriorate prematurely, the information can be transferred electronically with no loss of quality (as compared to microfilm which loses 10 to 20 percent of its quality when duplicated).

USING ELECTRONIC IMAGES IN COURT

In one trial court proceeding, records were scanned using an electronic imaging system and presented to witnesses on computer terminals. Most witnesses were reluctant to identify the documents as the ones they signed, prepared or used. As a result, the court was unable to use records from the optical disk system in evidence.

While some may argue that this case indicates electronic imaging records are not admissible into evidence, nothing could be further from the truth. In reality, the judge and attorneys felt quite comfortable with the legal status of these records. The problem was a psychological one, rather than a legal one. Witnesses were forced to testify from records displayed on a screen rather than in the familiar paper format. These people had never seen the records on a screen and, therefore, felt uncomfortable confirming their authenticity. Similarly, we would expect that witnesses would have difficulty testifying from a reader displaying a microfilm image, even though the microfilm is clearly legal as evidence.

Other trial courts have successfully used electronic imaging technology to present documentary evidence. Participating judges believe that this technology will simplify the presentation to documents to the court and witness, speed up the trial and reduce costs. Parties must cooperate when using this technology and proper procedures must be established.

Most judges and witness will need a paper version of the electronic images for their own use. We can expect little opposition to records produced by optical disk systems provided that the paper prints are submitted to the court. Your decision to use the technology will then be based on the cost and operational issues, not legal ones.

THE NEED FOR A TEST CASE

Some people have indicated that a court "test case" would be necessary to establish the legality of records produced from electronic imaging systems for purposes of evidence. As of 1994, several trial courts have accepted records produced from electronic imaging systems. Since there have not been any reported problems with using the technology for evidence, no cases have yet been appealed. An appellate decision confirming the propriety of the technology for evidence constitutes the "test case" that skeptics still want before relying on the technology and destroying the paper records.

The Internal Revenue Service of the United States has considered the legal questions regarding the submission of optical disk records into evidence. In a memorandum dated September 4, 1987, the Associate Chief Counsel of Litigation for the Internal Revenue Service reviewed the concern of the Assistant Commissioner that a test case may be necessary to determine the admissibility of such records into evidence. In the memorandum, the Associate Chief Legal Counsel clearly indicated that no test case was necessary since operable laws (the Uniform Rules of Evidence and the UPA in the federal domain) would be adequate to ensure the admissibility of these records. The Internal Revenue Service is now developing an electronic imaging system to store tax returns.

Even if a test case did take place, the results would not be binding on a court in your state. For example, if the test case took place in California, the results would not be binding in any other court in the United States or in federal jurisdiction. It is also expected that such a decision would not be important enough for review by the Supreme Court of a state or by the Supreme Court of the United States. Similarly, a decision by one federal circuit court is not binding on any other circuit court.

A test case is not needed to establish the legality of optical disk records. The prevailing laws and rules of evidence are clear enough to establish legal principles regarding this technology that would be affirmed at trial or on appeal.

Regulation

Those jurisdictions that have adopted the UPA will permit records from an electronic imaging system to be maintained for regulatory purposes. The uniform law clearly states that a reproduction made under the law "is as admissible in evidence as the original itself in any judicial or administrative proceeding."

Normally, when state and federal regulatory agencies require that you keep records, you may keep them in any form, unless the agency states a specific form. Some agencies have developed requirements regarding the size, layout and quality of microfilm records. Few agencies have not yet adopted requirements related to electronic images.

In the absence of any specific regulatory requirements in this area, those states that have adopted the UPA would permit electronic images to be utilized for regulatory proceedings. Those states that have not adopted the UPA would also permit records to be maintained using this process, unless the regulatory agencies prohibit or restrict this practice.

The UPA has been adopted as a statute, rather than a regulation or rule of evidence. Regulatory agencies, therefore, could not impose regulations that prohibit the use of electronic imaging systems.

The UPA, however, does state that the original paper records may be destroyed after reproduction "unless its preservation is required by law." Since regulations are "laws," regulatory agencies could prohibit the destruction of the original paper records after they have been scanned by an optical disk system or unless the images conform to prescribed requirements. Such requirements would have to be explicitly stated to be enforceable.

FEDERAL RULES AND REGULATIONS

For a period of several years, most federal agencies refrained from issuing regulations explicitly authorizing the use of imaging technology and setting forth the conditions under which they would deem its use in keeping with good practice. In recent years, the trend has substantially changed. Many federal agencies, including such important entities as the Securities and Exchange Commission, the Nuclear Regulatory Commission and the Internal Revenue Service have weighed in with regulations authorizing the use of imaging for required recordkeeping and setting forth terms and conditions that they would deem acceptable.

Among the first to authorize imaging was the Nuclear Regulatory Commission. In 1988, the Commission recognized the use of optical disk records for holders of construction permits and licensees of nuclear reactors:

***See* Appendix B. for details regarding United State federal laws.Generic Letter 88-18 dated October 20, 1988 to all licensees of operating reactors and holders of construction permits**

PLANT RECORD STORAGE ON OPTICAL DISKS (GENERIC LETTER 88-18)

The NRC has been requested by two utilities and an NSSS to approve the use of optical disk document imaging systems for the storage and retrieval of record copies of quality assurance records. The purpose of this generic letter is to inform addressees that the staff approves the use of this method of recordkeeping when appropriate quality assurance controls are applied.

Appendix B of 10 CFR 50, under criterion XVII, "Quality Assurance Records," establishes requirements for a recordkeeping system, and chapter 17 of the Standard Review Plan (NUREG-0800) expounds on these requirements. The purpose of the recordkeeping system is to ensure that records are available when needed. ANSI N45.2.9-1974, "Requirements for Collection, Storage, and Maintenance of Quality Assurance Records for Nuclear Power Plants," as endorsed by Regulatory Guide 1.88 (Rev. 2) and Basic Requirements 17, Supplement 17S-1, and Appendix 17A-1 of ANSI/ASME-NQA-1 1983 edition, "Quality Assurance Program Requirements for Nuclear Facilities," as endorsed by Regulatory Guide 1.28 (Rev. 3) both describe quality assurance controls regarding records. Appropriate quality controls for an optical disk document imaging system include the following:

- The optical disk technology does not allow deletion or modification of record images.
- The image of each record is written onto two optical disks.
- The legibility of each record image is verified to ensure that the image is legible on both disks. If the image is illegible, the hard copy record is maintained as the record copy.
- One optical disk is stored in the document imaging system for on-line retrieval.
- The second (backup) optical disk is stored in a records storage facility meeting the requirements of ANSI N45.2.9-1974 for single copy storage or in a separate remote location.
- To ensure permanent retention of records, the records stored on an optical disk are acceptably copied onto a new optical disk before the manufacturer's certified useful life of the original disk is exceeded. This includes verification of the records so copied.
- Periodic random inspections of images stored on optical disks are performed to verify that there has been no degradation of image quality.
- If the optical disk imaging system in use is to be replaced by an incompatible new system, the records stored on the old system's disk are acceptably converted into the new system before the old system is taken out of service. This includes verification of the records so copied.

See Appendix B for details.

The Commodity Futures Trading Commission has also establishing a regulation addressing optical disk records. Their regulation, however, is limited to using the technology to store computer data — computer output laser disk (COLD) — in place of paper printouts or computer output microfilm. The regulation does not address maintaining electronic images of paper records.

In 1993, the Securities and Exchange Commission issued a "no-action letter" that grants regulated broker-dealers permission to use WORM ("write once, read many times") optical disks for storing required records. Language in the letter gave the indication that the agency deemed WORM to be synonymous with ablative technology.

In 1997, this no-action letter was effectively replaced by regulations codified in 17 CFR Part 240, which clarified the agency's position. The explicit WORM requirement, as well and the implied ablative requirement, are now gone. Instead, the new regulation requires that the media be nonrewritable and noneraseable, and the system conform to stated requirements:

17 CFR 240.17a-4

Preservation of Records and Reports of Certain Stabilizing Activities

§ 240.17a-4 Records to be preserved by certain exchange members, brokers and dealers.

* * * * *

(f) The records required to be maintained and preserved pursuant to Secs. 240.17a-3 and 240.17a-4 may be immediately produced or reproduced on "micrographic media" (as defined in this section) or by means of "electronic storage media" (as defined in this section) that meet the conditions set forth in this paragraph and be maintained and preserved for the required time in that form.

(1) For purposes of this section:

(i) The term micrographic media means microfilm or microfiche, or any similar medium; and

(ii) The term electronic storage media means any digital storage medium or system and, in the case of both paragraphs (f)(1)(i) and (f)(1)(ii) of this section, that meets the applicable conditions set forth in this paragraph (f).

(2) If electronic storage media is used by a member, broker, or dealer, it shall comply with the following requirements:

(i) The member, broker, or dealer must notify its examining authority designated pursuant to section 17(d) of the Act (15 U.S.C. 78q(d)) prior to employing electronic storage media. If employing any electronic storage media other than optical disk technology (including CD-ROM), the member, broker, or dealer must notify its designated examining authority at least 90 days prior to employing such storage media. In either case, the member, broker, or dealer must provide its own representation or one from the storage medium vendor or other third party with appropriate expertise that the selected storage media meets the conditions set forth in this paragraph (f)(2).

(ii) The electronic storage media must:

(A) Preserve the records exclusively in a non-rewriteable, non-erasable format;

(B) Verify automatically the quality and accuracy of the storage media recording process;

(C) Serialize the original and, if applicable, duplicate units of storage media, and time-date for the required period of retention the information placed on such electronic storage media; and

(D) Have the capacity to readily download indexes and records preserved on the electronic storage media to any medium acceptable under this paragraph (f) as required by the Commission or the self-regulatory organizations of which the member, broker, or dealer is a member.

(3) If a member, broker, or dealer uses micrographic media or electronic storage media, it shall:

(i) At all times have available, for examination by the staffs of the Commission and self-regulatory organizations of which it is a member, facilities for immediate, easily readable projection or production of micrographic media or electronic storage media images and for producing easily readable images.

(ii) Be ready at all times to provide, and immediately provide, any facsimile enlargement which the Commission or its representatives may request.

(iii) Store separately from the original, a duplicate copy of the record stored on any medium acceptable under Sec. 240.17a-4 for the time required.

(iv) Organize and index accurately all information maintained on both original and any duplicate storage media.

(A) At all times, a member, broker, or dealer must be able to have such indexes available for examination by the staffs of the Commission and the self-regulatory organizations of which the broker or dealer is a member.

(B) Each index must be duplicated and the duplicate copies must be stored separately from the original copy of each index.

(C) Original and duplicate indexes must be preserved for the time required for the indexed records.

(v) The member, broker, or dealer must have in place an audit system providing for accountability regarding inputting of records required to be maintained and preserved pursuant to Secs. 240.17a-3 and 240.17a-4 to electronic storage media and inputting of any changes made to every original and duplicate record maintained and preserved thereby.

(A) At all times, a member, broker, or dealer must be able to have the results of such audit system available for examination by the staffs of the Commission and the self-regulatory organizations of which the broker or dealer is a member.

(B) The audit results must be preserved for the time required for the audited records.

> (vi) The member, broker, or dealer must maintain, keep current, and provide promptly upon request by the staffs of the Commission or the self-regulatory organizations of which the member, broker, or broker-dealer is a member all information necessary to access records and indexes stored on the electronic storage media; or place in escrow and keep current a copy of the physical and logical file format of the electronic storage media, the field format of all different information types written on the electronic storage media and the source code, together with the appropriate documentation and information necessary to access records and indexes.
>
> (vii) For every member, broker, or dealer exclusively using electronic storage media for some or all of its record preservation under this section, at least one third party ("the undersigned"), who has access to and the ability to download information from the member's, broker's, or dealer's electronic storage media to any acceptable medium under this section, shall file with the designated examining authority for the member, broker, or dealer the following undertakings with respect to such records:
>
> The undersigned hereby undertakes to furnish promptly to the U.S. Securities and Exchange Commission ("Commission"), its designees or representatives, upon reasonable request, such information as is deemed necessary by the Commission's or designee's staff to download information kept on the broker's or dealer's electronic storage media to any medium acceptable under Rule 17a-4.
>
> Furthermore, the undersigned hereby undertakes to take reasonable steps to provide access to information contained on the broker's or dealer's electronic storage media, including, as appropriate, arrangements for the downloading of any record required to be maintained and preserved by the broker or dealer pursuant to Rules 17a-3 and 17a-4 under the Securities Exchange Act of 1934 in a format acceptable to the Commission's staff or its designee. Such arrangements will provide specifically that in the event of a failure on the part of a broker or dealer to download the record into a readable format and after reasonable notice to the broker or dealer, upon being provided with the appropriate electronic storage medium, the undersigned will undertake to do so, as the Commission's staff or its designee may request.

Regulated broker-dealers now have more discretion to select a technology that meets the criteria. In the absence of other guidance, perhaps systems can now be used that meet the technology by utilizing hardware, software or a combined set of safeguards. However, since these regulation still restrict the type of media used, those entities regulated by the SEC will not have the system design options available to other organizations.

IMPACT OF TAX REGULATIONS

See Chapter 2 for details related to IRS Revenue Ruling 81-46 affecting microfilm and Chapter 3 for details related to IRS Revenue Procedure 91-59 affecting data processing. _See also_ Appendix B for the full text of these IRS regulations. IRS has indicated that a future revenue procedure would address electronic imaging technology.

Prior to 1997, the Internal Revenue Service had not specifically indicated whether or not imaging technology was acceptable for the Service's purposes. Other statements such as Revenue Ruling 81-46 (Microfilm) or Revenue Procedure 91-59 (Data Processing), gave some guidance as to the Service's attitude, so taxpayers might reasonably have anticipated that both requirements should be followed, when appropriate, for this technology..

In 1997, the Internal Revenue Service stated its views on electronic imaging records in Revenue Procedure 97-22.

Revenue Procedure 97-22

Revenue Procedure 97-22 presents acceptable criteria for an electronic imaging system to be in compliance with tax law and the Service's requirements. In keeping with IRS's past practice of acceptance of advanced media and systems, Revenue Procedure 97-22 sets forth a set of criteria which largely mirror good business practice and impose few or no additional or onerous requirements:

Internal Revenue Service, Revenue Procedure 97-22.

> **SECTION 4. ELECTRONIC STORAGE SYSTEM REQUIREMENTS**
>
> **.01 General Requirements**
>
> (1) An electronic storage system must ensure an accurate and complete transfer of the hardcopy or computerized books and records to an electronic storage media. The electronic storage system must also index, store, preserve, retrieve, and reproduce the electronically stored books and records.
>
> (2) An electronic storage system must include:
>
> (a) reasonable controls to ensure the integrity, accuracy, and reliability of the electronic storage system;
>
> (b) reasonable controls to prevent and detect the unauthorized creation of, addition to, alteration of, deletion of, or deterioration of electronically stored books and records;
>
> (c) an inspection and quality assurance program evidenced by regular evaluations of the electronic storage system including periodic checks of electronically stored books and records;
>
> (d) a retrieval system that includes an indexing system (within the meaning of section 4.02 of this revenue procedure); and

(e) the ability to reproduce legible and readable hardcopies (within the meaning of section 4.01(3) of this revenue procedure) of electronically stored books and records.

(3) All books and records reproduced by the electronic storage system must exhibit a high degree of legibility and readability when displayed on a video display terminal and when reproduced in hardcopy. The term "legibility" means the observer must be able to identify all letters and numerals positively and quickly to the exclusion of all other letters or numerals. The term "readability" means that the observer must be able to recognize a group of letters or numerals as words or complete numbers. The taxpayer must ensure that the reproduction process maintains the legibility and readability of the electronically stored document.

(4) The information maintained in an electronic storage system must provide support for the taxpayer's books and records (including books and records in an automated data processing system). For example, the information maintained in an electronic storage system and the taxpayer's books and records must be cross-referenced in a manner that provides an audit trail between the general ledger and the source document(s).

(5) For each electronic storage system used, the taxpayer must maintain, and make available to the Service upon request, complete descriptions of:

(a) the electronic storage system, including all procedures relating to its use; and

(b) the indexing system (see section 4.02 of this revenue procedure).

(6) At the time of an examination, or for the tests described in section 5 of this revenue procedure, the taxpayer must:

(a) retrieve and reproduce (including hardcopies if requested)electronically stored books and records; and

(b) provide the Service with the resources (e.g., appropriate hardware and software, personnel, documentation, etc.) necessary to locate, retrieve, read, and reproduce (including hardcopies) any electronically stored books and records.

(7) An electronic storage system must not be subject, in whole or in part, to any agreement (such as a contract or license) that would limit or restrict the Service's access to and use of the electronic storage system on the taxpayer's premises (or any other place where the electronic storage system is maintained), including personnel, hardware, software, files, indexes, and software documentation.

(8) The taxpayer must retain electronically stored books and records so long as their contents may become material in the administration of the Internal Revenue laws under section 1.6001- 1(e).

(9) The taxpayer may use more than one electronic storage system. In that event, each electronic storage system must meet the requirements of this revenue procedure. Electronically stored books and records that are contained in an electronic storage system with respect to which the taxpayer ceases to maintain the hardware and the software necessary to satisfy the conditions of this revenue procedure will be deemed destroyed by the taxpayer, unless the electronically stored books and records remain available to the Service in conformity with this revenue procedure.

(10) Taxpayers may use reasonable data compression or formatting technologies as part of their electronic storage system so long as the requirements of this revenue procedure are satisfied.

.02 Requirements of an Indexing System

(1) For purposes of this revenue procedure, an "indexing system" is a system that permits the identification and retrieval for viewing or reproducing of relevant books and records maintained in an electronic storage system. For example, an indexing system might consist of assigning each electronically stored document a unique identification number and maintaining a separate database that contains descriptions of all electronically stored books and records along with their identification numbers. In addition, any system used to maintain, organize, or coordinate multiple electronic storage systems is treated as an indexing system under this revenue procedure. The requirement to maintain an indexing system will be satisfied if the indexing system is functionally comparable to a reasonable hardcopy filing system. The requirement to maintain an indexing system does not require that a separate electronically stored books and records description database be maintained if comparable results can be achieved without a separate description database.

(2) Reasonable controls must be undertaken to protect the indexing system against the unauthorized creation of, addition to, alteration of, deletion of, or deterioration of any entries.

.03 Recommended Practices

The implementation of records management practices is a business decision that is solely within the discretion of the taxpayer. Records management practices may include the labeling of electronically stored books and records, providing a secure storage environment, creating back-up copies, selecting an off-site storage location, retaining hardcopies of books or records that are illegible or that cannot be accurately or completely transferred to an electronic storage system, and testing to confirm records integrity.

The key requirements can be summarized as follows:

- reasonable measures to ensure system and data integrity and accuracy
- reasonable measures to prevent unauthorized or improper access and alterations to data
- adequate system documentation
- adequate legibility of printouts
- audit and quality assurance procedures

Revenue Procedure 97-22 does not specify or recommend any type of electronic imaging system nor any storage media such as WORM (write once read many times). Instead, taxpayers should implement "reasonable procedures" to be in compliance.

As with all electronic records, IRS expects that digital information be available at the time of the tax audit. To comply, parties contemplating the use of an imaging system for tax records must ensure that when they convert to a new system, media or data format that they convert the old electronic images into a new machine-readable format for IRS audit. Procedure for combating "technological obsolescence" for records still subject to tax audit must be provided for in the long-term system design and funding.

Some organizations have been reluctant to destroy their original, paper records after scanning until there is a test case or definitive statement on the legality of electronic imaging. The Internal Revenue Service is such a powerful agency and regulates more records than any other agency. The agency's explicit approval of electronic imaging technology, with minimal restrictions, will go a long way to broaden the widespread acceptance of this technology, both by the public and other government agencies.

Federal Acquisition Regulations

The Federal Acquisition Regulations now permit government contractors to utilize electronic imaging technology or electronic records. The previous requirements for microfilm records have been eliminated.

See Appendix B, *Federal Acquisition Regulation*, 48 CFR 4.703 for requirements for most federal contracts. *See also* 10 USC 2313 for a similar provision that affects only armed forces contracts.

CHAPTER 1 — FEDERAL ACQUISITION REGULATION

PART 4 — ADMINISTRATIVE MATTERS

SUBPART 4.7 — CONTRACTOR RECORDS RETENTION

§ 4.703 Policy.

* * * * *

(c) Nothing in this section shall be construed to preclude a contractor from duplicating or storing original records in electronic form unless they contain significant information not shown on the record copy. Original records need not be maintained or produced in an audit if the contractor or subcontractor provides photographic or electronic images of the original records and meets the following requirements:

(1) The contractor or subcontractor has established procedures to ensure that the imaging process preserves accurate images of the original records, including signatures and other written or graphic images, and that the imaging process is reliable and secure so as to maintain the integrity of the records.

(2) The contractor or subcontractor maintains an effective indexing system to permit timely and convenient access to the imaged records.

(3) The contractor or subcontractor retains the original records for a minimum of one year after imaging to permit periodic validation of the imaging systems.

(d) If the information described in paragraph (a) of this section is maintained on a computer, contractors shall retain the computer data on a reliable medium for the time periods prescribed. contractors may transfer computer data in machine readable form from one reliable computer medium to another. Contractors' computer data retention and transfer procedures shall maintain the integrity, reliability, and security of the original computer data. Contractors shall also retain an audit trail describing the data transfer. For the record retention time periods prescribed, contractors shall not destroy, discard, delete, or write over such computer data.

Government

Many states have approved or are developing requirements governing the use of optical disk technology by government agencies. The optical disk medium has not been considered archival or permanent in nature. Unfortunately, the only definition of archival existing in the United States is the methylene blue test performed on silver halide microfilm to determine archival quality. No comparable standards exist for magnetic media or optical disk.

Many government records must be kept for long periods of time or permanently. These records are maintained historically to preserve the actions of government for later research and analysis. Previously, state and federal archivists have insisted that records for this purpose be preserved either in paper form or on microfilm that has been tested for archival quality. Now, agencies in the federal government and most states can use the technology provided that they following certain requirements.

GOVERNMENT - UNITED STATES FEDERAL

The National Archives and Records Administration approved electronic imaging technology for federal government records:

National Archives and Records Administration, NARA Bulletin 93-3. *See* Appendix B for details.

4. Interpretation.

a. Because of the hardware and software dependence of current optical disk systems and the absence of standards that ensure the portability of data from one system to another, NARA cannot accession permanent records stored on optical disks at this time. Until the development of data portability standards, permanent records stored on optical disks must be transferred to the National Archives on paper, microforms, magnetic tape, or 3480 class tape cartridges. Microforms must conform to the requirements of 36 CFR Part 1230. Magnetic tapes and 3480 class tape cartridges must conform to the requirements of 36 CFR 1228.188.

b. Reminding agencies of the requirements for transferring permanent records to the National Archives is not intended to discourage the use of optical disk technology. NARA recognizes the potential benefits of this technology for storing and retrieving large quantities of information. Agencies also may be able to use digital image enhancement for poor quality originals.

c. Agencies may use optical disk systems for the storage and retrieval of permanent records while the records remain in an agency's legal custody. However, no permanent records may be destroyed after copying onto an optical disk without NARA's approval. Normally, after permanent records have been copied onto an optical disk, they should be transferred to a Federal records center or to the Office of the National Archives. In some cases, NARA may authorize agencies to destroy permanent records after copying onto an optical disk provided that the agency agrees to convert the disk images to a medium acceptable to NARA at the time of transfer to NARA's legal custody.

d. Permanent records stored originally on optical disk must be converted to a medium acceptable to NARA at the time of transfer to NARA's legal custody.

e. Records appraised by NARA as temporary may be stored on any medium, including optical disks, that ensures maintenance of the information until its authorized disposal. This means that conversion of such temporary records to optical disks, and disposal of the original paper or other media, do not require NARA's approval.

f. Analog videodiscs that typically contain photographs are one type of optical disk that can be accessioned into the National Archives, provided that they do not require any interactive software or nonstandardized equipment. Original photographs appraised as permanent and copied onto a videodisc must be scheduled for transfer to the National Archives along with a copy of the videodisc. Likewise, compact disks used for digital audio playback also can be accessioned into the National Archives because they use a standard player and require no special software.

* * * * *

Each federal agency can develop the system that best meets its needs. However, records transferred to a federal records center must first be converted to a format accepted by NARA if the agency maintained them in a different format.

See **Appendix B, National Archives and Records Administration Bulletin No. 94-4, July 20, 1994.**

In 1994, the National Archives and Records Commission modified its requirements by permitting the use of CD-ROM media for transferring permanent federal records in electronic form to the National Archives.

NARA BULLETIN NO. 94-4 DATED July 20, 1994

* * * * *

4. *Agency action.*

a. Agencies are authorized to transfer CD-ROM's which include fielded data files or text files scheduled to be preserved in the National Archives that are:

(1) in conformance to the International Standards Organization (ISO) 9660 standard;

(2) in compliance with the American Standard Code for Information Interchange (ASCII) standard as defined in the Federal Information Processing Standard 1-2 (11/14/84);

(3) not dependent on control characters or codes which are not defined in the ASCII character set;

(4) not compressed unless the software to decompress the files is provided;

(5) individually addressable; and

(6) in compliance with the documentation requirements of 36 CFR 1228.188.

b. In some cases, permanently valuable electronic records which an agency disseminates on CD-ROM exist on other media, such as magnetic tape. In such cases, the agency and NARA will mutually agree on the most appropriate medium for transfer of the records to the National Archives.

c. Agencies should transfer the CD-ROM's with the necessary documentation for those files that are to be accessioned into the Center for Electronic Records.

* * * * *

See Appendix B, National Archives and Records Administration Bulletin No. 94-4, July 20, 1994.

The National Archives and Records Commission modified its requirements related to the use of electronic imaging technology. Besides CD-ROM media for maintaining and reproducing records as part of an electronic imaging system, other media is now approved for video and audio recordings. Although NARA continues to encourage federal agencies to develop electronic imaging systems, it continues to place some restrictions on the use of optical disk or other alternate media for storage of electronic images.

NARA BULLETIN NO. 94-5 DATED JULY 20, 1994

* * * * *

4. Interpretation.

a. At this time, NARA will accept permanent records for transfer to the National Archives on the following types of optical media:

(1) Optical disks which meet the requirements of NARA Bulletin 94-4, Use of Compact Disk-Read Only Memory (CD-ROM) medium to transfer records to the National Archives;

(2) Analog videodisks that typically contain photographs, provided that they do not require any interactive software or nonstandardized equipment. Original photographs appraised as permanent and copied onto a videodisc must be scheduled for transfer to the National Archives along with a copy of the videodisc; and

(3) Audio compact disks.

b. NARA is continuing to study the technical concerns with long-term storage of permanent records on optical media, including migration of data to next generation equipment. NARA may make exceptions to this limited accessioning policy on a case-by-case basis before revising the policy in the future.

c. NARA encourages Federal agencies in using optical disk technology to enhance their information management operations. NARA recognizes the potential benefits of this technology for storing and retrieving large quantities of information. NARA encourages agencies to inform NARA of significant current or anticipated uses of optical media.

d. Agencies may use optical disk systems for the storage and retrieval of permanent records while the records remain in an agency's legal custody. However, agencies must obtain NARA approval before destroying original permanent or unscheduled records that have been copied onto an optical disk. (This includes permanent records approved for transfer to the National Archives on CD-ROM under the provisions of NARA Bulletin 94-4.) Approval for destruction will be dependent upon the following:

(1) The usefulness of the form transferred to NARA in comparison to the original; and

(2) The nature of the media used to transfer the records to NARA. The transfer of permanent records stored on optical disks to the legal custody of the National Archives of the United States must be on a medium acceptable to NARA at the time of the transfer.

After permanent records have been copied onto an optical disk, if the records are no longer needed for current business in the agency, the records should be transferred to a Federal records center or, in the case of records on an electronic media, to the National Archives.

* * * * *

GOVERNMENT - STATE

Texas adopted legislation that allows optical disk records and the destruction of the original paper only for short-term records (retention under 10 years). Optical disk may be used to store long-term or permanent records but the original paper records must be preserved in paper or microfilm form.

Texas, Government Code

TITLE 6. — RECORDS.

SUBTITLE B. — COUNTY RECORDS.

CHAPTER 194. — STORAGE OF COUNTY RECORDS BY MICROFILMING OR BY OPTICAL DATA STORAGE PROCESS.

§ 194.0025. Authorization of Optical Data Storage Process.

(a) For the purposes described by Section 194.002(a), a county clerk or clerk of the county court may adopt and use an optical data storage process for the storage of records by optical disk.

(b) This chapter applies, to the extent feasible, to the optical data storage process, the optical disk used in that process, and the records stored by that process in a manner equivalent to the manner in which this chapter applies to a microfilm process, the film used in that process, and the records stored by that process.

SUBTITLE C. — RECORDS PROVISIONS APPLYING TO MORE THAN ONE TYPE OF LOCAL GOVERNMENT.

CHAPTER 205. — ELECTRONIC STORAGE OF RECORDS.

§ 205.001. Definitions.

In this chapter:

(1) "Electronic storage" means the maintenance of local government record data in the form of digital electronic signals on a computer hard disk, magnetic tape, optical disk, or similar machine-readable medium.

* * * * *

§ 205.007. Electronic Storage Authorization Requests.

(a) Before the electronic storage of any local government record data of permanent value or, if stipulated in commission rules, any local government record data whose retention period is at least 10 years on a records retention schedule issued by the commission, an electronic storage authorization request shall be submitted to the director and librarian for approval.

§ 205.008. Destruction of Source Documents.

(a) The source document, if any, for electronically stored local government record data covered by section 205.007(a) may be destroyed or returned to the person who filed it for record if the electronic storage authorization request is approved.

(b) The magnetic tape, optical disk, or similar medium containing the local government record data and the hardware and software necessary to provide access to it must be retained by the local government or be available to the local government until expiration of the retention period for all source documents, subject to the rules adopted in this chapter.

(c) The source document, if any, for electronically stored local government record data not covered by Section 205.007(a) may be destroyed before the expiration of the retention period for the source document in a records retention schedule issued by the commission if the magnetic tape, optical disk, or similar medium and hardware and software necessary to provide access to local government record data on the media are retained for the retention period in the schedule. Conversely, the magnetic tape, optical disk, or similar medium may be erased, written over, or destroyed before the expiration of the retention period for a source document for local government record data not covered in Section 205.007(a), if the source document, if any, is retained until the expiration of the retention period or, if the source document has already been destroyed, paper or microfilm copies are generated from the magnetic tape, optical disk, or similar medium before destruction or erasure and retained until the expiration of the retention period for the source document.

California adopted laws for the preservation of state, county and district records maintained on optical disk systems. The law requires that the medium "not permit additions, deletions, or changes to the original document" and complies with minimum national standards or guidelines for recording records.

California, Government Code

TITLE 2. GOVERNMENT OF THE STATE OF CALIFORNIA.

DIVISION 3. EXECUTIVE DEPARTMENT.

PART 5.5. DEPARTMENT OF GENERAL SERVICES.

CHAPTER 5. STATE RECORDS.

Article 4. Disposal of Records.

§ 14756. Microfilming of public records; Certification.

The public records of any state agency may be microfilmed, electronically data imaged, or otherwise photographically reproduced and certified upon the written authorization of the head of the agency. The microfilming, electronic data imaging, or photographic reproduction shall be made in compliance with the minimum standards or guidelines, or both, as recommended by the American National Standards Institute or the Association for Information and Image Management for recording permanent records or nonpermanent records, whichever applies.

The certification of each reproduction or set of reproductions shall be in accordance with the standards, or have the approval, of the Attorney General. The certification shall contain a statement of the identify, description, and disposition or location of the records reproduced, the date, reason, and authorization for such reproduction, and such other information as the Attorney General requires.

The certified reproductions shall be deemed to be original public records for all purposes, including introduction in courts of law and state agencies.

TITLE 3. GOVERNMENT OF COUNTIES

DIVISION 2. OFFICERS

PART 2. BOARD OF SUPERVISORS

CHAPTER 1. ORGANIZATION

§ 25105. Reproduction of board records; Minimum standards.

The board of supervisors may authorize the use of photographs, microphotographs, electronic data-processing records, optical disks, or any other medium which does not permit additions, deletions, or changes to the original document, or photocopies of all records, books and minutes of the board.

(a) Each photograph, microphotographic, or photocopy shall be made in a manner and on paper which will comply with the minimum standards or guidelines, or both, as recommended by the American National Standards Institute or the Association for Information and Image Management for recording of permanent records or nonpermanent records, whichever applies. Every reproduction shall be deemed and considered a transcript, exemplification, or certified copy, as the case may be, of the original. Each roll of microfilm shall be deemed and constitute a book and shall be designated and numbered, and provision shall be made for preserving, examining, and using it. A duplicate of each roll of microfilm shall be made and kept in a safe and separate place.

(b) Electronic data-processing records, records recorded on optical disks, and records recorded on any other medium shall comply with the minimum standards or guidelines, or both, as recommended by the American National Standards Institute or the Association for Information and Image Management. A duplicate copy of any authorized record reproduced in compliance with the minimum standards or guidelines, or both, as recommended by the American National Standards Institute or the Association for Information and Image Management for recording of permanent or nonpermanent records, whichever applies, shall be deemed an original.

(c) In the event the authorization provided herein is granted, the personal signatures required by § 25103 may be produced by the authorized process, and the reproduced signatures shall be deemed to satisfy the requirement of § 25103.

Kansas agencies, complying with the specified requirements, may produce optical disk records and destroy the originals.

Kansas Statutes Annotated

CHAPTER 45. — LAWS, JOURNALS AND PUBLIC INFORMATION.

Article 4. — Public Records Preservation.

§ 45-412. Microphotographic or optical disc copies of originals; original record destruction, when.

(a) The state archivist shall prepare recommendations, to be approved by the state records board, based on the current standards of the federal government and the American National Standards Institute, for the quality of film or optical disc, proper arrangement of materials, suitable filming or other image reproduction techniques and equipment, quality of photographic or optical disc images, film processing results, and film or optical disc storage conditions which should be achieved or utilized by state and local agencies in making microphotographic or optical disc copies of government records with enduring value pursuant to K.S.A. 12-122, 19-250, or 75-3506, and amendments thereto. Whenever microphotographic or optical disc copies of records with enduring value fail to meet the standards recommended by the state archivist and approved by the state records board, the state archivist shall urge state and local agencies to retain the original records.

(b) Whenever photographs, microphotographs or other reproductions on film or optical disc have been prepared pursuant to K.S.A. 75-3506, and amendments thereto, and have been placed in conveniently accessible files and provisions made for preserving, examining and using the same, and when a negative copy of the film or a master copy of the optical disc has been deposited in a secure place where it will not be subject to use except in making additional positive copies, any state agency, with the approval of the state records board or as authorized by the retention and disposition schedules, may cause the original records from which the photographs, microphotographs or other reproductions on film or optical disc have been made, or any part thereof, to be destroyed. Such records shall not be destroyed and shall be retained by the agency or transferred to the state archives or temporarily to another suitable place designated by the board, if the board judges such materials to have been of enduring value in their original form.

Even though the laws in many states do not permit the destruction of paper records after the electronic images have been produced, government agencies may still use this technology, but may be required to maintain the original paper records. Even if the optical disk system does not conform to government legal standards, the records should still be admissible in evidence.

State archives will also develop standards for these technologies. Unless specific standards for creation, maintenance and disposition are followed, the archives will not grant permission to the government agencies to destroy the original paper records. As a practical matter, archives remain reluctant to accept electronic records for permanent retention, including computer disks, tapes, and optical disks. In some states, government records scheduled for long-term or permanent retention will have to be maintained in either paper or archival microfilm format. As a result, government agencies will still be able to use the optical disk technology to manage information more effectively, but cannot use the technology to replace paper or microfilm records.

TECHNOLOGICAL OBSOLESCENCE

The concerns raised by archivists will probably remain the same even when optical disk or other media is certified for long-term retention. The problem relates more to the practical problem of "technological obsolescence" - the loss of information or the loss of the ability to read the information due to the evolution of and the ultimate obsolescence of the disk formats and equipment over time. This is a different issue than the loss of the disk's ability to retain information.

As a technology develops, new disk read/write equipment and disk formats will be developed. Imaged information must periodically be transferred to new, current formats or, alternative, compatible equipment would have to be to ensure readability in the future. Even if consistent standards for image and media formats could be developed, the technology will continue to evolve. It will, therefore, be impossible and impractical to maintain information on a specific media for long-term retention without transferring the information to another system.

One solution to the long-term or archival problem facing government (and other industries requiring long-term retention of records) could addressed by the development of low-cost computer output microfilm units for graphic images. At least one vendor offers this equipment at a reasonable cost of $36,000 per unit.

Graphics COM enables image information from the imaging system to be stored in an appropriate order on low-cost, archival microfilm. By utilizing a standardized microfilm format (analog format) for long-term retention of information once it becomes inactive, the optical or magnetic media would no longer be needed and may be destroyed or reused (e.g., erasable media). If the information becomes active in the future, the microfilm could be scanned and the electronic images recreated.

Without this technology, electronic imaging systems may not be used by some government agencies to replace paper records for long-term storage. Instead, the technology may only be used for active management and retrieval of short-term information, not long-term preservation. If electronic imaging is used for long-term records, the records must also be maintained in either paper or archival microfilm form.

International

While statutes and rules of evidence determine the legality of electronic imaging in the United States, court decisions will probably determine its legality in other countries. Countries outside the United States often rely on an evolutionary judicial process similar to the British Common Law system. Basically, rules of evidence evolve through court decisions over a period of time. When judges consistently reach the same conclusion, a principle of law is established.

Most countries outside the United States have yet to address the legal issues related to electronic imaging. In fact, some are still groping with legal questions regarding microfilm and other duplicate records. Few have dealt with issues related to computer records. In this environment, you can expect great uncertainties regarding the legality of electronic imaging for many years to come.

The United States also operates under a legal principle that all actions are permitted unless they are specifically prohibited or regulated by law. Other countries may not permit certain activities unless they are specifically permitted by law. As a result, some countries outside the United States will prohibit the use of optical court records until such time as they are specifically permitted by law. This evolutionary process could take many years.

Outside the United States and other common law countries, you can expect few other countries to embrace the legal acceptance of electronic imaging in the near future. The technology certainly can be used for effective management and retrieval of information. Visible records produced by the technology, however, may be questioned in evidence. Rarely will government agencies permit you to use the technology and destroy the original paper records.

In spite of the previous comments, however, the following laws seem to be broad enough so as to permit the use of any records technology, including electronic imaging systems, even though electronic imaging is not specifically mentioned:

Australia

EVIDENCE AMENDMENT ACT OF 1978

PART 3A. — ADMISSIBILITY OF BUSINESS RECORDS.

7A. (1) In this Part, unless the contrary intention appears — "business" includes —

(a) any business, profession, occupation, calling, trade or undertaking whether or not engaged in or carried on for profit and whether engaged in or carried on in Australia or elsewhere, including any business, profession, occupation, calling, trade or undertaking engaged in or carried on by the Crown in right of the Commonwealth or of a State; and

(b) the administration of the government of the Commonwealth, of a State, of a Territory or of another country, whether carried on in Australia or elsewhere;

* * * * *

"document" includes —

(a) a book, plan, paper, parchment, film or other material on which there is writing or printing, or on which there are marks, symbols or perforations having a meaning for persons qualified to interpret them;

(b) a disc, tape, paper, film or other device from which sounds or images are capable of being reproduced; and

(c) any other record of information;

* * * * *

7K. (1) For the purposes of section 7B —

(a) a statement in the document may, as prescribed or by leave of the court, be proved by the production of a copy of the document, or of the material part of the document;

(b) a statement in a document that is designed to be used to reproduce the statement in the form of a visible display or of sound may be proved by reproducing the statement in that form in the presence of the court; and

(c) a statement in the record of information made by the use of a computer may be proved by the production of a document produced by the use of a computer containing the statement in a form that can be understood by sight.

(2) For the purposes of section 7E, the absence of a record of the happening of an event in the record of information made by the use of a computer may be proved by the production of a document produced by the use of a computer containing a statement based on the absence of such a record.

(3) Where a person proposes to prove, or proves, a statement in a document otherwise than by producing the document, the court may require that the document be produced or be made available to the court or to other parties for examination or testing and, if the document is not so produced or made available, may reject the statement or, if it is in evidence, exclude it.

(4) Where a person proposes to prove, or proves, a statement by reproducing the statement in the form of a visible display or of sound, the court may direct a record of the statement to be produced and, if the record is not produced, may reject the statement or, if it is in evidence, exclude it.

(5) For the purposes of this section, "computer" means any device for storing or processing information.

Canada. ***Also see*** **Chapter 5. Standards, Guidelines and Proposed Laws for Canadian standards for documentary evidence.**

CHAPTER 1. — NATIONAL ARCHIVES OF CANADA

* * * * *

2. In this Act,

* * * * *

"record" includes any correspondence, memorandum, book, plan, map, drawing, diagram, pictorial or graphic work, photograph, film, microform, sound recording, videotape, machine readable record, and any other documentary material, regardless of physical form or characteristics, and any copy thereof.

* * * * *

CHAPTER C-5. — CANADA EVIDENCE.

Documentary Evidence

CHAPTER C-44. — CANADA BUSINESS CORPORATIONS ACT.

22. (1) All registers and other records required by this Act to be prepared and maintained may be in a bound or looseleaf form or in a photographic film form, or may be entered or recorded by any system of mechanical or electronic data processing or any other information storage device that is capable of reproducing any required information in intelligible written form within a reasonable time.

* * * * *

Germany

COMMERCIAL CODE OF MAY 10th, 1897

§ 44. Document storage; storage period.

(1) Every merchant is obligated to store the following documents in order:

(1) commercial business records, inventories, balance sheets as well as the instructions and other organizational documents necessary for interpreting such documents,
(2) incoming business correspondence,
(3) copies of outgoing business correspondence,
(4) the original records on the basis of which entries were made in the books to be kept by him pursuant to § 38 subsection (1).

(2) Business correspondence comprises only such records which pertain to a commercial transaction.

(3) With the exception of the balance sheet, the documents listed in subsection (1) can also be stored on film or on other data storage records, if this complies with generally accepted accounting principles and it is assured that the reproductions or data

(1) facsimilate the incoming business correspondence and original records and concur with the other documents with regard to content when they are made legible
(2) are available during the period of storage and can be made legible at any time within a reasonable period of time.

Where records were produced in a data storage record form by reason of § 43 subsection (4) sentence 1, the data can also be stored in a printout form instead of the data storage materials. The printed records can also be stored pursuant to sentence 1.

(4) The records listed in subsection (1) number 1 are to be stored for ten years, the other records listed in subsection (1) for six years.

(5) The period of storage begins with the close of the calendar year in which the last entry in the commercial record is made, the inventory prepared, the balance sheet approved, the business correspondence is received or sent or the original record has come into existence.

§ 47a. The production of documents from film or data storage material.

One who can only produce stored documents in the form of a film or other data storage copy, is obligated at his own expense to make available the devices necessary to make the documents legible; in so far as necessary he must, at his own expense, print the records or furnish reproductions which can be read without auxiliary devices.

Italy

THE ITALIAN CIVIL CODE

TITLE 2. — EVIDENCE.

CHAPTER 2. — DOCUMENTARY EVIDENCE.

Section 4. — Mechanical Reproductions.

2712. Mechanical reproductions. Photographic or cinematographic reproductions, phonographic recordings and, in general, all other mechanical representations of facts or things, constitute full evidence of the facts or things represented, if the persons against whom they are offered do not deny their correspondence to the actual facts or things concerned.

United Kingdom

LICENSED DEALERS (CONDUCT OF BUSINESS) RULES 1983

AUTHORITY: PREVENTION OF FRAUD (INVESTMENTS) ACT 1958

CROSS-HEADING: PART 3 BOOKS, ACCOUNTS AND DOCUMENTS TO BE KEPT BY THE HOLDER OF A PRINCIPAL'S LICENSE IN RELATION TO ANY DEALING IN SECURITIES

Section 26. Computer, etc. records; confidentiality of records.

(1) Any requirements in rules 20 to 24 for a holder of a principal's license to keep books, accounts and other documents for a particular purpose and containing particular items of information shall be taken to be satisfied by recording the matters in question otherwise than in a legible form so long as the recording is capable of being reproduced without delay in a legible form sufficient for that purpose and containing that information.

* * * * *

CIVIL EVIDENCE ACT 1968

CROSS-HEADING: PART 1. — HEARSAY EVIDENCE.

Section 6. Provisions supplementary to ss 2 to 5.

(1) Where in any civil proceeding a statement contained in a document is proposed to be given in evidence by virtue of section 2, 4 or 5 of this Act it may, subject to any rules of court, be proved by the production of that document or (whether or not that document is still in existence) by the production of a copy of that document, or of the material part thereof, authenticated in such manner as the court may approve.

(2) For the purpose of deciding whether or not a statement is admissible in evidence by virtue of section 2, 4 or 5 of this Act, the court may draw any reasonable inference from the circumstances in which the statement was made or otherwise came into being or from any other circumstances, including, in the case of a statement contained in a document, the form and contents of that document.

(3) In estimating the weight, if any, to be attached to a statement admissible in evidence by virtue of section 2, 3, 4, or 5 of this Act regard shall be had to all the circumstances from which any inference can reasonably be drawn as to the accuracy or otherwise of the statement and, in particular —

* * * * *

(c) in the case of a statement falling within section 5(1) of this Act, to the question whether or not the information which the information contained in the statement reproduces or is derived from was supplied to the relevant computer, or recorded for the purpose of being supplied thereto, contemporaneously with the occurrence or existence of the facts dealt with in that information, and to the question whether or not any person concerned with the supply of information to that computer, or with the operation of that computer or any equipment by means of which the document containing the statement was produced by it, had any incentive to conceal or misrepresent the facts.

* * * * *

Chapter 5 Standards, Guidelines and Proposed Laws

Law and the Public Interest

For additional information the legal requirements for records that promote the public interests *see* Appendix E for the AIIM *Performance Guideline* (ANSI/AIIM TR-31).

State legislatures and Congress prepare statutes that specify legal requirements that regulated organizations must follow. These statutes generally authorize state and federal regulatory agencies to prepare rules and regulations related to the statutes.

Rules and regulations specify detailed requirements, interpret the authorizing statutes, and set guidelines for determining compliance. In the recordkeeping area, these rules and regulations could indicate that certain records must be created, maintained for specified periods of time, maintained in a specified form, and made available for government inspectors or auditors.

Through the election of state legislatures and Congress, we empower our representatives to approve laws that "promote the public interest". However, the public interest does not just include the subject matter addressed by the particular laws. It also includes the impact these laws will have on those required to comply,

Clearly, lawmakers have a legitimate interest to ensure that organizations maintain required records to enable government to fulfill its legal responsibility. By requiring the public to submit information and maintain records, government can determine the impact of the laws and verify compliance.

But the degree of burden placed on the public through recordkeeping laws should be balanced against the relative costs and benefits to society of the entire legislative and regulatory scheme.

When laws establish unique and unnecessary requirements for records and information management systems, a significant and sometimes onerous burden may be placed on the public. Organizations conducting business in numerous jurisdictions and subject to numerous laws face an even greater burden to identify, understand, and implement the multitude of complex and even contradictory requirements.

Unnecessary and inappropriate recordkeeping requirements significantly increase the cost of compliance. In practical terms, increased costs results in lower taxable income, and, subsequently, lower taxes paid to support government and government-sponsored activities.

For this reason, the cost of recordkeeping requirements must be balanced between the need for these requirements to foster the public interest versus the cost or burden to the public for compliance. Those laws that exhibit an appropriate balance promote the public interest. Those laws that create unnecessary costs and burdens, may actually violate the public interest — even though the intent of the law and the subject matter affected reflects legitimate public needs.

GOALS OF RECORDKEEPING REQUIREMENTS

Recordkeeping requirements are established in either statutes or regulations to accomplish specific purposes. Some of the more common purposes are the following:

- *Information gathering.* When developing new statutes or regulations, lawmakers need information in order to determine the type and scope of new laws. It is therefore appropriate for government to require organizations to maintain information that would be relevant for this process. The typical cost to an organization to provide necessary information would be small versus the huge cost for government to commission consultants and other information-gathering organizations to accomplish this task. The information also enables lawmakers to develop laws that reflect real problems and solutions.

- *Rulemaking.* The information received from regulated entities as well as from the independent judgment of government agencies provide the basis for new rules and regulations. Often, proposed rules will be made available to those affected for comments and suggestions.

- *Compliance monitoring*. The information maintained by regulated organizations help government agencies determine whether an organization is complying with the law. For example, the Internal Revenue Service can compare information and tax returns to other information gathered from independent sources to determine whether the amount of taxes paid corresponds with the amount the agency believes is appropriate. While the information may not completely determine an issue, it is useful to alert the agency whether additional investigation or audit is appropriate.

- *Auditing*. Government will typically audit a segment of the regulated organizations on a regular basis, and audit others that are suspected of non-compliance. The records maintained by an organization serve as the primary basis for determining whether an organization complies with the law. Failure to keep required records prevents government from properly conducting an audit and determining compliance. For this reason, failure to maintain required records will result in severe fines and penalties and could cause an organization to cease operations.

- *Enforcement*. Information maintained by organizations helps government determine whether enforcement actions are necessary and also determine the impact of previous enforcement measures.

- *Education*. Rules and regulations tend to provide industry with guidance regarding appropriate recordkeeping practices. Small business, in particular, can often benefit from the guidelines provided by government to improve internal operations while complying with the law. Government often models new legislation and regulations on existing good practices in an industry.

- *Notice*. Published recordkeeping requirements inform the regulated public about the types of requirements with which they will be expected to comply. Fines, penalties, and other adverse consequences can only be imposed by government after adequate notice as to what is expected. When a law is too vague, government may be barred from enforcement since the regulated organization was never placed on "notice" of what was expected.

- *Standardization*. Both the public and government can benefit from the cost savings and efficiency resulting from standardization. Recordkeeping requirements often specify certain requirements to either force or encourage an industry to standardize certain practices. With standardized practices, government auditors and investigators can more quickly and efficiently accomplish their task, information can be submitted to government in standardized formats, and regulated entities may benefit from reduced cost and improved operations.

LAWS AFFECTING RECORDKEEPING REQUIREMENTS

Lawmakers have enacted voluminous statutes and regulations that specify recordkeeping requirements that they deem necessary to promote the public interest. Some laws establish uniform requirements similar to those that have been adopted by federal and state jurisdictions; others represent the unique perceptions of an individual jurisdiction. The Federal Paperwork Reduction Act balances the needs of government agencies versus the needs of regulated organizations.

Uniform Laws

Many jurisdictions have adopted uniform laws that have been approved by the National Conference of Commissioners on Uniform State Laws to promote uniformity in state laws where uniformity is deemed desirable and practical. Some of these uniform laws address issues of records as evidence, reproduction of records and records retention:

The Uniform Rules of Evidence. The Uniform Rules of Evidence establish the principles under which records can be admitted into evidence. The rules specify the requirements of evidence for creating and maintaining original records and for reproducing records. Records can be introduced into evidence if they are records of an act or event, produced at or near the time of the event, by or from somebody with knowledge, in the regular course of business, and presented into evidence by a custodian or other qualified person. Duplicate records, using any duplication technology, may be introduced into evidence (whether or not the originals exist) if they "accurately reproduce the original".

The Uniform Photographic Copies of Business and Public Records As Evidence Act. This uniform law permits duplicate records to be prepared in the regular course of business and the original records destroyed in the regular course of business, provided that the duplicates "accurately reproduce the original". In addition, duplicate records can be used for any "administrative proceeding" — generally including any quasi-judicial administrative proceeding or any other regulatory purpose. This uniform law is both a rule of evidence and a rule of business conduct.

The Uniform Records Retention Act was developed by the Association of Records Managers and Administrators in 1987.

The Uniform Preservation of Private Business Records Act. This uniform law specifies that any records required to be kept in the jurisdiction, for which no specific retention period is stated, may be destroyed after three years from creation. The uniform law also specifies that duplicate records produced by "any technology that accurately reproduces the original" meets the requirements of any laws in the jurisdiction that requires that records be kept. This uniform law is primarily a law affecting business conduct, although the principle may be used to indicate principles that can also facilitate the introduction of records in evidence. The original uniform law or the "Uniform Records Retention Act" has been enacted in three additional jurisdictions since 1989.

The uniform laws have facilitated the standardization of legal principles related to recordkeeping in a large number of jurisdictions. A majority of states and the federal government have adopted the Uniform Rules of Evidence and Uniform Photographic Copies of Business and Public Records As Evidence Act. To date, seven states have adopted the Uniform Preservation of Private Business Records Act and several more are considering or will consider this Act in the future. The uniform law process has tended to promote consistency through the introduction of thoughtful legislation designed to meet the public interest and reduce the burdens on regulated organizations.

Unique State and Federal Laws

Most recordkeeping laws will not be uniform. Instead, they reflect the unique ideas, language, needs and peculiarities of the jurisdiction or agency responsible for writing and approving the laws. For example, each state will develop its own unique language and requirements for recordkeeping laws in the areas of employment, health and safety, tax, industry regulation, and other activities being regulated. As a result, each jurisdiction will vary in terms of the type of information required to be kept, the form of information, the status of duplicate records, the use of specific types of technology, the records retention periods and practically all other aspects of recordkeeping imaginable.

An organization responsible for maintaining records in multiple jurisdictions will therefore be faced with a multitude of different and sometimes competing requirements. Their information systems must be flexible enough to comply with all these requirements and, yet, provide the information needed by the organization for its internal purposes in a cost-effective manner. Even if all these laws affecting an organization specify "reasonable" requirements, an organization doing business in multiple jurisdictions still faces an exceedingly difficult burden to identify and comply with the multitude of requirements. In reality, many recordkeeping provisions are not "reasonable" and impose severe and conflicting requirements on an organization.

A few federal agencies, however, have adopted unique regulations that have resulted in the equivalent of nationwide uniform laws. The Internal Revenue Service, for example, has published revenue procedures in the area of microfilm and computer records that has led to some "quasi-uniform" guidelines that several states have followed for state tax records. Similarly, the federal Office of Wage and Hour, Equal Opportunity Commission, and Occupational Safety and Health Administration have promulgated regulations that have sometimes been adopted by some states without change or with only minor changes. These examples, however, represent the exception to the rule.

Title 44, United States Code, Chapter 35

The Federal Paperwork Reduction Act

The Federal Paperwork Reduction Act represents the shining example of a law that forces government to balance between the needs of government and the needs of the regulated organizations. Under this Act of Congress, federal agencies must "minimize the control of burdens associated with the collection of information by federal agencies from individuals, businesses, and other private institutions, in state and local government". Federal agencies must comply with this Act in order for their regulations to be enforceable.

See 5 CFR 1320.

The Federal Paperwork Reduction Act authorizes the Office of Management and Budget to promulgate rules to implement the Act. OMB lists the situations when it will require a federal agency to justify the recordkeeping burdens being placed on regulated entities:

§ 1320.6 General information collection guidelines

> Unless the agency is able to demonstrate that such collection of information is necessary to satisfy statutory requirements or other substantial needs, OMB will not approve a collection of information:
>
> * * * * *
>
> (f) Requiring respondents to retain records, other than health, medical, or tax records for more than three years;
>
> * * * * *
>
> (j) Requiring respondents to maintain and provide information in a format other than that in which the information is customarily maintained.

Section 1320.6(f) addresses the same issue covered by the Uniform Preservation of Private Business Records Act — the records retention period for legally required records for which records retention periods have not been stated. In the Federal Paperwork Reduction Act, OMB must specifically approve and the agency must justify records retention requirements that exceed three years. This section appears to permit the destruction of records after three years when federal regulation requires records to be kept but does not specify a record retention period.

The Federal Paperwork Reduction Act also prohibits federal agencies from issuing regulations that require records to be kept in unusual or extraordinary forms — "in a format other than that in which the information is customarily maintained". This would prohibit a federal agency from specifying that record be kept on a particular type of record media, unless that record media is customarily used. The Act permits the public to respond to proposed new federal regulations by either writing the sponsoring regulatory agency or contacting OMB directly. OMB will determine whether the regulation complies with the Federal Paperwork Reduction Act by determining the burden being placed on the public. For definition purposes, "burden" is defined as the following:

> **Definitions.**
>
> "Burden" means the total time, effort, or financial resources required to respond to a collection of information, including that to read or hear instructions; to develop, modify, construct, or assemble any materials or equipment; conduct tests, inspections, polls, observations, or the like necessary to obtain information; to organize the information in the requested format; to review its accuracy and the appropriateness of its manner of presentation; and to maintain, disclose or report the information.
>
> The time and financial resources necessary to comply with the collection of information that would be incurred by persons in the normal course of their activities (e.g., in compiling, maintaining business records), will be excluded from the "burden" if the agency demonstrates that the reporting and recordkeeping activities needed to comply are usual and customary.
>
> * * * * *
>
> "Collection of information" means the obtaining or soliciting of information by the agency from ten or more persons by means of identical questions, whether such collection of information is mandatory or voluntary or required to obtain a benefit. For purposes of this definition, the "obtaining or soliciting of information" includes any requirement or request for persons to obtain, maintain, retain, report, or publicly disclose information. * * *

Unfortunately, no state has adopted the equivalent of the Paperwork Reduction Act. With this safeguard, any state agency may prepare and implement regulations that place onerous burdens on the public without any restrictions on their exercise of power.

FACTORS AFFECTING THE BURDENS IMPOSED BY LAWS

Lawmakers in one jurisdiction generally attempt to refrain from developing laws that conflict with other laws in the same jurisdiction or laws that fail to protect the public interest. The lawmakers in other jurisdictions operate under different laws and may interpret the public interest differently.

Rules and regulations developed by regulatory agencies cannot explicitly violate a statute or constitutional provision. A regulatory agency, especially in the states, is free, however, to regulate in areas authorized by the granting statute that is not prohibited by these types of legal constraints.

Lawmakers will consider a variety of legal approaches to achieve the regulatory purpose. Many factors will be weighed to determine the scope and degree of regulation in their final law. Significant consideration should be given to the burden that the regulation places on the public versus the benefits recognized by the public by full compliance.

The federal government has enacted the Federal Paperwork Reduction Act to establish a formal process to identify the burdens placed on the public by recordkeeping provisions and determine the level of recordkeeping that establishes the minimum burden on the public while fulfilling the regulatory purposes. The states and territories have not established a comparable, formal procedure to achieve this goal — possibly, due to the cost of monitoring state regulation.

An overly burdensome regulation can create significant harm to the public. For example, when a regulated organization is required to keep large quantities of records that would not normally be needed by the organization to conduct daily business, the organization incurs costs (e.g., staff, space, and equipment) to achieve this purpose. These costs will be reflected as expenses to the organization. It will also result in legitimate tax deductions on its tax return, reducing the organization's taxable income. As a result of the excessive burden placed by such a regulation, the organization will pay less taxes than it would with a less burdensome regulation. If a large number of organizations are affected by the regulation, the net loss in tax revenues to the jurisdiction would result in harm to the public that far exceeds the benefits gained by compliance with the regulation.

For these reasons, laws should only establish the minimum level of burden on regulated organizations necessary to achieve the regulatory purpose. Complex, inconsistent and expensive requirements may negate the benefits expected by lawmakers.

APPROPRIATE RECORDKEEPING REQUIREMENTS

Statutes and regulations specifying recordkeeping provisions should conform with the following principles to promote the public interest:

- *Laws should reflect the regulatory need, not technical system details*. Laws should focus on the regulatory needs (discussed earlier in this article) rather than details of specific information technology systems. Clearly, technology will change over time, rendering laws obsolete when specific technologies or approaches are enumerated. Legislators and regulators should identify the performance criteria or functional capabilities of the systems and not specify particular technologies nor approaches.

- *Laws should permit organizations to establish information technology systems that best meet their needs*. The public interest is best served when organizations develop systems that best meet their needs at the lowest possible cost. The systems must also meet the needs of government at the lowest possible cost to taxpayers.

  In 1985, the Federal Communication Commission eliminated almost all records retention requirements for telephone companies believing that a well-operated telephone company will retain records long enough to meet its own business needs. FCC argued that the normal business retention period will normally be adequate to also meet government needs. This philosophy has proven appropriate in the telephone industry and should be expanded greatly to other industries and jurisdictions.

- Laws should not discourage the use of any particular technology or approach, including the reproduction of records and destruction of the original records, except where a compelling need for the original records exist. Laws that discourage the reproduction of records and show preference for original records violate the public interest. When government establishes cumbersome and burdensome requirements before records can be reproduced, many potential users will be discouraged or dissuaded from adopting those systems.

Modern reproduction systems offer the opportunity to reproduce records and store them in multiple locations. In case of disaster or even attempted fraud, at least one set of records will probably remain available to government to perform its regulatory function. If records exist only in original form, due to burdensome or restrictive government requirements, government cannot perform its regulatory purpose when these records cease to exist as a result of natural disaster.

In a few instances, such as negotiable instruments, original records may be necessary to prevent fraud or abuse. But, few other records are needed in original form.

Modern technology systems often provide a series of passwords, audit trails, physical security and other methods for protecting the security of information. These measures help ensure the reliability of information and help prevent potential fraud. Paper records systems, on the other hand, rarely include any measure of security and are susceptible to fraud by even unsophisticated users. For this reason, government should permit regulated organizations to use systems that improve the security and integrity of information, resulting in improved information also available to government.

Standards and Guidelines

AIIM PERFORMANCE GUIDELINE

***See* Appendix E for the AIIM *Performance Guideline* (ANSI/AIIM TR-31).**

The Association for Information and Image Management (AIIM) mobilized a Task Force from 1991 through 1994 to examine the performance requirements of a records and information management system to ensure the admissibility of records in evidence or the acceptability of records by regulatory agencies. The result was a four-part report entitled Performance Guideline for Legal Acceptance of Records Produced by Information Technology Systems:

- Part I of the reports deals exclusively with performance guidelines for the admissibility of records in evidence.
- Part II addresses legal acceptance of records by government agencies.
- Part III provides implementation guidelines.
- Part IV provides a new proposed uniform law and model rule for implementation by government.

The Task Force consisted of lawyers, managers, vendors, system users, consultants and other interested parties from both government and the private sector. As the first step, they reviewed existing legal requirements for both evidence and regulation. They also examined available information related to legal requirements for records and information management systems.

The performance guideline will initially be published as an AIIM "technical report". After extensive review and analysis, it is hoped that the performance guidelines will ultimately be adopted as national standards in the United States. In addition, the project resulted in proposed uniform laws and model rules that, if adopted by the states or federal government, could become legal requirements.

The performance guideline responds to the multitude of legal requirements facing both the public and private sector. It also responds to a problem raised by even the uniform laws regarding technologies that did not exist at the time the uniform laws were adopted. Even though most uniform laws incorporate "any technology", they do not specify technologies such as electronic imaging technology or specify appropriate technologies that may be used for original records.

The applicability of the performance guideline is as follows:

See Performance Guideline, **Part I**

3.4 Applicability.

The guideline applies to records produced by information technology systems regardless of the physical characteristics of the record media or technology employed. This includes records produced by any technique employing an information technology system as defined above.

For purposes of this performance guideline, a new set of definitions were developed for such common terms as "record", "original record", "duplicate record", and "information technology system":

See Performance Guideline, **Section 3.3.**

3.3 Definitions

The following definitions apply to the process or system assessment criteria set forth below:

3.3.1 Record: Information preserved by any technique in any medium, now known, or later developed, that can be recognized by ordinary human sensory capabilities either directly or with the aid of technology.

3.3.2 Original record: A record prepared in the first instance or any counterpart intended to have the same effect by a person executing or issuing it. If data are stored in a computer or similar device, any printout or other output readable by sight shown to reflect the data accurately is an "original".

3.3.3 Duplicate record: A record that is produced by the same impression as the original, or from the same matrix, or by any other technique that accurately reproduces the original.

3.3.4 Information technology system: Any process or system that employs a mechanical, photo-optical, magnetic, electronic or other technological device for producing or reproducing records.

***See Performance Guideline,* Part I, Section 3.5.**

The performance guideline specifies factors for assessing the legal acceptance of records produced by any technology system. The quality of the records "relates to the ability of the information technology system to reliably produce and preserve records so that they may be used or recognized by the intended audience." Original records, for example, may "preserve information over time in the identical or functionally equivalent form to the original information." Duplicate records, on the other hand, must "accurately reproduce the originals to the extent that "information that is readable and recognizable on the originals should be readable and recognizable on the duplicates."

In order to produce accurate records, the guidelines provide specific recommendations related to the characteristics and components of the system. In order to meet legal requirements, the records must be produced as part of a regularly conducted business activity, by methods to ensure or enhance their accuracy, within a reasonably short time of the event.

The process or system used to produce the records will be critical for controlling the preparation of the records. Three key components need to be included to successfully withstand challenges to the trustworthiness of the records and information management program as a whole:

- *Procedures*: Procedures specify the methods for creating, modifying, duplicating, destroying or otherwise managing the records in a consistent and defensible manner.

- *Training*: Formal training of staff related to system operation and procedures raises a strong presumption that the staff knew what they needed to do and did in fact correctly follow procedures.

- *Audit*: Audit confirms that the process or system produces accurate results by comparing the procedures with the actual results. Audit trails specifically confirm what procedures were followed and can identify unauthorized or suspicious activity.

Documentation of the procedures, training and audit must also be kept to verify details about the process or system used to produce the records.

The performance guideline addresses a variety of other issues that have been raised regarding the legal status of records:

- Records must be maintained for the period required by the organization's records retention program, regardless of the life expectation of the media or technology used. For example, media with a short life expectancy can be used for maintaining long-term records, provided that a method is developed for recopying or reconstituting the media so that the records will exist for the requisite period.

- Regardless of the technology used, records must be submitted to courts and regulatory agencies in a form acceptable by those groups. Currently, any organization should expect to convert its records to paper form or to another form accepted by those groups. Some government agencies, for example, require data to be submitted on magnetic tape.

- The records and information management program must be available for review by outside parties, including court and government representatives, to review for accuracy.

- "Image enhancement" does not affect the legal status of records provided that the techniques do not change the information content of the records.

If the requirements of the performance guideline have been met, the records should be admissible in evidence and acceptable by regulatory agencies. However, until the guidelines or other proposed uniform laws become law, you should still review prevailing state and federal law to determine whether any provision exists that is contrary to the guidelines. In most cases, however, adherence to the performance guideline will result in compliance with state and federal laws related to records and information management.

See **Appendix C, United States — State Requirements, New Mexico, Performance Guideline for the Legal Acceptance of Records Produced by Information Technology Systems**

The State of New Mexico has already adopted a version of the performance guideline for state government records. This action converts the status of the performance guideline to a legally enforceable obligation to those state government agencies affected.

Part III provides recommendations for implementing Part I and II of the performance guidelines. It describes the process followed by several groups that successfully changed the laws regarding information technology systems in their states.

Part IV provides a model rule that jurisdictions can adopt for government records or recordkeeping systems of regulated organizations. This part also includes the following model law that may be adopted to clarify the status of information technology systems for regulatory purposes and to place some constraints on regulations affecting information technology systems:

The Uniform Records Act

§ 1. Definitions

The following definitions are used in this Act:

Record Information preserved by any technique in any media, now known or later developed.

Original records A record prepared in the first instance; a record derived from other records or any counterpart intended to have the same effect. If data are stored on a computer or similar device, any printout or other output readable by sight shown to reflect the data accurately is an "original."

Duplicate record A record that accurately reproduced the original.

Information technology system Any process or system that employs a mechanical, photo-optical, magnetic, electronic, or other technological device for producing or reproducing records.

§ 2. Records retention period

Records required to be created or kept by the laws of this state may be destroyed after three years from the time of creation unless the law establishes a specific different retention period or a specific procedure to be followed prior to destruction that results in a different retention period.

§ 3. Form of record

Original and duplicate records may be produced by any process or system, including any information technology system, regardless of the physical characteristics of the record media or technology employed. Retention of duplicate records produced under the laws of this state constitutes compliance with any laws of this state requiring that records be created or kept.

§ 4. Records requirements specified by law

No law in this state requiring records to be created or kept may specify that records be kept longer than three years, restrict the media used to maintain records, restrict the information technology system used to create or duplicate records, or require the maintenance of original records unless express, documented findings conclude that the law is necessary to satisfy specific statutory requirements or to meet other compelling needs of the government or the public. Laws may specify the data or information to be maintained, the form and content of information to be submitted to government, the requirement that records be available for inspection and audit by government, and other requirements necessary to facilitate law enforcement and government operation.

§ 5. Scope

This Act shall apply to records prepared by private individuals, partnerships, corporations or any other associations, whether carried on for profit or not, and to any government entity operating under the laws of this state.

§ 6. Uniformity of interpretation

This Act shall be so interpreted and construed as to effectuate its general purpose to make uniform the law of those states which enact it.

§ 7. Short title.

This Act will be cited as the Uniform Records Act.

§ 8. Effective date

This act shall become effective on (insert date) and shall apply to all records created before and after that date.

Until the performance guideline has been enacted as part of a statute, regulation or rule, it does not have the status of law. However, since the provisions reflect prevailing law in the United States, adherence to the performance guideline should enable an organization to comply with most state and federal laws.

CANADA DOCUMENTARY EVIDENCE STANDARDS

Permission had not been received at the time of publication to reproduce the text of Canadian General Standards Board revised National Standard of Canada entitled *Microfilm and Electronic Images As Documentary Evidence* (CAN/CGSB-72.11-93).

Instead of uniform laws, Canada has developed a unique and effective approach to standardization of records and information management systems for purposes of evidence. Canadian rules of evidence specify that reproductions of records may be admitted in place of the original records (even if the original records have been destroyed) if certain procedural safeguards have been met. In particular, the Evidence Acts recognize that reproductions produced under "national standards" improve the accuracy of the reproductions, justifying the destruction of the original records in the "usual and ordinary course of business". The national standards create a quasi-legal standard against which the courts will determine the accuracy of the reproductions and whether they will be admitted into evidence.

This document specifies the standards for producing microfilm and electronic images for admissibility in evidence and the appropriate procedures for destruction of original records. The document provides extensive detail and recommendations for making an accurate reproduction using either technology.

AMERICAN BAR ASSOCIATION POSITION ON LEGAL STANDARDS FOR ELECTRONIC RECORDS

See **Appendix E.**

The American Bar Association House of Delegates approved Resolution Number 115 that supports the development of legal standards to "encourage the use of information in electronic form:"

> The American Bar Association supports action by federal and state governments, international organizations, and private entities to:
>
> a) facilitate and promote the orderly development of legal standards to encourage the use of information in electronic form, including appropriate legal and professional education;
>
> b) encourage the use of appropriate and properly implemented security techniques, procedures and practices to assure the authenticity and integrity of information in electronic form; and
>
> c) recognize that information in electronic form, where appropriate, may be considered to satisfy legal requirements regarding a writing or signature to the same extent as information on paper or in other conventional forms, when appropriate security techniques, practices, and procedures have been adopted.

Appendices

The following symbols are used to identify each type of law in the Appendix:

- ☞ Evidence
- ✪ Government
- ✍ Regulation

Appendix A United States — Uniform Laws

The following Uniform Laws were prepared by the National Conference of Commissioners on Uniform State Laws. Differences may exist between the original versions and the versions finally adopted by the states.

Source: Uniform Business Records As Evidence Act

UNIFORM BUSINESS RECORDS AS EVIDENCE ACT.

§ 1. "Business" defined.

The term "business" shall include every kind of business, profession, occupation, calling or operation of institutions, whether carried on for profit or not.

§ 2. Business records as evidence.

A record of an act, condition or event, shall in so far as relevant, be competent evidence if the custodian or other qualified witness testifies to its identity and the mode of its preparation, and if it was made in the regular course of business, at or near the time of the act, condition or event, and if, in the opinion of the court, the sources of information, method and time of preparation were such as to justify its admission.

§ 3. Construction.

This chapter shall be so interpreted and construed as to effectuate its general purpose to make uniform the law of those states which enact it.

§ 4. Short title.

This chapter may be cited as the "Uniform Business Records as Evidence Act."

The following states have adopted this Uniform Law:

Arizona	New York
California	North Dakota
Connecticut	Ohio
Idaho	Pennsylvania
Minnesota	Rhode Island
Missouri	South Carolina
New Jersey	Vermont

Source: Uniform Photographic Copies of Business and Public Records As Evidence Act

UNIFORM PHOTOGRAPHIC COPIES OF BUSINESS AND PUBLIC RECORDS AS EVIDENCE ACT.

§ 1. Admissibility of reproduced records in evidence.

If any business, institution, member of a profession or calling, or any department or agency of government, in the regular course of business or activity has kept or recorded any memorandum, writing, entry, print, representation or combination thereof, of any act, transaction, occurrence or event, and in the regular course of business has caused any or all of the same to be recorded, copied or reproduced by any photographic, photostatic, microfilm, micro-card, miniature photographic, or other process which accurately reproduces or forms a durable medium for so reproducing the original, the original may be destroyed in the regular course of business unless held in a custodial or fiduciary capacity or unless its preservation is required by law. Such reproduction, when satisfactorily identified, is as admissible in evidence as the original itself in any judicial or administrative proceeding whether the original is in existence or not and an enlargement or facsimile of such reproduction is likewise admissible in evidence if the original reproduction is in existence and available for inspection under direction of court. The introduction of a reproduced record, enlargement or facsimile, does not preclude admission of the original.

§ 2. Interpretation.

This act shall be so interpreted and construed as to effectuate its general purpose of making uniform the law of those states which enact it.

§ 3. Short title.

This act may be cited as the "Uniform Photographic Copies of Business and Public Records as Evidence Act."

[The following jurisdictions have adopted this uniform law. Check the federal version in Appendix B. and the state versions in Appendix C. for variations.]

Alabama
Arkansas
Arizona
California
Colorado
Connecticut
Georgia
Idaho
Illinois
Iowa
Kansas
Kentucky
Maine
Maryland
Massachusetts
Michigan
Minnesota
Nebraska
Nevada
New Hampshire
New York
North Carolina
North Dakota
Pennsylvania
South Carolina
South Dakota
United States
Utah
Vermont
Virgin Islands
Virginia
Washington
West Virginia
Wisconsin

Source: Uniform Preservation of Private Business Records Act

UNIFORM PRESERVATION OF PRIVATE BUSINESS RECORDS ACT

§ 1. Definitions.

As used in this Act:

"Business" includes every kind of private business, profession, occupation, calling or operation of private institutions, whether carried on for profit or not.

"Person" means an individual, partnership, corporation, or any other association.

"Records" or "Business Records" include books of account, vouchers, documents, canceled checks, payrolls, correspondence, records of sales, personnel, equipment and production, reports relating to any or all of such records, and other business papers.

"Reproduction" means a reproduction or durable medium for making a reproduction obtained by any photographic, photostatic, microfilm, micro-card, miniature photographic or other process which accurately reproduces or forms a durable medium for so reproducing the original.

§ 2. Period of preservation.

Unless a specific period is designated by law for their preservation, business records which persons by the laws of this state are required to keep or preserve may be destroyed after the expiration of three years from the making of such records without constituting an offense under such laws. [This section does not apply to minute books of corporations nor to records of sales or other transactions involving weapons, poisons or other dangerous articles or substances capable of use in the commission of crimes.]

§ 3. Preservation of reproductions.

If in the regular course of business a person makes reproductions of original business records, the preservation of such reproductions constitutes compliance with any laws of this State requiring that business records be kept or preserved.

§ 4. Destruction of records by state officers.

Nothing in this Act shall be construed to diminish the authority of an officer of this State under existing law to permit the destruction of business records.

§ 5. Uniformity of interpretation.

This Act shall be so interpreted and construed as to effectuate its general purpose to make uniform the law of those states which enact it.

§ 6. Short title.

This act may be cited as the Uniform Preservation of Private Business Records Act.

The following have adopted this Uniform Law:

Colorado
Georgia
Illinois
Maryland
New Hampshire
Oklahoma
Texas

Source: Uniform Rules of Evidence

UNIFORM RULES OF EVIDENCE

Article VIII. Hearsay.

Rule 801. Definitions.

The following definitions apply under this article:

(a) *Statement.* A "statement" is (1) an oral or written assertion or (2) nonverbal conduct of a person, if it is intended by the person to be an assertion.

(b) *Declarant.* A "declarant" is a person who makes a statement.

(c) *Hearsay.* "Hearsay" is a statement other than one made by the declarant while testifying at the trial or hearing, offered in evidence to prove the truth of the matter asserted.

(d) *Statements which are not hearsay.* A statement is not hearsay if—

(1) Prior statement by witness. The declarant testifies at the trial or hearing and is subject to cross-examination concerning the statement, and the statement is (A) inconsistent with the declarant's testimony, and was given under oath subject to the penalty of perjury at a trial, hearing, or other proceeding, or in a deposition, or (B) consistent with the declarant's testimony and is offered to rebut an express or implied charge against the declarant of recent fabrication or improper influence or motive, or (C) one of identification of a person made after perceiving the person; or

(2) Admission by party-opponent. The statement is offered against a party and is (A) the party's own statement in either an individual or representative capacity or (B) a statement of which the party has manifested an adoption or belief in its truth, or (C) a statement by a person authorized by the party to make a statement concerning the subject, or (D) a statement by the party's agent or servant concerning a matter within the scope of the agency or employment, made during the existence of the relationship, or (E) a statement by a coconspirator of a party during the course and in furtherance of the conspiracy.

Rule 802. Hearsay Rule.

Hearsay is not admissible except as provided by law or by these rules.

Rule 803. Hearsay exceptions; availability of declarant immaterial.

The following are not excluded by the hearsay rule, even though the declarant is available as a witness:

* * * * *

(5) Recorded recollection. A memorandum or record concerning a matter about which a witness once had knowledge but now has insufficient recollection to enable him to testify fully and accurately, shown to have been made or adopted by the witness when the matter was fresh in the witness' memory and to reflect that knowledge correctly. If admitted, the memorandum or record may be read into evidence but may not itself be received as an exhibit unless offered by an adverse party.

(6) Records of regularly conducted activity. A memorandum, report, record, or data compilation, in any form, of acts, events, conditions, opinions, or diagnoses, made at or near the time by, or from information transmitted by, a person with knowledge, if kept in the course of a regularly conducted business activity, and if it was the regular practice of that business activity to make the memorandum, report, record, or data compilation, all as shown by the testimony of the custodian or other qualified witness, unless the source of information or the method or circumstances of preparation indicate lack of trustworthiness. The term "business" as used in this paragraph includes business, institution, association, profession, occupation, and calling of every kind, whether or not conducted for profit.

(7) Absence of entry in records kept in accordance with the provisions of paragraph (6). Evidence that a matter is not included in the memoranda, reports, records, or data compilations, in any form, kept in accordance with the provisions or paragraph (6), to prove the nonoccurrence or nonexistence of the matter, if the matter was of a kind of which a memorandum, report, record, or data compilation was regularly made and preserved, unless the sources of information or other circumstances indicate lack of trustworthiness.

(8) Public records and reports. Records, reports, statements, or data compilations in any form of a public office or agency setting forth its regularly conducted and regularly recorded activities, or matters observed pursuant to duty imposed by law and as to which there was a duty to report, or factual findings resulting from an investigation made pursuant to authority granted by law. The following are not within this exception to the hearsay rule: (i) investigative reports by police and other law enforcement personnel; (ii) investigative reports prepared by or for a government, a public office, or an agency when offered by it in a case in which it is a party; (iii) factual findings offered by the government in criminal cases; (iv) factual findings resulting from special investigation of a particular complaint, case, or incident; and (v) any matter as to which the sources of information or other circumstances indicate lack of trustworthiness.

(9) Records of vital statistics. Records or data compilations, in any form, of births, fetal deaths, deaths, or marriages, if the report thereof was made to a public office pursuant to requirements of law.

(10) Absence of public record or entry. To prove the absence of a record, report, statement, or data compilation, in any form, or the nonoccurrence or nonexistence of a matter of which a record, report, statement, or data compilation, in any form, was regularly made and preserved by a public office or agency, evidence in the form of a certification in accordance with Rule 902, or testimony, that diligent search failed to disclose the record, report, statement, or data compilation, or entry.

(11) Records of religious organizations. Statements of births, marriages, divorces, death, legitimacy, ancestry, relationship by blood or marriage, or other similar facts of personal or family history, contained in a regularly kept record of a religious organization.

(12) Marriage, baptismal, and similar certificates. Statements of fact contained in a certificate that the maker performed a marriage or other ceremony or administered a sacrament, made by a clergyman, public official, or other person authorized by the rules or practices of a religious organization or by law to perform the act certified, and purporting to have been issued at the time of the act or within a reasonable time thereafter.

(13) Family records. Statements of fact concerning personal or family history contained in family Bibles, genealogies, charts, engravings on rings, inscriptions on family portraits, engravings on urns, crypts, or tombstones, or the like.

(14) Records of documents affecting an interest in property. The record of a document purporting to establish or affect an interest in property, as proof of the content of the original recorded document and its execution and delivery by each person by whom it purports to have been executed, if the record is a record of a public office and an applicable statute authorizes the recording of documents of that kind in that office.

(15) Statements in documents affecting an interest in property. A statement contained in a document purporting to establish or affect an interest in property if the matter stated was relevant to the purpose of the document, unless dealings with the property since the document was made have been inconsistent with the truth of the statement or the purport of the document.

(16) Statements in ancient documents. Statements in a document in existence twenty years or more the authenticity of which is established.

(17) Market reports, commercial publications. Market quotations, tabulations, lists, directories, or other published compilations, generally used and relied upon by the public or by persons in particular occupations.

(18) Learned treatises. To the extent called to the attention of an expert witness upon cross-examination or relied upon by expert witness in direct examination, statements contained in published treatises, periodicals, or pamphlets on a subject of history, medicine, or other science or art, established as a reliable authority by testimony or admission of the witness or by other expert testimony or by judicial notice. If admitted, the statements may be read into evidence but may not be received as exhibits.

* * * * *

Article IX. Authentication and Identification.

Rule 901. Requirements of Authentication or Identification.

(a) General provision. The requirement of authentication or identification as a condition precedent to admissibility is satisfied by evidence sufficient to support a finding that the matter in question is what its proponent claims.

(b) Illustrations. By way of illustration only, and not by way of limitation, the following are examples of authentication or identification conforming with the requirements of this rule:

* * * * *

(7) Public records or reports. Evidence that a writing authorized by law to be recorded or filed and in fact recorded or filed in a public office, or a purported public record, report, statement, or data compilation, in any form, is from the public office where items of this nature are kept.

(8) Ancient documents or data compilation. Evidence that a document or data compilation, in any form, (A) is in such condition as to create no suspicion concerning its authenticity, (B) was in a place where it, if authentic, would likely be, and (C) has been in existence 20 years or more at the time it is offered.

(9) Process or system. Evidence describing a process or system used to produce a result and showing that the process or system produces an accurate result.

Rule 902. Self-authentication.

Extrinsic evidence of authenticity as a condition precedent to admissibility is not required with respect to the following:

(1) Domestic public documents under seal. A document bearing a seal purporting to be that of the United States, or of any State, district, Commonwealth, territory, or insular possession thereof, or the Panama Canal Zone, or the Trust Territory of the Pacific Islands, or of a political subdivision, department, officer, or agency thereof, and a signature purporting to be an attestation or execution.

(2) Domestic public documents not under seal. A document purporting to bear the signature in his official capacity of an officer or employee of any entity included in paragraph (1) hereof, having no seal, if a public officer having a seal and having official duties in the district or political subdivision of the officer or employee certifies under seal that the signer has the official capacity and that the signature is genuine.

(3) Foreign public documents. A document purporting to be executed or attested in his official capacity by a person authorized by the laws of a foreign country to make the execution or attestation, and accompanied by a final certification as to the genuineness of the signature and official position (A) of the executing or attesting person, or (B) of any foreign official whose certificate of genuineness of signature and official position relates to the execution or attestation or is in a chain of certificates of genuineness of signature and official position relating to the execution or attestation. A final certification may be made by a secretary of embassy or legation, consul general, consul, vice consul, or consular agent of the United States, or a diplomatic or consular official of the foreign country assigned or accredited to the United States. If reasonable opportunity has been given to all parties to investigate the authenticity and accuracy of official documents, the court may, for good cause shown, order that they be treated as presumptively authentic without final certification or permit them to be evidenced by an attested summary with or without final certification.

(4) Certified copies of public records. A copy of an official record or report or entry therein, or of a document authorized by law to be recorded or filed and actually recorded or filed in a public office, including data compilations in any form, certified as correct by the custodian or other person authorized to make the certification, by certificate complying with paragraph (1), (2), or (3) of this rule or complying with paragraph (1), (2), or (3) of this rule or complying with any Act of Congress or rule prescribed by the Supreme Court pursuant to statutory authority.

(5) Official publications. Books, pamphlets, or other publications purporting to be issued by public authority.

(6) Newspapers and periodicals. Printed materials purporting to be newspapers or periodicals.

(7) Trade inscriptions and the like. Inscriptions, signs, tags, or labels purporting to have been affixed in the course of business and indicating ownership control, or origin.

(8) Acknowledged documents. Documents accompanied by a certificate of acknowledgment executed in the manner provided by law by a notary public or other officer authorized by law to take acknowledgments.

(9) Commercial paper and related documents. Commercial paper, signatures thereon, and documents relating thereto to the extent provided by general commercial law.

(10) Presumptions under Acts of Congress. Any signature, document or other matter declared by Act of Congress to be presumptively or prima facie genuine or authentic.

Article X. Contents of Writings, Recordings, and Photographs.

Rule 1001. Definitions.

For purposes of this Article the following definitions are applicable:

(1) Writings and recordings. "Writings" and "recordings" consist of letters, words, sounds, or numbers, or their equivalent, set down by handwriting, typewriting, printing, photostating, photographing, magnetic impulse, mechanical or electronic recording, or other form of data compilation.

(2) Photographs. "Photographs" include still photographs, X-ray films, video tapes, and motion pictures.

(3) Original. An "original" of a writing or recording is the writing or recording itself or any counterpart intended to have the same effect by a person executing or issuing it. An "original" of a photograph includes the negative or any print therefrom. If data are stored in a computer or similar device, any printout or other output readable by sight, shown to reflect the data accurately, is an "original."

(4) Duplicate. A "duplicate" is a counterpart produced by the same impression as the original, or from the same matrix, or by means of photography, including enlargements and miniatures, or by mechanical or electronic rerecording, or by chemical reproduction, or by other equivalent techniques which accurately reproduces the original.

Rule 1002. Requirement of original.

To prove the content of a writing, recording, or photograph, the original writing, recording, or photograph is required, except as otherwise provided in these rules or by [rules adopted by the Supreme Court of this State or by] Act of Congress.

Rule 1003. Admissibility of duplicates.

A duplicate is admissible to the same extent as an original unless (1) a genuine question is raised as to the authenticity of the original or (2) in the circumstances it would be unfair to admit the duplicate in lieu of the original.

Rule 1004. Admissibility of other evidence of contents.

The original is not required, and other evidence of the contents of a writing, recording, or photograph is admissible if:

(1) Originals lost or destroyed. All originals are lost or have been destroyed, unless the proponent lost or destroyed them in bad faith; or

(2) Original not obtainable. No original can be obtained by any available judicial process or procedure; or

(3) Original in possession of opponent. At a time when an original was under the control of the party against whom offered, that party was put on notice, by the pleadings or otherwise, that the contents would be a subject of proof at the hearing, and that party does not produce the original at the hearing; or

(4) Collateral matters. The writing, recording, or photograph is not closely related to a controlling issue.

Rule 1005. Public records.

The contents of an official record, or of a document authorized to be recorded or filed and actually recorded or filed, including data compilations in any form, if otherwise admissible, may be proved by copy, certified as correct in accordance with Rule 902 or testified to be correct by a witness who has compared it with the original. If a copy complying with the foregoing cannot be obtained by the exercise of reasonable diligence, then other evidence of the contents may be given.

Rule 1006. Summaries.

The contents of voluminous writings, recordings, or photographs which cannot conveniently be examined in court may be presented in the form of a chart, summary, or calculation. The originals, or duplicates, shall be made available for examination or copying, or both, by other parties at a reasonable time and place. The court may order that they be produced in court.

The following jurisdictions have adopted the Uniform Rules of Evidence:

Alabama
Alaska
Arizona
Arkansas
Colorado
Delaware
Florida
Guam
Hawaii
Idaho
Indiana
Iowa
Kentucky
Louisiana
Maine
Maryland
Michigan
Minnesota
Mississippi
Missouri
Montana
Nebraska
Nevada
New Hampshire
New Jersey
New Mexico
North Carolina
North Dakota
Ohio
Oklahoma
Oregon
Puerto Rico
Rhode Island
South Carolina
South Dakota
Tennessee
Texas
United States
Utah
Vermont
Washington
West Virginia
Wisconsin
Wyoming

Appendix B United States — Federal Requirements

Country:	**United States — Federal**
Source:	**United States Code**

TITLE 10. ARMED FORCES

SUBTITLE A. GENERAL MILITARY LAW

PART 4. SERVICE, SUPPLY, AND PROCUREMENT

CHAPTER 137. PROCUREMENT GENERALLY.

Citation:	**10 USC 2313**

✍ **§ 2313. Examination of records of contractor.**

(a) *Agency Authority.* — (1) The head of an agency, acting through an authorized representative, is authorized to inspect the plant and audit the records of —

(A) a contractor performing a cost-reimbursement, incentive, time-and-materials, labor-hour, or price-redeterminable contract, or any combination of such contracts, made by that agency under this chapter; and

(B) a subcontractor performing any cost-reimbursement, incentive, time-and-materials, labor-hour, or price-redeterminable subcontract or any combination of such subcontracts under a contract referred to in subparagraph (A).

(2) The head of an agency, acting through an authorized representative, is authorized, for the purpose of evaluating the accuracy, completeness, and currency of certified cost or pricing data required to be submitted pursuant to § 2306a of this title with respect to a contract or subcontract, to examine all records of the contractor or subcontractor related to —

(A) the proposal for the contract or subcontract;

(B) the discussions conducted on the proposal;

(C) pricing of the contract or subcontract; or

(D) performance of the contract or subcontract.

(b) *DCAA Subpoena Authority.* — (1) The Director of the Defense Contract Audit Agency (or any successor agency) may require by subpoena the production of the records of a contractor that the Secretary of Defense is authorized to audit or examine under subsection (a).

(2) Any such subpoena, in he case of contumacy or refusal to obey, shall be enforceable by order of an appropriate United States district court.

(3) The authority provided by paragraph (1) may not be redelegated.

(4) The Director (or any successor official) shall submit an annual report to the Secretary of Defense on the exercise of such authority during the preceding year and the reasons why such authority was exercised in any instance. The Secretary shall forward a copy of such report to the Committees on Armed Services of the Senate and House of Representatives.

(c) *Comptroller General Authority.* — (1) Except as provided in paragraph (2), each contract awarded after using procedures other than sealed bid procedures shall provide that the Comptroller General and his representatives are authorized to examine any records of the contractor, or any of its subcontractors, that directly pertain to, and involve transactions relating to, the contract or subcontract.

(2) Paragraph (1) does not apply to a contract or subcontract with a foreign contractor or foreign subcontractor if the had of the agency concerned determines, with the concurrence of the Comptroller General or his designee, that the application of that paragraph to the contract or subcontract would not be in the public interest. However, the concurrence of the Comptroller General or his designee is not required —

(A) where the contractor or subcontractor is a foreign government or agency thereof or is precluded by the laws of the country involved from making its records available for examination; and

(B) where the head of the agency determines, after taking into account the price and availability of the property and services from United States sources that the public interest would be best served by not applying paragraph (1).

(3) Paragraph (1) may not be construed to require a contractor or subcontractor to create or maintain any record that the contractor or subcontractor does not maintain in the ordinary course of business or pursuant to another provision of law.

(d) *Limitation on Preaward Audits Relating to Indirect Costs.* — (1) The head of an agency may not perform a preaward audit to evaluate proposed indirect costs under any contract, subcontract, or modification to be entered into in accordance with this chapter in any case in which the contracting officer determines that the objectives of the audit can reasonably be met by accepting the results of an audit conducted by any other department or agency of the Federal Government within one year preceding the date of the contracting officer's determination.

(e) *Limitation.* — The authority of the head of an agency under subsection (a), and the authority of the Comptroller General under subsection (c), with respect to a contract or subcontract shall expire three years after final payment under such contract or subcontract.

(f) *Inapplicability to Certain Contracts.* This section does not apply to the following contracts:

(1) Contracts for utility services at rates not exceeding those established to apply uniformly to the public, plus any applicable reasonable connection charge.

(2) A contract or subcontract that is for an amount not greater than the simplified acquisition threshold.

(g) *Forms of Original Record Storage.* — Nothing in this section shall be construed to preclude a contractor from duplicating or storing original records in electronic form.

(h) *Use of Images of Original Records.* — The head of an agency shall not require a contractor or subcontractor to provide original records in an audit carried out pursuant to this section if the contractor or subcontractor provides photographic or electronic images of the original records and meets the following requirements:

(1) The contractor or subcontractor has established procedures to ensure that the imaging process preserves the integrity, reliability, and security of the original records.

(2) The contractor or subcontractor maintains an effective indexing system to permit timely and convenient access to the imaged records.

(3) The contractor or subcontractor retains the original records for a minimum of one year after imaging to permit periodic validation of the imaging systems.

(i) *Records Defined.* — In this section, the term "records" includes books, documents, accounting procedures and practices, and other data, regardless of type and regardless of whether such items are in written form, in the form of computer data, or in any other form.

TITLE 12. BANKS AND BANKING

CHAPTER 16. FEDERAL DEPOSIT INSURANCE CORPORATION

Citation: 12 USC 1829b

✍ § 1829b. Retention of records by insured depository institution(s).

* * * * *

(d) Reproduction of checks, drafts, and other instruments; record of transactions; identity of party

Each insured depository institution(s) shall make, to the extent that the regulations of the Secretary so require —

(1) a microfilm or other reproduction of each check, draft, or similar instrument drawn on it and presented to it for payment; and

(2) a record of each check, draft, or similar instrument received by it for deposit or collection, together with an identification of the party for whose account it is to be deposited or collected, unless the insured depository institution(s) has already made a record of the party's identity pursuant to subsection (c) of this section.

* * * * *

(g) Retention period

Any type of record or evidence required under this section shall be retained for such period as the Secretary may prescribe for the type in question. Any period so prescribed shall not exceed six years unless the Secretary determines, having regard for the purposes of this section, that a longer period is necessary in the case of a particular type of record or evidence.

* * * * *

TITLE 28. JUDICIARY AND JUDICIAL PROCEDURE

PART 5. PROCEDURE

CHAPTER 115. EVIDENCE; DOCUMENTARY

Citation: 28 USC 1732

☞ § 1732. Record made in regular course of business; photographic copies

If any business, institution, member of a profession or calling, or any department or agency of government, in the regular course of business or activity has kept or recorded any memorandum, writing, entry, print, representation or combination thereof, of any act, transaction, occurrence, or event, and in the regular course of business has caused any or all of the same to be recorded, copied, or reproduced by any photographic, photostatic, microfilm, micro-card, miniature photographic, or other process which accurately reproduces or forms a durable medium for so reproducing the original, the original may be destroyed in the regular course of business unless its preservation is required by law. Such reproduction, when satisfactorily identified, is as admissible in evidence as the original itself in any judicial or administrative proceeding whether the original is in existence or not and an enlargement or facsimile of such reproduction is likewise admissible in evidence if the original reproduction is in existence and available for inspection under direction of court. The introduction of a reproduced record, enlargement, or facsimile does not preclude admission of the original. This subsection shall not be construed to exclude from evidence any document or copy thereof which is otherwise admissible under the rules of evidence.

TITLE 28 APPENDIX. FEDERAL RULES OF EVIDENCE FOR UNITED STATES COURTS AND MAGISTRATES

ARTICLE X. CONTENTS OF WRITINGS, RECORDINGS, AND PHOTOGRAPHS

Citation: 28 USC Rule 1001

☞ Rule 1001. Definitions

For purposes of this article the following definitions are applicable:

(1) *Writings and recordings.* — "Writings" and "recordings" consist of letters, words, or numbers, or their equivalent, set down by handwriting, typewriting, printing, photostating, photographing, magnetic impulse, mechanical or electronic recording, or other form of data compilation.

(2) *Photographs.* — "Photographs" include still photographs, X-ray films, video tapes, and motion pictures.

(3) *Original.* — An "original" of a writing or recording is the writing or recording itself or any counterpart intended to have the same effect by a person executing or issuing it. An "original" of a photograph includes the negative or any print therefrom. If data are stored in a computer or similar device, any printout or other output readable by sight, shown to reflect the data accurately, is an "original."

(4) *Duplicate.* — A "duplicate" is a counterpart produced by the same impression as the original, or from the same matrix, or by means of photography, including enlargements and miniatures, or by mechanical or electronic re-recording, or by chemical reproduction, or by other equivalent techniques which accurately reproduces the original.

Citation: 28 USC Rule 1002

☞ Rule 1002. Requirement of Original

To prove the content of a writing, recording, or photograph, the original writing, recording, or photograph is required, except as otherwise provided in these rules or by Act of Congress.

Citation: 28 USC Rule 1003

☞ Rule 1003. Admissibility of Duplicates

A duplicate is admissible to the same extent as an original unless (1) a genuine question is raised as to the authenticity of the original or (2) in the circumstances it would be unfair to admit the duplicate in lieu of the original.

Citation: 28 USC Rule 1004

☞ Rule 1004. Admissibility of Other Evidence of Contents

The original is not required, and other evidence of the contents of a writing, recording, or photograph is admissible if—

(1) *Originals lost or destroyed.* — All originals are lost or have been destroyed, unless the proponent lost or destroyed them in bad faith; or

(2) *Original not obtainable.* — No original can be obtained by any available judicial process or procedure; or

(3) *Original in possession of opponent.* — At a time when an original was under the control of the party against whom offered, that party was put on notice, by the pleadings or otherwise, that the contents would be a subject of proof at the hearing, and that party does not produce the original at the hearing; or

(4) *Collateral matters.* — The writing, recording, or photograph is not closely related to a controlling issue.

Citation: 28 USC Rule 1005

☞ Rule 1005. Public records.

The contents of an official record, or of a document authorized to be recorded or filed and actually recorded or filed, including data compilations in any form, if otherwise admissible, may be proved by copy, certified as correct in accordance with Rule 902 or testified to be correct by a witness who has compared it with the original. If a copy complying with the foregoing cannot be obtained by the exercise of reasonable diligence, then other evidence of the contents may be given.

Citation: 28 USC Rule 1006

☞ Rule 1006. Summaries

The contents of voluminous writings, recordings, or photographs which cannot conveniently be examined in court may be presented in the form of a chart, summary, or calculation. The originals, or duplicates, shall be made available for examination or copying, or both, by other parties at reasonable time and place. The court may order that they be produced in court.

Citation: 28 USC Rule 1007

☞ Rule 1007. Testimony or Written Admission of Party

Contents of writings, recordings, or photographs may be proved by the testimony or deposition of the party against whom offered or by that party's written admission, without accounting for the nonproduction of the original.

TITLE 44. PUBLIC PRINTING AND DOCUMENTS

CHAPTER 35. COORDINATION OF FEDERAL INFORMATION POLICY

Citation: 44 USC 3501

✪ § 3501 Purposes.

The purposes of this chapter are to —

(1) minimize the paperwork burden for individuals, small businesses, educational and nonprofit institutions, Federal contractors, State, local and tribal governments, and other persons resulting from the collection of information by or for the Federal Government;

(2) ensure the greatest possible public benefit from and maximize the utility of information created, collected, maintained, used, shared and disseminated by or for the Federal government;

(3) coordinate, integrate, and to the extent practicable and appropriate, make uniform Federal information resources management policies and practices as a means to improve the productivity, efficiency, and effectiveness of Government programs, including the reduction of information collection burdens on the public and the improvement of service delivery to the public;

(4) improve the quality and use of Federal information to strengthen decision-making, accountability, and openness in Government and society;

(5) minimize the cost to the Federal Government of the creation, collection, maintenance, use, dissemination, and disposition of information;

(6) strengthen the partnership between the Federal Government and State, local, and tribal governments by minimizing the burden and maximizing the utility of information created, collected, maintained, used, disseminated, and retained by or for the Federal Government;

(7) provide for the dissemination of public information on a timely basis, on equitable terms, and in a manner that promotes the utility of the information to the public and makes effective use of information technology;

(8) ensure that the creation, collection, maintenance, use, dissemination, and disposition of information by or for the Federal Government is consistent with applicable laws, including laws relating to—

(A) privacy and confidentiality, including section 552a of title 5;

(B) security of information, including the Computer Security Act of 1987 (Public Law 100-235); and

(C) access to information, including section 552 of title 5;

(9) ensure the integrity, quality, and utility of the Federal statistical system;

(10) ensure that information technology is acquired, used, and managed to improve performance of agency missions, including the reduction of information collection burdens on the public; and

(11) improve the responsibility and accountability of the Office

of Management and Budget and all other Federal agencies to Congress and to the public for implementing the information collection review process, information resources management, and related policies and guidelines established under this chapter.

Citation: **44 USC 3502**

✪ § 3502. Definitions.

As used in this chapter —

(1) the term "agency" means any executive department, military department, Government corporation, Government controlled corporation, or other establishment in the executive branch of the Government (including the Executive Office of the President), or any independent regulatory agency, but does not include—

(A) the General Accounting Office;

(B) Federal Election Commission;

(C) the governments of the District of Columbia and of the territories and possessions of the United States, and their various subdivisions; or

(D) Government-owned contractor-operated facilities, including laboratories engaged in national defense research and production activities;

(2) the term "burden" means time, effort or financial resources expended by persons to generate, maintain, or provide information to or for a Federal agency, including the resources expended for—

(A) reviewing instructions;

(B) acquiring, installing, and utilizing technology and systems;

(C) adjusting the existing ways to comply with any previously applicable instructions and requirements;

(D) searching data sources;

(E) completing and reviewing the collection of information; and

(F) transmitting, or otherwise disclosing the information;

(3) the term "collection of information"—

(A) means the obtaining, causing to be obtained, soliciting, or requiring the disclosure to third parties of the public, of facts or opinions by or for an agency, regardless of form or format, calling for either—

(i) answers to identical questions posed to, or identical reporting or recordkeeping requirements imposed on, ten or more persons, other than agencies, instrumentalities, or employees of the United States; or

(ii) answers to questions posed to agencies, instrumentalities, or employees of the United States which are to be used for general statistical purposes; and

(B) shall not include a collection of information described under section 3518(c)(1);

(4) the term "Director" means the Director of the Office of Management and Budget;

(5) the term "independent regulatory agency" means the Board of Governors of the Federal Reserve System, the Commodity Futures Trading Commission, the Consumer Product Safety Commission, the Federal Communications Commission, the Federal Deposit Insurance Corporation, the Federal Energy Regulatory Commission, the Federal Housing Finance Board, the Federal Maritime Commission, the Federal Trade Commission, the Interstate Commerce Commission, the Mine Enforcement Safety and Health Review Commission, the National Labor Relations Board, the Nuclear Regulatory Commission, the Occupational Safety and Health Review Commission, the Postal Rate Commission, the Securities and Exchange Commission, and any other similar agency designated by statute as a Federal independent regulatory agency or commission;

(6) the term "information resources" means information and related resources, such as personnel, equipment, funds, and information technology;

(7) the term "information resources management" means the process of managing information resources to accomplish agency missions and to improve agency performance, including through the reduction of information collection burdens on the public;

(8) the term "information system" means a discrete set of information resources organized for the collection, processing, maintenance, use, sharing, dissemination, or disposition of information;

(9) the term "information technology" has the meaning given that term in section 5002 of the Clinger-Cohen Act of 1996 but does not include national security systems as defined in section 5142 of that Act;

(10) the term "person" means an individual, partnership, association, corporation, business trust, or legal representative, an organized group of individuals, a State, territorial, tribal, or local government or branch thereof, or a political subdivision of a State, territory, tribal, or local government or a branch of a political subdivision;

(11) the term "practical utility" means the ability of an agency to use information, particularly the capability to process such information in a timely and useful fashion;

(12) the term "public information" means any information, regardless of form or format, that an agency discloses, disseminates, or makes available to the public;

(13) the term "recordkeeping requirement" means a requirement imposed by or for an agency on persons to maintain specified records, including a requirement to—

(A) retain such records;

(B) notify third parties, the Federal Government, or the public of the existence of such records;

(C) disclose such records to third parties, the Federal Government, or the public; or

(D) report to third parties, the Federal Government, or the public regarding such records; and

(14) the term "penalty" includes the imposition by an agency or court of a fine or other punishment; a judgment for monetary damages or equitable relief; or the revocation, suspension, reduction, or denial of a license, privilege, right, grant, or benefit.

Citation: **44 USC 3503**

✪ § 3503. Office of Information and Regulatory Affairs

(a) There is established in the Office of Management and Budget an office to be known as the Office of Information and Regulatory Affairs.

(b) There shall be at the head of the Office an Administrator who shall be appointed by the President, by and with the advice and consent of the Senate. The Director shall delegate to the Administrator the authority to administer all functions under this chapter (44 USCS 3501 et seq.), except that any such delegation shall not relieve the Director of responsibility for the administration of such functions. The Administrator shall serve as principal adviser to the Director on Federal information policy.

Citation: **44 USC 3504**

✪ § 3504. Authority and functions of Director.

(a)(1) The Director shall oversee the use of information resources to improve the efficiency and effectiveness of governmental operations to serve agency missions, including burden reduction and service delivery to the public. In performing such oversight, the Director shall—

(A) develop, coordinate and oversee the implementation of Federal information resources management policies, principles, standards, and guidelines; and

(B) provide direction and oversee—

(i) the review and approval of the collection of information and the reduction of the information collection burden;

(ii) agency dissemination of and public access to information;

(iii) statistical activities;

(iv) records management activities;

(v) privacy, confidentiality, security, disclosure, and sharing of information; and

(vi) the acquisition and use of information technology.

(2) The authority of the Director under this chapter shall be exercised consistent with applicable law.

(b) With respect to general information resources management policy, the Director shall—

(1) develop and oversee the implementation of uniform information resources management policies, principles, standards, and guidelines;

(2) foster greater sharing, dissemination, and access to public information, including through—

(A) the use of the Government Information Locator Service; and

(B) the development and utilization of common standards for information collection, storage, processing and communication, including standards for security, interconnectivity and interoperability;

(3) initiate and review proposals for changes in legislation, regulations, and agency procedures to improve information resources management practices;

(4) oversee the development and implementation of best practices in information resources management, including training; and

(5) oversee agency integration of program and management functions with information resources management functions.

(c) With respect to the collection of information and the control of paperwork, the Director shall—

(1) review and approve proposed agency collections of information;

(2) coordinate the review of the collection of information associated with Federal procurement and acquisition by the Office of Information and Regulatory Affairs with the Office of Federal Procurement Policy, with particular emphasis on applying information technology to improve the efficiency and effectiveness of Federal procurement, acquisition and payment, and to reduce information collection burdens on the public;

(3) minimize the Federal information collection burden, with particular emphasis on those individuals and entities most adversely affected;

(4) maximize the practical utility of and public benefit from information collected by or for the Federal Government; and

(5) establish and oversee standards and guidelines by which agencies are to estimate the burden to comply with a proposed collection of information.

(d) With respect to information dissemination, the Director shall develop and oversee the implementation of policies, principles, standards, and guidelines to—

(1) apply to Federal agency dissemination of public information, regardless of the form or format in which such information is disseminated; and

(2) promote public access to public information and fulfill the purposes of this chapter, including through the effective use of information technology.

(e) With respect to statistical policy and coordination, the Director shall—

(1) coordinate the activities of the Federal statistical system to ensure—

(A) the efficiency and effectiveness of the system; and

(B) the integrity, objectivity, impartiality, utility, and confidentiality of information collected for statistical purposes;

(2) ensure that budget proposals of agencies are consistent with system-wide priorities for maintaining and improving the quality of Federal statistics and prepare an annual report on statistical program funding;

(3) develop and oversee the implementation of Governmentwide policies, principles, standards, and guidelines concerning—

(A) statistical collection procedures and methods;

(B) statistical data classification;

(C) statistical information presentation and dissemination;

(D) timely release of statistical data; and

(E) such statistical data sources as may be required for the administration of Federal programs;

(4) evaluate statistical program performance and agency compliance with Governmentwide policies, principles, standards and guidelines;

(5) promote the sharing of information collected for statistical purposes consistent with privacy rights and confidentiality pledges;

(6) coordinate the participation of the United States in international statistical activities, including the development of comparable statistics;

(7) appoint a chief statistician who is a trained and experienced professional statistician to carry out the functions described under this subsection;

(8) establish an Interagency Council on Statistical Policy to advise and assist the Director in carrying out the functions under this subsection that shall—

(A) be headed by the chief statistician; and

(B) consist of—

(i) the heads of the major statistical programs; and

(ii) representatives of other statistical agencies under rotating membership; and

(9) provide opportunities for training in statistical policy functions to employees of the Federal Government under which—

(A) each trainee shall be selected at the discretion of the Director based on agency requests and shall serve under the chief statistician for at least 6 months and not more that 1 year; and

(B) all costs of the training shall be paid by the agency requesting training.

(f) With respect to records management, the Director shall—

(1) provide advice and assistance to the Archivist of the United States and the Administrator of General Services to promote coordination in the administration of chapters 29, 31, and 33 of this title with the information resources management policies, principles, standards, and guidelines established under this chapter;

(2) review compliance by agencies with—

(A) the requirements of chapters 29, 31, and 33 of this title; and

(B) regulations promulgated by the Archivist of the United

States and the Administrator of General Services; and

(3) oversee the application of records management policies, principles, standards, and guidelines, including requirements for archiving information maintained in electronic format, in the planning and design of information systems.

(g) With respect to privacy and security, the Director shall—

(1) develop and oversee the implementation of policies, principles, standards, and guidelines on privacy, confidentiality, security, disclosure and sharing of information collected or maintained by or for agencies;

(2) oversee and coordiante compliance with sections 552 and 552a of title 5, sections 20 and 21 of the National Institute of Standards and Technology Act (15 U.S.C. 278g-3 and 278g-4), section 5131 of the Clinger-Cohen Act of 1996, and sections 5 and 6 of the Computer Security Act of 1987 (40 U.S.C. 759 note), and related information management laws; and

(3) require Federal agencies, consistent with the standards and guidelines promulgated under section 5131 of the Clinger-Cohen Act of 1996 and sections 5 and 6 of the Computer Security Act of 1987 (40 U.S.C. 759 note), to identify and afford security protections commensurate with the risk and magnitude of the harm resulting from the loss, misuse, or unauthorized access to or modification of information collected or maintained by or on behalf of an agency.

(h) With respect to Federal information technology, the Director shall—

(1) in consultation with the Director of the National Institute of Standards and Technology and the Administrator of General Services—

(A) develop and oversee the implementation of policies, principles, standards, and guidelines for information technology functions and activities of the Federal Government, including periodic evaluations of major information systems; and

(B) oversee the development and implementation of standards under section 5131 of the Clinger-Cohen Act of 1996;

(2) monitor the effectiveness of, and compliance with, directives issued under the Clinger-Cohen Act of 1996 and directives issued under section 110 of the Federal Property and Administrative Services Act of 1949 (40 U.S.C. 757);

(3) coordinate the development and review by the Office of Information and Regulatory Affairs of policy associated with Federal procurement and acquisition of information technology with the Office of Federal Procurement Policy;

(4) ensure, through the review of agency budget proposals, information resources management plans and other means—

(A) agency integration of information resources management plans, program plans and budgets for acquisition and use of information technology; and

(B) the efficiency and effectiveness of inter-agency information technology initiatives to improve agency performance and the accomplishment of agency missions; and

(5) promote the use of information technology by the Federal Government to improve the productivity, efficiency, and effectiveness of Federal programs, including through dissemination of public information and the reduction of information collection burdens on the public.

Source: Code of Federal Regulations

TITLE 1. GENERAL PROVISIONS

Agency: Administrative Committee of the Federal Register

PART 18. PREPARATION AND TRANSMITTAL OF DOCUMENTS GENERALLY

Citation: 1 CFR 18.4

✍ **§ 18.4 Form of document.**

* * * * *

(c) Original documents submitted by telecommunication and authenticated by digital signatures consistent with applicable Federal standards and Office of the Federal Register technical specifications may be accepted for publication.

Citation: 1 CFR 18.7

✍ **§ 18.7 Signature.**

* * * * *

Documents submitted under Sec. 18.4(c) may be authenticated as original documents by digital signatures.

TITLE 7. AGRICULTURE

Agency: Department of Agriculture
Food and Consumer Service

SUBCHAPTER C. FOOD STAMP AND FOOD DISTRIBUTION PROGRAM

PART 273. CERTIFICATION OF ELIGIBLE HOUSEHOLDS

Citation: 7 CFR 273.18

✍ **§ 273.18 Claims against households.**

* * * * *

(g) *Method of collecting payments.* * * *

(5) *Federal income tax refund offset program.* (i) *General requirements.* State agencies which choose to implement the Federal income tax refund offset program (FTROP) shall:

(A) Submit an amendment to their Plan of Operation as specified in Section 272.2(d)(1)(xii) of this chapter stating that they will comply with the requirements for FTROP and with the requirements for the Federal Salary Offset Program (salary offset). Such amendments shall be submitted to the appropriate FCS regional office no later than twelve months before the beginning of a State agency's first offset year.

(B) Submit data for FTROP to FCS in the record formats specified by FCS and/or the Internal Revenue Service (IRS), and according to schedules and by means of magnetic tape, electronic data transmission or other method specified by FCS.

(ii) *Claims referable for offset.* State agencies may submit for collection from Federal income tax refunds recipient claims which are past due and legally enforceable.

(A) Such claims must be:

(*1*) Only inadvertent household error claims or intentional Program violation claims. These claims shall be properly established according to the requirements of this section (which pertains to claims against households) and the requirements of section 273.16 (which pertains to disqualification for intentional Program violations). In addition, these claims shall be properly established no later than the date the State transmits its final request for IRS addresses for the particular offset year. Furthermore, the State agency shall have electronic records and/or paper documents showing that the claim was properly established. These records and documents include such items as claim demand letters, results of fair hearings, advance notices of disqualification hearings, results of such hearings, and records of payments.

* * * * *

Agency: Department of Agriculture
Consolidated Farm Service Agency

SUBCHAPTER C. REGULATIONS FOR WAREHOUSES

PART 735. COTTON WAREHOUSES

Citation: 7 CFR 735.17

✍ **§ 735.17 Copies of receipts.**

(a) At least one actual, skeleton, or microfilm copy of all receipts shall be made, and all copies, shall have clearly and conspicuously printed or stamped thereon the words "Copy — Not Negotiable."

(b) A copy of each receipt issued shall be retained by the warehouseman for a period of 1 year after December 31 of the year in which the corresponding original receipt is canceled.

(c) If copies are retained on microfilm, the warehouseman shall:

(1) Have available at all times facilities for immediate, easily readable projection of the microfilm and for producing easily readable facsimile enlargement;

(2) Arrange, index, and file the films in such a manner as to permit the immediate location of any particular microfilm record; and

(3) Be ready at all times to provide, and immediately provide, at the expense of the warehouseman, any facsimile enlargement of such microfilm copies which any authorized officers or agents of the Department of Agriculture may request.

DUTIES OF LICENSED WAREHOUSEMAN

Citation: 7 CFR 735.28

✍ **§ 735.28 Records to be kept in safe place.**

(a) Each warehouseman shall provide a metal fireproof safe, a fireproof vault, or fireproof compartment in which he shall keep, when not in actual use, all records, books, and papers pertaining to the licensed warehouse, including his current receipt book, copies of receipts issued, and canceled receipts except that with the written consent of the Administrator his representative, upon a showing by such warehouseman that it is not practicable to provide such fireproof safe, vault, or compartment he may keep such records, books, and papers in some other place of safety, approved by the Administrator or his representative.

(b) Each canceled receipt or microfilm copy of each canceled receipt shall be retained by the warehouseman for a period of 6 years after December 31 of the year in which the receipt is canceled and for such longer period as may be necessary for the purposes of any litigation which the warehouseman knows to be pending, or as may be required by the Administrator in particular cases to carry out the purposes of the Act.

(c) Canceled receipts shall be arranged by the warehouseman in numerical order and otherwise in such manner as shall be directed, for purposes of audit, by authorized officers or agents of the Department of Agriculture.

(d) If microfilm copies of canceled receipts are to be retained in lieu of canceled receipts, the warehouseman shall:

(1) Have available at all times facilities for immediate, easily readable projection of the microfilm and for producing easily readable facsimile enlargements.

(2) Arrange, index, and file the films in such a manner as to permit the immediate location of any particular microfilm copy; and

(3) Be ready at all times to provide, and immediately provide, at the expense of the warehouseman, any facsimile enlargement of such microfilm copies which any authorized officers or agents of the Department of Agriculture may request.

PART 782. END-USE CERTIFICATE PROGRAM

Citation: 7 CFR 782.12

✍ **§ 782.12 Filing FSA-750, End-Use Certificate for Wheat.**

* * * * *

(b) Importers may provide computer generated form FSA-750, provided such computer generated forms:

(1) Are approved in advance by KCCO,

(2) Contain a KCCO-assigned serial number, and

(3) Contain all of the information required in paragraphs (a)(1) through (a)(9).

(c) KCCO will accept form FSA-750 submitted through the following methods:

(1) Mail service, including express mail,

(2) Facsimile machine, and

(3) Other electronic transmissions, provided such transmissions are approved in advance by KCCO. The importer remains responsible for ensuring that electronically transmitted forms are received in accordance with paragraph (a).

* * * * *

(e) Distribution of form FSA-750 will be as follows:

(1) If form FSA-750 is submitted to KCCO in accordance with paragraph (c)(1);

(i) The original shall be forwarded to Kansas City Commodity Office, Warehouse License and Contract Division, P.O. Box 419205, Kansas City, MO 64141-6205, by the importer,

(ii) One copy shall be retained by the importer.

(2) If form FSA-750 is submitted to KCCO in accordance with paragraphs (c)(2) or (c)(3), the original form FSA-750 that is signed and dated by the importer in accordance with paragraph (d) shall be maintained by the importer,

(3) The importer shall provide a photocopy to the end user or, if the wheat is purchased for purposes of resale, the subsequent buyer(s).

* * * * *

Citation: 7 CFR 782.15

✍ **§ 782.15 Filing FSA-751, Wheat Consumption and Resale Report.**

* * * * *

(e) Filers may provide computer generated form FSA-751, provided such computer generated forms:

(1) Are approved in advance by KCCO, and

(2) Contain the information required in paragraphs (b)(1) through (b)(9) of this section.

(f) KCCO will accept form FSA-751 submitted through the following methods:

(1) Mail service, including express mail,

(2) Facsimile machine, and

(3) Other electronic transmissions, provided such transmissions are approved in advance by KCCO. The importer, end user, exporter, or subsequent buyer remains responsible for ensuring that electronically transmitted forms are received in accordance with this section.

(g) Distribution of form FSA-751 will be as follows:

(1) If form FSA-751 is submitted to KCCO in accordance with paragraph (f)(1) of this section:

(i) The original shall be forwarded to Kansas City Commodity Office, Warehouse License and Contract Division, P.O. Box 419205, Kansas City, MO 64141-6205, by the importer, end user, exporter, or subsequent buyer.

(ii) One copy shall be retained by the importer, end user, exporter, or subsequent buyer.

(2) If form FSA-751 is submitted to KCCO in accordance with paragraphs (f)(2) or (f)(3) of this section, the original form FSA-751 shall be maintained by the importer, end user, exporter, or subsequent buyer.

* * * * *

Agency: **Department of Agriculture**
Office of the Secretary

PART 1435. SUGAR PROGRAM

Subpart A. General Provisions

Citation: **7 CFR 1435.3**

✍ § 1435.3 Maintenance and inspection of records.

(a) CCC, as well as any other U.S. Government agency, has the right of access to the premises of any sugar beet processor, sugarcane processor, cane sugar refiner, or of any other person having custody of records that the examining agency deems necessary to verify compliance with the requirements of this part. The examining agency has the right to inspect, examine, and make copies of such books, records, accounts, and other written or electronic data as the examining agency deems relevant.

(b) Each sugar beet processor, sugarcane processor, and cane sugar refiner or any person having custody of the records shall retain such books, records, accounts, and other written or electronic data for not less than 3 years from the date:

(1) A loan is disbursed in accordance with subpart B;

(2) A marketing assessment is remitted to CCC in accordance with subpart C; and

(3) Market data are reported to CCC in accordance with subpart D.

Agency: **Rural Housing and Community Development Service**
Rural Business and Cooperative Development Service
Rural Utility Service, and Farm Service Agency

SUBCHAPTER H. PROGRAM REGULATIONS

PART 1942. ASSOCIATIONS

Subpart H. Development Grants For Community Domestic Water And Waste Disposal Systems

Citation: **7 CFR 1942 Exhibit C of Subpart H**

✍ § 1942 Exhibit C of Subpart H — Association Water or Sewer System Grant Agreement

* * * * *

N. Retain financial records, supporting documents, statistical records, and all other records pertinent to the grant for a period of at least three years after grant closing except that the records shall be retained beyond the three-year period if audit findings have not been resolved. Microfilm copies may be substituted in lieu of original records. The Grantor and the Comptroller General of the United States, or any of their duly authorized representatives, shall have access to any books, documents, papers, and records of the Grantee's government which are pertinent to the specific grant program for the purpose of making audits, examinations, excerpts and transcripts.

* * * * *

PART 1944. HOUSING

Subpart N. Housing Preservation Grants

Citation: **7 CFR 1944 Exhibit A of Subpart N**

✍ § 1944 Exhibit A of Subpart N — Housing Preservation Grant Agreement

Part C. Grantee Agrees

FmHA or its successor agency under Public Law 103-354 and grantee agree:

* * * * *

(c) Disposition of other nonexpendable property. When the grantee no longer needs the property, the property may be used for other activities in accordance with the following standards:

* * * * *

(ii) Nonexpendable personal property with a unit acquisition cost of $1,000 or more. * * *

* * * * *

(C) The grantee's property management standards for nonexpendable personal property shall include the following procedural requirements:

(1) Property records shall be maintained accurately and shall include:

(a) A description of the property.

(b) Manufacturer's serial number, model number, Federal stock number, national stock number, or other identification number.

(c) Sources of the property including grant or other agreement number.

(d) Whether title vests in the grantee or the Federal Government.

(e) Acquisition date (or date received, if the property was furnished by the Federal Government) and cost.

(f) Percentage (at the end of the budget year) of Federal participation in the cost of the project or program for which the property was acquired. (Not applicable to property furnished by the Federal Government).

(g) Location, use, and condition of the property and the date the information was reported.

(h) Unit acquisition cost.

(i) Ultimate disposition data, including date of disposal and sales price or the method used to determine current fair market value when a grantee compensates the Federal agency for its share.

(2) Property owned by the Federal Government must be marked to indicate Federal ownership.

(3) A physical inventory of property shall be taken and the results reconciled with the property records at least once every two years. Any differences between quantities determined by the physical inspection and those shown in the accounting records shall be investigated to determine the causes of the difference. The grantee shall, in connection with the inventory, verify the existence, current utilization, and continued need for the property.

(4) A control system shall be in effect to ensure adequate safeguards to prevent loss, damage, or theft of the property. Any loss, damage, or theft of nonexpendable property shall be investigated and fully documented; if the property was owned by the Federal Government the grantee shall promptly notify FmHA or its successor agency under Public Law 103-354.

* * * * *

2. To provide a financial management system which will include:

* * * * *

(b) Records which identify adequately the source and application of funds for grant-supported activities. Those records shall contain information pertaining to grant awards and authorizations, obligations, unobligated balances, assets, liabilities, outlays, and income.

* * * * *

(d) Accounting records supported by source documentation.

3. To retain financial records, supporting documents, statistical records, and all other records pertinent to the grant for a period of at least three years after the submission of the final Project Performance report pursuant to Part B(10)(c) of this Agreement except in the following situations:

(a) If any litigation, claim, audit, or investigation is commenced before the expiration of the three year period, the records shall be retained until all litigations, claims, audit or investigation findings involving the records have been resolved.

(b) Records for nonexpandable property acquired by FmHA or its successor agency under Public Law 103-354, the three year retention requirement is not applicable.

(c) When records are transferred to or maintained by FmHA or its successor agency under Public Law 103-354, the three year retention requirement is not applicable.

Microfilm copies may be substituted in lieu of original records. FmHA or its successor agency under Public Law 103-354 and the Comptroller General of the United States, or any of their duly authorized representatives, shall have access to any books, documents, papers, and records of the grantee which are pertinent to the specific grant program for the purpose of making audits, examinations, excerpts, and transcipts.

* * * * *

PART 1945. EMERGENCY

Subpart D. Emergency Loan Policies, Procedures and Authorizations

Citation: **7 CFR 1945.167**

✍ § 1945.167 Loan limitations and special provisions.

* * * * *

(g) Recordkeeping EM [emergency] borrowers receiving or indebted for EM loans of $100,000 or more are required to keep hard farm records on an approved format or use an accountant or a farm management service computer system as long as they are indebted for EM loans. EM emergency borrowers are required to retain these records for three years. (See Subpart B of Part 1924 of this chapter.)

* * * * *

PART 1948. RURAL DEVELOPMENT

Subpart B. Section 601 — Energy Impacted Area Development Assistance Program

Citation: **7 CFR Exhibit A of Subpart B**

✍ Subpart B Exhibit A — Grant Agreement — Growth Management and Housing Planning for Approved Designated Energy Impacted Areas

Part B. Grantee agrees —

* * * * *

(2) * * *

FmHA or its successor agency under Public Law 103-354 shall determine whether the property can be used to meet the agency's requirements. If not requirements exists within that agency, the availability of the property shall be reported, in accordance with the guidelines of the Federal Property Management Regulations (FPMR), to the General Services Administration by FmHa to determine whether a requirement for the property exists in other Federal agencies. FmHA or its successor agency under Public Law 103-354 shall issue instructions to the Grantee no later than 120 days after the Grantee request and the following procedures shall govern:

* * * * *

(c) *Property management standards for nonexpendable property.* The Grantee's property management standards for nonexpendable personal property shall include the following procedural requirements:

(1) Property records shall be maintained accurately and shall include:

(a) A description of the property.

(b) Manufacturer's serial number, model number, Federal stock number, national stock number, or other identification number.

(c) Sources of the property including grant or other agreement number.

(d) Whether title vests in the Grantee or the Federal Government.

(e) Acquisition date (or date received, if the property was furnished by the Federal Government) and cost.

(f) Percentage (at the end of the budget year) of Federal participation in the cost of the project or program for which the property was acquired. (Not applicable to property furnished by the Federal Government.)

(g) Location, use and condition of the property and the date the information was reported.

(h) Unit acquisition cost.

(i) Ultimate disposition data, including date of disposal and sales price or the method used to determine current fair market value where a Grantee compensates the Federal agency for its share.

* * * * *

(3) A physical inventory of property shall be taken and the results reconciled with the property records at least once every two years. Any differences between quantities determined by the physical inspection and those shown in the accounting records shall be investigated to determine the causes of the difference. * * *

* * * * *

2. To provide Financial Management Systems which will include:

* * * * *

(b) Records which identify adequately the source and application of funds for grant-supported activities. Those records shall contain information pertaining to grant awards and authorizations, obligations, unobligated balances, assets, liabilities, out-lays, and income.

* * * * *

(d) Accounting records supported by source documentation.

* * * * *

3. To retain financial records, supporting documents, statistical records, and all other records pertinent to the grant for a period of at least three years after closing except that the records shall be retained beyond the three-year period if audit findings have not been resolved. Microfilm copies may be substituted in lieu of original records. The Grantor and the Comptroller General of the United States, or any of their duly authorized representatives, shall have access to any books, documents, papers, and records of the Grantee which are pertinent to the specific grant program for the purpose of making audit, examination, excerpts, and transcripts.

* * * * *

Agency: **Department of Agriculture**
Office of Finance and Management

PART 3015. UNIFORM FEDERAL ASSISTANCE REGULATIONS

Subpart D. Record Retention and Access Requirements

Citation: **7 CFR 3015.22**

✍ § 3015.22 Starting date of retention period.

(a) *General.* The retention period starts from the date of the submission of the final expenditure report or, where USDA grant support is continued or renewed at annual or other intervals, the 3-year retention period for the records of each funding period starts on the day the recipient submits to USDA its annual or final expenditure report for that period. If an expenditure report has been waived, the 3-year retention period starts on the day the report would have been due. Exceptions to this paragraph are contained in paragraphs (b) through (d) of this section.

(b) *Equipment records.* The 3-year retention period for the equipment records required by Subpart R starts from the date of the equipment's disposition, replacement, or transfer at the direction of the awarding agency.

(c) *Records for income transactions after grant or subgrant support.* (1) In cases where USDA requires that program income (as defined in Appendix A) be applied to costs incurred after expiration or termination of grant or subgrant support, the 3-year retention period for these cost records starts from the end of the recipient's fiscal year in which the costs are incurred.

(2) Where USDA requires the disposition of copyright royalties or other program income earned after expiration or termination of grant or subgrant support, the 3-year retention period for those income records starts from the end of the recipient's fiscal year in which the income was earned. (See Subpart F, § 3015.44.)

(d) *Indirect cost rate proposals, cost allocation plans, etc.* — (1) *Applicability.* This paragraph applies to the following types of documents and their supporting records:

(i) Indirect cost rate computations or proposals;

(ii) Cost allocation plans; and

(iii) Any similar accounting computations of the rate at which a particular group of costs is chargeable (such as computer usage charge-back rates or composite fringe benefit rates).

(2) *If submitted for negotiation.* If the Federal government requires submission of the proposal; plan, or other computation for negotiation of the rate chargeable for particular costs, then the 3-year retention period for the plan, proposal or other computation and the supporting records starts from the date of such submission.

(3) *If not submitted for negotiation.* If the Federal government does not require submission of the proposal, plan, or other computation for negotiation of the rate chargeable for particular costs, then the 3-year retention period for the proposal, plan, or other computation and the supporting records starts from the end of the fiscal year covered by such proposal, plan, or other computation.

Citation: **7 CFR 3015.23**

✍ § 3015.23 Microfilm.

Copies made by microfilming, photocopying, or similar methods may be substituted for the original records.

PART 3019. UNIFORM ADMINISTRATIVE REQUIREMENTS FOR GRANTS AND AGREEMENTS WITH INSTITUTIONS OF HIGHER EDUCATION, HOSPITALS, AND OTHER NON-PROFIT ORGANIZATIONS

Subpart C. Post-Award Requirements

Citation: **7 CFR 3019.52**

✍ § 3019.52 Financial reporting.

(a) The following forms or such other forms as may be approved by OMB are authorized for obtaining financial information from recipients.

(1) *SF-269 or SF-269A, Financial Status Report.*

(i) Each Federal awarding agency shall require recipients to use the SF-269 or SF-269A to report the status of funds for all nonconstruction projects or programs. A Federal awarding agency may, however, have the option of not requiring the SF-269 or SF-269A when the SF-270, Request for Advance or Reimbursement, or SF-272, Report of Federal Cash Transactions, is determined to provided adequate information to meet its needs, except that a final SF-269 or SF-269A shall be required at the completion of the project when the SF-270 is used only for advances.

(ii) The Federal awarding agency shall prescribe whether the report shall be on a cash or accrual basis. If the Federal awarding agency requires accrual information and the recipient's accounting records are not normally kept on the accrual basis, the recipient shall not be required to convert its accounting system, but shall develop such accrual information through best estimates based on an analysis of the documentation on hand.

(iii) The Federal awarding agency shall determine the frequency of the Financial Status Report for each project or program, considering the size and complexity of the particular project or program. However, the report shall not be required more frequently than quarterly or less frequently than annually. A final report shall be required at the completion of the agreement.

(iv) The Federal awarding agency shall require recipients to submit the SF-269 or SF-269A (an original and no more than two copies no later than 30 days after the end of each specified reporting period for quarterly and semi-annual reports, and 90 calendar days for annual and final reports. Extensions of reporting due dates may be approved by the Federal awarding agency upon request of the recipient.

(2) *SF-272, Report of Federal Cash Transactions.*

(i) When funds are advanced to recipients the Federal awarding agency shall require each recipient to submit the SF-272 and, when necessary, its continuation sheet, SF-272a. The Federal awarding agency shall use this report to monitor cash advanced to recipients and to obtain disbursement information for each agreement with the recipients.

(ii) Federal awarding agencies may require forecasts of Federal cash requirements in the "Remarks" section of the report.

(iii) When practical and deemed necessary, Federal awarding agencies may require recipients to report in the "Remarks" section the amount of cash advances received in excess of three days. Recipients shall provide short narrative explanations of actions taken to reduce the excess balances.

(iv) Recipients shall be required to submit not more than the original and two copies of the SF-272 15 calendar days following the end of each quarter. The Federal awarding agencies may require a monthly report from those recipients receiving advances totaling $1 million or more per year.

(v) Federal awarding agencies may waive the requirement for submission of the SF-272 for any one of the following reasons:

(A) When monthly advances do not exceed $25,000 per recipient, provided that such advances are monitored through other forms contained in this section;

(B) If, in the Federal awarding agency's opinion, the recipient's accounting controls are adequate to minimize excessive Federal advances; or

(C) When the electronic payment mechanisms provide adequate data.

(b) When the Federal awarding agency needs additional information or more frequent reports, the following shall be observed.

(1) When additional information is needed to comply with legislative requirements, Federal awarding agencies shall issue instructions to require recipients to submit such information under the "Remarks" section of the reports.

(2) When a Federal awarding agency determines that a recipient's accounting system does not meet the standards in § 3019.21, additional pertinent information to further monitor awards may be obtained upon written notice to the recipient until such time as the system is brought up to standard. The Federal awarding agency, in obtaining this information, shall comply with report clearance requirements of 5 CFR part 1320.

(3) Federal awarding agencies are encouraged to shade out any line item on any report if not necessary.

(4) Federal awarding agencies may accept the identical information from the recipients in machine readable format or computer printouts or electronic outputs in lieu of prescribed formats.

(5) Federal awarding agencies may provide computer or electronic outputs to recipients when such expedites or contributes to the accuracy of reporting.

Agency: **Department of Agriculture**
Rural Development Administration

PART 4284. GRANTS

Subpart F. Rural Technology Development Grants

Citation: **7 CFR Exhibit A of Subpart F**

✍ Exhibit A of Subpart F — Agreement of Administrative Requirements for Rural Technology Development Grants

This exhibit contains information regarding the responsibilities of the grantee for receipt of grant funds under the Rural Technology Development Grant (RTDG) program. These requirements do not supersede the requirements for receipt of Federal funds as stated in 7 CFR parts 3015 and 3016; however, specific areas related to the program are cited below.

In consideration for the RTDG grant by RDA, grantee agrees to:

1. Cause the RTDG program to be completed within the total sums available to it, including grant funds, in accordance with the scope of work and any necessary modifications thereof prepared by grantee and approved by grantor.

2. Permit periodic inspection of the program operations by a representative of grantor.

3. Make the program available to all persons in grantee's service area without regard to race, color, national origin, religion, sex, marital status, age, physical or mental handicap.

4. Not use grant funds to replace any financial support previously provided or assured from any other source. The grantee agrees that the general level of expenditure by the grantee for the benefit of program area and/or program covered by this agreement shall be maintained and not reduced as a result of the Federal share funds received under this grant.

5. Provide financial management systems which will include:

(a) Accurate, current, and complete disclosure of the financial result of each grant.

(b) Records which identify adequately the source and application of funds for grant-supporting activities. Those records shall contain information pertaining to grant awards and authorizations, obligations, unobligated balances, assets, liabilities, outlays, and income.

(c) Effective control over and accountability for all funds. Grantee shall adequately safeguard all such assets and shall ensure that they are used solely for authorized purposes.

(d) Accounting records supported by source documentation.

6. Retain financial records, supporting documents, statistical records, and all other records pertinent to the grant for a period of at least 3 years after grant closing except that the records shall be retained beyond the 3-year period if audit findings have not been resolved. Microfilm copies may be substituted in lieu of original records. The grantor and the Comptroller General of the United States, or any of their duly authorized representatives, shall have access to any books, documents, papers, and records of the grantee which are pertinent to the specific grant program for the purpose of making audits, examinations, excerpts, and transcripts.

* * * * *

TITLE 8. ALIENS AND NATIONALITY

Agency: **Department of Justice**
Immigration and Naturalization Service

PART 274A. CONTROL OF EMPLOYMENT OF ALIENS

Subpart A. Employer Requirements

Citation: **8 CFR 274a.2**

✍ § 274a.2 erification of employment eligibility.

* * * * *

(b) *Employment verification requirements* —

* * * * *

(2) *Retention and inspection of Form I-9.* (i) Form I-9 must be retained by an employer or a recruiter or referrer for a fee for the following time periods:

(A) In the case of an employer, three years after the date of the hire or one year after the date the individual's employment is terminated, whichever is later; or

(B) In the case of a recruiter or referrer for a fee, three years after the date of hire.

(ii) Any person or entity required to retain Forms I-9 in accordance with this section shall be provided with at least three days notice prior to an inspection of the Forms I-9 by officers of the Service, the Special Counsel for Immigration-Related Unfair Employment Practices, or the Department of Labor. At the time of inspection, the Forms I-9 must be made available in their original form or on microfilm or microfiche at the location where the request for production was made. If Forms I-9 are kept at another location, the person or entity must inform the officer of the Service, the Special Counsel for the Immigration-Related Unfair Employment Practices, or the Department of Labor of the location where the forms are kept and make arrangements for the inspection. Inspections may be performed at an INS office. A recruiter or referrer for a fee who has designated an employer to complete the employment verification procedures may present a photocopy of the Form I-9 in lieu of presenting the Form I-9 in its original form or on microfilm or microfiche, as set forth in paragraph (b)(1)(iv) of this section. Any refusal or delay in presentation of the Forms I-9 for inspection is a violation of the retention requirements as set forth in § 274A(b)(3) of the Act. No Subpoena or warrant shall be required for such inspection, but the use of such enforcement tools is not precluded. In addition, if the person or entity has not complied with a request to present the Forms I-9, any Service officer listed in § 287.4 of this chapter may compel production of the Forms I-9 and any other relevant documents by issuing a subpoena. Nothing in this section is intended to limit the Service's subpoena power under § 235(a) of the Act.

(iii) The following standards shall apply to Forms I-9 presented on microfilm (or microfiche) submitted to an officer of the Service, the Special Counsel for Immigration-Related Unfair Employment Practices, or the Department of Labor: Microfilm, when displayed on a microfilm reader (viewer) or reproduced on paper must exhibit a high degree of legibility and readability. For this purpose, legibility is defined as the quality of a letter or numeral which enables the observer to positively and quickly identify it to the exclusion of all other letters or numerals. Readability is defined as the quality of a group of letters or numerals being recognizable as words or whole numbers. A detailed index of all microfilmed data shall be maintained and arranged in such a manner as to permit the immediate location of any particular record. It is the responsibility of the employer, recruiter or referrer for a fee:

(A) To provide for the processing, storage and maintenance of all microfilm and

(B) To be able to make the contents thereof available as required by law. The person or entity presenting the microfilm will make available a reader-printer at the examination site for the ready reading, location and reproduction of any record or records being retained on microfilm. Reader-printers made available to an officer of the Service, the Special Counsel for Immigration-Related Unfair Employment Practices, or the Department of Labor shall provide safety features and be in clean condition, properly maintained and in good working order. The reader-printers must have the capacity to display and print a complete page of information. A person or entity who is determined to have failed to comply with the criteria established by this regulation for the presentation of microfilm or microfiche to the Service, the Special Counsel for Immigration-Related Unfair Employment Practices, or the Department of Labor and at the time of the inspection does not present a properly completed Form I-9 for the employee, is in violation of § 274A(a)(1)(B) of the Act and § 274a.2(b)(2).

(3) *Copying of documentation.* An employer or a recruiter or referrer for a fee may, but is not required to, copy a document presented by an individual solely for the purpose of complying with the verification requirements of this section. If such copy is made, it must be retained with the Form I-9. The retention requirements in paragraph (b)(2) of this section do not apply to the photocopies. The copying of any such document and retention of the copy does not relieve the employer from the requirement to fully complete section 2 of the Form I-9. An employer, recruiter or referrer for a fee should not, however, copy the documents only of individuals of certain national origins or citizenship statuses. To do so may violate § 274B of the Act.

* * * * *

PART 299. IMMIGRATION FORMS

Citation: **8 CFR 299.4**

✍ § 299.4 Reproduction of Public Use Forms by public and private entities.

* * * * *

(b) *Requirements for electronic generation.* Public or private entities may electronically generate forms required for applying for a specific benefit, in compliance with the immigration and naturalization regulations, at their own expense. This includes forms that have been made available for purchase by the Superintendent of Documents, as listed in Sec. 299.3 provided that each form satisfies the following requirements:

(1) An electronic reproduction must be complete, containing all questions which appear on the official form. The wording and punctuation of all data elements and identifying information must match exactly. No data elements may be added or deleted. The sequence and format for each item on the form must be replicated to mirror the authorized agency form. Each item must be printed on the same page in the same location. Likewise, multiple-part sets may be printed as single sheets provided that the destination of the carbon copy is clearly identified on the bottom of the form. Private entities must reproduce forms on the same colored paper that is used on the official form. In the case of the Form I-20 A-B/I-20ID, Certificate of Eligibility for Nonimmigrant (F-1) Student Status — For Academic and Language Students, private entities may generate this form in single-page format rather than double-sided format, provided that the student's name, school, and date of birth is printed in a shaded box on the top of page 4 of the form, using the same type size and font style as the body of the form.

* * * * *

(3) The final form must be approved for use by the Director, Policy Directives and Instructions Branch. The form should be mailed to the address listed in paragraph (e) of this section for approval.

* * * * *

(d) Electronic printers that provide for near-letter-quality documents should be used to generate electronic forms. Dot matrix printers that are only capable of producing draft quality documents should not be used for form generation, but may be used for the entry of data in a preprinted form where appropriate.

(e) Any form with poor print quality or other defect which renders it illegible, difficult to read, or displays added or missing data elements, will be rejected by the Service. Any problems regarding the acceptability of a specific electronic version of a particular Service form may be brought to the attention of the Director, Policy Directives and Instructions Branch, 425 "I" Street, NW., Room 5307, Washington, DC 20536, telephone number (202) 514-3048.

TITLE 9. ANIMALS AND ANIMAL PRODUCTS

Agency: Department of Agriculture
Animal and Plant Health Inspection Service

SUBCHAPTER H. ANIMAL BREEDS

PART 151. RECOGNITION OF BREEDS AND BOOKS OF RECORD OF PUREBRED ANIMALS

Citation: 9 CFR 151.11

✍ § 151.11 Form of books of record.

(a) If a registry association has not published its book of record in printed form, a record in approved microfilm form which the Administrator finds provides a system for determining the recorded ancestry of the animals identified therein will be acceptable. When a registry association which has published its book of record in printed form ceases such publication and in lieu thereof publishes a microfilm record, the microfilm record shall commence with the first pedigree recorded by the association which is not in the printed volumes and shall otherwise be in approved form.

(b) A microfilm record will be approved under this part only if it is 16 mm. non-perforated safety film exposed at a reduction ratio not to exceed 24 diameters. All information on the original document shall be reproduced onto the microfilm so that it is clearly readable. The microfilm carton shall be indexed to state the numbers of the pedigree certificates on the roll of film it contains.

Agency: Department of Agriculture
Grain Inspection Packers and Stockyards Administration

PART 203. STATEMENTS OF GENERAL POLICY UNDER THE PACKERS AND STOCKYARDS ACT

Citation: 9 CFR 203.4

✍ § 203.4 Statement with respect to the disposition of records by packers, live poultry dealers, stockyard owners, market agencies and dealers.

(a) *Records to be kept.* Section 401 of the Packers and Stockyards Act (7 U.S.C. 221) provides, in part, that every packer, live poultry dealer, stockyard owner, market agency, and dealer shall keep such accounts, records and memoranda as fully and correctly disclose all transactions involved in his business, including the true ownership of such business by stockholding or otherwise. In order to properly administer the P&S Act, it is necessary that records be retained for such periods of time as may be required to permit the Grain Inspection, Packers and Stockyards Administration (Packers and Stockyards Programs) a reasonable opportunity to examine such records. Section 401 of the Act does not, however, provide for the destruction or disposal of records. Therefore, the Grain Inspection, Packers and Stockyards Administration (Packers and Stockyards Programs) has formulated this policy statement to provide guidance as to the periods of time after which records may be disposed of or destroyed.

(b) *Records may be disposed of after two years except as otherwise provided.* Except as provided in paragraph (c) of this section, each packer, live poultry dealer, stockyard owner, market agency, and dealer may destroy or dispose of accounts, records, and memoranda which contain, explain, or modify transactions in its business subject to the Act after such accounts, records, and memoranda have been retained for a period of two full years; *Provided,* That the following records made or kept by a packer may be disposed of after one year: cutting tests; departmental transfers; buyers' estimates, drive sheets; scale tickets received from others; inventory and products in storage; receiving records; trial balances; departmental overhead or expense recapitulations; bank statements; reconciliations and deposit slips; production or sale tonnage reports (including recapitulations and summaries of routes, branches, plants, etc.); buying or selling pricing instructions and price lists; correspondence; telegrams; teletype communications and memoranda relating to matters other than contracts, agreements, purchase or sales invoices, or claims or credit memoranda; and *Provided further,* That microfilm copies of records may be substituted for and retained in lieu of the actual records.

(c) *Retention for longer periods may be required.* The periods specified in paragraph (b) of this section shall be extended if the packer, live poultry dealer, stockyard owner, market agency, or dealer is notified in writing by the Administrator that specified records should be retained for a longer period pending the completion of any investigation or proceeding under the Act.

(d) *Unauthorized disposal of records.* If it is found that any person subject to the Act has disposed of accounts, records and memoranda which are necessary to fully and correctly disclose all transactions in its business prior to the period specified in this statement, consideration will be given to the issuance of a complaint charging a violation of section 401 of the Act and seeking an appropriate order. The administrative proceeding initiated will be conducted in accordance with the Rules of Practice Governing Formal Adjudicatory Proceedings Instituted by the Secretary (7 CFR 1.130 et seq.).

PART 205. CLEAR TITLE — PROTECTION FOR PURCHASERS OF FARM PRODUCTS

Citation: **9 CFR 205.101**

✍ § 205.101 Certification-request and processing.

* * * * *

(b) * * *

(11) * * *

(iii) All printed and electronic forms required to be used in connection with the system.

(c) * * *

(d) * * *

(e) To make changes to an existing certified central filing system, including changes necessitated or made possible by amendments to the Act, a written request to amend the existing certified central filing system must be filed together with such documents as are necessary to show that the system complies with the Act. The request must contain relevant new information consistent with the requirements specified elsewhere in this section.

Citation: **9 CFR 205.105**

✍ § 205.105 Master list and portion thereof distributed to registrants — format.

* * * * *

(b) Section (c)(2)(E) requires the portion to be distributed in "written or printed form." This means recording on paper by any technology in a form that can be read by humans without special equipment. The system may, however, honor requests from registrants to substitute recordings on any medium by any technology including, but not limited to, electronic recording on tapes or discs in machine-readable form, and on photographic recording on microfiche. It also includes, if requested by registrants, electronic transmissions whereby registrants can print their own paper copies.

* * * * *

Citation: **9 CFR 205.202**

✍ § 205.202 "Effective financing statement" or EFS.

* * * * *

(b) An EFS may be filed electronically provided a State allows electronic filing of financing statements without the signature of the debtor under applicable State law under provisions of the Uniform Commercial Code or may be a paper document. An electronically filed EFS need not be a paper document and need not be signed. If an original or reproduced paper document of an EFS is filed with the State, it must be signed by both the secured party and the debtor, and be filed by the secured party.

(c) Countermeasures against mishandling after filing, such as a requirement that a copy be date stamped and returned to the secured party, are discretionary with the State. If a State chooses to adopt such countermeasures, it is responsible for establishing procedures for recording the date and time when an EFS is received, and for meeting all legal requirements associated with filing and distributing information about security interests as required by Sec. 205.101.

Citation: **9 CFR 205.209**

✍ § 205.209 Amendment or continuation of EFS.

* * * * *

(c) The amendment must be filed in the same manner as the original filing. Note the requirement of section (c)(4)(E). The amendment may be filed electronically provided a State allows electronic filing of financing statements without the signature of the debtor underapplicable State law under provisions of the Uniform Commercial Code. An electronically filed amendment need not be signed. However, if an original or reproduced paper document is filed, the amendment must be signed by the secured party and the debtor, and be filed by the secured party.

* * * * *

Agency: **Department of Agriculture**
Food Safety and Inspection Service

PART 417. HAZARD ANALYSIS AND CRITICAL CONTROL POINT (HACCP) SYSTEMS

Citation: **9 CFR 417.5**

✍ § 417.5 Records.

(a) The establishment shall maintain the following records documenting the establishment's HACCP plan:

(1) The written hazard analysis prescribed in Sec. 417.2(a) of this part, including all supporting documentation;

(2) The written HACCP plan, including decisionmaking documents associated with the selection and development of CCP's and critical limits, and documents supporting both the monitoring and verification procedures selected and the frequency of those procedures.

(3) Records documenting the monitoring of CCP's and their critical limits, including the recording of actualtimes, temperatures, or other quantifiable values, as prescribed in the establishment's HACCP plan; the calibration of process-monitoring instruments; corrective actions, including all actions taken in response to a deviation; verification procedures and results; product code(s), product name or identity, or slaughter production lot. Each of these records shall include the date the record was made.

(b) Each entry on a record maintained under the HACCP plan shall be made at the time the specific event occurs and include the date and time recorded, and shall be signed or initialed by the establishment employee making the entry.

(c) Prior to shipping product, the establishment shall review the records associated with the production of that product, documented in accordance with this section, to ensure completeness, including the determination that all critical limits were met and, if appropriate, corrective actions were taken, including the proper disposition of product. Where practicable, this review shall be conducted, dated, and signed by an individual who did not produce the record(s), preferably by someone trained in accordance with Sec. 417.7 of this part, or the responsible establishment official.

(d) *Records maintained on computers.* The use of records

maintained on computers is acceptable, provided that appropriate controls are implemented to ensure the integrity of the electronic data and signatures.

(e) Record retention. (1) Establishments shall retain all records required by paragraph (a)(3) of this section as follows: for slaughter activities for at least one year; for refrigerated product, for at least one year; for frozen, preserved, or shelf-stable products, for at least two years.

(2) Off-site storage of records required by paragraph (a)(3) of this section is permitted after six months, if such records can be retrieved and provided, on-site, within 24 hours of an FSIS employee's request.

(f) *Official review.* All records required by this part and all plans and procedures required by this part shall be available for official review and copying.

TITLE 10. ENERGY

Agency:	Nuclear Regulatory Commission

PART 11. CRITERIA AND PROCEDURES FOR DETERMINING ELIGIBILITY FOR ACCESS TO OR CONTROL OVER SPECIAL NUCLEAR MATERIAL

Citation:	10 CFR 11.10

✍ § 11.10 Maintenance of records.

Each record required by this part must be legible throughout the retention period specified by each Commission regulation. The record may be the original or a reproduced copy or a microform provided that the copy or microform is authenticated by authorized personnel and that the microform is capable of producing a clear copy throughout the required retention period. The record may also be stored in electronic media with the capability for producing legible, accurate, and complete records during the required retention period. Records such as letters, drawing, specification, must include all pertinent information such as stamps, initials, and signatures etc. The licensee shall maintain adequate safeguards against tampering with and loss of records.

PART 20. STANDARDS FOR PROTECTION AGAINST RADIATION

Subpart O. Enforcement

Citation:	10 CFR Part 20 Appendix G

✍ Appendix G to 10 CFR Part 20 Requirements for Transfers of Low-Level Radioactive Waste Intended for Disposal at Licensed Land Disposal Facilities and Manifests

I. *Manifest*

A waste generator, collector, or processor who transports, or offers for transportation, low-level radioactive waste intended for ultimate disposal at a licensed low-level radioactive waste land disposal facility must prepare a Manifest (OMB Control Numbers 3150-0164, -0165, and -0166) reflecting information requested on applicable NRC Forms 540 (Uniform Low-Level Radioactive Waste Manifest (Shipping Paper)) and 541 (Uniform Low-Level Radioactive Waste Manifest (Container and Waste Description)) and, if necessary, on an applicable NRC Form 542 (Uniform Low-Level Radioactive Waste Manifest (Manifest Index and Regional Compact Tabulation)). NRC Forms 540 and 540A must be completed and must physically accompany the pertinent low-level waste shipment. Upon agreement between shipper and consignee, NRC Forms 541 and 541A and 542 and 542A may be completed, transmitted, and stored in electronic media with the capability for producing legible, accurate, and complete records on the respective forms. Licensees are not required by NRC to comply with the manifesting requirements of this part when they ship:

(a) LLW for processing and expect its return (i.e., for storage under their license) prior to disposal at a licensed land disposal facility;

(b) LLW that is being returned to the licensee who is the "waste generator" or "generator," as defined in this part; or

(c) Radioactively contaminated material to a "waste processor" that becomes the processor's "residual waste."

For guidance in completing these forms, refer to the instructions that accompany the forms. Copies of manifests required by this appendix may be legible carbon copies, photocopies, or computer printouts that reproduce the data in the format of the uniform manifest.

NRC Forms 540, 540A, 541, 541A, 542 and 542A, and the accompanying instructions, in hard copy, may be obtained from the Information and Records Management Branch, Office of Information Resources Management, U.S. Nuclear Regulatory Commission, Washington, DC 20555, telephone (301) 415-7232.

This appendix includes information requirements of the Department of Transportation, as codified in 49 CFR part 172. Information on hazardous, medical, or other waste, required to meet Environmental Protection Agency regulations, as codified in 40 CFR parts 259, 261 or elsewhere, is not addressed in this section, and must be provided on the required EPA forms. However, the required EPA forms must accompany the Uniform Low-Level Radioactive Waste Manifest required by this chapter.

As used in this appendix, the following definitions apply:

Chelating agent has the same meaning as that given in § 61.2 of this chapter.

Chemical description means a description of the principal chemical characteristics of a low-level radioactive waste.

Computer-readable medium means that the regulatory agency's computer can transfer the information from the medium into its memory.

Consignee means the designated receiver of the shipment of low-level radioactive waste.

Decontamination facility means a facility operating under a Commission or Agreement State license whose principal purpose is decontamination of equipment or materials to accomplish recycle, reuse, or other waste management objectives, and, for purposes of this part, is not considered to be a consignee for LLW shipments.

Disposal container means a container principally used to confine low-level radioactive waste during disposal operations at a land disposal facility (also see "high integrity container"). Note that for some shipments, the disposal container may be the transport package.

EPA identification number means the number received by a transporter following application to the Administrator of EPA as required by 40 CFR part 263.

Generator means a licensee operating under a Commission or Agreement State license who (1) is a waste generator as defined in this part, or (2) is the licensee to whom waste can be attributed within the context of the Low-Level Radioactive Waste Policy Amendments Act of 1985 (e.g., waste generated as a result of decontamination or recycle activities).

High integrity container (HIC) means a container commonly designed to meet the structural stability requirements of § 61.56

of this chapter, and to meet Department of Transportation requirements for a Type A package.

Land disposal facility has the same meaning as that given in § 61.2 of this chapter.

NRC Forms 540, 540A, 541, 541A, 542, and 542A are official NRC Forms referenced in this appendix. Licensees need not use originals of these NRC Forms as long as any substitute forms are equivalent to the original documentation in respect to content, clarity, size, and location of information. Upon agreement between the shipper and consignee, NRC Forms 541 (and 541A) and NRC Forms 542 (and 542A) may be completed, transmitted, and stored in electronic media. The electronic media must have the capability for producing legible, accurate, and complete records in the format of the uniform manifest.

Package means the assembly of components necessary to ensure compliance with the packaging requirements of DOT regulations, together with its radioactive contents, as presented for transport.

Physical description means the items called for on NRC Form 541 to describe a low-level radioactive waste.

Residual waste means low-level radioactive waste resulting from processing or decontamination activities that cannot be easily separated into distinct batches attributable to specific waste generators. This waste is attributable to the processor or decontamination facility, as applicable.

Shipper means the licensed entity (i.e., the waste generator, waste collector, or waste processor) who offers low-level radioactive waste for transportation, typically consigning this type of waste to a licensed waste collector, waste processor, or land disposal facility operator.

Shipping paper means NRC Form 540 and, if required, NRC Form 540A which includes the information required by DOT in 49 CFR part 172.

Source material has the same meaning as that given in § 40.4 of this chapter.

Special nuclear material has the same meaning as that given in § 70.4 of this chapter. *Uniform Low-Level Radioactive Waste Manifest* or *uniform manifest* means the combination of NRC Forms 540, 541, and, if necessary, 542, and their respective continuation sheets as needed, or equivalent.

Waste collector means an entity, operating under a Commission or Agreement State license, whose principal purpose is to collect and consolidate waste generated by others, and to transfer this waste, without processing or repackaging the collected waste, to another licensed waste collector, licensed waste processor, or licensed land disposal facility.

Waste description means the physical, chemical and radiological description of a low-level radioactive waste as called for on NRC Form 541.

Waste generator means an entity, operating under a Commission or Agreement State license, who (1) possesses any material or component that contains radioactivity or is radioactively contaminated for which the licensee foresees no further use, and (2) transfers this material or component to a licensed land disposal facility or to a licensed waste collector or processor for handling or treatment prior to disposal. A licensee performing processing or decontamination services may be a "waste generator" if the transfer of low-level radioactive waste from its facility is defined as "residual waste."

Waste processor means an entity, operating under a Commission or Agreement State license, whose principal purpose is to process, repackage, or otherwise treat low-level radioactive material or waste generated by others prior to eventual transfer of waste to a licensed low-level radioactive waste land disposal facility.

Waste type means a waste within a disposal container having a unique physical description (i.e., a specific waste descriptor code or description; or a waste sorbed on or solidified in a specifically defined media).

Information Requirements

A. *General Information*

The shipper of the radioactive waste, shall provide the following information on the uniform manifest:

1. The name, facility address, and telephone number of the licensee shipping the waste;
2. An explicit declaration indicating whether the shipper is acting as a waste generator, collector, processor, or a combination of these identifiers for purposes of the manifested shipment; and
3. The name, address, and telephone number, or the name and EPA identification number for the carrier transporting the waste.

B. *Shipment Information*

The shipper of the radioactive waste shall provide the following information regarding the waste shipment on the uniform manifest:

1. The date of the waste shipment;
2. The total number of packages/disposal containers;
3. The total disposal volume and disposal weight in the shipment;
4. The total radionuclide activity in the shipment;
5. The activity of each of the radionuclides H-3, C-14, Tc-99, and I-129 contained in the shipment; and
6. The total masses of U-233, U-235, and plutonium in special nuclear material, and the total mass of uranium and thorium in source material.

C. *Disposal Container and Waste Information*

The shipper of the radioactive waste shall provide the following information on the uniform manifest regarding the waste and each disposal container of waste in the shipment:

1. An alphabetic or numeric identification that uniquely identifies each disposal container in the shipment;
2. A physical description of the disposal container, including the manufacturer and model of any high integrity container;
3. The volume displaced by the disposal container;
4. The gross weight of the disposal container, including the waste;
5. For waste consigned to a disposal facility, the maximum radiation level at the surface of each disposal container;
6. A physical and chemical description of the waste;
7. The total weight percentage of chelating agent for any waste containing more than 0.1% chelating agent by weight, plus the identity of the principal chelating agent;
8. The approximate volume of waste within a container;
9. The sorbing or solidification media, if any, and the identity of the solidification media vendor and brand name;
10. The identities and activities of individual radionuclides contained in each container, the masses of U-233, U-235, and plutonium in special nuclear material, and the masses of uranium and thorium in source material. For discrete waste types (i.e., activated materials, contaminated equipment, mechanical filters, sealed source/devices, and wastes in solidification/stabilization media), the identities and activities of individual radionuclides associated with or contained on these waste types within a disposal container shall be reported;
11. The total radioactivity within each container; and
12. For wastes consigned to a disposal facility, the classification of the waste pursuant to § 61.55 of this chapter. Waste not meeting the structural stability requirements of § 61.56(b) of this chapter must be identified.

D. *Uncontainerized Waste Information*

The shipper of the radioactive waste shall provide the following information on the uniform manifest regarding a waste shipment delivered without a disposal container:

1. The approximate volume and weight of the waste;
2. A physical and chemical description of the waste;
3. The total weight percentage of chelating agent if the chelating agent exceeds 0.1% by weight, plus the identity of the principal chelating agent;
4. For waste consigned to a disposal facility, the classification of the waste pursuant to § 61.55 of this chapter. Waste not meeting the structural stability requirements of § 61.56(b) of this chapter must be identified;
5. The identities and activities of individual radionuclides contained in the waste, the masses of U-233, U-235, and plutonium in special nuclear material, and the masses of uranium and thorium in source material; and
6. For wastes consigned to a disposal facility, the maximum radiation levels at the surface of the waste.

E. *Multi-Generator Disposal Container Information*

This section applies to disposal containers enclosing mixtures of waste originating from different generators. (Note: The origin of the LLW resulting from a processor's activities may be attributable to one or more "generators" (including "waste generators") as defined in this part). It also applies to mixtures of wastes shipped in an uncontainerized form, for which portions of the mixture within the shipment originate from different generators.

1. For homogeneous mixtures of waste, such as incinerator ash, provide the waste description applicable to the mixture and the volume of the waste attributed to each generator.
2. For heterogeneous mixtures of waste, such as the combined products from a large compactor, identify each generator contributing waste to the disposal container, and, for discrete waste types (i.e., activated materials, contaminated equipment, mechanical filters, sealed source/devices, and wastes in solidification/stabilization media), the identities and activities of individual radionuclides contained on these waste types within the disposal container. For each generator, provide the following:

(a) The volume of waste within the disposal container;

(b) A physical and chemical description of the waste, including the solidification agent, if any;

(c) The total weight percentage of chelating agents for any disposal container containing more than 0.1% chelating agent by weight, plus the identity of the principal chelating agent;

(d) The sorbing or solidification media, if any, and the identity of the solidification media vendor and brand name if the media is claimed to meet stability requirements in 10 CFR 61.56(b); and

(e) Radionuclide identities and activities contained in the waste, the masses of U-233, U-235, and plutonium in special nuclear material, and the masses of uranium and thorium in source material if contained in the waste.

II. *Certification*

An authorized representative of the waste generator, processor, or collector shall certify by signing and dating the shipment manifest that the transported materials are properly classified, described, packaged, marked, and labeled and are in proper condition for transportation according to the applicable regulations of the Department of Transportation and the Commission. A collector in signing the certification is certifying that nothing has been done to the collected waste which would invalidate the waste generator's certification.

III. *Control and Tracking*

A. Any licensee who transfers radioactive waste to a land disposal facility or a licensed waste collector shall comply with the requirements in paragraphs A.1 through 9 of this section. Any licensee who transfers waste to a licensed waste processor for waste treatment or repackaging shall comply with the requirements of paragraphs A.4 through 9 of this section. A licensee shall:

1. Prepare all wastes so that the waste is classified according to § 61.55 and meets the waste characteristics requirements in § 61.56 of this chapter;
2. Label each disposal container (or transport package if potential radiation hazards preclude labeling of the individual disposal container) of waste to identify whether it is Class A waste, Class B waste, Class C waste, or greater then Class C waste, in accordance with § 61.55 of this chapter;
3. Conduct a quality assurance program to assure compliance with § § 61.55 and 61.56 of this chapter (the program must include management evaluation of audits);
4. Prepare the NRC Uniform Low-Level Radioactive Waste Manifest as required by this appendix;
5. Forward a copy or electronically transfer the Uniform Low-Level Radioactive Waste Manifest to the intended consignee so that either (i) receipt of the manifest precedes the LLW shipment or (ii) the manifest is delivered to the consignee with the waste at the time the waste is transferred to the consignee. Using both (i) and (ii) is also acceptable;
6. Include NRC Form 540 (and NRC Form 540A, if required) with the shipment regardless of the option chosen in paragraph A.5 of this section;
7. Receive acknowledgment of the receipt of the shipment in the form of a signed copy of NRC Form 540;
8. Retain a copy of or electronically store the Uniform Low-Level Radioactive Waste Manifest and documentation of acknowledgment of receipt as the record of transfer of licensed material as required by 10 CFR Parts 30, 40, and 70 of this chapter; and
9. For any shipments or any part of a shipment for which acknowledgment of receipt has not been received within the times set forth in this appendix, conduct an investigation in accordance with paragraph E of this appendix.

B. Any waste collector licensee who handles only prepackaged waste shall:

1. Acknowledge receipt of the waste from the shipper within one week of receipt by returning a signed copy of NRC Form 540;
2. Prepare a new manifest to reflect consolidated shipments that meet the requirements of this appendix. The waste collector shall ensure that, for each container of waste in the shipment, the manifest identifies the generator of that container of waste;
3. Forward a copy or electronically transfer the Uniform Low-Level Radioactive Waste Manifest to the intended consignee so that either:

(i) Receipt of the manifest precedes the LLW shipment or (ii) the manifest is delivered to the consignee with the waste at the time the waste is transferred to the consignee. Using both (i) and (ii) is also acceptable;

4. Include NRC Form 540 (and NRC Form 540A, if required) with the shipment regardless of the option chosen in paragraph B.3 of this section;
5. Receive acknowledgment of the receipt of the shipment in the form of a signed copy of NRC Form 540;
6. Retain a copy of or electronically store the Uniform Low-Level Radioactive Waste Manifest and documentation of acknowledgment of receipt as the record of transfer of licensed material as required by 10 CFR parts 30, 40, and 70 of this chapter;
7. For any shipments or any part of a shipment for which acknowledgment of receipt has not been received within the times set forth in this appendix, conduct an investigation in

accordance with paragraph E of this appendix; and

8. Notify the shipper and the Administrator of the nearest Commission Regional Office listed in appendix D of this part when any shipment, or part of a shipment, has not arrived within 60 days after receipt of an advance manifest, unless notified by the shipper that the shipment has been cancelled.

C. Any licensed waste processor who treats or repackages waste shall:

1. Acknowledge receipt of the waste from the shipper within one week of receipt by returning a signed copy of NRC Form 540;

2. Prepare a new manifest that meets the requirements of this appendix. Preparation of the new manifest reflects that the processor is responsible for meeting these requirements. For each container of waste in the shipment, the manifest shall identify the waste generators, the preprocessed waste volume, and the other information as required in paragraph I.E. of this appendix;

3. Prepare all wastes so that the waste is classified according to § 61.55 of this chapter and meets the waste characteristics requirements in § 61.56 of this chapter;

4. Label each package of waste to identify whether it is Class A waste, Class B waste, or Class C waste, in accordance with § § 61.55 and 61.57 of this chapter;

5. Conduct a quality assurance program to assure compliance with § § 61.55 and 61.56 of this chapter (the program shall include management evaluation of audits);

6. Forward a copy or electronically transfer the Uniform Low-Level Radioactive Waste Manifest to the intended consignee so that either:

(i) Receipt of the manifest precedes the LLW shipment or (ii) the manifest is delivered to the consignee with the waste at the time the waste is transferred to the consignee. Using both (i) and (ii) is also acceptable;

7. Include NRC Form 540 (and NRC Form 540A, if required) with the shipment regardless of the option chosen in paragraph C.6 of this section;

8. Receive acknowledgment of the receipt of the shipment in the form of a signed copy of NRC Form 540;

9. Retain a copy of or electronically store the Uniform Low-Level Radioactive Waste Manifest and documentation of acknowledgment of receipt as the record of transfer of licensed material as required by 10 CFR parts 30, 40, and 70 of this chapter;

10. For any shipment or any part of a shipment for which acknowledgment of receipt has not been received within the times set forth in this appendix, conduct an investigation in accordance with paragraph E of this appendix; and

11. Notify the shipper and the Administrator of the nearest Commission Regional Office listed in appendix D of this part when any shipment, or part of a shipment, has not arrived within 60 days after receipt of an advance manifest, unless notified by the shipper that the shipment has been cancelled.

D. The land disposal facility operator shall:

1. Acknowledge receipt of the waste within one week of receipt by returning, as a minimum, a signed copy of NRC Form 540 to the shipper. The shipper to be notified is the licensee who last possessed the waste and transferred the waste to the operator. If any discrepancy exists between materials listed on the Uniform Low-Level Radioactive Waste Manifest and materials received, copies or electronic transfer of the affected forms must be returned indicating the discrepancy;

2. Maintain copies of all completed manifests and electronically store the information required by 10 CFR 61.80(l) until the Commission terminates the license; and

3. Notify the shipper and the Administrator of the nearest Commission Regional Office listed in appendix D of this part when any shipment, or part of a shipment, has not arrived within 60 days after receipt of an advance manifest, unless notified by the shipper that the shipment has been cancelled.

E. Any shipment or part of a shipment for which acknowledgement is not received within the times set forth in this section must:

1. Be investigated by the shipper if the shipper has not received notification or receipt within 20 days after transfer; and

2. Be traced and reported. The investigation shall include tracing the shipment and filing a report with the nearest Commission Regional Office listed in Appendix D to this part. Each licensee who conducts a trace investigation shall file a written report with the appropriate NRC Regional Office within 2 weeks of completion of the investigation.

PART 25. ACCESS AUTHORIZATION FOR LICENSEE PERSONNEL

General Provisions

Citation: 10 CFR 25.13

✍ **§ 25.13 Records maintenance.**

* * * * *

(b) Each record required by this part must be legible throughout the retention period specified by each Commission regulation. The record may be the original or a reproduced copy or a microform provided that the copy or microform is authenticated by authorized personnel and that the microform is capable of producing a clear copy throughout the required retention period. The record may also be stored in electronic media with the capability for producing legible, accurate, and complete records during the required retention period. Records such as letters, drawings, specifications, must include all pertinent information such as stamps, initials, and signatures etc. The licensee shall maintain adequate safeguards against tampering with and loss of records.

PART 30. RULES OF GENERAL APPLICABILITY TO DOMESTIC LICENSING OF BYPRODUCT MATERIAL

RECORDS, INSPECTIONS, TESTS, AND REPORTS

Citation: 10 CFR 30.51

✍ **§ 30.51 Records.**

(a) Each person who receives byproduct material pursuant to a license issued pursuant to the regulations in this part and Parts 31 through 36 of this chapter shall keep records showing the receipt, transfer, and disposal of the byproduct material as follows:

(1) The licensee shall retain each record of receipt of byproduct material as long as the material is possessed and for three years following transfer or disposal of the material.

(2) The licensee who transferred the material shall retain each record of transfer for three years after each transfer unless a specific requirement in another part of the regulations in this chapter dictates otherwise.

(3) The licensee who disposed of the material shall retain each record of disposal of byproduct material until the Commission terminates each license that authorizes disposal of the material.

(b) The licensee shall retain each record that is required by the regulations in this part and Parts 31 through 36 of this chapter or by license condition for the period specified by the appropriate regulation or license condition. If a retention period is not otherwise specified by regulation or license condition, the record must be retained until the Commission terminates each license that authorizes the activity that is subject to the recordkeeping requirement.

(c)(1) Records which must be maintained pursuant to this part and Parts 31 through 36 of this chapter may be the original or a reproduced copy or microform is such reproduced copy or microform is duly authenticated by authorized personnel and the microform is capable of producing a clear and legible copy after storage for the period specified by Commission regulations. The record may also be stored in electronic media with the capability for producing legible, accurate, and complete records during the required retention period. Records such as letters, drawings, specification, must include all pertinent information such as stamps, initials, and signatures. The licensee shall maintain adequate safeguards against tampering with and loss of records.

* * * * *

PART 31. GENERAL DOMESTIC LICENSES FOR BYPRODUCT MATERIAL

Citation: 10 CFR 31.12

✍ § 31.12 Maintenance of records.

Each record required by this part must be legible throughout the retention period specified by each Commission regulation. The record may be the original or a reproduced copy or a microform provided that the copy or microform is authenticated by authorized personnel and that the microform is capable of producing a clear copy throughout the required retention period. The record may also be stored in electronic media with the capability for producing legible, accurate, and complete records during the required retention period. Records such as letters, drawings, specifications, must include all pertinent information such as letters, stamps, initials, and signatures etc. The licensee shall maintain adequate safeguards against tampering with and loss of records.

PART 32. SPECIFIC DOMESTIC LICENSES TO MANUFACTURE OR TRANSFER CERTAIN ITEMS CONTAINING BYPRODUCT MATERIAL

Citation: 10 CFR 32.3

✍ § 32.3 Maintenance of records.

Each record required by this part must be legible throughout the retention period specified by each Commission regulation. The record may be the original or a reproduced copy or a microform provided that the copy or microform is authenticated by authorized personnel and that the microform is capable of producing a clear copy throughout the required retention period. The record may also be stored in electronic media with the capability for producing legible, accurate, and complete records during the required retention period. Records such as letters, drawings, specifications, must include all pertinent information such as stamps, initials, and signatures etc. The licensee shall maintain adequate safeguards against tampering with and loss of records.

PART 34. LICENSES FOR RADIOGRAPHY AND RADIATION SAFETY REQUIREMENTS FOR RADIOGRAPHIC OPERATIONS

Citation: 10 CFR 34.4

✍ § 34.4 Maintenance of records.

Each record required by this part must be legible throughout the retention period specified by each Commission regulation. The record may be the original or a reproduced copy or a microform provided that the copy or microform is authenticated by authorized personnel and that the microform is capable of producing a clear copy throughout the required retention period. The record may also be stored in electronic media with the capability for producing legible, accurate, and complete records during the required retention period. Records such as letters, drawings, specifications, must include all pertinent information such as stamps, initials, and signatures etc. The licensee shall maintain adequate safeguards against tampering with and loss of records.

PART 35. MEDICAL USE OF BYPRODUCT MATERIAL

Subpart A. General Information

Citation: 10 CFR 35.5

✍ § 35.5 Maintenance of records.

Each record required by this part must be legible throughout the retention period specified by each Commission regulation. The record may be the original or a reproduced copy or a microform provided that the copy or microform is authenticated by authorized personnel and that the microform is capable of producing a clear copy throughout the required retention period. The record may also be stored in electronic media with the capability for producing legible, accurate, and complete records during the required retention period. Records such as letters, drawings, specifications, must include all pertinent information such as stamps, initials, and signatures etc. The licensee shall maintain adequate safeguards against tampering with and loss of records.

PART 40. DOMESTIC LICENSING OF SOURCE MATERIAL

RECORDS, REPORTS, AND INSPECTIONS

Citation: 10 CFR 40.61

✍ § 40.61 Records.

(a) Each person who receives source or byproduct material pursuant to a license issued pursuant to the regulations in this part shall keep records showing the receipt, transfer, and disposal of this source or byproduct material as follows:

(1) The licensee shall retain each record of receipt of source or byproduct material as long as the material is possessed and for three years following transfer or disposition of the source or byproduct material.

(2) The licensee who transferred the material shall retain each record of transfer or source or byproduct material until the Commission terminates each license that authorizes the activity that is subject to the recordkeeping requirement.

(3) The licensee shall retain each record of disposal of source or byproduct material until the Commission terminates each license that authorizes the activity that is subject to the

recordkeeping requirement.

(4) If source of byproduct material is combined or mixed with other licensed material and subsequently treated in a manner that makes direct correlation of a receipt record with a transfer, export, or disposition record impossible, the licensee may use evaluative techniques (such as first-in-first-out), to make the records that are required by this Part account for 100 percent of the material received.

(b) The licensee shall retain each record that is required by the regulations in this part or by license condition for the period specified by the appropriate regulation or license condition. If a retention period is not otherwise specified by regulation or license condition, each record must be maintained until the Commission terminates the license that authorizes the activity that is subject to the recordkeeping requirement.

(c)(1) Records which must be maintained pursuant to this part may be the original or reproduced copy or microform if the reproduced copy or microform is duly authenticated by authorized personnel and the microform is capable of producing a clear and legible copy after storage for the period specified by Commission regulations. The record may also be stored in electronic media with the capability for producing legible, accurate, and complete records during the required retention period. Records such as letters, drawings, specifications, must include all pertinent information such as stamps, initials, and signatures. The licensee shall maintain adequate safeguards against tampering with and loss of records.

(2) If there is a conflict between the Commission's regulations in this part, license condition, or other written Commission approval or authorization pertaining to the retention period for the same type of record, the retention period specified in the regulations in this part for such records shall apply unless the Commission, pursuant to § 40.14 of this part, has granted a specific exemption from the record retention requirements specified in the regulations in this part.

PART 50. DOMESTIC LICENSING OF PRODUCTION AND UTILIZATION FACILITIES

INSPECTIONS, RECORDS, REPORTS, NOTIFICATIONS

Citation: 10 CFR 50.71

✍ **§ 50.71 Maintenance of records, making of reports.**

(a) Each licensee and each holder of a construction permit shall maintain all records and make all reports, in connection with the activity, as may be required by the conditions of the license or permit or by the rules, regulations, and orders of the Commission in effectuating the purposes of the Act, including section 105 of the Act. Reports must be submitted in accordance with § 50.4.

(b) With respect to any production or utilization facility of a type described in § § 50.21(b) or 50.22, or a testing facility, each licensee and each holder of a construction permit shall submit its annual financial report, including the certified financial statements, to the Commission, as specified in § 50.4, upon issuance of the report.

(c) Records that are required by the regulations in this part, by license condition, or by technical specifications, must be maintained for the period specified by the appropriate regulation, license condition, or technical specification. If a retention period is not otherwise specified, these records must be retained until the Commission terminates the facility license.

(d)(1) Records which must be maintained pursuant to this part may be the original or a reproduced copy or microform if such reproduced copy or microform is duly authenticated by authorized personnel and the microform is capable of producing a clear and legible copy after storage for the period specified by Commission regulations. The record may also be stored in electronic media with the capability of producing legible, accurate, and complete records during the required retention period. Records such as letters, drawings, specifications, must include all pertinent information such as stamps, initials, and signatures. The licensee shall maintain adequate safeguards against tampering with and loss of records.

(2) If there is a conflict between the Commission's regulations in this part, license condition, or technical specification, or other written Commission approval or authorization pertaining to the retention period for the same type of record, the retention period specified in the regulations in this part for such records shall apply unless the Commission, pursuant to § 50.12 of this part, has granted a specific exemption from the record retention requirements specified in the regulations in this part.

* * * * *

PART 55. OPERATORS' LICENSES

Subpart F. Licenses

Citation: 10 CFR 55.59

✍ **§ 55.59 Requalification.**

* * * * *

(c) *Requalification program requirements.* * * *

* * * * *

(5) *Records.* The requalification program documentation must include the following:

(i) The facility licensee shall maintain records documenting the participation of each licensed operator and senior operator in the requalifications program. The records must contain copies of written examinations administered, the answers are given by the licensee, and the results of evaluations and documentation of operating tests and of any additional training administered in areas in which an operator or senior operator has exhibited deficiencies. The facility licensee shall retain these records until the operator's or senior operator's license if renewed.

(ii) Each record required by this part must be legible throughout the retention period specified by each Commission regulation. The record may be the original or reproduced copy or a microform provided that the copy or a microform provided that the copy of microform is authenticated by authorized personnel and that the microform is capable of producing a clear copy throughout the required retention period.

(iii) If there is a conflict between the Commission's regulations in this part, and any license condition, or other written Commission approval or authorization pertaining to the retention period for the same type of record, the retention period specified for these records by the regulations in this part apply unless the Commission, pursuant to § 55.11, grants a specific exemption from this record retention requirement.

* * * * *

PART 61. LICENSING REQUIREMENTS FOR LAND DISPOSAL OF RADIOACTIVE WASTE

Subpart G. Records, Reports, Tests, and Inspections

Citation:	10 CFR 61.80

✍ § 61.80 Maintenance of records, reports, and transfers.

(a) Each licensee shall maintain any records and make any reports in connection with the licensed activities as may be required by the conditions of the license or by the rules, regulations, and orders of the Commission.

(b) Records which are required by the regulations in this part or by license conditions must be maintained for a period specified by the appropriate regulations in this chapter or by license condition. If a retention period is not otherwise specified, these records must be maintained and transferred to the officials specified in paragraph (e) of this section as a condition of license termination unless the Commission otherwise authorizes their disposition.

(c) Records which must be maintained pursuant to this part may be the original or a reproduced copy or a microform if this reproduced copy or microform is capable of producing copy that is clear and legible at the end of the required retention period. The record may also be stored in electronic media with the capability for producing legible, accurate, and complete records during the required retention period. Records such as letters, drawings, specifications, must include all pertinent information such as stamps, initials, and signatures. The licensee shall maintain adequate safeguards against tampering with and loss of records.

(d) If there is a conflict between the Commission's regulations in this part, license condition, or other written Commission approval or authorization pertaining to the retention period for the same type of records, the longest retention period specified takes precedence.

(e) Notwithstanding paragraphs (a) through (d) of this section, the licensee shall record the location and the quantity of radioactive wastes contained in the disposal site and transfer these records upon license termination to the chief executive of the nearest municipality, the chief executive of the county in which the facility is located, the county zoning board or land development and planning agency, the State governor and other State, local and Federal governmental agencies as designated by the Commission at the time of license termination.

(f) Following receipt and acceptance of a shipment of radioactive waste, the licensee shall record the date that the shipment is received at the disposal facility, the date of disposal of the waste, a traceable shipment manifest number, a description of any engineered barrier or structural overpack provided for disposal of the waste, the location of disposal at the disposal site, the containment integrity of the waste disposal containers as received, any discrepancies between materials listed on the manifest and those received, the volume of any pallets, bracing, or other shipping or onsite generated materials that are contaminated, and are disposed of as contaminated or suspect materials, and any evidence of leaking or damaged disposal containers or radiation or contamination levels in excess of limits specified in Department of Transportation and Commission regulations. The licensee shall briefly describe any repackaging operations of any of the disposal containers included in the shipment, plus any other information required by the Commission as a license condition. The licensee shall retain these records until the Commission transfers or terminates the license that authorizes the activities described in this section.

(g) Each licensee shall comply with the safeguards reporting requirements of § § 30.55, 40.64, 70.53 and 70.54 of this chapter is the quantities or activities of materials received or transferred exceed the limits of these section. Inventory reports required by these sections are not required for materials after disposal.

(h) Each licensee authorized to dispose of radioactive waste received from other persons shall file a copy of its financial report or a certified financial statements annually with the Commission in order to update the information base for determining financial qualifications.

(i)(1) Each licensee authorized to dispose of waste materials received from other persons, pursuant to this part, shall submit annual reports to the appropriate Commission regional office shown in Appendix D to 10 CFR part 20, with copies to the Director, Division of Waste Management, Office of Nuclear Material Safety and Safeguards, U.S. Nuclear Regulatory Commission, Washington, DC 20555. Reports must be submitted by the end of the first calendar quarter of each year for the preceding year.

(ii) The reports shall include (I) specification of the quantity of each of the principal radionuclides released to unrestricted areas in liquid and in airborne effluents during the preceding year, (ii) the results of the environmental monitoring program, (iii) a summary of licensee disposal unit survey and maintenance activities, (iv) a summary, by waste class, of activities and quantities of radionuclides disposed of, (v) any instances in which observed site characteristics were significantly different from those described in the application for a license; and (vi) any other information the Commission may require. If the quantities of radioactive materials released during the reporting period, monitoring results, or maintenance performed are significantly different from those expected in the materials previously reviewed as part of the licensing action, the report must cover this specifically.

(j) Each licensee shall report in accordance with the requirements of § 70.52 of this chapter.

(k) Any transfer of byproduct, source, and special nuclear materials by the licensee is subject to the requirements in § § 30.41, 40.51, and 70.42 of this chapter. Byproduct, source and special nuclear materials means materials as defined in these parts, respectively.

(l) In addition to the other requirements of this section, the licensee shall store, or have stored, manifest and other information pertaining to receipt and disposal of radioactive waste in an electronic recordkeeping system.

(1) The manifest information that must be electronically stored is —

(i) That required in 10 CFR part 20, appendix G, with the exception of shipper and carrier telephone numbers and shipper and consignee certifications; and

(ii) That information required in paragraph (f) of this section.

(2) As specified in facility license conditions, the licensee shall report the stored information, or subsets of this information, on a computer-readable medium.

PART 70. DOMESTIC LICENSING OF SPECIAL NUCLEAR MATERIAL

Special Nuclear Material Control, Records, Reports and Inspections

Citation: **10 CFR 70.51**

✍ **§ 70.51 Material balance, inventory, and records requirements.**

* * * * *

(b) Licensees subject to the recordkeeping requirements of § § 74.31, 74.33 and 74.59 of this chapter are exempt from the requirements of § 70.51(b)(1) through (5). Otherwise:

* * * * *

(1) Each licensee shall keep records showing the receipt, inventory (including location), disposal, acquisition, and transfer of all special nuclear material in his possession regardless of its origin or method of acquisition.

(2) Each record that is required by the regulations in this part or by license condition must be maintained and retained for the period specified by the appropriate regulation or license condition. If a retention period is not otherwise specified by regulation or license condition, the licensee shall retain the record until the Commission terminates each license that authorizes the activity that is subject to the recordkeeping requirement.

(3) Each records of receipt, acquisition, or physical inventory of special nuclear material that must be maintained pursuant to paragraph (b)(1) of this section must be retained as long as the licensee retains possession of the material and for three years following transfer of such material.

(4) [Reserved]

(5) Each record of transfer of special nuclear material to other persons must be retained by the licensee who transferred the material until the Commission terminates the license authorizing the licensee's possession of the material. Each record required by paragraph (e)(1)(v) of this section must be retained for three years after it is made.

(6) Each record of disposal of special nuclear material must be retained until the Commission terminates each license that authorizes the activity that is subject to the recordkeeping requirement.

(c) Each licensee who is authorized to possess at any one time special nuclear material in a quantity exceeding one effective kilogram of special nuclear material shall establish, maintain, and follow written material control and accounting procedures that are sufficient to enable the licensee to account for the special nuclear material in the licensee's possession under license. The licensee shall retain these procedures until the Commission terminates the license that authorizes possession of the material and retain any superseded portion of the procedures for three years after the portion is superseded.

(d) Except as required by paragraph (e) of this section, each licensee who is authorized to possess at any one time and location special nuclear material in a quantity totaling more than 350 grams of contained uranium-235, uranium-233, or plutonium, or any combination thereof, shall conduct a physical inventory of all special nuclear material in his possession under license at intervals not to exceed twelve months.

(e) Each licensee who is authorized to possess at any one time special nuclear material in a quantity exceeding one effective kilogram of strategic special nuclear material, or special nuclear material of moderate strategic significance, and to use such special nuclear material for activities other than those involved in the operation of a nuclear reactor licensed pursuant to Part 50 of this chapter or those involved in a waste disposal operation; as sealed sources; or as reactor irradiated fuels involved in research, development, and evaluation programs in facilities other than irradiated fuel reprocessing plants, shall:

(1) Maintain procedures that include items listed in paragraphs (e)(1)(i), (ii), (iii), (iv), (v), (vi), and (vii) of this section and retain each record required in these paragraphs for three years after the record is made.

* * * * *

(f) Each licensee subject to the requirements of paragraph (e) of this section shall:

(1) Establish physical inventory procedures to assure that:

(i) The quantity of special nuclear material associated with each item on inventory is a measured value;

(ii) Each item on inventory is listed and identified to assure that all items are listed and that no item is listed more than once;

(iii) Cutoff procedures for transfers and processing are established so that all quantities are inventoried and none are inventoried more than once;

(iv) Cutoff procedures for records and reports are established so that all transfers for the inventory and material balance interval and no others are included in the records; and

(v) Upon completion of the inventory, all book and inventory records, both total plant and material balance area, are reconciled with and adjusted to the physical inventory.

(2) Establish inventory procedures for sealed sources and containers or vaults containing special nuclear material that provide for:

(i) Identification and location of all such items;

(ii) Verification of the integrity of the tamper-safing devices for such items;

(iii) Reverification of identity and quantity of contained special nuclear material for each item not tamper-safed, or whose tamper-safing is found to have been compromised;

(iv) Verification of the correctness of the inventory records of identity and location for all such items; and

(v) Documentation in compliance with the requirements of paragraphs (f)(2)(i), (ii), (iii), and (iv) of this section. Each record documenting compliance with these requirements must be retained for three years after it is made.

(3) Establish inventory procedures for special nuclear material in process that provide for:

(i) Measurement of all quantities not previously measured by the licensee for element and fissile isotope; and

(ii) For all material whose content of element and fissile isotope has been previously measured by the licensee but for which the validity of such previously made measurements has not been assured by tamper-safing, verification of the quantity of contained element and fissile isotope by remeasurement.

(4) Conduct physical inventories according to written inventory instructions for each inventory which shall:

(i) Assign inventory duties and responsibilities;

(ii) Specify the extent to which each material balance area and process is to be shut down, cleaned out, and/or remain static;

(iii) Identify the basis for accepting previously made measurements and their limits of error;

(iv) Designate measurements to be made for inventory purposes and the procedures for making such measurements; and

(v) Identify the means by which material on inventory will be listed to assure that each item is inventoried and that there is no duplication.

(g) Each licensee subject to the requirements of paragraph (e) of this section shall submit to the Atomic Energy Commission for approval by March 6, 1974, a full description of the program intended to be used to enable the licensee to comply with that paragraph and the requirements set forth in paragraph (f) of this section. This program shall be followed by the licensee after May 6, 1974.

(h) Each licensee who determines that the requirements of paragraph (e) of this section will require modifications of his plant or equipment costing $500,000 or more may, by March 6, 1974, apply to the Atomic Energy Commission for an extension of time, not to exceed six additional months, for compliance with those requirements. Each application for extension shall include a description of the modifications to be made, a statement of estimated associated costs with substantiating evidence, and a schedule of the dates when the modifications will be commenced and completed.

(i)(1) Records which must be maintained pursuant to this part may be the original or a reproduced copy or microform is such reproduced copy or microform is duly authenticated by authorized personnel and the microform is capable of producing a clear and legible copy after storage for the period specified by the Commission regulations. The record may also be stored in electronic media with the capability for producing legible, accurate, and complete records during the required retention period. Records such as letters, drawings, specification, must include all pertinent information such as stamps, initials, and signatures. The licensee shall maintain adequate safeguards against tampering with and loss of records.

(2) If there is a conflict between the Commission's regulations in this part, license condition, or other written Commission approval or authorization pertaining to the retention period for the same type of record, the retention period specified in the regulations in this part for such records shall apply unless the Commission, pursuant to § 70.14, has granted a specific exemption from the record retention requirements specified in the regulations in this part.

PART 71. PACKAGING AND TRANSPORTATION OF RADIOACTIVE MATERIAL

Subpart A. General Provisions

Citation: 10 CFR 71.1

✍ § 71.1 Communications and records.

* * * * *

(b) Each record required by this part must be legible throughout the retention period specified by each Commission regulation. The record may be the original or a reproduced copy or a microform provided that the copy or microform is authenticated and that the microform is capable of producing a clear copy throughout the required retention period. The records may also be stored in electronic media with the capability for producing legible, accurate, and complete records during the required retention period. Records such as letters, drawings, specifications, must include all pertinent information such as stamps, initials, and signatures. The licensee shall maintain adequate safeguards against tampering with and loss of records.

PART 72. LICENSING REQUIREMENTS FOR THE INDEPENDENT STORAGE OF SPENT NUCLEAR FUEL AND HIGH-LEVEL RADIOACTIVE WASTE

Subpart D. Records, Reports, Inspections, and Enforcement

Citation: 10 CFR 72.72

✍ § 72.72 Material balance, inventory, and records requirements for stored materials.

(a) Each licensee shall keep records showing the receipt, inventory (including location), disposal, acquisition, and transfer of all spent fuel and high-level radioactive waste in storage. The records must include as a minimum the name of shipper of the material to the ISFSI or MRS, the estimated quantity of radioactive material per item (including special nuclear material in spent fuel), item identification and seal number, storage location, onsite movements of each fuel assembly or storage canister, and ultimate disposal. These records for spent fuel at an ISFSI or for spent fuel and high-level radioactive waste at an MRS must be retained for as long as the material is stored and for a period of five years after the material is disposed of or transferred out of the ISFSI or MRS.

(b) Each licensee shall conduct a physical inventory of all spent fuel and high-level radioactive waste in storage at intervals not to exceed twelve months unless otherwise directed by the Commission. The licensee shall retain a copy of the current inventory as a record until the Commission terminates the license.

(c) Each licensee shall establish, maintain, and follow written material control and accounting procedures that are sufficient to enable the licensee to account for material in storage. The licensee shall retain a copy of the current material control and accounting procedures until the commission terminates the license.

(d) Records of spent fuel and high-level radioactive waste in storage must be kept in duplicate. The duplicate set of records must be kept at a separate location sufficiently remote from the original records that a single event would not destroy both sets of records. Records of spent fuel transferred out of an ISFSI or of spent fuel or high-level radioactive waste transferred out of an MRS must be preserved for a period of five years after the date of transfer.

PART 73. PHYSICAL PROTECTION OF PLANTS AND MATERIALS

RECORDS AND REPORTS

Citation: 10 CFR 73.70

✍ § 73.70 Records.

Each record required by this part must be legible throughout the retention period specified by each Commission regulation. The record may be the original or a reproduced copy or a microform provided that the copy or microform is authenticated by authorized personnel and that the microform is capable of producing a clear copy throughout the required retention period. The record may also be stored in electronic media with the capability for producing legible, accurate, and complete records during the required retention period. Records such as letters, drawings, specifications, must include all pertinent information such as stamps, initials, and signatures. The licensee shall maintain adequate safeguards against tampering with and loss of records. Each licensee subject to the provisions of § § 73.20,

73.25, 73.26, 73.27, 73.45, 73.46, 73.55, or 73.60 shall keep the following records:

(a) Names and addresses of all individuals who have been designated as authorized individuals. The licensee shall retain this record of currently designated authorized individuals for the period during which the licensee possesses the appropriate type and quantity of special nuclear material requiring this record under each license that authorizes the activity that is subject to the recordkeeping requirement and, for three years thereafter. Copies of superseded material must be retained for three years after each change.

(b) Names, addresses, and badge numbers of all individuals authorized to have access to vital equipment or special nuclear material, and the vital areas and material access areas to which authorization is granted. The licensee shall retain the record of individuals currently authorized this access for the period during which the licensee possesses the appropriate type and quantity of special nuclear material requiring this record under each license that authorizes the activity that is subject to the recordkeeping requirement and for three years thereafter. Copies of superseded material must be retained for three years after each change.

(c) A register of visitors, vendors, and other individuals not employed by the licensee pursuant to § § 73.46(d)(13), 73.55(d)(6), or § 73.60. The licensee shall retain this register as a record for three years after the last entry is made in the register.

(d) A log indicating name, badge number, time of entry, and time of exit of all individuals granted access to a vital area except those individuals entering or exiting the reactor control room. The licensee shall retain this log as a record for three years after the last entry is made in the log.

(e) Documentation of all routine security tours and inspections, and of all tests, inspections, and maintenance performed on physical barriers, intrusion alarms, communications equipment, and other security related equipment used pursuant to the requirements of this part. The licensee shall retain the documentation for these events for three years from the date of documenting each event.

(f) A record at each onsite alarm annunciation location of each alarm, false alarm, alarm check, and tamper indication that identifies the type of alarm, location, alarm circuit, date, and time. In addition, details of response by facility guards and watchmen to each alarm, intrusion, or other security incident shall be recorded. The license shall retain each record for three years after the record is made.

(g) Shipments of special nuclear material subject to the requirements of this part, including names of carriers, major roads to be used, flight numbers in the case of air shipments, dates and expected times of departure and arrival of shipments, verification of communication equipment on board the transfer vehicle, names of individuals who are to communicate with the transport vehicle, container seal descriptions and identification and any other information to confirm the means utilized to comply with § § 73.25, 73.26, and 73.27. This information must be recorded prior to shipment. Information obtained during the course of the shipment such as reports of all communications, change of shipping plan including monitor changes, trace investigations and others shall also be recorded. The licensee shall retain each record about a shipment required by this paragraph (g) for three years after the record is made.

(h) Procedures for controlling access to protected areas and for controlling access to keys for locks used to protect special nuclear material. The licensee shall retain a copy of the current procedures as a record until the Commission terminates each license for which the procedures were developed and, if any portion of the procedure is superseded, retain the superseded material for three years after each change.

PART 74. MATERIAL CONTROL AND ACCOUNTING OF SPECIAL NUCLEAR MATERIAL

Subpart C. Special Nuclear Material of Low Strategic Significance

Citation: 10 CFR 74.31

✍ § 74.31 Nuclear material control and accounting for special nuclear material of low strategic significance.

(a) *General performance objectives.* Each licensee who is authorized to possess and use more than one effective kilogram of special nuclear material of low strategic significance, excluding sealed sources, at any site or contiguous sites subject to control by the licensee, other than a production or utilization facility licensed pursuant to Part 50 or Part 70 of this chapter, or operations involved in waste disposal, shall implement and maintain a Commission approved material control and accounting system that will achieve the following objectives:

(1) Confirm the presence of special nuclear material;

(2) Resolve indications of missing material; and

(3) Aid in the investigation and recovery of missing material.

* * * * *

(c) *System Capabilities.* To meet the general performance objectives of § 74.31(a), the material control and accounting system must include the capabilities described in paragraph (c)(1) through (8) of this section. The licensee shall:

(1) Establish, document, and maintain a management structure which assures clear overall responsibility for material control and accounting functions, independence from production responsibilities, separation of key responsibilities, and adequate review and use of critical material control and accounting procedures;

* * * * *

(d) *Recordkeeping.* Each licensee shall establish records that will demonstrate that the requirements of paragraph (c) of this section have been met and maintain these records for at least 3 years, unless a longer retention time is required by Part 75 of this chapter.

(2) Records which must be maintained pursuant to this part may be the original or a reproduced copy or a microform is such reproduced copy or microform is duly authenticated by authorized personnel and the microform is capable of producing a clear and legible copy after storage for the period specified by Commission regulations. The record may also be stored in electronic media with the capability for producing legible, accurate, and complete records during the required retention period. Records such as letters, drawings, specifications, must include all pertinent information such as stamps, initials, and signatures.

The licensee shall maintain adequate safeguards against tampering with and loss of records.

PART 75. SAFEGUARDS ON NUCLEAR MATERIAL — IMPLEMENTATION OF US/IAEA AGREEMENT

General Provisions

Citation:	10 CFR 75.6

✍ **§ 75.6 Maintenance of records and delivery of information, reports, and other communications.**

* * * * *

(e) Each record required by this part must be legible throughout the retention period specified by each Commission regulation. The record may be the original or a reproduced copy or a microform provided that the copy or microform is authenticated by authorized personnel and that the microform is capable of producing a clear copy throughout the required retention period. The record may also be stored in electronic media with the capability for producing legible, accurate, and complete record during the required retention period. Records such as letters, drawings, specification, must include all pertinent information such as stamps, initials, and signatures. The licensee shall maintain adequate safeguards against tampering with and loss of records.

PART 110. EXPORT AND IMPORT OF NUCLEAR EQUIPMENT AND MATERIAL

Subpart E. License Terms and Related Provisions

Citation:	10 CFR 110.53

✍ **§ 110.53 United States address, records, and inspections.**

(a) Each licensee shall have an office in the United States where papers may be served and where records required by the Commission will be maintained.

(b)(1) Each licensee shall maintain records concerning his exports or imports. The licensee shall retain these records for five years after each export or import except that byproduct material record must be retained for three years after each export or import.

(2) Records which must be maintained pursuant to this part may be the original or a reproduced copy or microform if such reproduced copy or microform is duly authenticated by authorized personnel and the microform is capable of producing a clear and legible copy after storage for the period specified by Commission regulations. The record may also be stored in electronic media with the capability for producing legible, accurate, and complete record during the required retention period. Records such as letters, drawings, specifications, must include all pertinent information such as stamps, initials, and signatures. The licensee shall maintain adequate safeguards against tampering with and loss of records.

(c) Each licensee shall permit the Commission to inspect his records, premises, and activities pertaining to his exports and imports when necessary to fulfill the requirements of the Atomic Energy Act.

Agency:	Department of Energy

SUBCHAPTER D. ENERGY CONSERVATION

PART 430. ENERGY CONSERVATION PROGRAM FOR CONSUMER PRODUCTS

Subpart B. Test Procedures

Citation:	10 CFR 430.24

✍ **§ 430.24 Units to be tested.**

* * * * *

(m) * * *

(6) Each request to DOE for reviewing an alternative rating method shall include:

(i) The name, address and telephone number of the official representing the manufacturer.

(ii) Complete documentation of the alternative rating procedure, including the computer code when a computer model is used.

(iii) Test data for two coils from two different coil families for two different condensing units. The tested capacities for the matched systems for the two condensing units shall differ by at lease a factor of two. Rating information for the mixed systems shall include the ratings from testing, and from the alternative rating method.

(iv) Complete test data, product information, and related information to allow DOE to verify the rating information submitted by the manufacturer.

* * * * *

SUBCHAPTER H. ASSISTANCE REGULATIONS

PART 600. FINANCIAL ASSISTANCE RULES

Subpart B. Uniform Administrative Requirements for Grants and Cooperative Agreements With Institutions of Higher Education, Hospitals, Other Non-Profit Organizations and Commercial Organizations

Reports and Records

Citation:	10 CFR 600.152

✍ **§ 600.152 Financial reporting.**

(a) The following forms or such other forms as may be approved by OMB are authorized for obtaining financial information from recipients.

(1) SF-269 or SF-269A, Financial Status Report.

(i) Recipients shall use the SF-269 or SF-269A to report the status of funds for all nonconstruction projects or programs, except that DOE has the option of not requiring the SF-269 or SF-269A when the SF-270, Request for Advance or Reimbursement, or SF-272, Report of Federal Cash Transactions, is determined to provide adequate information to meet DOE needs. However, a final SF-269 or SF-269A shall be required at the completion of the project when the SF-270 is used only for advances.

(ii) The terms and conditions of award shall prescribe whether the report shall be on a cash or accrual basis. DOE may require accrual reporting only if such reporting is required by program statute or rule. If the award requires accrual information and the recipient's accounting records are not normally kept on the accrual basis, the recipient shall not be required to convert its accounting system, but shall develop such accrual information through best estimates based on an analysis of the documentation on hand.

(iii) DOE shall determine the frequency of the Financial Status Report for each project or program, considering the size and complexity of the particular project or program. However, the report shall not be required more frequently than quarterly or less frequently than annually. A final report shall be required at the completion of the agreement.

(iv) DOE shall require recipients to submit the SF-269 or SF-269A (an original and no more than two copies) no later than 30 days after the end of each specified reporting period for quarterly and semi-annual reports, and 90 calendar days for annual and final reports. Extensions of reporting due dates may be approved by the DOE upon request of the recipient.

(2) SF-272, Report of Federal Cash Transactions.

(i) When funds are advanced, each recipient shall submit the SF-272 and, when necessary, its continuation sheet, SF-272a. DOE will use this report to monitor cash advanced to recipients and to obtain disbursement information for each agreement with the recipients.

(ii) Recipients shall forecast Federal cash requirements in the "Remarks" section of the report.

(iii) When practical and deemed necessary, DOE may require recipients to report in the "Remarks" section the amount of cash advances received in excess of three days. Recipients shall provide short narrative explanations of actions taken to reduce the excess balances.

(iv) Recipients shall be required to submit not more than the original and two copies of the SF-272 15 calendar days following the end of each quarter. DOE may require a monthly report from those recipients receiving advances totaling $1 million or more per year.

(v) DOE may waive the requirement for submission of the SF-272 for any one of the following reasons:

(A) When monthly advances do not exceed $25,000 per recipient, provided that such advances are monitored through other forms contained in this section;

(B) If, in the contracting officer's opinion, the recipient's accounting controls are adequate to minimize excessive Federal advances; or,

(C) When electronic payment mechanisms provide adequate data.

(b) When DOE needs additional information or more frequent reports, the following shall be observed:

(1) When additional information is needed to comply with legislative requirements, DOE shall issue instructions to require recipients to submit such information under the "Remarks" section of the reports.

(2) When DOE determines that a recipient's accounting system does not meet the standards in Section 600.121, additional pertinent information to further monitor awards may be obtained upon written notice to the recipient until such time as the system is brought up to standard. DOE, in obtaining this information, shall comply with report clearance requirements of 5 CFR Part 1320.

(3) Contracting officers are encouraged to shade out any line item on any report if not necessary.

(4) DOE may accept the identical information from the recipients in machine readable format or computer printouts or electronic outputs in lieu of prescribed formats.

(5) Computer or electronic outputs may be provided to recipients when that expedites or contributes to the accuracy of reporting.

Citation: 10 CFR 600.153

✍ § 600.153 Retention and access requirements for records.

(a) This section sets forth requirements for record retention and access to records for awards to recipients. DOE shall not impose any other record retention or access requirements upon recipients, unless such requirements are established in program regulations.

(b) Financial records, supporting documents, statistical records, and all other records pertinent to an award shall be retained for a period of three years from the date of submission of the final expenditure report or, for awards that are renewed quarterly or annually, from the date of the submission of the quarterly or annual financial report, as authorized by DOE. The only exceptions are the following:

(1) If any litigation, claim, or audit is started before the expiration of the 3-year period, the records shall be retained until all litigation, claims or audit findings involving the records have been resolved and final action taken.

(2) Records for real property and equipment acquired with Federal funds shall be retained for 3 years after final disposition.

(3) When records are transferred to or maintained by DOE, the 3-year retention requirement is not applicable to the recipient.

(4) Indirect cost rate proposals, cost allocations plans, and related records, for which retention requirements are specified in § 600.153(g).

(c) Copies of original records may be substituted for the original records if authorized by DOE.

(d) DOE shall request transfer of certain records to its custody from recipients when it determines that the records possess long term retention value. However, in order to avoid duplicate recordkeeping, DOE may make arrangements for recipients to retain any records that are continuously needed for joint use.

(e) DOE, the Inspector General, Comptroller General of the United States, or any of their duly authorized representatives, have the right of timely and unrestricted access to any books, documents, papers, or other records of recipients that are pertinent to the awards, in order to make audits, examinations, excerpts, transcripts and copies of such documents. This right also includes timely and reasonable access to a recipient's personnel for the purpose of interview and discussion related to such documents. The rights of access in this paragraph are not limited to the required retention period, but shall last as long as records are retained.

(f) Unless required by statute, DOE shall place no restrictions on recipients that limit public access to the records of recipients that are pertinent to an award, except when DOE can demonstrate that such records shall be kept confidential and would have been exempted from disclosure pursuant to the Freedom of Information Act (5 U.S.C. 552) if the records had belonged to DOE.

(g) Paragraphs (g)(1) and (g)(2) of this section apply to the following types of documents, and their supporting records: indirect cost rate computations or proposals, cost allocation plans, and any similar accounting computations of the rate at which a particular group of costs is chargeable (such as computer usage chargeback rates or composite fringe benefit rates).

(1) *If submitted for negotiation.* If the recipient submits to the Federal agency responsible for negotiating the recipient's indirect cost rate or the subrecipient submits to the recipient the proposal, plan, or other computation to form the basis for negotiation of the rate, then the 3-year retention period for its supporting records starts on the date of such submission.

(2) *If not submitted for negotiation.* If the recipient is not required to submit to the cognizant Federal agency or the subrecipient is not required to submit to the recipient the proposal, plan, or other computation for negotiation purposes, then the 3-year retention period for the proposal, plan, or other computation and its supporting records starts at the end of the fiscal year (or other accounting period) covered by the proposal, plan, or other computation.

(h) If, by the terms and conditions of the award, the recipient or subrecipient —

(1) Is accountable for program income earned or received after the end of the project period or after the termination of an award or subaward, or

(2) If program income earned during the project period is required to be applied to costs incurred after the end of the project period or after termination of an award or subaward, the record retention period shall start on the last day of the recipient's or subrecipient's fiscal year in which such income was earned or received or such costs were incurred. All other program income records shall be retained in accordance with § 600.153(b).

Agency:	**Department of Energy** **Office of Environment, Safety and Health**

PART 602. EPIDEMIOLOGY AND OTHER HEALTH STUDIES FINANCIAL ASSISTANCE PROGRAM

Citation:	**10 CFR 602.19**

✍ § 602.19 Records and Data

(a) In some cases, DOE will require submission of certain project records or data to facilitate mission-related activities. Recipients, therefore, must take adequate steps to ensure proper management, control, and preservation of all project records and data.

(b) Awardees must ensure that all project data is adequately documented. Documentation shall:

(1) Reference software used to compile, manage, and analyze data;

(2) Define all technical characteristics necessary for reading or processing the records;

(3) Define file and record content and codes;

(4) Describe update cycles or conditions and rules for adding or deleting information; and

(5) Detail instrument calibration effects, sampling and analysis, space and time coverage, quality control measures, data algorithms and reduction methods, and other activities relevant to data collection and assembly.

(c) Recipients agree to comply with designated DOE records and data management requirements, including providing electronic data in prescribed formats and retention of specified records and data for eventual transfer to the Comprehensive Epidemiologic Data Resource or to another repository, as directed by DOE. Recipients will provide, as part of the final report, a description of records and data compiled during the project along with a plan for its preservation or disposition.

(d) Recipients agree to make project records and data available as soon as possible when requested by DOE.

TITLE 11. FEDERAL ELECTIONS

Agency:	**Federal Election Commission**

PART 104. REPORTS BY POLITICAL COMMITTEES

Citation:	**11 CFR 104.18**

✍ § 104.18 Electronic filing of reports (2 U.S.C. 432(d) and 434(a)(11)).

(a) *General.* A political committee that files reports with the Commission, as provided in 11 CFR part 105, may choose to file its reports in an electronic format that meets the requirements of this section. If a committee chooses to file its reports electronically, and its first electronic report passes the Commission's validation program in accordance with paragraph (c) of this section, it must continue to file in an electronic format all reports covering financial activity for that calendar year, unless the Commission determines that extraordinary and unforeseeable circumstances have made it impracticable for the committee to continue filing electronically.

(b) *Format specifications.* Reports filed electronically shall conform to the technical specifications described in the Federal Election Commission's Electronic Filing Specifications Requirements. The data contained in the computerized magnetic media provided to the Commission shall be organized in the order specified by the Electronic Filing Specifications Requirements.

(c) *Acceptance of reports filed in electronic format.* (1) Each committee that submits an electronic report shall check the report against the Commission's validation program before it is submitted, to ensure that the files submitted meet the Commission's format specifications and can be read by the Commission's computer system. Each report submitted in an electronic format under this section shall also be checked upon receipt against the Commission's validation program. The Commission's validation program is available on request and at no charge.

(2) A report that does not pass the validation program will not be accepted by the Commission and will not be considered filed. If a committee submits a report that does not pass the validation program, the Commission will notify the committee that the report has not been accepted.

(d) *Amended reports.* If a committee files an amendment to a report that was filed electronically, it shall also submit the amendment in an electronic format. The committee shall submit a complete version of the report as amended, rather than just those portions of the report that are being amended. In addition, the amended report shall contain electronic flags or markings that point to the portions of the report that are being amended.

(e) *Signature requirements.* The committee's treasurer, or any other person having the responsibility to file a designation, report or statement under this subchapter, shall verify the report in one of the following ways: by submitting a signed certification on paper that is submitted with the computerized media; or by submitting a digitized copy of the signed certification as a separate file in the electronic submission. Each verification submitted under this section shall certify that the person has examined the report or statement and, to the best of the signatory's knowledge and belief, it is true, correct and complete. Any verification under this section shall be treated for all purposes (including penalties for perjury) in the same manner as a verification by signature on a report submitted in a paper format.

(f) *Schedules and forms with special requirements.* The following list of schedules, materials, and forms have special signature and other requirements and reports containing these documents shall include, in addition to providing the required data within the electronic report, either a paper copy submitted with the committee's electronic report or a digitized version submitted as a separate file in the electronic submission: Schedule C-1 (Loans and Lines of Credit From Lending Institutions), including copies of loan agreements required to be filed with that Schedule, Schedule E (Itemized Independent Expenditures), Form 5 (Report of Independent Expenditures Made and Contributions Received), and Form 8 (Debt Settlement Plan). The committee shall submit any paper materials together with the electronic media containing the committee's report.

(g) *Preservation of reports.* For any report filed in electronic format under this section, the treasurer shall retain a machine-readable copy of the report as the copy preserved under 11 CFR 104.14(b)(2). In addition, the treasurer shall retain the original signed version of any documents submitted in a digitized format under paragraphs (e) and (f) of this section.

PART 105. DOCUMENT FILING (2 U.S.C. 432(g))

Citation: 11 CFR 105.1

✍ § 105.1 Place of filing; House candidates and their authorized committees (2 U.S.C. 432(g)(1)).

All designations, statements, reports, and notices, as well as any modification(s) or amendment(s) thereto, required to be filed under 11 CFR parts 101, 102, and 104 by a candidate for nomination or election to the office of Representative in, or Delegate or Resident Commissioner to, the Congress, or by his or her authorized committee(s), shall be filed in original form with, and received by, the Federal Election Commission.

Citation: 11 CFR 105.5

✍ § 105.5 Transmittal of microfilm copies and photocopies of original reports filed with the Secretary of the Senate to the Commission (2 U.S.C. 432(g)(3)).

(a) Either a microfilmed copy or photocopy of all original designations, statements, reports, modifications or amendments required to be filed pursuant to 11 CFR 105.2 shall be transmitted by the Secretary of the Senate to the Commission as soon as possible, but in any case no later than two (2) working days after receiving such designations, statements, reports, modifications, or amendments.

(b) The Secretary of the Senate shall then forward to the Commission a microfilm copy and a photocopy of each designation, statement, and report, or any modification or amendment thereto, filed with the Secretary pursuant to 11 CFR 105.2.

(c) The Secretary of the Senate shall place a time and date stamp on each original designation, statement, report, modification or amendment received.

TITLE 12. BANKS AND BANKING

Agency: Department of the Treasury
Office of the Comptroller of the Currency

PART 1. INVESTMENT SECURITIES

Citation: 12 CFR 1.5

✍ § 1.5 Safe and sound banking practices; credit information required.

(a) A national bank shall adhere to safe and sound banking practices and the specific requirements of this part in conducting the activities described in Sec. 1.3. The bank shall consider, as appropriate, the interest rate, credit, liquidity, price, foreign exchange, transaction, compliance, strategic, and reputation risks presented by a proposed activity, and the particular activities undertaken by the bank must be appropriate for that bank.

(b) In conducting these activities, the bank shall determine that there is adequate evidence that an obligor possesses resources sufficient to provide for all required payments on its obligations, or, in the case of securities deemed to be investment securities on the basis of reliable estimates of an obligor's performance, that the bank reasonably believes that the obligor will be able to satisfy the obligation.

(c) Each bank shall maintain records available for examination purposes adequate to demonstrate that it meets the requirements of this part. The bank may store the information in any manner that can be readily retrieved and reproduced in a readable form.

Citation: 12 CFR 1.8

✍ § 1.8 Prudent banking judgment; credit information required.

(a) Every bank shall maintain in its files credit information adequate to demonstrate that it has exercised prudence in making the determinations and carrying out the transactions described in § § 1.4 and 1.5.

(b) The information may be stored in microfiche or in other similar manner which can be readily retrieved and copied in a readable form.

PART 7. INTERPRETIVE RULINGS

Subpart C. Bank Ownership Of Property

Citation: 12 CFR 7.3500

✍ § 7.3500 Use of data processing equipment and furnishing of data processing services.

It is the opinion of the Comptroller that, in general, data processing is a technology rather than a service distinct or different from the underlying services or functions to which the technology is applied. A national bank may use data processing equipment and technology to perform for itself and others all services expressly or incidentally authorized under the statutes applicable to national banks.

PART 12. RECORDKEEPING AND CONFIRMATION REQUIREMENTS FOR SECURITIES TRANSACTIONS

Citation: 12 CFR 12.3

✍ § 12.3 Recordkeeping.

(a) *General rule.* A national bank effecting securities transactions for customers shall maintain the following records for at least three years:

(1) *Chronological records.* An itemized daily record of each purchase and sale of securities maintained in chronological order, and including:

(i) Account or customer name for which each transaction was effected;

(ii) Description of the securities;

(iii) Unit and aggregate purchase or sale price;

(iv) Trade date; and

(v) Name or other designation of the broker/dealer or other person from whom the securities were purchased or to whom the securities were sold;

(2) *Account records.* Account records for each customer, reflecting:

(i) Purchases and sales of securities;

(ii) Receipts and deliveries of securities;

(iii) Receipts and disbursements of cash; and

(iv) Other debits and credits pertaining to transactions in securities;

(3) *Memorandum order.* A separate memorandum (order ticket) of each order to purchase or sell securities (whether executed or canceled), including:

(i) Account or customer name for which the transaction was effected;

(ii) Type of order (market order, limit order, or subject to special instructions);

(iii) Time the trader or other bank employee responsible for effecting the transaction received the order;

(iv) Time the trader placed the order with the broker/dealer, or if there was no broker/dealer, time the order was executed or canceled;

(v) Price at which the order was executed; and

(vi) Name of the broker/dealer utilized;

(4) *Record of broker/dealers.* A record of all broker/dealers selected by the bank to effect securities transactions and the amount of commissions paid or allocated to each broker during the calendar year; and

(5) *Notifications.* A copy of the written notification required by Secs. 12.4 and 12.5.

(b) *Manner of maintenance.* The records required by this section must clearly and accurately reflect the information required and provide an adequate basis for the audit of the information. Record maintenance may include the use of automated or electronic records provided the records are easily retrievable, readily available for inspection, and capable of being reproduced in a hard copy.

PART 21. MINIMUM SECURITY DEVICES AND PROCEDURES, REPORTS OF SUSPICIOUS ACTIVITIES, AND BANK SECRECY ACT COMPLIANCE PROGRAM

Subpart B. Reports of Suspicious Activities

Citation: 12 CFR 21.11

✍ § 21.11 Suspicious Activity Report.

(a) *Purpose and scope.* This section ensures that national banks file a Suspicious Activity Report when they detect a known or suspected violation of Federal law or a suspicious transaction related to a money laundering activity or a violation of the Bank Secrecy Act. This section applies to all national banks as well as any Federal branches and agencies of foreign banks licensed or chartered by the OCC.

(b) *Definitions.* For the purposes of this section:

(1) FinCEN means the Financial Crimes Enforcement Network of the Department of the Treasury.

(2) Institution-affiliated party means any institution-affiliated party as that term is defined in sections 3(u) and 8(b)(5) of the Federal Deposit Insurance Act (12 U.S.C. 1813(u) and 1818(b)(5)).

(3) SAR means a Suspicious Activity Report on the form prescribed by the OCC.

(c) *SARs required.* A national bank shall file a SAR with the appropriate Federal law enforcement agencies and the Department of the Treasury in accordance with the form's instructions, by sending a completed SAR to FinCEN in the following circumstances:

(1) *Insider abuse involving any amount.* Whenever the national bank detects any known or suspected Federal criminal violation, or pattern of criminal violations, committed or attempted against the bank or involving a transaction or transactions conducted through the bank, where the bank believes that it was either an actual or potential victim of a criminal violation, or series of criminal violations, or that the bank was used to facilitate a criminal transaction, and the bank has a substantial basis for identifying one of its directors, officers, employees, agents or other institution-affiliated parties as having committed or aided in the commission of a criminal act, regardless of the amount involved in the violation.

(2) *Violations aggregating $5,000 or more where a suspect can be identified.* Whenever the national bank detects any known or suspected Federal criminal violation, or pattern of criminal violations, committed or attempted against the bank or involving a transaction or transactions conducted through the bank and involving or aggregating $5,000 or more in funds or other assets where the bank believes that it was either an actual or potential victim of a criminal violation, or series of criminal violations or that it was used to facilitate a criminal transaction, and the bank has a substantial basis for identifying a possible suspect or group of suspects. If it is determined prior to filing this report that the identified suspect or group of suspects has used an alias, then information regarding the true identity of the suspect or group of suspects, as well as alias identifiers, such as drivers' license or social security numbers, addresses and telephone numbers, must be reported.

(3) *Violations aggregating $25,000 or more regardless of potential suspects.* Whenever the national bank detects any known or suspected Federal criminal violation, or pattern of criminal violations, committed or attempted against the bank or involving a transaction or transactions conducted through the bank and involving or aggregating $25,000 or more in funds or other assets where the bank believes that it was either an actual

or potential victim of a criminal violation, or series of criminal violations, or that the bank was used to facilitate a criminal transaction, even though there is no substantial basis for identifying a possible suspect or group of suspects.

(4) *Transactions aggregating $5,000 or more that involve potential money laundering or violate the Bank Secrecy Act.* Any transaction (which for purposes of this paragraph (c)(4) means a deposit, withdrawal, transfer between accounts, exchange of currency, loan, extension of credit, or purchase or sale of any stock, bond, certificate of deposit, or other monetary instrument or investment security, or any other payment, transfer, or delivery by, through, or to a financial institution, by whatever means effected) conducted or attempted by, at or through the national bank and involving or aggregating $5,000 or more in funds or other assets, if the bank knows, suspects, or has reason to suspect that:

(i) The transaction involves funds derived from illegal activities or is intended or conducted in order to hide or disguise funds or assets derived from illegal activities (including, without limitation, the ownership, nature, source, location, or control of such funds or assets) as part of a plan to violate or evade any law or regulation or to avoid any transaction reporting requirement under Federal law;

(ii) The transaction is designed to evade any regulations promulgated under the Bank Secrecy Act; or

(iii) The transaction has no business or apparent lawful purpose or is not the sort in which the particular customer would normally be expected to engage, and the institution knows of no reasonable explanation for the transaction after examining the available facts, including the background and possible purpose of the transaction.

(d) *Time for reporting.* A national bank is required to file a SAR no later than 30 calendar days after the date of the initial detection of facts that may constitute a basis for filing a SAR. If no suspect was identified on the date of detection of the incident requiring the filing, a national bank may delay filing a SAR for an additional 30 calendar days to identify a suspect. In no case shall reporting be delayed more than 60 calendar days after the date of initial detection of a reportable transaction. In situations involving violations requiring immediate attention, such as when a reportable violation is ongoing, the financial institution shall immediately notify, by telephone, an appropriate law enforcement authority and the OCC in addition to filing a timely SAR.

(e) *Reports to state and local authorities.* National banks are encouraged to file a copy of the SAR with state and local law enforcement agencies where appropriate.

(f) *Exceptions.* (1) A national bank need not file a SAR for a robbery or burglary committed or attempted that is reported to appropriate law enforcement authorities.

(2) A national bank need not file a SAR for lost, missing, counterfeit, or stolen securities if it files a report pursuant to the reporting requirements of 17 CFR 240.17f-1.

(g) *Retention of records.* A national bank shall maintain a copy of any SAR filed and the original or business record equivalent of any supporting documentation for a period of five years from the date of the filing of the SAR. Supporting documentation shall be identified and maintained by the bank as such, and shall be deemed to have been filed with the SAR. A national bank shall make all supporting documentation available to appropriate law enforcement agencies upon request.

(h) *Notification to board of directors* — (1) *Generally.* Whenever a national bank files a SAR pursuant to this section, the management of the bank shall promptly notify its board of directors, or a committee of directors or executive officers designated by the board of directors to receive notice.

(2) Suspect is a director or executive officer. If the bank files a SAR pursuant to paragraph (c) of this section and the suspect is a director or executive officer, the bank may not notify the suspect, pursuant to 31 U.S.C. 5318(g)(2), but shall notify all directors who are not suspects.

(i) *Compliance.* Failure to file a SAR in accordance with this section and the instructions may subject the national bank, its directors, officers, employees, agents, or other institution-affiliated parties to supervisory action.

(j) *Obtaining SARs.* A national bank may obtain SARs and the Instructions from the appropriate OCC District Office listed in 12 CFR part 4.

(k) *Confidentiality of SARs.* SARs are confidential. Any national bank or person subpoenaed or otherwise requested to disclose a SAR or the information contained in a SAR shall decline to produce the SAR or to provide any information that would disclose that a SAR has been prepared or filed, citing this section, applicable law (e.g., 31 U.S.C. 5318(g)), or both, and shall notify the OCC.

(l) *Safe harbor.* The safe harbor provision of 31 U.S.C. 5318(g), which exempts any financial institution that makes a disclosure of any possible violation of law or regulation from liability under any law or regulation of the United States, or any constitution, law, or regulation of any state or political subdivision, covers all reports of suspected or known criminal violations and suspicious activities to law enforcement and financial institution supervisory authorities, including supporting documentation, regardless of whether such reports are required to be filed pursuant to this section or are filed on a voluntary basis.

(iii) The transaction has no business or apparent lawful purpose or is not the sort of transaction in which the particular customer would normally be expected to engage, and the bank knows of no reasonable explanation for the transaction after examining the available facts, including the background and possible purpose of the transaction.

(b) *Time for reporting.* (1) A bank shall file the suspicious activity report no later than 30 calendar days after the date of initial detection of facts that may constitute a basis for filing a suspicious activity report. If no suspect was identified on the date of detection of the incident requiring the filing, a bank may delay filing a suspicious activity report for an additional 30 calendar days to identify a suspect. In no case shall reporting be delayed more than 60 calendar days after the date of initial detection of a reportable transaction.

(2) In situations involving violations requiring immediate attention, such as when a reportable violation is ongoing, the bank shall immediately notify, by telephone, an appropriate law enforcement authority and the appropriate FDIC regional office (Division of Supervision) in addition to filing a timely report.

(c) *Reports to state and local authorities.* A bank is encouraged to file a copy of the suspicious activity report with state and local law enforcement agencies where appropriate.

(d) *Exemptions.* (1) A bank need not file a suspicious activity report for a robbery or burglary committed or attempted, that is reported to appropriate law enforcement authorities.

(2) A bank need not file a suspicious activity report for lost, missing, counterfeit, or stolen securities if it files a report pursuant to the reporting requirements of 17 CFR 240.17f-1.

(e) *Retention of records.* A bank shall maintain a copy of any suspicious activity report filed and the original or business record equivalent of any supporting documentation for a period of five years from the date of filing the suspicious activity report. Supporting documentation shall be identified and maintained by the bank as such, and shall be deemed to have been filed with the suspicious activity report. A bank must make all supporting documentation available to appropriate law enforcement authorities upon request.

(f) *Notification to board of directors.* The management of a bank shall promptly notify its board of directors, or a committee thereof, of any report filed pursuant to this section. The term "board of directors" includes the managing official of an insured state-licensed branch of a foreign bank for purposes of this part.

(g) *Confidentiality of suspicious activity reports.* Suspicious activity reports are confidential. Any bank subpoenaed or otherwise requested to disclose a suspicious activity report or the information contained in a suspicious activity report shall decline to produce the suspicious activity report or to provide any information that would disclose that a suspicious activity report has been prepared or filed citing this part, applicable law (e.g., 31 U.S.C. 5318(g)), or both, and notify the appropriate FDIC regional office (Division of Supervision).

(H) *Safe Harbor.* The safe harbor provisions of 31 U.S.C. 5318(g), which exempts any bank that makes a disclosure of any possible violation of law or regulation from liability under any law or regulation of the United States, or any constitution, law or regulation of any state or political subdivision, cover all reports of suspected or known criminal violations and suspicious activities to law enforcement and financial institution supervisory authorities, including supporting documentation, regardless of whether such reports are filed pursuant to this part or are filed on a voluntary basis.

PART 22. LOANS IN AREAS HAVING SPECIAL FLOOD HAZARDS

Citation: 12 CFR 22.6

✍ § 22.6 Required use of standard flood hazard determination form.

(a) *Use of form.* A bank shall use the standard flood hazard determination form developed by the Director of FEMA (as set forth in Appendix A of 44CFR part 65) when determining whether the building or mobile home offered as collateral security for a loan is or will be located in a special flood hazard area in which flood insurance is available under the Act. The standard flood hazard determination form may be used in a printed, computerized, or electronic manner.

(b) *Retention of form.* A bank shall retain a copy of the completed standard flood hazard determination form, in either hard copy or electronic form, for the period of time the bank owns the loan.

Citation: 12 CFR 22.10

✍ § 22.10 Notice of servicer's identity.

(a) *Notice requirement.* When a bank makes, increases, extends, renews, sells, or transfers a loan secured by a building or mobile home located or to be located in a special flood hazard area, the bank shall notify the Director of FEMA (or the Director's designee) in writing of the identity of the servicer of the loan. The Director of FEMA has designated the insurance provider to receive the bank's notice of the servicer's identity. This notice may be provided electronically if electronic transmission is satisfactory to the Director of FEMA's designee.

(b) *Transfer of servicing rights.* The bank shall notify the Director of FEMA (or the Director's designee) of any change in the servicer of a loan described in paragraph (a) of this section within 60 days after the effective date of the change. This notice may be provided electronically if electronic transmission is satisfactory to the Director of FEMA's designee. Upon any change in the servicing of a loan described in paragraph (a) of this section, the duty to provide notice under this paragraph (b) shall transfer to the transferee servicer.

Agency: Federal Reserve System

PART 203. HOME MORTGAGE DISCLOSURE (REGULATION C)

Citation: 12 CFR Appendix A to Part 203

✍ Appendix A to Part 203 — Form and Instructions for Completion of HMDA Loan/Application Register

* * * * *

II. Required Format and Reporting Procedures

A. Institutions must submit data to their supervisory agencies in an automated, machine-readable form. The format must conform exactly to that of form FR HMDA-LAR, including the order of columns, column headings, etc. Contact your federal supervisory agency for information regarding procedures and technical specifications for automated data submission; in some cases, agencies also make software for automated data submission available to institutions. The data must be edited before submission, using the edits included in the agency-supplied software or equivalent edits in software available from vendors or developed in-house. (Institutions that report 25 or fewer entries on their HMDA-LAR may collect and report the data in paper form. An institution that submits its register in nonautomated form must send two copies that are typed or computer printed, and must use the format of form FR HMDA-LAR (but need not use the form itself). Each page must be numbered, and the total number of pages must be given (for example, "Page 1 of 3").)

B. The required data are to be entered in the register for each loan origination, each application acted on, and each loan purchased during the calendar year. Your institution should decide on the procedure it wants to follow — for example, whether to begin entering the required data when an application is received, or to wait until final action is taken (such as when a loan goes to closing or an application is denied). Keep in mind that an application is to be reported in the calendar year they go to closing; if an application has been approved but has not yet gone to closing at year end, report it the following year.

C. Your institution may collect the data on separate registers at different branches, or on separate registers for different loan types (such as for home purchase or home improvement loans, or for loans on multifamily dwellings). But make sure the application or loan numbers (discussed under paragraph V.A.1., below) are unique.

D. Entries need not be grouped on your register by MSA, or chronologically, or by census tract numbers, or in any other particular order.

E. Applications and loans must be recorded on your register within thirty calendar days after the end of the calendar quarter in which final action (such as origination or purchase of a loan, or denial or withdrawal of an application) is taken. The type of purchaser for loans sold need not be included in these quarterly updates.

* * * * *

PART 205. ELECTRONIC FUND TRANSFERS

Citation: 12 CFR 205.13

✍ § 205.13 Administrative enforcement.

* * * * *

(c) *Record retention.* (1) Evidence of compliance with the requirements imposed by the Act and this regulation shall be preserved by any person subject to the Act and this regulation for a period of not less than 2 years. Records may be stored by use of microfiche, microfilm, magnetic tape, or other methods capable of accurately retaining and reproducing information.

(2) Any person subject to the Act and this regulation that has actual notice that it is being investigated or is subject to an enforcement proceeding by an agency charged with monitoring that person's compliance with the Act and this regulation, or that has been served with notice of an action filed under section 910, 915, or 916(a) of the Act, shall retain the information required in paragraph (c)(1) of this section that pertains to the action or proceeding until final disposition of the matter, unless an earlier time is allowed by order of the agency or court.

PART 208. MEMBERSHIP OF STATE BANKING INSTITUTIONS IN THE FEDERAL RESERVE SYSTEM (REGULATION H)

Citation: **12 CFR 208.23**

✍ § 208.23 Loans in areas having special flood hazards.

* * * * *

(f) Required use of standard flood hazard determination form —(1) *Use of form.* A state member bank shall use the standard flood hazard determination form developed by the Director of FEMA (as set forth in Appendix A of 44 CFR part 65) when determining whether the building or mobile home offered as collateral security for a loan is or will be located in a special flood hazard area in which flood insurance is available under the Act. The standard flood hazard determination form may be used in a printed, computerized, or electronic manner.

(2) *Retention of form.* A state member bank shall retain a copy of the completed standard flood hazard determination form, in either hard copy or electronic form, for the period of time the bank owns the loan.

* * * * *

Agency: **Deposit Insurance Corporation**
Federal Deposit Insurance Corporation

PART 339. LOANS IN AREAS HAVING SPECIAL FLOOD HAZARDS

Citation: **12 CFR 339.6**

✍ § 339.6 Required use of standard flood hazard determination form.

(a) *Use of form.* A bank shall use the standard flood hazard determination form developed by the Director of FEMA (as set forth in Appendix A of 44 CFR part 65) when determining whether the building or mobile home offered as collateral security for a loan is or will be located in a special flood hazard area in which flood insurance is available under the Act. The standard flood hazard determination form may be used in a printed, computerized, or electronic manner.

(b) *Retention of form.* A bank shall retain a copy of the completed standard flood hazard determination form, in either hard copy or electronic form, for the period of time the bank owns the loan.

Agency: **Department of the Treasury**
Office of Thrift Supervision

PART 545. OPERATIONS

Citation: **12 CFR 545.13**

✍ § 545.13 Account records.

* * * * *

(c) *Use of collecting and paying agent.* A Federal savings association may authorize any bank that is a member of the Federal Deposit Insurance Corporation to prepare, sign and deliver evidence of accounts, to collect and transmit funds obtained from those accounts, and to maintain records with respect to such accounts. The Federal savings association may provide for issuance of duplicate certificates, bond, security and other protection in connection with such activities. A Federal savings association may also authorize any such institution to pay an account according to its terms.

PART 563. OPERATIONS

Citation: **12 CFR 563.170**

✍ § 563.170 Examinations and audits; appraisals; establishment and maintenance of records.

* * * * *

(c) *Establishment and maintenance of records.* To enable the Office to examine savings associations and affiliates and audit savings associations, affiliates, and service corporations pursuant to the provisions of paragraph (a) of this section, each savings association, affiliate, or service corporation shall establish and maintain such accounting and other records as will provide an accurate and complete record of all business it transacts, and the documents, files, and other material or property comprising said records shall at all times be available for such examination and audit wherever any of said records, documents, files, material, or property may be. Without any limitation on the generality of the foregoing sentence, at a minimum savings associations and service corporations ("lenders") shall establish and maintain the following records:

(1) *Records with respect to loans secured by real estate.* The records of a lender with respect to each loan that such lender makes on the security of real estate shall include:

(i) An application for the loan, signed by the borrower or its agent, in such form and containing such information as will disclose the purpose for which the loan is sought (for example, construction, purchase, refinancing) and the identify of any security property;

(ii) A note evidencing the borrower's obligation to repay the amount of the loan, executed by the borrower or its agent;

(iii) A copy of the deed of trust or mortgage instrument on said real estate or other document customarily used in the jurisdiction in which such real estate security is located evidencing the creation of a security interest in the real estate for the benefit of the lender which deed of trust, mortgage instrument, or other document has been signed by the borrower or the borrower's agent; and if the loan is made for the purpose of financing the purchase of the real estate security for the loan, a signed statement by the borrower or its agent, as a part of or as an attachment to the application for the loan, disclosing the purchase price of such real estate security;

(iv) One or more written appraisal reports, prepared at the request of the lender or its agent and for the lender's use, and signed prior to the approval of such application (except in the case of an approval conditioned upon obtaining an appraisal) that satisfies the requirements of part 564 of this chapter: *Provided, however,* That nothing in paragraph (c)(1)(iv) shall apply to property improvement loans, as that term is used in 24 CFR 200.167, insured by the Federal Housing Administration for which that agency does not require an appraisal or certification of valuation;

(v) A financial statement, which is current at the time that the loan application is made, signed by the borrower disclosing its financial ability to repay the loan, or a written credit report prepared by the lender or by others at the special instance and request of such lender;

(vi) Documentation showing when and by whom such loan was approved and any terms and conditions of such approval;

(vii) Documentation showing the date, amount, purpose, the recipient of every disbursement of the proceeds of such loan, and to the best of the lender's knowledge, any actual recipient of any proceeds when the stated recipient is acting as an agent or intermediary for another.

(viii) For each loan made for the purpose of developing or constructing improvement on real estate, inspection reports prepared by or for the lender or vouchers signed by the borrower or its agent demonstrating that the work for which each disbursement is sought has been completed.

(ix) An opinion signed by the lender's attorney, a title insurance policy, or other documentary evidence customarily used in the jurisdiction in which the real estate security is located affirming the quality and validity of the lender's lien on the real estate security for the loan; Provided, however, That such documentary evidence shall not be required with respect to any loan having Federal Housing Administration mortgage insurance as to which 24 CFR 203.390 and 203.402 re applicable, and any such loan may be considered to be secured by a first lien without new title evidence;

(x) Documentation showing that the lender, upon the closing of the loan furnished to the borrower a loan settlement statement setting forth in detail the charges or fees such borrower has paid or is obligated to pay to such lender or to any other concern or person in connection with such loan, which documentation shall include a copy of such loan settlement statement;

(xi) A record showing the status and current payment of taxes, assessments, insurance premiums, other charges on the security for the loan, and the loan security, as well as any amounts recovered pursuant to an insurance settlement of such loss;

(xii) Documentation evidencing any modifications of the original documents by which a security interest for the benefit of the lender was created, showing appropriate approval of each party to such modifications; and

(xiii) Documentation evidencing any release of any portion of the collateral pledged to secure the loan, showing the portion of the collateral released, the consideration, if any, paid to effect such release, and a record of the appropriate approval of each such release.

(2) *Records with respect to loans not secured by real estate.* The records of a lender with respect to each unsecured loan or loan not secured by real estate that such lender makes shall include the documents referred to in paragraphs (c)(1)(i), (c)(1)(ii), (c)(1)(v), (c)(1)(vi), and (c)(1)(vii) of this section. If the loan is secured by collateral other than real estate, the lender's records also shall include documents evidencing the creation and perfection of a security interest in the collateral, including any financing statement, as well as the documents referred to in paragraphs (c)(1)(xii) and (c)(1)(xiii) of this section. In addition, if the loan is made to a business entity, the lender's records shall include documentation showing whether the obligor on the loan is able to generate sufficient case flow to meet scheduled interest and debt reduction payments and, if not sufficient, the lender's records shall include documentation demonstrating the anticipated source of the borrower's payments.

(3) *Records with respect to loan purchases or participations.* (i) The records of a lender with respect to each loan that it purchases, in whole or in part, that is secured by real estate shall include copies of the documents referred to in paragraphs (c)(1)(i), through (c)(1)(v), (c)(1)(ix), and (c)(1)(xiii) of this section. A single lender purchasing a whole loan secured by real estate must retain documents evidencing the assignment to it of the mortgage or deed of trust.

(ii) The records of the lender with respect to loans it has purchased, in whole or in part, that are unsecured or secured by collateral other than real estate shall include copies of the documents referred to in paragraphs (c)(1)(i), (c)(1)(ii), and (c)(1)(v) of this section. If the loan is made to a business entity and is unsecured or secured by collateral other than real estate, copies of documentation of the obligor's cash flow or other anticipated source of the borrower's payments, as described in paragraph (c)(2) of this section, must be included. If the loan is secured by collateral other than real estate, the purchasing lender must retain copies of documents required by paragraph (c)(1)(xiii) of this section and those evidencing creation and perfection of a security interest for its benefit in the collateral, including any financing statement, signed by the borrower or its agent.

(iii) In addition to the requirements of paragraphs (c)(3)(i) and (c)(3)(ii) of this section a lender purchasing all or any part of any loan must retain the originator's or the selling lender's statement concerning whether, on the date the loan is purchased, the payments are current and, if not current, the period for which the loan is delinquent; any agreement concerning participation in or servicing of the loan; and a copy of the underwriting standards of the originator. In addition, a purchaser must retain the written agreement of the seller of the loan to provide access, upon request, to all loan documentation in its possession or control to the purchasing lender, the Office, its District Director, or the examinations and supervision staff, as well as the seller's written certification that copies of any documents concerning the loan provided to the loan purchaser are accurate and complete to the best of the seller's knowledge.

(4) *Records with respect to loans secured by timeshare accounts receivable.* In addition to the records required by the applicable provisions of paragraphs (c)(1), (c)(2), and (c)(3) of this section, the records of a lender concerning loan purchases, participations, or originations of loans secured by timeshare accounts receivable, including fee, right-to-use, or membership interests, shall include any additional documents necessary to make those records accurate and complete, as this requirement is interpreted by the Senior Deputy Director for Supervision (Operations).

(5) *Records with respect to property purchased subject to a lender's lien or a secured loan assumed by a third party.* When a property on which the lender has a lien securing an unpaid loan is sold to a third party and the lender releases the original borrower from such indebtedness, the records of the lender shall contain such documentation and records with respect to such third party and such transactions as are required by paragraphs (c)(1)(ii), (c)(1)(iii), (c)(1)(v), (c)(1)(vi), (c)(1)(xii), and (c)(1)(xiii) of this section.

(6) *Records with respect to loans sold.* The records of a lender with respect to each loan it sells, whether in whole or in part, shall include a signed opinion by such lender's attorney stating whether the terms of the sales agreement governing such sale provide for a sale without recourse.

(7) *Records with respect to the acquisition of mortgaged security.* A lender shall maintain a record which discloses every

instance that it commences action to acquire the real estate security for a loan, by foreclosure or otherwise, and the ultimate disposition of such action. Such record shall include identification of the real estate security and loan, shall itemize all fees and charges incurred in such action, shall name the recipient or recipients to whom any such fees and charges were paid, and shall identify the holder of title to such real estate as a result of such action.

(8) *Records with respect to accounts.* The records of a savings association with respect to each withdrawal or repurchasable share, investment certificate, deposit, or savings account it issues shall include the signature of the owner of such account or the duly authorized representative of such owner, together with a record reflecting the balance in such account. Notwithstanding the preceding requirement, no account signature card for a trust executed by its trustee(s) of information disclosing the names of the settlor or trustee(s) of the trust need be maintained in the records of a savings association.

(9) *Other records.* A lender shall establish and maintain such other records as are required by statute or by any other regulations to which the lender is subject.

(d) *Change in location of records.* A savings association shall not transfer the location of any of its general accounting or control records from its home office to a branch or service office, or from a branch or service office to its home office or to another branch or service office unless the savings association has sent prior written notice of such transfer to the District Director of the District in which the principal office of the savings association is located.

(e) *Use of data processing services for maintenance of records.* A savings association which determines to maintain any of its records by means of data processing services shall so notify the District Director of the District in which the principal office of such savings association is located, in writing, at least 90 days prior to the date on which such maintenance of records will begin. Such notification shall include identification of the records to be maintained by data processing services and a statement as to the location at which such records will be maintained. Any contract, agreement, or arrangement made by a savings association pursuant to which data processing services are to be performed for such savings association shall be in writing and shall expressly provide that the records to be maintained by such services shall at all times be available for examination and audit.

PART 572. LOANS IN AREAS HAVING SPECIAL FLOOD HAZARDS

Citation: 12 CFR 572.6

✍ § 572.6 Required use of standard flood hazard determination form.

(a) *Use of form.* A savings association shall use the standard flood hazard determination form developed by the Director of FEMA (as set forth in Appendix A of 44 CFR part 65) when determining whether the building or mobile home offered as collateral security for a loan is or will be located in a special flood hazard area in which flood insurance is available under the Act. The standard flood hazard determination form may be used in a printed, computerized, or electronic manner.

(b) *Retention of form.* A savings association shall retain a copy of the completed standard flood hazard determination form, in either hard copy or electronic form, for the period of time the savings association owns the loan.

Agency: Farm Credit Administration

PART 614. LOAN POLICIES AND OPERATIONS

Citation 12 CFR 614.4940

✍ § 614.4940 Required use of standard flood hazard determination form.

(a) *Use of form.* System institutions shall use the standard flood hazard determination form developed by the Director of FEMA (as set forth in Appendix A of 44 CFR part 65) when determining whether the building or mobile home offered as collateral security for a loan is or will be located in a special flood hazard area in which flood insurance is available under the 1968 Act. The standard flood hazard determination form may be used in a printed, computerized, or electronic manner.

(b) *Retention of form.* System institutions shall retain a copy of the completed standard flood hazard determination form, in either hard copy or electronic form, for the period of time the institution owns the loan.

Agency: National Credit Union Administration

SUBCHAPTER A. REGULATIONS AFFECTING CREDIT UNIONS

PART 749. RECORDS PRESERVATION PROGRAM

Citation: 12 CFR 749.1

✍ § 749.1 Implementation.

The financial officer of the credit union is responsible for storing duplicate vital records at a vital records center. This responsibility may be delegated.

(a) The Records Preservation Program must be operational within 6 months after the credit union's insurance certificate is issued.

(b) The vital records center is defined as any location far enough from the credit union's office to avoid the simultaneous loss of both sets of records in the event of disaster.

(c) Records must be stored every 3 months, within 30 days after the end of the 3 month period. Previously stored records may be destroyed when the current records are stored.

(d) A records preservation log will be maintained showing what records were stored, where the records were stored, when the records were stored, and who sent the records for storage.

(e) Stored records may be any format which can be used to reconstruct the credit union's records. Formats include paper originals, machine copies, micro film or fiche, magnetic tape, etc.

(f) Credit unions which have some or all of their records maintained by an off-site data processor are considered to be in compliance for the storage of those records.

PART 760. LOANS IN AREAS HAVING SPECIAL FLOOD HAZARDS

Citation: 12 CFR 760.6

✍ § 760.6 Required use of standard flood hazard determination form.

(a) *Use of form.* A credit union shall use the standard flood hazard determination form developed by the Director (as set forth in Appendix A of 44 CFR part 65) when determining whether the building or mobile home offered as collateral security for a loan is or will be located in a special flood hazard area in which flood insurance is available under the Act. The standard flood hazard determination form may be used in a printed, computerized, or electronic manner.

(b) *Retention of form.* A credit union shall retain a copy of the completed standard flood hazard determination form, in either hard copy or electronic form, for the period of time the credit union owns the loan.

TITLE 14. AERONAUTICS AND SPACE

Agency:	**Department of Transportation Federal Aviation Administration**

SUBCHAPTER C. AIRCRAFT

PART 21. CERTIFICATION PROCEDURES FOR PRODUCTS AND PARTS

Subpart M. Designated Alteration Station Authorization Procedures

Citation:	**14 CFR 21.493**

✍ § 21.493 Current records.

(a) The DAS shall maintain, at its facility, current records containing —

(1) For each product for which it has issued an STC under this subpart, a technical data file that includes any data and amendments thereto (including drawings, photographs, specifications, instructions, and reports) necessary for the STC;

(2) A list of products by make, model, manufacturer's serial number and, if applicable, any FAA identification, that have been altered under the DAS authorization; and

(3) A file of information from all available sources on alteration difficulties of products altered under the DAS authorization.

(b) The records prescribed in paragraph (a) of this section shall be —

(1) Made available by the DAS, upon the Administrator's request, for examination by the Administrator at any time; and

(2) In the case of the data file prescribed in paragraph (a)(1) of this section, identified by the DAS and sent to the Administrator as soon as the DAS no longer operates under this subpart.

PART 43. MAINTENANCE, PREVENTIVE MAINTENANCE, REBUILDING, AND ALTERATION

Citation:	**14 CFR 43.12**

✍ § 43.12 Maintenance records: Falsification, reproduction, or alteration.

(a) No person may make or cause to be made:

(1) Any fraudulent or intentionally false entry in any record or report that is required to be made, kept, or used to show compliance with any requirement under this part;

(2) Any reproduction, for fraudulent purpose, of any record or report under this part; or

(3) Any alteration, for fraudulent purpose, of any record or report under this part.

(b) The commission by any person of an act prohibited under paragraph (a) of this section is a basis for suspending or revoking the applicable airman, operator, or production certificate, Technical Standard Order Authorization, FAA-Parts Manufacturer Approval, or Product and Process Specification issued by the Administrator and held by that person.

SUBCHAPTER D. AIRMEN

PART 61. CERTIFICATION: PILOTS AND FLIGHT INSTRUCTORS

Subpart A. General

Citation:	**14 CFR 61.59**

✍ § 61.59 Falsification, reproduction, or alteration of applications, certificates, logbooks, reports, or records.

(a) No person may make or cause to be made —

(1) Any fraudulent or intentionally false statement on any application for a certificate, rating, or duplicate thereof, issued under this part;

(2) Any fraudulent or intentionally false entry in any logbook, record, or report that is required to be kept, made, or used, to show compliance with any requirement for the issuance, or exercise of the privileges, or any certificate or rating under this part;

(3) Any reproduction, for fraudulent purpose, of any certificate or rating under this part; or

(4) Any alteration of any certificate or rating under this part.

(b) The commission by any person of an act prohibited under paragraph (a) of this section is a basis for suspending or revoking any airman or ground instructor certificate or rating held by that person.

PART 63. CERTIFICATION: FLIGHT CREW MEMBERS OTHER THAN PILOTS

Subpart A. General

Citation:	**14 CFR 63.20**

✍ § 63.20 Applications, certificates, logbooks, reports, and records; falsification, reproduction, or alteration.

(a) No person may make or cause to be made —

(1) Any fraudulent or intentionally false statement on any application for a certificate or rating under this part;

(2) Any fraudulent or intentionally false entry in any logbook, record, or report that is required to be kept, made, or used, to show compliance with any requirement for any certificate or rating under this part;

(3) Any reproduction, for fraudulent purpose, of any certificate or rating under this part; or

(4) Any alteration of any certificate or rating under this part.

(b) The commission by any person of an act prohibited under paragraph (a) of this section is a basis for suspending or revoking any airman or ground instructor certificate or rating held by that person.

PART 65. CERTIFICATION: AIRMEN OTHER THAN FLIGHT CREWMEMBERS

Subpart A. General

Citation: 14 CFR 65.20

✍ § 65.20 Applications, certificates, logbooks, reports, and records: Falsification, reproduction, or alteration.

(a) No person may make or cause to be made —

(1) Any fraudulent or intentionally false statement on any application for a certificate or rating under this part;

(2) Any fraudulent or intentionally false entry in any logbook, record, or report that is required to be kept, made, or used, to show compliance with any requirement for any certificate or rating under this part;

(3) Any reproduction, for fraudulent purpose, of any certificate or rating under this part; or

(4) Any alteration of any certificate or rating under this part.

(b) The commission by any person of an act prohibited under paragraph (a) of this section is a basis for suspending or revoking any airman or ground instructor certificate or rating held by that person.

PART 67. MEDICAL STANDARDS AND CERTIFICATION

Subpart A. General

Citation: 14 CFR 67.20

✍ § 67.20 Applications, certificates, logbooks, reports, and records: Falsification, reproduction, or alteration.

(a) No person may make or cause to be made —

(1) Any fraudulent or intentionally false statement on any application for a medical certificate under this part;

(2) Any fraudulent or intentionally false entry in any logbook, record, or report that is required to be kept, made, or used, to show compliance with any requirement for any medical certificate under this part;

(3) Any reproduction, for fraudulent purpose, of any medical certificate under this part;

(4) Any alteration of any medical certificate under this part.

(b) The commission by any person of an act prohibited under paragraph (a) of this section is a basis for suspending or revoking any airman, ground instructor, or medical certificate or rating held by that person.

SUBCHAPTER G. AIR CARRIERS AND OPERATORS FOR COMPENSATION OR HIRE: CERTIFICATION AND OPERATIONS

PART 121. OPERATING REQUIREMENTS: DOMESTIC, FLAG, AND SUPPLEMENTAL OPERATIONS

Subpart V. Records and Reports

Citation: 14 CFR 121.683

✍ § 121.683 Crewmember and dispatcher record.

(a) Each certificate holder shall —

(1) Maintain current records of each crewmember, and each aircraft dispatcher (domestic and flag air carriers only), that show whether the crewmember complies with this applicable sections of chapter, including, but not limited to, proficiency and route checks, airplane and route qualifications, training, any required physical examinations, and flight time records; and

(2) Record each action taken concerning the release from employment or physical or professional disqualification of any flight crewmember or aircraft dispatcher (domestic and flag air carriers only) and keep the record for at least six months thereafter.

(b) Supplemental air carriers and commercial operators: Each supplemental air carrier and commercial operator shall maintain the records required by paragraph (a) of this section at its principal operations base, or at another location used by it and approved by the Administrator.

(c) Computer record systems approved by the Administrator may be used in complying with the requirements of paragraph (a) of this section.

PART 125. CERTIFICATION AND OPERATIONS: AIRPLANES HAVING A SEATING CAPACITY OF 20 OR MORE PASSENGERS OR A MAXIMUM PAYLOAD CAPACITY OF 6,000 POUNDS OR MORE

Subpart L. Records and Reports

Citation: 14 CFR 125.401

✍ § 125.401 Crewmember record.

(a) Each certificate holder shall —

(1) Maintain current records of each crewmember that show whether or not that crewmember complies with this chapter (e.g., proficiency checks, airplane qualifications, any required physical examinations, and flight time records); and

(2) Record each action taken concerning the release from employment or physical or professional disqualification of any flight crewmember and keep the record for at least 6 months thereafter.

(b) Each certificate holder shall maintain the records required by paragraph (a) of this section at its principal operations base, or at another location used by it and approved by the Administrator.

(c) Computer record systems approved by the Administrator may be used in complying with the requirements of paragraph (a) of this section.

SUBCHAPTER I. AIRPORTS

PART 152. AIRPORT AID PROGRAM

Subpart D. Accounting and Reporting Requirements

Citation: 14 CFR 152.309

✍ § 152.309 Availability of sponsor's records.

(a) The sponsor or planning agency shall allow any authorized representative of the Administrator, the Secretary of Transportation, or the Comptroller General of the United States access to any of its books, documents, papers, and records that are pertinent to grants received under this part for the purposes of accounting and audit.

(b) The sponsor or planning agency shall allow appropriate FAA or DOT representatives to make progress audits at any time during the project, upon reasonable notice to the sponsor or planning agency.

(c) If audit findings have not been resolved, the applicable records shall be retained by the sponsor or planning agency until those findings have been resolved.

(d) Records for nonexpendable property that was acquired with Federal funds shall be retained for three years after final disposition of the property.

(e) Microfilm copies of original records may be substituted for original records with the approval of the FAA.

(f) If the FAA determines that certain records have long-term retention value, the FAA may require transfer of custody of those records to the FAA.

Agency: **Department of Transportation**
Office of the Secretary

SUBCHAPTER A. ECONOMIC REGULATIONS

PART 221. TARIFFS

Subpart W. Electronically Filed Tariffs

Citation: **14 CFR 221.251**

✍ § 221.251 Applicability of the subpart.

(a) Any carrier, consistent with the provisions of this subpart, and Part 221 generally, may file its international passenger fares tariffs electronically in machine-readable form as an alternative to the filing of printed paper tariffs as provided for elsewhere in Part 221. This subpart applies to all carriers and tariff publishing agents and may be used by either if the carrier or agent complies with the provisions of Subpart W. Any carrier or agent that files electronically under this subpart must transmit to the Department the Remainder of the tariff in a form consistent with Part 221, Subparts A-V on the same day that the electronic tariff would be deemed received under § 221.270(b).

(b) To the extent that Subpart W is inconsistent with the remainder of Part 221, Subpart W shall govern the filing of electronic tariffs. In all other respects, Part 221 remains in full force and effect.

Citation: **14 CFR 221.260**

✍ § 221.260 Requirements for filing.

(a) No carrier or filing agent shall file an electronic tariff unless, prior to filing, it has signed a maintenance agreement or agreements, furnished by the Department of Transportation, for the maintenance and security of the on-line tariff database.

(b) No carrier or agent shall file an electronic tariff unless, prior to filing, it has submitted to the Department's Office of International Aviation Tariffs Division, and received approval of, an application containing the following commitments:

* * * * *

(2) The filer shall provide, maintain and install in the Public Reference Room at the Department (as may be required from time to time) one or more CRT devices and printers connected to its on-line tariff database. The filer shall be responsible for the transportation, installation, and maintenance of this equipment and shall agree to indemnify and hold harmless the Department and the U.S. Government from any claims or liabilities resulting from defects in the equipment, its installation or maintenance.

* * * * *

(6) The filer shall ensure that the Department shall have the sole ability to approve or disapprove electronically any tariff filed with the Department and the ability to note, record and retain electronically the reasons for approval or disapproval. The carrier or agent shall not make any changes in data or delete data after it has been transmitted electronically, regardless of whether it is approved, disapproved, or withdrawn. The filer shall be required to make data fields available to the Department in any record which is part of the on-line tariff database.

(7) The filer shall maintain all fares filed with the Department and all Departmental approvals, disapprovals and other actions, as well as all Departmental notations concerning such approvals, disapprovals or other actions, in the on-line tariff database for a period of two (2) years after the fare becomes inactive. After this period of time, the carrier or agent shall provide the Department, free of charge, with a copy of the inactive data on a machine-readable tape or other mutually acceptable electronic medium.

* * * * *

(9) Should the filer terminate its business or cease filing tariffs electronically, it shall provide to the Department on a machine-readable tape or other mutually acceptable electronic medium, contemporaneously with the cessation of such business, a complete copy of its on-line tariff database.

* * * * *

(11) The file shall afford any authorized Departmental official full, free, and uninhibited access to its facilities, databases, documentation, records, and application programs, including support functions, environmental security, and accounting data, for the purpose of ensuring continued effectiveness of safeguards against threats and hazards to the security or integrity of its electronic tariffs, as defined in this subpart.

* * * * *

Citation: **14 CFR 221.275**

✍ § 221.275 Requirement for filing paper tariffs.

(a) Any tariff, or revision thereto, filed in paper format which accompanies, governs, or otherwise affects, a tariff filed electronically, must be received by the Department on the same date that a tariff or revision thereto, is filed electronically with the Department under § 221.270(b). Further, such paper tariff, or revision thereto, shall be filed in accordance with the requirements of Subparts A-V of Part 221. No tariff or revision thereto, filed electronically under this subpart, shall contain an effective date which is at variance with the effective date of the supporting paper tariff, except as authorized by the Department.

(b) Any printed justifications, or other information accompanying a tariff, or revision thereto, filed electronically under this subpart, must be received by the Department on the same date as any tariff, or revision thereto, filed electronically.

(c) If a filer submits a filing which fails to comply with paragraph (a) of this section, or if the filer fails to submit the information in conformity with paragraph (b) of this section, the filing will be subject to rejection, denial, or disapproval, as applicable.

Citation: **14 CFR 221.400**

✍ § 221.400 Discontinuation of electronic tariff system.

In the event that the electronic tariff system is discontinued, or the source of the data is changed, or a filer discontinues its business, all electronic data records prior to such date shall be provided immediately to the Department, free of charge, on a machine-readable tape or other mutually acceptable electronic medium.

Citation: 14 CFR 221.500

✍ § 221.500 Filing of paper tariffs required.

(a) After approval of any application filed under § 221.260 of this subpart to allow a filer to file tariffs electronically, the filer in addition to filing electronically must continue to file printed tariffs as required by Subparts A-V of Part 221 for a period of 90 days, or until such time as the Department shall deem such filing no longer to be necessary: Provided, That during the period specifically by this section the filed printed tariff shall continue to be the official tariff.

(b) Upon notification to the filer that it may commence to file its tariffs solely in an electronic mode, concurrently with the implementation of filing electronically the filer shall:

(1) Furnish the Department with a copy of all the existing effective and prospective records on a machine-readable tape or other mutually acceptable electronic medium accompanied by an affidavit attesting to the accuracy of such records; and

(2) Simultaneously cancel such records from the paper tariff in the manner prescribed by Subparts A-V of Part 221.

PART 249. PRESERVATION OF AIR CARRIER RECORDS

Subpart A. General Instructions

Citation: 14 CFR 249.2

✍ § 249.2 Definitions.

For the purposes of this part:

Authorized representatives of the DOT means any persons, including special agents and auditors, designated by the DOT to perform inspections, audits, or examinations within the purview of the DOT authority.

Certificated air carrier means the holder of a certificate of public convenience and necessity issued by the Department of Transportation under 49 U.S.C. 41102 or a certificate for all-cargo air service issued by the Department of Transportation under 49 U.S.C. 41103.

Final adjudication means the expiration date of the last possible period of review or reconsideration of a given case, by the DOT or by a court, that is provided by applicable statute or regulation.

Open mail rate period means the time interval between the date of institution of a new mail rate proceeding or the start of service over a new route for which no mail rate has previously been fixed, and the date upon which a DOT order setting the final mail rate becomes legally effective.

Pending case means any case that the DOT is empowered to hear before its final adjudication.

Records include all documents that are related to, or constitute integral links in developing the history of, or facts regarding, financial transactions or physical operations of a particular segment, operating division, or entire system of the carrier's operations. The term includes any copy of initially prepared documents which bear approvals, comments, or notations which were added and are of significance to a full explanation of recorded facts or information. The term records means not only accounting records in a limited technical sense but all other evidentiary accounts of events such as memoranda, correspondence, working sheets, tabulating equipment listings punched cards, computer-produced listings, microfilm, and magnetic storage media (i.e., magnetic tapes, disks). The term *records* also means microform and/or tape reproductions of documents made as authorized by this subpart. In addition, the term records includes any of the above-described materials coming into the possession of the air carrier through merger, consolidation, succession, transfer, or other acquisition.

Supporting papers (records) means any group of documentary papers, such as memoranda, correspondence, working sheets, etc., that assist in upholding the accuracy or clarity of related records.

Citation: 14 CFR 249.3

✍ § 249.3 Preservation of records.

(a) All records listed in 249.20 and 249.21 may be preserved on either paper or nonerasable microfilm (see § 249.4). However, a paper or microfilm record need not be created to satisfy the requirements of this part if the record is initially prepared in a machine-readable medium such as punched cards, magnetic tapes, and disks. The records maintained in machine-readable media and the underlying data used in their preparation shall be preserved for the periods prescribed in 249.20 and 249.21. A paper or microfilm record shall not be destroyed after transfer to a machine-readable medium before expiration of the prescribed period: however, a waiver permitting the early destruction of paper or microfilm records transferred to a machine-readable medium may be granted by the Chief, Data Requirements Division, Office of the Comptroller, when it is demonstrated by the requesting carrier that the substantive purpose of the retention requirement will be met by retention of the information in machine-readable form (see § 249.10).

(b) Each record kept in a machine-readable medium shall be accompanied by a statement clearly indicating the type of data included in the record and certifying that the information contained in it is complete and accurate. This statement shall be executed by a person having personal knowledge of the facts contained in the records. The records shall be indexed and retained in such a manner so that they are easily accessible, and the carrier shall have the facilities available to locate, identify and reproduce the records in readable form without loss of clarity. Authorized representatives of the Board shall be given immediate access to the carrier's facilities upon request.

(c) If any record which must be retained under the provisions of 249.20 and 249.21 is included as an exhibit to another document which must also be retained, the carrier need only keep in its files one copy of the record to satisfy these record retention requirements. In these cases, the carrier shall establish adequate cross-references to assist in locating the record.

(d) The provisions in this part do not excuse noncompliance with requirements of any other governmental body, Federal or State, prescribing longer retention periods for any records.

Citation: 14 CFR 249.4

✍ § 249.4 Photographic copies.

(a) Any record may be transferred to nonerasable microfilm (including microfiche, computer output microfilm, and aperture cards) at any time. Records so maintained on microfilm shall satisfy the minimum requirements listed in paragraphs (b) through (f) of this section.

(b) The microfilm shall be of a quality that can be easily read and that can be reproduced in paper similar in size to an original without loss of clarity or detail during the periods the records are required to be retained in § § 249.20 and 249.21.

(c) Microfilm records shall be indexed and retained in such a manner as will render them readily accessible, and the company shall have facilities available to locate, identify and read the microfilm and reproduce in paper form. Authorized representatives of the DOT shall be given immediate access to these facilities upon request.

(d) Any significant characteristic, feature, or other attribute which microfilm will not preserve shall be clearly indicated at the beginning of each roll of film or series of microfilm records if applicable to all records on the roll or series, or on the individual record, as appropriate.

(e) The printed side of printed forms need not be microfilmed for each record if nothing has been added to the printed matter common to all such forms, but an identified specimen of the form shall be on the film for reference.

(f) Each roll of film or series of microfilm records shall include a microfilm of a certificate stating that the photographs are direct and facsimile reproductions of the original records and they have been made in accordance with prescribed regulations. Such a certificate shall be executed by a person having personal knowledge of these facts. Where the microfilm is computer output, the microfilm certificate shall state that the information is complete and accurate.

Citation: **14 CFR 249.6**

✍ § 249.6 Destruction of records.

(a) Upon the expiration of the period of preservation prescribed in this regulation, records may be destroyed at the option of the carrier.

(b) Unless otherwise specified, duplicate copies of records may be destroyed at any time if they contain no significant information not shown on the originals.

SUBCHAPTER B. PROCEDURAL REGULATIONS

PART 302. RULES OF PRACTICE IN PROCEEDINGS

Subpart A. Rules Of General Applicability

Citation: **14 CFR 302.3**

✍ § 302.3 Filing of documents.

(a) *Filing address, date of filing, hours.* Documents required by any section of this part to be filed with DOT shall be filed with the Documentary Services Division of Transportation, Washington, D.C. 20590. Such documents shall be deemed to be filed on the date on which they are actually received by DOT. The hours of DOT for the receipt of filings are from 9:00 a.m. to 5:30 p.m., eastern standard or daylight saving time, whichever is in effect in the District of Columbia at the time, Monday to Friday, inclusive, except on legal holidays.

(b) *Formal specifications of documents.* (1) Documents filed under this part must be on white paper not larger than 8 1/2 by 11 inches, including any tables, charts and other documents that may be included. Ink must be dark enough (but may not be green) to provide substantial contrast for scanning and photographic reproduction. Text must be double-spaced (except for footnotes and long quotations, which may be single-spaced), using type not smaller than 12 point. The left margin must be at least 1 1/2 inches; all other margins must be at least 1 inch. The title page and first page must bear a clear date and all subsequent pages must bear a page number and abbreviated heading. In order to facilitate automated processing in document sheet feeders, documents of more than one page should be held together with removable metal clips or similar retainers. Original documents may not be bound in any form or include tabs, except in cases assigned by order to an Administrative Law Judge for hearing, in which case the filing requirements will be set by order. Section 302.31 contains additional requirements as to the contents and style of briefs.

(2) To facilitate indexing, a filer should include in or provide with each document: the docket title and subject; the relevant operating administration before which the application or request is filed; the identity of the filer; the title of the specific action being requested; and the name and address of the designated agent, and so identified, on file for official service. The Docket Management Facility has an Expedited Processing Sheet that filers can use to assist in this index input.

(3) *Reproduction of documents.* Papers may be reproduced by any duplicating process, provided all copies are clear and legible. Appropriate notes or other indications shall be used, so that the existence of any matters shown in color on the original will be accurately indicated on all copies.

* * * * *

Filers are encouraged to submit one of the required true copies (except for counterparts of Agreement CAB 18900) in electronic form on a 3 1/2 inch floppy disk, labeled to show the filer's and representative's names, the docket number (if known) or space for it, and document title. The electronic submission must be in one of the following formats: Microsoft Word (or RTF), WordPerfect, Excel, Lotus 123, or ASCII text. The disk must be accompanied by a signed certification that it is a true copy of the executed original document.

(d) *Table of contents.* All documents filed under this part consisting of twenty or more pages must contain a subject index of the matter in such document, with page references.

(e) Reserved.

(f) *Official docket copy.* With respect to all documents filed under this part that are scanned, the electronic scanned record produced by the Department shall thereafter be the official docket copy of the document and any subsequent copies generated by the Department's electronic records system will be usable for admission as record copies in any proceeding before the Department.

Agency: **National Aeronautics and Space Administration**

PART 1260. GRANTS AND COOPERATIVE AGREEMENTS

Subpart 4. Research Grant And Cooperative Agreement Provisions

Citation: **14 CFR 1260.406**

✍ § 1260.406 Financial management.

(a) The Grantee shall maintain books and accounting records, in accordance with the principles set forth in the documents listed in paragraph 405 of the NASA Grant and Cooperative Agreement Handbook in a manner sufficient to reflect properly all direct and indirect costs incurred or anticipated as a result of commitments made during the period of the grant. Microfilm records are acceptable.

(b) Financial records, supporting documents, statistical records, and all other records pertinent to this Grant shall be retained for a period of 3 years, except that:

(1) If any litigation, claim or audit is started before the expiration of the 3-year period, the records shall be retained until all litigation, claims, or audit findings involving the records have been resolved, and

(2) Records for nonexpendable property acquired with Grant funds shall be retained for 3 years after its final disposition.

(c) *Records.* Financial records, supporting documents, statistical records, and all other records (or microfilm copies) pertinent to this grant shall be retained for a period of 3 years, except that (1) If any litigation, claim, or audit is started before the expiration of the 3-year period, the records shall be retained until all litigation, claims, or audit findings involving the records have been resolved, and (2) Records for nonexpendable property acquired with grant funds shall be retained for 3 years after its final disposition. The retention period starts from the date of the submission of the final Federal Cash Transactions Report (SF—72). The Administrator of NASA and the Comptroller General of the United States, or any of their duly authorized representatives, shall have access to any pertinent books, documents, papers, and records of the Grantee and of subrecipients to make audits, examinations, excerpts, and transcripts. All of the foregoing provisions shall apply to any subrecipient performing substantive work under this grant.

PART 1273. UNIFORM ADMINISTRATIVE REQUIREMENTS FOR GRANTS AND COOPERATIVE AGREEMENTS TO STATE AND LOCAL GOVERNMENTS

Subpart C. Post-Award Requirements

Reports, Records, Retention, and Enforcement

Citation: **14 CFR 1273.41**

✍ § 1273.41 Financial reporting.

(a) *General.* (1) Except as provided in paragraphs (a) (2) and (5) of this section, grantees will use only the forms specified in paragraphs (a) through (e) of this section, and such supplementary or other forms as may from time to time be authorized by OMB, for:

(i) Submitting financial reports to Federal agencies, or

(ii) Requesting advances or reimbursements when letters or credit are not used.

(2) Grantees need not apply the forms prescribed in this section in dealing with their subgrantees. However, grantees shall not impose more burdensome requirements on subgrantees.

(3) Grantees shall follow all applicable standard and supplemental Federal agency instructions approved by OMB to the extent required under the Paperwork Reduction Act of 1980 for use in connection with forms specified in paragraphs (b) through (e) of this section. Federal agencies may issue substantive supplementary instructions only with the approval of OMB. Federal agencies may shade out or instruct the grantee to disregard any line item that the Federal agency finds unnecessary for its decisionmaking purposes.

(4) Grantees will not be required to submit more than the original and two copies of forms required under this part.

(5) Federal agencies may provide computer outputs to grantees to expedite or contribute to the accuracy of reporting. Federal agencies may accept the required information from grantees in machine usable format or computer printouts instead of prescribed forms.

(6) Federal agencies may waive any report required by this section if not needed.

(7) Federal agencies may extend the due date of any financial report upon receiving a justified request from a grantee.

(b) *Financial Status Report* — (1) *Form.* Grantees will use Standard Form 269 or 269A, Financial Status Report, to report the status of funds for all nonconstruction grants and for construction grants when required in accordance with paragraph § 1273.41(e)(2)(iii) of this section.

(2) *Accounting basis.* Each grantee will report program outlays and program income on a cash or accrual basis as prescribed by the awarding agency. If the Federal agency requires accrual information and the grantee's accounting records are not normally kept on the accrual basis, the grantee shall not be required to convert its accounting system but shall develop such accrual information through and analysis of the documentation on hand.

(3) *Frequency.* The Federal agency may prescribe the frequency of the report for each project or program. However, the report will not be required more frequently than quarterly. If the Federal agency does not specify the frequency of the report, it will be submitted annually. A final report will be required upon expiration or termination of grant support.

(4) *Due date.* When reports are required on a quarterly or semiannual basis, they will be due 30 days after the reporting period. When required on an annual basis, they will be due 90 days after the grant year. Final reports will be due 90 days after the expiration or termination of grant support.

(c) *Federal Cash Transactions Report* — (1) *Form.* (i) For grants paid by letter or credit, Treasury check advances or electronic transfer of funds, the grantee will submit the Standard Form 272, Federal Cash Transactions Report, and when necessary, its continuation sheet, Standard Form 272a, unless the terms of the award exempt the grantee from this requirement.

(ii) These reports will be used by the Federal agency to monitor cash advanced to grantees and to obtain disbursement or outlay information for each grant from grantees. The format of the report may be adapted as appropriate when reporting is to be accomplished with the assistance of automatic data processing equipment provided that the information to be submitted is not changed in substance.

(2) *Forecasts of Federal cash requirements.* Forecasts of Federal cash requirements may be required in the "Remarks" section of the report.

(3) *Cash in hands of subgrantees.* When considered necessary and feasible by the Federal agency, grantees may be required to report the amount of cash advances in excess of three days' needs in the hands of their subgrantees or contractors and to provide short narrative explanations of actions taken by the grantee to reduce the excess balances.

(4) *Frequency and due date.* Grantees must submit the report no later than 15 working days following the end of each quarter. However, where an advance either by letter of credit or electronic transfer of funds is authorized at an annualized rate of one million dollars or more, the Federal agency may require the report to be submitted within 15 working days following the end of each month.

(d) *Request for advance or reimbursement* — (1) *Advance payments.* Requests for Treasury check advance payments will be submitted on Standard Form 270, Request for Advance or Reimbursement. (This form will not be used for drawdowns under a letter of credit, electronic funds transfer or when Treasury check advance payments are made to the grantee automatically on a predetermined basis.)

(2) *Reimbursements.* Requests for reimbursement under nonconstruction grants will also be submitted on Standard Form 270. (For reimbursement requests under construction grants, see paragraph (e)(1) of this section.)

(3) The frequency for submitting payment requests is treated in § 1273.41(b)(3).

(e) *Outlay report and request for reimbursement for construction programs.*

(1) Grants that support construction activities paid by

reimbursement method.

(i) Requests for reimbursement under construction grants will be submitted on Standard Form 271, Outlay Report and Request for Reimbursement for Construction Programs. Federal agencies may, however, prescribe the Request for Advance or Reimbursement form, specified in § 1273.41(d), instead of this form.

(ii) The frequency for submitting reimbursement requests is treated in § 1273.41(b)(3).

(2) Grants that support construction activities paid by letter of credit, electronic funds transfer or Treasury check advance.

(i) When a construction grant is paid by letter of credit, electronic funds transfer or Treasury check advances, the grantee will report its outlays to the Federal agency using Standard Form 271, Outlay Report and Request for Reimbursement for Construction Programs. The Federal agency will provide any necessary special instruction. However, frequency and due date shall be governed by § 1273.41(b) (3) and (4).

(ii) When a construction grant is paid by Treasury check advances based on periodic requests from the grantee, the advances will be requested on the form specified in § 1273.41(d).

(iii) The Federal agency may substitute the Financial Status Report specified in § 1273.41(b) for the Outlay Report and Request for Reimbursement for Construction Programs.

(3) *Accounting basis.* The accounting basis for the Outlay Report and Request for Reimbursement for Construction Programs shall be governed by § 1273.41(b)(2).

Citation: 14 CFR 1273.42

✍ § 1273.42 Retention and access requirements for records.

(a) *Applicability.* (1) This section applies to all financial and programmatic records, supporting documents, statistical records, and other records of grantees or subgrantees which are:

(i) Required to be maintained by the terms of this part, program regulations or the grant agreement, or

(ii) Otherwise reasonably considered as pertinent to program regulations or the grant agreement.

(2) This section does not apply to records maintained by contractors or subcontractors. For a requirement to place a provision concerning records in certain kinds of contracts, see § 1273.36(I)(10).

(b) *Length of retention period.* (1) Except as otherwise provided, records must be retained for three years from the starting date specified in paragraph (c) of this section.

(2) If any litigation, claim, negotiation, audit or other action involving the records has been started before the expiration of the 3-year period, the records must be retained until completion of the action and resolution of all issues which arise from it, or until the end of the regular 3-year period, whichever is later.

(3) To avoid duplicate recordkeeping, awarding agencies may make special arrangements with grantees and subgrantees to retain any records which are continuously needed for joint use. The awarding agency will request transfer of records to its custody when it determines that the records possess long-term retention value. When the records are transferred to or maintained by the Federal agency, the 3-year retention requirement is not applicable to the grantee or subgrantee.

(c) *Starting date of retention period* — (1) *General.* When grant support is continued or renewed at annual or other intervals, the retention period for the records of each funding period starts on the day the grantee or subgrantee submits to the awarding agency its single or last expenditure report for that period. However, if grant support is continued or renewed quarterly, the retention period for each year's records starts on the day the grantee submits its expenditure report for the last quarter of the Federal fiscal year. In all other cases, the retention period starts on the day the grantee submits its final expenditure report. If an expenditure report has been waived, the retention period starts on the day the report would have been due.

(2) *Real property and equipment records.* The retention period for real property and equipment records starts from the date of the disposition or replacement or transfer at the direction of the awarding agency.

(3) *Records for income transactions after grant or subgrant support.* In some cases grantees must report income after the period of grant support. Where there is such a requirement, the retention period for the records pertaining to the earning of the income starts from the end of the grantee's fiscal year in which the income is earned.

(4) *Indirect cost rate proposals, cost allocations plans, etc.* This paragraph applies to the following types of documents, and their supporting records: indirect cost rate computations or proposals, cost allocation plans, and any similar accounting computations of the rate at which a particular group of costs is chargeable (such as computer usage chargeback rates or composite fringe benefit rates).

(i) If submitted for negotiation. If the proposal, plan, or other computation is required to be submitted to the Federal Government (or to the grantee) to form the basis for negotiation of the rate, then the 3-year retention period for its supporting records starts from the date of such submission.

(ii) *If not submitted for negotiation.* If the proposal, plan, or other computation is not required to be submitted to the Federal Government (or to the grantee) for negotiation purposes, then the 3-year retention period for the proposal plan, or computation and its supporting records starts from end of the fiscal year (or other accounting period) covered by the proposal, plan, or other computation.

(d) *Substitution of microfilm.* Copies made by microfilming, photocopying, or similar methods may be substituted for the original records.

(e) *Access to records* — (1) *Records of grantees and subgrantees.* The awarding agency and the Comptroller General of the United States, or any of their authorized representatives, shall have the right of access to any pertinent books, documents, papers, or other records of grantees and subgrantees which are pertinent to the grant, in order to make audits, examinations, excerpts, and transcripts.

(2) *Expiration of right of access.* The rights of access in this section must not be limited to the required retention period but shall last as long as the records are retained.

(f) *Restrictions on public access.* The Federal Freedom of Information Act (5 U.S.C. 552) does not apply to records unless required by Federal, State, or local law, grantees and subgrantees are not required to permit public access to their records.

Agency: National Aeronautics and Space Administration

PART 1274. COOPERATIVE AGREEMENTS WITH COMMERCIAL FIRMS

Subpart F. Reports and Records

Citation: 14 CFR 1274.601

✍ § 1274.601 Retention and access requirements for records.

(a) This subpart sets forth requirements for record retention and access to records for awards to Recipients.

(b) Financial records, supporting documents, statistical records, and all other records pertinent to an award shall be retained for a period of three years from the date of submission of the final invoice. The only exceptions are the following:

(1) If any litigation, claim, or audit is started before the expiration of the 3-year period, the records shall be retained until all litigation, claims or audit findings involving the records have been resolved and final action taken.

(2) Records for real property and equipment acquired with Federal funds shall be retained for 3 years after final disposition.

(3) When records are transferred to or maintained by NASA, the 3-year retention requirement is not applicable to the Recipient.

(4) Indirect cost rate proposals, cost allocations plans, etc. as specified in paragraph (g) of this section.

(c) Copies of original records may be substituted for the original records if authorized by NASA.

(d) NASA shall request transfer of certain records to its custody from Recipients when it determines that the records possess long term retention value. However, in order to avoid duplicate record keeping, NASA may make arrangements for Recipients to retain any records that are continuously needed for joint use.

(e) NASA, the Inspector General, Comptroller General of the United States, or any of their duly authorized representatives, have the right of timely and unrestricted access to any books, documents, papers, or other records of Recipients that are pertinent to the awards, in order to make audits, examinations, excerpts, transcripts and copies of such documents. This right also includes timely and reasonable access to a Recipient's personnel for the purpose of interview and discussion related to such documents. The rights of access in this paragraph are not limited to the required retention period, but shall last as long as records are retained.

(f) Unless required by statute, NASA shall not place restrictions on Recipients that limit public access to the records of Recipients that are pertinent to an award, except when NASA can demonstrate that such records shall be kept confidential and would have been exempted from disclosure pursuant to the Freedom of Information Act (5 U.S.C. 552) if the records had belonged to NASA.

(g) This paragraph (g) applies to the following types of documents, and their supporting records: indirect cost rate computations or proposals, cost allocation plans, and any similar accounting computations of the rate at which a particular group of costs is chargeable (such as computer usage chargeback rates or composite fringe benefit rates).

(1) If submitted for negotiation. If the Recipient submits to NASA or the subrecipient submits to the Recipient the proposal, plan, or other computation to form the basis for negotiation of the rate, then the 3-year retention period for its supporting records starts on the date of such submission.

(2) If not submitted for negotiation. If the Recipient is not required to submit to NASA or the subrecipient is not required to submit to the Recipient the proposal, plan, or other computation for negotiation purposes, then the 3-year retention period for the proposal, plan, or other computation and its supporting records starts at the end of the fiscal year (or other accounting period) covered by the proposal, plan, or other computation.

TITLE 15. COMMERCE AND FOREIGN TRADE

Agency:	**Department of Commerce Bureau of Export Administration**

SUBCHAPTER C. EXPORT ADMINISTRATION REGULATIONS

PART 742. CONTROL POLICY-CCL BASED CONTROLS

This Supplement sets forth the security conditions and safeguard plans for the export, reexport, or in-country transfer of high performance computers that may be imposed by BXA to certain destinations. The licensing policies for the export, reexport, or in-country transfer of high performance computers are set forth in § 742.12 of this part.

(a) *Safeguard conditions.* Following interagency review of the application, the Bureau of Export Administration (BXA) will instruct the exporter to submit a safeguard plan signed by the ultimate consignee and certified by the export control authorities of the importing country (see Certification by export control authorities of importing country in this Supplement). The safeguard plan must indicate that the ultimate consignee agrees to implement those safeguards required by the BXA as a condition of issuing the license. BXA will inform exporters concerning which of the following safeguards will be imposed as license conditions:

* * * * *

(8) The security personnel will undertake the following measures under the guidance of the exporter's representatives:

* * * * *

(v) The inspection of usage logs daily to ensure conformity with the conditions of the license and the retention of records of these logs for at least a year;

* * * * *

Supplement No. 3 to Part 742-High Performance

Citation:	**15 CFR 742.12**

✍ § 742.12 High performance computers.

(a) *License and recordkeeping requirements.* (1) This section contains special provisions for exports, reexports, and certain intra-country transfers of high performance computers, including software, and technology. This section affects the following ECCNs: 4A001, 4A002, 4A003, 4D001, 4D002, and 4E001. It applies to computers with a Composite Theoretical Performance (CTP) greater than 2000, stated in Million Theoretical Operations Per Second (MTOPS). Licenses are required under this section for ECCN's having an "XP" under "Reason for Control" when License Exception CTP is not available (see § 740.3(e) of the EAR). License requirements reflected in this section are based on particular destinations, end-users, or end-uses. For the calculation of CTP, see the Technical Note that follows the Advisory Notes for Category 4 in the Commerce Control List. Note that License Exception CTP contains restrictions on access by nationals of certain countries, and on reexports and transfers of computers.

(2) In recognition of the strategic and proliferation significance of high performance computers, a license is required for the export or reexport of high performance computers to destinations, end-users, and end-uses, as specified in this section and

on the CCL. These license requirements supplement requirements that apply for other control reasons, such as nuclear nonproliferation provided in § 742.3 of the EAR. The license requirements described in this 742.12 are not reflected on the Country Chart (Supplement No. 1 to part 738 of the EAR). Four Computer Country Tiers have been established for the purposes of these controls. Countries included in Computer Tiers 1, 2, and 3 are listed in License Exception CTP in § 740.3(e) of the EAR. Computer Tier 4 consists of Cuba, Iran, Iraq, Libya, North Korea, Sudan, and Syria.

(3) Exporters must keep accurate records of each export to any destination of a computer with a CTP equal to or greater than 2,000 MTOPS, irrespective of whether the export is made under License Exception or otherwise. These records will be made available to the U.S. Government upon request. The records will include the following information:

(i) Date of shipment;

(ii) Name and address of the end-user and each intermediate consignee;

(iii) CTP of each computer in shipment;

(iv) Volume of computers in shipment;

(v) Dollar value of shipment; and

(vi) End-Use.

* * * * *

PART 748. APPLICATIONS (CLASSIFICATION, ADVISORY, AND LICENSE) AND DOCUMENTATION

Citation: **15 CFR 748.10**

✍ § 748.10 Import and End-User Certificates.

(a) *Scope.* There are a variety of Import and End-User Certificates currently in use by various governments. The control exercised by the government issuing the Import or End-User Certificate is in addition to the conditions and restrictions placed on the transaction by BXA. The laws and regulations of the United States are in no way modified, changed, or superseded by the issuance of an Import or End-User Certificate. This section describes exceptions and relationships true for both Import and End-User Certificates, and applies only to transactions involving national security controlled items destined for one of the countries identified in § 748.9(b)(2) of this part.

(b) *Import or End-User Certificate.* An Import or End-User Certificate must be obtained, unless your transaction meets one of the exemptions stated in § 748.9(a) of this part, if:

(1) Any items on your license application are controlled for national security reasons (NS),

(2) The ultimate destination is a country listed in 748.9(b)(2) of this part; and

(3) Your license application involves the export of items classified in a single entry on the CCL, the total value of which exceeds $5,000.

(i) Your license application may list several separate CCL entries. If any entry controlled for national security reasons exceeds $5,000, then an Import or End-User Certificate must be obtained covering all items controlled for national security reasons on your license application;

(ii) If your license application involves a lesser transaction that is part of a larger order for items controlled for national security reasons in a single ECCN exceeding $5,000, an Import or End-User Certificate must be obtained.

(iii) You may be specifically requested by BXA to obtain an Import Certificate for a transaction valued under $5,000.

(c) *How to obtain an Import or End-User Certificate.* (1) Applicants must request that the importer (e.g., ultimate consignee or purchaser) obtain the Import or End-User Certificate, and that it be issued covering only those items that are controlled for national security reasons. Importers should not be requested to obtain an Import or End-User Certificate for items that are controlled for reasons other than national security. Upon receipt, the importer must transmit the original document to the applicant.

(2) The applicant's name must appear on the Import or End-User Certificate submitted to BXA as either the applicant, supplier, or order party. The Import Certificate may be made out to either the ultimate consignee or the purchaser, even though they are different parties, as long as both are located in the same country.

Note to paragraph (c) of this section: You should furnish the consignee with the item description contained in the CCL to be used in applying for the Import or End-User Certificate. It is also advisable to furnish a manufacturer's catalog, brochure, or technical specifications if the item is new.

(3) If your transaction requires support of a PRC End-User Certificate, you must ensure the following information is included on the PRC End-User Certificate signed by an official of the Department of Science and Technology of the Ministry of Foreign Trade and Economic Cooperation (MOFTEC) with MOFTEC's seal affixed to it:

(i) Title of contract and contract number (optional);

(ii) Names of importer and exporter;

(iii) End-User and end-use;

(iv) Description of the item, quantity and dollar value; and

(v) Signature of the importer and date.

(d) *Where to obtain Import and End-User Certificates.* See Supplement No. 4 to this part for a list of the authorities administering the Import Certificate/Delivery Verification and End-User Certificate Systems in other countries.

(e) *Triangular symbol on International Import Certificates.* (1) In accordance with international practice, the issuing government may stamp a triangular symbol on the International Import Certificate (IIC). This symbol is notification that the importer does not intend to import or retain the items in the country issuing the certificate, but that, in any case, the items will not be delivered to any destination except in accordance with the export regulations of the issuing country.

(2) If you receive an IIC bearing a triangular symbol, you must identify all parties to the transaction on the license application, including those located outside the country issuing the IIC. If the importer declines to provide you with this information, you may advise the importer to provide the information directly to BXA, through a U.S. Foreign Commercial Service office, or in a sealed envelope to you marked "To be opened by BXA only".

(f) *Multiple license applications supported by one certificate.* An Import or End-User Certificate may cover more than one purchase order and more than one item. Where the certificte includes items for which more than one license application will be submitted, you must include in Block 24 on your application, or in an attachment to each license application submitted against the certificate, the following certification:

I (We) certify that the quantities of items shown on this license application, based on the Certificate identified in Block 13 of this license application, when added to the quantities shown on all other license applications submitted to BXA based on the same Certificate, do not total more than the total quantities shown on the above cited Certificate.

(g) *Submission of Import and End-User Certificates.* If a PRC End-User Certificate is required for your proposed transaction, you must submit the original certificate with your license application. Copies will not be accepted. All other certificates must be retained on file by the applicant in accordance with the recordkeeping provisions of part 762 of the EAR, and not submitted with the license application.

(h) *Alterations.* After an Import or End-User Certificate is issued by a foreign government, no corrections, additions, or alterations may be made on the Certificate by any person. If you desire to explain any information contained on the Certificate, you may attach a signed statement to the Certificate.

(i) *Request for Delivery Verification.* BXA will, on a selective basis, require Delivery Verification documents for shipments supported by Import Certificates. You will be notified if Delivery Verification is required at the time of issuance of the license. Please refer to § 748.13 of this part for detailed information on these procedures.

(j) *Retention procedures.* You must retain on file the original copy of any certificate issued in support of a license application submitted to BXA, unless the original is submitted with the license application. All recordkeeping provisions contained in part 762 of the EAR apply to this requirement, except that reproductions may not be substituted for the officially authenticated original in this instance.

PART 762. RECORDKEEPING

Citation: 15 CFR 762.1

✍ **§ 762.1 Scope.**

In this part, references to the EAR are references to 15 CFR chapter VII, subchapter C.

(a) *Transactions subject to this part.* The recordkeeping provisions of this part apply to the following transactions:

(1) Transactions involving restrictive trade practices or boycotts described in part 760 of the EAR;

(2) Exports of commodities, software, or technology from the United States and any known reexports, transshipment, or diversions of items exported from the United States;

(3) Exports to Canada, if, at any stage in the transaction, it appears that a person in a country other than the United States or Canada has an interest therein, or that the item involved is to be reexported, transshipped, or diverted from Canada to another foreign country; or

(4) Any other transactions subject to the EAR, including, but not limited to, the prohibitions against servicing, forwarding and other actions for or on behalf of end-users of proliferation concern contained in § § 734.2(b)(7) and 744.6 of the EAR. This part also applies to all negotiations connected with those transactions, except that for export control matters a mere preliminary inquiry or offer to do business and negative response thereto shall not constitute negotiations, unless the inquiry or offer to do business proposes a transaction that a reasonably prudent exporter would believe likely to lead to a violation of the EAA, the EAR or any order, license or authorization issued thereunder.

(b) *Persons subject to this part.* Any person subject to the jurisdiction of the United States who, as principal or agent (including a forwarding agent), participates in any transaction described in paragraph (a) of this section, and any person in the United States or abroad who is required to make and maintain records under any provision of the EAR, shall keep and maintain all records described in § 762.2 of this part that are made or obtained by that person and shall produce them in a manner provided by § 762.6 of this part.

Citation: 15 CFR 762.2

✍ **§ 762.2 Records to be retained.**

(a) *Records required to be retained.* The records required to be retained under this part 762 include the following:

(1) Export control documents, as defined in part 772 of the EAR;

(2) Memoranda;

(3) Notes;

(4) Correspondence;

(5) Contracts;

(6) Invitations to bid;

(7) Books of account;

(8) Financial records;

(9) Restrictive trade practice or boycott documents and reports, and

(10) Other records pertaining to the types of transactions described in § 762.1(a) of this part, which are made or obtained by a person described in § 762.1(b) of this part.

(b) *Records retention references.* Paragraph (a) of this section describes records that are required to be retained. Other parts, sections, or supplements of the EAR which require the retention of records or contain recordkeeping provisions, include, but are not limited to the following:

(1) Part 736, General Prohibitions;

(2) § 732.6, Steps for other requirements;

(3) § 740.1, Introduction (to License Exceptions);

(4) § 742.12(a)(3), High Performance Computers;

(5) Supplement No. 3 to part 742 High Performance Computers, Safeguards and Related Information;

(6) § 740.7, Humanitarian donations (NEED);

(7) § 748.4(a), Disclosure and substantiation of facts on license applications;

(8) § 748.6, General instructions for license applications;

(9) § 748.9, Support documents for license applications;

(10) § 748.10, Import and End-user Certificates;

(11) § 748.11, Statement by Ultimate Consignee and Purchaser;

(12) § 748.13, Delivery Verification (DV);

(13) § 748.2(c), Obtaining forms; mailing addresses;

(14) § 750.7, Issuance of license;

(15) § 750.8, Revocation or suspension of license;

(16) § 750.9, Duplicate licenses;

(17) § 750.10, Transfer of licenses for export;

(18) § 752.7, Direct shipment to customers;

(19) § 752.9, Action on SCL applications;

(20) § 752.10, Changes to the SCL;

(21) § 752.11, Internal Control Programs;

(22) § 752.12, Recordkeeping requirements;

(23) § 752.13, Inspection of records;

(24) § 752.14, System reviews;

(25) § 752.15, Export clearance;

(26) § 754.4, Unprocessed western red cedar;

(27) § 758.1(b)(3), Record and proof of agent's authority;

(28) § 758.3, Shipper's Export Declaration;

(29) § 758.6, Destination control statements;

(30) § 760.6, Restrictive Trade Practices and Boycotts;

(31) § 762.2, Records to be retained;

(32) § 764.2, Violations;

(33) § 764.5, Voluntary self-disclosure; and

(34) § 766.10, Subpoenas.

Citation: 15 CFR 762.3

✍ § 762.3 Records exempt from recordkeeping requirements.

(a) The following types of records have been determined to be exempt from the recordkeeping requirement procedures:

(1) Export information page;
(2) Special export file list;
(3) Vessel log from freight forwarder;
(4) Inspection certificate;
(5) Warranty certificate;
(6) Guarantee certificate;
(7) Parking material certificate;
(8) Goods quality certificate;
(9) Notification to customer of advance meeting;
(10) Letter of indemnity;
(11) Financial release form;
(12) Financial hold form;
(13) Export parts shipping problem form;
(14) Draft number log;
(15) Expense invoice mailing log;
(16) Financial status report;
(17) Bank release of guarantees;
(18) Cash sheet;
(19) Commission payment back-up;
(20) Commissions payable worksheet;
(21) Commissions payable control;
(22) Check request forms;
(23) Accounts receivable correction form;
(24) Check request register;
(25) Commission payment printout;
(26) Engineering fees invoice;
(27) Foreign tax receipt;
(28) Individual customer credit status;
(29) Request for export customers code forms;
(30) Acknowledgement for receipt of funds;
(31) Escalation development form;
(32) Summary quote;
(33) Purchase order review form;
(34) Proposal extensions;
(35) Financial proposal to export customers; and
(36) Sales summaries.

(b) [Reserved]

Citation: 15 CFR 762.4

✍ § 762.4 Original records required.

The regulated person must maintain the original records in the form in which that person receives or creates them unless that person meets all of the conditions of § 762.5 of this part relating to reproduction of records. If the original record does not meet the standards of legibility and readability described in § 762.5 of this part and the regulated person intends to rely on that record to meet the recordkeeping requirements of the EAR, that person must retain the original record.

Citatation: 15 CFR 762.5

✍ § 762.5 Reproduction of original records.

(a) The regulated person may maintain reproductions instead of the original records provided all of the requirements of paragraph (b) of this section are met.

(b) In order to maintain the records required by § 762.2 of this part, the regulated persons defined in § 762.1 of this part may use any photographic, photostatic, miniature photographic, micrographic, automated archival storage, or other process that completely, accurately, legibly and durably reproduces the original records (whether on paper, microfilm, or through electronic digital storage techniques). The process must meet all of the following requirements, which are applicable to all systems:

(1) The system must be capable of reproducing all records on paper.

(2) The system must record and be able to reproduce all marks, information, and other characteristics of the original record, including both obverse and reverse sides of paper documents in legible form.

(3) When displayed on a viewer, monitor, or reproduced on paper, the records must exhibit a high degree of legibility and readability. (For purposes of this section, legible and legibility mean the quality of a letter or numeral that enable the observer to identify it positively and quickly to the exclusion of all other letters or numerals. Readable and readability mean the quality of a group of letters or numerals being recognized as complete words or numbers.)

(4) The system must preserve the initial image (including both obverse and reverse sides of paper documents) and record all changes, who made them and when they were made. This information must be stored in such a manner that none of it may be altered once it is initially recorded.

(5) The regulated person must establish written procedures to identify the individuals who are responsible for the operation, use and maintenance of the system.

(6) The regulated person must establish written procedures for inspection and quality assurance of records in the system and document the implementation of those procedures.

(7) The system must be complete and contain all records required to be kept by this part or the regulated person must provide a method for correlating, identifying and locating records relating to the same transaction(s) that are kept in other record keeping systems.

(8) The regulated person must keep a record of where, when, by whom, and on what equipment the records and other information were entered into the system.

(9) Upon request by the Office of Export Enforcement, the Office of Antiboycott Compliance, or any other agency of competent jurisdiction, the regulated person must furnish, at the examination site, the records, the equipment and, if necessary, knowledgeable personnel for locating, reading, and reproducing any record in the system.

(c) *Requirements applicable to systems based on the storage of digital images.* For systems based on the storage of digital images, the system must provide accessibility to any digital image in the system. With respect to records of transactions, including those involving restrictive trade practices or boycott requirements or requests. The system must be able to locate and reproduce all records relating to a particular transaction based on any one of the following criteria:

(1) The name(s) of the parties to the transaction;

(2) Any country(ies) connected with the transaction; or

(3) A document reference number that was on any original document.

(d) *Requirements applicable to a system based on photographic processes.* For systems based on photographic, photostatic, or miniature photographic processes, the regulated person must maintain a detailed index of all records in the system that is arranged in such a manner as to allow immediate location of any particular record in the system.

Citation: 15 CFR 762.6

✍ § 762.6 Period of retention.

(a) *Five year retention period.* All records required to be kept by the EAR must be retained for five years from the latest of the following times:

(1) The export from the United States of the item involved in the transaction to which the records pertain or the provision of financing, transporting or other service for or on behalf of end-users of proliferation concern as described in § § 736.2(b)(7) and 744.6 of the EAR;

(2) Any known reexport, transshipment, or diversion of such item;

(3) Any other termination of the transaction, whether formally in writing or by any other means; or

(4) In the case of records of pertaining to transactions involving restrictive trade practices or boycotts described in part 760 of the EAR, the date the regulated person receives the boycott-related request or requirement.

(b) *Destruction or disposal of records.* If the Bureau of Export Administration or any other government agency makes a formal or informal request for a certain record or records, such record or records may not be destroyed or disposed of without the written authorization of the agency concerned. This prohibition applies to records pertaining to voluntary disclosures made to BXA in accordance with § 765.5(c)(4)(ii) and other records even if such records have been retained for a period of time exceeding that required by paragraph (a) of this section.

Citation: 15 CFR 762.7

✍ § 762.7 Producing and inspecting records.

(a) *Persons located in the United States.* Persons located in the United States may be asked to produce records that are required to be kept by any provision of the EAR, or any license, order, or authorization issued thereunder and to make them available for inspection and copying by any authorized agent, official, or employee of the Bureau of Export Administration, the U.S. Customs Service, or any other agency of the U.S. Government, without any charge or expense to such agent, official, or employee. The Office of Export Enforcement and the Office of Antiboycott Compliance encourage voluntary cooperation with such requests. When voluntary cooperation is not forthcoming, the Office of Export Enforcement and the Office of Antiboycott Compliance are authorized to issue subpoenas for books, records, and other writings. In instances where a person does not comply with a subpoena, the Department of Commerce may petition a district court to have a subpoena enforced.

(b) *Persons located outside of the United States.* Persons located outside of the United States that are required to keep records by any provision of the EAR or by any license, order, or authorization issued thereunder shall produce all records or reproductions of records required to be kept, and make them available for inspection and copying upon request by an authorized agent, official, or employee of the Bureau of Export Administration, the U.S. Customs Service, or a Foreign Service post, or by any other accredited representative of the U.S. Government, without any charge or expense to such agent, official or employee.

PART 772. INDIVIDUAL VALIDATED LICENSES AND AMENDMENTS

Citation: 15 CFR 772.4

✍ § 772.4 How to apply for a validated license.

* * * * *

(b) *Applying electronically for a validated license.* An individual validated license may be applied for electronically by an applicant that has been authorized to do so in accordance with this Part. An authorization to submit license applications electronically may be limited or withdrawn by the Department of Commerce at any time.

* * * * *

(4) *Maintenance of records.* An applicant company shall maintain a log, either manually or electronically, specifying the date and time of each electronic submission, the ECCNs of commodities on each electronic submission, and the name of the employee or agent submitting the license application. This log may not be altered. Written corrections must be made in a manner that does not erase or cover original entries. If the log is maintained electronically, corrections may only be made as notations.

* * * * *

PART 775. DOCUMENTATION REQUIREMENTS

Citation: 15 CFR 775.9

✍ § 775.9 Documents accompanying applications.

* * * * *

(b) *Availability of original.* The Bureau of Export Administration may demand the original of any copy of a document retained in the applicant's files as required by this part 775. Such original must be kept and made available for inspection in accordance with the provisions of § 787.13.of this subchapter. To ensure compliance with this recordkeeping requirement, the Office of Export Licensing will require applicants, on a random basis, to submit specific supporting documents that have been retained on file.

* * * * *

PART 787. ENFORCEMENT

Citation: 15 CFR 787.13

✍ § 787.13 Recordkeeping.

(a) *Transactions subject to this regulation.* This section applies to — (1) transactions involving restrictive trade practice or boycott requirements or requests, (2) exports of commodities or technical data from the United States and any known reexports, transshipments, or diversions of commodities or technical data originally exported from the United States, or (3) any other transactions subject to these Regulations, regardless of whether the export of reexport is made, or proposed to be made, by any person with or without authorization by a validated license, a general license, or any other export authorization. This section also applies to all negotiations connected with those transactions, except that for export control matters a mere preliminary inquiry or offer to do business and negative response thereto shall not constitute negotiations, unless the inquiry or offer to do business proposes a transaction which a reasonably prudent exporter would believe likely to lead to a violation of export orders or regulations. It also applies to any exports to Canada, if, at any stage in the transactions it appears that a person in a country other than the United States or Canada has an interest therein or that the commodity or technical data involved is to be reexported, transshipped, or diverted from Canada to another foreign country.

(b) *Persons subject to this regulation.* Any person subject to the jurisdiction of the United States who, as principal or agent (including a forwarding agent), participates in any transaction described in paragraph (a) of this section, and any person in the United States or abroad who is required to make and keep records under any provisions of the Export Administration regulations, shall keep all the records described in paragraph (c) of this section, which are made or obtained by that person, and shall produce them in the manner provided in paragraph (f) of this section.

(c) *Records to be kept.* The records to be kept under this section shall include export control documents, as defined in § 770.2, memoranda, notes, correspondence, contracts, invitations to bid, books of account, financial records, restrictive trade practice or boycott documents and reports, and other written matter pertaining to the transactions described in paragraph (a) of this section, which are made or obtained by a person described in paragraph (b) of this section. In addition to the records required to be kept by this section, other sections of the Regulations require the retention records, including but not limited to § § 768.2, 769.6, 771.9, 771.10, 771.12, 771.17, 771.19, 771.22, 771.24, 771.25, 772.1, 772.4, 772.5, 772.6, 772.7, 772.8, 772.10, 772.11, 772.13, 773.2, 773.3, 773.7, 773.8, 773.9, 774.3, 774.7, 775.2, 775.3, 775.4, 775.5, 775.7, 776.4, 776.6, 776.7, 776.8, 776.9, 776.10, 776.11, 776.12, 778.6, 778.7, 779.4, 779.8, 779.9, 786.2, 786.3, 786.5, 786.6 and 791.2. The revocation or revision of any provision of the Export Administration Regulations which requires the making and keeping of records shall not be retroactive in effect unless specifically provided and shall not affect the original requirement to keep these records for the prescribed period.

(d) *Reproduction of records* — (1) *Definition.* "Reproduction" for the purpose of this paragraph (d) is defined to include any photographic, photostatic, micrographic, miniature photographic or other process which completely, accurately and durably reproduces the original record.

(2) *Use of reproductions.* Reproductions may not be substituted for original documents with respect to all categories of records required to be retained under any provisions of the Export Administration Regulations or of any order, until all of the following conditions are met:

(i) The original documents have been retained for twelve months after the beginning of the retention period set forth in paragraph (e) of this section or an exception has been granted under the provisions of paragraph (g) of this section.

(ii) All significant information, marks and/or other characteristics on the original document must be clearly visible and legibly reproduced.

(iii) Appropriate facilities must be provided and maintained for the preservation of the reproduced records during the retention period and for the ready location and inspection of the records, including a projector for viewing films, if needed.

(e) *Period of retention.(1) Two-year general requirement.* Except as indicated in paragraph (e)(2) of this section, records required under this section shall be kept for a period of two years from the latest of the following times:

(i) The export from the United States; or

(ii) Any known reexport, transshipment, or diversion; or

(iii) Any other termination of the transaction, whether formally in writing or by any other means. It may be advisable to maintain records longer than the mandatory two-year retention period because the statute of limitations for criminal actions brought under the Export Administration Act of 1979 and its predecessor Acts is five years (18 U.S.C. 3282). The statute for administrative compliance proceedings is also five years (28 U.S.C. 2462).

(2) *Retention requirements exceeding two years*—(i) *Three years.* Records relating to restrictive trade practice or boycott requests must be kept for a period of three years from the latest of the times indicated in paragraph (e)(1) of this section. (See § 769.6(b)(8) of this subchapter.)

(ii) *Five years.* The following records must be kept for a period of five years from the latest of the times indicated in paragraph (e)(1) of this section:

(A) Shipper's Export Declarations covering exports made under a Project License, as required by § 773.2(f)(1) of this subchapter—the three-year retention period specified in § 30.11 of the Foreign Trade Statistics Regulations (15 CFR 30.11) does not apply to Declarations covering exports made under a Project License;

(B) Records required for exports under the Distribution License, as required by § 773.3 of this subchapter;

(C) Records required for exports under the Service Supply Procedure, as required by § 773.7 of this subchapter;

(D) Supporting documentation that must be retained in the applicant's files, as required by § 772.11 and § 774.3 and part 775 of this subchapter.

(3) *Destruction or disposal of records.* If the Department of Commerce or any other Government agency makes a formal or informal request for a certain record or records, such record or records may not be destroyed or disposed of without the written authorization of the agency concerned. This prohibition applies even if such records have been retained for a period of time exceeding that required by paragraph (e)(1) or (e)(2) of this section.

(f) *Producing and inspecting records.* (1) Persons within the United States may be requested to produce records which are required to be kept by any provision of the Export Administration Regulations or by any order, and to make them available for inspection and copying by any authorized agent, official or employee of the Bureau of Export Administration, the U.S. Customs Service, or the U.S. Government, without any charge or expense to such agent, official or employee. The Office of Export Enforcement and the Office of Antiboycott Compliance encourage voluntary cooperation with such requests. When voluntary cooperation is not forthcoming, the Office of Export Enforcement and the Office of Antiboycott Compliance are authorized to issue subpoenas for books, records, and other writings. In instances where a person does not comply with a subpoena, the Department of Commerce may petition a district court to have the subpoena enforced.

(2) Every person abroad, required to keep records by any provision of the Export Administration Regulations or by any order, shall produce all records or reproductions of records required to be kept, and make them available for inspection and copying upon request by an authorized agent, official, or employee of the Bureau of Export Administration, the U.S. Customs Service, or a U.S. Foreign Service post, or by any other accredited representative of the U.S. Government, without any charge or expense to such agent, official or employee. Persons located outside the United States who fail to comply with certain requests, including requests to produce documents, may be subject to orders denying export privileges. (See § 787.8.)

(g) *Requests for exceptions to recordkeeping requirements* — (1) *Effect of exception.* Recordkeeping entities (as defined in paragraph (b) of this section) wishing to maintain records on micrographic systems prior to the second year of the retention period may request an exception to the recordkeeping requirements. An exception, if granted, permits the recordkeeping entity or substitute micrographic records for original documents for the full retention period.

(2) *Basis for consideration.* When reviewing requests for exceptions, the Office of Export Licensing, in consultation with the Office of Export Enforcement or the Office of Antiboycott Compliance, will take into consideration the requestor's previous performance with respect to general export control matters and antiboycott matters, respectively.

(3) *Guidelines for micrographic systems.* To maintain records under this exception, a micrographic system shall have the following minimum requirements:

(i) The system shall provide commercial permanence of all records.

(ii) The system shall provide for frequent quality control inspection to ensure readability of all records.

(iii) Micrographed records must have a degree of legibility and readability, when displayed on a viewer and when reproduced on paper, equal to that of the original records. (See section 5 of IRS Revenue Procedure No. 81-46, 1981-40 C.B. 6 concerning technical standards of micrographed records.)

(iv) A detailed index of all micrographic data shall be maintained, and arranged in such a manner as to permit the immediate location of any particular record, location of all documents relating to a given transaction, and determination of disposition of corresponding original documents.

(4) *Submission of requests for exception.* (i) The recordkeeping entity shall submit requests for exceptions involving general export matters to: Office of Export Licensing, Bureau of Export Administration, U.S. Department of Commerce, P. O. Box 273, Washington, DC 20044.

(ii) The recordkeeping entity shall submit requests for exceptions involving antiboycott matters to: Office of Antiboycott Compliance, Bureau of Export Administration, U. S. Department of Commerce, 14th Street and Constitution Ave., NW., Room H3886, Washington, DC 20230.

(iii) The requesting firm shall include in the request:

(A) Data on the proposed micrographic system, including specific information as to how the system conforms to requirements set forth in paragraph (g)(3) of this section;

(B) A statement concerning intended disposition of corresponding original documents; and

(C) Samples of records to be kept on the system.

(5) *Micrographing records under an exception.* Upon receiving written notice that an exception has been granted under this paragraph (g), the recordkeeping entity may substitute micrographic reproductions for only those records *already* in the retention period and approved under the exception. Originals of records that have not entered the retention period must be kept until the retention period begins (as set forth in § 769.6(b)(8) and paragraph (e) of this section) and micrographed records may then be substituted for the originals.

(6) *Disposition of original documents.* The recordkeeping entity shall include with micrographed records a signed document indicating final disposition of original documents, and the date of final disposition.

(7) *Revocation of exception.* The Department of Commerce may revoke an individual exception at any time if it determines that the firm has acted improperly, or for other good cause. A decision to revoke this exception may be appealed under the provisions of Part 789 of these regulations.

(h) *Records exempt from recordkeeping requirements.* The following kinds of records have been determined to be exempt from recordkeeping requirements:

Export Information Page;
Special Export Price List;
Vessel Log from Freight Forwarder;
Inspection Certificate;
Warranty Certificate;
Guarantee Certificate;
Packing Material Certificate;
Goods Quality Certificate;
Notification to Customer of Advance Mailings;
Letter of Indemnity;
Financial Release Form;
Financial Hold Form;
Export Parts Shipment Problem Form;
Draft Number Log;
Expense Invoice Mailing Log;
Financial Status Report;
Bank Release of Guarantee;
Cash Sheet;
Commission Payment Back-up;
Commissions Payable Worksheet;
Commissions Payable Control;
Check Request Forms;
Accounts Receivable Correction Form;
Check Request Register;
Commission Payment Printout;
Engineering Fees Invoice;
Foreign Tax Receipt;
Individual Customer Credit Status;
Request for Export Customers Code Forms;
Acknowledgment for Receipt of Funds;
Escalation Development Form;
Summary Quote;
Purchase Order Review Form;
Proposal Extensions;
Financial Proposal to Export Customers;
Sales Summaries

TITLE 17. COMMODITY AND SECURITIES EXCHANGE

Agency: **Commodity Futures Trading Commission**

PART 1. GENERAL REGULATIONS UNDER THE COMMODITY EXCHANGE ACT

Recordkeeping

Citation: **17 CFR 1.31**

✍ § 1.31 Books and records; keeping and inspection.

(a)(1) All books and records required to be kept by the Act or by these regulations shall be kept for a period of five years from the date thereof and shall be readily accessible during the first 2 years of the 5-year period. All such books and records shall be open to inspection by any representative of the Commission or the United States Department of Justice.

(2) A copy of any book or record required to be kept by the Act or by these regulations shall be provided, at the expense of the person required to keep the book or record, to a Commission representative upon the representative's request. Instead of furnishing a copy, such person may provide the original book or record for reproduction, which the representative may temporarily remove from such person's premises for this purpose. All copies or originals shall be provided promptly.

Upon request, the Commission representative shall issue a receipt provided by such person for any copy or original book or record received.

At the request of the Commission representative, such person shall, upon the return thereof, issue a receipt for any copy or original book or record returned by the representative.

(b) Reproductions on microfilm, microfiche and optical disk may be substituted for hard copy as follows:

(1) Computer, accounting machine or business machine generated records may be immediately produced or reproduced on microfilm and kept in that form; other records may be immediately produced or reproduced on microfilm and kept in that form. Computer generated records may be immediately

produced on optical disk in conformity with the requirements of paragraph (d) of this section and kept in that form.

(2) Except as provided herein, for all other books and records, microfilm or microfiche reproductions thereof may be substituted for the hard copies for the final three years of the five-year period. Trading cards and written customer orders, required to be kept pursuant to § 1.35(a-1)(1), (a-1)(2) and (d), must be retained in hard-copy form for the full five-year period.

(c) If microfilm, microfiche or optical disk substitution for hard copy is made, the person required to keep such records shall;

(1) At all times have on their premises and make available upon request to representatives of the Commission or the Department of Justice:

(i) Facilities for easily readable projection of the microfilm or microfiche, or display of information stored on optical disk, that allow immediate examination of their records:

(ii) If the records are preserved on microfilm or microfiche, facilities for immediately producing complete, accurate and easily readable facsimile enlargements of the records; and

(iii) If the records are preserved on optical disk, facilities for immediately producing complete, accurate and easily readable hard copies of the records and the means to provide, immediately upon request, any Commission or Department of Justice representative with copies of the records on Commission compatible machine-readable media as defined in § 15.00(l)(1) and (2).

(2) In order to permit the immediate location of any particular record:

(i) Arrange, index and file microfilm or microfiche and preserve the index and file in such a manner as to permit the immediate location of any particular record; and

(ii) Create a directory structure for files of records and an index for records on optical disk, and preserve the files, index and directory structure in such a manner as to permit the immediate location of any particular record. Directory structures must organize and locate computer files and an index must distinguish, identify and locate records in the same file. In addition, persons must maintain on their premises at all times current, accurate and complete hard copies of such directory structures and indices for examination by representatives of the Commission of the Department of Justice. Such hard copies must be preserved for 5 years.

(3) Be ready at all times to provide, and immediately provide, at the expense of the person required to keep such records, any hard copy or facsimile enlargement of such records, and for records stored on optical disk, copies of such records on approved machine-readable media as defined in § 15.00(l)(1) and (2) which any representative of the Commission or U. S. Department of Justice may request. Records on machine-readable media must use a format and coding structure specified in the request; and

(4) Keep only Commission-required records on the same disk. Storage of a non-Commission-required record shall be deemed a waiver of any; privilege, claim of confidentiality, or other objection to disclosure with respect to the non-Commission-required record.

(d) *Optical Storage Systems* — Any optical storage system used to preserve records under paragraph (b) of this section must allow for the preservation of the records required under this Section using non-rewritable WORM (write once read many) media. All records preserved on optical medial pursuant to paragraph (b) of this section must be preserved on non-rewritable WORM media. The technology must have write-verify capabilities that continuously and automatically verifies the quality and accuracy of the information stored and automatically corrects quality and accuracy defects.

(1) The system must:

(i) Use removable disks;

(ii) Serialize the disks;

(iii) Using a permanent and non-erasable time-date, it must time-date all files of information placed on the disk, reflecting the computer run time of the file of information; and

(iv) Write files in ASCII or EBCDIC format.

(2) Persons using optical storage systems must maintain on their premises, keep current, grant access to and surrender promptly, upon request by representatives of the Commission or the Department of Justice, all information necessary to read, convert to hard copy and download records stored in optical storage units, including directory structures and indices. This shall include but not be limited to a copy of logical file formats and field formats of all different files written on optical disks, the hardware make and model and operating system software version and release level of the computer system hosting the storage device and identity of the device driver used to write the optical media, including the release level, and if records are written in an ASCII or EBCDIC format other than standard non-compressed ASCII or EBCDIC, documentation of the method used to encode data proving a thorough descriptions of any compression algorithm, including the physical file format and conversion routines to transform the records to a non-compressed ASCII or EBCDIC format.

Citation: **17 CFR 1.35**

✍ § 1.35 Records of cash commodity, futures, and option transactions.

(a) *Futures commission merchants, introducing brokers, and members of contract markets.* Each futures commission merchant, introducing broker, and member of a contract market shall keep full, complete, and systematic records, together with all pertinent data and memoranda, of all transactions relating to its business of dealing in commodity futures, commodity options, and cash commodities. Each futures commission merchant, introducing broker, and member of a contract market shall retain the required records, data, and memoranda in accordance with the requirements of § 1.31, and produce them for inspection and furnish true and correct information and reports as to the contents or the meaning thereof, when and as requested by any authorized representative of the Commission or the United States Department of Justice. Included among such records shall be all orders (filled, unfilled, or canceled), trading cards, signature cards, street books, journals, ledgers, canceled checks, copies of confirmations, copies of statements of purchase and sale, and all other records, data and memoranda which have been prepared in the course of its business of dealing in commodity futures, commodity options, and cash commodities. Among such records each member of a contract markets must retain and produce for inspection are all documents on which trade information is originally recorded, whether or not such documents must be prepared pursuant to the rules or regulations of either the Commission or the contract market. For purposes of this section, such documents are referred to as "original source documents."

(a-1) *Futures commission merchants, introducing brokers, and members of contract markets: Recording of customers' and option customers' orders.* (1) Each futures commission merchant and each introducing broker receiving a customer's or option customer's order shall immediately upon receipt thereof prepare a written record of such order, including the account identification and order number, and shall record thereon, by time — stamp or other timing device, the date and time, to the nearest minute, the order is received, and in addition, for option customers' orders, the time, to the nearest minute, the order is transmitted for execution.

(2) Except as provided in paragraph (a)(3) of this section, each member of a contract market who on the floor of such contract market receives a customer's or option customer's order which is not in the form of a written record including the account identification, order number and the date and time, to the nearest minute, such order was transmitted or received on the floor of such contract market, shall immediately upon receipt thereof prepare a written record of such order in non-erasable ink, including the account identification and order number and shall record thereon, by time-stamp or other timing device, the date and time, to the nearest minute, the order is received.

(3) The requirements of paragraph (a)(2) of this section shall not apply if the member's commodity futures customer is another member of such contract market present on the floor thereof at the time the order is received, and the member receiving and executing such order immediately upon the execution thereof, notes on his trading card or other record maintained in accordance with the requirements of paragraph (d) of this section, the time of execution, to the nearest minute.

(4) Each member of a contract market reporting the execution of a customer's or option customer's order from the floor of a contract market shall record on a written record of such order, including the account identification and order number, by time-stamp or other timing device, the date and time, to the nearest minute, such report of execution was made. Each member of a contract market shall submit the written records of customer orders to contract market personnel or the clearing member responsible for the collection of orders prepared pursuant to this paragraph as required by contract market rules adopted in accordance with paragraph (j)(1) of this section. The execution price and other information reported on such order tickets must be written in non-erasable ink.

(a-2)(1) *Futures commission merchants, introducing brokers, and members of contract markets.* Upon request of the contract market, the Commission, or the United States Department of Justice, each futures commission merchant, introducing broker, and member of a contract market shall request from its customers and, upon receipt thereof, provide to the requesting body documentation of cash transactions underlying exchanges of futures for cash commodities or exchanges of futures in connection with cash commodity transactions.

(2) *Customers.* Each customer of a futures commission merchant, introducing broker, or member of a contract market shall create, retain, and produce upon request of the contract market, the Commission, or the United States Department of Justice documentation of cash transactions underlying exchanges of futures for cash commodities or exchanges of futures in connection with cash commodity transactions.

(3) *Contract markets.* Every contract market shall adopt rules which require its members to provide documentation of cash transactions underlying exchanges of futures for cash commodities or exchanges of futures in connection with cash commodity transactions upon request of the contract market.

(4) Documentation. For the purposes of this paragraph, documentation means those documents customarily generated in accordance with cash market practices which demonstrate the existence and nature of the underlying cash transactions, including, but not limited to, contracts, confirmation statements, telex printouts, invoices, and warehouse receipts or other documents of title.

(b) *Futures commission merchants, introducing brokers, and clearing members of contract markets.* Each futures commission merchant and each clearing member of a contract market and, for purposes of paragraph (b)(3) of this section, each introducing broker, shall, as a minimum requirement, prepare regularly and promptly, and keep systematically and in permanent form, the following:

(1) A financial ledger record which will show separately for each customer or option customer all charges against and credits to such customer's or option customer's account, including but not limited to customer funds deposited, withdrawn, or transferred, and charges or credits resulting from losses or gains on closed transactions;

(2) A record of transactions which will show separately for each account (including proprietary accounts):

(i) All commodity futures transactions executed for such account, including the date, price, quantity, market, commodity and future; and

(ii) All commodity option transactions executed for such account, including the date, whether the transaction involved a put or call, expiration date, quantity, underlying contract for future delivery or underlying physical, strike price, and details of the purchase price of the option, including premium, mark-up, commission and fees; and

(3) A record or journal which will separately show for each business day complete details of:

(i) All commodity futures transactions executed on that day, including the date, price, quantity, market, commodity, future and the person for whom such transaction was made;

(ii) All commodity option transactions executed on that day, including the date, whether the transaction involved a put or call, the expiration date, quantity, underlying contract for future delivery, or underlying physical, strike price, details of the purchase price of the option, including premium, mark-up, commission and fees and the person for whom the transaction was made; and

(iii) In the case of an introducing broker, the record or journal required by this paragraph (b)(3) shall also include the futures commission merchant carrying the account for which each commodity futures and commodity option transaction was executed on that day.

Provided, however, that where reproductions on microfilm, microfiche or optical disk are substituted for hard copy in accordance with the provisions of § 1.31(b) of third part, the requirements of paragraphs (b)(1) and (b)(2) of this section will be considered met if the person required to keep such records is ready at all times to provide, and immediately provides in the same city as that in which such person's commodity or commodity option books and records are maintained, at the expense of such person, reproduced copies which show the records as specified in paragraphs (b)(1) and (b)(2) of this section, on request of any representative of the Commission or the U.S. Department of Justice.

(c) *Clearing members of contract markets.* In the daily record or journal required to be kept under paragraph (b)(3) of this section, each clearing member of a contract market shall also show the floor broker or floor trader executing each transaction, the opposite floor broker or floor trader, and the opposite clearing member with whom it was made.

(d) *Members of contract markets.* (1) Each member of a contract market who, in the place provided by the contract market for the meeting of persons similarly engaged, executes purchases or sales of any commodity for future delivery or commodity option on or subject to the rules of such contract market, shall prepare regularly and promptly a trading card or other record showing such purchases and sales. Such trading card or record shall show the member's name, the name of the clearing member, transaction date, time (as specified in rules of the contract market which comply with the requirements of this section), quantity, and, as applicable, underlying commodity, contract for future delivery or physical, price or premium, delivery month or expiration date, whether the transaction involved a put or a call, and strike price. Such trading card or other record shall also clearly identify the opposite floor broker or floor trader with whom the transaction was executed, and the opposite clearing member is made known to the member).

(2) Each member of a contract market recording purchases and sales on trading cards must record such purchases and sales in exact chronological order of execution on sequential lines of the trading card without skipping lines between trades; Provided, however; That if lines remain after the last execution recorded on a trading card, the remaining lines must be marked through.

(3) Each member of a contract market must identify on his trading cards in the manner prescribed by the rules of the contract market the purchases and sales executed during the opening and closing periods designated by the contract market pursuant to paragraph (j)(7) of this section.

(4) Trading cards prepared by a member of a contract market pursuant to contract market values must contain:

(i) Pre-printed member identification or other unique identifying information which would permit the trading cards of one member to be distinguished from those of all other members;

(ii) Pre-printed sequence number to permit the intra-day sequencing of the cards; and

(iii) Unique and pre-printed identifying information which would distinguish each of the trading cards prepared by the member from other such trading cards for no less than a one-week period.

(5) Trading cards prepared by a member of a contract market and collected pursuant to paragraph (j)(1) of this section must be timestamped promptly to the nearest minute upon collection by either the contract market or the relevant clearing member.

(6) Each member of a contract market shall be accountable for all trading cards prepared pursuant to contract market rules in exact numerical sequence, whether or not such trading cards are relied on as original source documents.

(7) Trading records prepared by a member of a contract market pursuant to contract market rules must:

(i) Be submitted in accordance with contract market rules adopted pursuant to paragraph (j)(1) of this section; and

(ii) Be completed in non-erasable ink. A member may correct any errors bycrossing out erroneous information without obliterating or otherwise making illegible any of the originally recorded information. With regard to trading cards only, a member may correct erroneous information by rewriting the trading card; provided, however, that the member must submit a ply of the trading card, or in the absence of plies the original trading card, that is subsequently rewritten in accordance with contract market rules which set forth the required collection schedule for trading cards and provided further that the member is accountable for any trading card that subsequently is rewritten pursuant to paragraph (d)(6) of this section.

(8) Each member of a contract market must use a new trading card at the beginning of each designated 30-minute interval required by paragraph (j)(1) of this section (or such lesser interval as may be determined appropriate by the applicable contract market) or as may be required pursuant hereto.

(e) *Contract markets.* Each contract market shall maintain or cause to be maintained by its clearing organization a single records which shall show for each futures or option trade: the transaction date, time (as described in paragraph (g) of this section), quantity, and, as applicable, underlying commodity, contract for future delivery or physical, price or premium, delivery month or expiration date, whether the transaction involved a put or a call, strike price, floor broker or floor trader buying, clearing member buying, floor broker or floor trader selling, clearing member selling, and symbols indicating the buying and selling customer or option customer types. The customer and option customer type indicators shall show, with respect to each person executing the trade, whether such person:

(1) Was trading for his own account;

(2) Was trading for his clearing member's house account;

(3) Was trading for another member present on the exchange floor, or an account controlled by such other member; or

(4) Was trading for any other type of customer or option customer. The record required by this paragraph (e) shall also show, by appropriate and uniform symbols, any transaction which is made non-competitively in accordance with written rules of the contract market which have been submitted to and approved by the Commission in accordance with the provisions of § 1.38, and trades cleared on dates other than the date of execution. Except as otherwise approved by the Commission for good cause shown, the record required by this paragraph (e) shall be maintained in a format and coding structure approved by the Commission (i) in hard copy or on microfilm as specified in § 1.31 and (ii) for 60 days in computer-readable form on compatible magnetic tapes or discs.

(f) Each contract market shall provide for the identification of floor brokers, floor traders, and clearing members, in the records required to be kept under paragraphs (c), (d), and (e) of this section, by the use of a distinctive, nonvariable designation for each such floor broker, floor trader, and clearing member.

(g) *Time of trade execution.* For purposes of paragraph (e) of this section:

(1) The actual time of the execution of each side of a transaction must be obtained, or

(2) if a contract market identifies and records the time of a transaction, a single actual time of execution for both sides of the transaction may be obtained. Actual times of execution shall be stated in increments of no more than one minute in length. If a contract market submits rules to the Commission, in accordance with the provisions of section 5a(12) of the Act and § 1.41, defining and separately identifying opening and closing time periods, the contract market may, for purposes of paragraph (e) of this section, use those time periods for trades occurring during the opening and closing periods. Contract market rules in effect prior to the effective date of this paragraph (g) upon which a contract market intends to rely in complying herewith must be submitted for this purpose to the Commission in accordance with the provisions of section 5a(12) of the Act and § 1.41.

(h) *Contract market price change register.* Each contract market shall establish and maintain a record of all changes in the price of futures or option transactions executed on the floor of the contract market. This record shall include the time of all changes in price to the nearest ten seconds.

* * * * *

(j) *Contract markets.* Each contract market must maintain in effect rules which require that:

(1) Trading records prepared by a member of the contract market pursuant to paragraphs (a-1) and (d) of this section be submitted to contract market personnel or the clearing member within 15 minutes of designated intervals not to exceed 30 minutes, commencing with the beginning of each trading session. The time period permitted for the submission of trading records after the close of trading in each market shall not exceed 15 minutes from the close. Such documents should nevertheless be collected as often as is practicable by the contract market or relevant clearing member. Such contract market rules need not, however, require that those original source documents which

cannot be relied upon by the contract market or clearing member for clearing purposes be submitted pursuant to this paragraph. Each contract market shall submit a written report to the Commission no later than nine months after the effective date of this paragraph describing with particularity the contract market's system(s) in place to comply with this paragraph and the level of compliance achieved to date.

(2) Trading cards collected pursuant to this paragraph must be timestamped promptly to the nearest minute upon collection by either the contract market or relevant clearing member.

(3) A member of the contract market must use a new trading card at the beginning of each designated 30-minute interval required by paragraph (j)(1) of this section.

(4) A member of the contract market must record trades in the manner prescribed by paragraph (d)(2) of this section.

(5) Trading cards prepared by a member of the contract market must contain the identifying information prescribed in paragraph (d)(4) of this section.

(6) A member of the contract market must be accountable for all trading cards prepared pursuant to contract market rules in exact numerical sequence, whether or not such trading cards are relied on as original source documents.

(7) A member of this contract market must identify on his trading card trades executed during opening and closing periods either by drawing a line on the trading card to separate those trades from others recorded thereon or by some other method. Each contract market must designate as opening and closing periods for this purpose those periods upon which the opening and closing trading ranges are based for each of its markets.

(8) A member of the contract market must complete trades in non-erasable ink in the manner prescribed by paragraph (d)(7)(ii) of this section.

(k) *Collection of trading cards in intervals not to exceed 15 minutes.* The Commission, in its discretion, may publish a schedule in the Federal Register no earlier than 11 months after paragraph (j)(1) of this section becomes effective, indicating when the records required to be submitted pursuant to that paragraph must be submitted to contract market personnel or the clearing member within 15 minutes of designated intervals not to exceed 15 minutes, commencing with the beginning of each trading session.

(l) A contract market which can demonstrate that it currently has available hand-held terminals or such other automated means for the recordation of trades which can eliminate the opportunity for improper alteration or fabrication of trading record, may petition the Commission for an exception from Regulations 1.35(a-1)(2) and (4), (d), (j) or (k), as appropriate.

PART 4. COMMODITY POOL OPERATORS AND COMMODITY TRADING ADVISORS

Subpart B. Commodity Pool Operators

Citation:	17 CFR 4.23

✍ § 4.23 Recordkeeping.

Each commodity pool operator registered or required to be registered under the Act must make and keep the following books and records in an accurate, current and orderly manner at its main business office and in accordance with § 1.31. All books and records required by this section except those required by paragraphs (a)(3), (a)(4), (b)(1), (b)(2) and (b)(3) must be made available to participants for inspection and copying during normal business hours at the main business office of the pool operator. Upon request, copies must be sent by mail to any participant within five business days if reasonable reproduction and distribution costs are paid by the pool participant. If the commodity pool operator's main business office is outside of the United States, its territories or possessions, then upon the request of a Commission representative, the pool operator must provide such books and records as requested at the place in the United States, its territories or possessions designated by the representative within 72 hours after the pool operator receives the request.

(a) Concerning the commodity pool:

(1) An itemized daily record of each commodity interest transaction of the pool, showing the transaction date, quantity, commodity interest, and, as applicable, price or premium, delivery month or expiration date, whether a put or a call, strike price, underlying contract for future delivery or underlying physical, the futures commission merchant carrying the account and the introducing broker, if any, whether the commodity interest was purchased, sold, exercised, or expired, and the gain or loss realized.

(2) A journal of original entry or other equivalent record showing all receipts and disbursements of money, securities and other property.

(3) The acknowledgment specified in § 4.21(b) for each participant in the pool.

(4) A subsidiary ledger or other equivalent record for each participant in the pool showing the participant's name and address and all funds, securities and other property that the pool received from or distributed to the participant.

(5) Adjusting entries and any other records of original entry or their equivalent forming the basis of entries in any ledger.

(6) A general ledger or other equivalent record containing details of all asset, liability, capital, income and expense accounts.

(7) Copies of each confirmation of a commodity interest transaction of the pool, each purchase and sale statement and each monthly statement for the pool received from a futures commission merchant.

(8) Cancelled checks, bank statements, journals, ledgers, invoices, computer generated records, and all other records, data and memoranda prepared or received in connection with the operation of the pool.

(9) The original or a copy of each report, letter, circular, memorandum, publication, writing, advertisement or other literature or advice (including the texts of standardized oral presentations and of radio, television, seminar or similar mass media presentations) distributed or caused to be distributed by the commodity pool operator to any existing or prospective pool participant or received by the pool operator from any commodity trading advisor of the pool, showing the first date of distribution or receipt if not otherwise shown on the document.

(10) A Statement of Financial Condition as of the close of (i) each regular monthly period if the pool had net assets of $500,000 or more at the beginning of the pool's fiscal year, or (ii) each regular quarterly period for all other pools. The Statement must be completed within 30 days after the end of that period.

(11) A Statement of Income (Loss) for the period between (i) the later of: (A) the date of the most recent Statement of Financial Condition furnished to the Commission pursuant to § 4.22(c), (B) April 1, 1979 or (C) the formation of the pool, and (ii) the date of the Statement of Financial Condition required by paragraph (a)(10) of this section. The Statement must be completed within 30 days after the end of that period.

(b) Concerning the commodity pool operator:

(1) An itemized daily record of each commodity interest transaction of the commodity pool operator and each principal thereof, showing the transaction date, quantity, commodity

interest, and, as applicable, price or premium, delivery month or expiration date, whether a put or a call, strike price, underlying contract for future delivery or underlying physical, the futures commission merchant carrying the account and the introducing broker, if any whether the commodity interest was purchased, sold, exercised, or expired, and the gain or loss realized.

(2) Each confirmation of a commodity interest transaction, each purchase and sale statement and each monthly statement furnished by a futures commission merchant to (i) the commodity pool operator relating to a personal account of the pool operator, and (ii) each principal of the pool operator relating to a personal account of such principal.

(3) Books and records of all other transactions in all other activities in which the pool operator engages. Those books and records must include cancelled checks, bank statements, journals, ledgers, invoices, computer generated records and all other records, data and memoranda which have been prepared in the course of engaging in those activities.

PART 18. REPORTS BY TRADERS

Citation: **17 CFR 18.06**

✍ § 18.06 Use of data-processing media.

Any trader may provide the required series '03 information on compatible data-processing punched cards, magnetic tapes, magnetic discs or computer printouts provided that the format and coding structure used thereon have been approved in writing by the Executive Director or his designee. Information provided by means of data processing punched cards, magnetic tapes or magnetic discs shall also be accompanied by a complete and accurate printout of the information.

PART 31. LEVERAGE TRANSACTIONS

Citation: **17 CFR 31.14**

✍ § 31.14 Recordkeeping.

(a) All books, records and other documents required to be kept by this part shall be kept in accordance with the provisions of § 1.31 of this chapter. In addition, information concerning leverage transactions shall be made available upon request of the Executive Director, the Director of the Division of Trading and Markets, the Director of the Division of Economic Analysis or the Director of the Division of Enforcement, or other designees, at a time and place and in such form and manner as may be specified in the request.

(b) Each leverage transaction merchant shall:

(1) Keep full, complete, and systematic records, together with all pertinent data and memoranda, of all transactions relating to leverage contracts, commodity futures, commodity options and cash commodities and furnish true and correct information and reports as to the contents or the meaning thereof when and as requested by any authorized representative of the Commission, designated self-regulatory organization, if any, or the U.S. Department of Justice. Included among such records shall be: All leverage contract orders; signature cards; journals; ledgers; canceled checks; bank statements; loan agreements; invoices; copies of confirmations; copies of statements of purchase, sale, repurchase, resale, liquidation, rescission and delivery; copies of month-end statements; monthly trial balances, and a monthly listing as described in paragraph (d) of this section; reports, letters and copies of disclosure statements signed by leverage customers as described in § 31.11; promotional material, circulars, memoranda, publications, writings, and all other literature or written advice distributed to leverage customers or prospective leverage customers; and all other records, data and memoranda which have been prepared in the course of the business of the leverage transaction merchant concerning leverage contracts, commodity futures, commodity options, and cash commodities.

(2) Keep a record in permanent form which shall show for each leverage customer's account carried by such leverage transaction merchant:

(i) The true name and address of the person for whom such account is carried;

(ii) The principal occupation and/or type of business of the person for whom such account is carried;

(iii) The name and address of any other person who assumes or purports to assume any financial responsibility for or operational control of such account; and

(iv) The names of the persons who have solicited and are responsible for each leverage customer's account.

(c) Each leverage transaction merchant shall, as a minimum requirement, prepare regularly and promptly, and keep systematically and in permanent form, the following:

(1) A financial ledger which will show separately for each leverage customer's account all charges against and credits to such leverage customer's account, including but not limited to, all charges and credits for purchases, repurchases, sales, resales, liquidations, rescissions and settlements by delivery of leverage contracts (including the corresponding transaction identification numbers) and all funds transferred, deposited into, or withdrawn from the leverage customer's account.

(2) A record of transactions which will show separately for each leverage customer's account in chronological sequence all leverage contracts entered into with such customer. This record will show for each transaction:

The date of the transaction; the commodity involved; a transaction identification number, the maturity date; the number of contracts; whether the transaction represents an initial purchase, initial sale, closing repurchase, closing resale, a liquidating transaction, a rescission or a delivery; and, if a closing or liquidating transaction or a rescission, the total amount realized.

(3) A daily record or journal which will show separately by leverage commodity complete details of all leverage transactions executed on that day, including the person for whom such transaction was made, the leverage commodity and contract involved, the number of leverage contracts, the transaction identification number for each leverage contract, whether the transaction was an initial purchase, repurchase, initial sale, resale, liquidating transaction, rescission or delivery and the total value of the transaction.

(4) The acknowledgment specified in § 31.11(a).

(5) A record of all notifications under § 31.11(h).

(6) Where reproductions on microfilm of the records required by this paragraph (c) are substituted for hard copy in accordance with the provisions of paragraph (a) of this section, the requirement of paragraphs (c)(1) and (c)(2) of this section will be considered met if the person required to keep such records is ready at all times to provide, and immediately provides at such time and place as required by the Commission and at the expense of such person, reproduced copies which show the records as specified in paragraphs (c)(1) and (c)(2) of this section, on request by any representative of the Commission, designated self-regulatory organization or the U.S. Department of Justice.

(d) Each leverage transaction merchant shall prepare, as of the close of the last business day of each calendar month, a listing of all open leverage contracts carried for leverage customer. Such listing shall be by leverage commodity and contract and separately by long leverage contracts and short leverage separately by long leverage contracts and short leverage contracts, and shall include the following details with respect to each leverage contract:

(1) The customer account identification number;

(2) The name of the leverage commodity and contract;

(3) The date of execution and the maturity date;

(4) The transaction identification number;

(5) The value of the leverage contract when initiated; and

(6) The unrealized profit or loss on each open leverage contract market to the market on the basis of the leverage transaction merchant's bid price for a long leverage contract and ask price for a short leverage contract.

Agency: **Securities and Exchange Commission**

PART 200. ORGANIZATION; CONDUCT AND ETHICS; AND INFORMATION AND REQUESTS

Citation: **17 CFR 200.80**

✍ **§ 200.80 Commission records and information.**

* * * * *

(c) * * *

(3) Electronic filings made through the Electronic Data Gathering, Analysis, and Retrieval system are publicly available through the Commission's Web site (http://www.sec.gov).

PART 228. INTEGRATED DISCLOSURE SYSTEM FOR SMALL BUSINESS ISSUERS

Citation: **17 CFR 228.502**

✍ **§ 228.502 (Item 502) Inside front and outside back cover pages of prospectus.**

* * * * *

(a) * * *

(2) If the small business issuer is a reporting company, state that the reports and other information filed by the small business issuer may be inspected and copied at the public reference facilities of the Commission in Washington D.C., and at some of its Regional Offices (include addresses), and that copies of such material can be obtained from the Public Reference Section of the Commission, 450 Fifth Street, N.W., Washington D.C. 20549, at prescribed rates. If the small business issuer is an electronic filer, state that the Commission maintains a Web site that contains reports, proxy and information statements and other information regarding issuers that file electronically with the Commission and state the address of such site (http://www.sec.gov); and

* * * * *

PART 229. STANDARD INSTRUCTIONS FOR FILING FORMS UNDER SECURITIES ACT OF 1933, SECURITIES EXCHANGE ACT OF 1934 AND ENERGY POLICY AND CONSERVATION ACT OF 1975-REGULATION S-K

Citation: **17 CFR 229.502**

✍ **§ 229.502 (Item 502) Inside front and outside back cover pages of prospectus.**

* * * * *

(a) * * *

(2) State that reports (and where the registrant is subject to sections 14(a) and 14(c) of the Exchange Act, proxy and information statements) and other information filed by the registrant can be inspected and copied at the public reference facilities maintained by the Commission in Washington, D.C., and at certain of its Regional Offices, and state the current address of each such facility (see § § 200.11(b) and 200.80(c) of this chapter), and that copies of such material can be obtained from the Public Reference Section of the Commission, 450 Fifth Street, N.W., Washington, D.C. 20549 at prescribed rates. If the registrant is an electronic filer, state that the Commission maintains a Web site that contains reports, proxy and information statements and other information regarding registrants that file electronically with the Commission and state the address of such site (http://www.sec.gov);

* * * * *

PART 230. GENERAL RULES AND REGULATIONS, SECURITIES ACT OF 1933

Citation: **17 CFR 230.120**

✍ **§ 230.120 Inspection of registration statements.**

Except for material contracts or portions thereof accorded confidential treatment pursuant to § 230.406, all registration statements are available for public inspection, during business hours, at the principal office of the Commission in Washington, D.C. Electronic registration statements made through the Electronic Data Gathering, Analysis, and Retrieval system are publicly available through the Commission's Web site (http://www.sec.gov).

* * * * *

Citation: **17 CFR 230.253**

✍ **§ 230.253 Offering circular.**

* * * * *

(b) *Presentation of information.*

* * * * *

(2) Where an offering circular is distributed through an electronic medium, issuers may satisfy legibility requirements applicable to printed documents by presenting all required information in a format readily communicated to investors.

* * * * *

Citation: **17 CFR 230.402**

✍ **§ 230.402 Number of copies; binding; signatures.**

* * * * *

(e) *Signatures.* Where the Act or the rules thereunder, including paragraphs (a) and (c) of this section, require a document filed with or furnished to the Commission to be signed, such document shall be manually signed, or signed using either typed signatures or duplicated or facsimile versions of manual signatures. Where typed, duplicated or facsimile signatures are used, each signatory to the filing shall manually sign a signature page or other document authenticating, acknowledging or otherwise adopting his or her signature that appears in the filing. Such document shall be executed before or at the time the filing is made and shall be retained by the registrant for a period of five years. Upon request, the registrant shall furnish to the Commission or its staff a copy of any or all documents retained pursuant to this section.

Citation:	17 CFR 230.420

✍ § 230.420 Legibility of prospectus.

* * * * *

(b) Where a prospectus is distributed through an electronic medium, issuers may satisfy legibility requirements applicable to printed documents, such as paper size, type size and font, bold-face type, italics and red ink, by presenting all required information in a format readily communicated to investors, and where indicated, in a manner reasonably calculated to draw investor attention to specific information.

Citation:	17 CFR 230.471

✍ § 230.471 Signatures to amendments.

* * * * *

(b) Where the Act or the rules thereunder require a document filed with or furnished to the Commission to be signed, such document shall be manually signed, or signed using either typed signatures or duplicated or facsimile versions of manual signatures. Where typed, duplicated or facsimile signatures are used, each signatory to the filing shall manually sign a signature page or other document authenticating, acknowledging or otherwise adopting his or her signature that appears in the filing. Such document shall be executed before or at the time the filing is made and shall be retained by the registrant for a period of five years. Upon request, the registrant shall furnish to the Commission or its staff a copy of any or all documents retained pursuant to this section.

Citation:	17 CFR 230.473

✍ § 230.473 Delaying amendments.

* * * * *

(c) * * * Any such amendment filed after the filing of the registration statement, any amendment altering the proposed date of public sale of the securities being registered, or any amendment filed pursuant to paragraph (b) of this section may be made by telegram, letter or facsimile transmission. * * *

* * * * *

Citation:	17 CFR 230.481

✍ § 230.481 Information required in prospectus.

* * * * *

(h) Where a prospectus is distributed through an electronic medium, issuers may satisfy legibility requirements applicable to printed documents, such as paper size, type size and font, bold-face type, italics and red ink, by presenting all required information in a format readily communicated to investors, and where indicated, in a manner reasonably calculated to draw investor attention to specific information.

Citation:	17 CFR 230.605

✍ § 230.605 Filing and use of the offering circular.

* * * * *

(c) * * *

(2) Where an offering circular is distributed through an electronic medium, issuers may satisfy legibility requirements applicable to printed documents by presenting all required information in a format readily communicated to investors.

* * * * *

PART 232. REGULATION S-T — GENERAL RULES AND REGULATIONS FOR ELECTRONIC FILINGS

Citation:	17 CFR 232.10

✍ § 232.10 Applications of part 232.

(a) This part, in conjunction with the EDGAR Filer Manual and the electronic filing provisions of applicable rules, regulations and forms, shall govern the electronic submission of documents filed or otherwise submitted to the Commission and shall be controlling for an electronic format document in the manner and respects provided in this part.

(b) A FORM ID (§ § 239.63, 249.446, 259.602, 269.7 and 274.402 o this chapter), the uniform application for access codes to file on EDGAR, shall be filed by each registrant, third party, or agent prior to becoming subject to mandated electronic filing.

NOTE: It is strongly urged that Forms ID be submitted to the Commission between three and six months prior to becoming subject to mandated electronic filing.

Citation:	17 CFR 232.11

✍ § 232.11 Definition of terms used in part 232.

Unless otherwise specifically provided, the terms used in Regulation S-T (part 232 of this chapter) have the same meanings as in the federal securities laws and the rules, regulations and forms promulgated thereunder. In addition, the following definition of terms apply specifically to electronic format documents and shall apply wherever they appear in laws, rules, regulations and forms governing such documents, unless the context otherwise specifies:

(a) *Business development company.* The term *business development company* has the meaning set forth in section 2(a)(48) of the Investment Company Act.

(b) *Direct transmission.* The term *direct transmission* means the transmission of one or more electronic submissions via a telephonic communication session.

(c) *EDGAR.* The term *EDGAR* (Electronic Data Gathering, Analysis, and Retrieval) means the computer system for the receipt, acceptance, review and dissemination of documents submitted in electronic format.

(d) *EDGAR Filer Manual.* The term *EDGAR Filer Manual* means the current version of the manual prepared by the Commission setting out the technical format requirements for an electronic submission.

Note: See Rule 301 of Regulations S-T (Sec. 232.301)

(e) *Electronic Filer.* The term *electronic filer* means a person or an entity that submits filings electronically pursuant to Rules 101, 901, 902 or 903 of Regulation S-T (§ § 232.101, 232.901, 232.902 or 232.903, respectively).

(f) *Electronic filing.* The term *electronic filing* means a document filed under the federal securities laws that is transmitted or delivered to the Commission in electronic format.

(g) *Electronic format.* The term *electronic format* means the computerized format of a documents prepared in accordance with the EDGAR Filer Manual.

(h) *Electronic submission.* The term *electronic submission* means any document, such as a filing, correspondence, or modular submission, or any discrete set of documents, transmitted or delivered to the Commission in electronic format.

(i) *Exchange Act.* The term *Exchange Act* means the Securities Exchange Act of 1934.

(j) *Header information.* The term *header information* means information designated by the EDGAR Filer Manual to precede the text of each electronic submission and document submitted therewith via EDGAR that identifies characteristics of the submission and documents in order to facilitate electronic processing by the EDGAR system.

(k) *Investment Company Act.* The term *Investment Company Act* means the Investment Company Act of 1940.

(l) *Modular submission.* The term *modular submission* means an electronic submission that contains one or more documents, or portions of a document, submitted for storage in the non-public EDGAR data storage area for purposes of subsequent inclusion in one or more electronic filings pursuant to Rule 501(a) of Regulation S-T (§ 232.501(a)).

(m) *Official filing.* The term *official filing* means a microfiche copy, prepared in compliance with the Commission's administrative regulations and other requirements, of a registration statement, report or other document filed under the federal securities laws, regarding of filing medium and exclusive of header information, tags and any other technical information required in an electronic filing.

(n) *Original.* The term *original*, when used or implied in the securities laws, rules, regulations or forms, includes the writing itself or any counterpart intended to have the same effect by a person executing or issuing it. If data are stored in a computer or similar device, any printout or other output readable by sight, shown to reflect the data accurately, is an original.

(o) *Paper format.* The term *paper format* means a paper document.

(p) *Phase-in date.* The term *phase-in date* means the date established by the Commission on and after which a registrant is required to submit filings electronically pursuant to Rule 101 of Regulation S-T (§ 232.101).

(q) *Public Utility Act.* The term *Public Utility Act* means the Public Utility Holding Company Act of 1935.

(r) *Registrant.* The term *registrant* means an issuer of securities for which a Securities Act registration statement is required to be filed and/or an issuer of securities with respect to which an Exchange Act registration statement or report is required to be filed and/or an investment company required to file an Investment Company Act registration statement or report.

(s) *Securities Act.* The term *Securities Act* means the Securities Act of 1933.

(t) *Segmented Filing.* The term *segmented filing* means an electronic format document assembled from segments previously submitted to the non-public EDGAR data storage for one-time inclusion in an electronic filing pursuant to Rule 501(b) of Regulation S-T (§ 232.501(b)).

(u) *Tag.* The term *tag* means an identifier that highlights specific information to EDGAR that is in the format required by the EDGAR Filer Manual.

(v) *Third party filer.* The term *third party filer* means any person or entity that files documents with the Commission with respect to another entity.

(w) *Trust Indenture Act.* The term *Trust Indenture Act* means the Trust Indenture Act of 1939.

Citation: 17 CFR 232.12

✍ § 232.12 Business hours of the Commission.

(a) *General.*The principal office of the Commission, at 450 Fifth Street, NW., Washington, DC 20549, is open each day, except Saturdays, Sundays, and federal holidays, from 9 a.m. to 5:30 p.m., Eastern Standard Time or Eastern Daylight Savings Time, whichever is currently in effect, *provided that* hours for the filing of documents pursuant to the Acts or the rules and regulations thereunder are as set forth in paragraphs (b) and (c) of this section.

(b) *Submissions made in paper or on magnetic tape or diskette.* Paper documents filed with or otherwise furnished to the Commission, as well as electronic filings and submissions on magnetic tape or diskette under cover of Form ET (§ § 239.62, 249.445, 259.601, 269.6 and 274.401 of this chapter), may be submitted to the Commission each day, except Saturdays, Sundays and federal holidays, from 8 a.m. to 5:30 p.m., Eastern Standard Time or Eastern Daylight Saving Time, whichever is currently in effect. Submissions on magnetic tape or diskette may be filed either at the address indicated in paragraph (a) of this section, or at the Commission's Operations Center, 6432 General Green Way, Alexandria, VA 22312-2413.

(c) *Submissions by Direct Transmission.* Electronic filings and other documents may be submitted by direct transmission to the Commission each day, except Saturdays, Sundays and federal holidays, from 8 a.m. to 10:30 p.m., Eastern Standard Time or Eastern Daylight Saving Time, whichever is currently in effect.

Citation: 17 CFR 232.13

✍ § 232.13 Date of filing; adjustment of filing date.

(a) *General.* (1) Except as provided in paragraph (b) of this section, the business day on which a filing is received by the Commission shall be the date of filing thereof, if:

(i) All requirements of the Acts and rules applicable to such filing have been complied with;

(ii) The filing conforms to the applicable standards regarding electronic format in the EDGAR Filer Manual; and

(iii) With respect to Securities Act filings, the required fee payment has been confirmed, *provided that* the failure to pay an insignificant amount of the feel at the time of the filing, as a result of a *bona fide* error, shall not affect the date of filing.

(2) If the conditions of paragraph (a)(1) of this section are otherwise satisfied, all filings submitted by direct transmission commencing on or before 5:30 p.m. Eastern Standard Time or Eastern Daylight Saving Time, whichever is currently in effect, shall be deemed filed on the same business day, and all filings submitted by direct transmission commencing after 5:30 p.m. Eastern Standard Time or Eastern Daylight Time, whichever is currently in effect, shall be deemed filed as of the next business day.

(3) Notwithstanding paragraph (a)(2) of this section, any registration statement or any post-effective amendment thereto filed pursuant to Rule 462(b) (§ 230.462(b) of this chapter) by direct transmission commencing on or before 10 p.m. Eastern Standard Time or Eastern Daylight Savings Time, whichever is currently in effect, shall be deemed filed on the same business day.

NOTE: Electronic filings that have an automatic or immediate effective date must be deemed filed, as provided in paragraph (a) of this section, before any waiting period for automatic effectiveness commences or before the filing becomes immediately effective, whichever applies.

(b) *Adjustment of the filing date.* If an electronic filer in good faith attempts to file a document with the Commission in a timely manner but the filing is delayed due to technical difficulties beyond the electronic filer's control, the electronic filer may request an adjustment of the filing date of such document. The Commission, or the staff acting pursuant to delegated authority, may grant the request if it appears that such adjustment is appropriate and consistent with the public interest and the protection of investors.

(c) *Payment of fees*. Fees required with respect to a filing that is submitted electronically shall be paid in accordance with the procedures set forth in Instructions for Filing Fees — Rule 3a of the Commission's Informal and Other Procedures (§ 202.3a of this chapter).

NOTE. All filing fees paid by electronic filers must be submitted to the lockbox depository, as provided in Rule 3a, including those pertaining to documents filed in paper pursuant to a hardship exemption.

(d) Where the Commission's rules, schedules and forms provide that a document may be "mailed for filing with the Commission" at the same time it is published, furnished, sent or given to security holders or others, an electronic filer may file the document with the Commission electronically before or on the date the document is published, furnished, sent or given, or if such publication or distribution does not occur on a business day of the Commission, as soon as practicable on the next business day. Any associated time periods shall be calculated on the basis of the publication or distribution date (as applicable), and not on the basis of the date of filing.

ELECTRONIC FILING REQUIREMENTS

Citation: 17 CFR 232.101

✍ § 232.101 Mandated electronic submissions and exceptions.

(a) *Mandated electronic submissions.*

(1) The following filings, including any related correspondence and supplemental information, except as otherwise provided, shall be submitted in electronic format:

(i) Registration statements and prospectuses filed pursuant to the Securities Act (15 U.S.C. 77a, et seq.) or registration statements filed pursuant to Sections 12(b) or 12(g) of the Exchange Act (15 U.S.C. 78l(b) or (g));

(ii) Statements and applications filed with the Commission pursuant to the Trust Indenture Act (15 U.S.C. 77aaa, *et seq.*), other than applications for exemptive relief filed pursuant to Section 304(c) (15 U.S.C. 77ddd(c)) on Form T-4 (§ 269.4 of this chapter) and Section 310(b)(1)(ii) (15 U.S.C. 77jjj(b)(1)(ii)) of that Act;

(iii) Statements, reports and schedules filed with the Commission pursuant to Sections 13, 14, or 15(d) of the Exchange Act (15 U.S.C. 78m, n, and o(d)), except Form 13F (§ 249.325 of this chapter), provided that if a registrant's first mandated electronic filing would be an annual report on Form 10-K (§ 249.310 of this chapter) or Form 10-KSB (§ 249.310b of this chapter) such annual report may, at the option of the registrant, be submitted in paper format;

(iv) Documents filed with the Commission pursuant to Sections 8, 17, 20, and 30 of the Investment Company Act (15 U.S.C. 80a-8, 80a-17, 80a-20, and 80a-29); *provided, however*, that in no event shall any submissions under Section 6(c), 8(f), or 17(g) of the Act (15 U.S.C. 80a-6(c), 80a-8(f), or 80a-17(g)) or documents related to applications for exemptive relief under any section of the Act be made in electronic format; and

(v) Documents filed with the Commission pursuant to the Public Utility Act (15 U.S.C. 79a *et seq.*).

(2) The following amendments to filings, including any related correspondence and supplemental information except as otherwise provided, shall be submitted as follows:

(i) Any amendment to a filing by or relating to a registrant required to file electronically, including any amendment to a paper filing, shall be submitted in electronic format;

(ii) The first electronic amendment to a paper format Schedule 13D (§ 240.13d-101 of this chapter) or Schedule 13G (§ 240.13d-102 of this chapter) shall restate the entire text of the Schedule 13D or 13G (§ 240.13d-101 or § 240.13d-102 of this chapter), but previously filed paper exhibits to such Schedules are not required to be restated electronically. See Rule 102 (§ 232.102) regarding amendments to exhibits previously filed in paper format.

(3) Supplemental information shall be submitted in electronic format except as provided in paragraph (c)(2) of this section. The information shall be stored in the non-public EDGAR data storage area as correspondence. Supplemental information that is submitted in electronic format shall not be returned.

NOTE: Failure to submit a required electronic filing pursuant to this paragraph (a), as well as any required confirming electric copy of a paper filing made in reliance on a hardship exemption, as provided in Rules 201 and 202 of Regulation S-T (§ § 232.201 and 232.202), will result in ineligibility to use Forms S-2, S-3, S-8, F-2 and F-3 (see § § 239.12, 239.13, 239.16b, 239.32 and 239.33 of this chapter, respectively), restrict incorporation by reference of the document submitted in paper (see Rule 303 of Regulation S-T (§ 232.303)), or toll certain time periods associated with tender offers (see Rule 13e-4(f)(12) (§ 240.13e-4(f)(12) of this chapter) and Rules 14e-1(e) (§ 240.14e-1(e) of this chapter)).

(b) *Permitted electronic submissions.* The following documents may be submitted to the Commission in electronic format, at the option of the electronic filer:

(1) Annual Reports to Security Holders furnished for the information of the Commission pursuant to Rule 14a-3(c) (§ 240.14a-3(c) of this chapter) and Rule 14c-3(b) (§ 240.14c-3(b) of this chapter);

(2) Notices of exempt solicitation furnished for the information of the Commission pursuant to Rule 14a-6(g) (§ 240.14a-6(g) of this chapter).

(3) Form 11-K (§ 249.311 of this chapter). Registrants who satisfy their Form 11-K filing obligations by filing amendments to Forms 10-K or 10-KSB, as provided by Rule 15d-21 (§ 240.15d-21 of this chapter), also may choose to file such amendments in paper or electronic format;

(4) Forms 3, 4 and 5 (§ § 249.103, 249.104 and 249.105 of this chapter);

(5) Form 144 (§ 239.144 of this chapter), where the issuer of the securities is subject to the reporting requirements of Section 13 or 15(d) of the Exchange Act (15 U.S.C. 78m or 78o(d), respectively);

(6) Periodic reports and reports with respect to issuances of primary obligations filed by the International Bank for Reconstruction and Development pursuant to Section 15(a) of the Bretton Woods Agreements Act [22 U.S.C. 286k-1(a)] and part 285 of Title 17 of the Code of Federal Regulations;

(7) Reports on Form 13F (§ 249.325 of this chapter), filed with the Commission by institutional investment managers as required by Section 13(f)(1) (15 U.S.C. 78m(f)(1)) of, and Rule 13f-1 (§ 240.13f-1 of this chapter) under, the Exchange Act on magnetic tape in the format described in Form 13F-E (§ 249.326 of this chapter); and

(8) Exhibits to Form N-SAR (§ 274.101 of this chapter), except that the Financial Data Schedule required under Rule

483 under the Securities Act of 1933 (§ 230.483 of this chapter) shall be filed in electronic format.

(c) *Documents to be submitted in paper only.* The following shall not be submitted in electronic format:

(1)(i) Confidential treatment requests and the information with respect to which confidential treatment is requested;

(ii) Preliminary proxy materials and information statements with respect to a matter specified in Item 14 of Schedule 14A (§ 240.14a-101 of this chapter) for which confidential treatment has been requested in the manner prescribed by Rule 14a-6(e)(2) (§ 240.14a-6(e)(2) of this chapter) or Rule 14c-5(d)(2) (§ 240.14c-5(d)(2) of this chapter);

(2) Supplemental information, if the submitter requests that the information be protected from public disclosure under the Freedom of Information Act (5 U.S.C. 552) pursuant to a request for confidential treatment under Rule 83 (§ 200.83 of this chapter) or if the submitter requests that the information be returned after staff review and the information is of the type typically returned by the staff pursuant to Rule 418(b) of Regulation C (§ 230.418(b) of this chapter) or Rule 12b-4 of Regulation 12B (§ 240.12b-4 of this chapter);

(3) Shareholder proposals and all related correspondence submitted pursuant to Rule 14a-8 of the Exchange Act (§ 240.14a-8 of this chapter);

(4) No-action and interpretive letter requests (§ 200.81 of this chapter and 15 U.S.C. 78*l*(h));

(5) Form SR (§ 239.61 of this chapter);

(6) Applications for exemptive relief filed pursuant to Sections 304(d), 310(b) and 310(b)(1)(ii) of the Trust Indenture Act and applications under Section 304(c) of that Act on Form T-4;

(7) Filings related to offerings exempt from registration under the Securities Act of 1933, including filings made pursuant to Regulation A (§ § 230.251-230.264 of this chapter), Regulation B (§ § 230.300-230.346 of this chapter), Regulation D (§ § 230.501-230.508 of this chapter), Regulation E (§ § 230.601-230.610a of this chapter) and Regulation F (§ § 230.651-230.656 of this chapter), as well as filings on Form 144 (239.144 of this chapter) where the issuer of the securities is not subject to the reporting requirements of Section 13 or 15(d) of the Exchange Act (15 U.S.C. 78m or 78o(d), respectively);

(8) Promotional and Sales Material submitted pursuant to Securities Act Industry Guide 5 (§ 229.801(e) of this chapter) or otherwise supplementally furnished for review by the staff of the Division of Corporation Finance; and sales literature submitted under Rule 24b-2 of the Investment Company Act (§ 270.24b-2 of this chapter);

(9) Documents and symbols in a foreign language (see Rule 306 of Regulation S-T (§ 232.306));

(10) Exchange Act filings submitted to the Division of Market Regulation;

(11) Documents relating to investigations and litigation submitted pursuant to the Subpart D of Part 201 of this chapter;

(12) Submissions under Sections 6(c), 8(f), 17(g), and 33 of the Investment Company Act (15 U.S.C. 80a-6(c), 80a-8(f), 80a-17(g), and 80a-32) and documents related to applications for exemptive relief under any section of the Act;

(13) Annual Reports to Security Holders furnished by Public Utility Holding Companies under Exhibit A to Form U5S (§ 259.5s of this chapter) or under rule 29 (§ 250.29 of this chapter);

(14) Reports to State Commissions, if furnished by Public Utility Holdings Companies under Exhibit E to Form U5S (§ 259.5s of this chapter); and

(15) Maps furnished by Public Utility Holding Companies under Exhibits E to Forms U5B and U-1 (§ § 259.5b and 259.101 of this chapter).

(16) Form F-6 (§ 239.36 of this chapter);

(17) Annual reports filed with the Commission by indenture trustees pursuant to Section 313 of the Trust Indenture Act (15 U.S.C. 77mmm);

(18) Applications for an exemption from Exchange Act reporting obligations filed pursuant to Section 12(h) of the Exchange Act (15 U.S.C. 78ll(h)); and

(19) Written information concerning employee benefit plans required to be filed with the Commission pursuant to Rule 16b-3(b)(2)(ii) of the Exchange Act (§ 240.16b-3(b)(2)(ii) of this chapter).

Citation: 17 CFR 232.102

✍ § 232.102 Exhibits.

(a) Exhibits to an electronic filing that have not previously been filed with the Commission shall be filed in electronic format, absent a hardship exemption. Previously filed exhibits, whether in paper or electronic format, may be incorporated by reference into an electronic filing to the extent permitted by § 228.10(f) and § 229.10(d) of this chapter), Rule 411 under the Securities Act (§ 230.411 of this chapter), Rule 12b-23 or 12b-32 under the Exchange Act (§ 240.12b-23 or § 240.12b-32 of this chapter), Rule 22 under the Public Utility Holding Company Act (§ 250.22 of this chapter), Rules 0-4, 8b-23, and 8b-32 under the Investment Company Act (§ 270.0-4, § 270.8b-23 and § 270.8b-32 of this chapter) and Rule 303 of Regulation S-T (§ 232.303). An electronic filer may, at its option, restate in electronic format an exhibit incorporated by reference that originally was filed in paper format.

Note to paragraph a: Exhibits to a Commission schedule filed pursuant to Section 13 or 14(d) of the Exchange Act may be filed in paper under cover of Form SE where such exhibits previously were filed in paper (prior to a registrant's becoming subject to mandated electronic filing or pursuant to a hardship exemption) and are required to be refiled pursuant to the schedule's general instructions. See Rule 311(b) of Regulation S-T (17 CFR 232.311(b)).

(b) Amendments to all exhibits shall be filed in electronic format, absent a hardship exemption.

(c) Notwithstanding any other provisions of this section, an electronic filer shall, upon amendment, restate in electronic format its articles of incorporation, by-laws or investment advisory agreement (in the case of a registered investment company or a business development company).

(d) Each electronic filing requiring exhibits shall contain an exhibit index, which should immediately precede the exhibits filed with the document. The index shall list each exhibit filed. Whenever an exhibit is filed in paper pursuant to a temporary or continuing hardship exemption, the letter "P" shall be placed next to the listed exhibit in the exhibit index to reflect that the exhibit was filed in paper pursuant to such exemption. Whenever an electronic confirming copy of an exhibit is filed pursuant to a temporary hardship exemption, the electronic filer shall place the designation "CE" next to the listed exhibit in the exhibit index.

(e) Notwithstanding the provisions of paragraphs (a) through (d) of this section, after the date which is three years following a registrant's phase-in date, any incorporation by reference by a registered investment company or a business development company shall relate only to documents which have been filed in electronic format, unless:

(1) The document has been filed in paper pursuant to a hardship exemption (§ § 232.201 and 232.202 of this chapter) and any required confirming copy has been submitted or

(2) The document is an exhibit, filed in paper in accordance

with applicable rules, to Form N-SAR being incorporated by reference only into another Form N-SAR filing.

(f) Persons submitting filings electronically under the Public Utility Act shall not be subject to paragraph (c) of this section.

Citation: 17 CFR 232.103

✍ § 232.103 Liability for transmission errors or omissions in documents filed via EDGAR.

An electronic filer shall not be subject to the liability and anti-fraud provisions of the federal securities laws with respect to an error or omission in an electronic filing resulting solely from electronic transmission errors beyond the control of the filer, whether transmission is by magnetic tape, diskette, or direct transmission, where the error or omission is corrected by the filing of an amendment in electronic format as soon as reasonably practicable after the electronic filer becomes aware of the error or omission.

HARDSHIP EXEMPTIONS

Citation: 17 CFR 232.201

✍ § 232.201 Temporary hardship exemption.

(a) If an electronic filer experiences unanticipated technical difficulties preventing the timely preparation and submission of an electronic filing, the electronic filer may file the subject filing, under cover of Form TH (§ § 239.65, 249.447, 259.604, 269.10 and 274.404 of this chapter), in paper format no later than one business day after the date on which the filing was to be made.

(1) A microfiche copy of the paper format document shall be the official filing of the registrant for purposes of the federal securities laws.

(2) The following legend shall be set forth in capital letters on the cover page of the paper format document:

IN ACCORDANCE WITH RULE 201 OF REGULATION S-T, THIS (SPECIFY DOCUMENT) IS BEING FILED IN PAPER PURSUANT TO A TEMPORARY HARDSHIP EXEMPTION

(3) Signatures to the paper format document may be in typed form rather than manual format. See Rule 302 of Regulation S-T (§ 232.302). All other requirements relating to paper format filings shall be satisfied.

(4) If the exemption pertains to a document filed pursuant to section 13(a) or 15(d) of the Exchange Act (15 U.S.C. 78m and 78o(d)) or section 30 of the Investment Company Act and the paper format document is filed in the manner specified in paragraph (a) of this section, the filing shall be deemed to have been filed by its required due date.

NOTES: 1. Where a temporary hardship exemption relates to an exhibit only, the paper format exhibit shall be filed under cover of Form SE (§ § 239.64, 249.444, 259.603, 269.8, and 274.403 of this chapter).

2. Filers unable to submit a report within a prescribed time period because of electronic difficulties shall comply with the provisions of this section and shall not use Form 12b-25 (§ 249.322 of this chapter) as a notification of late filing.

(b) An electronic format copy of the filed paper format document shall be submitted to the Commission within six business days of filing the paper six business days of filing the paper format document. The electronic format version shall contain the following statement in capital letters at the top of the first page of the document:

THIS DOCUMENT IS A COPY OF THE (SPECIFY DOCUMENT) FILED ON (DATE) PURSUANT TO A RULE 201 TEMPORARY HARDSHIP EXEMPTION

NOTE: Failure to submit the confirming electronic copy of a paper filing made in reliance on the temporary hardship exemption, as required in paragraph (b) of this section, will result in ineligibility to use Forms S-2, S-3, S-8, F-2 and F-3 (*see* § § 239.12, 239.13, 239.16b, 239.32 and 239.33 of this section, respectively), restrict corporation by reference of the document submitted in paper (*see* Rule 303 of Regulation S-T (§ 232.303)), and toll certain time periods associated with tender offers (*see* Rule 13e-4(f)(12) (§ 240.13e-4(f)(12) of this chapter) and Rule 14e-1(e) (§ 240.14e-1(e) of this chapter).

Citation: 17 CFR 232.202

✍ § 232.202 Continuing hardship exemption.

(a) An electronic filer may apply in writing for a continuing hardship exemption if all or part of a filing or group of filings otherwise to be filed in electronic format cannot be so filed without undue burden or expense. Such written application shall be made at least ten business days prior to the required due date of the filing(s) or the proposed filing date, as appropriate, or within such shorter period as may be permitted. The written application shall contain the information set forth in paragraph (b) of this section.

(1) The application shall not be deemed granted until the applicant is notified by the Commission or the staff.

(2) If the Commission, or the staff acting pursuant to delegated authority, denies the application for a continuing hardship exemption, the electronic filer shall file the required document in electronic format on the required due date or the proposed filing date or such other date as may be permitted.

(3) If the Commission, or the staff acting pursuant to delegated authority, determines that the grant of the exemption if appropriate and consistent with the public interest and the protection of investors and so notifies the applicant, the electronic filer shall follow the procedures set forth in paragraph (c) of this section.

(b) The request for the continuing hardship exemption shall include, but not be limited to, the following:

(1) The reason(s) that the necessary hardware and software is not available without unreasonable burden and expense;

(2) The burden and expense involved to employ alternative means to make the electronic submission; and/or

(3) The reasons for not submitting electronically the document or group of documents, as well as justification for the requested time period.

(c) If the request is granted, the electronic filer shall submit the document or group of documents for which the continuing hardship exemption is granted in paper format on the required due date specified in the applicable form, rule or regulations, or the proposed filing date, as appropriate. The following legend shall be placed in capital letters at the top of the cover page of the paper format document(s):

IN ACCORDANCE WITH RULE 202 OF REGULATION S-T, THIS (SPECIFY DOCUMENT) IS BEING FILED IN PAPER PURSUANT TO A CONTINUING HARDSHIP EXEMPTION

(d) If a continuing hardship exemption is granted for a limited time period, the grant may be conditioned upon the filing of the document or group of documents that is the subject of the exemption in electronic format upon the expiration of the period for which the exemption is granted.

NOTE: Where a continuing hardship exemption is granted with respect to an exhibit only, the paper format exhibit shall be filed under cover of Form SE (§ § 239.64, 249.444, 259.603,

269.8 and 274.403 of this chapter).

PREPARATION OF ELECTRONIC SUBMISSIONS

Citation: 17 CFR 232.301

✍ § 232.301 EDGAR Filer Manual.

Electronic filings shall be prepared in the manner prescribed by the EDGAR Filer Manual, promulgated by the Commission, which sets out the technical formatting requirements for electronic submissions. The January 1995 edition of the EDGAR Filer Manual: Guide for Electronic Filing with the U.S. Securities and Exchange Commission (Release 4.40) is incorporated into the Code of Federal Regulations by reference, which action was approved by the Director of the Federal Register in accordance with 5 U.S.C. 552(a) and 1 CFR Part 51. Compliance with the requirements found therein is essential to the timely receipt and acceptance of documents filed with or otherwise submitted to the Commission in electronic format. Paper copies of the EDGAR Filer Manual may be obtained at the following address: Public Reference Room, U.S. Securities and Exchange Commission, Mail Stop 1-2, 450 5th Street NW., Washington, DC 20549. They also may be obtained from Disclosure Incorporated by calling (800) 638-8241. Electronic format copies are available through the EDGAR electronic bulletin board. Information on becoming an EDGAR E-mail/electronic bulletin board subscriber is available by contacting CompuServe Inc. at (800) 848-8199.

Citation: 17 CFR 232.302

✍ § 232.302 Signatures.

(a) Signatures to or within an electronic submission shall be in typed form rather than manual format. When used in connection with an electronic filing, the term "signature" means an electronic entry in the form of a magnetic impulse or other form of computer data compilation of any letter or series of letters comprising a name, executed, adopted or authorized as a signature.

(b) Each signatory to an electronic filing shall manually sign a signature page or other document authenticating, acknowledging or otherwise adopting his or her signature that appears in typed form within the electronic filing. Such document shall be executed before or at the time the electronic filing is made and shall be retained by the filer for a period of five years. Upon request, an electronic filer shall furnish to the Commission or its staff a copy of any or all documents retained pursuant to this section.

(c) Where the Commission's rules require a registrant to furnish to a national securities exchange or national securities association paper copies of a document filed with the Commission in electronic format, signatures to such paper copies may be in typed form.

Citation: 17 CFR 232.303

✍ § 232.303 Incorporation by reference.

(a) The following documents shall not be incorporated by reference into an electronic filing:

(1) Any document filed in paper in violation of mandated electronic filing requirements;

(2) Any document filed in paper pursuant to a temporary hardship exemption for which a required confirming electronic copy has not been submitted.

(3) For a registered investment company or a business development company making an electronic submission more than three years after its phase-in date, documents that have not been filed in electronic format, unless:

(i) The document has been filed in paper pursuant to a hardship exemption (§ § 232.201 and 232.202 of this chapter) and any required confirming copy has been submitted or

(ii) The document is an exhibit, filed in paper in accordance with applicable rules, to Form N-SAR being incorporated by reference into another Form N-SAR filing.

(4) Any Financial Data Schedule required under Rule 483 under the Securities Act of 1933 (§ 230.483 of this chapter).

(b) If any portion of the annual or quarterly report to security holders is incorporated by reference into any electronic filing, such portion of the annual or quarterly report to security holders shall be filed in electronic format as an exhibit to the filing, as required by Item 601(b)(13) of Regulation S-K (§ 229.601(b)(13) of this chapter) and Item 601(b)(13) of Regulation S-B (§ 228.601(b)(13) of this chapter).

Citation: 17 CFR 232.304

✍ § 232.304 Graphic, image and audio material.

(a) If a filer includes graphic, image or audio material in a document delivered to investors and others that cannot be reproduced in an electronic filing, the electronically filed version of that document shall include a fair and accurate narrative description, tabular representation or transcript of the omitted material. Such descriptions, representations or transcripts may be included in the text of the electronic filing at the point where the graphic, image or audio material is presented in the delivered version, or they may be listed in an appendix to the electronic filing. Immaterial differences between the delivered and electronically filed versions, such as pagination, color, type size or style, or corporate logo need not be described.

(b)(1) The graphic, image and audio material in the version of a document delivered to investors and others shall be deemed part of the electronic filing and subject to the liability and antifraud provisions of the federal securities laws.

(2) * * *

(c) An electronic filer shall retain for a period of five years a copy of each publicly distributed document, in the format used, that contains graphic, image or audio material where such material is not included in the version filed with the Commission. The five-year period shall commence as of the filing date, or the date that appears on the document, whichever is later. Upon request, an electronic filer shall furnish to the Commission or its staff a copy of any or all of the documents contained in the file.

* * * * *

Citation: 17 CFR 232.305

✍ § 232.305 Number of characters per line; tabular and columnar information.

The narrative portion of a document shall not exceed 80 characters per line, including blank spaces, and shall not be presented in multi-column newspaper format. Non-narrative information (*e.g.,* financial statements) may be presented in tabular or columnar format and may exceed 80 positions only if it is tagged as specified in the EDGAR File Manual. In no event shall information presented in tabular or columnar format exceed 132 positions wide.

Citation: 17 CFR 232.306

✍ § 232.306 Foreign language documents and symbols.

(a) Foreign language documents shall not be filed with the Commission in electronic format. A fair and accurate English translation of any required document shall be filed. A written representation to that effect shall be included in the English translation document and the representation shall be signed by a designated officer in the manner set forth in Rule 302 of Regulation S-T (§ 232.302). Upon request, any foreign language document otherwise required to be filed shall be provided to the Commission or the staff.

Note: With respect to submission of an electronic filer's latest annual budget required to be filed as Exhibit B in Form 18 (§ 249.218 of this chapter) or as Exhibit (c) in Form 18-K (§ 249.318 of this chapter), for foreign governments and political subdivisions thereof, if an English version of such filer's last annual budget as presented to its legislative body has been prepared, it shall be filed electronically. If no such version has been prepared, the budget need not be filed, but shall be provided to the Commission upon request.

(b) Foreign currency denominations shall be expressed in words or letters in the English language rather than representative symbols.

Citation: 17 CFR 232.307

✍ § 232.307 Bold face type; red ink.

Provisions requiring presentation of information in bold face type or in red ink shall be satisfied in an electronic format document by presenting such information in capital letters.

Citation: 17 CFR 232.308

✍ § 232.308 Type size and font; legibility.

Provisions relating to type size, font and other legibility requirements shall not apply to electronic format documents.

Citation: 17 CFR 232.309

✍ § 232.309 Paper size; binding; sequential numbering; number of copies.

(a) Requirements as to paper size, binding, and sequential page numbering shall not apply to electronic format documents.

(b) An electronic format document, submitted in the manner prescribed by the EDGAR Filer Manual, shall satisfy any requirement that more than one copy of such document be filed with or provided to the Commission.

Citation: 17 CFR 232.310

✍ § 232.310 Marking changed material.

Provisions requiring the marking of changed materials shall be satisfied by inserting the tag <R> before and the tag <\R> following a paragraph containing changed material. Financial statements and notes thereto need not be marked for changed material.

Citation: 17 CFR 232.311

✍ § 232.311 Documents submitted in paper under cover of Form SE.

Form SE (§ § 239.64, 249.444, 259.603, 269.8, and 274.403 of this chapter) shall be filed as a paper cover sheet to the following documents submitted to the Commission in paper:

(a) Exhibits filed in paper pursuant to a hardship exemption shall be filed under cover of Form SE. See Rules 201 and 202 of Regulations S-T (§ § 232.201 and 232.202).

(b) Exhibits to a Commission schedule filed pursuant to Section 13 or 14(d) of the Exchange Act may be filed in paper under cover of Form SE where such exhibits previously were filed in paper (prior to a registrant's becoming subject to mandated electronic filing or pursuant to a hardship exemption) and are required to be refiled pursuant to the schedule's general instructions.

(c) Exhibits consisting of all or portions of an annual statement provided to state insurance regulators (e.g., Schedules O and P), required to be filed pursuant to Item 601(b)(28) of Regulation S-B or Regulation S-K (§ 228.601(b)(28) or § 229.601(b)(28) of this chapter, respectively), may be filed in paper under cover of Form SE.

(d) Exhibits to Form N-SAR (§ 274.101 of this chapter), other than the Financial Data Schedule required under Rule 483 under the Securities Act of 1933 (§ 230.483 of this chapter), may be filed in paper under cover of Form SE.

(e) Annual Reports to Security Holders furnished by Public Utility Holding Companies as Exhibit A to Form U5S (§ 259.5s of this chapter) or under rule 29 (§ 250.29 of this chapter) shall be filed in paper under cover of Form S-E.

(f) Reprots to State Commissions, if furnished by Public Utility Holding Companies as Exhibit E to Form U5S (§ 259.5s of this chapter), shall be filed in paper under cover of Form S-E.

(g) Maps furnished by Public Utility Holding Companies under Exhibits E to Forms U5B and U-1 (§ 259.5b and 259.101 of this chapter) shall be filed in paper under cover of Form S-E.

(h) The Form SE shall be submitted in the following manner:

(1) If the subject of a temporary hardship exemption is an exhibit only, the exhibit shall be filed under cover of Form SE no later than one business day after the date the exhibit was to be filed electronically.

(2) An exhibit filed pursuant to a continuing hardship exemption, or any other document filed in paper under cover of Form SE (other than an exhibit filed pursuant to a temporary hardship exemption), as allowed by paragraphs (a) through (c) of this section, may be filed up to six business days prior to, or on the date of filing of, the electronic format document to which it relates but shall not be filed after such filing date. If a paper document is submitted in this manner, requirements that the documents be filed with, provided with or accompany the electronic filing shall be satisfied.

(i) Any requirements as to delivery or furnishing the information to persons other than the Commission shall not be affected by this section.

FINANCIAL DATA SCHEDULE

Citation: 17 CFR 232.401

✍ § 232.401 Financial Data Schedule.

A Financial Data Schedule shall be submitted as an exhibit to the filing(s) to which it relates in accordance with Item 601(c) of Regulation S-K (§ 229.601(c) of this chapter), Item 601(c) of

Regulation S-B (§ 228.601(c) of this chapter) or Rule 483(e) (§ 230.483(e) of this chapter).

NOTE: An electronic filer's failure to furnish a Financial Data Schedule will not prevent acceptance of the filing for which the Schedule is required. However, inasmuch as the Schedule may be used by the Commission staff in its review of the filing, processing of the filing may be delayed pending filing of the Schedule. Further, electronic filers that have not filed a required Financial Data Schedule will be ineligible to use Form S-2, Form S-3 and Form S-8 (§ § 239.12, 239.13 and 239.16b of this chapter, respectively).

Citation: 17 CFR 232.402

✍ § 232.402 Liability for Financial Data Schedule.

A Financial Data Schedule shall not be deemed filed for purposes of section 11 of the Securities Act (15 U.S.C. 77k), section 18 of the Exchange Act (15 U.S.C. 78r), section 16 of the Public Utility Act (15 U.S.C. 79p), section 323 of the Trust Indenture Act (15 U.S.C. 77www), or section 34(b) of the Investment Company Act (15 U.S.C. 80a-33(b)), or otherwise be subject to the liabilities of such sections, and shall not be deemed a part of a registration statement to which it relates. The Financial Data Schedule shall, however, be subject to all other liability and anti-fraud provisions of the Acts. An electronic filer that accurately extracts the Financial Data Schedule information from its financial statements, financial statement schedules, or disclosures prepared in response to applicable industry guides, shall not be liable, under the Securities Act, the Exchange Act or the Trust Indenture Act for such extracted information, *provided that* the extracted data was not materially false or misleading in the underlying financial statements, financial statement schedules, or disclosures prepared in response to applicable industry guides.

EDGAR FUNCTIONS

Citation: 17 CFR 232.501

✍ 232.501 Modular submissions and segmented filings.

An electronic data filer that subscribes to the optional EDGAR electronic mail service may use the following procedures to submit information on the EDGAR system for subsequent inclusion in an electronic filing.

(a) *Modular submissions.* (1) One or more electronic format documents may be submitted for storage in the non-public EDGAR data storage area as a modular submission for subsequent inclusion in one or more electronic submissions.

(2) An electronic filer shall be permitted a maximum of ten modular submissions in the non-public EDGAR data storage areas at any time, not to exceed a total of one megabyte of digital information. If an electronic filer attempts to submit a modular filing which would cause either of these limits to be exceeded, EDGAR will suspend the modular submission and notify the electronic filer by electronic mail. After six business days, the modular submissions held in suspense will be deleted from the system.

(3) A modular submission may be corrected or amended only by resubmitting the entire modular transmission.

(b) *Segmented filings.* (1) Segments of a document intended to become an electronic filing may be submitted to the non-public EDGAR data storage area for assembly as a segmented filing.

(2) Segments shall be submitted no more than six business days in advance of the anticipated filing data and are not limited in number or size. They may be submitted from several geographic locations by more than one filing entity. Segments may be included in only one electronic filing. Once used, segments will be removed from the non-public EDGAR data storage area. The assembly of segments into a segmented filing shall be effected pursuant to the applicable provisions of the EDGAR Filer Manual. If segments are not prepared in accordance with the EDGAR Filer Manual, the filing will not be constructed. The filing date of the segmented filing shall be the date upon which the filing is assembled and satisfies the requirements of Rule 13(a) of Regulation S-T (§ 232.13(a)).

(3) Segments may be corrected or amended only by resubmitting the entire segment.

(c) A modular submission or segment shall not:

(1) Be publicly available;

(2) Be deemed filed with the Commission for purposes of Securities Act section 11 (15 U.S.C. 77k), Exchange Act section 18 (15 U.S.C. 78r), Public Utility Act section 16 (15 U.S.C. 79p), Trust Indenture Act section 323 (15 U.S.C. 77www), or Investment Company Act section 34(b) (15 U.S.C. 80a-33(b)) prior to its inclusion in a filing; or

(3) Be deemed to constitute an official filing prior to its inclusion in a filing under the federal securities laws. Once a modular submission or segment has been included in an electronic filing, the liability and anti-fraud provisions of the Securities Act, the Exchange Act, the Trust Indenture Act, the Public Utility Act and the Investment Company Act shall apply to the electronic filing.

TRANSITION TO ELECTRONIC FILING

Citation: 17 CFR 232.901

✍ § 232.901 Division of Corporation Finance EDGAR Transition.

(a) *Registrant electronic submissions.* Registrants whose filings are subject to review by the Division of Corporation Finance, except for foreign private issuers and foreign governments, shall be subject to the electronic filing requirements of this part in accordance with the registrant phase-in schedule published by the Commission, including any amendments thereto.

(1) All other public companies, except for foreign private issuers and foreign governments, shall become subject to the electronic filing requirements of this part, including any company that makes a registered offering under the Securities Act or that comes subject to the reporting requirements of the Exchange Act, at the same time the last group of companies in the phase-in schedule becomes subject to mandated electronic filing.

(2) A registrant may request to participate in a phase-in group other than the group established by the Commission for the registrant. If such a request is granted by the Commission, or by the staff pursuant to Rule 30-1(m) of the Rules of Organization and Management (§ 200.30-1(m) of this chapter), the registrant shall become subject to the mandated filing requirements of Rule 101 of Regulation S-T (§ 232.101) on the phase-in date applicable to the group to which it has been reassigned.

Note to paragraph (a): Registrants become subject to mandated electronic filing on their phase-in date. Consequently, all documents required to be filed in electronic format pursuant to Rule 101 of Regulation S-T (§ 232.101) filed on or after a registrant's phase-in date must be filed electronically, absent a hardship exemption, even if the transaction to which a filing relates was commenced in paper before the phase-in date and is still in process on the registrant's phase-in date. See Rule 101(a)(1)(iii) of Regulation S-T, that provides for optional paper filing of a

Form 10-K or 10-KSB if it is the first document filed after a registrant's phase-in date.

(b) *Third party filers.* Any third party filing made pursuant to Section 13 or 14 of the Exchange Act with respect to a registrant that is subject to mandated electronic filing shall be filed in electronic format.

(c) *Electronic filings involving both a paper filer and an electronic filer.* Filings involving both a paper filer and an electronic filer shall be made as follows:

(1) *Cash tender offers and proxy contests.* Where a paper filer commences a cash tender offer or proxy contest (including a solicitation in opposition) with respect to an electronic filer, submissions by both filers relating to the transaction shall be in electronic format. Where an electronic filer commences a cash tender offer or proxy contest with respect to a paper filer, the electronic filer is permitted, but not required, to submit all filings in electronic format. If the electronic filer elects to file in electronic format in connection with the transaction, all related submissions by the electronic filer must be in electronic format. If the electronic filer elects to file in electronic format, the paper filer is permitted, but not required, to submit all filings in electronic format. If the paper filer elects to file in electronic format, the paper filer shall continue to make all filings relating to that transaction in electronic format.

(2)(i) *Securities Act registered business combinations.* Where a paper filer engages in an exchange offer, merger, or other business combination involving a Securities Act registration statement filed by that entity with respect to an electronic filer, submissions by both parties relating to that transaction shall be in electronic format. Where an electronic filer engages in an exchange offer, merger, or other business combination involving a Securities Act registration statement filed by that entity with respect to a paper filer, the electronic filer shall submit all filings in electronic format. The paper filer is permitted, but not required, to submit all filings in electronic format. If the paper filer elects to file in electronic format, the paper filer shall continue to make all filings relating to that transaction in electronic format.

(ii) *Cash mergers involving joint proxy statements.* Where a paper filer and an electronic filer seek a cash merger involving a joint proxy statement, submissions by both parties relating to that transaction shall be in electronic format.

(3) *Co-registrants.* Where a paper filer and an electronic filer are co-registrants with respect to an offering required to be registered under the Securities Act, the registration statement shall be filed in electronic format. Co-registrants that become subject to the reporting requirements of section 13(a) or 15(d) (15 U.S.C. 78m and 78o(d)) of the Exchange Act shall submit all reports in electronic format if one of the registrants is an electronic filer.

(4) *Schedule 13D and 13G.* Where a paper filer is required to file a Schedule 13D or 13G (§ § 240.13d-101 and 240.132-102 of this chapter) relating to an electronic filer in accordance with paragraph (b) of this section, the Schedule 13D or 13G shall be filed in electronic format. Where an electronic filer is required to file a Schedule 13D or 13G relating to a paper filer, the Schedule 13D or 13G may be filed in electronic format.

Note to paragraph (c)(4): While companies subject to mandated electronic filing generally may choose to electronically file Schedules 13D and 13G with respect to a paper filer, domestic electronic filers are restricted from doing so with respect to foreign private issuers because EDGAR currently requires an IRS tax identification number to be inserted for the subject company as a prerequisite to acceptance of the filing. Such filings should be made in paper until the EDGAR system is modified to process them electronically.

(d) *Paper Copies of Electronic Filings.* Electronic filers, including third party filers, shall submit to the Commission a paper copy of their first electronic filing, as follows:

(1) The paper copy shall be either a document that meets the requirements of the applicable Commission rules and regulations for paper filings or a paper printout of the electronic filing. If the copy being submitted is the paper printout of the electronic filing, the header information specified in the EDGAR Filer Manual shall be omitted to ensure that confidential information contained in the header remains non-public.

(2) The paper copy shall be sent to the following address: OFIS Filer Support, SEC Operations Center, 6432 General Green Way, Alexandria, VA 22312-2413. The paper copy shall be received by the Commission no later than six business days after the electronic filing. The following legend shall be typed, printed or stamped in capital letters at the top of the cover page of the paper copy:

THIS PAPER DOCUMENT IS BEING SUBMITTED PURSUANT TO RULE 901(d) OF REGULATION S-T.

(3) Signatures are not required for conforming paper format documents submitted pursuant to paragraph (d) of this section.

Citation: **17 CFR 232.902**

✍ § 232.902 Division of Investment Management EDGAR Transition.

(a) *Registrant transition to electronic submission via EDGAR.* Registrants whose filings are subject to review by the Division of Investment Management shall be subject to the electronic filing requirements of this Part ("phased in") in accordance with the phase-in schedule established and published by the Commission, including any amendments thereto (the "Phase-In Schedule"). At the conclusion of phase in, all remaining registered investment companies or business development companies shall be subject to the electronic filing requirements of this part.

Note to paragraph (a): Registrants become subject to mandated electronic filing on their phase-in date. Consequently, all documents required to be filed in electronic format pursuant to Rule 101 of Regulation S-T (§ 232.101) filed on or after a registrant's phase-in date must be filed electronically, absent a hardship exemption, even if the transaction to which a filing relates was commenced in paper before the phase-in date and is still in process on the registrant's phase-in date. See paragraph (e) of this section, that provides for optional paper filing of certain filings under Rule 497 under the Securities Act of 1933 (§ 230.497 of this chapter).

(b) *Phase-in rule for investment companies.* (1) Each registered investment company or business development company listed on the Phase-In Schedule is deemed to have the phase-in date assigned to the group in which it is included as listed on the schedule, or as may be designated by the Commission.

(2) For any investment company not listed on the Phase-In Schedule (including any company that subsequently registers under the Investment Company Act):

(i) An open-end or closed-end management investment company that has the same investment adviser or a unit investment trust that has the same depositor, as a registrant that is listed on the Phase-In Schedule shall have the same phase-in date as the registrant listed on the schedule.

(ii) A closed-end management investment company that does not have an investment advisor shall have the same phase-in data as a registrant having an investment adviser that is, or is affiliated with, the principal underwriter of the unlisted registrant.

(3) A registrant not listed on the Phase-In Schedule that has more than one investment adviser shall be deemed to have the same investment adviser as a registrant that is listed on the schedule if any of its investment advisers, other than sub-advisers, are investment advisers to the listed registrant.

(4) A registrant that is not phased in that subsequently changes its investment adviser to one that is the investment advise of a registrant that is phase in shall be deemed to be phase in at the time it changes its investment adviser.

(5) A registrant that is phased in that subsequently changes its investment adviser to one that is the investment adviser of a registrant that is not phased in shall remain phased in.

(c) *Phase-in rule for public utility filers.* When a Public Utility Filer is phase in to electronic filing in accordance with the Commission's published phase-in schedule, it will be considered phased in for purposes of all filings submitted to the Commission under the Public Utility Act, except as otherwise provided, and all such filings shall be submitted electronically, absent a hardship exemption granted by the Commission. In addition, a subsidiary company of a phased-in public-utility holding company shall be required, absent a hardship exemption granted by the Commission, to submit all required filings under the Public Utility Act electronically. Any Public Utility Filer that does not make Securities Act or Exchange Act filings and is not part of a holding company system previously phased in will be deemed to have the same phase-in date for electronic filing as the final phase-in group of registrants whose filings are subject to review by the Division of Corporation Finance.

(d) *Reassignment of phase-in group.* The Commission may, in its discretion, grant or deny a request by a registrant to participate in a phase-in group other than the group established under (b)(1) or (2) above.

(e) *Required Electronic Filing for Phased-in Filers.* A registrant that is phased in, under either the mandatory electronic filing provisions of paragraphs (a), (b), or (c) or by reassignment under paragraph (d) of this section, shall file electronically all filings which are mandated electronic submissions under Rule 101 of Regulation S-T (§ 232.101 of this chapter) and which are made on or after a registrant's phase-in date, provided, however that a registrant need not file electronically a filing, after the registrant's phase-in date, under Rule 497 under the Securities Act of 1933 (§ 230.497 of this chapter) that relates solely to a registration statement or post-effective amendment filed prior to the registrant's phase-in date and is submitted for the purpose of filing the definitive prospectus and/or statement of additional information for that registration statement or amendment. A registrant submitting electronically a Rule 497 filing for the purpose of "stickering" its prospectus and/or statement of additional information need not submit electronically the prospectus and/or statement of additional information to which the "sticker" relates, provided that the text of the prospectus and/or statement of additional information has already been filed electronically as a public document.

(f) *Electronic filings involving both a paper filer and an electronic filer.* Filings involving both a paper filer and an electronic filer shall be made as set forth in this section, *provided, however,* that the following provisions shall not affect a filer's phase-in date for mandatory electronic filing.

(1) *Cash tender offers and proxy contests.* Where a paper filer commences a cash tender offer or proxy contest (including a solicitation in opposition) with respect to an electronic filer, submissions by both filers relating to the transaction shall be in electronic format Where an electronic filer commences a cash tender offer or proxy contest with respect to a paper filer, the electronic filer is permitted, but not required, to submit all filings in electronic format. If the electronic filer elects to file in electronic format in connection with the transaction, all related submission must be in electronic format. If the electronic filer elects to file in electronic format, the paper filer is permitted, but not required, to submit all filings in electronic format. If the paper filer elects to file in electronic format, the paper filer shall continue to make all filings relating to that transaction in electronic format.

(2) *Securities Act registered business combinations.* Where a paper filer engages in an exchange offer, merger, or other business combination involving a Securities Act registration statement filed by that entity with respect to an electronic filer, submissions by both parties relating to that transaction shall be in electronic format. Where an electronic filer engages in an exchange offer, merger, or other business combination involving a Securities Act registration statement filed by that entity with respect to a paper filer, the electronic filer shall submit all filings in electronic format. The paper filer is permitted, but not required, to submits all filings in electronic format. If the paper filer elects to file in electronic format, the paper filer shall continue to make all filings relating to that transaction in electronic format.

(3) *Schedule 13D and 13G.* Where a paper filer is required to file a Schedule 13D or 13G (§ § 240.13d-101 and 240.13d-102 of this chapter) relating to an electronic filer in accordance with paragraph (b) of this section, the Schedule 13D or 13G shall be filed in electronic format. Where an electronic filer is required to file a Schedule 13D or 13G relating to a paper filer, the Schedule 13D or 13G may be filed in electronic format.

(g) *Paper Copies of Electronic Filings.* Electronic filers, including third party filers, shall submit to the Commission a paper copy of their first electronic filing, as follows:

(1) The paper copy shall be either a document that meets the requirements of the applicable Commission rules and regulations for paper filings or a paper print-out of the electronic filing. If the copy being submitted is the paper printout of the electronic filing, the header information specified in the EDGAR Filer Manual shall be omitted to ensure that confidential information contained in the header remains non-public.

(2) The paper copy shall be sent to the following address: OFIS Filer Support, SEC Operations Center, 6432 General Green Way, Alexandria, Virginia 22312-2413. The paper copy shall be received by the Commission no later than six business days after the electronic filing. The following legend shall be typed, printed or stamped in capital letters at the top of the cover page of the paper copy:

THIS PAPER DOCUMENT IS BEING SUBMITTED PURSUANT TO RULE 902(g) OF REGULATION S-T.

(3) Manual signatures are not required for conforming paper format documents submitted pursuant to paragraph (g) of this section.

(4) A filer that elects to file electronically forms permitted to be filed electronically in advance of a filer's mandatory phase-in date shall not be required to submit a paper copy of each electronic filing until the filer becomes subject to mandatory electronic filing.

Citation: **17 CFR 232.903**

✍ § 232.903 Division of Investment Management electronic submissions during transition.

In addition to the electronic submission requirements set forth in rule 101 of Regulation S-T (§ 232.101), the following provisions shall apply during the mandatory electronic filing phase-in period:-

(a) Permitted electronic submissions — (1) Filings by investment companies. Prior to its phase-in date, a filer that is a

registered investment company or a business development company may, but is not required to, submit Form N-SAR (§ 274.101 of this chapter) in electronic format, *provided that* if the filer elects to file Form N-SAR in electronic format, all subsequent amendments to the subject Form N-SAR shall be filed in electronic format.

(2) *Public Utility Act Filings.* Prior to its phase-in date, a filer submitting filings under the Public Utility Act may, but is not required to, submit those filings in electronic format *provided that,* if the filer elects to submit a filing in electronic format, all subsequent amendments to the subject filing shall be filed in electronic format.

(3) *Form 13F.* An institutional investment manager required by section 13(f)(1) (15 U.S.C. 78m(f)(1)) of, and rule 13f-1 (§ 240.13f-1 of this chapter) under, the Exchange Act to file a report on Form 13F (§ 249.235 of this chapter) with the Commission may file that report on magnetic tape in the format described in Form 13F-E (§ 249.326 of this chapter) *provided that,* if the filer elects to submit a filing in electronic format, all subsequent amendments to the subject filing shall be filed in electronic format.

(b) *Amendments to paper filings* — (1) *Filings by investment companies.* Unless otherwise specifically provided in rules or instructions pertaining to the submission of a specific form, amendments to filings filed in paper prior to the phase-in date of a registrant that is a registered investment company or a business development company shall be submitted in electronic format in accordance with rule 101 of Regulation S-T (§ 232.101). The subject filing, as amended, including any exhibit that has been previously filed only in paper and which is incorporated by reference into the filing, shall be filed electronically in its entirety, except as otherwise permitted under rules 102(b), (c), and (e) and Regulation S-T (§ § 232.102(b), (c) and (e)).

(2) *Public Utility Act Filings.* Unless otherwise specifically provided in rules or instructions pertaining to the submission of a specific form, amendments to filings under the Public Utility Act filed in paper prior to the phase-in date of the filer shall be submitted in electronic format in accordance with rules 101 and 102 of Regulation S-T (§ § 232.101 and 232.102).

PART 240. GENERAL RULES AND REGULATIONS SECURITIES EXCHANGE ACT OF 1934

Subpart A. Rules And Regulations Under the Securities Exchange Act Of 1934

Citation: 17 CFR 240.12b-11

✍ § 240.12b-11 Number of copies; signatures; binding.

* * * * *

(d) *Signatures.* Where the Act or the rules, forms, reports or schedules thereunder, including paragraph (b) of this section, require a document filed with or furnished to the Commission to be signed, such document shall be manually signed, or signed using either typed signatures or duplicated or facsimile versions of manual signatures. Where typed, duplicated or facsimile signatures are used, each signatory to the filing shall manually sign a signature page or other document authenticating, acknowledging or otherwise adopting his or her signature that appears in the filing. Such document shall be executed before or at the time the filing is made and shall be retained by the filer for a period of five years. Upon request, the filer shall furnish to the Commission or its staff a copy of any or all documents retained pursuant to this section.

Citation: 17 CFR 240.12b-12

✍ § 240.12b-12 Requirements as to paper, printing and language.

* * * * *

(e) Where a statement or report is distributed to investors through an electronic medium, issuers may satisfy legibility requirements applicable to printed documents, such as paper size and type size and font, by presenting all required information in a format readily communicated to investors.

Citation: 17 CFR 240.13e-3

✍ § 240.13e-3 Going private transactions by certain issuers or their affiliates.

* * * * *

(e) * * *

(3) * * *

Instructions to paragraph (e)(3).

1. * * *

2. * * *

3. If the information delivered to security holders is distributed through an electronic medium and the legend required by paragraph (e)(3)(ii) is included, issuers may satisfy the legibility requirement relating to type size and font by presenting the legend in any manner reasonably calculated to draw security holder attention.

* * * * *

Citation: 17 CFR 240.14a-3

✍ § 240.14a-3 Information to be furnished to security holders.

* * * * *

(b) * * *

(2) * * *

* * * * *

(ii) Where the annual report to security holders is delivered through an electronic medium, issuers may satisfy legibility requirements applicable to printed documents, such as type size and font, by presenting all required information in a format readily communicated to investors.

* * * * *

Citation: 17 CFR 240.14c-4

✍ § 240.14c-4 Presentation of information in information statement.

* * * * *

(d) Where an information statement is delivered through an electronic medium, issuers may satisfy legibility requirements applicable to printed documents, such as type size and font, by presenting all required information in a format readily communicated to investors.

Citation: 17 CFR 240.14d-1

✍ § 240.14d-1 Scope of and definitions applicable to Regulations 14D and 14E.

* * * * *

(d) *Signatures.* Where the Act or the rules, forms, reports or schedules thereunder require a document filed with or furnished to the Commission to be signed, such document shall be manually signed, or signed using either typed signatures or duplicated or facsimile versions of manual signatures. Where typed, duplicated or facsimile signatures are used, each signatory to the filing shall manually sign a signature page or other document authenticating, acknowledging or otherwise adopting his or her signature that appears in the filing. Such document shall be executed before or at the time the filing is made and shall be retained by the filer for a period of five years. Upon request, the filer shall furnish to the Commission or its staff a copy of any or all documents retained pursuant to this section.

Citation: 17 CFR 240.16a-3

✍ § 240.16a-3 Reporting transactions and holdings.

* * * * *

(i) *Signatures.* Where Section 16 of the Act, or the rules or forms thereunder, require a document filed with or furnished to the Commission to be signed, such document shall be manually signed, or signed using either typed signatures or duplicated or facsimile versions of manual signatures. Where typed, duplicated or facsimile signatures are used, each signatory to the filing shall manually sign a signature page or other document authenticating, acknowledging or otherwise adopting his or her signature that appears in the filing. Such document shall be executed before or at the time the filing is made and shall be retained by the filer for a period of five years. Upon request, the filer shall furnish to the Commission or its staff a copy of any or all documents retained pursuant to this section.

Preservation of Records and Reports of Certain Stabilizing Activities

Citation: 17 CFR 240.17a-4

✍ § 240.17a-4 Records to be preserved by certain exchange members, brokers and dealers.

(a) Every member, broker and dealer subject to § 240.17a-3 shall preserve for a period of not less than 6 years, the first 2 years in an easily accessible place, all records required to be made pursuant to § 240.17a-3(a) (1), (2), (3), and (5).

(b) Every such broker and dealer shall preserve for a period of not less than 3 years, the first two years in an accessible place:

(1) All records required to be made pursuant to § 240.17a-3(a) (4), (6), (7), (8), (9), and (10).

(2) All check books, bank statements, cancelled checks and cash reconciliations.

(3) All bills receivable or payable (or copies thereof), paid or unpaid, relating to the business of such member, broker or dealer, as such.

(4) Originals of all communications received and copies of all communications sent by such member, broker or dealer (including inter-office memoranda and communications) relating to his business as such.

(5) All trial balances, computations of aggregate indebtedness and net capital (and working papers in connection therewith), financial statements, branch office reconciliations, and internal audit working papers, relating to the business of such member, broker or dealer, as such.

(6) All guarantees of accounts and all powers of attorney and other evidence of the granting of any discretionary authority given in respect of any account, and copies of resolutions empowering an agent to act on behalf of a corporation.

(7) All written agreements (or copies thereof) entered into by such member, broker or dealer relating to his business as such, including agreements with respect to any account.

(8) Records which contain the following information in support of amounts included in the report prepared as of the audit date on Form X-17A-5 (§ 249.617 of this chapter) Part II or Part IIA and in annual audited financial statements required by § 240.17a-5(i)(xv):

(i) Money balance position, long or short, including description, quantity, price and valuation of each security including contractual commitments in customers' accounts, in cash and fully secured accounts, partly secured accounts, unsecured accounts, and in securities accounts payable to customers;

(ii) Money balance and position, long or short, including description, quantity, price and valuation of each security including contractual commitments in non-customers' accounts, in cash and fully secured accounts, partly secured and unsecured accounts, and in securities accounts payable to non-customers;

(iii) Position, long or short, including description, quantity, price and valuation of each security including contractual commitments included in the Computation of Net Capital as commitments, securities owned, securities owned not readily marketable, and other investments owned not readily market-able;

(iv) Amount of secured demand note, description of collateral securing such secured demand note including quantity, price and valuation of each security and cash balance securing such secured demand note;

(v) Description of futures commodity contracts, contract value on trade date, market value, gain or loss, and liquidating equity or deficit in customers' and non-customers' accounts;

(vi) Description of futures commodity contracts, contract value on trade date, market value, gain or loss and liquidating equity or deficit in trading and investment accounts;

(vii) Description, money balance, quantity, price and valuation of each spot commodity position or commitments in customers' and non-customers' accounts;

(viii) Description, money balance, quantity, price and valuation of each spot commodity position or commitments in trading and investment accounts;

(ix) Number of shares, description of security, exercise price, cost and market value of put and call options including short out of the money options having no market or exercise value, showing listed and unlisted put and call options separately;

(x) Quantity, price, and valuation of each security underlying the haircut for undue concentration made in the Computation for Net Capital;

(xi) Description, quantity, price and valuation of each security and commodity position or contractual commitment, long or short, in each joint account in which the broker or dealer has an interest, including each participant's interest and margin deposit;

(xii) Description, settlement date, contract amount, quantity, market price, and valuation for each aged failed to deliver requiring a charge in the Computation of Net Capital pursuant to § 240.15c3-1;

(xiii) Detail relating to information for possession or control requirements under § 240.15c3-3 and reported on the schedule in Part II or IIA of Form X-17A-5 (§ 249.617 of this chapter);

(xiv) Detail of all items, not otherwise substantiated, which are charged or credited in the Computation of Net Capital pursuant to § 240.15c3-1, such as cash margin deficiencies, deductions related to securities values and undue concentration, aged securities differences and insurance claims receivable; and

(xv) Other schedules which are specifically prescribed by the Commission as necessary to support information reported as required by § 240.17a-5.

(9) The records required to be made pursuant to § 240.15c3-3(d)(4).

(c) Every such member, broker and dealer shall preserve for a period of not less than 6 years after the closing of any customer's account any account cards or records which relate to the terms and conditions with respect to the opening and maintenance of such account.

(d) Every such member, broker and dealer shall preserve during the life of the enterprise and of any successor enterprise all partnership articles or, in the case of a corporation, all articles of incorporation or charter, minute books and stock certificate books.

(e) Every such member, broker and dealer shall maintain and preserve in an easily accessible place:

(1) All records required under paragraph (a)(12) of § 240.17a-3 until at least three years after the "associated person" has terminated his employment and any other connection with the member, broker or dealer.

(2) All records required under paragraph (a)(13) of § 240.17a-3 until at least three years after the termination of employment or association of those persons required by § 240.17f-2 to be fingerprinted; and

(3) All records required pursuant to paragraph (a)(15) of § 240.17a-3 for the life of the enterprise.

(4) All records required pursuant to paragraph (a)(14) of § 240.17a-3 for three years.

(f) The records required to be maintained and preserved pursuant to Secs. 240.17a-3 and 240.17a-4 may be immediately produced or reproduced on "micrographic media" (as defined in this section) or by means of "electronic storage media" (as defined in this section) that meet the conditions set forth in this paragraph and be maintained and preserved for the required time in that form.

(1) For purposes of this section:

(i) The term micrographic media means microfilm or microfiche, or any similar medium; and

(ii) The term electronic storage media means any digital storage medium or system and, in the case of both paragraphs (f)(1)(i) and (f)(1)(ii) of this section, that meets the applicable conditions set forth in this paragraph (f).

(2) If electronic storage media is used by a member, broker, or dealer, it shall comply with the following requirements:

(i) The member, broker, or dealer must notify its examining authority designated pursuant to section 17(d) of the Act (15 U.S.C. 78q(d)) prior to employing electronic storage media. If employing any electronic storage media other than optical disk technology (including CD-ROM), the member, broker, or dealer must notify its designated examining authority at least 90 days prior to employing such storage media. In either case, the member, broker, or dealer must provide its own representation or one from the storage medium vendor or other third party with appropriate expertise that the selected storage media meets the conditions set forth in this paragraph (f)(2).

(ii) The electronic storage media must:

(A) Preserve the records exclusively in a non-rewriteable, non-erasable format;

(B) Verify automatically the quality and accuracy of the storage media recording process;

(C) Serialize the original and, if applicable, duplicate units of storage media, and time-date for the required period of retention the information placed on such electronic storage media; and

(D) Have the capacity to readily download indexes and records preserved on the electronic storage media to any medium acceptable under this paragraph (f) as required by the Commission or the self-regulatory organizations of which the member, broker, or dealer is a member.

(3) If a member, broker, or dealer uses micrographic media or electronic storage media, it shall:

(i) At all times have available, for examination by the staffs of the Commission and self-regulatory organizations of which it is a member, facilities for immediate, easily readable projection or production of micrographic media or electronic storage media images and for producing easily readable images.

(ii) Be ready at all times to provide, and immediately provide, any facsimile enlargement which the Commission or its representatives may request.

(iii) Store separately from the original, a duplicate copy of the record stored on any medium acceptable under Sec. 240.17a-4 for the time required.

(iv) Organize and index accurately all information maintained on both original and any duplicate storage media.

(A) At all times, a member, broker, or dealer must be able to have such indexes available for examination by the staffs of the Commission and the self-regulatory organizations of which the broker or dealer is a member.

(B) Each index must be duplicated and the duplicate copies must be stored separately from the original copy of each index.

(C) Original and duplicate indexes must be preserved for the time required for the indexed records.

(v) The member, broker, or dealer must have in place an audit system providing for accountability regarding inputting of records required to be maintained and preserved pursuant to Secs. 240.17a-3 and 240.17a-4 to electronic storage media and inputting of any changes made to every original and duplicate record maintained and preserved thereby.

(A) At all times, a member, broker, or dealer must be able to have the results of such audit system available for examination by the staffs of the Commission and the self-regulatory organizations of which the broker or dealer is a member.

(B) The audit results must be preserved for the time required for the audited records.

(vi) The member, broker, or dealer must maintain, keep current, and provide promptly upon request by the staffs of the Commission or the self-regulatory organizations of which the member, broker, or broker-dealer is a member all information necessary to access records and indexes stored on the electronic storage media; or place in escrow and keep current a copy of the physical and logical file format of the electronic storage media, the field format of all different information types written on the electronic storage media and the source code, together with the appropriate documentation and information necessary to access records and indexes.

(vii) For every member, broker, or dealer exclusively using electronic storage media for some or all of its record preservation under this section, at least one third party ("the undersigned"), who has access to and the ability to download information from the member's, broker's, or dealer's electronic storage media to any acceptable medium under this section, shall file with the designated examining authority for the member, broker, or dealer the following undertakings with respect to such records:

The undersigned hereby undertakes to furnish promptly to the U.S. Securities and Exchange Commission ("Commission"), its designees or representatives, upon reasonable request, such information as is deemed necessary by the Commission's or designee's staff to download information kept on the broker's or or dealer's electronic storage media to any medium acceptable under Rule 17a-4.

Furthermore, the undersigned hereby undertakes to take reasonable steps to provide access to information contained on the broker's or dealer's electronic storage media, including, as appropriate, arrangements for the downloading of any record required to be maintained and preserved by the broker or dealer pursuant to Rules 17a-3 and 17a-4 under the Securities Exchange Act of 1934 in a format acceptable to the Commission's staff or its designee. Such arrangements will provide specifically that in the event of a failure on the part of a broker or dealer to download the record into a readable format and after reasonable notice to the broker or dealer, upon being provided with the appropriate electronic storage medium, the undersigned will undertake to do so, as the Commission's staff or its designee may request.

(g) If a person who has been subject to § 240.17a-3 ceases to transact a business in securities directly with others than members of a national securities exchange, or ceases to transact a business in securities through the medium of a member of a national securities exchange, or ceases to be registered pursuant to section 15 of the Securities Exchange Act of 1934 as amended (48 Stat. 895, 49 Stat. 1377; 15 U.S.C. 78o), such person shall, for the remainder of the periods of time specified in this section, continue to preserve the records which he theretofore preserved pursuant to this section.

(h) For purposes of transactions in municipal securities by municipal securities brokers and municipal securities dealers, compliance with Rule G-9 of the Municipal Securities Rulemaking Board will be deemed to be in compliance with this section.

(i) If the records required to be maintained and preserved pursuant to the provisions of § § 240.17a-3 and 240.17a-4 are prepared or maintained by an outside service bureau, depository, bank which does not operate pursuant to § 240.17a-3(b)(2), or other recordkeeping service on behalf of the member, broker or dealer required to maintain and preserve such records, such outside entity shall file with the Commission a written undertaking in form acceptable to the Commission, signed by a duly authorized person, to the effect that such records are the property of the member, broker or dealer required to maintain and preserve such records and will be surrendered promptly on request of the member, broker or dealer and including the following provision:

With respect to any books and records maintained or preserved on behalf of [BD], the undersigned hereby undertakes to permit examination of such books and records at any time or from time to time during business hours by representatives or designees of the Securities and Exchange Commission, and to promptly furnish to said Commission or its designee true, correct, complete and current hard copy of any or all or any part of such books and records.

Agreement with an outside entity shall not relieve such member, broker or dealer from the responsibility to prepare and maintain records as specified in this section or in § 240.17a-3.

(j) Every member, broker or dealer subject to this section shall furnish promptly to a representative of the Commission such legible, true and complete copies of those records of the member, broker or dealer, which are required to be preserved under this section, as are requested by the representative of the Commission.

Citation: 17 CFR 240.17a-6

✍ ✪ § 240.17a-6 Right of national securities exchange, national securities association, registered clearing agency or the Municipal Securities Rulemaking Board to destroy or dispose of documents.

(a) Any document kept by or on file with a national securities exchange, national securities association, registered clearing agency or the Municipal Securities Rulemaking Board pursuant to the Act or any rule or regulation thereunder may be destroyed or otherwise disposed of by such exchange, association, clearing agency or the Municipal Securities Rulemaking Board at the end of five years or at such earlier date as is specified in a plan for the destruction or disposition of any such documents if such plan has been filed with the Commission by such exchange, association, clearing agency or the Municipal Securities Rulemaking Board and has been declared effective by the Commission.

(b) Such plan may provide that any such document may be transferred to microfilm or other recording medium after such time as specified in the plan and thereafter be maintained and preserved in that form. If a national securities exchange, association, clearing agency or the Municipal Securities Rulemaking Board uses microfilm or other recording medium it shall:(1) Be ready at all times to provide, and immediately provide, easily readable projection of the microfilm or other recording medium and easily readable hard copy thereof;

(2) Provide indexes permitting the immediate location of any such document on the microfilm or other recording medium; and

(3) In the case of microfilm, store a duplicate copy of the microfilm separately from the original microfilm for the time required.

(c) For the purposes of this rule a plan filed with the Commission by a national securities exchange, association, clearing agency or the Municipal Securities Rulemaking Board shall not become effective unless the Commission, having due regard for the public interest and for the protection of investors, declares the plan to be effective. The Commission in its declaration may limit the applications, reports, and documents as to which it shall apply, and may impose any other terms and conditions to the plan and to the period of its effectiveness which it deems necessary or appropriate in the public interest or for the protection of investors.

Citation: 17 CFR 240.17f-2

✍ § 240.17f-2 Fingerprinting of securities industry personnel.

* * * * *

(d) *Record maintenance* — (1) *Maintenance of processed fingerprint cards and other related information.* Every member of a national securities exchange, broker, dealer, registered transfer agent and registered clearing agency shall maintain the processed fingerprint card or any substitute record when such card is not returned after processing, together with any information received from the Attorney General or its designee, for every person required to be fingerprinted under section 17(f)(2) of the Securities Exchange Act of 1934 and for persons who have complied with this section pursuant to paragraph (b) or (c) of this section. Every substitute record shall state the name of the person whose fingerprint card was submitted to the Attorney General of the United States, the name of the member of a national securities exchange, broker, dealer, registered transfer agent or registered clearing agency that submitted the fingerprint card, the name of the person or organization that rolled the fingerprints, the date on which the fingerprints were rolled, and the date the fingerprint card was submitted to the Attorney General of the United States. The processed fingerprint card and every other substitute record containing the information required by this paragraph, together with any information received from the Attorney General of the United States, shall be kept in an easily accessible place at the organization's principal office and shall be made available upon request to the Commission, the appropriate regulatory agency (if not the Commission) or other designated examining authority. The organization's principal office must provide to the regional, branch or satellite office actually employing the person written evidence that the person's fingerprints have been processed by the FBI, and must provide to that office a copy of any criminal history record information received from the FBI. All fingerprint cards, records and information required to be maintained under this paragraph shall be retained for a period of not less than three years after termination of that person's employment or relationship with the organization.

(2) *Record maintenance by designated examining authorities.* The records required to be maintained and preserved by a member of a national securities exchange, broker, or dealer pursuant to the requirements of paragraph (d)(1) of this section may be maintained and preserved on behalf of that member, broker, or dealer by a self-regulatory organization that is also the designated examining authority for that member, broker or dealer, Provided That the self-regulatory organization has filed in accordance with 240.17f-2(c) a fingerprinting plan or amendments to an existing plan concerning the storage and maintenance of records and that plan, as amended, has been declared effective by the Commission, and Provided Further That:

(i) Such records are subject at any time, or from time to time, to reasonable periodic, special or other examinations by representatives of the Commission; and

(ii) The self-regulatory organization furnishes to the Commission, upon demand, at either the principal office or at the regional office complete, correct and current hard copies of any and all such records.

(3) *Reproduction of records on microfilm.* The records required to be maintained pursuant to paragraph (d)(1) of this section may be produced or reproduced on microfilm and preserved in that form. If such microfilm substitution for hard copy is made by a member of a national securities exchange, broker, dealer, registered transfer agent or registered clearing agency, or by a self-regulatory organization maintaining and storing records pursuant to paragraph (d)(2) of this section, it shall at all times:

(i) Have available for examination by the Commission, the appropriate regulatory agency (if not the Commission) or other designated examining authority, facilities for the immediate, easily readable projection of the microfilm and for the production of easily readable and legible facsimile enlargements;

(ii) File and index the films in such a manner as to permit the immediate location and retrieval of any particular record;

(iii) Be ready to provide, and immediately provide, any facsimile enlargement which the Commission, the appropriate regulatory agency (if not the Commission) or other designated examining authority by their examiners or other representatives may request; and

(iv) For the period for which the microfilm records are required to be maintained, stored separately from the original microfilm records a copy of the microfilm records.

(e) *Notice requirement.* Every member of a national securities exchange, broker, dealer, registered transfer agent and registered clearing agency that claims one or more of the exemptions in paragraph (a)(1) of this section shall make and keep current a statement entitled "Notice Pursuant to Rule 17f-2" containing the information specified in paragraph (e)(1) of this section.

* * * * *

(2) *Record maintenance.* A copy of the Notice required to be made and kept current under paragraph (e) of this section shall be kept in an easily accessible place at the organization's principal office and at the office employing the persons for whom exemptions are claimed and shall be made available upon request for inspection by the Commission, appropriate regulatory agency (if not the Commission) or other designated examining authority.

(3) *Exemption from the notice requirement.* A registered transfer agent that performs transfer agent functions only on behalf of itself as an issuer and that receives fewer than 500 items for transfer and fewer than 500 items for processing during any six consecutive months shall be exempt from the Notice requirement of paragraph (c) of this section.

Citation: 17 CFR 240.17Ad-7

✍ § 240.17Ad-7 Record retention.

(a) The records required by § 240.17Ad-6(a)(1), (3)(i), (6) or (11) shall be maintained for a period of not less than two years, the first six months in an easily accessible place.

(b) The records required by § 240.17Ad-6(a) (2), (3)(ii), (4), (5) or (7) shall be maintained for a period of not less than two years, the first year in an easily accessible place.

(c) The records required by § 240.17Ad-6(a) (8), (9) and (10) and (b) shall be maintained in an easily accessible place during the continuance of the transfer agency and shall be maintained for one year after termination of the transfer agency.

(d) The records required by § 240.17Ad-6(c) shall be maintained for a period of not less than six years, the first six months in an easily accessible place.

(e) Every registered transfer agent shall maintain in an easily accessible place:

(1) All records required under § 240.17f-2(d) until at least three years after the termination of employment of those persons required by § 240.17f-2 to be fingerprinted; and

(2) All records required pursuant to § 240.17f-2(e).

(f) The records required to be maintained pursuant to § 240.17Ad-6 may be produced or reproduced on microfilm and be preserved in that form for the time required by § 240.17Ad-7. If such microfilm substitution for hard copy is made by a registered transfer agent, it shall:

(1) At all times have available for examination by the Commission and the appropriate regulatory agency for such transfer agent, facilities for immediate, easily readable projection of the microfilm and for producing easily readable facsimile enlargements;

(2) Arrange the records and index and file the films in such a manner as to permit the immediate location of any particular record;

(3) Be ready at all times to provide, and immediately provide, any facsimile enlargement which the Commission and the appropriate regulatory agency by their examiners or other representatives may request; and

(4) For the period for which the microfilmed records are required to be maintained, store separately from the original microfilm records a copy of the microfilm records.

(g) If the records required to be maintained and preserved by a registered transfer agent pursuant to the requirements of 240.17Ad-6 and 240.17Ad-7 are maintained and preserved on behalf of the registered transfer agent by an outside service bureau, other recordkeeping service or the issuer, the registered transfer agent shall obtain, from such outside service bureau, other recordkeeping service or the issuer, an agreement, in writing, to the effect that:

(1) Such records are subject at any time, or from time to time, to reasonable periodic, special, or other examinations by representatives of the Commission and the appropriate regulatory agency for such registered transfer agent if it is not the Commission; and

(2) The outside service bureau, recordkeeping service, or issuer will furnish to the Commission and the appropriate regulatory agency, upon demand, at either the principal office or at any regional office, complete, correct and current hard copies of any and all such records.

(h) When a registered transfer agent ceases to perform transfer agent functions for an issue, the responsibility of such transfer agent under § 240.17Ad-7 to retain the records required to be made and kept current under § 240.17Ad-6(a) (1), (6), (9), (10) and (11), (b) and (c) shall end upon the delivery of such records to the successor transfer agent.

Citation: 17 CFR 240.24b-2

✍ § 240.24b-2 Nondisclosure of information filed with the Commission and with any exchange.

Preliminary Note

Confidential treatment requests shall be submitted in paper format only, whether or not the filer is required to submit a filing in electronic format.

* * * * *

PART 257. PRESERVATION AND DESTRUCTION OF RECORDS OF REGISTERED PUBLIC UTILITY HOLDING COMPANIES AND OF MUTUAL AND SUBSIDIARY SERVICE COMPANIES

Citation: 17 CFR 257.1

✍ § 257.1 General instructions.

(a) *Scope of regulations.* The General Instructions and Schedule apply to any holding company, except an electric or gas utility company, registered as a holding company under the Public Utility Holding Company Act of 1935, and to companies found by the Commission, pursuant to § 250.88 to meet the requirements of Section 13 of the Act as mutual subsidiary service companies.

(1) Company means a service company subject to § 250.93, or a holding company subject to § 250.26, which is not an electric utility company or a gas utility company, and any predecessor or inactive or dissolved associate company, the records of which are in the possession or control of such company.

(2) Records include any records prepared, maintained or held by any agent or employee of a company, including any such records of a stock transfer agent, registrar, paying agent, indenture trustee or other person employed by a company to perform services with respect to the securities of the company, insofar as such person is accountable to the company or to its security holders for such records. The specification in the schedule of a record related to a type of transaction includes all documents and correspondence, not redundant or duplicative of other records retained, needed to explain or verify such transaction. Supporting documents such as checks or vouchers, which are separately scheduled may, nevertheless, be destroyed in accordance with the schedule for their respective class, when the company determines that the lapse of time has made it unlikely that it will need to prove the details evidenced thereby.

(3) Any company subject to this regulation, which, as agent, operator, lessor or otherwise, maintains or has possession of any records relating to the operation, property or obligations of an electric or gas utility company or natural gas company or a nuclear licensee, as defined in the Federal Power Act, the Natural Gas Act, the Atomic Energy Act or the laws of any state within which such utility company operates, shall comply with the laws or regulations as to record retention and destruction which would apply to such records if they were records of such utility company or licensee.

(4) Except for the certifications, indices and cross references specified herein, the regulation shall not be construed as requiring the preparation or maintenance of records not required to be prepared or maintained by other rules or regulations of the Commission.

(5) The regulation shall not excuse compliance with any other lawful requirement for the preservation of records for periods longer than those prescribed in the regulation.

(6) Duplicate copies of records which contain no significant information not shown on the copy preserved may be destroyed at any time. If the same document would be required under more than one scheduled item, such as an indenture also included as an exhibit in a filing required to be retained, only one copy need be preserved if cross references are substituted for the additional copies.

(7) Notwithstanding the provisions of the regulation, the Commission may, upon the request of any company, authorize the destruction of any specified records of such company and the Commission, on its own motion or on the motion of any regulatory agency, may direct that records which would be useful in developing facts relevant to any transaction recorded by the company be preserved for such period as the Commission may specify.

* * * * *

(c) *Protection and storage of records.* The company shall provide reasonable protection from damage by fire, flood, and other hazards for records required by the regulation to be preserved and, in the selection of storage space, safeguard such records from unnecessary exposure to deterioration from excessive humidity, dryness, or lack of proper ventilation.

(d) *Index of records.* At each office of the company where records are kept or stored, such records as are required by the regulation to be preserved shall be so arranged, filed, and currently indexed that such records shall be readily available for inspection by authorized representatives of regulatory agencies concerned.

(e) *Definition of record media.* (1) The data constituting the records listed in the schedules may be retained in any of the media forms in Figure 1 of this section, if the media selected has a standard life expectancy equal to or in excess of the specified retention period. In cases where media regeneration to achieve full length of period retention becomes necessary, the company shall take such action as prudence calls for and notify the Commission immediately thereafter. The specifications in Figure 1 are generic. At the request of a company, the Commission may authorize alternative media reasonably equivalent to those specified.

(2) If the media form of the record retained is other than a readable paper copy, then reader and/or printer equipment and related printout programs, if required, shall be provided by the company for data reference.

(3) The media form initially selected for the record becomes the "original" for that particular record. If subsequent conditions (e.g., improved media life expectancy, increased company resources, increased securities sales) require and the remaining

retention period permits a change in the media forms, the company may convert to another media and dispose of its old equipment, provided the certification processes described in paragraph (f) of this section are observed and data referencing capability is maintained.

Figure 1. Record Media

Record media/form	Comments and standards
1. Paper and card stock (hardcopy).	For each document, paper stock should be selected with a life expectancy equal to or greater than the retention period specified for that document.
2. Tape: a. Magnetic (including video tape).	Assumes storage in a controlled environment with a temperature and humidity range of 60°-80° F. and 40-60%, respectively.
b. Punched.	For each record, tape media (paper, mylar, metallic base) should be selected with a life expectancy equal to or greater than the retention period for that record.
3. Microforms: a. Microfilm, including Computer Output Microfilm ("COM"), microfiche jackets, and aperture cards).	Assumes processing to standards and storage in a controlled environment with a temperature and humidity range of 60°-80° F. and 40-50% respectively. (Ref. American National Standards Institute ("ANSI") standards PH 5.4—1970, PH 1.41—1976, PH 1.28—1979, Ph 1.43—1981, or most current standards as accepted by the National Archives for use by Federal agencies. (See 41 CFR. 101-11.5).
b. Metallic recording data strips.	Same storage conditions as for microfilm.

(f)*Microform, tape and computer output certification.* — (1) As the initial recording media —

}(A) The series is prepared in accordance with written standard procedures developed, or accepted general business practices followed, by the company that ensure the integrity of record series that are the product of computer output; and

(B) Such procedures include the name or title of the official responsible for validating or confirming the data contained in the record series and confirming that a particular computer output record series was produced in accordance with the standard procedures or practices.

(iii) Each tape record series shall be externally labeled and there shall be prepared for that series an introduction stating the record series title, date prepared, the name of the official responsible for validating or confirming the data contained therein and an index where appropriate. Each record series shall be closed with a clear and standard notation indicating the completion of that series and the date.

(2) Conversion from other media — (i) Each microform record series shall include, as an integral part, a certificate(s) stating that the microforms are direct and facsimile reproductions of the original records and that they have been made in accordance with prescribed instructions. Such certificate(s) shall be executed by a person(s) having personal knowledge of the facts covered thereby.

(ii) Each microform record series shall commence and end with a statement as to the nature and arrangement of the records reproduced, and the date. Rolls of film shall not be cut except to produce jacketed microfiche. Supplemental or retaken film, whether of misplaced or omitted documents or of portions of microform found to be defective, shall be attached to the beginning of the microform record series. If supplemental or retaken film of misplaced or omitted documents, or of portions of microfilm found to be defective, are attached to the microfilm record series, the certificate described in paragraph (f)(l)(i) shall cover the supplemental or retaken film and shall state the reasons for the attachment.

When a retrieval system (e.g., image count indexing ("blipping")) is used, the supplemental or retaken film may be attached at the end of the series, if the provisions at the beginning of the series advise the viewer of the location of the problem frames and the supplemental or retaken images.

(iii) If, in accordance with the provisions of paragraph (g) of this section, the company elects to convert records to the tape media, the same certification provisions specified in paragraph (f)(l)(iii) of this section must be provided in the conversion program.

(g) *Change of media for existing records.* Those records prepared and maintained under previous regulations in a paper media and whose remaining retention period falls within the life expectancy range of any of the media detailed in Figure 1, may be converted to that media at the company's option, provided the applicable certification processes described in paragraph (f) of this section are observed and an audit referencing capability maintained.

(h) *Media.* (1) All records created or maintained in a media shall —

(i) Be prepared, arranged, classified, identified, and indexed as to permit the subsequent location, examination, and reproduction of the record to a readable media;

(ii) Be stored in such a manner as to provide reasonable protection from hazards such as fire, flood, theft, etc., and be maintained in a controlled environment; and

(iii) Be regenerated, including proper certification, when damaged.

(2) The company shall be prepared to furnish, at its own expense, standard facilities for reading media and shall additionally provide, if the Commission so directs, copies of records in a readable form.

(3) All film stock shall be of approved operationally-permanent-record microcopying type, which meets the current specifications of the American National Standards Institute.

(4) Punched cards, tape or similar media used as intermediate records or steps in data processing for assembling data to be posted to the records of the company or used in a report or study can be destroyed at the option of the company.

(i) *Destruction of Records.* The destruction of the records permitted to be destroyed under the provisions of the regulations in this part may be performed in any manner elected by the company. Precautions should be taken, however, to macerate or otherwise destroy the legibility of records, the content of which is forbidden by law to be divulged to unauthorized persons.

(j) *Premature destruction or loss of records.* When records are destroyed or lost before the expiration of the prescribed period of retention, a statement listing, as far as may be determined, the records destroyed and describing the circumstances of accidental or other premature destruction or loss shall be filed with the Commission within ninety (90) days from the date of discovery of such destruction or loss.

* * * * *

PART 270. RULES AND REGULATIONS, INVESTMENT COMPANY ACT OF 1940

Citation: 17 CFR 270.7d-1

✍ **§ 270.7d-1 Specification of conditions and arrangements of Canadian management investment companies requesting order permitting registration.**

* * * * *

(b) An application filed pursuant to this section shall contain, inter alia, the following undertakings and agreements of the applicant:

* * * * *

(8) Applicant's Charter and By Laws, taken together, will contain, so long as applicant is registered under the act in substance the following:

* * * * *

(iii) Applicant will maintain the original or duplicate copies of its books and records at the office of its custodian or other office located within the United States.

* * * * *

(viii) Any contract entered into between the applicant and its investment adviser and principal underwriter will contain provisions in compliance with the requirements of sections 15, 17(i) and 31 and the rules thereunder, and require that the investment adviser maintain in the United States its books and records or duplicate copies thereof relating to applicant.

Citation: 17 CFR 270.8b-12

✍ **§ 270.8b-12 Requirements as to paper, printing and language.**

* * * * *

(f) Where a registration statement or report is distributed through an electronic medium, issuers may satisfy legibility requirements applicable to printed documents, such as paper size, type size and font, bold-face type, italics and red ink, by presenting all required information in a format readily communicated to investors, and where indicated, in a manner reasonably calculated to draw investor attention to specific information.

Citation: 17 CFR 270.31a-1

✍ **§ 270.31a-1 Records to be maintained by registered investment companies, certain majority-owned subsidiaries thereof, and other persons having transactions with registered investment companies.**

(a) Every registered investment company, and every underwriter, broker, dealer, or investment adviser which is a majority-owned subsidiary of such a company, shall maintain and keep current the accounts, books, and other documents relating to its business which constitute the record forming the basis for financial statements required to be filed pursuant to Section 30 of the Investment Company Act of 1940 and of the auditor's certificates relating thereto.

(b) Every registered investment company shall maintain and keep current the following books, accounts, and other documents:

(1) Journals (or other records of original entry) containing an itemized daily record in detail of all purchases and sales of securities (including sales and redemptions of its own securities), all receipts and deliveries of securities (including certificate numbers if such detail is not recorded by custodian or transfer agent), all receipts and disbursements of cash and all other debits and credits. Such records shall show for each such transaction the name and quantity of securities, the unit and aggregate purchase or sale price, commission paid, the market on which effected, the trade date, the settlement date, and the name of the person through or from whom purchased or received or to whom sold or delivered. In the case of a money market fund, also identify the provider of any put (as defined in § 270.2a-7(a)(16) or guarantee with respect to a portfolio security and give a brief description of the nature of the put (*e.g.*, unconditional demand feature, conditional demand feature, guarantee, letter of credit, or bond insurance) and, in a subsidiary portfolio investment record, provide the complete legal name and accounting and other imformation (including sufficient information to calculate coupons, accruals, maturities, puts, and calls) necessary to identify, value, and account for each investment.

(2) General and auxiliary ledgers (or other records) reflecting all assets, liability, reserve, capital, income and expense accounts, including:

(i) Separate ledger accounts (or other records) reflecting the following (a) Securities in transfer; (b) Securities in physical possession; (c) Securities borrowed and securities loaned; (d) Monies borrowed and monies loaned (together with a record of the collateral therefor and substitutions in such collateral); (e) Dividends and interest received; (f) Dividends receivable and interest accrued.

Instruction. (a) and (b) of this subdivision shall be stated in terms of securities quantities only; (c) and (d) of this subdivision shall be stated in dollar amounts and securities quantities as appropriate; (e) and (f) of this subdivision shall be stated in dollar amounts only.

(ii) Separate ledger accounts (or other records) for each portfolio security, showing (as of trade dates) (a) the quantity and unit and aggregate price for each purchase, sale, receipt, and delivery of securities and commodities for such accounts, and (b) all other debits and credits for such accounts. Securities positions and money balances in such ledger accounts (or other records) shall be brought forward periodically but not less frequently than at the end of fiscal quarters.

Any portfolio security, the salability of which is conditioned, shall be so noted. A memorandum record shall be available setting forth, with respect to each portfolio security account, the amount and declaration ex-dividend, and payment dates of each dividend declared thereon.

(iii) Separate ledger accounts (or other records) for each broker-dealer bank or other person with or through which transactions in portfolio securities are effected, showing each purchase or sale of securities with or through such persons, including details as to the date of the purchase or sale, the quantity and unit and aggregate price of such securities, and the commissions or other compensation paid to such persons. Purchases or sales effected during the same day at the same price may be aggregated.

(iv) Separate ledger accounts (or other records), which may be maintained by a transfer agent or registrar, showing for each shareholder of record of the investment company the number of shares of capital stock of the company held. In respect of share accumulation accounts (arising from periodic investment plans, dividend reinvestment plans, deposit of issued shares by the owner thereof, etc.), details shall be available as to the dates and number of shares of each accumulation, and except with respect to already issued shares deposited by the owner thereof, prices of each such accumulation.

(3) A securities record or ledger reflecting separately for each portfolio security as of trade date all "long" and "short" positions carried by the investment company for its own account and showing the location of all securities long and the off-setting position to all securities short. The record called for by this paragraph shall not be required in circumstances under which all portfolio securities are maintained by a bank or banks or a member or members of a national securities exchange as custodian under a custody agreement or as agent for such custodian.

(4) Corporate charters, certificates of incorporation or trust agreements, and by-laws, and minute books of stockholders' and directors' or trustees' meetings; and minute books of directors' or trustees' committee and advisory board or advisory committee meetings.

(5) A record of each brokerage order given by or in behalf of the investment company for, or in connection with, the purchase or sale of securities, whether executed or unexecuted. Such record shall include the name of the broker, the terms and conditions of the order and of any modification or cancellation thereof, the time of entry or cancellation, the price at which executed, and the time of receipt of report of execution. The record shall indicate the name of the person who placed the order in behalf of the investment company.

(6) A record of all other portfolio purchases or sales showing details comparable to those prescribed in paragraph (b)(5) of this section.

(7) A record of all puts, calls, spreads, straddles, and other options in which the investment company has any direct or indirect interest or which the investment company has granted or guaranteed; and a record of any contractual commitments to purchase, sell, receive or deliver securities or other property (but not including open orders placed with broker-dealers for the purchase or sale of securities, which may be cancelled by the company on notices without penalty or cost of any kind); containing, at least, an identification of the security, the number of units involved, the option price, the date of maturity, the date of issuance, and the person to whom issued.

(8) A record of the proof of money balances in all ledger accounts (except shareholder accounts), in the form of trial balances. Such trial balances shall be prepared currently at least once a month.

(9) A record for each fiscal quarter, which shall be completed within ten days after the end of such quarter, showing specifically the basis or bases upon which the allocation of orders for the purchase and sale of portfolio securities to named brokers or dealers and the division of brokerage commissions or other compensation on such purchase and sale orders among named persons were made during such quarter. The record shall indicate the consideration given to (i) sales of shares of the investment company by brokers or dealers, (ii) the supplying of services or benefits by brokers or dealers to the investment company, its investment adviser or principal underwriter or any persons affiliated therewith, and (iii) any other considerations other than the technical qualifications of the brokers and dealers as such. The record shall show the nature of the services or benefits made available, and shall describe in detail the application of any general or specific formula or other determinant used in arriving at such allocation of purchase and sale orders and such division of brokerage commissions or other compensation. The record shall also include the identities of the persons responsible for the determination of such allocation and such division of brokerage commissions or other compensation.

(10) A record in the form of an appropriate memorandum identifying the person or persons, committees, or groups authorizing the purchase or sale of portfolio securities. Where an authorization is made by a committee or group, a record shall be kept of the names of its members who participated in the authorization. There shall be retained as part of the record required by this paragraph any memorandum, recommendation, or instruction supporting or authorizing the purchase or sale of portfolio securities. The requirements of this paragraph are applicable to the extent they are not met by compliance with the requirements of paragraph (b)(4) of this section.

(11) Files of all advisory material received from the investment adviser, any advisory board or advisory committee, or any other persons from whom the investment advice, other than material which is furnished solely through uniform publications distributed generally.

(12) The term "other records" as used in the expressions "journals (or other records of original entry)" and "ledger accounts (or other records)" shall be construed to include, where appropriate, copies of voucher checks, confirmations, or similar documents which reflect the information required by the applicable rule or rules in appropriate sequence and in permanent form, including similar records developed by the use of automatic data processing systems.

(c) Every underwriter, broker, or dealer which is a majority-owned subsidiary of a registered investment company shall maintain in the form prescribed therein such accounts, books and other documents as are required to be maintained by brokers and dealers by rule adopted under section 17 of the Securities Exchange Act of 1934.

(d) Every depositor of any registered investment company, and every principal underwriter for any registered investment company other than a closed-end investment company, shall maintain such accounts, books and other documents as are required to be maintained by brokers and dealers by rule adopted under section 17 of the Securities Exchange Act of 1934, to the extent such records are necessary or appropriate to record such person's transactions with such registered investment company.

(e) Every investment advisor which is a majority-owned subsidiary of a registered investment company shall maintain in the form prescribed therein such accounts, books and other documents as are required to be maintained by registered investment advisers by rule adopted under section 204 of the Investment Advisers Act of 1940.

(f) Every investment adviser not a majority-owned subsidiary of a registered investment company shall maintain such accounts, books and other documents as are required to be maintained by registered investment advisers by rule adopted under section 204 of the Investment Advisers Act of 1940, to the extent such records are necessary or appropriate to record such person's transactions with such registered investment company.

Citation: 17 CFR 270.31a-2

✍ **§ 270.31a-2 Records to be preserved by registered investment companies, certain majority-owned subsidiaries thereof, and other persons having -transactions with registered investment companies.**

(a) Every registered investment company shall:

(1) Preserve permanently, the first two years, in an easily accessible place, all books and records required to be made pursuant to paragraphs (1) through (4) of § 270.31a-1(b);

(2) Preserve for a period not less than six years from the end of the fiscal year in which any transactions occurred, the first two years in an easily accessible place, all books and records required to be made pursuant to paragraphs (5) through (12) or § 270.31a-1(b) and all vouchers, memoranda, correspondence, checkbooks, bank statements, cancelled checks, cash

reconciliations, cancelled stock certificates, and all schedules evidencing and supporting each computation of net asset value of the investment company shares, and other documents required to be maintained by § 270.31a-1(a) and not enumerated in 270.31a-1(b).

(3) Preserve for a period not less than 6 years from the end of the fiscal year last used, the first 2 years in an easily accessible place, any advertisement, pamphlet, circular, form letter or other sales literature addressed to or intended for distribution to prospective investors.

(b) Every underwriter, broker, or dealer which is a majority-owned subsidiary of a registered investment company shall preserve for the periods prescribed therein such accounts, books and other documents as are required to be preserved by brokers and dealers by rule adopted under section 17 of the Securities Exchange Act of 1934.

(c) Every depositor of any registered investment company, and every principal underwriter for any registered investment company other than a closed-end company, shall preserve for a period of not less than six years such accounts, books and other documents as are required to be maintained by brokers and dealers by rule adopted under section 17 of the Securities Exchange Act of 1934, to the extent such records are necessary or appropriate to record such person's transactions with such registered investment company.

(d) Every investment adviser which is a majority-owned subsidiary of a registered investment company shall preserve for the periods prescribed therein such accounts, books and other documents as are required to be preserved by investment advisers by rule adopted under section 204 of the Investment Advisers Act of 1940.

(e) Every investment adviser not a majority-owned subsidiary of a registered investment company shall preserve for a period of not less than six years such accounts, books and other documents as are required to be maintained by registered investment advisers by rule adopted under section 204 of the Investment Advisers Act of 1940, to the extent such records are necessary or appropriate to record such person's transactions with such registered investment company.

(f)(1) The records required to be maintained and preserved under paragraphs (a) through (d) of Rule 31a-1 and paragraphs (a) through (c) of Rule 31a-2 may be immediately produced or reproduced on photographic film or, as provided in paragraph (f)(2) of this section, on magnetic tape, disk, or other computer storage medium, and be maintained and preserved for the required time in that form. If such records are produced or reproduced by photographic film or computer storage medium by, or on behalf of, an investment company, such investment company shall:

(i) Arrange the records and index and file the films or computer storage medium in such a manner as to permit the immediate access and retrieval of any particular record;

(ii) Be ready at all times to provide, and promptly provide, any facsimile enlargement of film or computer printout or copies of the computer storage medium that the Commission, by its examiners or other representatives, or the directors of such investment company may request;

(iii) Store separately from the original one other copy of the photographic film or computer storage medium for the time required;

(iv) With respect to records stored on computer storage medium, maintain procedures for maintenance and preservation of, and access to, records so as to reasonably safeguard records from loss, alteration, or destruction; and

(v) With respect to records stored on photographic film, at all times have available for examination of its records by the Commission, pursuant to section 31 of the Investment Company Act of 1940, or by the directors of such investment company, facilities for immediate, easily readable projection of the photographic film and for producing easily readable facsimile enlargements.

(2) Under paragraph (f)(1) of this section, an investment company may maintain and preserve on computer tape, disk, or other computer storage medium records that, in the ordinary course of the investment company's business, are created by, or on behalf of, the investment company on electronic media or are received by, or on behalf of, the investment company solely on electronic media or by electronic data transmission.

(3) Notwithstanding the provisions of paragraphs (a) through (e) of this section, any record, book or other document may be destroyed in accordance with a plan previously submitted to and approved by the Commission. A plan shall be deemed to have been approved by the Commission if notice to the contrary has not been received within 90 days after submission of the plan to the Commission.

PART 275. RULES AND REGULATIONS, INVESTMENT ADVISERS ACT OF 1940

Citation: 17 CFR 275.204-2

✍ **§ 275.204-2 Books and records to be maintained by investment advisers.**

(a) Every investment adviser who makes use of the mails or of any means or instrumentality of interstate commerce in connection with his or its business as an investment adviser (other than one specifically exempted from registration pursuant to section 203(b) of the Act) shall make and keep true, accurate and current the following books and records relating to his investment advisory business:

(1) A journal or journals, including cash receipts and disbursements, records, and any other records of original entry forming the basis of entries in any ledger.

(2) General and auxiliary ledgers (or other comparable records) reflecting asset, liability, reserve, capital, income and expense accounts.

(3) A memorandum of each order given by the investment adviser for the purchase or sale of any security, of any instruction received by the investment adviser concerning the purchase, sale, receipt or delivery of a particular security, and of any modification or cancellation of any such order or instruction. Such memoranda shall show the terms and conditions of the order, instruction, modification or cancellation; shall identify the person connected with the investment adviser who recommended the transaction to the client and the person who placed such order; and shall show the account for which entered, the date of entry, and the bank, broker or dealer by or through whom executed where appropriate. Orders entered pursuant to the exercise of discretionary power shall be so designated.

(4) All check books, bank statements, cancelled checks and cash reconciliations of the investment adviser.

(5) All bills or statements (or copies thereof), paid or unpaid, relating to the business of the investment adviser as such.

(6) All trial balances, financial statements, and internal audit papers relating to the business of such investment adviser.

(7) Originals of all written communications received and copies of all written communications sent by such investment adviser relating to (i) any recommendation made or proposed to be made and any advice given or proposed to be given, (ii) any receipt, disbursement or delivery of funds or securities, or (iii) the placing or execution of any order to purchase or sell any

security; Provided, however, (a) That the investment adviser shall not be required to keep any unsolicited market letters and other similar communications of general public distribution not prepared by or for the investment adviser, and (b) that if the investment adviser sends any notice, circular or other advertisement offering any report, analysis, publication or other investment advisory service to more than 10 persons, the investment adviser shall not be required to keep a record of the names and addresses of the persons to whom it was sent; except that if such notice, circular or advertisement is distributed to persons named on any list, the investment adviser shall retain with the copy of such notice, circular or advertisement a memorandum describing the list and the source thereof.

(8) A list or other record of all accounts in which the investment adviser is vested with any discretionary power with respect to the funds, securities or transactions of any client.

(9) All power of attorney and other evidences of the granting of any discretionary authority by any client to the investment adviser, or copies thereof.

(10) All written agreements (or copies thereof) entered into by the investment adviser with any client or otherwise relating to the business of such investment adviser as such.

(11) A copy of each notice, circular, advertisement, newspaper article, investment letter, bulletin or other communication recommending the purchase or sale of a specific security, which the investment adviser circulates or distributes, directly or indirectly, to 10 or more persons (other than investment supervisory clients or persons connected with such investment adviser), and if such notice, circular, advertisement, newspaper article, investment letter, bulletin, or other communication does not state the reasons for such recommendation, a memorandum of the investment adviser indicating the reasons therefor.

(12)(i) A record of every transaction in a security in which the investment adviser or any advisory representative (as hereinafter defined) of such investment adviser has, or by reason of such transaction acquires, any direct or indirect beneficial ownership, except (A) transactions effected in any account over which neither the investment adviser nor any advisory representative of the investment adviser has any direct or indirect influence or control; and (B) transactions in securities which are direct obligations of the United States. Such record shall state the title and amount of the security involved; the date and nature of the transaction (i.e., purchase, sale or other acquisition or disposition); the price at which it was effected; and the name of the broker, dealer or bank with or through whom the transaction was effected. Such record may also contain a statement declaring that the reporting or recording of any such transaction shall not be construed as an admission that the investment adviser or advisory representative has any direct or indirect beneficial ownership in the security. A transaction shall be recorded not later than 10 days after the end of the calendar quarter in which the transaction was effected.

* * * * *

(13)(i) Notwithstanding the provisions of paragraph (a)(12) of this section above, where the investment adviser is primarily engaged in a business or businesses other than advising registered investment companies or other advisory clients, a record must be maintained of every transaction in a security in which the investment adviser or any advisory representative (as hereinafter defined) of such investment adviser has, or by reason of such transaction acquires, any direct or indirect beneficial ownership, except (A) transactions effected in any account over which neither the investment adviser nor any advisory representative of the investment adviser has any direct or indirect influence or control; and (B) transactions in securities which are direct obligations of the United States. Such record shall state the title and amount of the security involved; the date and nature of the transaction (i.e., purchase, sale or other acquisition or disposition); the price at which it was effected; and the name of the broker, dealer or bank with or through whom the transaction was effected. Such record may also contain a statement declaring that the reporting or recording of any such transaction shall not be construed as an admission that the investment adviser or advisory representative has any direct or indirect beneficial ownership in the security. A transaction shall be recorded not later than 10 days after the end of the calendar quarter in which the transaction was effected.

* * * * *

(14) A copy of each written statement and each amendment or revision thereof, given or sent to any client or prospective client of such investment adviser in accordance with the provisions of Rule 204-3 under the Act, and a record of the dates that each written statement, and each amendment or revision thereof, was given, or offered to be given, to any client or prospective client who subsequently becomes a client.

(15) All written acknowledgments of receipt obtained from clients pursuant to § 275.206(4)-3(a)(2)(iii)(B) and copies of the disclosure documents delivered to clients by solicitors pursuant to 275.206(4)-3.

(b) If an investment adviser subject to paragraph (a) of this section has custody or possession of securities or funds of any client, the records required to be made and kept under paragraph (a) of this section shall include:

(1) A journal or other record showing all purchases, sales, receipts and deliveries of securities (including certificate numbers) for such accounts and all other debits and credits to such accounts.

(2) A separate ledger account for each such client showing all purchases, sales, receipts and deliveries of securities, the date and price of each purchase and sale, and all debits and credits.

(3) Copies of confirmation of all transactions effected by or for the account of any such client.

(4) A record for each security in which any such client has a position, which record shall show the name of each such client having any interest in such security, the amount or interest of each such client, and the location of each such security.

(c) Every investment adviser subject to paragraph (a) of this section who renders any investment supervisory or management service to any client shall, with respect to the portfolio being supervised or managed and to the extent that the information is reasonably available to or obtainable by the investment adviser, make and keep true, accurate and current:

(1) Records showing separately for each such client the securities purchased and sold, and the date, amount and price of each such purchase and sale.

(2) For each security in which any client has a current position, information from which the investment adviser can promptly furnish the name of each such client, and the current amount or interest of such client.

(d) Any books or records required by this section may be maintained by the investment adviser in such manner that the identity of any client to whom such investment adviser renders investment supervisory services is indicated by numerical or alphabetical code or some similar designation.

(e)(1) All books and records required to be made under the provisions of paragraphs (a) to (c)(1) of this section shall be maintained and preserved in an easily accessible place for a period of not less than five years from the end of the fiscal year during which the last entry was made on such record, the first two years in an appropriate office of the investment adviser.

(2) Partnership articles and any amendments thereto, articles of incorporation, charters, minute books, and stock certificate books of the investment adviser and of any predecessor, shall be maintained in the principal office of the investment adviser and preserved until at least three years after termination of the enterprise.

(f) An investment adviser subject to paragraph (a) of this section, before ceasing to conduct or discontinuing business as an investment adviser shall arrange for and be responsible for the preservation of the books and records required to be maintained and preserved under this section for the remainder of the period specified in this section, and shall notify the Commission in writing, at its principal office, Washington, D.C., 20549, of the exact address where such books and records will be maintained during such period.

(g) After a record or other document has been preserved for two years a photograph on film may be substituted for the balance of the required time.

(h)(1) Any book or other record made, kept, maintained and preserved in compliance with 240.17a-3 and 240.17a-4 of this chapter under the Securities Exchange Act of 1934, which is substantially the same as the book or other record required to be made, kept, maintained and preserved under this section, shall be deemed to be made, kept, maintained and preserved in compliance with this section.

(2) A record made and kept pursuant to any provision of paragraph (a) of this section, which contains all the information required under any other provision of paragraph (a) of this section, need not be maintained in duplicate in order to meet the requirements of the other provision of paragraph (a) of this section.

(i) As used in this section the term "discretionary power" shall not include discretion as to the price at which or the time when a transaction is or is to be effected, if, before the order is given by the investment adviser, the client has directed or approved the purchase or sale of a definite amount of the particular security.

(j)(1) Except as provided in paragraph (j)(3) hereof, each non-resident investment adviser registered or applying for registration pursuant to Section 203 of the Act shall keep, maintain and preserve, at a place within the United States designated in a notice from him as provided in paragraph (j)(2) of this section true, correct, complete and current copies of books and records which he is required to make, keep current, maintain or preserve pursuant to any provisions of any rule or regulation of the Commission adopted under the Act.

(2) Except as provided in paragraph (j)(3) of this section, each nonresident investment adviser subject to this paragraph (j) shall furnish to the Commission a written notice specifying the address of the place within the United States where the copies of the books and records required to be kept and preserved by him pursuant to paragraph (j)(1) hereof are located. Each non-resident investment adviser registered or applying for registration when this paragraph becomes effective shall file such notice within 30 days after such rule becomes effective. Each non-resident investment adviser who files an application for registration after this paragraph becomes effective shall file such notice with such application for registration.

(3) Notwithstanding the provisions of paragraphs (j)(1) and (j)(2) of this section, a non-resident investment adviser need not keep or preserve within the United States copies of the books and records referred to in said paragraphs (j)(1) and (j)(2), if:

(i) Such non-resident investment adviser files with the Commission, at the time or within the period provided by paragraph (j)(2) of this section, a written undertaking, in form acceptable to the Commission and signed by a duly authorized person, to furnish to the Commission upon demand, at its principal office in Washington, D.C., or at any Regional Office of the Commission designated in such demand, true, correct, complete and current copies of any or all of the books and records which he is required to make, keep current, maintain or preserve pursuant to any provision of any rule or regulation of the Commission adopted under the Act, or any part of such books and records which may be specified in such demand. Such undertaking shall be in substantially the following form:

> The undersigned hereby undertakes to furnish at its own expense to the Securities and Exchange Commission at its principal office in Washington, D.C. or at any Regional Office of said Commission specified in a demand for copies of books and records made by or on behalf of said Commission, true, correct, complete and current copies of any or all, or any part, of the books and records which the undersigned is required to make, keep current or preserve pursuant to any provision of any rule or regulation of the Securities and Exchange Commission under the Investment Advisers Act of 1940. This undertaking shall be suspended during any period when the undersigned is making, keeping current, and preserving copies of all of said books and records at a place within the United States in compliance with Rule 204-2(j) under the Investment Advisers Act of 1940. This undertaking shall be binding upon the undersigned and the heirs, successors and assigns of the undersigned, and the written irrevocable consents and powers of attorney of the undersigned, its general partners and managing agents filed with the Securities and Exchange Commission shall extend to and cover any action to enforce same.

(ii) Such non-resident investment adviser furnishes to the Commission, at his own expense 14 days after written demand therefor forwarded to him by registered mail at his last address of record filed with the Commission and signed by the Secretary of the Commission or such person as the Commission may authorize to act in its behalf, true, correct, complete and current copies of any or all books and records which such investment adviser is required to make, keep current or preserve pursuant to any provision of any rule or regulation of the Commission adopted under the Act, or any part of such books and records which may be specified in said written demand. Such copies shall be furnished to the Commission at its principal office in Washington, D.C., or at any Regional Office of the Commission which may be specified in said written demand.

(4) For purposes of this rule the term "non-resident investment adviser" shall have the meaning set out in § 275.0-2(d)(3) under the Act.

TITLE 18. CONSERVATION OF POWER AND WATER RESOURCES

Agency: **Department of Energy**
Federal Energy Regulatory Commission

SUBCHAPTER B. REGULATIONS UNDER THE FEDERAL POWER ACT

PART 12. SAFETY OF WATER POWER PROJECTS AND PROJECT WORKS

Subpart B. Reports and Records

Citation: **18 CFR 12.12**

✍ § 12.12 Maintenance of records.

(a) *Kinds of records.* (1) *General Rule.* Except as provided in paragraph (a)(2) of this section, the applicant or licensee must maintain as permanent project records in addition to those required in Part 125 of this chapter, the following information:

(i) Engineering and geological data relating to design, construction, maintenance, repair, or modification of the project, including design memoranda and drawings, laboratory and other testing reports, geologic data (such as maps, sections, or logs of exploratory borings or trenches, foundation treatment, and excavation), plans and specifications, inspection and quality control reports, "as built" construction drawings, designers' operating criteria, photographs, and any other data necessary to demonstrate that construction, maintenance, repair, or modification of the project has been performed in accordance with plans and specifications;

(ii) Instrumentation observations and data collected during construction, operation, or maintenance of the project, including continuously maintained tabular records and graphs illustrating the data collected pursuant to § 12.41; and

(iii) The operational and maintenance history of the project, including:

(A) The dates, times, nature, and causes of any complete or partial unscheduled shut-down, suspension of project operations, or reservoir filling restrictions related to the safety of the project or project works; and

(B) Any reports of project modifications, conditions affecting the safety of the project or project works, or deaths or serious injuries at the project.

(2) *Exception.* The applicant or licensee is not required to maintain as permanent project records any information specified in paragraph (a)(1) of this section that was or reasonably would have been prepared before the applicant or licensee acquired control of the project and that the applicant or the licensee never acquired or reasonably could have acquired.

(b) *Location of records* — (1) *Original records.* The applicant or licensee must maintain the originals of all permanent project records at a central location, such as the project site or the main business office of the applicant or licensee, secure from damage from any conceivable failure of the project works and convenient for inspection. The applicant or licensee must keep the Regional Engineer advised of the location of the permanent project records.

(2) *Record copies.* If the originals of the permanent project records are maintained at a central location other than the project site, the applicant or licensee must maintain at the project site copies of at least the project Exhibit G or L (design drawings), instrumentation data, and operational history that are necessary to the safe and efficient operation of the project.

(3) In accordance with the provisions of Part 125 of this chapter, the applicant or licensee may maintain original records, or record copies at the project site, in microform, if appropriate equipment is readily available to view the records.

(c) *Transfer of records.* If the project is taken over by the United States at the end of a license term or the Commission issues a new license to a different licensee, the prior licensee must transfer the originals of all permanent project records to the custody of the administering Federal agency or department or to the new licensee.

PART 33. APPLICATION FOR SALE, LEASE, OR OTHER DISPOSITION, MERGER OR CONSOLIDATION OF FACILITIES, OR FOR PURCHASE OR ACQUISITION OF SECURITIES OF A PUBLIC UTILITY

Citation: **18 CFR 33.2**

✍ § 33.2 Contents of application.

Each such applicant shall set forth in its application to the Commission, in the manner and form and in the order indicated, the following information which should insofar as possible be furnished as to said applicant and each company whose facilities or securities are involved:

* * * * *

(l) A form of notice suitable for publication in the Federal Register, as well as a copy of the same notice in electronic format (in either ASCII text, WordPerfect 5.1 for DOS or WordPerfect 5.2 for Windows format) on a 3 1/2 " diskette marked with the name of the applicant and the words "Notice of Filing," which will briefly summarize the facts contained in the application in such way as to acquaint the public with its scope and purpose.

* * * * *

PART 34. APPLICATION FOR AUTHORIZATION OF THE ISSUANCE OF SECURITIES OR THE ASSUMPTION OF LIABILITIES

Citation: **18 CFR 34.3**

✍ § 34.3 Contents of application for issuance of securities.

* * * * *

(k) A form of notice suitable for publication in the Federal Register, as well as a copy of the same notice in electronic format (in either ASCII text, WordPerfect 5.1 for DOS or WordPerfect 5.2 for Windows format) on a 3 1/2 " diskette marked with the name of the applicant and the words "Notice of Filing," setting forth:

(1) The legal name of the applicant;

(2) The securities offered for issuance including the proposed issue date; and

(3) The comment procedure.

* * * * *

PART 35. FILING OF RATE SCHEDULES

Citation: **18 CFR 35.8**

✍ § 35.8 Comments by interested parties.

(a) *Form of notice for Federal Register.* The public utility shall file a form of notice suitable for publication in the Federal Register, as well as a copy of the same notice in electronic format (in either ASCII text, WordPerfect 5.1 for DOS or WordPerfect 5.2 for Windows format) on a 3 1/2 " diskette marked with the name of the applicant and the words "Notice of Filing," which shall be in the following form:

* * * * *

PART 36. RULES CONCERNING APPLICATIONS FOR TRANSMISSION SERVICES UNDER SECTION 211 OF THE FEDERAL POWER ACT

Citation: **18 CFR 36.1**

✍ § 36.1 Notice provisions applicable to applications for transmission services under section 211 of the Federal Power Act.

* * * * *

(b) * * *

(1) A form of notice suitable for publication in the Federal Register, as well as a copy of the same statement in electronic format (in either ASCII text, WordPerfect 5.1 for DOS or WordPerfect 5.2 for Windows format) on a 3 1/2 " diskette marked with the name of the applicant and the words "Notice of Filing."

* * * * *

PART 37. OPEN ACCESS SAME-TIME INFORMATION SYSTEMS AND STANDARDS OF CONDUCT FOR PUBLIC UTILITIES

Citation: 18 CFR 37.1

✍ § 37.1 Applicability.

This part applies to any public utility that owns, operates, or controls facilities used for the transmission of electric energy in interstate commerce and to transactions performed under the pro forma tariff required in part 35 of this chapter.

Citation: 18 CFR 37.2

✍ § 37.2 Purpose.

(a) The purpose of this part is to ensure that potential customers of open access transmission service receive access to information that will enable them to obtain transmission service on a non-discriminatory basis from any Transmission Provider. These rules provide standards of conduct and require the Transmission Provider (or its agent) to create and operate an Open Access Same-time Information System (OASIS) that gives all users of the open access transmission system access to the same information.

(b) The OASIS will provide information by electronic means about available transmission capability for point-to-point service and will provide a process for requesting transmission service. OASIS will enable Transmission Providers and Transmission Customers to communicate promptly requests and responses to buy and sell available transmission capacity offered under the Transmission Provider's tariff.

Citation: 18 CFR 37.5

✍ § 37.5 Obligations of Transmission Providers and Responsible Parties.

(a) Each Transmission Provider is required to provide for the operation of an OASIS, either individually or jointly with other Transmission Providers, in accordance with the requirements of this Part. The Transmission Provider may delegate this responsibility to a Responsible Party such as another Transmission Provider, an Independent System Operator, a Regional Transmission Group, or a Regional Reliability Council.

(b) A Responsible Party must:

(1) Provide access to an OASIS providing standardized information relevant to the availability of transmission capacity, prices, and other information (as described in this part) pertaining to the transmission system for which it is responsible; and

(2) Shall operate the OASIS in compliance with the standardized procedures and protocols found in OASIS Standards and Communication Protocols, which can be obtained from the Public Reference and Files Maintenance Branch, Room 2A, Federal Energy Regulatory Commission, 888 First Street NE., Washington, DC 20426.

(c) Transmission Providers must provide "read only" access to the OASIS to Commission staff and the staffs of State regulatory authorities, at no cost, after such staff members have complied with the requisite registration procedures.

Citation: 18 CFR 37.6

✍ § 37.6 Information to be posted on an OASIS.

(a) The information posted on the OASIS must be in such detail as to allow Transmission Customers to:

(1) Make requests for transmission services offered by Transmission Providers, Resellers and other providers of ancillary services;

(2) View and download in standard formats, using standard protocols, information regarding the transmission system necessary to enable prudent business decision making;

(3) Post, view, upload and download information regarding available products and desired services;

(4) Clearly identify the degree to which their transmission service requests or schedules were denied or interrupted; and

(5) Obtain access, in electronic format, to information to support available transmission capability calculations and historical transmission service requests and schedules for various audit purposes.

(b) *Posting transmission capability.* The transmission capability that is expected to be available on the Transmission Provider's system (ATC) and the total transmission capability (TTC) of that system shall be calculated and posted for each Posted Path as set out in this section.

(1) *Definitions.* For purposes of this section the terms listed below have the following meanings:

(i) Posted path means any control area to control area interconnection; any path for which service is denied, curtailed or interrupted for more than 24 hours in the past 12 months; and any path for which a customer requests to have ATC or TTC posted. For this last category, the posting must continue for 180 days and thereafter until 180 days have elapsed from the most recent request for service over the requested path. For purposes of this definition, an hour includes any part of an hour during which service was denied, curtailed or interrupted.

(ii) Constrained posted path means any posted path having an ATC less than or equal to 25 percent of TTC at any time during the preceding 168 hours or for which ATC has been calculated to be less than or equal to 25 percent of TTC for any period during the current hour or the next 168 hours.

(iii) Unconstrained posted path means any posted path not determined to be a constrained posted path.

(2) Calculation methods, availability of information, and requests. (i) Information used to calculate any posting of ATC and TTC must be dated and time-stamped and all calculations shall be performed according to consistently applied methodologies referenced in the Transmission Provider's transmission tariff and shall be based on current industry practices, standards and criteria.

(ii) On request, the Responsible Party must make all data used to calculate ATC and TTC for any constrained posted paths publicly available (including the limiting element(s) and the cause of the limit (e.g., thermal, voltage, stability)) in electronic form within one week of the posting. The information is required to be provided only in the electronic format in which it was created, along with any necessary decoding instructions, at a cost limited to the cost of reproducing the material. This information is to be retained for six months after the applicable posting period.

(iii) System planning studies or specific network impact studies performed for customers to determine network impacts are to be made publicly available in electronic form on request and a list of such studies shall be posted on the OASIS. A study is required to be provided only in the electronic format in which it was created, along with any necessary decoding instructions, at a cost limited to the cost of reproducing the material. These studies are to be retained for two years.

(3) *Posting.* The ATC and TTC for all Posted Paths must be posted in megawatts by specific direction and in the manner prescribed in this subsection.

(i) Constrained posted paths —

(A) *For Firm ATC and TTC.* (*1*) The posting shall show ATC and TTC for a 30-day period. For this period postings shall be: by the hour, for the current hour and the 168 hours next following; and thereafter, by the day. If the Transmission Provider charges separately for on-peak and off-peak periods in its tariff, ATC and TTC will be posted daily for each period.

(*2*) Postings shall also be made by the month, showing for the current month and the 12 months next following.

(*3*) If planning and specific requested transmission studies have been done, seasonal capability shall be posted for the year following the current year and for each year following to the end of the planning horizon but not to exceed 10 years.

(B) *For Non-Firm ATC and TTC.* The posting shall show ATC and TTC for a 30-day period by the hour and days prescribed under paragraph (b)(3)(i)(A)(*1*) of this section and, if so requested, by the month and year as prescribed under paragraph (b)(3)(i)(A)(*2*) and (*3*) of this section.

(C) *Updating Posted Information for Constrained Paths.*

(*1*) The capability posted under paragraphs (b)(3)(i) (A) and (B) of this section must be updated when transactions are reserved or service ends or whenever the TTC estimate for the Path changes by more than 10 percent.

(*2*) All updating of hourly information shall be made on the hour.

(ii) *Unconstrained Posted Paths.* (A) Postings of ATC and TTC shall be by the day, showing for the current day and the next six days following and thereafter, by the month for the 12 months next following. If the Transmission Provider charges separately for on-peak and off-peak periods in its tariff, ATC and TTC will be posted for the current day and the next six days following for each period. These postings are to be updated whenever the ATC changes by more than 20 percent of the Path's TTC.

(B) If planning and specific requested transmission studies have been done, seasonal capability shall be posted for the year following the current year and for each year following until the end of the planning horizon but not to exceed 10 years.

(c) *Posting Transmission Service Products and Prices.* (1) Transmission Providers must post prices and a summary of the terms and conditions associated with all transmission products offered to Transmission Customers.

(2) Transmission Providers must provide a downloadable file of their complete tariffs in the same electronic format as the tariff that is filed with the Commission.

(3) A Transmission Provider, within 24 hours of agreeing to sell transmission service to a non-affiliate at a discount (as measured from when ATC must be adjusted in response to the transaction), must post on the OASIS (and make available for download) information describing the transaction (including price, quantity, and any other relevant terms and conditions) and shall keep such information posted on the OASIS for at least 30 days. A record of the transaction must be retained and kept available as part of the audit log required in § 37.7. With respect to any discount offered to its own power customers or its affiliates, the Transmission Provider must, at the same time, post on the OASIS an offer to provide the same discount to all Transmission Customers on the same path and on all unconstrained transmission paths.

(4) Customers choosing to use the OASIS to offer for resale transmission capacity they have purchased must post relevant information to the same OASIS as used by the one from whom the Reseller purchased the transmission capacity. This information must be posted on the same display page, using the same tables, as similar capability being sold by the Transmission Provider, and the information must be contained in the same downloadable files as the Transmission Provider's own available capability. A customer reselling transmission capacity without the use of an OASIS must, nevertheless, inform the original Transmission Provider of the transaction within the time limits prescribed by the "Sale or Assignment of Transmission Service" section of the pro forma tariff.

(d) *Posting Ancillary Service Offerings and Prices.* (1) Any ancillary service required to be provided or offered under the pro forma tariff prescribed by part 35 of this chapter must be posted with the price of that service.

(2) A Transmission Provider, within 24 hours of agreeing to sell an ancillary service to a non-affiliate at a discount, must post on the OASIS (and make available for download) information describing the transaction (including price, quantity, and any other relevant terms and conditions) and shall keep such information posted on the OASIS for at least 30 days. A record of the transaction must be retained and kept available as part of the audit log required in § 37.7. As to discounts for ancillary services, if a Transmission Provider offers a rate discount to an affiliate, or attributes a discounted ancillary service rate to its own transactions, the Transmission Provider must, at the same time, post on the OASIS an offer to provide the same discount to all eligible customers.

(3) Any other interconnected operations service offered by the Transmission Provider may be posted, with the price for that service.

(4) Any entity offering an ancillary service shall have the right to post the offering of that service on the OASIS if the service is one required to be offered by the Transmission Provider under the pro forma tariff prescribed by part 35 of this chapter. Any entity may also post any other interconnected operations service voluntarily offered by the Transmission Provider. Postings by customers and third parties must be on the same page, and in the same format, as postings of the Transmission Provider.

(e) *Posting Specific Transmission Service Requests and Responses.* (1) *General rules.* (i) All requests for transmission service offered by Transmission Providers under the pro forma tariff must be made on the OASIS. Requests for transmission service, and the responses to such requests, must be conducted in accordance with the Transmission Provider's tariff, the Federal Power Act, and Commission regulations.

(ii) In processing a request for transmission or ancillary service, the Responsible Party shall post the following information: the date and time when the request is made, its place in any queue, the status of that request, and the result (accepted, denied, withdrawn).

(iii) The identity of the parties will be masked-if requested-during the negotiating period and for 30 days from the date when the request was accepted, denied or withdrawn.

(2) Posting when a request for transmission service is denied.

(i) When a request for service is denied, the Responsible Party must provide the reason for that denial as part of any response to the request.

(ii) Information to support the reason for the denial, including the operating status of relevant facilities, must be maintained for 60 days and provided, upon request, to the potential Transmission Customer.

(iii) Any offer to adjust operation of the Transmission Provider's System to accommodate the denied request must be posted and made available to all Transmission Customers at the same time.

(3) *Posting when a transaction is curtailed or interrupted.* (i) When any transaction is curtailed or interrupted, the

curtailment or interruption must be posted (with the identities of the parties masked as required in § 37.6(e)(1)(iii)) and must state the reason why the transaction could not be continued or completed.

(ii) Information to support any such curtailment or interruption, including the operating status of the facilities involved in the constraint or interruption, must be maintained for 60 days and provided, upon request, to the curtailed or interrupted customer.

(iii) Any offer to adjust the operation of the Transmission Provider's system to restore a curtailed or interrupted transaction must be posted and made available to all curtailed and interrupted Transmission Customers at the same time.

(f) *Posting Transmission Service Schedules Information.* Information on transmission service schedules must be recorded by the entity scheduling the transmission service and must be available on the OASIS for download. Transmission service schedules must be posted no later than seven calendar days from the start of the transmission service.

(g) *Posting Other Transmission-Related Communications.* (1) The posting of other communications related to transmission services must be provided for by the Responsible Party. These communications may include "want ads" and "other communications" (such as using the OASIS as a Transmission-related conference space or to provide transmission-related messaging services between OASIS users). Such postings carry no obligation to respond on the part of any market participant.

(2) The Responsible Party is responsible for posting other transmission-related communications in conformance with the instructions provided by the third party on whose behalf the communication is posted. It is the responsibility of the third party requesting such a posting to ensure the accuracy of the information to be posted.

(3) Notices of transfers of personnel shall be posted as described in § 37.4(b)(2).

Citation: **18 CFR 37.7**

✍ § 37.7 Auditing Transmission Service Information.

(a) All OASIS database transactions, except other transmission-related communications provided for under § 37.6(g)(2), must be stored, dated, and time stamped.

(b) Audit data must remain available for download on the OASIS for 90 days. The audit data are to be retained and made available upon request for three years from the date when they are first posted.

Citation: **18 CFR 37.8**

✍ § 37.8 Implementation schedule for OASIS requirements; phases.

Each Transmission Provider must develop or participate in an OASIS that meets the requirements of this part and that is in operation by November 1, 1996. Each Transmission Provider must be in compliance with the standards of conduct prescribed in § 37.4 by November 1, 1996.

SUBCHAPTER C. ACCOUNTS, FEDERAL POWER ACT

PART 125. PRESERVATION OF RECORDS OF PUBLIC UTILITIES AND LICENSEES

Citation: **18 CFR 125.2**

✍ § 125.2 General instructions.

(a) *Scope of this part.* (1) The regulations in this part apply to all books of account and other records prepared by or on behalf of the public utility or licensee. See subsection 64 of the schedule for those records which come into possession of the public utility or licensee in connection with the acquisition of property, such as purchase, consolidation, merger, etc.

(2) The regulations in this part shall not be construed as excusing compliance with any other lawful requirements for the preservation of records for periods longer than those prescribed herein.

(3) Unless otherwise specified in the schedule (§ 125.3), duplicate copies of records may be destroyed at any time: *Provided, however,* That such duplicate copies contain no significant information not shown on the originals.

(4) Records other than those listed in the schedule may be destroyed at the option of the public utility or licensee: *Provided, however,* That records which are used in lieu of those listed shall be preserved for the periods prescribed for the records used for substantially similar purposes. And, provided further, That retention of records pertaining to added services, functions, plant, etc., the establishment of which cannot be presently foreseen, shall conform to the principles embodied herein.

(5) Notwithstanding the provisions of the Records Retention Schedule, the Commission may, upon the request of the Company, authorize a shorter period of retention for any record listed therein upon a showing by the Company that preservation of such record for a longer period is not necessary or appropriate in the public interest or for the protection of investors or consumers.

(b) *Designation of supervisory official.* Each public utility or licensee subject to the regulations in this part shall designate one or more persons with official responsibility to supervise the utility's or licensee's program for preservation and the authorized destruction of its records.

(c) *Protection and storage of records.* The public utility or licensee shall provide reasonable protection for records subject to the regulations in this part from damage by fire, floods, and other hazards and, in the selection of storage spaces, safeguards the records from unnecessary exposure to deterioration from excessive humidity, dryness, or lack of proper ventilation.

(d) *Definition of record media.* (1) For the purpose of these regulations, the data constituting the records listed in the schedule may be retained in any of the media forms in Figure 1 of this section, provided that the media selected has a standard life expectancy equal to or in excess of the specified retention period. However, records supporting plant and licensed project cost shall be retained in their original form, unless microfilmed. (See general instruction (j), for periods of retention.) In no instance, except in emergencies, will media regeneration to achieve the full length of period retention be allowed without Commission approval of the request of the company. In emergency cases management shall take such action as prudence calls for and notify the Commission immediately thereafter.

(2) If the media form of the record retained is other than a readable paper copy, then reader and/or printer equipment and related printout programs, if required, shall be provided by the utility for data reference.

(3) The media form initially selected for the record becomes the "original" for that particular record. If subsequent

conditions (e.g. improved media life expectancy, increased utility resources, environmental factors) require and the remaining retention period permits a change in the media forms, the utility may convert to another media and dispose of its old equipment, provided the certification processes described in paragraph (e) of this section are observed and data referencing capability is maintained

Figure 1.—Record Media

Record media/form	Media expected life	Comments and standards
1. Paper and card stock (hardcopy)	Archival permanency.	For each document, paper stock should be selected with a life expectancy equal to or greater than the retention period specified for that document.
2. Tape: Magnetic (including video tape).	5 years	Assumes storage in a controlled environment with a temperature and humidity range of 60°-80° F. and 40-60%, respectively. (Ref. instruction (g) for specific storage conditions.)
Punched	Archival permanency.	For each record, tape media (paper, mylar, metallic base) should be selected with a life expectancy equal to or greater than the retention period specified for that record.
3. Microforms: a. Microfilm, including Computer Output Microfilm (COM), microfiche jackets, and aperture cards.	do	Assumes processing to standards and storage in a controlled environment with a temperature and humidity range of 60-80° F. and 40-50% respectively. (Ref. American National Standards Institute (ANSI) standards PH 5.4— 1970, PH 1.41—1976, PH 1.28— 1979, Ph 1.43— 1981, or most current standards as accepted by the National Archives for use by Federal agencies. See 41 CFR. 101-11.5)
b. Updatable type.	Dependent on use of Media	For temporary records not requiring archival permanency so long as the microform or film selected has a life expectancy equal to, or greater than, the retention period for that record. Same storage conditions as for microfilm.
c. Metallic recording data strips.	Archival permanency.	Same storage conditions as for microfilm.

(e) *Microform, tape and computer output certification.* (1) As the initial recording media —

(i) Except as provided in paragraph (e)(1)(ii) of this section each microform record series:

(A) shall contain, at the beginning, a microform introduction stating the title of the record series, the date prepared, the name of the official responsible for validating or confirming the data contained therein; and

(B) shall be closed with a clear and standard microform notation indicating the completion of the series and the date.

(ii) If an official permanent record series is a computer output product (i.e., output paper or microfilm, jacketed microfiche, or aperture cards), any certification that may otherwise be required under paragraph (e)(1)(i) of this section is not required if:

(A) The series is prepared in accordance with written standard procedures developed, or accepted general business practices followed, by the company that ensure the integrity of record series that are the product of computer output; and

(B) Such procedures or practices include the name or title of the official responsible for validating or confirming the data contained in the record series and confirming that a particular computer output record series was produced in accordance with the standard procedures or practices.

(iii) If after validation, supplemental data and/or corrections (i.e., resulting from computer programming) are required, said microform may be produced separately or as a part of the series rerun, but shall be affixed to the original microform certificate as described in paragraph (e)(1)(i) of this section.

(iv) Each tape record series shall be externally labeled and shall include, as a basic part of the program, at the beginning of that series an introduction stating the record series title, date prepared, the name of the official responsible for validating or confirming the data contained therein and an index where appropriate. Each record series shall be closed with a clear and standard notation indicating the completion of that series and the date.

(2) Conversion from other media —

(i) Each microform record series shall include, as an integral part, a certificate(s) stating that the microforms are direct and facsimile reproductions of the original records and that they have been made in accordance with prescribed instructions. Such certificate(s) shall be executed by a person(s) having personal knowledge of the facts covered thereby.

(ii) Each microform record series shall commence and end with a statement as to the nature and arrangement of the records reproduced, and the date. Rolls of film shall not be cut except to produce jacketed microfiche. Supplemental or retaken film, whether of misyaced or omitted documents or of portions of microform found to be defective, shall be attached to the beginning of the microform record series. However, if a retrieval system using such methods as, for example, image count indexing or "blipping" is used, the supplemental or retaken film may be attached at the end of the series, if provisions at the beginning of the series advise the viewer of the location of the problem frames and the location of the supplemental or retaken frames. If supplemental or retaken film of misplaced or omitted documents, or of portions of microform found to be defective, are attached to the microform record series, the certificate described in paragraph (e)(1)(i) of this section shall cover the supplemental or retaken film and shall state the reasons for the attachment.

(iii) If, in accordance with the provisions of paragraph (f) of this section, the utility or licensee elects to convert records to the tape media, the same certification provisions specified in paragraph (e)(1)(iii) of this section must be provided in the conversion program.

(f) *Change of media for existing records.* Those records prepared and maintained under previous regulations in a paper media and whose remaining retention period falls within the life expectancy range of any of the media detailed in Figure 1, may be converted to that media at the public utility's and/or licensee's option, provided the applicable certification processes described in paragraph (e) of this section are observed and an audit referencing capability maintained.

(g) *Media.* (1) All records created or maintained in a media and a format other than readable entries on paper shall:

(i) Be prepared, arranged, classified, identified, and indexed as to permit the subsequent location, examination, and reproduction of the record to a readable media;

(ii) Be stored in such a manner as to provide reasonable protection from hazards such as fire, flood, theft, etc.; and be maintained in a controlled environment;

(iii) Be regenerated, including proper certification, when damaged. (Also see § 125.2(d)(1).)

(2) The company shall be prepared to furnish, at its own expense, standard facilities for reading media and shall additionally provide, if the Commission so directs, copies of record in a readable form.

(3) All film stock shall be of approved operational-permanent-record microcopying type, which meets the current specifications of the American National Standards Institute.

(h) *Destruction of records.* The destruction of the records permitted to be destroyed under the provisions of the regulations in this part may be performed in any manner elected by the public utility or licensee concerned. Precautions should be taken, however, to macerate or otherwise destroy the legibility of records, the content of which is forbidden by law to be divulged to unauthorized persons.

(i) *Premature destruction or loss of records.* When records are destroyed or lost before the expiration of the prescribed period of retention, a certified statement listing, as far as may be determined, the records destroyed and describing the circumstances of accidental or other premature destruction or loss shall be filed with the Commission within ninety (90) days from the date of discovery of such destruction.

(j) *Schedule of records and periods of retention.* The schedule of records, § 125.3, shows the period of time that designated records shall be preserved. However, records related to plant shall be retained a minimum of 25 years unless accounting adjustments resulting from reclassification and original cost studies have been approved by the regulatory commission having jurisdiction, and either (1) continuing plant inventory records are maintained (see Definition No. 8, "Continuing Plant Inventory Records", Parts 101 and 104 of this subchapter), or (2) unitization of construction costs appear in work orders, except that those relating to the construction of licensed projects, or additions or betterments thereto for which the Commission has not determined the actual legitimate original cost are to be retained until such cost has been determined. Additionally, all records which affect the determination of amortization reserves related to licensed projects shall be retained until Commission determination and final adjudication is made.

(k) *Retention periods designated "Destroy at option".* Use of the retention period, "Destroy at option," in the regulations in this part constitutes authorization for such destruction under the conditions specified for the particular types of records, only if such optional destruction is appropriate to limited managerial interest in such records and if such optional destruction is not in conflict with other legal retention requirements or usefulness of such records in satisfying pending regulatory actions or directives.

(l) *Records of services performed by associated companies.* The public utility or licensee to which the regulations in this part apply shall assure the availability of records of services performed by associated companies for the periods indicated herein, as are necessary, to support the cost of services rendered to it by an associated company.

(m) *Index of records.* At each office of the public utility or licensee where records are kept or stored, such records as are herein required to be preserved shall be so arranged, filed, and currently indexed that they may be readily identified and made available to representatives of the Commission.

(n) *Schedule of notes.* (1) For the purpose of the regulation, a stockholder's account may be treated as a closed account at the time that such stockholder ceases to be a holder of record of the particular class and series of stock of the company and the 6-year retention period prescribed herein shall run from that date. If such person subsequently acquires shares of capital stock of the company and thus again becomes a stockholder of the company, the record of such acquisition shall be treated as a new stockholder account.

(2) The terms "bonds" and "debentures," as used in captions (a) through (f) of this item, shall include all debt securities, such as bonds, debentures or notes other than debt securities which evidence temporary borrowings and which are expected to be repaid out of the proceeds of the sale of longer term securities. Typical of such temporary debt securities as described in 4(i) would be notes issued to banks evidencing temporary working capital and construction loans.

(3) Canceled bonds and debentures and paid interest coupons pertaining thereto may be destroyed, provided that a certificate of destruction giving full descriptive reference to the documents destroyed shall be made by the person or persons authorized to perform such destruction and shall be retained by the company for the period herein prescribed. The certificate of destruction evidencing the destruction of paid interest coupons pertaining to bonds or debentures need not contain a listing of the bond or debenture serial numbers pertaining to such paid interest coupons. When documents represent debt secured by mortgage, the certificate of destruction shall also be authorized by a representative of the trustee(s) acting in conjunction with the person or persons destroying the documents or shall have the trustee(s) acceptance thereon. The certificate of destruction above described may be destroyed 6 years after the payment and discharge of the bonds or debentures or interest coupons described in such certificate.

(4) If a retention period is prescribed elsewhere in the schedule with respect to any document which is included as an exhibit to any filing retained pursuant to the requirements of this item, the company need retain only one copy of such document in its files provided appropriate cross references are established.

(5) Life or mortality study data for depreciation purposes shall be retained for 25 years or for 10 years after plant is retired, whichever is longer.

PART 154. RATE SCHEDULES AND TARIFFS

Subpart A. General Provisions and Conditions

Citation: 18 CFR 154.4

✍ § 154.4 Electronic and paper media.

(a) *General rule.* All statements filed pursuant to subpart D of this part, and all workpapers in spreadsheet format, and tariff sheets other than those in Volume No. 2, must be submitted on electronic media. Filings pursuant to this part 154 must also include the prescribed number of paper copies. Tariffs, rate schedules, and contracts, or parts thereof, and material related thereto, including any change in rates, notice of cancellation or termination, and certificates of adoption, must be submitted to the Commission in an original and 5 paper copies, except that filings pursuant to subpart D of this part must be submitted in an original and 12 paper copies.

(b) All filings must be signed in compliance with the following.

(1) The signature on a filing constitutes a certification that: The signer has read the filing signed and knows the contents of the paper copies and electronic media; the paper copies contain the same information as contained on the electronic media; the contents as stated in the copies and on the electronic media are true to the best knowledge and belief of the signer; and, the signer possesses full power and authority to sign the filing.

(2) A filing must be signed by one of the following:

(i) The person on behalf of whom the filing is made;

(ii) An officer, agent, or employee of the governmental authority, agency, or instrumentality on behalf of which the filing is made; or,

(iii) A representative qualified to practice before the Commission under 385.2101 of this chapter who possesses authority to sign.

(c) Electronic media suitable for Commission filings are listed in the instructions for each form and filing. Lists of suitable electronic media are available upon request from the Commission. The formats for the electronic filing and paper copy can be obtained at the Federal Energy Regulatory Commission, Public Information and Reference Branch, 888 First Street, NE., Washington, D.C. 20426.

(d) *Where to file.* The electronic media, the paper copies and accompanying transmittal letter must be submitted in one package to: Office of the Secretary, Federal Energy Regulatory Commission, 888 First Street, NE., Washington, D.C. 20426.

(e) *Waiver.* A natural gas company may request a waiver of the requirement to submit filings by electronic media, by filing an original and 5 copies of a request for waiver. The request must demonstrate that the natural gas company does not have, and is unable to acquire, the technical capability to file the information on electronic media.

Subpart C — Procedures for Changing Tariffs

Citation: 18 CFR 154.209

✍ § 154.209 Form of notice for FEDERAL REGISTER.

The company must file a form of notice suitable for publication in the Federal Register. The company must also submit a copy of the notice on a separate 3 1/2" diskette in ASCII format. Each diskette must be labelled with the name of the company and the words "notice of filing." The notice must be in the following form:

United States of America Federal Energy Regulatory Commission

(Name of Company)

Docket number

Notice of Proposed Changes in FERC Gas Tariff (or Notice of Compliance Filing)

Take notice that on (date),(name of company) tendered for filing as part of its FERC Gas Tariff, Volume No. (number), the following tariff sheets, to become effective (insert effective date). (List tariff sheets). [The following language in the first paragraph applies only to compliance filings.] (Name of company) asserts that the purpose of this filing is to comply with the Commission's order issued (insert issue date), in (docket). [The following language in the first paragraph applies only to rate change filings.] The proposed changes would (increase/decrease) revenues from jurisdictional service by (dollar amount) based on the 12-month period ending (date), as adjusted. [For proposed changes other than changed rates and charges, the company must state concisely the nature of these changes.][The company must briefly describe the reasons for the proposed changes in the second paragraph.]

Any person desiring to be heard or to protest this filing should file a motion to intervene or protest with the Federal Energy Regulatory Commission, Washington, DC 20426, in accordance with § 385.214 and § 385.211 of the Commission's rules and regulations. All such motions or protests must be filed on or before (insert date 12 days after filing date). Protests will be considered by the Commission in determining the appropriate action to be taken, but will not serve to make protestants parties to the proceeding. Any person wishing to become a party must file a motion to intervene. Copies of this filing are on file with the Commission and are available for public inspection in the Public Reference Room.

Exhibit A-Diskette Filing Procedures

Diskette(s) containing the information specified for each record ID of the tariff filing filed with the FERC must conform with the following requirements:

(1) The character code for representing all data should be the American National Standard Code for Information Interchange (ASCII) as defined in FIPS PUB 1-2. An exception will be made for the cents (›) symbol, which should be coded as hexadecimal 8B, or decimal 155, as defined in the IBM-US (PC-8) symbol set. Note that there are symbol sets which define it differently.

(2) The definitions, instructions, and schedule ID/record ID data layouts for this form specify explicitly the data items to be reported and the sequence for recording the information on the diskette(s). The information required for a tariff filing should be recorded on the diskette(s) exactly as specified in the data layout for each schedule/record and in accordance with the general instructions.

(3) All tariff sheets filed under a given docket number should all be included in the same "file" or data set, if possible. (Large files may be split as a matter of convenience or diskette size limitation). The file should be named: "TFMMDDYY.ASC" where "TF" stands for "Tariff Filing", and "MMDDYY" is the two digit month, day, and year the tariff filing is submitted. If more than one tariff filing is made on the same day, the subsequent filings should be given file names "TFMMDDYY.BSC", "TFMMDDYY.CSC", etc., where "BSC" indicates the second filing of the day, "CSC" the third filing, etc. The file name for each submission should be included in the transmittal letter accompanying the respondent's filing.

(4) Each logical record must be terminated by a CR (ASCII carriage return-13 decimal, OD hexadecimal). An ASCII line feed (LF) following a CR is accepted but not required as part of termination. Do Not pad the end of data records with spaces.

(5) Do not omit any numeric item. Numeric items do not require leading zeros unless specifically noted in the description of the data item. See the General Instructions of this form for detailed instructions for recording numeric data on the diskette(s).

(6) When refiling a diskette only to correct an electronic data error on the electronic version of a tariff sheet and not in the paper version, use the same file name, pagination and submittal date.

(7) Each diskette must state on the label that tariff sheets are enclosed. If more than one diskette is necessary to accommodate a filing, the diskettes should be numbered 1 of N, 2 of N, etc., where N is the total number of diskettes.

SUBCHAPTER F. ACCOUNTS, NATURAL GAS ACT

PART 225. PRESERVATION OF RECORDS OF NATURAL GAS COMPANIES

Citation:	18 CFR 225.2

§ 225.2 General instructions.

(a) *Scope of this part.* (1) The regulations in this part apply to all books of account and other records prepared by or on behalf of the natural gas company. See subsection 64 of the schedule for those records which come into possession of the natural gas company in connection with the acquisition of property, such as purchase, consolidation, merger, etc.

(2) The regulations in this part shall not be construed as excusing compliance with any other lawful requirement for the preservation of records for periods longer than those prescribed herein.

(3) Unless otherwise specified in the schedule (§ 225.3), duplicate copies of records may be destroyed at any time: Provided, however, That such duplicate copies contain no significant information not shown on the originals.

(4) Records other than those listed in the schedule may be destroyed at the option of the natural gas company: Provided, however, That records which are used in lieu of those listed shall be preserved for the periods prescribed for the records used for substantially similar purposes. And, provided further, That retention of records pertaining to added services, functions, plant, etc., the establishment of which cannot be presently foreseen, shall conform to the principles embodied herein.

(5) Notwithstanding the provisions of the Records Retention Schedule, the Commission may, upon the request of the company, authorize a shorter period of retention for any record listed therein upon a showing by the company that preservation of such record for a longer period is not necessary or appropriate in the public interest or for the protection of investors or consumers.

(b) *Designation of supervisory official.* Each natural gas company subject to the regulations in this part shall designate one or more persons with official responsibility to supervise the natural gas company's program for preservation and the authorized destruction of its records.

(c) *Protection and storage of records.* The natural gas company shall provide reasonable protection for records subject to the regulations in this part from damage by fires, floods, and other hazards and, in the selection of storage spaces, safeguard the records from unnecessary exposure to deterioration from excessive humidity, dryness, or lack of proper ventilation.

(d) *Definition of record media.* (1) For the purpose of these regulations, the data constituting the records listed in the schedule may be retained in any of the media forms in Figure 1 below, provided that the media selected has a standard life expectancy equal to or in excess of the specified retention period. However, records supporting plant cost shall be retained in their original form unless microfilmed. (See general instructions (j), for periods of retention.) In no instance, except in emergencies, will media regeneration to achieve the full length of period retention be allowed without Commission approval of the request of the company. In emergency cases, management shall take action as prudence calls for and notify the Commission immediately thereafter.

Figure 1.— Record Media

Record Media/form	Media expected life	Comments and standards
1. Paper and card stock (hardcopy).	Archival permanency.	For each document, paper stock should be selected with a life expectancy equal to or greater than the retention period specified for that document.
2. Tape: Magnetic (including video tape).	5 years	Assumes storage in a controlled environment with a temperature and humidity range of 60°-80° F. and 40-60%, respectively. (Ref. instruction (g)for specific storage conditions.)
Punched	Archival permanency.	For each record, tape media (paper, mylar, metallic base) should be selected with a life expectancy equal to or greater than the retention period specified for that record.
3. Microforms: a. Microfilm, including Computer Output Microfilm (COM), microfiche jackets, and aperture cards.	do	Assumes process to standards and storage in a controlled environment with a temperature and humidity range of 60-80 degrees F. and 40-50% respectively. (Ref. American National Standards Institute (ANSI) standards PH 5.4 — 1970, PH 1.41 — 1976, PH 1.28 — 1979, Ph 1.43 — 1981, or most current standards as accepted by the National Archives for use be Federal agencies. See 41 CFR. 101-11.5)
b. Updatable type.	Dependent on use of Media	For temporary records not requiring archival permanency so long as the microform or film selected has a life expectancy equal to, or greater than, the retention period for that record. Same storage conditions as for microfilm.
c. Metallic recording data strips.	Archival Permannency.	Same storage conditions as for microfilm.

(2) If the media form of the record retained is other than a readable paper copy, then reader and/or printer equipment and related printout programs, if required, shall be provided by the utility for data reference.

(3) The media form initially selected for the record becomes the "original" for that particular record. If subsequent conditions (e.g., improved media life expectancy, increased company resources, environmental factors) require and the remaining retention period permits a change in the media forms the company may convert to another media and dispose of its old equipment, provided the certification processes described in paragraph (3) of this section are observed and data referencing capability is maintained.

(e) *Microform and tape certification.* (1) As the initial recording media —

(i) Except as provided in paragraph (e)(1)(ii) of this section, each microform record series:

(A) Shall contain, at the beginning, a microform introduction stating the title of the record series, the date prepared, the name of the official responsible for validating or confirming the data contained therein; and

(B) Shall be closed with a clear and standard microform

notation indicating the completion of the series and the date.

(ii) If an official permanent record series is a computer output product (i.e., output paper or microfilm, jacketed microfiche, or aperture cards), any certification that may otherwise be required under paragraph (e)(1)(i) of this section is not required if:

(A) The series is prepared in accordance with written standard procedures developed, or accepted general business practices followed, by the company that ensure the integrity of record series that are the product of computer output; and

(B) Such procedures or practices include the name or title of the official responsible for validating or confirming the data contained in the record series and confirming that a particular computer output record series was produced in accordance with the standard procedures or practices.

(iii) If after validation, supplemental data and/or corrections (i.e., resulting from computer programming) are required, said microform may be produced separately or as a part of the series rerun, but shall be affixed to the original microform certificate as described in subparagraph (1)(i) of this paragraph.

(iv) Each tape record series shall be externally labeled and shall include, as a basic part of the program, at the beginning of that series an introduction stating the record series title, date prepared, the name of the official responsible for validating or confirming the data contained therein, and an index where appropriate. Each record series shall be closed with a clear and standard notation indicating the completion of that series and the date.

(2) Conversion from other media —

(i) Each microform record series shall include, as an integral part, a certificate(s) stating that the microforms are direct and facsimile reproductions of the original records and that they have been made in accordance with prescribed instructions. Such certificate(s) shall be executed by a person(s) having personal knowledge of the facts covered thereby.

(ii) Each microform record series shall commence and end with a statement as to the nature and arrangement of the records reproduced, and the date. Rolls of film shall not be cut except to produce jacketed microfiche. Supplemental or retaken film, whether of misplaced or omitted documents or of portions of microform found to be defective, shall be attached to the beginning of the microform record series. However, if a retrieval system using such methods as, for example, image count indexing or "blipping" is used, the supplemental or retaken film may be attached at the end of the series if provisions at the beginning of the series advise the viewer of the location of the problem frames and the location of the supplemental or retaken frames. If supplemental or retaken film of misplaced or omitted documents, or of portions of microform found to be defective, are attached to the microform record series, the certificate described in paragraph (e)(1)(i) of this section shall cover the supplemental or retaken film and shall state the reasons for the attachment.

(iii) If, in accordance with the provisions of paragraph (f) of this section, the natural gas company elects to convert records to the tape media, the same certification provision specified in paragraph (e)(1)(iii) of this section must be provided in the conversion program.

(f) *Change of media for existing records*. Those records prepared and maintained under previous regulations in a paper media and whose remaining retention period falls within the life expectancy range of any of the media detailed in Figure 1, may be converted to that media at the natural gas company's option, provided the applicable certification processes described in paragraph (e) of this section are observed and an audit referencing capability maintained.

(g) *Media*. (1) All records created or maintained in a media and a format other than readable entries on paper shall:

(i) Be prepared, arranged, classified, identified, and indexed as to permit the subsequent location, examination, and reproduction of the record to a readable media;

(ii) Be stored in such a manner as to provide reasonable protection from hazards such as fire, flood, theft, etc.; and maintained in a controlled environment;

(iii) Be regenerated, including proper certification, when damaged. (Also see § 225.2(d)(1).)

(2) The company shall be prepared to furnish, at its own expense, standard facilities for reading media and shall additionally provide, if the Commission so directs, copies of the record in a readable form.

(3) All film stock shall be of approved operationally-permanent-record micro-copying type, which meets the current specifications of the American National Standards Institute.

(h) *Destruction of records*. The destruction of the records permitted to be destroyed under the provisions of the regulations in this part may be performed in any manner elected by the natural gas company concerned. Precautions should be taken, however, to macerate or otherwise destroy the legibility of records, the content of which is forbidden by law to be divulged to unauthorized persons.

(i) *Premature destruction or loss of records*. When records are destroyed or lost before the expiration of the prescribed period of retention, a certified statement listing, as far as may be determined, the records destroyed and describing the circumstances of accidental or other premature destruction or loss shall be filed with the Commission within ninety (90) days from the date of discovery of such destruction.

(j) *Schedule of records and periods of retention*. The schedule of records, § 225.3, shows the period of time that designated records shall be preserved. However, records related to plant shall be retained a minimum of 25 years unless accounting adjustments resulting from reclassification and original cost studies have been approved by the regulatory commission having jurisdiction, and either (1) continuing plant inventory records are maintained (see Definition No. 8, "Continuing Plant Inventory Records," Parts 201 and 204 of this subchapter), or (2) unitization of construction costs appear in work orders.

(k) *Retention periods designated "Destroy at option"*. Use of the retention period, "Destroy at option," in the regulations in this part constitutes authorization for such destruction under the conditions specified for the particular types of records, only if such optional destruction is appropriate to limited managerial interest in such records and if such optional destruction is not in conflict with other legal retention requirements or usefulness of such records in satisfying pending regulatory actions or directives.

(l) *Records of services performed by associated companies*. The natural gas company to which the regulations in this part apply shall assure the availability of records of services performed by associated companies for the periods indicated herein, as are necessary, to support the cost of services rendered to it by an associated company.

(m) *Index of records*. At each office of the natural gas company where records are kept or stored, such records as are herein required to be preserved shall be so arranged, filed and currently indexed that they may be readily identified and made available to representatives of the Commission.

(n) *Schedule of notes*: (1) For the purposes of the regulation, a stockholder's account may be treated as a closed account at the time that such stockholder ceases to be a holder of record of the particular class and series of stock of the company and the 6-year retention period prescribed herein shall run from that date. If such person subsequently acquires shares of capital stock of the company and thus again becomes a stockholder of the company, the record of such acquisition shall be treated as a new stockholder account.

(2) The terms "bonds" and "debentures," as used in paragraphs (a) through (f) of this section, shall include all debt securities, such as bonds, debentures, or notes other than debt securities which evidence temporary borrowings and which are expected to be repaid out of the proceeds of the sale of longer term securities. Typical of such temporary debt securities as described in 4(i) would be notes issued to banks evidencing temporary working capital and construction loans and gas storage loans.

(3) Canceled bonds and debentures and paid interest coupons pertaining thereto may be destroyed, provided that a certificate of destruction giving full descriptive reference to the documents destroyed shall be made by the person or persons authorized to perform such destruction and shall be retained by the company for the period herein prescribed. The certificate of destruction evidencing the destruction of paid interest coupons pertaining to bonds or debentures need not contain a listing of the bond or debenture serial numbers pertaining to such paid interest coupons. When documents represent debt secured by mortgage, the certificate of destruction shall also be authorized by a representative of the trustee(s) acting in conjunction with the person or persons destroying the documents or shall have the trustee(s) acceptance hereon. The certificate of destruction above described may be destroyed 6 years after the payment and discharge of the bonds or debentures or interest coupons described in such certificate.

(4) If a retention period is prescribed elsewhere in the schedule with respect to any document which is included as an exhibit to any filing retained pursuant to the requirements of this item, the company need retain only one copy of such document in its files provided appropriate cross references are established.

(5) Life or mortality study data for depreciation purposes shall be retained for 25 years or for 10 years after plant is retired, whichever is longer.

* * * * *

SUBCHAPTER G. APPROVED FORMS, NATURAL GAS ACT

PART 250. FORMS

Citation: 18 CFR 250.16

✍ § 250.16 Format of compliance plan for transportation services and affiliate transactions.

(a) *Who must comply.* An interstate natural gas pipeline that transports natural gas for others pursuant to Subparts B, G, or H of Part 284 or pursuant to Subparts A or E of Part 157 and is affiliated, as that term is defined in § 161.2 of this chapter, in any way with a marketing or brokering entity, except a pipeline that does not conduct any transactions with its affiliated marketer must:

(1) File FERC Form No. 592 in the manner prescribed in paragraph (b) of this section.

(2) Maintain and provide the information specified in paragraph (c) of this section, and

(3) Maintain all information required under this section from the time the information is received until July 31, 1994.

PART 284. CERTAIN SALES AND TRANSPORTATION OF NATURAL GAS UNDER THE NATURAL GAS POLICY ACT OF 1978 AND RELATED AUTHORITIES

Subpart A. General Provisions and Conditions

Citation: 18 CFR 284.7

✍ § 284.7 Rates.

* * * * *

(c) *Rate design.* * * *

* * * * *

(6) *Discount reports.* (i) A pipeline that provides either firm or interruptible transportation service at a discounted rate must file within 15 days of the close of the billing period a report containing the following information:

(A) the full legal name of the shipper being provided the discount;

(B) any corporate affiliation between the transporting pipeline and the shipper;

(C) the maximum rate or fee; and

(D) the rate or fee actually charged during the billing period.

(ii) The requirements of this section do not apply to discounts relating to the release of capacity under § 284.243, unless the release is permanent.

(iii) The discount report information must be provided in electronic format according to specifications that can be obtained at the Federal Energy Regulatory Commission, Division of Information Services, Public Reference and Files Maintenance Branch, Washington, DC 20426.

Citation: 18 CFR 284.8

✍ § 284.8 Firm transportation service.

* * * * *

(b) * **

(3) An interstate pipeline that offers transportation service on a firm basis under subpart B or G of this part must provide all shippers with equal and timely access to information relevant to the availability of such service, including, but not limited to, the availability of capacity at receipt points, on the mainline, at delivery points, and in storage fields, and whether the capacity is available directly from the pipeline or through capacity release. The information must be provided on an Electronic Bulletin Board with the features prescribed in Sec. 284.10(a) and as required by Sec. 284.10(b).

* * * * *

Citation: 18 CFR 284.9

✍ § 284.9 Interruptible transportation service.

* * * * *

(b) * * *

(3) An interstate pipeline that offers transportation service on an interruptible basis under subpart B or G of this part must provide all shippers with equal and timely access to information relevant to the availability of such service. The information must be provided on an Electronic Bulletin Board with the features prescribed in Sec. 284.10(a) and as required by Sec. 284.10(b).

* * * * *

Citation: 18 CFR 284.10

✍ § 284.10 Standards for Pipeline Business Operations and Communications.

(a) *Electronic Bulletin Boards.* An interstate pipeline that is required by this chapter or by its tariff to display information on an Electronic Bulletin Board must provide for the following features on its board:

(1) Downloading by users;

(2) Daily back-up of information displayed on the board, which must be available for user review for at least three years;

(3) Purging of information on completed transactions from current files;

(4) Display of most recent entries ahead of information posted earlier; and

(5) On-line help, a search function that permits users to locate all information concerning a specific transaction, and a menu that permits users to separately access the notices of available capacity, the marketing affiliate discount information, the marketing affiliate capacity allocation log, and the standards of conduct information.

(b) Incorporation by Reference of Business Practice and Electronic Communication Standards. (1) An interstate pipeline that transports gas under subpart B or G of this part must comply with the following business practice and electronic communication standards promulgated by the Gas Industry Standards Board, which are incorporated herein by reference:

(i) Nominations Related Standards (Version 1.0, June 14, 1996);

(ii) Flowing Gas Related Standards (Version 1.0, June 14, 1996);

(iii) Invoice Related Standards (Version 1.0, June 14, 1996); and

(iv) Capacity Release Related Standards (Version 1.0, June 14, 1996).

(2) This incorporation by reference was approved by the Director of the Federal Register in accordance with 5 U.S.C. 552(a) and 1 CFR part 51. Copies of these standards may be obtained from the Gas Industry Standards Board, 1100 Louisiana, Suite 4925, Houston, TX 77002. Copies may be inspected at the Federal Energy Regulatory Commission, Public Reference and Files Maintenance Branch, 888 First Street, NE., Washington, DC 20426 and at the Office of the

Subpart B — Certain Transportation by Interstate Pipelines

Citation: 18 CFR 284.106

✍ § 284.106 Reporting requirements.

(a) *Notice of bypass.* An interstate pipeline that provides transportation (except storage) under § 284.102 to a customer that is located in the service area of a local distribution company and will not be delivering the customer's gas to that local distribution company, must file with the Commission, within thirty days after commencing such transportation, a statement that the interstate pipeline has notified the local distribution company and the local distribution company's appropriate regulatory agency in writing of the proposed transportation prior to commencement.

(b) *Semi-annual storage report.* Within 30 days of the end of each complete storage injection and withdrawal season, the interstate pipeline must file with the Commission a report of storage activity provided under the authority of either § 284.102 or § 284.223, as applicable. The report must be signed under oath by a senior official, consist of an original and five conformed copies, and contain a summary of storage injection and withdrawal activities to include the following:

* * * * *

(c) *Index of customers.* (1) Each calendar quarter, subsequent to the initial implementation of this provision, an interstate pipeline must provide for electronic dissemination of an index of all its firm transportation and storage customers under contract as of the first day of the calendar quarter. Electronic dissemination will be by placing a file, adhering to the requirements set forth by the Commission, on the pipeline's electronic bulletin board in a format which can be downloaded from the electronic bulletin board. The pipeline must also submit the electronic file to the Commission.

(2) Until an interstate pipeline is in compliance with the reporting requirements of this paragraph, the pipeline must comply with the index of customer requirements applicable to transportation and sales under Part 157, set forth under § 154.111 (b) and (c) of this chapter.

(3) For each customer receiving firm transportation or storage service, the index must include the information listed below:

(i) the full legal name of the customer;

(ii) the rate schedule number of the service being provided;

(iii) the contract effective date;

(iv) the contract expiration date;

(v) for transportation service, maximum daily contract quantity (specify unit of measurement);

(vi) for storage service, maximum storage quantity (specify unit of measurement).

(4) The information included in the quarterly index must be available on the electronic bulletin board until the next quarterly index is established. The electronic files must be archived for at least three years.

(5) The requirements of this section do not apply to contracts which relate solely to the release of capacity under § 284.243, unless the release is permanent.

(6) The requirements for the electronic index can be obtained at the Federal Energy Regulatory Commission, Division of Information Services, Public Reference and Files Maintenance Branch, Washington, DC 20426.

PART 292. REGULATIONS UNDER SECTIONS 201 AND 210 OF THE PUBLIC UTILITY REGULATORY POLICIES ACT OF 1978 WITH REGARD TO SMALL POWER PRODUCTION AND COGENERATION

Citation: 18 CFR 292.207

✍ § 292.207 Procedures for obtaining qualifying status.

* * * * *

(b) * * *

(4) *Notice.* (i) Applications for certification filed under paragraph (b) of this section must include a form of notice of the request for certification suitable for publication in the Federal Register, as well as a copy of the samenotice in electronic format (in either ASCII text, WordPerfect 5.1 for DOS or WordPerfect 5.2 for Windows format) on a 3 1/2 " diskette marked with the name of the applicant and the words "Notice of Filing."

* * * * *

PART 300. CONFIRMATION AND APPROVAL OF THE RATES OF FEDERAL POWER MARKETING ADMINISTRATIONS

Citation: **18 CFR 300.10**

✍ § 300.10 Application for confirmation and approval.

(a) *General provisions* — (1) *Contents of filing.* Any application under this subpart for confirmation and approval of rate schedules must include, as described in this section a letter of request for rate approval, a form of notice suitable for publication in the Federal Register, as well as a copy of the same notice in electronic format (in either ASCII text, WordPerfect 5.1 for DOS or WordPerfect 5.2 for Windows format) on a 3 1/2" diskette marked with the name of the applicant and the words "Notice of Filing," the rate schedule, a statement of revenue and related costs, the order, if any, placing the rates into effect on an interim basis, the Administrator's Record of Decision or explanation of the rate development process, supporting documents, a certification, and technical supporting information and analysis.

* * * * *

SUBCHAPTER P. REGULATIONS UNDER THE INTERSTATE COMMERCE ACT

PART 348. OIL PIPELINE APPLICATIONS FOR MARKET POWER DETERMINATIONS

Citation: **18 CFR 348.2**

✍ § 348.2 Procedures.

(a) A carrier must file, as provided in § 341.1 of this chapter, an original plus fourteen copies of its application, including its statement of position, statements, and related material, and a letter of transmittal and must submit its application on an electronic medium. The formats for the electronic filing and the paper copy can be obtained at the Federal Energy Regulatory Commission, Division of Public Information, 825 North Capitol Street, N.E., Washington, D.C. 20426. A carrier must submit with its application any request for privileged treatment of documents and information under § 388.112 of this chapter and a proposed form of protective agreement. In the event the carrier requests privileged treatment under § 388.112 of this chapter, it must file the original and three copies of its application with the information for which privileged treatment is sought and 11 copies of the application without the information for which privileged treatment is sought.

(b) A carrier must provide a copy of its letter of transmittal and its proposed form of protective agreement to each shipper and subscriber on or before the day the material is transmitted to the Commission for filing.

(c) A letter of transmittal must describe the market-based rate filing, including an identification of each rate that would be market-based, and the pertinent tariffs or supplement numbers, state if a waiver is being requested and specify the statute, section, subsection, regulation, policy or order requested to be waived. Letters of transmittal must be certified pursuant to § 341.2(c)(2) of this chapter and acknowledgment must be requested pursuant to § 341.2(c)(3) of this chapter.

(d) An interested person must make a written request to the carrier for a copy of the carrier's complete application within 20 days after the filing of the application. The request must include an executed copy of the protective agreement. Any objection to the proposed form of protective agreement must be filed under § 385.212 of this chapter.

(e) A carrier must provide a copy of the complete application to the requesting person within seven days after receipt of the written request and an executed copy of the protective agreement.

(f) A carrier must provide copies as required by paragraphs (b) and (e) of this section by first-class mail or by other means of transmission agreed upon in writing.

(g) Any intervention or protest to the application must be filed within 60 days after the filing of the application and must be filed pursuant to § § 343.2 (a) and (b) of this chapter. A protest must also be telefaxed if required by § 343.3(a) of this chapter.

(h) A protest filed against an application for a market power determination must set forth in detail the grounds for opposing the carrier's application, including responding to its position and information and, if desired, presenting information pursuant to § 348.1(c).

(i) After expiration of the date for filing protests, the Commission will issue an order in which it will summarily rule on the application or, if appropriate, establish additional procedures and the scope of the investigation.

SUBCHAPTER R. APPROVED FORMS, INTERSTATE COMMERCE ACT

PART 356. PRESERVATION OF RECORDS

Citation: **18 CFR 356.6**

✍ § 356.6 Preservation of records.

(a) All records listed in § 356.11 may be preserved in either hard-copy paperstock or nonerasable microfilm (see § 356.8). However, a paperstock or microfilm record need not be created to satisfy the requirements of this part if the particular records are initially prepared on nonerasable media such as punched cards, magnetic tapes and disks. The records maintained in nonreadable media and the underlying data used in their preparation shall be preserved for the periods prescribed in § 356.11. In no case shall a paperstock or microfilm record be destroyed after transfer to nonreadable media before expiration of the prescribed periods of retention without Commission approval (see § 356.7).

(b) Each nonreadable form of media shall be accompanied by a statement clearly indicating the type of data included in the media and certifying that the information contained therein is complete and accurate. This statement shall be executed by a person having personal knowledge of the facts contained in the records. The records shall be indexed and retained in such a manner as will render them readily accessible, and the company shall have facilities available to locate, identify and reproduce the records on paper similar in size to the original without loss of clarity.

Citation: **18 CFR 356.8**

✍ § 356.8 Photographic copies.

(a) Any record may be transferred to nonerasable microfilm (including microfiche, computer output microfilm, and aperture cards) at any time. Records so maintained on microfilm shall satisfy the minimum requirements listed in paragraphs (b) through (f) of this section.

(b) The microfilm used shall be of a quality that can be easily read and that reproduction in paperstock can be similar in size of an original without loss of clarity of detail during the periods the records are required to be retained in § 356.11.

(c) Microfilm records shall be indexed and retained in such a manner as will render them readily accessible, and the company shall have facilities available to locate, identify and read the microfilm and reproduce in paper form.

(d) Any significant characteristic, feature, or other attribute which microfilm will not preserve shall be clearly indicated at the beginning of each roll of film or series of microfilm records if applicable to all records on the roll or series, or on the individual record, as appropriate.

(e) The printed side of printed forms need not be microfilmed for each record if nothing has been added to the printed matter common to all such forms, but an identified specimen of the form shall be on the film for reference.

(f) Each roll of film or series of microfilm records shall include a microfilm of a certificate stating that the photographs are direct and facsimile reproductions of the original records and they have been made in accordance with prescribed regulations. Such a certificate shall be executed by a person having personal knowledge of the facts covered therein. Where the microfilm is computer output microfilm the certificate shall state that the information is complete and accurate.

TITLE 19. CUSTOMS DUTIES

Agency:	**Department of the Treasury** **United States Customs Service**

PART 4. VESSELS IN FOREIGN AND DOMESTIC TRADES

Citation:	**19 CFR 4.8**

✍ **§ 4.8 Preliminary entry.**

Preliminary entry allows a U.S. or foreign vessel arriving under circumstances which require it to formally enter, to discharge cargo, passengers, or baggage prior to making formal entry. The granting of preliminary entry may be accomplished electronically pursuant to an authorized electronic data interchange system, or by other means of communication approved by the Customs Service. Preliminary entry must be made in compliance with § 4.30 of this part. The granting of preliminary vessel entry by the Customs Service may be conditioned upon the presentation of a completed Customs Form 1300 (Master's Certificate on Preliminary Entry) to Customs during discretionary vessel boarding, or upon the filing with Customs of a Customs Form 1300 or its equivalent by electronic or other means in instances where vessels are not boarded.

LANDING AND DELIVERY OF CARGO

Citation:	**19 CFR 4.30**

✍ **§ 4.30 Permits and special licenses for unlading and lading.**

(a) Except as prescribe in paragraph (f), (g), or (k) of this section or in § 123.8 of this chapter, and except in the case of a vessel exempt from entry or clearance under 19 U.S.C. 288, no passengers, cargo, baggage, or other article shall be unladen from a vessel which arrives directly or indirectly from any port or place outside the Customs territory of the U.S., including the adjacent waters (see § 4.6 of this part), or from a vessel which transits the Panama Canal and no cargo, baggage, or other article shall be laden on a vessel destined to a port or place outside the Customs territory of the U.S., including the adjacent waters (see § 4.6 of this part) if Customs supervision of such lading is required, until the port director shall have issued a permit or special license therefore on Customs Form 3171 or electronically pursuant to an authorized electronic data interchange system or other means of communication approved by the Customs Service.

* * * * *

(b) Application for a permit or special license shall be made by the master, owner, or agent of the vessel on Customs Form 3171, or electronically pursuant to an authorized electronic data interchange system or other means of communicaiton approved by the Customs Service, and shall specifically indicate the type of service desired at that time, unlesss a term permit or term special license has been issued. Arrangements, in the case of a term permit or term special license, shall be made locally so that the proper Customs officer will be notified during official hours in advance of the rendering of the services as to the nature of the services desired and the exact times they will be needed. An agent of a vessel may limit his application to operations involved in the entry and unlading of the vessel or to operations involved in its lading and clearance.Such limitaion shall be specifically noted on the application.

* * * * *

PART 10. ARTICLES CONDITIONALLY FREE, SUBJECT TO A REDUCED RATE, ETC.

Citation:	**19 CFR 10.62b**

✍ **§ 10.62b Aircraft turbine fuel.**

(a) *General.* Unless otherwise provided, aircraft turbine fuel withdrawn from a Customs bonded warehouse for use under section 309, Tariff Act of 1930, as amended (19 U.S.C. 1309), may be commingled with domestic or other aircraft turbine fuel after such withdrawal only if such commingling is approved by the appropriate Customs official for the port where the commingling occurs. The appropriate Customs official may approve such commingling if the fueling system in which the commingling will occur contains adequate physical safeguards to prevent the possible unauthorized entry into the Customs territory of the bonded fuel. Such commingled fuel must be accounted for in the same 24-hour period in which it was commingled and must be —

(1) Exported within that 24-hour period;

(2) Used under section 309 within that 24-hour period; or

(3) Entered or withdrawn for consumption, with duty deposited, as required under the applicable regulations (see part 144 of this chapter).

(b) *Duty-free withdrawal from warehouse of aircraft turbine fuel under section 557(a), Tariff Act of 1930, as amended (19 U.S.C. 1557(a)).* Turbine fuel intended for use as supplies on aircraft under section 309, Tariff Act of 1930, as amended, and withdrawn from a Customs bonded warehouse shall be entitled to the privileges provided for in section 309 if an amount equal to or exceeding the quantity of such fuel is established, as provided for in paragraph (c) of this section, to have been used on aircraft qualifying for the privileges provided for in section 309 within 30 days after the withdrawal of the fuel from the Customs bonded warehouse. Withdrawal of aircraft turbine fuel under this paragraph shall be in accordance with the procedures in § § 10.59 through 10.64, unless otherwise provided in this section. Withdrawals under this paragraph shall be annotated with the term "Withdrawal under 19 CFR 10.62b(b)".

(c) *Establishment of use of fuel by qualifying aircraft.* (1) The person withdrawing aircraft turbine fuel under paragraph (b) of this section shall establish that an aircraft qualifying for the privileges provided for in section 309, Tariff Act of 1930, as amended, used fuel in an amount equal to or exceeding the quantity of the fuel withdrawn which is not entered and upon which duties are not paid by submitting to Customs, within the time provided in paragraph (d) of this section, either —

(i) Records prepared in the normal course of business effecting the transfer to identified (e.g., by aircraft company name, flight number, flight origin and destination, and date of flight) aircraft of fuel in an amount equal to or exceeding the quantity of the fuel withdrawn which is not entered and on which duties are not paid and objective evidence that the aircraft to which the fuel was transferred were actually used in trade qualifying for the privileges provided in section 309, Tariff Act of 1930, as amended; or

(ii) A certification (documentary or electronic) that:

(A) All of the fuel withdrawn was intended for use on aircraft entitled to the privileges provided for in section 309;

(B) Within 30 days of the date of withdrawal from warehouse, an amount of fuel equal to or exceeding the quantity of the fuel withdrawn which is not entered and on which duties are not paid was transferred as supplies to aircraft entitled to the privileges provided for in section 309;

(C) All of the aircraft, to which the fuel which is not entered and on which duties are not paid was transferred as supplies, were used in a trade provided for in section 309; and

(D) The person making the certification possesses evidence (documentary or electronic) available for Customs inspection at a named place which supports each of the above statements.

(2) Upon request by Customs, the person who submits the certification provided for in paragraph (c)(1) of this section shall promptly provide the evidence required to support the claim for treatment under this section (including the records described in § 10.62b(c)(1)(i)) and § § 10.62 and 19.6(d) and each of the statements in the certification.

(d) *Time for establishment of use of fuel by qualifying aircraft.* The person withdrawing aircraft turbine fuel under paragraph (b) of this section shall submit the records or certification provided for in paragraph (c) of this section by the 40th day after the date of withdrawal of the fuel unless the fuel was withdrawn under a blanket withdrawal under paragraph (g) of this section. If the fuel was withdrawn under a blanket withdrawal, the person withdrawing aircraft turbine fuel under this section shall submit the records or certification provided for in paragraph (c) of this section by the 40th day after all of the fuel covered by the blanket permit to withdraw has been withdrawn.

(e) *Treatment of turbine fuel withdrawn but not used on qualifying aircraft within 30 days.* If turbine fuel is withdrawn from a Customs bonded warehouse under paragraph (b) of this section but fuel in an amount less than the quantity withdrawn is established to have been used within 30 days of the date of withdrawal from warehouse on aircraft qualifying for the privileges provided for in section 309, Tariff Act of 1930, as amended, a withdrawal for consumption shall be filed and duties shall be deposited for the excess of fuel so withdrawn over that used on aircraft so qualifying. Such withdrawal shall be filed and such duties shall be deposited by the 40th day after the date of withdrawal of the fuel in accordance with the procedures in § 144.38 of this chapter. Interest shall be payable and deposited with such duties, calculated from the date of withdrawal at the rate of interest established under 26 U.S.C. 6621.

(f) *Liquidated damages.* Failure to account for turbine fuel withdrawn under paragraphs (b) through (h) of this section shall result in liquidated damages against the person withdrawing the turbine fuel, as provided for under § 113.62 of this chapter. Such failure to account for turbine fuel includes:

(1) The failure to timely file the withdrawal for consumption and payment of duty, with interest, on the quantity of fuel so withdrawn in excess of the quantity of fuel established to have been used on qualifying aircraft within 30 days of withdrawal, as provided for in paragraph (e) of this section;

(2) The failure to timely file the evidence or certification establishing such use of the fuel which is not entered and on which duties are not paid, as provided for in paragraph (c) of this section; or

(3) The failure to promptly provide the evidence required to support the claim for treatment under paragraph (b) of this section, upon request by Customs, as provided for in paragraph (c)(2) of this section.

(g) *Blanket withdrawals.* Blanket withdrawals, as provided for in § § 10.62 and 19.6(d), may be used for withdrawals from warehouse under section 557(a), Tariff Act of 1930, as amended, and paragraphs (b) through (h) of this section, under the procedures provided in § § 10.62 and 19.6(d) except that —

(1) Application by the withdrawer for a blanket permit to withdraw shall be on the warehouse entry, or on the warehouse entry/entry summary when used as an entry, annotated with the words "Some or all of the merchandise will be withdrawn under blanket permit per § § 10.62, 10.62b, and 19.6(d).";

(2) Turbine fuel withdrawn under a blanket permit as authorized in this paragraph may be delivered at a port other than the port of withdrawal;

(3) Customs acceptance of a properly completed application for a blanket permit to withdraw, on the warehouse entry or warehouse entry/entry summary, will constitute approval of the blanket permit to withdraw;

(4) A copy of the approved blanket permit to withdraw will be delivered to the warehouse proprietor, whereupon fuel may be withdrawn under the terms of the blanket permit;

(5) The withdrawal document to be placed in the proprietor's permit file folder (see § 19.6(d)(2)) will be a commercially acceptable document of receipt (such as a "withdrawal ticket") issued by the warehouse proprietor, identified with a unique alpha-numeric code and containing the following information:

(i) Identity of withdrawer;

(ii) Identity of warehouse and tank from which fuel is withdrawn;

(iii) Date of withdrawal;

(iv) Type of merchandise withdrawn; and

(v) Quantity of merchandise withdrawn.

(6) The date of withdrawal, for purposes of calculating the 30-day period in which fuel must be used on qualifying aircraft under this section, shall be the date on which physical removal of the fuel from the warehouse commences;

(7) The blanket permit summary prepared by the proprietor as provided for in § 19.6(d)(4) shall be prepared when all of the fuel covered by the blanket permit has been withdrawn and shall account for all merchandise withdrawn under the blanket permit, as required by § 19.6(d)(4), by stating, in summary form, the unique alpha-numeric codes and information required in paragraph (g)(5) of this section, as well as the identity of the warehouse entry to which the withdrawal is attributed;

(8) The certification on the blanket permit summary (see § 19.6(d)(4)) shall be that the merchandise listed thereunder was withdrawn in compliance with § § 10.62, 10.62b, and 19.6(d); and

(9) The person withdrawing aircraft turbine fuel under these blanket procedures shall submit the records or certification provided for in § 10.62b(c) by the 40th day after all of the fuel covered by the blanket permit has been withdrawn (see § 10.62b(d)). At the discretion of the port director for the port where blanket withdrawal was approved, submission of the

records and evidence required to establish use of the fuel on qualifying aircraft may be required to be submitted electronically, in a format compatible with Customs electronic recordkeeping systems.

(h) *Recordkeeping.* The person withdrawing aircraft turbine fuel from warehouse under this section is subject to the recordkeeping requirements in 19 U.S.C. 1508 and 1509, as provided for in part 162 of this chapter.

PART 111. CUSTOMHOUSE BROKERS

Subpart C. Duties and Responsibilities of Customhouse Brokers

Citation: **19 CFR 111.23**

✍ **§ 111.23 Retention of Records.**

(a) *Place and period of retention.* (1) *Place.* The records, as defined in § 111.1(f), and required by § § 111.21 and 111.22 to be kept by a broker, shall be retained within the Customs district to which they relate, unless an exemption has been granted for centralized accounting records under paragraph (e) of this section.

(2) *Period.* The records described in paragraph (a)(1) of this section, other than powers of attorney, shall be retained for at least 5 years after the date of entry. Powers of attorney shall be retained until revoked, and revoked powers of attorney and letters of revocation shall be retained for 5 years after either the date of revocation or the date the client ceases to be an "active client" as defined in 111.29(b)(2)(ii). When merchandise is withdrawn from a bonded warehouse, copies of papers relating to the withdrawal shall be retained for 5 years from the date of withdrawal of the last merchandise withdrawn under the entry.

(b) *Microfilming of records.* A broker, with the approval of the district director for the district in which he has been granted a permit and the records are located, may maintain on microfilm or similar medium, in lieu of an original, any records other than powers of attorney required to be retained under the provisions of paragraph (a) of this section, at any time after the entry to which these records pertain has been liquidated, upon the following conditions:

(c) *Standard required for microfilming.* Brokers microfilming their records shall maintain the integrity of the original records by insuring that the microfilm copies are true reproductions or the original records and serve the purpose for which such records were created. The following shall be observed in any microfilming;

(1) Copies shall contain all significant record detail shown on the original.

(2) Copies of the records, on either roll microfilm or unit microfilm systems, shall be so arranged, identified, and indexed that any individual document or component of the records can be located with reasonable facility.

(3) Any indexes, registers or other finding aids shall be microfilmed at the beginning of the records to which they relate.

(d) *Other methods of reproduction for record retention.* If approved by the district director in which a broker has been granted a permit and in which he has records located, a broker may use, in lieu of original documents, methods of reproduction other than microfilm, including microfiche, for the reproduction of records, provided the requirements of paragraphs (b) and (c) of this section are met. While original powers of attorney must be retained, copies also may be retained.

(e) *Exemption.* (1) *Applicability.* The procedure to maintain financial records on a centralized system basis is available to brokers who have been granted permits to do business in more than one district.

(2) *Request.* A written request for authorization to maintain financial records on a centralized system basis shall be submitted to the regional commissioner responsible for the region in which the centralized records are to be maintained. The written request shall include:

(i) The address at which the broker desires to maintain the centralized accounting records. This location must be within a district where the broker has been granted a permit.

(ii) A detailed statement describing all the records of financial transactions to be maintained at the centralized location, the methodology of record maintenance, a description of any automated data processing to be applied, and a list of all the broker's customs business activity locations.

(iii) An agreement that if the authorization is granted, no change in the records, the manner of recordkeeping, or the location at which they will be maintained, will be made unless approved by Customs. Each request for a change requires prior approval in the same manner as prescribed above.

(iv) An agreement to comply with § 111.22.

(v) An agreement that all financial records pertaining to customs transactions will be made available to Customs for complete inspection in accordance with § 111.25 and § 162.1d of this Chapter after reasonable notice in writing has been provided.

(3) *Approval.* After the broker's request has been received and reviewed by the regional commissioner, he shall advise the broker, in writing, of his decision whether to authorize the broker to maintain financial records on a centralized system basis. If the regional commissioner denies the request he shall advise the broker of the reasons. Denial shall be without prejudice to reapply for an exemption. If the request involves records from districts not within the jurisdiction of the regional commissioner of the region where the request was filed, the regional commissioner should consult with the other affected regional commissioners before acting on the request.

(f) *Withdrawal of exemption.* Whenever an audit by Customs indicates that a broker to whom an exemption has been granted is not keeping records in accordance with the requirements of paragraph (e) of this section, the regional commissioner who granted the exemption shall notify the broker, in writing, of the audit finding(s). The regional commissioner shall provide the broker with 30 days from the date of notification to respond to the audit finding(s) unless a shorter period is deemed necessary. If the broker fails to respond, or if the regional commissioner determines that a broker has not responded satisfactorily to the audit finding(s), the regional commissioner shall withdraw the exemption by notice in writing. The withdrawal shall not become effective until 30 days after the date of mailing of the notice. The broker shall thereafter keep and maintain records as required by paragraph (a) of this section.

(g) *Reproduction of centralized accounting records.* The regional commissioner for the region in which a broker has been granted an exemption to maintain financial records on a centralized system basis, provided in paragraph (e) of this section, is responsible for approving requests for the reproduction of centralized financial records provided under paragraphs (b) and (d) of this section.

PART 162. RECORDKEEPING, INSPECTION, SEARCH, AND SEIZURE

Subpart A. Recordkeeping, Inspection, Examination, and Search

Citation: 19 CFR 162.1a

✍ § 162.1a Definitions.

When used in § § 162.1a through 162.1i, the following terms shall have the meaning indicated:

(a) *Records*. "Records" means:

(1) Statements, declarations, books, papers, correspondence, accounts, technical data, automated record storage devices (e.g., magnetic discs and tapes), computer programs necessary to retrieve information in a usable form, and other documents which:

(i) Pertain to any importation, or to the information contained in the documents required by law or regulation under the Tariff Act of 1930, as amended, in connection with the entry of merchandise;

(ii) Are of the type normally kept in the ordinary course of business; and

(iii) Are sufficiently detailed:

(A) To establish the right to make entry,

(B) To establish the correctness of any entry,

(C) To determine the liability of any person for duties and taxes due, or which may be due, the United States,

(D) To determine the liability of any person for fines, penalties, and forfeitures, and

(E) To determine whether the person has complied with the laws and regulations administered by the Customs Service; and

(2) Any other documents required under laws or regulations administered by the Customs Service.

(b) *Third-party recordkeeper.* "Third-party recordkeeper" means any Customs broker, attorney, or accountant.

(c) *Summons*. "Summons" means any summons issued under this subpart which requires either the production of records or the giving of testimony, or both.

(d) *Technical data*. "Technical data" includes records, diagrams, and other data with regard to a business or an engineering or exploration operation, whether conducted inside or outside the United States, and whether on paper, cards, photographs, blueprints, tapes, microfiche, film, or other media.

PART 181. NORTH AMERICAN FREE TRADE AGREEMENT

Subpart B. Export Requirements

Citation: 19 CFR 181.12

✍ § 181.12 Maintenance and availability of records.

(a) *Maintenance of records* — (1) *General*. An exporter or producer in the United States who completes and signs a Certificate of Origin shall maintain in the United States, for five years after the date on which the Certificate was signed, all records relating to the origin of a good for which preferential tariff treatment may be claimed in Canada or Mexico, including records associated with:

(i) The purchase of, cost of, value of, and payment for, the good that is exported from the United States;

(ii) The purchase of, cost of, value of, and payment for, all materials, including indirect materials, used in the production of the good that is exported from the United States; and

(iii) The production of the good in the form in which the good is exported from the United States.

(2) *Method of maintenance*. The records referred to in paragraph (a) of this section shall be maintained in accordance with the Generally Accepted Accounting Principles applied in the United States and may be maintained in hard-copy form, on microfilm or microfiche or in automated record storage devices (for example, magnetic discs and tapes) if associated computer programs are available to facilitate retrieval of the data in a usable form.

(b) *Availability of records* — (1) *To Customs*. For purposes of determining compliance with the provisions of this part, the records required to be maintained under this section shall be made available for examination and inspection by the port director or other appropriate Customs officer in the same manner as provided in § 162.1d of this chapter in the case of U.S. importer records.

(2) *To the Canadian or Mexican customs administration.* If a U.S. exporter or producer receives notification of, and consents to, an origin verification visit by the Canadian or Mexican customs administration under Article 506 of the NAFTA (see § 181.74(e) of this part), such consent shall constitute agreement by the U.S. exporter or producer to make available to an officer of that customs administration all records required to be maintained under this section and to provide facilities for the inspection thereof. If, during the course of an origin verification of a U.S. producer, the Canadian or Mexican customs administration finds that the U.S. producer has failed to maintain its records in accordance with the Generally Accepted Accounting Principles applied in the United States, that customs administration will so inform the U.S. producer in writing and will give the U.S. producer 60 calendar days to conform the records to those Principles. If a U.S. exporter or producer fails to maintain records or make records available to the Canadian or Mexican customs administration in accordance with the provisions of this section, or if a U.S. producer fails to conform its records to Generally Accepted Accounting Principles as provided in this paragraph, the Canadian or Mexican customs administration may deny preferential tariff treatment to the good that is the subject of the verification visit.

Subpart C. Import Requirements

Citation: 19 CFR 181.22

✍ § 181.22 Maintenance of records and submission of Certificate by importer.

(a) *Maintenance of records*. Each importer claiming preferential tariff treatment for a good imported into the United States shall maintain in the United States, for five years after the date of entry of the good, all documentation relating to the importation of the good. Such documentation shall include a copy of the Certificate of Origin and any other relevant records as specified in § 162.1a(a) of this chapter.

(b) *Submission of Certificate*. An importer who claims preferential tariff treatment on a good under § 181.21 of this part shall provide, at the request of the port director, a copy of each Certificate of Origin pertaining to the good which is in the possession of the importer. A Certificate of Origin submitted to Customs under this paragraph or under § 181.32(b)(3) of this part:

(1) Shall be on Customs Form 434, including privately-printed copies thereof, or on such other form as approved by the Canadian or Mexican customs administration, or, as an alternative to Customs Form 434 or such other approved form, in an approved computerized format or such other medium or format

as is approved by the Office of Field Operations, U.S. Customs Service, Washington, DC 20229. An alternative format must contain the same information and certification set forth on Customs Form 434;

(2) Shall be signed by the exporter or by the exporter's authorized agent having knowledge of the relevant facts;

(3) Shall be completed either in the English language or in the language of the country from which the good is exported. If the Certificate is completed in a language other than English, the importer shall also provide to the port director, upon request, a written English translation thereof;

(4) Shall be accepted by Customs for four years after the date on which the Certificate was signed by the exporter or producer; and

(5) May be applicable to:

(i) A single importation of a good into the United States, including a single shipment that results in the filing of one or more entries and a series of shipments that results in the filing of one entry; or

(ii) Multiple importations of identical goods into the United States that occur within a specified period, not exceeding 12 months, set out therein by the exporter or producer.

(c) *Acceptance of Certificate.* A Certificate of Origin shall be accepted by the port director as valid for the purpose set forth in § 181.11(a) of this part, provided that the Certificate is completed, signed and dated in accordance with the requirements of paragraph (b) of this section. If the port director determines that a Certificate is illegible or defective or has not been completed in accordance with paragraph (b) of this section, the importer shall be given a period of not less than five working days to submit a corrected Certificate. Acceptance of a Certificate will result in the granting of preferential tariff treatment to the imported good unless, in connection with an origin verification initiated under subpart G of this part or based on a pattern of conduct within the meaning of § 181.76(c) of this part, the port director determines that the imported good does not qualify as an originating good or should not be accorded such treatment for any other reason as specifically provided for elsewhere in this part. A Certificate shall not be accepted in connection with subsequent importations during a period referred to in paragraph (b)(5)(ii) of this section if, based on an origin verification under subpart G of this part, the port director determined that a previously imported identical good covered by the Certificate did not qualify as an originating good.

(d) *Certificate not required* — (1) *General.* Except as otherwise provided in paragraph (d)(2) of this section, an importer shall not be required to have a Certificate of Origin in his possession for:

(i) An importation of a good for which the port director has in writing waived the requirement for a Certificate of Origin because the port director is otherwise satisfied that the good qualifies for preferential tariff treatment under the NAFTA;

(ii) A non-commercial importation of a good; or

(iii) A commercial importation of a good whose value does not exceed US $2,500, provided that, unless waived by the port director, the producer, exporter, importer or authorized agent includes on, or attaches to, the invoice or other document accompanying the shipment the following signed statement:

I hereby certify that the good covered by this shipment qualifies as an originating good for purposes of preferential tariff treatment under the NAFTA. Check One:

Importer
Exporter
Importer
Agent
Name
Title
Address
Signature and Date

(2) *Exception.* If the port director determines that an importation described in paragraph (d)(1) of this section forms part of a series of importations that may reasonably be considered to have been undertaken or arranged for the purpose of avoiding a certification requirement set forth in this part, the port director shall notify the importer in writing that for that importation the importer must have in his possession a valid Certificate of Origin to support the claim for preferential tariff treatment. The importer shall have 30 calendar days from the date of the written notice to obtain a valid Certificate, and a failure to timely obtain the Certificate will result in denial of the claim for preferential tariff treatment. For purposes of paragraph (d)(2) of this section, a "series of importations" means two or more entries covering goods arriving on the same day from the same exporter and consigned to the same person.

TITLE 20. EMPLOYEES' BENEFITS

Agency:	**Department of Labor** **Employment and Training Administration**

PART 627. GENERAL PROVISIONS GOVERNING PROGRAMS UNDER TITLES I, II, AND III OF THE ACT

Subpart D. Administrative Standards

Citation:	**20 CFR 627.455**

✍ **§ 627.455 Reports required.**

(a) *General.* The Governor shall report to DOL pursuant to instructions issued by DOL. Reports shall be submitted no more frequently than quarterly, in accordance with section 165(f) of the Act, and within 45 calendar days after the end of the report period. Additional reporting requirements for title III are set forth at § 631.15 of this chapter.

(b) A recipient may impose different forms or formats, shorter due dates, and more frequent reporting requirements on subrecipients, however, the recipient is required to meet the reporting requirements imposed on it by DOL.

(c) DOL may provide computer outputs to recipients to expedite or contribute to the accuracy of reporting. DOL may accept the required information from recipients in electronically reported format or computer printouts instead of prescribed forms.

(d) *Financial reports.* (1) Financial reports for programs under titles I, II, and III shall be submitted to DOL by each State quarterly and by program year of appropriation.

(2) Each recipient shall report program outlays on an accrual basis. If the recipient's accounting records are not normally kept on the accrual basis, the recipient shall develop such accrual information through an analysis of the documentation on hand.

(3) A final financial report is required 90 days after the expiration of a funding period (see § 627.485 of this part, Closeout).

(4) Pursuant to section 104(b)(13) of the Act, the SDA shall annually report to the Governor. Among other items, this report shall include information on the extent to which the SDA has met the goals for the training and training-related placement of women in nontraditional employment.

Citation: 20 CFR 627.460

✍ § 627.460 Requirements for records.

(a) Records, including the records identified in section 165(g) of the Act, shall be retained in accordance with section 165(e) of the Act. In establishing the time period of record retention requirements for records of subrecipients, the State may either:

(1) Impose the time limitation requirement of section 165(e) of the Act; or

(2) Require that subrecipient records for each funding period be retained for 3 years after the subrecipient submits to the awarding agency its final expenditure report for that funding period. Records for nonexpendable property shall be retained for a period of three years after final disposition of the property.

(b) The Governor shall ensure that the records under this section shall be retained beyond the prescribed period if any litigation or audit is begun or if a claim is instituted involving the grant or agreement covered by the records. In these instances, the Governor shall ensure that the records shall be retained until the litigation, audit, or claim has been finally resolved.

(c) In the event of the termination of the relationship with a subrecipient, the Governor or SDA or title III SSG shall be responsible for the maintenance and retention of the records of any subrecipient unable to retain them.

(d) *Record storage.* Records shall be retained and stored in a manner which will preserve their integrity and admissibility as evidence in any audit or other proceeding. The burden of production and authentication of the records shall be on the custodian of the records.

(e) *Federal and awarding agencies' access to records* — (1) *Records of recipients and subrecipients.* The awarding agency, the Department of Labor (including the Department of Labor's Office of Inspector General), and the Comptroller General of the United States, or any of their authorized representatives, have the right of timely and reasonable access to any books, documents, papers, computer records, or other records of recipients and subrecipients that are pertinent to the grant, in order to conduct audits and examinations, and to make excerpts, transcripts, and photocopies of such documents. This right also includes timely and reasonable access to recipient and subrecipient personnel for the purpose of interview and discussion related to such documents.

(2) *Expiration of right of access.* The right of access in this section is not limited to the required retention period but shall last as long as the records are retained.

TITLE 21. FOOD AND DRUGS

Agency: Department of Health and Human Services
Food and Drug Administration

SUBCHAPTER A. GENERAL

PART 58. GOOD LABORATORY PRACTICE FOR NONCLINICAL LABORATORY STUDIES

Subpart J. Records and Reports

Citation: 21 CFR 58.195

✍ § 58.195 Retention of records.

(a) Record retention requirements set forth in this section do not supersede the record retention requirements of any other regulations in this chapter.

(b) Except as provided in paragraph (c) of this section, documentation records, raw data and specimens pertaining to a nonclinical laboratory study and required to be made by this part shall be retained in the archive(s) for whichever of the following periods is shortest:

(1) A period of at least 2 years following the date on which an application for a research or marketing permit, in support of which the results of the nonclinical laboratory study were submitted, is approved by the Food and Drug Administration. This requirement does not apply to studies supporting notices of claimed investigational exemption for new drugs (IND'S) or applications for investigational device exemptions (IDE'S), records of which shall be governed by the provisions of paragraph (b)(2) of this section.

(2) A period of at least 5 years following the date on which the results of the nonclinical laboratory study are submitted to the Food and Drug Administration in support of an application for a research or marketing permit.

(3) In other situations (e.g., where the nonclinical laboratory study does not result in the submission of the study in support of an application for a research or marketing permit), a period of at lest 2 years following the date on which the study is completed, terminated, or discontinued.

(c) Wet specimens (except those specimens obtained from mutagenicity tests and wet specimens of blood, urine, feces, and biological fluids), samples of test or control articles, and specially prepared material, which are relatively fragile and differ markedly in stability and quality during storage, shall be retained only as long as the quality of the preparation affords evaluation. In no case shall retention be required for longer periods than those set forth in paragraphs (a) and (b) of this section.

(d) The master schedule sheet, copies of protocols, and records of quality assurance inspections, as required by § 58.35(c) shall be maintained by the quality assurance unit as an easily accessible system of records for the period of time specified in for the period of time specified in paragraphs (a) and (b) of this section.

(e) Summaries of training and experience and job descriptions required to be maintained by § 58.29(b) may be retained along with all other testing facility employment records for the length of time specified in paragraphs (a) and (b) of this section.

(f) Records and reports of the maintenance and calibration and inspection of equipment, as required by § 58.63(b) and (c), shall be retained for the length of time specified in paragraph (b) of this section.

(g) Records required by this part may be retained either as original records or as true copies such as photocopies, microfilm, microfiche, or other accurate reproductions of the original records.

* * * * *

PART 123. FISH AND FISHERY PRODUCTS

Subpart A. General Provisions

Citation: 21 CFR 123.9

✍ § 123.9 Records.

(a) *General requirements.* All records required by this part shall include:

(1) The name and location of the processor or importer;

(2) The date and time of the activity that the record reflects;

(3) The signature or initials of the person performing the operation; and

(4) Where appropriate, the identity of the product and the

production code, if any. Processing and other information shall be entered on records at the time that it is observed.

(b) *Record retention.* (1) All records required by this part shall be retained at the processing facility or importer's place of business in the United States for at least 1 year after the date they were prepared in the case of refrigerated products and for at least 2 years after the date they were prepared in the case of frozen, preserved, or shelf-stable products.

(2) Records that relate to the general adequacy of equipment or processes being used by a processor, including the results of scientific studies and evaluations, shall be retained at the processing facility or the importer's place of business in the United States for at least 2 years after their applicability to the product being produced at the facility.

(3) If the processing facility is closed for a prolonged period between seasonal packs, or if record storage capacity is limited on a processing vessel or at a remote processing site, the records may be transferred to some other reasonably accessible location at the end of the seasonal pack but shall be immediately returned for official review upon demand.

(c) *Official review.* All records required by this part and all plans and procedures required by this part shall be available for official review and copying at reasonable times.

(d) *Public disclosure.* (1) Subject to the limitations in paragraph (d)(2) of this section, all plans and records required by this part are not available for public disclosure unless they have been previously disclosed to the public as defined in § 20.81 of this chapter or they relate to a product or ingredient that has been abandoned and they no longer represent a trade secret or confidential commercial or financial information as defined in § 20.61 of this chapter.

(2) However, these records and plans may be subject to disclosure to the extent that they are otherwise publicly available, or that disclosure could not reasonably be expected to cause a competitive hardship, such as generic-type HACCP plans that reflect standard industry practices.

(e) *Tags.* Tags as defined in § 123.3(t) are not subject to the requirements of this section unless they are used to fulfill the requirements of § 123.28(c).

(f) *Records maintained on computers.* The maintenance of records on computers is acceptable, provided that appropriate controls are implemented to ensure the integrity of the electronic data and signatures.

SUBCHAPTER C. DRUGS; GENERAL

PART 211. CURRENT GOOD MANUFACTURING PRACTICE FOR FINISHED PHARMACEUTICALS

Subpart J. Records and Reports

Citation: 21 CFR 211.180

✍ § 211.180 General requirements.

(a) Any production, control, or distribution record that is required to be maintained in compliance with this part and is specifically associated with a batch of a drug product shall be retained for at least 1 year after the expiration date of the batch or, in the case of certain OTC drug products lacking expiration dating because they meet the criteria for exemption under § 211.137, 3 years after distribution of the batch.

(b) Records shall be maintained for all components, drug product containers, closures, and labeling for at least 1 year after the expiration date or, in the case of certain OTC drug products lacking expiration dating because they meet the criteria for exemption under 211.137, 3 years after distribution of the last lot of drug product incorporating the component or using the container, closure, or labeling.

(c) All records required under this part, or copies of such records, shall be readily available for authorized inspection during the retention period at the establishment where the activities described in such records occurred. These records or copies thereof shall be subject to photocopying or other means of reproduction as part of such inspection. Records that can be immediately retrieved from another location by computer or other electronic means shall be considered as meeting the requirements of this paragraph.

(d) Records required under the part may be retained either as original records or as true copies such as photocopies, microfilm, microfiche, or other accurate reproductions of the original records. Where reduction techniques, such as microfilming are used, suitable reader and photocopying equipment shall be readily available.

(e) Written records required by this part shall be maintained so that data therein can be used for evaluating, at least annually, the quality standards of each drug product to determine the need for changes in drug product specifications or manufacturing or control procedures. Written procedures shall be established and followed for such evaluations and shall include provisions for:

(1) A review of a representative number of batches, whether approved or rejected, and, where applicable, records associated with the batch.

(2) A review of complaints, recalls, returned or salvaged drug products, and investigations conducted under § 211.192 for each drug product.

(f) Procedures shall be established to assure that the responsible officials of the firm, if they are not personally involved in or immediately aware of such actions, are notified in writing of any investigations conducted under 211.198,211.204, or 211.208 of these regulations, any recalls, reports of inspectional observations issued by the Food and Drug Administration, or any regulatory actions relating to good manufacturing practices brought by the Food and Drug Administration.

PART 225. CURRENT GOOD MANUFACTURING PRACTICE FOR MEDICATED FEEDS

Subpart E. Records and Reports

Citation: 21 CFR 225.115

✍ § 225.115 Complaint files.

* * * * *

(b) The medicated feed manufacturer shall maintain on the premises a file which contains the following information:

(1) The original or copy of a record of each oral and written complaint received relating to the safety and effectiveness of the product produced. The record shall include the date of the complaint, the complainant's name and address, name and lot or control number or date of manufacture of the medicated feed involved, and the specific details of the complaint. This record shall also include all correspondence from the complainant and/or memoranda of conversation with the complainant, and a description of all investigations made by the manufacturer and of the method of disposition of the complaint.

(2) For medicated feeds requiring an approved Medicated Feed Application (Form FDA-1900), records and reports of clinical and other experience with the drug shall be maintained and reported, appropriately identified with the number(s) of the Form FDA-1900 to which they relate, to the Center for

Veterinary Medicine, 7500 Standish Place, Rockville, MD 20855, in duplicate, pursuant to § 510.301 of this chapter.

SUBCHAPTER D. DRUGS FOR HUMAN USE

PART 431. CERTIFICATION OF ANTIBIOTIC DRUGS

Subpart C. Records And Reports

Citation: 21 CFR 431.62

✍ **§ 431.62 Records retention.**

At the option of the person having control of records required to be kept by any regulation in this Part 431, photostatic or other permanent reproductions may be substituted for such records after the first 2 years of the holding period.

PART 433. EXEMPTIONS FROM ANTIBIOTIC CERTIFICATION AND LABELING REQUIREMENTS

Subpart D. Records and Reports

Citation: 21 CFR 433.30

✍ **§ 433.30 Records retention.**

At the option of the person having control of records required to be kept by any regulation in this Part 433, photostatic or other permanent reproductions may be substituted for such records after the first 2 years of the holding period.

SUBCHAPTER F. BIOLOGICS

PART 600. BIOLOGICAL PRODUCTS: GENERAL

Subpart D. Reporting of Adverse Experiences

Citation: 21 CFR 600.80

✍ **§ 600.80 Postmarketing reporting of adverse experiences.**

(a) *Definitions.* The following definitions of terms apply to this section:

Adverse experience means any adverse event associated with the use of a biological product in humans, whether or not considered product related, including the following: an adverse event occurring in the course of the use of a biological product in professional practice; an adverse event occurring from overdose of the product, whether accidental or intentional; an adverse event occurring from abuse of the product; an adverse event occurring from withdrawal of the product; and any failure of expected pharmacological action.

Blood Component for this purpose has the same meaning as defined in § 606.3(c) of this chapter.

Increased frequency means an increase in the rate of occurrence of a particular adverse biological product experience, e.g., an increased number of reports of a particular adverse biological product experience after appropriate adjustment for biological product exposure.

Serious means an adverse experience associated with the use of a biological product that is fatal or life-threatening, is permanently disabling, requires inpatient hospitalization, or is a congenital anomaly, cancer, or overdose.

Unexpected means an adverse biological product experience that is not listed in the current labeling for the product and includes an event that may be symptomatically and pathophysiologically related to an event listed in the labeling, but differs from the event because of greater severity or specificity. For example, under this definition, hepatic necrosis would be unexpected (by virtue of greater severity) if the labeling only referred to elevated hepatic enzymes or hepatitis. Similarly, cerebral thromboembolism and cerebral vasculitis would be unexpected (by virtue of greater specificity) if the labeling only listed cerebral vascular accidents.

(b) *Review of adverse experiences.* Any person having a product license under § 601.20 of this chapter shall promptly review all adverse experience information pertaining to its product obtained or otherwise received by the licensed manufacturer from any source, foreign or domestic, including information derived from commercial marketing experience, postmarketing clinical investigations, postmarketing epidemiological/surveillance studies, reports in the scientific literature, and unpublished scientific papers.

(c) *Reporting requirements.* The licensed manufacturer shall report to FDA adverse experience information, as described in this section. The licensed manufacturer shall submit two copies of each report described in this section for nonvaccine biological products, to the Center for Biologics Evaluation and Research (HFM-210), Food and Drug Administration, 1401 Rockville Pike, Suite 200 N., Rockville, MD 20852-1448. Submit all vaccine adverse experience reports to: Vaccine Adverse Event Reporting System (VAERS), P.O. Box 1100, Rockville, MD 20849-1100. FDA may waive the requirement for the second copy in appropriate instances.

(1) *Fifteen-day Alert reports.* (i) The licensed manufacturer shall report each adverse experience that is both serious and unexpected, regardless of source, as soon as possible but in any case within 15 working days of initial receipt of the information. These reports are required to be submitted, for nonvaccine biological products, on a form designated by FDA or a suitable format containing all of the data elements in the FDA designated reporting form, and, for vaccines on a VAERS form. The licensed manufacturer shall promptly investigate all adverse experiences that are the subject of these 15-day Alert reports and shall submit followup reports within 15 working days of receipt of new information or as requested by FDA. If additional information is not obtainable, a followup report may be required that describes briefly the steps taken to seek additional information and the reasons why it could not be obtained. These 15-day Alert reports and followups to them are required to be submitted under separate cover and may not be included, except for summary or tabular purposes, in a periodic report.

(ii) The licensed manufacturer shall review periodically (at least as often as the periodic reporting cycle) the frequency of reports of adverse biological product experiences that are both serious and expected and reports of therapeutic failure (lack of effect), regardless of source, and report any significant increase in frequency as soon as possible but in any case within 15 working days of determining that a significant increase in frequency exists. Upon written notice, FDA may require that licensed manufacturers review the frequency of reports of serious, expected adverse biological product experiences at intervals different than the periodic reporting cycle. Reports of a significant increase in frequency are required to be submitted in narrative form (including the time period on which the increased frequency is based, the method of analysis, and the interpretation of the results), rather than using the form designated by FDA. Fifteen-day Alert reports based on increased frequency are required to be submitted under separate cover and may not be included, except for summary purposes, in a periodic report.

(iii) The requirements of paragraphs (c)(1)(i) and (c)(1)(ii) of this section, concerning the submission of Fifteen-day Alert reports, shall also apply to any person other than the licensed manufacturer of the final product whose name appears on the label of a licensed biological product as a manufacturer, packer, distributor, shared manufacturer, joint manufacturer, or any other participant involved in divided manufacturing. In order to avoid unnecessary duplication in the initial and followup submission of reports to FDA, the obligations of a manufacturer other than the licensed manufacturer, may be met by submitting all reports to the licensed manufacturer of the final product. If a manufacturer other than the licensed manufacturer elects to submit reports to the licensed manufacturer rather than to FDA, it shall submit each report to the licensed manufacturer within 3 working days of its receipt, and the licensed manufacturer shall then comply with the requirements of this section. Under this circumstance, the manufacturer shall maintain a record of this action which shall include:

(A) A copy of all adverse biological product experience reports submitted to the licensed manufacturer,

(B) Date the report was received by the manufacturer,

(C) Date the report was submitted to the licensed manufacturer,

(D) Name and address of the licensed manufacturer.

(iv) Each report submitted under this paragraph shall bear prominent identification as to its contents, i.e., "15-day Alert report" or "15-day Alert report-followup."

(2) *Periodic adverse experience reports.* (i) The licensed manufacturer shall report each adverse experience not reported under paragraph (c)(1)(i) of this section at quarterly intervals, for 3 years from the date of issuance of the product license, and then at annual intervals. The licensed manufacturer shall submit each quarterly report within 30 days of the close of the quarter (the first quarter beginning on the date of issuance of the product license) and each annual report within 60 days of the anniversary date of the issuance of the product license. Upon written notice, FDA may extend or reestablish the requirement that a licensed manufacturer submit quarterly reports, or require that the licensed manufacturer submit reports under this section at different times than those stated. Followup information to adverse experiences submitted in a periodic report may be submitted in the next periodic report.

(ii) Each periodic report shall contain:

(A) A narrative summary and analysis of the information in the report and an analysis of the 15-day Alert reports submitted during the reporting interval (all 15-day Alert reports being appropriately referenced by the licensed manufacturer's patient identification number, adverse reaction term(s), and date of submission to FDA);

(B) A form designated for Advèrse Experience Reporting by FDA for each adverse experience not reported under paragraph (c)(1)(i) of this section (with an index consisting of a line listing of the licensed manufacturer's patient identification number and adverse reaction term(s)); and

(C) A history of actions taken since the last report because of adverse experiences (for example, labeling changes or studies initiated).

(iii) Periodic reporting, except for information regarding 15-day Alert reports, does not apply to adverse experience information obtained from postmarketing studies (whether or not conducted under an investigational new drug application), from reports in the scientific literature, and from foreign marketing experience.

(d) *Scientific literature.* (1) A 15-day Alert report based on information from the scientific literature shall be accompanied by a copy of the published article. The 15-day Alert reporting requirements in paragraph (c)(1)(i) of this section (i.e., serious, unexpected adverse experiences) apply only to reports found in scientific and medical journals either as case reports or as the result of a formal clinical trial. The 15-day Alert reporting requirements in paragraph (c)(1)(ii) of this section (i.e., a significant increase in frequency of a serious, expected adverse experience or of a therapeutic failure) apply only to reports found in scientific and medical journals either as the result of a formal clinical trial, or from epidemiologic studies or analyses of experience in a monitored series of patients.

(2) As with all reports submitted under paragraph (c)(1)(i) of this section, reports based on the scientific literature shall be submitted on the reporting form designated by FDA or comparable format as prescribed by paragraph (f) of this section. In cases where the licensed manufacturer believes that preparing the form designated by FDA constitutes an undue hardship, the licensed manufacturer may arrange with the Division of Biostatistics and Epidemiology (HFM-210) for an acceptable alternative reporting format.

(e) *Postmarketing studies.* (1) Licensed manufacturers are not required to submit a 15-day Alert report under paragraph (c) of this section for an adverse experience obtained from a postmarketing clinical study (whether or not conducted under a biological investigational new drug application) unless the licensed manufacturer concludes that there is a reasonable possibility that the product caused the adverse experience.

(2) The licensed manufacturer shall separate and clearly mark reports of adverse experiences that occur during a postmarketing study as being distinct from those experiences that are being reported spontaneously to the licensed manufacturer.

(f) *Reporting forms.* (1) Except as provided in paragraphs (c)(1)(ii), and (f)(3) of this section, the licensed manufacturer shall complete the reporting form designated by FDA (FDA-3500A, or, for vaccines, a VAERS form) for each report of an adverse experience.

(2) Each completed form should refer only to an individual patient or single attached publication.

(3) Instead of using a designated reporting form, a licensed manufacturer may use a computer-generated form or other alternative format (e.g., a computer-generated tape or tabular listing) provided that:

(i) The content of the alternative format is equivalent in all elements of information to those specified in the form designated by FDA; and

(ii) the format is approved in advance by MEDWATCH: The FDA Medical Products Reporting Program; or, for alternatives to the VAERS Form, by the Division of Biostatistics and Epidemiology.

(4) Copies of the reporting form designated by FDA (FDA-3500A) for nonvaccine biological products may be obtained from the Center for Biologics Evaluation and Research (address above). Additional supplies of the form may be obtained from the Consolidated Forms and Publications Distribution Center, 3222 Hubbard Rd., Landover, MD 20785. Supplies of the VAERS form may be obtained from VAERS by calling 1-800-822-7967.

(g) *Multiple reports.* A licensed manufacturer should not include in reports under this section any adverse experiences that occurred in clinical trials if they were previously submitted in the product license application. If a report refers to more than one biological product marketed by a licensed manufacturer, the licensed manufacturer should submit the report to the license for the product listed first in the report.

(h) *Patient privacy.* For nonvaccine biological products, a licensed manufacturer should not include in reports under this section the names and addresses of individual patients; instead, the licensed manufacturer should assign a unique code number to each report, preferably not more than eight characters in length. The licensed manufacturer should include the name of the reporter from whom the information was received. The names of patients, health care professionals, hospitals, and geographical identifiers in adverse experience reports are not releasable to the public under FDA's public information regulations in part 20 this of chapter. For vaccine adverse experience reports, these data will become part of the CDC Privacy Act System 09-20-0136, "Epidemiologic Studies and Surveillance of Disease Problems." Information identifying the person who received the vaccine or that person's legal representative will not be made available to the public, but may be available to the vaccinee or legal representative.

(i) *Recordkeeping*. The licensed manufacturer shall maintain for a period of 10 years records of all adverse experiences known to the licensed manufacturer, including raw data and any correspondence relating to the adverse experiences.

(j) *Guideline*. FDA has prepared a guideline for the submission of reports of adverse experiences and suggested followup investigation of reports.

(k) *Revocation of license*. If a licensed manufacturer fails to establish and maintain records and make reports required under this section with respect to a licensed biological product, FDA may revoke the product license for such a product in accordance with the procedures of § 601.5 of this chapter.

(l) *Exemptions*. Manufacturers of the following listed products are not required to submit adverse experience reports under this section:(1) Whole blood or components of whole blood.

(2) In vitro diagnostic products, including assay systems for the detection of antibodies or antigens to retroviruses. These products are subject to the reporting requirements for devices.

(m) *Disclaimer*. A report or information submitted by a licensed manufacturer under this section (and any release by FDA of that report or information) does not necessarily reflect a conclusion by the licensed manufacturer or FDA that the report or information constitutes an admission that the biological product caused or contributed to an adverse effect. A licensed manufacturer need not admit, and may deny, that the report or information submitted under this section constitutes an admission that the biological product caused or contributed to an adverse effect. For purposes of this provision, this paragraph also includes any person reporting under paragraph (c)(1)(iii) of this section.

SUBCHAPTER H. MEDICAL DEVICES

PART 820. GOOD MANUFACTURING PRACTICE FOR MEDICAL DEVICES: GENERAL

Subpart J. Records

Citation: **21 CFR 820.180**

✍ § 820.180 General requirements.

All records required by this part shall be maintained at the manufacturing establishment or other location that is reasonably accessible to responsible officials of the manufacturer and to employees of the Food and Drug Administration designated to perform inspections. Such records shall be available for review and copying by such employees. Except as specifically provided elsewhere, the following general provisions shall apply to all records required by this part.

(a) *Confidentiality*. Those records deemed confidential by the manufacturer may be marked to aid the Food and Drug Administration in determining whether information may be disclosed under the public information regulation in Part 20 of this chapter.

(b) *Record Retention period*. All required records pertaining to a device shall be retained for a period of time equivalent to the design and expected life of the device, but in no case less than 2 years from the date of release for commercial distribution by the manufacturer. Photostatic or other reproductions of records required by this part may be used.

Citation: **21 CFR 820.195**

✍ § 820.195 Critical devices, automated data processing.

When automated data processing is used for manufacturing or quality assurance purposes, adequate checks shall be designed and implemented to prevent inaccurate data output, input, and programming errors.

Agency: **Department of Justice**
Drug Enforcement Administration

PART 1304. RECORDS AND REPORTS OF REGISTRANTS

General Information

Citation: **21 CFR 1304.04**

✍ § 1304.04 Maintenance of records and inventories.

(a) Every inventory and other records required to be kept under this part shall be kept by the registrant and be available, for at least 2 years from the date of such inventory or records, for inspection and copying by authorized employees of the Administration, except that financial and shipping records (such as invoices and packing slips but not executed order forms subject to § 1305.13 of this chapter) may be kept at a central location, rather than at the registered location, if the registrant has notified the Administration of his intention to keep central records. Written notification must be submitted by registered or certified mail, return receipt requested, in triplicate, to the Special Agent in Charge of the Administration in the area in which the registrant is located. Unless the registrant is informed by the Special Agent in Charge that permission to keep central records is denied, the registrant may maintain central records commencing 14 days after receipt of his notification by the Special Agent in Charge.

All notifications must include:

(1) The nature of the records to be kept centrally.

(2) The exact location where the records will be kept.

(3) The name, address, DEA registration number and type of DEA registration of the registrant whose records are being maintained centrally.

(4) Whether central records will be maintained in a manual, or computer readable form.

(b) All registrants that are authorized to maintain a central recordkeeping system shall be subject to the following conditions:

(1) The records to be maintained at the central record location shall not include executed order forms, prescriptions and/or inventories which shall be maintained at each registered location.

(2) If the records are kept on microfilm, computer media or in any form requiring special equipment to render the records easily readable, the registrant shall provide access to such equipment with the records. If any code system is used (other than pricing information), a key to the code shall be provided to make the records understandable.

(3) The registrant agrees to deliver all or any part of such records to the registered location within two business days upon

receipt of a written request from the Administration for such records, and if the Administration chooses to do so in lieu of requiring delivery of such records to the registered location, to allow authorized employees of the Administration to inspect such records at the central location upon request by such employees without a warrant of any kind.

(4) In the event that a registrant fails to comply with these conditions, the Special Agent in Charge may cancel such central recordkeeping authorization, and all other central recordkeeping authorizations held by the registrant without a hearing or other procedures. In the event of a cancellation of central recordkeeping authorizations under this paragraph the registrant shall, within the time specified by the Special Agent in Charge, comply with the requirements of this section that all records be kept at the registered location.

(c) Registrants need not notify the Special Agent in Charge or obtain central recordkeeping approval in order to maintain records on an in-house computer system.

(d) ARCOS participants who desire authorization to report from other than their registered locations must obtain a separate central identifier. Request for central reporting identifiers will be submitted to: ARCOS Unit, P.O. Box 28293, Central Station, Washington, D.C. 20005.

(e) All central recordkeeping permits previously issued by the Administration will expire on September 30, 1980. Registrants who desire to continue maintaining central records will make notification to the local Special Agent in Charge as provided in paragraph (a) of this section.

(f) Each registered manufacturer, distributor, importer, narcotic treatment program and compounder for narcotic treatment program shall maintain inventories and records of controlled substances as follows:

(1) Inventories and records of controlled substances listed in Schedules I and II shall be maintained separately from all of the records of the registrant; and

(2) Inventories and records of controlled substances listed in Schedules III, IV and V shall be maintained either separately from all other records of the registrant or in such form that the information required is readily retrievable from the ordinary business records of the registrant.

(g) Each registered individual practitioner required to keep records and institutional practitioner shall maintain inventories and records of controlled substances in the manner prescribed in paragraph (f) of this section.

(h) Each registered pharmacy shall maintain the inventories and records of controlled substances as follows:

(1) Inventories and records of all controlled substances listed in Schedules I and II shall be maintained separately from all other records of the pharmacy, and prescriptions for such substances shall be maintained in a separate prescription file; and

(2) Inventories and records of controlled substances listed in Schedules III, IV, and V shall be maintained either separately from all other records of the pharmacy or in such form that the information required is readily retrievable from ordinary business records of the pharmacy, and prescriptions for such substances shall be maintained either in separate prescription file for controlled substances listed in Schedules III, IV and V only or in such form that they are readily retrievable from the other prescription records of the pharmacy. Prescriptions will be deemed readily retrievable if, at the time they are initially filed, the face of the prescription is stamped in red ink in the lower right corner with the letter "C" no less than 1-inch high and filed either in the prescription file for controlled substances listed in Schedules I and II or in the usual consecutively numbered prescription file for non-controlled substances.

PART 1306. PRESCRIPTIONS

CONTROLLED SUBSTANCES LISTED IN SCHEDULES III AND IV

Citation: 21 CFR 1306.22

✍ **§ 1306.22 Refilling of prescriptions.**

* * * * *

(b) As an alternative to the procedures provided by subsection (a), an automated data processing system may be used for the storage and retrieval of refill information for prescription orders for controlled substances in Schedule III and IV, subject to the following conditions:

* * * * *

(3) Documentation of the fact that the refill information entered into the computer each time a pharmacist refills an original prescription order for a Schedule III or IV controlled substance is correct must be provided by the individual pharmacist who makes use of such a system. If such a system provides a hardcopy printout of each day's controlled substance prescription order refill data, that printout shall be verified, dated, and signed by the individual pharmacist who refilled such a prescription order. The individual pharmacist must verify that the data indicated is correct and then sign this document in the same manner as he would sign a check or legal document (e.g., J.H. Smith, or John H. Smith). This document shall be maintained in a separate file at that pharmacy for a period of two years from the dispensing date. This printout of the day's controlled substance prescription order refill data must be provided to each pharmacy using such a computerized system within 72 hours of the date on which the refill was dispensed. It must be verified and signed by each pharmacist who is involved with such dispensing. In lieu of such a printout, the pharmacy shall maintain a bound log book, or separate file, in which each individual pharmacist involved in such dispensing shall sign a statement (in the manner previously described) each day, attesting to the fact that the refill information entered into the computer that day has been reviewed by him and is correct as shown. Such a book or file must be maintained at the pharmacy employing such a system for a period of two years after the date of dispensing the appropriately authorized refill.

* * * * *

TITLE 24. HOUSING AND URBAN DEVELOPMENT

Agency: Department of Housing and Urban Development
Office of the Secretary

PART 84. GRANTS AND AGREEMENTS WITH INSTITUTIONS OF HIGHER EDUCATION, HOSPITALS, AND OTHER NON-PROFIT ORGANIZATIONS

Subpart C. Post-Award Requirements

Reports and Records

Citation: 24 CFR 84.52

✍ **§ 84.52 Financial reporting.**

(a) The following forms or such other forms as may be approved by OMB are authorized for obtaining financial information from recipients.

(1) *SF-269 or SF-269A, Financial Status Report.*

(i) HUD requires recipients to use the SF-269 or SF-269A to report the status of funds for all nonconstruction projects or programs. HUD has the option of not requiring the SF-269 or SF-269A when the SF-270, Request for Advance or Reimbursement, or SF-272, Report of Federal Cash Transactions, is determined to provide adequate information to meet its needs, except that a final SF-269 or SF-269A shall be required at the completion of the project when the SF-270 is used only for advances.

(ii) HUD shall prescribe whether the report shall be on a cash or accrual basis. If HUD requires accrual information and the recipient's accounting records are not normally kept on the accrual basis, the recipient shall not be required to convert its accounting system, but shall develop such accrual information through best estimates based on an analysis of the documentation on hand.

(iii) HUD shall determine the frequency of the Financial Status Report for each project or program, considering the size and complexity of the particular project or program. However, the report shall not be required more frequently than quarterly or less frequently than annually. A final report shall be required at the completion of the agreement.

(iv) HUD requires recipients to submit the SF-269 or SF-269A (an original and no more than two copies) no later than 30 days after the end of each specified reporting period for quarterly and semi-annual reports, and 90 calendar days for annual and final reports. Extensions of reporting due dates may be approved by HUD upon request of the recipient.

(2) *SF-272, Report of Federal Cash Transactions.*

(i) When funds are advanced to recipients HUD shall require each recipient to submit the SF-272 and, when necessary, its continuation sheet, SF-272a. HUD shall use this report to monitor cash advanced to recipients and to obtain disbursement information for each agreement with the recipients.

(ii) HUD may require forecasts of Federal cash requirements in the "Remarks" section of the report.

(iii) When practical and deemed necessary, HUD may require recipients to report in the "Remarks" section the amount of cash advances received and retained in excess of three days. Recipients shall provide short narrative explanations of actions taken to reduce the excess balances.

(iv) Recipients shall be required to submit not more than the original and two copies of the SF-272 15 calendar days following the end of each quarter. HUD may require a monthly report from those recipients receiving advances totaling $1 million or more per year.

(v) HUD may waive the requirement for submission of the SF-272 for any one of the following reasons:

(A) When monthly advances do not exceed $25,000 per recipient, provided that such advances are monitored through other forms contained in this section;

(B) If, in HUD's opinion, the recipient's accounting controls are adequate to minimize excessive Federal advances; or

(C) When the electronic payment mechanisms provide adequate data.

(b) When HUD needs additional information or more frequent reports, the following shall be observed.

(1) When additional information is needed to comply with legislative requirements, HUD shall issue instructions to require recipients to submit such information under the "Remarks" section of the reports.

(2) When HUD determines that a recipient's accounting system does not meet the standards in § 84.21, additional pertinent information to further monitor awards may be obtained upon written notice to the recipient until such time as the system is brought up to standard. HUD, in obtaining this information, shall comply with report clearance requirements of 5 CFR part 1320.

(3) HUD will shade out any line item on any report if not necessary.

(4) HUD may accept the identical information from the recipients in machine readable format or computer printouts or electronic outputs in lieu of prescribed formats.

(5) HUD may provide computer or electronic outputs to recipients when such expedites or contributes to the accuracy of reporting.

Agency: **Department of Housing and Urban Development**
Office of Assistant Secretary for Housing-Federal Housing Commissioner

SUBCHAPTER A. GENERAL

PART 200. INTRODUCTION TO FHA PROGRAMS

Subpart G. Restrictions On Use of Assisted Housing

Citation: **24 CFR 200.182**

✍ § 200.182 Evidence of citizenship or eligible alien status.

* * * * *

(d) *Retention of evidence.* A photocopy of each document (or original if released by the person submitting the document), and a signed verification consent form, shall be retained by the owner or mortgagee to whom the evidence is submitted. However, a photocopy need not be made or retained of any document bearing an identifying serial number if a record of the serial number and other necessary identifying information is made and retained in such manner as shall be prescribed by the Department.

* * * * *

SUBTITLE B. REGULATIONS RELATING TO HOUSING AND URBAN DEVELOPMENT

SUBCHAPTER B. MORTGAGE AND LOAN INSURANCE PROGRAMS UNDER NATIONAL HOUSING ACT AND OTHER AUTHORITIES

PART 208. ELECTRONIC TRANSMISSION OF REQUIRED DATA FOR CERTIFICATION AND RECERTIFICATION AND SUBSIDY BILLING PROCEDURES FOR MULTIFAMILY SUBSIDIZED PROJECTS

Citation: **24 CFR 208.108**

✍ § 208.108 Requirements.

(a) *Projects specified in § 208.104(a) that are automated.* Project owners of applicable projects under § 208.104(a) who currently use an automated software package to process certifications and recertifications and to provide subsidy billings to HUD must update their software packages and begin electronic transmission of that data in a HUD specified format by March 21, 1994. These project owners are required to transmit data collected for the 12 months preceding March 21, 1994, as well as data collected on or after this date. Data collected for the 12 months preceding March 21, 1994, is to include only the tenant's most recent "complete certification" (move-in, initial certification, interim recertification, or annual recertification). When the most recent certification for a tenant is a partial certification (gross rent change, unit transfer, or correction), both the complete and partial certifications must be transmitted.

(b) *Projects specified in § 208.104(a) that are not automated.* Nonautomated project owners and agents (those owners and agents that currently prepare the certification, recertification, and subsidy billing forms manually) of applicable projects under § 208.104(a) must:

(1) Complete the search and either obtain the necessary hardware or software, or sign service contracts;

(2) Complete their data loading; and

(3) Begin electronic transmission by May 20, 1994. These project owners are required to transmit data collected for the 12 months preceding May 20, 1994, as well as data collected on or after this date. Data collected for the 12 months preceding May 20, 1994, is to include only the tenant's most recent "complete certification" (move-in, initial certification, interim recertification, or annual recertification). When the most recent certification for a tenant is a partial certification (gross rent change, unit transfer, or correction), both the complete and partial certifications must be transmitted.

(c) *Projects specified in § 208.104(b).* (1) Project owners. Project owners of applicable projects under § 208.104(b) must electronically transmit data for certification, recertification and subsidy billing procedures in a HUD specified format to the contract administrator. These project owners are required to transmit data collected for the 12 months preceding September 23, 1994, as well as data collected on or after that date. Data collected for the 12 months preceding September 23, 1994 is to include only the tenant's most recent "complete certification" (move-in, initial certification, interim recertification, or annual recertification). When the most recent certification for a tenant is a partial certification (gross rent change, unit transfer, or correction), both the complete and partial certifications must be transmitted.

(2) *Contract administrators.* State housing finance and development agencies and Public Housing Agencies that serve as the subsidy contract administrator must accept the electronic transmission of the HUD forms listed below in § 208.108(e) from the projects they administer, and electronically transmit that data to HUD in a HUD specified format after appropriate review and correction of the data.

(d) *Projects specified in § 208.104(c).* Project owners of applicable projects under § 208.104(c) must electronically transmit data for certification, recertification and subsidy billing procedures to HUD in a HUD specified format. In the case of partially assisted section 202 projects, owners are required to electronically transmit data only for subsidized units. These project owners are required to transmit data collected for the 12 months preceding the effective date of the rule, as well as data collected on or after the effective date of the rule. Data collected for the 12 months preceding September 23, 1994 is to include only the tenant's most recent "complete certification" (move-in, initial certification, interim recertification, or annual recertification). When the most recent certification for a tenant is a partial certification (gross rent change, unit transfer, or correction), both the complete and partial certifications must be transmitted.

(e) *Data to be transmitted.* Electronic transmission consists of data transmitted from the HUD-50059, 50059 worksheets, 52670 and 52670A, Parts 1 and 2 and 52671 A through D correctly formatted in accord with the HUD data requirements and in lieu of the hard copy forms.

Agency:	**Department of Housing and Urban Development** **Office of Assistant Secretary for Public and Indian Housing**

PART 908. ELECTRONIC TRANSMISSION OF REQUIRED FAMILY DATA FOR PUBLIC HOUSING, INDIAN HOUSING, AND THE SECTION 8 RENTAL CERTIFICATE, RENTAL VOUCHER, AND MODERATE REHABILITATION PROGRAMS

Citation:	**24 CFR 908.101**

✍ § 908.101 Purpose.

The purpose of this part is to require Housing Agencies (HAs) that operate public housing, Indian housing, or Section 8 Rental Certificate, Rental Voucher and Moderate Rehabilitation programs to electronically submit certain data to HUD for those programs. This electronically submitted data is required for HUD Forms HUD-50058, Family Report, and HUD-50058-FSS, Family Self-Sufficiency Addendum.

Citation:	**24 CFR 908.104**

✍ § 908.104 Requirements.

(a) *Automated HAs.* Housing agencies that currently use automated software packages to transmit Forms HUD-50058 and HUD-50058-FSS information by tape or diskette to the Department's data processing contractor must convert to telephonic electronic transmission of that data in a HUD specified format by June 30, 1995.

(b) *Nonautomated HAs.* Housing agencies that currently prepare and transmit the HUD-50058 and HUD-50058-FSS information to HUD paper must:

(1) Complete a vendor search and obtain either:

(i) The necessary hardware and software required to develop and maintain an in-house automated data processing system (ADP) used to generate electronic submission of the data for these forms via telephonic network; or

(ii) A service contract for the operation of an automated system to generate electronic submission of the data for these forms via telephonic network;

(2) Complete their data loading; and

(3) Begin electronic transmission by March 2, 1996.

(c) *Electronic transmission of data.* Electronic transmission of data consists of submission of all required data fields (correctly formatted) from the forms HUD-050058 and HUD-50058-FSS telephonically, in accordance with HUD instructions. Regardless of whether an HA obtains the ADP system itself or contracts with a service bureau to provide the system, the software must be periodically updated to incorporate changes or revisions in legislation, regulations, handbooks, notices, or HUD electronic transmission data format requirements.

(d) *Service contract.* HAs that determine that the purchase of hardware and/or software is not cost effective may contract out the electronic data transmission function to organizations that provide such services, including, but not limited to the following organizations: local management associations and management agents with centralized facilities. HAs that contract out the electronic transmission function must retain the ability to monitor the day-to-day operations of the project at the HA site and be able to demonstrate the ability to the relevant HUD Field Office.

(e) Notwithstanding the provisions of paragraphs (a) and (b) of this section, the Department may approve transmission of the data by tape or diskette if it determines that the cost of telephonic transmission would be excessive.

Citation: **24 CFR 908.108**

✍ § 908.108 Cost.

(a) *General.* The costs of the electronic transmission of the correctly formatted data, including either the purchase and maintenance of computer hardware or software, or both, the cost of contracting for those services, or the cost of centralizing the electronic transmission function, shall be considered Section 8 Administrative expenses, or eligible public and Indian housing operating expenses that can be included in the public and Indian housing operating budget. At the HA's option, the cost of the computer software may include service contracts to provide maintenance or training, or both.

(b) *Sources of funding.* For public and Indian housing, costs may be covered from operating subsidy for which the HA is already eligible, or the initial cost may be covered by funds received by the HA under HUD's Comprehensive Improvement Assistance Program (CIAP) or Comprehensive Grant Program (CGP). For Section 8 programs, the costs may be covered from ongoing administrative fees or the Section 8 operating reserve.

Citation: **24 CFR 908.112**

✍ § 908.112 Extension of time.

The HUD Field Office may grant an HA an extension of time, of a reasonable period, for implementation of the requirements of § 908.104, if it determines that such electronic submission is infeasible because of one of the following:

(a) Lack of staff resources;

(b) Insufficient financial resources to purchase the required hardware, software or contractual services; or

(c) Lack of adequate infrastructure, including, but not limited to, the inability to obtain telephone service to transmit the required data.

Agency: **Department of Housing and Urban Development**

PART 3500. REAL ESTATE SETTLEMENT PROCEDURES ACT

24 CFR 3500.17

✍ § 3500.17 Escrow accounts.

* * * * *

(l) *System of recordkeeping.* (1) Each servicer shall keep records, which may involve electronic storage, microfiche storage, or any method of computerized storage, so long as the information is easily retrievable, reflecting the servicer's handling of each borrower's escrow account. The servicer's records shall include, but not be limited to, the payment of amounts into and from the escrow account and the submission of initial and annual escrow account statements to the borrower.

(2) The servicer responsible for servicing the borrower's escrow account shall maintain the records for that account for a period of at least five years after the servicer last serviced the escrow account.

(3) A servicer shall provide the Secretary with information contained in the servicer's records for a specific escrow account, or for a number or class of escrow accounts, within 30 days of the Secretary's written request for the information. The servicer shall convert any information contained in electronic storage, microfiche or computerized storage to paper copies for review by the Secretary.

(i) To aid in investigations, the Secretary may also issue an administrative subpoena for the production of documents, and for the testimony of such witnesses as the Secretary deems advisable.

(ii) If the subpoenaed party refuses to obey the Secretary's administrative subpoena, the Secretary is authorized to seek a court order requiring compliance with the subpoena from any United States district court. Failure to obey such an order of the court may be punished as contempt of court.

(4) Borrowers may seek information contained in the servicer's records by complying with the provisions set forth in 12 U.S.C. 2605(e) and § 3500.21(f).

(5) After receiving a request (by letter or subpoena) from the Department for information relating to whether a servicer submitted an escrow account statement to the borrower, the servicer shall respond within 30 days. If the servicer is unable to provide the Department with such information, the Secretary shall deem that lack of information to be evidence of the servicer's failure to submit the statement to the borrower.

TITLE 25 — INDIANS

Agency: **Department of the Interior**
Bureau of Indian Affairs

SUBCHAPTER G. FINANCIAL ACTIVITIES

PART 141. BUSINESS PRACTICES ON THE NAVAJO, HOPI AND ZUNI RESERVATIONS

Subpart F — Enforcement Powers, Procedures and Remedies

Citation: **25 CFR 141.58**

✍ § 141.58 Records, reports, and obligations of reservation business owners.

* * * * *

(c) The business owner or an employee shall record all sales and purchases whether for cash or credit. If the business is on the Navajo Reservation the owner or an employee shall supply the customer with a copy of the sale transaction containing a description of the article purchased or sold, the date of the transaction, and the price. A cash register receipt complies with this paragraph for grocery or dry goods purchases for cash.

(d) The licensee shall keep a duplicate copy of any writing required by paragraph (c) of this section for a period of not less than three (3) years and shall provide the customer or the customer's representative one copy of those writings upon request.

SUBCHAPTER M. INDIAN SELF-DETERMINATION AND EDUCATION ASSISTANCE ACT PROGRAM

PART 276. UNIFORM ADMINISTRATIVE REQUIREMENTS FOR GRANTS

Citation: 25 CFR 276.5

✍ § 276.5 Recordkeeping.

(a) The Bureau shall not impose record retention requirements over and above those established by the grantee except that financial records, supporting documents, statistical records, and all other records pertinent to a Bureau grant, or to any subgrant (or negotiated contract exceeding $2500) under a grant, shall be retained for a period of three years, with the following qualifications: (1) The records shall be retained beyond the three-year period if audit findings have not been resolved.

(2) Records for nonexpendable property which was acquired with Bureau grant funds shall be retained for three years after its final disposition.

(3) When grant records are transferred to or maintained by the Bureau, the three-year retention requirement is not applicable to the grantee.

(b) The retention period starts from the date of submission of the final expenditure report or, for grants which are renewed annually, from the date of the submission of the annual expenditure report.

(c) Grantees are authorized, if they desire, to substitute microfilm copies in lieu of original records.

(d) The Bureau shall request transfer of certain records to its custody from grantees when it determines that the records possess long-term retention value. However, in order to avoid duplicate recordkeeping the Bureau may make arrangements with the grantee for the grantee to retain any records which are continuously needed for joint use.

(e) The Secretary of the Interior and the Comptroller General of the United States, or any of their duly authorized representatives shall have access to any books, documents, papers, and records of the grantees and their subgrantees which are pertinent to a specific grant program for the purpose of making audit, examination, excerpts, transcripts and copies at government expense.

(f) Unless otherwise required by law, the Bureau shall not place restrictions on grantees which will limit public access to the grantee's records created as part of the grant except when records must remain confidential. Following are some of the reasons for withholding records: (1) prevent a clearly unwarranted invasion of personal privacy;

(2) Specifically required by statute or Executive Order to be kept secret;

(3) Commercial or financial information obtained from a person or firm on a privileged or confidential basis.

Agency: Department of the Interior
Bureau of Indian Affairs

Agency: Department of Health And Human Services
Indian Health Service

PART 900. CONTRACTS UNDER THE INDIAN SELF-DETERMINATION AND EDUCATION ASSISTANCE ACT

Subpart F. Standards for Tribunal Organization Management Systems

Citation: 25 CFR 900.41

✍ § 900.41 How long must an Indian tribe or tribal organization keep management system records?

The Indian tribe or tribal organization must retain financial, procurement and property records for the minimum periods described below. Electronic, magnetic or photographic records may be substituted for hard copies.

(a) *Financial records.* Financial records include documentation of supporting costs incurred under the contract. These records must be retained for three years from the date of submission of the single audit report to the Secretary.

(b) *Procurement records.* Procurement records include solicitations, purchase orders, contracts, payment histories and records applicable of significant decisions. These records must be retained for three years after the Indian tribe or tribal organization or subcontractors make final payment and all other pending matters are closed.

(c) *Property management records.* Property management records of real and personal property transactions must be retained for three years from the date of disposition, replacement, or transfer.

(d) *Litigation, audit exceptions and claims.* Records pertaining to any litigation, audit exceptions or claims requiring management systems data must be retained until the action has been completed.

TITLE 26. Internal Revenue

Agency: Department of the Treasury
Internal Revenue Service

PART 1. INCOME TAXES

Citation: 26 CFR 1.6045-1

✍ § 1.6045-1 Returns of information of brokers and barter exchanges.

* * * * *

(c) *Reporting by brokers—(1) Requirement of reporting.* Any broker shall, except as otherwise provided, report in the manner prescribed in this section.

(2) *Sales required to be reported.* Except as provided in paragraphs (c)(3), (c)(5), (g), and (p)(1), a broker shall make a return of information with respect to each sale by a customer of the broker effected by the broker in the ordinary course of a trade or business in which the broker stands ready to effect sales to be made by others.

(3) *Exceptions.* The exceptions set forth in paragraph (c)(3) of § 5f.6045-1 of this chapter apply to sales effected on or after May 29, 1984. For an exception for certain sales of agricultural

commodities and certificates issued by the Commodity Credit Corporation after January 1, 1993, see paragraph (c)(7) of this section. With respect to sales effected before May 29, 1984, the exceptions provided in § 1.6045-1(c)(3) (as contained in the CFR edition revised as of April 1, 1984) apply.

Editorial Note: At 57 FR 53032, Nov. 6, 1992 paragraph (c)(3) of § 1.6045-1 was revised (above), effective January 1, 1993. At 57 FR 58984, Dec. 14, 1992 paragraph (c)(3) was revised (below), effective July 1, 1983. The IRS will publish a document in the FEDERAL REGISTER clarifying this discrepancy.

(3) *Exceptions.*—(i)*In general.* Except as provided in paragraph (c)(3)(ii) of this section, the exceptions set forth in paragraph (c)(3) of § 5f.6045-1 of this chapter apply to sales effected on or after May 29, 1984. For an exception for certain sales of agricultural commodities and certificates issued by the Commodity Credit Corporation after January 1, 1993, see paragraph (c)(7) of this section. With respect to sales effected before May 29, 1984, the exceptions provided in § 1.6045-1(c)(3)(as containded in the CFR edition revised as of April 1, 1984) apply.

(ii) *Excepted sales.* No return of information is required with respect to a sale effected by a broker for a customer if the sale is an excepted sale. For this purpose, a sale is an excepted sale if it is so designated by the Internal Revenue Service in a revenue ruling or revenue procedure published in the Internal Revenue Bulletin. (See § 601.601(d)(2)(ii)(*b*) of this chapter).

* * * * *

(l) *Use of magnetic media*—(1) *In general.*. Except as otherwise provided by paragraphs (l) (2) and (3), a broker or a barter exchange required to file returns of information under this section, shall, in lieu of filing Form 1099 for such year, file such returns of information on magnetic media authorized by the Commissioner and shall follow the appropriate revenue procedures for such magnetic media filing in lieu of following Form 1099 instructions.

(2) *Exception for undue hardship.* (i) The Commissioner may authorize a broker or barter exchange to file returns of information on Form 1099 instead of on magnetic media if undue hardship is shown on an application filed with the appropriate Internal Revenue Service Center.

(ii) In the case of a person who is a broker or barter exchange on July 1, 1983, an applicaiton to file returns of information on Form 1099 must be filed on or before September 15, 1983. In the case of a person who becomes a broker or barter exchange after July 1, 1983, such application must be filed by the end of the second month following the month in which such person becomes a broker or barter exchange.

(3) *Transitional rule.* A broker or barter exchange may submit returns of information on Form 1099 for reporting periods that:

(i) End before January 1, 1984; or

(ii) Begin before 30 days after the date on which a timely filed request to file returns of information on Form 1099 is denied.

(m) *Reporting on options transactions.* [Reserved]

(n) *Reporting on bond discounts.* [Reserved]

(o) *Additional reporting by stock transfer agents.* [Reserved]

* * * * *

(q) * * * With regard to paragraph (l) of this section, see section 6011(e) of the Internal Revenue Code for information returns required to be filed after December 31, 1989, and before January 1, 1997; and see Sec. 1.6045-1T(l) for information returns required to be filed after December 31, 1996.

Citation: 26 CFR 1.6045-2

✍ § 1.6045-2 Furnishing statement required with respect to certain substitute payments.

(a) *Requirement of furnishing statements*—(1) *In general.* Any broker (as defined in paragraph (a)(4)(ii) of this section) that transfers securities (as defined in § 1.6045-1(a)(3)) of a customer (as defined in paragraph (a)(4)(iii) of this section) for use in a short sale and receives on behalf of the customer a substitute payment (as defined in paragraph (a)(4)(i) shall, except as otherwise provided, furnish a statement to the customer identifying such payment as being a substitute payment.

(2) *Special rule for transfers for broker's own use.* Any broker that borrows securities of a customer for use in a short sale entered into for the broker's own account shall be deemed to have transferred the stock to itself and received on behalf of the customer any substitute payment made with respect to the transferred securities, and shall be required to furnish a statement with respect to such payments in accordance with paragraph (a)(1) of this section.

(3) *Special rule for furnishing statements to individual customers with respect to payments in lieu of dividends*—(i) *In general.* Except as otherwise provided, a broker that receives a substitute payment in lieu of a dividend on behalf of a customer who is an individual ("individual customer") need not furnish a statement to the customer.

(ii) *Exception for certain dividends.* Any broker that receives on behalf of an individual customer a substitute payment in lieu of—

(A) An exempt-interest dividend (as defined in paragraph (a)(4)(vii) of this section);

(B) A capital gain dividend (as defined in paragaph (a)(4)(vi) of this section);

(C) A distribution treated as a return of capital under section 301(c)(2) or (c)(3); or

(D) An FTC dividend (as defined in paragraph (a)(4)(viii) of this section) shall furnish a statement to the individual customer identifying the payment as being a substitute payment as prescribed by this section, provided that the broker has reason to know not later than the record date of the dividend payment that the payment is a substitute payment in lieu of an exempt-interest dividend, a capital gain dividend, a distribution treated as a return of capital, or an FTC dividend.

* * * * *

(b) *Exceptions*—(1) *Minimal payments.* No statement is required to be furnished under section 6045(d) or this section to any customer if the aggregate amount of the substitute payments received by a broker on behalf of the customer during a calendar year for which a statement must be furnished is less than $10.

(2) *Exempt recipients*—(i) *In general.* A statement shall not be required to be furnished with respect to substitute payments made to a broker on behalf of—

(A) An organization exempt from taxation under section 501(a),

(B) An individual retirement plan,

(C) The United States, a possession of the United States, or an instrumentality or a political subdivision or a wholly-owned agency of the foregoing,

(D) A State, the District of Columbia, or a political subdivision or wholy-owned agency or instrumentality of either of the foregoing.

(E) A foreign government or a political subdivision thereof, or

(F) An international organization.

(ii) *Determination of whether a person is described in paragraph (b)(2)(i) of this section.* The determination of whether a person is described in paragraph (b)(2)(i) of this section shall be made in the manner provided in § 5f.6045-1(c)(3)(i)(B) of the Temporary Income Tax Regulations under the Tax Equity and Fiscal Responsibility Act of 1982.

(3) *Exempt foreign persons.* A statment shall not be required to be furnished with respect to substitute payments made to a broker on behalf of a person that is an exempt foreign person as described in § 1.6045-1(g)

(c) *Form of statement.* A broker shall furnish the statement required by paragraph (a) of this section on Form 1099. The statement must show the aggregate dollar amount of all substitute payments received by the broker on behalf of a customer (for which the broker is required to furnish a statement) during a calendar year, and such other information as may be required by Form 1099. A statement shall be considered to be furnished to a customer if it is mailed to the customer at the last address of the customer known to the broker.

* * * * *

(g) *Reporting by brokers*—(1) *Requirement of reporting.* Any broker required to furnish a statement under paragraph (a) of this section shall report on Form 1096 showing such information as may be required by From 1096, in the form, manner, and number of copies required by Form 1096. With respect to each customer for which a broker is required to furnish a statement, the broker shall make a return of information on Form 1099, in the form, manner and number of copies required by Form 1099.

(2) *Use of magnetic media.* Brokers not receiving an undue hardship exception under paragraph (l)(2) of § 1.6045-1 shall file the returns required by this paragraph on magnetic media in accordance with paragraph(l)(1) of § 1.6045-1.

* * * * *

(i) * * * With regard to paragraph (g)(2) of this section, see section 6011(e) of the Internal Revenue Code for information returns required to be filed after December 31, 1989, and before January 1, 1997; and see Sec. 1.6045-2T(g)(2) for information returns required to be filed after December 31, 1996.

Except as otherwise provided by paragraphs (l) (2) and (3), a broker or a barter exchange required to file returns of information under this section, shall, in lieu of filing Form 1099 for such year, file such returns of information on magnetic media authorized by the Commissioner and shall follow the appropriate revenue procedures for such magnetic media filing in lieu of following Form 1099 instructions.

Citation: 26 CFR 1.6045-2T

✍ § 1.6045-2T Furnishing statement required with respect to certain substitute payments (temporary).

(a) through (g)(1) [Reserved] For further guidance, see Sec. 1.6045-2 (a) through (g)(1).

(g)(2) *Use of magnetic media.* For information returns filed after December 31, 1996, see Sec. 301.6011-2T of this chapter for rules relating to filing information returns on magnetic media and for rules relating to waivers granted for undue hardship. For information returns filed prior to January 1, 1997, see Sec. 1.6045-2(g)(2).

PART 301. PROCEDURE AND ADMINISTRATION

Citation: 26 CFR 301.6011-2T

✍ § 301.6011-2T Required use of magnetic media (temporary).

This section applies to information returns required to be filed after December 31, 1996. For information returns required to be filed after December 31, 1989, and before January 1, 1997, see section 6011(e) of the Internal Revenue Code and Sec. 301.6011-2.

(a) *Meaning of terms.* The following definitions apply for purposes of this section:

(1) *Magnetic media.* The term magnetic media means any magnetic media permitted under applicable regulations, revenue procedures, or, in the case of returns filed with the Social Security Administration, Social Security Administration publications. These generally include magnetic tape, tape cartridge, and diskette, as well as other media (such as electronic filing) specifically permitted under the applicable regulations, procedures, or publications.

(2) and (3) [Reserved] For further guidance, see Sec. 301.6011-2(a) (2) and (3).

(b) *Returns required on magnetic media.* (1) If the use of Form 1042-S, 1098, 1099 series, 5498, 8027, W-2G, or other form treated as a form specified in this paragraph (b)(1) is required by the applicable regulations or revenue procedures for the purpose of making an information return, the information required by the form must be submitted on magnetic media, except as otherwise provided in paragraph (c) of this section. Returns on magnetic media must be made in accordance with applicable revenue procedures or publications. See Sec. 601.601(d)(2)(ii)(b) of this chapter. Pursuant to these procedures, the consent of the Commissioner of Internal Revenue (or other authorized officer or employee of the Internal Revenue Service) to a magnetic medium must be obtained by submitting Form 4419 (Application for Filing Information Returns Magnetically/Electronically) prior to submitting a return described in this paragraph (b)(1) on the magnetic medium.

(2) If the use of Form W-2 (Wage and Tax Statement), Form 499R-2/W-2PR (Withholding Statement), Form W-2VI (U.S. Virgin Islands Wage and Tax Statement), Form W-2GU (Guam Wage and Tax Statement), Form W-2AS (American Samoa Wage and Tax Statement), or other form treated as a form specified in this paragraph (b)(2) is required for the purpose of making an information return, the information required by the form must be submitted on magnetic media, except as otherwise provided in paragraph (c) of this section. Returns described in this paragraph (b)(2) must be made in accordance with applicable Social Security Administration procedures or publications (which may be obtained from the local office of the Social Security Administration).

(3) [Reserved] For further guidance, see Sec. 301.6011-2(b)(3).

(c) *Exceptions*—(1) *Low-volume filers/250-threshold*—(i) *In general.* No person is required to file information returns on magnetic media unless the person is required to file 250 or more returns during the calendar year. Persons filing fewer than 250 returns during the calendar year may make the returns on the prescribed paper form, or, alternatively, such persons may make returns on magnetic media in accordance with paragraph (b) of this section.

(ii) [Reserved] For further guidance, see Sec. 301.6011-2(c)(1)(ii).

(iii) *No aggregation.* Each type of information return

described in paragraphs (b) (1) and (2) of this section is considered a separate return for purposes of this paragraph (c)(1). Therefore, the 250-threshold applies separately to each type of form required to be filed.

(iv) *Examples.* The provisions of paragraph (c)(1)(iii) of this section are illustrated by the following examples:

Example 1. For the calendar year ending December 31, 1996, Company X is required to file 200 returns on Form 1099-INT and 350 returns on Form 1099-MISC. Company X is not required to file Forms 1099-INT on magnetic media but is required to file Forms 1099-MISC on magnetic media.

Example 2. During the calendar year ending December 31, 1996, Company Y has 275 employees in Puerto Rico and 50 employees in American Samoa. Company Y is required to file Forms 499R-2/W-2PR on magnetic media but is not required to file Forms W-2AS on magnetic media.

Example 3. For the calendar year ending December 31, 1996, Company Z files 300 original returns on Form 1099-DIV and later files 70 corrected returns on Form 1099-DIV. Company Z is required to file the original returns on magnetic media. However, Company Z is not required to file the corrected returns on magnetic media because the corrected returns fall under the 250-threshold. See Sec. 301.6721-1(a)(2)(ii).

(2) *Waiver.* (i) The Commissioner may waive the requirements of this section if hardship is shown in a request for waiver filed in accordance with this paragraph (c)(2)(i). The principal factor in determining hardship will be the amount, if any, by which the cost of filing the information returns in accordance with this section exceeds the cost of filing the returns on other media. Notwithstanding the foregoing, if an employer is required to make a final return on Form 941, or a variation thereof, and expedited filing of Forms W-2, Forms 499R-2/W-2PR, Forms W-2VI, Forms W-2GU, or Form W-2AS is required, the unavailability of the specifications for magnetic media filing will be treated as creating a hardship. See Sec. 31.6071(a)-1(a)(3)(ii). A request for waiver must be made in accordance with applicable revenue procedures or publications. See Sec. 601.601(d)(2)(ii)(b) of this chapter. Pursuant to these procedures, a request for waiver should be filed at least 45 days before the due date of the information return in order for the Service to have adequate time to respond to the request for waiver. The waiver will specify the type of information return and the period to which it applies and will be subject to such terms and conditions regarding the method of reporting as may be prescribed by the Commissioner.

(ii) The Commissioner may prescribe rules that supplement the provisions of paragraph (c)(2)(i) of this section.

(c)(3) and (4) [Reserved]. For further guidance, see Sec. 301.6011-2(c) (3) and (4).

(d) and (e) [Reserved] For further guidance, see Sec. 301.6011-2 (d) and (e).

(f) *Failure to file.* If a person fails to file an information return on magnetic media when required to do so by this section, the person is deemed to have failed to file the return. In addition, if a person making returns on a paper form under paragraph (c) of this section fails to file a return on machine-readable paper form when required to do so by this section, the person is deemed to have failed to file the return. See sections 6652, 6693, and 6721 for penalties for failure to file certain returns. See also section 6724 and the regulations under section 6721 for the specific rules and limitations regarding the penalty imposed under section 6721 for failure to file on magnetic media.

(g) *Effective date.* (1) [Reserved] For further guidance, see Sec. 301.6011-2(g)(1).

(2) Paragraphs (a)(1), (b) (1) and (2), (c)(1) (i), (iii), and (iv), (c)(2), and (f) of this section are effective for information returns required to be filed after December 31, 1996. For information returns required to be filed after December 31, 1989, and before January 1, 1997, see section 6011(e) of the Internal Revenue Code and Sec. 301.6011-2.

PART 31. EMPLOYMENT TAXES AND COLLECTION OF INCOME TAX AT SOURCE

Citation: 26 CFR 31.3402(f)(5)-1

✍ § 31.3402(f)(5)-1 Form and contents of withholding exemption certificates.

(a) *Form W-4.* * * * Blank copies of paper Forms W-4 will be supplied to employers upon request to the Internal Revenue Service. * * *

(b) *Invalid Form W-4.* * * *

(c) *Electronic Form W-4* — (1) *In general.* An employer may establish a system for its employees to file withholding exemption certificates electronically.

(2) *Requirements* — (i) *In general.* The electronic system must ensure that the information received is the information sent, and must document all occasions of employee access that result in the filing of a Form W-4. In addition, the design and operation of the electronic system, including access procedures, must make it reasonably certain that the person accessing the system and filing the Form W-4 is the employee identified in the form.

(ii) Same information as paper Form W-4. The electronic filing must provide the employer with exactly the same information as the paper Form W-4.

(iii) *Jurat and signature requirements.* The electronic filing must be signed by the employee under penalties of perjury.

(A) *Jurat.* The jurat (perjury statement) must contain the language that appears on the paper Form W-4. The electronic program must inform the employee that he or she must make the declaration contained in the jurat and that the declaration is made by signing the Form W-4. The instructions and the language of the jurat must immediately follow the employee's income tax withholding selections and immediately precede the employee's electronic signature.

(B) *Electronic signature.* The electronic signature must identify the employee filing the electronic Form W-4 and authenticate and verify the filing. For this purpose, the terms "authenticate" and "verify" have the same meanings as they do when applied to a written signature on a paper Form W-4. An electronic signature can be in any form that satisfies the foregoing requirements. The electronic signature must be the final entry in the employee's Form W-4 submission.

(iv) *Copies of electronic Forms W-4.* Upon request by the Internal Revenue Service, the employer must supply a hardcopy of the electronic Form W-4 and a statement that, to the best of the employer's knowledge, the electronic Form W-4 was filed by the named employee. The hardcopy of the electronic Form W-4 must provide exactly the same information as, but need not be a facsimile of, the paper Form W-4.

(3) *Effective date* — (i) *In general.* This paragraph applies to all withholding exemption certificates filed electronically by employees on or after January 2, 1997.

(ii) Special rule for certain Forms W-4. In the case of an electronic system that precludes the filing of Forms W-4 required on commencement of employment and Forms W-4 claiming more than 10 withholding exemptions or exemption from withholding, the requirements of paragraph (c)(2)(iii) of this section will be treated as satisfied if the Form W-4 is filed electronically before January 1, 1999.

TITLE 27. ALCOHOL, TOBACCO PRODUCTS AND FIREARMS

Agency: **Department of the Treasury**
Bureau of Alcohol, Tobacco and Firearms

SUBCHAPTER A. LIQUORS

PART 18. PRODUCTION OF VOLATILE FRUIT-FLAVOR CONCENTRATE

Subpart F. Records and Reports

Citation: **27 CFR 18.62**

✍ § 18.62 Record of transfer.

When concentrate, juice, or fruit mash is transferred from the concentrate plant premises, the proprietor shall prepare, in duplicate, a record of transfer. The record of transfer may consist of a commercial invoice, bill of lading, or any other similar document. The proprietor shall forward the original of the record of transfer to the consignee and retain the copy as a record. Each record of transfer shall show the following information:

(a) Name, registry number, and address of the concentrate plant;

(b) Name and address of the consignee;

(c) Kind (by fruit from which produced) and description of product, e.g. grape concentrate, concentrated grape juice, unconcentrated grape juice, grape mash;

(d) Quantity (in wine gallons); and

(e) For concentrate, percent of alcohol by volume.

Citation: **27 CFR 18.64**

✍ § 18.64 Photographic copies of records.

Proprietors may record, copy, or reproduce records required by this part by an process which accurately reproduces or forms a durable medium for reproducing the original of records. Whenever records are reproduced under this section, the reproduced records will be preserved in conveniently accessible files, and provisions will be made for examining, viewing, and using the reproduced record the same as if it were the original record. The reproduced record will be treated and considered for all purposes as though it were the original record. All provisions of law and regulation applicable to the original record are applicable to the reproduced record.

PART 19. DISTILLED SPIRITS PLANTS

Subpart W. Records and Reports

General

Citation: **27 CFR 19.723**

✍ § 19.723 Maintenance and preservation of records.

(a) *Place of maintenance.* Records required by this part shall be prepared and kept by the proprietor at the plant where the operation or transaction occurs and shall be available for inspection by any ATF officer during business hours.

(b) *Reproduction of original records.* (1) Whenever any record, because of its condition, becomes unsuitable for its intended or continued use the proprietor shall reproduce such record, by a process approved by the regional director (compliance) under § 19.725 for reproducing records, and such reproduction shall be treated and considered for all purposes as though it were the original record.

(2) All provisions of law applicable to the original record shall be applicable to such reproductions.

(c) *Retention of records.* (1) Records required by this part shall be preserved for a period of not less than three years from the date thereof or the date of the last entry required to be made thereon, whichever is later. However, the regional director (compliance) may require records to be kept for an additional period not exceeding three years in any case where such retention is deemed necessary or advisable for the protection of the revenue.

(2) The period for retention of records prescribed in paragraph (c)(1) of this section shall not apply to copies of outstanding approved formulas or to copies of formulas which form the basis for claims for credit or refund of taxes on spirits returned to bonded premises. A copy of any such formula shall be kept by the proprietor at the plant where spirits are processed subject to the formula or at the plant where such spirits are received.

(d) *Data processing.* (1) Notwithstanding any other provision of this section, record data maintained on data processing equipment may be kept at a location other than the plant premises if the original transaction (source) records required by § § 19.736-19.779 are kept available for inspection at the plant premises.

(2) Data which has been accumulated on cards, tapes, discs, or other accepted record media must be retrievable within five business days.

(3) The applicable data processing program shall be made available for examination if requested by an ATF officer.

Citation: **27 CFR 19.725**

✍ § 19.725 Photographic copies of records.

(a) *Application.* Proprietors who desire to record, copy or reproduce records, required by this part, by any process which accurately reproduces or forms a durable medium for so reproducing the original of such records, shall apply to the regional director (compliance) for permission to do so, describing:

(1) The records to be reproduced.

(2) The reproduction process to be employed.

(3) The manner in which the reproductions are to be preserved, and

(4) The provisions to be made for examining, viewing, and using such reproductions.

(b) *Approval.* The regional director (compliance) shall not approve any application unless the manner of preservation of the reproductions and the provisions for examining, viewing, and using such reproductions are satisfactory.

(c) *Conditions.* Whenever records are reproduced under this section, the reproduced records shall be preserved in conveniently accessible files, and provisions shall be made for examining, viewing, and using the reproduced records the same as if it were the original record, and it shall be treated and considered for all purposes as though it were the original record. All provisions of law and regulations applicable to the original shall be applicable to the reproduced records. As used in this section, "original record" shall mean the record required by this part to be maintained or preserved by the proprietor, even though it may be an executed duplicate or other copy of the document.

PART 20. DISTRIBUTION AND USE OF DENATURED ALCOHOL AND RUM

Subpart P. Records and Reports

Citation: 27 CFR 20.268

✍ **§ 20.268 Photographic copies of records.**

(a) *General.* Permittees may record, copy, or reproduce required records. Any process may be used which accurately reproduces the original record, and which forms a durable medium for reproducing and preserving the original record.

(b) *Copies of records treated as original records.* Whenever records are reproduced under this section, the reproduced records will be preserved in conveniently accessible files, and provisions will be made for examining, viewing, and using the reproduced records the same as if they were the original record, and they will be treated and considered for all purposes as though they were the original record. All provisions of law and regulations applicable to the original are applicable to the reproduced record. As used in this section, "original record" means the record required by this part to be maintained or preserved by the permittee, even though it may be an executed duplicate or other copy of the document.

PART 22. DISTRIBUTION AND USE OF TAX-FREE ALCOHOL

Subpart J. Recovery of Tax-Free Alcohol

Citation: 27 CFR 22.165

✍ **§ 22.165 Photographic copies of records.**

(a) *General.* Permittees may record, copy, or reproduce required records. Any process may be used which accurately reproduces the original record, and which forms a durable medium for reproducing and preserving the original record.

(b) *Copies of records treated as original records.* Whenever records are reproduced under this section, the reproduced records shall be preserved in conveniently accessible files, and provisions shall be made for examining, viewing, and using the reproduced records the same as if they were the original record, and they shall be treated and considered for all purposes as though they were the original record. All provisions of law and regulations applicable to the original are applicable to the reproduced record. As used in this section, "original record" means the record required by this part to be maintained or preserved by the permittee, even though it may be an executed duplicate or other copy of the document.

PART 25. BEER

Subpart U. Records and Reports

Citation: 27 CFR 25.300

✍ **§ 25.300 Retention and preservation of records.**

(a) *Place of maintenance.* Records required by this part will be prepared and kept by the brewer at the brewery where the operation or transaction occurs and will be available for inspection by any ATF officer during business hours.

(b) *Reproduction of original records.* Whenever any record, because of its condition, becomes unsuitable for its intended or continued use, the brewer shall reproduce the record by a process under § 25.301. The reproduced record will be treated and considered for all purposes as though it were the original record, and all provisions of law applicable to the original are applicable to the reproduction.

(c) *Retention of records.* Records required by this part will be preserved for a period of not less than three years from the date thereof or the date of the last entry required to be made thereon, whichever is later. The regional director (compliance) may require records to be kept for an additional period not exceeding three years in any case where such retention is deemed necessary or advisable for the protection of the revenue.

(d) *Data Processing.* (1) Notwithstanding any other provision of this section, record data maintained on data processing equipment may be kept at a location other than the brewery if the original transaction (source) records required by § § 25.292-25.298 are kept available for inspection at the brewery.

(2) Data which has been accumulated on cards, tapes, discs, or other accepted record media will be retrievable within five business days.

(3) The applicable data processing program will be made available for examination if requested by an ATF officer.

Citation: 27 CFR 25.301

✍ **§ 25.301 Photographic copies of records.**

(a) *General.* Brewers may record, copy, or reproduce records required by this part. Brewers may use any process which accurately reproduces the original records and which forms a durable medium for reproducing and preserving the original record.

(b) *Copies of records treated as original records.* Whenever records are reproduced under this section, the reproduced records will be preserved in conveniently accessible files, and provisions will be made for examining, viewing and using the reproduced records the same as if it were the original record, and it will be treated and considered for all purposes as though it were the original record. All provisions of law and regulations applicable to the original are applicable to the reproduced record. As used in this section, "original record" means the record required by this part to be maintained or preserved by the brewer, even though it may be an executed duplicate or other copy of the document.

SUBCHAPTER M. ALCOHOL, TOBACCO AND OTHER EXCISE TAXES

PART 178. COMMERCE IN FIREARMS AND AMMUNITION

Subpart H. Records

Citation: 27 CFR 178.125

✍ **§ 178.125 Record of receipt and disposition.**

(a) *Ammunition received by licensed dealers.* Each licensed dealer shall maintain records of all ammunition (except .22 caliber rimfire) received for the purpose of sale or distribution. Such record may consist of invoices or other commercial records which shall be filed in an orderly manner separate from other commercial records maintained, and be readily available for inspection. Such record shall (1) show the name of the manufacturer and the transferor, and the type, caliber or gauge, and quantity of the ammunition acquired in the transaction, and the date of such acquisition, and (2) be retained on the licensed premises of the dealer for a period of not less than two years following the date of the acquisition.

(b) *Ammunition received by licensed collectors.* Each

licensed collector shall maintain records of all ammunition (except .22 caliber rimfire) acquired as curios or relics for the collection. Such records may consist of invoices or other commercial records which shall be filed in an orderly manner separate from other commercial records maintained, and be readily available for inspection. Such records shall show the information required by paragraph (a) of this section and be retained in the same manner.

(c) *Ammunition disposition* — (1) *Sales to nonlicensees.* The sale or other disposition of ammunition, or of an ammunition curio or relic, shall be recorded in a bound record at the time a transaction is made, except that no record need be maintained for the sale of shotgun ammunition, .22 caliber rimfire ammunition, ammunition suitable for use only in rifles generally available in commerce, or component parts of these types of ammunition. Sales or other dispositions of ammunition which are interchangeable between rifles and pistols or revolvers (for example, .45 Pistol or Revolver), except .22 caliber rimfire, must be recorded. The bound record shall be maintained in chronological order by date of sale or disposition of the ammunition, and shall be retained on the licensed premises of the licensee for a period not less than two years following the date of the recorded sales or disposition of the ammunition.

The bound record entry shall show:

(i) The date of the transaction;

(ii) The name of the manufacturer;

(iii) The caliber or gauge (or the type of ammunition component);

(iv) The quantity of ammunition (or component);

(v) The name, address, and date of birth of the nonlicensee; and

(vi) The method used to establish the identity of the ammunition purchaser.

The format required for the bound records is as follows: Date; Manufacturer; Caliber, gauge, or type of component; No. of boxes; Purchaser; Name and address; Date of birth; Enter a (x) in the "known" column if the purchaser is personally known to you. Otherwise, establish the purchaser's identification; Known; Driver's license; Other type (specify).

However, when a commercial record is made at the time a transaction is made, a licensee may delay making an entry into the bound record if the provisions of paragraph (d) of this section are complied with.

(2) *Sales to licensees.* Sales or other dispositions of all ammunition from a licensee to another licensee shall be recorded and maintained in the manner prescribed in § 178.122(b) for importers.

(d) *Commercial records of ammunition sales.* When a commercial record is made at the time of sale or other disposition of ammunition, or of an ammunition curio or relic, and such record contains all information required by the bound record prescribed by paragraph (c) of this section, the licensed dealer or licensed collector transferring the ammunition or ammunition curio or relic, may, for a period not exceeding 7 days following the date of such transfer, delay making the required entry into such bound record: Provided, That the commercial record pertaining to the transfer is; (1) maintained by the licensed dealer or licensed collector separate from other commercial documents maintained by such licensee, and (2) is readily available for inspection on the licensed premises until such time as the required entry into the bound record is made.

(e) *Firearms receipt and disposition.* Each licensed dealer and each licensed collector shall enter into a record each receipt and disposition of firearms or firearms curios or relics.

(f) *Commercial records of firearms received.* When a commercial record is held by a licensed dealer or licensed collector showing his acquisition of a firearm or firearm curio or relic, and such record contains all acquisition information required by the bound record prescribed by paragraph (e) of this section, the licensed dealer or licensed collector acquiring such firearm or curio or relic, may, for a period not exceeding seven days following the date of such acquisition, delay making the required entry into such bound record:

Provided, That the commercial record is, until such time as the required entry into the bound record is made (1) maintained by the licensed dealer or licensed collector separate from other commercial documents maintained by such licensee, and (2) is readily available for inspection on the licensed premises: Provided, further, That when disposition is made of a firearm or firearm curio or relic not entered in the bound record under the provisions of this paragraph, the licensed dealer or licensed collector making such disposition shall enter all required acquisition information regarding the firearm or firearm curio or relic in the bound record at the time such transfer or disposition is made.

(g) *Alternate records.* Notwithstanding the provisions of paragraph (c) and (e) of this section, the regional regulatory administrator may authorize alternate records to be maintained by a licensed dealer or a licensed collector to record his acquisition and disposal of firearms and ammunition, or curios and relics, when it is shown by the licensed dealer or the licensed collector that such alternate records will accurately and readily disclose the required information. A licensed dealer or licensed collector who proposes to use alternate records shall submit a letter application, in duplicate, to the regional regulatory administrator and shall describe the proposed alternate records and the need therefor. Such alternate records shall not be employed by the licensed dealer or the licensed collector until approval in such regard is received from the regional regulatory administrator.

(h) *Requirements for importers and manufacturers.* Each licensed importer and licensed manufacturer selling or otherwise disposing of firearms or ammunition to nonlicensees shall maintain such records of such transactions as are required of licensed dealers and licensed collectors by this section.

PART 194. LIQUOR DEALERS

Subpart O. Prescribed Records and Reports, and Posting of Signs

Period of Retention

Citation: **27 CFR 194.238**

✍ **§ 194.238 Photographic copies of records.**

(a) *General.* Dealers may record, copy, or reproduce records required by this part. Dealers may use any process which accurately reproduces the original record, and which forms a durable medium for reproducing and preserving the original record.

(b) *Copies of records treated as original records.* Whenever records are reproduced under this section, the produced records will be preserved in conveniently accessible files, and provisions will be made for examining, viewing, and using the reproduced record the same as if it were the original record, and it will be treated and considered for all purposes as though it were the original record. All provisions of law and regulations applicable to the original record are applicable to the reproduced record. As used in this section, "original record" means the record required by this part to be maintained or preserved by the dealer, even though it may be an executed duplicate or other copy of the document.

PART 275. IMPORTATION OF CIGARS, CIGARETTES, AND CIGARETTE PAPERS AND TUBES

Subpart G. Puerto Rican Cigars, Cigarettes, and Cigarette Papers and Tubes, Brought Into the United States

Citation:	27 CFR 275.115a

✍ **§ 275.115a Payment of tax by electronic fund transfer.**

* * * * *

(c) *Remittance.*

* * * * *

(3) When the taxpayer directs the bank to effect an electronic fund transfer message as required by paragraph (b)(2) of this section, any transfer data record furnished to the taxpayer, through normal banking procedures, will serve as the record of payment, and shall be retained as part of required records.

* * * * *

PART 285. MANUFACTURE OF CIGARETTE PAPERS AND TUBES

Subpart C. Taxes

Citation:	27 CFR 285.27

✍ **§ 285.27 Payment of tax by electronic fund transfer.**

* * * * *

(c) *Remittance.*

* * * * *

(3) When the taxpayer directs the bank to effect an electronic fund transfer message as required by paragraph (b)(2) of this section, any transfer data records furnished to the taxpayer, through normal banking procedures, will serve as the record of payment, and shall be retained as part of required records.

* * * * *

PART 290. EXPORTATION OF CIGARS, CIGARETTES,

Subpart G. Operations by Export Warehouse Proprietors

Citation:	27 CFR 290.142

✍ **§ 290.142. Records.**

Every export warehouse proprietor shall keep at his warehouse complete and adequate records of the date, kind, and quantity of tobacco products, and cigarette papers and tubes received, removed, transferred, destroyed, lost, or returned to manufacturers or to customs warehouse proprietors. In addition to such records, the export warehouse proprietor shall retain a copy of each notice, Form 2149 or 2150, received from a manufacturer, another export warehouse proprietor, or customs warehouse proprietor from whom tobacco products, and cigarette papers and tubes are received, and a copy of each notice, Form 2150, covering the tobacco products, and cigarette papers and tubes removed from his warehouse. The entries for each day in the records maintained or kept under this section shall be made by the close of the business day following that on which the transactions occur. No particular form of records is prescribed, but the information required shall be readily ascertainable. Such records and copies of the notices, Forms 2149 and 2150, shall be retained for 2 years following the close of the calendar year in which the shipments were received or removed and shall be made available for inspection by any ATF officer upon his request.

TITLE 29. LABOR

Agency:	Department of Labor Wage and Hour Division

SUBCHAPTER A. REGULATIONS UNDER SECTION 15C OF THE SECURITIES EXCHANGE ACT OF 1934

PART 516. RECORDS TO BE KEPT BY EMPLOYERS

Introductory

Citation:	29 CFR 516.1

✍ **§ 516.1 Form of records; scope of regulations.**

(a) *Form of records.* No particular order or form of records is prescribed by the regulations in this part. However, every employer subject to any provisions of the Fair Labor Standards Act of 1938, as amended (hereinafter referred to as the "Act"), is required to maintain records containing the information and data required by the specific sections of this part. The records may be maintained and preserved on microfilm or other basic source document of an automatic word or data processing memory provided that adequate projection or viewing equipment is available, that the reproductions are clear and identifiable by date or pay period and that extensions or transcriptions of the information required by this part are made available upon request.

(b) *Scope of regulations.* The regulations in this part are divided into two subparts. (1) Subpart A of this part contains the requirements generally applicable to all employers employing covered employees, including the requirements relating to the posting of notices, the preservation and location of records, and the recordkeeping requirements for employers of employees to whom both the minimum wage provision of section 6 or the minimum wage provisions of section 6 and the overtime pay provisions of section 7(a) of the Act apply. In addition, section 516.3 contains the requirements relating to executive, administrative, and professional employees (including academic administrative personnel or teachers in elementary or secondary schools), and outside sales employees.

(2) Subpart B of this part deals with the information and data which must be kept for employees (other than executive, administrative, etc., employees) who are subject to any of the exemptions provided in the Act. This section also specifies the records needed for deductions from and additions to wages for "board, lodging, and other facilities," industrial homeworkers and employees whose tips are credited toward wages. The sections in Subpart B of this part require the recording of more, less, or different items of information or data than required under the generally applicable recordkeeping requirements of Subpart A.

(c) *Relationship to other recordkeeping and reporting requirements.* Nothing in 29 CFR Part 516 shall excuse any party from complying with any recordkeeping or reporting requirement imposed by any other Federal, State or local law, ordinance, regulation or rule.

SUBCHAPTER C. OTHER LAWS

PART 825. THE FAMILY AND MEDICAL LEAVE ACT OF 1993

Subpart E. What Records Must be Kept to Comply With the FMLA?

Citation: **29 CFR 825.500**

✍ § 825.500 What records must an employer keep to comply with the FMLA?

(a) FMLA provides that covered employers shall make, keep, and preserve records pertaining to their obligations under the Act in accordance with the recordkeeping requirements of section 11(c) of the Fair Labor Standards Act (FLSA) and in accordance with these regulations. FMLA also restricts the authority of the Department of Labor to require any employer or plan, fund or program to submit books or records more than once during any 12-month period unless the Department has reasonable cause to believe a violation of the FMLA exists or the DOL is investigating a complaint. These regulations establish no requirement for the submission of any records unless specifically requested by a Departmental official.

(b) *Form of records.* No particular order or form of records is required. These regulations establish no requirement that any employer revise its computerized payroll or personnel records systems to comply. However, employers must keep the records specified by these regulations for no less than three years and make them available for inspection, copying, and transcription by representatives of the Department of Labor upon request. The records may be maintained and preserved on microfilm or other basic source document of an automated data processing memory provided that adequate projection or viewing equipment is available, that the reproductions are clear and identifiable by date or pay period, and that extensions or transcriptions of the information required herein can be and are made available upon request. Records kept in computer form must be made available for transcription or copying.

(c) *Items required.* Covered employers who have eligible employees must maintain records that must disclose the following:

(1) Basic payroll and identifying employee data, including name, address, and occupation; rate or basis of pay and terms of compensation; daily and weekly hours worked per pay period; additions to or deductions from wages; and total compensation paid.

(2) Dates FMLA leave is taken by FMLA eligible employees (e.g., available from time records, requests for leave, etc., if so designated). Leave must be designated in records as FMLA leave; leave so designated may not include leave required under State law or an employer plan which is not also covered by FMLA.

(3) If FMLA leave is taken by eligible employees in increments of less than one full day, the hours of the leave.

(4) Copies of employee notices of leave furnished to the employer under FMLA, if in writing, and copies of all general and specific written notices given to employees as required under FMLA and these regulations (see § 825.301(c)). Copies may be maintained in employee personnel files.

(5) Any documents (including written and electronic records) describing employee benefits or employer policies and practices regarding the taking of paid and unpaid leaves.

(6) Premium payments of employee benefits.

(7) Records of any dispute between the employer and an eligible employee regarding designation of leave as FMLA leave, including any written statement from the employer or employee of the reasons for the designation and for the disagreement.

(d) Covered employers with no eligible employees must maintain the records set forth in paragraph (c)(1) above.

(e) Covered employers in a joint employment situation (see § 825.106) must keep all the records required by paragraph (c) of this section with respect to any primary employees, and must keep the records required by paragraph (c)(1) with respect to any secondary employees.

(f) If FMLA-eligible employees are not subject to FLSA's recordkeeping regulations for purposes of minimum wage or overtime compliance (i.e., not covered by or exempt from FLSA), an employer need not keep a record of actual hours worked (as otherwise required under FLSA, 29 CFR 516.2(a)(7)), provided that:

(1) eligibility for FMLA leave is presumed for any employee who has been employed for at least 12 months; and

(2) with respect to employees who take FMLA leave intermittently or on a reduced leave schedule, the employer and employee agree on the employee's normal schedule or average hours worked each week and reduce their agreement to a written record maintained in accordance with paragraph (b) of this section.

(g) Records and documents relating to medical certifications, recertifications or medical histories of employees or employees' family members, created for purposes of FMLA, shall be maintained as confidential medical records in separate files/records from the usual personnel files, and if ADA is also applicable, such records shall be maintained in conformance with ADA confidentiality requirements (see 29 CFR § 1630.14(c)(1)), except that:

(1) Supervisors and managers may be informed regarding necessary restrictions on the work or duties of an employee and necessary accommodations;

(2) First aid and safety personnel may be informed (when appropriate) if the employee's physical or medical condition might require emergency treatment; and

(3) Government officials investigating compliance with FMLA (or other pertinent law) shall be provided relevant information upon request.

Agency: **Equal Employment Opportunity Commission**

SUBCHAPTER B. STATEMENT OF GENERAL POLICY OR INTERPRETATION NOT DIRECTLY RELATED TO REGULATIONS

PART 1602. RECORDKEEPING AND REPORTING REQUIREMENTS UNDER TITLE VII AND THE ADA

Subpart C. Recordkeeping By Employers

Citation: **29 CFR 1602.13**

✍ § 1602.13 Records as to racial or ethnic identify of employees.

Employers may acquire the information necessary for completion of Items 5 and 6 of Report EEO-1 either by visual surveys of the work force, or at their option, by the maintenance of post-employment records as to the identity of employees where the same is permitted by State law. In the latter case, however, the Commission recommends the maintenance of a permanent record as to the racial or ethnic identity of an individual for purpose of completing the report form only where the employer keeps such records separately from the employee's basic personnel form or other records available to those responsible for personnel decisions, e.g. as part of an automatic data processing system in the payroll department.

TITLE 30. MINERAL RESOURCES

Agency:	**Department of Labor** **Mine Safety and Health Administration**

SUBCHAPTER N. Metal and Nonmetal Mine Safety and Health

PART 75. MANDATORY SAFETY STANDARDS — UNDERGROUND COAL MINES

Subpart D. Ventilation

Citation:	**30 CFR 75.310**

✍ § 75.310 Installation of main mine fans.

(a) Each main mine fan shall be —

(1) Installed on the surface in an incombustible housing;

(2) Connected to the mine opening with incombustible air ducts;

(3) Equipped with an automatic device that gives a signal at the mine when the fan either slows or stops. A responsible person designated by the operator shall always be at a surface location at the mine where the signal can be seen or heard while anyone is underground. This person shall be provided with two-way communication with the working sections and work stations where persons are routinely assigned to work for the majority of a shift;

(4) Equipped with a pressure recording device or system. Mines permitted to shut down main mine fans under § 75.311 and which do not have a pressure recording device installed on main mine fans shall have until March 11, 1997 to install a pressure recording device or system on all main mine fans. If a device or system other than a circular pressure recorder is used to monitor main mine fan pressure, the monitoring device or system shall provide a continuous graph or continuous chart of the pressure as a function of time. At not more than 7-day intervals, a hard copy of the continuous graph or chart shall be generated or the record of the fan pressure shall be stored electronically. When records of fan pressure are stored electronically, the system used to store these records shall be secure and not susceptible to alteration and shall be capable of storing the required data. Records of the fan pressure shall be retained at a surface location at the mine for at least 1 year and be made available for inspection by authorized representatives of the Secretary and the representative of miners;

* * * * *

(c) If a main mine fan monitoring system is used under § 75.312, the system shall —

(1) Record, as described in paragraph (a)(4) the mine ventilating pressure;

(2) Monitor bearing temperature, revolutions per minute, vibration, electric voltage, and amperage;

(3) Provide a printout of the monitored parameters, including the mine ventilating pressure within a reasonable period, not to exceed the end of the next scheduled shift during which miners are underground; and

(4) Be equipped with an automatic device that signals when —

(i) An electrical or mechanical deficiency exists in the monitoring system; or

(ii) A sudden increase or loss in mine ventilating pressure occurs.

(5) Provide monitoring, records, printouts, and signals required by paragraphs (c)(1) through (c)(4) at a surface location at the mine where a responsible person designated by the operator is always on duty and where signals from the monitoring system can be seen or heard while anyone is underground. This person shall be provided with two-way communication with the working sections and work stations where persons are routinely assigned to work for the majority of a shift.

* * * * *

Citation:	**30 CFR 75.312**

✍ § 75.312 Main mine fan examinations and records.

(a) To assure electrical and mechanical reliability of main mine fans, each main mine fan and its associated components, including devices for measuring or recording mine ventilation pressure, shall be examined for proper operation by a trained person designated by the operator. Examinations of main mine fans shall be made at least once each day that the fan operates, unless a fan monitoring system is used. No examination is required on any day when no one, including certified persons, goes underground, except that an examination shall be completed prior to anyone entering the mine.

(b)(1) If a main mine fan monitoring system is used, a trained person designated by the operator shall-

(i) At least once each day review the data provided by the fan monitoring system to assure that the fan and the fan monitoring system are operating properly. No review is required on any day when no one, including certified persons, goes underground, except that a review of the data shall be performed prior to anyone entering the underground portion of the mine. Data reviewed should include the fan pressure, bearing temperature, revolutions per minute, vibration, electric voltage, and amperage; and

(ii) At least every 7 days-

(A) Test the monitoring system for proper operation; and

(B) Examine each main mine fan and its associated components to assure electrical and mechanical reliability of main mine fans.

(2) If the monitoring system malfunctions, the malfunction shall be corrected, or paragraph (a) of this section shall apply.

(c) At least every 31 days, the automatic fan signal device for each main mine fan shall be tested by stopping the fan. Only persons necessary to evaluate the effect of the fan stoppage or restart, or to perform maintenance or repair work that cannot otherwise be made while the fan is operating, shall be permitted underground. Notwithstanding the requirement of § 75.311(b)(3), underground power may remain energized during this test provided no one, including persons identified in § 75.311(b)(1), is underground. If the fan is not restarted within 15 minutes, underground power shall be deenergized and no one shall enter any underground area of the mine until the fan is restarted and an examination of the mine is conducted as described in § 75.360 (b) through (e) and the mine has been determined to be safe.

(d) At least every 31 days, the automatic closing doors in multiple main mine fan systems shall be tested by stopping the fan. Only persons necessary to evaluate the effect of the fan stoppage or restart, or to perform maintenance or repair work that cannot otherwise be made while the fan is operating, shall be permitted underground. Notwithstanding the provisions of § 75.311, underground power may remain energized during this test provided no one, including persons identified in

§ 75.311(b)(1), is underground. If the fan is not restarted within 15 minutes, underground power shall be deenergized and no one shall enter any underground area of the mine, until the fan is restarted and an examination of the mine is conducted as described in § 75.360 (b) through (e) and the mine has been determined to be safe.

(e) Circular main mine fan pressure recording charts shall be changed before the beginning of a second revolution.

(f)(1) *Certification.* Persons making main mine fan examinations shall certify by initials and date at the fan or another location specified by the operator that the examinations were made. Each certification shall identify the main mine fan examined.

(2) Persons reviewing data produced by a main mine fan monitoring system shall certify by initials and date on a printed copy of the data from the system that the review was completed. In lieu of certification on a copy of the data, the person reviewing the data may certify electronically that the review was completed. Electronic certification shall be by handwritten initials and date in a computer system so as to be secure and not susceptible to alteration.

(g)(1) *Recordkeeping.* By the end of the shift on which the examination is made, persons making main mine fan examinations shall record all uncorrected defects that may affect the operation of the fan that are not corrected by the end of that shift. Records shall be maintained in a secure book that is not susceptible to alteration or electronically in a computer system so as to be secure and not susceptible to alteration.

(2) When a fan monitoring system is used in lieu of the daily fan examination-

(i) The certified copies of data produced by fan monitoring systems shall be maintained separate from other computer-generated reports or data; and

(ii) A record shall be made of any fan monitoring system malfunctions, electrical or mechanical deficiencies in the monitoring system and any sudden increase or loss in mine ventilating pressure. The record shall be made by the end of the shift on which the review of the data is completed and shall be maintained in a secure book that is not susceptible to alteration or electronically in a computer system so as to be secure and not susceptible to alteration.

(3) By the end of the shift on which the monthly test of the automatic fan signal device or the automatic closing doors is completed, persons making these tests shall record the results of the tests. Records shall be maintained in a secure book that is not susceptible to alteration or electronically in a computer system so as to be secure and not susceptible to alteration.

(h) *Retention period.* Records, including records of mine fan pressure and the certified copies of data produced by fan monitoring systems, shall be retained at a surface location at the mine for at least 1 year and shall be made available for inspection by authorized representatives of the Secretary and the representative of miners.

75.342 Methane monitors.

(a)(1) MSHA approved methane monitors shall be installed on all face cutting machines, continuous miners, longwall face equipment, loading machines, and other mechanized equipment used to extract or load coal within the working place.

(2) The sensing device for methane monitors on longwall shearing machines shall be installed at the return air end of the longwall face. An additional sensing device also shall be installed on the longwall shearing machine, downwind and as close to the cutting head as practicable. An alternative location or locations for the sensing device required on the longwall shearing machine may be approved in the ventilation plan.

(3) The sensing devices of methane monitors shall be installed as close to the working face as practicable.

(4) Methane monitors shall be maintained in permissible and proper operating condition and shall be calibrated with a known air-methane mixture at least once every 31 days. To assure that methane monitors are properly maintained and calibrated, the operator shall:

(i) Use persons properly trained in the maintenance, calibration, and permissibility of methane monitors to calibrate and maintain the devices.

(ii) Maintain a record of all calibration tests of methane monitors. Records shall be maintained in a secure book that is not susceptible to alteration or electronically in a computer system so as to be secure and not susceptible to alteration.

(iii) Retain the record of calibration tests for 1 year from the date of the test. Records shall be retained at a surface location at the mine and made available for inspection by authorized representatives of the Secretary and the representative of miners.

(b)(1) When the methane concentration at any methane monitor reaches 1.0 percent the monitor shall give a warning signal.

(2) The warning signal device of the methane monitor shall be visible to a person who can deenergize the equipment on which the monitor is mounted.

(c) The methane monitor shall automatically deenergize the machine on which it is mounted when-

(1) The methane concentration at any methane monitor reaches 2.0 percent; or

(2) The monitor is not operating properly.

Citation: 30 CFR 75.360

✍ § 75.360 Preshift examination.

* * * * *

(e) *Certification.* At each working place examined, the person doing the preshift examination shall certify by initials, date, and the time, that the examination was made. In areas required to be examined outby a working section, the certified person shall certify by initials, date, and the time at enough locations to show that the entire area has been examined.

(f) *Recordkeeping.* A record of the results of each preshift examination, including a record of hazardous conditions and their locations found by the examiner during each examination and of the results and locations of air and methane measurements, shall be made on the surface before any persons, other than certified persons conducting examinations required by this subpart, enter any underground area of the mine. The results of methane tests shall be recorded as the percentage of methane measured by the examiner. The record shall be made by the certified person who made the examination or by a person designated by the operator. If the record is made by someone other than the examiner, the examiner shall verify the record by initials and date by or at the end of the shift for which the examination was made. A record shall also be made by a certified person of the action taken to correct hazardous conditions found during the preshift examination. All preshift and corrective action records shall be countersigned by the mine foreman or equivalent mine official by the end of the mine foreman's or equivalent mine official's next regularly scheduled working shift. The records required by this section shall be made in a secure book that is not susceptible to alteration or electronically in a computer system so as to be secure and not susceptible to alteration.

(g) *Retention period.* Records shall be retained at a surface location at the mine for at least 1 year and shall be made available for inspection by authorized representatives of the Secretary and the representative of miners.

Citation: 30 CFR 75.363

✍ § 75.363 Hazardous conditions; posting, correcting and recording.

(a) Any hazardous condition found by the mine foreman or equivalent mine official, assistant mine foreman or equivalent mine official, or other certified persons designated by the operator for the purposes of conducting examinations under this subpart D, shall be posted with a conspicuous danger sign where anyone entering the areas would pass. A hazardous condition, other than one detected during a preshift examination or an examination conducted following a fan stoppage and restart under § 75.313(d)(1)(i), shall be corrected immediately or the area shall remain posted until the hazardous condition is corrected. If the condition creates an imminent danger, everyone except those persons referred to in section 104(c) of the Act shall be withdrawn from the area affected to a safe area until the hazardous condition is corrected. Only persons designated by the operator to correct or evaluate the condition may enter the posted area.

(b) A record shall be made of any hazardous condition found. This record shall be kept in a book maintained for this purpose on the surface at the mine. The record shall be made by the completion of the shift on which the hazardous condition is found and shall include the nature and location of the hazardous condition and the corrective action taken. This record shall not be required for shifts when no hazardous conditions are found or for hazardous conditions found during the preshift or weekly examinations inasmuch as these examinations have separate recordkeeping requirements.

(c) The record shall be made by the certified person who conducted the examination or a person designated by the operator. If made by a person other than the certified person, the certified person shall verify the record by initials and date by or at the end of the shift for which the examination was made. Records shall be countersigned by the mine foreman or equivalent mine official by the end of the mine foreman's or equivalent mine official's next regularly scheduled working shift. The record shall be made in a secure book that is not susceptible to alteration or electronically in a computer system so as to be secure and not susceptible to alteration.

(d) *Retention period.* Records shall be retained at a surface location at the mine for at least 1 year and shall be made available for inspection by authorized representatives of the Secretary and the representative of miners.

Citation: 30 CFR 75.364

✍ § 75.364 Weekly examination.

(a) *Worked-out areas.* (1) At least every 7 days, a certified person shall examine unsealed worked-out areas where no pillars have been recovered by traveling to the area of deepest penetration; measuring methane and oxygen concentrations and air quantities and making tests to determine if the air is moving in the proper direction in the area. The locations of measurement points where tests and measurements will be performed shall be included in the mine ventilation plan and shall be adequate in number and location to assure ventilation and air quality in the area. Air quantity measurements shall also be made where the air enters and leaves the worked-out area. An alternative method of evaluating the ventilation of the area may be approved in the ventilation plan.

(2) At least every 7 days, a certified person shall evaluate the effectiveness of bleeder systems required by § 75.334 as follows:

(i) Measurements of methane and oxygen concentrations and air quantity and a test to determine if the air is moving in its proper direction shall be made where air enters the worked-out area.

(ii) Measurements of methane and oxygen concentrations and air quantity and a test to determine if the air is moving in the proper direction shall be made immediately before the air enters a return split of air.

(iii) At least one entry of each set of bleeder entries used as part of a bleeder system under § 75.334 shall be traveled in its entirety. Measurements of methane and oxygen concentrations and air quantities and a test to determine if the air is moving in the proper direction shall be made at the measurement point locations specified in the mine ventilation plan to determine the effectiveness of the bleeder system.

(iv) In lieu of the requirements of paragraphs (a)(2)(i) and (iii) of this section, an alternative method of evaluation may be specified in the ventilation plan provided the alternative method results in proper evaluation of the effectiveness of the bleeder system.

(b) *Hazardous conditions.* At least every 7 days, an examination for hazardous conditions at the following locations shall be made by a certified person designated by the operator:

(1) In at least one entry of each intake air course, in its entirety, so that the entire air course is traveled.

(2) In at least one entry of each return air course, in its entirety, so that the entire air course is traveled.

(3) In each longwall or shortwall travelway in its entirety, so that the entire travelway is traveled.

(4) At each seal along return and bleeder air courses and at each seal along intake air courses not examined under § 75.360(b)(5).

(5) In each escapeway so that the entire escapeway is traveled.

(6) On each working section not examined under § 75.360(b)(3) during the previous 7 days.

(7) At each water pump not examined during a preshift examination conducted during the previous 7 days.

(c) *Measurements and tests.* At least every 7 days, a certified person shall-

(1) Determine the volume of air entering the main intakes and in each intake split;

(2) Determine the volume of air and test for methane in the last open crosscut in any pair or set of developing entries or rooms, in the return of each split of air immediately before it enters the main returns, and where the air leaves the main returns; and

(3) Test for methane in the return entry nearest each set of seals immediately after the air passes the seals.

(d) Hazardous conditions shall be corrected immediately. If the condition creates an imminent danger, everyone except those persons referred to in § 104(c) of the Act shall be withdrawn from the area affected to a safe area until the hazardous condition is corrected.

(e) The weekly examination may be conducted at the same time as the preshift or on-shift examinations.

(f) (1) The weekly examination is not required during any 7 day period in which no one enters any underground area of the mine.

(2) Except for certified persons required to make examinations, no one shall enter any underground area of the mine if a weekly examination has not been completed within the previous 7 days.

(g) *Certification.* The person making the weekly examinations shall certify by initials, date, and the time that the examination was made. Certifications and times shall appear at enough locations to show that the entire area has been examined.

(h) *Recordkeeping.* At the completion of any shift during

which a portion of a weekly examination is conducted, a record of the results of each weekly examination, including a record of hazardous conditions found during each examination and their locations, the corrective action taken, and the results and location of air and methane measurements, shall be made. The results of methane tests shall be recorded as the percentage of methane measured by the examiner. The record shall be made by the person making the examination or a person designated by the operator. If made by a person other than the examiner, the examiner shall verify the record by the initials and date by or at the end of the shift for which the examination was made. The record shall be countersigned by the mine foreman or equivalent mine official by the end of the mine foreman's or equivalent mine official's next regularly scheduled working shift. The records required by this section shall be made in a secure book that is not susceptible to alteration or electronically in a computer system so as to be secure and not susceptible to alteration.

(i) *Retention period.* Records shall be retained at a surface location at the mine for at least 1 year and shall be made available for inspection by authorized representatives of the Secretary and the representative of miners.

Citation: 30 CFR 75.1911

✍ § 75.1911 Fire suppression systems for diesel-powered equipment and diesel fuel transportation units.

* * * * *

(i) Each fire suppression system shall be tested and maintained in accordance with the manufacturer's recommended inspection and maintenance program and as required by the nationally recognized independent testing laboratory listing or approval, and be visually inspected at least once each week by a person trained to make such inspections.

(j) *Recordkeeping.* Persons performing inspections and tests of fire suppression systems under paragraph (i) shall record when a fire suppression system does not meet the installation or maintenance requirements of this section.

(1) The record shall include the equipment on which the fire suppression system did not meet the installation or maintenance requirements of this section, the defect found, and the corrective action taken.

(2) Records are to be kept manually in a secure manner not susceptible to alteration or recorded electronically in a secured computer system that is not susceptible to alteration.

(3) Records shall be maintained at a surface location at the mine for one yearand made available for inspection by an authorized representative of the Secretary and miners' representatives.

Citation: 30 CFR 75.1912

✍ § 75.1912 Fire suppression systems for permanent underground diesel fuel storage facilities.

* * * * *

(h) Each fire suppression system shall be tested and maintained in accordance with the manufacturer's recommended inspection and maintenance program and as required by the nationally recognized independent testing laboratory listing or approval, and be visually inspected at least once each week by a person trained to make such inspections.

(i) *Recordkeeping.* Persons performing inspections and tests of fire suppression systems under paragraph (h) shall record when a fire suppression system does not meet the installation or maintenance requirements of this section.

(1) The record shall include the facility whose fire suppression system did not meet the installation or maintenance requirements of this section, the defect found, and the corrective action taken.

(2) Records are to be kept manually in a secure manner not susceptible to alteration or recorded electronically in a secured computer system that is not susceptible to alteration.

(3) Records shall be maintained at a surface location at the mine for one year and made available for inspection by an authorized representative of the Secretary and miners' representatives.

(j) All miners normally assigned to the active workings of the mine shall be instructed about the hazards inherent to the operation of the fire suppression systems and, where appropriate, the safeguards available for each system.

PART 210. FORMS AND REPORTS

Subpart B. Oil and Gas, and OCS Sulphur — General

Citation: 30 CFR 210.50

✍ § 210.50 Required recordkeeping.

Information required by the MMS shall be filed using the forms prescribed in this Subpart, which are available from MMS. Records may be maintained in microfilm, microfiche, or other recorded media that is easily reproducible and readable.

Subpart E. Solids Minerals, General

Citation: 30 CFR 210.200

✍ § 210.200 Required recordkeeping.

Information required by the Minerals Management Service (MMS) shall be filed using the forms prescribed in this subpart, copies of which are available from MMS. Instructions on the completion of these forms are provided in the Payor Handbook — Solid Minerals, also available from MMS. Records and supporting data may be maintained in hardcopy, microfilm, microfiche, or other recorded media that is readily available and readable.

PART 212. RECORDS AND FILES MAINTENANCE

Subpart B. Oil and Gas, and OCS Sulphur — General

Citation: 30 CFR 212.51

✍ § 212.51 Records and files maintenance.

(a) *Records.* Each lessee, operator, revenue payor, or other person shall make and retain accurate and complete records necessary to demonstrate that payments of rentals, royalties, net profit shares, and other payments related to offshore and onshore Federal and Indian oil and gas leases are in compliance with lease terms, notices, and orders. Records covered by this section include those specified by lease terms, regulations, and orders, and by the various parts of this Chapter. Records also include computer programs, automated files, and supporting systems documentation used to produce automated reports or magnetic tape submitted to the Minerals Management Service (MMS) for use in its Auditing and Financial System (AFS) and Production Accounting and Auditing System (PAAS).

(b) *Period for keeping records.* Lessees, operators, revenue payors, or other persons required to keep records under this

Section shall maintain and preserve them for 6 years from the day on which the relevant transaction recorded occurred unless the Secretary notifies the recordholder of an audit or investigation involving the records and that they must be maintained for a longer period. When an audit or investigation is underway, records shall be maintained until the recordholder is released in writing from the obligation to maintain the records. Lessees, operators, revenue payors, or other persons shall maintain the records generated during the period for which they have paying or operating responsibility on the lease for a period of 6 years.

(c) *Inspection of records*. The lessee, operator, revenue payor, or other person required to keep records shall be responsible for making the records available for inspection. Records shall be provided at a business location of the lessee, operator, revenue payor, or other person during normal business hours upon the request of any officer, employee or other party authorized by the Secretary. Lessees, operators, revenue payors, and other persons will be given a reasonable period of time to produce historical records.

TITLE 31. MONEY AND FINANCE: TREASURY

Agency:	**Department of the Treasury** **Monetary Offices**

PART 103. FINANCIAL RECORDKEEPING AND REPORTING OF CURRENCY AND FOREIGN TRANSACTIONS

Subpart C. Records Required to Be Maintained

Citation:	**31 CFR 103.33**

✍ § 103.33 Records to be made and retained by financial institutions.

* * * * *

(e) *Banks*. Each agent, agency, branch, or office located within the United States of a bank is subject to the requirements of this paragraph (e) with respect to a funds transfer in the amount of $3,000 or more:

(1) *Recordkeeping requirements*. (i) For each payment order that it accepts as an originator's bank, a bank shall obtain and retain either the original or a microfilm, other copy, or electronic record of the following information relating to the payment order:

* * * * *

(ii) For each payment order that it accepts as an intermediary bank, a bank shall retain either the original or a microfilm, other copy, or electronic record of the payment order.

(iii) For each payment order that it accepts as a beneficiary's bank, a bank shall retain either the original or a microfilm, other copy, or electronic record of the payment order.

* * * * *

(6) *Exceptions*. * * *

(i) * * *

(A) A bank;

(B) A wholly-owned domestic subsidiary of a bank chartered in the United States;

(C) A broker or dealer in securities;

(D) A wholly-owned domestic subsidiary of a broker or dealer in securities;

(E) The United States;

(F) A state or local government; or

(G) A federal, state or local government agency or instrumentality; and

(ii) Funds transfers where both the originator and the beneficiary are the same person and the originator's bank and the beneficiary's bank are the same bank.

(f) *Nonbank financial institutions*. Each agent, agency, branch, or office located within the United States of a financial institution other than a bank is subject to the requirements of this paragraph (f) with respect to a transmittal of funds in the amount of $3,000 or more:

(1) *Recordkeeping requirements*. (i) For each transmittal order that it accepts as a transmittor's financial institution, a financial institution shall obtain and retain either the original or a microfilm, other copy, or electronic record of the following information relating to the transmittal order:

* * * * *

(ii) For each transmittal order that it accepts as an intermediary financial institution, a financial institution shall retain either the original or a microfilm, other copy, or electronic record of the transmittal order.

(iii) for each transmittal order that it accepts as a recipient's financial institution, a financial institution shall retain either the original or a microfilm, other copy, or electronic record of the transmittal order.

* * * * *

(6) *Exceptions*. * * *

(i) * * *

(A) A bank;

(B) A wholly-owned domestic subsidiary of a bank chartered in the United States;

(C) A broker or dealer in securities;

(D) A wholly-owned domestic subsidiary of a broker or dealer in securities;

(E) The United States;

(F) A state or local government; or

(G) A federal, state or local government agency or instrumentality; and

(ii) Transmittals of funds where both the transmittor and the recipient are the same person and the transmittor's financial institution and the recipient's financial institution are the same broker or dealer in securities.

Citation:	**31 CFR 103.34**

✍ § 103.34 Additional records to be made and retained by banks.

(a)(1) With respect to each certificate of deposit sold or redeemed after May 31, 1978, or each deposit or share account opened with a bank after June 30, 1972, a bank shall, within 30 days from the date such a transaction occurs or an account is opened, secure and maintain a record of the taxpayer identification number of the customer involved; or where the account or certificate is in the names of two or more persons, the bank shall secure the taxpayer identification number of a person having a financial interest in the certificate or account. In the event that a bank has been unable to secure, within the 30-day period specified, the required identification, it shall nevertheless not be deemed to be in violation of this section if (i) it has made a reasonable effort to secure such identification, and (ii) it maintains a list containing the names, addresses, and account numbers of those persons from whom it has been unable to secure such identification, and makes the names, addresses, and account numbers of those persons available to the Secretary as directed by him. A bank acting as an agent for another person in the purchase or redemption of a certificate of deposit issued by another bank is responsible for obtaining and recording the required taxpayer identification, as well as for maintaining the records referred to in paragraphs (b) (11) and (12) of this section. The issuing bank can satisfy the recordkeeping requirement by recording the name and address of the agent together with a description of the instrument and the date of the transaction.

Where a person is a non-resident alien, the bank shall also record the person's passport number or a description of some other government document used to verify his identity.

(2) The 30-day period provided for in paragraph (a)(1) of this section shall be extended where the person opening the account has applied for a taxpayer identification or social security number on Form SS-4 or SS-5, until such time as the person maintaining the account has had a reasonable opportunity to secure such number and furnish it to the bank.

(3) A taxpayer identification number required under paragraph (a)(1) of this section need not be secured for accounts or transactions with the following: (i)Agencies and instrumentalities of Federal, State, local or foreign governments; (ii) judges, public officials, or clerks of courts of record as custodians of funds in controversy or under the control of the court; (iii) aliens who are (A) ambassadors, ministers, career diplomatic or consular officers, or (B) naval, military or other attaches of foreign embassies and legations, and for the members of their immediate families; (iv) aliens who are accredited representatives of international organizations which are entitled to enjoy privileges, exemptions and immunities as an international organization under the International Organization Immunities Act of December 29, 1945 (22 U.S.C. sec. 288), and the members of their immediate families; (v) aliens temporarily residing in the United States for a period not to exceed 180 days; (vi) aliens not engaged in a trade or business in the United States who are attending a recognized college or university or any training program, supervised or conducted by any agency of the Federal Government; (vii) unincorporated subordinate units of a tax exempt central organization which are covered by a group exemption letter, (viii) a person under 18 years of age with respect to an account opened as a part of a school thrift savings program, provided the annual interest is less than $10; (ix) a person opening a Christmas club, vacation club and similar installment savings programs provided the annual interest is less than $10; and (x) non-resident aliens who are not engaged in a trade or business in the United States. In instances described in paragraphs (a)(3), (viii) and (ix) of this section, the bank shall, within 15 days following the end of any calendar year in which the interest accrued in that year is $10 or more use its best effort to secure and maintain the appropriate taxpayer identification number or application form therefor.

(4) The rules and regulations issued by the Internal Revenue Service under section 6109of the Internal Revenue Code of 1954 shall determine what constitutes a taxpayer identification number and whose number shall be obtained in the case of an account maintained by one or more persons.

(b) Each bank shall, in addition, retain either the original or a microfilm or other copy or reproduction of each of the following:

(1) Each document granting signature authority over each deposit or share account, including any notations, if such are normally made, of specific identifying information verifying the identity of the signer (such as a driver's license number or credit card number);

(2) Each statement, ledger card or other record on each deposit or share account, showing each transaction in, or with respect to, that account;

(3) Each check, clean draft, or money order drawn on the bank or issued and payable by it, except those drawn for $100 or less or those drawn on accounts which can be expected to have drawn on them an average of at least 100 checks per month over the calendar year or on each occasion on which such checks are issued, and which are (i) dividend checks, (ii) payroll checks, (iii) employee benefit checks, (iv) insurance claim checks, (v) medical benefit checks, (vi) checks drawn on government agency accounts, (vii) checks drawn by brokers or dealers in securities, (viii) checks drawn on fiduciary accounts, (ix) checks drawn on other financial institutions, or (x) pension or annuity checks;

(4) Each item in excess of $100 (other than bank charges or periodic charges made pursuant to agreement with the customer), comprising a debit to a customer's deposit or share account, not required to be kept, and not specifically exempted, under paragraph (b) (3) of this section;

(5) Each item, including checks, drafts, or transfers of credit, of more than $10,000 remitted or transferred to a person, account or place outside the United States;

(6) A record of each remittance or transfer of funds, or of currency, other monetary instruments, checks, investment securities, or credit, of more than $10,000 to a person, account or place outside the United States;

(7) Each check or draft in an amount in excess of $10,000 drawn on or issued by a foreign bank which the domestic bank has paid or presented to a nonbank drawee for payment;

(8) Each item, including checks, drafts or transfers of credit, of more than $10,000 received directly and not through a domestic financial institution, by letter, cable or any other means, from a bank, broker or dealer in foreign exchange outside the United States;

(9) A record of each receipt of currency, other monetary instruments, investment securities or checks, and of each transfer of funds or credit, of more than $10,000 received on any one occasion directly and not through a domestic financial institution, from a bank, broker or dealer in foreign exchange outside the United States; and

(10) Records prepared or received by a bank in the ordinary course of business, which would be needed to reconstruct a demand deposit account and to trace a check in excess of $100 deposited in such account through its domestic processing system or to supply a description of a deposited check in excess of $100. This subparagraph shall be applicable only with respect to demand deposits.

(11) A record containing the name, address, and taxpayer identification number, if available, of the purchaser of each certificate of deposit, as well as a description of the instrument, a notation of the method of payment, and the date of the transaction.

(12) A record containing the name, address and taxpayer identification number, if available, of any person presenting a certificate of deposit for payment, as well as a description of the instrument and the date of the transaction.

(13) Each deposit slip or credit ticket reflecting a transaction in excess of $100 or the equivalent record for direct deposit or other wire transfer deposit transactions. The slip or ticket shall record the amount of any currency involved.

Citation: **31 CFR 103.35**

✍ § 103.35 Additional records to be made and retained by brokers or dealers in securities.

(a)(1) With respect to each brokerage account opened with a broker or dealer in securities after June 30, 1972, by a person residing or doing business in the United States or a citizen of the

United States, such broker or dealer shall within 30 days from the date such account is opened, secure and maintain a record of the taxpayer identification number of the person maintaining the account; or in the case of an account of one or more individuals, such broker or dealer shall secure and maintain a record of the social security number of an individual having a financial interest in that account. In the event that a broker or dealer has been unable to secure the identification required within the 30-day period specified, it shall nevertheless not be deemed to be in violation of this section if: (i) It has made a reasonable effort to secure such identification, and (ii) it maintains a list containing the names, addresses, and account numbers of those persons from whom it has been unable to secure such identification, and makes the names, addresses, and account numbers of those persons available to the Secretary as directed by him. Where a person is a nonresident alien, the broker or dealer in securities shall also record the person's passport number or a description of some other government document used to verify his identity.

(2) The 30-day period provided for in paragraph (a)(1) of this section shall be extended where the person opening the account has applied for a taxpayer identification or social security number on Form SS-4 or SS-5, until such time as the person maintaining the account has had a reasonable opportunity to secure such number and furnish it to the broker or dealer.

(3) A taxpayer identification number for a deposit or share account required under paragraph (a)(1) of this section need not be secured in the following instances: (i) Accounts for public funds opened by agencies and instrumentalities of Federal, State, local or foreign governments, (ii) accounts for aliens who are (a) ambassadors, ministers, career diplomatic or consular officers, or (b) naval, military or other attaches of foreign embassies and legations, and for the members of their immediate families; (iii) accounts for aliens who are accredited representatives to international organizations which are entitled to enjoy privileges, exemptions and immunities as an international organization under the International Organization Immunities Act of December 29, 1945 (22 U.S.C. sec. 288), and the members of their immediate families; (iv) aliens temporarily residing in the United States for a period not to exceed 180 days, (v) aliens not engaged in a trade or business in the United States who are attending a recognized college or university or any training program, supervised or conducted by any agency of the Federal Government, and (vi) unincorporated subordinate units of a tax exempt central organization which are covered by a group exemption letter.

(b) Each broker or dealer in securities shall, in addition, retain either the original or microfilm or other copy or reproduction of each of the following:

(1) Each document granting signature or trading authority over each customer's account;

(2) Each record described in § 240.17a-3(a) (1), (2), (3), (5), (6), (7), (8), and (9) of Title 17, Code of Federal Regulations;

(3) A record of each remittance or transfer of funds, or of currency, checks, other monetary instruments, investment securities, or credit, of more than $10,000 to a person, account, or lace, outside the United States;

(4) A record of each receipt of currency, other monetary instruments, checks, or investment securities and of each transfer of funds or credit, of more than $10,000 received on any one occasion directly and not through a domestic financial institution, from any person, account, or place outside the United States.

Citation: 31 CFR 103.36

✍ **§ 103.36 Additional records to be made and retained by casinos.**

(a) With respect to each deposit of funds, account opened or line of credit extended after the effective date of these regulations, a casino shall, at the time the funds are deposited, the account is opened or credit is extended, secure and maintain a record of the social security number of the person involved. Where the deposit, account or credit is in the names of two or more persons, the casinos shall secure the social security number of each person having a financial interest in the deposit, account or line of credit. In the event that a casino has been unable to secure the required social security number, it shall not be deemed to be in violation of this section if (1) it has made a reasonable effort to secure such number and (2) it maintains a list containing the names and permanent addresses of those persons from whom it has been unable to obtain social security numbers and makes the names and addresses of those persons available to the Secretary upon request. Where a person is a nonresident alien, the casino shall also record the person's passport number or a description of some other government document used to verify his identity.

(b) In addition, each casino shall retain either the original or a microfilm or other copy or reproduction of each of the following:

(1) A record of receipt (including but not limited to funds for safekeeping or front money) of funds by the casino for the account (credit or deposit) of any person. The record shall include the name, permanent address and social security number of the person from whom the funds were received, as well as the date and amount of the funds received. If the person from whom the funds were received is a non-resident alien, the person's passport number or a description of some other government document used to verify the person's identity shall be obtained and recorded.

(2) A record of each bookkeeping entry comprising a debit or credit to a customer's deposit account or credit account with the casino;

(3) Each statement, ledger card or other record of each deposit account or credit account with the casino, showing each transaction (including deposits, receipts, withdrawals, disbursements or transfers) in or with respect to, a customer's deposit account or credit account with the casino;

(4) A record of each extension of credit in excess of $2500, the terms and conditions of such extension of credit, and repayments. The record shall include the customer's name, permanent address, social security number, and the date and amount of the transaction (including repayments). If the customer or person for whom the credit extended is a non-resident alien, his passport number or description of some other government document used to verify his identity shall be obtained and recorded;

(5) A record of each advice, request or instruction received or given by the casino for itself or another person with respect to a transaction involving a person, account or place outside the United States (including but not limited to communications by wire, letter, or telephone). If the transfer outside the United States is on behalf of a third party, the record shall include the third party's name, permanent address, social security number, signature, and the date and amount of the transaction. If the transfer is received from outside the United States on behalf of a third party, the record shall include the third party's name, permanent address, social security number, signature, and the date and amount of the transaction. If the person for whom the

transaction is being made is a non-resident alien the record shall also include the person's name, his passport number or a description of some other government document used to verify his identity.

(6) Records prepared or received by the casino in the ordinary course of business which would be needed to reconstruct a person's deposit account or credit account with the casino or to trace a check deposited with the casino through the casino's records to the bank of deposit.

(7) All records, documents or manuals required to be maintained by a casino under state and local laws or regulations.

(8) All records which are prepared or used by a casino to monitor a customer's gaming activity.

(c)(1) Casinos which input, store, or retain, in whole or in part, for any period of time, any record required to be maintained by § 103.33 or this section on computer disk, tape, or other machine-readable media shall retain the same on computer disk, tape, or machine-readable media.

(2) All indexes, books, programs, record layouts, manuals, formats, instructions, file descriptions, and similar materials which would enable a person readily to access and review the records that are described in § 103.33 and this section and that are input, stored, or retained on computer disk, tape, or other machine-readable media shall be retained for a period of time such records are required to be retained.

Citation: **31 CFR 103.37**

✍ § 103.37 Additional records to be made and retained by currency dealers or exchangers.

(a)(1) After July 7, 1987, each currency dealer or exchanger shall secure and maintain a record of the taxpayer identification number of each person for whom a transaction account is opened or a line of credit is extended within 30 days after such account is opened or credit line extended. Where a person is a non-resident alien, the currency dealer or exchanger shall also record the person's passport number or a description of some other government document used to verify his identity. Where the account or credit line is in the names of two or more persons, the currency dealer or exchanger shall secure the taxpayer identification number of a person having a financial interest in the account or credit line. In the event that a currency dealer or exchanger has been unable to secure the identification required within the 30-day period specified, it shall nevertheless not be deemed to be in violation of this section if:

(i) It has made a reasonable effort to secure such identification, and

(ii) It maintains a list containing the names, addresses, and account or credit line numbers of those persons from whom it has been unable to secure such identification, and makes the names, addresses, and account or credit line numbers of those persons available to the Secretary as directed by him.

(2) The 30-day period provided for in paragraph (a)(1) of this section shall be extended where the person opening the account or credit line has applied for a taxpayer identification or social security number on Form SS-4 or SS-5, until such time as the person maintaining the account or credit line has had a reasonable opportunity to secure such number and furnish it to the currency dealer or exchanger.

(3) A taxpayer identification number for an account or credit line required under paragraph (a)(1) of this section need not be secured in the following instances:

(i) Accounts for public funds opened by agencies and instrumentalities of Federal, State, local or foreign governments,

(ii) Accounts for aliens who are —

(A) Ambassadors, ministers, career diplomatic or consular officers, or

(B) Naval, military or other attaches of foreign embassies, and legations, and for members of their immediate families,

(iii) Accounts for aliens who are accredited representatives to international organizations which are entitled to enjoy privileges, exemptions, and immunities as an international organization under the International Organizations Immunities Act of December 29, 1945 [22 U.S.C. 288], and for the members of their immediate families.

(iv) Aliens temporarily residing in the United States for a period not to exceed 180 days.

(v) Aliens not engaged in a trade or business in the United States who are attending a recognized college or any training program, supervised or conducted by an agency of the Federal Government, and

(vi) Unincorporated subordinate units of a tax exempt central organization which are covered by a group exemption letter.

(b) Each currency dealer or exchanger shall retain either the original or a microfilm or other copy or reproduction of each of the following:

(1) Statements of accounts from banks, including paid checks, charges or other debit entry memoranda, deposit slips and other credit memoranda representing the entries reflected on such statements;

(2) Daily work records, including purchase and sales slips or other memoranda needed to identify and reconstruct currency transactions with customers and foreign banks;

(3) A record of each exchange of currency involving transactions in excess of $1000, including the name and address of the customer (and passport number or taxpayer identification number unless received by mail or common carrier) date and amount of the transaction and currency name, country, and total amount of each foreign currency;

(4) Signature cards or other documents evidencing signature authority over each deposit or security account, containing the name of the depositor, street address, taxpayer identification number (TIN) or employer identification number (EIN) and the signature of the depositor or of a person authorized to sign on the account (if customer accounts are maintained in a code name, a record of the actual owner of the account);

(5) Each item, including checks, drafts, or transfers of credit, of more than $10,000 remitted or transferred to a person, account or place outside the United States;

(6) A record of each receipt of currency, other monetary instruments, investment securities and checks, and of each transfer of funds or credit, or more than $10,000 received on any one occasion directly and not through a domestic financial institution, from any person, account or place outside the United States;

(7) Records prepared or received by a dealer in the ordinary course of business, that would be needed to reconstruct an account and trace a check in excess of $100 deposited in such account through its internal recordkeeping system to its depository institution, or to supply a description of a deposited check in excess of $100;

(8) A record maintaining the name, address and taxpayer identification number, if available, of any person presenting a certificate of deposit for payment, as well as a description of the instrument and date of transaction;

(9) A system of books and records that will enable the currency dealer or exchanger to prepare an accurate balance sheet and income statement.

Citation: 31 CFR 103.38

✍ § 103.38 Nature of records and retention period.

(a) Wherever it is required that there be retained either the original or a microfilm or other copy or reproduction of a check, draft, monetary instrument, investment security, or other similar instrument, there shall be retained a copy of both front and back of each such instrument or document, except that no copy need be retained of the back of any instrument or document which is entirely blank or which contains only standardized printed information, a copy of which is on file.

(b) Records required by this subpart to be retained by financial institutions may be those made in the ordinary course of business by a financial institution. If no record is made in the ordinary course of business of any transaction with respect to which records are required to be retained by this subpart, then such a record shall be prepared in writing by the financial institution.

(c) The rules and regulations issued by the Internal Revenue Service under 26 U.S.C. § 6109 determine what constitutes a taxpayer identification number and whose number shall be obtained in the case of an account maintained by one or more persons.

(d) All records that are required to be retained by this Part shall be retained for a period of five years. Records or reports required to be kept pursuant to an order issued under § 103.26 of this part shall be retained for the period of time specified in such order, not to exceed five years. All such records shall be filed or stored in such a way as to be accessible within a reasonable period of time, taking into consideration the nature of the record, and the amount of time expired since the record was made.

* * * * *

Agency: Department of the Treasury
Bureau of the Public Debt

PART 330. REGULATIONS GOVERNING PAYMENT UNDER SPECIAL ENDORSEMENT OF UNITED STATES SAVINGS BONDS AND UNITED STATES SAVINGS NOTES (FREEDOM SHARES)

Citation: 31 CFR 330.5

✍ § 330.5 Evidence of owner's authorization to affix special endorsement.

* * * * *

(c) *Record of authorization.* Agents should maintain such records as may be necessary to establish the receipt of, and compliance with, instructions supporting the special endorsement. If the agent elects to make notations on the backs of the securities to serve as a record, the Bureau of the Public Debt will undertake to produce, on request, photocopies of such securities at any time up to 10 years after the redemption date. However, the Bureau does not assume responsibility for the adequacy of such notations, for the legibility of any photocopy, or for failure to produce a photocopy from its records.

* * * * *

TITLE 33. NAVIGATION AND NAVAGABLE WATERS

Agency: Department of Transportation
Coast Guard

SUBCHAPTER K. SECURITY OF VESSELS

PART 120. SECURITY OF PASSENGER VESSELS

Subpart C. Plans and Procedures for Vessel Security

Citation: 33 CFR 120.300

✍ § 120.300 Plan: General.

(a) Each operator of a vessel subject to this part shall for each such vessel develop and maintain, in writing, an appropriate Vessel Security Plan that —

(1) Is unique to the vessel;

(2) Articulates the program required by Sec. 120.200; and

(3) Includes an appendix, for each port in which the vessel embarks or disembarks passengers, that contains port-specific security information.

(b) The Plan must be developed and maintained in accordance with the guidance in IMO MSC Circular 443, and must address security for periods of low, medium, and high threats, to —

(1) Deter unauthorized access to the vessel and its restricted areas;

(2) Deter the introduction of prohibited weapons, incendiaries, or explosives aboard the vessel;

(3) Encourage vigilance, as well as general awareness of security, aboard the vessel;

(4) Provide adequate training to members of the crew for security aboard the vessel;

(5) Coordinate responsibilities for security with the operator of each terminal at which the vessel embarks or disembarks passengers; and

(6) Provide information to members of the crew and to law-enforcement personnel, in case of an incident affecting security.

(c) The operator shall amend the Plan to address any known deficiencies.

(d) The operator shall restrict the distribution, disclosure, and availability of information contained in the plan to those persons with an operational need to know.

PART 128. SECURITY OF PASSENGER TERMINALS

Subpart C. Plans and Procedures for Terminal Security

Citation: 33 CFR 128.300

✍ § 128.300 Plan: General.

(a) Each operator of a passenger terminal subject to this part shall develop and maintain, in writing, for each such terminal of which it is the operator, an appropriate Terminal Security Plan that articulates the program required by Sec. 128.200.

(b) The Plan must be developed and maintained in accordance with the guidance in IMO MSC Circular 443 and must address the security of passengers, of members of crews of passenger vessels subject to Part 120 of this chapter, and of employees of the terminal, by establishing procedures, for periods of low, medium, and high threats, to —

(1) Deter unauthorized access to the terminal and its restricted areas and to any passenger vessel moored at the terminal;

(2) Deter the introduction of prohibited weapons,

incendiaries, and explosives into the terminal and its restricted areas and onto any passenger vessel moored at the terminal;

(3) Encourage vigilance, as well as general awareness of security, at the terminal;

(4) Provide adequate training to employees of the terminal for security at the terminal;

(5) Coordinate responsibilities for security with the operator of each vessel that embarks or disembarks passengers at the terminal; and

(6) Provide information to employees of the terminal and to law-enforcement personnel, in case of an incident affecting security.

(c) The operator shall amend the Plan to address any known deficiencies.

(d) The operator shall restrict the distribution, disclosure, and availability of information contained in the Plan to those persons with an operational need to know.

TITLE 34. EDUCATION

Agency:	**Department of Education** **Office of the Secretary**

PART 99. FAMILY EDUCATIONAL RIGHTS AND PRIVACY

Citation:	**34 CFR 99.3**

✍ § 99.3 What definitions apply to these regulations?

* * * * *

Disclosure means to permit access to or the release, transfer, or other communication of personally identifiable information contained in education records to any party, by any means, including oral, written, or electronic means.

* * * * *

Record means any information recorded in any way, including, but not limited to, handwriting, print, computer media, video or audio tape, film, microfilm, and microfiche.

* * * * *

Agency:	**Department of Education** **Office of Elementary and Secondary Education**

PART 222. IMPACT AID PROGRAMS

Subpart A. General

Citation:	**34 CFR 222.21**

✍ § 222.21 What requirements must a local educational agency meet concerning Federal acquisition of real property within the local educational agency?

(a) For an LEA with an otherwise approvable application to be eligible to receive financial assistance under section 8002, the LEA must meet the requirements in subpart A of these regulations and § 222.22, and, unless otherwise provided by statute as meeting the requirements in section 8002(a)(1)(C), document—

(1) That the United States owns or has acquired "eligible Federal property" within the LEA, that has an aggregate assessed value of 10 percent or more of the assessed value of—

(i) All real property in that LEA, based upon the assessed values of the eligible Federal property and of all real property (including that Federal property) on the date or dates of acquisition of the eligible Federal property; or

(ii) All real property in the LEA as assessed in the first year preceding or succeeding acquisition, whichever is greater, only if—

(A) The assessment of all real property in the LEA is not made at the same time or times that the Federal property was so acquired and assessed; and

(B) State law requires an assessment be made of property so acquired; or

(2)(i) That, as demonstrated by written evidence from the United States Forest Service satisfactory to the Secretary, the LEA contains between 20,000 and 60,000 acres of land that has been acquired by the United States Forest Service between 1915 and 1990; and

(ii) That the LEA serves a county chartered by State law in 1875 or 1890.

(b) "Federal property" described in section 8002(d) (certain transferred property) is considered to be owned by the United States for the purpose of paragraph (a) of this section.

(c) If, during any fiscal year, the United States sells, transfers, is otherwise divested of ownership of, or relinquishes an interest in or restriction on, eligible Federal property, the Secretary redetermines the LEA's eligibility for the following fiscal year, based upon the remaining eligible Federal property, in accordance with paragraph (a) of this section. This paragraph does not apply to a transfer of real property by the United States described in section 8002(d).

(d) Except as provided under paragraph (a)(2) of this section, the Secretary's determinations and redeterminations of eligibility under this section are based on the following documents:

(1) For a new section 8002 applicant or newly acquired eligible Federal property, only upon—

(i) Original records as of the time(s) of Federal acquisition of real property, prepared by a legally authorized official, documenting the assessed value of that real property; or

(ii) Facsimiles of those records such as microfilm or other reproduced copies.

(2) For a redetermination of an LEA's eligibility under section 8002(a)(1), only upon—

(i) Records described in paragraph (d)(1) of this section; or

(ii) Department records.

(e) The Secretary does not base the determination or redetermination of an LEA's eligibility under this section upon secondary documentation such as estimates, certifications, or appraisals.

Subpart J. Impact Aid Administrative Hearings and Judicial Review under Section 8011 of the Act

Citation:	**34 CFR 222.154**

✍ § 222.154 How must written submissions under this subpart be filed?

(a) All written submissions under this subpart must be filed by hand-delivery, mail, or facsimile transmission. The Secretary discourages the use of facsimile transmission for documents longer than five pages.

(b) If agreed upon by the parties, a party may serve a document upon the other party or parties by facsimile transmission.

(c) The filing date for a written submission under this subpart is the date the document is—

(1) Hand-delivered;

(2) Mailed; or

(3) Sent by facsimile transmission.

(d) A party other than the Department filing by facsimile transmission is responsible for confirming that a complete and legible copy of the document was received by the Department, including by the administrative law judge (ALJ).

(e) If a document is filed by facsimile transmission, the Secretary or ALJ, as applicable, may require the filing of a follow-up hard copy by hand-delivery or by mail within a reasonable period of time.

Subpart K. Determinations under Section 8009 of the Act

Citation: **34 CFR 222.165**

✍ § 222.165 What procedures does the Secretary follow after making a determination under section 8009?

(a) *Request for hearing.* (1) A State or LEA that is adversely affected by a determination under section 8009 and this subpart and that desires a hearing regarding that determination must submit a written request for a hearing within 30 days of receipt of the determination. The time within which a request must be filed may not be extended unless the Secretary, or the Secretary's delegatee, extends the time in writing at the time notice of the determination is given.

(2) A request for a hearing in accordance with this section must specify the issues of fact and law to be considered.

(3) If an LEA requests a hearing, it must furnish a copy of the request to the State. If a State requests a hearing, it must furnish a copy of the request to all LEAs in the State.

(b) *Right to intervene.* Any LEA or State that is adversely affected by a determination shall have the right of intervention in the hearing.

(c) *Time and place of hearing.* The hearing is held at a time and place fixed by the Secretary or the Secretary's delegatee (with due regard to the mutual convenience of the parties).

(d) Counsel. In all proceedings under this section, all parties may be represented by counsel.

(e) *Proceedings.* The Secretary refers the matter in controversy to an administrative law judge (ALJ) appointed under 5 U.S.C. 3105.

(f) *Filing requirements.* (1) Any written submission under this section must be filed by hand-delivery, mail, or facsimile transmission. The Secretary discourages the use of facsimile transmission for documents longer than five pages.

(2) If agreed upon by the parties, service of a document may be made upon the other party by facsimile transmission.

(3) The filing date for a written submission under this section is the date the document is —

(i) Hand-delivered;

(ii) Mailed; or

(iii) Sent by facsimile transmission, followed by a mailed hard copy.

(4) A party filing by facsimile transmission is responsible for confirming that a complete and legible copy of the document was received by the Department.

(g) *Procedural rules.* (1) If, in the opinion of the ALJ, no dispute exists as to a material fact the resolution of which would be materially assisted by oral testimony, the ALJ shall afford each party to the proceeding an opportunity to present its case —

(i) In whole or in part in writing; or

(ii) In an informal conference after affording each party sufficient notice of the issues to be considered.

(2) With respect to hearings involving a dispute as to a material fact the resolution of which would be materially assisted by oral testimony, the ALJ shall afford the following procedures to each party:

(i) Sufficient notice of the issues to be considered at the hearing.

(ii) An opportunity to make a record of the proceedings.

(iii) An opportunity to present witnesses on the party's behalf.

(iv) An opportunity to cross-examine other witnesses either orally or through written interrogatories.

(h) *Decisions.* The ALJ shall make an initial decision based upon written findings, which shall be forwarded to the Secretary. The Secretary may, by appropriate notification to the parties, determine to review it or certify it as the final decision of the Secretary without further proceedings. Written notice of the initial decision shall be sent to all parties. In any case in which the Secretary modifies or reverses the initial decision, a notice of that action shall be accompanied by a written statement of the grounds for the reversal or modification. Notice of the final decision of the Secretary is served upon all parties to the hearing, the hearing panel and any LEA that may be adversely affected.

(i) *Corrective Action.* (1) Within 30 days after a determination by the Secretary that a State has been in violation of section 8009 unless the determination is timely appealed by the State, the State shall provide satisfactory written assurances that it will undertake appropriate corrective action if necessary.

(2) A State found by the Secretary to have been in violation of section 8009 following a hearing shall provide, within 30 days after disposal of the hearing request (such as by a final decision issued under this subpart or withdrawal of the hearing request), satisfactory assurances that it is taking corrective action, if necessary.

(3) At any time during a hearing under this subpart, a State may provide the Secretary appropriate assurances that it will undertake corrective action if necessary. The Secretary or the ALJ, as applicable, may stay the proceedings pending completion of corrective action.

Agency: **Department of Education**
Office of Postsecondary Education

PART 668. STUDENT ASSISTANCE GENERAL PROVISIONS

Citation: **34 CFR 668.24**

✍ § 668.24 Record retention and examinations.

(a) *Program records.* An institution shall establish and maintain, on a current basis, any application for title IV, HEA program funds and program records that document —(1) Its eligibility to participate in the title IV, HEA programs;

(2) The eligibility of its educational programs for title IV, HEA program funds;

(3) Its administration of the title IV, HEA programs in accordance with all applicable requirements;

(4) Its financial responsibility, as specified in this part;

(5) Information included in any application for title IV, HEA program funds; and

(6) Its disbursement and delivery of title IV, HEA program funds.

(b) *Fiscal records.* (1) An institution shall account for the receipt and expenditure of title IV, HEA program funds in accordance with generally accepted accounting principles.

(2) An institution shall establish and maintain on a current basis — (i) Financial records that reflect each HEA, title IV program transaction; and

(ii) General ledger control accounts and related subsidiary accounts that identify each title IV, HEA program transaction and separate those transactions from all other institutional financial activity.

(c) *Required records.* (1) The records that an institution must maintain in order to comply with the provisions of this section include but are not limited to — (i) The Student Aid Report (SAR) or Institutional Student Information Record (ISIR) used to determine eligibility for title IV, HEA program funds;

(ii) Application data submitted to the Secretary, lender, or guaranty agency by the institution on behalf of the student or parent;

(iii) Documentation of each student's or parent borrower's eligibility for title IV, HEA program funds;

(iv) Documentation relating to each student's or parent borrower's receipt of title IV, HEA program funds, including but not limited to documentation of — (A) The amount of the grant, loan, or FWS award; its payment period; its loan period, if appropriate; and the calculations used to determine the amount of the grant, loan, or FWS award;

(B) The date and amount of each disbursement or delivery of grant or loan funds, and the date and amount of each payment of FWS wages;

(C) The amount, date, and basis of the institution's calculation of any refunds or overpayments due to or on behalf of the student; and

(D) The payment of any refund or overpayment to the title IV, HEA program fund, a lender, or the Secretary, as appropriate;

(v) Documentation of and information collected at any initial or exit loan counseling required by applicable program regulations;

(vi) Reports and forms used by the institution in its participation in a title IV, HEA program, and any records needed to verify data that appear in those reports and forms; and

(vii) Documentation supporting the institution's calculations of its completion or graduation rates under Secs. 668.46 and 668.49.

(2) In addition to the records required under this part — (i) Participants in the Federal Perkins Loan Program shall follow procedures established in 34 CFR 674.19 for documentation of repayment history for that program;

(ii) Participants in the FWS Program shall follow procedures established in 34 CFR 675.19 for documentation of work, earnings, and payroll transactions for that program; and

(iii) Participants in the FFEL Program shall follow procedures established in 34 CFR 682.610 for documentation of additional loan record requirements for that program.

(d) *General.* (1) An institution shall maintain required records in a systematically organized manner.

(2) An institution shall make its records readily available for review by the Secretary or the Secretary's authorized representative at an institutional location designated by the Secretary or the Secretary's authorized representative.

(3) An institution may keep required records in hard copy or in microform, computer file, optical disk, CD-ROM, or other media formats, provided that — (i) Except for the records described in paragraph (d)(3)(ii) of this section, all record information must be retrievable in a coherent hard copy format or in other media formats acceptable to the Secretary;

(ii) An institution shall maintain the Student Aid Report (SAR) or Institutional Student Information Record (ISIR) used to determine eligibility for title IV, HEA program funds in the format in which it was received by the institution, except that the SAR may be maintained in an imaged media format;

(iii) Any imaged media format used to maintain required records must be capable of reproducing an accurate, legible, and complete copy of the original document, and, when printed, this copy must be approximately the same size as the original document;

(iv) Any document that contains a signature, seal, certification, or any other image or mark required to validate the authenticity of its information must be maintained in its original hard copy or in an imaged media format; and

(v) Participants in the Federal Perkins Loan Program shall follow procedures established in 34 CFR 674.19 for maintaining the original promissory notes and repayment schedules for that program.

(4) If an institution closes, stops providing educational programs, is terminated or suspended from the title IV, HEA programs, or undergoes a change of ownership that results in achange of control as described in 34 CFR 600.31, it shall provide for — (i) The retention of required records; and

(ii) Access to those records, for inspection and copying, by the Secretary or the Secretary's authorized representative, and, for a school participating in the FFEL Program, the appropriate guaranty agency.

(e) *Record retention.* Unless otherwise directed by the Secretary — (1) An institution shall keep records relating to its administration of the Federal Perkins Loan, FWS, FSEOG, or Federal Pell Grant Program for three years after the end of the award year for which the aid was awarded and disbursed under those programs, provided that an institution shall keep —(i) The Fiscal Operations Report and Application to Participate in the Federal Perkins Loan, FSEOG, and FWS Programs (FISAP), and any records necessary to support the data contained in the FISAP, including "income grid information," for three years after the end of the award year in which the FISAP is submitted; and

(ii) Repayment records for a Federal Perkins loan, including records relating to cancellation and deferment requests, in accordance with the provisions of 34 CFR 674.19;

(2)(i) An institution shall keep records relating to a student or parent borrower's eligibility and participation in the FFEL or Direct Loan Program for three years after the end of the award year in which the student last attended the institution; and

(ii) An institution shall keep all other records relating to its participation in the FFEL or Direct Loan Program, including records of any other reports or forms, for three years after the end of the award year in which the records are submitted; and

(3) An institution shall keep all records involved in any loan, claim, or expenditure questioned by a title IV, HEA program audit, program review, investigation, or other review until the later of —(i) The resolution of that questioned loan, claim, or expenditure; or

(ii) The end of the retention period applicable to the record.

(f) *Examination of records.* (1) An institution that participates in any title IV, HEA program and the institution's third-party servicer, if any, shall cooperate with an independent auditor, the Secretary, the Department of Education's Inspector General, the Comptroller General of the United States, or their authorized representatives, a guaranty agency in whose program the institution participates, and the institution's accrediting agency, in the conduct of audits, investigations, program reviews, or other reviews authorized by law.

(2) The institution and servicer must cooperate by — (i) Providing timely access, for examination and copying, to requested records, including but not limited to computerized records and records reflecting transactions with any financial institution with which the institution or servicer deposits or has deposited any title IV, HEA program funds, and to any pertinent books, documents, papers, or computer programs; and

(ii) Providing reasonable access to personnel associated with the institution's or servicer's administration of the title IV, HEA programs for the purpose of obtaining relevant information.

(3) The Secretary considers that an institution or servicer has failed to provide reasonable access to personnel under paragraph (f)(2)(ii) of this section if the institution or servicer — (i) Refuses to allow those personnel to supply all relevant information;

(ii) Permits interviews with those personnel only if the institution's or servicer's management is present; or

(iii) Permits interviews with those personnel only if the interviews are tape recorded by the institution or servicer.

(4) Upon request of the Secretary, or a lender or guaranty agency in the case of a borrower under the FFEL Program, an institution or servicer promptly shall provide the requester with any information the institution or servicer has respecting the last known address, full name, telephone number, enrollment information, employer, and employer address of a recipient of title IV funds who attends or attended the institution.

PART 674. FEDERAL PERKINS LOAN PROGRAM

Citation: 34 CFR 674.19

✍ § 674.19 Fiscal procedures and records.

* * * * *

(c) *Records and reporting.* (1) An institution must establish and maintain on a current basis financial records that reflect all program transactions. The institution must establish and maintain general ledger control accounts and related subsidiary accounts that identify each program transaction and separate those transactions from all other institutional financial activity.

(2) The institution must also establish and maintain program and fiscal records that —

(i) Are reconciled at least monthly;

(ii) Identify each student's account and status;

(iii) Show the eligibility of each student aided under the program;

(iv) Show the amount of need and how the need was met for each student; and

(v) Identify the administrator who determined the need.

(3) Each year an institution must submit a Fiscal-Operations Report plus other information the Secretary requires. The institution must comply with requirements to insure the information reported is accurate and must submit it on the form and at the time specified by the Secretary.

(d) *Retention of records* — (1) Records. Each institution must keep intact and accessible records of the receipt and expenditure of Federal funds, including all accounting records and original and supporting documents necessary to document how the funds are spent.

(2) *Period of retention.* Except for loan records and audit questions, an institution must keep records for an award year for five years after it submits its Fiscal-Operations Report for that year.

(3) *Loan records.* (i) An institution must maintain a repayment history for each borrower. This repayment history must show the date and amount of each repayment over the life of the loan. It must also indicate the amount of each repayment credited to principal and interest respectively.

(ii) This history must also show the date, nature, and result of each contact with the borrower or proper endorser in the collection of an overdue loan. The institution must include in the repayment history copies of all correspondence to or from the borrower and endorser, except routine bills, routine overdue notices, and routine form letters.

(iii) An institution must retain repayment records, including cancellation and deferment requests, for at least 5 years from the date of the loan's assignment or final repayment or cancellation.

(4) *Microfilm copies.* An institution may substitute microfilm copies for original records in meeting the requirements of this section.

(5) *Audit questions.* An institution must keep records in any claim or expenditure questioned by Federal audit until resolution of any audit questions. However, the institution does not have to retain records beyond 5 years if the actions taken by the United States to recover funds are barred by the Federal statute of limitation in 28 U.S.C. 2415(b).

(e) * * *

(4) * * *

(v) An institution may keep the records required in this section on microforms, optical disk, other comparable imaging technology, or in computer format. If an institution keeps its records in computer format, it shall maintain, in either hard copy, microforms, optical disk, or other comparable imaging technology, the source documents supporting the computer input.

* * * * *

(f) *Separate records.* An institution need not maintain separate records for National Defense Student Loans and National Direct Student Loans except for loan cancellation records.

* * * * *

(i) *Safekeeping.* An institution must keep promissory notes and student loan ledgers in good order in a locked, fire proof container. Only authorized personnel may have access to these documents.

PART 675. FEDERAL WORK-STUDY PROGRAMS

Subpart A. Federal Work-Study Program

Citation: 34 CFR 675.19

✍ § 675.19 Fiscal procedures and records.

* * * * *

(b) *Records and reporting.* (1) An institution must establish and maintain on a current basis financial records that reflect all program transactions. The institution must establish and maintain general ledger control accounts and related subsidiary accounts that identify each program transaction and separate those transactions from all other institutional financial activity.

(2) The institution must also establish and maintain program and fiscal records that —

(i) Include a certification that each student has worked and earned the amount being paid. The student's supervisor, an official of the institution or off-campus agency, must sign the certification. The certification shall include or be supported by, for students paid on an hourly basis, a time record showing the hours each student worked in clock time sequence, or the total hours worked per day;

(A) For students paid on an hourly basis, a time record showing the hours each student worked; and

(B) For all students, a statement of whether the work was performed in a satisfactory manner.

(ii) Include a payroll voucher containing sufficient information to support all payroll disbursements;

(iii) Include a noncash contribution record to document any payment of the institution's share of the student's earnings in the form of services and equipment (see § 675.27(a));

(iv) Identify each student's account and status;

(v) Show the eligibility of each student aided under the program;

(vi) Show the amount of need and how the need was met for each student;

(vii) Identify the administrator who determined the need; and

(viii) Are reconciled at least monthly.

(3) Each year an institution must submit a Fiscal-Operations Report plus other information the Secretary requires. The institution must comply with requirements to insure the information reported is accurate and must submit it on the form and at the time specified by the Secretary.

(c) *Retention of records.* (1) *Records.* Each institution must keep intact and accessible records of the receipt and expenditure of Federal funds, including all accounting records and original and supporting documents necessary to document how the funds are spent.

(2) *Period of Retention.* Except for audit questions, an institution must keep records for an award year for five years after it submits its Fiscal-Operations Reports for that year.

(3) An institution may keep the records required in this section on microforms, optical disk, other comparable imaging technology, or in computer format. If an institution keeps its records in computer format, it shall maintain, in either hard copy, microforms, optical disk, or other comparable imaging technology, the source documents supporting the computer input.

(4) *Audit questions.* An institution must keep records in any claim or expenditure questioned by Federal audit until resolution of any audit questions. However, the institution does not have to retain records beyond 5 years if the actions taken by the United States to recover funds are barred by the Federal statute of limitation in 28 U.S.C. 2415(b).

* * * * *

PART 676. FEDERAL SUPPLEMENTAL EDUCATIONAL OPPORTUNITY GRANT PROGRAM

Citation: **34 CFR 676.19**

✍ **§ 676.19 Fiscal Procedures and Records.**

* * * * *

(b) *Records and reporting.* (1) An institution shall establish and maintain on a current basis financial records that reflect all program transactions. The institution shall establish and maintain general ledger control accounts and related subsidiary accounts that identify each program transaction and separate those transactions from all other institutional financial activity.

(2) The institution shall also establish and maintain program and fiscal records that —

(i) Are reconciled at least monthly;

(ii) Identify each student's account and status;

(iii) Show the eligibility of each student aided under the program; and

(iv) Show how the need was met for each student.

(3) The institution shall maintain on file all SEOG applications for those students it reports on the Fiscal Operations Report and Application to Participate in the Perkins Loan, SEOG, and CWS Programs (FISAP).

(4) The institution shall maintain all records supporting its application for funds under this part.

(5) Each year an institution shall submit a Fiscal Operation Report plus other information the Secretary requires. The institution shall insure that the information reported is accurate and shall submit it on the form and at the time specified by the Secretary.

(c) *Retention of records.* — (1) *Records.* Each institution shall keep intact and accessible records of the application, and receipt, and the expenditure of Federal funds, including all accounting records and original and supporting documents necessary to document how the funds are spend.

(2) *Period of retention.* Except for audit questions, an institution shall keep records for an award year for five years after it submits its FISAP for that year.

(3) An institution may keep the records required in this section on microforms, optical disk, other comparable imaging technology, or in computer format. If an institution keeps its records in computer format, it shall maintain, in either hard copy, microforms, optical disk, or other comparable imaging technology, the source documents supporting the computer input

(4) *Audit questions.* An institution shall keep records on any claim or expenditure questioned by Federal audit or program review until any audit questions are resolved.

PART 682. FEDERAL FAMILY EDUCATION LOAN (FFEL) PROGRAM

Subpart D. Administration of the Federal Family Education Loan Programs By a Guaranty Agency

Citation: **34 CFR 682.414**

✍ **§ 682.414 Records, reports, and inspection requirements for guarantee agency programs.**

(a) *Records.* (1)(i) The guaranty agency shall maintain current, complete, and accurate records of each loan that it holds, including, but not limited to, the records described in paragraph (a)(1)(ii) of this section. The records must be maintained in a system that allows ready identification of each loan's current status, updated at least once every 10 business days. Any reference to a guaranty agency under this section includes a third-party servicer that administers any aspect of the FFEL programs under a contract with the guaranty agency, if applicable.

(ii) The agency shall maintain —

(A) All documentation supporting the claim filed by the lender;

(B) Notices of changes in a borrower's address;

(C) A payment history showing the date and amount of each payment received from or on behalf of the borrower by the guaranty agency, and the amount of each payment was attributed to principal, accrued interest, and collection costs and other charges, such as late charges;

(D) A collection history showing the date and subject of each communication between the agency and the borrower or endorser relating to collection of a defaulted loan, each communication between the agency and a credit bureau regarding the loan, each effort to locate a borrower whose address was unknown at any tie, and each request by the lender for preclaims and supplemental preclaims assistance to the loan;

(E) Documentation regarding any wage garnishment actions initiated by the agency on the loan;

(F) Documentation of any matters relating to the collection of the loan by tax-refund offset; and

(G) Any additional records that are necessary to document its rights to receive or retain payments made by the Secretary under this part and the accuracy of reports it submits to the Secretary.

(2) The guarantee agency shall retain records for each loan for at least five years after the loan is paid in full or has been determined to be uncollectible in accordance with the agency's write-off procedures. For the purpose of this section, the term "paid in full" includes loans paid by the Secretary due to the

borrower's death (or student's death in the case of a PLUS loan), the borrower's permanent and total disability or bankruptcy, the discharge of the borrower's loan obligation because of attendance at a closed school, or because the student's eligibility to borrow had been falsely certified by the school.

(3)(i) The guaranty agency shall require a participating lender to maintain current, complete, and accurate records of each loan that it holds, including, but not limited to, the records described in paragraph (a)(3)(ii) of this section. The records must be maintained in a system that allows ready identification of each loan's current status.

(ii) The lender shall keep —

(A) A copy of the loan application;

(B) A copy of the signed promissory note, including the repayment instruments;

(C) The repayment schedule;

(D) A record of each disbursement of loan proceeds;

(E) Notices of changes in a borrower's address and status as at least a half-time student;

(F) Evidence of the borrower's eligibility for a deferment;

(G) The documents required for the exercise of forbearance;

(H) Documentation of the assignment of the loan;

(I) A payment history showing the date and amount of each payment received from or on behalf of the borrower, and the amount of each payment which was attributed to principal, interest, late charges, and other costs;

(J) A collection history, showing the date and subject of each communication between the lender and the borrower or endorser relating to collection of a delinquent loan, each communication other than regular reports by the lender showing that an account is current, between the lender and a credit bureau regarding the loan, each effort to locate a borrower whose address was unknown at any time and each request by the lender for preclaims assistance on the loan; and

(K) Any additional records that are necessary to document the validity of a claim against the guarantee or the accuracy of reports submitted under this part.

(iii) Except as provided in paragraph (a)(3)(iv) of this section, a lender shall retain the records required for each loan for not less than five years following the date the loan is repaid in full by the borrower or the lender is reimbursed on a claim. However, in particular cases the Secretary or the guaranty agency may require the retention of records beyond this minimum period.

(iv) A lender shall retain a copy of the audit report for not less than five years after the report is issued.

(4)(i) A guaranty agency or lender may store the records specified in paragraphs (a)(3)(ii)(C)-(K) of this section on microfilm, optical disk, or other machine readable format.

(ii) A lender or guaranty agency holding a promissory note shall retain the original note until the loan is paid in full or assigned to the Secretary. When a loan is paid in full by the borrower, the lender or guaranty agency shall either return the original note to the borrower or notify the borrower under an alternate procedure that is acceptable under State law, that the loan is paid in full, and retain a copy for the prescribed period.

(iii) Either the lender or guaranty agency shall retain the original loan application and, until the loan is fully repaid, the promissory note.

* * * * *

Subpart E. Federal Guaranteed Student Loan Programs

Citation: 34 CFR 682.515

§ 682.515 Records, reports, and inspection requirements for Federal GSL Program lenders.

(a) *Records.* (1) A lender shall keep complete and accurate records of each loan that it holds, including but not limited to the records described in § 682.414(a)(3)(ii). The records must be maintained in a system that allows ready identification of the current status of each loan.

(2) A lender shall retain the records required for each loan for not less than five years following the date the loan is repaid in full by the borrower or the lender is reimbursed on a claim. However, in particular cases the Secretary may require the retention of records beyond this minimum period.

(3)(i) The lender may store the records specified in 682.414(a)(3)(ii)(C)-(K) on microfilm or computer format.

(ii) The holder of the promissory note shall retain the original note and repayment instrument until the loan is fully repaid. At that time the lender shall return the original note and repayment instrument to the borrower, and retain copies for the prescribed period.

(iii) The lender shall retain the original or a copy of the loan application.

* * * * *

Subpart F. Requirements, Standards, and Payments for Participating Schools

Citation: 34 CFR 682.610

§ 682.610 Administrative and fiscal requirements for participating schools.

(a) *General.* Each school shall —

(1) Establish and maintain proper administrative and fiscal procedures and all necessary records as set forth in the regulation in this part in 34 CFR 668 in order to —

(i) Protect the rights of students and parent borrowers;

(ii) Protect the United States from unreasonable risk of loss; and

(iii) Comply with any specific requirements in those regulations; and

(2) Submit all reports required by this part and 34 CFR Part 668 to the Secretary.

(b) Loan record requirements. In addition to records required by 34 CFR Part 668, for each loan received under this part by or on behalf of its student, a school shall maintain a copy of the loan application and a record of —

(1) The name of the lender;

(2) The address of the lender;

(3) The amount of the loan and the period of attendance for which the loan was intended;

(4) The data used to construct an individual student budget or the school's itemized standard budget used in calculating the student's estimated cost of attendance.;

(5) The amount of the student's tuition and fees paid for the loan period and the date the student paid the tuition and fees;

(6) In the case of a GSLP loan for which the borrower applies for interest benefits under § 682.301, the data used to determine the student's adjusted gross family income and the student's expected family contribution, and the corresponding certification by the school to the lender;

(7) In the case of a GSLP loan —

(i) The date the school received such loan disbursement and the amount of that disbursement;

(ii) The date the school endorsed each loan check; and

(iii) The date or dates of transmittal of the loan proceeds by the school to the student; and

(8) A record of the student's job placement, if known.

* * * * *

(d) Record-retention requirements. Unless otherwise directed by the Secretary, the school or its successors —

(1) Shall keep all records required under the regulations in this part for five years following the last day of the period for which the loan was intended;

(2) Shall keep for five years after their completion copies of reports and other forms used by the school relating to the GSLP or the PLUS Program;

(3) Shall provide, in the event of the school's closure, termination, suspension, or change of ownership, for the retention of the records and reports required by the regulations in this part and for access by the Secretary or his authorized representatives to those records and reports; and

(4) May keep records and copies of reports on microfilm or in computer format.

(e) Inspection requirements. Upon request, a school shall afford the Secretary, a guarantee agency, and any of their duly authorized representatives, access to its records in order to verify the accuracy of its reports or the school's compliance with the Act and applicable regulations.

PART 690. FEDERAL PELL GRANT PROGRAM

Subchapter A. Scope, Purpose and General Definitions

Citation: 34 CFR 690.2

✍ **§ 690.2 Definitions.**

(b) * * * Payment Data: An electronic or magnetic record that is provided to the Secretary by an institution showing a student's expected family contribution, cost of attendance, enrollment status, and student disbursement information.

* * * * *

Electronic Data Exchange: An electronic exchange system between the central processor and an institution under which—

(1) A student is able to transmit his or her application information to the central processor through his or her institution and an ISIR is transmitted back to the institution;

(2) A student through his or her institution is able to transmit any changes in application information to the central processor; and

(3) An institution is able to receive an ISIR from the central processor for a student.

Enrollment status: Full-time, three-quarter-time, half-time, or less-than-half-time depending on a student's credit-hour work load per academic term at an institution using semesters, trimesters, quarters, or other academic terms and measuring progress by credit hours.

* * * * *

Institutional Student Information Record (ISIR): A paper document or a computer-generated electronic record that the central processor transmits to an institution that includes an applicant's —

(1) Personal identification information;

(2) Application data used to calculate the applicant's EFC; and

(3) EFC calculated by the central processor.

Less-than-half-time student: An enrolled student who is carrying less than half the work load of the appropriate minimum requirement outlined in the institution's definition of a full-time student.

* * * * *

Payment Data: An electronic or magnetic record that is provided to the Secretary by an institution showing a student's expected family contribution, cost of attendance, enrollment status, and student disbursement information.

* * * * *

Subpart G. Administration of Grant Payments

Citation: 34 CFR 690.82

✍ **§ 690.82 Maintenance and retention of records.**

(a) Each institution shall maintain adequate records (including those related to verification), which include the fiscal and accounting records that are required under § 690.81, records required for audits in 34 CFR 668.23, the SAR or ISIR of each student who received a Federal Pell Grant, and records indicating —

(1) The eligibility of all enrolled students who have submitted valid SARs to the institution or for whom the institution has received valid ISIRs;

* * * * *

(8) Documentation of a student's eligibility for any part of a second Scheduled Federal Pell Grant award in any award year.

(b) Each institution shall retain any completed applications and any other documents submitted by a student to the institution under § 690.14(c) if the application information is transmitted to the Secretary under EDE and is processed by the Secretary.

* * * * *

(e) An institution may substitute microform copies or other media formats acceptable to the Secretary, as published in a notice in the Federal Register, in lieu of original records in meeting the requirements of this section.

TITLE 36. PARKS, FORESTS, AND PUBLIC PROPERTY

Agency: National Archives and Records Administration

SUBCHAPTER B. RECORDS MANAGEMENT.

PART 1220. FEDERAL RECORDS; GENERAL

Subpart A. General Provisions

Citation 36 CFR 1220.14

✍ **§ 1220.14 General definitions.**

* * * * *

File means an arrangement of records. The term is used to denote papers, photographs, photographic copies, maps, machine-readable information or other recorded information regardless of physical form or characteristics accumulated or maintained in filing equipment, boxes, or machine-readable media, or on shelves, and occupying office or storage space.

* * * * *

Recordkeeping system is a manual or automated system in which records are collected, organized, and categorized to facilitate their preservation, retrieval, use, and disposition.

* * * * *

PART 1222. CREATION AND MAINTENANCE OF FEDERAL RECORDS

Subpart B. Program Requirements

Citation: 36 CFR 1222.20

✍ § 1222.20 Agency responsibilities.

(a) The head of each Federal agency, in meeting the requirements of 44 U.S.C. 2904, 3101, and 3102, shall observe the responsibilities and standards set forth in this part. Agencies are also subject to regulations issued by the General Services Administration (GSA) in 41 CFR chapter 201.

(b) Each Federal agency shall:

(1) Assign to one or more offices of the agency the responsibility for the development and implementation of agency-wide programs to identify, develop, issue, and periodically review recordkeeping requirements for records for all agency activities at all levels and locations in all media including paper, microform, audiovisual, cartographic, and electronic (including those created or received using electronic mail);

(2) Integrate programs for the identification, development, issuance, and periodic review of recordkeeping requirements with other records and information resources management programs of the agency, including the requirement of close coordination between the office designated in 36 CFR 1222.20(b)(1) and the office assigned overall records management responsibility in accordance with 36 CFR 1220.40, if the two are different;

(3) Issue a directive(s) establishing program objectives, responsibilities, and authorities for agency recordkeeping requirement. Copies of the directive(s) (including subsequent amendments or supplements) shall be disseminated throughout the agency, as appropriate, and a copy shall be sent to NARA (NI);

(4) Establish procedures for the participation of records management officials in developing new or revised agency programs, processes, systems, and procedures in order to ensure that adequate recordkeeping requirements are established and implemented;

(5) Ensure that adequate training is provided to all agency personnel on policies, responsibilities, and techniques for the implementation of recordkeeping requirements and the distinction between records and nonrecord materials, regardless of media, including those materials created by individuals using computers to send or receive electronic mail.

(6) Develop and implement records schedules for all records created and received by the agency and obtain NARA approval of the schedules in accordance with 36 CFR part 1228;

(7) Ensure compliance with applicable governmentwide policies, procedures, and standards relating to recordkeeping requirements as may be issued by the Office of Management and Budget, the General Services Administration, the National Archives and Records Administration, The National Institute of Standards and Technology, or other agencies, as appropriate;

(8) Review recordkeeping requirements, as part of the periodic information resources management reviews required by 44 U.S.C. 3506, or the periodic records management evaluations required by 36 CFR 1220.54, in order to validate their currency and to ensure that recordkeeping requirements are being implemented.

(9) Remind all employees annually of the agency's recordkeeping policies and of the sanctions provided for the unlawful removal or destruction or Federal records (18 U.S.C. 2071).

Subpart C. Standards for Agency Recordkeeping Requirements

Citation: 36 CFR 1222.32

✍ § 1222.32 General requirements.

Agencies shall identify, develop, issue, and periodically review their recordkeeping requirements for all agency operations and for records in all media, including those records created or received on electronic mail systems. Recordkeeping requirements shall:

(a) Identify and prescribe specific categories of documentary materials to be systematically created or received and maintained by agency personnel in the course of their official duties;

(b) Prescribe the use of materials and recording techniques that ensure the preservation of records as long as they are needed by the Government;

(c) Prescribe the manner in which these materials shall be maintained wherever held; and

(d) Distinguish records from nonrecord materials and, with the approval of the Archivist of the United States, prescribe action for the final disposition of agency records when they are no longer needed for current business.

Citation: 36 CFR 1222.34

✍ § 1222.34 Identifying Federal records.

(a) *General.* To ensure that complete and accurate records are made and retained in the Federal Government, it is essential that agencies distinguish between records and nonrecord materials by the appropriate application of the definition of records (see 44 U.S.C. 3301 and 36 CFR 1220.14) to agency documentary materials. Applying the definition of records to most documentary materials created or received by agencies presents few problems with agencies have established and periodically updated recordkeeping requirements covering all media and all agency activities at all levels and locations.

(b) *Record status.* Documentary materials are records when they meet both of the following conditions:

(1) They are made or received by an agency of the United States Government or Federal law or in connection with the transaction of agency business; and

(2) They are preserved or are appropriate for preservation as evidence of agency organization and activities or because of the value of the information they contain.

(c) *Working files and similar materials.* Working files, such as preliminary drafts and rough notes, and other similar materials shall be maintained for purposes of adequate and proper documentation if:

(1) They were circulated or made available to employees, other than the creator, for official purposes such as approval, comment, action, recommendation, follow-up, or to communicate with agency staff about agency business; and

(2) They contain unique information, such as substantive annotations or comments included therein, that adds to a proper understanding to the agency's formulation and execution of

basic policies, decisions, actions, or responsibilities.

(d) *Record status of copies.* The determination as to whether a particular document is a record does not depend upon whether it contains unique information. Multiple copies of the same document and documents containing duplicative information, including messages created or received on electronic mail systems, may each have record status depending on how they are used to transact agency business. See paragraph (f)(2) of this section concerning the nonrecord status of extra copies.

(e) *Electronic mail messages.* Messages created or received on electronic mail systems may meet the definition of record in 44 USC 3301.

(f) *Nonrecord materials.* Nonrecord materials are Government-owned documentary materials that do not meet the conditions of record status (see § 1222.34(b)) or that are specifically excluded from status as records by statute (see 44 U.S.C. 3301):

(1) Library and museum material (but only if such material is made or acquired and preserved solely for reference or exhibition purposes);

(2) Extra copies of documents (but only if the sole reason such copies are preserved is for convenience of reference); and

(3) Stocks of publications and of processed documents. (Each agency shall create and maintain serial or record sets of its publications and processed documents, as evidence of agency activities and for the information they contain, including annual reports, brochures, pamphlets, books, handbooks, posters and maps.)

(g) *Agency responsibilities.* Agencies shall take appropriate action to ensure that all staff are capable of identifying Federal records. For electronic mail systems, agencies shall ensure that all staff are informed of the potential record status of messages, transmittal and receipt data, directories, and distribution lists.

Citation: **36 CFR 1222.50**

✍ § 1222.50 Records maintenance.

(a) Agencies shall prescribe an appropriate records maintenance program so that complete records are filed or otherwise identified and preserved, records can be found when needed, the identification and retention of permanent records are facilitated, and permanent and temporary records are physically segregated or, for electronic records, segregable.

(b) Each Federal agency, in providing for effective controls over the maintenance of records, shall:

(1) Establish and implement standards and procedures for classifying, indexing, and filing records as set forth in GSA or NARA handbooks;

(2) Formally specify official file locations for records in all media and prohibit the maintenance of records at unauthorized locations;

(3) Formally specify which officials are responsible for maintenance and disposition of electronic records and which computer systems are used for recordkeeping;

(4) Standardize reference service procedures to facilitate the finding, charging out, and refiling of paper, audiovisual, and cartographic and architectural records, and to ensure that reference to electronic records minimizes the risk of unauthorized additions, deletions, or alterations;

(5) Make available to all agency employees published standards, guides, and instructions designed for easy reference and revision;

(6) Review its records maintenance program periodically to determine its adequacy; audit a representative sample of its paper, audiovisual, electronic, cartographic, and architectural files for duplication, misclassification, or misfiles;

(7) Maintain microform, audiovisual, and electronic records in accordance with 36 CFR parts 1230, 1232, and 1234, respectively;

(8) Establish and implement procedures for maintaining records and nonrecord materials separately; ensure that record materials generated electronically are clearly identified as records and protected from unauthorized change or deletion for the length of their scheduled retention period; and

(9) Establish and implement procedures for the separate maintenance of any personal papers in accordance with § 1222.36.

PART 1228. DISPOSITION OF FEDERAL RECORDS

Citation: **36 CFR 1228.1**

✍ § 1228.1 Scope of part.

This part sets policies and establishes standards, procedures, and techniques for the disposition of all Federal records in accordance with 44 U.S.C. chapters 21, 29, 31, and 33. The disposition of documentary materials created or acquired by a Federal agency, regardless of physical form or characteristics, is controlled by this part if any of the following conditions are met:

(a) The materials are created or received in the course of business and contain information related to the organization, functions, policies, decisions, procedures, operations, or other official activities of the agency. Also included is documentation of oral exchanges such as telephone conversations and meetings during which policy was discussed or formulated or other significant activities of the agency are planned, discussed, or transacted.

(b) The creation, retention, or disposition of the materials is mandated by statute or agency or other Federal regulations, directives, policies, or procedures.

(c) The materials are controlled, maintained, preserved, processed, filed, or otherwise handled following established agency procedures for records.

(d) The material contains unique information, such as substantive annotations, including drafts, transmittal sheets, and final documents or other materials circulated or made available to employees other than the creator for official purposes, such as approval, comment, action, recommendation, follow-up, or to keep agency staff informed regarding agency business.

(e) The material was created or received on an electronic mail system and it meets the definition of record. For specific instructions on the disposition of records created or received on electronic mail systems, see 36 CFR 1234.32.

PART 1230. MICROGRAPHIC RECORDS MANAGEMENT

Subpart A. General

Citation: **36 CFR 1230.1**

✪ § 1230.1. Scope of part.

This part provides standards for using micrographic technology in the creation, use, storage, retrieval, preservation, and disposition of Federal records.

Citation: **36 CFR 1230.2**

✪ § 1230.2. Authority.

As provided in 44 U.S.C. Chapters 29 and 33, the Archivist of the United States is authorized to establish standards for the reproduction of records by photographic and microphotographic processes with a view to the disposal of original records; to establish uniform standards within the Government for the creation, storage, use, and disposition of processed microform records; and to establish, maintain, and operate centralized microfilming services for Federal agencies.

Citation: 36 CFR 1230.3

✪ § 1230.3. Publications incorporated by reference.

(a) *General.* The following publications cited in this section are hereby incorporated by reference into Part 1230. They are available from the issuing organization at the addresses listed in this section. They are also available for inspection at the Office of the Federal Register, 800 North Capitol Street NW., Suite 700, Washington, DC. This incorporation by reference was approved by the Director of the Federal Register in accordance with 5 U.S.C. 552(a) and 1 CFR part 51. These materials are incorporated as they exist in the date of the approval, and a notice of any change in these materials will be published in the Federal Register.

(b) *American National Standards Institute (ANSI) and International (ISO)* ANSI and ISO standards cited in this part are available from the American National Standards Institute, 11 West 42nd St., New York City, NY 10036.

ANSI/NAPM IT9.1-1992, Imaging Media (Film) — Silver-Gelatin Type — Specifications for Stability.

ANSI IT9.2-1991, Imaging Media — Photographic Processed Films, Plates, and Papers — Filing Enclosures and Storage Containers.

ANSI IT9.5-1988, Imaging Media (Film) — Ammonia-Processed Diazo Films — Specifications for Stability.

ANSI PH1.43-1985, Photography (Film) — Processed Safety Film — S

ANSI PH1.67-1985, Photography (Film) — Processed Vesicular Film — for Stability.

ANSI/ISO 5/2-1985, ANSI PH2.19-1086, Photography (Sensitometry) — Densit Measurements — Geometric Conditions for Transmission Density.

ANSI/ISO 5/3-1984, ANSI PH2.18-1985, Photography (Sensitometry)§ Density Measurements — Special Conditions.

ISO 3334-1989, Micrographics — ISO resolution chart test No. 2 — Description and use.

(c) *Association of Information and Image Management (AIIM) Standards.* The following AIIM standards are available from the Association for Information and Image Management, 1100 Wayne Avenue, Suite 1100, Silver Spring, MD 20910.

ANSI/AIIM MS1-1989, Recommended Practices for Alphanumeric Computer-Output Microforms — Operational Practices for Inspection and Quality Control.

ANSI/AIIM MS5-1985, Micrographics — Microfiche.

ANSI/AIIM MS14-1988, Specifications for 16mm and 35mm Roll Microfilm.

ANSI/AIIM MS19-1987, Recommended Practice for Identification of Microforms.

ANSI/AIIM MS23-1983, Practice for Operational Procedures/Inspection and Quality Control of First Generation, Silver-Gelatin Microfilm of Documents.

ANSI/AIIM MS32-1987, Microrecording of Engineering Source Documents on 35mm Microfilm.

ANSI/AIIM MS41-1988, Unitized Microfilm Carriers (Aperture, Camera, Copy, and Image Cards).

ANSI/AIIM MS43-1988, Recommended Practice for Operational Procedures/Inspection and Quality Control of Duplicate Microforms of Documents and From COM.

AIIM Special Interest Package (SIP) No. 34, July, 1987, Microspots and Aging Blemishes.

(d) *National Institute of Standards and Technology (NIST) publications.* The following publication is available from the National Institute of Standards and Technology, Office of Standards Reference Materials, Rm. B311 Chemistry, Gaithersburg, MD 20899.

NIST-SRM 1010a, Microcopy Resolution Test Chart (ISO Test Chart No. 2), certified June 1, 1990.

Citation: 36 CFR 1230.4

✪ § 1230.4. Definitions.

For the purpose of this part the following definitions shall apply:

Archival microfilm. A photographic film that meets the standards described in § 1230.14 and that is suitable for the preservation of permanent records when stored in accordance with § 1230.20(a). Such film must conform to film designated as LE 500 in ANSI/NAPM IT9.1-1992.

Background density. The opacity of the area of the microform not containing information.

Computer assisted retrieval (CAR) system. A records storage and retrieval system, normally microfilm-based, that uses a computer for indexing, automatic markings such as blips or bar codes for identification, and automatic devices for reading those markings and, in some applications, for transporting the film for viewing.

Computer Output Microfilm (COM). Microfilm containing data produced by a recorder from computer generated signals.

Facility. An area set aside for equipment and operations required in the production or reproduction of microforms either for internal use or for the use of other organizational elements of the Federal Government.

Microfilm. (a) Raw (unexposed and unprocessed) fine-grain, high resolution photographic film with characteristics that make it suitable for use in micrographics;

(b) The process of recording microimages on film; or

(c) A fine-grain, high resolution photographic film containing an image greatly reduced in size from the original.

Microform. A term used for any form containing microimages.

Microimage. A unit of information such as a page of text or a drawing, that has been made too small to be read without magnification.

Permanent record. Any record (see definition in 44 U.S.C. 3301) that has been determined by the Archivist of the United States to have sufficient historical or other value to warrant its continued preservation by the Government.

Temporary record. Any record approved by the Archivist of the United States for disposal, either immediately or after a specified retention period. Temporary records may warrant microfilming for economies of storage and distribution.

Unscheduled record. Any record that has not been appraised by NARA, i.e., a record that has neither been approved for disposal nor designated as permanent by the Archivist of the United States in accordance with part 1228 of this chapter.

Use or work copies. Duplicates of original film which are prepared for use as reference copies or as duplication masters for recurring or large-scale duplication. These copies are not to be confused with the preservation master copies which are stored under the conditions in § 1230.20 and which are not to be used for reference purposes.

Subpart B. Program Requirements

Citation: **36 CFR 1230.7**

✪ § 1230.7 Agency responsibilities.

The head of each Federal agency must ensure that the management of microform records incorporates the following elements:

(a) Assigning responsibility to develop and implement an agencywide program for managing all records on microform media and notifying the National Archives and Records Administration (NI), Washington, DC 20408 of the name and title of the person assigned the responsibility.

(b) Integrating the management of microform records with other records and information resources management programs of the agency.

(c) Incorporating microform records management objectives, responsibilities, and authorities in pertinent agency directives and disseminating them throughout the agency as appropriate.

(d) Establishing procedures for addressing records management concerns, including recordkeeping and disposition requirements, before approving new microform records systems or enhancements to existing systems.

(e) Ensuring that adequate training is provided for the managers and users of microform records.

(f) Developing and securing NARA approval of records schedules covering microform records, and ensuring proper implementation of the schedule provisions.

(g) Ensuring that computerized indexes associated with microform records, such as in a computer-assisted retrieval (CAR) systems, are scheduled in accordance with part 1234 of this chapter.

(h) Reviewing the agency's program periodically to ensure compliance with NARA standards in this part for the creation storage, use, inspection, and disposition of microform records.

Subpart C. Standards for Microfilming Records.

Citation: **36 CFR 1230.10**

✪ § 1230.10. Disposition authorization.

(a) *Permanent or unscheduled records.* Agencies must schedule the disposition of both source documents (originals) and microforms by submitting Standard Form (SF) 115. Request for Records Disposition Authority, to NARA in accordance with part 1228 of this chapter. Source documents may not be disposed of before NARA authorization is received. The original records shall not be destroyed after microfilming when NARA determines that the original records have intrinsic value or when NARA concludes that the microforms present reference problems because of the access restrictions, including security classification, or other characteristics of the original records.

(1) Agencies using microfilming methods and procedures meeting the standards in § 1230.14 shall include on the SF 115 the following certification:

"This certifies that the records described on this form were (or will be) microfilmed in accordance with the standards set forth in 36 CFR part 1230."

(2) Agencies using microfilming methods, materials and procedures that do not meet the standards in § 1230.14(a) shall include on the SF 115 a description of the system and standards used.

(3) Agencies proposing to retain and store the silver original microforms of permanent records after disposal of the original records shall include on the SF 115 a statement that the agency's storage conditions shall comply with the standards of § 1230.20 and that the inspections required by § 1230.22 will be performed.

(b) *Temporary records.* Agencies do not need to obtain further NARA approval before disposing of scheduled temporary records that have been microfilmed. The approved retention period for temporary records shall be applied to microform copies of such records; the original records shall be destroyed upon verification of the microfilm, unless legal requirements preclude early destruction of the originals.

Citation: **36 CFR 1230.12**

✪ § 1230.12. Preparatory steps prior to filming.

(a) The integrity of the original records authorized for disposal shall be maintained by ensuring that the microforms are adequate substitutes for the original records and serve the purpose for which such records were created or maintained. Copies shall be complete and contain all information shown on the originals.

(b) The records shall be arranged, identified, and indexed so that any particular document or component of the records can be located. Each microform roll or fiche shall include accurate titling information on a titling target or header. At a minimum, titling information shall include the name of the agency and organization; the title of the records; the number or identifier for each unit of film; the security classification, if any; and the inclusive dates, names, or other data identifying the records to be included on a unit of film. For fiche, complete titling information may be placed as a microimage in frame 1 if the information will not fit on the header.

(c) Each microform shall contain an identification target showing the date of filming. When necessary to give the film copy better legal standing, the target shall also identify the person authorizing the microfilming. See ANSI/AIIM MS19-1987 for standards for identification targets.

(d) The following formats are mandatory standards for microforms.

(1) *Roll film* — (i) *Source documents.* The formats described in ANSI/AIIM MS14-1988 must be used for microfilming source documents on 16mm and 35mm roll film. A reduction ratio no greater than 1:24 is recommended for typewritten or correspondence type of documents. See ANSI/AIIM MS23-1991 for determining the appropriate reduction ratio and format for meeting the image quality requirements. When microfilming on 35mm film for aperture card applications, the format dimensions in AIIM/MS19-1987, Table 1 are mandatory, the aperture card format "D Aperture" shown in ANSI/AIIM MS41-1988, Figure 1 must be used. The components of the aperture card, including the paper and adhesive, must conform to the requirements of ANSI IT9.2-1001. The 35mm film used in the aperture card application must conform to film designated in LE 500 in ANSI/NAPM IT9.1-1992.

(ii) *COM.* Computer output microfilm (COM) generated images shall be the simplex mode described in ANSI/AIIM MS14-1988 at an effective ratio of 1:24 or 1:48 depending on the application.

(2) *Microfiche.* For microfilming source documents or computer generated information (COM) on microfiche, the appropriate formats and reduction ratios prescribed in ANSI/AIIM MS5-1990 must be used as specified for the size and quality of the documents being filmed. See ANSI/AIIM MS23-1991 for determining the appropriate reduction ratio and format for meeting the image quality requirement.

(e) *Index placement.* — (1) *Source documents.* When filming original (source) documents, all indexes, registers, or other finding aids, if microfilmed, shall be placed either in the first frames of the first roll of film or in the last frames of the last roll of film of a series or in the last frames of the last microfiche or microfilm jacket of a series.

(2) *COM.* Computer-generated microforms shall have the indexes following the data on a roll of film or in the last frames of a single microfiche, or the last frames of the last fiche in a series. Other index locations may be used only if dictated by special system constraints.

Citation: 36 CFR 1230.14

✪ § 1230.14. Film and image requirements for permanent records or unscheduled records.

(a) *Application.* The following standards apply to the microfilming of permanent records where the original paper record will be destroyed or otherwise disposed of. Systems that produce original permanent records on microfilm with no paper originals, such as computer output microfilm (COM), must be designed so that they produce microfilm which meets the standards of this section. Unscheduled records from systems such as COM must also meet the standards of this section. Prior NARA approval of a SF 115 is required before unscheduled paper records are disposed of after microfilming.

(b) *Film stock standards.* Only polyester-based silver gelatin type film that conforms to ANSI/NAPM IT9.1-1992 for LE 500 film must be used in all applications.

(c) *Processing standards.* Microforms shall be processed so that the residual thiosulfate ion concentration will not exceed 0.014 grams per square meter in accordance with ANSI/NAPM IT9.1-1992. Processing shall be in accordance with processing procedures in ANSI/AIIM MS1-1989 and MS23-1991.

(d) *Quality standards* — (1) *Resolution* — (i) *Source documents.* The method for determining minimum resolution on microforms of source documents shall conform to the Quality Index Methods for determining resolution and anticipated losses when duplicating as described in ANSI/AIIM MS23-1991 and MS43-1988. Resolution tests shall be performed using a NIST-SRM 1010a, Microcopy Resolution Test Chart (a calibrated and certified photographic reproduction) as specified in ISO 3334-1991 (the standard practices for using the test chart), and the patterns will be read following the instructions of ISO 3334-1991. The character used to determine the height used in the Quality Index formula shall be the smallest character used to display information. A Quality Index of five is required at the third generation level.

(ii) *COM.* Computer output microfilm (COM) shall meet the requirements of ANSI/AIIM MS1-1988.

(2) *Background density of images.* The background ISO standard visual diffuse transmission density on microforms shall be appropriate to the type of documents being filmed. The procedure for density measurement is described in ANSI/AIIM MS23-1991 and the densitometer shall be in accordance with ANSI/ISO 5/3-1984, for spectral conditions and ANSI IT2.19-1990, for geometric conditions for transmission density. Recommended visual diffuse transmission background densities for images of documents are as follows:

Classification	Description of document	Background density
Group 1	High-quality, high-contrast printed books, periodicals, and black typing	1.3-1.5
Group 2	Fine-line originals, black opaque pencil writing, and documents with small high-contrast printing	1.15-1.4
Group 3	Pencil and ink drawings, faded printing, and very small printing, such as footnotes at the bottom of a printed page	1.0-1.2
Group 4	Low-contrast manuscripts and drawings, graph paper with pale, fine-colored lines; letters typed with a worn ribbon; and poorly printed, faint documents	0.8-1.0
Group 5	Poor-contrast documents (special exception)	0.7-0.85

Recommended visual diffuse transmission densities for computer generated images are as follows:

Film type	Process	Density measurement method	Min. Dmax.°	Max. Dmin.°	Minimum density difference
Silver gelatin	Conventional	Printing or diffuse	0.75	0.15	0.60
Silver gelatin	Full reversal	Printing	1.50	0.20	1.30

°Character of line density, measured with a microdensitometer or by comparing the film under a microscope with an image of a known density.

(3) *Base plus fog density of films.* The base plus fog density of unexposed, processed films should not exceed 0.10. When a tinted base film is used, the density will be increased. The difference must be added to the values given in the tables in paragraph (d)(2) of this section.

(4) *Line or Stroke Width.* Due to optical limitations in most photographic systems, film images of thin lines appearing in the original documents will tend to fill in as a function of their width and density. Therefore, as the reduction ratio of a given system is increased, the background density shall be reduced as needed to ensure that the copies produced will contain legible characters.

Citation: 36 CFR 1230.16

✪ § 1230.16. Film and image requirements for temporary records, duplicates, and user copies.

(a) *Temporary records with a retention period over 99 years.* Agencies must follow the film and image requirements in § 1230.14.

(b) *Other temporary records.* Agencies must select an appropriate film stock that meets agency needs for temporary microforms to be kept for less than 100 years and ensures the preservation of the microforms for their full retention period. NARA does not require use of particular standards for processing microfilm of such temporary records; agencies may consult appropriate ANSI standards or manufacturer's instructions.

Subpart D. Standards for the Storage, Use and Disposition of Microform Records.

Citation: 36 CFR 1230.20

✪ § 1230.20. Storage.

(a) *Permanent and unscheduled records.* The extended term storage conditions specified in ANSI IT9.11-1991 and ANSI IT9.2-1991 are required for storing permanent and unscheduled microform records, except that the relative humidity of the storage area must be a constant 35% RH, plus or minus 5%. Non-silver copies of permanent or unscheduled microforms must not be stored in the same storage area as silver gelatin originals or duplicate copies.

(b) *Temporary records.* Temporary microform records must be stored under conditions that will ensure their preservation and for their full retention period. Agencies may consult ANSI IT9.11-1991 and ANSI IT9.2-1991 to determine appropriate storage conditions; however, NARA does not require adherence to this standard for temporary records.

Citation: 36 CFR 1230.22

✪ § 1230.22. Inspection.

(a) *Permanent and unscheduled records.*

(1) Master films of permanent records microfilmed in order to dispose of the original records, master films of permanent records originally created on microfilm, and other master films scheduled for transfer to the National Archives, must be inspected by the agency creating the film when the films are 2 years old and, until they are transferred to a Federal records center or to the National Archives, every 2 years thereafter. The inspection must be made in accordance with ANSI/AIIM MS45-1990.

(2) Microforms cannot be accepted for deposit with the National Archives of the United States until the first inspection (occurring after the microforms are 2 years old) has been performed. Permanent microforms may be transferred to a Federal records center only after the agency has performed the first inspection or has certified that the microforms will be inspected by the agency, an agency contractor, or the Federal records center (on a reimbursable basis) when they become 2 years old.

(3) To facilitate inspection, an inventory of microfilm must be maintained, listing each microform series/publication by production date, producer, processor, format, and results of previous inspections.

(4) The elements of the inspection shall consist of:

(i) An inspection for aging blemishes following the guidelines in the AIIM/AIIM MS45-1990;

(ii) A rereading of resolution targets;

(iii) A remeasurement of density; and

(iv) A certification of the environmental conditions under which the microforms are stored, as specified in § 1230.20(a).

(5) An inspection report must be prepared, and a copy must be furnished to NARA in accordance with § 1230.26(b). The inspection report must contain:

(i) A summary of the inspection findings, including:

(A) A list of batches by year that includes the identification numbers of microfilm rolls and microfiche in each batch;

(B) The quantity of microforms inspected;

(C) An assessment of the overall conditions of the microforms;

(D) A summary of any defects discovered, e.g., redox blemishes or base deformation; and

(E) A summary of corrective action taken.

(ii) A detailed inspection log created during the inspection that contains the following information:

(A) A complete description of all records inspected (title, roll or fiche number or other unique identifier for each unit of film inspected; security classification, if any; and inclusive dates, names, or other data identifying the records on the unit of film);

(B) The date of inspection;

(C) The elements of inspection (see subparagraph (a)(4) of this section);

(D) Any defects uncovered; and

(E) The corrective action taken.

(6) An agency having in its custody a master microform that is deteriorating, as shown by the inspection, shall prepare a silver duplicate in accordance with § 1230.14 to replace the deteriorating master. The duplicate film will be subject to the 2-year inspection requirement before transfer to a Federal Records Center or to the National Archives.

(7) Inspection must be performed in an environmentally controlled area in accordance with ANSI/AIIM MS45-1990.

(b) *Temporary records.* Inspection by sampling procedures described in § 1230.22(a) is recommended but not required.

Citation: 36 CFR 1230.24

✪ § 1230.24. Use of microform records.

(a) The silver gelatin original microform or duplicate silver gelatin microform crated in accordance with § 1230.14 of this part (archival microform) must not be used for reference purposes. Duplicates must be used for reference and for further duplication on a recurring basis or for large-scale duplication, as well as for distribution of records on microform. Agency procedures must ensure that the archival microform remains clear and undamaged during the process of making a duplicating master.

(b) Agencies retaining the original record in accordance with an approved records disposition schedule may apply agency standards for the use of microform records.

Citation: 36 CFR 1230.26

✪ § 1230.26. Disposition of microform records.

The disposition of microform records shall be carried out in the same manner prescribed for other types of records in part 1228 of this chapter with the following additional requirements:

(a) The silver gelatin original (or duplicate silver gelatin microform created in accordance with § 1230.14) plus one microform copy of each permanent record microfilmed by an agency, must be transferred to an approved agency records center, the National Archives of the United States, or to a Federal records center, at the time that the records are to be transferred in accordance with the approved records disposition schedule, SF 258, or other authorization for transfer. Non-silver copies must be packaged separately from silver gelatin original or silver duplicate microform copy and labeled clearly as non-silver copies.

(b) The microforms shall be accompanied by:

(1) Information identifying the agency and organization; the title of the records; the number of identifier for each unit of film; the security classification, if any; the inclusive dates, names, or other data identifying the records to be included on a unit of film;

(2) Any finding aids relevant to the microform that are not contained in the microform; and

(3) The inspection log forms and inspection reports required by § 1230.22(and (6).

(c) The information required in this paragraph (b) shall be attached to the SF 135 when records are being transferred to a

Federal records center and to the SF 258 when records are being transferred to the legal custody of the National Archives.

PART 1234. ELECTRONIC RECORDS MANAGEMENT.

Subpart A. General

Citation:	36 CFR 1234.1

✍ § 1234.1 Scope of part.

This part establishes the basic requirements related to the creation, maintenance, use, and disposition of electronic records. Electronic records include numeric, graphic, and text information, which may be recorded on any medium capable of being read by a computer and which satisfies the definition of a record. This includes, but is not limited to, magnetic media, such as tapes and disks, and optical disks. Unless otherwise noted, these requirements apply to all electronic information systems, whether on microcomputers, minicomputers, or main-frame computers, regardless of storage media, in network or stand-alone configurations. This part also covers creation, maintenance and use, and disposition of Federal records created by individuals using electronic mail applications.

Citation:	36 CFR 1234.2

✍ § 1234.2 Definitions.

Basic records management terms are defined in 36 CFR 1220.14. As used in part 1234 —

Data base means a set of data, consisting of at least one data file, that is sufficient for a given purpose.

Data base management system means a software system used to access and retrieve data stored in a data base.

Data file means related numeric, textual, or graphic information that is organized in a strictly prescribed form and format.

Electronic information system. A system that contains and provides access to computerized Federal records and other information.

Electronic mail message. A document created or received on an electronic mail system including brief notes, more formal or substantive narrative documents, and any attachments, such as word processing and other electronic documents, which may be transmitted with the message.

Electronic mail system. A computer application used to create, receive, and transmit messages and other documents. Excluded from this definition are file transfer utilities (software that transmits files between users but does not retain any transmission data), data systems used to collect and process data that have been organized into data files or data bases on either personal computers or mainframe computers, and word processing documents not transmitted on an e-mail system.

Electronic record means any information that is recorded in a form that only a computer can process and that satisfied the definition of a Federal record in 44 USC 3301.

Electronic recordkeeping system. An electronic system in which records are collected, organized, and categorized to facilitate their preservation, retrieval, use, and disposition.

Text documents means narrative or tabular documents, such as letters, memorandums, and reports, in loosely prescribed form and format.

Transmission and receipt data. (1) *Transmission data.* Information in electronic mail systems regarding the identities of sender and addressee(s), and the date and time messages were sent.

(2) *Receipt data.* Information in electronic mail systems regarding date and time of receipt of a message, and/or acknowledgment of receipt or access by addressee(s).

Subpart B. Program Requirements.

Citation:	36 CFR 1234.10

✪ § 1234.10. Agency responsibilities.

The head of each Federal agency shall ensure that the management of electronic records incorporates the following elements:

(a) Assigning responsibility to develop and implement an agencywide program for the management of all records created, received, maintained, used, or stored on electronic media; and notifying the National Archives and Records Administration, Office of Records Administration (NI), Washington, DC 20408 and the General Services Administration, Regulations Branch (KMPR), Washington, DC 20405, of the name and title of the person assigned the responsibility.

(b) Integrating the management of electronic records with other records and information resources management programs of the agency.

(c) Incorporating electronic records management objectives, responsibilities, and authorities in pertinent agency directives and disseminating them throughout the agency as appropriate.

(d) Establishing procedures for addressing records management requirements, including recordkeeping requirements and disposition, before approving new electronic records systems or enhancements to existing systems.

(e) Ensuring that adequate training is provided for users of electronic mail systems on recordkeeping requirements, the distinction between Federal records and nonrecord materials, procedures for designating Federal records, and moving or copying records for inclusion in an agency recordkeeping system.

(f) Ensuring tht adequate training is provided for users of electronic information system in the operation, care, and handling of the equipment, software, and media used in the system.

(g) Developing and maintaining up-to-date documentation about all electronic records systems that is adequate to: Specify all technical characteristics necessary for reading or processing the records; identify all defined inputs and outputs of the system; define the contents of the files and records; determine restrictions on access and use; understand the purpose(s) and function(s) of the system; describe update cycles or conditions and rules for adding information in it, or deleting information; and ensure the timely, authorized disposition of the records.

(h) Specifying the location, manner, and media in which electronic records will be maintained to meet operational and archival requirements, and maintaining inventories of electronic records systems to facilitate disposition.

(i) Developing and securing NARA approval of records disposition schedules, and ensuring implementation of their provisions.

(j) Specifying the methods of implementing controls over national security-classified sensitive proprietary, and Privacy Act records stored and used electronically.

(k) Establishing procedures to ensure that the requirements of this part are applied to those electronic records that are created or maintained by contractors.

(l) Ensuring compliance with applicable Governmentwide policies, procedures, and standards such as those issued by the Office of Management and Budget, the General Accounting Office, the General Services Administration, the National

Archives and Records Administration, and the National Institute of Standards and Technology.

(m) Reviewing electronic information system periodically for conformance to established agency procedures, standards, and policies as part of the periodic reviews required by 44 U.S.C. 3506. The review should determine if the records have been properly identified and described, and whether the schedule descriptions and retention periods reflect the current informational content and use. If not, or if substantive changes have been made in the structure, design, codes, purposes, or uses of the system, submit an SF 115, Request for Records Disposition Authority, to NARA.

Subpart C. Standards for the Creation, Use, Preservation, and Disposition of Electronic Records

Citation: 36 CFR 1234.20

✪ § 1234.20. Creation and use of data files.

(a) For electronic information systems that produce, use, or store data files, disposition instructions for the data shall be incorporated into the system's design.

(b) Agencies shall maintain adequate an up-to-date technical documentation for each electronic information system that produces, uses, or stores data files. Minimum documentation required is a narrative description of the system; physical and technical characteristics of the records, including a record layout that describes each field including its name, size, starting or relative position, and a description of the form of the data (such as alphabetic, zoned decimal, packed decimal, or numeric), or a data dictionary or the equivalent information associated with a data base management system including a description of the relationship between data elements in data bases; and any other technical information needed to read or process the records.

Citation: 36 CFR 1234.22

✪ § 1234.22. Creation and use of text documents.

(a) Electronic recordkeeping systems that maintain the official file copy of text documents on electronic media shall met the following minimum requirements:

(1) Provide a method for all authorized users of the system to retrieve desired documents, such as an indexing or text search system;

(2) Provide an appropriate level of security to ensure integrity of the documents;

(3) Provide a standard interchange format when necessary to permit the exchange of documents on electronic media between agency computers using different software/operating systems and the conversion or migration of documents on electronic media from one system to another, and

(4) Provide for the disposition of the documents including, when necessary, the requirements for transferring permanent records to NARA (see § 1228.188 of this chapter).

(b) Before a document is created electronically on electronic recordkeeping systems that will maintain the official file copy on electronic media, each document shall be identified sufficiently to enable authorized personnel to retrieve, protect, and carry out the disposition of documents in the system. Appropriate identifying information for each document maintained on the electronic media may include: office of origin, file code, key words for retrieval, addressee (if any), signature, author, date, authorized disposition (coded or otherwise), and security classification (if applicable). Agencies shall ensure that records maintained in such systems can be correlated with related records on paper, microform, or other media.

Citation: 36 CFR 1234.24

✍ § 1234.24 Standards for managing electronic mail records.

Agencies shall manage records created or received on electronic mail systems in accordance with the provisions of this chapter pertaining to adequacy of documentation, recordkeeping requirements, agency records management responsibilities, and records disposition (36 CFR parts 1220, 1222, and 1228).

(a) Agency instructions on identifying and preserving electronic mail messages will address the following unique aspects of electronic mail:

(1) Some transmission data (names of sender and addressee(s) and date the message was sent) must be preserved for each electronic mail record in order for the context of the message to be understood. Agencies shall determine if any other transmission data is needed for purposes of context.

(2) Agencies that use an electronic mail system that identifies users by codes or nicknames or identifies addressees only by the name of a distribution list shall instruct staff on how to retain names on directories or distributions lists to ensure identification of the sender and addressee(s) of messages that are records.

(3) Agencies that use an electronic mail system that allows users to request acknowledgments or receipts showing that a message reached the mailbox or inbox of each addressee, or that an addressee opened the message, shall issue instructions to e-mail users specifying when to request such receipts or acknowledgments for recordkeeping purposes and how to preserve them.

(4) Agencies with access to external electronic mail systems shall ensure that Federal records sent or received on these systems are preserved in the appropriate recordkeeping system and that reasonable steps are taken to capture available transmission and receipt data needed by the agency for recordkeeping purposes.

(5) Some e-mail systems provide calendars and task lists for users. These may meet the definition of Federal record. Calendars that meet the definition of Federal records are to be managed in accordance with the provisions of General Records Schedule 23, Item 5.

(6) Draft documents that are circulated on electronic mail systems may be records if they meet the criteria specified in 36 CFR 1222.34.

(b) Agencies shall consider the following criteria when developing procedures for the maintenance of electronic mail records in appropriate recordkeeping systems, regardless of format.

(1) Recordkeeping systems that include electronic mail messages must:

(i) Provide for the grouping of related records into classifications according to the nature of the business purposes the records serve;

(ii) Permit easy and timely retrieval of both individual records and files or other groupings of related records;

(iii) Retain the records in a usable format for their required retention period as specified by a NARA-approved records schedule;

(iv) Be accessible by individuals who have a business need for information in the system;

(v) Preserve the transmission and receipt data specified in agency instructions; and

(vi) Permit transfer of permanent records to the National Archives and Records Administration (see 36 CFR 1228.188 and 36 CFR 1234.32(a)).

(2) Agencies shall not store the recordkeeping copy of electronic mail messages that are Federal records only on the electronic mail system, unless the system has all of the features specified in paragraph (b)(1) of this section. If the electronic mail system is not designed to be a recordkeeping system, agencies shall instruct staff on how to copy Federal records from the electronic mail system to a recordkeeping system.

(c) Agencies that maintain their electronic mail records electronically shall move or copy them to a separate electronic recordkeeping system unless their system has the features specified in paragraph (b)(1) of this section. Because they do not have the features specified in paragraph (b)(1) of this section, backup tapes should not be used for recordkeeping purposes. Agencies may retain records from electronic mail systems in an off-line electronic storage format (such as optical disk or magnetic tape) that meets the requirements described at 36 CFR 1234.30(a). Agencies that retain permanent electronic mail records scheduled for transfer to the National Archives shall either store them in a format and on a medium that conforms to the requirements concerning transfer at 36 CFR 1228.188 or shall maintain the ability to convert the records to the required format and medium at the time transfer is scheduled.

(d) Agencies that maintain paper files as their recordkeeping systems shall print their electronic mail records and the related transmission and receipt data specified by the agency.

Citation: 36 CFR 1234.26

✪ § 1234.26. Judicial use of electronic records.

Electronic records may be admitted in evidence to Federal courts for use in court proceedings (Federal Rules of Evidence 803(8)) if trustworthiness if established by thoroughly documenting the recordkeeping system's operation and the controls imposed upon it. Agencies should implement the following procedures to enhance the legal admissibility of electronic records.

(a) Document that similar kinds of records generated and stored electronically are created by the same processes each time and have a standardized retrieval approach.

(b) Substantiate that security procedures prevent unauthorized addition, modification or deletion of a record and ensure system protection against such problems as power interruptions.

(c) Identify the electronic media on which records are stored throughout their life cycle, the maximum time span that records remain on each storage medium, and the NARA-approved disposition of all records.

(d) Coordinate all of the above with legal counsel and senior IRM and records management staff.

Citation: 36 CFR 1234.28

✪ § 1234.28. Security of electronic records.

Agencies shall implement and maintain an effective records security program that incorporates the following:

(a) Ensures that only authorized personnel have access to electronic records.

(b) Provides for backup and recovery of records to protect against information loss.

(c) Ensures that appropriate agency personnel are trained to safeguard sensitive or classified electronic records.

(d) Minimizes the risk of unauthorized alteration or erasure of electronic records.

(e) Ensures that electronic records security is included in computer systems security plans prepared pursuant to the Computer Security Act of 1987 (40 USC 759 note).

Citation: 36 CFR 1234.30

✪ § 1234.30. Selection and maintenance of electronic records storage media.

(a) Agencies shall select appropriate media and systems for storing agency records throughout their life, which met the following requirements:

(1) Permit easy retrieval in a timely fashion;

(2) Facilitate distinction between record and nonrecord material;

(3) Retain the records in a usable format until their authorized disposition date; and

(4) When appropriate, meet requirements for transferring permanent records to NARA (see § 1228.188 of this chapter).

(b) The following factors shall be considered before selecting a storage medium or converting from one medium to another:

(1) The authorized life of the records, as determined during the scheduling process;

(2) The maintenance necessary to retain the records;

(3) The cost of storing and retrieving the records;

(4) The records density;

(5) The access time to retrieve stored records;

(6) The portability of the medium (that is, selecting a medium that will run on equipment offered by multiple manufacturers) and the ability to transfer the information from one medium to another (such as from optical disk to magnetic tape); and

(7) Whether the medium meets current applicable Federal Information Processing Standards.

(c) Agencies should avoid the use of floppy disks for the exclusive long-term storage of permanent or unscheduled electronic records.

(d) Agencies shall ensure that all authorized users can identify and retrieve information stored on diskettes, removable disks, or tapes by establishing or adopting procedures for external labeling.

(e) Agencies shall ensure that information is not lost because of changing technology or deterioration by converting storage media to provide compatibility with the agency's current hardware and software. Before conversion to a different medium, agencies must determine that the authorized disposition of the electronic records can be implemented after conversion.

(f) Agencies shall back up electronic records on a regular basis to safeguard against the loss of information due to equipment malfunctions or human error. Duplicate copies of permanent or unscheduled records shall be maintained in storage areas separate from the location of the records that have been copies.

(g) *Maintenance of magnetic computer tape.* — (1) Agencies shall test magnetic computer tapes no more than 6 months prior to using them to store electronic records that are unscheduled or scheduled for permanent retention. This test should verify that the tape is free of permanent errors and in compliance with the National Institute of Standards of Technology or industry standards.

(2) Agencies shall maintain the storage and test areas for computer magnetic tapes containing permanent and unscheduled records at the following temperatures and relative humidities:

Constant temperature — 62 to 68 °F.

Constant relative humidity — 35% to 45%.

(3) Agencies shall rewind under controlled tension all tapes containing unscheduled and permanent records every 3 1/2 years.

(4) Agencies shall annually read a statistical sample of all reels of magnetic computer tape containing permanent and unscheduled records to identify any loss of data and to discover and correct the causes of data loss. In tape libraries with 1800 or fewer reels, a 20% sample or a sample size of 50 reels, whichever is larger, should be read. In tape libraries with more than

1800 reels, a sample of 384 reels should be read. Tapes with 10 or more errors should be replaced and, when possible, lost data shall be restored. All other tapes which might have been affected by the same cause (i.e., poor quality tape, high usage, poor environment, improper handling) shall be read and corrected as appropriate.

(5) Agencies shall copy permanent or unscheduled data on magnetic tapes before the tapes are 10 years old onto tested and verified new tapes.

(6) External labels (or the equivalent automated tape management system) for magnetic tapes used to store permanent or unscheduled electronic records shall provide unique identification for each reel, including the name of the organizational unit responsible for the data, system title, and security classification, if applicable. Additionally, the following information shall be maintained for (but not necessarily attached to) each reel used to store permanent or unscheduled electronic records: file title(s); dates of creation; dates of coverage; the recording density; type of internal labels; volume serial number if applicable; number of tracks; character code/software dependency; information about block size; and reel sequence number, if the file is part of a multi-reel set. For numerical data files, include record format and logical record length, if applicable; data set name(s) and sequence, if applicable, and number of records for each data set.

(7) Agencies shall prohibit smoking and eating in magnetic computer tape storage libraries and test or evaluation areas that contain permanent or unscheduled records.

(h) *Maintenance of direct access storage media.*

(1) Agencies shall issue written procedures for the care and handling of direct access storage media which draw upon the recommendations of the manufacturers.

(2) External labels for diskettes or removal disks used when processing or temporarily storing permanent or unscheduled records shall include the following information: name of the organizational unit responsible for the records, descriptive title of the contents, dates of creation, security classification, if applicable, and identification of the software and hardware used.

Citation: 36 CFR 1234.32

✪ § 1234.32. Retention and disposition of electronic records.

Agencies shall establish policies and procedures to ensure that electronic records and their documentation are retained as long as needed by the Government. These retention procedures shall include provisions for:

(a) Scheduling the disposition of all electronic records, as well as related documentation and indexes, by applying General Records Schedules (particularly GRS 20 or GRS 23) as appropriate or submitting an SF 115, Request for Records Disposition Authority, to NARA (see part 1228 of this chapter). The information in electronic information systems, including those operated for the Government by a contractor, shall be scheduled as soon as possible but no later than one year after implementation of the system.

(b) Transferring a copy of the electronic records and any related documentation and indexes to the National Archives at the time specified in the records disposition schedule in accordance with instructions found in § 1228.188 of this chapter. Transfer may take place at an earlier date if convenient for both the agency and the National Archives and Records Administration.

(c) Establishing procedures for regular recopying, reformatting, and other necessary maintenance to ensure the retention and usability of electronic records throughout their authorized life cycle (see § 123.428).

(d) Electronic mail records may not be deleted or otherwise disposed of without prior disposition authority from NARA (44 U.S.C. 3303a). This applies to the original version of the record that is sent or received on the electronic mail system and any copies that have been transferred to a recordkeeping system. See 36 CFR part 1228 for records disposition requirements.

(1) *Disposition of records on the electronic mail system.* When an agency has taken the necessary steps to retain the record in a recordkeeping system, the identical version that remains on the user's screen or in the user's mailbox has no continuing value. Therefore, NARA has authorized deletion of the version of the record on the electronic mail system under General Records Schedule 20, Item 14, after the record has been preserved in a recordkeeping system along with all appropriate transmission data.

(2) *Records in recordkeeping systems.* The disposition of electronic mail records that have been transferred to an appropriate recordkeeping system is governed by the records schedule or schedules that control the records in that system. If the records in the system are not scheduled, the agency shall follow the procedures at 36 CFR part 1228.

Citation: 36 CFR 1234.34

✪ § 1234.34. Destruction of electronic records.

Electronic records may be destroyed only in accordance with a records disposition schedule approved by the Archivist of the United States, including General Records Schedules. At a minimum each agency shall ensure that:

(a) Electronic records scheduled for destruction are disposed of in a manner that ensures protection of any sensitive proprietary, or national security information.

(b) Magnetic recording media previously used for electronic records containing sensitive, proprietary, or national security information are not reused if the previously recorded information can be compromised by reuse in any way.

(c) Agencies shall establish and implement procedures that specifically address the destruction of electronic records generated by individuals employing electronic mail.

PART 1236. MANAGEMENT OF VITAL RECORDS

Subpart B. Vital Records

Citation: 36 CFR 1236.26

✍ § 1236.26 Protection of vital records.

Agencies shall take appropriate measures to ensure the survival of the vital records or copies of vital records in case of emergency or disaster. In the case of electronic records, this requirement is met if the information needed in the event of emergency or disaster is available in a copy made for general security purposes, even when the copy contains other information.

(a) *Duplication.* Computer backup tapes created in the normal course of system maintenance or other electronic copies that may be routinely created in the normal course of business may be used as the vital record copy. For hard copy records, agencies may choose to make microform copies. Standards for the creation, preservation and use of microforms are found in 36 CFR part 1230, Micrographic Records Management. The Computer Security Act of 1987 (40 U.S.C. 759, Pub. L. 100-235), OMB Circular A-130, and 36 CFR part 1234, Electronic Records Management, and 41 CFR part 201, subchapter B, Management and Use of Information and Records, specify protective measures and standards for electronic records.

(b) *Storage*. When agencies choose duplication as a protection method, the copy of the vital record stored off-site is normally a duplicate of the original record. Designating and using duplicate copies of original records as vital records facilitates destruction or deletion of obsolete duplicates when replaced by updated copies, whereas original vital records must be retained for the period specified in the agency records disposition schedule. The agency may store the original records off-site if protection of original signatures is necessary, or if it does not need to keep the original record at its normal place of business.

(c) *Storage considerations*. Agencies need to consider several factors when deciding where to store copies of vital records. Copies of emergency operating vital records need to be accessible in a very short period of time for use in the event of an emergency or disaster. Copies of legal and financial rights records may not be needed as quickly. In deciding where to store vital records copies, agencies shall treat records that have the properties of both categories, that is, emergency operating and legal and financial rights records, as emergency operating records.

(1) Under certain circumstances, Federal records centers (FRC's) may store copies of emergency operating vital records. FRC's will store small volumes of such records, but may not be able to provide storage for large collections or ones requiring constant recycling of the vital records, except under reimbursable agreement. Prior to preparing the records for shipment, the agency must contact the FRC to determine if the center can accommodate the storage requirements and return copies in an acceptable period of time.

(2) The off-site copy of legal and financial rights vital records may be stored at an off-site agency location or, in accordance with § 1228.156 of this chapter, at an FRC.

(3) When using an FRC for storing vital records that are duplicate copies of original records, the agency must specify on the SF 135, Records Transmittal and Receipt, that they are vital records (duplicate copies) and the medium on which they are maintained. The agency shall also periodically cycle (update) them by removing obsolete items and replacing them with the most recent version, when necessary.

(4) Agencies that transfer permanent, original vital records maintained on electronic or microform media to the custody of the National Archives may designate such records as their off-site copy. That designation may remain in effect until the information in such transferred records is superseded or becomes obsolete.

Citation: 36 CFR 1236.28

✍ § 1236.28 Disposition of original vital records.

The disposition of original vital records is governed by records schedules approved by NARA (see part 1228, Disposition of Federal Records). Original records that are not scheduled may not be destroyed or deleted.

SUBCHAPTER C. PUBLIC AVAILABILITY AND USE

PART 1254. AVAILABILITY OF RECORDS AND DONATED HISTORICAL MATERIALS

Subpart F. Microfilming Archival Records

Citation: 36 CFR 1254.90

✍ § 1254.90 General.

(a) This subpart establishes rules and procedures governing the use of privately owned microfilm equipment to film archival records and donated historical materials in the National Archives Building, the Washington National Records Center, the regional archives, and the Presidential Libraries.

(b) Persons or organizations wishing to microfilm Federal agency records in the custody of a Federal Records Center should contact the director of the Center about procedures for obtaining permission to film those records.

(c) Federal agencies needing to microfilm archival records in support of the agency's mission must contact the Assistant Archivist for the National Archives, as soon as possible after the need is identified, for information concerning standards and procedures for microfilming archival records.

Citation: 36 CFR 1254.92

✍ § 1254.92 Requests to microfilm records and donated historical materials.

(a) Requests to microfilm archival records or donated historical materials (except donated historical materials under the control of the Office of Presidential Libraries) in the National Archives Building, the Washington National Records Center, or the regional archives must be made in writing to the Assistant Archivist for the National Archives (NM), NARA, Washington, DC 20408. Requests to microfilm records or donated historical materials in a Presidential Library or donated historical materials in the National Archives Building under the control of the Office of Presidential Libraries must be made in writing to the Assistant Archivist for Presidential Libraries (NL), NARA, Washington, DC 20408. OMB control number 3095-0017 has been assigned to the information collection contained in this section.

(b) Request to use privately owned microfilm equipment should be submitted six months in advance of the proposed starting date of the microfilming project. Requests submitted with less advance notice will be considered and may be approved if space is available for the cameras in the area set aside for private microfilming and if the records require minimal preparation for filming. Only one microfilming project may be included in a request. NARA will not accept additional requests from an individual or organization to microfilm records in a NARA facility while NARA is evaluating an earlier request from that individual or organization to microfilm records at that facility. NARA will establish the number of camera spaces available to a single project based upon the total number of projects approved for filming at that time.

(c) The request must include:

(1) A description of the documents to be copied which includes the following elements:

(i) Agency of origin or, for donated historical materials, title of the collection,

(ii) Title of series or file segment;

(iii) Date span; and

(iv) Estimated volume in number of pages or cubic feet.

(2) The estimated amount of time (work-days) that the microfilm copying project will take; the date that the requester would like to begin the project; and the number of persons who would require training [see § 1254.100(b)].

(3) The number and a description of the equipment that will be used for copying including:

(i) The name of the manufacturer and model number; and

(ii) The type of light source to be employed (fluorescent, tungsten, or electronic flash) and if electronic flash (i.e., strobe) or fluorescent, whether the light source is filtered to omit ultraviolet radiation.

(4) A statement of the procedures which will be followed to ensure that all pages are copied, that the images on the microfilm are legible, and that the microfilm is properly processed. At a minimum, the procedures should meet the requirements specified in Part 1230 of this Chapter regarding the microfilming of permanent records.

(d) The requester must agree to credit the National Archives or the particular Presidential Library having custody of the original documents. The credit must appear at the beginning of a microfilm publication and in any publicity material or descriptions of the publication.

(1) If the original documents are Federal records, the requester must agree to include on the film this statement: "The documents reproduced in this publication are among the records of the (name or agency) in the custody of the National Archives of the United States. No copyright is claimed in these official U.S. Government records."

(2) If the original documents are donated historical materials, the requester must agree to include on the film this statement: "The documents reproduced in this publication are donated historical materials from (name of donor) in the custody of the (name of Presidential Library or National Archives). The National Archives administers them in accordance with the requirements of the donor's deed of gift and the U.S. Copyright Law Title 17, U.S.C.".

(e) If the person or organization producing the film plans to copyright the microfilm publication, the National Archives and Records Administration must be given a royalty-free worldwide license to sell the publication seven years after filming at the NARA facility is completed, or earlier if there is no commercial distributor.

Citation: **36 CFR 1254.94**

✍ § 1254.94 Criteria for granting the requests.

(a) NARA will evaluate the requests on the basis of this extent to which completion of a proposed project would further NARA's efforts to preserve and to make available to the public the historically valuable records of the Government.

(b) NARA will approve only requests to microfilm a complete body of documents, such as an entire series or a major continuous segment of a very large series which is reasonably divisible. Microfilming a complete body of documents means that all documents within the file unit(s) to be microfilmed will be consecutively copied, from the first to the last page, not skipping any pages in between except for pages that are exact duplicates or blank pages that are not included in a pagination scheme.

(c) NARA will normally approve only requests which include assurances that the project will adhere to the specifications in Part 1230 of this Chapter which concern microfilm stock standards, index placement, and microfilm processing for permanent records.

(d) NARA will approve only requests which specify that NARA will receive a first generation silver halide duplicate negative containing no splices made from the original camera negative of the microform record created in accordance with Part 1230 of this Chapter.

(1) NARA may use this duplicate negative microform to make duplicate preservation and reference copies. The copies may be made available for NARA and public use in NARA facilities and programs.

(2) NARA may also sell copies of the microform seven years after filming at the NARA facility is completed, or earlier if there is no commercial distributor. NARA may choose to add its own editorial material to the microform copies which NARA distributes or sells.

(e) NARA will not approve any request that does not include all of the information required by § 1254.92.

(f) NARA will normally not approve requests to microfilm documents:

(1) Which have previously been microfilmed and made available to the public;

(2) Which have been approved for microfilming by another party; or

(3) Which NARA plans to film as a NARA microfilm publication or which relate closely to other documents previously microfilmed or approved for microfilming by NARA. Exceptions to this provision may be granted at the discretion of NARA.

(g) NARA will normally not approve requests to microfilm the following categories of documents:

(1) Documents which include documents with general or specific restrictions on access that preclude their reproduction;

(2) Documents which include documents which are known to be protected by copyright;

(3) Documents of high intrinsic value which may be handled only by authorized NARA personnel;

(4) Documents in vulnerable physical condition;

(5) Documents having high research demand and which would have to be denied to others for an extended period of time during the microfilming process. Where possible, NARA will assist requesters in developing filming schedules that avoid the need to close documents for a lengthy period of time; and

(6) Oversize documents, bound volumes, and other formats that would be subject to excessive stress and possible damage from special equipment planned to be used by the requester, as well as documents fastened with grommets, heavy duty staples, miscellaneous fasteners, or wafers and other adhesives that cannot be removed without tearing or breaking documents.

(h) NARA will normally not approve requests from persons or organizations who have failed to produce usable microfilm or to honor commitments made in previous requests, or who have had a previous permission to microfilm documents rescinded because of their conduct.

(i) NARA will not approve requests to microfilm documents in NARA facilities in which there is insufficient space available for private microfilming. NARA will not move documents from a facility lacking space for private microfilming to another NARA facility for that purpose.

(j) Federal agencies microfilming records in support of the agency's mission may use the space set aside for private microfilming. Agency microfilming takes precedence over private microfilming when there is insufficient space to accommodate both at the same time.

Citation: 36 CFR 1254.96

✍ § 1254.96 Microfilm preparation.

(a) As part of its evaluation of a request to microfilm documents, NARA will determine the amount of microfilm preparation that NARA must do before the documents can be microfilmed and the estimated cost of such preparation. The fees for microfilm preparation will be based on direct salary costs (including benefits) and supply costs when NARA staff performs the work. When the work is performed by a NARA contractor, the fees will be the cost to NARA. Microfilm preparation includes:

(1) Verifying or correcting the ,arrangement of documents after withdrawn items are inviewed and refiled when appropriate;

(2) Screening the documents for possible restrictions on use;

(3) Declassifying security classified documents;

(4) Removing document fasteners from documents when the fasteners can be removed without damage to the documents; and

(5) Taking any document conservation actions that must be accomplished in order to film the documents, such as documents flattening or mending.

(b) NARA will provide the requester detailed information on the fees for microfilm preparation in the letter of approval. Payment of fees will be made in accordance with § 1258.14 of this Chapter. When a body of documents will require extensive microfilm preparation, a different payment schedule may be established at the discretion of NARA.

Citation: 36 CFR 1254.98

✍ § 1254.98 Equipment standards.

(a) Equipment must be designed for the microfilming of documents in roll form or standard fiche form and be operable from a table top. Only planetary type camera equipment may be used. Automatic feed devices may not be used. Book cradles or other specialized equipment designed for use with bound volumes, oversized documents, or other formats will be approved by the Office of the National Archives on a case-by-case basis.

(b) The power consumption of the equipment normally must not exceed 1.2 kilowatts. Power normally available is 115 volts, 60 hz. Requests for electricity exceeding that normally available must be made at least 90 days in advance.

(c) Equipment having clamps or other devices to exert pressure upon or to affix the document to any surface in a way that might damage the document may not be used.

(d) The equipment must not use a heat generating light source in close enough proximity to the documents to result in their physical distortion or degradation. All sources of ultraviolet light must be filtered.

Citation: 36 CFR 1254.100

✍ § 1254.100 Microfilming procedures.

(a) Equipment used must conform to the equipment standards in 1254.98.

(b) Documents must be handled in accordance with the training and instructions provided by NARA personnel so that documents are not damaged during copying and so that their original order is maintained. Only persons who have attended NARA training will be permitted to handle the documents or supervise microfilming operations. Training will be offered only in Washington, DC.

(c) Documents from only one file unit may be microfilmed at a time.

(d) Documents may not be left unattended on the copying equipment or elsewhere.

(e) Under normal microfilming conditions, actual copying time per sheet must not exceed 30 seconds.

(f) Any lights used with the camera must be turned off when the camera is not in actual operation.

(g) Microfilm equipment may be operated only in the presence of the research room attendant or a designated NARA employee.

(h) The equipment normally should be in use each working day that it is in a NARA facility. The director of the NARA facility (as defined in § 1252.2 of this Chapter) will decide when equipment must be removed because of lack of regular use. The equipment must be promptly removed upon request of the facility director.

(i) NARA assumes no responsibility for loss or damage to microfilm equipment or supplies left unattended.

(j) NARA will inspect the microform output at scheduled intervals during the project to verify that the processed film meets the microfilm preparation and filming standards required by Part 1230 of this Chapter. To enable NARA to properly inspect the film, NARA must receive the film within 5 days after it has been processed. The person or organization producing the microfilm will provide NARA with a silver halide duplicate negative of the filmed records (see 1254.94(d)) according to the schedule shown in (k). If the processed film does not meet the standards, NARA may require that the records be refilmed.

(k) When 10,000 or fewer images are filmed, the person or organization producing the microfilm will provide NARA with a silver halide duplicate negative upon completion of the project. When the project involves more that 10,000 images, a silver halide duplicate negative of the first completed roll or segment of the project reproducing this image count will be provided to NARA for evaluation; subsequent completed segments of the project, in quantities approximating 100,000 or fewer images, will be provided to NARA within 30 days after filming unless NARA approved other arrangements.

Citation: 36 CFR 1254.102

✍ § 1254.102 Rescinding permission.

NARA may, at any time, rescind permission to microfilm records:

(a) If the person or organization fails to comply with the microfilming procedures in § 1254.100;

(b) If inspection of the processed microfilm reveals persistent problems with the quality of the filming or processing;

(c) If the person or organization fails to proceed with the microfilming or project as indicated in the request, or

(d) If the microfilming project is having an unanticipated adverse effect on the condition of the documents or the space set aside in the NARA facility for microfilming.

TITLE 37. PATENTS, TRADEMARKS, AND COPYRIGHTS

Agency: Department of Commerce
Patent and Trademark Office

PART 1. RULES OF PRACTICE IN PATENT CASES

Citation: 37 CFR 1.52

✍ § 1.52 Language, paper, writing, margins.

(a) The application, any amendments or corrections thereto, and the oath or declaration must be in the English language except as provided for in Sec. 1.69 and paragraph (d) of this section, or be accompanied by a verified translation of the application and a translation of any corrections or amendments into the English language. All papers which are to become a part of the permanent records of the Patent and Trademark Office must be legibly written either by a typewriter or mechanical printer in permanent dark ink or its equivalent in portrait orientation on flexible, strong, smooth, non-shiny, durable, and white paper. All of the application papers must be presented in a form having sufficient clarity and contrast between the paper and the writing thereon to permit the direct reproduction of readily legible copies in any number by use of photographic, electrostatic, photo-offset, and microfilming processes and electronic reproduction by use of digital imaging and optical character recognition. If the papers are not of the required quality, substitute typewritten or mechanically printed papers of suitable quality will be required. See Sec. 1.125 for filing substitute typewritten or mechanically printed papers constituting a substitute specification when required by the Office.

(b) Except for drawings, the application papers (specification, including claims, abstract, oath or declaration, and papers as provided for in this part and also papers subsequently filed, must have each page plainly written on only one side of a sheet of paper, with the claim or claims commencing on a separate sheet and the abstract commencing on a separate sheet. See Secs. 1.72(b) and 1.75(h). The sheets of paper must be the same size and either 21.0 cm. by 29.7 cm. (DIN size A4) or 21.6 cm. by 27.9 cm. (8 1/2 by 11 inches). Each sheet must include a top margin of at least 2.0 cm. (3/4 inch), a left side margin of at least 2.5 cm. (1 inch), a right side margin of at least 2.0 cm. (3/4 inch), and a bottom margin of at least 2.0 cm. (3/4 inch), and no holes should be made in the sheets as submitted. The lines of the specification, and any amendments to the specification, must be 1 1/2 or double spaced. The pages of the specification including claims and abstract must be numbered consecutively, starting with 1, the numbers being centrally located above or preferably, below, the text. See Sec. 1.84 for drawings.

* * * * *

Citation: 37 CFR 1.96

✍ § 1.96 Submission of computer program listings.

(a) *General.* Descriptions of the operation and general content of computer program listings should appear in the description portion of the specification. A computer program listing for the purpose of this section is defined as a printout that lists in appropriate sequence the instructions, routines, and other contents of a program for a computer. The program listing may be either in machine or machine-independent (object or source) language which will cause a computer to perform a desired procedure or task such as solve a problem, regulate the flow of work in a computer, or control or monitor events. Computer program listings may be submitted in patent applications as set forth in paragraphs (b) and (c) of this section.

(b) Material which will be printed in the patent. If the computer program listing is contained on ten printout pages or less, it must be submitted either as drawings or as part of the specification.

(1) *Drawings.* If the listing is submitted as drawings, it must be submitted in the manner and complying with the requirements for drawings as provided in Sec. 1.84. At least one figure numeral is required on each sheet of drawing.

(2) *Specification.* (i) If the listing is submitted as part of the specification, it must be submitted in accordance with the provisions of Sec. 1.52, at the end of the description but before the claims.

(ii) Any listing submitted as part of the specification must be direct printouts (i.e., not copies) from the computer's printer with dark solid black letters not less than 0.21 cm. high, on white, unshaded and unlined paper, and the sheets should be submitted in a protective cover. Any amendments must be made by way of submission of substitute sheets.

(c) As an appendix which will not be printed. If a computer program listing printout is eleven or more pages long, applicants must submit such listing in the form of microfiche, referred to in the specification (see Sec. 1.77(a)(6)). Such microfiche filed with a patent application is to be referred to as a "microfiche appendix." The "microfiche appendix" will not be part of the printed patent. Reference in the application to the "microfiche appendix" must be made at the beginning of the specification at the location indicated in Sec. 1.77(a)(6). Any amendments thereto must be made by way of revised microfiche.

(1) *Availability of appendix.* Such computer program listings on microfiche will be available to the public for inspection, and microfiche copies thereof will be available for purchase with the file wrapper and contents, after a patent based on such application is granted or the application is otherwise made publicly available.

(2) *Submission requirements.* Except as modified or clarified in this paragraph (c)(2), computer-generated information submitted as a "microfiche appendix" to an application shall be in accordance with the standards set forth in 36 CFR part 1230 (Micrographics).

(i) Film submitted shall be a first generation (camera film) negative appearing microfiche (with emulsion on the back side of the film when viewed with the images right-reading).

(ii) Reduction ratio of microfiche submitted should be 24:1 or a similar ratio where variation from said ratio is required in order to fit the documents into the image area of the microfiche format used.

(iii) At least the left-most third (50 mm. x 12 mm.) of the header or title area of each microfiche submitted shall be clear or positive appearing so that the Patent and Trademark Office can apply an application number and filing date thereto in an eye-readable form. The middle portion of the header shall be used by applicant to apply an eye-readable application identification such as the title and/or the first inventor's name. The attorney's docket number may be included. The final right-hand portion of the microfiche shall contain sequence information for the microfiche, such as 1 of 4, 2 of 4, etc.

(iv) Additional requirements which apply specifically to microfiche of filmed paper copy:

(A) The first frame of each microfiche submitted shall contain a test target.

(B) The second frame of each microfiche submitted must contain a fully descriptive title and the inventor's name as filed.

(C) The pages or lines appearing on the microfiche frames

should be consecutively numbered.

(D) Pagination of the microfiche frames shall be from left to right and from top to bottom.

(E) At a reduction of 24:1, resolution of the original microfilm shall be at least 120 lines per mm. (5.0 target).

(F) An index, when included, should appear in the last frame (lower right-hand corner when data is right-reading) of each microfiche.

(v) Microfiche generated by Computer Output Microfilm.

(A) The first frame of each microfiche submitted should contain a resolution test frame.

(B) The second frame of each microfiche submitted must contain a fully descriptive title and the inventor's name as filed.

(C) The pages or lines appearing on the microfiche frames should be consecutively numbered.

(D) It is preferred that pagination of the microfiche frames be from left to right and top to bottom but the alternative, i.e., from top to bottom and from left to right, is also acceptable.

(E) An index, when included, should appear on the last frame (lower right-hand corner when data is right-reading) of each microfiche.

Agency: **Department of Commerce**
Assistant Secretary for Technology Policy

PART 401. RIGHTS TO INVENTIONS MADE BY NONPROFIT ORGANIZATIONS AND SMALL BUSINESS FIRMS UNDER GOVERNMENT GRANTS, CONTRACTS, AND COOPERATIVE AGREEMENTS

Citation: **37 CFR 401.2**

✍ **§ 401.2 Definitions.**

* * * * *

(k) The term electronically filed means any submission of information transmitted by an electronic or optical-electronic system.

(l) The term electronic or optical-electronic system means a software-based system approved by the agency for the transmission of information.

* * * * *

Citation: **37 CFR 401.16**

✍ **§ 401.16 Electronic filing.**

Unless otherwise requested or directed by the agency,

(a) the written report required in (c)(1) of the standard clause in § 401.14(a) may be electronically filed;

(b) the written election required in (c)(2) of the standard clause in § 401.14(a) may be electronically filed; and

(c) the close-out report in (f)(1) and the information identified in (f)(2) and (f)(3) of § 401.5 may be electronically filed.

TITLE 40— PROTECTION OF ENVIRONMENT

Agency: **Environmental Protection Agency**

SUBCHAPTER C. AIR PROGRAMS

PART 58. AMBIENT AIR QUALITY SURVEILLANCE

Subpart A.General Provisions

Citation: **40 CFR 58.1**

✍ **§ 58.1 Definitions.**

* * * * *

(p) *Aerometric Information Retrieval System (AIRS) — Air Quality Subsystem (AQS)* is EPA's computerized system for storing and reporting of information relating to ambient air quality data.

(q) *Storage and Retrieval of Aerometric Data (SAROAD)* system is a computerized system which stores and reports information relating to ambient air quality. The SAROAD system has been replaced with the AIRS-AQS system; however, the SAROAD data reporting format continues to be used by some States and local air pollution agencies as an interface to AIRS on an interim basis.

* * * * *

Subpart C. State and Local Air Monitoring Stations (SLAMS)

Citation: **40 CFR 58.28**

✍ **§ 58.28 SLAMS data submittal.**

The State shall submit all of the SLAMS data according to the same data submittal requirements as defined for NAMS in section 58.35. The State shall also submit any portion or all of the SLAMS data to the appropriate Regional Administrator upon request.

Subpart D. National Air Monitoring Stations (NAMS)

Citation: **40 CFR 58.35**

✍ **§ 58.35 NAMS data submittal.**

(a) The requirements of this section apply to those stations designated as both SLAMS and NAMS by the network description required by § § 58.20 and 58.30.

(b) The State shall report to the Administrator all ambient air quality data for SO_2, CO, O3, NO_2, Pb, and PM-10 and information specified by the AIRS Users Guide (Volume II, Air Quality Data Coding, and Volume III, Air Quality Data Storage) to be coded into the AIRS-AQS format. Such air quality data and information must be submitted directly to the AIRS-AQS via either electronic transmission or magnetic tape, in the format of the AIRS-AQS, and in accordance with the quarterly schedule described in paragraph (c) of this section.

(c) The specific quarterly reporting periods are January 1-March 31, April 1-June 30, July 1-September 30, and October 1-December 31. The data and information reported for each reporting period must:

(1) Contain all data and information gathered during the reporting period.

(2) Be received in the AIRS-AQS within 90 days after the end of the quarterly reporting period. For example, the data for the reporting period January 1-March 31, 1994 are due on or before June 30, 1994.

(d) Air quality data submitted for each reporting period must be edited, validated, and entered into the AIRS-AQS for updating (within the time limits specified in paragraph (c) of this section) pursuant to appropriate AIRS-AQS procedures. The procedures for editing and validating data are described in the AIRS Users Guide, Volume II Air Quality Data Coding.

(e) This section does not permit a State to exempt those SLAMS which are also designated as NAMS from all or any of the reporting requirements applicable to SLAMS in Section 58.26.

PART 60. STANDARDS OF PERFORMANCE FOR NEW STATIONARY SOURCES

Subpart WWW. Standards of Performance for Municipal Solid Waste Landfills

Citation: **40 CFR 60.758**

✍ § 60.758 Recordkeeping requirements.

Except as provided in § 60.752(b)(2)(i)(B),

(a) Each owner or operator of an MSW landfill subject to the provisions of § 60.752(b) shall keep for at least 5 years up-to-date, readily accessible, on-site records of the maximum design capacity, the current amount of solid waste in-place, and the year-by-year waste acceptance rate. Off-site records may be maintained if they are retrievable within 4 hours. Either paper copy or electronic formats are acceptable.

(b) Each owner or operator of a controlled landfill shall keep up-to-date, readily accessible records for the life of the control equipment of the data listed in paragraphs (b)(1) through (b)(4) of this section as measured during the initial performance test or compliance determination. Records of subsequent tests or monitoring shall be maintained for a minimum of 5 years. Records of the control device vendor specifications shall be maintained until removal.

(1) Where an owner or operator subject to the provisions of this subpart seeks to demonstrate compliance with § 60.752(b)(2)(ii):

(i) The maximum expected gas generation flow rate as calculated in § 60.755(a)(1). The owner or operator may use another method to determine the maximum gas generation flow rate, if the method has been approved by the Administrator.

(ii) The density of wells, horizontal collectors, surface collectors, or other gas extraction devices determined using the procedures specified in § 60.759(a)(1).

(2) Where an owner or operator subject to the provisions of this subpart seeks to demonstrate compliance with § 60.752(b)(2)(iii) through use of an enclosed combustion device other than a boiler or process heater with a design heat input capacity greater than 44 megawatts:

(i) The average combustion temperature measured at least every 15 minutes and averaged over the same time period of the performance test.

(ii) The percent reduction of NMOC determined as specified in § 60.752(b)(2)(iii)(B) achieved by the control device.

(3) Where an owner or operator subject to the provisions of this subpart seeks to demonstrate compliance with § 60.752(b)(2)(iii)(B)(1) through use of a boiler or process heater of any size: a description of the location at which the collected gas vent stream is introduced into the boiler or process heater over the same time period of the performance testing.

(4) Where an owner or operator subject to the provisions of this subpart seeks to demonstrate compliance with § 60.752(b)(2)(iii)(A) through use of an open flare, the flare type (i.e., steam-assisted, air-assisted, or nonassisted), all visible emission readings, heat content determination, flow rate or bypass flow rate measurements, and exit velocity determinations made during the performance test as specified in § 60.18; continuous records of the flare pilot flame or flare flame monitoring and records of all periods of operations during which the pilot flame of the flare flame is absent.

(c) Each owner or operator of a controlled landfill subject to the provisions of this subpart shall keep for 5 years up-to-date, readily accessible continuous records of the equipment operating parameters specified to be monitored in § 60.756 as well as up-to-date, readily accessible records for periods of operation during which the parameter boundaries established during the most recent performance test are exceeded.

(1) The following constitute exceedances that shall be recorded and reported under § 60.757(f):

(i) For enclosed combustors except for boilers and process heaters with design heat input capacity of 44 megawatts (150 million British thermal unit per hour) or greater, all 3-hour periods of operation during which the average combustion temperature was more than 28 oC below the average combustion temperature during the most recent performance test at which compliance with § 60.752(b)(2)(iii) was determined.

(ii) For boilers or process heaters, whenever there is a change in the location at which the vent stream is introduced into the flame zone as required under paragraph (b)(3)(i) of this section.

(2) Each owner or operator subject to the provisions of this subpart shall keep up-to-date, readily accessible continuous records of the indication of flow to the control device or the indication of bypass flow or records of monthly inspections of car-seals or lock-and-key configurations used to seal bypass lines, specified under § 60.756.

(3) Each owner or operator subject to the provisions of this subpart who uses a boiler or process heater with a design heat input capacity of 44 megawatts or greater to comply with § 60.752(b)(2)(iii) shall keep an up-to-date, readily accessible record of all periods of operation of the boiler or process heater. (Examples of such records could include records of steam use, fuel use, or monitoring data collected pursuant to other State, local, Tribal, or Federal regulatory requirements.)

(4) Each owner or operator seeking to comply with the provisions of this subpart by use of an open flare shall keep up-to-date, readily accessible continuous records of the flame or flare pilot flame monitoring specified under § 60.756(c), and up-to-date, readily accessible records of all periods of operation in which the flame or flare pilot flame is absent.

(d) Each owner or operator subject to the provisions of this subpart shall keep for the life of the collection system an up-to-date, readily accessible plot map showing each existing and planned collector in the system and providing a unique identification location label for each collector.

(1) Each owner or operator subject to the provisions of this subpart shall keep up-to-date, readily accessible records of the installation date and location of all newly installed collectors as specified under § 60.755(b).

(2) Each owner or operator subject to the provisions of this subpart shall keep readily accessible documentation of the nature, date of deposition, amount, and location of asbestos-containing or nondegradable waste excluded from collection as provided in § 60.759(a)(3)(i) as well as any nonproductive areas excluded from collection as provided in § 60.759(a)(3)(ii).

(e) Each owner or operator subject to the provisions of this subpart shall keep for at least 5 years up-to-date, readily accessible records of all collection and control system exceedances of the operational standards in § 60.753, the reading in the subsequent month whether or not the second reading is an exceedance, and the location of each exceedance.

PART 63. NATIONAL EMISSION STANDARDS FOR HAZARDOUS AIR POLLUTANTS FOR SOURCE CATEGORIES

Citation: 40 CFR 63.642

✍ **§ 63.642 General standards.**

(a) Each owner or operator of a source subject to this subpart is required to apply for a part 70 or part 71 operating permit from the appropriate permitting authority. If the EPA has approved a State operating permit program under part 70, the permit shall be obtained from the State authority. If the State operating permit program has not been approved, the source shall apply to the EPA Regional Office pursuant to part 71.

(b) [Reserved]

(c) Table 6 of this subpart specifies the provisions of subpart A of this part that apply and those that do not apply to owners and operators of sources subject to this subpart.

(d) Initial performance tests and initial compliance determinations shall be required only as specified in this subpart.

(1) Performance tests and compliance determinations shall be conducted according to the schedule and procedures specified in this subpart.

(2) The owner or operator shall notify the Administrator of the intention to conduct a performance test at least 30 days before the performance test is scheduled.

(3) Performance tests shall be conducted according to the provisions of § 63.7(e) except that performance tests shall be conducted at maximum representative operating capacity for the process. During the performance test, an owner or operator shall operate the control device at either maximum or minimum representative operating conditions for monitored control device parameters, whichever results in lower emission reduction.

(4) Data shall be reduced in accordance with the EPA-approved methods specified in the applicable section or, if other test methods are used, the data and methods shall be validated according to the protocol in Method 301 of appendix A of this part.

(e) Each owner or operator of a source subject to this subpart shall keep copies of all applicable reports and records required by this subpart for at least 5 years except as otherwise specified in this subpart. All applicable records shall be maintained in such a manner that they can be readily accessed within 24 hours. Records may be maintained in hard copy or computer-readable form including, but not limited to, on paper, microfilm, computer, floppy disk, magnetic tape, or microfiche.

(f) All reports required under this subpart shall be sent to the Administrator at the addresses listed in § 63.13 of subpart A of this part. If acceptable to both the Administrator and the owner or operator of a source, reports may be submitted on electronic media.

* * * * *

PART 75. CONTINUOUS EMISSION MONITORING

Citation: 40 CFR 75.16

✍ **§ 75.16 Special provisions for monitoring emissions from common, bypass, and multiple stacks for SO_2 emissions and heat input determinations.**

(a) * * *

(2) * * *

(ii) * * *

(B) Install, certify, operate, and maintain an SO_2 continuous emission monitoring system and flow monitoring system in the duct from each Phase II or nonaffected unit; calculate SO_2 mass emissions from the Phase I units as the difference between SO_2 mass emissions measured in e common stack and SO_2 mass emissions measured in the ducts of the Phase II and nonaffected units; record and report the calculated SO_2 mass emissions from the Phase I units, not to be reported as an hourly average value less than zero; and combine emissions for the Phase I units for compliance purposes; or

(C) Install, certify, operate, and maintain an SO_2 continuous emission monitoring system and flow monitoring system in the duct from each Phase I or nonaffected unit; calculate SO_2 mass emissions from the Phase II units as the difference between SO_2 mass emissions measured in the common stack and SO_2 mass emissions measured in the ducts of the Phase I and nonaffected units, not to be reported as an hourly average value less than zero; and combine emissions for the Phase II units for recordkeeping and compliance purposes; or

* * * * *

(b) * * *

(2) * * *

(ii) * * *

(B) Install, certify, operate, and maintain an SO_2 continuous emission monitoring system and flow monitoring system in the duct from each nonaffected unit; determine SO_2 mass emissions from the affected units as the difference between SO_2 mass emissions measured in the common stack and SO_2 mass emissions measured in the ducts of the nonaffected units, not to be reported as an hourly average value less than zero; and combine emissions for the Phase I and Phase II affected units for recordkeeping and compliance purposes; or

* * * * *

(e) * * *

(5) The owner or operator of an affected unit with a diluent monitor and a flow monitor installed on a common stack to determine heat input at the common stack may choose to apportion the heat input from the common stack to each affected unit utilizing the common stack by using either of the following two methods, provided that all of the units utilizing the common stack are combusting fuel with the same F-factor found in section 3 of appendix F of this part. The heat input may be apportioned either by using the ratio of load (in MWe) for each individual unit to the total load for all units utilizing the common stack or by using the ratio of steam flow (in 1000 lb/hr) for each individual unit to the total steam flow for all units utilizing the common stack.

Citation: 40 CFR 75.32

✍ **§ 75.32 Determination of monitoring data availability for standard missing data procedures.**

(a) * * *

(3) The owner or operator shall include all unit operating

hours, and all monitor operating hours for which quality-assured data were recorded by a certified primary monitor; a certified redundant or non-redundant backup monitor or a reference method for that unit; or by an approved alternative monitoring system under subpart E of this part when calculating percent monitor data availability using Equation 8 or 9. No hours from more than three years (26,280 clock hours) earlier shall be used in Equation 9. For a unit that has accumulated less than 8,760 unit operating hours in the previous three years (26,280 clock hours), replace the words "during previous 8,760 unit operating hours" in Equation 9 with "in the previous three years" and replace "8,760" with "total unit operating hours in the previous three years." The owner or operator of a unit with an SO_2 monitoring system shall, when SO_2 emissions are determined in accordance with Secs. 75.11(e)(1) or (e)(2), exclude hours in which a unit combusts only natural gas (or gaseous fuel with a sulfur content no greater than natural gas) from calculations of percent monitor data availability for SO_2 pollutant concentration monitors, as provided in Sec. 75.30(d).

* * * * *

Citation: 40 CFR 75.55

✍ § 75.55 General recordkeeping provisions for specific situations.

* * * * *

(b) * * *

(3) For units with add-on SO_2 or NO_x emission controls following the provisions of Secs. 75.34 (a)(1) or (a)(2), the owner or operator shall, for each hour of missing SO_2 or NO_x emission data, record:

(i) Parametric data which demonstrate the proper operation of the add-on emission controls, as described in the quality assurance/quality control program for the unit. The parametric data shall be maintained on site, and shall be submitted upon request to the Administrator, an EPA Regional office, State, or local agency;

(ii) A flag indicating either that the add-on emission controls are operating properly, as evidenced by all parameters being within the ranges specified in the quality assurance/quality control program, or that the add-on emission controls are not operating properly;

* * * * *

(e) Specific SO_2 emission record provisions during the combustion of gaseous fuel.

(1) If SO_2 emissions are determined in accordance with the provisions in Sec. 75.11(e)(2) during hours in which only natural gas (or gaseous fuel with a sulfur content no greater than natural gas) is combusted in a unit with an SO_2 continuous emission monitoring system, the owner or operator shall record the information in paragraph (c)(3) of this section in lieu of the information in Secs. 75.54 (c)(1) and (c)(3), for those hours.

(2) The provisions of this paragraph apply to a unit which, in accordance with the provisions of Sec. 75.11(e)(3) uses an SO_2 continuous emission monitoring system to determine SO2 emissions during hours in which only natural gas or gaseous fuel with a sulfur content no greater than natural gas is combusted in the unit. If the unit sometimes burns only natural gas (or gaseous fuel with a sulfur content no greater than natural gas) as a primary and/or backup fuel, and at other times combusts higher-sulfur fuels such as coal or oil as primary and/or backup fuel(s), then the owner or operator shall keep records on-site, suitable for inspection, of the type(s) of fuel(s) burned during each period of missing SO_2 data, and the number of hours that each type of fuel was combusted in the unit during each missing data period. This recordkeeping requirement does not apply to an affected unit that burns natural gas (or gaseous fuel with a sulfur content no greater than natural gas) exclusively, nor does it apply to a unit that burns such gaseous fuel(s) only during unit startup.

* * * * *

Citation: 40 CFR 75.56

✍ § 75.56 Certification, quality assurance and, quality control record provisions.

* * * * *

(c) For units with add-on SO_2 and NO_x emission controls following the provisions of Secs. 75.34(a)(1) or (a)(2), the owner or operator shall keep the following records on-site in the quality assurance/quality control plan required by section 1 in appendix B of this part:

(1) A list of operating parameters for the add-on emission controls, including parameters in Sec. 75.55 (b), appropriate to the particular installation of add-on emission controls; and

(2) The range of each operating parameter in the list that indicates the add-on emission controls are properly operating.

(d) The owner or operator shall meet the requirements of paragraphs (a) and (b) of this section on and after January 1, 1996. The owner or operator shall meet the requirements of paragraph (c) of this section on and after January 1, 1998.

Subpart G. Reporting Requirements

Citation: 40 CFR Part 75 Appendix A

✍ Appendix A to Part 75

* * * * *

4. Data Acquisition and Handling Systems

* * * * *

For an excepted monitoring system under appendix D or E of this part, data acquisition and handling systems shall:

(1) Read and record the full range of fuel flowrate through the upper range value;

(2) Calculate and record intermediate values necessary to obtain emissions, such as mass fuel flowrate and heat input rate;

(3) Calculate and record emissions in units of the standard (lb/hr of SO_2, lb/mmBtu of NO_x);

(4) Predict and record NO_x emission rate using the heat input rate and the NO_x/heat input correlation developed under appendix E of this part;

(5) Calculate and record all missing data substitution values specified in appendix D or E of this part; and

(6) Provide a continuous, permanent record of all measurements and required information as an ASCII flat file capable of transmission via an IBM-compatible personal computer diskette or other electronic media.

* * * * *

Citation:	40 CFR Part 75 Appendix B

✍ Appendix B to Part 75. Quality Assurance and Quality Control Procedures

1. Quality Control Program

* * * * *

1.6 Parametric Monitoring for Units With Add-On Emission Controls

The owner or operator shall keep a written (or electronic) record including a list of operating parameters for the add-on SO_2 or NO_x emission controls, including parameters in Sec. 75.55(b), and the range of each operating parameter that indicates the add-on emission controls are operating properly.

The owner or operator shall keep a written (or electronic) record of the parametric monitoring data during each hour of each SO_2 or NO_x missing data period.

* * * * *

PART 80. REGULATION OF FUELS AND FUEL ADDITIVES

Terms and Conditions Memorandum for Submission of Reformulated Gasoline (RFG) and Anti-Dumping Reports via Electronic Data Interchange (EDI)

I. Introduction

A. EDI, Defined

Electronic Data Interchange (EDI) is the transmission, in a standard syntax, of unambiguous information between computers of independent organizations.

B. Acceptance of Electronically Submitted Reports in Lieu of Paper Documents, Generally

Under the reporting provisions for the reformulated gasoline (RFG) and anti-dumping program at 40 CFR 80.75(n) and 80.105(d), reports shall be "submitted on forms and following procedures specified by the Administrator" by a specified date and shall be signed and certified as correct by either the owner or a responsible corporate officer[1] of the reporting entity.

EPA has announced its intent to permit RFG and anti-dumping reporting via EDI (as substitution for paper reports) in the Federal Register notice and will accept such electronically filed reports provided the reporting party signs and abides by the provisions of the "Terms and Conditions Memorandum for Submission of Reformulated Gasoline (RFG) and Anti-Dumping Reports via Electronic Data Interchange (EDI)" (hereafter referred to as the "Terms and Conditions Memorandum" or simply as "this memorandum"). The Federal Register notice is part and parcel to this Memorandum and is incorporated herein by reference.

The technical requirements are contained in "Reformulated Gasoline and Anti-Dumping Program Electronic Data Interchange Technical Guideline," (hereafter referred to as the "technical guidance document") which is part and parcel to this memorandum and is incorporated herein by reference. (This memorandum, the Federal Register notice, and the technical guidance are sometimes collectively referred to as "the agreement.")

From time to time and due to technological change or technical necessity, EPA may update the technical guidance document. EPA will provide reasonable notice of any such changes to the reporting party.

C. Standards for Documents

The reporting party who has signed the Terms and Conditions Memorandum may electronically transmit to EPA any of the transaction sets for RFG and the anti-dumping program. These transaction sets are identified in the technical guidance document. The reporting party must use only those transaction sets approved for general use by the American National Standards Institute (ANSI) Accredited Standards Committee (ASC) X.12.

D. System Requirements

Reporting parties who wish to submit reports via EDI are responsible for maintaining the equipment, software, services, and testing necessary to effectively and reliably transmit and receive documents. The reporting party may use the EPA VAN or a VAN interconnected with the EPA VAN. The current EPA VAN is identified in the technical guidance.

E. Security Procedures

EPA and the reporting party must protect electronic data and Personal Identification Numbers (PINs) from unauthorized access, alteration, loss, destruction and/or disclosure to ensure, at a minimum, the same level of protection required for paper documents. This protection must extend beyond the transactions themselves to any files or data bases that contain information conveyed via EDI.

In order to reasonably protect electronically submitted reports, EPA will maintain security procedures to protect data and messages against the risk of unauthorized access, alteration, loss or destruction. All information claimed by the reporting party as "confidential business information" party will be subject to additional safeguards and procedures consistent with 40 CFR Part 2 and with established Agency procedures for protection of such information. It is the responsibility of a responsible corporate officer of the reporting party to provide, in writing and on company letterhead, a list of those authorized representatives to receive individual PINs and to identify a responsible corporate officer to receive the company PIN. EPA will only issue PINs to the responsible corporate officer and such properly designated authorized representatives. It is the responsibility of a responsible corporate officer of the reporting party to notify EPA in writing and on company letterhead of any changes which necessitate changes, deletions, or issuance of [a] new individual or company PIN[s]. The reporting party agrees to use all reasonable efforts to maintain the confidentiality of PINs.

F. Failure to Conduct EDI

Circumstances may arise which render the reporting party unable to submit RFG and anti-dumping reports via EDI. Such circumstances may include, but are not limited to, so-called "acts of God."

Nothing herein is intended to relieve the reporting party of the obligation to file a timely report. If a report cannot be filed in a timely manner via EDI, then the reporting party must submit a paper document as required by 40 CFR 80.75 and 80.105.

II. Subject Responsible corporate officer:

Reporting party:(Company name as registered with EPA)

EPA RFG Company Registration number:

Corporate Address:(as registered with EPA)

(List of facilities who will report via EDI to be included in Part V, below.)

III. Terms and Conditions

The reporting party who has signed this Terms and Conditions Memorandum to submit reports via EDI, agrees to use only those transaction sets approved for general use by the American National Standards Institute ("ANSI") Accredited Standards Committee ("ASC") X.12 and in accordance with the requirements of the technical guidance and the Federal Register notice. The reporting party further agrees:

(a) That both company and individual PINs shall be included on each and every report submitted and that such inclusion of the PINs constitutes the signature and certification that the report is correct within the meaning of 40 CFR 80.75(n)(2) and 80.105(d)(3) for that report and constitutes a "signed document" within the meaning of this Memorandum.

(b) That electronically submitted RFG reports (i.e., RFG reports submitted via EDI) are equivalent to, and in substitution for, paper documents and that any document properly transmitted pursuant to this Memorandum, the technical guidance, and the Federal Register notice, shall be considered to be a "writing" or "in writing," and any such document when containing, or to which there is affixed, a signature ("signed documents") shall be deemed for all purposes to have been "signed" and to constitute an "original" when printed from electronic files or records established and maintained in the normal course of business.

(c) Not to contest the validity or enforceability of signed documents under the provisions of any applicable law relating to whether certain agreements are to be in writing or signed by the party to be bound thereby. Signed documents, if introduced into evidence on paper in any judicial, arbitration, mediation or administrative proceedings, will be admissible as between the parties to the same extent and under the same conditions as other business records originated and maintained in documentary form. Neither party shall contest the admissibility of copies of signed documents under either the business records exception to the hearsay rule or the best evidence rule on the basis that the signed documents were not originated or maintained in documentary form.

(d) To provide and maintain the equipment, software, services, and testing necessary to effectively and reliably transmit and receive documents and to accept responsibility for interfacing the EDI application to the EDI system and be responsible for all problems at the application level, including, but not limited to, wrong or missing fields or wrong data in fields.

(e) To safeguard electronic data from tampering and unauthorized disclosure to ensure, at a minimum, the same level of protection required for paper documents.

(f) To safeguard Personal Identification Numbers (PINs) and to notify EPA of any loss of or compromising of a PIN[2] and to treat all individual PINs as non-transferrable. EPA will issue no PINs without the written request of a responsible corporate officer on letterhead, consistent with the requirements of Paragraph V, below.

(g) That no document will be considered to have been received by EPA until it is accessible to EPA at its receipt computer. No document shall be of any legal effect until it is received. Upon receipt of any report, EPA will promptly (i.e., within five [5] business days) and properly submit a functional acknowledgment in return. The functional acknowledgment will constitute conclusive evidence that a report has been properly received by EPA. If a functional acknowledgment is not received in return for a document transmitted to EPA, then the reporting party who transmitted the document shall be responsible for re-sending the document.

(h) To retransmit any document for which a functional acknowledgment was not received. Such re-transmission is to occur within five (5) days of request by EPA.

(i) To maintain records and archives of documents sent and received for not less than five (5) years[3] Such archives must include a complete record of the data interchanged representing the messages between the parties (i.e., the transaction or data log).

(j) To promptly notify EPA of any inability to properly conduct EDI[4] and to file paper reports on forms provided by EPA or under circumstances where an electronic report cannot be filed by the applicable regulatory deadline.

(k) To notify EPA, in writing, of any information for which the party claims business confidentiality.[5]

IV. Acceptance and Duration of Agreement

This Memorandum and the Federal Register notice and the technical guidance constitute the complete agreement of the parties relating to the matters specified in this agreement and supersede all prior representations or agreements, whether oral or written, with respect to such matters. No oral modification or waiver of any of the provisions of this agreement shall be binding on either party. As the parties develop additional capabilities respecting EDI, additional addenda may be added to this agreement. Each addendum shall be signed and dated by both the reporting party and EPA. The date of the last signature shall be the effective data, and each addendum shall be appended to this agreement. This agreement is for the benefit of, and shall be binding upon, the reporting party and its respective successors and assigns.

Acceptance by the reporting party of this Terms and Conditions Memorandum is upon return of the original agreement, signed by a responsible corporate officer, to the Director, Field Operations and Support Division (6406J), Environmental Protection Agency, 401 M Street SW., Washington, DC 20460.

This Terms and Conditions memorandum is effective upon the date indicated in Section VII, below. The agreement shall remain in effect until terminated by either the reporting party or EPA. Termination shall require 30 days written notice, specifying the effective date of the termination. If the reporting party wishes to terminate this agreement, written notice shall be sent to the Director, Field Operations and Support Division, at the above listed address. Such written notice shall be on company letterhead and signed by a responsible corporate officer.

Any termination shall not affect the respective obligations or rights of the parties arising under this Memorandum or the Federal Register notice and technical guidance document, which are part and parcel to this Memorandum. Termination of this agreement shall not affect any action required to complete or implement Messages which are sent prior to such termination. Emergency temporary termination of computer connections may be made to protect data from illegal access or other incidental damage.

V. List of Reporting Facilities and Authorized Representatives to Receive Individual PINs

The responsible corporate officer agrees to submit in writing, on company letterhead, a list of "Authorized Representatives" to submit reformulated gasoline and anti-dumping reports and the facilities for which these representatives are authorized to reports. Such list shall include appropriate company and facility identification number(s) (issued by EPA), as well as the address, phone number, and title of each authorized representative. All requests for changes or deletions of company or individual PINs or changes in authorized representatives must be submitted in writing, on company letterhead, and signed by a responsible corporate officer.

VI. Confidential Business Information

Some information required to be submitted under "Table 2" or "the detail area" of the transaction sets, as identified in the technical guidance may be claimed as business confidential by the reporting party. The responsible corporate officer representing the reporting party may claim confidentiality as to "Table 2" or "detail area" information for those reports required to be filed for calendar year 1995 by initialing this clause. A reporting party may also notify EPA of a claim of confidentiality in a separate writing addressed to the Director, Field Operations and Support Division, 401 M Street, SW. (6406-J), Washington, DC 20460. Beginning with the report due on May 31, 1996, parties will be able to claim business confidentiality through the electronic reporting format. The reporting party will receive timely notice of such procedures, which will be included in an update to the technical guidance document.

Initials of Responsible Corporate Officer

VII. Acceptance

The terms and conditions set forth above are hereby accepted and agreed to by the Reporting Party. Upon receipt of this properly signed Terms and Conditions Memorandum and the list of reporting facilities and authorized representatives, EPA will issue PINs and accept electronic reports from the Reporting Party.

Signature of Responsible Corporate Officer

Printed/Typed Name of Responsible Corporate Officer

Company Name

Date

The statutory authority for today's notice is granted to EPA by § § 211(c) and (k) and § 301(a) of the Clean Air Act as amended, 42 U.S.C. 7545(c) and (k) and 7601(a)

[1] The term "responsible corporate officer" as used here, means an officer of the corporation as defined by the incorporation laws of the state in which the corporation is incorporated or a representative of the corporation who has been delegated the authority in writing to certify RFG and Anti-dumping reports by such a responsible corporate officer.

[2] EPA will promptly issue within fourteen (14) business days a new PIN upon request of the regulated party.

[3] Examples of documents sent and received include all outgoing transmissions and incoming functional acknowledgments.

[4] Notification does not relieve the party of any reporting requirements under the RFG regulation.

[5] EPA recognizes that information required to be submitted under "Table 2" or "the detail area" of the transaction sets may be claimed as business confidential by the reporting party. For reports due for calendar year 1995, the party may claim confidentiality for the information contained in "Table 2" or "the detail area" by initialing the clause in Section VI. Beginning with the report due May 31, 1996, the party must claim confidentiality with respect to each EDI submission.

Citation: 40 CFR 80.157

✍ § 80.157 Volumetric additive reconciliation (VAR), equipment calibration, and recordkeeping requirements under the interim detergent program.

This section contains requirements for automated detergent blending facilities and hand-blending detergent facilities. All gasolines and all PRC intended for use in gasoline must be additized, unless otherwise noted in supporting VAR records, and must be accounted for in VAR records. The VAR reconciliation standard is attained under this section when the actual concentration of detergent used per VAR formula record equals or exceeds the lowest additive concentration (LAC) specified for that detergent pursuant to Sec. 80.141(c)(3), or, if appropriate, under Sec. 80.141(d). A separate VAR formula record must be created for leaded gasoline additized with a detergent registered for use only with leaded gasoline, or used at a concentration that is registered as effective for leaded gasoline only. Detergent so used must be accurately and separately measured, either through the use of a separate storage tank, a separate meter, or some other measurement system that is able to accurately distinguish its use. Recorded volumes of gasoline, detergent, and PRC must be expressed to the nearest gallon (or smaller units), except that detergent volumes of five gallons or less must be expressed to the nearest tenth of a gallon (or smaller units). However, if the blender's equipment cannot accurately measure to the nearest tenth of a gallon, then such volumes must be rounded downward to the next lower gallon. PRC included in the reconciliation must be identified. Each VAR formula record must also contain the following information:

(a) *Automated blending facilities*. In the case of an automated detergent blending facility, for each VAR period, for each detergent storage system and each detergent in that storage system, the following must be recorded:

(1) The manufacturer and commercial identifying name of the detergent additive package being reconciled, and the LAC specified in the detergent registration for use with the applicable type of gasoline (i.e., unleaded or leaded). The LAC must be expressed in terms of gallons of detergent per thousand gallons of gasoline or PRC, and expressed to four digits. If the specified LAC is only effective for use with leaded gasoline, the record must so indicate. If the detergent storage system which is the subject of the VAR formula record is a proprietary system under the control of a customer, this fact must be indicated on the record.

(2) The total volume of detergent blended into gasoline and PRC, in accordance with one of the following paragraphs, as applicable.

(i) For a facility which uses in-line meters to measure detergent usage, the total volume of detergent measured, together with supporting data which includes one of the following: the beginning and ending meter readings for each meter being measured, the metered batch volume measurements for each meter being measured, or other comparable metered measurements. The supporting data may be supplied on the VAR formula record or in the form of computer printouts or other comparable VAR supporting documentation.

(ii) For a facility which uses a gauge to measure the inventory of the detergent storage tank, the total volume of detergent shall be calculated from the following equation:

Detergent Volume=(A)-(B)+(C)-(D)

Where:

A=Initial detergent inventory of the tank

B=Final detergent inventory of the tank

C=Sum of any additions to detergent inventory

D=Sum of any withdrawals from detergent inventory for purposes other than the additization of gasoline or PRC.

The value of each variable in this equation must be separately recorded on the VAR formula record. In addition, a list of each detergent addition included in variable C and a list of each detergent withdrawal included in variable D must be provided, either on the formula record or as VAR supporting documentation.

(3) The total volume of gasoline plus PRC to which detergent has been added, together with supporting data which includes one of the following: The beginning and ending meter measurements for each meter being measured, the metered batch volume measurements for each meter being measured, or other comparable metered measurements. The supporting data may be supplied on the VAR formula record or in the form of computer printouts or other comparable VAR supporting documentation. If gasoline has intentionally been overadditized in anticipation of the later addition of unadditized PRC, then the total volume of gasoline plus PRC recorded must include the expected amount of unadditized PRC to be added later. In addition, the amount of gasoline which was overadditized for this purpose must be specified.

(4) The actual detergent concentration, calculated as the total volume of detergent added (pursuant to paragraph (a)(2) of this section), divided by the total volume of gasoline plus PRC (pursuant to paragraph (a)(3) of this section). The concentration must be calculated and recorded to four digits.

(5) A list of each detergent concentration rate initially set for the detergent that is the subject of the VAR record, together with the date and description of each adjustment to any initially set concentration. The concentration adjustment information may be supplied on the VAR formula record or in the form of computer printouts or other comparable VAR supporting documentation. No concentration setting is permitted below the applicable LAC, except as may be modified pursuant to Sec.

80.141(d) or as described in paragraph (a)(7) of this section.

(6) The dates of the VAR period, which shall be no longer than thirty-one days. If the VAR period is contemporaneous with a calendar month, then specifying the month will fulfill this requirement; if not, then the beginning and ending dates and times of the VAR period must be listed. The times may be supplied on the VAR formula record or in supporting documentation. Any adjustment to any detergent concentration rate more than 10 percent over the concentration rate initially set in the VAR period shall terminate that VAR period and initiate a new VAR period, except as provided in paragraph (a)(7) of this section.

(7) The concentration setting for a detergent injector may be set below the applicable LAC, or it may be adjusted more than 10 percent above the concentration initially set in the VAR period without terminating that VAR period, provided that:

(i) The purpose of the change is to correct a batch misadditization prior to the end of the VAR period and prior to the transfer of the batch to another party, or to correct an equipment malfunction; and

(ii) The concentration is immediately returned after the correction to a concentration that fulfills the requirements of paragraphs (a)(5) and (6) of this section; and

(iii) The blender creates and maintains documentation establishing the date and adjustments of the correction; and

(iv) If the correction is initiated only to rectify an equipment malfunction, and the amount of detergent used in this procedure is not added to gasoline in the compliance period, then this amount is subtracted from the detergent volume listed on the VAR formula record.

(8) If unadditized gasoline has been transferred from the facility, other than bulk transfers from refineries or pipelines to non-retail outlets or non-WPC facilities, the total amount of such gasoline must be specified.

(b) *Non-automated facilities.* In the case of a facility in which hand blending or any other non-automated method is used to blend detergent, for each detergent and for each batch of gasoline and each batch of PRC to which the detergent is being added, the following shall be recorded:

(1) The manufacturer and commercial identifying name of the detergent additive package being reconciled, and the LAC specified in the detergent registration for use with the applicable type of gasoline (i.e., unleaded or leaded). The LAC must be expressed in terms of gallons of detergent per thousand gallons of gasoline or PRC, and expressed to four digits. If the specified LAC is only effective for use with leaded gasoline, the record must so indicate.

(2) The date of the additization that is the subject of the VAR formula record.

(3) The volume of added detergent.

(4) The volume of the gasoline and/or PRC to which the detergent has been added. If gasoline has intentionally been overadditized in anticipation of the later addition of unadditized PRC, then the total volume of gasoline plus PRC recorded must include the expected amount of unadditized PRC to be added later. In addition, the amount of gasoline which was overadditized for this purpose must be specified.

(5) The brand (if known), grade, and leaded/unleaded status of gasoline, and/or the type of PRC.

(6) The actual detergent concentration, calculated as the volume of added detergent (pursuant to paragraph (b)(3) of this section), divided by the volume of gasoline and/or PRC (pursuant to paragraph (b)(4) of this section). The concentration must be calculated and recorded to four digits.

* * * * *

(d) *Electronically-generated VAR formula and supporting records.*

(1) Electronically-generated records are acceptable for VAR formula records and supporting documentation (including PTDs), provided that they are complete, accessible, and easily readable. VAR formula records must also be stored with access and audit security, which must restrict to a limited number of specified people those who have the ability to alter or delete the records. In addition, parties maintaining records electronically must make available for EPA use the hardware and software necessary to review the records.

(2) Electronically-generated VAR formula records may use an electronic user identification code to satisfy the signature requirements of paragraph (c)(1) of this section, provided that:

(i) The use of the ID is limited to the record creator; and

(ii) A paper record is maintained, which is signed and dated by the VAR formula record creator, acknowledging that the use of that particular user ID on a VAR formula record is equivalent to his/her signature on the document.

(e) Automated detergent blenders must calibrate their detergent equipment once in each calendar half year, with the acceptable calibrations being no less than one hundred twenty days apart. Equipment recalibration is also required each time the detergent package is changed, unless written documentation indicates that the new detergent package has the same viscosity as the previous detergent package. Detergent package change calibrations may be used to satisfy the semiannual requirement provided that the calibrations occur in the appropriate half calendar year and are no less than one hundred twenty days apart.

(f) The following VAR supporting documentation must also be created and maintained:

(1) For all automated detergent blending facilities, documentation reflecting performance of the calibrations required by paragraph (e) of this section, and any associated adjustments of the automated detergent equipment;

(2) For all hand-blending facilities which are terminals, a record specifying, for each calendar month, the total volume in gallons of transfers from the facility of unadditized base gasoline;

(3) For all detergent blending facilities, product transfer documents for all gasoline, detergent and detergent-additized PRC transferred into or out of the facility; in addition, bills of lading, transfer, or sale for all unadditized PRC transferred into the facility;

(4) For all automated detergent blending facilities, documentation establishing the brands (if known) and grades of the gasoline which is the subject of the VAR formula record;

(5) For all hand blending detergent blenders, the documentation, if in the party's possession, supporting the volumes of gasoline, PRC, and detergent reported on the VAR formula record; and

(6) For all detergent blending facilities, documentation establishing the curing of a batch or amount of misadditized gasoline or PRC, or the curing of a use restriction on the additized gasoline or PRC, and providing at least the following information: the date of the curing procedure; the problem that was corrected; the amount, name, and LAC of the original detergent used; the amount, name, and LAC of the added curing detergent; and the actual detergent concentration attained in, and the volume of, the total cured product.

(g) *Document retention and availability.* All detergent blenders shall retain the documents required under this section for a period of five years from the date the VAR formula records and supporting documentation were created, and shall deliver them upon request to the EPA Administrator or the Administrator's authorized representative.

(1) Except as provided in paragraph (g)(3) of this section, automated detergent blender facilities and hand-blender facilities which are terminals, which physically blend detergent into gasoline, must make immediately available to EPA, upon request, the preceding twelve months of VAR formula records plus the preceding two months of VAR supporting documentation.

(2) Except as provided in paragraph (g)(3) of this section, other hand-blending detergent facilities which physically blend detergent into gasoline must make immediately available to EPA, upon request, the preceding two months of VAR formula records and VAR supporting documentation.

(3) Facilities which have centrally maintained records at other locations, or have customers who maintain their own records at other locations for their proprietary detergent systems, and which can document this fact to the Agency, may have until the start of the next business day after the request to supply VAR supporting documentation, or longer if approved by the Agency.

(4) In this paragraph (g) of this section, the term immediately available means that the records must be provided, electronically or otherwise, within approximately one hour of EPA's request, or within a longer time frame as approved by EPA.80.170 Volumetric additive reconciliation (VAR), equipment calibration, and recordkeeping requirements.

This section contains requirements for automated detergent blending facilities and hand-blending detergent facilities. All gasoline and all PRC intended for use in gasoline must be additized unless otherwise noted in supporting VAR records, and must be accounted for in VAR records. The VAR reconciliation standard is attained under this section when the actual concentration of detergent used per VAR formula record equals or exceeds the applicable LAC certified for that detergent pursuant to Sec. 80.161(b)(3)(ix) or, if appropriate, Sec. 80.161(d). If a given detergent package has been certified under more than one certification option pursuant to Sec. 80.163, then a separate VAR formula record must be created for gasoline or PRC additized on the basis of each certification and its respective LAC. In such cases, the amount of the detergent used under different certification options must be accurately and separately measured, either through the use of a separate storage tank, a separate meter, or some other measurement system that is able to accurately distinguish its use. Recorded volumes of gasoline, detergent, and PRC must be expressed to the nearest gallon (or smaller units), except that detergent volumes of five gallons or less must be expressed to the nearest tenth of a gallon (or smaller units). However, if the blender's equipment cannot accurately measure to the nearest tenth of a gallon, then such volumes must be rounded downward to the next lower gallon. PRC included in the reconciliation must be identified. Each VAR formula record must also contain the following information:

(a) *Automated blending facilities*. In the case of an automated detergent blending facility, for each VAR period, for each detergent storage system and each detergent in that storage system, the following must be recorded:

(1) The manufacturer and commercial identifying name of the detergent additive package being reconciled, the LAC, and any use restriction applicable to the LAC. The LAC must be expressed in terms of gallons of detergent per thousand gallons of gasoline or PRC, and expressed to four digits. If the detergent storage system which is the subject of the VAR formula record is a proprietary system under the control of a customer, this fact must be indicated on the record.

(2) The total volume of detergent blended into gasoline and PRC, in accordance with one of the following paragraphs (a)(2)(i) or (ii) of this section, as applicable.

(i) For a facility which uses in-line meters to measure detergent usage, the total volume of detergent measured, together with supporting data which includes one of the following: the beginning and ending meter readings for each meter being measured, the metered batch volume measurements for each meter being measured, or other comparable metered measurements. The supporting data may be supplied on the VAR formula record or in the form of computer printouts or other comparable VAR supporting documentation.

(ii) For a facility which uses a gauge to measure the inventory of the detergent storage tank, the total volume of detergent shall be calculated from the following equation:

Detergent Volume=(A)-(B)+(C)-(D)

Where:

A=Initial detergent inventory of the tank

B=Final detergent inventory of the tank

C=Sum of any additions to detergent inventory

D=Sum of any withdrawals from detergent inventory for purposes other than the additization of gasoline or PRC.

The value of each variable in this equation must be separately recorded on the VAR formula record. In addition, a list of each detergent addition included in variable C and a list of each detergent withdrawal included in variable D must be provided, either on the formula record or as VAR supporting documentation.

(3) The total volume of gasoline plus PRC to which detergent has been added, together with supporting data which includes one of the following: the beginning and ending meter measurements for each meter being measured, the metered batch volume measurements for each meter being measured, or other comparable metered measurements. The supporting data may be supplied on the VAR formula record or in the form of computer printouts or other comparable VAR supporting documentation. If gasoline has intentionally been overadditized in anticipation of the later addition of unadditized PRC, then the total volume of gasoline plus PRC recorded must include the expected amount of unadditized PRC to be added later. In addition, the amount of gasoline which was overadditized for this purpose must be specified.

(4) The actual detergent concentration, calculated as the total volume of detergent added (pursuant to paragraph (a)(2) of this section), divided by the total volume of gasoline plus PRC (pursuant to paragraph (a)(3) of this section). The concentration must be calculated and recorded to four digits.

(5) A list of each detergent concentration rate initially set for the detergent that is the subject of the VAR record, together with the date and description of each adjustment to any initially set concentration. The concentration adjustment information may be supplied on the VAR formula record or in the form of computer printouts or other comparable VAR supporting documentation. No concentration setting is permitted below the applicable certified LAC, except as may be modified pursuant to Sec. 80.161(d) or as described in paragraph (a)(7) of this section.

(6) The dates of the VAR period, which shall be no longer than thirty-one days. If the VAR period is contemporaneous with a calendar month, then specifying the month will fulfill this requirement; if not, then the beginning and ending dates and times of the VAR period must be listed. The times may be supplied on the VAR formula record or in supporting documentation. Any adjustment to any detergent concentration rate more than 10 percent over the concentration rate initially set in the VAR period shall terminate that VAR period and initiate a new VAR period, except as provided in paragraph (a)(7) of this section.

(7) The concentration setting for a detergent injector may be set below the applicable LAC, or it may be adjusted more than

10 percent above the concentration initially set in the VAR period without terminating that VAR period, provided that:

(i) The purpose of the change is to correct a batch misadditization prior to the end of the VAR period and prior to the transfer of the batch to another party, or to correct an equipment malfunction; and

(ii) The concentration is immediately returned after the correction to a concentration that fulfills therequirements of paragraphs (a) (5) and (6) of this section; and

(iii) The blender creates and maintains documentation establishing the date and adjustments of the correction; and

(iv) If the correction is initiated only to rectify an equipment malfunction, and the amount of detergent used in this procedure is not added to gasoline within the compliance period, then this amount is subtracted from the detergent volume listed on the VAR formula record.

(8) If unadditized gasoline has been transferred from the facility, other than bulk transfers from refineries or pipelines to non-retail outlets or non-WPC facilities, the total amount of such gasoline must be specified.

(b) *Non-automated facilities.* In the case of a facility in which hand blending or any other non-automated method is used to blend detergent, for each detergent and for each batch of gasoline and each batch of PRC to which the detergent is being added, the following shall be recorded:

(1) The manufacturer and commercial identifying name of the detergent additive package being reconciled, the LAC, and any use restriction applicable to the LAC. The LAC must be expressed in terms of gallons of detergent per thousand gallons of gasoline or PRC, and expressed to four digits.

(2) The date of the additization that is the subject of the VAR formula record.

(3) The volume of added detergent.

(4) The volume of the gasoline and/or PRC to which the detergent has been added. If gasoline has intentionally been overadditized in anticipation of the later addition of unadditized PRC, then the total volume of gasoline plus PRC recorded must include the expected amount of unadditized PRC to be added later. In addition, the amount of gasoline which was overadditized for this purpose must be specified.

(5) The brand (if known), grade, and leaded/unleaded status of gasoline, and/or the type of PRC.

(6) The actual detergent concentration, calculated as the volume of added detergent (pursuant to paragraph (b)(3) of this section), divided by the volume of gasoline and/or PRC (pursuant to paragraph (b)(4) of this section). The concentration must be calculated and recorded to four digits.

(c) Every VAR formula record created pursuant to paragraphs (a) and (b) of this section shall contain the following:

(1) The signature of the creator of the VAR record;

(2) The date of the creation of the VAR record; and

(3) A certification of correctness by the creator of the VAR record.

(d) *Electronically-generated VAR formula and supporting records.*

(1) Electronically-generated records are acceptable for VAR formula records and supporting documentation (including PTDs), provided that they are complete, accessible, and easily readable. VAR formula records must also be stored with access and audit security, which must restrict to a limited number of specified people those who have the ability to alter or delete the records. In addition, parties maintaining records electronically must make available to EPA the hardware and software necessary to review the records.

(2) Electronically-generated VAR formula records may use an electronic user identification code to satisfy the signature requirements of paragraph (c)(1) of this section, provided that:

(i) The use of the ID is limited to the record creator; and

(ii) A paper record is maintained, which is signed and dated by the VAR formula record creator, acknowledging that the use of that particular user ID on a VAR formula record is equivalent to his/her signature on the document.

(e) Automated detergent blenders must calibrate their detergent equipment once in each calendar half year, with the acceptable calibrations being no less than one hundred twenty days apart. Equipment recalibration is also required each time the detergent package is changed, unless written documentation indicates that the new detergent package has the same viscosity as the previous detergent package. Detergent package change calibrations may be used to satisfy the semiannual requirement provided that the calibrations occur in the appropriate half calendar year and are no less than one hundred twenty days apart.

(f) The following VAR supporting documentation must also be created and maintained:

(1) For all automated detergent blending facilities, documentation reflecting performance of the calibrations required by paragraph (e) of this section, and any associated adjustments of the automated detergent equipment;

(2) For all hand-blending facilities which are terminals, a record specifying, for each VAR period, the total volume in gallons of transfers from the facility of unadditized base gasoline;

(3) For all detergent blending facilities, product transfer documents for all gasoline, detergent and detergent-additized PRC transferred into or out of the facility; in addition, bills of lading, transfer, or sale for all unadditized PRC transferred into the facility;

(4) For all automated detergent blending facilities, documentation establishing the brands (if known) and grades of the gasoline which is the subject of the VAR formula record; and

(5) For all hand blending detergent blenders, the documentation, if in the party's possession, supporting the volumes of gasoline, PRC, and detergent reported on the VAR formula record.

(6) For all detergent blending facilities, documentation establishing the curing of a batch or amount of misadditized gasoline or PRC, or the curing of a use restriction on the additized gasoline or PRC, and providing at least the following information: the date of the curing procedure; the problem that was corrected; the amount, name, and LAC of the original detergent used; the amount, name, and LAC of the added curing detergent; and the actual detergent concentration attained in, and the volume of, the total cured product.

(g) *Document retention and availability.* All detergent blenders shall retain the documents required under this section for a period of five years from the date the VAR formula records and supporting documentation are created, and shall deliver them upon request to the EPA Administrator or the Administrator's authorized representative.

(1) Except as provided in paragraph (g)(3) of this section, automated detergent blender facilities and hand-blender facilities which are terminals, which physically blend detergent into gasoline, must make immediately available to EPA, upon request, the preceding twelve months of VAR formula records plus the preceding two months of VAR supporting documentation.

(2) Except as provided in paragraph (g)(3) of this section, other hand-blending detergent facilities which physically blend detergent into gasoline must make immediately available to EPA, upon request, the preceding two months of VAR formula records and VAR supporting documentation.

(3) Facilities which have centrally maintained records at other locations, or have customers who maintain their own

records at other locations for their proprietary detergent systems, and which can document this fact to the Agency, may have until the start of the next business day after the EPA request to supply VAR supporting documentation, or longer if approved by the Agency.

(4) In this paragraph (g) of this section, the term immediately available means that the records must be provided, electronically or otherwise, within approximately one hour of EPA's request, or within a longer time frame as approved by EPA.

PART 85. CONTROL OF AIR POLLUTION FROM MOTOR VEHICLES AND MOTOR VEHICLE ENGINES

Subpart S. Recall Regulations

Citation: **40 CFR 85.1806**

✍ **§ 85.1806 Records and reports.**

(a) The manufacturer shall provide to the Administrator a copy of all communications which relate to the remedial plan directed to dealers and other persons who are to perform the repair under the remedial plan. Such copies shall be mailed to the Administrator contemporaneously with their transmission to dealers and other persons who are to perform the repair under the remedial plan.

(b) The manufacturer shall provide for the establishment and maintenance of records to enable the administrator to conduct a continuing analysis of the adequacy of the recall campaign. The records shall include, for each class or category of vehicle or engine, but need not be limited to, the following:

(1) Recall campaign number as designated by the manufacturer.

(2) Date owner notification was begun, and date completed.

(3) Number of vehicles or engines involved in the recall campaign.

(4) Number of vehicles or engines known or estimated to be affected by the nonconformity.

(5) Number of vehicles or engines inspected pursuant to the remedial plan.

(6) Number of inspected vehicles found to be affected by the nonconformity.

(7) Number of vehicles actually receiving repair under the remedial plan.

(8) Number of vehicles determined to be unavailable for inspection or repair under the remedial plan due to exportation, theft, scrapping or for other reasons (specify).

(9) Number of vehicles or engines determined to be ineligible for remedial action due to a failure to properly maintain or use such vehicles or engines.

* * * * *

(e) The manufacturer shall maintain in a form suitable for inspection, such as computer information storage devices or card files, lists of the names and addresses of vehicles or engine owners.

(1) To whom notification was given;

(2) Who received remedial repair or inspection under the remedial plan; and

(3) When eligibility for repair is conditioned on proper maintenance or use, that were determined not to qualify for such remedial action.

(f) The records described in paragraph (e) of this section shall be made available to the Administrator upon request.

(g) The records and reports required by this section shall be retained for not less than 5 years.

Subpart T. Emission Defect Reporting Requirements

Citation: **40 CFR 85.1904**

✍ **§ 85.1904 Voluntary emissions recall report; quarterly reports.**

* * * * *

(d) The manufacturer shall maintain in a form suitable for inspection, such as computer information storage devices or card files, the names and addresses of vehicles or engine owners:

(1) To whom notification was given;

(2) Who received remedial repair or inspection under the remedial plan; and

(3) Who were determined not to qualify for such remedial action when eligibility is conditioned on proper maintenance or use.

* * * * *

PART 86. CONTROL OF AIR POLLUTION FROM NEW MOTOR VEHICLES AND NEW MOTOR VEHICLE ENGINES: CERTIFICATION AND TEST PROCEDURES

✍

Subpart E. Emission Regulations for 1978 and Later New Motorcycles, General Provisions

Citation: **40 CFR 86.440-78**

✍ **§ 86.440-78 Maintenance of records.**

(a) The manufacturer of any motorcycle subject to any of the standards or procedures prescribed in this subpart shall establish, maintain and retain the following adequately organized and indexed records:

(1) *General records.* (i)(A) Identification and description of all certification vehicles for which testing is required under this subpart.

(B) A description of all emission control systems which are installed on or incorporated in each certification vehicle.

(C) A description of all procedures used to test each such certification vehicle.

(ii) A properly completed application, following the format prescribed by the U.S. EPA for the appropriate year of production, fulfills each of the requirements of this paragraph.

(2) *Individual records.* (i) A brief history of each motorcycle used for certification under this subpart including:

(A) (1) In the case where a current production engine is modified for use in a certification vehicle, a description of the process by which the engine was selected and of the modification made.

(2) In the case where the engine for a certification vehicle is not derived from a current production engine, a general description of the build-up of the engine (e.g., experimental heads were cast and machined according to supplied drawings, etc.)

(3) In both cases above, a description of the origin and selection process for the carburetor, fuel system, emission control system components, and exhaust after treatment device shall be included.

(4) The required description shall specify the steps taken to assure that the certification vehicle with respect to its engine, drive train, fuel system, emission control system components, exhaust after treatment device, vehicle mass, or any other device or component that can reasonably be expected to influence exhaust emissions, will be representative of production vehicles, and that either all components and/or vehicle

construction processes, component inspection and selection techniques, and assembly techniques employed in constructing such vehicles are reasonably likely to be implemented for production vehicles, or they are as closely analogous as practicable to planned construction and assembly processes.

(B) A complete record of all emission tests performed (except tests performed by EPA directly) including test results, the date and purpose of each test, and the distance accumulated on the vehicle.

(C) The date of each service accumulation run, listing the distance accumulated.

(D) [Reserved].

(E) A record and description of all maintenance and other servicing performed, giving the date of the maintenance or service and the reason for it.

(F) A record and description of each test performed to diagnose engine or emissions control system performance, giving the date and time of the test and the reason for it.

(G) [Reserved].

(H) A brief description of any significant events affecting the vehicle during any time in the period covered by the history, not described by an entry under one of the previous headings, including such extraordinary events as vehicle accidents or dynamometer runaway.

(ii) Each such history shall be started on the date that the first of any of the selection or build-up activities in paragraph (a)(2)(i)(A) of this section occurred with respect to the certification vehicle, shall be updated each time the operational status of the vehicle changes or additional work is performed on it, and shall be kept in a designated location.

(3) All records, other than routine emission test records, required to be maintained under this subpart shall be retained by the manufacturer for a period of six (6) years after the issuance of all certificates of conformity to which they relate. Routine emission test records shall be retained by the manufacturer for a period of one (1) year after issuance of all certificates of conformity to which they relate. Records may be retained as hard copy or reduced to microfilm, punch cards, etc., depending on the record retention procedures of the manufacturer; *Provided* that, in every case, all the information contained in the hard copy shall be retained.

Subpart G. Selective Enforcement Auditing of New Light-Duty Vehicles

Citation: **40 CFR 86.605-88**

✍ § 86.605-88 Maintenance of records; submittal of information.

(a) The manufacturer of any new motor vehicle subject to any of the standards or procedures prescribed in this part shall establish, maintain and retain the following adequately organized and indexed records:

(1) *General records.* (i) A description of all equipment used to test vehicles in accordance with § 86.608 pursuant to a test order issued under this subpart, including the following information:

(A) Dynamometer.

(*1*) Inertia loading.

(*2*) Road load power absorption at 50 m.p.h.

(*3*) Manufacturer, model and serial number.

(B) Constant Volume Sampler.

(*1*) Pressure of the mixture of exhaust and dilution air entering the positive displacement pump, pressure increase across the pump, and the temperature set point of the temperature control system.

(*2*) Number of revolutions of the positive displacement pump accumulated while test is in progress and exhaust samples are being collected.

(*3*) Humidity of dilution air.

(*4*) Manufacturer, model, type and serial number.

(C) Instrumentation.

(*1*) Manufacturer, model and serial number for each analyzer.

(*2*) Pertinent information such as tuning gain, ranges and calibration data.

(*3*) Identification of zero, span, exhaust gas and dilution air sample traces.

(*4*) Temperature set point of heated sample line and heated hydrocarbon detector temperature control system (for diesel vehicles only).

(D) Test cell.

(*1*) Barometric pressure, ambient temperature and humidity.

(*2*) Date and time of day.

(ii) In lieu of recording test equipment information, reference to a vehicle test cell number may be used, with the advance approval of the Administrator; Provided, the test cell records show the pertinent information.

(2) *Individual records.* These records pertain to each audit conducted pursuant to this subpart.

(i) The location where audit testing was performed, and the date and time for each emissions test.

(ii) The number of miles on the test vehicle when the test began and ended.

(iii) The names of supervisory personnel responsible for the conduct of the audit.

(iv) A record and description of any repairs performed prior to and/or subsequent to approval by the Administrator, giving the date and time of the repair, the reason for it, the person authorizing it, and the names of the supervisory personnel responsible for the repair.

(v) The dates when the test vehicles were shipped from the assembly plant or the storage facility and when they were received at the testing facility.

(vi) The drive wheel tire pressure and the inertia weight class for each test vehicle, and the actual curb weight for each test vehicle required to be weighed pursuant to a test order.

(vii) A complete record of all emission tests performed pursuant to this subpart (except tests performed by EPA directly) including all individual worksheets and/or other documentation relating to each test, or exact copies thereof.

(viii) A brief description of all significant audit events, commencing with the test vehicle selection process, but not described by any other subparagraph under paragraph (a)(2) of this section, including such extraordinary events as vehicle accident.

(ix) A paper copy of the driver's trace for each test.

(3) Additional required records for diesel vehicles.

(4) The manufacturer shall record test equipment description, pursuant to paragraph (a)(1) of this section, for each test cell that is used to perform emission testing under this subpart.

(b) All records required to be maintained under this subpart shall be retained by the manufacturer for a period of one (1) year after completion of all testing in response to a test order. Records may be retained as hard copy or reduced to microfilm, punch cards, etc., depending upon the record retention procedures of the manufacturer: *Provided,* That in every case all the information contained in the hard copy shall be retained.

(c) The manufacturer shall, pursuant to a request made by the Administrator, submit to the Administrator the following information with regard to vehicle production:

(1) Number of vehicles, by configuration and assembly plant, scheduled for production for the time period designated in the request.

(2) Number of vehicles, by configuration and assembly plant, produced during the time period designated in the request which are complete for introduction into commerce.

(d) Nothing in this section shall limit the Administrator's discretion to require the manufacturer to retain additional records or submit information not specifically required by this section.

(e) All reports, submissions, notifications and requests for approvals made under this subpart shall be addressed to:

Director, Manufacturers Operations Division EN-340, U.S. Environmental Protection Agency, 401 M Street, SW, Washington, D.C. 20460.

Subpart K. Selective Enforcement Auditing of New Heavy-Duty Engines and Light-Duty Trucks

Citation: 40 CFR 86.1005-88

✍ § 86.1005-88 Maintenance of records; submittal of information.

(a) The manufacturer of any new gasoline-fueled or diesel heavy-duty engine or light-duty truck subject to any of the provisions of this subpart shall establish, maintain, and retain the following adequately organized and indexed records:

(1) *General records.* A description of all equipment used to test engines or vehicles in accordance with § 86.1008-84 pursuant to a test order issued under this subpart specifically:

(i) If testing heavy-duty gasoline engines, the equipment requirements specified in § § 86.1306-84 and 86.1506-84 of this part;

(ii) If testing heavy-duty diesel engines, the equipment requirements specified in § § 86.1306-84, 86.884-8 and 86.884-9 of this part;

(iii) If testing light-duty gasoline-fueled trucks, the equipment requirements specified in § § 86.106 (excluding all references to evaporative and particulate emission testing) and 86.1506-84 of this part; and

(iv) If testing light-duty diesel trucks, the equipment requirements specified in § 86.106 (excluding all references to evaporative emission testing) of this part.

(2) *Individual records.* These records pertain to each audit conducted pursuant to this subpart.

(i) The date, time, and location of each test;

(ii) The number of hours of service accumulated on the engine or the number of miles on the vehicle when the test began and ended;

(iii) The names of all personnel, including supervisory personnel, involved in the conduct of the audit;

(iv) A record and description of any repairs performed prior to and/or subsequent to approval by the Administrator, giving the date and time of the repair, the reason for it, the person authorizing it, and the names of all personnel involved in the supervising and performance of the repair;

(v) The date when the engine or vehicle was shipped from the assembly plant or associated storage facility and when it was received at the testing facility;

(vi) A complete record of all emission tests performed pursuant to this subpart (except test performed by EPA directly), including all individual worksheets and/or other documentation relating to each test, or exact copies thereof, specifically —

(A) If testing heavy-duty gasoline engines, the record requirements specified in § § 86.1344-88 and 86.1542-84 of this part;

(B) If testing heavy-duty diesel engines, the record requirements specified in § § 86.1344-88 and 86.884-10;

(C) If testing light-duty gasoline-fueled trucks, the record requirements specified in § § 86.142-82 and 86.1542-84 of this part; and

(D) If testing light-duty diesel trucks, the record requirements specified in § 86.142-82 of this part; and

(vii) A brief description of any significant audit events commencing with the test engine or vehicle selection process, but not described by any subparagraph under paragraph (a)(2) of this section, including such extraordinary events as engine damage during shipment or vehicle accident.

(viii) A paper copy of the driver's trace for each test.

(3) The manufacturer shall record test equipment description, pursuant to paragraph (a)(1) of this section, for each test cell that can be used to perform emission testing under this subpart.

(b) The manufacturer shall retain all records required to be maintained under this subpart for a period of one (1) year after completion of all testing in response to a test order. Records may be retained as hard copy or reduced to microfilm, punch cards, etc., depending upon the manufacturer's record retention procedure: Provided, That in every case all the information contained in the hard copy is retained.

* * * * *

PART 90. CONTROL OF EMISSIONS FROM NONROAD SPARK-IGNITION ENGINES

Subpart E. Gaseous Exhaust Test Procedures

Citation: 40 CFR 90.412

✍ § 90.412 Data logging.

(a) A computer or any other automatic data collection (ADC) device(s) may be used as long as the system meets the requirements of this subpart.

(b) Determine from the data collection records the analyzer responses corresponding to the end of each mode.

(c) Record data at a minimum of rate of one Hz (one time per second).

(d) Determine the final value for power by averaging the individually calculated power points for each value of speed and torque recorded during the sampling period. As an alternative, the final value for power can be calculated from the average values for speed and torque, collected during the sampling period.

(e) Determine the final value for CO_2, CO, HC, and NO_x concentrations by averaging the concentration of each point taken during the sample period for each mode.

Citation: 40 CFR 90.413

✍ § 90.413 Exhaust sample procedure-gaseous components.

(a) *Automatic data collection equipment requirements.* The analyzer response may be read by automatic data collection (ADC) equipment such as computers, data loggers, and so forth. If ADC equipment is used, the following is required:

(1) For dilute grab ("bag") sample analysis, the analyzer response must be stable at greater than 99 percent of the final reading for the dilute exhaust sample. The ADC must store a single value representing the average chart deflection over a 10-second stabilized period. Alternatively, the ADC may store the individual instantaneous chart deflections collected over a 10-second stabilized period.

(2) For continuous analysis systems, the ADC must store a single value representing the average integrated concentration over a measurement period. Alternatively, the ADC may store

the individual instantaneous values collected during the measurement period.

(3) The chart deflections or average integrated concentrations required in paragraphs (a)(1) and (a)(2) of this section may be stored on long-term computer storage devices such as computer tapes, storage discs, punch cards, or they may be printed in a listing for storage. In either case a chart recorder is not required and records from a chart recorder, if they exist, need not be stored.

(4) If ADC equipment is used to interpret analyzer values, the ADC equipment is subject to the calibration specifications of the analyzer as if the ADC equipment is part of analyzer system.

(b) Data records from any one or a combination of analyzers may be stored as chart recorder records.

(c) *Grab sample analysis.* For dilute grab sample analysis perform the following procedure:

(1) Calibrate analyzers using the procedure described in § 90.326.

(2) Record the most recent zero and span response as the pre-analysis values.

(3) Measure and record HC, CO, CO_2, and NO_x concentrations in the exhaust sample bag(s) and background sample bag(s) using the same flow rates and pressures.

(4) Good engineering practice dictates that exhaust emission sample bag analyzer readings below 15 percent of full scale should generally not be used.

(5) A post-analysis zero and span calibration check of each range must be performed and the values recorded. The number of events that may occur between the pre- and post-checks is not specified. However, the difference between pre-analysis zero and span values (recorded in paragraph (c)(2) or (c)(3) of this section) versus those recorded for the post-analysis check may not exceed the zero drift limit or the span drift limit of two percent of full-scale chart deflection for any range used. Otherwise the analysis is void.

(d) *Continuous sample analysis.* For continuous sample analysis perform the following procedure:

(1) Calibrate analyzers using the procedure described in § 90.326.

(2) Leak check portions of the sampling system that operate at negative gauge pressures when sampling and allow heated sample lines, filters, pumps, and so forth to stabilize at operating temperature.

(3) Option: Determine the HC hang-up for the FID or HFID sampling system:

(i) Zero the analyzer using zero gas introduced at the analyzer port.

(ii) Flow zero gas through the overflow sampling system. Check the analyzer response.

(iii) If the overflow zero response exceeds the analyzer zero response by two percent or more of the FID or HFID full-scale deflection, hang-up is indicated and corrective action must be taken (see paragraph (e) of this section).

(iv) The complete system hang-up check specified in paragraph (e) of this section is recommended as a periodic check.

(4) If necessary, recalibrate analyzer using the procedure specified in paragraph (d)(1) of this section.

(5) Good engineering practice dictates that analyzers used for continuous analysis should be operated such that the measured concentration falls between 15 percent and 100 percent of full scale.

(6) Record the most recent zero and span response as the pre-analysis values.

(7) Collect background HC, CO, CO_2, and NO_x in a sample bag (for dilute exhaust sampling only, see § 90.422).

(8) Perform a post-analysis zero and span check for each range used at the conditions specified in paragraph (d)(1) of this section. Record these responses as the post-analysis values.

(9) Neither the zero drift nor the span drift between the pre-analysis and post-analysis checks on any range used may exceed three percent for HC, or two percent for NO_x, CO, and CO_2, of full-scale chart deflection, or the test is void. (If the HC drift is greater than three percent of full-scale chart deflection, HC hang-up is likely.)

(10) Determine background levels of HC, NO_x, CO, or CO_2 (for dilute exhaust sampling only) by the grab ("bag") technique outlined in paragraph (c) of this section.

(e) *Hydrocarbon hang-up.* If HC hang-up is indicated, the following procedure may be performed:

(1) Fill a clean, evacuated sample bag with background air.

(2) Zero and span the HFID at the analyzer ports.

(3) Analyze the background air sample bag through the analyzer ports.

(4) Analyze the background air through the entire sample probe system.

(5) If the difference between the readings obtained is two ppm or more, clean the sample probe and the sample line.

(6) Reassemble the sample system, heat to specified temperature, and repeat the procedure in paragraphs (e)(1) through (e)(5) of this section.

Subpart F. Selective Enforcement Auditing

Citation: 40 CFR 90.505

✍ **§ 90.505 Maintenance of records; submittal of information.**

(a) The manufacturer of any new nonroad engine subject to any of the provisions of this subpart shall establish, maintain, and retain the following adequately organized and indexed records:

(1) *General records.* A description of all equipment used to test engines, as specified in subpart D of this part, in accordance with § 90.508 pursuant to a test order issued under this subpart.

(2) *Individual records.* These records pertain to each audit conducted pursuant to this subpart and shall include:

(i) The date, time, and location of each test;

(ii) The number of hours of service accumulated on the engine when the test began and ended;

(iii) The names of all supervisory personnel involved in the conduct of the audit;

(iv) A record and description of any repairs performed prior to and/or subsequent to approval by the Administrator, giving the date, associated time, justification, name(s) of the authorizing personnel, and names of all supervisory personnel responsible for the conduct of the repair;

(v) The date the engine was shipped from the assembly plant, associated storage facility or port facility and date the engine was received at the testing facility;

(vi) A complete record of all emission tests performed pursuant to this subpart (except tests performed directly by EPA), including all individual worksheets and/or other documentation relating to each test, or exact copies thereof, to be in accordance with the record requirements specified in § § 90.405, 90.406, 90.418, and/or 90.425 as applicable.

(vii) A brief description of any significant audit events commencing with the test engine selection process, but not described under paragraph (a)(2) of this section, including such extraordinary events as engine damage during shipment.

(3) The manufacturer shall record test equipment description, pursuant to paragraph (a)(1) of this section, for each test cell that can be used to perform emission testing under this subpart.

(b) The manufacturer shall retain all records required to be maintained under this subpart for a period of one year after completion of all testing in response to a test order. Records may be retained as hard copy or reduced to microfilm, floppy disc, and so forth, depending upon the manufacturer's record retention procedure, provided that in every case all the information contained in the hard copy is retained.

(c) The manufacturer shall, upon request by the Administrator, submit the following information with regard to engine production:

(1) Projected U.S. sales data for each engine configuration within each engine family for which certification is requested;

(2) Number of engines, by configuration and assembly plant, scheduled for production for the time period designated in the request;

(3) Number of engines, by configuration and by assembly plant, storage facility or port facility, scheduled to be stored at facilities for the time period designated in the request; and

(4) Number of engines, by configuration and assembly plant, produced during the time period designated in the request that are complete for introduction into commerce.

(d) Nothing in this section limits the Administrator's discretion in requiring the manufacturer to retain additional records or submit information not specifically required by this section.

(e) The manufacturer shall address all reports, submissions, notifications, and requests for approvals made under this subpart to: Director, Manufacturers Operations Division, U.S. Environmental Protection Agency, 6405-J, 401 M Street S.W., Washington, D.C. 20460.

PART 91. CONTROL OF EMISSIONS FROM MARINE SPARK-IGNITION ENGINES

Subpart E. Gaseous Exhaust Test Procedures

Citation: **40 CFR 91.412**

✍ § 91.412 Data logging.

(a) A computer or any other automatic data collection (ADC) device(s) may be used as long as the system meets the requirements of this subpart.

(b) Determine from the data collection records the analyzer responses corresponding to the end of each mode.

(c) Record data at a minimum of one Hz (one time per second).

(d) Determine the final value for power by averaging the individually calculated power points for each value of speed and torque recorded during the sampling period. As an alternative, the final value for power can be calculated from the average values for speed and torque, collected during the sampling period.

(e) Determine the final value for CO_2, CO, HC, and NO_x concentrations by averaging the concentration of each point taken during the sample period for each mode.

Citation: **40 CFR 91.413**

✍ § 91.413 Exhaust sample procedure — gaseous components.

(a) *Automatic data collection equipment requirements.* The analyzer response may be read by automatic data collection (ADC) quipment such as computers, data loggers, etc. If ADC equipment is used the following is required:

(1) For dilute grab ("bag") analysis, the analyzer response must be stable at greater than 99 percent of the final reading for the dilute exhaust sample bag. A single value representing the average chart deflection over a 10-second stabilized period shall be stored.

(2) For continuous analysis systems, a single value representing the average integrated concentration over a cycle shall be stored. Alternatively, the ADC may store the individual instantaneous values collected during the measurement period.

(3) The chart deflections or average integrated concentrations required in paragraphs (a)(1) and (a)(2) of this section may be stored on long-term computer storage devices such as computer tapes, storage discs, punch cards, and so forth, or they may be printed in a listing for storage. In either case a chart recorder is not required and records from a chart recorder, if they exist, need not be stored.

(4) If ADC equipment is used to interpret analyzer values, the ADC equipment is subject to the calibration specifications of the analyzer as if the ADC equipment is part of analyzer system.

(b) Data records from any one or a combination of analyzers may be stored as chart recorder records.

(c) *Grab sample analysis.* For dilute grab sample analysis perform the following sequence:

(1) Calibrate analyzers using the procedure described in Sec. 91.326.

(2) Record the most recent zero and span response as the pre-analysis value.

(3) Measure HC, CO, CO_2, and NO_x background concentrations in the sample bag(s) and background sample bag(s) using the same flow rates and pressures.

(4) Good engineering practice dictates that analyzers used for continuous analysis should be operated such that the measured concentration falls between 15 percent and 100 percent of full scale.

(5) A post-analysis zero and span check of each range must be performed and the values recorded. The number of events that may occur between the pre and post checks is not specified. However, the difference between pre-analysis zero and span values (recorded in paragraph (c)(5) or (c)(6) of this section) versus those recorded for the post-analysis check may not exceed the zero drift limit or the span drift limit of 2 percent of full scale chart deflection for any range used. Otherwise the test is void.

(d) *Continuous sample analysis.* For continuous sample analysis, perform the following sequence:

(1) Calibrate analyzers using the procedures described in Sec. 91.326.

(2) Leak check portions of the sampling system that operate at negative gauge pressures when sampling, and allow heated sample lines, filters, pumps, and so forth to stabilize at operating temperature.

(3) Option: Determine the hang-up for the FID or HFID sampling system:

(i) Zero the analyzer using zero air introduced at the analyzer port.

(ii) Flow zero air through the overflow sampling system. Check the analyzer response.

(iii) If the overflow zero response exceeds the analyzer zero response by two percent or more of the FID or HFID full-scale deflection, hang-up is indicated and corrective action must be taken (see paragraph (e) of this section).

(iv) The complete system hang-up check specified in paragraph (f) of this section is recommended as a periodic check.

(4) Obtain a stable zero reading.

(5) Good engineering practice dictates that analyzers used for continuous analysis should be operated such that the measured concentration falls between 15 percent and 100 percent of full scale.

(6) Record the most recent zero and span response as the pre-analysis values.

(7) Collect background HC, CO, CO_2, and NO_x in a sample bag (for dilute exhaust sampling only, see Sec. 91.422).

(8) Perform a post-analysis zero and span check for each range used at the conditions specified in paragraph (d)(1) of this section. Record these responses as the post-analysis values.

(9) Neither the zero drift nor the span drift between the pre-analysis and post-analysis checks on any range used may exceed three percent for HC, or two percent for NO_x, CO, and CO_2, of full scale chart deflection, or the test is void. (If the HC drift is greater than three percent of full-scale chart deflection, hydrocarbon hang-up is likely.)

(10) Determine background levels of NO_x, CO, or CO_2 (for dilute exhaust sampling only) by the grab ("bag") technique outlined in paragraph (c) of this section.

(e) *Hydrocarbon hang-up.* If HC hang-up is indicated, the following sequence may be performed:

(1) Fill a clean sample bag with background air.

(2) Zero and span the HFID at the analyzer ports.

(3) Analyze the background air sample bag through the analyzer ports.

(4) Analyze the background air through the entire sample probe system.

(5) If the difference between the readings obtained is two ppm or more, clean the sample probe and the sample line.

(6) Reassemble the sample system, heat to specified temperature, and repeat the procedure in paragraphs (e)(1) through (e)(5) of this section.

SUBCHAPTER E. PESTICIDE PROGRAMS

PART 171. CERTIFICATION OF PESTICIDE APPLICATORS

Citation:	40 CFR 171.11

✍ § 171.11 Federal certification of pesticide applicators in States or on Indian Reservations where there is no approved State or Tribal certification plan in effect.

(a) *Applicability.* This section applies to persons in any State and on any Indian Reservation where, because there is no approved State or Tribal certification plan in effect, the Administrator implements an EPA plan for the Federal certification of applicators of restricted use pesticides.

* * * * *

(c) *Certification of commercial applicators* — * * *

* * * * *

(7) *Recordkeeping requirements.* (i) Each self-employed certified commercial applicator, each firm employing a certified commercial applicator, and each person who contracts with a certified commercial applicator (or his or her employer) to have a restricted use pesticide applied on property owned or operated by another person shall keep and maintain at their principal place of business true and accurate records of the use of restricted use pesticides, providing the following information:

(A) Name and address of the person for whom the pesticide was applied;

(B) Location of the pesticide application;

(C) Target pest(s);

(D) Specific crop or commodity, as appropriate, and site, to which the pesticide was applied;

(E) Year, month, day, and time of application;

(F) Trade name and EPA registration number of the pesticide applied;

(G) Amount of the pesticide applied and percentage of active ingredient per unit of the pesticide used; and

(H) Type and amount of the pesticide disposed of, method of disposal, date(s) of disposal, and location of the disposal site.

(ii) Availability of required records. Each certified commercial applicator shall keep all records required under this paragraph current and shall make such records available for inspection and copying by representatives of EPA for a period of at least two years from the date of use of the pesticide.

* * * * *

(g) *Pesticide dealer reporting and recordkeeping requirements, availability of records, and failure to comply* — * * *

* * * * *

(2) *Recordkeeping requirement.* Recordkeeping is required when making restricted use pesticides available to:

(i) *Certified applicators.* Each restricted use pesticide retail dealer shall maintain at each individual dealership records of each transaction where a restricted use pesticide is made available for use by that dealership to a certified applicator. Record of each such transaction shall be maintained for a period of 24 months after the date of the transaction, and shall include the following information:

(A) Name and address of the residence or principal place of business of each person to whom the pesticide was made available for use.

(B) The certification number on the document evidencing that person's certification, the State (or other governmental unit) that issued the document, the expiration date of the certification, and the categories in which the applicator is certified, if appropriate.

(C) The product name, EPA registration number, and the State special local need registration number, granted under section 24(c) of the FIFRA (if any) on the label of the pesticide.

(D) The quantity of the pesticide made available for use in the transaction.

(E) The date of the transaction.

(ii) *Uncertified persons.* No dealer or dealership may make a restricted use pesticide available to an uncertified person unless he can document that the restricted use pesticide will be used by a certified applicator, and he maintains the records required in this subsection. Each restricted use pesticide retail dealer shall maintain records at each individual dealership of each transaction where a restricted use pesticide was made available to an uncertified person for use by a certified applicator. Records of each such transaction shall be maintained for a period of 24 months after the date of the transaction, and shall include the following information:

(A) The name and address of the residence or principal place of business of the uncertified person to whom the restricted use pesticide is made available for use by a certified applicator.

(B) The name and address of the residence or principal place of business of the certified applicator who will use the restricted use pesticide.

(C) The certified applicator's certification number, the State (or other governmental unit) that issued his certification document, the expiration date of the certification, and the categories in which the applicator is certified, if appropriate.

(D) The product name, EPA registration number, and the State special local need registration number, granted under section 24(c) of the FIFRA (if any) on the label of the pesticide.

(E) The quantity of the pesticide made available for use in the transaction.

(F) The date of the transaction.

(G) At the time of each transaction, EPA recommends that the dealer obtain the information required in paragraph (g)(2)(ii) (A) through (C) of this section and assure himself that the restricted use pesticide is made available for use by a certified applicator by examining one of the following sets of documents:

(*1*) The original of the certified applicator's certification document, and a driver's license or other State, county, or Tribal identification document issued to the uncertified person to whom the restricted use pesticide is made available.

(*2*) A photocopy or facsimile of the certified applicator's certification document, together with a statement signed by the certified applicator authorizing the uncertified person to purchase the restricted use pesticide on his behalf, and a driver's license or other State, county, or Tribal identification document issued to the uncertified person to whom the restricted use pesticide is made available.

(*3*) A photocopy or facsimile of the certified applicator's certification document, together with a copy of a signed contract or agreement, between the uncertified person to whom the restricted use pesticide is being made available for use and the identified certified applicator, which provides for the use of the restricted use pesticide by the identified certified applicator, and a driver's license or other State, county, or Tribal identification document issued to the uncertified person to whom the restricted use pesticide is made available.

(3) *Availability of required records.* Each pesticide dealer shall, upon request of any officer or employee of EPA duly designated by the Administrator, furnish or permit such person at all reasonable times to have access to and copy all records required to be maintained under this section.

(4) *Failure to comply.* Any person who fails to comply with the provisions of this rule may be subject to civil or criminal sanctions, under section 14 of the Act, or 18 U.S.C. 1001. Violations include failure to submit or falsification of any report required under this paragraph, failure to maintain or falsification of records as required under this section, and making available for restricted use to a person who is not a certified commercial applicator other than in accordance with these regulations and section 3(d) of the amended FIFRA or rules promulgated thereunder.

SUBCHAPTER G. NOISE ABATEMENT PROGRAMS

PART 205. TRANSPORTATION EQUIPMENT NOISE EMISSION CONTROLS

Subpart E. Motorcycle Exhaust Systems

Citation: **40 CFR 205.172**

✍ § 205.172 Maintenance of records; submittal of information.

(a) Except as otherwise provided in regulation, the manufacturer of any new exhaust system subject to any of the standards or procedures prescribed in this subpart must establish, maintain and retain the following adequately organized and indexed records:

(1) General records;

(i) Identification and description by category parameters of all exhaust systems in the manufacturer's product line;

(ii) A description of any procedures other than those contained in this subpart used to perform noise emission tests on any test exhaust system;

(iii) A record of the calibration of the acoustical instrumentation as is described in Appendix I;

(iv) A record of the date of manufacture of each exhaust system subject to this subpart, keyed to the serial number.

(2) Individual records for test exhaust systems:

(i) A complete record of all noise emission tests performed for Production Verification and Selective Enforcement Audit (except tests performed by EPA directly), including all individual worksheets and other documentation or exact copies relating to each test;

(ii) A record of the information recorded as described in Appendix I; and

(iii) A record and description of all repairs, maintenance and other servicing which were performed before successful testing of the exhaust system pursuant to these regulations and which could affect the noise emission of the exhaust system, giving the date and time of the maintenance or service, the reason for it, the person authorizing it, and the names of supervisory personnel responsible for the conduct of the maintenance or service.

(3) A properly filed production verification report following the format prescribed by the Administrator in § 205.168-3 fulfills the requirements of paragraphs (a)(1) (i) and (ii) of this section.

(4) All records required to be maintained under this subpart must be retained by the manufacturer for a period of three (3) years from the production verification date. Records may be retained as hard copy or alternatively reduced to microfilm, punch cards, etc., depending on the record retention procedures of the manufacturer; however, when an alternative method is used, all information contained in the hard copy must be contained in the copy made by the alternative method.

(b) The manufacturer must, upon request, submit to the Administrator the following information with regard to new exhaust system production:

(1) Number of exhaust systems, by category, scheduled for production for the time period designated in the request.

(2) Number of exhaust systems, by category, produced during the time period designated in the request.

(c) The reporting requirements of this regulation will no longer be effective after five (5) years from the last effective date of this regulation. However, the requirements will remain in effect if the Administrator is taking appropriate steps to repromulgate or modify the reporting requirements at that time.

SUBCHAPTER Q. ENERGY POLICY

PART 600. FUEL ECONOMY OF MOTOR VEHICLES

Subpart A. Fuel Economy Regulations for 1977 And Later Model Year Automobiles — General Provisions

Citation: **40 CFR 600.005-81**

✍ § 600.005-81 Maintenance of records and right of entry.

The provisions of this section are applicable to all fuel economy data vehicles. Certification vehicles are required to meet the provisions of § 86.007-77:

(a) The manufacturer of any new motor vehicle subject to any of the standards or procedures prescribed in this part shall establish, maintain, and retain the following adequately organized and indexed records:

(1) *General records.* (i) Identification and description of all vehicles for which data are submitted to meet the requirements of this part.

(ii) A description of all procedures used to test each vehicle.

(iii) A copy of the information required to be submitted under 600.006 fulfills the requirements of paragraph (a)(1)(i) of this section.

(2) *Individual records.* (i) A brief history of each vehicle for which data are submitted to meet the requirements of this part,

in the form of a separate booklet or other document for each separate vehicles, in which must be recorded:

(A) The steps taken to ensure that the vehicle with respect to its engine, drive train, fuel system, emission control system components, exhaust after treatment device, vehicle weight, or any other device or component, as applicable, will be representative of production vehicles. In the case of electric vehicles, the manufacturer should describe the steps taken to ensure that the vehicle with respect to its electric traction motor, motor controller, battery configuration, or any other device or component, as applicable, will be representative of production vehicles.

(B) A complete record of all emission tests performed under Part 86, all fuel economy tests performed under Part 600 (except tests actually performed by EPA personnel), and all electric vehicle tests performed according to procedures promulgated by DOE, including all individual worksheets and other documentation relating to each such test or exact copies thereof; the date, time, purpose, and location of each test; the number of miles accumulated on the vehicle when the tests began and ended; and the names of supervisory personnel responsible for the conduct of the tests.

(C) A description of mileage accumulated since selection of buildup of such vehicles including the date and time of each mileage accumulation listing both the mileage accumulated and the name of each driver, or each operator of the automatic mileage accumulation device, if applicable. Additionally, a description of mileage accumulated prior to selection or buildup of such vehicle must be maintained in such detail as is available.

(D) If used, the record of any devices employed to record the speed of mileage, or both, of the test vehicle in relationship to time.

(E) A record and description of all maintenance and other servicing performed, within 2,000 miles prior to fuel economy testing under this part, giving the date and time of the maintenance or service, the reason for it, the person authorizing it, and the names of supervisory personnel responsible for the conduct of the maintenance or service. A copy of the maintenance information to be submitted under § 600.006-81 fulfills the requirements of this paragraph.

(F) A brief description of any significant events affecting the vehicle during any time of the period covered by the history not described in an entry under one of the previous headings including such extraordinary events as vehicle accidents or driver speeding citations or warnings.

(3) The manufacturer shall retain all records required under this subpart for a period of five years after the end of the model year to which they relate. Records may be retained as hard copy or reduced to microfilm, punch cards, etc., depending on the record retention procedures of the manufacturer, provided that in every case all the information contained in hard copy shall be retained.

* * * * *

SUBCHAPTER R. TOXIC SUBSTANCES CONTROL ACT

PART 710. INVENTORY REPORTING REGULATIONS

Citation: 40 CFR 710.32

✍ **§ 710.32 Information to be reported.**

* * * * *

(b) *Reporting by magnetic media.* Any person who chooses to report information to EPA by means of magnetic media must submit the information prescribed in paragraph (c) of this section. Magnetic media submitted in response to this subpart must meet EPA specifications, as described in the instruction booklet available from EPA at the address set forth in § 710.39(b).

(c) *Information to be reported.* Persons reporting information under this subpart must report the following:

(1) The name, company, address, city, State, Zip code, and telephone number of a person who will serve as technical contact for the respondent company, and will be able to answer questions about the information submitted by the company to EPA. Persons reporting by means of magnetic media must submit this information on the reporting form available from EPA at the address set forth in § 710.39.

(2) A certification statement signed and dated by an authorized official of the respondent company. Persons reporting by means of magnetic media must submit this information on the reporting form available from EPA at the address set forth in § 710.39.

(3) The specific chemical name and Chemical Abstracts Service (CAS) Registry Number of each chemical substance for which reporting is required under this subpart. A respondent to this subpart may use other chemical identification numbers in lieu of CAS Registry Numbers when a CAS Registry Number is not known to the respondent as provided in the instruction booklet identified in § 710.39(b), including EPA-designated Accession Numbers for confidential substances, EPA-assigned numbers for *bona fide* or Premanufacture Notification submissions or Test Market Exemption Applications, or original Inventory form numbers.

(4) The name, street address, city, State, and Zip code of each site at which 10,000 pounds (4,540 kilograms) or more of a chemical substance for which reporting is required under this subpart is manufactured or imported. (The site for a person who imports a chemical substance is the site of the operating unit within the person's organization which is directly responsible for importing the substance and which controls the import transaction, and may in some cases be the organization's headquarters office in the U.S.) A respondent to this subpart must include the appropriate Dun & Bradstreet Number for each plant site reported.

(5) A statement for each substance for which information is being submitted indicating whether the substance is manufactured in the United States or imported into the United States.

(6)A statement for each substance for which information is being submitted indicating whether the substance is site-limited.

(7) The total volume (in pounds) of each subject chemical substance manufactured or imported at each site. This amount must be reported to two significant figures of accuracy provided that the reported figures are within (plus or minus)10 percent of the actual volume.

Subpart J. Records and Reports

Citation: 40 CFR 792.195

✍ **§ 792.195 Retention of records.**

(a) Record retention requirements set forth in this section do not supersede the record retention requirements of any other regulations in this subchapter.

(b)(1) Except as provided in paragraph (c) of this section, documentation records, raw data, and specimens pertaining to a study and required to be retained by this part shall be retained in the archive(s) for a period of at least ten years following the effective data of the applicable final test rule.

(2) In the case of negotiated testing agreements, each agreement will contain a provision that, except as provided in

paragraph (c) of this section, documentation records, raw data, and specimens pertaining to a study and required to be retained by this part shall be retained in the archive(s) for a period of at least ten years following the publication date of the acceptance of a negotiated test agreement.

(3) In the case of testing submitted under section 5, except for those items listed in paragraph (c) of this section, documentation records, raw data, and specimens pertaining to a study should be retained in the archive(s) for a period of at least five years following the date on which the results of the study are submitted to the Agency.

(c) Wet specimens, samples of test or control substances, and specially prepared material (e.g., histochemical, electron microscopic, blood mounts, teratological preparation, and uteri from dominant lethal mutagenesis tests), which are relatively fragile and differ markedly in stability and quality during storage, shall be retained only as long as the quality of the preparation affords evaluation. In no case shall retention be required for longer period than those set forth in paragraph (b) of this section.

(d) The master schedule sheet, copies of protocols, and records of quality assurance inspections, as required by § 792.35(c) shall be maintained by the quality assurance unit as an easily accessible system of records for the period of time specified in paragraph (b) of this section.

(e) Summaries of training and experience and job descriptions required to be maintained by § 792.29(b) may be retained along with all other testing facility employment records for length of time specified in paragraph (b) of this section.

(f) Records and reports of the maintenance and calibration and inspection of equipment, as required by § 792.63(b) and (c), shall be retained for the length of time specified in paragraph (b) of this section.

(g) If a facility conducting testing or an archive contracting facility goes out of business, all raw data, documentation, and other material specified in this section shall be transferred to the archives of the sponsor of the study. The EPA shall be notified in writing of such a transfer.

(h) Specimens, samples, or other nondocumentary materials need not be retained after EPA has notified in writing the sponsor or testing facility holding the materials that retention is no longer required by EPA. Such notification normally will be furnished upon request after EPA or FDA has completed an audit of the particular study to which the materials relate and EPA has concluded that the study was conducted in accordance with this part.

(i) Records required by this part may be retained either as original records or as true copies such as photocopies, microfilm, microfiche, or other accurate reproductions of the original records.

TITLE 41. PUBLIC CONTRACTS AND PROPERTY MANAGEMENT

Agency: General Services Administration

PART 105-72. UNIFORM ADMINISTRATIVE REQUIREMENTS FOR GRANTS AND AGREEMENTS WITH INSTITUTIONS OF HIGHER EDUCATION, HOSPITALS, AND OTHER NON-PROFIT ORGANIZATIONS

Subpart 105-72.60. Post-Award Requirements/Reports and Records

Citation: 41 CFR 105-72.602

✍ § 105-72.602 Financial reporting.

(a) The following forms or such other forms as may be approved by OMB are authorized for obtaining financial information from recipients.

(1) *SF-269 or SF-269A, Financial Status Report.*

(i) Each Federal awarding agency shall require recipients to use the SF-269 or SF-269A to report the status of funds for all nonconstruction projects or programs. A Federal awarding agency may, however, have the option of not requiring the SF-269 or SF-269A when the SF-270, Request for Advance or Reimbursement, or SF-272, Report of Federal Cash Transactions, is determined to provide adequate information to meet its needs, except that a final SF-269 or SF-269A shall be required at the completion of the project when the SF-270 is used only for advances.

(ii) The Federal awarding agency shall prescribe whether the report shall be on a cash or accrual basis. If the Federal awarding agency requires accrual information and the recipient's accounting records are not normally kept on the accrual basis, the recipient shall not be required to convert its accounting system, but shall develop such accrual information through best estimates based on an analysis of the documentation on hand.

(iii) The Federal awarding agency shall determine the frequency of the Financial Status Report for each project or program, considering the size and complexity of the particular project or program. However, the report shall not be required more frequently than quarterly or less frequently than annually. A final report shall be required at the completion of the agreement.

(iv) The Federal awarding agency shall require recipients to submit the SF-269 or SF-269A (an original and no more than two copies) no later than 30 days after the end of each specified reporting period for quarterly and semiannual reports, and 90 calendar days for annual and final reports. Extensions of reporting due dates may be approved by the Federal awarding agency upon request of the recipient.

(2) *SF-272, Report of Federal Cash Transactions.*

(i) When funds are advanced to recipients the Federal awarding agency shall require each recipient to submit the SF-272 and, when necessary, its continuation sheet, SF-272a. The Federal awarding agency shall use this report to monitor cash advanced to recipients and to obtain disbursement information for each agreement with the recipients.

(ii) Federal awarding agencies may require forecasts of Federal cash requirements in the "Remarks" section of the report.

(iii) When practical and deemed necessary, Federal awarding agencies may require recipients to report in the "Remarks" section the amount of cash advances received in excess of three days. Recipients shall provide short narrative explanations of actions taken to reduce the excess balances.

(iv) Recipients shall be required to submit not more than the original and two copies of the SF-272, 15 calendar days following the end of each quarter. The Federal awarding agencies may require a monthly report from those recipients receiving advances totaling $1 million or more per year.

(v) Federal awarding agencies may waive the requirement for submission of the SF-272 for any one of the following reasons:

(A) When monthly advances do not exceed $25,000 per recipient, provided that such advances are monitored through other forms contained in this section;

(B) If, in the Federal awarding agency's opinion, the recipient's accounting controls are adequate to minimize excessive Federal advances; or,

(C) When the electronic payment mechanisms provide adequate data.

(b) When the Federal awarding agency needs additional information or more frequent reports, the following shall be observed.

(1) When additional information is needed to comply with legislative requirements, Federal awarding agencies shall issue instructions to require recipients to submit such information under the "Remarks" section of the reports.

(2) When a Federal awarding agency determines that a recipient's accounting system does not meet the standards in § 105-72.301, additional pertinent information to further monitor awards may be obtained upon written notice to the recipient until such time as the system is brought up to standard. The Federal awarding agency, in obtaining this information, shall comply with report clearance requirements of 5 CFR part 1320.

(3) Federal awarding agencies are encouraged to shade out any line item on any report if not necessary.

(4) Federal awarding agencies may accept the identical information from the recipients in machine readable format or computer printouts or electronic outputs in lieu of prescribed formats.

(5) Federal awarding agencies may provide computer or electronic outputs to recipients when such expedites or contributes to the accuracy of reporting.

TITLE 42. PUBLIC HEALTH

Agency:	**Department of Health and Human Services Public Health Service**

SUBCHAPTER D. GRANTS

PART 60. HEALTH EDUCATION ASSISTANCE LOAN PROGRAM

Subpart D. The Lender and Holder

Citation:	**42 CFR 60.42**

✍ § 60.42 Records, reports, inspection, and audit requirements for HEAL lenders and holders.

(a) *Records.* (1) A lender or holder must keep complete and accurate records of each HEAL loan which it holds. The records must be organized in a way that permits them to be easily retrievable and allows the ready identification of the current status of each loan. The required records include:

(i) The loan application;

(ii) The original promissory note;

(iii) The repayment schedule agreement;

(iv) Evidence of each disbursement of loan proceeds;

(v) Notices of changes in a borrower's address and status as a full-time student;

(vi) Evidence of the borrower's eligibility for a deferment;

(vii) The borrower's signed statement describing his or her rights and responsibilities in connection with a HEAL loan;

(viii) The documents required for the exercise of forbearance;

(ix) Documentation of the assignment of the loan; and

(x) Evidence of a borrower's creditworthiness, including the borrower's credit report.

(2) The lender or holder must maintain for each borrower a payment history showing the date and amount of each payment received on the borrower's behalf, and the amounts of each payment attributable to principal and interest. A lender or holder must also maintain for each loan a collection history showing the date and subject of each communication with a borrower or endorser for collection of a delinquent loan. Furthermore, a lender or holder must keep any additional records which are necessary to make any reports required by the Secretary.

(3) A lender or holder must retain the records required for each loan for not less than 5 years following the date the loan is repaid in full by the borrower. However, in particular cases the Secretary may require the retention of records beyond this minimum period. A lender or holder must keep the original copy of an unpaid promissory note, but may store all other records in microform or computer format.

(4) The lender or holder must maintain accurate and complete records on each HEAL borrower and related school activities required by the HEAL program. All HEAL records shall be maintained under security and protected from fire, flood, water leakage, other environmental threats, electronic data system failures or power fluctuations, unauthorized intrusion for use, and theft.

(b) *Reports.* A lender or holder must submit reports to the Secretary at the time and in the manner required by the Secretary.

(c) *Inspections.* Upon request, a lender or holder must afford the Secretary, the Comptroller General of the United States, and any of their authorized representatives access to its records in order to assure the correctness of its reports.

(d) The lender or holder must comply with the Department's biennial audit requirements of section 705 of the Act.

(e) Any lender or holder who has information which indicates potential or actual commission of fraud or other offenses against the United States, involving these loan funds, must promptly provide this information to the appropriate Regional Office of Inspector General for Investigation.

Subpart E. The School

Citation:	**42 CFR 60.56**

✍ § 60.56 Records.

(a) In addition to complying with the requirements of section 739(b) of the Act, each school must maintain an accurate, complete, and easily retrievable record with respect to each student who has a HEAL loan. The record must contain all of the following information:

(1) Student's name, address, academic standing and period of attendance;

(2) Name of the HEAL lender, amount of the loan, and the period for which the HEAL loan was intended;

(3) If a noncitizen, documentation of the student's alien registration status.

(4) Amount and source of other financial assistance received by the student during the period for which the HEAL loan was made;

(5) Date the school receives the HEAL check or draft and the

date it either gives it to the student or returns it to the lender (if the school is not the lender);

(6) Date the school disburses the loan to a student (if the school is the lender);

(7) Date the school signs the loan check or draft (if the school is a copayee);

(8) Amount of tuition, fees, and other charges paid by the student to the school for the academic period covered by the loan and the dates of payment;

(9) Photocopy of each HEAL check or draft received by the student;

(10) Documentation of each entrance interview, including the date of the entrance interview and the signature of the borrower indicating that the entrance interview was conducted;

(11) Documentation of the exit interview, including the date of the exit interview and the signature of the borrower indicating that the exit interview was conducted, or documentation of the date that the school mailed exit interview materials to the borrower if the borrower failed to report for the exit interview;

(12) A photocopy made by the school of the borrower's I-151 or I-551, if the borrower is required to possess such identification by the United States, or other documentation, if obtained by the school, to verify citizenship status and Social Security number (e.g., a certified copy of the borrower's birth certificate or a photocopy made by the school of the borrower's original Social Security card or copy issued by the Federal Government);

(13) Documentation of the calculations made which compare the financial resources of the applicant with the cost of his or her education at the school;

(14) Copy(s) of the borrower's financial aid transcript(s);

(15) The standard budget used for the student, the documentation to support the basis for any deviations made to the standard budget;

(16) Copies of all correspondence between the school and the borrower or between the school and the lender or its assignee regarding the loan;

* * * * *

(18) Expected postgraduate destination of borrower.

(b) The school must maintain the record for not less than 5 years following the date the student graduates, withdraws or fails to enroll as a full time student. The school may store the records in microform or computer format.

(c) The school must comply with the Department's biennial audit requirements of section 705 of the Act.

(d) The school must develop and follow written procedures for the receipt, verification of amount, and disbursements of HEAL checks or drafts. These procedures must be maintained in the school's policies and procedures manuals or other general office records.

Agency: **Department of Health and Human Services**
Health Care Financing Administration

SUBCHAPTER B. MEDICARE PROGRAM

PART 413. PRINCIPLES OF REASONABLE COST REIMBURSEMENT; PAYMENT FOR END-STAGE RENAL DISEASE SERVICES; OPTIONAL PROSPECTIVELY DETERMINED PAYMENT RATES FOR SKILLED NURSING FACILITIES

Citation: **42 CFR 413.24**

✍ § 413.24 Adequate cost data and cost finding.

* * * * *

(f) *Cost reports.* * * *

(4) *Electronic submission of cost reports.* (i) As used in this paragraph, "provider" means a hospital, skilled nursing facility, or home health agency.

(ii) Effective for cost reporting periods beginning on or after October 1, 1989, for hospitals, and cost reporting periods ending on or after February 1, 1997, for skilled nursing facilities and home health agencies, a provider is required to submit cost reports in a standardized electronic format. The provider's electronic program must be capable of producing the HCFA standardized output file in a form that can be read by the fiscal intermediary's automated system. This electronic file, which must contain the input data required to complete the cost report and the data required to pass specified edits, is forwarded to the fiscal intermediary for processing through its system.

(iii) The fiscal intermediary stores the provider's as-filed electronic cost report and may not alter that file for any reason. The fiscal intermediary makes a "working copy" of the as-filed electronic cost report to be used, as necessary, throughout the settlement process (that is, desk review, processing audit adjustments, final settlement, etc). The provider's electronic program must be able to disclose if any changes have been made to the as-filed electronic cost report after acceptance by the intermediary. If the as-filed electronic cost report does not pass all specified edits, the fiscal intermediary rejects the cost report and returns it to the provider for correction. For purposes of the requirements in paragraph (f)(2) of this section concerning due dates, an electronic cost report is not considered to be filed until it is accepted by the intermediary.

(iv) Effective for cost reporting periods ending on or after September 30, 1994, for hospitals, and cost reporting periods ending on or after, February 1, 1997, for skilled nursing facilities and home health agencies, a provider must submit a hard copy of a settlement summary, a statement of certain worksheet totals found within the electronic file, and a statement signed by its administrator or chief financial officer certifying the accuracy of the electronic file or the manually prepared cost report. During a transition period, skilled nursing facilities and home health agencies must submit a hard copy of the completed cost report forms in addition to the electronic file. The following statement must immediately precede the dated signature of the provider's administrator or chief financial officer:

I hereby certify that I have read the above certification statement and that I have examined the accompanying electronically filed or manually submitted cost report and the Balance Sheet Statement of Revenue and Expenses prepared by ________ (Provider Name(s) and Number(s)) for the cost reporting period beginning ________ and ending ________ and that to the best of my knowledge and belief, this report and statement are true, correct, complete and prepared from the books and records of the provider in accordance with applicable instructions, except as noted. I further certify that I am familiar with the laws and regulations regarding the provision of health care services, and that the services identified in this cost report were provided in compliance with such laws and regulations.

(v) A provider may request a delay or waiver of the electronic submission requirement in paragraph (f)(4)(ii) of this section if this requirement would cause a financial hardship or if the provider qualifies as a low or no Medicare utilization provider. The provider must submit a written request for delay or waiver with necessary supporting documentation to its intermediary no later than 30 days after the end of its cost reporting period. The intermediary reviews the request and forwards it, with a recommendation for approval or denial, to HCFA central office within 30 days of receipt of the request. HCFA central office either approves or denies the request and notifies the intermediary within 60 days of receipt of the request.

* * * * *

SUBCHAPTER D. PEER REVIEW ORGANIZATIONS

PART 476. ACQUISITION, PROTECTION, AND DISCLOSURE OF PEER REVIEW INFORMATION

Subpart B. Utilization and Quality Control Peer Review Organizations (PROs)

PRO Responsibilities

Citation: 42 CFR 476.115

✍ § 476.115 Requirements for maintaining confidentiality.

(a) *Responsibilities of PRO officers and employees.* The PRO must provide reasonable physical security measures to prevent unauthorized access to PRO information and to ensure the integrity of the information, including those measures needed to secure computer files. Each PRO must instruct its officers and employees and health care institution employees participating in PRO activities of their responsibility to maintain the confidentiality of information and of the legal penalties that may be imposed for unauthorized disclosure of PRO information.

(b) *Responsible individuals within the PRO.* The PRO must assign a single individual the responsibility for maintaining the system for assuring the confidentiality of information within the PRO review system. That individual must notify HCFA of any violations of these regulations.

(c) *Training requirements.* The PRO must train participants of the PRO review system in the proper handling of confidential information.

(d) *Authorized access.* An individual participating in the PRO review system on a routine or ongoing basis must not have authorized access to confidential PRO information unless that individual—

(1) Has completed a training program in the handling of PRO information in accordance with paragraph (c) of this section or has received comparable training from another source; and

(2) Has signed a statement indicating that he or she is aware of the legal penalties for unauthorized disclosure.

(e) *Purging of personal identifiers.* (1) The PRO must purge or arrange for purging computerized information, patient records and other noncomputerized files of all personal identifiers as soon as it is determined by HCFA that those identifiers are no longer necessary.

(2) The PRO must destroy or return to the facility from which it was collected confidential information generated from computerized information, patient records and other noncomputerized files when the PRO determines that the maintenance of hard copy is no longer necessary to serve the specific purpose for which it was obtained or generated.

(f) *Data system procedures.* The PRO must assure that organizations and consultants providing data services to the PRO have established procedures for maintaining the confidentiality of PRO information in accordance with requirements defined by the PRO and consistent with procedures established under this part.

SUBCHAPTER E. STANDARDS AND CERTIFICATION

PART 482. CONDITIONS OF PARTICIPATION FOR HOSPITALS

Subpart C. Basic Hospital Functions

Citation: 42 CFR 482.24

✍ § 482.24 Condition of participation: Medical record services.

The hospital must have a medical record service that has administrative responsibility for medical records. A medical record must be maintained for every individual evaluated or treated in the hospital.

(a) *Standard: Organization and staffing.* The organization of the medical record service must be appropriate to the scope and complexity of the services performed. The hospital must employ adequate personnel to ensure prompt completion, filing, and retrieval of records.

(b) *Standard: Form and retention of record.* The hospital must maintain a medical record for each inpatient and outpatient. Medical records must be accurately written, promptly completed, properly filed and retained, and accessible. The hospital must use a system of author identification and record maintenance that ensures the integrity of the authentication and protects the security of all record entries.

(1) Medical records must be retained in their original or legally reproduced form for a period of at least 5 years.

(2) The hospital must have a system of coding and indexing medical records. The system must allow for timely retrieval by diagnosis and procedure, in order to support medical care evaluation studies.

(3) The hospital must have a procedure for ensuring the confidentiality of patient records. Information from or copies of records may be released only to authorized individuals, and the hospital must ensure that unauthorized individuals cannot gain access to or alter patient records. Original medical records must be released by the hospital only in accordance with Federal or State laws, court orders, or subpoenas.

(c) *Standard: Content of record.* The medical record must contain information to justify admission and continued hospitalization, support the diagnosis, and describe the patient's progress and response to medications and services.

(1) All entries must be legible and complete, and must be authenticated and dated promptly by the person (identified by name and discipline) who is responsible for ordering, providing, or evaluating the service furnished.

(i) The author of each entry must be identified and must authenticate his or her entry.

(ii) Authentication may include signatures, written initials or computer entry.

(2) All records must document the following as appropriate:

(i) Evidence of a physical examination, including a health

history, performed no more than 7 days prior to admission or within 48 hours after admission.

(ii) Admitting diagnosis.

(iii) Results of all consultative evaluations of the patient and appropriate findings by clinical and other staff involved in the care of the patient.

(iv) Documentation of complications, hospital acquired infections, and unfavorable reactions to drugs and anesthesia.

(v) Properly executed informed consent forms for procedures and treatments specified by the medical staff, or by Federal or State law if applicable, to require written patient consent.

(vi) All practitioners' orders, nursing notes, reports of treatment, medication records, radiology, and laboratory reports, and vital signs and other information necessary to monitor the patient's condition.

(vii) Discharge summary with outcome of hospitalization, disposition of case, and provisions for follow-up care.

(viii) Final diagnosis with completion of medical records within 30 days following discharge.

Citation: 42 CFR 482.26

✍ § 482.26 Condition of participation: Radiologic services.

The hospital must maintain, or have available, diagnostic radiologic services. If therapeutic services are also provided, they, as well as the diagnostic services, must meet professionally approved standards for safety and personnel qualifications.

(a) *Standard: Radiologic services.* The hospital must maintain, or have available, radiologic services according to needs of the patients.

(b) *Standard: Safety for patients and personnel.* The radiologic services, particularly ionizing radiology procedures, must be free from hazards for patients and personnel.

(1) Proper safety precautions must be maintained against radiation hazards. This includes adequate shielding for patients, personnel, and facilities, as well as appropriate storage, use, and disposal of radioactive materials.

(2) Periodic inspection of equipment must be made and hazards identified must be promptly corrected.

(3) Radiation workers must be checked periodically, by the use of exposure meters or badge tests, for amount of radiation exposure.

(4) Radiologic services must be provided only on the order of practitioners with clinical privileges or, consistent with State law, of other practitioners authorized by the medical staff and the governing body to order the services.

(c) *Standard: Personnel.* (1) A qualified full-time, part-time, or consulting radiologist must supervise the ionizing radiology services and must interpret only those radiologic tests that are determined by the medical staff to require a radiologist's specialized knowledge. For purposes of this section, a radiologist is a doctor of medicine or osteopathy who is qualified by education and experience in radiology.

(2) Only personnel designated as qualified by the medical staff may use the radiologic equipment and administer procedures.

(d) *Standard: Records.* Records of radiologic services must be maintained.

(1) The radiologist or other practitioner who performs radiology services must sign reports of his or her interpretations.

(2) The hospital must maintain the following for at least 5 years.

(i) Copies of reports and printouts.

(ii) Films, scans, and other image records, as appropriate.

PART 483. CONDITIONS OF PARTICIPATION AND REQUIREMENTS FOR LONG TERM CARE FACILITIES

Subpart B. Requirements for Long Term Care Facilities

Citation: 42 CFR 483.10

✍ § 483.10 Level A requirement: Resident rights.

* * * * *

(b) *Level B requirement: Notice of rights and services.* (1) The facility must inform the resident both orally and in writing in a language that the resident understands of his or her rights and all rules and regulations governing resident conduct and responsibilities during the stay in the facility. Such notification must be made prior to or upon admission and during the resident's stay. Receipt of such information, and any amendments to it, must be acknowledged in writing;

(2) The resident has the right to inspect and purchase photocopies of all records pertaining to the resident, upon written request and 48 hours notice to the facility;

* * * * *

TITLE 43. PUBLIC LANDS: INTERIOR

Agency: Department of the Interior
Office of the Secretary

PART 12. ADMINISTRATIVE AND AUDIT REQUIREMENTS AND COST PRINCIPLES FOR ASSISTANCE PROGRAMS

Subpart F. Uniform Administrative Requirements for Grants and Agreements With Institutions of Higher Education, Hospitals, and Other Non-Profit Organizations

Reports and Records

Citation: 43 CFR 12.952

✍ § 12.952 Financial reporting.

(a) The following forms or such other forms as may be approved by OMB are authorized for obtaining financial information from recipients.

(1) *SF-269 or SF-269A, Financial Status Report.*

(i) Each Federal awarding agency will require recipients to use either the SF-269 or SF-269A to report the status of funds for all nonconstruction projects or programs. A Federal awarding agency may, however, have the option of not requiring the SF-269 or SF-269A when the SF-270, Request for Advance or Reimbursement, or SF-272, Report of Federal Cash Transactions, is determined to provide adequate information to meet its needs, except that a final SF-269 or SF-269A shall be required at the completion of the project when the SF-270 is used only for advances.

(ii) The Federal awarding agency shall prescribe whether the report shall be on a cash or accrual basis. If the Federal awarding agency requires accrual information and the recipient's accounting records are not normally kept on an accrual basis, the recipient shall not be required to convert its accounting system, but shall develop accrual information through best estimates based upon an analysis of the documentation on hand.

(iii) The Federal awarding agency shall determine the frequency of the Financial Status Report for each project or program, considering the size and complexity of the particular project or program. However, the report shall not be required more frequently than quarterly or less frequently than annually. A final report shall be required at the completion of the agreement.

(iv) The Federal awarding agency shall require recipients to submit the SF-269 or SF-269A (an original and no more than two copies) no later than 30 days after the end of each specified reporting period for quarterly and semi-annual reports, and 90 calendar days for annual and final reports. Extensions of reporting due dates may be approved by the Federal awarding agency upon request by the recipient.

(2) *SF-272, Report of Federal Cash Transactions.*

(i) When funds are advanced to recipients, the Federal awarding agency shall require each recipient to submit the SF-272 and, when necessary, its continuation sheet, SF-272a. The Federal awarding agency shall use this report to monitor cash advanced to recipients and to obtain disbursement information for each agreement with the recipients.

(ii) Federal awarding agencies may require forecasts of Federal cash requirements in the "Remarks" section of the report.

(iii) When practical and deemed necessary, Federal awarding agencies may require recipients to report in the "Remarks" section the amount of cash advances received in excess of three days. Recipients shall provide short narrative explanations of actions taken to reduce the excess balances.

(iv) Recipients shall be required to submit not more than the original and two copies of the SF-272 15 calendar days following the end of each quarter. The Federal awarding agencies may require a monthly report from those recipients receiving advances totaling $1 million or more per year.

(v) Federal awarding agencies may waive the requirement for submission of the SF-272 for any one of the following reasons:

(A) When monthly advances do not exceed $25,000 per recipient, provided that the advances are monitored through other forms contained in this section;

(B) If, in the Federal awarding agency's opinion, the recipient's accounting controls are adequate to minimize excessive Federal advances; or

(C) When the electronic payment mechanisms provide adequate data.

(b) When the Federal awarding agency needs additional information or more frequent reports, the following shall be observed;

(1) When additional information is needed to comply with legislative requirements, Federal awarding agencies shall issue instructions to require recipients to submit such information under the "Remarks" section of the reports.

(2) When a Federal awarding agency determines that a recipient's accounting system does not meet the standards in Section 12.921, additional pertinent information to further monitor awards may be obtained upon written notice to the recipient until such time as the system is brought up to standard. The Federal awarding agency, in obtaining this information, shall comply with report clearance requirements of 5 CFR part 1320.

(3) Federal awarding agencies are encouraged to shade out any line item or any report if not necessary.

(4) Federal awarding agencies may accept the identical information from the recipients in machine readable format or computer printouts or electronic outputs in lieu of prescribed formats.

(5) Federal awarding agencies may provide computer or electronic outputs to recipients when such action expedites or contributes to the accuracy of reporting.

TITLE 45. PUBLIC WELFARE

Agency: **Department of Health and Human Services General Administration**

PART 74. UNIFORM ADMINISTRATIVE REQUIREMENTS FOR AWARDS AND SUBAWARDS TO INSTITUTIONS OF HIGHER EDUCATION, HOSPITALS, OTHER NONPROFIT ORGANIZATIONS, AND COMMERCIAL ORGANIZATIONS; AND CERTAIN GRANTS AND AGREEMENTS WITH STATES, LOCAL GOVERNMENTS AND INDIAN TRIBAL GOVERNMENTS

Subpart C. Post-Award Requirements

Financial and Program Management

Citation: **45 CFR 74.26**

✍ § 74.26 Non-Federal audits.

(a)(1) Recipients and subrecipients that are institutions of higher education, hospitals affiliated with institutions of higher education, and other nonprofit organizations shall be subject to the audit requirements contained in OMB Circular A-133, "Audits of Institutions of Higher Education and Other Non-Profit Institutions." (See Appendix I to this part.)

(2) Recipients and subrecipients that are commercial organizations have two options regarding audits:

(i) A financial related audit (as defined in the Government Auditing Standards, GPO Stock #020-000-00-265-4) of a particular award in accordance with Government Auditing Standards, in those cases where the recipient receives awards under only one HHS program; or, if awards are received under multiple HHS programs, a financial related audit of all HHS awards in accordance with Government Auditing Standards; or

(ii) An audit that meets the requirements contained in OMB Circular A-133.

(3) Commercial organizations that receive annual HHS awards totaling less than OMB Circular A-133'a audit requirement threshold are exempt from requirements for a non-Federal audit for that year, but records must be available for review by appropriate officials of Federal agencies.

* * * * *

(d)(1) All copies of audit reports required by this section shall be submitted to: Department of Health and Human Services, Office of Inspector General, National External Audit Review Center, Lucas Place, Room 514, 323 West 8th Street, Kansas City, MO 64105.

(2) The HHS Office of Inspector General will distribute copies as appropriate within HHS. Recipients, therefore, are not required to send their audit reports to any other HHS officials. Recipients shall provide their Employer Identification Numbers (EIN) on the cover page of reports and submit along with the printed reports a computer disk containing the entire contents of the audit report or at least the information in the report relating to HHS awards.

Reports and Records

Citation: **45 CFR 74.52**

✍ § 74.52 Financial reporting.

(a) The following forms are used for obtaining financial information from recipients:

(1) *SF-269 or SF-269A, Financial Status Report.*

(i) The HHS awarding agency will require recipients to use either the SF-269 (long form) or SF-269A to report the status of funds for all nonconstruction projects or programs. The SF-269 shall always be used if income has been earned. The awarding agency may, however, waive the SF-269 or SF-269A requirement when the PMS-270, Request for Advance or Reimbursement, or PMS-272, Report of Federal Cash Transactions, will provide adequate information to meet its needs, except that a final SF-269 or SF-269A shall be required at the completion of the project when the PMS-270 is used only for advances.

(ii) If the HHS awarding agency requires accrual information and the recipient's accounting records are not normally kept on the accrual basis, the recipient shall not be required to convert its accounting system, but shall develop such accrual information through best estimates based on an analysis of the documentation on hand.

(iii) The HHS awarding agency will determine the frequency of the Financial Status Report for each project or program, considering the size and complexity of the particular project or program. However, the report will not be required more frequently than quarterly or less frequently than annually except under § 74.14. A final report shall be required at the completion of the agreement.

(iv) Recipients shall submit the SF-269 and SF-269A (an original and two copies) no later than 30 days after the end of each specified reporting period for quarterly and semi-annual reports, and 90 calendar days for annual and final reports. Extensions of reporting due dates may be approved by the HHS awarding agency upon request of the recipient.

(2) PMS-272, Report of Federal Cash Transactions.

(i) When funds are advanced to recipients, the HHS awarding agency requires each recipient to submit the PMS-272 and, when necessary, its continuation sheet, PMS-272A through G. The HHS awarding agency uses this report to monitor cash advanced to recipients and to obtain disbursement information for each agreement with the recipients.

(ii) The HHS awarding agency may require forecasts of Federal cash requirements in the "Remarks" section of the report.

(iii) Recipients shall submit the original and two copies of the PMS-272 15 calendar days following the end of each quarter. The HHS awarding agency may require a monthly report from those recipients receiving advances totaling $1 million or more per year.

(iv) The HHS awarding agency may waive the requirement for submission of the PMS-272 for any one of the following reasons:

(A) When monthly advances do not exceed $25,000 per recipient, provided that such advances are monitored through other forms contained in this section;

(B) If, in HHS' opinion, the recipient's accounting controls are adequate to minimize excessive Federal advances; or, (C) When the electronic payment mechanisms provide adequate data.

(b) When the HHS awarding agency needs additional information or more frequent reports, the following shall be observed.

(1) When additional information is needed to comply with legislative requirements, the HHS awarding agency will issue instructions to require recipients to submit that information under the "Remarks" section of the reports.

(2) When HHS determines that a recipient's accounting system does not meet the standards in § 74.21, additional pertinent information to further monitor awards may be obtained, without regard to § 74.4, upon written notice to the recipient until such time as the system is brought up to standard. In obtaining this information, the HHS awarding agencies comply with report clearance requirements of 5 CFR part 1320, " Controlling Paperwork Burdens on the Public."

(3) The HHS awarding agency may accept the identical information from a recipient in machine readable format or computer printouts or electronic outputs in lieu of prescribed formats.

(4) The HHS awarding agency may provide computer or electronic outputs to recipients when such action expedites or contributes to the accuracy of reporting.

Agency: **Corporation for National and Community Service**

PART 2541. UNIFORM ADMINISTRATIVE REQUIREMENTS FOR GRANTS AND COOPERATIVE AGREEMENTS TO STATE AND LOCAL GOVERNMENTS

Subpart E. Reports, Records, Retention and Enforcement

Citation: **45 CFR 2541.410**

✍ § 2541.410 Financial reporting.

(a) *General.* — (1) Except as provided in paragraphs (a) (2) and (5) of this section, grantees will use only the forms specified in paragraphs (a) through (e) of this section, and such supplementary or other forms as may from time to time be authorized by OMB, for:

(i) Submitting financial reports to Federal agencies; or

(ii) Requesting advances or reimbursements when letters of credit are not used.

(2) Grantees need not apply the forms prescribed in this section in dealing with their subgrantees. However, grantees shall not impose more burdensome requirements on subgrantees.

(3) Grantees shall follow all applicable standard and supplemental Federal agency instructions approved by OMB to the extent required under the Paperwork Reduction Act of 1980 for use in connection with forms specified in paragraphs (b) through (e) of this section. Federal agencies may issue substantive supplementary instructions only with the approval of OMB. Federal agencies may shade out or instruct the grantee to disregard any line item that the Federal agency finds unnecessary for its decision making purposes.

(4) Grantees will not be required to submit more than the original and two copies of forms required under this part.

(5) Federal agencies may provide computer outputs to grantees to expedite or contribute to the accuracy of reporting. Federal agencies may accept the required information from grantees in machine usable format or computer printouts instead of prescribed forms.

(6) Federal agencies may waive any report required by this section if not needed.

(7) Federal agencies may extend the due date of any financial report upon receiving a justified request from a grantee.

(b) *Financial Status Report.* — (1) *Form.* Grantees will use Standard Form 269 or 269A, Financial Status Report, to report the status of funds for all nonconstruction grants and for construction grants when required in accordance with paragraph (e)(2)(iii) of this section.

(2) *Accounting basis.* Each grantee will report program outlays and program income on a cash or accrual basis as prescribed by the awarding agency. If the Federal agency requires accrual information and the grantee's accounting records are not normally kept on the accrual basis, the grantee shall not be required to convert its accounting system but shall develop such accrual information through an analysis of the documentation on hand.

(3) *Frequency.* The Federal agency may prescribe the frequency of the report for each project or program. However, the

report will not be required more frequently than quarterly. If the Federal agency does not specify the frequency of the report, it will be submitted annually. A final report will be required upon expiration or termination of grant support.

(4) *Due date.* When reports are required on a quarterly or semiannual basis, they will be due 30 days after the reporting period. When required on an annual basis, they will be due 90 days after the grant year. Final reports will be due 90 days after the expiration or termination of grant support.

(c) *Federal Cash Transactions Report.* — (1) *Form.* (i) For grants paid by letter or credit, Treasury check advances or electronic transfer of funds, the grantee will submit the Standard Form 272, Federal Cash Transactions Report, and when necessary, its continuation sheet, Standard Form 272a, unless the terms of the award exempt the grantee from this requirement.

(ii) These reports will be used by the Federal agency to monitor cash advanced to grantees and to obtain disbursement or outlay information for each grant from grantees. The format of the report may be adapted as appropriate when reporting is to be accomplished with the assistance of automatic data processing equipment provided that the information to be submitted is not changed in substance.

(2) *Forecasts of Federal cash requirements.* Forecasts of Federal cash requirements may be required in the "Remarks" section of the report.

(3) *Cash in hands of subgrantees.* When considered necessary and feasible by the Federal agency, grantees may be required to report the amount of cash advances in excess of three days' needs in the hands of their subgrantees or contractors and to provide short narrative explanations of actions taken by the grantee to reduce the excess balances.

(4) *Frequency and due date.* Grantees must submit the report no later than 15 working days following the end of each quarter. However, where an advance either by letter of credit or electronic transfer of funds is authorized at an annualized rate of one million dollars or more, the Federal agency may require the report to be submitted within 15 working days following the end of each month.

(d) *Request for advance or reimbursement.* — (1) *Advance payments.* Requests for Treasury check advance payments will be submitted on Standard Form 270, Request for Advance or Reimbursement. (This form will not be used for drawdowns under a letter of credit, electronic funds transfer or when Treasury check advance payments are made to the grantee automatically on a predetermined basis.)

(2) *Reimbursements.* Requests for reimbursement under nonconstruction grants will also be submitted on Standard Form 270. (For reimbursement requests under construction grants, see paragraph (e)(1) of this section.)

(3) The frequency for submitting payment requests is treated in paragraph (b)(3) of this section.

(e) *Outlay report and request for reimbursement for construction programs.* —

(1) *Grants that support construction activities paid by reimbursement method.*

(i) Requests for reimbursement under construction grants will be submitted on Standard Form 271, Outlay Report and Request for Reimbursement for Construction Programs. Federal agencies may, however, prescribe the Request for Advance or Reimbursement form, specified in paragraph (d) of this section, instead of this form.

(ii) The frequency for submitting reimbursement requests is treated in paragraph (b)(3) of this section.

(2) *Grants that support construction activities paid by letter of credit, electronic funds transfer or Treasury check advance.* (i) When a construction grant is paid by letter of credit, electronic funds transfer or Treasury check advances, the grantee will report its outlays to the Federal agency using Standard Form 271, Outlay Report and Request for Reimbursement for Construction Programs. The Federal agency will provide any necessary special instruction. However, frequency and due date shall be governed by paragraphs (b) (3) and (4) of this section.

(ii) When a construction grant is paid by Treasury check advances based on periodic requests from the grantee, the advances will be requested on the form specified in paragraph (d) of this section.

(iii) The Federal agency may substitute the Financial Status Report specified in paragraph (b) of this section for the Outlay Report and Request for Reimbursement for Construction Programs.

(3) *Accounting basis.* The accounting basis for the Outlay Report and Request for Reimbursement for Construction Programs shall be governed by paragraph (b)(2) of this section.

Citation: **45 CFR 2541.420**

✍ § 2541.420 Retention and access requirements for records.

(a) *Applicability.* (1) This section applies to all financial and programmatic records, supporting documents, statistical records, and other records of grantees or subgrantees which are:

(i) Required to be maintained by the terms of this part, program regulations or the grant agreement; or

(ii) Otherwise reasonably considered as pertinent to program regulations or the grant agreement.

(2) This section does not apply to records maintained by contractors or subcontractors. For a requirement to place a provision concerning records in certain kinds of contracts, see § 2541.360(i)(10).

(b) *Length of retention period.* (1) Except as otherwise provided, records must be retained for three years from the starting date specified in paragraph (c) of this section.

(2) If any litigation, claim, negotiation, audit or other action involving the records has been started before the expiration of the 3-year period, the records must be retained until completion of the action and resolution of all issues which arise from it, or until the end of the regular 3-year period, whichever is later.

(3) To avoid duplicate recordkeeping, awarding agencies may make special arrangements with grantees and subgrantees to retain any records which are continuously needed for joint use. The awarding agency will request transfer of records to its custody when it determines that the records possess long-term retention value. When the records are transferred to or maintained by the Federal agency, the 3-year retention requirement is not applicable to the grantee or subgrantee.

(c) *Starting date of retention period.* — (1) *General.* When grant support is continued or renewed at annual or other intervals, the retention period for the records of each funding period starts on the day the grantee or subgrantee submits to the awarding agency its single or last expenditure report for that period. However, if grant support is continued or renewed quarterly, the retention period for each year's records starts on the day the grantee submits its expenditure report for the last quarter of the Federal fiscal year. In all other cases, the retention period starts on the day the grantee submits its final expenditure report. If an expenditure report has been waived, the retention period starts on the day the report would have been due.

(2) *Real property and equipment records.* The retention period for real property and equipment records starts from the date of the disposition or replacement or transfer at the direction of the awarding agency.

(3) *Records for income transactions after grant or subgrant support.* In some cases grantees must report income after the period of grant support. Where there is such a requirement, the retention period for the records pertaining to the earning of the income starts from the end of the grantee's fiscal year in which the income is earned.

(4) *Indirect cost rate proposals, cost allocations plans, etc.* This paragraph applies to the following types of documents, and their supporting records: indirect cost rate computations or proposals, cost allocation plans, and any similar accounting computations of the rate at which a particular group of costs is chargeable (such as computer usage charge back rates or composite fringe benefit rates).

(i) If submitted for negotiation. If the proposal, plan, or other computation is required to be submitted to the Federal Government (or to the grantee) to form the basis for negotiation of the rate, then the 3-year retention period for its supporting records starts from the date of such submission.

(ii) If not submitted for negotiation. If the proposal, plan, or other computation is not required to be submitted to the Federal Government (or to the grantee) for negotiation purposes, then the 3-year retention period for the proposal plan, or computation and its supporting records starts from end of the fiscal year (or other accounting period) covered by the proposal, plan, or other computation.

(d) *Substitution of microfilm.* Copies made by microfilming, photocopying, or similar methods may be substituted for the original records.

(e) *Access to records.* — (1) *Records of grantees and subgrantees.* The awarding agency and the Comptroller General of the United States, or any of their authorized representatives, shall have the right of access to any pertinent books, documents, papers, or other records of grantees and subgrantees which are pertinent to the grant, in order to make audits, examinations, excerpts, and transcripts.

(2) *Expiration of right of access.* The rights of access in this section must not be limited to the required retention period but shall last as long as the records are retained.

(f) *Restrictions on public access.* The Federal Freedom of Information Act (5 U.S.C. 552) does not apply to records. Unless required by Federal, State, or local law, grantees and subgrantees are not required to permit public access to their records.

PART 2543. GRANTS AND AGREEMENTS WITH INSTITUTIONS OF HIGHER EDUCATION, HOSPITALS, AND OTHER NON-PROFIT ORGANIZATIONS

Subpart C. Post-Award Requirements

Reports and Records

Citation: 45 CFR 2543.52

✍ § 2543.52 Financial reporting.

(a) The following forms or such other forms as may be approved by OMB are authorized for obtaining financial information from recipients.

(1) SF-269 or SF-269A, Financial Status Report.

(i) Each Federal awarding agency shall require recipients to use the SF-269 or SF-269A to report the status of funds for all nonconstruction projects or programs. A Federal awarding agency may, however, have the option of not requiring the SF-269 or SF-269A when the SF-270, Request for Advance or Reimbursement, or SF-272, Report of Federal Cash Transactions, is determined to provide adequate information to meet its needs, except that a final SF-269 or SF-269A shall be required at the completion of the project when the SF-270 is used only for advances.

(ii) The Federal awarding agency shall prescribe whether the report shall be on a cash or accrual basis. If the Federal awarding agency requires accrual information and the recipient's accounting records are not normally kept on the accrual basis, the recipient shall not be required to convert its accounting system, but shall develop such accrual information through best estimates based on an analysis of the documentation on hand.

(iii) The Federal awarding agency shall determine the frequency of the Financial Status Report for each project or program, considering the size and complexity of the particular project or program. However, the report shall not be required more frequently than quarterly or less frequently than annually. A final report shall be required at the completion of the agreement.

(iv) The Federal awarding agency shall require recipients to submit the SF-269 or SF-269A (an original and no more than two copies) no later than 30 days after the end of each specified reporting period for quarterly and semi-annual reports, and 90 calendar days for annual and final reports. Extensions of reporting due dates may be approved by the Federal awarding agency upon request of the recipient.

(2) SF-272, Report of Federal Cash Transactions.

(i) When funds are advanced to recipients the Federal awarding agency shall require each recipient to submit the SF-272 and, when necessary, its continuation sheet, SF-272a. The Federal awarding agency shall use this report to monitor cash advanced to recipients and to obtain disbursement information for each agreement with the recipients.

(ii) Federal awarding agencies may require forecasts of Federal cash requirements in the "Remarks" section of the report.

(iii) When practical and deemed necessary, Federal awarding agencies may require recipients to report in the "Remarks" section the amount of cash advances received in excess of three days. Recipients shall provide short narrative explanations of actions taken to reduce the excess balances.

(iv) Recipients shall be required to submit not more than the original and two copies of the SF-272 15 calendar days following the end of each quarter. The Federal awarding agencies may require a monthly report from those recipients receiving advances totaling $1 million or more per year.

(v) Federal awarding agencies may waive the requirement for submission of the SF-272 for any one of the following reasons:

(A) When monthly advances do not exceed $25,000 per recipient, provided that such advances are monitored through other forms contained in this section;

(B) If, in the Federal awarding agency's opinion, the recipient's accounting controls are adequate to minimize excessive Federal advances; or,

(C) When the electronic payment mechanisms provide adequate data.

(b) When the Federal awarding agency needs additional information or more frequent reports, the following shall be observed.

(1) When additional information is needed to comply with legislative requirements, Federal awarding agencies shall issue instructions to require recipients to submit such information under the "Remarks" section of the reports.

(2) When a Federal awarding agency determines that a recipient's accounting system does not meet the standards in Section § 2543.21, additional pertinent information to further monitor awards may be obtained upon written notice to the recipient until such time as the system is brought up to standard. The Federal awarding agency, in obtaining this information, shall comply with report clearance requirements of 5 CFR part 1320.

(3) Federal awarding agencies are encouraged to shade out any line item on any report if not necessary.

(4) Federal awarding agencies may accept the identical information from the recipients in machine readable format or computer printouts or electronic outputs in lieu of prescribed formats.

(5) Federal awarding agencies may provide computer or electronic outputs to recipients when such expedites or contributes to the accuracy of reporting.

TITLE 46. SHIPPING

Agency:	**Department of Transportation Coast Guard**

SUBCHAPTER A. PROCEDURES APPLICABLE TO THE PUBLIC

PART 4. MARINE CASUALTIES AND INVESTIGATIONS

Subpart 4.05. Notice Of Marine Casualty and Voyage Records

Citation:	**46 CFR 4.05-15**

✍ § 4.05-15 Voyage records, retention of.

(a) The owner, agent, master, or person in charge of any vessel involved in a marine casualty shall retain such voyage records as are maintained by the vessel, such as both rough and smooth deck and engine room logs, bell books, navigation charts, navigation work books, compass deviation cards, gyro records, stowage plans, records of draft, aids to mariners, night order books, radiograms sent and received, radio logs, crew and passenger lists, articles of shipment, official logs and other material which might be of assistance in investigating and determining the cause of the casualty. The owner, agent, master, other officer or person responsible for the custody thereof, shall make these records available upon request, to a duly authorized investigating officer, administrative law judge, officer or employee of the Coast Guard.

(b) The investigating officer may substitute photostatic copies of the voyage records referred to in paragraph (a) of this section when they have served their purpose and return the original records to the owner or owners thereof.

PART 14. SHIPMENT AND DISCHARGE OF MERCHANT MARINERS

Subpart B. Shipment of Merchant Mariners

Citation:	**46 CFR 14.207**

✍ § 14.207 Content and form of shipping articles.

(a)(1) The content and form of shipping articles for each vessel of the United States of 100 gross tons or more upon a foreign or intercoastal voyage must conform to the present shipping articles, form CG-705A, which meets the requirements of 46 U.S.C. 10302, 10303, 10304, and 10305. The articles must identify the nature of the voyage and specify at least the name, the number of the license or merchant mariner's document, the capacity of service, the time due on board to begin work, and the name and address of the next of kin of, and the wages due to each merchant mariner, either who was discharged or whose services were otherwise terminated during the month.

(2) The content and form of articles for each such vessel upon a coastwise voyage (including a voyage on the Great Lakes) must also conform to the present shipping articles, form CG-705A, which meet the requirements of 46 U.S.C. 10502. The articles must specify at least the matter identified by paragraph (a)(1) of this section, except that they must not specify the wages due to the mariner. The wages section of the form shall be left blank for coastwise voyages.

(b) Any shipping company that manually prepares the articles may, upon request, obtain Shipping Articles, Form CG-705A, from any Officer in Charge, Marine Inspection (OCMI), of the Coast Guard.

(c) Any company that electronically prepares the articles may, upon request submitted to either address in Sec. 14.103, obtain a copy of software developed by the Coast Guard to produce articles in the proper format. Alternatively, a company may develop its own software or buy it off the shelf; but, in either of these cases, it must secure approval of the software from the National Maritime Center at either address in Sec. 14.103.

Citation:	**46 CFR 14.209**

✍ § 14.209 Preparation of shipping articles at beginning of voyage.

Each master or individual in charge of a vessel when shipping articles are required shall prepare an original and two copies of the articles. The original and one copy must be signed by the master or individual in charge and by each merchant mariner; but the second copy must not be signed by any of them.

Citation:	**46 CFR 14.213**

✍ § 14.213 Report of shipment of merchant mariner.

(a) When a vessel of the United States sails upon a foreign, intercoastal, or coastwise voyage (excluding a voyage on the Great Lakes), each master or individual in charge shall, at the commencement of the voyage, send one copy of shipping articles, signed by the master and by each merchant mariner, to the owner, charterer, or managing operator. The master shall keep the original throughout the voyage and enter in it all charges made to the crew during the voyage.

(b) (1) When a vessel of the United States sails exclusively on the Great Lakes, each master or individual in charge shall, at the commencement of the season, or once the vessel is put into service, whichever occurs earlier, send one copy of articles, signed by the master and by each mariner, to the owner, charterer, or managing operator.

(2) The master or individual in charge shall every 60 days send supplementary particulars of engagement covering each mariner engaged during this period, signed by the master and by each mariner, to the owner, charterer, or managing operator.

(3) The master of individual in charge shall, at the close of the season, or once the vessel is withdrawn from service, whichever occurs later, send articles, signed by the master and by each mariner, to the owner, charterer, or managing operator.

(c) When a vessel of the United States sales exclusively on bays or sounds, each master or individual in charge shall, at least every 60 days, send articles, signed by the master and by each mariner, to the owner, charter, or managing operator.

(d) Any person who fails to comply with the requirements of this section is subject to a civil penalty of $5,000.

Subpart C. Discharge of Merchant Mariners

Citation: 46 CFR 14.305

✍ § 14.305 Entries in continuous discharge book.

If the merchant mariner holds a continuous discharge book, the master or individual in charge of the vessel shall make the proper entries in it.

Citation: 46 CFR 14.309

✍ § 14.309 Entries in shipping artjcles at end of voyage.

(a) Each master or individual in charge of a vessel shall, for each merchant mariner being discharged from the vessel, prepare a certificate of discharge and two copies; whether by writing or typing them on the prescribed form with permanent ink or generating them from computer in the prescribed format; and shall sign them with permanent ink. The prescribed format for a certificate of discharge is the same as the present form CG-719A (Rev. 8-80). The left portion of the form has the mariner's printed name, signature, citizenship, and merchant mariner's document number; the certification statement, date and the master's signature. The right portion of the form contains the rate/rank the mariner is serving on the voyage, date and place of shipment, date and place of discharge, name of the vessel, name of the operating company, official number of the vessel, class of the vessel, and the nature of the voyage.

(b) Each mariner being discharged shall sign the certificate and both copies with permanent ink.

(c) When the mariner leaves the vessel, the master or individual in charge shall give the original certificate to the mariner.

(d) Except as directed by Sec. 14.313, the shipping company shall keep both copies of the certificate.

(e) The company shall provide copies of certificates of discharge to the mariner and the Coast Guard upon request.

Citation: 46 CFR 14.311

✍ § 14.311 Report of discharge of merchant mariner.

(a) At the end of each foreign, intercoastal, and coastwise voyage by a vessel of the United States, or of each voyage by such a vessel that sails exclusively on bays or sounds (or by such a vessel at the close of the season on the Great Lakes, or once the vessel is withdrawn from service there, whichever occurs later), the shipping company shall electronically transmit the data from the certificates of discharge via modem to an electronic address which the shipping company may request from the National Maritime Center.

(b) If the data is submitted manually, the shipping companies shall provide the data for foreign and intercoastal voyages at the end of each voyage. For coastwise voyages or of each voyage by such a vessel that sails exclusively on bays or sounds (or by such a vessel at the close of the season of the Great Lakes, or once the vessel is withdrawn from service there, whichever occurs later), the shipping companies shall submit a copy of each certificate of discharge to the address in Sec. 14.103(a) at least once per calendar month.

Citation: 46 CFR 14.313

✍ § 14.313 Storage of shipping articles and of certificates of discharge.

(a) Each shipping company shall keep all original shipping articles and copies of all certificates of discharge for 3 years. After 3 years the shipping companies shall prepare the original shipping articles in alphabetical order by vessel name and send to the address in Sec. 14.103(a) for storage at the Federal Records Center at Suitland, Maryland. The company may dispose of the copies of certificates of discharge. The Coast Guard will dispose of copies of certificates submitted manually, once the data are entered into its sea-service database and are validated.

(b) Each shipping company that goes out of business or merges with another company shall send all original articles to the address in Sec. 14.103(a) within 30 days of the transaction.

(c) The shipping company must provide copies of shipping articles and certificates of discharge to the mariner and the Coast Guard upon request.

Subpart D. Oceanographic Research Vessels

Citation: 46 CFR 14.407

✍ § 14.407 Reports.

(a) The owner, charterer, managing operator, master, or individual in charge of each oceanographic research vessel of 100 gross tons or more shall maintain a record of the employment, discharge, or termination of service of every merchant mariner in the crew. At least every 6 months, the person maintaining this record shall transmit it to the Coast Guard, either manually, in the form of a copy of a certificate of discharge, or electronically.

(b) The owner, charterer, managing operator, master, or individual in charge of the vessel shall keep original shipping articles and a copy of each certificate ready for review by the Coast Guard or the concerned mariner upon request. After January 3, 1997, the Coast Guard will no longer keep either original articles or copies of certificates; it will keep only electronic records of employment.

(c) The master or individual in charge of the vessel shall ensure that every entry made in the articles agrees with the corresponding entry made in a continuous discharge book, on a certificate, or in any other proof of sea service furnished to the mariner.

(d) Each oceanographic company shall keep all original articles and copies of all certificates for 3 years. After that each such company shall send all articles to the address in Sec. 14.103(a).

(e) Each oceanographic company that goes out of business or merges with another company shall send all original articles to the address in Sec. 14.103(a) within 30 days of the transaction.

Agency: Department of Transportation
Maritime Administration

PART 380. PROCEDURES

Subpart C. Records Retention Schedule

Citation: 46 CFR 380.21

✍ § 380.21 Reproduction.

(a) The records described in § 380.24 may be microfilmed or otherwise reproduced in lieu of their retention in original form: *Provided*, that such reproductions shall not be made prior to completion of the audit of such records by the Administration.

(b) The following standards are established for reproduction processes:

(1) *Microfilm.* The film stock used in making photographic or microphotographic copies shall comply with Interim Federal Standard No. 125 covering photographic film and processed photographic film. The microfilm shall be regularly inspected for aging in accordance with Handbook 96, entitled, "Inspection of Processed Photographic Record Films for Aging Blemishes," published by the U.S. Department of Commerce, National Bureau of Standards. If blemishes are detected, a duplicate copy of the roll or print shall be made immediately.

(2) *Photocopy.* Electrostatic or wet processes only.

TITLE 47. TELECOMMUNICATIONS

Agency: Federal Communications Commission

PART 1. PRACTICE AND PROCEDURE

Citation: 47 CFR 1.52

✍ ☞ **§ 1.52 Subscription and verification.**

The original of all petitions, motions, pleadings, briefs, and other documents filed by any party represented by counsel shall be signed by at least one attorney of record in his individual name, whose address shall be stated. A party who is not represented by an attorney shall sign and verify the document and state his address. Either the original document, or an electronic reproduction of such original document containing the facsimile signature of the attorney or unrepresented party is acceptable for filing. If a facsimile copy of a document is filed, the signatory shall retain the original until the Commission's decision is final and no longer subject to judicial review. Except when otherwise specifically provided by rule or statute, documents signed by the attorney for a party need not be verified or accompanied by affidavit. The signature or electronic reproduction thereof by an attorney constitutes a certificate by him that he has read the document; that to the best of his knowledge, information and belief there is good ground to support it; and that it is not interposed for delay. If the original of a document is not signed or is signed with intent to defeat the purpose of this section, or an electronic reproduction does not contain a facsimile signature, it may be stricken as sham and false, and the matter may proceed as though the document had not been filed. An attorney may be subjected to appropriate disciplinary action, pursuant to § 1.24, for a willful violation of this rule or if scandalous or indecent matter is inserted.

Subpart E. Complaints, Applications, Tariffs, and Reports Involving Common Carriers

Applications

Citation: 47 CFR 1.743

✍ **§ 1.743 Who may sign applications.**

(a) Except as provided in paragraph (b) of this section, applications, amendments thereto, and related statements of fact required by the Commission must be signed by the applicant, if the applicant is an individual; by one of the partners, if the applicant is a partnership; by an officer or duly authorized employee, if the applicant is a corporation; or by a member who is an officer, if the applicant is an unincorporated association. Applications, amendments, and related statements of fact filed on behalf of eligible government entities such as states and territories of the United States, their political subdivisions, the District of Columbia, and units of local government, including incorporated municipalities, must be signed by a duly elected or appointed official who is authorized to do so under the laws of the applicable jurisdiction.

* * * * *

(e) "Signed," as used in this section, means an original handwritten signature, except that by public notice in the Federal Register the Common Carrier Bureau may allow signature by any symbol executed or adopted by the applicant with the intent that such symbol be a signature, including symbols formed by computer-generated electronic impulses.

PART 22. PUBLIC MOBILE SERVICES

Subpart A. Scope and Authority

Citation: 47 CFR 22.99

✍ **§ 22.99 Definitions.**

Terms used in this part have the following meanings:

Air-Ground Radiotelephone Service. A radio service in which common carriers are authorized to offer and provide radio telecommunications service for hire to subscribers in aircraft.

Airborne station. A mobile station in the Air-Ground Radiotelephone Service authorized for use on aircraft while in flight or on the ground.

Antenna structure. A structure comprising an antenna, the tower or other structure that exists solely to support antennas, and any surmounting appurtenances (attachments such as beacons or lightning rods).

Antenna. A device that converts radio frequency electrical energy to radiated electromagnetic energy and vice versa; in a transmitting station, the device from which radio waves are emitted.

Archival quality microfiche. A silver halide master microfiche or a copy made on silver halide film.

* * * * *

Subpart B. Application Requirements and Procedures

Citation: 47 CFR 22.105

✍ **§ 22.105 Written applications, standard forms, microfiche, magnetic disks.**

Except for authorizations granted under the emergency conditions set forth in section 308 of the Communications Act of 1934, as amended (47 U.S.C. 308), the FCC may grant authorizations only upon written application (FCC Form 401) received by it. A separate written application is required for each authorization. Applicants shall submit any documents, exhibits, or other written statements of fact that the FCC may require in determining whether to grant, deny or dismiss an application.

Table B-1. — Standard Forms for the Public Mobile Services

Purpose of filing	Form No.	Title of form
application for new or modified station	401	Application for Mobile Radio Service Authorization
major amendment to pending application application for partial assignment of authorization application for renewal of authorization	405	Application for Renewal of Station License
application for airborne mobile authorization	409	Application for Airborne Mobile Radiotelephone Authorization.
application for assignment of authorization	430	Licensee Qualification Report
notification of completion of construction notification of minor modification of station	489	Notification of Commencement of Service or of Additional or Modified Facilities
application for consent to transfer of control	490	Application for Assignment of Authorization or Consent to Transfer of Control of Licensee

(a) *Formal applications, amendments and notifications.* Except as provided in paragraph (b) of this section, applications, amendments and notifications must be filed using the standard forms listed in paragraph (c) of this section.

(b) *Informal applications, amendments and notifications.* Applications, amendments and notifications in letter or document form may be accepted for filing, if none of the standard forms listed in this section are prescribed for or clearly applicable for the intended purpose. Such informal applications, amendments and notifications must be submitted in duplicate, with a caption clearly stating the name of the filer, nature of the filing, the Public Mobile service involved, the call sign of the relevant existing station, if any, and the file number of the relevant pending application, if any, and must contain all necessary technical data and exhibits.

(c) *Standard forms.* Standard forms may be obtained in small quantities from the FCC. Standard forms may be reproduced and the copies used. Computer-generated standard forms may also be used after approval by the FCC staff. Standard forms used for applications, amendments, notifications and reports in the Public Mobile Services are listed in Table B-1 of this section.

(d) *Microfiche required.* All filings and submissions related to stations in the Public Mobile Services, including applications (including exhibits and attachments), notifications, amendments, reports, correspondence and pleadings must be submitted in microfiche form, except as provided in paragraphs (d)(1) and (g) of this section.

(1) Emergency filings, such as requests for special temporary authority, need not be submitted in microfiche form. Filings and submissions (other than standard application forms) that are no longer than three pages need not be submitted in microfiche form. Standard application forms must be submitted in microfiche forms, even if they comprise three pages or less.

(2) Three microfiche copies of each filing or submission must be submitted, except that, for initial Phase I unserved area applications in the Cellular Radiotelephone Service (see § 22.949), two microfiche copies must be submitted. Each microfiche copy must be a complete copy of the signed paper original. Each microfiche must be a 148 mm by 105 mm negative (clear transparent characters appearing on a background providing sufficient contrast to make legible copies) at 24x or 27x reduction. At least one of the microfiche copies must be a silver halide camera master or a copy made on silver halide film such as Kodak Direct Duplicatory Film. Microfiche must be placed in paper microfiche envelopes and submitted in a 5" by 7 1/2" envelope. Applicants must leave Row "A" (the first row for page images) of the first microfiche blank for FCC use.

(3) The following information must be printed on the mailing envelope, the microfiche envelope, and the title area at the top of the microfiche:

(i) For notifications, amendments, reports, correspondence, pleadings and applications, other than initial applications in the Cellular Radiotelephone Service — the name of the applicant, the city and state of the application and the call sign of the station, if the application refers to an existing station.

(ii) For initial applications in the Cellular Radiotelephone Service — the name of the applicant, the market name, the market number, and the channel block.

(4) The microfiche copies of opposition and reply pleadings may be submitted after the required paper originals, in accordance with § 1.45 of this chapter.

(e) *Paper original required.* The paper originals of notifications, amendments, reports, correspondence and applications, other than initial Phase I unserved area applications in the Cellular Radiotelephone Service, must be submitted at the same time as the microfiche required by paragraph (d) of this section. The paper originals of initial Phase I unserved area applications selected in random selection processes must be submitted 7 days after the release of the public notice announcing the tentative selectee. The paper originals of opposition and reply pleadings must be submitted within the time frames established by § 1.45 of this chapter. Each paper original must be stamped "ORIGINAL" on the top page. In addition to the paper original, paper copies of pleadings must be submitted as required by § 1.51 of this chapter.

(f) *Correspondence.* Correspondence concerning a submitted application must clearly identify the name of the filer, nature of the filing, the Public Mobile service involved, the call sign of the relevant existing station, if any, and the file number (if assigned) of the relevant pending application. Correspondence may be sent directly to Mobile Services Division, Common Carrier Bureau, Federal Communications, Washington, DC 20554.

(g) *Magnetic disks.* To assist the FCC in maintaining an accurate technical licensing database, applicants are encouraged to submit the technical and administrative data contained in applications and notifications on magnetic disks. Applicants may also submit, in lieu of the microfiche required by paragraph (d) of this section, entire applications and notifications on magnetic disks, by including graphics files containing the images of the signed paper originals.

(1) Each application must be submitted on a separate labeled standard 3 1/4" magnetic disk, formatted to be readable by high-density floppy drives operating under MS-DOS (3.X or later compatible versions). A copy of each disk must also be submitted (2 identical disks per application).

(2) [Reserved]

Note: Paragraph (g) of § 22.105 is not effective until further notice.

SUBCHAPTER B. COMMON CARRIER SERVICES

PART 42. PRESERVATION OF RECORDS OF COMMUNICATION COMMON CARRIERS

General Instructions

Citation:	47 CFR 42.5

✍ § 42.5 Preparation and preservation of reproductions of original records.

(a) Each carrier may use a retention medium of its choice to preserve records in lieu of original records, provided that they observe the requirements of paragraphs (b) and (c) of this section.

(b) A paper or microfilm record need not be created to satisfy the requirements of this part if the record is initially prepared in machine-readable medium such as punched cards, magnetic tapes, and disks. Each record kept in a machine-readable medium shall be accompanied by a statement clearly indicating the type of data included in the record and certifying that the information contained in it has been accurately duplicated. This statement shall be executed by a person duplicating the records. The records shall be indexed and retained in such a manner that they are easily accessible, and the carrier shall have the facilities available to locate, identify and reproduce the records in readable form without loss of clarity.

(c) Records may be retained on microfilm provided they meet the requirements of the Federal Business Records Act (28 U.S.C. § 1732).

PART 61. TARIFFS

Citation:	47 CFR 61.52

✍ § 61.52 Form, size, type, legibility, etc.

* * * * *

(c) Local exchange carriers shall file all tariff publications and associated documents, such as transmittal letters, requests for special permission, and cost support documents, electronically in accordance with the requirements established by the Chief, Common Carrier Bureau.

PART 63. EXTENSION OF LINES AND DISCONTINUANCE, REDUCTION, OUTAGE AND IMPAIRMENT OF SERVICE BY COMMON CARRIERS; AND GRANTS OF RECOGNIZED PRIVATE OPERATING AGENCY STATUS

Citation:	47 CFR 63.53

✍ § 63.53 Form.

(a) Applications under Section 214 of the Communications Act shall be submitted on paper not more than 21.6 cm (8.5 in) wide and not more than 35.6 cm (14 in) long with a left-hand margin of 4 cm (1.5 in). This requirement shall not apply to original documents, or admissible copies thereof, offered as exhibits or to specially prepared exhibits. The impression shall be on one side of the paper only and shall be double-spaced, except that long quotations shall be single-spaced and indented. All papers, except charts and maps, shall be typewritten or prepared by mechanical processing methods, other than letter press, or printed. The foregoing shall not apply to official publications. All copies must be clearly legible.

(b) Applications submitted under Section 214 of the Communications Act for international services may be submitted on computer diskettes pursuant to a filing manual compiled by the International Bureau, but a paper copy of the application with the original signature must accompany the diskette. The manual will specify the type and format of the computer diskettes and the reporting and procedural requirements for such applications.

(c) Applications submitted under Section 214 of the Communications Act for international services and any related pleadings that are in a foreign language shall be accompanied by a certified translation in English.

SUBCHAPTER C. BROADCAST RADIO SERVICES

PART 73. RADIO BROADCAST SERVICES

Subpart H. Rules Applicable to All Broadcast Stations

Citation:	47 CFR 73.1226

✍ § 73.1226 Availability to FCC of station logs and records.

The following shall be made available to any authorized representative of the FCC upon request:

(a) Station records and logs shall be made available for inspection or duplication at the request of the FCC or its representative. Such logs or records may be removed from the licensee's possession by an FCC representative or, upon request, shall be mailed by the licensee to the FCC by either registered mail, return receipt requested, or certified mail, return receipt requested. The return receipt shall be retained by the licensee as part of the station records until such records or logs are returned to the licensee. A receipt shall be furnished when the logs or records are removed from the licensee's possession by an FCC representative and this receipt shall be retained by the licensee as part of the station records until such records or logs are returned to the licensee. When the FCC has no further need for such records or logs, they shall be returned to the licensee. The provisions of this rule shall apply solely to those station logs and records which are required to be maintained by the provisions of this chapter.

(1) Logs and records stored on microfilm, microfiche or other data-storage systems are subject to the requirements pertaining thereto found in § 73.1840(b).

(b) Where records or logs are maintained as the official records of a recognized law enforcement agency and the removal of the records from the possession of the law enforcement agency will hinder its law enforcement activities, such records will not be removed pursuant to this section if the chief of the law enforcement agency promptly certifies in writing to the FCC that removal of the logs or records will hinder law enforcement activities of the agency, stating insofar as feasible the basis for his decision and the date when it can reasonably be expected that such records will be released to the FCC.

(c) The following contracts, agreements, or understandings, which need not be filed with the FCC (per § 73.3613, Filing of contracts), must be kept at the station and made available for inspection by any authorized representative of the FCC upon request:

(1) Contracts relating to the sale of broadcast time to "time brokers" for resale.

(2) FM subchannel leasing agreements for subsidiary communications.

(3) Time sales contracts with the same sponsor for 4 or more hours per day, except where the length of the events (such as athletic contests, musical programs, and special events) broadcast pursuant to the contract is not under control of the station.

(4) Contracts with chief operators or other engineering personnel.

Citation: 47 CFR 73.1840

✍ § 73.1840 Retention of logs.

(a) Any log required to be kept by station licensees shall be retained by them for a period of 2 years. However, logs involving communications incident to a disaster or which include communications incident to or involved in an investigation by the FCC and about which the licensee has been notified, shall be retained by the licensee until specifically authorized in writing by the FCC to destroy them. Logs incident to or involved in any claim or complaint of which the licensee has notice shall be retained by the licensee until such claim or complaint has been fully satisfied or until the same has been barred by statute limiting the time for filing of suits upon such claims.

(b) Logs may be retained on microfilm, microfiche or other data-storage systems subject to the following conditions:

(1) Suitable viewing-reading devices shall be available to permit FCC inspection of logs pursuant to § 73.1226, availability to FCC of station logs and records.

(2) Reproduction of logs, stored on data-storage systems, to full-size copies, is required of licensees if requested by the FCC or the public as authorized by FCC rules. Such reproductions must be completed within 2 full work days of the time of the request.

(3) Corrections to logs shall be made:

(i) Prior to converting to a data-storage system pursuant to the requirements of § 73.1800(c) and (d), (§ 73.1800, General requirements relating to logs).

(ii) After converting to a data-storage system, by separately making such corrections and then associating with the related data-stored logs. Such corrections shall contain sufficient information to allow those reviewing the logs to identify where corrections have been made, and when and by whom the corrections were made.

(4) Copies of any log required to be filed with any application; or placed in the station's local public inspection file as part of an application; or filed with reports to the FCC must be reproduced in fullsize form when complying with these requirements.

Citation: 47 CFR 73.3526

✍ § 73.3526 Local public inspection file of commercial stations.

(a) *Records to be maintained.* Every applicant for a construction permit for a new station in the commercial broadcast services shall maintain for public inspection a file containing the material described in paragraph (a)(1) of this section. Every permittee or licensee of an AM, FM or TV station in the commercial broadcast services shall maintain for public inspection a file containing the material described in paragraphs (a)(1), (2), (3), (4), (5), (6), (7), and (10) of this section. In addition, every permittee or licensee of a TV station shall maintain for public inspection a file containing material described in paragraph (a)(8) of this section; every permittee or licensee of an AM or FM station shall maintain for public inspection a file containing material described in (a)(9) of this section. The material to be contained in the file is as follows:

(1) A copy of every application tendered for filing, with respect to which local public notice is required to be given under the provisions of § 73.3580 or § 73.3594; and all exhibits, letters and other documents tendered for filing as part thereof; all amendments thereto, copies of all documents incorporated therein by reference, all correspondence between the FCC and the applicant pertaining to the application after it has been tendered for filing, and copies of Initial Decisions and Final Decisions in hearing cases pertaining thereto, which according to the provisions of § § 0.451 through 0.461 of the rules are open for public inspection at the offices of the FCC. Information incorporated by reference which is already in the local file need not be duplicated if the entry making the reference sufficiently identifies the information so that it may be found in the file, and if there has been no change in the document since the date of filing and the applicant, after making the reference so states. If petitions to deny are filed against the application, and have been duly served on the applicant, a statement that such a petition has been filed shall appear in the local file together with the name and address of the party filing the petition. The file shall also contain a copy of every written citizen agreement. For purposes of this section, a citizen agreement is a written agreement between a broadcast applicant, permittee, or licensee, and one or more citizens or citizen groups, entered for primarily noncommercial purposes. This definition includes those agreements that deal with goals or proposed practices directly or indirectly affecting station operation in the public interest, in areas such as Appendix B — but not limited to — community ascertainment, programming, and employment. It excludes common commercial agreements such as advertising contracts, union, employment, and personal services contracts; network affiliations, syndication, program supply contracts and so on. However, the mere inclusion of commercial terms in a primarily noncommercial agreement — such as a provision for payment of fees for future services of the citizen — parties (see "Report and Order," Docket 19518, 57 FCC 2d 494 1976) — would not cause the agreement to be considered commercial for purposes of this section.

Note. — Applications tendered for filing on or before May 13, 1965, which are subsequently designated for hearing after May 13, 1965, with local notice being given pursuant to the provisions of § 73.3594, and material related to such applications, need not be placed in the file required to be kept by this section. Applications tendered for filing after May 13, 1965, which contain major amendments to applications tendered for filing on or before May 13, 1965, with local notice of the amending application being given pursuant to the provisions of 73.3580, need not be placed in the file required to be kept by this section.

(2) A copy of every application tendered for filing by the licensee or permittee for such station which is not included in paragraph (a)(1) of this section and which involves changes in program service, which requests an extension of time in which to complete construction of a new station, or which requests consent to involuntary assignment or transfer, or to voluntary assignment or transfer not resulting in a substantial change in ownership or control and which may be applied for on FCC Form 316; and copies of all exhibits, letters, and other documents filed as part thereof, all amendments thereto, all correspondence between the FCC and the applicant pertaining to the application after it has been tendered for filing, and copies of all documents incorporated therein by reference, which according to the provisions of § § 0.451 through 0.461 of the rules are open for public inspection at the offices of the FCC. Information incorporated by reference which is already in the local file need not be duplicated if the entry making the reference sufficiently identifies the information so that it may be found in the file, and there has been no change in the document since the date of filing and the licensee, after making the reference, so states. If petitions to deny are filed against the application, and have been duly served on the applicant, a statement that such a petition has been filed shall appear in the local file together with the name and address of the party filing the petition.

Note. — The engineering section of the applications mentioned in paragraphs (a)(1) and (2) of this section, and material related to the engineering section, need not be kept in the file required to be maintained by this paragraph. If such engineering section contains service contour maps submitted with that section, copies of such maps and information (State, county, city, street, address, or other identifying information) showing main studio and transmitter location shall be kept in the file.

(3) A copy of every ownership report or supplemental ownership report filed by the licensee or permittee for such station after May 13, 1986, pursuant to the provisions of this part; and copies of all exhibits, letters, and other documents filed as part thereof, all amendments thereto, all correspondence between the permittee or licensee and the FCC pertaining to the reports after they have been filed, and all documents incorporated therein by reference, including contracts listed in such reports in accordance with the provisions of § 73.3615(a)(4)(i) and which according to the provisions of § § 0.451 through 0.461 of the rules are open for public inspection at the offices of the FCC. Information incorporated by reference which is already in the local file need not be duplicated if the entry making the reference sufficiently identifies the information so that it may be found in the file, and if there has been no change in the document since the date of filing and the licensee or permittee, after making the reference so states.

(4) Such records as are required to be kept by § 73.1940 concerning broadcasts by candidates for public office.

(5) A copy of every annual employment report filed by the licensee or permittee for such station pursuant to the provisions of this part; and copies of all exhibits, letters and other documents filed as part thereof, all amendments thereto, and all correspondence between the permittee or licensee and the FCC pertaining to the reports after they have been filed and all documents incorporated therein by reference and which according to the provisions of § § 0.451 through 0.461 of the rules are open for public inspection at the offices of the FCC.

(6) The Public and Broadcasting — A Procedure Manual (see FCC 74-942.39 FR 32288, September 5, 1974).

(7) Letters received from members of the public as are required to be retained by § 73.1202.

(8) For commercial TV broadcast stations every three months a list of at least 5 to 10 community issues addressed by the station's programming during the preceding 3 month period. The list is filed by the tenth day of each calendar quarter (e.g., July 10, October 10, January 10 and April 10) and should include a record of programming for the 3 preceding calendar months (e.g., the list filed by October 10 would be a record of programming from July 1 through September 30). The list shall include a brief narrative describing how each issue was treated. The description of the program should include, but is not limited to, the time, date and duration of each program, the title, and the type of programming in which the issue was treated. (e.g., public service announcements, a call-in program with a public official, etc.) These lists are to be retained for the entire license renewal period.

Note. — The first quarterly filing is to include at least the past three months of a station's programming performance. If the last annual problems/programs list was filed more than three months prior to October 1, 1984, the licensee must place in its public inspection file an issues/programs list encompassing the period of time between its last annual filing and October 1, 1984.

(9) For commercial AM and FM broadcast stations every three months a list of at least 5 to 10 community issues addressed by the station's programming during the preceding 3 month period. The list is to be filed by the tenth day of each calendar quarter (e.g., January 10, April 10, July 10 and October 10). The list shall include a brief narrative describing how each issue was treated, i.e., public service announcements or programs, giving a description of the programs including time, date and duration of each program. These lists are to be retained for the entire license renewal period.

Note. — The first quarterly filing is to include at least the past 3 months of a station's programming performance. If the last annual issues/programs list was filed more than 3 months prior to July 1, 1984, the licensee must place in its public inspection file an issues/programs list encompassing the period of time between its last annual filing and July 1, 1984.

(10) Each applicant for renewal of license shall within 7 days of the last day of broadcast of the local public notice of filing announcements required pursuant to § 73.3580(h), place in the station's local public inspection file a statement certifying compliance with this requirement. The dates and times that the pre-filing and post filing notices were broadcast and the text thereof shall be made part of the certifying statement.

(b) *Responsibility in case of assignment or transfer.* (1) In cases involving applications for consent to assignment of broadcast station construction permits or licenses, with respect to which public notice is required to be given under the provisions of § 73.3580 or 73.3594, the file mentioned in paragraph (a) of this section shall be maintained by the assignor. If the assignment is consented to by the FCC and consummated, the assignee shall maintain the file commencing with the date on which notice of the consummation of the assignment is filed with the FCC. The file maintained by the assignee shall cover the period both before and after the time when the notice of consummation of assignment was filed. The assignee is responsible for obtaining copies of the necessary documents from the assignor or from the FCC files.

(2) In cases involving applications for consent to transfer of control of a permittee or licensee of a broadcast station, the file mentioned in paragraph (a) of this section shall be maintained by the permittee or licensee.

(c) *Station to which reports pertain.* The file need contain only applications, ownership reports, and related material that concern the station for which the file is kept. Applicants, permittees, and licensees need not keep in the file copies of such applications, reports and material which pertain to other stations with regard to which they may be applicants, permittees, or licensees, except to the extent that such information is reflected in the materials required to be kept under the provisions of this section.

(d) *Location of records.* The file shall be maintained at the main studio of the station, where such studio is located in the community to which the station is licensed, or any accessible place (such as a public registry for documents or an attorney's office) in the community to which the station is or is proposed to be licensed, and shall be available for public inspection at any time during regular business hours.

(e) *Period of retention.* The records specified in paragraph (a)(4) of this section shall be retained for periods specified in § 73.1940 (2 years). The manual specified in paragraph (a)(6) of this section shall be retained indefinitely. The letters specified in paragraph (a)(7) of this section shall be retained for the period specified in § 73.1202 (3 years). The issues/programs list specified in paragraphs (a)(8) and (9) of this section shall be retained for the term of license (5 and 7 years for TV and radio respectively). The certification specified in paragraph (a)(10) of this section shall be retained for the period specified in § 73.3580 (for as long as the application to which it refers). The records specified in paragraphs (a)(1), (2), (3), and (5) of this section shall be retained as follows: (1) The applicant for a construction permit for a new station shall maintain such a file so long as the application is pending before the FCC or any proceeding involving that application is pending before the courts. (If the application is granted, paragraph (e)(2) of this section shall apply.)

(2) The permittee or licensee shall maintain such a file so long as an authorization to operate the station is outstanding, and shall permit public inspection of the material as long as it is retained by the licensee even though the request for inspection is made after the conclusion of the required retention period specified in this paragraph. However, material which is voluntarily retained after the required retention time may be kept in a form and place convenient to the licensee, and shall be made available to the inquiring party, in good faith after written request, at a time and place convenient to both the party and the licensee. Applications and related material placed in the file shall be retained for a period of 7 years from the date the application is tendered for filing with the FCC with two exceptions: First, engineering material pertaining to a former mode of operation need not be retained longer than 3 years after a station commences operation under a new or modified mode; and second, all of the material shall be retained for whatever longer period is necessary to comply with the following requirements:

(i) Material shall be retained until final FCC action on the section renewal application following the application or other material in question; and

(ii) Material having a substantial bearing on a matter which is the subject of a claim against the licensee, or relating to an FCC investigation or a complaint to the FCC of which the licensee has been advised, shall be retained until the licensee is notified in writing that the material may be discarded, or, if the matter is a private one, the claim has been satisfied or is barred by statute of limitations. Where an application or related material incorporates by reference material in earlier applications and material concerning programming and related matters (section IV and related material), the material so referred to shall be retained as long as the application referring to it. If a written agreement is not incorporated in an application tendered for filing with the FCC, the starting date of the retention period for that agreement is the date the agreement is executed.

(f) Copies of any material required to be in the public file of any applicant for a construction permit, or permittee or licensee of any commercial TV or radio station shall be available for machine reproduction upon request made in person, provided the requesting party shall pay the reasonable cost of reproduction. Requests for machine copies shall be fulfilled at a location specified by the applicant, permittee or licensee, within a reasonable period of time which, in no event, shall be longer than seven days unless reproduction facilities are unavailable in the applicant's, permittee's, or licensee's community. The applicant, permittee or licensee is not required to honor requests made by mail, but may do so if it chooses.

(g) Statements of a commercial television station's election with respect to either must-carry or retransmission consent as defined in § 76.64 of this chapter shall be retained in the public file of the television station for the duration of the three year election period to which the statement applies.

Citation: 47 CFR 73.3527

✍ § 73.3527 Location public inspection file of noncommercial educational stations.

(a) *Records to be maintained.* Every applicant for a construction permit for a new station in the noncommercial educational broadcast services shall maintain for public inspection a file containing the material in paragraph (a)(1) of this section. Every permittee or licensee of a station in the noncommercial educational broadcast services shall maintain for public inspection a file containing the material described in paragraphs (a)(1) through (9) of this section. The material to be contained in the file is as follows:

(1) A copy of every application tendered for filing with respect to which local public notice is required to be given under the provisions of § 73.3580 or § 73.3594; and all exhibits, letters and other documents tendered for filing as part thereof, all amendments thereto, copies of all documents incorporated therein by reference, all correspondence between the FCC and the applicant pertaining to the application after it has been tendered for filing, and copies of Initial Decisions and Final Decisions in hearing cases pertaining thereto, which according to the provisions of § § 0.451 through 0.461 of the rules are open for public inspection at the offices of the FCC. Information incorporated by reference which is already in the local file need not be duplicated if the entry making the reference sufficiently identifies the information so that it may be found in the file, and if there has been no change in the document since the date of filing and the applicant, after making the reference, so states. If petitions to deny are filed against the application, and have been duly served on the applicant, a statement that such a petition has been filed shall appear in the local file together with the name and address of the party filing the petition.

Note. — Applications tendered for filing on or before May 13, 1965, which were subsequently designated for hearing after May 13, 1965, with local notice being given pursuant to the provisions of § 73.3594, and material related to such applications, need not be placed in the file required to be kept by this section. Materials tendered for filing after May 13, 1965, which contain major amendments to applications tendered for filing on or before May 13, 1965, which local notice of the amending application being given pursuant to the provisions of § 73.3580, need not be placed in the file required to be kept by this section.

(2) A copy of every application tendered for filing by the licensee or permittee for such station after May 13, 1965, pursuant to the provisions of this part, which is not included in paragraph (a)(1) of this section and which involves changes in program service, which requests an extension of time in which to complete construction of a new station, or which requests consent to involuntary assignment or transfer, or to voluntary assignment or transfer not resulting in a substantial change in ownership or control and which may be applied for on FCC Form 316; and copies of all exhibits, letters, and other documents filed as part thereof, all amendments thereto, all correspondence between the FCC and the applicant pertaining to the application after it has been tendered for filing, and copies of all documents incorporated therein by reference, which according to the provisions of § § 0.451 through 0.461 of the rules are open for public inspection at the offices of the FCC. Information incorporated by reference which is already in the local file need not be duplicated if the entry making the reference sufficiently identifies the information so that it may be found in the file, and there has been no change in the document since the date of filing and the licensee, after making the reference, so states. If petitions to deny are filed against the application, and have been duly served on the applicant, a statement that such a petition has been filed shall appear in the local file together with the name and address of the party filling the petition.

Note. — The engineering section of the applications mentioned in paragraphs (a)(1) and (2) of this section, and material related to the engineering section, need not be kept in the file required to be maintained by this paragraph. If such engineering section contains service contour maps submitted with that section, copies of such maps and information (State, county, city, street, address, or other identifying information) showing main studio and transmitter location shall be kept in the file.

(3) A copy of contracts listed in ownership reports filed in accordance with the provisions of § 73.3615(e) and which according to the provisions of § § 0.451 through 0.461 of the rules are open for public inspection at the offices of the FCC. Information incorporated by reference which is already in the local file need not be duplicated if the entry making the reference sufficiently identifies the information so that it may be found in the file, and if there has been no change in the document since the date of filing and the licensee or permittee, after making the reference, so states.

(4) Such records as are required to be kept by § 73.1940, "Broadcasts by candidates for public office."

(5) A copy of every annual employment report filed by the licensee or permittee for such station pursuant to the provisions of this Part; and copies of all exhibits, letters and other documents filed as part thereof, all amendments thereto, all correspondence between the permittee or licensee and the FCC pertaining to the reports after they have been filed and all documents incorporated therein by reference and which; according to the provisions of § § 0.451 through 0.461 of the rules, are open for public inspection at the office of the FCC.

(6) The Public and Broadcasting: Revised Edition (see FCC 74-942, 39 FR 32288, September 5, 1974).

(7) For nonexempt noncommercial educational broadcast stations, every three months a list of at least 5 to 10 community issues addressed by the station's programming during the preceding 3 month period. The list is filed by the tenth day of each calendar quarter (e.g., July 10, October 10, January 10 and April 10) and should include a record of programming of the 3 preceding calendar months (e.g., the list filed by July 10 would be a record of programming from April 1 through June 30). The list shall include a brief narrative describing how each issue was treated. The description of the program should include, but is not limited to, the time, date and duration of each program, the title, the type of programming in which the issue was treated. (e.g., public service announcements, a call-in program with a public official, etc.) These lists are to be retained for the entire license renewal period.

Note 1. — The first quarterly filing is to include at least the past three months of a station's programming performance. If the last annual issues/programs list was filed more than three months prior to October 1, 1984, the licensee must place in its public inspection file an issues/programs list encompassing the period of time between its last annual filing and October 1, 1984.

Note 2. — For purposes of paragraph (a)(7) of this section, exempt applicants, permittees or licensees include those whose existing or prospective facilities are Class D FM stations or whose programming is wholly "Instructional."

(8) The lists of donors supporting specific programs.

(9) Each applicant for renewal of license shall, within 7 days of the last day of broadcast of the local public notice of filing announcements required pursuant to § 73.3580(h), place in the station's local public inspection file a statement certifying compliance with this requirement. The dates and times that the pre-filing and post-filing notices were broadcast and the test thereof shall be made part of the certifying statement.

(b) *Responsibility in case of assignment or transfer.* (1) In cases involving applications for consent to assignment of broadcast station construction permits or licenses, with respect to which public notice is required to be given under the provisions of § 73.3580 or 73.3594, the file mentioned in paragraph (a) of this section shall be maintained by the assignor. If the assignment is consented to by the FCC and consummated, the assignee shall maintain the file commencing with the date on which notice of the consummation of the assignment is filed with the FCC. The file maintained by the assignee shall cover the period both before and after the time when the notice of consummation of assignment was filed. The assignee is responsible for obtaining copies of the necessary documents from the assignor or from the FCC files.

(2) In cases involving applications for consent to transfer of control of a permittee or licensee of a broadcast station, the file mentioned in paragraph (a) of this section shall be maintained by the permittee or licensee.

(c) *Station to which records pertain.* The file need contain only applications, ownership reports, and related material that concern the station for which the file is kept. Applicants, permittees, and licensees need not keep in the file copies of such applications, reports and material which pertain to other stations with regard to which they may be applicants, permittees, or licensees, except to the extent that such information is reflected in the materials required to be kept under the provisions of this section.

(d) *Location of records.* The file shall be maintained at the main studio of the station, where such studio is located in the community to which the station is licensed, or at any accessible place (such as a public registry for documents or an attorney's office) in the community to which the station is or is proposed to be licensed, and shall be available for public inspection at any time during regular business hours.

(e) *Period of retention.* The records specified in paragraph (a)(4) of this section shall be retained for periods specified in § 73.1940 (2 years). The manual specified in paragraph (a)(6) of this section shall be retained indefinitely. The letters specified in paragraph (a)(7) of this section shall be retained for the period specified in § 73.1202 (3 years). The "significant treatment of community issues" list specified in paragraphs (a)(8) and (9) of this section shall be retained for the term of license (5 and 7 years for TV and radio, respectively). The certification specified in paragraph (a)(10) of this section shall be retained for the period specified in § 73.3580 (for as long as the application to which it refers). The records specified in paragraphs (a)(1), (2), (3), and (5) of this section shall be retained, as follows:

(1) The applicant for a construction permit for a new station shall maintain such a file so long as the proceeding in which that application was filed is pending before the FCC or any proceeding involving that application is pending before the courts. (If the application is granted, paragraph (e)(2) of this section shall apply.)

(2) The permittee or licensee shall maintain a file of such records so long as an authorization to operate the station is outstanding, and shall permit public inspections of the material as long as it is retained by the licensee even though the request for inspection is made after the conclusion of the required retention period specified in this subparagraph. However, material which is voluntarily retained after the required retention time may be kept in a form and place convenient to the licensee, and shall be made available to the inquiring party, in good faith after written request, at a time and place convenient to both the party and the licensee. Applications and related material placed in the file shall be retained for a period of 7 years from the date the application is tendered for filing with the FCC with two exceptions: First, engineering material pertaining to a former mode of operation need not be retained longer than 3 years after a station commences operation under a new or modified mode; and second, all of the material shall be retained for whatever longer period is necessary to comply with the following requirements:

(i) Material shall be retained until final FCC action on the second renewal application following the application or other material in question; and

(ii) Material having a substantial bearing on a matter which is the subject of a claim against the licensee, or relating to an FCC investigation or a complaint to the FCC of which the licensee has been advised, shall be retained until the licensee is notified in writing that the material may be discarded, or, if the matter is a private one, the claim has been satisfied or is barred by statutes of limitations. Where an application or related material incorporates by reference material in an earlier application and material concerning programming and related matters (section IV and related material), the material so referred to shall be retained as long as the application referring to it.

(f) Copies of any material required to be in the public file of any applicant for a construction permit, or permittee or licensee of any commercial TV or radio station shall be available for machine reproduction upon request made in person, provided the requesting party shall pay the reasonable cost of reproduction. Requests for machine copies shall be fulfilled at a location specified by the applicant, permittee or licensee, within a reasonable period of time which, in no event, shall be longer than seven days unless reproduction facilities are unavailable in the applicant's, permittee's, or licensee's community. The applicant, permittee or licensee is not required to honor requests made by mail, but may do so if it chooses.

(g) Noncommercial television stations requesting mandatory carriage on any cable system pursuant to § 76.56 of this chapter shall place a copy of such request in its public file and shall retain both the request and relevant correspondence for the duration of any period to which the statement applies.

PART 76. CABLE TELEVISION SERVICE

Subpart H. General Operating Requirements

Citation: **47 CFR 76.305**

✍ **§ 76.305 Records to be maintained locally by cable system operators for public inspection.**

(a) *Records to be maintained.* The operator of every cable television system having 1000 or more subscribers shall maintain for public inspection a file containing a copy of all records which are required to be kept by § 76.207 (political file); § 76.221(f) (sponsorship identification); and § 76.79 (EEO records available for public inspection); 76.225(c) (commercial records for children's programming); 76.601(c) (proof-of-performance test data); 76.601(e) (signal leakage logs and repair records) and § 76.701(h) (records for leased access).

(1) A record shall be kept of each test and activation of the Emergency Alert System (EAS) procedures pursuant to the requirements of part 11 of this chapter and the EAS Operating Handbook. These records shall be kept for three years.

(2) [Reserved]

(b) *Location of records.* The public inspection file shall be maintained at the office which the system operator maintains for the ordinary collection of subscribers charges, resolution of subscriber complaints, and other business or at any accessible place in the community served by the system unit(s) (such as a public registry for documents or an attorney's office). The public inspection file shall be available for public inspection at any time during regular business hours.

(c) The records specified in paragraph (a) of this section shall be retained for the periods specified in § § 76.207, 76.221(f), 76.79, 76.225(c), 76.601(c) and 76.601(e), respectively.

(d) *Reproduction of records.* Copies of any material in the public inspection file shall be available for machine reproduction upon request made in person, provided the requesting party shall pay the reasonable cost of reproduction. Requests for machine copies shall be fulfilled at a location specified by the system operator, within a reasonable period of time, which in no event shall be longer than seven days. The system operator is not required to honor requests made by mail but may do so if it chooses.

SUBCHAPTER D. SAFETY AND SPECIAL RADIO SERVICES

PART 87. AVIATION SERVICES

Subpart C. Operating Requirements and Procedures

Operating Procedures

Citation: **47 CFR 87.103**

✍ **§ 87.103 Posting station license.**

(a) *Stations at fixed locations.* The license or a photocopy must be posted or retained in the station's permanent records.

* * * * *

PART 90. PRIVATE LAND MOBILE RADIO SERVICES

Subpart N. Operating Requirements

Citation: **47 CFR 90.437**

✍ **§ 90.437 Posting station licenses.**

* * * * *

(b) Entities authorized under this part must make available either a clearly legible photocopy of the authorization for each base or fixed station at a fixed location at every control point of the station or an address or location where the current authorization may be found.

* * * * *

TITLE 48. FEDERAL ACQUISITION REGULATIONS SYSTEM

Agency: **Department of Defense**
National Aeronautics and Space Administration

CHAPTER 1. FEDERAL ACQUISITION REGULATION

SUBCHAPTER A. GENERAL

PART 4. ADMINISTRATIVE MATTERS

Subpart 4.7. Contractor Records Retention

Citation: **48 CFR 4.703**

✍ **§ 4.703 Policy.**

(a) Except as stated in 4.703(b), contractors shall make available records, which includes books, documents, accounting procedures and practices, and other data, regardless of type and regardless of whether such items are in written form, in the form of computer data, or in any other form, and other supporting evidence to satisfy contract negotiation, administration, and audit requirements of the contracting agencies and the Comptroller General for (1) 3 years after final payment or, for certain records, (2) the period specified in 4.705 through 4.705-3, whichever of these periods expires first.

(b) Contractors shall make available the foregoing records and supporting evidence for a longer period of time than is required in 4.703(a) if —

(1) A retention period longer than that cited in 4.703(a) is specified in any contract clause; or

(2) The contractor, for its own purposes, retains the foregoing documents and supporting evidence for a longer period. Under this circumstance, the retention period shall be the period of the contractor's retention or 3 years after final payment, whichever period expires first.

(3) The contractor does not meet the original 90-day due date for submission of final indirect cost rate proposals specified in subparagraph (d)(2) of the clause at 52.216-7, Allowable Cost and Payment, and subparagraph (c)(2) of the clause at § 52.216-13, Allowable Cost and Payment — Facilities. Under these circumstances, the retention periods in 4.705 shall be automatically extended one day for each day the proposal is not submitted after the original 90-day due date.

(c) Nothing in this section shall be construed to preclude a contractor from duplicating or storing original records in electronic form unless they contain significant information not shown on the record copy. Original records need not be maintained or produced in an audit if the contractor or subcontractor provides photographic or electronic images of the original records and meets the following requirements:

(1) The contractor or subcontractor has established procedures to ensure that the imaging process preserves accurate images of the original records, including signatures and other written or graphic images, and that the imaging process is reliable and secure so as to maintain the integrity of the records.

(2) The contractor or subcontractor maintains an effective indexing system to permit timely and convenient access to the imaged records.

(3) The contractor or subcontractor retains the original records for a minimum of one year after imaging to permit periodic validation of the imaging systems.

(d) If the information described in paragraph (a) of this section is maintained on a computer, contractors shall retain the computer data on a reliable medium for the time periods prescribed. Contractors may transfer computer data in machine readable form from one reliable computer medium to another. Contractors' computer data retention and transfer procedures shall maintain the integrity, reliability, and security of the original computer data. Contractors shall also retain an audit trail describing the data transfer. For the record retention time periods prescribed, contractors shall not destroy, discard, delete, or write over such computer data.

Subpart 4.8. Government Contract Files

Citation: **48 CFR 4.800**

✍ § 4.800 Scope of subpart.

This subpart prescribes requirements for establishing, maintaining, and disposing of contract files for all contractual actions. The application of this subpart to small purchases and other simplified procedures covered by part 13 is optional. See also documentation requirements in 13.160(c).

Citation: **48 CFR 4.802**

✍ § 4.802 Contract files.

(a) A contract file should generally consist of —

(1) The contracting office contract file, which shall document the basis for the acquisition and the award, the assignment of contract administration (including payment responsibilities), and any subsequent actions taken by the contracting officer;

(2) The contract administration office contract file, which shall document actions reflecting the basis for and the performance of contract administration and responsibilities; and

(3) The paying office contract file, which shall document actions prerequisite to, substantiating, and reflecting contract payments.

(b) Normally, each file should be kept separately; however, if appropriate, any or all of the files may be combined; e.g., if all functions or any combination of the functions are performed by the same office.

(c) Files shall be maintained at organization levels that shall ensure —

(1) Effective documentation of contract actions;

(2) Ready accessibility to principal users;

(3) Minimal establishment of duplicate and working files;

(4) The safeguarding of classified documents; and

(5) Conformance with agency regulations for file location and maintenance.

(d) If the contract files or file segments are decentralized (e.g., by type or function) to various organizational elements or to other outside offices, responsibility for their maintenance shall be assigned. A central control and, if needed, a locator system should be established to ensure the ability to locate promptly any contract files.

(e) Contents of contract files that are proprietary or source selection information as defined in 3.104-4 shall be protected from disclosure to unauthorized persons (see 3.104-5).

(f) Agencies may retain contract files in any medium (paper, electronic, microfilm, etc.) or any combination of media, as long as the requirements of this subpart are satisfied.

Citation: **48 CFR 4.805**

✍ § 4.805 Storage, handling, and disposal of contract files.

(a) Agencies shall prescribe procedures for the handling, storing, and disposing of contract files. Such procedures shall take into account documents held in other than paper format, such as microfilm and various electronic media. The original medium on which the document was created may be changed to facilitate storage as long as the requirements of part 4, law and other regulations are satisfied. The process used to create and store records must record and reproduce the original document, including signatures and other written and graphic images completely, accurately, and clearly. Data transfer, storage, and retrieval procedures shall protect the original data from alteration. Unless law or other regulations require signed originals to be kept, they may be destroyed after the record copies on alternate media and copies reproduced from the record copy are verified to be accurate, complete and clear representations of the originals. Agency procedures for contract file disposal shall include provisions that the documents specified in paragraph (b) of this section shall not be destroyed before the times indicated. When original documents have been converted to alternate media for storage, the requirements in paragraph (b) of this section shall apply to the record copies on the alternate media instead of the original documents.

(b) If administrative records are mixed with program records and cannot be economically segregated, the entire file should be kept for the period of time approved for the program records. Similarly, if documents, specified below, are part of a subject or case file which documents activities different from those specified below, they should be treated in the same manner as the files of which they are a part.

Document	Retention Period
(1) Records pertaining to exceptions or protests, claims for or against the United States, investigations, cases pending or in litigation, or similar matters.	Until final clearance or settlement, or until the retention period otherwise specified for the document in paragraphs (b)(2) through (13) below is completed, whichever is later.
(2) Signed originals of construction contracts over $2,000 and all other contracts over $25,000.	6 years and 3 months after initial payment.
(3) Signed originals of justifications and approvals and determinations and findings required by part 6, and copies of supporting documents and data.	6 years and 3 months after final payment.
(4) Signed originals of construction contracts of $2,000 or less and all other contracts of $25,000 or less.	3 years after final payment.
(5) Unsuccessful offers or quotations that pertain to contracts using simplified acquisition procedures.	Retain 1 year after the date of award or until final payment, whichever is later; but if the contracting officer determines that the files have future value to the Government, retain as long as advisable.
(6) Contract status (progressing), expediting, and production surveillance records.	6 months after final payment.
(7) Rejected engineering change proposals.	6 months after final payment.
(8) Labor compliance records, including equal employment opportunity records.	3 years after final payment.
(9) Documents pertaining generally to the contractor as described at 4.801(c)(3).	Until superseded or obsolete.
(10) Records or documents other than those in paragraphs 4.805(b)(1)-(9) of this section pertaining to contracts using simplified acquisitions procedures.	1 year after final payment.
(11) Records or documents other than those in paragraphs 4.805(b)(1)-(10) of this section pertaining to contracts not using simplified acquisition procedures.	6 years and 3 months after final payment.
(12) Files for cancelled solicitations (see 4.801(c)(1)).	5 years after cancellation.
(13) Solicited and unsolicited unsuccessful offers and quotations above the simplified acquisition threshold:	
(i) When filed separately from contract case files.	Until contract completion date.
(ii) When filed with contract case files.	6 years and 3 months after final payment.

(c) Documents listed in paragraph (b)(1) under "Document" shall not be destroyed until final clearance or settlement.

SUBCHAPTER H. CLAUSES AND FORMS

PART 52. SOLICITATION PROVISIONS AND CONTRACT CLAUSES

Subpart 52.2. Texts of Provisions and Clauses

Citation: 48 CFR 52.214-26

✍ § 52.214-26 Audit and Records-Sealed Bidding.

As prescribed in 14.201-7(a), inserting the following clause:
Audit and Records-Sealed Bidding (Oct 1995)

(a) As used in this clause, records includes books, documents, accounting procedures and practices, and other data, regardless of type and regardless of whether such items are in written form, in the form of computer data, or in any other form.

(b) *Cost or pricing data.* If the Contractor has been required to submit cost or pricing data in connection with the pricing of any modification to this contract, the Contracting Officer, or an authorized representative of the Contracting Officer, in order to evaluate the accuracy, completeness, and currency of the cost or pricing data, shall have the right to examine and audit all of the Contractor's records, including computations and projections, related to-

(1) The proposal for the modification;

(2) The discussions conducted on the proposal(s), including those related to negotiating;

(3) Pricing of the modification; or

(4) Performance of the modification.

(c) Comptroller General. In the case of pricing any modification, the Comptroller General of the United States, or an authorized representative, shall have the same rights as specified in paragraph (b) of this clause.

(d) *Availability.* The Contractor shall make available at its office at all reasonable times the materials described in reproduction, until 3 years after final payment under this contract, or for any other period specified in Subpart 4.7 of the Federal Acquisition Regulation (FAR). FAR Subpart 4.7, Contractor Records Retention, in effect on the data of this contract, is incorporated by reference in its entirety and made a part of this contract.

(1) If this contract is completely or partially terminated, the records relating to the work terminated shall be made available for 3 years after any resulting final termination settlement.

(2) Records pertaining to appeals under the Disputes clause or to litigation or the settlement of claims arising under or relating to the performance of this contract shall be made available until disposition of such appeals, litigation, or claims.

(e) The Contractor shall insert a clause containing all the provisions of this clause, including this paragraph (e), in all subcontracts expected to exceed the threshold in FAR 15.804-2(a)(1) for submission of cost or pricing data.

(End of clause)

Citation: 48 CFR 52.215-2

✍ § 52.215-2 Audit and Records-Negotiation.

As prescribed in 15.106-1(b), insert the following clause:
Audit and Records-Negotiation (Oct 1995)

(a) As used in this clause, records includes books, documents, accounting procedures and practices, and other data, regardless of type and regardless of whether such items are in written form, in the form of computer data, or in any other form.

(b) *Examination of costs.* If this is a cost-reimbursement, incentive, time-and-materials, labor-hour, or price redeterminable contract, or any combination of these, the Contractor shall maintain and the Contracting Officer, or an authorized representative of the Contracting Officer, shall have the right to examine and audit all records and other evidence sufficient to reflect properly all costs claimed to have been incurred or anticipated to be incurred directly or indirectly in performance of this contract. This right of examination shall include inspection at all reasonable times of the Contractor's plants, or parts of them, engaged in performing the contract.

(c) *Cost or pricing data.* If the Contractor has been required to submit cost or pricing data in connection with any pricing action relating to this contract, the Contracting Officer, or an authorized representative of the Contracting Officer, in order to evaluate the accuracy, completeness, and currency of the cost or pricing data, shall have the right to examine and audit all of the Contractor's records, including computations and projections, related to-

(1) The proposal for the contract, subcontract, or modification;

(2) The discussions conducted on the proposal(s), including those related to negotiating;

(3) Pricing of the contract, subcontract, or modification; or

(4) Performance of the contract, subcontract or modification.

(d) *Comptroller General* — (1) The Comptroller General of the United States, or an authorized representative, shall have access to and the right to examine any of the Contractor's directly pertinent records involving transactions related to this contract or a subcontract hereunder.

(2) This paragraph may not be construed to require the Contractor or subcontractor to create or maintain any record that the Contractor or subcontractor does not maintain in the ordinary course of business or pursuant to a provision of law.

(e) *Reports.* If the Contractor is required to furnish cost, funding, or performance reports, the Contracting Officer or an authorized representative of the Contracting Officer shall have the right to examine and audit the supporting records and materials, for the purpose of evaluating (1) the effectiveness of the Contractor's policies and procedures to produce data compatible with the objectives of these reports and (2) the data reported.

(f) *Availability.* The Contractor shall make available at its office at all reasonable times the records, materials, and other evidence described in paragraphs (a), (b), (c), (d), and (e) of this clause, for examination, audit, or reproduction, until 3 years after final payment under this contract or for any shorter period specified in Subpart 4.7, Contractor Records Retention, of the Federal Acquisition Regulation (FAR), or for any longer period required by statute or by other clauses of this contract. In addition —

(1) If this contract is completely or partially terminated, the records relating to the work terminated shall be made available for 3 years after any resulting final termination settlement; and

(2) Records relating to appeals under the Disputes clause or to litigation or the settlement of claims arising under or relating to this contract shall be made available until such appeals, litigation, or claims are finally resolved.

(g) The Contractor shall insert a clause containing all the terms of this clause, including this paragraph (a), in all subcontracts under this contract that exceed the simplified acquisition threshold in FAR Part 13, and —

(1) That are cost-reimbursement, incentive, time-and-materials, labor-hour, or price-redeterminable type or any combination of these;

(2) For which cost or pricing data are required; or

(3) That require the subcontractor to furnish reports as discussed in paragraph (e) of this clause.

The clause may be altered only as necessary to identify properly the contracting parties and the Contracting Officer under the Government prime contract.(End of clause)

Agency: **Department of Defense**

SUBCHAPTER A. GENERAL

PART 204. ADMINISTRATIVE MATTERS

Citation: **48 CFR 204.670-5**

✍ § 204.670-5 Departmental data collection point responsibilities.

Departmental data collection points —

(a) Collect DD Forms 350 and 1057 data provided by their contracting activities;

(b) Electronically record the data in accordance with the instructions for recording and editing developed by WHS-DIOR with the majority agreement of the departments/agencies and prescribed by the Director of Defense Procurement; and

(c) Submit monthly reports (noncumulative) to Washington Headquarters Services, ATTN: DIOR, within 18 days after the close of the reporting period, except the due date for September may be extended for no more than ten days. Reports control symbols, DD-P&L(M) 1014 and DD-P&L(M) 1015, respectively, apply to reports submitted to WHS-DIOR for DD Form 350 actions and DD Form 1057.

SUBCHAPTER E. GENERAL CONTRACTING REQUIREMENTS

PART 227. PATENTS, DATA, AND COPYRIGHTS

Citation: **48 CFR 227.4**

✍ § 227.4 Technical Data, Other Data, Computer Software, and Copyrights

[Readers interested in this section should consult the source document.]

SUBCHAPTER H. CLAUSES AND FORMS

PART 252. SOLICITATION PROVISIONS AND CONTRACT CLAUSES

Inspection And Manner of Doing Work (Apr 1982)

Citation: **48 CFR 252.227**

✍ § 252.227 Rights in technical data and computer software.

[Readers interested in this section should consult the source document.]

TITLE 49. TRANSPORTATION

Agency:	**Department of Transportation Office of the Secretary**

PART 40. PROCEDURES FOR TRANSPORTATION WORKPLACE DRUG TESTING PROGRAMS

Subpart B — Drug Testing

Citation:	**49 CFR 40.29**

✍ § 40.29 Laboratory analysis procedures.

(a) *Security and chain of custody.* (1) Drug testing laboratories shall be secure at all times. They shall have in place sufficient security measures to control access to the premises and to ensure that no unauthorized personnel handle specimens or gain access to the laboratory process or to areas where records are stored. Access to these secured areas shall be limited to specifically authorized individuals whose authorization is documented. With the exception of personnel authorized to conduct inspections on behalf of Federal agencies for which the laboratory is engaged in urine testing or on behalf of DHHS, all authorized visitors and maintenance and service personnel shall be escorted at all times. Documentation of individuals accessing these areas, dates, and time of entry and purpose of entry must be maintained.

* * * * *

(g) *Reporting results.* * * *

* * * * *

(8) Unless otherwise instructed by the employer in writing, all records pertaining to a given urine specimen shall be retained by the drug testing laboratory for a minimum of 2 years.

(h) *Long-term storage.* Long-term frozen storage (-20 °C or less) ensures that positive urine specimens will be available for any necessary retest during administrative or disciplinary proceedings. Drug testing laboratories shall retain and place in properly secured long-term frozen storage for a minimum of 1 year all specimens confirmed positive, in their original labeled specimen bottles. Within this 1-year period, an employer (or other person designated in a DOT agency regulation) may request the laboratory to retain the specimen for an additional period of time, but if no such request is received the laboratory may discard the specimen after the end of 1 years, except that the laboratory shall be required to maintain any specimens known to be under legal challenge for an indefinite period.

* * * * *

(m) *Documentation.* The drug testing laboratories shall maintain and make available for at least 2 years documentation of all aspects of the testing process. This 2-year period may be extended upon written notification by a DOT agency or by any employer for which laboratory services are being provided. The required documentation shall include personnel files on all individuals authorized to have access to specimens; chain of custody documents; quality assurance/quality control records, procedure manuals; all test data (including calibration curves and any calculations used in determining test results); reports; performance records on performance testing; performance on certification inspections; and hard copies of computer-generated data. The laboratory shall maintain documents for any specimen under legal challenge for an indefinite period.

(n) *Additional requirements for certified laboratories.* — (1) *Procedure manual.* Each laboratory shall have a procedure manual which includes the principles of each test preparation of reagents, standards and controls, calibration procedures, derivation of results, linearity of methods, sensitivity of methods, cutoff values, mechanisms for reporting results, controls criteria for unacceptable specimens and results, remedial actions to be taken when the test systems are outside of acceptable limits, reagents of expiration dates, and references. Copies of all procedures and dates on which they are in effect shall be maintained as part of the manual.

* * * * *

(3) *Instruments and equipment.* * * *

(ii) There shall be written procedures for instrument set-up and normal operation, a schedule for checking critical operating characteristics for all instruments, tolerance limits for acceptable function checks and instructions for major trouble shooting and repair. Records shall be available on preventative maintenance.

(4) *Remedial actions.* There shall be written procedures for the actions to be taken when systems are out of acceptable limits or errors are detected. There shall be documentation that these procedures are followed and that all necessary corrective actions are taken. There shall also be in place systems to verify all stages of testing and reporting and documentation that these procedures are followed.

* * * * *

Agency:	**Department of Transportation Research and Special Programs Administration**

SUBTITLE B. OTHER REGULATIONS RELATING TO TRANSPORTATION

SUBCHAPTER C. HAZARDOUS MATERIALS REGULATIONS

PART 178. SPECIFICATIONS FOR PACKAGINGS

Subpart J. Specifications for Containers for Motor Vehicle Transportation

Citation:	**49 CFR 178.337-18**

✍ § 178.337-18 Certification.

* * * * *

(b) The owner shall retain the copy of the data report and certificates and related papers in his files throughout his ownership of the cargo tank motor vehicle and for at least one year thereafter; and in the event of change in ownership, retention by the prior owner of nonfading photographically reproduced copies will be deemed to satisfy this requirement. Each motor carrier using the cargo tank motor vehicle, if not the owner thereof, shall obtain a copy of the data report and certificate and retain them in his files during the time he uses the cargo tank motor vehicle and for at least one year thereafter.

PART 199. DRUG AND ALCOHOL TESTING

Citation:	**49 CFR 199.25**

✍ § 199.25 Reporting of anti-drug testing results.

* * * * *

(d) Each report shall be signed by the Operator's anti-drug manager or designated representative. RSPA will allow the operator the option of sending the report on the computer disk provided by RSPA. If this option is used, a signature page attesting to the validity of the information on the computer disk must be sent to the address in paragraph (b) of this section.

* * * * *

Citation: 49 CFR 199.229

✍ § 199.229 Reporting of alcohol testing results.

* * * * *

(c) Each report, required under this section, shall be submitted to the Office of Pipeline Safety, Research and Special Programs Administration, Department of Transportation, room 2335, 400 Seventh Street, SW., Washington, DC 20590. RSPA will allow the operator the option of sending the report on the computer disk provided by RSPA. If this option is used, a signature page attesting to the validity of the information on the computer disk must be sent to the address in this section.

* * * * *

Agency: Department of Transportation
Federal Railroad Administration

PART 217. RAILROAD OPERATING RULES

Subpart A. General

Citation: 49 CFR 217.9

✍ § 217.9 Program of operational tests and inspections; recordkeeping.

(a) *Requirement to conduct operational tests and inspections.* Each railroad to which this part applies shall periodically conduct operational tests and inspections to determine the extent of compliance with its code of operating rules, timetables, and timetable special instructions in accordance with a written program retained at its system headquarters and at the division headquarters for each division where the tests are conducted.

(b) *Written program of operational tests and inspections.* On or after November 21, 1994, or 30 days before commencing operations, whichever is later, each railroad to which this part applies shall retain one copy of its current program for periodic performance of the operational tests and inspections required by paragraph (a) of this section and one copy of each subsequent amendment to such program. These records shall be retained at the system headquarters of the railroad and at the division headquarters for each division where the tests are conducted, for three calendar years after the end of the calendar year to which they relate. These records shall be made available to representatives of the Federal Railroad Administration for inspection and copying during normal business hours. The program shall —

(1) Provide for operational testing and inspection under the various operating conditions on the railroad;

(2) Describe each type of operational test and inspection adopted, including the means and procedures used to carry it out;

(3) State the purpose of each type of operational test and inspection;

(4) State, according to operating divisions where applicable, the frequency with which each type of operational test and inspection is conducted;

(5) Begin within 30 days after November 21, 1994, or the date of commencing operations, whichever is later; and

(6) Include a schedule for making the program fully operative within 210 days after it begins.

(c) *Records of individual tests and inspections.* Each railroad to which this part applies shall keep a record of the date, time, place, and result of each operational test and inspection that was performed in accordance with its program. Each record shall specify the officer administering the test and inspection and each employee tested. These records shall be retained at the system headquarters of the railroad and at the division headquarters for each division where the tests are conducted for one calendar year after the end of the calendar year to which they relate. These records shall be made available to representatives of the Federal Railroad Administration for inspection and copying during normal business hours.

(d) *Annual summary on operational tests and inspections.* Before March 1 of each calendar year, each railroad to which this part applies, except for a railroad with less than 400,000 total manhours, shall retain, at each of its division headquarters and at the system headquarters of the railroad, one copy of a written summary of the following with respect to its previous year's activities: The number, type, and result of each operational test and inspection, stated according to operating divisions where applicable, that was conducted as required by paragraphs (a) and (b) of this section. These records shall be retained for three calendar years after the end of the calendar year to which they relate and shall be made available to representatives of the Federal Railroad Administration for inspection and copying during normal business hours.

(e) *Electronic recordkeeping.* Each railroad to which this part applies is authorized to retain by electronic recordkeeping the information prescribed in paragraphs (b) through (d) of this section, provided that all of the following conditions are met:

(1) The railroad adequately limits and controls accessibility to such information retained in its electronic database system and identifies those individuals who have such access;

(2) The railroad has a terminal at the system headquarters and at each division headquarters;

(3) Each such terminal has a desk-top computer (i.e., monitor, central processing unit, and keyboard) and either a facsimile machine or a printer connected to the computer to retrieve and produce information in a usable format for immediate review by FRA representatives;

(4) The railroad has a designated representative who is authorized to authenticate retrieved information from the electronic system as true and accurate copies of the electronically kept records; and

(5) The railroad provides representatives of the Federal Railroad Administration with immediate access to these records for inspection and copying during normal business hours and provides printouts of such records upon request.

Citation: 49 CFR 217.11

✍ § 217.11 Program of instruction on operating rules; recordkeeping; electronic recordkeeping.

(a) To ensure that each railroad employee whose activities are governed by the railroad's operating rules understands those rules, each railroad to which this part applies shall periodically instruct each such employee on the meaning and application of the railroad's operating rules in accordance with a written program retained at its system headquarters and at the division headquarters for each division where the employee is instructed.

(b) On or after November 21, 1994, or 30 days before commencing operations, whichever is later, each railroad to which this part applies shall retain one copy of its current program for the periodic instruction of its employees as required by paragraph (a) of this section and one copy of each subsequent amendment to that program. The system headquarters of the railroad shall retain one copy of all these records; the division headquarters for each division where the employees are instructed shall retain one copy of all portions of these records that the division applies and enforces. These records shall be made available to representatives of the Federal Railroad Administration for inspection and copying during normal business hours. This program shall —

(1) Describe the means and procedures used for instruction of the various classes of affected employees;

(2) State the frequency of instruction and the basis for determining that frequency;

(3) Include a schedule for completing the initial instruction of employees who are employed when the program begins;

(4) Begin within 30 days after November 21, 1994, or the date of commencing operations, whichever is later; and

(5) Provide for initial instruction of each employee hired after the program begins.

(c) Each railroad to which this part applies is authorized to retain by electronic recordkeeping its program for periodic instruction of its employees on operating rules provided that the requirements stated in § 217.9(e)(1) through (5) of this part are satisfied.

PART 225. RAILROAD ACCIDENTS/INCIDENTS: REPORTS CLASSIFICATION, AND INVESTIGATIONS

Citation: **49 CFR 225.25**

✍ § 225.25 Recordkeeping.

(a) Each railroad shall maintain either the Railroad Employee Injury and/or Illness Record (Form FRA F 6180.98) or an alternative railroad-designed record as described in paragraph (b) of this section of all reportable and accountable injuries and illnesses of its employees that arise from the operation of the railroad for each railroad establishment where such employees report to work, including, but not limited to, an operating division, general office, and major installation such as a locomotive or car repair or construction facility.

(b) The alternative railroad-designed record may be used in lieu of the Railroad Employee Injury and/or Illness Record (Form FRA F 6180.98) described in paragraph (a) of this section. Any such alternative record shall contain all of the information required on the Railroad Employee Injury and/or Illness Record. Although this information may be displayed in a different order from that on the Railroad Employee Injury and/or Illness Record, the order of the information shall be consistent from one such record to another such record. The order chosen by the railroad shall be consistent for each of the railroad"s reporting establishments. Railroads may list additional information on the alternative record beyond the information required on the Railroad Employee Injury and/or Illness Record. The alternative record shall contain, at a minimum, the following information:

(1) Name of railroad;

(2) Case/incident number;

(3) Full name of railroad employee;

(4) Date of birth of railroad employee;

(5) Gender of railroad employee;

(6) Social security number of railroad employee;

(7) Date the railroad employee was hired;

(8) Home address of railroad employee; include the street address, city, State, ZIP code, and home telephone number with area code;

(9) Name of facility where railroad employee normally reports to work;

(10) Address of facility where railroad employee normally reports to work; include the street address, city, State, and ZIP code;

(11) Job title of railroad employee;

(12) Department assigned;

(13) Specific site where accident/incident/exposure occurred; include the city, county, State, and ZIP code;

(14) Date and time of occurrence; military time or AM/PM;

(15) Time employee's shift began; military time or AM/PM;

(16) Whether employee was on premises when injury occurred;

(17) Whether employee was on or off duty;

(18) Date and time when employee notified company personnel of condition; military time or AM/PM;

(19) Name and title of railroad official notified;

(20) Description of the general activity this employee was engaged in prior to the injury/illness/condition;

(21) Description of all factors associated with the case that are pertinent to an understanding of how it occurred. Include a discussion of the sequence of events leading up to it; and the tools, machinery, processes, material, environmental conditions, etc., involved;

(22) Description, in detail, of the injury/illness/condition that the employee sustained, including the body parts affected. If a recurrence, list the date of the last occurrence;

(23) Identification of all persons and organizations used to evaluate or treat the condition, or both. Include the facility, provider and complete address;

(24) Description of all procedures, medications, therapy, etc., used or recommended for the treatment of the condition.

(25) Extent and outcome of injury or illness to show the following as applicable:

(i) Fatality—enter date of death;

(ii) Restricted work; number of days; beginning date;

(iii) Occupational illness; date of initial diagnosis;

(iv) Instructions to obtain prescription medication, or receipt of prescription medication;

(v) If missed one or more days of work or next shift, provide number of work days; and beginning date;

(vi) Medical treatment beyond "first aid";

(vii) Hospitalization for treatment as an inpatient;

(viii) Multiple treatments or therapy sessions;

(ix) Loss of consciousness;

(x) Transfer to another job or termination of employment;

(26) Each railroad shall indicate if the Railroad Injury and Illness Summary (Continuation Sheet) (FRA Form F 6180.55a) has been filed with FRA for the injury or illness. If FRA Form F 6180.55a was not filed with FRA, then the railroad shall provide an explanation of the basis for its decision.

(27) The reporting railroad shall indicate if the injured or ill railroad employee was provided an opportunity to review his or her file; and

(28) The reporting railroad shall identify the preparer's name; title; telephone number with area code; and the date the log entry was completed.

(c) Each railroad shall provide the employee, upon request, a copy of either the completed Railroad Employee Injury and/or Illness Record (Form FRA F 6180.98) or the alternative railroad-designed record as described in paragraphs (a) and (b) of this section as well as a copy of any other form, record or report filed with FRA or held by the railroad pertaining to the employee's injury or illness.

(d) Each railroad shall maintain the Initial Rail Equipment Accident/Incident Record (Form FRA F 6180.97) or an alternative railroad-designed record as described in paragraph (e) of this section of reportable and accountable collisions, derailments, fires, explosions, acts of God, or other events involving the operation of railroad on-track equipment, signals, track, or track equipment

(standing or moving) that result in damages to railroad on-track equipment, signals, tracks, track structures, or roadbed, including labor costs and all other costs for repairs or replacement in kind for each railroad establishment where workers report to work, including, but not limited to, an operating division, general office, and major installation such as a locomotive or car repair or construction facility.

(e) The alternative railroad-designed record may be used in lieu of the Initial Rail Equipment Accident/Incident Record (Form FRA F 6180.97). Any such alternative record shall contain all of the information required on the Initial Rail Equipment Accident/Incident Record. Although this information may bedisplayed in a different order from that on the Initial Rail Equipment Accident/Incident Record, the order of the information shall be consistent from one such record to another such record. The order chosen by the railroad shall be consistent for each of the railroad's reporting establishments. Railroads may list additional information in the alternative record beyond the information required on the Initial Rail Equipment Accident/Incident Record. The alternative record shall contain, at a minimum, the following information:

(1) Date and time of accident;

(2) Reporting railroad, and accident/incident number;

(3) Other railroad, if applicable, and other railroad's accident/incident number;

(4) Railroad responsible for track maintenance, and that railroad's incident number;

(5) Type of accident/incident (derailment, collision, etc.);

(6) Number of cars carrying hazardous materials that derailed or were damaged; and number of cars carrying hazardous materials that released product;

(7) Division;

(8) Nearest city or town;

(9) State;

(10) Milepost (to the nearest tenth);

(11) Specific site;

(12) Speed (indicate if actual or estimate);

(13) Train number or job number;

(14) Type of equipment (freight, passenger, yard switching, etc.);

(15) Type of track (main, yard, siding, industry);

(16) Total number of locomotives in train;

(17) Total number of locomotives that derailed;

(18) Total number of cars in train;

(19) Total number of cars that derailed;

(20) Total amount of damage in dollars to equipment based on computations as described in the "FRA Guide for Preparing Accidents/Incidents Reports";

(21) Total amount of damage in dollars to track, signal, way and structures based on computations as described in the "FRA Guide for Preparing Accidents/Incidents Reports";

(22) Primary cause;

(23) Contributing cause;

(24) Persons injured and persons killed, broken down into the following classifications: worker on duty—employee; employee not on duty; passenger on train; nontrespasser—on railroad property; trespasser; worker on duty—contractor; contractor—other; worker on duty—volunteer; volunteer—other; and nontrespasser—off railroad property;

(25) Narrative description of the accident;

(26) Whether the accident/incident was reported to FRA;

(27) Preparer's name, title, telephone number with area code, and signature; and

(28) Date the report was completed.

(f) Each railroad shall enter each reportable and accountable injury and illness and each reportable and accountable rail equipment accident/incident on the appropriate record, as required by paragraphs (a) through (e) of this section, as early as practicable but no later than seven working days after receiving information or acquiring knowledge that an injury or illness or rail equipment accident/incident has occurred.

(g) The records required under paragraphs (a) through (e) of this section may be maintained at the local establishment or, alternatively, at a centralized location. If the records are maintained at a centralized location, but not through electronic means, then a paper copy of the records that is current within 35 days of the month to which it applies shall be available for that establishment. If the records are maintained at a centralized location through electronic means, then the records for that establishment shall be available for review in a hard copy format within four business hours of FRA's request. FRA recognizes that circumstances outside the railroad's control may preclude it from fulfilling the four-business-hour time limit. In these circumstances, FRA will not assess a monetary penalty against the railroad for its failure to provide the requested documentation provided the railroad made a reasonable effort to correct the problem.

(h) A listing of all reported injuries and occupational illnesses for the previous month shall be posted in a conspicuous location at and for each railroad establishment within 30 days after expiration of the month during which the injuries and illnesses occurred. For purposes of this paragraph, this list is required to be posted only at those establishments that are in continual operation for a minimum of 90 calendar days; otherwise the list shall be posted at the next higher organizational level establishment. This listing shall be posted and shall remain continuously displayed for the next twelve consecutive months. Incidents reported for employees at that establishment shall be displayed in date sequence. The listing shall contain, at a minimum, the following information:

(1) Name and address of the establishment;

(2) Calendar year of the cases being displayed;

(3) Incident number used to report case;

(4) Date of the injury or illness;

(5) Location of incident;

(6) Regular job title of employee injured or ill;

(7) Description of the injury or condition;

(8) Number of days employee absent from work at time of posting;

(9) Number of days of work restriction for employee at time of posting;

(10) If fatality —enter date of death;

(11) Annual average number of railroad employees reporting to this establishment;

(12) Preparer's name, title, telephone number with area code, and signature; and

(13) Date the report was completed.

(14) When there are no reportable injuries or occupational illnesses associated with an establishment for that month, the listing shall make reference to this fact.

Citation: 49 CFR 225.37

✍ § 225.37 Magnetic media transfer and electronic submission.

(a) A railroad has the option of submitting the following reports, updates, and amendments by way of magnetic media (computer diskette or magnetic tape), or by means of electronic submission over telephone lines or other means:

(1) The Rail Equipment Accident/Incident Report (Form FRA F 6180.54);

(2) the Railroad Injury and Illness Summary (Form FRA F 6180.55);

(3) the Railroad Injury and Illness Summary (Continuation Sheet)

(Form FRA F 6180.55a);

(4) the Highway-Rail Grade Crossing Accident/Incident Report (Form FRA F 6180.57); and

(5) the Batch Control Form (Form FRA F 6180.99).

(b) Each railroad utilizing the magnetic media option shall submit to FRA the following:

(1) the computer diskette or magnetic tape;

(2) the Batch Control Form (Form FRA F 6180.99); and

(3) a notarized hard copy of the Railroad Injury and Illness Summary (Form FRA F 6180.55), signed by the railroad's reporting officer.

(c) Each railroad utilizing the electronic submission option shall submit to FRA the following:

(1) the Batch Control Form (Form FRA F 6180.99) which is submitted to an FRA-designated computer; and

(2) a notarized hard copy of the Railroad Injury and Illness Summary (Form FRA F 6180.55), signed by the railroad's reporting officer.

(d) Each railroad employing either the magnetic media or electronic submission option, shall submit its monthly reporting data for the reports identified in paragraph (a) of this section in a year-to-date file format as described in the "FRA Guide for Preparing Accidents/Incidents Reports."

(e) In addition to fulfilling the requirements stated in paragraph (b) through (d) of this section, each railroad initially utilizing either the magnetic media or electronic submission option, shall submit the hard copy report(s) for each accident/incident it reports by such means. FRA will continually review the railroad"s submitted hard copy reports against the data it has submitted electronically, or by means of magnetic media. Once the magnetic media or electronic submission is in total agreement with the submitted hard copies of the reports for three consecutive reporting months, FRA will notify the railroad, in writing, that submission of the hard copy reports, except for the notarized Railroad Injury and Illness Summary, is no longer required.

PART 234. GRADE CROSSING SIGNAL SYSTEM SAFETY

Subpart D. Maintenance, Inspection, and Testing Maintenance Standards

Citation: 49 CFR 234.273

✍ § 234.273 Results of inspections and tests.

(a) Results of inspections and tests made in compliance with this part shall be recorded on forms provided by the railroad, or by electronic means, subject to approval by the Associate Administrator for Safety. Each record shall show the name of the railroad, AAR/DOT inventory number, place and date, equipment tested, results of tests, repairs, replacements, adjustments made, and condition in which the apparatus was left.

(b) Each record shall be signed or electronically coded by the employee making the test and shall be filed in the office of a supervisory official having jurisdiction. Records required to be kept shall be made available to FRA as provided by 49 U.S.C. 20107 (formerly Sec. 208 of the Federal Railroad Safety Act of 1970 (45 U.S.C. 437)).

(c) Each record shall be retained until the next record for that test is filed but in no case for less than one year from the date of the test.

PART 236. INSTALLATION, INSPECTION, MAINTENANCE, AND REPAIR OF SYSTEMS, DEVICES AND APPLIANCES

Subpart A. Rules and Instructions: All Systems

Citation: 49 CFR 236.110

✍ § 236.110 Results of tests.

Results of tests made in compliance with § § 236.109 to 236.102, inclusive; 236.376 to 236.387, inclusive; 236.576; 236.577; and 236.586 to 236.589, inclusive, shall be recorded on preprinted or computerized forms provided by the railroad. Such forms shall show the name of the railroad, place and date, equipment tested, results of tests, repairs, replacements, adjustments made, and condition in which the apparatus was left. Each record shall be signed by the employee making the test and shall be filed in the office of a supervisory official having jurisdiction. Results of tests made in compliance with § 236.587 shall be retained for 92 days. Results of all other tests listed in this section shall be retained until the next record is filed but in no case less than one year.

Agency: Department of Transportation
Federal Highway Administration

SUBCHAPTER B. FEDERAL MOTOR CARRIER SAFETY REGULATIONS

PART 390. FEDERAL MOTOR CARRIER SAFETY REGULATIONS; GENERAL

Subpart B. General Requirements and Information

Citation: 49 CFR 390.31

✍ § 390.31 Copies of records or documents.

(a) All records and documents required to be maintained under this subchapter must be preserved in their original form for the periods specified, unless the records and documents are suitably photographed and the microfilm is retained in lieu of the original record for the required retention period.

(b) To be acceptable in lieu of original records, photographic copies of records must meeting the following minimum requirements:

(1) Photographic copies shall be no less readily accessible than the original record or document as normally filed or preserved would be and suitable means or facilities shall be available to locate, identify, read, and reproduce such photographic copies.

(2) Any significant characteristic, feature or other attribute of the original record or document, which photography in black and white will not preserve, shall be clearly indicated before the photograph is made.

(3) The reverse side of printed forms need not be copies if nothing has been added to the printed matter common to all

such forms, but an identified specimen of each form shall be on the film for reference.

(4) Film used for photographing copies shall be of permanent record-type meeting in all respects the minimum specifications of the National Bureau of Standards, and all processes recommended by the manufacturer shall be observed to protect it from deterioration or accidental destruction.

(5) Each roll of film shall include a microfilm of a certificate or certificates stating that the photographs are direct or facsimile reproductions of the original records. Such certificate(s) shall be executed by a person or persons having personal knowledge of the material covered thereby.

(c) All records and documents required to be maintained under this subchapter may be destroyed after they have been suitably photographed for preservation.

(d) *Exception.* All records except those requiring a signature may be maintained through the use of computer technology provided the motor carrier can produce, upon demand, a computer printout of the required data.

Subpart C. Intermodal Transportation

Citation: 49 CFR 390.54

✍ § 390.54 Notification and certification.

(a) If the initial carrier is a motor carrier, before any person tenders a container or trailer subject to this subpart having a projected gross cargo weight (inclusive of packing material and pallets) of more than 10,000 pounds or 4,536 kilograms, such person shall notify the initial carrier of the projected gross cargo weight and a reasonable description of the contents of the container or trailer. The notification may be communicated by electronic transmission or telephone.

(b) At or before the time any person tenders a loaded container or trailer subject to this subpart, such person shall provide a certification to the initial carrier.

(1) If the initial carrier is a motor carrier, the certification shall be provided in a tangible form.

(2) The certification may be transmitted electronically, provided that the certification can be reproduced in a tangible form.

(3) A carrier, agent of a carrier, broker, customs broker, freight forwarder, warehouseman, and terminal operator shall not be considered to be tendering a loaded container or trailer unless such person loads the container or trailer or issues the certification on the basis of information available from the person who loads the container or trailer.

(c) The certification shall include:

(1) The title "INTERMODAL CERTIFICATION";

(2) The identification number of the container or trailer;

(3) The actual gross cargo weight, including the unit of measurement, of the contents of the container or trailer, including packing material and pallets;

(4) A reasonable description of the contents;

(5) The name and company of the person tendering the loaded container or trailer; and

(6) The date.

(d) *Signature.* The certification required by paragraph (c) of this section:

(1) Must be legibly signed by the person or representative tendering the loaded container or trailer; and

(2) May be legibly signed manually, by typewriter, or other mechanical means.

(e) The required elements of a certification shall be legible and in the English language.

(f) No person may provide false or erroneous information in a certification.

Intermodal Certification

Identification number:
Gross cargo weight:
Reasonable description:
(Name and company of the person tendering the loaded container or trailer)
(Signature of the person tendering the loaded container or trailer)
(Date)

Citation: 49 CFR 390.56

✍ § 390.56 Duty of motor carrier.

(a) No motor carrier may provide transportation of a loaded container or trailer subject to this subpart prior to receiving the certification required by § 390.54 in a tangible form.

(b) The certification in a tangible form shall accompany the loaded container or trailer during transportation by a motor carrier.

Citation: 49 CFR 390.58

✍ § 390.58 Forwarding and retention of certification.

(a) A carrier, agent of a carrier, broker, customs broker, freight forwarder, warehouseman, or terminal operator that receives the certification required by § 390.54 in the course of intermodal transportation shall forward the certification to a subsequent carrier transporting the loaded container or trailer.

(1) If received in a tangible form, the certification may be converted into an electronic format.

(2) If received as a separate document, the certification may be incorporated into a shipping document corresponding to the loaded container or trailer.

(3) The person who converts a certification into an electronic format and/or incorporates a certification into a shipping document corresponding to the loaded container or trailer shall state in writing that the conversion and/or incorporation was performed accurately. Such statement shall take the following form: "Electronic Format and/or Incorporation by John Doe, X Company, Month/Day/Year." Such statement shall appear immediately after the certification of the person tendering the loaded container or trailer.

(b) The certification may be forwarded by electronic transmission provided that all subsequent motor carriers receive the certification in a tangible form.

(c) The forwarding of any certification required or statement authorized by this section does not constitute a verification or affirmation of the accuracy or completeness of the certification or statement.

(d) Any person who tenders a loaded container or trailer that is transported by a motor carrier, and each motor carrier transporting a loaded container or trailer shall maintain a copy of the certification for a period of one year from the date of the tendering. Certifications may be maintained electronically if the certification can be reproduced in a tangible form.

PART 398. TRANSPORTATION OF MIGRANT WORKERS

Citation: 49 CFR 398.3

✍ **§ 398.3 Qualifications of drivers or operators.**

* * * * *

(b) *Minimum physical requirements.* No person shall drive, nor shall any motor carrier require or permit any person to drive, any motor vehicle unless such person possesses the following minimum qualifications:

* * * * *

(8) *Certificate of physical examination*: Every motor carrier shall have in its files at its principal place of business for every driver employed or used by it a legible certificate of a licensed doctor of medicine or osteopathy based on a physical examination as required by paragraph (b)(7) of this section or a legible photographically reproduced copy thereof, and every driver shall have in his possession while driving, such a certificate or a photographically reproduced copy thereof covering himself/herself.

* * * * *

Agency: Department of Transportation
National Highway Traffic Safety Administration

SUBCHAPTER B. SAFETY APPROVAL OF CARGO CONTAINERS

PART 576. RECORD RETENTION

Citation: 49 CFR 576.6

✍ **§ 576.6 Records.**

Records to be retained by manufacturers under this part include all documentary materials films, tapes, and other information-storing media that contain information concerning malfunctions that may be related to motor vehicle safety. Such records include, but are not limited to, communications from vehicle users and memoranda of user complaints; reports and other documents, including material generated or communicated by computer, telefax or other electronic means, that are related to work performed under, or claims made under, warranties; service reports or similar documents, including electronic transmissions, from dealers or manufacturer's field personnel; and any lists, compilations, analyses, or discussions of such malfunctions contained in internal or external correspondence of the manufacturer, including communications transmitted electronically.

Citation: 49 CFR 576.7

✍ **§ 576.7 Retention.**

Duplicate copies need not be retained. Information may be reproduced or transferred from one storage medium to another (e.g. from paper files to microfilm) as long as no information is lost in the reproduction or transfer, and when so reproduced or transferred the original form may be treated as a duplicate.

PART 580. ODOMETER DISCLOSURE REQUIREMENTS

Citation: 49 CFR 580.8

✍ **§ 580.8 Odometer disclosure statement retention.**

* * * * *

(c) Dealers and distributors of motor vehicles who are granted a power of attorney by their transferor pursuant to § 580.13, or by their transferee pursuant to § 580.14, shall retain for five years a photostat, carbon, or other facsimile copy of each power of attorney that they receive. They shall retain all powers of attorney at their primary place of business in an order that is appropriate to business requirements and that permits systematic retrieval.

Agency: Department of Transportation
Surface Transportation Board

PART 1104. FILING WITH THE BOARD-COPIES-VERIFICATIONS-SERVICE-PLEADINGS, GENERALLY

Citation: 49 CFR 1104.3

✍ **§ 1104.3 Copies.**

(a) * * * In addition to the paper copies required to be filed with the Board, 3 copies of:

(1) Textual submissions of 20 or more pages; and

(2) All electronic spreadsheets should be submitted on 3.5 inch, IBM compatible formatted diskettes or QIC-80 tapes. Textual materials must be in WordPerfect 5.1 format, and electronic spreadsheets must be in LOTUS 1-2-3 release 5 or earlier format. One copy of each such computer diskette or tape submitted to the Board should, if possible, be provided to any other party requesting a copy.

* * * * *

PART 1114. EVIDENCE; DISCOVERY

Citation: 49 CFR 1114.30

✍ **§ 1114.30 Production of documents and records and entry upon land for inspection and other purposes.**

(a) *Scope.* Any party may serve on any other party a request:

(1) To produce and permit the party making the request to inspect any designated documents (including writings, drawings, graphs, charts, photographs, phonograph records, tapes, and other data compilations from which information can be obtained, translated, if necessary, with or without the use of detection devices into reasonably usable form), or to inspect and copy, test, or sample any tangible things which are in the possession, custody, or control of the party upon whom the request is served, but if the writings or data compilations include privileged or proprietary information or information the disclosure of which is proscribed by the Act, such writings or data compilations need not be produced under this rule but may be provided pursuant to Sec. 1114.26(b) of this part; or

(2) To permit, subject to appropriate liability releases and safety and operating considerations, entry upon designated land or other property in the possession or control of the party upon whom the request is served for the purpose of inspecting and measuring, surveying, photographing, testing, or sampling the

property or any designated object or operation thereon.

(b) *Procedure.* Any request filed pursuant to this rule should set forth the items to be inspected either by individual item or by category and describe each item and category with reasonable particularity. The request should specify a reasonable time, place, and manner of making the inspection and performing the related acts.

Agency: Interstate Commerce Commission

SUBCHAPTER C. ACCOUNTS, RECORDS AND REPORTS

PART 1220. PRESERVATION OF RECORDS

Citation: 49 CFR 1220.3

✍ § 1220.3 Preservation of records.

(a) All records may be preserved on hardcopy paper stock, microfilm or other forms of micrographics. It is not necessary to create paperstock or micrographic media if the records are initially prepared on machine — readable media such as punch cards, magnetic tape, disks and so on. However, these machine-readable media shall be preserved for the required retention periods.

(b) Each machine-readable form of media shall be accompanied by a statement clearly indicating the type of data included in the media. This statement shall be executed by a person having personal knowledge of the facts contained in the records. The records shall be indexed and retained in such a manner as will render them readily accessible. The company shall have facilities available to locate, identify and reproduce legible paper copies of the records.

(c) Any record may be transferred to micrographics (including microfiche, computer output microfilm, and aperture cards) at any time. Records so maintained shall satisfy the minimum requirements listed in paragraphs (b) through (f) of this section.

(d) The micrographics used shall be of a quality that can be easily read and that reproduction in paperstock can be similar in size of an original and sufficient clarity of detail during the period the records are required to be retained.

(e) These records shall be indexed and retained in such a manner as will render them readily accessible, and the company shall have facilities available to locate, identify and read the microfilm, and reproduce in paper form.

(f) Any significant characteristic, feature, or other attribute which micrographic media will not preserve shall be clearly indicated at the beginning of the applicable micrographic records as appropriate.

(g) The printed side of forms, such as instructions, need not be preserved for each record as long as the printed matter is common to all such forms and an identified specimen of the form is maintained on the film for reference.

TITLE 50. WILDLIFE AND FISHERIES

Agency: Department of Commerce
National Oceanic and Atmospheric Administration

PART 679. FISHERIES OF THE EXCLUSIVE ECONOMIC ZONE OFF ALASKA

Subpart A. General

Citation: 50 CFR 679.5

✍ § 679.5 Recordkeeping and reporting.

(a) *General requirements* — (1) *Applicability, Federal fisheries permit.* The following must comply with the recordkeeping and reporting requirements of this section:

(i) Any catcher vessel, mothership, catcher/processor, or tender vessel, 5 net tons or larger, that is 60 ft (18.3 m) and over LOA, and is required to have a Federal fisheries permit under Sec. 679.4.

(ii) Any shoreside processor, mothership, or buying station that receives groundfish from vessels required to have a Federal fisheries permit under Sec. 679.4. A shoreside processor, mothership, or buying station subject to recordkeeping and reporting requirements must report all groundfish and prohibited species received, including:

(A) Fish received from vessels not required to have a Federal fisheries permit.

(B) Fish received under contract for handling or processing for another processor.

(2) *Applicability, Federal processor permit.* Any processor that retains groundfish is responsible for complying with the applicable recordkeeping and reporting requirements of this section.

(3) *Responsibility.* The operator of a catcher vessel, catcher/processor, mothership, or buying station receiving from a catcher vessel and delivering to a mothership (hereafter referred to as the operator) and the manager of a shoreside processor or buying station receiving from a catcher vessel and delivering to a shoreside processor (hereafter referred to as the manager) are each responsible for complying with the applicable recordkeeping and reporting requirements of this section. In addition, the owner of a vessel, shoreside processor, or buying station must ensure that the operator, manager, or representative (see paragraph (b) of this section) complies with these requirements and is responsible for compliance.

(4) *Groundfish logbooks and forms.* The Regional Director will prescribe and provide groundfish logbooks and forms required under this section as shown in Table 9 of this part. The operator or manager must use these logbooks and forms or obtain approval from the Regional Director to use electronic versions of the logbooks and forms.

(5) Participant identification information. The operator or manager must record on all required records, reports, and logbooks:

(i) The name of the catcher vessel, catcher/processor, mothership, shoreside processor, or buying station as displayed in official documentation.

(ii) If a vessel, the Federal fisheries permit number and ADF&G vessel number (if applicable).

(iii) If a processor, the Federal processor permit number and ADF&G processor number.

(iv) If a buying station, the name and ADF&G vessel number (if applicable) of the buying station; the name, ADF&G

processor number, and Federal processor permit number of associated processor.

(v) If a shoreside processor or buying station delivering to a shoreside processor, the geographic location of operations.

(vi) If a representative, the name, daytime business telephone number (including area code), fax or telex number, and the COMSAT number (if applicable) of the representative.

(6) *Maintenance of records.* (i) The operator or manager must maintain all records, reports, and logbooks in a legible, timely, and accurate manner; in English; if handwritten, in indelible ink; if computer-generated, a printed, paper copy; and based on A.l.t.

(ii) The operator or manager must account for each day of the fishing year, starting with January 1 and ending with December 31, and the time periods must be consecutive in the logbook.

(iii) When applicable, the operator or manager must record in each report, form, and logbook the following information:

(A) *Page number.* Number the pages in each logbook consecutively, beginning with page one and continuing throughout the logbook for the remainder of the fishing year, except that the manager of a shoreside processor must number the DCPL pages within Part I and Part II separately, beginning with page one.

(B) Date, presented as month-day-year.

(C) Time, in military format to the nearest hour, A.l.t.

(D) Position coordinates, latitude and longitude to the nearest minute (Optional: Record to the nearest second or fraction of minute).

(E) Reporting area codes, given in Figures 1 and 3 of this part.

(F) Species codes, each target species, the "other species" category, and prohibited species under Sec. 679.21(b), using the species codes given in Table 2 of this part.

(G) Original/revised report. If a report is the first one submitted to the Regional Director for a given date, gear type, and reporting area, the report should be labeled, "ORIGINAL REPORT." If the report is a correction to a previously submitted report for a given date, gear type, and reporting area, the report should be labelled, "REVISED REPORT."

(H) *Weights.* Landings, product, and discards of groundfish and herring must be recorded in pounds or to the nearest 0.01 mt on all forms and logbooks.

(7) *Active and inactive periods.* The operator or manager must, in the DFL, DCL, or DCPL:

(i) Account for each day of the fishing year by indicating active and inactive periods as defined under Sec. 679.2.

(ii) Use a separate logbook page for each day of an active period.

(iii) Indicate on one page the first and last day of an inactive period.

(iv) Indicate all fishing activity, which is defined for each type of vessel as follows:

(A) If a catcher vessel — harvest or discard of groundfish.

(B) If a catcher/processor — harvest, discard, or processing of groundfish.

(C) If a mothership or shoreside processor — receipt, discard, or processing of groundfish.

(D) If a buying station — receipt, discard, or delivery of groundfish.

(v) If in an active period and conducting fishing activity, the operator or manager must record:

(A) The gear type used to harvest the groundfish. If a catcher vessel or catcher/processor and using hook-and-line longline gear, the average number of hooks per skate.

(B) The reporting area code where gear retrieval was completed; whether gear retrieval was in Federal or Alaska State waters.

(C) If a catcher vessel, whether a NMFS-certified observer is aboard the vessel. If a catcher/processor, mothership, or shoreside processor, the number of NMFS-certified observers aboard or on site.

(D) The number of crew, except for certified observer(s).

(E) Whether harvest is under a CDQ program; if yes, the CDQ number.

(F) If a catcher vessel or buying station, the name and ADF&G processor number of the mothership or shoreside processor to which groundfish deliveries were made.

(vi) If in an active period and not conducting fishing activity, the operator or manager must indicate "NO FISHING ACTIVITY" and briefly describe the reason.

(8) *Landings information.* The manager of a shoreside processor must:

(i) Record and report groundfish landings by species codes and product codes as defined in Tables 1 and 2 of this part for each reporting area, whether from Alaska State waters or Federal waters, gear type, and CDQ number.

(ii) Record in the DCPL each day on the day such landings occur, the following additional information:

(A) The daily combined scale weight of landings retained for processing from a catcher vessel or any associated buying station, in pounds or to at least the nearest 0.01 mt.

(B) If more than one page is used during a weekly reporting period, the total amount of landings carried forward from the previous page.

(C) At the end of each weekly reporting period, the cumulative total weight, calculated by adding the daily totals and total carried forward for that week.

(iii) If no landings occurred, write "NO LANDINGS" for that day.

(9) *Product information.* The operator of a catcher/processor or mothership or the manager of a shoreside processor must, where required:

(i) Record and report groundfish products by species codes, product codes, and product designations as defined in Tables 1 and 2 of this part for each reporting area, whether in Alaska State waters or Federal waters, gear type, and CDQ number.

(ii) Record in the DCPL each day on the day such production occurs, the daily total, balance brought forward (except for shoreside processor), and cumulative total fish product weight for each product of groundfish in pounds, or to at least the nearest 0.01 mt.

(iii) If no production occurred, write "NO PRODUCTION" for that day.

(10) *Discarded/donated species information* — (i) *General.* The operator or manager must record and report discards and donations by species codes and discard product codes as defined in Tables 1 and 2 of this part for each reporting area, whether in Alaska State waters or Federal waters, gear type, and CDQ number.

(A) The operator or manager must record the estimated daily total, balance brought forward, and cumulative total round fish weight in the DFL, DCL, or DCPL each day on the day discards and donations occur for each discard or donation of groundfish species, groundfish species groups, and Pacific herring in pounds, or to at least the nearest 0.01 mt.

(B) The operator or manager must record the estimated daily total balance brought forward, and cumulative total numbers in the DFL, DCL, or DCPL each day on the day discards or donations occur for each discard and donation of Pacific salmon, steelhead trout, halibut, king crab, and Tanner crab.

(C) If there were no discards or donations, write "NO DISCARDS", "0", or "ZERO" for that day.

(ii) *Catcher vessel discards/donations.* (A) For deliveries of unsorted codends, the catcher vessel is exempt from recording discards in the DFL and from submittal of the blue logsheet (discards copy) for that delivery. The operator of the catcher vessel is required to check the box entitled "unsorted codend," and the blue DFL logsheet (discards copy) remains in the DFL.

(B) For presorted deliveries or in the event a catcher vessel has "bled" a codend prior to delivery to a processor, the operator of the catcher vessel must check the "presorted delivery" box, enter the amount of discards or donations by species, and submit the blue DFL logsheet (discards copy) to the mothership, buying station, or shoreside processor with each harvest delivery.

(iii) *Buying station discards/donations.* (A) The operator or manager of a buying station must record in the DCL on a daily basis on the day discard occurs, all discards or donations that occur after receipt of harvest from a catcher vessel and prior to delivery of harvest to a mothership or shoreside processor.

(B) If a blue DFL logsheet is received from a catcher vessel and contains reports of discards or donations, the operator or manager of a buying station must record in the DCL the discards and donations on the day the DFL logsheet is received from the catcher vessel.

(iv) *Catcher/processor discards/donations.* The operator of a catcher/processor must record in the DCPL on the day discards or donations occur, all discards or donations that occur prior to harvest, during harvest, and during processing.

(v) *Mothership or shoreside processor discards/donations.* (A) The operator of a mothership or manager of a shoreside processor must record in the DCPL on a daily basis on the day discards or donations occur, all discards or donations that occur on site after receipt of groundfish, and all discards or donations that occur during processing of groundfish.

(B) If an unsorted codend is received from a catcher vessel, the catcher vessel is not required to submit a blue discard logsheet to the mothership or shoreside processor. The operator of a mothership or manager of a shoreside processor must sort the catch received from the unsorted codends and must record the discards by species in the DCPL as discard at sea on the day the harvest is received from the catcher vessel.

(C) If discards are reported on a blue DFL logsheet from a catcher vessel delivering a presorted codend or if a catcher vessel reports an amount bled at sea, the operator of a mothership or manager of a shoreside processor must record in the DCPL the discards on the day the DFL logsheet is received from the catcher vessel.

(D) If a yellow DCL logsheet is received from a buying station anddiscards or donations are reported, the operator of a mothership or manager of a shoreside processor must record in the DCPL the discards or donations on the day the DCL logsheet is received from the buying station.

(11) *Contract processing.* (i) The manager of a shoreside processor or operator of a mothership who receives groundfish to be handled or processed under contract for another processor or business entity must report these fish to the Regional Director consistently throughout a fishing year using one of the following two methods:

(A) Record landings (if applicable), discards, and products of contract-processed groundfish routinely in the DCPL without separate identification; or

(B) Record landings (if applicable), discards, and products of contract-processed groundfish in a separate DCPL identified by the name, Federal processor permit number, Federal fisheries permit number (if applicable), and ADF&G processor code of the associated business entity.

(ii) If contract-processed groundfish records are kept separately from the routine DCPL, the operator of the mothership or manager of the shoreside processor must summarize and report that information on a WPR identified by the name, Federal processor permit number, Federal fisheries permit number (if applicable), and ADF&G processor code of the associated business entity.

(12) *Alteration of records.* (i) The operator, manager, or any other person may not alter or change any entry or record in a logbook, except that an inaccurate or incorrect entry or record may be corrected by lining out the original and inserting the correction, provided that the original entry or record remains legible.

(ii) No person except an authorized officer may remove any original page of any logbook.

(13) *Inspection of records.* The operator or manager must make all logbooks, reports, and forms required under this section available for inspection upon the request of an authorized officer.

(14) *Submittal of logbooks, reports and forms* — (i) *Logbooks.* (A) The operator of a catcher vessel, catcher/processor, or mothership, or the manager of a shoreside processor must submit the yellow logsheets on a quarterly basis to the NMFS Alaska Fisheries Science Center, Logbook Program, Seattle, WA, as follows: First quarter, by May 1 of that fishing year; second quarter, by August 1 of that fishing year; third quarter, by November 1 of that fishing year; and fourth quarter, by February 1 of the following fishing year.

(B) During an inactive period that extends across two or more successive quarters, the operator or manager must complete two logsheets: One to indicate the last day of the first inactive quarter and the next page to indicate the first day of the second inactive quarter.

(ii) *Reports and forms.* Reports and forms may be submitted by the operator or manager by:

(A) Using the NMFS printed form and faxing it to the fax number on the form; or

(B) Transmitting a data file with required information and forms to NMFS by modem or satellite (specifically INMARSAT standards A, B, or C).

(15) *Record retention* — (i) *Original.* (A) The operator of a catcher vessel, catcher/processor, or mothership, and the manager of a shoreside processor, must retain the original (white) copy of all logbooks and a paper copy of all reports and forms, including those reports and forms that were originally submitted electronically and must make these documents available for inspection by an authorized officer:

(*1*) On site until the end of the fishing year during which the records were made and for as long thereafter as fish or fish products recorded in the logbook, reports, and forms are retained.

(*2*) For 3 years after the end of the fishing year during which the records were made.

(B) The operator or manager of a buying station must retain the original (white) copy of all DCLs on site until the buying station has concluded receiving groundfish from a catcher vessel for delivery to a shoreside processor or mothership and for as long as fish and fish products recorded in the DCL are retained by the buying station.

(ii) *Yellow DCL logsheet.* The operator of a mothership or manager of a shoreside processor must retain a photocopy of the yellow DCL logsheets submitted to NMFS under paragraph (a)(14) of this section that were received from associated buying stations until the mothership or shoreside processor receives the original DCL.

(iii) *Blue DFL logsheet.* (A) The operator of a mothership and the manager of a shoreside processor must retain the blue DFL logsheets (discard reports) submitted to them by operators of catcher vessels through the last day of the fishing year during which the records were made.

(B) The operator or manager of a buying station must submit

to the mothership or shoreside processor any blue logsheets (discard report) received from catcher vessels delivering groundfish to the buying station.

(iv) *Pink DCL logsheet.* The operator or manager of a buying station must retain the pink DCL logsheets for 3 years after the end of the fishing year during which the records were made.

(16) *Integration of buying station records.* (i) The operator or manager of a buying station must maintain a separate DCL for each mothership or shoreside processor to which the buying station delivers groundfish during a fishing year.

(ii) The operator or manager of a buying station must submit upon delivery of catch the yellow DCL logsheets to the shoreside processor or mothership to which it delivers groundfish, along with the blue DFL logsheets and ADF&G fish tickets or catch receipts for that delivery.

(iii) Upon conclusion of receiving groundfish for a shoreside processor or mothership, the operator or manager of a buying station must submit the original DCL to the manager of a shoreside processor or operator of a mothership to which deliveries were made.

(iv) If the mothership or shoreside processor receives fish from a buying station, the operator of the mothership or manager of the shoreside processor must incorporate all of the DCL information into the DCPL.

(b) *Representative.* The operator of a catcher vessel, mothership, catcher/processor, or buying station delivering to a mothership or manager of a shoreside processor or buying station delivering to a shoreside processor may identify one person to fill out and sign the logbook, complete the recordkeeping and reporting forms, or both, and to identify the contact person for inquiries from NMFS. Designation of a representative under this paragraph does not relieve the owner, operator, or manager of responsibility for compliance under paragraph (a)(3) of this section.

(c) *Catcher vessel DFL and catcher/processor DCPL* — (1) *Pair trawls.* If two catcher vessels are dragging a trawl between them (pair trawl), a separate DFL must be maintained by each vessel. Each vessel operator must log the amount of the catch retained by that vessel and any fish discarded by the vessel.

(2) *Time limit and submittal.* (i) The operator of a catcher vessel or catcher/processor must record in the DFL or DCPL, the time, position, and estimated groundfish catch weight within 2 hours after gear retrieval.

(ii) The operator of a catcher vessel must record all other informationrequired in the DFL by noon of the day following gear retrieval.

(iii) The operator of a catcher/processor must record all other information required in the DCPL by noon of the day following completion of production.

(iv) The operator of a catcher vessel must submit the blue DFL logsheets with delivery of the harvest to the operator of a mothership or a buying station delivering to a mothership, or to the manager of a shoreside processor or buying station delivering to a shoreside processor.

(v) Notwithstanding other time limits, the operator of a catcher vessel must record all information required in the DFL within 2 hours after the vessel's catch is offloaded.

(vi) Notwithstanding other time limits, the operator of a catcher/processor must record all information required in the DCPL within 2 hours after the vessel's catch is offloaded.

(3) *Information required* — (i) *General.* The operator of a catcher vessel or catcher/processor must record on each page:

(A) Page number as described in paragraph (a)(6)(iii)(A) of this section.

(B) The start date and end date of the fishing trip.

(C) If a catcher vessel, the vessel name and ADF&G vessel registration number.

(D) If a catcher/processor, the name, ADF&G processor number, and Federal processor number of the catcher/processor.

(E) The signature of the operator of the catcher vessel or catcher/processor.

(F) Whether catcher vessel or catcher/processor is in an active or inactive period as described in paragraph (a)(7) of this section.

(ii) *Haul/set information.* The operator of a catcher vessel or catcher/processor must record the following for each haul or set:

(A) Date (month-day-year).

(B) The number of haul or set, by sequence; begin time and position coordinates of gear deployment; average sea depth and average gear depth, recorded to the nearest meter or fathom.

(C) The date, time, and position coordinates of gear retrieval. If the vessel is using longline hook-and-line gear, the number of skates set. If the vessel is using longline pot or single pot gear, the total number of pots set.

(D) The estimated total round fish weight of the groundfish catch.

(E) The species code of the intended target species from Table 2 of this part.

(F) The estimated IFQ sablefish amounts in the "comments" column.

(iii) Discard/donated species information. The operator of a catcher vessel or catcher/processor must record discard/donation information as described in paragraph (a)(10) of this section.

(iv) *Catcher vessels.* If a catcher vessel, the operator must record:

(A) The date of delivery.

(B) The name, ADF&G processor code, and ADF&G fish ticket number(s) provided by the operator of the mothership or buying station delivering to a mothership, or the manager of a shoreside processor or buying station delivering to a shoreside processor.

(v) *Catcher/processors.* If a catcher/processor, the operator must record product information as set forth in paragraph (a)(9) of this section.

(d) *Buying station DCL* — (1) *Time limits.* (i) The operator or manager of each buying station subject to this part must record entries in the DCL as to catcher vessel delivery information within 2 hours after completion of receipt of the groundfish.

(ii) All other information required in the DCL must be recorded by noon of the day following the day the receipt of groundfish was completed or discard occurred.

(2) *Information required* — (i) *General.* The operator or manager of a buying station must record for each page:

(A) Page number as described in paragraph (a)(6)(iii)(A) of this section.

(B) The date.

(C) The buying station name and, if a vessel, the ADF&G vessel number.

(D) The operator's or manager's signature.

(E) Whether the buying station is in an active or inactive period as described in paragraph (a)(7) of this section.

(F) The name and ADF&G processor code of the mothership or shoreside processor to which groundfish deliveries were made.

(G) The number of crew.

(ii) *Groundfish deliveries.* The operator or manager of a buying station must record the following information for each delivery of groundfish:

(A) The ADF&G fish ticket number issued to each catcher vessel delivering groundfish. If a fish ticket was not issued, the catch receipt number of the transaction.

(B) Whether blue DFL logsheets were received from the catcher vessel delivering the groundfish.

(C) The time when receipt of groundfish catch was completed.

(D) The name and ADF&G vessel registration number of the catcher vessel delivering the groundfish.

(E) The total groundfish delivery weight.

(iii) *Discard/donated species information.* The operator or manager of the buying station must record discard/donation information as described in paragraph (a)(10) of this section.

(e) *Mothership DCPL* — (1) *Time limits.* (i) The operator of each mothership must record entries in the DCPL as to catcher vessel or buying station delivery information within 2 hours after completion of the groundfish receipt.

(ii) All other information required in the DCPL must be recorded by noon of the day following the day the catch receipt, discard, or production occurred.

(2) *Information required* — (i) *General.* The operator of each mothership must record on each page:

(A) Page number as described in paragraph (a)(6)(iii)(A) of this section.

(B) The date.

(C) The name, ADF&G processor number, and Federal processor number.

(D) The operator's signature.

(E) Whether mothership is in an active or inactive period as described in paragraph (a)(7) of this section.

(ii) *Deliveries.* The operator or each mothership must record for each delivery:

(A) Whether delivery is from a catcher vessel or a buying station.

(B) The name and ADF&G vessel registration number (if applicable) of the catcher vessel or buying station delivering the groundfish.

(C) The time and position coordinates of the mothership when groundfish catch is received.

(D) The estimated total ground fish weight of the groundfish catch.

(E) The ADF&G fish ticket number issued to each catcher vessel delivering groundfish. If a fish ticket is not issued, record the catch receipt number of the transaction.

(iii) *Discard/donation.* The operator of each mothership must record discard/donation information as described in paragraph (a)(10) of this section.

(iv) *Production information.* The operator of each mothership must record product information as described in paragraph (a)(9) of this section.

(f) *Shoreside processor DCPL* — (1) *Time limits.* (i) The manager of each shoreside processor must record in the DCPL all catcher vessel or buying station delivery information within 2 hours after completion of the groundfish receipt.

(ii) All other information required in the DCPL must be recorded by noon of the day following the day the catch receipt, discard, or production occurred.

(2) *Information required* — (i) *Part IA.* The manager of each shoreside processor must record on each page:

(A) If a page is for an individual day, the date. If a page is for 1 week, the week-ending date. See also paragraph (a)(6)(iii)(A) of this section.

(B) Participant identification information as described in paragraph (a)(5) of this section.

(C) The signature of the manager.

(D) Whether the shoreside processor is in an active or inactive period as described in paragraph (a)(7) of this section.

(ii) *Part IB.* The manager of each shoreside processor must record the following information for each delivery:

(A) Date and time when receipt of groundfish catch was completed.

(B) Whether delivery is from catcher vessel or buying station.

(C) Whether blue DFL logsheets were submitted by catcher vessel.

(D) The name and ADF&G vessel registration number (if applicable) of the catcher vessel or buying station delivering the groundfish.

(E) The total scale weight of groundfish delivery in pounds or to the nearest 0.01 mt.

(F) The ADF&G fish ticket number issued to the catcher vessel delivering groundfish. If a fish ticket is not issued, record the catch receipt number of the transaction.

(iii) Landings information, Part IC. The manager must record:

(A) The date next to the appropriate day of the week (SUN through SAT).

(B) Landings information as described in paragraph (a)(8) of this section.

(iv) Discarded/donated species information (Part ID). The manager of each shoreside processor must record:

(A) The date next to the appropriate day of the week (SUN through SAT).

(B) Discard information, as described in paragraph (a)(10) of this section.

(v) *Part II.* The manager of each shoreside processor must record:

(A) Page numbers must be consecutive within Part II, beginning with page one for the first day product was produced after the start of the fishing year and continuing throughout the section for the remainder of the fishing year.

(B) The name, ADF&G processor code number, and Federal processor number of shoreside processor.

(C) The signature of the manager of the shoreside processor.

(D) *Product information.* (1) The week-ending date.

(2) The management area (BSAI or GOA).

(3) The date next to the appropriate day of the week (SUN through SAT).

(4) Product information as described in paragraph (a)(9) of this section.

(g) *Groundfish Product Transfer Report (PTR)* — (1) *Applicability.*

(i) The operator of a mothership or catcher/processor or the manager of a shoreside processor must record each transfer of groundfish product on a separate PTR.

(ii) The manager of a shoreside processor must report on a PTR those fish products that are subsequently transferred to an offsite meal reduction plant.

(iii) The operator of a mothership or catcher/processor or manager of a shoreside processor must report on a PTR, daily sales or transfer of groundfish to vessels for bait. Individual sales of groundfish for bait purposes during a day may be aggregated when recording the amount of product leaving a facility that day.

(2) *Time limits and submittal.* The operator of a mothership or catcher/processor or manager of a shoreside processor must:

(i) Record all product transfer information on a PTR within 2 hours of the completion of the transfer.

(ii) Submit by fax a copy of each PTR to the Regional Director within 24 hours of completion of transfer.

(3) *Information required* — (i) *General.* The operator of a mothership or catcher/processor or manager of a shoreside processor must record on each page of a PTR:

(A) Whether the PTR is an original or revised report, as described in paragraph (a)(6)(iii)(G) of this section.

(B) Page numbers must be numbered consecutively, starting with the first transfer of the fishing year as page 1 +and continuing throughout the remainder of the fishing year.

(C) "RECEIPT," if product (including raw fish) is received; "OFFLOAD," if product (including raw fish) is offloaded from a mothership or catcher/processor; "SHIPMENT," if product (including raw fish) is shipped from a shoreside processor.

(D) Representative identification information, as described in paragraph (a)(5)(vi) of this section.

(E) If a catcher/processor or mothership, the participant identification information as described in paragraph (a)(5) of this section and USCG documentation number. If a shoreside processor, the participant identification information as described in paragraph (a)(5) of this section.

(ii) *Transfer information.* The operator of a catcher/processor or mothership or manager of a shoreside processor must record on each page the following information for each transfer:

(A) If another vessel is involved with the transfer, the name and call sign of the vessel receiving or delivering groundfish or groundfish products.

(B) If a mothership or catcher/processor and the transfer takes place in port, the port of landing and country, if a foreign location.

(C) If the transfer is made to an agent, the agent's name. For purposes of this section, "agent" is defined as the transport company, the buyer, or the distributor.

(D) *Intended first destination of product.* (1) If an offload or shipment, the intended destination of the vessel or agent receiving the groundfish or groundfish product.

(2) If an offload or shipment has several destinations, the first intended destination.

(3) If offload or shipment has a single destination but requires loading on multiple vans, trucks, or airline flights, the transfer may be recorded on a single PTR page.

(E) *Date and time of product transfer* — (1) *Start date.* The date, as described in paragraph (a)(6)(iii)(B) of this section, and time, as described in paragraph (a)(6)(iii)(C) of this section, the transfer starts.

(2) *Finish date.* The date and time the transfer is completed, as follows:

(i) If shipment is an individual van load or flight, the date and time when each shipment leaves the plant.

(ii) If shipment involves multiple vans or trucks, the date and time when loading of vans or trucks is completed for each day.

(iii) If shipment involves airline flights, record date, as described in paragraph (a)(6)(iii)(B) of this section, and time, as described in paragraph (a)(6)(iii)(C) of this section, when the last airline flight shipment of the day leaves the plant.

(F) *Position transferred.* If a catcher/processor or mothership and transfer of product is made at sea, the transfer position coordinates.

(iii) Products and quantities offloaded, shipped, or received. The operator of a catcher/processor or mothership or manager of a shoreside processor must record the following information:

(A) If a catcher/processor or mothership, the Harvest Zone code of the area in which groundfish were harvested as defined in Table 8 of this part.

(B) The species code and product code for each product transferred as defined in Tables 1 and 2 of this part.

(C) The number of cartons or production units transferred.

(D) The average net weight of one carton for each species and product code in kilograms or pounds.

(E) The total net weight (fish product weight, to the nearest 0.01 mt) of the products transferred.

(iv) *Total or partial offload.* If a catcher/processor or mothership, whether the transfer is a total or partialoffload. If partial offload, the total fish product weight, to the nearest 0.01 mt, of the products (by harvest zone, species and product codes) remaining on board after this transfer.

(h) *Check-in/check-out report* — (1) *Applicability* — (i) *Transit between reporting areas.* If a vessel is transiting through a reporting area and is not fishing or receiving fish, a check-in or check-out report is not required from that area.

(ii) *Multiple vessel operations categories* — (A) *Check-in report.* If a catcher/processor is functioning simultaneously as a mothership in the same reporting area, the operator must submit a separate check-in report for each vessel operations category.

(B) *Check-out report.* Upon completion of each activity, the operator must submit a check-out report for each vessel operations category.

(2) *Time limits and submittal* — (i) *Check-in report (BEGIN message)* — (A) *Catcher/processor.* Before the operator of a catcher/processor commences harvest of groundfish in Alaska State or Federal waters of any reporting area except 300, 400, 550, or 690, the operator must submit by fax a check-in report (BEGIN message) to the Regional Director.

(B) *Mothership or buying station delivering to a mothership.* Before the operator of a mothership or buying station delivering to a mothership commences receipt of groundfish from Alaska State or Federal waters of any reporting area except 300, 400, 550, or 690, the operator must submit by fax a check-in report (BEGIN message) to the Regional Director.

(C) *Shoreside processor or buying station delivering to a shoreside processor.* Before the manager of a shoreside processor or buying station delivering to a shoreside processor commences receipt of groundfish from Alaska State or Federal waters of any reporting area except 300, 400, 550, or 690, the manager must submit by fax a check-in report to the Regional Director.

(ii) *Check-out report (CEASE message)* — (A) *Catcher/processor.* If a catcher/processor departs a reporting area or moves between Alaska State and Federal waters in a reporting area, and gear retrieval is complete from that area, the operator must submit by fax a check-out report to the Regional Director within 24 hours after departing a reporting area or leaving either the Alaska State or Federal part of a reporting area.

(B) *Mothership or buying station delivering to a mothership.* If a mothership or buying station delivering to a mothership completes receipt of groundfish, the operator must submit by fax a check-out report to the Regional Director within 24 hours after departing a reporting area or leaving either the Alaska State or Federal part of a reporting area.

(C) *Shoreside processor.* If a shoreside processor, the manager must submit by fax a check-out report to the Regional Director within 48 hours after the end of the applicable weekly reporting period that a shoreside processor ceases to process groundfish for the fishing year or has not processed groundfish for more than one weekly reporting period.

(D) Buying station delivering to a shoreside processor. If a buying station delivering to a shoreside processor, the manager must submit by fax a check-out report to the Regional Director within 48 hours after the applicable weekly reporting period that a buying station delivering to a shoreside processor ceases to receive or deliver groundfish for the fishing year or has not received or delivered groundfish for more than one weekly reporting period.

(E) *End of fishing year.* If a check-out report has not previously been submitted during a fishing year, the operator or manager must submit a check-out report at the end of that fishing year, December 31.

(3) *Information required* — (i) *General.* The operator of a catcher/processor, mothership, or buying station delivering to a mothership or the manager of a shoreside processor or buying station delivering to a shoreside processor must record on each page:

(A) Whether it is an original or revised report as described in paragraph (a)(6)(iii)(G) of this section.

(B) Participant identification information as described in paragraph (a)(5) of this section.

(C) Representative identification information as described in paragraph (a)(5)(vi) of this section.

(D) For a mothership or catcher/processor, the processor type and gear type used to harvest the groundfish. If groundfish are received by a mothership in the same reporting area from more than one gear type, or if groundfish are caught by a catcher/processor in the same reporting area using more than one gear type, the operator must submit a separate form for each gear type.

(E) Whether harvest is under a CDQ Program; if yes, the CDQ number.

(F) If a buying station, the number of crew on the last day of the reporting week.

(ii) *BEGIN message*. The operator of a catcher/processor, mothership, or buying station delivering to a mothership or the manager of a shoreside processor or buying station delivering to a shoreside processor must record:

(A) For a catcher/processor, date and time that gear is deployed. For a mothership, date and time that receipt of groundfish begins.

(B) For a catcher/processor, position coordinates where gear is set. For a mothership, position coordinates where groundfish receipt begins.

(C) For a catcher/processor, the reporting area code of gear deployment and whether gear deployment was in Federal or Alaska State waters. For a mothership or buying station delivering to a mothership, the reporting area code where groundfish receipt begins and whether receipt of groundfish occurred in Federal or Alaska State waters.

(D) For a shoreside processor, the date receipt of groundfish will begin, whether checking in for the first time in fishing year or checking in to restart receipt and processing of groundfish after filing a check-out report.

(E) For a mothership or catcher/processor, the primary and secondary species expected to be harvested. For a buying station, the intended primary target expected to be harvested. A change in intended target species within the same reporting area does not require a new BEGIN message.

(iii) *CEASE message*. The operator of a catcher/processor, mothership, or buying station delivering to a mothership or the manager of a shoreside processor or buying station delivering to a shoreside processor must report:

(A) If a catcher/processor, mothership or buying station delivering to a mothership, the date, time and position coordinates where the vessel departed the reporting area or moved to Federal waters from Alaska State waters within a reporting area, or vice versa.

(B) If a shoreside processor or buying station delivering to a shoreside processor, the date that receipt of groundfish ceased.

(iv) *Fish or fish product held at plant*. The manager of a shoreside processor must report the weight of the fish or fish products in pounds or to the nearest 0.01 mt by species and product codes.

(i) *Weekly Production Report (WPR)* — (1) *Applicability*. (i) The operator of a catcher/processor or mothership or the manager of a shoreside processor must submit a WPR for any week the mothership, catcher/processor, or shoreside processor is checked in pursuant to paragraph (h)(2)(i) of this section.

(ii) The operator of a vessel that is authorized to conduct operations as both a catcher/processor and as a mothership must submit separate WPRsto report production and discard as a catcher/processor and production and discard as a mothership.

(2) *Time limits and submittal*. The operator or manager must submit a WPR by fax to the Regional Director by 1200 hours, A.l.t., on the Tuesday following the end of the applicable weekly reporting period.

(3) *Information required* — (i) *General*. The operator of a catcher/processor or mothership, or the manager of a shoreside processor must record on each page:

(A) Whether an original or revised report, as described in paragraph (a)(6)(iii)(G) of this section.

(B) Participant identification information as described in paragraph (a)(5) of this section.

(C) Representative identification information as described in paragraph (a)(5)(vi) of this section and date WPR was completed.

(D) If a mothership or catcher/processor, the processor type and gear type used to harvest the groundfish.

(E) Whether harvest is under a CDQ Program; if yes, the CDQ number.

(F) The week-ending date.

(G) The primary and secondary target codes for the next week.

(H) If a mothership or catcher/processor, the number of crew on the last day of the reporting week.

(ii) *Landings information*. The manager of a shoreside processor must report landings information as described in paragraph (a)(8) of this section.

(iii) *Discarded/donated species information (Part ID)*. The operator of a catcher/processor or mothership, or the manager of a shoreside processor must report discard/donated species information as described in paragraph (a)(10) of this section.

(iv) *Product information*. The operator of a catcher/processor or mothership, or the manager of a shoreside processor must report product information as described in paragraph (a)(9) of this section.

(v) *Catcher vessel delivery information*. If ADF&G fish tickets are issued, the operator of the mothership or manager of the shoreside processor must list the fish ticket numbers issued to catcher vessels for the weekly reporting period.

(j) *Daily Production Report (DPR)* — (1) *Notification*. If the Regional Director determines that DPRs are necessary to avoid exceeding a groundfish TAC or prohibited species bycatch allowance, NMFS may require submission of DPRs from motherships, catcher/processors, and shoreside processors for reporting one or more specified species, in addition to a WPR. NMFS will publish notification in the Federal Register specifying the fisheries that require DPRs and the dates that submittal of DPRs are required.

(2) *Applicability*. (i) If a catcher/processor, mothership, or shoreside processor is checked in to the specified reporting area and is harvesting, receiving, processing, or discarding the specified species or is receiving reports from a catcher vessel of discard at sea of the specified species, the operator of catcher/processor or mothership or the manager of a shoreside processor must submit a DPR.

(ii) The operator of a catcher/processor or mothership or the manager of a shoreside processor must use a separate DPR for each gear type, processor type, and CDQ number.

(3) *Time limit and submittal*. The operator or manager must submit a DPR by fax to the Regional Director by 1200 hours, A.l.t., the day following each day of landings, discard, or production.

(4) *Information required* — (i) *General*. The operator of a catcher/processor or mothership, or the manager of a shoreside processor must record on each page:

(A) Whether it is an original or revised report as described in paragraph (a)(6)(iii)(G) of this section.

(B) Participant identification information as described in paragraph (a)(5) of this section, and processor type.

(C) Representative identification information as described in paragraph (a)(5)(vi) of this section.

(D) The gear type used to harvest the groundfish, date landings were received, and Federal reporting area where landings were harvested.

(E) Whether harvest is under a CDQ Program; if yes, the CDQ number.

(ii) *Landings information.* The manager of a shoreside processor must report landings information as described in paragraph (a)(8) of this section.

(iii) *Product information.* The operator of a mothership or catcher/processor must report product information as described in paragraph (a)(9) of this section.

(iv) *Discard/donated species information.* The operator of a mothership or catcher/processor and the manager of a shoreside processor must report discard/donated species information as described in paragraph (a)(10) of this section.

(k) *U.S. Vessel Activity Report (VAR)*—(1) *Applicability.* The operator of a catcher vessel, catcher/processor, or mothership regulated under this part must submit a VAR by fax to NMFS Alaska Enforcement Division, Juneau, AK, before the vessel crosses the seaward boundary of the EEZ off Alaska or crosses the U.S.-Canadian international boundary between Alaska and British Columbia.

(2) *Information required*—(i) *General.* The operator of each catcher vessel, catcher/processor, or mothership must record on each page:

(A) Whether an original or revised report as described in paragraph (a)(6)(iii)(G) of this section.

(B) Participant identification information as described in paragraph (a)(5) of this section.

(C) Representative identification information as described in paragraph (a)(5)(vi) of this section, and date VAR was completed.

(D) If the vessel is crossing into the seaward boundary of the EEZ off Alaska or crossing the U.S.-Canadian international boundary between Alaska and British Columbia, the operator must indicate "return" report.

(E) If the vessel is crossing out of the seaward boundary of the EEZ off Alaska or crossing the U.S.-Canadian international boundary between Alaska and British Columbia into Canadian waters, the operator must indicate "depart" report.

(F) Port of landing.

(G) Whether the vessel is returning from fishing or departing to fish in the Russian Zone.

(H) Date and time the vessel will cross the seaward boundary of the EEZ off Alaska or the U.S.-Canadian international boundary between Alaska and British Columbia.

(I) Latitude and longitude at the point of crossing the seaward boundary of the EEZ off Alaska or U.S.-Canadian international boundary between Alaska and British Columbia.

(ii) *Fish or fish products.* The operator of a catcher vessel, catcher/processor, or mothership must record the fish or fish product on board the vessel when crossing the seaward boundary of the EEZ off Alaska or U.S.-Canadian international boundary as follows:

(A) The Harvest Zone code of the area in which groundfish were harvested as defined in Table 8 of this part.

(B) The species code and product code for each species on board as defined in Tables 1 and 2 of this part.

(C) The fish product weight of products on board in pounds or to the nearest 0.01 mt.

(l) *IFQ recordkeeping and reporting requirements.* In addition to the recordkeeping and reporting requirements in this section and as specified in part 301 of this title, the following reports are required.

(1) *IFQ landings report* — (i) *Prior notice of IFQ landing.* The operator of any vessel making an IFQ landing mustnotify the Alaska Region, NMFS, no less than 6 hours before landing IFQ halibut or IFQ sablefish, unless permission to commence an IFQ landing within 6 hours of notification is granted by a clearing officer.

(A) Notification of an IFQ landing must be made to the toll-free telephone number specified on the IFQ permit between the hours of 0600 hours, A.l.t., and 2400 hours, A.l.t.

(B) Notification must include: Name and location of the registered buyer(s) to whom the IFQ halibut or IFQ sablefish will be landed, vessel identification, estimated weight of the IFQ halibut or IFQ sablefish that will be landed, identification number(s) of the IFQ card(s) that will be used to land the IFQ halibut or IFQ sablefish, and anticipated date and time of landing.

(ii) *Registered buyer reports IFQ landings.* (A) A registered buyer must report an IFQ landing in the manner prescribed on the registered buyer permit within 6 hours after all such fish are landed and prior to shipment or departure of the delivery vessel from the landing site.

(B) An IFQ landing may be made only between the hours of 0600 hours, A.l.t., and 1800 hours, A.l.t., unless permission to land at a different time is granted in advance by a clearing officer. An IFQ landing may continue after this time period if it were started during the period.

(iii) *Verification and inspection.* (A) Each IFQ landing and all fish retained on board the vessel making an IFQ landing are subject to verification, inspection, and sampling by authorized officers, clearing officers, or observers. Each IFQ halibut landing is subject to sampling for biological information by persons authorized by the IPHC.

(B) A copy of all reports and receipts required by this section must be retained by registered buyers and be made available for inspection by an authorized officer or a clearing officer for a period of 3 years.

(iv) *Information required.* Information contained in a complete IFQ landing report shall include: Date, time, and location of the IFQ landing; names and permit numbers of the IFQ card holder and registered buyer; product type landed; and fish product weight of sablefish and halibut landed.

(2) *IFQ shipment report* — (i) *Applicability.* Each registered buyer, other than those conducting dockside sales, must report on a shipment report any shipments or transfers of IFQ halibut and IFQ sablefish to any location other than the location of the IFQ landing.

(ii) *Submittal.* (A) A shipment report must be submitted to the Chief, RAM Division, prior to shipment or transfer, in a manner prescribed on the registered buyer permit.

(B) A shipment report must specify: Species and product type being shipped, number of shipping units, fish product weight, names of the shipper and receiver, names and addresses of the consignee and consignor, mode of transportation, and intended route.

(iii) *Registered buyer.* A registered buyer must assure that:

(A) Shipments of IFQ halibut or IFQ sablefish from that registered buyer in Alaska or in any IFQ regulatory area to a destination outside Alaska or outside an IFQ regulatory area do not commence until the shipment report is received by the Alaska Region, NMFS.

(B) A copy of the shipment report or a bill of lading that contains the same information accompanies the shipment to all points of sale in Alaska and to the first point of sale outside of Alaska.

(iv) *Dockside sale and outside landing.* (A) A person holding a valid IFQ permit, IFQ card, and registered buyer permit may conduct a dockside sale of IFQ halibut or IFQ sablefish to a person who has not been issued a registered buyer permit.

(B) The person making such an IFQ landing must submit an IFQ landing report in the manner prescribed in paragraph (l)(1) of this section before any fish are sold, transferred, or removed from the immediate vicinity of the vessel with which they were harvested.

(C) A receipt that includes the date of sale or transfer, the registered buyer permit number, and the fish product weight of the sablefish or halibut transferred must be issued to each individual receiving IFQ halibut or IFQ sablefish through a dockside sale.

(D) A person holding a valid IFQ permit, IFQ card, and registered buyer permit may conduct a IFQ landing outside an IFQ regulatory area or the State of Alaska to a person who does not hold a registered buyer permit. The person making such an IFQ landing must submit an IFQ landing report in the manner prescribed in paragraph (l)(1) of this section.

(v) *Transshipment.* (A) No person may transship processed IFQ halibut or IFQ sablefish between vessels without authorization by a clearing officer. Authorization must be obtained for each instance of transshipment.

(B) An IFQ transshipper's request for authorization to transship must be received by a clearing officer at least 24 hours before the transshipment is intended to occur.

(3) *IFQ vessel clearance* — (i) *Applicability.* A person who makes an IFQ landing at any location other than in an IFQ regulatory area or in the State of Alaska must obtain prelanding written clearance of the vessel and provide the weight of IFQ halibut and IFQ sablefish on board to the clearing officer.

(ii) *State of Alaska.* A vessel obtaining prelanding written clearance at a port in the State of Alaska must obtain that clearance prior to departing the waters of the EEZ adjacent to the jurisdictional waters of the State of Alaska, the territorial sea of the State of Alaska, or the internal waters of the State of Alaska.

(iii) *State other than Alaska.* (A) A vessel obtaining prelanding written clearance at a port in a state other than Alaska must provide a departure report to NMFS, Alaska Region, prior to departing the waters of the EEZ adjacent to the jurisdictional waters of the State of Alaska, the territorial sea of the State of Alaska, or the internal waters of the State of Alaska.

(B) The departure report must include the weight of the IFQ halibut or IFQ sablefish on board and the intended date and time the vessel will obtain prelanding written clearance at that port in a state other than Alaska.

(iv) *Foreign port other than Canada.* A vessel operator who lands IFQ species in a foreign port must first obtain vessel clearance from a clearing officer located at a primary port in the State of Alaska.

(v) *Canadian ports.* No person shall make an IFQ landing in Canada other than at the ports of Port Hardy, Prince Rupert, or Vancouver, British Columbia.

(vi) *Reporting requirements.* (A) A vessel operator must land and report all IFQ species on board at the same time and place as the first landing of any species harvested during a fishing trip.

(B) Any person requesting a vessel clearance must have valid IFQ and registered buyer permits and one or more valid IFQ cards on board that indicate that IFQ holdings are equal to or greater than all IFQ halibut and IFQ sablefish on board, and must report the intended date, time, and location of IFQ landing.

(C) Any person granted a vessel clearance must submit an IFQ landing report, required under this section, for all IFQ halibut, IFQ sablefish, and products thereof that are on board the vessel at the first landing of any fish from the vessel.

(vii) *Inspection.* A vessel seeking clearance is subject to inspection of all fish, log books, permits, and other documents on board the vessel, at the discretion of the clearing officer.

(viii) *Primary ports.* Unless specifically authorized on a case-by-case basis, vessel clearances will be issued only by clearing officers at the following primary ports:

* * * * *

Citation: 50 CFR 679.50

✍ §679.50 Groundfish Observer Program applicable through December 31, 1997.

* * * * *

(f) * * *

(1) * * *

(iii) * * *

(B) * * *

(*1*) *Hardware and software.* Providing for use by the observer a personal computer in working condition that contains a full 486DX 66Mhz or greater capacity processing chip, at least 16 megabytes of RAM, at least 75 megabytes of free hard disk storage, DOS version 6.0 or a successor version of the DOS operating system, Windows 3.1, 3.11, or Windows95 (or equivalent and compatible software approved by NMFS), a mouse, and a 3.5-inch floppy disk drive. The computer equipment specified in this paragraph (B) must be connected to either an INMARSAT Standard C unit capable of transmitting binary files or a communication device that provides a point-to-point modem connection to the NMFS host computer and supports one or more of the following protocols: ITU V.22, ITU V.22bis, ITU V.32, ITU V.32bis, or ITU V.34. Those processors that use other than an INMARSAT Standard C unit must have at least a 28.8kbs Hayes-compatible modem. The above-specified hardware and software requirements do not apply to processors that do not process groundfish.

* * * * *

(2) * * *

(iii) * * *

(B) * * *

(*1*) *Hardware and software.* Making available for use by the observer a personal computer in working condition that contains a full 486DX 66Mhz or greater capacity processing chip, at least 16 megabytes of RAM, at least 75 megabytes of free hard disk storage, DOS version 6.0 or a successor version of the DOS operating system, Windows 3.1, 3.11, or Windows95 (or equivalent and compatible software approved by NMFS), at least a 28.8kbs Hayes-compatible modem, a mouse, and a 3.5-inch floppy disk drive. The computer equipment specified in this paragraph (B) must be connected to a communication device that provides a point-to-point modem connection to the NMFS host computer and supports one or more of the following protocols: ITU V.22, ITU V.22bis, ITU V.32, ITU V.32bis, or ITU V.34. The above-specified hardware and software requirements do not apply to processors that do not process groundfish.

* * * * *

Source: Revenue Procedures
Agency: Department of the Treasury
Internal Revenue Service

Rev. Proc. 81-46

✍ § 1. Purpose.

.01 The purpose of this revenue procedure is to update Rev. Proc. 76-43, 1976-2 C.B. 667, which sets forth the conditions under which microfilm (including microfiche) reproduction of general books of account will be considered books and records within the meaning of section 6001 of the Internal Revenue Code. General books of account include cash books, journals, voucher registers, ledgers, etc., and supporting records of detail.

§ 2. Changes.

.01 Previous sections 3.02 and 3.03 requiring (1) permission from the Internal Revenue Service to establish a microfilm system and (2) the Service's review of such system have been eliminated.

.02 Section 5.01 revises previous section 4.01 to eliminate specific standards of microfilm systems.

.03 Section 4.03 has been added to provide that those taxpayers considered not in compliance with this revenue procedure may be subject to all applicable penalties under sub-title F of the Code.

§ 3. Background.

.01 Rev. Rul. 75-265, 1975-2 C.B. 460, holds that microfilm reproduction of general books of account and supporting records of detail will be considered books and records within the meaning of section 6001 of the Code when such books are maintained in accordance with Rev. Proc. 75-33, 1975-2 C.B. 559. Rev. Proc. 75-33 was superseded by Rev. Proc. 76-43.

.02 In undertaking a system of micrographic reproduction of books and records, the taxpayer is responsible for the integrity and availability of the books and records, and for a quality that is sufficient to establish the amount of gross income, deductions, credits, or other matters required to be shown in any return of tax or information.

.03 If a taxpayer uses microfilm, books, records, statements, and returns to which section 6001 of the Code applies, they are required to be authentic, accessible, and readable.

§ 4. Procedure.

.01 Taxpayers who want to keep books and records on microfilm must meet the requirements set forth in section 5 of this revenue procedure (1) if they have a micrographic system that includes the ability to produce records on microfilm directly on-line from the computer or off-line from magnetic tape, or (2) if they have records photographed onto microfilm from original documents, "hard copy" printouts, etc.

.02 Taxpayers whose micrographic systems do not meet the requirements of section 5 will be considered not in compliance with section 6001 of the Code and section 1.6001 of the Income Tax Regulations

.03 Taxpayers whose micrographic systems are found to be not in compliance with this revenue procedure may be subject to all applicable penalties under subtitle F of the Code.

§ 5. Requirements.

.01 The following requirements apply to microfilm:

1. Taxpayers must set forth in writing the procedures governing the establishment of a microfilm system, and the individuals who are responsible for maintaining and operating the microfilm system with appropriate authorization from the Board of Directors, general partner(s), or owner, whichever is applicable;
2. The microfilm system must be complete and must be used consistently in the regularly conducted activity of the business;
3. Taxpayers must establish procedures with appropriate documentation so the original document can be followed through the micrographic system;
4. Taxpayers must establish internal procedures for inspection and quality assurance;
5. Taxpayers are responsible for the effective identification, processing, storage, and preservation of microfilm, making it readily available for as long as the contents may become material in the administration of any Internal Revenue law;
6. Taxpayers must keep a record of where, when, by whom, and on what equipment the microfilm was produced;
7. When displayed on a microfilm reader (viewer) or reproduced on paper, the material must exhibit a high degree of legibility and readability. For this purpose, legibility is defined as the quality of a letter or numeral that enables the observer to identify it positively and quickly to the exclusion of all other letters or numerals. Readability is defined as the quality of a group of letters or numerals being recognizable as words or complete numbers;
8. A detailed index of all microfilmed data must be maintained and arranged in a manner that permits the immediate location of any particular record;
9. All microfilming and processing duplication, quality control, storage, identification, and inspection must meet industry standards as set forth by the American National Standards Institute, National Micrographics Association, or National Bureau of Standards;
10. The taxpayer must make available upon the Service's request a reader/printer in good working order at the examination site for reading, locating, and reproducing any record maintained on microfilm; and
11. If any part of the taxpayer's books and records are maintained in any machine-sensible data medium (for example, magnetic tape or magnetic disk) prior to microfilming, the taxpayer must contact the local District Director to get an automatic data processing records evaluation under Rev. Rul. 71-20, 1971-1 C.B. 392.

§ 6. Effect on other documents.

.01 Microfilm books of account are another class of records added to those described in Rev. Proc. 64-12, 1964-1 (Part 1) C.B. 672, if produced by an automatic data processing system. Rev. Proc. 64-12 is amplified. Rev. Proc. 76-43 is superseded.

Rev. Proc. 83-6

§ 1. Purpose and Background

The purpose of this revenue procedure is to make clear that Rev. Proc. 81-46, 1981-2 C.B. 621, governs the microfilm (including microfiche) reproduction of Form W-6, Individual Certificate of Exemption, and Form W-7, Certificate of Exemption — Other Than Individuals.

This clarification is necessary due to the enactment of new provisions of the Internal Revenue Code providing for income tax withholding from payments of interest, dividends, and patronage dividends. Such provisions were enacted by the Tax Equity and Fiscal Responsibility Act of 1982, 1982-2 C.B. 462, 550.

* * * * *

§ 2. Application

Rev. Proc. 81-46 specifically sets forth conditions under which microfilm reproductions of general books of account and supporting records of detail will be considered books and records within the meaning of section 6001 of the Code. These conditions also apply to microfilm reproductions of Forms W-6 and W-7. So long as the requirements set forth in Rev. Proc. 81-46 are complied with, microfilm reproductions of Forms W-6 and W-7, or acceptable substitutes as permitted by section 35.3452(f)-1(b)(2) of the Temporary Employment Tax Regulations, will be accepted.

Rev. Proc. 86-19

[Note: The Internal Revenue Service replaced this section with Rev. Proc. 91-59 in 1993.]

Rev. Proc. 87-11

✍ § 1. Purpose

This revenue procedure states the Internal Revenue Service (the Service) requirements relating to acceptable privately designed and printed or computer-prepared substitute federal tax return forms, (i.e., Forms 1040, 1040A, 1040EZ, 1120, 1120A, 940, 941, etc.) and computer-generated substitute schedules or forms to be attached thereto. It also authorizes the use of reproductions of official forms and gives direction for the proper completion of returns.

✍ § 2. Scope

This revenue procedure is the guide for preparing substitutes for most printed, computer-prepared and computer-generated tax forms. This procedure does not include guidance for Form 1040-ES, Form 5498, Form 1096, the Form 1099 series, Form W-9 and the Form W-2 series. (See Sec. 18 and 19 to obtain guidance for the excluded forms.)

[Consult the Revenue Procedure for the complete text if this section appears relevant.]

Rev. Proc. 87-38

✍ § 1. Purpose

The purpose of this revenue procedure is two fold: to state the requirements of the Internal Revenue Service regarding the reproduction, private design, and printing of substitute federal tax return Form 1040-ES, Estimated Tax for Individuals, in lieu of the official form; and to state the Service's requirements regarding the acceptance of computer-generated Forms 1040-ES. Also, beginning with Forms 1040-ES for 1988, all substitutes must be laser printed and scannable by the Service.

[Consult the Revenue Procedure for the complete text if this section appears relevant.]

Rev. Proc. 87-47

✍ § 1. Purpose

.01 The purpose of this revenue procedure is to update Rev. Proc. 86-13, 1986-1 C.B. 535, (IRS Pub. 1245), which outlines the requirements and conditions for submitting certain Forms W-4, Employee's Withholding Allowance Certificate, on magnetic tape to the Internal Revenue Service (IRS), National Computer Center (NCC). It also makes certain other changes based on new requirements contained in The Tax Reform Act of 1986.

.02 Employers may submit all information on magnetic tape; or a combination of tape records and paper documents is acceptable, provided there is no duplications or omission of documents.

[Consult the Revenue Procedure for the complete text if this section appears relevant.]

Rev. Proc. 88-43

✍ § 1. Purpose

.01 The purpose of this revenue procedure is to provide general rules for filing and to state the requirements of the Internal Revenue Service (IRS) and the Social Security Administration (SSA) relating to substitutes for Form W-2, Wage and Tax Statement, Form W-2P, Statement for Recipients of Annuities, Pensions, Retired Pay, or IRA Payments, and Form W-3, Transmittal of Income and Tax Statements. This revenue procedure also contains general rules for filing Forms W-2, W-2P, and W-3. Preparers should also refer to the Instructions for Forms W-2 and W-2P and Form W-3 for additional information on how to complete these forms. See Section 5.03 below for information on ordering the official IRS forms and instructions.

.02 This revenue procedure supersedes Rev. Proc. 87-;25, 1987-1 C.B. 721.

§ 2 Nature of Changes

.01 Various editorial changes were made.

.02 Left and right margins on Forms W-2, W-2P and W-3 were changed. Left margin is now .35 inch, right margin is .15 inch. (see Exhibits)

.03 The use of chemical transfer paper is acceptable on Form W-2 and W-2P (Copy A) so long as the specification in Section 7.15 are met.

.04 Payers who file on magnetic media are reminded NOT to submit the same information to SSA on paper Forms W-2 and W-2P (Copy A)

§ 3. General Rules for Filing Forms W-2 and W-2p

.01 Employers and payers (hereafter and where applicable collectively referred to as payers) MUST use magnetic media for filing if the payer will file 250 or more 1988 Forms W-2 (Copy A) or W-2P (Copy A0 with the Social Security Administration. This requirements applies unless the payer establishes that filing on magnetic media will result in undue hardship and requests a waiver of the requirement from the IRS. To request a one year waiver of the magnetic media filing requirement, submit Form 8508, Request for Waiver From Filing Information Returns on Magnetic Media, to: Magnetic Media Reporting, National Computer Center, P. O. Box 1359, Martinsburg, WV 25401-1359. Requests must be submitted at least 90 days before the due date of the return. * * * Payers who file Forms W-2 and W-2P information on magnetic media MUST NOT send the same data to SSA on paper Forms W-2 and W-2P. This would result in duplicate reporting of wage data. Since many states and localities accept Forms W-2 and W-2P data on magnetic media, savings may be obtained if magnetic media is used for filing with both SSA and state or local agencies.

.02 Magnetic media users can design their own statements to give to employees, pensioners, annuitants, recipients of retired pay, recipients of IRA (Individual Retirement Account) payments, and recipients of disability income (hereafter and where applicable collectively referred to as payees). Payee statements designed by payers must comply with the requirements of Sections 6, 8, 9 and 10 shown below.

* * * * *

.04 Payers using magnetic media are cautioned to obtain the most recent Technical Information Bulletins and supplements due to possible changes in the specifications and procedures.

.05 Payers not using magnetic media must file Copy A of Form W-2 or Copy A of Form W-2P with SSA on either an official form or a privately printed substitute paper form meeting the specifications shown below.

* * * * *

Rev. Proc. 91-59

✍ § 1. Purpose

.01 The purpose of this revenue procedure is to update Rev. Proc. 86-19, 1986-1 C.B. 558, and to specify the basic requirements that the Internal Revenue Service considers to be essential in cases where a taxpayer's records are maintained within an Automatic Data Processing (ADP) system. Rev. Proc. 86-19 provides guidelines for record requirements to be followed in cases where part or all of the accounting records are maintained within an ADP system. References to ADP systems include all accounting and/or financial systems and subsystems that process all or part of a taxpayer's transactions, records, or data by other than manual methods.

.02 The technology of automatic data processing has evolved rapidly, and new methods and techniques are constantly being devised and adopted. The requirements set forth in Section 5 of this revenue procedure are intended to ensure that all machine-sensible records generated by a taxpayer's ADP system are retained so long as they may become material in the administration of any internal revenue law. These requirements will be modified and amended as needed to keep pace with developments in ADP systems.

✍ § 2. Background.

.01 Section 6001 of the Code provides that every person liable for any tax imposed by the Code, or for the collection thereof, shall keep such records as the Secretary may from time to time prescribe.

.02 Rev. Rul. 71-20, 1971-1 C.B. 392, establishes that all machine-sensible data media used for recording, consolidating, and summarizing accounting transactions and records within a taxpayer's ADP system are records within the meaning of section 6001 of the Code and section 1.6001-1 of the Income Tax Regulations, and are required to be retained so long as the contents may be material in the administration of any internal revenue law.

✍ § 3. Scope.

.01 This revenue procedure encompasses all types of data processing systems, including, but not limited to, microcomputer systems, Data Base Management Systems (DBMS), and all systems using Electronic Data Interchange (EDI) technology. For purposes of this revenue procedure: DBMS means a software system that creates, controls, retrieves, and provides accessibility to data stored in a data base; and EDI technology means the computer-to-computer exchange of business information.

.02 The utilization of a service bureau, time-sharing service, or value-added network does not relieve the taxpayer of the responsibilities described in this revenue procedure.

.03 A taxpayer with assets of $10 million or more at the end of its taxable year shall comply with the record retention requirements of Rev. Rul. 71-20 and the provisions of this revenue procedure. For purposes of this revenue procedure, a controlled group of corporations, as defined in section 1563 of the Code, will be considered to be one corporation and all assets of all members of the group will be aggregated

.04 A taxpayer that has assets of less than $10 million shall comply with the record retention requirements of Rev. Rul. 71-20 and the provisions of this revenue procedure if any of the following conditions exist:

(1) information required by section 6001 of the Code is not in the hardcopy books and records, but is available in machine-sensible records;

(2) machine-sensible records were used for computations that cannot be reasonably verified or recomputed without using a computer (e.g., Last-In, First-Out (LIFO) inventories); or

(3) the taxpayer is notified by the District Director that machine-sensible records must be retained to meet the requirements of section 6001 of the Code.

.05 The requirements of this revenue procedure pertain to all matters under the jurisdiction of the Commissioner of Internal Revenue including, but not limited to, income, excise, employment, and estate and gift taxes, as well as employee plans and exempt organizations.

.06 The requirements of this revenue procedure are applicable to the machine-sensible records generated by a Controlled Foreign Corporation (CFC), a domestic corporation that is 25 percent foreign-owned, and foreign corporation engaged in a trade or business within the United States at any time during a taxable year because the definition of "records" in section 964(c), 982(d), 6038A, and 6038C of the Code and the regulations thereunder has the same meaning as "records" as used in section 6001 of the Code and section 1.6001-1(a) of the regulations.

.07 Machine-sensible records used by an insurance company to determine losses incurred under section 832(b)(5) of the Code shall be retained in accordance with the requirements of this revenue procedure and Rev. Proc. 75- 56, 1975-2 C.B. 596. For this purpose, the machine- sensible files for a particular taxable year include the files for that year and the seven preceding years, all of which must be retained so long as they are material to the examination of the return. *See* section 5.06 for a discussion of materiality.

.08 The requirements of this revenue procedure are applicable to any sections of the Code that have unique or specific recordkeeping requirements. For example, machine-sensible records maintained by the taxpayer to meet the requirements of section 274(d) relating to the amount, time, and place of a business expense must meet the requirements of this revenue procedure.

✍ § 4. District Director Authority.

.01 In the case of a taxpayer that has less than $10 million in assets at the end of its taxable year, the District Director may notify a taxpayer that machine-sensible records must be retained to meet the requirements of section 6001 of the Code, and that Rev. Rul. 71-20 and the provisions of this revenue procedure apply to that taxpayer. Subsequent failure to comply with this notification may result in the imposition of the penalties described in section 7.

.02 The District Director has the authority to enter into or revoke a record retention limitation agreement with the taxpayer to modify or waive all or any of the specific requirements in this revenue procedure. The taxpayer remains subject to all requirements of this revenue procedure that are not specifically modified or waived by a record retention limitation agreement. A taxpayer that has questions regarding the application of this revenue procedure to a specific factual situation should contact the appropriate District Director.

(1) A record retention limitation agreement does not apply to a subsidiary company acquired, or accounting and tax systems added, subsequent to the completion of the record evaluation (see section 3.03 below) upon which the agreement is based. All machine-sensible records produced by a subsequently acquired company or a subsequently added accounting and tax system whose contents may be or may become material in the administration of the Code shall be retained by the taxpayer who signed the agreement until a new evaluation is conducted by the District Director.

(2) Upon the disposition of a subsidiary, the files being retained for the Service by, or for, the disposed subsidiary shall be retained by the taxpayer until a new evaluation can be made by the District Director.

.03 To determine if a taxpayer may limit its retention of machine-sensible records, a record evaluation may be conducted by the District Director. This evaluation of the data processing and accounting systems may be initiated by the District Director or requested by the taxpayer, and is not an "examination," "investigation," or "inspection" of the books and records within the meaning of section 7605(b) of the Code because the evaluation is not directly related to the determination of tax liability for a particular taxable period.

,04 The District Director may periodically initiate tests to establish the authenticity, readability, completeness, and integrity of the machine-sensible records retained as required by this revenue procedure. These tests may include the testing of EDI and/or other procedures, and a review of the internal controls and security procedures associated with the creation and storage of the records. These tests are not an "examination," "investigation," or "inspection" of the books and records within the meaning of section 7605(b) of the Code because these tests are not directly related to the determination of tax liability for a particular taxable period.

✍ § 5. Machine-Sensible Recordkeeping Requirements.

.01 All machine-sensible records whose contents may be or may become material to the administration of the Code shall be retained by the taxpayer. The retained records shall be in a retrievable format that provides the information necessary to determine the correct tax liability. The taxpayer shall ensure that the details and the source documents underlying any summary accounting data may be easily identified and made available to the Service upon request.

.02 Documentation that provides a complete description of the ADP portion of the accounting system, including all subsystems and files that feed into the accounting system, shall be retained and made available to the Service upon request. The statements and illustrations as to the scope of operations shall be sufficiently detailed to indicate:

(1) the application being performed;

(2) the procedures employed in each application;

(3) the controls used to ensure accurate and reliable processing; and

(4) the controls used to prevent the unauthorized addition, alteration, or deletion of retained records.

.03 The following specific documentation for all retained files shall also be kept:

(1) record formats (including the meaning of all "codes" used to represent information);

(2) flowcharts for a system and a program;

(3) label descriptions;

(4) source program listings of programs that created the retained files;

(5) detailed charts of accounts (for specific periods);

(6) evidence that periodic checks of the retained records that are prescribed in section 5.08 were performed; and

(7) evidence that the retained records reconcile to the books and the tax return. This reconciliation shall establish the relationship between the total of the amounts in the retained records by account to the account totals in the books and to the tax return.

04. Any changes to the ADP system which affects the accounting system and/or subsystems, together with their effective dates, shall be documented in order to preserve an accurate chronological record. This documentation shall include any changes to software or systems and any changes to the formats of files.

Audit trails should be designed to insure that details underlying the summary accounting data, such as invoices and vouchers, may be easily identified and made available to the Service upon request.

.05 In addition to the documentation described in section 5.02 through 5.04, the Service may require that the taxpayer furnish any other evidence (*e.g.*, internal audit reports) that pertains to the authenticity and integrity of the records.

.06 Machine-sensible records are required to be retained until their contents are no longer material to the administration of the Code. At a minimum, this materiality continues until the expiration of the statute of limitations, including extensions, for each tax year. In certain situations, records should be kept for a longer period of time. For example, records that pertain to fixed assets, loses incurred under section 832(b)(5) of the Code, and LIFO inventories should be kept for longer period of time.

.07 All machine-sensible records that must be retained shall be clearly labeled and stored in a secure environment. For example, supplemental labels with the statement "Tax Year 19XX Records — Retain for IRS until ______" or "Retain for IRS, Consult Tax Manager Before Releasing" should be used and affixed to each tape reel, cartridge, disk pack, diskette, or other device being retained, and a retention date should be written on the internal label. Back-up copies of machine-sensible records retained for the service should be stored at an off-site location. The Service recommends that taxpayers refer to the National Archives and Record Administration's (NARA) standards for additional guidance on the maintenance and storage of electronic records. *See*, Standards for the Creation, Use, Preservation, and Disposition of Electronic Records, 36 C.F.R. Ch. XII, Part 1234, Subpart C (1990).

.08 The taxpayer shall make periodic checks on all records retained for the Service. The Service recommends using the NARA standard for making periodic checks of retained machine-sensible records. *See*, 36 C.F.R. § 1234.28(g)(4) (199). In general, this standard requires a recordkeeper to annually select and test a random sample of all reels of magnetic tape to identify any loss of data, and to discover and correct the causes of the data loss. In libraries with 1800 or fewer storage units (*e.g.*, magnetic tape reels), a 20 percent random sample or a sample size of 50 units, whichever is larger, shall be read. In libraries with more than 1800 units, a sample of 384 units shall be read.

.09 If any machine-sensible records required to be retained are lost, destroyed, damaged, or found to be incomplete or materially inaccurate, the taxpayer shall report this to the District Director and recreate the files within a reasonable period of time.

.10 Although the NARA sampling standard referred to in section 5.08 is specifically for magnetic computer tape, the Service recommends that all retained machine-sensible media be randomly sampled and tested as described by NARA. A taxpayer whose data maintenance practices conform with the NARA standards and who loses only a portion of the data from a particular storage unit will not be subject to the penalties described in section 7. However, this taxpayer remains responsible for substantiating the information on its return as required by section 6001 of the Code.

.11 The taxpayer must be able to process the retained records at the time of a Service examination. Processing shall include the ability to print a hardcopy of any record. When the data processing system that created the records is being replaced by a system with which the records would be incompatible, the taxpayer shall convert pre-existing records to a format that is compatible with the new system. Any changes in the ability to process the retained records shall be reported to the District

Director.

.12 The taxpayer shall provide the Service, at the time of an examination, with computer resources (*e.g.*, terminal access, computer time, personnel, etc.) that are necessary for the processing of the retained records. Failure to provide these resources will be a failure to maintain books and records under section 6001 of the Code.

.13 The use of a DBMS necessitates the implementation of procedures to ensure that appropriate records and documentation are retained. A taxpayer is in compliance with the provisions of this revenue procedure if a sequential file exists and is available to the Service. The sequential file shall contain the detail necessary to identify the underlying source documents. The process to create a sequential file should be reviewed by the District Director prior to destruction of the DBMS records. Section 5.01 through 5.12 of this procedure shall apply to the resultant sequential file(s).

.14 In addition to the documentation described in section 5.02 through 5.05, the following documentation pertaining to each DBMS system shall be retained:

(1) Data Base Description (DBD);

(2) Record layout of each segment with respect to the fields in the segment;

(3) Systems Control Language;

(4) Program Specification Block (PSB); and

(5) Program Communication Block (PCB).

.15 In order to be in compliance with this revenue procedure, a taxpayer that uses EDI technology must retain machine-sensible records that, in combination with any other records (*e.g.*, the underlying contracts, price lists, and price changes), contain all of the detailed information required by section 6001 of the Code. The extent of the detail in the retained electronic and other records, if any, must be equivalent to the level of detail contained in an acceptable paper record. For example, the retained records for an electronic invoice must contain identification of the vendor by name, invoice date, product description, quantity purchased, price, etc. The taxpayer may capture this information at any level within the accounting system provided that the audit trail, authenticity, and integrity of the retained records can be established.

✍ § 6. Impact on Hardcopy Recordkeeping Requirements.

.01 Except as otherwise provided in this section, the provisions of this revenue procedure do not relieve taxpayers of the responsibility to retain hardcopy records that are created or received in the ordinary course of business as required by existing law and regulations. Hardcopy records may be retained in microfiche or microfilm format in accordance with the requirements outlined in Rev. Proc. 81-46, 1981-2 C.B. 621. These records are not a substitute for the machine-sensible records required to be retained by this revenue procedure.

.02 Hardcopy records generated at the time of a transaction (*e.g.*, credit card receipts) need not be retained if all the details relating to the transaction are subsequently received by the taxpayer in an EDI transaction and are retained by the taxpayer in accordance with this revenue procedure.

.03 If hardcopy records are not produced or received in the ordinary course of transacting business (as may be the case when utilizing EDI technology), or are not retained pursuant to section 6.02, hardcopy printouts of computerized records need not be created unless requested by the Service. These requests may be made either at the time of an examination or in conjunction with the testing described in section 4.04.

.04 Computer printouts that are created for validation, control, or other temporary purposes need not be retained.

✍ § 7. Penalties.

The District Director may issue a Notice of Inadequate Records pursuant to section 1.6001-1(d) of the regulations if machine-sensible records are not properly retained as required by this revenue procedure. Failure to comply with the provisions of this revenue procedure may also result in the imposition of an accuracy related civil penalty under section 6662(a) of the Code that is attributable to negligence or disregard of rules or regulations as provided under section 6662(b)(1). A criminal penalty under section 7203 may also be applicable. See Rev. Rul. 81-205, 1981-2 C.B. 225, which explains the applicability of the predecessor of section 6662(a) civil penalty and the section 7203 criminal penalty.

✍ § 8. Effect on Other Revenue Procedures.

Rev. Proc. 86-19 is superseded for taxable years beginning after December 31, 1991. However, if a taxpayer complies with this revenue procedure for prior taxable years, the taxpayer will be treated as having complied with Rev. Proc. 86-19 for those years.

✍ § 9. Effective date.

This revenue procedure is effective for taxable years beginning after December 31, 1991.

Rev. Proc. 97-22

§ 1. Purpose

This revenue procedure provides guidance to taxpayers that maintain books and records by using an electronic storage system that either images their hard copy (paper) books and records, or transfers their computerized books and records, to an electronic storage media, such as an optical disk. Records maintained in an electronic storage system that complies with the requirements of this revenue procedure will constitute records within the meaning of section 6001 of the Internal Revenue Code.

§ 2. Background

.01 Section 6001 provides that every person liable for any tax imposed by the Code, or for the collection thereof, must keep such records, render such statements, make such returns, and comply with such rules and regulations as the Secretary may from time to time prescribe. Whenever necessary, the Secretary may require any person, by notice served upon that person or by regulations, to make such returns, render such statements, or keep such records, as the Secretary deems sufficient to show whether or not that person is liable for tax.

.02 Section 1.6001-1(a) of the Income Tax Regulations provides that, except for farmers and wage-earners, any person subject to income tax, or any person required to file a return of information with respect to income, must keep such books and records, including inventories, as are sufficient to establish the amount of gross income, deductions, credits, or other matters required to be shown by that person in any return of such tax or information.

.03 Section 1.6001-1(e) provides that the books or records required by section 6001 must be kept available at all times for inspection by authorized internal revenue officers or employees, and must be retained so long as the contents thereof may become material in the administration of any internal revenue law.

§ 3. Scope

01 This revenue procedure applies to taxpayers who maintain books and records using an "electronic storage system." An electronic storage system is a system to prepare, record, transfer, index, store, preserve, retrieve, and reproduce books and records by either: (1) electronically imaging hard copy documents to an electronic storage media; or (2) transferring computerized books and records to an electronic storage media using a technique such as "COLD" (computer output to laser disk), which allows books and records to be viewed or reproduced without the use of the original program.

.02 The requirements of this revenue procedure pertain to all matters under the jurisdiction of the Commissioner of Internal Revenue including, but not limited to, income, excise, employment, and estate and gift taxes, as well as employee plans and exempt organizations.

.03 A taxpayer's use of a third party (such as a service bureau or time-sharing service) to provide the taxpayer with an electronic storage system for its books and records does not relieve the taxpayer of the responsibilities described in this revenue procedure.

.04 Except as otherwise provided in this revenue procedure, all requirements of section 6001 that apply to hardcopy books and records apply as well to books and records that are stored electronically pursuant to this revenue procedure.

§ 4. Electronic Storage System Requirements

01 General Requirements

(1) An electronic storage system must ensure an accurate and complete transfer of the hardcopy or computerized books and records to an electronic storage media. The electronic storage system must also index, store, preserve, retrieve, and reproduce the electronically stored books and records.

(2) An electronic storage system must include:

(a) reasonable controls to ensure the integrity, accuracy, and reliability of the electronic storage system;

(b) reasonable controls to prevent and detect the unauthorized creation of, addition to, alteration of, deletion of, or deterioration of electronically stored books and records;

(c) an inspection and quality assurance program evidenced by regular evaluations of the electronic storage system including periodic checks of electronically stored books and records;

(d) a retrieval system that includes an indexing system (within the meaning of section 4.02 of this revenue procedure); and

(e) the ability to reproduce legible and readable hardcopies (within the meaning of section 4.01(3) of this revenue procedure) of electronically stored books and records.

(3) All books and records reproduced by the electronic storage system must exhibit a high degree of legibility and readability when displayed on a video display terminal and when reproduced in hardcopy. The term "legibility" means the observer must be able to identify all letters and numerals positively and quickly to the exclusion of all other letters or numerals. The term "readability" means that the observer must be able to recognize a group of letters or numerals as words or complete numbers. The taxpayer must ensure that the reproduction process maintains the legibility and readability of the electronically stored document.

(4) The information maintained in an electronic storage system must provide support for the taxpayer's books and records (including books and records in an automated data processing system). For example, the information maintained in an electronic storage system and the taxpayer's books and records must be cross-referenced in a manner that provides an audit trail between the general ledger and the source document(s).

(5) For each electronic storage system used, the taxpayer must maintain, and make available to the Service upon request, complete descriptions of:

(a) the electronic storage system, including all procedures relating to its use; and

(b) the indexing system (see section 4.02 of this revenue procedure).

(6) At the time of an examination, or for the tests described in section 5of this revenue procedure, the taxpayer must:

(a) retrieve and reproduce (including hardcopies if requested) electronically stored books and records; and

(b) provide the Service with the resources (e.g., appropriate hardware and software, personnel, documentation, etc.) necessary to locate, retrieve, read, and reproduce (including hardcopies) any electronically stored books and records.

(7) An electronic storage system must not be subject, in whole or in part, to any agreement (such as a contract or license) that would limit or restrict the Service's access to and use of the electronic storage system on the taxpayer's premises (or any other place where the electronic storage system is maintained), including personnel, hardware, software, files, indexes, and software documentation.

(8) The taxpayer must retain electronically stored books and records so long as their contents may become material in the administration of the Internal Revenue laws under section 1.6001- 1(e).

(9) The taxpayer may use more than one electronic storage system. In that event, each electronic storage system must meet the requirements of this revenue procedure. Electronically stored books and records that are contained in an electronic storage system with respect to which the taxpayer ceases to maintain the hardware and the software necessary to satisfy the conditions of this revenue procedure will be deemed destroyed by the taxpayer, unless the electronically stored books and records remain available to the Service in conformity with this revenue procedure.

(10) Taxpayers may use reasonable data compression or formatting technologies as part of their electronic storage system so long as the requirements of this revenue procedure are satisfied.

.02 Requirements of an Indexing System

(1) For purposes of this revenue procedure, an "indexing system" is a system that permits the identification and retrieval for viewing or reproducing of relevant books and records maintained in an electronic storage system. For example, an indexing system might consist of assigning each electronically stored document a unique identification number and maintaining a separate database that contains descriptions of all electronically stored books and records along with their identification numbers. In addition, any system used to maintain, organize, or coordinate multiple electronic storage systems is treated as an indexing system under this revenue procedure. The requirement to maintain an indexing system will be satisfied if the indexing system is functionally comparable to a reasonable hardcopy filing system. The requirement to maintain an indexing system does not require that a separate electronically stored books and records description database be maintained if comparable results can be achieved without a separate description database.

(2) Reasonable controls must be undertaken to protect the indexing system against the unauthorized creation of, addition to, alteration of, deletion of, or deterioration of any entries.

.03 Recommended Practices

The implementation of records management practices is a business decision that is solely within the discretion of the taxpayer. Records management practices may include the labeling of electronically stored books and records, providing a secure storage environment, creating back-up copies, selecting an off-site storage location, retaining hardcopies of books or records that are illegible or that cannot be accurately or completely transferred to an electronic storage system, and testing to confirm records integrity.

§ 5. District Director Testing

.01 The District Director may periodically initiate tests of a taxpayer's electronic storage system. These tests may include an evaluation (by actual use) of a taxpayer's equipment and software, as well as the procedures used by a taxpayer to prepare, record, transfer, index, store, preserve, retrieve, and reproduce electronically stored documents. In some instances, the District Director may choose to review the internal controls, security procedures, and documentation associated with the taxpayer's electronic storage system.

.02 The tests described in section 5.01 of this revenue procedure are not an "examination," "investigation," or "inspection" of the books and records within the meaning of section 7605(b), or a prior audit for purposes of section 530 of the Revenue Act of 1978, 1978-3 (Vol.1) C.B. 119, as amended by section 1122 of the Small Business Job Protection Act of 1996, because these tests are not directly related to the determination of the tax liability of a taxpayer for a particular taxable period.

.03 The District Director must inform the taxpayer of the results of any tests under this section.

§ 6. Compliance

.01 A taxpayer's electronic storage system that meets the requirements of this revenue procedure will be treated as being in compliance with the recordkeeping requirements of section 6001 and the regulations thereunder.

.02 A taxpayer's electronic storage system that fails to meet the requirements of this revenue procedure may be treated as not being in compliance with the recordkeeping requirements of section 6001 and the regulations thereunder. See section 9 of this revenue procedure for applicable penalties. However, even though a taxpayer's electronic storage system fails to meet the requirements of this revenue procedure, the penalties described in section 9 of this revenue procedure may not apply if the taxpayer maintains its original books and records, or maintains its books and records in micrographic form in conformity with Rev. Proc. 81-46,1981-2 C.B. 621.

§ 7. Destruction and Deletion of Original Books and Records

This revenue procedure permits the destruction of the original hardcopy books and records and the deletion of the original computerized records(other than "machine-sensible" records required to be retained by Rev.Proc. 91-59, 1991-2 C.B. 841), after the taxpayer:

(1) has completed its own testing of the electronic storage system that establishes that hardcopy or computerized books and records are being reproduced in compliance with all the provisions of this revenue procedure; and

(2) has instituted procedures that ensure its continued compliance with all the provisions of this revenue procedure.

§ 8. Impact on Machine-Sensible Records

The provisions of this revenue procedure regarding electronically stored books and records do not relieve taxpayers of the responsibility of retaining any other books and records required to be retained under section6001. Such other books and records may include "machine-sensible" records required to be retained by Rev. Proc. 91-59 in connection with the taxpayer's use of an automatic data processing (ADP) system.

§ 9. Penalties

The District Director may issue a Notice of Inadequate Records pursuant to section 1.6001-1(d) if the taxpayer's books and records are available only as electronically stored books and records and the taxpayer's electronic storage system fails to meet the requirements of this revenue procedure. Taxpayers whose electronic storage system fails to meet the requirements of this revenue procedure may also be subject to applicable penalties under subtitle F of the Code, including the section 6662(a) accuracy-related civil penalty and the section 7203 willful failure criminal penalty.

§ 10. Internal Revenue Service Office Contact

The principal author of this notice is Celia Gabrysh of the Office of the Assistant Chief Counsel (Income Tax and Accounting). For further information regarding this notice, contact Ms. Gabrysh on (202) 622-4940(not a toll-free call).

.01 Questions regarding this revenue procedure should be directed to the Office of the Assistant Commissioner (Examination). The telephone number for this office is (202)622-5480 (not a toll- free number). Written questions should be addressed to:

Assistant Commissioner (Examination)
Attention: CP:EX
Internal Revenue Service
1111 Constitution Ave., N.W.
Washington, D.C. 20224

.02 Questions regarding the application of this revenue procedure to a specific factual situation should be directed to the appropriate District Director.

Source: Revenue Rulings

Rev. Rul. 71-20

✍ Advice has been requested whether punched cards, magnetic tapes, disks, and other machine-sensible data media used in the automatic data processing of accounting transactions constitute records within the meaning of section 6001 of the Internal Revenue Code of 1954 and section 1.6001-1 of the Income Tax Regulations.

In the typical situation the taxpayer maintains records within his automatic data processing (ADP) system. Daily transactions are recorded on punched cards and processed by the taxpayer's computer which prints daily listings and accumulates the individual transaction records for a month's business on magnetic tapes. At the month's end the tapes are used to print out monthly journals, registers, and subsidiary ledgers and to prepare account summary totals entered on punched cards. The summary data from these cards is posted to the general ledger and a monthly printout is generated to reflect opening balances, summary total postings, and closing balances. At the year's end several closing ledger runs are made to record adjusting entries. In other situations taxpayers use punched cards, disks, or other machine-sensible data media to store accounting information.

Section 6001 of the Code provides that every person liable for any tax imposed by the Code, or for the collection thereof, shall keep such records as the Secretary of the Treasury or his delegate may from time to time prescribe.

Section 1.6001-1(a) of the Income Tax Regulations provides that any person subject to income tax shall keep such permanent books of account of records, including inventories, as are sufficient to establish the amount of gross income, deductions, credits, or other matters required to be shown by such person in any return of such tax.

Section 1.6001-1(e) of the regulations provides that the books and records required by this section shall be retained so long as the contents thereof may become material in the administration of any internal revenue law.

It is held that punched cards, magnetic tapes, disks, and other machine- sensible data media used for recording, consolidating, and summarizing accounting transactions and records within a taxpayer's automatic data processing system are records within the meaning of section 6001 of the Code and section 1.6001-1 of the regulations and are required to be retained so long as the contents may become material in the administration of any internal revenue law.

However, where punched cards are used merely as a means of input to the system and the information is duplicated on magnetic tapes, disks, or other machine-sensible records, such punched cards need not be retained.

It is recognized that ADP accounting systems will vary from taxpayer to taxpayer and, usually, will be designed to fit the specific needs of the taxpayer. Accordingly, taxpayers who are in doubt as to which records are to be retained or who desire further information should contact their District Director for assistance.

Rev. Rul. 80-272

Law and Analysis

* * * * *

✍ Section 4997 of the Code provides that each taxpayer liable for tax under section 4986, each partnership, trust, or estate producing domestic crude oil, each purchaser of domestic crude oil, and each operator of a well from which domestic crude oil was produced, shall keep such records, make such returns and furnish such information with respect to such oil as the Secretary may by regulations prescribe.

Under section 150.4997-1(b) of the Temporary Excise Tax Regulations under the Crude Oil Windfall Profit Tax Act of 1980, * * * The records shall be kept at all times available for inspection by authorized internal revenue officers or employees and shall be retained so long as the contents thereof may become material in the administration of any internal revenue law.

Holding

Punched cards, magnetic tapes, disks, and other machine-sensible data media used for recording, consolidating, and summarizing accounting transactions and records within a taxpayer's automatic data processing system are records within the meaning of section 4997 of the Code and section 150.4997-1(b) of the regulations and are required to be retained so long as the contents may become material in the administration of any internal revenue law. However, where punched cards are used merely as a means of input to the system and the information is duplicated on magnetic tapes, disks, or other machine-sensible records, such punched cards need not be retained.

It is recognized that ADP accounting systems will vary from taxpayer to taxpayer and, usually, will be designed to fit the specific needs of the taxpayer. Accordingly, taxpayers who are in doubt as to which records are to be retained or who desire further information should contact their district director for assistance.

* * * * *

Agency: Municipal Securities Rulemaking Board
Source: MSRB Manual — General Rules

Rule G-9. Preservation of Records

* * * * *

(e) *Method of Record Retention.* Whenever a record is required to be preserved by this rule, such record may be retained either as an original or as a copy or other reproduction thereof, or on microfilm, electronic or magnetic tape, or by the other similar medium of record retention, provided that such municipal securities broker or municipal securities dealer shall have available adequate facilities for ready retrieval and inspection of any such record and for production of easily readable facsimile copies thereof and, in the case of records retained on microfilm, electronic or magnetic tape, or other similar medium of record retention, duplicates of such records shall be stored separately from each other for the periods of time required by this rule.

Agency: Securities and Exchange Commission
Source: No Action Letter Dated June 18, 1993

[The June 18, 1993 No Action Letter has been rendered ineffective by the 1997 revisions to 17 CFR 240.17a-4.]

Source: Bulletins
Agency: National Archives and Records Administration

NARA BULLETIN NO. 92-4

TO: Heads of Federal agencies
SUBJECT: Use of 3480 class tape cartridges to store permanent computer data

1. **Purpose.** This bulletin announces a change in NARA policy to authorize the use of 3480 class tape cartridges for the storage of permanent electronic records and for their transfer to the National Archives. NARA regulations (36 CFR 1228.188(a)) are being updated to reflect this revised policy.

2. **Expiration date.** This bulletin will remain in effect until May 31, 1994.

3. **Background.** Currently, NARA accepts electronic records for accessioning into the National Archives of the United States only on one-half inch, seven or nine track reel-to-reel magnetic tape. Agencies can continue to use reel-to-reel magnetic tape for storage and transfer. However, a growing number of Federal agencies are storing electronic records on 3480 class tape cartridges. After carefully evaluating this situation, NARA has concluded that 3480 class tape cartridges are a reliable storage medium for permanent electronic records.

4. **Agency action.**

a. Agencies are authorized to transfer permanent electronic records to the National Archives on 3480 class tape cartridges that meet the American National Standard based on the IBM format. The magnetic tape and cartridge for information interchange must be 18-track, parallel, 12.65 mm (1/2 inch), and 1491 cpmm (37,871 cpi).

b. All maintenance requirements of 36 CFR 1234.28(g) apply to 3480 class tape cartridges.

5. **NARA action.** NARA will copy the contents of 3480 class tape cartridges at the time of accessioning and return them to the agency unless the agency indicates that it does not want the cartridges returned.

6. **Questions.** Questions concerning this policy may be directed

to the Center for Electronic Records (NNX), National Archives, Washington, DC 20408, 202-501-5565 (local or FTS 2000).

DON W. WILSON
Archivist of the United States

NARA BULLETIN NO. 93-3

December 4, 1992
To: Heads of Federal Agencies
Subject: Use of optical disk systems to store permanent Federal records

1. **Purpose**. This bulletin restates NARA policy regarding the use of optical disk technology for the storage of permanent records that are designated for preservation as part of the National Archives of the United States. The same policy applies to unscheduled records that may be appraised as permanent.

2. **Expiration date**. This bulletin will remain in effect until November 30, 1993.

3. **Background**.

a. A growing number of Federal agencies have begun using optical disk systems to store Federal records. Several agencies have inquired about current NARA policy on the use of optical disks in records management. They want to know whether NARA regulations permit the use of optical disk for storing records and whether NARA will accession permanent records stored on optical disks.

b. This bulletin is restatement of the policy announced in NARA bulletin 91-2, which expired on September 30, 1992. The guidance provided in that bulletin has been updated to add 3480 class magnetic tape cartridges as a medium for transferring to the National Archives permanent records stored on optical disks.

4. **Interpretation**.

a. Because of the hardware and software dependence of current optical disk systems and the absence of standards that ensure the portability of data from one system to another, NARA cannot accession permanent records stored on optical disks at this time. Until the development of data portability standards, permanent records stored on optical disks must be transferred to the National Archives on paper, microforms, magnetic tape, or 3480 class tape cartridges. Microforms must conform to the requirements of 36 CFR Part 1230. Magnetic tapes and 3480 class tape cartridges must conform to the requirements of 36 CFR 1228.188.

b. Reminding agencies of the requirements for transferring permanent records to the National Archives is not intended to discourage the use of optical disk technology. NARA recognizes the potential benefits of this technology for storing and retrieving large quantities of information. Agencies also may be able to use digital image enhancement for poor quality originals.

c. Agencies may use optical disk systems for the storage and retrieval of permanent records while the records remain in an agency's legal custody. However, no permanent records may be destroyed after copying onto an optical disk without NARA's approval. Normally, after permanent records have been copied onto an optical disk, they should be transferred to a Federal records center or to the Office of the National Archives. In some cases, NARA may authorize agencies to destroy permanent records after copying onto an optical disk provided that the agency agrees to convert the disk images to a medium acceptable to NARA at the time of transfer to NARA's legal custody.

d. Permanent records stored originally on optical disk must be converted to a medium acceptable to NARA at the time of transfer to NARA's legal custody.

e. Records appraised by NARA as temporary may be stored on any medium, including optical disks, that ensures maintenance of the information until its authorized disposal. This means that conversion of such temporary records to optical disks, and disposal of the original paper or other media, do not require NARA's approval.

f. Analog videodiscs that typically contain photographs are one type of optical disk that can be accessioned into the National Archives, provided that they do not require any interactive software or nonstandardized equipment. Original photographs appraised as permanent and copied onto a videodisc must be scheduled for transfer to the National Archives along with a copy of the videodisc. Likewise, compact disks used for digital audio playback also can be accessioned into the National Archives because they use a standard player and require no special software.

5. **Agency action**. Agencies seeking authorization to destroy permanent records after copying onto optical disks must submit a Standard Form 115, Request for Records Disposition Authority, to NARA's Office of Records Administration (NIR), Washington, DC 20408. The agency must certify on the SF 115 that it will convert the optical disk images to paper, microform, magnetic tape, or 3480 class tape cartridge that meets the standards specified in Subchapter B of 36 CFR Chapter XII before transfer to NARA's legal custody.

6. **NARA action**. Industry standards for data portability among optical disk systems are now under development that, when implemented, may enable the National Archives to accession permanent records stored on optical disks. NARA will continue to monitor developments in optical disk technology that may permit a modification of current policy regarding the accessioning of optical disks. Agencies are encouraged to inform NARA of significant uses of optical disk technology.

7. **Questions**. Questions concerning this policy may be directed to the Office of Records Administration, Agency Services Division (NIA), Washington, DC 2048, 202-501-6000.

DON W. WILSON
Archivist of the United States

NARA BULLETIN NO. 94-4

July 20, 1994
TO: Heads of Federal Agencies
Subject: Use of Compact Disk-Read Only Memory (CD-ROM) Medium to Transfer Records to the National Archives

1. *Purpose*. This bulletin announces that the National Archives and Records Administration authorizes the limited use of the CD-ROM medium for the transfer of permanent electronic records to the National Archives. NARA regulation 36 CFR 1228.188 "Transfer of Machine Readable Records to the National Archives" will be revised to reflect this procedure.

2. *Expiration Date*. This bulletin will remain in effect until July 31, 1996.

3. *Background*.

a. Currently, NARA accepts electronic records for transfer and accessioning into the National Archives of the United States only on one-half inch, seven or nine track reel-to-reel magnetic tape and 3480 class tape cartridges, as defined in 36 CFR 1228.88.

b. A growing number of Federal agencies are publishing materials on the CD-ROM medium. The CD-ROM medium is acceptable for the transfer of electronic records to the National Archives under the condition that are specified in paragraph 4 of this bulletin.

c. CD-ROM medium may store a variety of files to serve a range of functions. This bulletin addresses only CD-ROM's which include files that have been scheduled for transfer to the preservation in the National Archives in accordance with NARA-approved records disposition schedule. These CD-ROM's also may contain other files which do not have to conform to the criteria listed below.

4. *Agency action.*

a. Agencies are authorized to transfer CD-ROM's which include fielded data files or text files scheduled to be preserved in the National Archives that are:

(1) in conformance to the International Standards Organization (ISO) 9660 standard;

(2) in compliance with the American Standard Code for Information Interchange (ASCII) standard as defined in the Federal Information Processing Standard 1-2 (11/14/84);

(3) not dependent on control characters or codes which are not defined in the ASCII character set;

(4) not compressed unless the software to decompress the files is provided;

(5) individually addressable; and

(6) in compliance with the documentation requirements of 36 CFR 1228.188.

b. In some cases, permanently valuable electronic records which an agency disseminates on CD-ROM exist on other media, such as magnetic tape. In such cases, the agency and NARA will mutually agree on the most appropriate medium for transfer of the records to the National Archives.

c. Agencies should transfer the CD-ROM's with the necessary documentation for those files that are to be accessioned into the Center for Electronic Records.

5. *NARA action.*

a. For those files on the CD-ROM which meet the criteria in paragraph 4a, NARA will assume responsibility for their preservation.

b. Upon request and subject to legal restrictions, NARA will provide access to any electronic records preserved in the National Archives and will replicate them on any medium offered by NARA for copies of accessioned electronic records. Legal restrictions include copyright, licensing, or special distribution agreements.

c. NARA will provide copies of any copyrighted software contained on a CD-ROM only when there is an applicable license provided to do so or the software has been placed in the public domain.

d. NARA will continue to evaluate criteria for accessioning permanent records on CD-ROM to determine how the criteria may be expanded or otherwise revised. NARA may make exceptions to this limited accessioning policy on a case-by-case basis before revising the policy in a future NARA bulletin.

6 *Questions.* Questions concerning this bulletin may be directed to the National Archives and Records Administration, Center for Electronic Records (NSX), 8601 Adelphi Road, College Park, MD 20740-6001, (301) 713-6630.

TRUDY HUSKAMP PETERSON
Acting Archivist of the United States

NARA BULLETIN NO. 94-5

July 20, 1994
TO: Heads of Federal Agencies
SUBJECT: Use of optical disk systems to store Federal records

1. *Purpose.* This bulletin states NARA policy regarding the use of optical disk technology for the storage of permanent records that are designed for preservation as part of the National Archives of the United States. The same policy applies to unscheduled records.

2. *Expiration date.* This bulletin will remain in effect until July 31, 1996.

3. *Background.*

a. A growing number of Federal agencies are using optical disk systems for the management and dissemination of Federal information. Additional guidance has been requested from NARA concerning the relationship of NARA regulations on the management of Federal records to uses of optical disk technology.

b. This bulletin clarifies NARA policies on optical disks and records management and references additional NARA guidance and policies.

4. *Interpretation.*

a. At this time, NARA will accept permanent records for transfer to the National Archives on the following types of optical media:

(1) Optical disks which meet the requirements of NARA Bulletin 94-4, Use of Compact Disk-Read Only Memory (CD-ROM) medium to transfer records to the National Archives;

(2) Analog videodisks that typically contain photographs, provided that they do not require any interactive software or nonstandardized equipment. Original photographs appraised as permanent and copied onto a videodisc must be scheduled for transfer to the National Archives along with a copy of the videodisc; and

(3) Audio compact disks.

b. NARA is continuing to study the technical concerns with long-term storage of permanent records on optical media, including migration of data to next generation equipment. NARA may make exceptions to this limited accessioning policy on a case-by-case basis before revising the policy in the future.

c. NARA encourages Federal agencies in using optical disk technology to enhance their information management operations. NARA recognizes the potential benefits of this technology for storing and retrieving large quantities of information. NARA encourages agencies to inform NARA of significant current or anticipated uses of optical media.

d. Agencies may use optical disk systems for the storage and retrieval of permanent records while the records remain in an agency's legal custody. However, agencies must obtain NARA approval before destroying original permanent or unscheduled records that have been copied onto an optical disk. (This includes permanent records approved for transfer to the National Archives on CD-ROM under the provisions of NARA Bulletin 94-4.) Approval for destruction will be dependent upon the following:

(1) The usefulness of the form transferred to NARA in comparison to the original; and

(2) The nature of the media used to transfer the records to NARA. The transfer of permanent records stored on optical disks to the legal custody of the National Archives of the United States must be on a medium acceptable to NARA at the time of the transfer.

After permanent records have been copied onto an optical disk, if the records are no longer needed for current business in the agency, the records should be transferred to a Federal records center or, in the case of records on an electronic media, to the National Archives.

e. Records appraised by NARA as temporary may be stored on any medium, including optical disks, that ensures that maintenance of the information until expiration of its authorized retention period. This means that conversion of such temporary records to optical disks, and disposal of the original paper or records to optical disks, and disposal of the original paper or other media, do not require NARA's approval.

5. *Agency action.*

a. Agencies seeking authorization to destroy permanent records after copying onto optical disks must submit a Standard Form 115, Request for Records Disposition Authority, to NARA's Office of Records Administration (NIR), 8601 Adelphi Road, College Park, MD 20740-6001. The agency must certify on the SF 115 that either the optical disks meet the requirements of NARA Bulletin 94-4 or that the agency will convert the optical disk images to a medium that meets the standards specified in Subchapter B of 36 CFR Chapter XII before transfer to NARA's legal custody.

b. Agencies proposing the transfer of permanent records in CD-ROM format to the National Archives under the criteria specified in NARA Bulletin 94-4 must submit a Standard Form 115, Request for Records Disposition Authority, to NARA's Office of Records Administration (NIR), 8601 Adelphi Road, College Park, MD 20740-6001. This requirement does not apply to records which are already scheduled in electronic format for transfer to the National Archives of the United States.

c. Agencies must obtain NARA approval for disposition scheduling for videodisks and audio compact disks by submitting a Standard Form 115 for any Federal records contained on those media. The SF 115 should be submitted to NARA's Office of Records Administration (NIR), 8601 Adelphi Road, College Park, MD 20740-6001.

6. *Questions.* Questions concerning this policy, including exceptions to the limited accessioning policy, may be directed to the National Archives of Records Administration, Office of Records Administration, 8601 Adelphi Road, College Park, MD 20740-6001, 301-713-7100.

TRUDY HUSKAMP PETERSON
Acting Archivist of the United States

Agency: Nuclear Regulatory Commission

Source: Generic Letter 88-18 dated October 20, 1988

TO: ALL LICENSEES OF OPERATING REACTORS AND HOLDERS OF CONSTRUCTION PERMITS
SUBJECT: PLANT RECORD STORAGE ON OPTICAL DISKS (GENERIC LETTER 88-18)

The NRC has been requested by two utilities and an NSSS to approve the use of optical disk document imaging systems for the storage and retrieval of record copies of quality assurance records. *The purpose of this generic letter is to inform addressees that the staff approves the use of this method of recordkeeping when appropriate quality assurance controls are applied.*

Appendix B of 10 CFR 50, under criterion XVII, "Quality Assurance Records," establishes requirements for a recordkeeping system, and chapter 17 of the Standard Review Plan (NUREG-0800) expounds on these requirements. The purpose of the recordkeeping system is to ensure that records are available when needed. ANSI N45.2.9-1974, "Requirements for Collection, Storage, and Maintenance of Quality Assurance Records for Nuclear Power Plants," as endorsed by Regulatory Guide 1.88 (Rev. 2) and Basic Requirements 17, Supplement 17S-1, and Appendix 17A-1 of ANSI/ASME-NQA-1 1983 edition, "Quality Assurance Program Requirements for Nuclear Facilities," as endorsed by Regulatory Guide 1.28 (Rev. 3) both describe quality assurance controls regarding records. Appropriate quality controls for an optical disk document imaging system include the following:

The optical disk technology does not allow deletion or modification of record images.

The image of each record is written onto two optical disks.

The legibility of each record image is verified to ensure that the image is legible on both disks. If the image is illegible, the hard copy record is maintained as the record copy.

One optical disk is stored in the document imaging system for on-line retrieval.

The second (backup) optical disk is stored in a records storage facility meeting the requirements of ANSI N45.2.9-1974 for single copy storage or in a separate remote location.

To ensure permanent retention of records, the records stored on an optical disk are acceptably copied onto a new optical disk before the manufacturer's certified useful life of the original disk is exceeded. This includes verification of the records so copied.

Periodic random inspections of images stored on optical disks are performed to verify that there has been no degradation of image quality.

If the optical disk imaging system in use is to be replaced by an incompatible new system, the records stored on the old system's disk are acceptably converted into the new system before the old system is taken out of service. This includes verification of the records so copied.

**Source: Armstrong v. Executive Office of the President
1 F.3d 1271 (D.C.Cir. 1993)**

Before MIKVA, Chief Judge; WALD and HENDERSON, Circuit Judges.

Opinion for the Court filed Per Curiam.

PER CURIAM: This consolidated appeal presents us with important questions of federal agencies' statutory obligations to manage electronic questions of federal agencies' statutory obligations to manage electronic records as well as issues related to the appropriate use of the civil contempt power to coerce conformity with district court orders.

In the flagship portion of the appeal, defendants-appellants — the Executive Office of the President ("EOP"), the Office of Administration, the National Security Council ("NSC"), the White House Communications Agency, and Trudy Peterson, Acting Archivist of the United States — challenge the district court's conclusion that EOP and NSC guidelines for managing electronic documents do not comport with Federal Records Act ("FRA" or the "Act") requirements. More specifically, these government agencies and officials contend that, contrary to the court's ruling, they have, in the past, reasonably discharged their FRA obligations by instructing employees to print out a paper version of any electronic communications that falls within the statutory definition of a "record" by managing the receipt.

The defendants also appeal the district court's order holding them in civil contempt of its prior order enjoining the Archivist to "take all necessary steps" to preserve federal records and requiring the defendant agencies not to remove, alter, or delete any information until the Archivist takes action to prevent the destruction of federal records. More specifically, they contest that (1) the defendant agencies failed to issue adequate recordkeeping instructions to employees in the four months after their former guidelines were held invalid and (2) the transfer of nearly 6,000 backup tapes to the Archivist "adversely affected" those tapes. Because the district court orders on which the contempt citation rests did not specify that the defendants had an affirmative duty to create new guidelines by a date certain, the district court abused its discretion in holding the defendants in contempt at least in part because of their failure to issue such guidelines within four months. We remand to allow the district court to determine whether, in light of the tapes, its second ground, the failure to preserve these tapes, by itself, justifies a contempt citation.

Finally, we are presented with a cross-appeal. The plaintiffs-cross-appellants — Scott Armstrong, the National Security Archive, and several other researchers and nonprofit organizations — take issue with the district court's conclusion that federal courts have no authority to review NSC and Office of Science and Technology Policy ("OSTP") guidelines differentiating federal records subject to the FRA from presidential records subject to the President Records Act ("PRA"), 44 U.S.C. s 2201 et. seq. Contrary to the district court, we conclude that the PRA allows limited review to assure that guidelines defining presidential records do not improperly sweep in nonpresidential records. Accordingly, we remand to the district court to determine whether the relevant NSC and OSTP directives categorize nonpresidential records as subject to the PRA.

I. BACKGROUND

A. Statutory Framework

Federal agencies' records creation, management, and disposal duties are set out in a collection of statutes known collectively as the Federal Records Act. See 44 U.S.C. ss 2101 et seq., 2901 et seq., 3101 et seq., 3301 et seq. The FRA, Congress informs, is intended to assure, among other things, "[a]ccurate and complete documentation of the policies and transactions of the Federal Government," "[c]ontrol of the quantity and quality of records produced by the Federal Government," and "[j]udicious preservation and disposal of records." 44 U.S.C. s 2902(1), (2), (5); see also Armstrong v. Bush, 924 F.2d 282, 292 (D.C.Cir.1991) ("Armstrong I") (the FRA is intended to guarantee that agencies' records management programs "strike a balance `between developing efficient and effective records management, and the substantive need for Federal records'") (quoting S. REP. NO. 1326, 94th Cong., 2d Sess. 2 (1976)). To achieve those ends, the FRA burdens the heads of federal agencies with several obligations. Most basically, each agency head must "make and preserve records containing adequate and proper documentation of the organization, functions, policies, decisions, procedures and essential transactions of the agency and designed to furnish the information necessary to protect the legal and financial rights of the Government and of persons directly affected by the agency's activities." 44 U.S.C. s 3101. Moreover, under the Act, agency chiefs must also "establish and maintain an active, continuing program for . . . economical and efficient [records] management," id. s 3102, and "establish safeguards against the removal or loss of records [the agency head] determines to be necessary and required by regulations of the Archivist." Id. s 3105; see also Armstrong I, 924 F2d at 293 (noting that these provisions, as well as others furnished "law to apply" under the Administrative Procedure Act ("APA"), see 5 U.S.C. s 701(a)(2), and thus permitted judicial review of agency recordkeeping guidelines' conformity with the FRA).

Besides assigning specific duties to agency heads, the FRA prescribes the exclusive mechanism for disposal of federal records. See 44 U.S.C. s 3314 (no records may be "alienated or destroyed" except in accordance with the FRA's provisions). For these purposes, "records" are defined as

> all books, papers, maps, photographs, machine readable [i.e., electronic] materials, or other documentary materials, regardless of physical form or characteristics, made or received by an agency of the United States Government under Federal law or in connection with the transaction or public business and preserved or appropriate for preservation by that agency . . . as evidence of the organization, functions, policies, decisions, procedures, operations, or other activities of the Government or because of the informational value of data in them. Library and museum material made or acquired and preserved solely for reference or exhibition purposes, extra copies of documents preserved only for convenience of reference, and stocks of publications and of processed documents are not included.

Id. s 3301. If a document qualifies as a record, the FRA prohibits an agency from discarding it by fiat. See American Friends Service Committee v. Webster, 720 F.2d 29 62 (D.C.Cir.1983) ("Congress did not intend to grant [the agency] . . . a blank check for records disposal."). Instead, the FRA requires the agency to procure the approval of the Archivist before disposing of any record. Cf. id. at 63. Normally, that approval may be obtained in one of two ways. First, an agency may submit a schedule of records sought to be discarded to the Archivist, who will sign off on the records' destruction only if she concludes that they do no "have sufficient administrative, legal, research, or other value to warrant their continued preservation." 44 U.S.C. s 3303a(a). Second, the agency may jettison certain common types of records pursuant to disposal schedules promulgated in advance by the Archivist (the disposal schedules are, of course, designed to take into account the FRA's goal of preserving documents of "administrative, legal, research, or other value"). Id. s 3303a(d).

Under the FRA, the Archivist's duties are not limited to judging the suitability of record for disposal. In addition, the Archivist must provide guidance and assistance to Federal agencies with respect to ensuring adequate and proper documentation of the policies and transactions of the Federal Government and ensuring proper records disposition," id. s 2904(a), "promulgate standards, procedures, and guidelines with respect to records management," id. s 2904(c)(1), and "conduct inspections or surveys of the records and the records management programs and practices within and between Federal agencies." Id. s 2904(c)(7). The Archivist also plays a key role in the FRA's enforcement scheme. If the discovers that an FRA provision has been or is being breached, the Archivist must (1) inform the agency head of the violation and suggest corrections and (2) if ameliorative measures are not undertaken with reasonable time, submit a written report to Congress and the President. Id. s 2115(b). Also, should the Archivist become aware of any "actual, impending, or threatened unlawful removal, defacing, alteration, or destruction of records in the custody of [an] agency," she must notify the agency head of the problem and assist the agency head in initiating an action through the Attorney General for the recovery of wrongfully removed records or for other legal redress. Id. s 2905(a); see also id. s 3106 (requiring agency heads to notify the Archivist of any unlawful destruction or removal of records and placing upon them an independent duty to seek legal action through the Attorney General to recover the records). If the agency head is recalcitrant in pursuing legal remedies, the Archivist herself is to (1) request the Attorney General to initiate action and (2) inform Congress that she has made that request. Id. s 2905(a); see also Armstrong I, 924 F.2d at 295 (holding that "if the agency head or Archivist does nothing while an agency official destroys or removes records in contravention of agency guidelines and directives, private litigants may bring suit to require the agency head and Archivist to fulfill their statutory duty to notify Congress and ask the Attorney General to initiate legal action").

B. The NSC and EOP Electronic Communications Systems

Since the mid-1980s, the NSC and the EOP have utilized electronic communications systems to improve their operational efficiency. These systems allow employees to create and share electronic appointment calendars as well as to transfer and edit word processing documents, but it is their electronic mail (or "e-mail") capacity that has racked up the most mileage. The 1,300 federal employees with access to the EOP and NSC electronic mail systems can, and apparently do, utilize them to relay lengthy substantive — even classified — "notes" that, in content, are often indistinguishable from letters or memoranda. But, in contrast to its paper cousin, e-mail can be delivered nearly instantaneously at any time of the day or week. And, in contrast to telephone conversations, e-mail automatically creates a complete record of the exact information users send and receive.

Other attributes of the EOP and NSC electronic mail systems are also relevant here. First, these systems give recipients the option of storing notes in their personal electronic "log." After receiving a message, a user may instruct the computer to delete the note; otherwise, it will be stored in her log for later used. Second, both the recipient and the author of a note can print out a "hard copy" of the electronic message containing essentially all the information displayed on the computer screen. That paper rendering will not, however, necessarily include all the information held in the computer memory as part of the electronic document. Directories, distribution lists, acknowledgments of receipts and similar materials do not appear on the computer screen — and thus are not reproduced when users print out the information that appears on the screen. Without this "non-screen" information, a later reader may not be able to glean from the hard copy such basic facts as who sent or received a particular message or when it was received. For example, if a note is sent to individuals on a distribution list already in the computer, the hard copy may well include only a generic reference to the distribution list (e.g., "List A", not the names of the individuals on the list who received the document. Consequently, if only the hard copy is preserved in such situations, essential transmittal information relevant to a fuller understanding of the context and import of an electronic communication will simply vanish. A final relevant fact here is that the individual note logs are not the only electronic repositories for information on the e-mail system. The defendant agencies periodically create backup tapes — snapshots of all the material stored on these electronic communications systems at a given time — that can be used later for retrieval purposes.

C. Procedural History

On January 19, 1989, the final day of the Reagan Presidency, the National Security Archive filed several freedom of Information Act ("FOIA"), 5 U.S.C. s 552, requests for all the material stored on the EOP and NSC electronic communications systems from their installation in the mid-1980s up to that time. Simultaneously, the plaintiffs filed this suit for a declaration that the electronic documents contained on the NSC and EOP electronic communication systems and backup tapes were federal and presidential records and an injunction prohibiting those documents' destruction. After agreeing to preserve the electronic tapes, the defendants filed a motion in the district court for dismissal or, in the alternative, for summary judgment. After that motion was denied, see Armstrong v. Bush, 721 F.Supp. 343 (D.D.C.1989), this court, on the interlocutory appeal, settled several threshold issues in the litigation. Specifically, we held that the plaintiffs had standing to assert these claims because they were within the zone of interests of the records management provisions of the PRA and the FRA, see Armstrong I, 924 F.2d at 287-88, but that the President was not an agency under the APA and that the PRA impliedly precluded judicial review of the President's record creation, management, and disposal decisions under that statute. See id. at 288-91. We said, however, that the plaintiffs could seek judicial review of (1) agency guidelines' conformity to the FRA and (2) the agency heads' and Archivist's discharge or removal of federal records. See id. at 291-96. We then remanded the case to allow for supplementation of the records as to the precise guidance — written and oral — that the defendant agencies had given employees. See id. at 296-97.

On remand, the parties developed an extensive record, including a Joint Statement of Facts (the "Joint Statement"), and, on January 6, 1993, the district court issued its ruling on all the FRA issues raised by the plaintiffs (the plaintiffs; FOIA claims remain undecided). See Armstrong v. Executive Office of the President, 810 F.Supp. 335 (D.D.C.1993). In that ruling, the district court first addressed whether the communications stored in these electronic communications systems constituted federal records. Because the FRA's definition of "records" includes material "regardless of physical form or characteristics," the court concluded that substantive communications otherwise meeting the definition of federal "records" that had been saved on the electronic mail came within the FRS's purview. See id. at 340-41.

The court then found that the defendant's current practices for electronic records management were deficient in two key respects. First, assuming arguendo that the defendant agencies unequivocally informed their staffs to print out all on-screen information of any electronic note that qualified as a federal record (an assumption that the plaintiffs have vigorously contested throughout this litigation), that instruction was not adequate to met the FRA's requirements because the "electronic material . . . [is] qualitatively different than a copy printed out in paper form." Id. at 341. The district court emphasized that unless employees also printed out the transmittal information stored in the computer but not appearing on screen, the hard copies preserved in the paper files would not necessarily contain all the important items retained in the electronic system. See id. ("A paper copy of the electronic material does not contain all of the information included in the electronic version."); see also Appellants' Brief at 22 ("[The defendant agencies] do not require that all information related to an electronic message be preserved, but only that information that is captured when the message screen is printed or incorporated into a written memorandum."). Specifically, data "regarding who has received the information and when the information was received" might well be omitted form the paper versions. 810 F.Supp. at 341; see also id. at 346-47 (discussing NSC guidance).

The court found a second flaw in the agencies' records management practices: they failed to provide for any supervision of agency employees' electronic recordkeeping practices. Noting that (1) the

National Archives Records Management Handbook provided that only "records officers" should determine the status of FRA records and (2) the defendant agencies supervise staffers' management of paper, but not electronic records, the court concluded that the defendants' failure to supervise employees' electronic recordkeeping was arbitrary and capricious. See id. at 343; see also id. at 347 (discussing NSC guidance).

Finally, the district court refused to adjudicate plaintiffs' claim that the NSC guidelines did not adequately distinguish between federal and presidential records. The court found that our holding in Armstrong I precluded judicial review of any guideline affecting the status of a presidential record. See id. at 347-48.

To implement its decision, the district court issued a multipart declaratory and injunctive order. The order, as amended, first declared that the defendant agencies' current guidelines were arbitrary and capricious and contrary to law. See Amended Order, Armstrong v. Executive Office of the President, No. 89-142 (D.D.C. Jan. 11, 1993). Second, it enjoined the Archivist to "seek the assistance of the Attorney General with notice to Congress, and take all necessary steps to preserve, without erasure, all electronic Federal Records generated at the defendant Agencies." Id. Finally, it enjoined all the defendants "from removing, deleting, or altering information on their electronic communications systems until such time as the Archivist takes action . . . to prevent the destruction of federal records, including those records saved on backup tapes." Id. In response to an emergency motion by the defendants, this court stayed this last requirement to the extent of allowing the agencies to "remove, delete, or alter" information so long as it was preserved elsewhere in identical form. See Armstrong v. Executive Office of the President, No. 93-5002 (D.D.Cir. Jan. 15, 1993).

On May 21, 1993, on petition of the plaintiffs, the district court found the defendants in civil contempt. See Armstrong v. Executive Office of the President, No. 89-142 (D.D.C. May 21, 1993). First, it found that interim guidance issued by the defendants in the wake of the court's invalidation of their old guidelines was inadequate. Accordingly, the court reasoned, the defendants were in contempt for not substantially complying with its orders requiring the agencies to preserve all records. See id., slip opinion ("slip op.") at 5-13. Second, the court held that the conditions surrounding the January 19, 1993, inauguration-eve transfer of backup tapes from the White House to the National Archives, as well as the Archivist's subsequent failure to recopy Reagan-era backup tapes nearing the end of their natural lifespan, violated the court's order requiring preservation of the tapes. This treatment of the backup tapes, including the failure to recopy deteriorating tapes, thus furnished an additional basis for the contempt citation. See id. at 17-21. The court then set out a list of specific acts that the defendants were required to undertake by June 21, 1993 to purge themselves of contempt; if the defendants failed to accomplish them, fines of $50,000 a day would be doubled in subsequent weeks, would be imposed until the defendants cleansed themselves of their contempt. See Order, Armstrong v. Executive Office of the President, No. 89-142 (D.D.C. May 21, 1993).

Following oral argument on June 15, 1993, this court stayed the district court's contempt sanctions pending the outcome of this appeal. See Armstrong v. Executive Office of the President, No. 93-5002, et al. (D.C.Cir. June 15, 1993).

THE VALIDITY OF CURRENT NSC AND EOP GUIDELINES

A. The Instruction to Print "Hard-Copy" Paper Versions

We first address appellants' contention that the district court erred in finding that their pre-January-order instruction to print on-screen information from electronic federal records was inconsistent with the FRA. This question implicates two parts of this case. First, if the agencies' policy of printing on-screen information did not result in "papering" all federal records material, then at least some federal records will be permanently lost or destroyed unless the electronic backup records, currently being retained pursuant to the district court's orders, are preserved. This circumstance alone creates the predicate for an order requiring the Archivist and the relevant agency heads to take the statutorily prescribed steps to prevent the destruction of those tapes. Second, if this "print screen" policy — which was still in effect at the time the district court ruled in January — is inadequate under the FRA, then the district court appropriately issued a declaratory judgment invalidating its future use.

In proceeding to the decision on this point, we adopt the district courts' assumption, based on the appellants' submissions, that both the EOP and the NSC have consistently instructed employees, either orally or in writing, that when any electronic document meets the definition of a federal record, the employee should either print out the information that appears on her computer screen or incorporate that material into a written memorandum. See Appellants' Brief at 7-8; see also id. at 22 ("[The agencies] do not require that all information related to an electronic message be preserved, but only that information that is captured when the message screen is printed or incorporated into a written memorandum.").

Accepting appellants' factual predicate, however, does not leas us to their legal conclusion that such an approach satisfied the Act. Our analysis is a straightforward one. We begin with the apparently undisputed proposition that the EOP and NSC electronic communications systems can create, and have created, documents that constitute federal records under the FRA. The FRA contemplates that documents qualifying as records may be stripped of that status only if they are "extra copies of documents preserved only for convenience of reference." 44 U.S.C. s 3301. Applied to this case, that means that the mere existence of the paper print-outs does not affect the record status of the electronic materials unless the paper versions include all significant material contained in the electronic records. Otherwise, the two documents cannot accurately be termed "copies" — identical twins — but are, at most, "kissing cousins." Since the record shows that the two versions of the documents may frequently be only cousins — perhaps distant ones at that — the electronic documents retain their status as federal records after the creation of the paper print-outs, and all of the FRA obligations concerning the management and preservation of records still apply. See, e.g., id. s 3105 (requiring agency heads to "establish safeguards against the removal or loss" of "records"); id. s 3314 (stating that "records" may only be "alienated or destroyed" in accordance with FRA provisions, i.e., with the approval of the Archivist).

To qualify as a record under the FRA, a document must satisfy a two-pronged test. It must be (1) "made or received by an agency of the United States Government under Federal law or in connection with the transaction of public business" and (2) "preserved or appropriate for preservation by that agency . . . as evidence of the organization, functions, policies, decisions, procedures, operations, or other activities of the Government or because of the informational value of data in [it]." Id. s 3301. The appellants do not contest the fact that many, if not all, of the communications relayed over the electronic system satisfy the "public transaction" element of this test. At oral argument, the government appeared to acknowledge that the "preserved or appropriate for preservation" criterion was satisfied as well for some documents on the system.

To the extent that any question remains, we reject the appellants' argument, on brief, that agency head have sweeping discretion to decide which documents are "appropriate for preservation" (since we reject this contention, we do not consider whether the disputed documents have also been "preserved"). The appellants have stipulated that the electronic communications systems "contain information on the organization, functions, policies, decisions, procedures, operations, and other activities" of the agencies. Joint Statement P. 64. Such documents could only fail to qualify as records if, despite their content, the agency has the inherent discretion to consider them en masse as not "appropriate for preservation . . . as evident of [the government's] organizations, functions, policies, decisions, procedures, operations or other activities." 44 U.S.C. s 3301 (emphasis added), an odd proposition to assert in this case since the agency heads admit they have never surveyed the contents of the electronic systems. See Joint Statement P 67 ("neither the EOP nor the NSC ha[s] conducted any formal examination, inspection, or survey to determine the types of communications recorded on the system, or the amount of information on the organization, functions, policies, decisions, procedures or other activities of the EOP or NSC recorded in [electronic] files."); cf. American Friends, 720 F.2d at 65. In any case, while the agency undoubtedly does have some discretion to decide if a particular document satisfied the statutory definition of a record, see Armstrong I, 924 F.2d at 297, n.14, the statute surely cannot be read to allow the agency by fiat to declare "inappropriate for preservation" an entire set of substantive e-mail documents generated by two administrations over a seven-year period. Cf. American Friends, 720 F.2d at 41 ("Congress was certainly aware that agencies, left to themselves, have a built-in incentive to dispose of records relating to [their] `mistakes'. . . . "). Indeed, to conclude that agencies have broad discretion to exempt seven years of substantive documents from record status would flout our prior holding in Armstrong I that the FRA furnishes sufficient "law to apply" to permit judicial review of agency guidelines relating to the management of federal records. See Armstrong I, 924 F.2d at 293 (noting that the FRA contains a "detailed definition of the `records' that agencies must preserve") (emphasis added); see also id. ("although the FRA understandably leaves the details of records management to the discretion of individual agency heads, it does contain several specific requirements . . . . ").

Having established that the electronic communications systems contain preservable records, we turn finally to the question of whether the government has the discretion to convert only part of the electronic records to paper and then manage only the partial paper records in accordance with the FRA and the Archivist's regulations. The question answers itself. Only one FRA provision exists that would even arguable sanction a document, once denominated a federal record, shedding that appellation at a later point. That provision states that "extra copies of documents preserved only for convenience of reference" are not "records." 44 U.S.C. s 3301. But it is too tight a fit for the government to shoehorn the electronic records at issue here into that exception. Even assuming, without of course deciding, that one set of parallel documents retained in a different records system in a different medium than another set may be classified as a "cop[y]" under the FRA and thus subject to unobstructed destruction, the electronic records would still not qualify as "full reproduction[s] or transcription[s]; imitation[s] of a prototype; . . . duplicate[s]," WEBSTER'S NEW UNIVERSAL UNABRIDGED DICTIONARY 404 (2d ed.1979), of the paper print-outs. This is because important information present in the e-mail system, such as who sent a document, who received it, and when that person received it, will not always appear on the computer screen and so will not be preserved on the paper print-out. See Joint Statement P 46 ("When printed on paper, a[n] [e-mail] not will not always identify the sender(s) and recipient(s) of a note by name. Instead, the sender(s) or recipient(s) may be identified only by (a) userid [i.e., user identification]; (b) nickname; or (c) the title given to a distribution list identifying several individuals. Identifying the names of the sender(s) or recipient(s) for such notes requires reference to the distribution lists or directories maintained only in electronic form." (emphasis added; record citations omitted); see also id. at P 47 ("If requested, [the electronic communications system] will provide the sender of a note with a confirmation that it has been received, called an `acknowledgment.' The acknowledgment records the date and time the addressee of the note opened his or her electronic mail. This information on the date and time the note is received does not appear on the paper copy of the notes when it is printed-out.") (record citations omitted). Since employees had never been — at least until the time of the district court's January order — instructed to include these integral parts of the electronic record in any paper print-out, there is no way we can conclude that the original electronic records are mere "extra copies" of the paper print-outs. Cf. National Archives and Records Administration, Managing Electronic Records 19 (1990) ("Most agencies have decided to meet their recordkeeping requirements for documents that are created by using word processing or electronic mail or messaging by printing those documents in hard copy. The success of this approach depends upon a clear understanding by all employees of the obligation to print and file all record material." (emphasis added).

Our refusal to agree with the government that electronic records are merely "extra copies" of the paper versions amounts to far more than judicial nitpicking. Without the missing information, the paper print-outs — akin to traditional memoranda with the "to" and "from" cut off and even the "received" stamp pruned away — are dismembered documents indeed. Texts alone may be of quite limited utility to researchers and investigators studying the formulation and dissemination of significant policy initiatives at the highest reaches of our government. See 810 F.Supp. at 341 (noting that the omitted information may be "of tremendous historical value in demonstrating what agency personnel were involved in making a particular policy decision and what officials knew, and when they knew it"). The "[t]omorrow, and tomorrow, and tomorrow" of government will be allowed to "creep in [their] petty pace from day to day" without benefit of the "last syllable of recorded time." WILLIAM SHAKESPEARE, MACBETH, Act V, scene v, line 19. In our view, as well as the district judge's, the practice of retaining only the amputated paper print-outs is flatly inconsistent with Congress' evident concern with preserving a complete record of government activity for historical and other uses. See 44 U.S.C. s 2902(1) (listing first among Act's goals the "[a]ccurate and complete documentation of the policies and transactions of the Federal Government"); see also Armstrong I, 924 F.2d at 288 (noting the "expressed statutory goal of preserving records for historical purposes"); American Friends, 720 F.2d at 57 (describing the FRA's legislative history as demonstrating that "Congress intended, expected, and positively desired private researchers . . . to have access to the documentary history of the federal government"); cf. 36 C.F.R. s 1222.38 ("Agency recordkeeping requirements shall prescribe the creation and maintenance of records of the transaction of agency business that are sufficient to: . . . (e) Document the formulation and execution of basic policies and decisions and the taking of necessary actions, including all significant decisions and commitments reached orally (person to person, by telecommunications, or in conference)."). Perhaps that is why, in this court, the appellants seem to have abandoned their former heavy reliance on this theory.

Before us they plead an alternative, related, but no more compelling theory of statutory compliance: "that the extra information that plaintiffs argue must be preserved in fact not always 'appropriate for preservation' as evidence of an agency's essential transactions, and that printing the actual message text on the computer screen is normally sufficient for adequate documentation of the agency's business. Since the printed copy is identical to what is on the computer screen, the electronic version of the message that remains is a copy that is nonrecord within the meaning of the statute." Reply Brief for Appellants at 9. In other words, the appellants content that given the broad discretion vested in the agencies by the FRA, they may reasonably determine that some parts of a record document — the so-called "extra information" — are not "appropriate for preservation"; thus, after the creation of the paper records, the electronic version is a "copy" because the paper record contains all the material worth preserving from the electronic files.

This appeal to discretion, however, relies in the main on snippets of language from different parts of the FRA pasted together in ways incompatible with the overall design of the Act. As noted above, the "appropriate for preservation" phrase in the definition of "records" at most allows the agency some discretion in deciding whether a document meets that definition in the first place. See 44 U.S.C. s 3301 (providing that federal "records" must be, inter alia, "preserved or appropriate for preservation by that agency . . . as evidence of the organization, functions, policies, decisions, procedures, operations, or other activities of the Government or because of the informational value of data in them"). It does not, as appellants imply, grant agencies the discretion to automatically lop off a predesignated part of a whole series of documents that qualify as records (nor would it allow the wholesale destruction of the directories and similar materials if they were perceived to be independent records, see supra note 8). In substance the appellants are claiming that it satisfies the Act to preserve a second version of a record that it satisfies the Act to preserve a second version of a record that is an approximation of the first version if it includes all the material that, in their view, is "appropriate for preservation." Even if this argument made sense with respect to a particular document, it cannot be accepted across the board for seven years of records documenting high-level government decisionmaking. Further, as our discussion above makes clear, it cannot be squared with the FRA's "extra copies" provision. The Act explicitly provides an "out" of the system for a federal record only when a second version is identical to — i.e., an "extra copy" of — the first. There is no provision accepting abbreviated or summary versions of the original as the only record if the summary contains all material deemed "appropriate for preservation."

Equally unconvincing is the appellants' suggestion that Congress' directive to preserve "adequate documentation" of agencies' "essential transactions" justifies their practice of retaining only the "substantive information" displayed on the computer screen. The phrases "adequate documentation" and "essential transactions" are lifted from 44 U.S.C. s 3101, which states: "The head of each Federal agency shall make a preserve records containing adequate and proper documentation of the organization, functions, policies, decisions, procedures and essential transactions of the agency and designed to furnish the information necessary to protect the legal and financial rights of the Government and of persons directly affected by the agency's activities." The purpose of this provision, by its own terms, is to place a general obligation on agency leaders to create and then retain a baseline inventory of "essential" records. See American Friends, 720 F.2d at 54; see also id. at 56 (summarizing legislative history of this provision and concluding that it provided an enforceable "across-the-board requirement" that agencies retain certain types of records); S. REP. NO. 2140, 81st Cong., 2d Sess. 15 (1950) (this provision "provides a general declaration by the Congress [to maintain adequate records]". Other parts of the FRA, however, go on to prescribe more particularized duties for agency head that reach beyond their general obligation to "adequately document" core agency functions. In particular, the Act includes (1) a separate definition of the term "records" that the appellants acknowledge sweeps in many of the electronic communications at issue here — whether or not preservation of those documents is necessary to maintain "adequate documentation" of "essential transactions" — and (2) other statutory provisions that mandate that all records — again, whether or not related to "adequate documentation" of "essential transactions" — be managed and retained in accordance with explicit statutory directives. See 44 U.S.C. s 3314 ("[R]ecords . . . may not be alienated or destroyed except under this chapter.") (emphasis added); see also id. s 3105 (agency heads must "establish safeguards against the removal or loss of records") (emphasis added). In sum, appellants' arguments fail to detour us from the analytical path we started down and now come close to finishing: (1) substantive e-mail communications satisfy the FRA definition of "records"; (2) the lone FRA provision for terminating their status as such requires that they be merely "extra copies" of other documents preserved elsewhere; and (3) since there are often fundamental and meaningful differences in content between paper and electronic versions of these documents, the electronic versions do not lose their status as records and must be managed and preserved in accordance with the FRA.

Contrary to appellants' assertions, the conclusion that agencies must retain and manage these electronic documents in no way collides with Congress' oft-expressed intent to balance complete documentation with efficient, streamlined recordkeeping. See, e.g., S. REP. NO. 2140, 81st Cong. 2d Sess. 4 (1950) ("It is well to emphasize that records come into existence, or should do so, not in order to . . . satisfy the archival needs of this and future generations, but first of all to serve the administrative and executive purposes of the organization that creates them."). Our decision does not require that agencies, in appellants' words, save "every scrap of paper" they create. Not all scribbles and off-the-cuff comments will qualify as federal records. Nor do we saddle agencies with any new obligations to make additional documents in order to satisfy the needs of researchers or investigators. Cf. Armstrong I, 924 F.2d at 288 ("[P]laintiffs do not seek the creation of any new records, but rather ask only that the records already created be appropriately classified and disposed of. . . ."); S. REP. NO. 1326, 94th Cong., 2d Sess. 8 (1976) (emphasizing the need for economy in records creation because that is where 80% of total recordkeeping costs are incurred). Finally, or decision leaves undisturbed the agencies' ability to purge identical electronic records from their files by acting, with the Archivist's approval, to dispose of those documents that lack "sufficient administrative, legal, research, or other value to warrant their continued preservation." 44 U.S.C. s 3303(a); see also Fed.Reg. 19,216 (1990) (Archivist notes that the burden of managing electronic records "can be reduced significantly by promptly scheduling all electronic records, thus limiting the application of [regulatory] requirements to the very small percentage of records that are scheduled as permanent").

In sum, we find that the district court was fully justified in concluding that appellants' recordkeeping guidance was not in conformity with the Act.

B. Supervision of Electronic Recordkeeping Practices

Appellants also dispute the district court's finding that their records management practices were arbitrary and capricious in failing to provide for supervision or auditing of employees' electronic recordkeeping practices by knowledgeable records management personnel. Specifically, appellants contend that they reasonably discharged their obligation to "safeguard" federal records by assigning records managers the task of providing oral and written guidance to agency personnel and making those recordkeeping experts available for resolution of specific problems.

The FRA explicitly requires each agency head to establish such safeguards against the removal or loss of federal records as she "determines to be necessary and required by regulations of the Archivist." 44 U.S.C. s 3105; see also 36 C.F.R. s 1220.2 ("Federal agency records management programs must be in compliance with regulations promulgated by [the Archivist]."). In this case, the agency heads clearly failed to discharge this obligation.

The Archivist's regulations provide:

The head of each Federal agency shall ensure that the management of electronic records incorporates the following elements: . . .

(1) Reviewing electronic records systems periodically for conformance to established agency procedures, standards, and policies . . . The review should determine if the records have been properly identified and described, and whether the schedule descriptions and retention periods reflect the current information content and use . . . .

Id. s 1234.10 (emphasis added). The Archivist has defined an "electronic records system" as "any information system that produces, manipulates, or stores Federal records by suing a computer." Id. s 1234.2 (emphasis added). As previously discussed, the electronic communication systems used by the EOP and the NSC do produce federal records, and it follows that agencies have an obligation under the Archivist's guidelines to undertake periodic reviews to assure that "established agency procedures, standards, and policies," including instructions as to what constitutes a record, are being adhered to. Moreover, the relevant regulations make clear that they apply to all electronic systems used by agency employees to create electronic records, not just, as appellants suggest, to "official" agency electronic records systems. See id. s 1234.1 ("Unless otherwise noted, [this section's] requirements apply to all electronic records systems, whether on microcomputers, minicomputers, or mainframe computers, regardless of storage media, in network or stand-alone configurations."); cf. id. s 1234.22 (listing specific requirements for electronic records systems "that maintain the official file copy of text documents on electronic media"). Moreover, to the extent there is any residual doubt on this question, we think that the agencies' own action in undertaking some review of employees' paper records before those employees exit government service and the common sense insight that an adequate program for ensuring records preservation must include some ongoing inspections and evaluations tip that balance against the government and lead to the conclusion that oversight is necessary as part of "an agencywide program for the management of all records created, received, maintained, used or stored on electronic media." Id. s 1234.10(a).

On that basis, we affirm the district court's holding that the defendant agencies must undertake some periodic review of their employees' electronic recordkeeping practices.

III. THE DISTRICT COURT'S CIVIL CONTEMPT ORDER

Next, the appellants appeal from the district court's May 21, 1993 civil contempt order. The district court found that the appellants "in contempt of this Court's Orders of January 6 and 11, 1993, and the Order of the United States Court of Appeals for the District of Columbia dated January 15, 1993" in two respects: (1) "for failing to promulgate new, appropriate, and proper recordkeeping regulations for electronic federal records to replace those regulations struck down by this Court on January 6, 1993" and (2) "because the transfer of 5,839 tapes from the Defendant agencies to the Archivist has adversely affected the condition of the tapes and the information stored therein" which was "contrary to this Court's Orders to preserve the tapes and federal records contained on them." Order, Armstrong v. Bush, No. 89-142 (D.D.C. May 21, 1992). The court further ordered that, unless the appellants should "purge themselves of this finding of contempt" by "tak[ing] appropriate action by 4:00 p.m. on June 21, 1993," they would be subject to a fine of $50,000 for each day of noncompliance during the first week, to be doubled to $100,000 per day the second week and $200,000 per day the third week, "with increases in such sanctions reserved thereafter for any further noncompliance with Court Orders." id. at 2-3. The appellants assert that the contempt finding must be reversed because, inter alia, the district court's first ground, the failure to promulgate new regulations, was not a violation of the cited orders and therefore cannot support civil contempt. "The standard of review on an appeal from a finding of contempt is whether the District Court abused its discretion." International Ass'n of Machinists and Aerospace Workers v. Eastern Airlines, Inc., 849 F.2d 1481, 1486 (D.D.Cir.1988). We agree with the appellants that the contempt finding, as articulated, was an abuse of discretion because it rests in part on an impermissible ground.

As a preliminary matter, we reject the appellee's jurisdictional argument that the May 21, 1993 order is not an appealable one because it "imposes only a conditional sanction for failure to comply with a preexisting order." See Appellees' Contempt Brief at 13. As both the Eleventh Circuit and the Second Circuit have concluded, "'Being placed under the threat of future sanction is a present sanction'" and an order so threatening "'imposes a present remedy and hence is appealable.'" United States v. O'Rourke, 943 F.2d 180, 186 (2d Cir.1991) (quoting Sizzler Family Steak House v. Western Sizzler Steak House, Inc., 793 F.2d 1529, 1533 n.2 (11th Cir.1986)) (emphasis in original). We agree and therefore proceed to the merits of the contempt appeal.

"There can be no question that courts have inherent power to enforce compliance with their lawful orders through civil contempt." Shillitani v. United States, 384 U.S. 364, 370 (1966). Nevertheless, "civil contempt will lie only if the putative contemnor has violated an order that is clear and unambiguous," Project B.A.S.I.C. v. Kemp, 947 F.2d 11, 16 (1st Cir.1991), and the violation must be proved by "clear and convincing evidence. Washington-Baltimore Newspaper Guild, Local 35 v. Washington Post Co., 626 F.2d 1029, 1031 (D.C.Cir.1980). The district court's first ground for its contempt findings, however, did not involve violation of any court order. The district court's January 11, 1993 order did not expressly direct the appellants to promulgate new regulations, but merely issued "a Declaratory Judgment that the guidelines issued by and at the direction of the Defendant Agencies are inadequate and not reasonable and are arbitrary and capricious and contrary to law in that they permit the destruction of records contrary to the Federal Records Act." Amended Order, Armstrong v. Bush, 89-142 (D.D.C. Jan. 11, 1993). As the Supreme Court has observed: "[E]ven through a declaratory judgment has 'the force and effect of a final judgment,' 28 U.S.C. s 2201, it is a much milder form of relief than an injunction. Though it may be persuasive, it is not ultimately coercive; noncompliance with it may be inappropriate, but is not contempt." Steffel v. Thompson, 415

U.S. 452, 471 (1974) (quoting Perez v. Ledesma, 401 U.S. 82, 125-26 (1971) (Brennan, J., concurring)). Thus, because the appellants were never directly ordered to promulgate new regulations, we must reverse the district court's contempt finding which was based in part on their failure to do so. Cf. Spallone v. United States, 492 U.S. 265, 276-77 (1990) (reversing contempt finding against individual city councilmembers for city's violation of consent decree where "the individual city councilmembers . . . were not parties to the action" and "although the injunctive portion of that decree was directed not only to the city but to 'its officers, agents, employees, successors and all persons in active concert with any of them,' . . . the remaining parts of the decree ordering affirmative steps were directly only to the city"); International Longshoresmen's Ass'n, Local 1291 v. Philadelphia Marine Trade Ass'n, 389 U.S. 64, 76 (1967) (reversing opinion upholding contempt finding for violating order that "did not state in 'specific . . . terms' that the acts that it required or prohibited") (quoting FED. R. CIV. P. 65(d)). Accordingly, we vacate the contempt order and remand to the district court the consider whether its second ground, the failure to preserve the tapes, by itself, justifies a finding of contempt, taking into account all efforts that have or will then have been made to assure the tapes' integrity.

* * * * *

CONCLUSION

To recap: We affirm the district court's decision that the EOP and NSC electronic records management guidelines violate the FRA, reverse the district court's civil contempt finding, and remand to allow the district court to determine whether the challenged NSC and OSTP guidelines inaccurately classify some documents are presidential records.

So ordered.

Appendix C United States — State Requirements

State: Alabama
Source: Code of Alabama

TITLE 5. BANKS AND FINANCIAL INSTITUTIONS

CHAPTER 4A. RETENTION OF BANK RECORDS

Citation: AC 5-4A-1

☞ **§ 5-4A-1. Generally.**

(a) Every bank shall retain its business records for such periods as may be prescribed by regulation adopted pursuant to Section 5-2A-9.

(b) Any bank may dispose of any records which have been retained for the period prescribed by the superintendent.

(c) Any bank may cause any or all books and records at any time in its custody and books and records relating to trusts, estates and other fiduciary accounts, to be reproduced by photostatic, photographic, or microphotographic process, or by any other generally recognized reproduction process, and reproduction so made, whether enlarged or not, shall have the same force and effect as the original thereof and be admitted in evidence equally with the original.

TITLE 12. COURTS.

CHAPTER 21. EVIDENCE AND WITNESSES.

Article 1. General Provisions.

Division 1. Evidence.

Subdivision 1. Generally.

Citation: AC 12-21-5

☞ **§ 12-21-5. Copy of hospital records — Admissibility.**

When the original would be admissible in any case or proceeding in a court in the state, a certified copy of the hospital records of any hospital organized or operated under or pursuant to the laws of Alabama, including records of admission, medical, hospital, occupational, disease, injury and disability histories, temperature and other charts, X rays and written interpretions thereof, pictures, photographs, files, written orders, directions, findings and reports and interpretations of physicians, doctors, surgeons, pathologists, radiologists, specialists, dentists, technicians and nurses, as well as of all employees of such hospital, forming a part of such hospital records as to the health, condition, state, injuries, sickness, disease, mental, physical and nervous disorders, duration and character of disabilities, diagnosis, prognosis, progress, wounds, cuts, contusions, lacerations, breaks, loss of blood, incisions, operations, injuries, examinations, tests, transfusions, hospitalization and duration thereof, medication, medicines, supplies, treatment and care and the cost, expenses, fees and charges therefor and thereof, a part of, or shown on or in, said hospital records of any patient in said hospital, when certified and affirmed by the custodian of said hospital records as provided in Section 12-21-7, shall be admissible in evidence, without further proof in any court in the state where admissible, if and when said hospital records were made and kept in the usual and regular course of business of said hospital and it was in the regular course of business of said hospital to make and keep said records and that said records were made at the time of such acts, transactions, occurrences or events therein referred to occurred or arose or were made, or within a reasonable time thereafter.

Citation: AC 12-21-6

☞ **§ 12-21-6. Copy of hospital records — subpoena duces tecum; inspection; form; weight.**

(a) A certified copy of said hospital records may be procured by any litigant in any court of competent jurisdiction in the state by subpoena duces tecum, and when any such subpoena duces tecum is issued for said hospital records, the custodian of said hospital records shall prepare a copy of said hospital records as provided in this subsection and securely seal the same in an envelope or other container and date and fill out and sign a certificate in substantially the form provided in Section 12-21-7 and place on, or securely fasten said certificate to the outside of, said envelope or container in which said copy of said hospital records are placed and deliver the same to the clerk or register of the court hearing, or to hear or to try, the case or proceeding in which the records are sought, and he shall not otherwise be required to appear in court unless thereafter ordered to do so by the court. The copy of the hospital records shall not be open to inspection or copy by other persons than the parties to the case or proceeding and their attorneys until ordered published by the court trying the case at the time of the trial. When so prepared and certified, the copy of said hospital records shall be admissible in evidence in any court in the state, if and when admissible, in *prima facie* proof of the facts therein shown just as if otherwise verified and just as if the copy were the original. The copy of the hospital records may be photostated, photographed or made by microphotographic plate or film, or otherwise made, so long as clear and easily legible. All the circumstances of the making of such hospital records, including lack of personal knowledge of the entrant or maker of such hospital records, may otherwise be shown to affect the weight of such hospital records, but this shall not affect their admissiblity.

Citation: AC 12-21-44

☞ **§ 12-21-44. Writings or records made in the regular course of business — Photostatic, photographic or microphotographic plate or film of originals, or prints thereof; rights thereto when original not available.**

(a) Any writing or record, whether in the form of an entry in a book or otherwise, made as a memorandum or record of any act, transaction, occurrence or event, if it was made in the regular course of any business and it was in the regular course of the business to make such memorandum or record at the time of such act, transaction, occurrence or event, or within a reasonable time thereafter, may be photostated, or it may be photographed or microphotographed on plate or film; and such photostat, photographic or microphotographic plate or film, or print thereof, whether enlarged or not, shall be deemed to be an original record and shall be admissible in evidence in proof of said act, transaction, occurrence or event in all instances that the original record might have been admissible and shall be presumed to be a true and correct reproduction of the original record it purports to represent. All other circumstances of the making of such writing or record, or of such photostat, photographic or microphotographic plate or film or print thereof, whether enlarged or not, including lack of personal knowledge by the entrant or maker, may be shown to affect its weight, but they shall not affect its admissibility.

(b) Whenever any writing or record, whether in the form of an entry in a book or otherwise, made as a memorandum or record of any act, transaction, occurrence or event has been photostated, photographed or microphotographed on plate or film, any party having the right to have the original record preserved or to an inspection of the original writing or record, or other rights in connection therewith, shall have the same rights as to the photostat, photographic or microphotographic plate or film, or prints made therefrom, in the event the original is not available. The custodian of such plate or film shall provide for the ready location of particular records so reproduced on plate or film and shall provide a projector or other convenient means for viewing the records so reproduced by those entitled thereto, and said custodian shall furnish a legible print or copy of such plate or film to such persons as are entitled to a copy of the original record. Nothing contained in this subsection shall be construed to allow the destruction or other disposition of original records which by statutory enactment now are, or hereafter may be, required to be preserved for inspection or for other purposes.

(c) For the purposes of this section, the term "business" shall mean and include any private business, industry, profession, occupation or calling of any kind. The term "record" or "records" as used in this section shall mean and include any writing or record as described in subsection (a) of this section, heretofore made or which may be made after May 21, 1951.

TITLE 16. EDUCATION.

CHAPTER 1. GENERAL PROVISIONS

Citation: AC 16-1-3

✪ **§ 16-1-3. Photographing or microphotographing records — Authorized; force and effect.**

The State Superintendent of Education and each of the several city and county superintendents of education may cause any records, documents, books, papers or writing made, acquired or received as required by law to be photographed or microphotographed, on plate or film. Such photographs, microfilms or prints made therefrom, when duly authenticated by the custodian thereof, shall have the same force and effect at law as the original record, or of a record made by any other legally authorized means, and may be offered in like manner and shall be received in evidence in any court where such original record, or record made by other legally authorized means, could have been so introduced and received.

Citation: AC 16-1-4

✪ **§ 16-1-4. Photographing or microphotographing records — Destruction of records photographed, etc.; retention of photographs.**

The State Superintendent of Education and each of the several city and county superintendents of education may destroy or cause to be disposed of any record, document, books, papers or other writing which have been photographed or microphotographed. Such photographs or microphotograph shall be retained and kept in lieu of such records, documents, books or papers required to be kept or maintained. However, no record or other written matter authorized under the provisions of section 16-1-3 to be photographed or microphotographed may be destroyed of otherwise disposed of until the copy has been processed and checked with the original for accuracy, and no city or county superintendent of education shall destroy or dispose of any record or other written matter without first obtaining the approval of the State Superintendent of Education.

The State Superintendent of Education may, however, classify such records and other written matter and authorize the destruction of certain classes of records or other written matter upon their being photographed or microphotographed, and may prescribe the period for which records of certain classes must be retained after having been photographed or microphotographed before such records are destroyed.

TITLE 25. INDUSTRIAL RELATIONS AND LABOR.

CHAPTER 4. UNEMPLOYMENT COMPENSATION.

Article 6. Administration

Citation: AC 25-4-116

✍ ☞ **§ 25-4-116. Employment Records.**

Every employing unit shall keep true and accurate work records containing such information as is necessary for the administration of this chapter. Such records shall be open to inspection and be subject to being copied by the director or his authorized representatives at any reasonable time and as often as may be necessary. The director, an appeals tribunal, any member of the board of appeals created by the industrial relations law or any authorized representative of the director may require from such employer or employing unit such reports covering persons employed by him or it, or employment, wages, hours, unemployment and related matters as are necessary to the effective administration of this chapter. Information thus obtained shall be held confidential, except to the extent necessary for the proper presentation of the contest of a claim, and shall not be published or be open to public inspection in any manner revealing the employers' or employing units' identity. Any person violating any provision of this section shall be fined not less than $20.00 nor more than $200.00 or imprisoned for not longer than 30 days or both. All letters, reports, communications and other matters, written or oral, from employer or employee to each other or to the director or any of his agents, representatives or employees, or to any official or board functioning under this chapter, which shall have been written, sent, delivered or made in connection with the requirements and administration of this chapter, shall be absolutely privileged and shall not be made the subject matter or basis for any civil action for slander or libel in any court. The director may cause to be made such summaries, compilations, photographs, duplications or reproductions of any records, reports or transcripts thereof or canceled benefit payment checks as he may deem advisable for the effective and economical preservation of the information contained therein, and such summaries, compilations, photographs, duplications or reproductions, duly authenticated, shall be admissible in any proceeding under this chapter if the original record or records would have been admissible therein. The director may provide by regulations for the destruction or disposition, after reasonable periods, of any records, reports, transcripts or reproductions thereof or other papers in his custody, the preservation of which is no longer necessary for the establishment of contribution liability or benefit rights or for any purpose necessary for the proper administration of this chapter, including any required audit thereof.

TITLE 41. STATE GOVERNMENT.

CHAPTER 6. DEPARTMENT OF ARCHIVES AND HISTORY.

Article 1. General Provisions.

Citation: AC 41-6-11

✪ **§ 41-6-11. Provision of certified copies of books, records, etc., surrendered to department.**

When books, records, documents, original papers and newspaper files have been surrendered in accordance with § 41-6-10, copies therefrom shall be made and certified by the director upon the application of any person interested, which certificate shall have all the force and effect as if made by the officer originally in the custody of them and for which the same fees shall be charged, to be collected in advance.

CHAPTER 13. PUBLIC RECORDS.

Article 1. General Provisions.

Citation: AC 41-13-1

✪ **§ 41-13-1. Definitions.**

As used in this article, the term "public records" shall include all written, typed or printed books, papers, letters, documents and maps made or received in pursuance of law by the public officers of the state, counties, municipalities and other subdivisions of government in the transactions of public business and shall also include any record authorized to be made by any law of this state belonging or pertaining to any court of record or any other public record authorized by law or any paper, pleading, exhibit or other writing filed with, in or by any such court, office or officer.

Citation: AC 41-13-4

✪ **§ 41-13-4. Assistance of public officials in preserving, filing, etc., of public records by department of archives and history.**

The department of archives and history may examine into the condition of public records and shall at the request of the custodian thereof give advice and assistance to any public official in the solution of his problems of preserving, filing and making available the public records in his custody.

Citation: AC 41-13-5

✪ **§ 41-13-5. Destruction.**

Any public records, books, papers, newspapers, files, printed books, manuscripts or other public records which have no significance, importance or value may, upon the advice and recommendation of the custodian thereof and upon the further advice, recommendation and consent of the state or local government records commission are hereby authorized and empowered to make such orders, rules, and regulations as may be necessary or proper to carry the provision of this section into effect.

Article 2. State and County Records Commissions.

Citation: AC 41-13-21

✪ **§ 41-13-21. Duties.**

The state records commission shall be charged with the responsibility of determining which state records shall be permanently preserved because of historical value, which state records may be destroyed or otherwise disposed of after they have been microfilmed and which state records may be destroyed or otherwise disposed of without microfilming. The commission may classify the different types of records accordingly.

No state officer or agency head shall cause any state record to be destroyed or otherwise disposed of without first obtaining approval of the state records commission; provided, however, that records of the courts within the unified judicial system may be disposed of in the manner and in accordance with such procedures as may be prescribed by rule of the supreme court, after consultation with the state records commission. Any such retention schedule prescribed by rule of the supreme court pertaining to records of the unified judicial system shall be deemed sufficient authorization for disposal and shall supersede any prior retention schedule with respect to such records, other provisions of the law to the contrary notwithstanding.

Citation: AC 41-13-23

✪ **§ 41-13-23. Local government commission to make determination as to county, municipal, etc., records to be preserved or destroyed, etc., after microfilming; classification of records; officials not to cause destruction, etc., of records without prior approval of commission.**

The local government records commission shall be charged with the responsibility of determining which county, municipal, and other local government records shall be permanently preserved because of historical value and which county, municipal, and other local government records may be destroyed or otherwise disposed of after they have been microfilmed. The commission may classify the different types of records accordingly.

No county, municipal, and other local government official shall cause any county, municipal, and other local government record to be destroyed or otherwise disposed of without first obtaining the approval of the local government records commission.

Article 3. Photographing or Microphotographing of Records.

Citation: AC 41-13-40

✪ ☞ **§ 41-13-40. Photographing or microphotographing of records, books, files, etc.; admissibility in evidence, etc., of photographs, microfilms, etc.**

The head of any office, court, commission, board, institution, department or agency of the state or of any political subdivision thereof may cause any record, document, plat, court file, book, map, paper, or writing made, acquired or received as required by law to be photographed or microphotographed on plate or film. Such photographs, microfilms or prints made therefrom, when duly authenticated by the custodian thereof, shall have the same force and effect at law as the original record or of a record made by any other legally authorized means and may be offered in like manner and shall be received in evidence in any court where such original record or record made by other legally authorized means could have been so introduced and received; provided, that the provisions of this article shall not apply to the state department of pensions and security, the state health department, the state board of health, the state department of industrial relations or to any other office, court, commission, board, institution, department or agency of the state which is otherwise authorized by law to provide for the photographing or microphotographing of its records.

Citation: AC 41-13-41

✪ **§ 41-13-41. Photographing or microphotographing of state records centralized in department of archives and history; charges for photographing or microphotographing.**

The photographing or microphotographing of public records, except the public records of counties, municipalities and other political subdivisions of the state of Alabama, shall be centralized in the department of archives and history. The department of archives and history is authorized to charge any office, court, commission, board, institution, department or agency of the state for the photographing or microphotographing of public records belonging to that office, court, commission, board, institution, department or agency. Such charge shall be on a cost basis.

Citation: AC 41-13-42

✪ **§ 41-13-42. Purchase or lease of photographic or microphotographic equipment and supplies by department of archives and history authorized; appropriation of funds therefore.**

The department of archives and history is hereby authorized to purchase or lease photographic or microphotographic equipment and supplies necessary to carry out the duties prescribed in this article.

There is hereby appropriated out of the general fund of the state an amount sufficient to cover the cost of purchase or lease of such equipment and supplies, such appropriation to be released only upon the approval of the governor.

Citation: AC 41-13-43

✪ **§ 41-13-43. Appropriation of funds by counties or municipalities for photographing or microphotographing of public records authorized.**

The county commission of any county or municipality may appropriate an amount sufficient to cover the cost of photographing or microphotographing the public records belonging to that county or municipality.

Citation: AC 41-13-44

✪ **§ 41-13-44. State and county officials, etc., not to destroy, etc., public records until microfilmed copies processed and checked for accuracy.**

No state or county official or employee shall destroy, dispose of or cause to be destroyed or disposed of any public record that has been microfilmed under the provisions of this article until the microfilm copy has been processed and checked with the original for accuracy.

Source: Alabama Rules of Evidence

ARTICLE X. CONTENTS OF WRITINGS

☞ **Rule 1001. Definitions.**

For purposes of this article the following definitions are applicable:

(1) *Writings.* — "Writings" consist of letters, words, or numbers, or their equivalent, set down by handwriting, typewriting, printing, photostating, photographing, or other form of data compilation.

(2) *Original.* — An "original" of a writing is the writing itself or any counterpart intended to have the same effect by a person executing or issuing it. If data are stored in a computer or similar device, any printout or other output readable by sight, shown to reflect the data accurately, is an "original"

(3) *Duplicate.* — A "duplicate" is a counterpart produced by the same impression as the original, or from the same matrix, or by means of photography, or by equivalent technique which accurately reproduces the original.

☞ **Rule 1003. Admissibility of Duplicates.**

A duplicate is admissible to the same extent as an original unless (1) a genuine question is raised as to the authenticity of the original or (2) in the circumstances it would be unfair to admit the duplicate in lieu of the original.

☞ Rule 1005. Public Records.

The contents of an official record, or of a document authorized to be recorded or filed and actually recorded or filed, including data compilations in any form, if otherwise admissible, may be proved by copy, certified as correct in accordance with Rule 902 or testified to be correct by a witness who has compared it with the original. If a copy which complies with the foregoing cannot be obtained by the exercise of reasonable diligence, then other evidence of the contents may be given.

Agency:	**Alabama Department of Archives and History**
Source:	**Technical Leaflet No. 1 dated October 1988**

STANDARD FOR MICROFILMING PERMANENT RECORDS

Citation:	**Technical Leaflet No. 1**

✪ INTRODUCTION

Micrographics is defined as the techniques associated with the production, handling, and use of microforms. When properly produced these microforms become valuable tools in any records program. They reduce storage cost, increase protection of the vital information, and are more durable than the original document.

This technical leaflet has been developed to address the technical standards required for the archival microfilming of permanent records. Microfilm containing permanent records must meet these standards before the destruction of the original records can be authorized by either the State or Local Government Records Commissions. This leaflet covers the primary areas of "archival" concern; selection of supplies and equipment; standards to ensure the long-term preservation of the microfilm; proper steps to ensure the integrity and authenticity of the records by the use of proper documentation targets; protection of the microfilm by proper storage procedures; and production of legible duplicates for reference use.

GETTING STARTED: SELECTION OF FILM AND EQUIPMENT

The first step in any micrographics project is the selection of the format for filing, film size, and equipment. The size of the microformat depends primarily on the size, tonal contrast, and fineness of detail of the materials to be filmed. It would be inappropriate to microfilm engineering drawings on 16mm roll film, for example, since the reduction required would be too great for satisfactory reproduction or good legibility. Oversize documents are generally produced on 35mm film. It is also desirable and necessary to match the quality of the original material both to the type of film and the reproduction equipment. Oversized handwritten journals should be filmed on a 35mm planetary camera at a reduction that matches the reduction capabilities of the reader printer to be used during reference.

The most important requirement of the State or Local Government Record Commission is the use of silver halide safety base film (as specified by the Association for Information and Image Management in AIIM TR6-1985 Guidelines for Microfilming Public Records on Silver Halide Film for any records with a retention requirement in excess of twenty-five years. Agencies using microfilm systems that do not produce an original microfilm that meets these standards for permanent records must immediately make a silver duplicate negative or silver master positive in order to satisfy the standards for records designated for long-term retention by the State and Local Government Records Commission.

The Alabama Department of Archives and History can provide assistance when selecting format, film size, and appropriate equipment. Contact the Records Service Center at 242-4306 for assistance.

ENSURING LONG-TERM PRESERVATION

For microfilm to be of "archival quality" it must meet the national standards established by the American National Standards Institute (ANSI). Copies of these standards can be purchased directly through ANSI or from the Association for Information and Image Management. A list of these standards and information on where to order them is provided in the Appendix. The most useful publication is ANSI/AIIM MS23-1981 Practice for Operational Procedures/Inspection and Quality Control of First-Generation Silver-Gelatin Microfilm of Documents The three major elements to be measured against established standards are resolution, density, and chemical residual level. Each of these elements should be measured at the appropriate intervals suggested below.

Resolution

Resolution is the ability of a film to reproduce fine details sharply. Resolution is usually measured by photographing five copies of Resolution Chart 1010A (issued by ANSI) in accordance with a prescribed procedure. This test should be performed on each roll of film.

These resolution charts measure the performance of the equipment and the method and quality of film processing. When these charts are examined through a loupe or microscope, the lines and spaces of each pattern must be clearly separate. The reduction ratio multiplied by the number of the smallest pattern clearly distinguished equals the resolution in terms of lines per millimeter. The standard resolution for a film produced on a planetary camera should be 100 lines per millimeter, and film produced on a rotary camera should have a resolution of 86 or more lines per millimeter. It should be noted that planetary and rotary testing targets differ. Proper resolution is a significant factor in the production of high quality film.

Density

Background density is the degree of opacity of the noninformation area of an image. Density is measured by an instrument called a densitometer.

To measure density, a photographic image of a document clear of all lines must be produced on each roll of film. This density target is then located on the film and placed on a densitometer. The densitometer transmits light through the film and measures the density. The minimum standard is .85 and the maximum standard is 1.30. As a general rule, density should be maintained midway between the minimum and maximum standard, depending on the type of material being filmed. The inspector should be alert for density readings that vary from frame to frame, a problem caused by exposure problems in the camera or processor. If this occurs the equipment should be inspected. Density readings should be taken on each roll of film. If the base fog density is measured, the readings for quality film should be .10 or less.

Chemical Residue

Sodium thiosulfate, referred to as hypo, is the principal

residual chemical from file processing which can impair image permanence.

The maximum concentration allowable is 1.4 milligrams per square centimeter of film.

The methylene blue test is employed to check for harmful residual chemicals which might impair the archival permanence of silver halide films. This procedures should be applied soon after processing and always within two weeks. If there is a delay beyond the two-week period, thiosulfate may break down into polythionates which are not detectable by this test. These second polythionates also contribute to the destruction of the silver images. ANSI PH.8-1985 Standard for Photography (Chemicals) Residual Thiosulfate and Other Chemicals in Films, Plates, and Papers, Determination and Measurement outlines the frequency requirements of these tests.

Documentation of these test results should be requested in writing when contracting with outside vendors.

ASSURING THE INTEGRITY AND AUTHENTICITY OF THE ORIGINAL RECORDS

Preparation and Image Placement

Preparation is an important and necessary step in microfilming. Once the documents are filmed the order of the materials cannot be changed. Irregular or unsymmetrical image placement is also an annoyance to the user and a detriment to the efficiency of the production of paper copies. Consideration of both areas should be given prior to filming.

Proper Documentation

Targets are signals photographed throughout a roll of film. Their purpose is to present users with certain information about the original materials and/or about the technical details of the microforms themselves. They are an essential part of technical and bibliographic control. All microfilm should include similar documentation. The following sequence is a suggested format.

ROLL NUMBER

This target identifies the roll.

START

This target should have the word START printed in large letters, clearly indicating the beginning of the film.

CREDIT

This target should have the name and address of the state or local agency producing or sponsoring the film.

TITLE PAGE
(Primary Bibliographic)

This target should identify the record series being filmed. A record series consists of records grouped together physically because they relate to a particular function, result from the same activity, or have a particular form. Examples include case files, vouchers, or employee personnel files.

RESOLUTION TARGET

This testing target is very important in measuring the quality of the film. It is usually made up of five test charts mounted on a large sheet of paper. Prepared targets are also available from several suppliers. A list of these suppliers in included in the Appendix.

DENSITY TARGET

This target should be a sheet of paper free of lines and the exact size and color of these documents. The density reading taken from this target must conform to ANSI standards.

CERTIFICATE OF AUTHENTICITY

This target should state that the records contained on the roll of film are exact copies of the original records and are complete. A signature of the appropriate authority should also be included. This documentation is necessary for legal verification.

FLASH

This target allows the viewer to scan the film and easily locate the specific file by alerting that the next target will contain the specific file title.

SECONDARY TITLE
(Secondary Bibliographic)

This target should identify the specific file, volume, or data span that is to be filmed. In the case of personnel files an example would be the "File of Jones, John."

DOCUMENTS

The actual documents are then filmed followed by a flash and a secondary bibliographic target for each new file or volume filmed within the roll.

To facilitate roll identification it is recommended that the title target be refilmed at the end of the roll of film. Each roll of film should have at least eighteen inches of blank film at each end for convenience in threading the microviewer.

Inspection

The final step in assuring the integrity of a film is to perform a document-by-document inspection. It is important to ensure that each document is legible prior to the destruction of the originals, otherwise valuable information will be lost.

Retakes

Any document missing or not legible should be refilmed and spliced onto the film, using a similar retake documentation sequence.

1 - Retake Notice
2 - Order for Retakes
3 - Documents to be Refilmed
4 - End of Retake

It is recommended that all retakes be spliced at the head of the roll following the start target. Only those materials designated for microfilm splicing should be used.

PRODUCTION OF USER COPIES

The first product of any microfilm system is the camera film or master film. The master film is the first generation. A copy from the original is a second generation. A copy produced from the duplicate copy is a third generation.

The first generation master film should be placed in a proper storage facility and used only for producing a user copy.

Duplicate copies can be either positive or negative at the discretion of the user.

STORING FILMS

Microfilm must be stored in an environmentally controlled area in which the relative humidity remains constant between 35 and 40 percent; the temperature is between 60 and 70 degrees Fahrenheit with a fluctuation of no more than 5 degrees; and the air is filtered to removed acidic gases. ANSI

PH1.43-1983 Photography (film) - Storage of Processed Safety Film covers in detail the standards for storage.

The storage containers should be properly identified by agency, record series, date filmed, and name of producer. Such information will help identify films if they develop severe problems that require the removal from the security vault. If a problem, such as mold growth, appears on a film, all films from that producer would need to be checked in order to prevent contamination.

The Department of Archives and History can help you with the storage of your permanent microfilms.

Microfilm rolls should not be overfilled or held tightly wound by rubber bands. Instead, small slips of acid free paper secured by string should be used. Suppliers are listed in the Appendix.

Microfilm can be the answer to many archival and records administrative needs. However, this tool can only be successful if produced in accordance to the standards described herein. We hope this technical leaflet has provided assistance to your organization. If more help is needed please contact the Alabama Department of Archives and History's Records Service Center at 715 Shady Street, Montgomery, Alabama 36130 or phone 242-4306.

Source: **Technical Leaflet No. 2 dated October 1988**

STANDARDS FOR MICROGRAPHICS LABORATORY CERTIFICATION

Citation: **Technical Leaflet No. 2**

✪ INTRODUCTION

The Alabama State and Local Government Records Commissions with the Alabama Department of Archives and History have established a certification program for microfilm laboratories filming Alabama public records. The laboratory certification program of the Records Management Division of the Alabama Department of Archives and History is designed to make clear what the State and Local Government Records Commissions believe to be acceptable minimum standards for producing long-term microfilm and to recognize the laboratories that meet these standards. Under Alabama law and the regulations of these Commissions, original copies of public records cannot be disposed of after microfilming unless the microfilm meets standards that ensure its durability. Application can be made to the Records Service Center, 715 Shady Street, Montgomery, Alabama 36130.

Certification must be renewed annually and is granted to either public funded or private microfilm labs without discrimination except for the quality of micrographic work as outlined in the standards described below.

CERTIFICATION REQUIREMENTS

Film Requirements

Silver halide safety base film must be used when filming records with a retention requirement in excess of twenty-five years.

Targets

Documentation Targets

Each roll of film must contain proper, preferably typed, documentation targets. These targets facilitate the use of the film and support its legal admissibility in a court of law. Agencies may determine the specific wording, sequence, or combination of documentation for their targets. The minimum documentation required on each individual roll of microfilm should include some form of the following targets.

START

This target, which indicates the beginning of the roll contains the words *START, HEAD*, or large, clearly printed letters.

CERTIFICATE OF AUTHENTICITY

This target states that the records contained on the roll of film are accurate and complete reproductions of the original records. If a set of records — case files, for example — is not filmed in its entirety, this target should also include the standards used to define what records were filmed and should identify those records removed from the files prior to microfilming. This document signed and dated by the camera operator provides legal verification of the information contained on the roll of film.

TITLE PAGE

This target identifies the records series being filmed. A record series consists of records grouped together physically because they relate to a particular function, result from the same activity, or have a particular form. Examples include case files, budgets, or employee personnel files (for additional information see the State Records Manual or the Local Records Guide).

CREDIT AND FILMING DATE

This target gives the name and address of the agency producing the film and the date of filming.

END

This target, which indicates the end of the roll, contains the words "END" or "TAIL" in large, clearly printed letters.

Quality Control Technical Targets

Testing targets to evaluate compliance with resolution and density standards are required on each roll of film that contains permanent public records or with a retention greater than twenty-five years.

RESOLUTION TARGET

This testing target is very important in measuring the quality of the film. The target is used to determine the ability of the film to reproduce fine details. It is usually made up of five test charts mounted on a large sheet of paper. It is not acceptable to use photocopied resolution charts. Resolution can only be measured using skillfully printed test charts that are available from various micrographic suppliers. The minimum standard resolution for a film produced on a planetary camera should be 100 or more lines per millimeter, and film produced on a rotary camera should have a resolution of 86 or more lines per millimeter.

DENSITY TARGET

This target should be a sheet of paper free of lines and the exact size and color of the documents. The target is used to determine the proper amount of contrast within an image, which is necessary to ensure clear sharp images. Density is measured by an instrument called a densitometer. The minimum standard is .85 and the maximum is 1.30. The ideal density is 1.10.

The Archives' technical leaflet, "Standards for Microfilming Permanent Records," outlines the recommended sequence and use of these required targets as well as other useful ones. Copies of these tares are also available from the Archives.

Quality Control Procedures

Methylene Blue Test

The final evaluation of a film's archival quality is the testing for residual chemicals after processing. High concentrations of these chemicals on silver halide films will impair the archival permanence of the film. The methylene blue test determines the amount of residual chemicals on the film. This test must be conducted within two weeks of processing a roll of film. A ten square centimeter of clear unexposed film is used as the test sample. The maximum concentration allowable is 1.4 milligrams per square centimeter of film.

Inspection Procedures

To verify the integrity of the film including the legibility of the reproduced documents, each roll of film must be inspected frame-by-frame. This procedure is especially important if the original records are scheduled for destruction.

Proper Retake Practices

The procedures outlined in the technical leaflet "Standards for Microfilming Permanent Records," including the use of targets, should be followed whenever correcting filming errors. Splicing methods should conform to AIIM MS18-9184 Standard for Micrographics — Splices for Imaged Film — Dimensions and Operational Constraints Heat-welded splices should be used on films containing permanent records.

PRESERVATION OF SILVER SECURITY FILMS

A laboratory must provide for the preservation of the silver security copy (the original camera negative, if possible) in a facility that meets the environmental standards. If a lab cannot meet these standards, it must arrange for the deposit of the original camera negative or a second generation silver copy in a preservation storage facility. The application for certification must be submitted with a written statement from the preservation storage facility outlining its archival storage standards and certifying its compliance with ANSI standards.

The Alabama Department of Archives and History contracts with a commercial preservation facility for the storage of its security films. Any Alabama government agency can transmit security films to the Department of Archives and History for deposit into this facility. This service is provided free of charge.

SELECTION OF PUBLIC RECORDS FOR MICROFILMING

State and local government agencies whose micrographic laboratories seek certification must comply with established guidelines concerning records disposition, including the selection of records for microfilming. These guidelines are outlined in the State or Local Government Records Manual, available from the Department of Archives and History. Specifically, records intended for reproduction on microfilm should first be identified and designated for filming on records schedules approved by the Department of Archives and History and the State or Local Government Records Commissions. This step ensures that agencies will not waste money either with unneeded microfilming or a microfilming format inappropriate for the particular records series.

Furthermore, records of special importance may be required on records schedules to meet additional preservation microfilming standards. In compliance with nationally-recognized preservation microfilming standards, the camera negatives of these identified records will be designated as the security microfilm copy and used only to generate a duplicate silver halide negative. (This duplication service is available at cost from the Alabama Department of Archives and history.) Only the duplicate silver halide negative will then be used to produce reference (diazo or vesicular) copies of the film.

DESTRUCTION OF MICROFILMED PERMANENT RECORDS

In accordance with the procedures of the State and Local Government Records Commissions and in compliance with approved retention schedules, the microfilm copies of all permanent records must comply with these certification standards before the original documents may be authorized for destruction.

APPLYING FOR CERTIFICATION

Applications for certification are available from the Records Services Center. Send the application and two rolls of microfilm processed within the last fourteen days as a test sample to the Records Services Center.

A certificate will be issued to the laboratory upon the successful completion of the evaluation. The certification will be valid for one year from the date issued and may be contingent upon the submission of periodical samples for continued monitoring. In applying for certification designation, a micrographic laboratory agrees to follow the above standards and procedures for the filming of any public records with a retention greater than twenty-five years. If a microfilm sample does not meet the certification requirements, the staff of the Archives will be available to provide technical assistance to the laboratory.

For more information on the certification program, please contact the Records Service Center, 715 Shady Street, Montgomery, Alabama 36130, telephone 205/242-4306.

Citation: **Technical Leaflet No. 3**

✪ CERTIFICATION REQUIREMENTS FOR SYSTEMS USING DIGITAL IMAGING TECHNOLOGIES TO MAINTAIN LONG-TERM GOVERNMENT RECORDS

INTRODUCTION

Government officials are legally obligated to create and maintain records that adequately document government business. Records provide evidence of government operations and serve as a mechanism of accountability to the citizenry. Government officials, therefore, are responsible for ensuring that their records, regardless of storage medium (i.e., paper, microfilm, magnetic tape, or digital optical disk), are usable for as long as they are needed to satisfy record keeping requirements. Public officials should also be aware of specific code requirements specifying particular record formats that may prohibit the sole reliance on digital imaging technologies. For more information on the identification of and compliance with specific record keeping requirements, such as records disposition, records storage formats, and legal admissibility, contact the Government Records Division of the Alabama Department of Archives and History (ADAH) at (334) 242-4452.

Digital imaging technologies can provide many benefits: ease of records retrieval, rapid response to user requests, multiple user access to information, and reduced space requirements. Digital imaging systems also create an array of new and often very complex problems. Particularly important are issues concerning access to records of long-term value. The State and Local Government Records Commissions define record of long-term value as those that must be available for agency use for ten years or more.

According to Alabama law the State and Local Government Records Commissions may issue guidelines, rules, and regulations concerning the destruction or other disposition of government records (Code of Alabama 1975, Section 41-13-5). This technical leaflet revises the Commissions' policy, adopted in 1989, regarding the use of digital imaging technologies for storing government records identified for long-term retention. This current policy also applies to any government records not covered by Commission-approved disposition guidelines.

In 1988, the Commissions established a certification program for microfilm laboratories filming Alabama government records of long-term value. This program has helped ensure that, when public records are maintained on microfilm and the original paper records are destroyed, the public interest will be protected by the assurance of durable, quality microfilm. Because of increased interest and use of digital imaging technologies for the storage of long-term government records, the Alabama State and Local Government Records Commissions, with support from the Alabama Department of Archives and History, have established a certification program for digital imaging systems. This certification program is designed to establish minimum criteria for systems that store records of long-term value using digital imaging technologies.

The Commissions' requirements for the preservation of long-term records are not intended to discourage the use of digital imaging technologies. The Commissions and ADAH recognize the potential administrative benefits of this technology. At the same time, the Commissions have a legal responsibility — along with the custodial agency — for ensuring that the state and public's interests in government records of long-term value are adequately protected.

The Commissions have issued separate guidelines to assist public officials in planning for the use of digital imaging technologies for long-term public records in Alabama — Technical Leaflet No. 4, Guidelines for the Use of Digital Imaging Technologies for Long-Term Government Records in Alabama This leaflet is available from the Government Record Division of the Alabama Department of Archives and History.

CERTIFICATION REQUIREMENTS

This certification program is of greatest value when used during the system design phase and prior to system implementation. This pre-implementation review will help assure that a new system being planned will meet the certification requirements. Certification may also be granted to systems that are currently in operation, provided those systems also meet the requirements.

Certification must be renewed annually to ensure the compliance with system requirements that provide for the continued accessibility of long-term government records. Certification applications (see enclosed form) from state and local government agencies should be sent to the Government Records Division, Alabama Department of Archives and History, P. O. Box 300100, Montgomery, Alabama 36130-0100.

If the agency does not have Commission approval through the certification program to use a digital imaging system to store records of long-term value, the agency must provide for their security and preservation by: (1) maintaining the records of microfilm, the life expectancy of which meets the retention requirements of the records and conforms to American National Standards Institute (ANSI) standards and has been produced by a certified micrographics laboratory (as outlined in Technical Leaflet No. 2, Standards for Micrographics Laboratory Certification or (2) maintaining the original paper records.

For a digital imaging system to be certified, a government office must provide written evidence that the following requirements can be met prior to system implementation or are being met for established systems:

1. The system has output capacity to another medium or device (i.e., to another digital optical disk, microfilm, or paper) from which all records in the system not specifically authorized for early destruction can be read. Although the Commissions are not requiring the creation of duplicate security copies of long-term records, agencies should create security copies of mission critical records.
2. Other installed devices exist, either in the responsible agency or in another location, to allow access to the records in case the system is down or in the event of an emergency.
3. The system is vendor-supported either by the original vendor or another vendor who can provide system support.
4. For a new system, the agency will migrate forward all earlier records of the program not scheduled for approved early destruction or not retained in an approved long-term medium. For existing systems, the agency recognizes its future responsibility to migrate long-term records to the next version or system it will install.

The application for certification is a form attached. It should be sent to the Government Records Division of the Alabama Department of Archives and History, where it will be reviewed by staff of the department, who also provide staff support for the State and Local Government Records Commissions. For additional information on certification requirements, contact the Government Records Division at (334) 242-4452.

Citation: Technical Leaflet No. 4 dated October 1994

✪ GUIDELINES FOR THE USE OF DIGITAL IMAGING TECHNOLOGIES FOR LONG-TERM GOVERNMENT RECORDS IN ALABAMA

INTRODUCTION

Public officials are responsible by law for ensuring that their records of long-term value are protected and accessible. This responsibility applies regardless of the records storage media. These guidelines are for use by public officials in the design of responsible digital imaging systems that may be used for creating or maintaining records of long-term value.

The guidelines are advisory in character and are not intended to serve as a rigid set of requirements. National technical standards, established practices, and research in the professional literature form the basis for these guidelines. The leaflet is designed to identify critical issues for public officials to consider in designing, selecting, implementing, and operating digital imaging technologies. These issues are especially important for systems used for mission critical records or for records of long-term value (records that must be available for agency use for ten years or more).

Digital imaging technology continues to change at a rapid rate. No system is generally accepted as the standard. To allow the use of these systems for long-term records while the technical environment is still so fluid, the State and Local Government Records Commissions have established a system certification program. The purpose of this program is to ensure that each system provides continued access to the records of long-term value maintained in the system.

The certification program provides for a review of the system's access capability on an annual basis. Unless a system is certified, the original versions of long-term records scanned into the system may not be approved for destruction. For information on the Commission's certification program for digital imaging systems, contact the Government Records Division of the Alabama Department of Archives and History at (334) 242-4452 and ask for a copy of Technical Leaflet No. 3, Certification Requirements for Systems Using Digital Imaging Technologies to Maintain Long-Term Government Records

The recommendations for this set of guidelines are listed in order of their implementation.

GUIDELINES

RECORDS SYSTEMS ANALYSIS

Recommendation 1: Prior to selecting a digital imaging system, conduct a records systems analysis to determine and document existing and planned agency information needs.

A records systems analysis is the crucial first step in determining the need for a digital imaging system. The analysis assesses existing operations to determine what records are best suited for digital imaging applications. There are cases where implementation without adequate analysis has led to operational problems and the loss of records. In other cases, it may be that records creation and retrieval processes can be restructured to improve operational efficiency. The records systems analysis should include an evaluation of the record keeping activity and requirements of the agency, a comparison of other media alternatives such as microforms or offsite storage of paper records, and a cost comparison analysis.

Program managers, information systems managers, and records management/archival specialists should participate in the analysis. The latter are important participants because they can assist in incorporating record keeping requirements into the system design. For more information on the identification of an compliance with state record keeping requirements, contact the Government Records Division at (334) 242-4452.

SYSTEM SPECIFICATIONS AND SELECTION

Recommendation 2: Require an open systems architecture for digital imaging applications or require vendors to provide a bridge to systems with non-proprietary configurations.

Although the term open systems architecture is defined in various ways, public officials should follow a system design approach that permits future component upgrades with minimal degradation of system functions. This open system architecture allows the system to be upgraded over time without a significant risk of records loss. It also supports the importing and exporting of digital images to and from other sources. One key factor in achieving an open systems architecture is the adoption of non-proprietary standards. The flexibility of an open systems architecture helps enable records of long-term value to be accessed and transferred from one open system to another.

Recommendation 3: Where data longevity or records integrity is a primary concern use a recording medium that is not rewritable.

Write Once Read Many (WORM) and Computer Output to Laser Disk (COLD) are two examples of media that are not rewritable. Digital images stored on these digital optical disks cannot be erased or modified — a desirable system characteristic to help preserve the integrity of long-term records.

Recommendation 4. Use a non-proprietary digital image file format. If using a proprietary format, provide a bridge to a non-proprietary digital image file format.

A digital file format is a structured container for information about each digital image file and the image data. Information about the digital image file includes, but is not limited to, its name, width, length, resolution, and compression technique. The computer needs this information to interpret the digital image. It is essential to use a non-proprietary image file format to ensure the ability to transfer successfully digital images between different systems or when a system is upgraded or modified.

ANSI/AIIM MS53-1993,Standard Recommended Practice - File Format for Storage and Exchange of Images - Bi-Level Image File Format: Part I details a standards definition for file formats. Because ANSI/AIIM MS53 is a relatively new recommended practice, there is not an agreed-upon, industry-wide image format standard. Many digital imaging systems use the Tagged Image File Format, or TIFF. Because different versions of TIFF exist, use the most generic version of TIFF that is available. Comprehensive documentation of the digital image file format, including TIFF, is recommended.

Recommendation 5: Use International Telecommunications Union (ITU) Group 3 and Group 4 compression techniques or have the vendor provide a bridge to these techniques (formerly the Consultative Committee on International Telegraphy and Telephony [CCITT]).

The large file sizes of typical scanned documents require digital image compression to support data transmission and to promote storage efficiency. Today most digital imaging systems use standard compression algorithms to "shrink" images. Standard compression techniques are instrumental in ensuring a migration strategy for records needed for long-term use. Two international standards are currently available. Using compression techniques conforming to any of these specifications will increase the likelihood that the images can be used with other technologies or migrated between systems.

Recommendation 6: When determining document scanning resolution, consider data storage requirements, document scanning throughput rates, and the accurate reproduction of the image. Validate vendor claims using a sampling of the agency's documents.

A digitized image consists of black and white dots or picture elements (pixels) measured in dots per inch (dpi). The higher the number of dpi, the higher the legibility of the reproduced image. Images scanned at higher dpi rates. however, use more storage on the disk and may require longer scanning times. The selection of scanning density involves a trade-off between image clarity, storage capacity, and speed.

When selecting a scanner, ask the vendor to perform a quality test on a broad sampling of documents at various dpi settings so that an appropriate end-to-end throughput rate and resolution can be determined.

For good quality images in scanning modern office records, use a scanning density of at least 300 dpi. A higher scanning density (600 dpi or above) is appropriate for deteriorating documents, engineering drawings, maps, or documents with background detail. The display resolution of the inspection/verification monitor and printer should match the scanning density of the document scanner.

When scanning continuous tone images, such as photographs, maps, and illustrations, use gray scale or color imaging technology.

Recommendation 7: Select equipment that conforms to the standard methodology for media error detection and correction. The system should provide techniques for monitoring and reporting verification of the records stored on a digital optical disk, and the systems administrator should actively follow the status of these monitors.

Digital imaging technology uses two methods within the Error Detection and Correction (EDAC) system to minimize digital image recording and retrieval errors. The first method uses error correction codes to detect and correct data read errors automatically. The second employs error correction code software to determine if an when the utilization of error correction codes is approaching a critical point. Monitoring the error correction status information provides an audit trail to measure the progress and degree of disk degradation. Tracking error correction trends will indicate an appropriate timetable for recopying disks.

The Association for Information and Image Management's Standards Committee has developed a standardized methodology for reporting the error rate data to the operating system for user evaluations. ANSI/AIIM MS59-1994, Use of Media Error monitoring and Reporting Techniques for Verification of the Information Stored on an Optical Disk, describes these standards. Another precaution administrators can take against losing records of long-term value because of defective disks is to require the use of digital optical disks with a guaranteed minimum post-write life of twenty years.

Recommendation 8: Specify that the Small Computer Systems Interface (SCSI) command "Write and Verify" is used when writing data to digital optical disks.

The "Write and Verify" command, available within the Small Computer System Interface (SCSI), is valuable for accessing how accurately the scanned information is transferred from the central processing unit of the computer to the digital optical disk. "Write and Verify" requires verification from the system that the digital image is correctly written to the disk and provides additional protection for continued access to long-term records.

Recommendation 9: Use an indexing data base that provides for efficient retrieval, ease of use, and up-to-date information about the digital images stored in the system. The indexing data base should be selected after an analysis of agency operations and user needs.

Reliable access to scanned images depends on an accurate, up-to-date index data base. Indexing a digital images involves linking descriptive image information with header file information. Normally, index data is manually key-entered using the original documents or the scanned images, either at the time of image capture or later in the production process. Index data verification, in which data base entries are compared with the original source documents for completeness and accuracy, is crucial because an erroneous index term may result in the inability to retrieve related images.

Recommendation 10: Provide specific plans for an ongoing process of migrating the records of long-term value from older to newer hardware and software.

Agencies must ensure that their records of long-term value are continually accessible. Systems as physical devices could be operational for ten years or more, but system technology will often be superseded within two to three years. If the system stores record with retention periods exceeding the life span of the hardware and software, it is essential that the administrator plan for future data migration. A migration strategy documents how an organization will transfer long-term records from one generation or hardware and/or software to another generation without losing system functionality. The strategy should be written and available with current system documentation.

Current strategies for migrating digital imaging system records include: upgrading equipment as technology evolves and periodically recopying disks as required; recopying optical disks based upon projected longevity and/or periodic verification of the records, or; transferring the data from an obsolete generation of optical disks to a newly-emerging technology, in some cases bypassing the intermediate generation that is mature, but at risk of becoming obsolete.

SYSTEM IMPLEMENTATION

Recommendation 11: Assign a permanent staff member as systems administrator and require the vendor to provide a project director during the installation and training periods. The assignment of a qualified staff member, preferably with systems administration experience, is critical to the effective implementation and maintenance of a digital imaging system. The systems administrator should be responsible for overall project management and the development and maintenance of written system documentation, which describes the requirements, capabilities, limitations, design, operation, and maintenance of the digital imaging system. Making a vendor representative responsible for installing the equipment and training the systems administrator and other appropriate agency staff will help to ensure successful implementation of the system.

Recommendation 12: Establish operational practices and provide technical and administrative documentation to ensure the future usability of the system, continued access to records of long-term value, and a sound foundation for assuring the system's legal integrity. It is the responsibility of office administrators, rather than vendors and manufacturers, to maintain written documentation of systems procedures, including access and security policies and procedures. Security and access policies should be developed to protect the system and the records from alteration or unauthorized use.

In regard to legal admissibility and trustworthiness, records stored on a digital imaging system should be treated no differently than records stored on magnetic disk or tape. The key is for the systems administrator to become familiar with how the rules of evidence apply to such records. Procedural controls should be established and followed to protect the integrity of the records.

These procedural controls should be documented and should reflect requirements for the legal acceptance of records as outlined in AIIM TR31-1992, Performance Guideline for the Legal Acceptance of Records Produced by Information Technology Systems This AIIM Performance Guideline stresses the importance of specifying the processes used to create the records, demonstrating that records are produced and relied upon in the regular course of business, establishing quality control and audit procedures, conducting formal training programs, and providing written documentation for each procedure. Case histories indicate that system requirements for good archival maintenance are consistent with the requirements for the admission of records under the "rules of evidence" laws. Records administrators should be familiar with how the rules of evidence apply to Alabama's public records. Policies and procedures should be followed to protect the integrity of long-term records.

Recommendation 13: Perform a visual quality control evaluation of each scanned image and related index data. Write the scanned image to optical media only after the evaluation process is completed.

To help ensure the integrity of long-term records stored on the system, staff members should perform a visual quality evaluation of each index entry and scanned image before writing the digital image to optical media. Overall system quality control is best when the scanned image is temporarily stored on magnetic media, permitting corrections through rescans as needed. Depending on the system configuration, corrections may be performed at the scanner capture station or at designated inspection/rescan workstations. Training and supervision of the operations staff is a key factor in maintaining acceptable image and index quality as well as user satisfaction with the system.

When the system is operational, a routine scanning quality test, as outlined in ANSI/AIIM MS44-1088, Recommended Practice for Quality Control of Image Scanners, should be performed on a weekly or monthly basis.

Recommendation 14: Design backup procedures to create security copies of digitized images and their related index records.

System component liability is critical to system success. Prolonged or repetitive downtime can seriously affect office operations. Creating a duplicate copy of records in another format or another system is an effective method of ensuring access to long-term information. Backup copies also support system integrity and legal admissibility requirements. The government office may select the backup storage medium (optical, magnetic, paper, or microfilm) that best meets the office's records requirements. Security copies of the records should be stored in an offsite, environmentally-stable location.

Recommendation 15: Provide adequate environmental conditions for the digital optical disks.

Even in an optimum environment, digital optical disks are susceptible to deterioration. Adverse storage conditions, especially high humidity, can cause rapid deterioration of the media. A prudent storage guideline for digital optical disk is to adhere to the temperature and humidity levels recommended for magnetic media storage. Technical specialists recommend a stable environment, with a temperature between 65 and 75 degrees and a relative humidity between 30 and 50 per cent. Digital optical disks should never be stored in direct sunlight nor placed near sources of heat.

Digital optical disks are affected by dust, debris, and fingerprints. Plastic cartridges should never be removed; nor should the cartridge shutter be opened to expose the digital optical disk's recording surface. Because the disk must be protected from warping, disks should not be subject to pressure and should be stored in an upright position when not in the disk drive.

Recommendation 16: Budget annually between fifteen and twenty per cent of the original system acquisition cost for upgrades, training, and maintenance.

Administrative managers should be aware of the high cost of maintaining and upgrading digital imaging systems. Unless these costs are factored into the continuing support of system maintenance and improvement, the system is in danger of becoming obsolete and requiring a far greater cost outlay to restore its effectiveness. Also, records stored in an outdated system tend to be at greater risk than those in a well-supported system.

IF YOU NEED ASSISTANCE

The Government Records Division staff of the Alabama Department of Archives and History provides assistance to state and local government agencies regarding the record administration considerations affecting the design and implementation of digital imaging systems. Questions or comments concerning digital imaging technologies, or this technical leaflet, may be directed to the Government Records Division, Alabama Department of Archives and History, P. O. Box 300100, Montgomery, Alabama 36130-0100, (334) 242-4452. Technical assistance questions concerning the design and implementation of digital imaging technologies should be directed to the Data Systems Management Division, Department of Finance, P. O. Box 303854, Montgomery, Alabama 36130-3854, (334) 242-3100.

State: Alaska
Source: Alaska Statutes

TITLE 6. BANKS AND FINANCIAL INSTITUTIONS.

CHAPTER 40. PREMIUM FINANCING ACT.

Article 2. Operations.

Citation: AS 6.40.100

✍ § 6.40.100. Recordkeeping; examination of records.

(a) A licensee shall maintain records of its premium finance transactions, including the insurance agents through which the licensee provides loans to residents of this state and the records shall be open to examination and investigation by the commissioner at the office of the licensee. All records pertaining to insurance contracts financed by state residents shall be maintained or readily available in the licensee's office. The commissioner may, at any reasonable time, require the licensee to bring records pertaining to premium finance agreements to the commissioner's office for examination. The expenses incurred by the department in conducting an examination shall be charged to an paid by the licensee in accordance with AS 06.01.010.

(b) A licensee shall preserve its records of premium finance transactions, including cards used in a card system, for at three years after making the final entry relating to any premium finance agreement. The preservation of records in photographic form constitutes compliance with this requirement.

(c) Each licensee shall, on or before March 15 of each year, file a report with the department containing information as the department may reasonably require concerning the business and operations during the preceding calendar year of each licensed place of business conducted by the licensee. The report shall be made under oath, shall be in the form prescribed by the department, and shall be kept available as a public record.

TITLE 9. CODE OF CIVIL PROCEDURE

Chapter 25. Evidence, Presumptions, Public Records, and Privileges.

Article 2. Public Records.

Citation: AS 09.25.115

☞ § 09.25.115. Electronic services and products.

(a) Notwithstanding AS 09.25.110(b) - (d) to the contrary, upon request and payment of a fee established under (b)of this section, a public agency may provide electronic services and products involving public records to members of the public. A public agency is encouraged to make information available in usable electronic formats to the greatest extent feasible. The activities authorized under this section may not take priority over the primary responsibilities of a public agency.

(b) The fee for electronic services and products must be based on recovery of the actual incremental costs of providing the electronic services and products, and a reasonable portion of the costs associated with building and maintaining the information system of the public agency. The fee may be reduced or waived by the public agency if the electronic services and products are to be used for a public purpose, including public agency program support, nonprofit activities, journalism, and academic research. Fee reductions and waivers shall be uniformly applied among persons who are similarly situated.

(c) Notwithstanding (b) of this section, the fee for duplicating a public record in the electronic form kept by a public agency may not exceed the actual incremental costs of the public agency.

(d) Public agencies shall include in a contract for electronic services and products provisions that

(1) protect the security and integrity of the information system of the public agency and of information systems that are shared by public agencies; and

(2) limit the liablity of the public agency providing the services and products.

(e) Each public agency shall notify the state library distribution and data access center established under AS 14.56.090 of the electronic services and products.offered by the public agency to the public under this section. The notification must include a summary of the availale format options and the fees charged.

(f) When offering on-line access to an electronic file or data base, a public agency also shall provide without charge on-line acces to the electronic file or data base through one or more public terminals.

(g) Each public agency shall establish the fees for the electronic services and products provided under this section. The Telecommunications Information Council may cancel the fees established by a public agency in the executive branch, except the fees of the University of Alaska and the Alaska Railroad Corporation, if the council determines that the fees are unreasonably high.

(h) A public agency may not make electronic services and products available to one member of the public and withhold them from other members of the public.

(i) A public agency other than a municipality or the Alaska Railroad Corporation shall separately account for the fees received by the agency under this section and deposited in the general fund. The annual estimated balance in the account may be used by the legislature to make appropriations to the agency to carry out the activities of the agency.

Citation: AS 09.25.220

☞ § 09.25.220. Definitions for AS 09.25.100 - 09.25.220.

In AS 09.25.100 - 09.25.220, unless the context otherwise requires,

(1) "electronic services and products" means computer-related services and products provided by a public agency, including

(A) electronic manipulation of the data containded in public records in order to tailor the data to the person's request or to develop a product that meets the person's request;

(B) duplicating public records in alternative formats not used by a public agency, providing periodic updates of an electronic file or data base, or duplicating an electronic file or data base from a geographic information system;

(C) providing on-line access to an electronic file or data base;

(D) providing information that cannot be retrieved or generated by the existing computer programs of the public agency;

(E) providing functional electronic access to the information system of the public agency; in this subparagraph, "functional access" includes the capability for alphanumeric query and printing, graphic query and plotting, nongraphic data input and analysis and graphic data input and analysis;

(F) providing software developed by a public agency or developed by a private contractor for a public agency;

(G) generating maps or other standard or customized products from a electronic geographic information system;

(2) "public agency" means a political subdivision, department, institution, board, commission, division, authority, public corporation, council, committee, or other instrumentality of the state or a municipality; "public agency " includes the University of Alaska and the Alaska Railroad Corporation;

(3) "public records" means books, papers, files, accounts, writings, including drafts and memorializations of conversation, and other items, regardles of format, or physical characteristics, that are developed or received by a public agency, or by a private contractor for a public agency, and that are preserved for their informational value or as evidence of the organization or operation of the public agency; "public records" does not include proprietary software programs;

(4) "Telecommunications Information Council" means the Telecommunications Information Council established under AS 44.19.502.

TITLE 21. INSURANCE.

CHAPTER 66. TITLE INSURANCE COMPANIES.

Citation: AS 21.66.170

✍ § 21.66.170. Determination of insurability required.

(a) A policy or contract of title insurance may not be written until the title insurance company conducts or has conducted a reasonable search and examination of the title and has made a determination of insurability of title in accordance with its established underwriting practices. Evidence of the determination shall be preserved and retained in the files of the title insurance company or its agent for a period of not less than 15 years after the policy or contract of title insurance has been issued. In lieu of retaining the original evidence, the title insurance company or the title insurance limited producer, may, in the regular course of business, establish a system by which all or part of these writings are recorded copied, or reproduced by any photographic, photostatic, microfilm, microcard, miniature photographic, or other process that accurately reproduces or forms a durable medium for reproducing the original.

(b) This section does not apply to (1) a company assuming no primary liability in a contract of reinsurance; or (2) a company acting a a co-insurer if one of the other co-insuring companies has complied with this section.

TITLE 40. PUBLIC RECORDS AND RECORDERS.

CHAPTER 21. MANAGEMENT AND PRESERVATION OF PUBLIC RECORDS.

Article 1. Public Records.

Citation: AS 40.21.080

✪ § 40.21.080. Disposal of public records by political subdivision.

An official of a political subdivision of the state having legal custody of public records that are considered by the official to be without legal or administrative value or historical interest may compile lists of these records sufficiently detailed to identify them and submit the lists to the governing body of the political subdivision. The governing body may authorize the disposal and the method of disposal of the records in the list that it finds to be without legal or administrative value or historical interest. The governing body may also, upon request of the legal custodian of the records, authorize in advance the periodic disposal of routine records that the governing body considers to have no legal, administrative, or historical value. After receipt of written authorization from the governing body, the legal custodian of the records may dispose of the records. The legal custodian shall file in the office from which the records were drawn a descriptive list of the records disposed of and a record of the disposal itself. Copies of these documents shall be transmitted to the governing body, which shall file and preserve them.

Citation: AS 40.21.120

✪ § 40.21.120. Standards of clarity, accuracy, and permanency of copies.

When a public officer performing duties under this chapter is required or authorized by law to record, copy, recopy, or replace any public record, the officer may do so by photostatic, photographic, microphotographic, microfilm or other mechanical process that produces a clear, accurate and permanent copy or reproduction of the original record, in accordance with the latest standards approved for the reproduction of permanent records by the department.

Citation: AS 40.21.130

✪ § 40.21.130. Alteration and replacement of public records.

An original public record that is worn or damaged may be replaced by a reproduction made in accordance with this chapter. Certification by the agency having custody of the record that the replacement is a true and correct copy of the original shall appear at the end of the reproduction. When original public records are photographed or otherwise mechanically reproduced under the provisions of this chapter and the photographic or other mechanical reproductions are placed in conveniently accessible files and provisions made for preserving and using them, the original records from which they were made may be destroyed only with the approval of the state archivist.

Citation: AS 40.21.140

✪ § 40.21.140. Use of copies and replacements as evidence. ☞

Reproductions or replacements of records made under this chapter are considered original records for all purposes and are admissible in evidence as original records.

Article 2. General Provisions.

Citation: AS 40.21.150

✪ § 40.21.150. Definitions.

In this chapter, unless the contents otherwise requires,

(a) "agency" or "state agency" means a department, office, agency, state board, commission, public corporation or other organizational unit of or created under the executive branch of the state government, the term does not include the University of Alaska;

(b) "archives" means

(A) the noncurrent records of a state agency or political subdivision of the state preserved, after appraisal, because of their value; and referred to as archival material; also referred to as an archival agency;

(C) the building or part of a building where archival material is located; also referred to as an archival depository;

(3) "department" means the Department of Education;

(4) "local record" means a public record of a city or borough of any class, villages, district, authority or other political subdivision unless the record is designated or treated as a state record under state law.

(5) "record" means any document, paper, book, letter, drawing, map, plat, photo, photographic file, motion picture film, microfilm, microphotograph, exhibit, magnetic or paper tape, punched cared, or other document of any other material, regardless of physical form or characteristic, developed or received under law or in connection with the transaction of official business and preserved or appropriate for preservation by an agency or political subdivision, as evidence of the organization, function, policies, decisions, procedures, operations, or other activities of the state or political subdivision or because of the informational value in them; the term does not include library or museum material developed or acquired and preserved solely for reference, historical or exhibition purposes, extra copies of documents preserved solely for convenience of reference, or stocks of publications and processed documents;

(6) "records center" means a records depository in the department for the storage and disposition of noncurrent records;

(7) "state record" means a record of a department, office, commission, board, public corporation, or other agency of the state government, including a record of the legislature or a court and any other record designated or treated as a public record under state law.

TITLE 45. TRADE AND COMMERCE.

Chaper 55. Alaska Securities Act of 1959.

Article 5. General Provisions.

Citation: AS 45.55.970

✍ § 45.55.970. Administrative files and opinions.

(a) A document is filed when it is received by the administrator.

(b) The administrator shall keep a register of all applications for registration and registration statements which are or have ever been effective under this chapter and all denial, suspension, or revocation orders which have been entered under this chapter. The register shall be open for public inspection.

(c) The information contained in or filed with a registration statement, application, or report may be made available to the public under the regulations adopted by the administrator.

(d) Upon request and at the reasonable charges that the administrator prescribes, the administrator shall furnish to any person photostatic or other copies, certified under the seal of office if requested, of any entry in the register or any document which is a matter of public record. In a proceeding or prosecution under this chapter, a copy so certified is *prima facie* evidence of the contents of the entry or documents certified.

(e) The administrator may honor requests from interested persons for interpretative opinions.

Source: Alaska Rules of Evidence

ARTICLE X. WRITINGS.

☞ Rule 1001. Definitions

For purposes of this article the following definitions are applicable:

(1) *Writings and recordings.* — "Writings" and "recordings" consist of letters, words, or numbers, or their equivalent, set down by handwriting, typewriting, printing, photostating, photographing, magnetic impulse, mechanical or electronic recording, or other form of data compilation.

(2) *Photographs.* — "Photographs" include still photographs, X-ray films, video tapes, and motion pictures.

(3) *Original.* — An "original" of a writing or recording is the writing or recording itself or any counterpart intended to have the same effect by a person executing or issuing it. An "original" of a photograph includes the negative or any print therefrom. If data are stored in a computer or similar device, any printout or other output readable by sight, shown to reflect the data accurately, is an "original".

(4) *Duplicate.* — A "duplicate" is a counterpart produced by the same impression as the original, or from the same matrix, or by means of photography, including enlargements and miniatures, or by mechanical or electronic re-recording, or by chemical reproduction, or by other equivalent techniques which accurately reproduces the original.

☞ Rule 1003. Admissibility of Duplicates.

A duplicate is admissible to the same extent as an original unless (1) a genuine question is raised as to the authenticity of the original or (2) in the circumstances it would be unfair to admit the duplicate in lieu of the original.

☞ Rule 1005. Public Records.

The contents of an official record, or of a document authorized to be recorded or filed and actually recorded or filed, including data compilations in any form, if otherwise admissible, may be proved by copy, certified as correct in accordance with Rule 902 or testified to be correct by a witness who has compared it with the original. If a copy which complies with the foregoing cannot be obtained by the exercise of reasonable diligence, then other evidence of the contents may be given.

[See Appendix A. Uniform Rules of Evidence for additional provisions.]

Source: **Alaska Administrative Code**
Agency: **Department of Education**

TITLE 4. EDUCATION.

CHAPTER 59. ARCHIVES AND RECORDS MANAGEMENT SERVICES (ARMS).

Citation: **4 AAC 59.005**

✪ § 59.005. Retention and Preservation of Electronic Records.

(a) This section establishes the minimum requirements for the creation, use, maintenance, retention, preservation, and disposition of state records in an electronic format.

(b) A state agency shall

(1) establish internal procedures to comply with archives and records management requirements, including recordkeeping requirements and disposition, before the state agency approves new electronic records systems or enhances to its existing state systems;

(2) integrate the management of electronic records with other records and information resources management programs of that agency;

(3) identify any electronic record being created, used, received, or maintained in its office, to ensure that those records appear on that agency's records retention schedule;

(4) develop and maintain documentation about electronic records systems used by the agency that specify technical characteristics necessary for reading or processing the records; and

(5) retain its electronic records until a disposition period has been approved by the state archivist, the attorney general, the commissioner of administration, and the state agency head.

(c) The state archivist, in coöperation with the Department of Administration and the Telecommunications Information Council, will conduct a technology assessment every three years, beginning one year after the 10/2/94. This assessment must examine storage technology, hardware and software, systems applications, retrieval and other aspects of technology that are related to electronic recordkeeping and archival practice.

(d) Except as provided in (f) of this section, the state archivist will not accept in the state archives permanent records stored on optical disks. A permanent record copied onto an optical disk may not be destroyed without the state archivist's approval. An agency using optical media storage for records with retention periods of more than 10 years shall recopy optical media at lest every 10 years.

(e) State records determined by the state archivist as temporary may be stored on any medium, including optical disk, that ensures the maintenance of information until its disposal is authorized under (b) of this section.

(f) Analog videodiscs that typically contain photographs are one type of optical disk that may be accepted by the state archivist into the state archives, if they do not require any interactive software on nonstandardized equipment. Original photographs determined by the state archivist as permanent and copied onto a videodisc must be scheduled for transfer to the state archives along with a copy of the videodisc. Compacts disks used for digital audio playback also may be accepted by the state archivist into the state archives, if they use a standard player and require no special software.

Citation: **4 AAC 59.060**

✪ § 59.060. Microforms and Microform Systems.

(a) This section establishes the minimum requirements for the design, production, retention, and certification for microforms of state records.

(b) A state agency shall

(1) establish internal procedures that comply with AS 40.21, other state law, this chapter, and ARMS internal procedures for state agencies, including recordkeeping and disposition, before implementing new micrographic systems or modifying existing systems, and consult with ARMS staff when designing or modifying microform systems;

(2) identify any microforms created, used, received or maintained in its office to ensure that these records appear on the agency records retention schedule, and update the agency records retention schedule to include the microform copy when converting paper record;

(3) ensure that microforms meets or exceed the Association for Information and Image Management (AIIM) standards for archival quality; these standards are contained in Practice for Operational Procedures/Inspection and Quality Control of First-generation, Silver Microfilm of Documents, approved as of January 14, 1991, and adopted by reference in this paragraph;

(4) certify that microforms are authentic copies of original state records;

(5) index and label microforms according to ARMS

requirements and the agency records retention schedule;

(6) develop and maintain procedural information about the microform system, including software and hardware documentation if computer assisted retrieval systems are used; and

(7) transfer microforms to the state records center or state archives, or dispose of microforms according to the agency records retention schedule. (eff. 10/2/94, Register 131)

Agency: **Occupational Safety and Health Division**

TITLE 8. LABOR.

PART 4. OCCUPATIONAL SAFETY AND HEALTH DIVISION.

CHAPTER 61. OCCUPATIONAL SAFETY AND HEALTH.

ARTICLE 4. RECORDING AND REPORTING OCCUPATIONAL INJURIES AND ILLNESSES.

Citation: **8 AAC 61.230**

✍ § 61.230. Log of Occupational Injuries and Illnesses.

(a) Each employer shall maintain in each establishment a log of occupational injuries and illnesses on a calendar year basis.

(b) At all places where a log is maintained, sufficient information must be available to complete the log within six working days after receipt of notice that a recordable injury or illness has occurred.

(c) The log may be maintained at some other location if information for the log, current to within six days, is available at that other location and a copy of the log, current to within 45 days, is available at the location of the establishment.

(d) Recordable occupational injuries or illnesses are any occupational injuries or illnesses which result in

(1) fatalities, regardless of the time between the injury and death, or the length of the illness which led to the death;

(2) cases, other than fatalities, that result in lost workdays; and

(3) nonfatal cases without lost workdays which result in transfer of an employee to another job or termination of employment, or which require medical treatment (other than first aid), or which involve a loss of consciousness or restriction of work or motion. This category also includes any diagnosed occupational illnesses which are reported to the employer but are not classified as fatalities or lost workday cases.

(e) The employer shall maintain the log on department form DOSH 200 "Log and Summary of Occupational Injuries and Illnesses" or on a form that contains the information required to be kept on DOSH 200. If an equivalent to form DOSH 200 is used, such as a printout from data processing equipment, the information must be as readable and comprehensible to a person not familiar with the data processing equipment as the form DOSH 200 itself.

(f) For each injury or illness recorded in the log, the employer shall keep on file a copy of the department's Workmen's Compensation form 07ADL210 "Report of Occupational Injury or Illness," or DOSH 101, or a form that contains the information required to be kept on DOSH 101. This report or a copy thereof must be maintained at each establishment and be available at the establishment within six working days after the receipt of information by the employer that a recordable injury or illness has occurred.

* * * * *

Citation: **8 AAC 61.260**

✍ § 61.260. Retention of records.

(a) Records provided for in 8 AAC 61.230 and 8 AAC 61.240 (including form DOSH 200 and its predecessor forms, DOSH 100 and DOSH 102) must be retained in each establishment for five years following the end of the calendar year to which they relate.

(b) An employer who makes and keeps employee exposure records or employee medical records, or analyses of those records, pertaining to employee exposure to toxic substances or harmful physical agents, shall keep and preserve these records for the duration of employment of the employee to whom the record applies plus 30 years, with the following exceptions:

(1) health insurance claims records maintained separately from the employer's medical program and its records;

(2) blood or urine samples which are routinely discarded as a part of normal medical practice;

(3) records of voluntary employee assistance programs (alcohol, drug abuse, or personal counseling programs), if maintained separately from the employer's medical program and its records;

(4) background data to environmental monitoring or measuring, such as laboratory reports and worksheets, need only be retained for one year if the sampling results, the collection methodology, a description of the analytical and mathematical methods used and a summary of other background data relevant to interpretation of the result obtained are retained for at least 30 years; and

(5) materials safety data sheets and records concerning the identity of a substance or agent need not be retained if some record of the identity (chemical name if known) of the substance or agent, where it was used, and when it was used is retained for at least 30 years.

(c) Nothing in this section is intended to mandate the form, manner, or process by which an employer preserves a record so long as the information contained in the record is preserved and retrievable, except that X-ray films must be preserved in their original state.

State: **American Samoa**
Source: **American Samoa Code**

TITLE 4. EXECUTIVE.

CHAPTER 12. ARCHIVES AND RECORDS MANAGEMENT.

Citation: **ASC 4.1205**

✪ § 4.1205. Archivist — Duties and responsibilities.

The archivist shall adopt rules under the Administrative Procedure Act, 4.1001 et seq., which:

* * * * *

(E) the reproduction and maintenance of records by micrographic, photographic, magnetic or other processes. Reproductions made in compliance with these standards have the same force and effect as the originals would have and are treated as originals for audit, admissibility in evidence, and other similar purposes;

* * * * *

State: Arizona
Source: Arizona Revised Statutes

TITLE 11. COUNTIES.

CHAPTER 3. COUNTY OFFICERS.

Article 3. Recorder.

Citation: ARS 11-476

✪ § 11-476. Preservation of county records; transcription and certification.

A. When county records or indexes become defaced, worn or in a condition endangering their preservation, the board of supervisors shall procure appropriate books and require the recorder to transcribe such records and indexes with a standard permanent black ink, provided, the recorder may choose otherwise to preserve the records as provided in § 11-478 which procedure may be used in lieu of the provisions of this section at the option of the recorder.

B. The books or records when transcribed or reproduced shall conform to the original records as indexed. The designation of the transcribed books or records shall not be changed from the original. They shall be compared to the original and when found to be correctly transcribed or reproduced, the recorder and deputies transcribing, verifying or reproducing them shall officially certify at the end of the record, with the seal of the office affixed on the same page, the correctness of the transcriptions or reproductions, reciting the number of pages in the book, from on to the highest number.

C. Records so transcribed and certified shall be of the force and effect of the original records.

Citation: ARS 11-478

✪ § 11-478. Reproduction and microphotography of records.

The county recorder may cause any or all files or records in his official custody to be microphotographed or otherwise reproduced on film as in the case of original filings or recordings or both. Every such reproduction shall be deemed and considered an original, and a transcript, exemplification or reproduction thereof may be certified to by the recorder in like manner as the original.

Citation: ARS 11-479

✪ § 11-479. Destruction of records; requirements; exception.

A. The county recorder may destroy, under the provisions of § § 41-1339, 41-1343, 41-1344, 41-1345, 41-1345.01 and 41-1436 through 41-1351, any or all of the filed papers or record books created by handwriting, by typing on printed forms, by typewriting or by photographic methods in the recorder's official custody, except federal tax lien notices, if all of the following conditions exist:

1. The record, paper or document if photographed or reproduced by any other method under the direction and control of the county recorder on electronic media or film of a type approved for permanent record by the department of library, archives and public records.

2. The device used to reproduce such record, paper or document on film or electronic media is one which accurately and legibly reproduces the original thereof in all details.

3. The photographs or other reproductions on film or electronic media are made as accessible for public reference as the book records were.

4. A true copy of archival quality of such film or electronic media reproduction is kept in a safe and separate place for security purposes.

B. No page of any record, paper or document shall be destroyed if any such page cannot be reproduced on film or electronic media with full legibility. Every such unreproducible page shall be permanently preserved in a manner that will afford easy reference.

TITLE 12. COURTS AND CIVIL PROCEEDINGS.

CHAPTER 2. JUDICIAL OFFICERS AND EMPLOYEES.

Article 1. Clerk of the Supreme Court.

Citation: ARS 12-202.01

✪ § 12-202.01. Preservation and destruction of records.

A. The clerk of the supreme court may destroy or provide for the destruction of all documents, records, instruments, books, papers, depositions, exhibits and transcripts in any action or proceeding in the supreme court, or otherwise filed or deposited in the clerk's custody pursuant to rules adopted by the supreme court.

B. A photographic or electronic reproduction or image of any of the records described in this section, which has been certified by the person in charge of such reproduction as being an exact replica of the original, shall be received in evidence in all courts, and in hearings before any officer, board or commission having jurisdiction or authority to conduct such hearings, in like manner as the original.

C. The clerk shall notify the director of the department of library, archives and public records of records designated for destruction pursuant to court rules. The department, during the time prescribed by court rule, may review and inspect these records. During this time period, the department may remove any of these records for storage and retrieval.

Article 8. Clerk of the Superior Court.

Citation: ARS 12-282

✪ § 12-282. Custody of records filed; purging; destruction; microphotography; electronic imaging; evidence; withdrawal of voucher exemption.

A. The clerk shall keep custody at the county seat, and shall take charge of and safely keep and dispose of according to court rules, all books, papers and records which may be filed or deposited in custody.

B. The clerk may destroy all documents, records, instruments, books, papers, depositions, exhibits and transcripts in any action or proceeding in the superior court, or otherwise filed or deposited in custody pursuant to rules established by the supreme court.

C. The clerk shall notify the director of the department of library, archives and public records designated for destruction pursuant to court rules. The department, during the time prescribed by court rule, may review and inspect these records. During this time period, the department may remove any of these records for storage and retrieval.

D. A photographic or electronic reproduction or image of any of the records described in this section, which has been certified by the clerk in charge of such reproduction or imaging as being an exact replica of the original, shall be received in evidence in all courts, and in hearings before any officer, board or commission having jurisdiction or authority to conduct such hearings, in like manner as the original. A state or local agency shall accept any of the records under this subsection as a registration of a record or a procedure if the agency receives the record from the clerk of the superior court through electronic transmission and the electronically reproduced document states that the copy received is a full, true and correct copy of the original on file with the clerk of the court.

E. The clerk may produce an abstract of marriage in lieu of a reproduction of the recorded marriage license. An abstract of marriage shall include the name of the bride at the time of the marriage, the name of the groom, the date of the marriage and the date on which the marriage license was recorded.

F. Any voucher filed in support of an account by a trustee, a personal representative or any litigant may be withdrawn if a certified copy is retained on file. Pursuant to court rules the clerk may destroy the voucher or, if requested to do so, may deliver the voucher to the trustee, personal representative or litigant. No notification is necessary prior to destruction of such vouchers.

G. Section 8-247 is exempt from this section.

TITLE 16. ELECTIONS AND ELECTORS

CHAPTER 1. QUALIFICATIONS AND REGISTRATION OF ELECTORS.

Article 5. Registration Rolls.

Citation: ARS 16-162

✪ § 16-162. Retention of registration forms and record of cancellation.

The county recorder shall provide a means of retaining registration forms and records of cancellation of registration. The records shall be retained as prescribed by § § 41-1347 and 41-1351.

Citation: ARS 16-163

✪ § 16-163. Assignment of registrations to general county register; exception; notification to electors; filing of registration forms.

A. The county recorder shall, upon receipt of a registration in proper form, assign the registration record to its proper precinct and alphabetical arrangement in the general county register. The general county register shall be preserved permanently to reflect the registration as of each general election. After the general county register is revised to relect the valid registrations for the general election, the county recorder shall provide the department of library, archives and public records with a copy of the revised county register.

B. After placing the record of registration in the county general register, the county recorder shall notify the elector within thirty days in writing that his name appears in the general register.

C. If the notice that is sent is returned undeliverable, the county recorder may send an additional notice as prescribe by § 16-166, subsection A and that notice shall indicate that the elector must respond no later than twenty-nine days before the election at which the elector intends to vote.

D. All current original registration forms shall be filed countrywide or by precinct in alphabetical order by surname of elector. All original registration forms canceled, and all original applications for cancellation of registration received since the preceding general election, shall be separately filed and maintained. Computer output microfilm, listings or other electronic format media containing the information from the general county register after each general election shall be provided to the department of library, archives and public records and shall serve to fulfill the requirements of this subsection and § 16-164, subsection A.

Citation: ARS 16-168

✪ § 16-168. Precinct registers; date of preparation; contents; copies; reports; violation; classification.

A. By the tenth day preceding the primary, general and runoff elections the county recorder shall prepare from the original registration forms or from electronic media at least four lists that are printed or typed on paper of all qualified electors in each precinct in the county, and such lists shall be the official precinct registers.

B. The official precinct registers for use at the polling place shall contain at least the names in full, party preference, date of registration and residence address of each qualified elector in the respective precincts. Such names shall be in alphabetical order and, in a column to the left of the names, such names shall be numbered consecutively beginning with number 1 in each precinct register.

C. For purposes of transmitting voter reistration information as prescribed by this subsection, computer generated disks, tapes or other electronic media shall be the principal media. A county or state chairman who is eligible to receive copies of precinct registers as prescribed by this subsection may request that the recorder provide a paper copy of the precinct registers. The county recorder shall, in addition to preparing the official precinct registers, provide a means for mechanically or electronically reproducing the precinct registers and shall unless otherwise agreed deliver within eight days after the close of registration for the primary, general and runoff elections, without charge, on the same day one electronic media copy of each precinct register within the county to the county chairman and one electronic media copy to the state chairman of each party which has at least four candidates other than presidential electors appearing upon the ballot in that county at the current election. The county recorder shall also, upon request and without charge, deliver one electronic media copy of the precinct register to legislative council.

The county recorder of a county with a population of fewer than four hundred thousand persons shall, on the same day precinct registers are delivered to county chairmen, deliver one electronic media copy of each precinct register within the county to the state chairman of each party which has at least four candidates other than presidential electors appearing on the ballot in this state at the current election. The copies of the precinct registers shall be on magnetic computer disks or tape which shall include for each elector the following information:

1. Name in full and appropriate title.
2. Party preference.
3. Date of registration.
4. Residence address.
5. Mailing address, if different from residence address.
6. The zip code.
7. The telephone number if given.
8. Birth date.

9. Occupation.

10. Primary election and general election voting history for the prior four years and other information regarding registered voters which the county recorder maintains on magnetic computer disks or tape and which is public information.

D. The names on the precinct registers shall be in alphabetical order and any changes, additions or deletions to the precinct registers shall unless otherwise agreed be delivered to each county chairman and each state chairman at least quarterly and within ten business days of the close of each quarter in the same format and media as prescribed by subsection C of this section.

E. Precinct registers and other lists and information derived from registration forms may be used only for purposes relating to a political or political party activity, a political campaign or an election, for revising election district boundaries, or for any other purpose specifically authorized by law. The county recorder shall, upon a request for such use and within thirty days from receipt of such request, prepare additional copies of any precinct register and furnish them to any person requesting them upon payment of a fee equal to five cents for each name appearing on the register for a printed list and ten cents for each name for an electronic data medium, plus the cost of the blank computer tape or disk if furnished by the recorder, for each copy so furnished.

F. Any person in possession of a precinct register, in whole or part, or any reproduction of a precinct register, shall not permit such register to be used, bought, sold or otherwise transferred for any purpose except for uses otherwise authorized by this section. Any person violating the provisions of this subsection is guilty of a class 2 misdemeanor. Nothing in this subsection shall preclude public inspection of voter registration records.

G. The county recorder shall count the registered voters by political party by precinct, legislative district and congressional district as follows:

1. In even numbered years, the county recorder shall count all persons who are registered to vote as of:

(a) January 1.

(b) March 1.

(c) The last day on which a person may register to be eligible to vote in the next primary election.

(d) The last day on which a person may register to be eligible to vote in the next general election.

2. In odd numbered years, the county recorder shall count all persons who are registered to vote as of:

(a) January 1.

(b) April 1.

(c) July 1.

(d) October 1.

3. The county recorder shall count all persons who are registered to vote as of the last day on which a person may register to be eligible to vote in a second election if a second election is held pursuant to article V, § 1, Constitution of Arizona.

H. The county recorder shall report the totals to the secretary of state as soon as is practicable following each of the dates prescribed in subsection G, paragraphs 1 and 2 of this section. The report shall include completed registration forms returned in accordance with § 16-134, subsection B. The county recorder shall also provide the report in a uniform electronic computer media format that shall be agreed upon between the secretary of state and all county recorders. The secretary of state shall then prepare a summary report for the state and shall maintain that report as a permanent record.

I. The county recorder shall provide to the secretary of state a list of registered voters in the county, including the voter's name, date of birth and state of birth along with the count of registered voters pursuant to subsection G of this section. The list of registered voters is a public record and shall be in a format agreed upon between the secretary of state and each county recorder. The list shall be labeled to show that it is not an official listing of registered voters. The secretary of state shall compare the lists to identify persons registered in more than one county. If a person is registered in more than one county, the secretary of state shall notify, within fifteen days after receipt of the list, the county recorder in each county in which the person is registered except the county recorder in the county in which the person registered last. The notice shall include the date of the person's latest registration. After receiving this notice the county recorder shall cancel the person's registration as of the date of the newest registration and notify the person of the cancellation at the address provided by the secretary of state from the county of the latest registration.

Citation: ARS 16-173

✪ § 16-173. County recorder to file data processing system or program.

In each county in which an electronic data processing system or program is used for voter registration, the county recorder shall file with the board of supervisors a detailed and complete explanation of such data processing system or program and any subsequent revision thereof.

TITLE 28. TRANSPORTATION.

CHAPTER 1. DEFINITIONS AND PENALTIES.

Article 1. General Provisions.

Citation: ARS 28-110

✪ § 28-110. Duplication of records; notification of duplication; admissibility of duplications as originals; destruction of nonessential or obsolete records; computer storage of information; definitions.

A. The director may cause any writings, recordings and photographs kept by the department to be duplicated.

B. When such duplicates are placed in conveniently accessible files and provisions made for preserving, examining and using them, the director of the department of transportation may certify such fact to the director of the department of library, archives and public records, who shall thereafter, within ninety days, direct the disposal, archival storage or destruction of the records or papers.

C. A certified duplicate of the original writing, recordings or photographs shall be deemed to be an original writing, recording or photograph for all purposes and shall be admissible in evidence without further foundation in all courts or administrative agencies.

D. Upon certification by the director of the department of transportation of any obsolete or nonessential writings, recordings and photographs, which the director of the department of transportation determines are not of sufficient value to be preserved by being duplicated, the director of the department of library, archives and public records shall order their destruction within ninety days from the certification, but the director of the department of library, archives and public records may elect to have any such documents proposed to be destroyed transferred to the department of library, archives and public records upon request therefor, within the ninety day period.

E. The director may cause the information contained on any

original writing, recording or photograph or duplicate made pursuant to this section to be placed on computer storage devices, but the original writings, recordings and photographs or the copies shall be maintained by the department so long as required by law or the director deems necessary after which time the writings, recordings and photographs may be disposed of as provided in this section. Signatures on writings, recordings and photographs need not be placed on the computer storage devices.

F. A duplicate of the information placed on computer storage devices shall be deemed to be an original of the writing, recording or photograph for all purposes and shall be admissible in evidence without further foundation in all courts or administrative agencies if the following certification appears on each page:

This document is a certified duplicate of the information contained in the computer storage devices of the department of transportation, motor vehicle division, in accordance with Arizona Revised Statutes § 28-110, subsection F.

G. For purposes of this section:

1. "Duplicate" means a counterpart produced by any of the following:

(a) The same impression or from the same matrix as the original.

(b) Means of photograph, including enlargements and miniatures.

(c) Mechanical or electronic rerecording.

(d) Chemical reproduction.

(e) Any other equivalent technique that accurately reproduces the original.

2. "Original":

(a) Of a writing or recording means the writing or recording itself or any counterpart intended to have the same effect by the person executing or issuing it.

(b) Of a photograph means the negative or a print from the negative.

(c) Of data stored in a computer or similar device means a printout or other output that is readable by sight and that is shown to reflect the data accurately.

3. "Photographs" includes still photographs, x-ray films, videotapes and motion pictures.

4. "Writings" and "recordings" means letters, words or numbers or their equivalent that are set down by handwriting, typewriting, printing, photostating, photographing, magnetic impulse, mechanical or electronic recording or any other form of data compilation.

CHAPTER 1. STATE AGENCIES AND OFFICERS.

Article 1. Motor Vehicle Division.

Citation: ARS 28-211

✪ **§ 28-211. Filing, compiling and indexing records; preservation of applications and records.**

A. Whenever in this title an application or record is required to be filed, an index maintained or a record compiled, the director may, by rule, provide that such filing, indexing or compilation be accomplished by use of a computer so that on inquiry to the computer it will be capable of disclosing and reproducing all information required by law. Signatures on applications or records need not be stored.

B. When the director adopts rules pursuant to subsection A, the former requirement of filing, compiling or indexing need no longer be complied with, except as provided in subsection A of this section, but the applications or records from which the information was obtained shall be preserved so long as required by law or until a new application is filed by an applicant or a new record is received and the application or record is no longer needed to carry out the provisions of this title.

TITLE 39. PUBLIC RECORDS, PRINTING AND NOTICES.

CHAPTER 1. PUBLIC RECORDS.

Article 1. Requirements for Materials Used

Citation: ARS 39-101

✪ **§ 39-101. Permanent public records; quality; storage; violation; classification.**

A. Permanent public records of the state, a county, city or town, or other political subdivision of the state, shall be transcribed or kept on paper or other material which is of durable or permanent quality and which conforms to standards established by the director of the department of library, archives and public records.

B. Permanent public records transcribed or kept as provided in subsection A shall be stored and maintained according to standards for the storage of permanent public records established by the director of the department of library, archives and public records.

C. A public officer charged with transcribing or keeping such public records who violates this section is guilty of a class 2 misdemeanor.

TITLE 41. STATE GOVERNMENT.

CHAPTER 8. AGENCIES OF THE LEGISLATIVE DEPARTMENT.

Article 3. Department of Library, Archives and Public Records.

Citation: ARS 41-1344

✪ **§ 41-1344. Disagreement as to value of records.**

If the department of library, archives and public records determines, after consultation with the historical advisory commission, attorney general and auditor general, that any records in the custody of a public officer, other than a public officer of a county, municipality, district or other political subdivision, are of no legal, administrative, historical or other value, and the public officer having custody of the records or from whose office the records originated disagrees with the determination and opposes disposal of the records, the department may request the governor to make his determination as to whether the records should be disposed of in the interests of conservation of space, economy or safety.

Citation: ARS 41-1346

✪ **§ 41-1346. State and local public records management; definition; violation; classification.**

A. The head of each state and local agency shall:

1. Establish and maintain an active, continuing program for the economical and efficient management of the public records of the agency.

2. Make and maintain records containing adequate and proper documentation of the organization, functions, policies,

decisions, procedures and essential transactions of the agency designed to furnish information to protect the rights of the state and of persons directly effected by the agency's activities.

3. Submit to the director of the department of library, archives and public records, in accordance with established standards, schedules proposing the length of time each record series warrants retention for administrative, legal or fiscal purposes after it has been received by the agency.

4. Submit a list of public records in the agency's custody that are not needed in the transaction of current business and that are not considered to have sufficient administrative, legal or fiscal value to warrant their inclusion in established disposal schedules.

5. Submit to the director of the department of library, archives and public records lists of all essential pubic records in the custody of the agency.

6. Cooperate with the director of the department of library, archives and public records in the conduct of surveys.

7. Designate an individual within the agency to manage the records management program of the agency. The designated individual:

(a) Must be at a level of management sufficient to direct the records management program in an effective manner.

(b) Shall act as coordinator and liaison for the agency with the records management division of the department of library, archives and public records.

8. Comply with rules, regulations, standards and procedures issued by the director of the department of library, archives and public records.

B. The governing body of each county, city, town, or other political subdivision shall promote the principles of efficient records management for local public records. Such governing body shall, as far as practicable, follow the program established for the management of state records. The director of the department of library, archives and public records shall, upon request of the governing body, provide advice and assistance in the establishment of a local public records management program.

C. As used in this section, "records management" means the creation and implementation of systematic controls for records and information activities from the point where they are created or received through final disposition or archival retention, including distribution, use, storage, retrieval, protection and preservation.

D. A head of a state or local agency who violates this section is guilty of a class 2 misdemeanor.

Citation: ARS 41-1347

✪ § 41-1347. Preservation of public records.

A. All records made or received by public officials of this state in the course of their public duties are the property of the state. Except as provided in this article, the director of the department of library, archives and public records and every other custodian of public records shall carefully protect and preserve the records from deterioration, mutilation, loss or destruction and, when advisable, shall cause them to be properly repaired and renovated. All paper, ink and other materials used in public offices for the purpose of permanent records shall be of durable quality.

B. Records shall not be destroyed or otherwise disposed of by any agency of the state, unless it is determined by the department that the record has not further administrative, legal, fiscal, research or historical value. The original of any record reproduced pursuant to the provisions of § 41-1348 may be determined by the department of have no further administrative, legal, fiscal, research or historical value.

Citation: ARS 41-1348

✪ § 41-1348. Production and reproduction of records by agencies of the state and political subdivisions; admissibility; violation; classification.

A. Each agency of the state or any of its political subdivisions may implement a program for the production or reproduction by photography or other method of reproduction on film or electronic media of records in its custody, whether obsolete or current, and classify, catalogue and index such records for convenient reference. Such agency, prior to the institution of any such program of production or reproduction, shall obtain approval from the director of the department of library, archives and pubic records of the types of records to be produced or reproduced and of the methods of production, reproduction and storage and the equipment which the agency proposes to use in connection with the production, reproduction and storage.

B. Except as otherwise provided by law, records reproduced as provided in subsection A of this section are admissible in evidence.

C. The provisions of this section shall not be applicable to permit destruction of current original affidavits of registration as that term is used in § 16-163.

D. A head of an agency of this state or a political subdivision of this state who violates this section is guilty of a class 2 misdemeanor.

Citation: ARS 41-1350

✪ § 41-1350. Definition of records.

In this chapter, unless the context otherwise requires, "records" means all books, papers, maps, photographs, or other documentary materials, regardless of physical form or characteristics, including prints or copies of such items produced or reproduced on film or electronic media pursuant to § 41-1348, made or received by any governmental agency in pursuance of law or in connection with the transaction of public business and preserved or appropriate for preservation by the agency or its legitimate successor as evidence of the organization, functions, policies, decisions, procedures, operations or other activities of the government, or because of the informational and historical value of the data contained therein. Library or museum material made or acquired solely for reference or exhibition purposes, extra copies of documents preserved only for convenience of reference and stocks of publications or documents intended for sale or distribution to interested persons are not included within the definition of records as used in this chapter.

Source: Arizona Rules of Evidence

ARTICLE X. CONTENTS OF WRITINGS, RECORDINGS, AND PHOTOGRAPHS

☞ Rule 1001. Definitions

For purposes of this article the following definitions are applicable:

(1) *Writings and recordings.* — "Writings" and "recordings" consist of letters, words, or numbers, or their equivalent, set down by handwriting, typewriting, printing, photostating, photographing, magnetic impulse, mechanical or electronic recording, or other form of data compilation.

(2) *Photographs.* — "Photographs" include still photographs, X-ray films, video tapes, and motion pictures.

(3) *Original.* — An "original" of a writing or recording is the writing or recording itself or any counterpart intended to have the same effect by a person executing or issuing it. An "original" of a photograph includes the negative or any print therefrom. If data are stored in a computer or similar device, any printout or other output readable by sight, shown to reflect the data accurately, is an "original".

(4) *Duplicate.* — A "duplicate" is a counterpart produced by the same impression as the original, or from the same matrix, or by means of photography, including enlargements and miniatures, or by mechanical or electronic re-recording, or by chemical reproduction, or by other equivalent techniques which accurately reproduces the original.

☞ Rule 1003. Admissibility of Duplicates.

A duplicate is admissible to the same extent as an original unless (1) a genuine question is raised as to the authenticity of the original or (2) in the circumstances it would be unfair to admit the duplicate in lieu of the original.

[See Appendix A. Uniform Rules of Evidence for additional provisions.]

State: Arkansas
Source: Arkansas Code Annotated

TITLE 13. LIBRARIES, ARCHIVES, AND CULTURAL RESOURCES.

CHAPTER 4. PUBLIC RECORDS MANAGEMENT AND ARCHIVES.

Subchapter 1. General Provisions.

Citation: ACA 13-4-104

✪ § 13-4-104. Title to records.

(a) Agency records are hereby declared to be the property of the people of this state, and they shall not be stolen, expropriated, alienated, secreted, nor destroyed except as provided in this subchapter.

(b) Records shall be preserved, stored, transferred, destroyed, or otherwise disposed of only in accordance with the provisions of this subchapter.

(c)(1) Title to all current, semicurrent, and noncurrent records in the physical possession of an agency or those stored in a records center maintained by the state shall be vested in the agency.

(2) Title to all archives in the physical possession of the Arkansas History Commission shall be vested in the Arkansas History Commission.

(d)(1) Nothing in this subchapter shall be construed as in contravention of or in conflict with, nor as broadening or expanding, existing or subsequently enacted laws guaranteeing to the people of this state the rights of freedom of information or of public access to the records of the state.

(2) No current, semicurrent, or noncurrent records in the custody of any agency or in the state archives shall be designated, classified, regarded, or treated as confidential or as closed to public access, except in accordance with law.

(e) All records which by the laws of this state are declared to be confidential or restricted to specified use only shall not be open to the public except in the manner provided by law.

Citation: ACA 13-4-105

✪ § 13-4-105. State Records Commission created.

(a) There is hereby created a State Records Commission to be composed of the following members:

(1) The Governor, or his designee;

(2) The Secretary of State, or his designee;

(3) The Attorney General, or his designee;

(4)The Commissioner of State Lands, or his desingee;

(5) The Chief Justice of the Arkansas Supreme Court, or his designee;

(6) The Director of the Department of Finance and Administration, or his designee;

(7) The Director of the Department of Arkansas Heritage, or his designee;

(8) The State Historian, or his designee;

(9) The President of the Arkansas Historical Association, or designee; and

(10) One (1) member of the general public, who shall be appointed by and serve at the pleasure of the Governor.

(b)(1)(A) The commission shall elect from its membership a chair and such other officers as needed for the transaction of its business.

(B) The records manager shall serve as secretary of the commission but shall not have a vote.

(2) The commission shall meet at least once every three (3) months but may meet more often at the call of the chair.

(3) The commission shall establish rules and procedures for the conduct of its business.

(4) Members of the commission shall serve without compensation but may, to the extent moneys are appropriated therefor and subject to limitations established by the Department of Finance and Administration for reimbursement of state employees, be reimbursed for actual reasonable expenses incurred in the performance of their official duties.

(c)(1) The commission shall promulgate rules and regulations to establish standards for the State Records Management and Archives Program.

(2) The areas in which standards shall be developed shall include, but are not limited to, retention schedules for the control, preservation, protection, retention, and disposition of the records of agencies.

(3) In developing retention schedules, the commission shall determine from the State Historian which records are of archival value. Such records shall be transferred to the Arkansas History Commission.

Citation: ACA 13-4-106

✪ § 13-4-106. State Records Management and Archives Program created.

(a) There is hereby established a State Records Management and Archives Program.

(b) The program shall:

(1) Include a designation by the State Records Commission of those records which are to be maintained and preserved by agency officials; and

(2) May include the designation of such records centers as shall, from time to time, be required for the storage of semicurrent and noncurrent records of the agencies when the records have been scheduled for retention and disposal in the manner hereinafter provided.

(c)(1) There is hereby established an Office of Records Management within the Department of Finance and Administration under the direction of a records manager, who shall administer the State Records Management Program under the direction of the Director of the Department of Finance and Administration.

(2) The Office of Records Management shall administer the State Records Management and Archives Program and work with agencies to facilitate compliance with the provisions of this subchapter and the rules promulgated by the State Records Commission.

(d) The State Records Commission shall act in an advisory capacity to the Office of Records Management.

Subchapter 2. Electronic Court Records.

Citation: ACA 13-4-201

✪ § 13-4-201. Electronic reproduction of court records.

The circuit clerks, county clerks, and any public officers whose duty it is to make and maintain court records are authorized to use and employ an approved system of photographic recording, photostatic recording, microfilm, microcard, miniature photographic recording, digital compact disc, optical disc, and other processes which accurately reproduce or form a durable medium for reproducing the original.

Citation: ACA 13-4-202

✪ § 13-4-202. Requirements for format and storage of records.

When equipment necessary for such methods of recording is used to record court records, it shall meet all of the following requirements:

(1) The information retained shall be in a usable and accessible format capable of accurately reproducing the original over the time periods specified in § 13-10-101 et seq.;

(2) Operational procedures shall ensure that the authenticity, confidentiality, accuracy, reliability, and appropriate level of security are provided to safeguard the integrity of the information.

(3) Procedures shall be available for the backup, recovery, and storage of records to protect of those records against media destruction or deterioration and information loss; and

(4) A retention conversion-review schedule shall be established to ensure that electronically or optically stored information is reviewed for data conversion or recertification at least once every five (5) years or more frequently when necessary to prevent the physical loss of data or technological obsolescence of the medium.

Subchapter 3. County Records Retention.

Citation: ACA 13-4-301

✪ § 13-4-301. Retention required — Destruction.

(a) All counties of the State of Arkansas shall maintain the records named in this subchapter for the period of time provided for herein, after which time the records may be destroyed, but in no case shall said records be destroyed until at least one (1) year after an audit by the Division of Legislative Audit or any private auditor is completed and approved.

(b) No record of any kind over fifty (50) years old will be destroyed before written notice by the custodian of the records in question has been furnished to the Arkansas History Commission, describing the scope and nature of said records, at least sixty (60) days prior to the destruction of the records.

(c) Before any record shall be destroyed, the custodian of the record shall document the date and type of document.

(d) If a record is photgraphically transferred to other media of a permanent nature, the original documents may be destroyed.

TITLE 14. LOCAL GOVERNMENT.

SUBTITLE 1. GENERAL PROVISIONS.

CHAPTER 2. PUBLIC RECORDS GENERALLY.

Subchapter 1. General Provisions.

Citation: ACA 14-2-201

✪ § 14-2-201. Authority — Requirements.

(a) The head of any county or municipal department, commission, bureau, or board may cause any or all records kept by the official, department, commission, or board to be photographed, microfilmed, photostated, or reproduced on film.

(b) At the time of reproduction, the agency head shall attach his certificate to the record certifying that it is the original record, and the certificate shall be reproduced with the original.

(c)(1) The film or reproducing material shall be of durable material.

(2) The device used to reproduce the records on the film or material shall be such as to accurately reproduce and perpetuate the original records in all details.

Citation: ACA 14-2-202

✪ § 14-2-202. Copy of record — Admissibility.

(a) A photostatic copy, photograph, microfilm, or photographic film of original records shall be deemed to be an original record for all purposes and shall be admissible in evidence in all courts or administrative agencies.

(b) For all purposes recited in this section, a facsimile, exemplification, or certified copy thereof shall be deemed to be a transcript, exemplification, or certified copy of the original.

Citation: ACA 14-2-203

✪ § 14-2-203. Disposal, etc. of copied records.

Whenever photostatic copies, photographs, microfilms, or reproductions on films of public records shall be placed in conveniently accessible files and provision made for preserving, examining, and using them, the head of a county office or department or city office or department may certify those facts to the county court or to the mayor of a municipality, respectively, who shall have the power to authorize the disposal, archival storage, or destruction of the records.

Citation: ACA 14-19-250

✪ § 14-19-250. Reproduction and preservation of public records, other than court records; minimum standards.

The board of county commissioners in any county in the state may, by resolution, provide for and authorize any officer of the county to photograph, microphotograph or reproduce or to have photographed, microphotographed or reproduced on film any of the records, papers or documents which are by law placed in the custody and control of such officer, except court records, and to acquire necessary facilities and equipment, and to acquire, maintain and use all such appropriate containers and files as shall be necessary to accommodate and preserve the photographs, microphotographs or films so obtained. Such photographing, microphotographing or filming may be so authorized for the reproducing of lists and records in the usual day by official activities of any such officer, where to do so will greatly promote efficiency in the office, or as a method of preserving old or work records, papers or documents. The photographic film and prints or reproductions therefrom shall comply with federal standard No. 125a, dated April 24, 1958, or the latest revision thereof, issued pursuant to the federal property and administrative services act of 1949, and any amendments thereto, and the devices used to reproduce such records on such film shall be one which accurately reproduces the original thereof in all details.

TITLE 16. PRACTICE, PROCEDURE, AND COURTS.

SUBTITLE 4. EVIDENCE AND WITNESSES.

CHAPTER 41. UNIFORM RULES OF EVIDENCE.

ARTICLE X. CONTENTS OF WRITINGS, RECORDINGS, AND PHOTOGRAPHS.

☞ Rule 1001. Definitions

For purposes of this article the following definitions are applicable:

(1) *Writings and recordings.* — "Writings" and "recordings" consist of letters, words, or numbers, or their equivalent, set down by handwriting, typewriting, printing, photostating, photographing, magnetic impulse, mechanical or electronic recording, or other form of data compilation.

(2) *Photographs.* — "Photographs" include still photographs, X-ray films, video tapes, and motion pictures.

(3) *Original.* — An "original" of a writing or recording is the writing or recording itself or any counterpart intended to have the same effect by a person executing or issuing it. An "original" of a photograph includes the negative or any print therefrom. If data are stored in a computer or similar device, any printout or other output readable by sight, shown to reflect the data accurately, is an "original".

(4) *Duplicate.* — A "duplicate" is a counterpart produced by the same impression as the original, or from the same matrix, or by means of photography, including enlargements and miniatures, or by mechanical or electronic re-recording, or by chemical reproduction, or by other equivalent techniques which accurately reproduces the original.

☞ Rule 1003. Admissibility of duplicates.

A duplicate is admissible to the same extent as an original unless

(1) a genuine question is raised as to the authenticity or continuing effectiveness of the original or (2) in the circumstances it would be unfair to admit the duplicate in lieu of the original.

[See Appendix A. Uniform Rules of Evidence for additional provisions.]

CHAPTER 46. DOCUMENTARY EVIDENCE GENERALLY.

Citation: ACA 16-46-101

☞ § 16-46-101. Recordation of certain certified copies — Photographic copies of business and public records.

(a)(1) The clerk of any court of record may record any certified copy of any instrument by attaching the certified copy to his record book so as to make the copy be and become a part of the record to the extent that the copy cannot be detached, and the copy shall be legally recorded when the attachment has been made by the clerk. This subdivision shall apply to plats, blueprints, and photostatic copies only.

(2)(A) The county recorders, clerks of court of record, and any public officer whose duty it is to make public records are authorized to use and employ an approved system of photographic recording, photostatic recording, microfilm, microcard, miniature photographic recording, optical disk, or other process which accurately reproduces or forms a durable medium for reproducing the original when provided with equipment necessary for such method of recording.

(B) When any document is recorded by the means prescribed by subdivision (a)(2)(A) of this section, the original may be destroyed unless its preservation is required by law.

(b)(1) If any business, institution, member of a profession or calling, or any department or agency of government, in the regular course of business or activity has kept or recorded any memorandum, writing, entry, print, representation, or combination thereof, of any act, transaction, occurrence, or event, and in the regular course of business has caused any or all of the same to be recorded, copied, or reproduced by any photographic, photostatic, microfilm, microcard, miniature photographic, optical disk, electronic imaging or other process which accurately reproduces or forms a durable medium for so reproducing the original, the original may be destroyed in the regular course of business unless its preservation is required by law.

(2) The reproduction, when satisfactorily identified, is as admissible in evidence as the original itself in any judicial or administrative proceeding whether the original is in existence or not.

(3) An enlargement of facsimile of the reproduction is likewise admissible in evidence if the original reproduction is in existence and available for inspection under direction of the court.

(4) The introduction of a reproduced record, enlargement, or facsimile does not preclude admission of the original.

TITLE 25. STATE GOVERNMENT.

CHAPTER 18. PUBLIC RECORDS.

Citation: ACA 25-18-101

✪ ✍ ☞ § 25-18-101. Reproduction of records generally.

(a) For the purposes of this section, "business" means and includes business, industry, profession, occupation, and calling of every kind.

(b)(1) The head of any business or head of any state, county, or municipal department, commission, bureau, or board may cause any or all records kept by the official, department, commission board, or business to be photographed, microfilmed, photostated, or reproduced on film. At the time of reproduction, he shall attach his certificate to the record certifying that it is the original record, and the certificate shall be reproduced with the original.

(2) The film or reproducing material shall be of durable material, and the device used to reproduce records on the film or

material shall be such as to accurately reproduce and perpetuate the original records in all details.

(c)(1) The photostatic copy. photograph, microfilm, or photographic film of the original records shall be deemed to be an original record for all purposes and shall be admissible in all courts or administrative agencies.

(2) A facsimile, exemplification, or certified copy of a record for all purposes recited in this subsection (c) shall be deemed to be a transcript, exemplification, or certified copy of the original.

(d) Whenever photostatic copies, photographs, microfilms, or reproductions on films of public records kept by a state official, department, commission, or board shall be placed in conveniently accessible files, and provision made for preserving, examining, and using them, the head of the state department, commission, bureau, or board may certify those facts to the Governor, who shall have the power to authorize the disposal, archival storage, or destruction of the records or papers.

Citation: ACA 25-18-102

✪ § 25-18-102. Microfilming of records by Secretary of State.

(a) The Secretary of State is authorized and empowered to proceed to have microfilmed any state records and documents which, in his opinion, with the advice of the State Board of Finance and the heads of the various state departments, may be of the most importance from an historical and legal point of view.

(b) The microfilm records shall be properly indexed and placed in a fire-proof vault which will be available to all department heads, officials, employees, and the public. The operator-supervisor is directed to place the microfilm record of all state documents or records on the microfilm reader machine for the use of any citizens, officials, or employees of the state at their request.

(c) The Secretary of State is charged with the general direction of this microfilming program, provided the Governor may, by proclamation, transfer these duties to some other official or department.

Source: Arkansas Regulations
Agency: Department of Finance and Administration

Citation: AR GR-80

✍ § GR-80. Taxpayer to keep adequate records — Preservation of records — Estimated assessment:

A. It is the duty of every taxpayer to keep and preserve suitable records as are necessary to determine the proper amount of tax due. These records may consist of the following: sales invoices, sales tickets, sales billings, credit memoranda, cash register tapes, beginning and ending inventory records, purchase invoices, refund slips, and other records as will substantiate and prove the accuracy of the returns required to be filed. Records may be microfilmed or microfiched. However, proper facilities are to be provided for the ready inspection including machines for viewing and copying the records necessary to determine the proper amount of tax due.

B. All such records shall be preserved for a period of six years and shall be subject to examination by the Commissioner at any reasonable time.

C. In the event that such records are kept outside of the State of Arkansas in the usual course of business they shall be produced within the State of Arkansas upon proper demand by the Commissioner within a period of fifteen days after receipt of such demand.

D. If a taxpayer fails to preserve and maintain such records required by this regulation, the Commissioner may make an estimated assessment based upon information available to him as to the amount of tax due by the taxpayer. The burden of proof of refuting this estimated assessment is upon the taxpayer.

State: California
Source: Corporations Code

TITLE 1. CORPORATIONS.

DIVISION 2. NONPROFIT CORPORATIONS LAW.

PART 2. NONPROFIT PUBLIC BENEFIT CORPORATIONS.

CHAPTER 13. RECORDS, REPORTS AND RIGHTS OF INSPECTION.

Article 1. General Provisions.

Citation: CC 6310

✍ § 6310. Records; availability in written form.

If any record subject to inspection pursuant to this chapter is not maintained in written form, a request for inspection is not complied with unless and until the corporation at its expense makes such record available in written form. For the purposes of this chapter "written" or "in writing" also includes cathode ray tube and similar electronic communications methods.

Article 2. Required Records, Reports to Directors and Members

Citation: CC 6320

✍ § 6320. Books and records.

(a) Each corporation shall keep:

(1) Adequate and correct books and records of account;

(2) Minutes of the proceedings of its members, board and committees of the board; and

(3) A records of its members giving their names and addresses and the class of each membership held by each.

(b) Minutes shall be kept in written form. Other books and records shall be kept either in written form or in any other form capable of being converted into written form.

Source: Evidence Code

DIVISION 11. WRITINGS.

CHAPTER 2. SECONDARY EVIDENCE OF WRITINGS.

Article 1. Best Evidence Rule.

Citation: EC 1500.5

☞ § 1500.5. Printed representation of computer information or computer program used by or stored on computer or computer readable storage media; admissibility of evidence; presumption; burden of proof.

(a) Notwithstanding the provisions of Section 1500, a printed representation of computer information or a computer program which is being used by or stored on a computer or computer readable storage media shall be admissible to prove the existence and content of the computer information or computer program.

(b) Computer recorded information or computer programs, or copies of computer recorded information or computer programs, shall not be rendered inadmissible by the best evidence rule.

(c) Printed representations of computer information and computer programs will be presumed to be accurate representations of the computer information or computer programs that they purport to represent. This presumption, however, will be a presumption affecting the burden of producing evidence only. If any party to a judicial proceeding introduces evidence that such a printed representation is inaccurate or unreliable, the party introducing it into evidence will have the burden of proving, by a preponderance of evidence, that the printed representation is the best available evidence of the existence and content of the computer information or computer programs that it purports to represent.

(d) Subdivision (c) shall not apply to computer-generated official records certified in accordance with Section 452.5 or 1530.

Citation: EC 1511

☞ § 1511. Duplicates; admissibility.

A duplicate is admissible to the same extent as an original unless (a) a genuine question is raised as to the authenticity of the original or (b) in the circumstances it would be unfair to admit the duplicate in lieu of the original.

Article 3. Photographic Copies of Writings.

Citation: EC 1550

☞ § 1550. Photographic copies made as business records.

A nonerasable optical image reproduction provided that additions, deletions, or changes to the original document are not permitted by the technology, photostatic, microfilm, microcard, miniature photographic or other photographic copy or reproduction, or an enlargement thereof, of a writing is as admissible as the writing itself if the copy or reproduction was made and preserved as a part of the records of a business (as defined by Section 1270) in the regular course of that business. The introduction of the copy, reproduction, or enlargement does not preclude admission of the original writing if it is still in existence. A court may require the introduction of a hard copy printout of that document.

Citation: EC 1551

☞ § 1551. Photographic copies where original destroyed or lost.

A print, whether enlarged or not, from a photographic film (including a photographic plate, microphotographic film, photostatic negative, or similar reproduction) of an original writing destroyed or lost after such film was taken or a reproduction from an electronic recording of video images on magnetic surfaces is admissible as the original writing itself if, at the time of the taking of such film or electronic recording, the person under whose direction and control it was taken attached thereto, or to the sealed container in which it was placed and has been kept, or incorporated in the film or electronic recording, a certification complying with the provisions of Section 1531 and stating the date on which, and the fact that, it was so taken under his direction and control.

Source: Government Code

TITLE 2. GOVERNMENT OF THE STATE OF CALIFORNIA

DIVISION 3. EXECUTIVE DEPARTMENT

PART 2. CONSTITUTIONAL OFFICERS

CHAPTER 3. SECRETARY OF STATE.

Article 2. Duties.

Citation: GC 12164.5

✪ § 12164.5. Articles of incorporation and other corporate records, microphotographic film.

The Secretary of State may cause to be returned to the corporation to which they relate, or to be destroyed, the articles of incorporation and other corporate records filed in his office by any corporation, domestic or foreign, if the Secretary of State complies with both of the following requirements:

(a) He maintains for the use of the public a microphotographic film print or copy of each document, record, instrument, or paper so returned or destroyed, prepared in accordance with the procedure specified in Sections 1551 and 1531 of the Evidence Code.

(b) He promptly seals and stores at least one original negative of each such microphotographic film in such manner and place as reasonably to assure its preservation indefinitely against loss, theft, defacement, or destruction.

PART 5.5. DEPARTMENT OF GENERAL SERVICES

CHAPTER 5. STATE RECORDS

Article 4. Disposal of Records

Citation: GC 14756

✪ § 14756. Microfilming of public records; Certification.

The public records of any state agency may be microfilmed, electronically data imaged, or otherwise photographically reproduced and certified upon the written authorization of the head of the agency. The microfilming, electronic data imaging, or photographic reproduction shall be made in compliance with the minimum standards or guidelines, or both, as recommended by the American National Standards Institute or the Association of Information and Image Management for recording of permanent records or nonpermanent records, whichever applies.

The certification of each reproduction or set of reproductions shall be in accordance with the standards, or have the approval, of the Attorney General. The certification shall contain a statement of the identity, description, and disposition or location of the records reproduced, the date, reason, and authorization for such reproduction, and such other information as the Attorney General requires.

The certified reproductions shall be deemed to be original public records for all purposes, including introduction in courts of law and state agencies.

TITLE 3. GOVERNMENT OF COUNTIES

DIVISION 2. OFFICERS

PART 2. BOARD OF SUPERVISORS.

CHAPTER 1. ORGANIZATION.

Article 6. Clerk of the Board.

Citation: GC 25105

✪ § 25105. Reproduction of board records; Minimum standards.

The board of supervisors may authorize the use of photographs, microphotographs, electronic data-processing records, optical disks, or any other medium which does not permit additions, deletions, or changes to the original document, or photocopies of all records, books and minutes of the board.

(a) Each photograph, microphotographic, or photocopy shall be made in a manner and on paper which will comply with the minimum standards or guidelines, or both, as recommended by the American National Standards Institute or the Association for Information and Image Management for recording of permanent records or nonpermanent records, whichever applies. Every reproduction shall be deemed and considered a transcript, exemplification, or certified copy, as the case may be, of the original. Each roll of microfilm shall be deemed and constitute a book and shall be designated and numbered, and provision shall be made for preserving, examining, and using it. A duplicate of each roll of microfilm shall be made and kept in a safe and separate place.

(b) Electronic data-processing records, records recorded on optical disks, and records recorded on any other medium shall comply with the minimum standards or guidelines, or both, as recommended by the American National Standards Institute or the Association for Information and Image Management. A duplicate copy of any authorized record reproduced in compliance with the minimum standards or guidelines, or both, as recommended by the American National Standards Institute or the Association for Information and Image Management for recording of permanent or nonpermanent records, whichever applies, shall be deemed an original.

(c) In the event the authorization provided herein is granted, the personal signatures required by § 25103 may be produced by the authorized process, and the reproduced signatures shall be deemed to satisfy the requirement of § 25103.

CHAPTER 13. MISCELLANEOUS POWERS.

Citation: GC 26205

✪ § 26205. Destruction of records on request of county officer.

At the request of the county officer concerned, the board of supervisors of any county may authorize the destruction of any record, paper, or document which is not expressly required by law to be filed and preserved if all of the following conditions are complied with:

(a) The record, paper, or document is photographed, microphotographed, reproduced by electronically recorded video images on magnetic surfaces, recorded in the electronic data-processing system, recorded on optical disk, or reproduced on film or any other medium which does not permit additions, deletions, or changes to the original document of and is produced in compliance with the minimum standards or guidelines, or both, of the American National Standards Institute or the Association for Information and Image Management for recording of permanent records or nonpermanent records, whichever applies.

(b) The device used to reproduce the record, paper, or document on film, optical disk, or any other medium is one which accurately reproduces the original thereof in all details and which does not permit additions, deletions, or changes to the original document images.

(c) The photographs, microphotographs, electronically recorded video images on magnetic surfaces, records in the electronic data-processing system, records recorded on optical disk, or other reproductions on film or any other medium are place in conveniently accessible files and provision is made for preserving, examining, and using the files.

Notwithstanding any other provision of this section, destruction of the original records, papers, or documents is not authorized when the method of reproduction pursuant to this section is reproduction of electronically recorded video images on magnetic surfaces unless a duplicate videotape of the images is separately maintained. A duplicate copy of a record contained in the electronic data-processing system, on optical disk, or on any other medium which does not permit additions, deletions, or changes to the original document images shall also be separately maintained.

Citation: GC 26205.1

✪ § 26205.1. Destruction of records and other documents upon resolution of board of supervisors.

(a) The county officer having custody of nonjudicial public records, documents, instruments, books, and papers may cause to be destroyed any or all of the records, documents, instruments, books, and papers if all of the following conditions exist:

(1) The board of supervisors of the county has adopted a resolution authorizing the county officer to destroy records, documents, instruments, books, and papers pursuant to this subdivision. The resolution may impose such conditions, in addition to those specified in this subdivision, which the board of supervisors determines are appropriate.

(2) The county officer who destroys any record, document, instrument, book, or paper pursuant to the authority granted by this subdivision and a resolution of the board of supervisors adopted pursuant to paragraph (1) shall maintain for the use of the public a photographic or microphotographic film, electronic recorded video reproduction, a record contained in the electronic data-processing system, a record recorded on optical disk, a record recorded by any other medium which does not permit additions, deletions, or changes to the original document, or other duplicate of the record, document, instrument, book, or paper destroyed.

(3) The record, paper, or document is photographed, microphotographed, reproduced by electronically recorded video images on magnetic surfaces, recorded in the electronic data-processing system, recorded on optical disk or reproduced on film or any other medium which does not permit additions, deletions, or changes to the original document and is produced in compliance with the minimum standards of guidelines, or both, as recommended by the American National Standards Institute or the Association for Information and Image Management for recording of permanent records or nonpermanent records, whichever applies.

(b) Paragraphs (2) and 3 of subdivision (a) does not apply to records prepared or received other than pursuant to a state statute or county charter, or records which are not expressly required by law to be filed and preserved.

For the purposes of this section, every reproduction shall be deemed to be an original record and a transcript, exemplification, or certified copy of any reproduction shall be deemed to be a transcript, exemplification, or certified copy, as the case may be, of the original.

(c) The county clerk having custody of the original or a copy of the articles of any corporation may cause the destruction of any or all the documents. "Articles" includes the articles of incorporation, amendments thereto, amended articles, restated articles, certificate of incorporation, certificates of determination of preferences, dissolution certificates, merger certificates, and agreements of consolidation to merger.

(d) Notwithstanding any other provision of this section, destruction of the original records, papers, or documents is not authorized when the method of reproduction pursuant to this section is reproduction of electronically recorded video images on magnetic surfaces unless a duplicate video tape of the images is separately maintained. A duplicate copy of a record contained in the electronic data-processing system, on optical disk, or on any other medium which does not permit additions, deletions, or changes to the original document shall also be separately maintained.

Citation: GC 26205.5

✪ **§ 26205.5. Destruction of records on request of county recorder.**

At the request of the county recorder, the board of supervisors of any county may authorize the destruction of any or all of the filed papers or record books created by handwriting, typing on printed forms, by typewriting, or by photographic methods, in the recorder's official custody, if all of the following conditions are complied with:

(a) The record, paper, or document is photographed, microphotographed, reproduced by electronically recorded video images on magnetic surfaces, recorded in the electronic data-processing system, recorded on optical disk, reproduced on film or any other medium which does not permit additions, deletions, or changes to the original document, or reproduced under the direction and control of the county recorder on film, optical disk, or any other medium in compliance with the minimum standards or guidelines or both, as recommended by the American National Standards Institute or the Association for Information and Image Management for recording of permanent records or nonpermanent records, whichever applies.

(b) The device used to reproduce the record, paper, or document on film, optical disk, or any other medium is one which accurately and legibly reproduces the original thereof in all details; and which does not permit additions, deletions, or changes to the original document images.

(c) The photographs, microphotographs, or other reproductions on film, optical disk, or any other medium are made as accessible for public reference as the original records were.

(d) A true copy of the archival quality of the film, optical disk, or other medium reproductions shall be kept in a safe and separate place for security purposes.

However, no page of any record, paper, or document shall be destroyed if any page cannot be reproduced on film with full legibility. Every unreproducible page shall be permanently preserved in a manner that will afford easy reference.

For the purposes of this section, every reproduction shall be deemed to be an original record and a transcript, exemplification, or certified copy of any reproduction shall be deemed to be a transcript, exemplification, or certified copy, as the case may be, of the original.

PART 3. OTHER OFFICERS

CHAPTER 5. COUNTRY TREASURER

Article 1. Duties Generally

Citation: GC 27002.1

✪ **§ 27002.1. Photographic records of receipts and expenditures.**

(a) The treasurer may, in lieu of entering in books an account of the receipt and expenditure of all money received or paid out by him or her as provided in Section 27002, photograph, microphotograph, photocopy, or enter into an electric data processing system that utilizes optical transmission and filing, all receipts for money received by him or her and all warrants paid out by him or her.

(b) Every reproduction described in subdivision (a)shall be deemed and considered an original; and a transcript, exemplification, or certified copy of any of those reproductions shall be deemed and considered a transcript, exemplification, or certified copy, as the case may be, of the original.

(c) All reproductions described in subdivision (a) shall be properly indexed and placed in convenient, accessible files. Each roll of microfilm shall be deemed and constitute a book, and shall be designated and numbered, and provision shall be made for preserving, examining and using it.

A duplicate of each roll of microfilm shall be made and kept in a safe and separate place.

CHAPTER 6. RECORDERS.

Article 1. Duties Generally.

Citation: GC 27206

✪ **§ 27206. Federal tax liens; releases; destruction; microfilm copy of unreleased liens.**

The county recorder may destroy federal tax liens together with any release of said liens eight years after the lien was filed in his office; provided, a microfilm copy of each unreleased tax lien has been made and certified in the manner provided for in Section 1551 of the Evidence Code. All film used in the microphotography process shall comply with the minimum standards of quality approved by the United States Bureau of Standards. The original copy of the microfilm shall be kept in a safe and separate place for security purposes.

Article 4. Recording.

Citation: GC 27322.2

✪ **§ 27322.2. Use of systems as photographic reproduction process to record.**

A system of microphotography, optical disk, or reproduction by any other technique which does not permit additions, deletions, or changes to the original document may be used by the recorder as a photographic reproduction process to record some or all instruments, papers and notices that are required or permitted by law to be recorded or filed. All reproductions shall be made in compliance with the minimum standards or guidelines, or both, as recommended by the American National Standards Institute or the Association for Information and Image Management. A true copy of the document shall be kept in a safe and separate place which will reasonably assure its preservation for the duration of the retention prescribed by law against loss or destruction. A true copy of the document shall be arranged in a suitable place in the office of the recorder to facilitate public inspection.

Citation: 27322.3

✪ **§ 27322.3. Type of record books where microfilming used.**

If the recorded instruments or the record books in the office of the recorder have been microfilmed for preservation purposes, a type of record book may be used which will permit the removal of leaves in order that reproduction may be made in an efficient manner.

In order to microfilm or otherwise reproduce the record books for preservation purposes, permanently bound record books may be disassembled and after they have been copies such books shall be rebound in a type of record books which will permit the removal of leaves in order that reproduction may be made in an efficient manner.

Citation: GC 27322.4

✪ **§ 27322.4. Microphotography; files and records; reproduction deemed original.**

The county recorder may cause any or all files or records in his or her official custody to be microphotographed or otherwise reproduced pursuant to Section 27322.2 as in the case of original filings or recordings or both. Every reproduction shall be deemed and considered an original; and a transcript, exemplification or certified copy, as the case may be, of the original.

Citation: GC 27323

✪ **§ 27323. Segregation of instruments, etc., or recordation in one seres of books or films.**

The recorder may segregate the instruments, papers, and notices and record them in separate books, or sheets or rolls of film under titles of indices provided for in Article 2 of this chapter.

In lieu thereof the recorder may record any or all of the instruments, papers or notices in one general series of books or film to be called "official records." The series shall be numbered consecutively beginning with number one. The recording of instruments in "official records" imparts notice in like manner and effect as if the instruments were recorded in separate books or film.

If a system of microphotography is used to record any instruments, papers or notices, each original roll of film thereof kept by the recorder shall be given a separate number, and shall be called a "book," "film," "reel," or shall be similarly designated, and each page of such instrument paper or notice shall be similarly designated, and each page of such instrument, paper or notice shall be called a "page," "image" or similar designation. Whenever under any law it is required that an instrument, paper, or notice be identified or referred to as recorded in a book or page or both, it shall be sufficient for purposes of identification and of compliance with such law that reference be made to such instrument, paper, or notice by the designation adopted by the recorder pursuant to the provisions of this section.

TITLE 4. GOVERNMENT OF CITIES.

DIVISION 1. CITIES GENERALLY.

CHAPTER 1. GENERAL.

Article 4. Miscellaneous.

Citation: GC 34090

✪ **§ 34090. Destruction of city records; excepted records; construction.**

Unless otherwise provided by law, with the approval of the legislative body by resolution and the written consent of the city attorney the head of a city department may destroy any city record, document, instrument, book or paper, under his charge, without making a copy thereof, after the same is not longer required.

This section does not authorize the destruction of:

(a) Records affecting the title to real property or liens thereon.

(b) Court records.

(c) Records required to be kept by statute.

(d) Records less than two years old.

(e) The minutes, ordinances, or resolutions of the legislative body or of a city board or commission.

This section shall not be construed as limiting or qualifying in any manner the authority provided in Section 34090.5 for the destruction of record, documents, instruments, books and papers in accordance with the procedure therein prescribed.

Citation: GC 34090.5

✪ **§ 34090.5. Destruction of records; conditions.**

Notwithstanding the provisions of Section 34090, the city officer having custody of public records, documents, instruments, books, and papers, may, without the approval of the legislative body or the written consent of the city attorney, cause to be destroyed any or all of the records, documents, instruments, books, and papers, if all of the following conditions are complied with.

(a) The record, paper, or document is photographed, microphotographed, reproduced, by electronically recorded video images on magnetic surfaces, recorded in the electronic data-processing system, recorded on optical disk, reproduced on film or any other medium which does not permit additions, deletions, or changes to the original document, or reproduced on film, optical disk, or any other medium in compliance with the minimum standards or guidelines, or both, as recommended by the American National Standards Institute or the Association for Information and Image Management for recording of permanent records or nonpermanent records, whichever applies.

(b) The device used to reproduce the record, paper, or document on film, optical disk, or any other medium is one which accurately and legibly reproduces the original thereof in all details and which does not permit additions, deletions, or changes to the original document images.

(c) The photographs, microphotographs, or other reproductions on film, optical disk, or any other medium are made as accessible for public reference as the original records were.

(d) A true copy of archival quality of the film, optical disk, or any other medium reproductions shall be kept in a safe and separate place for security purposes.

However, no page of any record, paper, or document shall be destroyed if any page cannot be reproduced on film with full legibility. Every unreproducible page shall be permanently preserved in a manner that will afford easy reference.

For the purposes of this section, every reproduction shall be deemed to be an original record and a transcript, exemplification, or certified copy of any reproduction shall be deemed to be a transcript, exemplification, or certified copy, as the case may be, of the original.

Citation: GC 34090.7

✪ § 34090.7. Duplicate records less than two years old; destruction; video recording media.

Notwithstanding the provisions of Section 34090, the legislative body of a city may prescribe a procedure under which duplicates of city record less than two years old may be destroyed if they are no longer required.

For purposes of this section, video recording mediums, such as videotapes and films, shall be considered duplicate records if the city keeps another record, such as written minutes or an audio tape recording, of the event which is recorded in the video medium. However, a video recording medium shall not be destroyed or erased pursuant to this section for a period of at least 90 days after occurrence of the event recorded thereon.

TITLE 6. DISTRICTS.

DIVISION 1. GENERAL.

CHAPTER 7. DESTRUCTION OF RECORDS OF SPECIAL DISTRICTS.

Citation: GC 60200

✪ § 60200. Duplicate records, papers, or documents.

The legislative body of any special district may authorize at any time the destruction or disposition of any duplicate record, paper, or document, the original or a permanent photographic record of which is in the files of any officer or department of the district.

Citation: GC 60201

✪ § 60201. Records, papers or documents more than two years old and prepared or received other than pursuant to statute.

The legislative body of a district may authorize the destruction or disposition of any record, paper, or document which is more than two years old and which was prepared or received in any manner other than pursuant to state statute. Such records, papers, or documents need not be photographed, reproduced, or microfilmed prior to destruction and no copy thereof need be retained.

Citation: GC 60203

✪ § 60203. Records, papers, or documents to be filed; conditions.

The legislative body of a district may authorize the destruction of any record, paper, or document which is not expressly required by law to be filed and preserved if all of the following conditions are complied with:

(a) The record, paper, or document is photographed, microphotographed, reproduced by electronically recorded video images on magnetic surfaces, recorded in the electronic data-processing system, recorded on optical disk, reproduced on film or any other medium which does not permit additions, deletions, or changes to the original document in compliance with the minimum standards or guidelines, or both, as recommended by the American National Standards Institute or the Association for Information and Image Management for recording of permanent records or nonpermanent records, whichever applies.

(b) The device used to reproduce the record, paper, or document on film, optical disk, or any other medium is one which accurately reproduces the original thereof in all details, and which does not permit additions, deletions, or changes to the original document images.

(c) The photographs, microphotographs, or other reproductions on film, optical disk, or an other medium are placed in conveniently accessible files and provision is made for preserving, examining, and using the files.

For the purposes of this section, every reproduction shall be deemed to be an original record and a transcript, exemplification, or certified copy of any reproduction shall be deemed to be a transcript, exemplification, or certified copy, as the case may be, of the original.

TITLE 8. ORGANIZATION AND GOVERNMENT OF COURTS.

CHAPTER 1.4. MANAGEMENT OF TRIAL COURT RECORDS.

Citation: GC 68150

✪ § 68150. Preservation of trial court records; standards; copies; storage; accessibility of records.

(a) Trial court records may be preserved in any form of communication or representation, including optical, electronic, magnetic, microphotographic, or photographic media or other technology capable of accurately producing or reproducing the original record according to minimum standards or guidelines for the preservation and reproduction of the medium adopted by the American National Standards Institute or the Association for Information and Image Management.

Specifications for electronic recordings made as the official record of the oral proceedings shall be governed by the California Rules of Court.

(b) No additions, deletions, or changes shall be made to the content of the record. The records shall be indexed for convenient access.

(c) A copy of the record preserved or reproduced according to subdivisions (a) and (b) shall be deemed the original court record and may be certified as a correct copy of the original record.

(d) A court record preserved or reproduced in accordance with subdivisions (a) and (b) shall be stored in a manner and in a place that reasonably ensures its preservation against loss, theft, defacement, or destruction for the prescribed retention period under Section 68152. Electronic recordings made as the official record of the oral proceedings shall not require a backup copy unless otherwise specified in the California Rules of Court.

(e) The court record that was reproduced in accordance with subdivisions (a) and (b) may be disposed of in accordance with the procedure under Section 68153, unless it is subject to subdivision (f).

(f) The following court records may be preserved or reproduced under subdivisions (a) and (b) but shall also be preserved on paper, microfilm, or in another form of communication or representation approved by and in accordance with standards that are defined as archival by the American National Standards Institute for the duration of the record's retention period:

(1) The comprehensive historical and sample superior court records preserved for research under the California Rules of Court.

(2) Court records that are preserved permanently.

Court records that must be preserved longer than 10 years but not permanently may be reproduced on media other than paper or microfilm using technology authorized under subdivisions (a) and (b). However the records shall be reproduced before the expiration of their estimated lifespan for the medium in which they are stored as specified in subdivision (g).

(g) Instructions for access to data stored on a medium other than paper shall be documented. Each court shall conduct a periodic review of the media in which the court records are stored to assure that the storage medium is not obsolete and that current technology is capable of accessing and reproducing the records. The court shall reproduce records before the expiration of their estimated lifespan for the medium in which they are stored according to minimum standards and guidelines for the preservation and reproduction of the medium adopted by the American National Standards Institute or the Association for Information and Image Management.

(h) Court records preserved or reproduced under subdivisions (a) and (b) shall be made reasonably accessible to all members of the public for viewing and duplication as would the paper records. Reasonable provision shall be made for duplicating the records at cost. Cost shall consist of all costs associated with duplicating the records as determined by the court.

Citation: GC 68151

✪ § 68151. The following definitions apply to this chapter:

(a) "Court record" shall consist of the following:

(1) All filed papers and documents in the case folder; but if no case folder is created by the court, all filed papers and documents that would have been in the case folder if one had been created.

(2) Administrative records filed in an action or proceeding, depositions, paper exhibits, transcripts, including preliminary hearing transcripts, and tapes of electronically recorded proceedings filed, lodged, or maintained in connection with the case, unless disposed of earlier in the case pursuant to law.

(3) Other records listed under subdivision (j) of Section 68152.

(b) "Notice of destruction and no transfer" means that the clerk has given notice of destruction of the superior court records open to public inspection, and that there is not request and order for transfer of the records as provided in the California Rules of Court.

(c) "Final disposition of the case" means that an acquittal, dismissal, or order of judgment has been entered in the case or proceeding, the judgment has become final, and no postjudgment motions or appeals are pending in the case or for the reviewing court upon the mailing of notice of the issuance of the remittitur.

In a criminal prosecution, the order of judgment shall mean imposition of sentence, entry of an appealable order (including, but not limited to, an order granting probation, commitment of a defendant for insanity, or commitment of a defendant as a narcotics addict appealable under Section 1237 of the Penal Code), or forfeiture of bail without issuance of a bench warrant or calendaring of other proceedings.

(d) "Retain permanently" means that the original court records shall never be transferred or destroyed.

Citation: GC 68152

✪ § 68152. Destruction of records; notice; retention periods.

The trial court clerk may destroy court records under Section 68153 after notice of destruction and if there is not request and order for transfer of the records, except the comprehensive historical and sample superior court records preserved for research under the California Rules of Court, when the following times have expired after final disposition of the case in the categories listed:

(a) Adoption: retain permanently.

(b) Change of name; retain permanently.

(c) Other civil actions and proceedings, as follows:

(1) Except as otherwise specified: 10 years.

(2) Where a party appears by a guardian ad litem: 10 years after termination of the court's jurisdiction.

(3) Domestic violence: same period as duration of the restraining or other orders and any renewals, then retain the restraining or other orders as a judgment; 60 days after expiration of the temporary protective or temporary restraining order.

(4) Eminent domain: retain permanently.

(5) Family law, except as otherwise specified: 30 years.

(6) Harassment: same period as duration of the injunction and any renewals, then retain the injunction as a judgment; 60 days after expiration of the temporary restraining order.

(7) Mental health (Lanterman Development Disabilities Services Act and Lanterman-Petris-Short Act): 30 years.

(8) Paternity: retain permanently.

(9) Petition, except as otherwise specified: 10 years.

(10) Real property other than unlawful detainer: retain permanently if the action effects title or an interest in real property.

(11) Small claims: 10 years.

(12) Unlawful detainer: one year if judgment is for possession of the premises; 10 years if judgment is for money.

(d) Notwithstanding subdivision (c), any civil or small claims case in the trial court:

(1) Involuntarily dismissed by the court for delay in prosecution or failure to comply with state or local rules: one year.

(2) Voluntarily dismissed by a party without entry of judgment: one year.

Notation of this dismissal shall be made on the civil index of cases or on a separate dismissal index.

(e) Criminal.

(1) Capital felony (murder with special circumstances where the prosecution seeks the death penalty): retain permanently. If the charge is disposed of by acquittal or a sentence less than death, the case shall be reclassified.

(2) Felony, except as otherwise specified: 75 years.

(3) Felony, except capital felony, with court records from the initial complaint through the preliminary hearing or plea and for which the case file does not include final sentencing or other final disposition of the case because the case was bound over to the superior court: five years.

(4) Misdemeanor, except as otherwise specified: five years.

(5) Misdemeanor alleging a violation of the Vehicle Code, except as otherwise specified: three years.

(6) Misdemeanor alleging a violation of Section 23103, 23152, or 23153 of the Vehicle Code: seven years.

(7) Misdemeanor alleging a violation of Section 14601, 14601.1, 20002, 23104, or 23109 of the Vehicle Code: five years.

(8) Misdemeanor alleging a marijuana violation under subdivision (b), (c), (d), or (e) of Section 11357 of the Health and Safety Code, or subdivision (b) of Section 11360 of the Health and Safety Code in accordance with the procedure set forth in Section 11361.5 of the Health and Safety Code: records shall be

destroyed two years from the date of conviction or from the date of arrest if no conviction.

(9) Misdemeanor, infraction, or civil action alleging a violation of the regulation and licensing of dogs under Section 30951 to 30956, inclusive, of the Food and Agricultural Code or violation of any other local ordinance: three years.

(10) Infraction, except as otherwise specified: three years.

(11) Parking infractions, including alleged violation under the stopping, standing, and parking provisions set forth in Chapter 9 (commencing with Section 22500) of Division 11 of the Vehicle Code: two years.

(f) Habeas corpus: same period as period for retention of the records in the underlying case category.

(g) Juvenile.

(1) Dependent (Section 300 of the Welfare and Institutions Code): upon reaching age 28 or on written request shall be released to the juvenile five years after jurisdiction over the person has terminated under subdivision (a) of Section 826 of the Welfare and Institutions Code. Sealed records shall be destroyed upon court order five years after the records have been sealed pursuant to subdivision (c) of Section 389 of the Welfare and Institutions Code.

(2) Ward (Section 601 of the Welfare and Institutions Code): Upon reaching age 21 or on written request shall be released to the juvenile five years after jurisdiction over the person has terminated under subdivision (a) of Section 826 of the Welare and Institutions Code. Sealed records shall be destroyed upon court order five years after the records have been sealed under subdivision (d) of Section 781 of the Welfare and Institutions Code.

(3) Ward (Section 602 of the Welfare and Institions Code): upon reaching age 38 under subdivision (a) of Section 826 of the Welfare and Institutions Code. Sealed records shall be destroyed upon court order when the subject of the record reaches the age 38 under subdivision (d) of Section 781 of the Welfare and Institutions Code.

(4) Traffic and some nontraffic misdemeanors and infractions (Section 601 of the Welfare and Institutions Code): upon reaching age 21 or five years after jurisdiction over the person has terminated under subdivision (c) of Section 826 of the Welfare and Institutions Code. May be microfilmed or photocopied.

(5) Marijuana misdemeanor under subdivision (e) of Section 11357 of the Health and Safety Code in accordance with procedures specified in subdivision (a) of Section 11361.5 of the Health and Safety Code: upon reaching age 18 the records shall be destroyed.

(h) Probate.

(1) Conservatorship: 10 years after decree of termination.

(2) Guardianship: 10 years after the age of 18.

(3) Probate, including probated wills, except as otherwise specified: retain permanently.

(i) Court records of the appellate department of the trial court: five years.

(j) Other records.

(1) Applications in forma pauperis: same period as period for retention of the records in the underlying case category.

(2) Arrest warrant: same period as period for retention of the records in the underlying case category.

(3) Bench warrant: same period as period for retention of the records in the underlying case category.

(4) Bond: three years after exoneration and release.

(5) Coroner's inquest report: same period as period for retention of the records in the underlying case category; if no case, then permanent.

(6) Court orders not associated with an underlying case, such as orders for destruction of court records for telephone taps, or to destroy drugs, and other miscellaneous court orders: three years.

(7) Court reporter notes: 10 years after the notes have been taken in criminal and juvenile proceedings and five years after the notes have been taken in all other proceedings, except notes reporting proceedings in capital felony cases (murder with special circumstances where the prosecution seeks the death penalty and the sentence is death), including notes reporting the preliminary hearing, which shall be retained permanently, unless the Supreme Court on request of the court clerk authorizes the destruction.

(8) Electronic recordings made as the official record of the oral proceedings under the California Rules of Court: any time after final disposition of the case in infraction and misdemeanor proceedings, 10 years in all other criminal proceedings, and five years in all other proceedings.

(9) Electronic recordings not made as the official record of the oral proceeding under the California Rules of Court: any time either before or after final disposition of the case.

(10) Index, except as otherwise specified: retain permanently.

(11) Index for cases alleging traffic violations: same period as period for retention of the records in the underlying case category.

(12) Judgments within the jurisdiction of the superior court: retain permanently.

(13) Judgments within the jurisdiction of the municipal and justice court: same period as for retention of the records in the underlying case category.

(14) Minutes: same period as period for retention of the records in the underlying case category.

(15) Naturalization index: retain permanently.

(16) Ninety-day evaluation (under Section 1203.03 of the Penal Code): same period as period for retention of the records in the underlying case category, or period for completion or termination of probation, whichever is longer.

(17) Register of actions or docket: same period as period for retention of the records in the underlying case category, but in no event less than 10 years for civil and small claims cases.

(18) Search warrant: 10 years, except search warrants issued in connection with a capital felony case defined in paragraph (7), which shall be retained permanently.

(k) Retention of any court records under this section shall be extended as follows:

(1) By order of the court on its own motion, or on application of a party or any interested member of the public for good cause shown and on such terms as are just. No fee shall be charged for making the application.

(2) Upon application and order for renewal of the judgment to the extended time for enforcing the judgment

Citation: GC 68153

✪ § 68153. Order for destruction of records; methods and record of destruction

Upon order of the presiding judge of the court, court records open to public inspection and not ordered transferred under the procedures in the California Rules of Court, confidential records, and sealed records that are ready for destruction under Section 68152 may be destroyed. Destruction shall be by shredding, burial, burning, erasure, obliteration, recycling, or other method approved by the court, except confidential and sealed records, which shall not be buried or recycled unless the test of the records is first obliterated.

Notation of the date of destruction shall be made on the index of cases or on a separate destruction index. A list of the court records destroyed within the jurisdiction of the superior court shall be provided to the Judicial Council in accordance with the California Rules of Court.

Source: Penal Code

PART 4. PREVENTION OF CRIMES AND APPREHENSION OF CRIMINALS.

TITLE 1. INVESTIGATION AND CONTROL OF CRIMES AND CRIMINALS.

CHAPTER 1. INVESTIGATION IDENTIFICATION AND INFORMATION RESPONSIBILITIES OF THE DEPARTMENT OF JUSTICE.

Article 3. Criminal Identification and Statistics.

Citation: PC 11106

✪ § 11106. Retention of records; exceptions, registry.

In order to assist in the investigation of crime, the arrest and prosecution of criminals, and the recovery of lost, stolen, or found property, the Attorney General shall keep and properly file a complete record of all copies of fingerprints, copies of applications for licenses to carry firearms issued pursuant to § 12050, information reported to the Department of Justice pursuant to § 12053, dealers' records of sales of firearms, reports provided pursuant to § 12078, forms provided pursuant to § 12084, reports provided pursuant to § 12071 that are not dealers' records of sales of firearms, and reports of stolen, lost, found, pledged, or pawned property in any city or county of this state, and shall, upon proper application therefore, furnish to the officers mentioned in § 11105, hard copy printouts of those records as photographic, photostatic and nonerasable optically stored reproductions.

(b)(1) Notwithstanding subdivision (a), the Attorney General shall not retain or compile any information from reports filed pursuant to subdivision (a) of § 12078 for firearms that are not pistols, revolvers, or other firearms capable of being concealed upon the person, from forms submitted pursuant to § 12084 for firearms that are not pistols, revolvers, or other firearms capable of being concealed upon the person, or from dealers' records of sales for firearms that are not pistols, revolvers, or other firearms capable of being concealed upon the person. All copies of the forms submitted pursuant to § 12084 for firearms that are not pistols, revolvers, or other firearms capable of being concealed upon the person, or of the dealers' records of sales for firearms that are not pistols, revolvers, or other firearms capable of being concealed upon the person shall be destroyed within five days of the clearance by the Attorney Genera, unless the purchaser or transferor is ineligible to take possession of the firearm. All copies of the reports filed pursuant to subdivision (a) of § 12078 for firearms that are not pistols, revolvers, or other firearms capable of being concealed upon the person shall be destroyed within five days of the receipt by the Attorney General, unless retention is necessary for use in a criminal prosecution.

(2) A peace officer, the Attorney General, a Department of Justice employee designated by the Attorney General, or any authorized local law enforcement employee shall not retain or compile any information from a firearms transaction record, as defined in paragraph (5) of subdivision (c) of § 12071, for firearms that are not pistols, revolvers, or other firearms capable of being concealed upon the person unless retention or compilation is necessary for use in a criminal prosecution or in a proceeding to revoke a license issued pursuant to § 12071.

(3) A violation of this subdivision is a misdemeanor.

(c)(1) The Attorney General shall permanently keep and properly file and maintain all information reported to the Department of Justice pursuant to § § 12071, 12072, 12078, 12082, and 12084 or any other law, as to pistols, revolvers, or other firearms capable of being concealed upon the person and maintain a registry thereof.

(2) The registry shall consist of all of the following:

(A) The name, address, identification of, place of birth (state or country), complete telephone number, occupation, sex, description, and all legal names and aliases used by the owner or person being loaned the paı ticular pistol, revolver, or other firearm capable of being concealed upon the person as listed on the information provided to the department on the Record of Sale, the Law Enforcement Firearms Transfer (LEFT), as defined in § 12084, or reports made to the department pursuant to § 12078 or any other law.

(B) The name and address and other information (whether a dealer or a private party) from whom the owner acquired or the person being loaned the particular pistol, revolver, or other firearm capable of being concealed upon the person as listed on the information provided to the department on the Record of Sale, the LEFT, or reports made to the department pursuant to § 12078 or any other law.

(C) Any waiting period exemption applicable to the transaction which resulted in the owner of or the person being loaned the particular pistol, revolver, or other firearm capable of being concealed upon the person acquiring or being loaned that firearm.

(D) The manufacturer's name if stamped on the firearm; model name or number if stamped on the firearm; and, if applicable, the serial number, or number (if more than one serial number is stamped on the firearm), caliber, type of firearm, if the firearm is new or used, barrel length, and color of the firearm.

(3) Information in the registry referred to in the subdivision shall, upon proper application therefor, be furnished to the officers transferred to in § 11105 or to the person listed in the registry as the owner or person who is listed as being loaned the particular pistol, revolver, or other firearm capable of being concealed upon the person in the form of hard copy printouts of that information as photographic, photostatic, and nonerasable optically stored reproductions.

Citation: PC 11106.1

✪ § 11106.1. Photographic reproduction process; techniques, standards.

Any system of microphotography, optical disk, or reproduction by other techniques that do not permit additions, deletions, or changes to the original document, may be used by the Department of Justice as a photographic reproduction process to record some or all instruments, papers, photographs, and notices that are required or permitted by law to be recorded or filed. All storage medium shall comply with minimum standards of quality approved by the National Institute of Standards and Technology.

Citation: PC 11106.2

✪ § 11106.2. Reproduction of files and records by criminal justice agency.

Any criminal justice agency may cause any or all files or records in its official custody to be microphotographed or otherwise reproduced pursuant to Section 11106.1, as in the case of original filings or recordings, or both. Every reproduction shall be deemed and considered an original, and as a transcript exemplification or certified copy, as the case may be, of the original.

TITLE 3. CRIMINAL STATISTICS.

CHAPTER 2. CRIMINAL OFFENDER RECORD INFORMATION.

Article 1. Legislative findings and definitions.

Citation:	PC 13103

✪ **§ 13103. Destruction of Records; conditions.**

Notwithstanding any other provisions of law relating to retention of public records, any criminal justice agency may cause the original records filed pursuant to this chapter to be destroyed if all of the following requirements are met:

(a) The records have been reproduced onto microfilm or optical disk, or by any other techniques which do not permit additions, deletions, or changes to the original document.

(b) If the records have reproduced onto optical disk, at lease one year has elapsed since the date of registration of the records.

(c) The nonerasable storage medium used meets the minimum standards recommended by the National Institute of Standards and Technology for permanent record purposes.

(d) Adequate provisions are made to ensure that the nonerasable storage medium reflects additions or corrections to the records.

(e) A copy of the nonerasable storage medium is maintained in a manner which permits it to be used for all purposes served by the original record.

(f) A copy of the nonerasable storage medium has been stored at a separate physical location in a place and manner which will reasonably assure its preservation indefinitely against loss or destruction.

Citation:	PC 13104

✪ **§ 13104. Certified reproduction of records.**

Any certified reproduction of any record stored on a nonerasable storage medium under the provisions of this chapter shall be deemed to be a certification of the original record.

Source:	Public Utilities Code

DIVISION 6. MUNICIPAL UTILITY DISTRICTS ACT.

CHAPTER 6. POWERS AND FUNCTIONS OF DISTRICT.

Article 4. Property.

Citation:	PUC 12772

✪ **§ 12772. Disposition of old records; procedures.**

Whenever the board by resolution determines that any record, map, book, or paper in the possession of the district or any officer or employee thereof is of no further value to the district, the board may authorize its sale, destruction, or other disposition. Nothing in this section shall prevent the board from establishing procedures whereby categories of original records, maps, books, or papers designated by the board as having further value may be destroyed without further approval by the board if all of the following conditions are complies with:

(a) The records, maps, books, or papers are photographed, microphotographed, or reproduced on film of a type approved for permanent photographic records by the National Bureau of Standards.

(b) The device used to reproduce such records, maps, books, or papers on film is one which accurately and legibly reproduces the original thereof in all details.

(c) The photographs, microphotographs, or other reproductions on film are made as accessible for public reference as were the records, maps, books, or papers.

(d) A true copy of archival quality of such film reproductions shall be kept in a safe and separate place for security purposes.

No page of any records, maps, books, or papers shall be destroyed pursuant to such procedures if any such page cannot be reproduced on film with full legibility. Every such unreproducible page shall be permanently preserved in a manner that will afford easy reference.

Source:	Revenue and Taxation Code
Agency:	Franchise Tax Board

DIVISION 2. OTHER TAXES

PART 10.2. ADMINISTRATION OF FRANCHISE AND INCOME TAX LAWS

Article 3. General Provisions Applicable to All Persons

Citation:	R&TC 18621.5

✍ **§ 18621.5. Electronic imaging Technology; use and filing; form; requirements.**

(a) Any return, declaration, statement, or other document required to be made under this part, that is filed using electronic technology shall be in a form as the Franchise Tax Board may prescribe and shall be accompanied by a transmittal document signed in accordance with Section 18621 in the case of individuals, banks, or corporations, or subdivision (a) of Section 18633 in the case of a partnership.

(b) Notwithstanding any other provision of law, any return, declaration, statement, or other document otherwise required to be signed that is filed in a traditional medium and captured using electronic imaging technology shall be deemed to be valid original document upon reproduction to paper form by the Franchise Tax Board.

(c) "Electronic imaging technology" means a system of microphotography, optical disk, or reproduction by other technique does not permit additions, deletions, or changes to the original document. The system may include, but is not limited to, any magnetic media or other machine readable form.

(d) "Traditional medium" means any return, declaration, statement, or other document required to be made pursuant to this article other than those made using electronic imaging technology.

Source:	Welfare and Institutions Code

DIVISION 2. CHILDREN.

PART 1. DELINQUENTS AND WARDS OF THE JUVENILE COURT.

CHAPTER 2. JUVENILE COURT LAW.

Citation:	W&IC 826

✪ **§ 826. Release or destruction of court records; reproduction.**

* * * * *

(c) Juvenile court records in juvenile traffic matters, which include, all records and papers, any minute book entries, dockets and judgment dockets, may be destroyed after five years from the date on which the jurisdiction of the juvenile court over a minor is terminated, or when the minor reaches the age of 21 years, if the person was alleged or adjudged to be a person described by Section 601. Prior to such destruction the original record may be microfilmed or photocopied. Every such reproduction shall be deemed and considered an original; and a transcript, exemplification or certified copy of any such reproduction shall be deemed and considered a transcript, exemplification or certified copy, as the case may be, of the original.

Citation:	W&IC 826.5

✪ **§ 826.5. Reproduction of records pror to destruction.**

(a) Notwithstanding the provisions of Section 826, at any time before a person reaches the age when his or her records are required to be destroyed, the judge or clerk of the juvenile court or the probation officer may destroy all records and papers, the juvenile court record, any minute book entries, dockets, and judgment documents in the proceedings concerning the person as a minor if the records and papers, juvenile court record, any minute book entries, dockets, and judgment dockets are microfilmed or photocopied prior to destruction. Exhibits shall be destroyed as provided under Sections 1418, 1418.5, and 1419 of the Penal Code.

(b) Every reproduction shall be deemed and considered an original. A transcript, exemplification, or certified copy of any reproduction shall be deemed and considered a transcript, exemplification, or certified copy, as the case may be, of the original.

Source:	California Administrative Code
Agency:	Division of Labor Statistics and Research

TITLE 7. LABOR STATISTICS AND RESEARCH

CHAPTER 7. DIVISION OF LABOR STATISTICS AND RESEARCH

Subchapter 1. Occupational Injury or Illness Reports and Records

Article 1. Reporting of Occupational Injury or Illness

Citation:	CAC-L 14001

✍ **§ 14001. Employer.**

(a) Every employer shall file a complete report of every occupational injury or occupational illness to each employee which results in lost time beyond the date of such injury or illness or which requires medical treatment beyond first aid. As used in this subdivision, "lost time" means absence from work for a full day or shift beyond the date of the injury or illness, and "first aid" is any one-time treatment of minor scratches, cuts, burns, splinters, and so forth, which do not require the services of a physician, as defined in Labor Code Section 3209.3.

(b) Such report shall be made on Form 5020, Rev. 5, Employer's Report of Occupational Injury or Illness, reproduced in accordance with Section 14005, or by use of computer input media, prescribed by the Division and compatible with the Division's computer equipment.

(c) In the case of a self-insured employer, the report required by subdivision 14001(a) shall be filed directly with the Division within five days after the injury or illness has been reported to the employer. The report filed shall be the original of Form 5020, Rev. 5, or the computer input media prescribed by the Division. In addition, the self-insured employer shall transmit the doctor's report filed in accordance with Section 14003 to the Division within five days of receipt.

(d) In the case of an insured employer, the report required by subdivision 14001(a) shall be filed with the insurer within five days after the injury or illness has been reported to such insured employer. The report filed shall be the original of Form 5020, Rev. 5, or the computer input media prescribed by the Division.

Citation:	CAC-L 14002

✍ **§ 14002. Insurer.**

(a) Immediately upon receipt, the insurer shall transmit to the Division the employer's report required by subdivision 14001(a), which has been filed with the insurer within five days after the injury or illness has been reported to insured employers. The report filed shall be the original of Form 5020, Rev. 5, or the computer input media prescribed by the Division.

(b) In addition, the insurer shall transmit the doctor's report filed in accordance with Section 14003 to the Division within five days of receipt.

Citation:	CAC-L 14003

✍ **§ 14003. Physician.**

(a) Every physician, as defined in Labor Code Section 3209.3, who attends an inured employee shall file, within five days after initial examination, a complete report of every occupational injury or occupational illness to each such employee with the employer's insurer, or with the employer, if self-insured. The injured or ill employee, if able to do so, shall complete a portion of such report describing how the injury or illness occurred. Unless the report is transmitted on computer input media, the physician shall file the original signed report with the insurer or self-insured employer.

(b) If treatment is for pesticide poisoning or for a condition suspected to be pesticide poisoning, the physician shall also file a complete report directly with the Division within five days after initial treatment. In no case shall treatment administered for pesticide poisoning or suspected pesticide poisoning be deemed to be first aid treatment.

(c) The reports required by this Section shall be made on Form 5021, Rev. 3, Doctor's First Report of Occupational Injury or Illness, copies of which may be secured from the Division, upon a form reproduced in accordance with Section 14007, or by use of computer input media prescribed by the Division and compatible with the Division's computer equipment. However, reports may be submitted on prior revisions of Form 5021 until December 31, 1989.

(d) Physicians who use computerized data collection and reporting systems shall keep the injured worker's statement with the patient's medical records.

Agency: **State Board of Equalization**

TITLE 18. TAXATION.

MOTOR VEHICLE FUEL LICENSE TAX REGULATIONS

Article 6. Records.

Sales and Use Tax Regulations

Citation: **CAC-T 1698**

✍ § 1698. Records.

(a) General. Every seller, retailer, and person storing, using or otherwise consuming in this state tangible personal property purchased from a retailer, and every lessor and lessee of tangible personal property for use in this state, shall keep adequate and complete records showing:

(1) Gross receipts from sales or rental payments from leases of tangible personal property (including any services that are a part of the sale or lease) made within California irrespective of whether the seller or lessor regards the receipts as taxable or nontaxable.

(2) All deductions allowed by law and claimed in filing returns.

(3) Total purchase price of all tangible personal property purchased for sale or consumption or lease in California.

These records must include the normal books of account ordinarily maintained by the average prudent businessman engaged in the activity in question, together with all bills, receipts, invoices, cash register tapes, or other documents of original entry supporting the entries in the books of account as well as all schedules or working papers used in connection with the preparation of tax returns.

(b) Microfilm Records. Microfilm reproductions of general books of account, such as cash books, journals, voucher registers, ledgers, etc., are not acceptable in lieu of original records. However, microfilm reproductions of supporting records of details, such as sales invoices, purchase invoices, credit memoranda, etc., may be maintained providing the following conditions are met:

(1) Appropriate facilities are provided for preservation of the films for periods required.

(2) Microfilm rolls are indexed, cross referenced, labeled to show beginning and ending numbers or beginning and ending alphabetical listing of documents included, and are systematically filed.

(3) The taxpayer agrees to provide transcriptions of any information contained on microfilm which may be required for purposes of verification of tax liability.

(4) Proper facilities are provided for the ready inspection and location of the particular records, including modern projectors for viewing and copying the records.

A posting reference must be on each invoice. Credit memoranda must carry a reference to the document evidencing the original transaction. Documents necessary to support claimed exemptions from tax liability, such as bills of lading and purchase orders, must be maintained in an order by which they readily can be related to the transactions for which exemption is sought.

(c) Records Prepared by Automated Data Processing Systems. An ADP tax accounting system must have built into its program a method of producing visible and legible records which will provide the necessary information for verification of the taxpayer's tax liability.

(1) Recorded or Reconstructible Data. ADP records must provide an opportunity to trace any transaction back to the original source or forward to a final total. If detail printouts are not made of transactions at the time they are processed, then the system must have the ability to reconstruct these transactions.

(2) General and Subsidiary Books of Account. A general ledger, with source references, will be written out to coincide with financial reports for tax reporting periods. In cases where subsidiary ledgers are used to support the general ledger accounts, the subsidiary ledgers should also be written out periodically.

(3) Supporting Documents and Audit Trail. The audit trail should be designed so that the details underlying the summary accounting data may be identified and made available to the board upon request. The system should be so designed that supporting documents, such as sales invoices, purchase invoices, credit memoranda, etc., are readily available.

(4) Program Documentation. A description of the ADP portion of the accounting system should be available. The statements and illustrations as to the scope of operations should be sufficiently detailed to indicate, (A) the application being performed, (B) the procedures employed in each application (which, for example, might be supported by flow charts, block diagrams or other satisfactory description of the input or output procedures), and (C) the controls used to insure accurate and reliable processing. Important changes, together with their effective dates, should be noted in order to preserve an accurate chronological record.

(d) Records Retention. All records pertaining to transactions involving sales or use tax liability must be preserved for a period of not less than four years unless the State Board of Equalization authorizes in writing their destruction within a lesser period.

(e) Examination of Records. All of the above-described records must be made available for examination on request by the board or its authorized representatives.

(f) Failure to Maintain Records. Failure to maintain and keep complete and accurate records will be considered evidence of negligence or intent to evade the tax and may result in penalties or other appropriate administrative action.

Agency: **Employment Development Department**

TITLE 22. EMPLOYMENT DEVELOPMENT DEPARTMENT

ARTICLE 6. RECORDS, REPORTS AND CONTRIBUTION PAYMENTS.

Citation: **CAC-E 1085-2**

✍ § 1085-2. Required Work Records.

(a) Each employing unit shall establish and maintain records with respect to each worker performing services for it which shall indicate:

(1) The period covered by the pay period.

(2) For each worker:

(A) His or her name;

(B) Social security number;

(C) The date on which he or she was hired, rehired, or returned to work after temporary lay-off, and the last date when he or she performed any services;

(D) The place of his or her work which shall be shown in accordance with such forms and instructions as the department may approve.

(3) The remuneration paid to each worker for each pay period,

showing separately:
(A) Money paid;
(B) Cash value of all other remuneration received from the employing unit.
(C) Special payments in cash or kind for services other than those rendered exclusively in a given pay period such as annual bonuses, gifts, prizes, etc., showing the nature of such payments and the period during which the services were performed for which such special payments were made.
(4) All disbursement records which show payments to anyone who performed services.
(5) Such other information as may be necessary to enable the employing unit to determine the employee's total wages earned in each week.
(b) Each employing unit which considers that it is not an employer subject to the code or that it is engaged in exempt employment shall keep and maintain the records required of such employing units under this regulation for at least four years after the period to which the records relate.
(c) Each employer subject to the code shall keep and maintain the records required under this section for a period of at least four years after the date the contributions to which they relate become due, or the date the contributions are paid, whichever is the later.
(d) If an employing unit processes and maintains records in the form of magnetic media such as tapes or disks, then records include, but are not limited to, these magnetic devices or other machine sensible media.
(1) The procedures built into a computer's accounting program shall include a method of producing from punched cards, disk or tapes visible and legible records which will provide the necessary information for the verification of information required by this regulation.
(2) Magnetic media records which reflect payments for personal services shall be retained. Examples of such records include, but are not limited to, the following:
(A) Calendar year to date payroll master file.
(B) Vendor transaction history file.
(C) General ledger account distribution file.
(3) The records shall provide the opportunity to trace any transaction back to the original source for forward to a final total. The audit trail shall be designed so that the details underlying the summary accounting data, such as invoices and vouchers, may be identified and made available to the director upon request.
(4) A description of the electronic data processing portion of the accounting system shall be available. The statements and illustrations as to the scope of operations shall be sufficiently detailed to indicate (a) the application being performed, (b) the procedures employed in each application (which, for example, might be supported by flow charts, block diagrams or other satisfactory descriptions or input or output procedures), and (c) the controls used to ensure accurate and reliable processing. Important changes, together with their effective dates, shall be noted in order to preserve an accurate chronological record.
(5) Substitution of hard copy records maintained or magnetic media do not meet the requirements of this section.
(6) If an employer engages an outside service bureau to process and maintain any of the records described in this section then it is the responsibility of the employee to meet the requirements of this section.
(e) In the event the payroll records of an employing unit do not indicate the particular days during any week on which a worker performed services it shall be presumed in the absence of evidence to the contrary that the worker performed services on each day of such week.

State: Colorado
Source: Colorado Revised Statutes

TITLE 6. CONSUMER AND COMMERCIAL AFFAIRS

ARTICLE 17. UNIFORM RECORDS RETENTION ACT

Citation: CRS 6-17-101

✍ ✪ **6-17-101. Short title.**

This article shall be known and may be cited as the "Uniform Records Retention Act".

Citation: CRS 6-17-102

✍ ✪ **§ 6-17-102. Legislative declaration.**

The general assembly hereby finds that there is a need to minimize the paperwork burden associated with the retention of business records for individuals, small businesses, state and local agencies, corporations, and other persons, and there is a need to minimize the costs of collecting, maintaining, using, storing, and disseminating information and business records. The general assembly therefore finds that the provisions of this article are necessary to promote efficiency and economy.

Citation: CRS 6-17-103

✍ ✪ **§ 6-17-103. Definitions.**

As used in this article, unless the context otherwise requires:
(1) "Business records"means books of account; vouchers; documents, canceled checks; payrolls; correspondence; records of sales, personnel, equipment, and production; reports relating to any or all of such records; and other business papers.
(2) "Record" means any letter, word, sound, number, or its equivalent, set down by handwriting, typewriting, printing, photostating, photographing, magnetic impulse, mechanical, or electronic recording of other forms of data compilation. Unless otherwise specified, reproductions are records for purposes of this article.
(3) "Reproduction" means any counterpart produced by the same impression as the original or from the same matrix, or by means of photography, including enlargements and miniatures, or by mechanical or electronic rerecording or by chemical reproduction or by any equivalent technique which accurately reproduces the original.

Citation: CRS 6-17-104

✍ ✪ **§ 6-17-104. Records retention period.**

Any record required to be created or kept by any state or local law or regulation may be destroyed after three years from the date of creation, unless such law or regulation establishes a specified records retention period or a specific procedure to be followed prior to destruction.

Citation: CRS 6-17-105

✍ ✪ **§ 6-17-105. Form of record.**

Retention of reproductions produced pursuant to this article shall constitute compliance with any state or local law requiring that any record be created or kept.

Citation: CRS 6-17-106

✍ ✪ **§ 6-17-106. Scope of article.**

This article shall apply to all records prepared by private individuals, partnerships, corporations, or any other association, whether carried on for profit or not, and to any government entity operating under the laws of this state and shall apply to all records created before and after July 1, 1990.

TITLE 13. COURTS AND COURT PROCEDURE.

EVIDENCE

ARTICLE 26. UNIFORM PHOTOGRAPHIC RECORDS ACT.

Citation: CRS 13-26-102

☞ **§ 13-26-102. Business and public records as evidence.**

If any business, institution, or member of a profession or calling, or any department or agency of government in the regular course of business or activity keeps or records any memorandum, writing, entry, print, or representation, or combination thereof, of any act, transaction, occurrence, or event and in the regular course of business has caused any of the same to be recorded, copied, or reproduced by any photographic, photostatic, microfilm, microcard, miniature photographic, optical disk, or other form of mass storage, electronic imaging, electronic data processing, electronically transmitted facsimile, printout, or other reproduction of electronically stored data, or other process which accurately reproduces or forms a durable medium for reproducing the original, the original may be destroyed in the regular course of business unless held in a custodial or fiduciary capacity or unless its preservation is required by law. Such reproduction, when satisfactorily identified, is as admissible in evidence as the original itself in any judicial or administrative proceeding whether the original is in existence or not and an enlargement or facsimile of such reproduction is likewise admissible in evidence if the original reproduction is in existence and available for inspection under direction of court. The introduction of a reproduced record, enlargement, or facsimile does not preclude admission of the original. This shall not be construed to exclude from evidence any document or copy thereof which is otherwise admissible under the rules of evidence.

Citation: CRS 13-26-103

☞ **§ 13-26-103. Records of trust departments or companies not excepted.**

The records of the trust department of a bank or trust company are not such records as are excepted under the phrase "held in a custodial or fiduciary capacity" in section 13-26-102. The originals of such trust records may be reproduced at any time and destroyed at any time, if done in good faith and without wrongful intent. Neither the manner in which an original is destroyed, whether voluntarily or by casualty or otherwise, nor the fact that it may have been destroyed while it was held in a custodial or fiduciary capacity shall effect the admissibility of a reproduction.

TITLE 24. GOVERNMENT. STATE.

ARTICLE 80. STATE HISTORY, ARCHIVES, AND EMBLEMS.

Part 1. State Archives and Public Records.

Citation: CRS 24-80-101

✪ **§ 24-80-101. Definitions.**

As used in this part 1, unless the context otherwise requires:

(1) "Records" means all books, papers, maps, photographs, or other documentary materials, regardless of physical form or characteristics, made or received by any governmental agency in pursuance of law or in connection with the transaction of public business and preserved or appropriate for preservation by the agency or its legitimate successor as evidence of the organization, functions, policies, decisions, procedures, operations, or other activities of the government or because of the value of the official governmental data contained therein. As used in this part 1, the following are excluded from the definition of records:

(a) Materials preserved or appropriate for preservation because of the value of the data contained therein other than that of an official governmental nature or because of the historical value of the materials themselves;

(b) Library books, pamphlets, newspapers, or museum material made, acquired, or preserved for reference, historical, or exhibition purposes;

(c) Private papers, manuscripts, letters, diaries, pictures, biographies, books, and maps, including materials and collections previously owned by persons other than the state or any political subdivision thereof and transferred by them to the state historical society;

(d) Extra copies of publications or duplicated documents preserved for convenience of reference;

(e) Stocks of publications.

Citation: CRS 24-80-103

✪ **§ 24-80-103. Determination of value — disposition.**

Every public officer who has public records in his or her custody shall consult periodically with the department of personnel and the attorney general of the state, and such three officers shall determine whether the records in questions are of legal, administrative, or historical value. Those records unanimously determined to be of no legal, administrative, or historical value shall be disposed of by such method as such three officers may specify. A list of all records so disposed of, together with a statement certifying compliance with this part 1, signed by these three officers, shall be filed and preserved in the office from which the records were drawn and in the files of the department of personnel. Public records in the custody of the executive director of the department of personnel may be disposed of upon a similar determination by the attorney general, the executive director of the department of personnel, and the head of the agency from which the records were received, or its legal successor.

Citation: CRS 24-80-105

✪ **§ 24-80-105. Disposal of records.**

All public records of any public office, upon the termination of the existence and functions of that office, shall be checked by the executive director of the department of personnel and the attorney general and either disposed or transferred to the custody of the department of personnel, in accordance with the procedure of this part 1 and the findings of such two officers. When a public office is terminated or reduced by the transfer of its power and duties to another office or to other offices, its appropriate public records shall pass with the powers and duties so transferred.

Citation: CRS 24-80-106

✪ § 24-80-106. Protection of records.

The department of personnel and every other custodian of public records shall carefully protect and preserve them from deterioration, mutilation, loss, or destruction and, whenever advisable, shall cause them to be properly repaired and renovated. All paper, ink, and other materials used in public offices for the purpose of permanent records shall be of durable quality.

Citation: CRS 24-80-107

✪ § 24-80-107. Reproduction on film — evidence.

☞

(1) Any public officer of the state or any county, city, municipality, district or legal subdivision thereof may cause any or all records, papers, or documents kept by him to be photographed, microphotographed, or reproduced on film. Such photographic film shall comply with the minimum standards of quality approved for permanent photographic records by the national bureau of standards, and the device used to reproduce such records on such film shall be one which accurately reproduces the original thereof in all details. Such photographs, microphotographs, or photographic film shall be deemed to be original records for all purposes, including introduction in evidence in all courts or administrative agencies. A transcript, exemplification, or certified copy thereof, for all purposes recited in this section, shall be deemed to be a transcript, exemplification, or certified copy of the original.

(2) Whenever such photographs, microphotographs, or reproductions on film properly certified are placed in conveniently accessible files and provisions made for preserving, examining, and using the same, any such public officer may cause the original records from which the photographic or microphotographs have been made, or any part thereof, to be disposed of according to methods prescribed by sections 24-80-103 to 24-80-106. Such copies shall be certified by their custodian as true copies of the originals before the originals are destroyed or lost, and the copies so certified shall have the same force and effect as the originals. Copies of public records transferred from the office of their origin to the department of personnel, when certified by the executive director of the department of personnel or the assistant to the executive director, shall have the same legal force and effect as if certified by the original custodian of the records.

Citation: CRS 24-80-110

✪ § 24-80-110. Disagreement as to value of records.

In the event the attorney general and the executive director of the department of personnel determine that any records in the custody of a public officer including the executive director of the department of personnel, but not those in the custody of a public officer of any county, city, municipality, district, or political subdivision thereof, are of no legal, administrative, or, subject to section 24-80-211(1)(b) historical value, but the public officer having custody of said records or from whose office records originated fails to agree with such determination or refuses to dispose of said records, the attorney general and the executive director of the department of personnel may request the governor to make his or her determination as to whether said records should be disposed of in the interests of conservation of space, economy, or safety.

Source: Colorado Court Rules

CHAPTER 9. COURT ADMINISTRATION.

✪ Rule 79. Records.

(a) *Register of Actions*. The clerk shall keep a record known as the register of actions and shall enter therein those items set forth below. The register of actions may be in any of the following forms or styles:

(1) A page, sheet, or printed form in a book, case jacket, or separate file.

(2) A microfilm roll, film jacket, or microfiche card.

(3) Computer magnetic tape or magnetic disc storage, where the register of actions items appear on the terminal screen, or on a paper print-out of the screen display.

(4) Any other form or style prescribed by supreme court directive. A register of actions shall be prepared for each case or matter filed. The file number of each case or matter shall be noted one every page, film, or computer record whereon the first and all subsequent entries of actions are made. All papers filed with the clerk, all process issued and return made thereon, all costs, appearances, orders, verdicts, and judgments shall be noted chronologically in the register of actions. These notations shall be brief but shall show the nature of each paper filed or writ issued and the substance of each order or judgment of the court and of the returns showing execution of process. The notation of an order, or of the entry of judgment, shall show the date the order or judgment was ordered in open court, in chambers, or under the provisions of Rule 55 regarding default. When trial by jury has been demanded or ordered, the clerk shall enter the word jury on the page, film, or computer record assigned to that case.

* * * * *

(c) *Indices; Calendars*. The clerk shall keep suitable indices of all records as directed by the court. The clerk shall also keep, as directed by the court, calendars of all hearings and all cases ready for trial, which shall distinguish trials to a jury from trials to the court. Indices and calendars may be in any of the following forms or styles:

(1) A page or sheet in a book or separate file.

(2) A mechanical or hand-operated index machine or file card.

(3) Computer magnetic tape or magnetic disc storage, where the information appears on the terminal screen, or on a print-out of the screen display.

(4) Microfilm copies of 1, 2, and 3 above.

(5) Any other form or style prescribed by supreme court directive.

(d) Judgment Record. The clerk shall keep a judgment record in which a notation shall be made of every money judgment. The judgment record may be in any of the following forms or styles:

(1) A page or sheet in a book, case jacket, or separate file.

(2) Computer magnetic tape or magnetic disc storage, where the judgment and subsequent transactions appear on the terminal screen, or on a paper print-out of the screen display.

(3) Microfilm copies of 1 and 2 above.

(4) Any other form or style prescribed by supreme court directive.

* * * * *

Source: Colorado Rules of Evidence

ARTICLE X. CONTENTS OF WRITINGS, RECORDINGS AND PHOTOGRAPHS.

☞ Rule 1001. Definitions

For purposes of this article the following definitions are applicable:

(1) *Writings and recordings.* — "Writings" and "recordings" consist of letters, words, or numbers, or their equivalent, set down by handwriting, typewriting, printing, photostating, photographing, magnetic impulse, mechanical or electronic recording, or other form of data compilation.

(2) *Photographs.* — "Photographs" include still photographs, X-ray films, video tapes, and motion pictures.

(3) *Original.* — An "original" of a writing or recording is the writing or recording itself or any counterpart intended to have the same effect by a person executing or issuing it. An "original" of a photograph includes the negative or any print therefrom. If data are stored in a computer or similar device, any printout or other output readable by sight, shown to reflect the data accurately, is an "original".

(4) *Duplicate.* — A "duplicate" is a counterpart produced by the same impression as the original, or from the same matrix, or by means of photography, including enlargements and miniatures, or by mechanical or electronic re-recording, or by chemical reproduction, or by other equivalent techniques which accurately reproduces the original.

☞ Rule 1003. Admissibility of Duplicates.

A duplicate is admissible to the same extent as an original unless (1) a genuine question is raised as to the authenticity of the original or (2) in the circumstances it would be unfair to admit duplicate in lieu of the original.

[See Appendix A. Uniform Rules of Evidence for additional provisions.]

Source: Code of Colorado Regulations
Agency: Department of Revenue

✍ Regulation 26-116.

(a) *General.*

It is the duty of every person engaged or continuing in business in this state, for the transaction of which a license is required under this Part 1, and the duty of every lessor and lessee of tangible personal property for use in this state, to keep adequate and complete records. Unless the department authorizes an alternate method of recordkeeping in writing, these records should show:

(1) Gross receipts from sales, or rental payments from leases, of tangible personal property (including any services that are a part of the sale or lease) made in this state, irrespective of whether the seller or lessor regards the receipts to be taxable or nontaxable.

(2) All deductions allowed by law and claimed in filing returns.

(3) Total purchase price of all tangible personal property purchased for sale or consumption or lease in this state.

These records must include the normal books of account maintained by the ordinarily prudent businessman engaged in such business, together with all bills, receipts, invoices, cash register tapes, or other documents of original entry supporting the entries in the books of accounts together with all schedules or working papers used in connection with the preparation of tax returns.

(b) *Microfilm records.*

Records may be microfilmed; however, microfilm reproductions of general books of account, such as cash books, journals, voucher registers, ledgers, etc., are not acceptable as original records. Where microfilm reproductions of supporting records are maintained, such as sales invoices, purchase invoices, credit memoranda, etc., the following conditions must be met:

(1) Appropriate facilities are provided for preservation of the films for periods required.

(2) Microfilm rolls are indexed cross referenced, and labeled to show beginning and ending numbers and to show beginning and ending alphabetical listing of documents included, and are systematically filed.

(3) The taxpayer agrees to provide transcriptions of any information contained on microfilm which may be required for verification of tax liability.

(4) Proper facilities are provided for the ready inspection and location of the particular records, including machines for viewing and copying the records.

A posting reference must be on each invoice. Credit memoranda must carry a reference to the document evidencing the original transaction. Documents necessary to support claimed exemptions from tax liability, such as bills of lading and purchase orders, must be maintained in an order by which they readily can be related to the transaction for which exemption is sought.

(c) *Records prepared by automated data processing systems.*

An ADP tax accounting system must be capable of producing visible and legible records for verification of taxpayer's tax liability.

(1) *Recorded or reconstructible data.*

ADP records must provide an opportunity to trace any transaction back to the original source or forward to a final total. If detail printouts are not made of transactions at the time they are processed, the systems must have the ability to reconstruct these transactions.

(2) *General and Subsidiary Books of Account.*

A general ledger, with source references, will be written out to coincide with financial reports for tax reporting periods. In cases where subsidiary ledgers are used to support the general ledger accounts, the subsidiary ledgers should also be written out periodically.

(3) *Supporting Documents and Audit Trail.*

The audit trail should be designed so that the details underlying the summary accounting data may be identified and made available to the Department upon request. The system should be so designed that supporting documents, such as sales invoices, purchase invoices, credit memoranda, etc., are readily available.

(4) *Program Documentation.* A description of the ADP portion of the accounting system should be available. The statements and illustrations as to the scope of operations should be sufficiently detailed to indicate, (A) the application being performed, (B) the procedures employed in each application (which, for example, might be supported by flow charts, block diagrams, or other satisfactory description of the input or output procedures), and (C) the controls used to insure accurate and reliable processing. Important changes, together with their effective dates, should be noted in order to preserve an accurate chronological record.

(d) *Record Retention.* All records pertaining to transactions involving sales or use tax liability must be preserved for a period of not less than three years.

State: Connecticut
Source: Connecticut General Statutes

TITLE 7. MUNICIPALITIES.

CHAPTER 93. REGISTRARS OF VITAL STATISTICS.

Citation: CGS 7-51a

✪ **§ 7-51a. Copying of vital records for purposes of genealogical research.**

Notwithstanding the provisions of section 7-51, persons acting under the direction of a legally incorporated genealogical society shall be permitted to copy the vital records, including birth, death and marriage records and their indexes, of any municipality. The provisions of this section shall apply only to those vital records of a municipality which are not included in the Barbour Collection and which relate to events which occurred prior to the year 1900. All copies made under the provisions of this section shall be reduced to microfilm and shall be placed in the custody of the state's public records administrator who shall make such microfilm copies available to the public for purposes of genealogical research at the state library. If any vital records for the periods specified in this section have been microfilmed, the person having custody of the microfilm negatives shall permit their use for the purposes of this section. No expense arising from activities permitted under this section shall be paid by the state or any municipality. Nothing in this section shall be construed to be in derogation of any other right of public access to vital records conferred by any other provision of the general statutes.

TITLE 9. ELECTIONS.

CHAPTER 141. GENERAL PROVISIONS.

Citation: CGS 9-58

✪ **§ 9-58. Applications for enrollment; record of, disposal after five years.**

All applications for enrollment shall be arranged in alphabetical order and shall be preserved for by the registrars as a permanent record open to public inspection, except that any such application of an elector whose name has been removed from the registry list for a period of at least five years may be placed on microfilm, destroyed or otherwise disposed of, in the manner provided in section 7-109, by such registrars.

TITLE 17a. SOCIAL AND HUMAN SERVICES AND RESOURCES.

CHAPTER 319i. MENTALLY ILL PERSONS

Part II. Commitment. General Provisions.

Citation: CGS 17a-500

✪ **§ 17a-500. Court of probate to keep record of cases of persons with psychiatric disabilities.**

Each court of probate shall keep a record of the cases related to mentally ill persons with psychiatric disabilities coming before it under § § 17a-75 to 17a-83, inclusive, 17a-450 to 17a-484, inclusive, 17a-495 to 17a-528, inclusive, 17a-540 to 17a-550, inclusive, 17a-560 to 17a-576, inclusive, and 17a-615 to 17a-618, inclusive, and the disposition of them. It shall also keep on file the original application and certificate of physicians required by said sections, or a microfilm duplicate of such records in accordance with regulations issued by the probate court administrator. All records maintained in the courts of probate under the provisions of said sections shall be sealed and available only to the respondent or his or her counsel unless the court of probate, after hearing held with notice to the respondent, determines such records should be disclosed for cause shown.

TITLE 51. COURTS.

CHAPTER 871. COURTS.

Citation: CGS 51-36

✪ **§ 51-36. Microfilming, destruction and transferring of court records.**

(a) The chief court administrator may cause any and all court records, papers or documents other than records concerning title to land, required to be retained indefinitely or for a defined period of time by rules of court or directives promulgated by the Office of the Chief Court Administrator or statute, to be microfilmed. The device used to reproduce such records on film shall be one which accurately reproduces the original thereof in detail. Such microfilm shall be considered and treated the same as the original records, papers or documents, provided a certificate of authenticity appears on each roll of microfilm. A transcript, exemplification or certified copy thereof shall for all purposes be deemed to be a transcript, exemplification or certified copy of the original. The original court records, papers or documents so reproduced may be disposed of in such manner as approved by the Office of the Chief Court Administrator. For purposes of this subsection, microfilm shall include microcard, microfiche, microphotograph or any other process which actually reproduces or forms a durable medium for so reproducing the original.

(b) Any judge of the superior court may order that official records of evidence or judicial proceedings in said court, the court of common pleas or the circuit court taken more than ten years prior to the date of such order by any stenographer or official court reporter, be destroyed by the person having the custody thereof. All court records other than records concerning title to land may be destroyed in accordance with rules of court. Records concerning title to land shall not be subject to any such destruction. All court records may be transferred to any agency of this state or to any federal agency in accordance with rules of court or directives promulgated by the Office of the Chief Court Administrator, provided records in any action concerning title to land terminated by a final judgment affecting any right, title or interest in real property shall be retained for not less than forty years in the office of the clerk of the court location in which the judgment was rendered. Any other judicial department books, records, papers or documents may be destroyed or transferred to any agency of this state or to any federal agency in accordance with directives promulgated by the Office of the Chief Court Administrator.

TITLE 52. CIVIL ACTIONS.

CHAPTER 899. EVIDENCE.

Citation:	CGS 52-180

☞ § 52-180. **Admissibility of business entries and photographic copies.**

(a) Any writing or record, whether in the form of an entry in a book or otherwise, made as a memorandum or record of any act, transaction, occurrence or event, shall be admissible as evidence of the act, transaction, occurrence or event, if the trial judge finds that it was made in the regular course of any business, and that it was the regular course of the business to make the writing or recorded at the time of the act, transaction, occurrence or event or within a reasonable time thereafter.

(b) The writing or record shall not be rendered inadmissible by (1) a party's failure to produce as witnesses the person or persons who made the writing or record, or who have personal knowledge of the act, transaction, occurrence or event recorded or (2) the party's failure to show that such persons are unavailable as witnesses. Either of such facts and all other circumstances of the making of the writing or record, including lack or personal knowledge by the entrant or maker, may be shown to affect the weight of the evidence, but not to affect its admissibility.

(c) Except as provided in chapter 3, if any person in the regular course of business has kept or recorded any memorandum, writing, entry, print, representation or combination thereof, of any act, transaction, occurrence or event, and in the regular course of business has caused any or all of them to be recorded, copied or reproduced by any photographic, photostatic, microfilm, microcard, miniature photographic or other process which accurately reproduces or forms a durable medium for so reproducing the original, the original may be destroyed in the regular course of business unless its preservation is otherwise required by statute. The reproduction, when satisfactorily identified, shall be as admissible in evidence as the original in any judicial or administrative proceeding, whether the original is in existence or not, and an enlargement or facsimile of the reproduction shall be likewise admissible in evidence if the original reproduction is in existence and available for inspection under direction of court. The introduction of a reproduced record, enlargement or facsimile shall not preclude admission of the original.

(d) The term "business" shall include business, profession, occupation and calling of every kind.

Source:	CONNECTICUT STATE LIBRARY
Citation:	**GENERAL LETTER 94-1**

March 1, 1994

TO: ADMINISTRATIVE HEADS OF STATE AGENCIES; STATE AGENCY RECORDS MANAGEMENT LIAISON OFFICERS; ADMINISTRATIVE HEADS OF MUNICIPALITIES; TOWN CLERKS; ALL OTHER STATE AGENCY AND MUNICIPAL RECORDS CUSTODIANS AND RECORDS MANAGEMENT PERSONNEL

FROM: EUNICE B. DiBELLA
PUBLIC RECORDS ADMINISTRATOR

SUBJECT: OPTICAL IMAGING TECHNOLOGY AND PUBLIC RECORDS: POLICY STATEMENT

INTRODUCTION

The Office of the Public Records Administrator and State Archives issues this Statement under authority granted it by Sections 11-8, 11-8a and 7-109 of the *Connecticut General Statutes (CGS)*. The following provides a policy on the disposal of original public records reformatted on optical storage disks without hard copy or microfilm backup, recommendations for optical imaging systems in a government records setting, and legal guidelines. The Office recognizes that optical imaging is an important advance in records management and will continue to monitor this rapidly changing technology.

POLICY ON DISPOSAL OF ORIGINAL PUBLIC RECORDS

This Office will approve disposal authorizations for original public records reformatted on an optical imaging system only if the original records have an approved retention period of ten (10) years or less.

This Office will not approve disposal authorizations for original public records reformatted on an optical imaging system if their approved retention period is above ten (10) years or permanent or permanent/archival.

At this time, no national standards exist to ensure the longevity of information stored on optical disks or to guarantee access to that information. This Office advises public officials contemplating the purchase of imaging systems to make their selection within the context of a comprehensive records management program and to consider systems with the knowledge that hardware and software will change and that over time optical disks will deteriorate. The following recommendations for design, selection and operation of optical imaging systems will assist public officials and are based on current studies and guidelines.[1]

RECOMMENDATIONS FOR OPTICAL IMAGING SYSTEMS

A. Evaluating the Needs.

Remember that purchasing any optical system constitutes a large ongoing financial commitment to hardware, software, training, media and data conversion requirements. Reformatting information on optical imaging technology is most cost effective for a large quantity of records that are frequently retrieved. On the other hand, records which become inactive after a very short period of time may not be cost-effective candidates. Converting to, maintaining and using optical technology may be justified if the costs (hardware, software, personnel, media) are less than the cost of maintaining a current system for creating and storing public records. When planning a budget for converting data to an optical system, remember that scanning is a simple low-cost procedure. Indexing, which is crucial for locating information stored on disks, on the other hand, takes three to five times longer than scanning and consumes around 30% of the data conversion budget.

When evaluating the need for optical imaging technology, remember that hardware and software are changing rapidly. Currently there is no guarantee that optical disks written on one system can be read or will be read on other systems, inlcuding successive generations of one system. In other words, the technology suffers from incompatibility.

The technology may also become obsolete on account of continuous turnover in the hardware and software. If a user retains a system for many years, he/she may find that the vendor no longer provides technical support services and that replacement parts and supplies are not available.

The medium of optical disk technology is not "permanent." Carefully evaluate any claims that disks are permanent. Some studies estimate a life span at 10 to 20 years while others extend the estimate to 30 years. Therefore, at some point users will have to transfer data from older disks to new disks to avoid incompatibility, technological obsolescence, and/or the end of the medium's life span.

Finally, in evaluating the need for an optical system, consider the ramifications of the above-stated disposal policy of original public records reformatted on optical technology and the last section on legal issues.

B. Administration.

Assign a full-time staff member as system administrator, and require the vendor to provide a project director to work with the staff administrator during installation and training.

C. System Documentation.

In order to ensure efficient operation and ongoing retrieval of data, keep full documentation of the follwowing:

1. System design, including justification, cost-benefit analysis, and media alternatives
2. Hardware and software brand names, version numbers, and dates of installation, upgrades, replacements, and conversions
3. Data structure and content, including the file layout andata dictionaries
4. "Enhancement" algorithms
5. All operating procedures

D. Hardware and Software.

1. When selecting a system, require that a vendor provide a bridge by means of a platform or some other solution so that information on one system can be sent to another system to avoid incompatibility and to ensure that the information is readable.
2. Specifications for hardware and software should require vendors to continue to support and maintain their products.
3. Establish performance standards, make them part of specifications, and require vendors to support them with a substantial performance bond.
4. Consider systems that provide scanning resolution with sufficient density to produce a high-quality image.
5. Consider systems that use standard instead of proprietary compression algorithms so that future migrations of data will be more reliable.
6. Specify that vendors must supply programs or services to test the readability of disks periodically.
7. Require vendors to provide necessary bridges (hardware and software) to accomplish migrating information from an older onto a newer system.

E. Verification and Inspection.

Make visual inspecion a part of operational procedures in order to verify the completeness and accuracy of scanning after documents have been transferred to a disk.

F. Indexing.

Include in the system design an indexing component based on anticipated needs of future uses. Establish as an operational procedure an index check for accuracy at the time of creation of the index.

G. Labelling.

Label all disks, tapes, and other storage containers as completely as possible to ensure future use and accessibility.

H. Backup and Storage.

Make backups of all records and indexes, and store them off-site. Provide adequate facilities and environmental conditions for the current system and all backups.

I. Refreshment, Migration, and Conversion.

Operating procedures should include "refreshment" of all data and corollary indeces within the lifetime of a system, usually five (5), or at a maximum, ten(10) years.

J. Disaster Prevention and Recovery.

Develop and implement as part of operating procedures a comprehensive disaster prevention and recovery plan.

LEGAL ISSUES

Connecticut General Statutes, Section 52-180—"Admissibility of Business Entries and Photographic Copies," which allows for properly certified microfilm and other photographically reproduced records to be entered as evidence in court, does not specifically mention optical imaging technology. Records created by an optical imaging system are not photographic copies. Some states have changed their evidence statutes to include imaging systems. Connecticut has not done so.[2]

As of the date of this statement, we are unaware of any optical image that has gone to court to "test" its admissibility. That is to say, certified copies of records created by imaging systems have been accepted into evidence providing these copies meet the federal and state rules of evidence requirements. Future court action may affect the legal status of optical images.

Any state agency or municipality contemplating an imaging system should be aware of those issues. It is crucial that the guidelines outlined here be adopted to ensure the authenticity of the documents created. Consultation with appropriate legal counsel regarding rules of evidence would be advisable.

Optical imaging is dynamic technology and for that reason standards may change as the technology develops. This Office will attempt to monitor the situation and advise government agencies and municipalities as changes occur.[3]

[1] Association for Information and Image Management, *Technical Report for Information and Image Management: The Use of Optical Disks for Public Records,* AIIM TR25-1990, Silver Springs, MD, AIIM, 1990; Dick Harrington, "States' Optical Imaging Policies Reviewed," National Association of Government Archivists and Records Administrators, *Clearinghouse,* Vol. 8, No. 4 (Fall 1992), pp. 6-8; South Carolina Deparment of Archives and History, Archives and Records Management Division, *Optical Disk: Policy Statement and Recommended Practices,* Public Records Information Leaflet No. 13, February 3, 1992;New York State Archives and Records Administration, *Introduction to Optical Disk,* State Government Records Management Information Series, Albany, NY., The University of the State of New York, 1990; *Preservation of Historical Records,*Washington, DC, National Academy Press, 1986, pp. 71-76.

[2] Currently, these are the states of Missouri, Louisiana, and Virginia; plus Washington, DC.

[3] For further discussion of this question, consult the following: Donald S. Skupsky, JD,CRM, *Legal Requirements for Microfilm, Computer and Optical Disk Records,* Information Requirements Clearinghouse, Denver, CO, 1991; Keith Ninesling and Carly Masyr, "Optical Storage Systems,"*The Records and Retrieval Report,* Vol. 9, No, 3 (March 1993), Greenwood Publishing Group, Inc.; The National Archives and Records Administration and The National Association of Government Archives and Records Administrators, *Digital Imaging and Optical Media Storage Systems: Guidelines for State and Local Government Agencies, a joint report, December 1991.*

Source:	**CONNECTICUT STATE LIBRARY**
Citation:	**GENERAL LETTER 95-1**

June 1, 1995
TO: ADMINISTRATIVE HEADS OF STATE AGENCIES; STATE AGENCY RECORDS MANAGEMENT LIAISON OFFICERS; ADMINISTRATIVE HEADS OF MUNICIPALITIES; TOWN CLERKS; ALL OTHER STATE AGENCY AND MUNICIPAL RECORDS CUSTODIANS AND RECORDS MANAGEMENT PERSONNEL
FROM: EUNICE G. DiBELLA
PUBLIC RECORDS ADMINISTRATOR
SUBJECT: E-MAIL GUIDELINES FOR PUBLIC OFFICIALS

INTRODUCTION

The Office of the Public Records Administrator and State Archives issues this statement under authority granted it by Sections 11-8, 11-8a and 7-109 of the *Connecticut General Statutes.*

DEFINITION

E-mail refers to messages transmitted by computer technology. E-mail systems include messages, calendars, directories, distribution lists, attachments such as word-processing documents, and communications generated on external systems, the most familiar being the Internet. Like the telepone, E-mail provides instant communications, allowing the transmittal of up-to-date information. Like postal or interoffice mail, E-mail messages can be stored, though on electronic media, and are retrievable at a future date.[1]

E-MAIL AND PUBLIC RECORDS

When deciding what to do with E-mail messages, it is important to remember the statutory definition of public records:

Any recorded data or information relating to the conduct of the public's business prepared, owned, used, or received by a public agency, whether such data or information be handwritten, typed, tape-recorded, printed, photostated, photographed or *recorded by any method.*[2](Italics added.)

A message sent or received by E-mail in the conduct of public business is by law a *public record.*

RETENTION GUIDELINES

E-mail messages sent and received by public officials fall within three broad categories:

(1) Transitory non-records, including copies posted to several persons and casual and routine communications similar to telephone conversations;

(2) Public records with a less than Permanent retention period, and

(3) Public records with a Permanent or Permanent/Archival retention period.

Retention guidelines for each of these catagories follows:

(1) *Transitory*—Since these messages are not public records, there is *No Requirement.* Public officials and employees receiving such communications may *delete them immediately without obtaining the approval of the Office of the Public Records Administration and State Archives.*[3]

(2) *Less than Permanent*—Retention may be in the form of a hard copy print-out or computer-generated. If the record is electronically generated, the record creator must be able to interpret and retrieve the data for the minimum legal retention requirement. *Municipalities and state-agency officials may delete or destroy the records only after receiving signed approval from the Office of the Public Records Administrator.*

(3) *Permanent or Permanent/Archival*—Retention may be in the form of a hard-copy printout or microfilm which meets archival quality standards issued by this office.

State and local government officials and supervisors and State Agency Records Management Liaison Officers are responsible for instructing their employees in determining which E-mail messages fall in each of the three categories, in using retention schedules and in securing approval for destruction. Depending upon the function of the public record being generated by E-mail, state agencies and municipalities may take steps to institute procedures for routinely printing E-mail records, including *all* transmissions and receipt data in the system, and filing the printouts in the normal course of business.

LEGAL ISSUES

Public officials and employees should keep in mind that E-Mail messages sent as part of their workdays are not"private" but are discoverable communications. Since messages may be retained at different locations or levels of the system, users may be surprised to learn that indiscrete communications can be retrieved during formal discovery processes. Discretion, therefore, is an important consideration when using this or any other new technology to send, record and/or retain communications.[4]

CONCLUSION

E-mail is a new, rapidly evolving technology that has attracted the attention of the courts.[5] This office will monitor this changing technology and will communicate with public officials on implications for Connecticut's public records.

[1] Texas State Library, State and Local Records Management Division, *E-Mail and Records Management*, RMD Technical Bulletin No. 15 (December 1994), p. 1.

[2] *Connecticut General Statues* Section 1-18(d).

[3] For discussion of record and non-record materials, see Connecticut State Library, Office of the Public Records Administrator, *Records Management Manual: Statutes, Policies, and Procedures for Connecticut State Agencies.*

[4] David C. Jacobson, *et al.*, "Peril of the E-Mail Trail," *The National Law Journal*, "Corporate Counsel," Section C, January 16, 1995, pp. 1, 22-23; Marci Alborghetti, "What's in Your Computers May Hurt You in Court," *The Hartford Courant*, Business Weekly, October 24, 1994, p. 3; Texas State Library, *op. cit.*, pp. 2-3.

[5] Texas State Library, *ibid.*, p. 1.

State: Delaware
Source: Delaware Code Annotated

TITLE 8. CORPORATIONS.

CHAPTER 1. GENERAL CORPORATION LAW.

Subchapter 7. Meetings, Elections, Voting and Notice.

Citation: 8 DCA 224

✍ **§ 224. Form of records.**

Any records maintained by a corporation in the regular course of its business, including its stock ledger, books of account, and minute books, may be kept on, or be in the form of, punch cards, magnetic tape, photographs, microphotographs or any other information storage device, provided that the records so kept can be converted into clearly legible written form within a reasonable time. Any corporation shall so convert any records so kept upon the request of any person entitled to inspect the same. When records are kept in such manner, a clearly legible written form produced from the cards, tapes, photographs, microphotographs or other information storage device shall be admissible in evidence, and accepted for all other purposes, to the same extent as an original written record of the same information would have been, provided the written form accurately portrays the record.

TITLE 29. STATE GOVERNMENT.

PART 1. GENERAL PROVISIONS.

CHAPTER 5. STATE ARCHIVES AND HISTORICAL OBJECTS.

Citation: 29 DCA 502

✪ **§ 502. Definitions.**

As used in this subchapter, the following terms have the meanings indicated:

(1) "Public record" means any document, book photographic image, electronic data recording, paper, sound recording or other material regardless of physical form or characteristics, made or received pursuant to the law or ordinance in connection with the transaction of public business by any officer or employee of this State or any political subdivision thereof.

* * * * *

Citation: 29 DCA 504

✪ **§ 504. Duties of public officials and employees concerning public records.**

(a) It shall be the responsibility of every public official and employee to:

(1) Adequately document the transaction of public business and the services and programs for which such persons are responsible; to

(2) Retain and adequately protect all public records in their custody; and

(3) Cooperate with the Department, state and local government records commissions and records officers in the establishment and maintenance of an active and continuous program for the economical and efficient management of public records.

(b) No officer, member or employee of any agency of this State or any political subdivision thereof shall destroy, sell or otherwise dispose of any public record or printed public document or official correspondence in his care or custody or under his control without first having advised the Department of State of their nature and obtained its consent.

Citation: 29 DCA 516

✪ **§ 516. Responsibility of Department concerning records created or reproduced by photographic or microphotographic means; admissibility of photographic copies of records in evidence.**

(a) The Department shall be responsible for monitoring the use of photographic or microphotographic processes in the creation or duplication of public records.

(1) The Department shall enforce compliance with approved procedures and standards of quality, to be established by the Department pursuant to the provisions of this chapter, regarding creation and storage of public records by microphotography or other means.

(2) Destruction of original records which have been duplicated in this manner shall require the prior approval of the Department of State.

(b) Photographs, photocopies or microphotographs of any record photographed, photocopies or microphotographed as provided in this chapter shall have the same force and effect as the originals thereof would have had and shall be treated as originals for the purpose of their admissibility in evidence. Certified or authenticated copies of such photographs, photocopies or microphotographs or enlargements thereof shall be admitted in evidence equally with the original photographs, photocopies or microphotographs.

Citation: 29 DCA 517

✪ **§ 517. Standards for methods and materials used for public records.**

(a) All custodians of public records in this State and the political subdivisions thereof, whose duty it shall be to create any public record required by law, shall not use or permit to be used for recording purposes, any materials or methods which do no meet standards of quality established by the Department.

(b) The Department of State may require that certain records shall be kept on permanent-durable paper. The Department may require the microfilming of records that are not produced on permanent-durable paper.

(c) The Department shall make available, upon request, its standard of quality for methods and materials.

Source: Delaware Rules of Evidence

ARTICLE X. CONTENTS OF WRITINGS, RECORDINGS, AND PHOTOGRAPHS

☞ **Rule 1001. Definitions**

For purposes of this article the following definitions are applicable:

(1) *Writings and recordings.* — "Writings" and "recordings" consist of letters, words, or numbers, or their equivalent, set down by handwriting, typewriting, printing, photostating, photographing, magnetic impulse, mechanical or electronic recording, or other form of data compilation.

(2) *Photographs.* — "Photographs" include still photographs, X-ray films, video tapes, and motion pictures.

(3) *Original.* — An "original" of a writing or recording is the writing or recording itself or any counterpart intended to have the same effect by a person executing or issuing it. An "original" of a photograph includes the negative or any print therefrom. If data are stored in a computer or similar device, any printout or other output readable by sight, shown to reflect the data accurately, is an "original".

(4) *Duplicate.* — A "duplicate" is a counterpart produced by the same impression as the original, or from the same matrix, or by means of photography, including enlargements and miniatures, or by mechanical or electronic re-recording, or by chemical reproduction, or by other equivalent techniques which accurately reproduces the original.

☞ Rule 1003. Admissibility of Duplicates.

A duplicate is admissible to the same extent as an original unless (1) a genuine question is raised as to the authenticity of the original, or (2) in the circumstances it would be unfair to admit the duplicate in lieu of the original.

[See Appendix A. Uniform Rules of Evidence for additional provisions.]

State: District of Columbia
Source: District of Columbia Code

PART 1. GOVERNMENT OF DISTRICT.

TITLE 1. ADMINISTRATION.

CHAPTER 29. PUBLIC RECORDS MANAGEMENT.

Citation: DCC 1-2901

✪ § 1-2901. Definitions.

For the purposes of this chapter, the term:

* * * * *

(3) "Archival quality" means a quality of photographic reproduction consistent with standards specified by the American National Standards Institute.

* * * * *

Citation: DCC 1-2902

✪ § 1-2902. Establishment of District of Columbia Office of Public Records Management, Archival Administration, and Library of Government Information.

(a) There is established the District of Columbia Office of Public Records Management, Archival Administration, and Library of Governmental Information within the Office of the Secretary.

(b) The head of the Office shall be the Public Records Administrator of the District of Columbia who shall be appointed by the Mayor. The Administrator shall be qualified by training and experience in records and archives management. Other staff shall be appointed as necessary.

(c) Subject to the approval of the Mayor, the Administrator is authorized to adopt, alter, and use a seal which shall establish the authenticity or true copy of any public record in the Administrator's custody. A true copy shall then have the same force and effect as the original.

(d) Repealed.

(e) The Mayor shall issue rules and regulations to implement the provisions of this chapter pursuant to subchapter I of Chapter 15 of Title 1.

PART 5. GENERAL STATUTES.

TITLE 36. LABOR.

CHAPTER 12. OCCUPATIONAL SAFETY AND HEALTH.

Citation: DCC 36-1213

✍ § 36-1213. Recordkeeping and reporting.

(a) Each employer shall make, keep, preserve, and make available to the Mayor any records relating to this chapter that the Mayor may require, by rule, for the enforcement of this chapter or for the development of information regarding the causes and prevention of occupational accidents and illnesses. The rules may include provisions requiring employers to conduct periodic inspections.

(b) The Mayor shall promulgate rules requiring employers to maintain accurate records of and to make periodic reports on work-related deaths, injuries and illnesses, other than minor injuries requiring minimal treatment, regardless of whether minor injuries are reportable under Chapter 3 of Title 36.

(c) All employers, to the extent required by the Federal Act, shall maintain records and make reports to the Secretary of Labor in the same manner and to the same extent that would be required if no state plan were in effect under 29 U.S.C. 667(c).

(d) The mayor shall promulgate rules to require employers to maintain accurate records of employee exposure to any potentially toxic materials or harmful physical agents required to be monitored or measured under section 36-1208. The rules shall provide employees or other authorized representatives the right to observe the monitoring or measuring of potentially toxic materials or harmful physical agents and to access to the records. The rules shall make appropriate provisions for each employee, former employee, or the authorized representative of the employee or former employee to have access to the records on the exposure of the employee or former employee to toxic materials or harmful physical agents and to periodic summaries and other records required to be kept in the workplace under this chapter, except medical records of other employees and former employees. Information contained in records and reports concerning employee exposure to toxic substances may be made public and disseminated to employers, employees, or other representative organizations without disclosure of the name of individual who is the subject of the physical examination or special study.

(e) Each employers shall promptly notify each employee who has been or is being exposed to toxic materials or harmful physical agents in concentrations or at levels that exceed those prescribed by an applicable occupational safety and health rule promulgated under this chapter. Each employer shall promptly undertake to reduce the exposure to compliance levels and inform each employee who is being exposed of the corrective action being taken.

(f) Each employer shall notify the Mayor, within 24 hours, of an accident or occurrence that causes the death of an employee or a life threatening injury requiring the hospitalization of an employee.

(g) Each employer shall submit to the Mayor, within 10 days from the date of an injury or the date that the employer has knowledge of a disease or infection resulting from an injury, a duplicate copy of the report required to be made pursuant to section 36-228(c).

State: Florida
Source: Florida Statutes

TITLE 4. EXECUTIVE BRANCH.

CHAPTER 18. TREASURER

Citation: FS 18.20

✪ **§ 18.20. Treasurer to make reproductions of certain warrants, records, and documents.**

(1) All vouchers or checks heretofore or hereafter drawn by appropriate court officials of the several counties of the state against money deposited with the treasurer under the provisions of § 43.17, and paid by the treasurer, may be photographed, microphotographed or reproduced on film by the treasurer. Such photographic film shall be durable material and the device used to so reproduce such warrants, vouchers or checks shall be one which accurately reproduces the originals thereof in all detail; and such photographs, microphotographs or reproductions on film shall be placed in conveniently accessible and identified files and shall be preserved by the treasurer as a part of the permanent records of his office. When any such warrants, vouchers or checks have been so photographed, microphotographed or reproduced on film, and the photographs, microphotographs or reproductions on film thereof have been placed on files as a part of the permanent records of the office of the treasurer as aforesaid, the treasurer is authorized to return such warrants, vouchers or checks to the offices of the respective county officials who drew the same and such warrants, vouchers or checks shall be retained and preserved in such offices to which returned as a part of the permanent records of such offices.

(2) Such photographs, microphotographs or reproductions on film of said warrants, vouchers or checks shall be deemed to be original records for all purposes; and any copy or reproduction thereof made from such original film, duly certified by the treasurer as a true and correct copy or reproduction made from such film, shall be deemed to be a transcript, exemplification or certified copy of the original warrant, voucher or check such copy represents, and shall in all cases and in all courts and places be admitted and received in evidence with the like force and effect as the original thereof might be.

(3) The treasurer is also hereby authorized to photograph, microphotograph or reproduce on film, all records and documents of said office, as he may, in his discretion, select; and said treasurer is hereby authorized to destroy any of the said documents or records after they have been, photographed and filed and after audit of his office has been completed for the period embracing the dates of said documents and records.

(4) Photographs or microphotographs in the form of film or prints of any records made in compliance with the provisions of this section shall have the same force and effect as the originals thereof would have, and shall be treated as originals for the purpose of their admissibility in evidence. Duly certified or authenticated reproductions of such photographs or microphotographs shall be admitted in evidence equally with the original photographs or microphotographs.

TITLE 5. JUDICIAL BRANCH.

CHAPTER 28. CLERKS OF THE CIRCUIT COURTS.

Citation: FS 28.30

✪ **§ 28.30. Records; destruction; reproduction; electronic recordkeeping.**

(1) The purpose of this section and § 28.31 is to make available for the use of the clerks of the circuit court and the several counties of the state sufficient space to enable them to efficiently administer the affairs of office.

(2) The clerk of the circuit court of each county of the state is authorized to destroy and dispose of public records pursuant to the rules adopted by the Division of Library and Information Services of the Department of State pursuant to § 257.36.

(3) Each clerk of the circuit court is authorized to photograph, microphotograph, or reproduce on film, or to maintain in an electronic recordkeeping system, any public record that the clerk may select. Such photographs, microphotographs, or other reproductions on film or reproductions from an electronic recordkeeping system shall be admissible in evidence with the same force and effect as the originals. Duly certified or authenticated reproductions of such photographs, microphotographs, reproductions on film, or reproductions from an electronic recordkeeping system shall be admitted into evidence equally with the original photographs, microphotographs, reproductions on film, or reproductions from an electronic recordkeeping system.

(4) The clerk of the circuit court shall follow procedures for electronic recordkeeping in accordance with rules adopted by the Division of Library and Information Services of the Department of State.

(5) Except when otherwise provided by law or applicable rule, a document that is submitted to the clerk of the circuit court by electronic transmission is deemed filed when the document is received and the date and time are acknowledged by the clerk, as opposed to the date and time of transmission. The clerk is not liable for malfunctions or errors occurring in the transmission of documents for filing by electronic means.

TITLE 7. EVIDENCE.

CHAPTER 90. FLORIDA EVIDENCE CODE.

Citation: FS 90.803

☞ **§ 90.803. Hearsay exceptions; availability of declarant immaterial.**

The provision of section 90.802 to the contrary notwithstanding, the following are not inadmissible as evidence, even though the declarant is available as a witness:

* * * * *

(6) *Records of regularly conducted business activity.* — (a) A memorandum, report, record, or data compilation, in any form, of acts, events, conditions, opinion, or diagnosis, made at or near the time by, or from information transmitted by, a person with knowledge, if kept in the course of a regularly conducted business activity and if it was the regular practice of that business activity to make such memorandum, report, record, or data compilation, all as shown by the testimony of the custodian or other qualified witness, unless the sources of information or other circumstances show lack of trustworthiness. The term

"business" as used in this paragraph includes a business, institution, association, profession, occupation, and calling of every kind, whether or not conducted for profit.

(b) No evidence in the form of an opinion or diagnosis is admissible under paragraph (a) unless such opinion or diagnosis would be admissible under sections 90.701 - 90.705 if the person whose opinion is recorded were to testify to the opinion directly.

* * * * *

(7) *Absence of entry in records of regularly conducted activity.* — Evidence that a matter is not included in the memoranda, reports, records, or data compilations, in any form, of a regularly conducted activity to prove the nonoccurrence or nonexistence of the matter, if the matter was of a kind of which a memorandum, report, record, or data compilation was regularly made and preserved, unless the sources of information or other circumstances show lack of trustworthiness.

* * * * *

Citation: FS 90.951

☞ § 90.951. Definitions.

For purposes of this chapter:

(1) "Writings" and "recordings" include letters, words, or numbers, or their equivalent, set down by handwriting, typewriting, printing, photostating, photography, magnetic impulse, mechanical or electronic recording, or other form of data compilation, upon paper, wood, stone, recording tape, or other materials.

(2) "Photographs" include still photographs, x-ray films, videotapes, and motion pictures.

(3) An "original" of a writing or recording means the writing or recording itself, or any counterpart intended to have the same effect by a person executing or issuing it. An "original" of a photograph includes the negative or any print made from it. If data are stored in a computer or similar device, any printout or other output readable by sight and shown to reflect the data accurately is an "original."

(4) "Duplicate" includes:

(a) A counterpart produced by the same impression as the original, from the same matrix; by means of photography, including enlargements and miniatures; by mechanical or electronic re-recording; by chemical reproduction; or by other equivalent technique that accurately reproduces the original; or

(b) An executed carbon copy not intended by the parties to be an original.

Citation: FS 90.953

☞ § 90.953. Admissibility of duplicates.

A duplicate is admissible to the same extent as an original, unless:(1) The document or writing is a negotiable instrument as defined in § 673.1041, a security as defined in § 678.102, or any other writing that evidences a right to the payment of money, is not itself a security agreement or lease, and is of a type that is transferred by delivery in the ordinary course of business with any necessary endorsement or assignment.

(2) A genuine question is raised about the authenticity of the original or any other document or writing.

(3) It is unfair, under the circumstance, to admit the duplicate in lieu of the original.

CHAPTER 92. WITNESSES, RECORDS, AND DOCUMENTS.

Citation: FS 92.29

☞ ✪ § 92.29. Photographic or electronic copies.

Photographic reproductions or reproductions through electronic recordkeeping systems made by any federal, state, county, or municipal governmental board, department, or agency, in the regular course of business, of any original record, document, paper or instrument in writing or in an electronic recordkeeping system, which is, or may be, required or authorized to be made, filed, or recorded with that board, department, or agency shall in all cases and in all courts and places be admitted and received as evidence with a like force and effect as the original would be, whether said original record, document, paper, or instrument in writing or in an electronic recordkeeping system is in existence or not.

Citation: FS 92.295

☞ ✪ § 92.295. Copies of voter registration records.

Any reproduction of an original voter registration record stored pursuant to s. 98.461, whether microfilmed or maintained digitally or on electronic, magnetic, or optic media, which reproduction is certified by the supervisor or elections who is the custodian of the record, is admissible as evidence in any judicial or administrative proceeding in this state with the same effect as the original voter registration record, whether the original voter registration record exists or not.

TITLE 10. PUBLIC OFFICERS, EMPLOYEES AND RECORDS.

CHAPTER 119. PUBLIC RECORDS.

Citation: FS 119.031

✪ § 119.031. Keeping records in safe places; copying or repairing certified copies.

Insofar as practicable, custodians of vital, permanent, or archival records shall keep them in fireproof and waterproof safes, vaults, or rooms fitted with noncombustible materials and in such arrangement as to be easily accessible for convenient use. All public records should be kept in the buildings in which they are ordinarily used. Record books should be copies or repaired, renovated, or rebound if worn, mutilated, damaged, or difficult to read. Whenever any state, county, or municipal records are in need of repair, restoration, or rebinding, the head of such state agency, department, board, or commission, the board of county commissioners of such county, or the governing body of such municipality may authorize that such records be removed from the building or office in which such records are ordinarily kept for the length of time required to repair, restore, or rebind them. Any public official who causes a record book to be copied shall attest it and certify on oath that it is an accurate copy of the original book. The copy shall then have the force and effect of the original.

✪ § 119.041. Destruction of records regulated.

(1) Every public official shall systematically dispose of records no longer needed subject to the consent of the records and

information management program of the Division of Library and Information Services of the Department of State in accordance with § 257.36.

(2) Agency orders that comprise final agency action and that must be indexed or listed pursuant to § 120.53 have continuing legal significance; therefore, notwithstanding any other provision of this chapter or any provision of chapter 257, each agency shall permanently maintain records of such orders pursuant to the applicable rules and guidelines of the Department of State.

TITLE 14. TAXATION AND FINANCE.

CHAPTER 197. TAX COLLECTIONS, SALES, AND LIENS.

Citation: FS 197.202

✪ **§ 197.202. Destruction of 20-year-old tax receipts.**

The tax collector in each county of the state is authorized to destroy all duplicate tax receipts and microfilm of tax receipts on file in the tax collector's office as they become 20 years old. Tax receipts may be destroyed after 1 year if microfilmed.

TITLE 16. EDUCATION.

CHAPTER 238. RETIREMENT SYSTEM FOR SCHOOL TEACHERS.

Citation: FS 238.03

✪ **§ 238.03. Administration.**

* * * * *

(9) The division is authorized to photograph and reduce to microfilm as a permanent record, its ledger sheets showing the salary and contributions of members of the retirement system, also the records of deceased members of the system and thereupon to destroy the documents from which such films are photographed.

TITLE 18. PUBLIC LANDS AND PROPERTY.

CHAPTER 257. PUBLIC LIBRARIES AND STATE ARCHIVES.

Citation: FS 257.36

✪ **§ 257.36. Records and information management.**

* * * * *

(7) No record shall be destroyed or disposed of by any agency unless approval of the division is first obtained. The divisions shall adopt reasonable rules not inconsistent with this chapter which shall be binding on all agencies relating to the destruction and disposal of records. Such rules shall provide, but not be limited to:

(a) Procedures for complying and submitting to the division lists and schedules of records proposed for disposal.

(b) Procedures for the physical destruction or other disposal of records.

(c) Standards for the reproduction of records for security or with a view to the disposal of the original record.

TITLE 23. MOTOR VEHICLES.

CHAPTER 320. MOTOR VEHICLE LICENSES.

Citation: FS 320.833

☞ ✪ **§ 320.833. Retention, destruction, and reproduction of records.**

Records and documents of the Department of Highway Safety and Motor Vehicles, created in compliance with, and in the implementation of, chapters 319 and 320, shall be retained by the department as specified in record retention schedules established under the general provisions of chapter 119. Further, the department is hereby authorized:

(1) To destroy, or otherwise dispose of, those record and documents, in conformity with the approved retention schedules.

(2) To photograph, microphotograph, or reproduce on film, as authorized and directed by the approved retention schedules, whereby each page will be exposed in exact conformity with the original records and documents retained in compliance with the provisions of this section. Photographs or microphotographs in the form of film or print on any records, made in compliance with the provisions of this section, shall have the same force and effect as the originals thereof would have and shall be treated as originals for the purpose of their admissibility in evidence. Duly certified or authenticated reproductions of such photographs or microphotographs shall be admitted in evidence equally with the original photographs or microphotographs.

CHAPTER 321. HIGHWAY PATROL.

Citation: FS 321.23

☞ ✪ **§ 321.23. Public records; fees for copies; destruction of obsolete records; photographing records; effect as evidence.**

(1) The purpose of this section is to make available for the use of the Department of Highway Safety and Motor Vehicles sufficient floor space to enable it to efficiently administer the affairs of the department and to provide fees for copies of public records.

* * * * *

(4) The department is authorized to destroy reports, records, documents, papers and correspondence which are considered obsolete.

(5) The department is authorized to photograph, microphotograph, or reproduce on film such documents, records, reports as it may select. The photographs or microphotographs in the form of film or print of any records made in compliance with the provisions of this section shall have the same force and effect as the originals thereof would have and shall be treated as originals for the purpose of their admissibility in evidence. Duly certified or authenticated reproductions of such photographs or microphotographs shall be admitted in evidence equally with the original photographs or microphotographs.

TITLE 26. PUBLIC TRANSPORTATION.

CHAPTER 334. FLORIDA HIGHWAY CODE, FIRST PART HIGHWAY ADMINISTRATION.

Public Transportation

Citation: FS 334.196

☞ ✪ **§ 334.196. Authority of department to photograph or microphotograph records and to destroy original records; admissibility of photographs or microphotographs in evidence.**

(1) The department is authorized to photograph, microphotograph, or reproduce on film, whereby each page will be exposed in exact conformity with the original, all its documents, records, maps, data, and information of a permanent character. The department is further authorized to destroy any documents after they have been photographed and filed except the original minutes of the meetings of the former State Road Board and such title deeds, maps, easements, leases, and releases relating to the rights-of-way of the state roads and other property owned or leased by the department, which deeds, maps, easements, leases, and releases the department deems should be preserved in original form.

(2) Photographs or microphotographs in the form of film or print of any records made in compliance with the provisions of this section shall have the same force and effect as the originals for the purpose of their admissibility in evidence. Duly certified or authenticated reproductions of such photographs or microphotographs shall be admitted in evidence equally with original photographs or microphotographs.

TITLE 29. PUBLIC HEALTH

CHAPTER 382. VITAL STATISTICS.

Public Health

Citation: FS 382.004

☞ ✪ **§ 382.004. Microfilming and destroying records.**

(1) The department is authorized to photograph, microphotograph, reproduce on film, or reproduce by electronic means vital records in such a manner that the data on each page are in exact conformity with the original record.

(2) The department is hereby authorized to destroy any of the original vital records after they have been photographed or reproduced in exact conformity with the original record and after approval for destruction in accordance with chapter 257.

(3) Photographs, microphotographs, or reproductions of any record in the form of film, prints, or electronically produced certifications made in compliance with the provisions of this chapter shall have the same force and effect as the originals thereof, and shall be treated as originals for the purpose of their admissibility in any court or case where the documents have been duly certified by the department.

CHAPTER 402. HEALTH AND REHABILITATIVE SERVICES; MISCELLANEOUS PROVISIONS.

Citation: FS 402.19

☞ ✪ **§ 402.19. Photographing records; destruction of records; effect as evidence.**

The Department of Health and Rehabilitative Services may authorize each of the agencies under its supervision and control to photograph, microphotograph, or reproduce in film or prints, such correspondence, documents, records, data, or other information as the department shall determine, and which is not otherwise authorized to be reproduced under chapter 119, whether the same shall be of a temporary or permanent character and whether public, private, or confidential, including that pertaining to patients or inmates of the agencies, and to destroy any of said documents after they have been reproduced. Photographs or microphotographs in the form of film or prints made in compliance with the provisions of this section shall have the same force and effect as the originals thereof would have, and shall be treated as originals for the purpose of their admissibility in evidence. Duly certified or authenticated reproductions of such photographs or microphotographs shall be admitted in evidence equally with the original photographs or microphotographs.

TITLE 33. REGULATION OF TRADE, COMMERCE, INVESTMENTS AND SOLICITATIONS.

CHAPTER 517. SECURITIES TRANSACTIONS.

Citation: FS 517.313

☞ ✪ **§ 517.313. Destroying certain records; reproduction.**

(1) The department is authorized to photograph, microphotograph, or reproduce on film or prints documents, records, data, and information of a permanent character.

(2) The department is authorized to destroy any of said documents after audit of the office has been completed for the period embracing the dates of said instruments, after complying with the provisions of chapter 119.

(3) Duly certified or authenticated photographs or microphotographs in the form of film or prints of any records made in compliance with the provisions of this section shall have the same force and effect as the originals thereof would have and shall be treated as originals for the purpose of their admissibility as evidence.

TITLE 37. INSURANCE.

CHAPTER 624. INSURANCE CODE: ADMINISTRATION AND GENERAL PROVISIONS.

Citation: FS 624.312

☞ **§ 624.312. Reproductions and certified copies of records as evidence.**

(1) Photographs or microphotographs in the form of film or prints of documents and records made under § 624.311(3), or made under former § 624.311(3) before October 1, 1982, shall have the same force and effect as the originals thereof and shall be treated as originals for the purpose of their admissibility in evidence. Duly certified or authenticated reproductions of such photographs or microphotographs shall be as admissible in evidence as the originals.

(2) Upon the request of any person and payment of the applicable fee, the department shall give a certified copy of any record in its office which is then subject to public inspection.

(3) Copies of original records or documents in its office certified by the department shall be received in evidence in all courts as if they were originals.

TITLE 40. REAL AND PERSONAL PROPERTY.

CHAPTER 696. RECORD OF CONTRACTS; PHOTOGRAPHIC RECORDING.

Citation:	**FS 696.06**

✪ § 696.06. Photographic recording by county court judge.

(1) In every county in the state, the county court judge may record any and all instruments filed for record by photographic process, this phrase being used in its most general sense not excluding any photographic process heretofore or herafter devised, however designated, such as may be recommended by the county court judge from time to time and approved by the board of county commissioners, and the board of county commissioners shall provide out of the general revenue fund adequate equipment and supplies for making and preserving such records in accordance with the process so recommended and approved.

(2) Any instrument heretofore recorded and any action of the boards of county commissioners or county court judges heretofore performed in accordance with the provisions of this section shall be held good and valid.

Source:	**Florida Administrative Code**
Agency:	**Department of Revenue**

Citation:	**FAC 12B-5.008**

✍ § 12B-5.008 Preservation and Inspection of Records; Statute of Limitations; Tracking System.

(1) *Preservation of Records.* The Florida Department of Revenue has the power to prescribe the records to be kept by all persons subject to the taxes imposed by Part II of Ch. 206 and Part II of Ch. 212, F.S., and to prescribe all forms upon which reports shall be made to it and any other forms required for the proper administration of Ch. 206, F.S.

(2) *Record Retention.*

(a) Each licensee of motor fuel and special fuel shall maintain and keep, for a period of five (5) years, such record of motor fuel and special fuel purchased, received, acquired, used, transferred, loaned, sold and delivered within this state by said licensee, together with physical inventory records, purchase and sale invoices, receiving records, delivery tickets, loading tickets, bills of lading, resale and exemption certificates, and other pertinent records and papers, as may be required by the department for the reasonable administration of the motor fuel and special fuel tax laws of this state.

(b) Every person not a licensee of motor fuel or special fuel who purchases fuel taxable under Ch. 206 and Part II of Ch. 212, F.S., for the purposes of resale, shall maintain and keep for a period of five (5) years a record of fuel received, the amount of tax paid as part of the purchase price, together with delivery tickets, invoices, and bills of lading, and such other records as the department requires.

(c) Other recordkeeping requirements are summarized in § 95.091(3)(a)1., F.S.

(3) *Inspection.*

(a) All such records, books, papers, and other documents and equipment of licensees of motor fuel, dealers of special fuel, common carriers, and other persons who purchase or otherwise acquire motor fuel and/or special fuel in tank car, truck, or cargo lots and selling, using, consuming or otherwise disposing of the fuel in this state shall be open during normal business hours for inspection by the department to verify the truth and accuracy of any statement or report, to ascertain whether or not the tax imposed by Ch. 206 and Part II of Ch. 212, F.S., has been paid.

(b) The amount of any tax imposed under Ch. 206 and Part II of Ch. 212, F.S., may be determined and assessed for a period of five years after the tax becomes due and payable. The beginning of the five year period for determination and assessment of tax due shall be five years prior to the first day of the month in which a request for inspection and examination of the books and records has been made by the Department. The licensee shall have 60 days from the date of the Notice of Intent to audit books and records for Florida Taxes to have available for inspection all such books and records, including RESALE AND EXEMPTION CERTIFICATES. The Department is not required to issue a Notice of Intent to audit in situations involving emergency audits requested by taxpayers, or in distress or jeopardy situations.

(4) *Tracking System Reporting Requirements.*

(a) Any person who is required to file returns under § § 206.48, 206.08, 206.09 and 206.095, F.S., shall file supporting schedules of such returns on magnetic media or floppy disks. Magnetic tape or floppy disks specifications and file description may be obtained from the Division of Tax Processing, Bureau of Returns Processing, Attn: Bureau Chief, 5050 West Tennessee St., Tallahassee, FL 32314-7443, or call 904-488-7080.

(b) The magnetic media shall be labeled, indicating name of company, Florida fuel identification number, applied date, type of tax(es) included in tape (motor fuel, aviation, gasohol, special fuel). Magnetic tapes shall be identified by reel number, disk by identification number. Submitters of magnetic media shall file the face of the return and all required supporting schedules containing grand totals and the reel or disk identification number.

(c) Taxpayers wishing not to use magnetic media or to obtain permission to delay reporting on magnetic media shall submit a written request stating reasons why the required file types cannot be submitted. Send request to:

Division of Tax Processing
Bureau of Returns Processing
Attn: Bureau Chief
5050 West Tennessee St.
Tallahassee, FL 32314-7443
or call 904-488-7080

Agency:	**Florida Department of Labor and**
Employment	**Security**
	Division of Unemployment Compensation

Citation:	**FS 38F-3.003**

✍ § 38F-3.003 Procedures for Filing Documents

(1) The carrier shall ensure that all parts of all documents filed with the Division pursuant to this chapter are complete and legible. These documents shall be filed with the Division of Workers' Compensation, 2728 Centerview Drive, Suite 220, Forrest Building, Tallahassee, Florida 32399-0685, except as otherwise indicated. If a document is not complete and legible, the Division will return it to the carrier's address as provided for correction or completion.

(2) Carriers or employers shall respond to any written request for information by the Division no later than 14 days after receiving the request, except as otherwise provided in Title 38F. F.A.C.

(3) Instructions on or pertaining to forms which are promulgated under this chapter are also rules under this chapter. Forms must be completed according to instructions. Entities completing forms must include the Division assigned Carrier or Service Co/TPA Code #, where required.

(4) The carrier, where required, shall include on every document it submits to the Division the following information:

(a) the employee's name.

(b) the employee's social security number. If the employee does not have a social security number because the employee is an alien, the carrier shall instead use the number of the employee's Arrival and Departure card (Form I-94) or Alien Registration Receipt card (Form I-151). If the carrier is unable to ascertain the numbers, it shall send a written request to the Information Management Division at the address in subsection (1) to obtain a temporary internal file number until one of the above identifying numbers is obtained.

(c) the month, date and year of the employee's accident, in the following order: month/day/year. The Division shall return to the carrier any document on which the appropriate identification does not appear, and shall notify the carrier of its error or omission. The carrier shall make the correction and resubmit the document to the Division. The filing date of the document is the date the Division receives the corrected document. If the carrier reports an incorrect employee name, social security number or date of accident, it shall send an LES Form DWC-4 or electronic alternative pursuant to Rule 38F-3.0091(16), F.A.C. All subsequent filings must reflect the corrected information.

(5) A carrier shall supply each employer to which it provides coverage a supply of LES Form DWC-1, First Report of Injury or Illness, unless an alternative electronic reporting arrangement is in place, and LES Form DWC-1a, Wage Statement. The carrier name, address and telephone number must be preprinted or pre-stamped on each such form. As required by these rules, the carrier shall supply to employees LES Form DWC-40, Statement of Quarterly Earnings for Supplemental Income Benefits for dates of accident on or after 1/1/94, and LES Form DWC-3, Request for Wage Loss/Temporary Partial Benefits, for dates of accident prior to 1/1/94.

(6) Computer-generated versions of any form promulgated under this rule must appear in substantial conformity with the printed form in design, layout, field size and content. Computer-generated forms must contain all data elements required by the printed form. If the Division finds that the computer-generated form is not sufficiently similar to the printed form, if it fails to contain all data elements, or if it is unclear or confusing, the Division will return the form to the carrier and notify the carrier of the deficiency. The carrier shall make the correction and resubmit a corrected form to the Division. The filing date of the form is the date the Division receives the corrected form.

(7) A carrier wishing to use alternative electronic reporting methods, or to alter any existing approved alternative electronic reporting methods, must submit a written proposal to the Director of the Division of Workers' Compensation, who will review the proposal to ensure compliance with applicable statues and rules, and compatibility with the Division's systems. The Director shall inform the carrier in writing of the Division's determination. After the carrier has received written approval of its proposal, it may send documents to the Division according to the method set out in its proposal.

(8) Only those documents required by this or previous editions of Title 38F, F.A.C., shall be maintained in the Division's files.

(9) Any person or entity failing to timely send documents promulgated under this chapter is subject to civil penalties assessed by the Division according to the provisions of Rule Chapter 38F-24, F.A.C.

Citation: FAC 38F-3.004

✍ § 38F-3.004 First Report of Injury of Illness: Employer's Responsibility to Record and Report Accidents.

(1) An employer shall record all industrial injuries and diseases as follows:

(a) For a first aid case, the employer shall complete either:

1. LES Form DWC-1, First Report of Injury or Illness; or

2. A form which the Division has previously approved in writing.

(b) For a medical only case, lost time case, or death case, the employer shall complete either:

1. LES Form DWC-1, First Report of Injury or Illness;

2. An approved alternative electronic data reporting method.

(2) An employer shall report an industrial injury or illness to its carrier as follows:

(a) First Report of Injury:

1. An employer shall report all cases, except first aid cases, to its carrier within seven days after the employer's knowledge of an industrial injury or disease. The employer may inform the carrier either by telephone, by electronic medium, or by completing and submitting LES Form DWC-1. The employer shall not delay submitted the LES Form DWC-1 because the employee's signature if unavailable.

2. An employer is not required to report a first aid case to the carrier. If the case later becomes a medical only or lost time case, the employer shall inform the carrier within seven days after the employer's knowledge of the change. The employer may inform the carrier either by telephone, by electronic medium, or by submitting LES Form DWC-1. The employer shall complete the Employer section of LES Form DWC-1 and ensure that the Employee section is complete before submitting the form to the carrier.

3. When an employer submits to its carrier LES Form DWC-1, it shall provide a copy of the form to the employee or the employee's estate. If the information required in LES Form DWC-1 is reported to the carrier by telephone or electronic medium, the carrier shall mail the employee and the employer a paper version of an approved First Report of Injury or Illness within three business days. An approved First Report of Injury or Illness is an LES Form DWC-1, or an ACCORD-4 form, also known as LES Form IA-1, if the carrier is approved to electronically submit First Reports of Injury or Illness to the Division.

4. If an injury or illness results in the employee's death, the employer shall give notice by telephone, facsimile or telegram to the Division of Safety within 24 hours of the employer's knowledge of the death, and shall file LES Form DWC-1 with the carrier. The address of the Division of Safety is: State of Florida, Department of Labor and Employment Security, Division of Safety, 2002 Old St. Augustine Road, Building E, Suite 45, Tallahassee, Florida 32399-0663; the telephone number for purposes of reporting is (904) 488-3044.

(b) Wage Statements: Within fourteen days after the employer has knowledge of a lost time case, it shall report wage information to the carrier on LES Form DWC-1A, Wage Statement. The employer shall provide a copy of the form, and any corrected form, to the employee or the employee's estate.

(3) Employers shall retain a copy or electronic record of all information which must be maintained or reported under this section for not less than two years and six months.

Agency: Florida Public Service Commission

✪ FAC 25-6.015. Location and Preservation of Records.

(1) All records that a utility is required to keep by reason of these or other rules prescribed by the Commission shall be kept at the office or offices of the utility within this state, unless otherwise authorized by the Commission.

(2) Any utility authorized to keep its records outside of the state shall reimburse the Commission for the reasonable travel expense of the Commission's representative during any out-of-state audit.

(3) All records shall be preserved in accordance with the Federal Energy Regulatory Commission's regulations, Title 18, Subchapter C, Part 125, Code of Federal Regulations, entitled "Preservation of Records of Public Utilities and Licensees" as revised, April 1, 1991 which is hereby incorporated by reference into this rule, with the exception of Item 64 (Records of predecessors and former associates) of the Schedule of records and periods of retention contained in Title 18, Subchapter C, Section 125.3, Code of Federal Regulations. Instead, utilities shall retain records of acquired companies until permission for disposal is petitioned for and approved by the Florida Public Service Commission.

(a) However, all source documents retained as required by Title 18, Subchapter C, Part 125, Code of Federal Regulations shall be maintained in their original form for a minimum of three years, or for any lesser period of time specified for that type of record in Title 18, Subchapter C, Part 125, Code of Federal Regulations, after the date the document was created or received by the utility. This paragraph does not require the utility to create paper copies of documents where the utility would not otherwise do so in the ordinary course of its business. The Commission may waive the requirement that documents be retained in their original form upon a showing by a utility that it employs a storage and retrieval systems that consistently produces clear, readable copies that are substantially equivalent to the originals, and clearly reproduces handwritten notations on documents.

(b) The utility shall maintain written procedures governing the conversion of source documents to a storage and retrieval system, which procedures ensure the authenticity of documents and the completeness of records. Records maintained in the storage and retrieval system must be easy to search and easy to read.

RULES OF THE DEPARTMENT OF STATE, DIVISION OF LIBRARY AND INFORMATION SERVICES

CHAPTER 1B-26. RECORDS MANAGEMENT STANDARDS AND REQUIREMENTS

✪ § 1B-26.003. Electronic Recordkeeping.

(1) *Purpose*. These rules provide standards for public records which have a retention value of more than ten years which will be recorded and stored on electronic media. Public records are those as defined by § 119.011(1), Florida Statutes.

(2) *Authority*. The authority for the establishment of these rules is § 257.36(1) and (7)(c), Florida Statutes.

(3) *Scope*.

(a)1. These rules are applicable to all agencies as defined by § 119.011(2), Florida Statutes.

2. These rules establish the minimum requirements for the creation, utilization, maintenance, retention, preservation, storage and disposition of long-term and permanent electronic records, regardless of the media utilized.

3. Electronic records include numeric, graphic, and textual information which may be recorded in any machine readable media form which includes, but is not limited to, magnetic media, such as tapes and disks (hard or floppy), and optical disks.

4. These rules apply to all electronic records systems, including, but not limited to, microcomputers, minicomputers, mainframe computers, or optical image recording systems (regardless of storage media) in network or stand-alone configuration.

(b) Before records with a retention period of 10 years or less are committed to an electronic recordkeeping system, with the intent of destroying the original record, a cost benefit analysis shall be prepared and reviewed by the agency to insure that the project or system contemplated is cost effective. Public records with a retention value of 10 years or less, or which are kept voluntarily beyond the established retention period, which are committed to electronic recordkeeping systems, are not subject to the provisions of rules 1B-26.003 (10)(c), (d), (e) and (11)(a).

(c) Any electronic recordkeeping system not meeting the provisions of these rules may be utilized for long-term or permanent records provided the original public record is maintained or microfilmed in accordance with the provisions of Rule 1B-26.0021, Florida Administrative Code prior to disposition.

(4) *Intent*. In enacting these rules, the Department of State is cognizant of the fact that there may be instances where an agency may be utilizing electronic recordkeeping systems and destroying public records. The Department is further aware that it may not be possible to implement this rule in its entirety immediately upon its enactment, and it is not the by this rule to disrupt such recordkeeping practices provided that such agencies make no further disposition of public records without approval of the Division of Library and Information Services of the Department of State.

(5) *Definitions*. For the purpose of these rules:

(a) "Database" means an organized collection of automated information.

(b) "Database management system" means a set of software programs that controls the organization, storage and retrieval of data (fields, records and files) in a database. It also controls the security and integrity of the database.

(c) "Data file" means related numeric, textual, or graphic information that is organized in a prescribed form and format.

(d) "Electronic record" means any information that is recorded in machine readable form.

(e) "System design" means the design of the nature and content of input, files, procedures, and output and their interrelationships.

(f) "Information system" means the organized collection, processing, transmission, and dissemination of information in accordance with defined procedures, whether automated or manual.

(h) "Permanent or Long-term records" means any public records which have an established retention period of more than 10 years. See § 119.011(1), Florida Statutes for the definition of a public record. Each record series shall be considered on an individual basis by the Division of Library and Information Services in establishing this retention period. See Rule 1B-24.002(13), Florida Administrative Code for the definition of a record series.

(6) *Agency duties and responsibilities*. The head of each agency shall:

(a) Develop and implement a program for the management of records created, received, maintained, used, or stored on electronic media.

(b) Integrate the management of electronic records with other records and information resources management programs of the agency.

(c) Incorporate electronic records management objectives, responsibilities, and authorities in pertinent agency directives, or rules, as applicable.

(d) Establish procedures for addressing records management requirements, including recordkeeping requirements and disposition, before approving new electronic records systems or enhancements to existing systems.

(e) Provide training for users of electronic records systems in the operation, care, and handling of the equipment, software, and media used in the system.

(f) Develop and maintain documentation about electronic records systems used by the agency to specify technical characteristics necessary for reading or processing the records. Documentation for electronic records systems shall meet the following standards:

1.Standard. Each agency shall identify all inputs and outputs of the system; define the contents of the files and records; define policies on access and use; define the purpose and function of the system; define update cycles or conditions and rules for adding information to the system, changing information in it, or deleting information; and ensure the timely, authorized disposition of the records in accordance with Chapter 1B-24, Florida Administrative Code.

2. *Standard.* Each agency shall specify the location and media in which electronic records are maintained to meet retention requirements, and maintain inventories of electronic records systems to facilitate disposition.

3. *Standard.* Each agency which maintains public records in an electronic records system shall provide, to any person making a request pursuant to Chapter 119, Florida Statutes, a copy of any data in such records which is not specifically exempt. Said copy shall be on paper, disk, tape, optical disk, or any other electronic storage device or media requested by the person, if the agency currently maintains the record in that form, or as otherwise required by Chapter 119, Florida Statutes. Except as otherwise provided by state statute, the cost for providing a copy of such data shall be in accordance with the provisions of § 119.07(1)(a) & (b), Florida Statutes. Agencies should not reproduce, or permit reproduction of, or distribute copies of, copyrighted work or material to the public but shall permit public access to copyrighted work in the possession for examination and inspection purposes only.

4. *Standard.* Except as otherwise provided by law, no agency shall enter into a contract with, or otherwise obligate itself to, any person or entity if such contract or obligation impairs the right of the public under state law to inspect or copy the agency's nonexempt public records existing on-line in, or stored on a device or media used in connection with, a computer system or optical imaging system owned, leased or otherwise used by an agency in the course of its governmental functions.

5. *Standard.* Before any agency acquires or makes a major modification to any computer or imaging system, equipment or software to store or retrieve public records, it shall assure such proposed system, equipment or software adequately provides for the rights of the public to access public records under Chapter 119, Florida Statutes.

6. *Standard.* Each agency shall develop and obtain approval of records retention schedules, and ensure the implementation of their provisions as prescribed by Chapter 1B-24, Florida Administrative Code.

(7) *Creation and Use of Data Files.* For electronic records systems that produce, use, or store data files, disposition instructions for the data shall be incorporated into a system's design.

(a) *Standard.* Agencies shall maintain adequate and up-to-date technical documentation for each electronic records system. The minimum documentation required is:

1. a narrative description of the system;

2. the physical and technical characteristics of the records, including a record layout that describes each field including its name, size, starting or relative position, and description of the form of the data (such as alphabetic, decimal, or numeric), or a data dictionary or the equivalent information associated with a database management system including a description of the relationship between data elements in data bases;

3. for information coming from geographic information systems, the physical and technical characteristics of the records must be described including a data dictionary, a quality and accuracy report and a description of the graphic data structure, such as recommended by the federal Spatial Data Transfer Standards, and

4. any other technical information needed to read or process the records.

(8) *Creation and Use of Text Documents.* Electronic records systems that maintain the official file copy of text documents on electronic media shall meet the following minimum requirements:

(a)1. Provide a method for all authorized users of the system to retrieve desired documents;

2. Provide an appropriate level of security to ensure the integrity of the documents in accordance with the provisions of Chapter 44-4, Florida Administrative Code;

3. Identify the standard interchange format when necessary to permit the exchange of documents on electronic media between agency computers using different software/operating systems and the conversion or migration of documents on electronic media from one system to another. In the absence of other conversion capabilities, the word processing or text creation system should be able to import and export files in the ASCII format as prescribed by Federal Information Processing Standard Publication (FIPS PUB) Number 1-2; Title: Code For Information Interchange. Its Representation, Subsets, and Extensions, which is hereby incorporated by reference, and made a part of this rule. This publication is available from the National Technical Information Service (NTIS), 5285 Port Royal Road, U.S. Department of Commerce, Springfield, VA 22161; and

4. Provide for the disposition of the documents including, when appropriate, transfer to the Florida State Archives.

(b) *Standard.* Before an official file copy document is created on electronic records systems, the document shall be uniquely identified to enable authorized personnel to retrieve, protect, and carry out the disposition of documents in the system. Agencies shall ensure that records maintained in such systems can be correlated with related records on paper, microfilm, or other media.

(9) *Legal Authentication.* Agencies will implement the following procedures to enhance the legal admissibility of electronic records:

(a) Document that similar kinds of records generated and stored electronically are created by the same processes each time and have a standardized retrieval approach.

(b) Substantiate that security procedures prevent unauthorized addition, modification, or deletion of a record and ensure systems protection against such problems as power interruptions.

(c) Identify the electronic media on which records are stored throughout their life cycle, the maximum time span that records remain on each storage media, and the official retention requirements as approved by the Department of State.

(10) *Selection of Electronic Records Storage Media.* For storing public records throughout their life cycle, agencies shall select appropriate media and systems which meet the following requirements:

(a) Permit easy and accurate retrieval in a timely fashion, and;

(b) Retain the records in a usable format until their authorized disposition and, when appropriate, meet the requirements necessary for transfer to the Florida State Archives.

(c) Optical disks will be obtained only from vendors whose guarantee of 10 years or more of readability is based upon accelerated aging tests which are linked to specific locations of the disk surface.

(d) *Standard.* A scanning density with a minimum of 200 dots per inch will be required for recording normal office documents on optical disk.

(e) *Standard.* A scanning density with a minimum of 300 dots per inch will be required for engineering drawings, maps, and other documents with background detail.

(f) *Standard.* Any optical media application system will support either Group 3 or Group 4 compression techniques as specified in the Consultative Committee on International Telegraphy and Telephones "Blue Book, Volume 7.3", which is hereby incorporated by reference and made a part of this rule. This volume is available from the International Communications Union, Consultative Committee, Place des Nations, CH-1211, Geneva 20, Switzerland. If use of a proprietary compression technique is unavoidable, the vendor should be required to provide a gateway to either Group 3 or Group 4 compression techniques.

(g) The following factors are to be considered before selecting a storage media or converting from one media to another:

1. The authorized retention of the records as determined during the scheduling process;
2. The maintenance necessary to retain the records;
3. The cost of storing and retrieving the records;
4. The access time to retrieve stored records; and
5. The portability of the medium (that is, selecting a medium that will run on equipment offered by multiple manufacturers), and the ability to transfer the information from one medium to another such as, from optical disk to magnetic tape.

(h) Agencies will not use floppy disks for the exclusive storage of long-term or permanent records.

(i) Agencies will ensure that all authorized users can identify and retrieve information stored on diskettes, removable disks, tapes, or optical disks by establishing and adopting procedures for external labeling of the contents of such diskettes, disk tapes, or optical disks.

(j) Agencies will ensure that information is not lost due to changing technology or deterioration of storage media by converting storage media to provide compatibility with the agency's current hardware and software. Before conversion of information to a different media, agencies must determine that authorized disposition of the electronic records can be implemented after conversion.

(k) Agencies will back up electronic records on a regular basis to safeguard against the loss of information due to equipment malfunctions or human error. Duplicate copies of long-term or permanent records will be maintained in storage areas located in buildings separate from the location of the records that have been copied.

(11) *Maintenance of Electronic Records.*

(a) *Standard.* Agencies shall maintain all long-term and permanent backup/security electronic recording media in a storage facility, either on-site or off-site, with constant temperature (below 68 degrees Fahrenheit) and relative humidity (30 to 40 percent) controls.

(b) *Standard.* Agencies shall annually read a statistical sample of all electronic media containing long-term or permanent records to identify any loss of information and to discover and correct the cause of data loss.

(c) *Standard.* Agencies shall copy all long-term or permanent electronic records before the media are 10 years old onto tested and verified new media. The test will verify that the media is free of permanent errors.

(d) *Standard.* Agencies shall rewind tapes only when necessary. Stored tapes are to be rewound only immediately before use to restore proper tension to the tape. Only tapes with extreme cases of degradation should be rewound when they are discovered to avoid more permanent damage.

(e) *Standard.* Agencies shall prohibit smoking and eating in electronic media storage libraries and test or evaluate areas which contain long-term or permanent records.

(f) *Standard.* External labels (or the equivalent automated management system) for electronic recording media used to store long-term or permanent records shall provide unique identification for each storage media, including:

1. the name of the organizational unit responsible for the data;
2. system title, including the version number of the application;
3. special security requirements or restrictions on access, if any; and,
4. software in use at the time of creation.

(g) *Standard.* Additionally, the following information shall be maintained for each media used to store long-term or permanent electronic records:

1. file title;
2. dates of creation;
3. dates of coverage;
4. the recording density;
5. type of internal labels;
6. volume serial number, if applicable;
7. the number of tracks;
8. character code/software dependency;
9. information about block size, and;
10. sequence number, if the file is part of a multi-media set.

(12) *Retention of Electronic Records.* Agencies shall establish policies and procedures to ensure that electronic records and their documentation are retained as long as needed. These retention procedures will include provisions for:

(a) *Standard.* Scheduling the retention and disposition of all electronic records, as well as related access documentation and indexes, in accordance with the provisions of Chapter 1B-24, Florida Administrative Code.

(b) *Standard.* Transferring a copy of the electronic records and any related documentation and indexes to the Florida State Archives at the time specified in the records retention schedule, if applicable. Transfer may take place at an earlier date if convenient for both the agency and the Archives.

(c) *Standard.* Establishing procedures for regular recopying, reformatting, and other necessary maintenance to ensure the retention and usability of the electronic records throughout their authorized life cycle.

(13) *Destruction of Electronic Records.* Electronic records may be destroyed only in accordance with the provision of Chapter 1B-24, Florida Administrative Code. At a minimum each agency should ensure that:

(a) Electronic records schedule for destruction must be disposed of in a manner that ensures protection of any sensitive, proprietary, or security information; and,

(b) Magnetic recording media previously used for electronic records containing sensitive, proprietary, or security information are not reused if the previously recorded information can be compromised in any way by reuse.

State:	Georgia
Source:	Georgia Code Annotated

TITLE 15. COURTS.

CHAPTER 6. SUPERIOR COURTS.

Citation:	GCA 15-6-87

✪ **§ 15-6-87. Use of photostatic and photographic equipment.**

(a) The clerk of the superior court of any county of this state may install and use photostatic or other photographic equipment, including microfilm photographic equipment, and electronic or computer equipment for use in the filing, docketing, recording, copying, binding, indexing, certification and furnishing of copies, including certified copies, of any and all instruments, records, and proceedings or parts of the same of record or on file in the clerk's office, with the consent and permission only of the county governing authority. The equipment and supplies for the same may be provided by the proper and respective county authorities out of county funds.

(b) All provisions of law relating to the filing, docketing, recording, keeping, copying, binding, indexing, certification, and furnishing of copies of records, including certified copies, and those provisions relating to the amount of fees of officers in connection therewith, as far as may be consistent with this Code section, shall apply to such photostatic and photographic records and copies.

(c) The provisions of this Code section for the installation and use of the equipment enumerated in subsection (a) of this Code section shall be construed as permissive only and are cumulative of other laws. However, should such equipment be purchased as authorized in this Code section, the use of the equipment shall be mandatory insofar as practical.

(d) This code section shall not be construed to change or repeal any rule of court or provision of law relating to records on appeal or review in the courts of this state.

TITLE 24. EVIDENCE.

CHAPTER 5. BEST EVIDENCE RULE.

Citation:	GCA 24-5-26

☞ **§ 24-5-26. Reproductions made in regular course of business admissible; when enlargements or facsimiles admitted.**

Any photostatic, microphotographic, photographic, or non-erasable optical image reproduction of any original writing or record made in the regular course of business to preserve the writing or record shall be admissible in evidence in any proceeding in any court of this state and in any proceeding before any board, bureau, department, commission, or agency of the state, in lieu of and without accounting for the original of such writing or record, if such reproduction accurately reproduces or forms a durable medium for reproducing the original. Any enlargement or facsimile of such reproduction shall likewise be admissible if the original of the reproduction is in existence and available for inspection under direction of the court or the agency conducting the proceeding.

TITLE 50. STATE GOVERNMENT.

CHAPTER 18. STATE PRINTING AND DOCUMENTS.

Article 5. State Records Management.

Citation:	GCA 50-18-93

✪ **§ 50-18-93. Duties of department.**

It shall be the duty of the department to:

* * * * *

(2) Develop and issue procedures, rules, and regulations establishing standards for efficient and economical management methods relating to the creation, maintenance, utilization, retention, preservation, and disposition of records, and vital records programs;

* * * * *

Citation:	GCA 50-18-96

✪ **§ 50-18-96. Copies of records as primary evidence.**

Photostatic copies of records produced from microfilm and print-out copies of computer records shall be received in any court of this state as primary evidence of the recitals contained therein.

Article 6. Microforms.

Citation:	GCA 50-18-120

✪ **§ 50-18-120. Authority for establishment of standards.**

The authority for the establishment of microform standards shall be vested in the State Records Committee. All powers and duties of the State Records Committee as provided in Article 5 of this chapter shall be applicable to the establishment and maintenance of microform standards in this state. With respect to microform standards for the courts, the concurrence of the Administrative Office of the Courts shall be required for the establishment of such standards.

State:	Guam
Source:	Civil Code Annotated

TITLE 6. EVIDENCE.

DIVISION 1. GUAM RULES OF EVIDENCE

Article X. Contents of Writings, Recordings, and Photographs.

☞ **§ 1001. Definitions.**

For purposes of this article the following definitions are applicable:

(1) *Writings and recordings.* — "Writings and recordings" consist of letters, words, or numbers, or their equivalent, set down by handwriting, typewriting, printing, photostating, photographing, magnetic impulse, mechanical or electronic recordings, or other form of data compilation.

(2) *Photographs.* — "Photographs" include still photographs, X-ray films, video tapes, and motion pictures.

(3) *Original.* — An "original" of a writing or recording is the

writing or recording itself or any counterpart intended to have the same effect by a person executing or issuing it. An original of a photograph includes the negative or any print therefrom. If data are stored in a computer or similar device, any printout or other output readable by sight, shown to reflect the data accurately, is an "original".

(4) *Duplicate.* — A "duplicate" is a counterpart produced by the same impression as the original, or from the same matrix, or by means of photography, including enlargements and miniatures, or by mechanical or electronic re-recording, or by chemical reproduction, or by other equivalent techniques which accurately reproduces the original.

☞ § 1003. Admissibililty of Duplicates.

A duplicate is admissible to the same extent as an original unless (1) a genuine question is raised as to the authenticity of the original or (2) in the circumstances it would be unfair to admit the duplicate in lieu of the original.

However, circumstances shall not be used to prohibit the introduction of business records in microfilm form if the business keeping such records has adopted a policy of keeping the records in question in microfilm form at the time they are sought to be admitted in evidence, but any irregularities or doubts as to the authenticity of the evidence may be proven.

☞ § 1004. Admissibility Other Evidence of Contents.

The original is not required, and other evidence of the contents of a writing, recording, or photograph is admissible if—

(1) *Originals lost or destroyed.* All originals are lost or have been destroyed, unless the proponent lost or destroyed them in bad faith; or

(2) *Original not obtainable.* No original can be obtained by any available judicial process or procedure; or

(3) *Original in possession of opponent.* At a time when an original was under the control of the party against whom offered, he was put on notice, by the pleadings or otherwise, that the contents would be a subject of proof at the hearing, and he does not produce the original at the hearing; or

(4) *Collateral matters.* The writing, recording, or photograph is not closely related to a controlling issue.

State:	**Hawaii**
Source:	**Hawaii Revised Statutes**

TITLE 6. COUNTY ORGANIZATION AND ADMINISTRATION.

CHAPTER 92. PUBLIC AGENCY MEETINGS AND RECORDS.

Part 3. Copies of Records; Costs and Fees.

Citation: **HRS 92-29**

✪ § 92-29. Reproduction of public records on films.

Any public officer having the care and custody of any record, paper or document may cause the same to be photographed, microphotographed, or otherwise reproduced on film. The film shall be of durable material and the device used to reproduce the record, paper, or document on the film shall be one which accurately reproduces the original thereof in all details.

Citation: **HRS 92-30**

✪ § 92-30. Film deemed original record.

Such photograph, microphotograph, or reproduction on film shall be deemed to be an original for all purposes, including introduction in evidence in all courts or administrative agencies. A transcript, exemplification, facsimile, or certified copy thereof shall, for all purposes recited herein, be deemed to be a transcript, exemplification, facsimile, or certified copy of the original record.

Citation: **HRS 92-31**

☞ § 92-31. Disposition of original.

Such photograph, microphotograph, or reproduction on film shall be placed in conveniently accessible files and provisions made for preserving, examining and using the same. Thereafter, such public officer, having first received the written approval of the comptroller described in section 94-3, may cause such record, paper or document to be destroyed. The comptroller may require, as a prerequisite to the granting of such approval, that a reproduction or print of such photograph, microphotograph, or reproduction on film, be delivered into the custody of the public archives for safekeeping. The comptroller may also require the delivery into the custody of another governmental department or agency or a research library of any such record, paper, or document proposed to be destroyed under the provisions of this section.

TITLE 33. EVIDENCE.

CHAPTER 622. DOCUMENTARY EVIDENCE.

Part 5. Medical Records.

Citation: **HRS 622-58**

✪ § 622.58. Retention of medical records.

(a) Medical records may be computerized or minified by the use of microfilm or any other similar photographic process; provided that the method used creates an unalterable record. The health care provider shall retain medical records in the original or reproduced form for a minimum of seven years after the last data entry except in the case of minors whose records shall be retained during the period of minority plus seven years after the minor reaches the age of majority.

(b) Records exempt from the retention requirement are: public health mass screening records; pupils' health records and related school health room records; preschool screening program records; communicable disease reports; and mass testing epidemiological projects and studies records, including consents; topical fluoride application consents; psychological test booklets; laboratory copies of reports, pharmacy copies of prescriptions, patient medication profiles, hospital nutritionists' special diet orders, and similar records retained separately from the medical record but duplicated within it; public health nurses' case records that do not contain any physician's direct notations; social workers' case records; and diagnostic or evaluative studies for the department of education or other state agencies.

(c) X-ray films, electro-encephalogram tracings, and similar imaging records shall be retained for at least seven years, after which they may be presented to the patient or destroyed; provided that interpretations or separate reports of x-ray films, electro-encephalogram tracings, and similar imaging records shall be subject to subsection (e).

(d) Medical records may be destroyed after the seven-year retention period or after minification, in a manner that will preserve the confidentiality of the information in the record; provided that the health care provider retains basic information from each record destroyed. Basic information from the records of a physician or surgeon shall include the patient's name and birthdate, a list of dated diagnoses and intrusive treatments, and a record of all drugs prescribed or given. Basic information from the records of a health care facility, as defined in § 323D-2, shall include the patient's name and birthdate, dates of admission and discharge, names of attending physicians, final diagnosis, major procedures performed, operative reports, pathology reports, and discharge summaries.

(e) The health care provider, or the health care provider's successor, shall be liable for the preservation of basic information from the medical record for twenty-five years after the last entry, except in the case of minors, whose records shall be retained during the period of minority plus twenty-years after the minor reaches the age of majority. If the health care provider is succeeded by another entity, the burden of compliance with this section shall rest with the successor. Before a provider ceases operations, the provider shall make immediate arrangements, subject to the approval of the department of health, for the retention and preservation of the medical records in keeping with the intent of this section.

(f) For the purposes of this section, the term "health care provider" means as defined in § 671-1.

CHAPTER 626. HAWAII RULES OF EVIDENCE.

Citation: **HRS 626-Rule 1001**

☞ Rule 1001. Definitions

For purposes of this article the following definitions are applicable:

(1) *Writings and recordings.* — "Writings" and "recordings" consist of letters, words, or numbers, or their equivalent, set down by handwriting, typewriting, printing, photostating, photographing, magnetic impulse, mechanical or electronic recording, or other form of data compilation.

(2) *Photographs.* — "Photographs" include still photographs, X-ray films, video tapes, and motion pictures.

(3) *Original.* — An "original" of a writing or recording is the writing or recording itself or any counterpart intended to have the same effect by a person executing or issuing it. An "original" of a photograph includes the negative or any print therefrom. If data are stored in a computer or similar device, any printout or other output readable by sight, shown to reflect the data accurately, is an "original".

(4) *Duplicate.* — A "duplicate" is a counterpart produced by the same impression as the original, or from the same matrix, or by means of photography, including enlargements and miniatures, or by mechanical or electronic re-recording, or by chemical reproduction, or by other equivalent techniques which accurately reproduces the original.

Citation: **HRS 626-Rule 1003**

☞ Rule 1003 Admissibility of duplicates.

A duplicate is admissible to the same extent as an original unless (1) a genuine question is raised as to the authenticity of the original, or (2) in the circumstances it would be unfair to admit the duplicate in lieu of the original.

[See Appendix A. Uniform Rules of Evidence for additional provisions.]

State: **Idaho**
Source: **Idaho Code**

TITLE 9. EVIDENCE.

CHAPTER 3. PUBLIC WRITINGS.

Citation: **IC 9-328**

☞ § 9-328. Photographic or digital retention of records, disposition of originals.

Any state officer may receive or retain documents filed or recorded in his office on media other than paper, provided that the media comply with the standards set forth in this section. The originals of paper documents may be disposed of in accordance with the provisions of this section.

(1) A state officer may receive, file or record documents in his office in paper form. When permitted by law or administrative rule, a state officer may alternatively receive, file or record documents which are transmitted on other media or by electronic means, provided that the media or means or transmittal does not permit undetected additions, deletions or alterations of documents during transmittal. Such media and electronic means include, but are not limited to, facsimile (FAX), magnetic tape or disk, photographic film, optical disk and an electronically transmitted data stream.

(2) A state officer may retain a document in a different form or medium from that in which it is received, provided that the form or medium in which the document is retained results in a permanent record which may be accurately reproduced during the period for which the document must be retained.

(3) If a document is received in paper form or as an image of a paper document, e.g., film, FAX or other digitized image, it must be retained in a form or medium which permits accurate reproduction of the document in paper form. If the medium chosen for retention is photographic, all film used for capture or retention of images must meet the quality standards of the American National Standards Institute (ANSI). If the medium chosen for retention is digital, the permanent medium must preclude alteration or erasure of a document, and must permit reproduction on paper at a resolution not worse than two hundred (200) dots per inch.

(4) If a document is received as a data stream, it must be retained in a system which is secure against unauthorized or undetected alteration or deletion of data, and which provides for periodic back-up of data for off-site storage. The system must permit the document to be readily and intelligibly reproduced on paper.

(5) If a document is received in paper form or as an image of a paper document, and if the receiving state officer retains it in another form or medium as permitted in subsection (3) of this section, then the original of the document may be disposed of or returned to the sender, provided that such disposition or return is done pursuant to statute or an administrative rule promulgated under § 67-5751, Idaho Code.

(6) A document retained by a state officer in any form or medium permitted under this section shall be deemed to be an original public record for all purposes. A reproduction or copy of such a document, certified by the state officer, shall be deemed to be a transcript or certified copy of the original, and shall be admissible before any court or administrative hearing.

Citation: IC 9-331

☞ **§ 9-331. County officials replacing documents or books — Manner.**

Whenever any office of any county is required or authorized by law to record, copy, file, recopy or replace any document, plat, paper, written instrument, or book, on file or of record in his office, he may do so by photostatic, photographic, microphotographic, microfilm, optical scan or other process which produces a clear, accurate, and permanent copy or reproduction of the original document, plat, paper, written instrument, or record, in accordance with standards not less than those now approved for permanent records by the American National Standards Institute (ANSI).

Citation: IC 9-331A

☞ **§ 9-331A. Photographic or digital retention of county records — Disposition of originals.**

Any county officer may receive or retain records filed or recorded in his office on media other than paper, provided that the media comply with the standards set forth in this section. The originals of paper documents may be disposed of in accordance with the provisions of this section.

(1) A county officer may receive, file or record documents in his office in paper form. When permitted by law, a county officer may alternately receive, file or record documents which are transmitted on other media or by electronic means, provided that the medium or means of transmittal does not permit undetected additions, deletions, or alterations of documents during transmittal. Such media and electronic means include, but are not limited to, facsimile transmissions (FAX), magnetic tape or disk, photographic film, optical disk and an electronically transmitted data stream.

(2) A county officer may retain a document in a different form or medium from that in which it is received, provided that the form or medium in which the document is retained results in a permanent record which may be accurately reproduced during the period for which the document must be retained.

(3) If a document is received in paper form or as an image of a paper document, e.g. film, FAX, or other digitized image, it must be retained in a form or medium which permits accurate reproduction of the document in paper form. If the medium chosen for retention is photographic, all film used for capture or retention of images must meet the quality standards of the American National Standards Institute (ANSI). If the medium chosen for retention is digital, the permanent medium must preclude alteration or erasure of a document, and must permit reproduction on paper at a resolution not worse than two hundred (200) dots per inch.

(4) If a document is received as a data stream, it must be retained in a system which is secure against unauthorized or undetected alteration or deletion of data, and which provides for periodic backup of data for off-site storage. The system must permit the document to be readily and intelligibly reproduced on paper.

(5) If a document is received in paper form or as an image of a paper document, and if the receiving county officer retains it in another form or medium as permitted in subsection (3) of this section, then the original of the document may be disposed of or returned to the sender, provided that such disposition or return is done pursuant to statute.

(6) A document retained by a county officer in any form or medium permitted under this section shall be deemed to be an original public record for all purposes. A reproduction or copy of such a document, certified by the county officer, shall be deemed to be a transcript or certified copy of the original, and shall be admissible before any court or administrative hearing.

CHAPTER 4. PRIVATE WRITINGS.

Citation: IC 9-417

☞ ✍ **§ 9-417. Admissibility of reproduced records in evidence.**

If any business, institution, or member of a profession or calling, in the regular course of business or activity has kept or recorded any memorandum, writing, entry, print, representation or combination thereof, of any act, transaction, occurrence or event, and in the regular course of business has caused any or all of the same to be recorded, copied or reproduced by any photographic, optical imaging, photostatic, microfilm, micro-card, miniature photographic, or other process which accurately reproduces or forms a durable medium for so reproducing the original, the original may be destroyed in the regular course of business unless held in a custodial or fiduciary capacity and the principal or true owner has not authorized destruction or unless its preservation is required by law. Such reproduction, when satisfactorily identified, is as admissible in evidence as the original itself in any judicial or administrative proceeding whether the original is in existence or not and an enlargement or facsimile of such reproduction is likewise admissible in evidence if the original reproduction is in existence and available for inspection under the direction of court. The introduction of a reproduced record, enlargement or facsimile, does not preclude admission of the original. Approved February 28, 1995.

Citation: IC 9-419

☞ **§ 9-419. Short title.**

This law may be cited as the Uniform Photographic Copies of Business Records as Evidence Act.

Source: Idaho Court Administrative Rules

RULES GOVERNING THE ADMINISTRATION AND SUPERVISION OF THE UNIFIED AND INTEGRATED IDAHO JUDICIAL SYSTEM

Part 4. Court Records Required; Preservation, Destruction or Disposition of Court Records.

Citation: RULE 37

✪ **Rule 37. Preservation, destruction, or disposition of trial court records and property — Civil actions.**

(a) *General Standards.* (1) Courts using any type of microfilming process to create a permanent court record must follow the Idaho Standards for Microfilming Court records in order to ensure that the film is of archival quality. (2) Wherever in this rule it is required that a record be preserved, it may be preserved in the form of the original document or a microfilmed or other permanent copy thereof.

(b) *Destruction of Court Records.* All court documents to be preserved shall be preserved as prescribed in subsection (c) below. After a document has been preserved, it , and all other pleadings, motions, affidavits, orders, exhibits and documents of every nature, kind, and description in any action or proceeding may be destroyed pursuant to order of the administrative district judge. Such court order shall not be entered for at least one (1) year from the expiration of the time for appeal or determination of an appeal, or the determination of a proceeding following an appeal, whichever is later, unless otherwise specifically provided.

(c) *Preservation of certain documents.* The register of actions, the proof of service, the final order, judgment or decree, and the notice of intent to destroy exhibits in any civil action or special or other proceeding shall be preserved by the clerk of the court indefinitely. Additional court records shall be preserved as follows:

(1) *Probate proceedings.* The will, letters testamentary, letters intestate, inventory and appraisal, and any final decree or order shall be preserved indefinitely.

(2) *Guardianships and conservatorships.* All documents filed or lodged with the court shall be preserved for four (4) years after the guardianship or conservatorship is terminated.

(3) *Juvenile proceedings.* In Child Protective Act proceedings and Youth Rehabilitation Act proceedings, all reports to the court shall be preserved indefinitely.

(4) *Domestic relations cases involving children.* All documents filed or lodged with the court shall be preserved until two years after the youngest child reaches the age of majority, provided, however, child support payment records shall be preserved indefinitely.

(5) *Adoptions and terminations of parental rights.* The entire case file shall be preserved indefinitely.

(6) *Sealed cases.* Document in sealed cases may be preserved either in the form of the original document or a microfilmed or other permanent copy thereof; provided, however, that when preserved by microfilm, the microfilm shall be clearly designated as "sealed" or shall be maintained in a separate sealed area.

(d) *Destruction of recordings, stenographic records and tapes.* The administrative district judge of the district where the record is kept may order the destruction of all recordings, stenographic records and tapes of any court proceeding ten (10) years after the date of the proceeding; providing, however, the reporter's stenographic record may be destroyed immediately upon settlement of the reporter's transcript on appeal.

(e) *Disposition of Exhibits and Property.* This rule shall not prohibit a court from releasing exhibits at any time, or allowing the substitution of copies under such conditions as to assure the existence and availability of the exhibit in the event of an appeal.

(1) *Exhibits admitted in evidence.* Exhibits admitted in evidence or any other property used, displayed, or considered in connection with an action may be destroyed or disposed of by the clerk of the court pursuant to order of the court, after ten (10) days notice to the parties, when the exhibits or property are no longer necessary for the determination of the action or appeal of such action.

(2) *Exhibits marked, but not offered at trial.* Exhibits, marked but not offered at trial, may be returned at the conclusion of the trial to the party who had the exhibit marked or may be destroyed or disposed of by the clerk of the court pursuant to order of the court after ten (10) days notice to the parties.

(f) *Notice to Historical Society.* The court shall given written notice to the Idaho State Historical Society of the intent to destroy or dispose of any document or property. No document or property shall be disposed of or destroyed for 120 days following said notice unless the Idaho State Historical Society gives written notice to the court that it has no interest in obtaining or preserving said document or property.

(g) *Retention of original record.* Notwithstanding any other provision of this rule, the presiding judge of any case may order the original record of any part thereof be retained for a specific time period or indefinitely.

Citation: RULE 38

✪ **Rule 38. Preservation, destruction and disposition of trial court records and property — Criminal actions and infractions.**

(a) *General standards.* (1) Courts using any type of microfilming process to create a permanent record must follow the Idaho Standards for Microfilming Court Records in order to insure that the film is of archival quality. (2) Wherever in this rule, it is required that a record be preserved, it may be preserved either in the form of the original document or a microfilmed or other permanent copy thereof.

(b) *Destruction of Court Records.* Subject to section (d) below, no court records pertaining to a criminal conviction may be destroyed while a defendant is incarcerated or being held in any Idaho state or county institution in connection with the conviction to which the records pertain, nor while a defendant is participating in a court-ordered probation or rehabilitation program or is subject to conditions of parole in connection with the conviction to which the records pertain. The administrative district judge of any judicial district may order the destruction in all other cases of all pleadings, motions, affidavits and all other written documents of every nature, kind and description under the following conditions:

(1) *Criminal actions where a judgment of acquittal or dismissal of the charge against the defendant has been entered.* Destruction may be ordered one (1) year from the expiration of the time for appeal or from the determination of an appeal or from the determination of a proceeding following an appeal, provided the final determination results in dismissal or acquittal.

(2) *Any criminal action, including driving without privileges and driving or being in actual physical control of a motor vehicle while under the influence of alcohol, drugs or any other intoxicating substance, in which judgment has been entered prior to July 1, 1993.* Destruction can be ordered five (5) years from the expiration of the time for appeal or from the determination of an appeal or from the determination of a proceeding following an appeal, whichever is later; provided however, that the payment history shall be preserved on any action in which monies are due.

(3) *Any criminal action, including driving without privileges and driving or being in actual physical control of a motor vehicle while under the influence of alcohol, drugs or any other intoxicating substance, in which judgment has been entered on or after July 1, 1993.* Destruction can be ordered one (1) year from the expiration of the time for the appeal or from the determination of an appeal or from the determination of a proceeding following an appeal, whichever is later; provided however, that the payment history shall be preserved in any action in which monies are due.

(4) *Traffic offenses, other than driving without privileges and driving or being in actual physical control of a motor vehicle while under the influence of alcohol, drugs or any other intoxicating substance.* Destruction of all court records, except any existing register of actions, may be ordered one (1) year from the expiration of the time for appeal or from determination of an appeal or from determination of a proceeding following an appeal, whichever is later; provided, however, that the final judgment and sentence and payment history shall be preserved in actions in which monies are due.

(5) *Infractions.* Destruction of all records may be ordered one (1) year from the expiration of the time for appeal or from the determination of an appeal or from the determination of a proceeding following an appeal, whichever is later; provided,

however, that unpaid infraction citations shall be preserved for a period of three (3) years from the date of judgment.

(6) *Sealed cases.* Documents in sealed cases may be preserved either in the form of the original document or a microfilmed or other permanent copy thereof; provided, however, that when preserved by microfilm, the microfilm shall be clearly designated as "sealed" or shall be maintained in a separate sealed area.

(c) *Preservation of certain documents.* The register of actions, the original and any amended complaint or information, the notification of defendant's rights, the notice of subsequent penalties, the final judgment of conviction, the order withholding judgment, the judgment of acquittal or dismissal, and the notice of intent to destroy exhibits in any criminal action, including driving without privileges and driving or being in actual physical control of a motor vehicle while under the influence of alcohol, drugs or any other intoxicating substance, shall be preserved by the Clerk of Court indefinitely.

(d) *Destruction of recordings, stenographic records and tapes.* The administrative district judge of any judicial district may order the destruction of all recordings, stenographic records and tapes of any court proceeding ten (10) years after the date of the proceeding; provided, however, the reporter's stenographic record may be destroyed immediately upon settlement of the reporter's transcript on appeal.

(e) *Disposition of exhibits and property.* This rule shall not prohibit a court from releasing exhibits at any time, or allowing the substitution of copies under such conditions as to assure the existence and availability of the exhibit in the event of an appeal.

(1) *Exhibits admitted in evidence.*— Exhibits admitted in evidence or any other property used, displayed or considered in connection with an action may be destroyed or disposed of by the Clerk of the Court pursuant to order of the court, after ten (10) days notice to the parties, when the exhibits or property are no longer necessary for the determination of the action or appeal of such action.

(2) *Exhibits marked, but not offered at trial.*— Exhibits marked, but not offered at trial may be returned to the party who had the exhibit marked at the conclusion of the trial, or may be destroyed or disposed of by the Clerk of the Court pursuant to order of the court, after ten (10) days notice to the parties.

(f) *Notice to Historical Society.* The court shall give written notice to the Idaho State Historical Society of intent to destroy or dispose of any documents or property. No document or property shall be disposed of or destroyed for 120 days following said notice unless the Idaho State Historical Society gives written notice to the court that it has no interest in obtaining or preserving said document or property.

(g) *Retention of original record.* Notwithstanding any other provision of this rule, the presiding judge of any case may order the original record of any part thereof be retained for a specific time period or indefinitely.

Source: **Idaho Rules of Evidence**

ARTICLE X. CONTENTS OF WRITINGS, RECORDINGS, AND PHOTO.

☞ Rule 1001. Definitions.

For purposes of this article the following definitions are applicable:

(1) *Writings and recordings.* — "Writings" and "recordings" consist of letters, words, or numbers, or their equivalent, set down by handwriting, typewriting, printing, photostating, photographing, magnetic impulse, mechanical or electronic recording, or other form of data compilation.

(2) *Photographs.* — "Photographs" include still photographs, X-ray films, video tapes, and motion pictures.

(3) *Original.* — An "original" of a writing or recording is the writing or recording itself or any counterpart intended to have the same effect by a person executing or issuing it. An "original" of a photograph includes the negative or any print therefrom. If data are stored in a computer or similar device, any printout or other output readable by sight, shown to reflect the data accurately, is an "original".

(4) *Duplicate.* — A "duplicate" is a counterpart produced by the same impression as the original, or from the same matrix, or by means of photography, including enlargements and miniatures, or by mechanical or electronic re-recording, or by chemical reproduction, or by other equivalent techniques which accurately reproduces the original.

☞ Rule 1003. Admissibility of duplicates.

A duplicate is admissible to the same extent as an original unless (1) a genuine question is raised as to the authenticity or continuing effectiveness of the original or (2) in the circumstances it would be unfair to admit the duplicate in lieu of the original.

State: **Illinois**
Source: **Illinois Consolidated Statutes**

CHAPTER 5. GENERAL PROVISIONS

ACT 160. STATE RECORDS ACT

Citation: **5 ILCS 160/17**

✪ § 160/17. Disposal and reproduction of records — Regulations.

§ 17. Regardless of other authorization to the contrary, no record shall be disposed of by any agency of the State, unless approval of the State Records Commission is first obtained. The Commission shall issue regulations, not inconsistent with this Act, which shall be binding on all agencies. Such regulations shall establish procedures for compiling and submitting to the Commission lists and schedules of records proposed for disposal; procedures for the physical destruction or other disposition of records proposed for disposal; and standards for the reproduction of records by photography or microphotographic processes with the view to the disposal of the original records. Such standards shall relate to the quality of film used, preparation of the records for filming, proper identification matter on the records so that an individual document or series of document can be located on the film with reasonable facility, and that the copies contain all significant record detail, to the end that the photographic or microphotographic copies will be adequate.

Such regulations shall also provide that the State archivist may retain any records which the Commission has authorized to be destroyed, where they have a historical value, and that the State archivist may deposit them in the State Library or State historical museum or with a historical society, museum or library.

ACT 170. FILMED RECORDS REPRODUCTION ACT

Citation: 5 ILCS 170/2

✪ **§ 170/2. Reproduction of records on film.**

§ 2. Any public officer of the state may cause any or all records, papers or documents made or kept by him to be photographed, microphotographed or reproduced on film or by other processes which accurately reproduce or form a durable medium for reproducing the original. The reproduction of records by any photographic, microphotographic or silver halide processes, when such reproductions are to serve as permanent records, shall comply with the regulations and standards of the State Records Commission. Other durable media using machine readable techniques may be used as an alternative to film, provided the medium is non-erasable and cannot be altered once the original document has been recorded.

Citation: 5 ILCS 170/3

✪ **§ 170/3. Film or other process as original record.**

§ 3. Such photographs, microphotographs or photographic film or the result of any other process authorized by Section 2 shall be deemed to be an original record for all purposes, including introduction in evidence in all courts or administrative agencies. A transcript, exemplification or certified copy thereof shall, for all purposes recited herein, be deemed to be a transcript, exemplification, or certified copy of the original.

Citation: 5 ILCS 170/4

✪ **§ 170/4. Disposition of originals.**

§ 4. Whenever such photographs, microphotographs, or reproductions on film or the result of any other process authorized by Section 2 shall be placed in conveniently accessible files and provisions made for preserving, examining and using the same, any such public officer may, with the approval of the State Records Commission, cause the original records from which the photographs or microphotographs or other permanent record have been made or any part thereof to be disposed of according to methods prescribed by law.

CHAPTER 15. EXECUTIVE OFFICERS.

ACT 415. COMPTROLLER'S RECORDS ACT

Citation: 15 ILCS 415/1

✪ **§ 415/1. Comptroller may destroy records.**

§ 1. Comptroller may destroy records. After obtaining the approval of the State Records Commission, the State Comptroller may destroy any records made and kept by him. When applying to the State Records Commission for approval to destroy any records, the Comptroller shall accompany his request with a list and a brief description of the records to be destroyed. A copy of this list shall be sent to the Secretary of State before any records are destroyed. The Secretary of State shall examine this list to determine whether any of the records which the Comptroller proposes to destroy are of unusual historic value. If the Secretary of State determines that any of the records are of unusual historical value, he shall inform the Comptroller of his determination, and the Comptroller shall deposit such records in the State Archives rather than destroy them. Warrants and vouchers shall be retained by the Comptroller for at least 5 years after the date thereof and may thereafter be destroyed, but warrants must be reproduced as required by Section 3 before being destroyed.

Citation: 15 ILCS 415/3

✪ **§ 415/3. Records to be photographed or reproduced on film.**

§ 3. Records to be photographed or reproduced on film. The State Comptroller may have any records kept by him photographed, microfilmed, or otherwise reproduced on film prior to destruction; provided, that prior to the destruction of any warrants, the Comptroller shall have those warrants photographed, microfilmed or otherwise reproduced on film, in 2 copies.

Reproductions shall be placed in conveniently accessible files and provisions made for preserving, examining and using them.

CHAPTER 50. LOCAL GOVERNMENT

ACT 205. LOCAL RECORDS ACT

Citation: 50 ILCS 205/4

✪ **§ 205/4. Public records — Disposal — Duties of archivist.**

§ 4. All public records made or received by, or under the authority of, coming into the custody, control or possession of any officer or agency shall not be mutilated, destroyed, transferred, removed or otherwise damaged or disposed of, in whole or in part, except as provided by law.

Court records filed with the clerks of the Circuit Court shall be destroyed in accordance with the Supreme Court's General Administrative Order on Recordkeeping in the Circuit Courts. The clerks of the Circuit Courts shall notify the Supreme Court, in writing, specifying case records or other documents which they intend to destroy. The Supreme Court shall review the schedule of items to be destroyed and notify the appropriate Local Records Commission of the Court's intent to destroy such records. The Local Records Commission, within 90 days after receipt of the Supreme Court's notice, may undertake to photograph or microphotograph, or digitize electronically any or all such records and documents, or, in the alternative, may transport such original records to the State Archives or other storage location under its supervision.

The Archivist may accept for deposit in the State Archives or regional depositories official papers, drawings, maps, writings and records of every description of counties, municipal corporations, political subdivisions and courts of this State, when such materials are deemed by the Archivist to have sufficient historical or other value to warrant their continued preservation by the State of Illinois.

The officer or clerk depositing such records may, upon request, obtain from the Archivist, without charge, a certified copy or reproduction of any specific record, paper or document when such record, paper or document is required for public use.

CHAPTER 55. COUNTIES

ACT 5. COUNTIES CODE.

ARTICLE 3. OFFICERS AND EMPLOYEES

DIVISION 3-5. RECORDER

Citation:	55 ILCS 5/3-5025

✪ **§ 5/3-5025. Books.**

Every recorder shall keep the following books:

* * * * *

8. An index of all ordinances, petitions, assessment rolls, orders, judgments or other documents filed or recorded in respect of any drainage or special assessment matter sufficient to enable the public to identify all tracts involved therein and to locate all the documents which have been filed or recorded. The recorder may solicit the assistance of the State Records Commission in organizing and indexing these documents. Any recorder may install or contract for the use of a computerized system that will permit automated entry and indexing, alphabetically by document, of instruments filed in his or her office and that will provide both quick search and retrieval of such entries and hard copy print output, whether on paper or microfilm, of such entries as indexed. If such a computerized system has been in use in his or her office for at least 6 months and the recorder determines that it provides accurate and reliable indices that may be stored as permanent records, more quickly and efficiently than the system previously used, the recorder may thereafter discontinue the use of the manual system and use only the computerized system for such indices. In that event, references in this Division to books, records or forms as relate to such indices are intended to encompass and refer to the computer system and all materials and forms directly related to that system and its proper use. This Section is subject to the Local Records Act (50 ILCS 205/1 *et seq.*

CHAPTER 410. PUBLIC HEALTH.

ACT 530. MARRIAGE, DISSOLUTIONS, AND INVALIDITY RECORDS ACT.

Citation:	410 ILCS 530/2

☞ ✪ **§ 530/2. Reproduction — Copies.**

§ 2. The Department may cause the records of marriage, dissolution of marriage and declaration of invalidity of marriage established under this Act to be reproduced on microfilm for permanent retention.

Such microfilm shall comply with the minimum standards of quality approved for permanent photographic records by the National Bureau of Standards and the device used to reproduce such records on such film shall be one which accurately reproduces the original thereof in all its details.

Such microfilm or a computer print-out copy thereof, as provided herein shall be deemed to be an original record for all purposes, including introduction in evidence in all courts or administrative agencies. A transcript, exemplification, or certified copy thereof, shall, for all purposes recited herein, be deemed to be a transcript, exemplification, or certified copy of the original.

If the Department has records of marriage, divorce and annulment of marriage on computer tape, certified computer print-outs of such records shall have the same legal effect as certified copies of such documents would have for all purposes. Whenever such microfilm has been properly and permanently filed for use and safekeeping, the Department may cause the original records from which the microfilm reproduction was made to be destroyed.

The Department is authorized to furnish a copy of the microfilm or computer print-out of the records relating to marriages, dissolutions of marriages and declarations of invalidity of marriages in a particular county to the Clerk of any court of that county, provided that this is done without cost to the State.

The Department shall cause its records of marriage, dissolution of marriage and declaration of invalidity of marriage to be permanently preserved and safeguarded in its offices at Springfield. The Secretary of State shall provide suitable quarters for the administration and the permanent and safe preservation of all records returned to the Department under this Act.

CHAPTER 735. CIVIL PROCEDURE

ACT 5. CODE OF CIVIL PROCEDURE

ARTICLE VIII. EVIDENCE.

PART 4. ACCOUNT BOOKS AND RECORDS.

Citation:	735 ILCS 5/8-401

☞ **§ 5/8-401. Account books and records.**

Where in any action or proceeding, the claim or defense is founded on a book account or any other record or document, any party or interested person may testify to his or her account book, or any other record or document and the items therein contained; that the same is a book, record, or document of original entries, and that the entries therein were made by himself or herself, and are true and just; or that the same were made by a deceased person, or by a disinterested person, a non-resident person of the state at the time of the trial, and where made by such deceased or non-resident person in the usual course of trade, and of his or her duty or employment to the party so testifying; and thereupon the account book and entries or any other record or document shall be admitted as evidence in the cause. Where such book of original entries or any other record or document has been photographed, microphotographed, microfilmed, optical imaged, or otherwise reproduced either in the usual course of business, or pursuant to any statute of this State authorizing the reproduction of public records, papers or documents, and the reproduction, in either case, complies with the minimum standards of quality for permanent photographic records approved by the State Records Commission, then such reproduction shall be deemed to be an original record, book or document for all purposes, including introduction in evidence in all courts or administrative agencies.

CHAPTER 805. BUSINESS ORGANIZATIONS.

ACT 410. UNIFORM PRESERVATION OF PRIVATE BUSINESS RECORDS ACT

Citation:	805 ILCS 410/1

☞ **§ 410/1. Definitions.**

§ 1. As used in this Act,

"Business" includes every kind of private business, profession, occupation, calling or operation of private institutions, whether carried on for profit or not.

"Person" means an individual, partnership, corporation, or

any other association.

"Records" or "Business Records" include books of account, vouchers, documents, canceled checks, payrolls, correspondence, records of sales, personnel, equipment and production, reports relating to any or all of such records, and other business papers.

"Reproduction" means a reproduction or durable medium for making a reproduction obtained by any photographic, optical imaging, photostatic, microfilm, microcard, miniature photographic or other process which accurately reproduces or forms a durable medium for so reproducing the original.

Citation: 805 ILCS 410/3

✍ ☞ § 410/3. Reproductions — Preservation — Inspection — Enlargement — Admissibility.

§ 3. (a) If reproductions of original business records are made, the preservation of such reproductions constitutes compliance with any laws of this State requiring that business records be kept or preserved, subject to the following conditions:

(1) The reproductions shall be made in the regular course of business or pursuant to a general plan for making reproductions of records:

(2) Persons required to keep the records shall without expense to the State make the reproductions available during usual business hours to State officers or authorized employees entitled to inspect or examine the records by running or projecting the reproductions for the inspection or examination of such officers, or employees, and shall so run or project the reproductions as to make it possible for such officers or employees to make notes or copies thereof;

(3) Persons required to keep the records, upon the request of the State department or agency charged with the administration of the Act requiring the records to be kept, shall without expense to the State provide enlargements of the reproductions in approximately original size of any and all records to the possession of which the department or agency would be entitled if reproductions have not been made.

(b) A reproduction constituting compliance with laws requiring the keeping of records under subsection (a), or an enlargement of such reproduction, when satisfactorily identified, is admissible in evidence, in instances where the original record would be admissible, to prove the contents of the original record in any judicial or administrative proceeding concerned with the enforcement of the laws of this State.

Citation: 805 ILCS 410/4

✪ § 410/4. Authority of state officer to permit destruction.

§ 4. Nothing in this Act shall be construed to diminish the authority of an officer of this State under existing law to permit the destruction of business records.

CHAPTER 820. EMPLOYMENT.

ACT 405. UNEMPLOYMENT INSURANCE ACT

Citation: 820 ILCS 405/1801

✍ § 405/1801. Destruction of records by employing units.

§ 1801. Records which employing units are required to keep and preserve pursuant to the provisions of Section 1800 may be destroyed not less than five years after the making of such records, provided that if, within the time specified by Section 2207, a determination and assessment of contributions, interest or penalties is made, or an action for the collection of contributions, interest, or penalties is brought, records pertaining to the period or periods covered by such determination and assessment or action may not be destroyed until the determination and assessment or action has become final, or has been canceled or withdrawn.

If, in the regular course of business, an employing unit makes reproductions of any records which it is required to keep and preserve pursuant to the provisions of Section 1800, the preservation of such reproductions constitutes compliance with the provisions of this Section. For the purposes of this Section, "reproduction" means a reproduction or durable medium for making a reproduction obtained by any photographic, photostatic, microfilm, micro-card, miniature photographic or other process which accurately reproduces or forms a durable medium for so reproducing the original.

ILLINOIS SUPREME COURT RULES

Citation: SUPREME COURT RULE 236

☞ § 236. Admission of Business Records in Evidence.

(a) Any writing or record, whether in the form of any entry in a book or otherwise, made as a memorandum or record of any act, transaction, occurrence, or event, shall be admissible as evidence of the act, transaction, occurrence, or event, if made in the regular course of any business, and if it was the regular course of the business to make such a memorandum or record at the time of such an act, transaction, occurrence, or event or within a reasonable time thereafter. All other circumstances of the making of the writing or record, including lack of personal knowledge by the entrant or maker, may be shown to affect its weight, but shall not affect its admissibility. The term "business," as used in this rule, includes business, profession, occupation, and calling of every kind.

(b) Although medical records or police accident reports may otherwise be admissible in evidence under the law, subsection (a) of this rule does not allow such writings to be admitted as a record or memorandum made in the regular course of business.

Source: Illinois Administrative Code

CHAPTER I. SALES TAX.

SUBPART H. BOOKS AND RECORDS.

Citation: IAC 130.825

✍ § 130.825. Department Authorization to Destroy Records Sooner Than Would Otherwise be Permissible.

a) In all cases, the Department may, in writing, authorize the destruction of books and records and other papers prior to the expiration of the periods of time during which the taxpayer, except for such written authorization from the Department, is required to keep his books and records.

b) The Department may authorize destruction of records at the conclusion of an audit with respect to those records if the records are preserved in microfilm or microfiche and meet the following conditions:

1) Reproductions of all original records must be produced upon request by the Department or its authorized representatives.

2) Appropriate facilities are provided for preservation of the microfilm or microfiche for periods required.

3) Microfiche or microfilm records are indexed, cross referenced, labeled to show beginning and ending numbers or beginning and ending alphabetical listing of documents included, and are systematically filed.

4) The taxpayer agrees to provide transcriptions of any information contained on microfiche which may be required for purposes of verification of tax liability.

5) Proper facilities are provided for the ready inspection and location of the particular records, including projectors for viewing and copying the records.

6) A posting reference must be on each invoice. Credit memoranda must carry a reference to the document evidencing the original transaction. Documents necessary to support claimed exemptions from tax liability, such as bills of lading and purchase orders, must be maintained in an order by which they readily can be related to the transactions for which exemption is sought.

7) The taxpayer retains the microfilm or microfiche copies so long as the contents thereof may be material in the administration of any audit by the Department.

Agency: **Department of Employment Security**

TITLE 56. LABOR AND EMPLOYMENT.

CHAPTER 4. DEPARTMENT OF EMPLOYMENT SECURITY.

SUBCHAPTER C. RIGHTS AND DUTIES OF EMPLOYERS.

PART 2760. NOTICES, RECORDS, REPORTS.

Citation: **56 IAC 2760.140**

✍ § 2760.140. Use of electronic data processing media for quarterly reporting.

(a) The reports required by Sections 2760.120 and 2760.125 may be made by the use of an electronic data processing medium with the prior written approval of the Director. The Director shall approve the use of electronic data processing media for reporting if he finds that:

(1) All of the data required on the forms provided by the Director for quarterly reporting are also provided by the employer in the same format on the electronic data processing medium; and,

(2) The employer's electronically data processed reports are compatible and readable by the electronic data processing equipment used by the Director without the need for any programming adjustment by the Director.

(b) Any employer who was authorized by the Director before the effective date of this Section to submit his quarterly report on electronic data processing media may continue to do so without further approval by the Director.

(c) Any report approved by the Director for submissions by an electronic data processing medium must be accompanied by a certification, signed by the owner, partner or authorized officer or official, that the information submitted is true and correct to the best of his knowledge and belief and that no part of the contribution reported was or is to be deducted from the worker's wages.

Agency: **Secretary of State & State Archivist**

STATE RECORDS ACT AND STATE RECORDS COMMISSION RULES

Citation: **IAC 4400.10**

✪ § 4400.10. General.

a) The State Records Commission shall consist of the Secretary of State or his representative, who shall act as chairman; the State Historian, who shall act as secretary; the State treasurer, or his authorized representative; the Director of Central Management Services, or his authorized representative; The Attorney General, or his authorized representative; and the State Comptroller, or his authorized representative.

b) The Commission shall meet whenever called by the Chairman who shall have no vote on matters considered by the Commission.

c) All meetings of the Commission shall be open to the public and will be held in the conference room of the State Archives Building, unless otherwise stated in the call for the meeting.

d) It is the duty of the Commission to determine what records no longer have administrative, legal, fiscal, research, or historical value and should be destroyed or disposed of otherwise. The State Archivist may retain any records which the Commission has authorized to be destroyed, where they have a historical value, and may deposit them in the State Library or the State historical museum or with a historical society, museum or library.

e) No record shall be disposed of by any agency of the State, unless approval of the State Records Commission is first obtained.

f) The Commission reserves the right to review, modify, or revoke approved records schedules if any changes occur in the records' administrative, legal, fiscal, research or historical value after initial scheduling for destruction. Reviews, modifications and revocations of existing records schedules may only take place after the head of each agency involved receives written notice two weeks prior to the Commission meeting stating time, date, and place of meeting and the reason for the proposed review. Commission meeting date, times and locations will be posted in the Illinois State Archives two weeks prior to each meeting and will be publicized in accordance with the Open Meetings Act (Ill. Rev. Stat. 1983, ch. 102, pars 41 et seq.).

g) "Agency" means all parts, boards, and commissions of the executive branch of the State government including but not limited to all departments established by the Civil Administrative Code of Illinois, (Ill. Rev. Stat. 1983, ch. 127, pars. 1 et seq.) as heretofore or hereafter amended.

h) The head of each agency shall provide for compliance with provisions of these rules.

Citation: **IAC 4400.20**

✪ § 4400.20. Definitions.

a) "Records" means all books, papers, maps, photographs, or other official documentary materials, regardless of physical form or characteristics, made, produced, executed, or received by any agency in the State in pursuance of state law or in connection with the transaction of public business and preserved or appropriate for preservation by that agency or its successor as evidence of the organization, functions, policies, decisions, procedures, operations, or other activities of the State or of the State Government, or because of the informational data contained therein.

b) "Nonrecord material" means:

1) Material not filed as evidence of administrative activity or

for the informational content thereof.

2) Extra copies of documents preserved only for convenience of reference.

3) Stocks of printed or reproduced documents kept for supply purposes, where file copies have been retained for record purposes.

4) Books, periodicals, newspapers, posters, and other library and museum material made or acquired and preserved solely for reference or exhibition purposes.

5) Private materials neither made nor received by a State agency pursuant to state law or in connection with the transaction of public business.

6) Perforated, magnetized and photographically coded cards and tapes, provided that documents containing the same information have been filed in the same office and such cards and tapes were not prepared as evidence of administrative decisions or transactions subject to audit.

c) Whenever doubt arises whether certain papers are nonrecord materials, it should be presumed that they are records.

d) Nonrecord materials may be destroyed at any time by the agency in possession of such materials without the prior approval of the State Records Commission.

e) Permanent record film is a photographic camera original, or an exact copy of such an original film, so composed and treated that the image and support will have a maximum keeping quality under archival room storage conditions of temperature 65-70 degrees F. and humidity 30-40%.

f) Raw stock. Raw stock is sensitized photographic material that has not undergone the process of development.

Citation: IAC 4400.30

✪ § 4400.30. Procedures for Compiling and Submitting Lists and Schedules of Records of Disposal.

a) The head of each agency shall submit to the Commission lists or schedules or records in his custody that are not needed in the transaction of current business and that do not have sufficient administrative, legal, or fiscal value to warrant their further preservation.

1) Lists are applications for authority to destroy records that have accumulated.

2) Schedules are applications for continuing authority to destroy records after specified periods of time or the occurrence of specified events.

b) New lists or schedules are required whenever the informational contents of a record series are changed.

c) An original and two copies of all applications for authority to destroy records shall be submitted to the Commission on forms available from the State Records Commission, Archives Building, Springfield, Illinois, 62756.

d) Application for authority to destroy records shall be accomplished by samples of each record series proposed for destruction, which will be filed as permanent records of the State Records Commission. Blank forms and explanatory statements may be submitted in lieu of confidential records.

Citation: IAC 4400.40

✪ § 4400.40. Procedures for the Physical Destruction or Other Disposition of Records Proposed for Disposal.

a) Subject to statutory provisions, agencies may dispose of, records authorized for destruction by the Commission. All records, regardless of physical format or characteristics must be disposed of using the same procedures as followed for the disposition of original hard copy documents.

b) Thirty days prior to planned disposal or destruction of records so authorized by the Commission, the head of any agency doing so will submit a State Records Disposal Certificate to the Chairman of the State Records Commission, and proceed with such disposal only after a copy of that certificate has been reviewed and signed by the Chairman and returned to the head of the agency. The original copy of this disposal certificate will be kept in the files of the State Records Commission and the duplicate copy signed and returned by the Chairman shall be retained by the disposing agency for its files.

Citation: IAC 4400.50

✪ § 4400.50. Standards for the Reproduction of Records by Microphotographic Processes with a View to the Disposal of the Original Records.

a) Records proposed for microfilming must be on a list or retention schedule approved by the State Records Commission.

b) In submitting lists or schedules of records for which microfilm copies are to be substituted, the head of each agency shall certify that microfilm copies, made in accordance with standards of the State Records Commission, will be adequate substitutes for the original records.

c) Computer Output Microfilm (COM) is to be considered an original record and not a copy of an original record. Therefore, authentication requirements for source document microfilm as found in §§ 4400.50(f) and (g) do not apply to COM.

d) Quality of the film used. The film stock used, and the processing thereof, shall comply with the minimum standards of quality required by the State Records Commission as set forth in Section 4400.60 of these rules.

e) Preparation of the records for filming. All document in the file shall be microfilmed, unless their size or physical form prevents microfilming, in which case an explanation of their omission shall be microfilmed at the appropriate point on the roll of film and be worded substantially as follows: "(Item Description) was omitted from this roll of film becaus. It may be located." Any records not filmed shall be maintained by the agency or transferred to the Archives under terms specified on the approved records disposition schedule.

f) Integrity of the original records.

1) The integrity of the original records shall be preserved through a photographic process such that the camera original, or exact duplicates thereof, will be adequate substitutes for the original records in that they will serve the purposes for which such records were created or maintained and that such copies will contain all significant record detail needed for probable future reference.

2) Prior to microfilming, the original documents shall be so prepared, arranged, classified and indexed as to readily permit the subsequent location, examination and reproduction of the photographs thereof. Any significant characteristics of the records which would not reflect photographically (e.g., that the record is indistinct or that certain figures are of a color not suited to recording on microfilm) shall be indicated by means of an explanatory target inserted to guide the user. Any notations on the fact or reverse side of any document shall be photographed and identified as forming an integral part of the original document. A significant characteristic is any part of the record necessary for its interpretation, including all words, numbers and illustrations.

A) Each film roll, camera negative, or sheet (including 105MM continuous fiche rolls, but not COM) shall be identified by or contain the following targets:

i) A technical target for measuring Resolution.

ii) A film density target (8 1/2" x 11" bond paper).

iii) A roll number START target in characters that can be read without magnification.

iv) A TITLE target giving name of the office having custody of the records, a brief title of the record series, dates, file arrangement, and the number of the schedule approved by the State Records Commission authorizing the project.

v) Listed between the START file and END file targets must be explanatory targets for omission, deletion, misfiles, retakes, or any example given in § 4400.50(f)(2).

B) At the end of each roll/sheet of film, after the document images, shall be targets as follow:

i) An END target containing the number of the list or schedule approved by the State Records Commission authorizing the project.

ii) Roll number.

iii) Brief title of the record series.

iv) Beginning and ending file designations.

v) A camera operator's certificate as follows:

"I hereby certify that I have on this__ day of___, 19__ photographed the documents appearing on this roll of film, that they are true copies of the documents found in the record file described above, and that the integrity of the above described record file has been maintained on the film by microfilming each document in the exact order in which it was found in the file. Reproductions designed to serve as permanent records comply with the regulations and standards of the State Records Commission."

vi) Signature of the camera operator.

vii) A film density target (8 1/2" x 11") bond paper).

viii) A technical target for measuring Resolution.

g) Security microfilm shall have no breaks, cuts or splices in the body of the film, which shall be the area following the START target and preceding the Camera Operator's Certificate. However, a retake of a length of film may be spliced ahead of the START target or aft the Camera Operator's Certificate, providing that the retake be given its own START target and Camera Operator's Certificate. This shall be done in such a manner as not to overload a reel or cartridge. Exceptions to this rule are:

1) If the trailing end of a reel be fogged or unreadable, the camera operator shall be rephotograph the original document from a point 12 images in advance of the last readable image prior to the fogged or unreadable area. The retake will include a (camera operator's certificate) and will be spliced to the trailing end or the fogged or unreadable portion of the film.

2) When a court-ordered expungement of specific records is issued and deletions are made from the roll of film, the court expungement order and a certificate of deletion, illustrated below, must be photographed and the images spliced to the beginning of the film.

CERTIFICATE OF DELETION

This is to certify the deletion of microfilm images on this roll of microfilm, occurred due to Court Order #___, date___, signed by Judge___. No other images other than those listed in this order were deleted.

Signature of Officer

h) The camera used to microfilm the records shall be one which accurately reproduces the content of the original records with sufficient photographic contrast and resolution to be readable through three generations of reproductions.

i) Each roll of original film or camera negatives must be inspected after processing and before duplicate copies are made. The inspection must be conducted in such a manner as to reveal defects such as improper density, poor resolution, blurred or obscured images, improper document sequence, or improper identification targets. If a defect prohibits a clear, legible, hard copy print from the files, the original records must be rephotographed.

1) Randomly sampling the film, making sure that the samples include the beginning, middle, and end of the roll or microform. (It is suggested that this be done on all films as a minimum quality control.)

2) Visually inspecting the film by passing each image through a reader and checking for overlapping, double or folded images, or other types of problems that would impair retrieving any information on the microimages.

3) Performing all of (2) plus, counting the number of microimages on the film and comparing that against the number of documents that were to be microfilmed. (If the numbers coincide, the conclusion is made that every document has been microfilmed.)

4) Individually comparing each document with each microimage that was actually created. (This visual verification provides the highest assurance that every document has been properly filmed.)

j) If more than one percent of the original images need to be refilmed (approximately 30 images per roll), the entire roll must be refilmed.

k) Updateable Microfiche Systems:

An agency considering using such a system should first contact the State Records Unit to review the proposed application. The application will be approved if the updateable microfiche meets the following specifications:

1) each microfiche must have the specified targets at the beginning and end of each fiche as called for by § 4400.50(f)(2)(A) and (B).

2) each time a microfiche is updated, either a camera operator's certificate must be inserted at the end of the added documents or annotated reference to the original camera operator's certificate must appear on each added image.

3) only records bearing retention periods of ten years or less may be placed on updatable microforms.

4) if a court ordered expungement is necessary, a certificate of deletion must appear at the place of the deleted image.

l) Prior to the destruction of records microfilmed under the authority of approved records schedules, the agency shall file with the State Records Commission a statement of compliance with its standards governing the microfilming of records. The statement shall include:

1) Agency having custody of the records.

2) Date.

3) Title and inclusive dates of the record series.

4) The number of the list or schedule approved by the State Records Commission authorizing the project.

5) The following statement:

"I hereby certify that the film on which the records were reproduced complies with the standards given in § 4400.60 of the rules of the State Records Commission."

6) Signature of the microfilm project supervisor.

m) Each film carton shall be identified by a label or exterior marking indicating:

1) Roll number.

2) Name of office.

3) Title of the record series.

4) Names of the file units at the start of the roll, at space targets, and at the end of the roll.

5) The number of the application authorizing the microfilming of the record/record series.

n) Inspection

Security of Master films of permanent record microforms, and records microfilmed to dispose of the original record, shall be inspected every 2 years during their scheduled life. The inspection shall be made using a 1 percent randomly selected sample in the following categories: 70 percent — microforms not previously tested, 20 percent — microforms tested in the last inspection, and 10 percent — control group. The control group shall represent samples of microforms filmed through the most current.

Citation: IAC 4400.60

✪ § 4400.60. Minimum Standards of Quality for Permanent Record Photographic Original Microfilm Intended for Retention Periods in Excess of 10 Years.

a) These standards are concerned with both raw stock for permanent record films and with the processed film ready for storage. They are not restricted to microfilm but apply equally to motion picture films, roll films, and sheet films. No incorporation by reference in § 4400.60 includes any later amendments or editions.

b) All such film stock shall be of approved permanent type such as meets the minimum specifications of the American National Standards Institute (ANSI) as found in:

PH 1.25-1976
PH 1.28-1981
PH 1.41-1981

c) Every frame of microfilm shall be exposed and processed so that every line and character on the document appears on the microfilm with sufficient clarity to permit reproducibility through three successive generations of reproduction. With regard to operational procedures, inspection, and quality control of silver gelatin microfilm, ANSI/NMA MS23-1983, PH 1.25-1976, PH 1.28-1981, PH 1.41-1981 and PH 4.8-1978 shall apply.

d) The background photographic densities must be appropriate to the type of documents being filmed. Appropriate background densities are as follows:

Classification	Description of Documents	Background Density
Group 1	High-quality printed books, periodicals, and dense typing	1.30-1.50
Group 2	Fine-line originals, letters typed with a worn ribbon, pencil writing with a soft lead, and documents with small printing	1.15-1.40
Group 3	Pencil drawings, faded printing, graph paper with pale, fine colored lines, and very small printing such as footnotes	1.00-1.20
Group 4	Very weak pencil manuscripts and drawings, and poorly printed, faint documents	.90-1.10
Group 5	COM	1.50-2.00

State: Indiana
Source: Indiana Code

TITLE 4. STATE ADMINISTRATION.

ARTICLE 5. SECRETARY OF STATE.

CHAPTER 1. POWERS AND DUTIES — BOND

Citation: IC 4-5-1-2

✪ § 4-5-1-2. Keeping of documents — Transfer to commission on public records — Copying by micrographic techniques — Storage of micrographic copies.

(a) The secretary of state shall keep and preserve:

(1) the enrolled copy of the constitution of the state;

(2) the manuscripts containing the enrolled acts and joint resolutions of the general assembly;

(3) all the official bonds of state officers except his own bond; and

(4) all written contracts to which the state is a party, unless required to be deposited elsewhere; and

(5) any rule or other agency statement that is filed under IC 4-22-2.

(b) All documents described in subsection (a)(1), (a)(2), or (a)(5) may be transferred by the secretary of state to the commission on public records for safekeeping, and the commission shall receive and safely preserve them when transferred. The secretary of state and the commission on public records shall establish an indexing system so that the secretary of state, an agency, or the commission on public records can comply with a request under IC 5-14-3 to inspect or copy a transferred document described in subsection (a)(5), including the full text of a matter incorporated by reference into a document described in subsection (a)(5). The indexing system must at least [identify] transferred documents by the following:

(1) Indiana Administrative Code citation.

(2) Indiana Register document control number or volume and page number.

(3) Year of adoption.

(4) General subject matter.

(c) Regardless of whether a document is described in subsection (a)(1) or (a)(2) is transferred to the commission on public records under subsection (b), when deemed expedient or necessary for the preservation of the documents, the secretary of state may copy the documents by any micrographic technique, and the micrographic copies shall be stored in a place other than in the state capitol building or the Indiana state library.

(d) The secretary of state may copy in micrographic form the complete contents of each rule that is filed with the secretary of state's office under IC 4-22-2. Both the rule and the full text of matters incorporated by reference into the rule may be copied.

(e) Micrographic copies prepared under subsection (d) must conform with:

(1) the standards developed by the supreme court and the oversight commission on public records under IC 5-15-5.1-8; and

(2) the standards developed in an agreement between the secretary of state, the publisher of the Indiana Register, the governor, the attorney general, the Indiana library and historical department, and the commission on public records.

(f) The secretary of state may micrographically copy documents under subsection (d):

(1) in the micrographic laboratory operated by the commission of public records under IC 5-15-5.1-8;

(2) with equipment and technology operated by the secretary

of state or

(3) through a contract for services procured under IC 4-13.4.

(g) When a document is micrographically copied under this section, the original documents shall never be destroyed even if microfilmed. However, if the secretary of state has the capacity to make certifiable copies from a micrographic media prepared under subsection (d), the secretary of state may return to its originating agency the full text of any matter that is incorporated by reference into a rule and micrographically copied.

TITLE 5. STATE AND LOCAL ADMINISTRATION.

ARTICLE 15. PRESERVATION OF PUBLIC RECORDS

CHAPTER 1. REPRODUCTION OF RECORDS.

Citation: IC 5-15-1-1

✪ § 5-15-1-1. Reproduction authorized — Force and effect at law.

Sec. 1. (a) Any officer, office, court, commission, board, institution, department, agent or employee of the state, county, or any political subdivision being charged with the duty or authorized or required by law to record, preserve, keep, maintain or file any record, document, plat, paper or instrument-in-writing, may, whenever any such officer, office, court, commission, board, institution, department, agent, or employee of the state, county, or any political subdivision shall deem it necessary, for the purpose of recording or copying same; preserving and protecting same; reducing space required for storage or filing of same, or any similar purpose, have or cause to have any or all such records recorded, copied or reproduced by any photostatic, photographic, micrographic, electronic, or other process which correctly and accurately copies or reproduces, recreates, or forms a medium of copying or reproducing the original record, document, plat, paper or instrument-in-writing. Any officer, office, court, commission, board, institution, department, agent, or employee of the state may have or cause to have records recorded, copied, or reproduced under this subsection by any optical imaging process that correctly and accurately copies or reproduces, recreates, or from a medium of copying or reproducing the original record, document, plat, paper, or instrument-in-writing.

(b) The original filing record may be destroyed if:

(1) the record has been copied or is capable of being reproduced or recreated under subsection (a); and

(2) the commission on public records, as to state records, or the commission of public records of the respective county, as to records of counties and other local units of government, has decided to destroy the original record.

(c) Copies, recreations, or reproductions made under subsection (a):

(1) shall have the same force and effect at law as the original record destroyed under subsection (b); and

(2) shall be received in any court where the original record could have been so introduced;

if the recreations, copies or reproductions are properly certified as to authenticity and accuracy by a duly constituted official custodian of such records.

(d) All micrographics processes done under this chapter shall comply with the quality standards developed under IC 5-15-5.1-8.

(e) This section does not apply to the state court administration division of the supreme court.

CHAPTER 5.1. COMMISSION ON PUBLIC RECORDS.

Citation: IC 5-15-5.1-17

✪ § 5-15-5.1-17. Preservation of official books, records, documents and papers — Authority of officials and commission.

(a) A state, county, or other official may turn over to the commission, in accordance with the rules of the commission for permanent preservation, any official books, records, documents, original papers, newspaper files, or printed books or materials not in current use in his office.

(b) Subject to subsection (c), the commission may make a copy, by photography or in any other way, of any official book, record, document, original paper, newspaper, or printed book or material in any county, city, or other public office for preservation in the state archives. County, city, and other officials shall permit such copies to be made of the books, records, documents, and papers in their respective offices.

(c) The commission shall copy the official copy of the rules (including incorporated matters filed under IC 4-22-2-21) retained by the secretary of state under IC 4-5-1-2. Any duplicate original copy possessed by another agency is not a critical record and may not be copied. If the secretary of state prepares micrographic copies of these documents under IC 4-5-1-2 and the copies are in a form that meets the specifications of the commission, the commission shall arrange with the secretary of state to obtain the number of copies needed by the commission, rather than copying the documents as part of a separate program.

TITLE 34. CIVIL PROCEDURE.

ARTICLE 3. EVIDENCE.

CHAPTER 15. RECORDS — PHOTOCOPY OF BUSINESS RECORDS DEEMED AN ORIGINAL RECORD.

Citation: IC 34-3-15-1

☞ ✍ § 34-3-15-1. Business records — Preservation by photographic process — Disposal of original.

Any business may cause any or all records kept by such business to be recorded, copied or reproduced by any photographic, photostatic, miniature photographic, or optical imaging process which correctly, accurately and permanently copies, reproduces or forms a medium for copying or reproducing the original record on a film or other durable material, and such business may thereafter dispose of the original record.

Citation: IC 34-3-15-2

☞ ✍ § 34-3-15-2. Photographic or optical image copies — Admissibility in evidence.

Any such photographic, photostatic, miniature photographic, or optical image copy or reproduction shall be deemed to be an original record for all purposes and shall be treated as an original record in all courts or administrative agencies for the purpose of its admissibility in evidence. A facsimile, exemplification or certified copy of any such photographic or optical image copy or reproduction shall, for all purposes, be deemed a facsimile, an exemplification or certified copy of the original record.

CHAPTER 15.5. HOSPITAL MEDICAL RECORDS.

Citation: IC 34-3-15.5-5

☞ **§ 34-3-15.5-5. Photostatic copies — Admissibility in evidence.**

Notwithstanding the hearsay rule, photostatic copies of hospital medical records certified under section 6 [34-3-15.5-6] of this chapter are admissible into evidence in any civil action or administrative proceeding without testimony from the custodian of the hospital medical records, subject to all other objections.

Citation: IC 34-3-15.5-6

☞ **§ 34-3-15.5-6. Records requested by subpoena — Production of copies.**

(a) When a:

(1) Subpoena coupled with a request under Rule 34 of the Indiana Rules of Trial Procedure;

(2) Subpoena coupled with a patient's written authorization under section 4 [IC 34-3-15.5-4] of this chapter; or

(3) Court order;

requiring the production of a hospital medical record is served upon any hospital employee, and the hospital has received an authorization that complies with section 4 [34-3-15.5-4] of this chapter to release the patient's medical record, the hospital employee with custody of the original hospital medical record may elect, in lieu of personally appearing and producing the original hospital medical record, to furnish the requesting party or the party's attorney with a photostatic copy of the hospital medical record, certified in accordance with subsection (c).

(b) If the hospital has elected to proceed under subsection (a), the hospital employee with custody of the original hospital medical records shall, upon receipt of payment for the reproduction of the hospital medical records, promptly delivery, by certified mail or personal delivery, copies of the hospital medical records specified in the subpoena to the person specified in the subpoena.

(c) The hospital employee's certification of the hospital medical records under this section must:

(1) Be signed by the hospital employee with custody of the hospital medical records; and

(2) Include:

(A) The full name of the patient;

(B) The patient's medical record number;

(C) The number of pages in the hospital medical record; and

(D) A statement in substantially the following form:

"The copies of records for which this certification is made are true and complete reproductions of the original or microfilmed hospital medical records that are housed in — (name of hospital). The original records were made in the regular course of business, and it was the regular course of — (name of hospital) to make the records at or near the time of the matter recorded. This certification is given pursuant to IC 34-3-15.5-6 by the custodian of the records in lieu of the custodian's personal appearance."

(d) The hospital shall:

(1) Place the copies of the hospital medical records in an envelope or wrapper; and

(2) Write or type on the envelope or wrapper:

(A) The words "Confidential Medical Records";

(B) The title and number of the action or proceeding; and

(C) The name and business telephone number of the hospital employee making the certification.

(e) If the hospital does not have the hospital medical records or has only a part of the hospital medical records specified in the subpoena, the hospital employee with custody of the original hospital medical records shall:

(1) Execute an affidavit, either notarized or by affirmation, stating that the hospital does not have or has only a part of the subpoenaed hospital medical records; and

(2) Follow the procedures in subsections (a), (b), (c), and (d) in delivering the part of the hospital medical records that are in the hospital's possession.

(f) This subsection applies to a medical record or a part of a record that is confidential under 42 U.S.C. 290dd-3, 42 U.S.C. 290ee-3, or the regulations adopted under those statutes. The hospital employee with custody of the original medical records shall:

(1) Execute a verified affidavit:

(A) Identifying the record or part of the record that is confidential; and

(B) Stating that the confidential record or part of the record will only be provided under the federal procedure for production of the record; and

(2) Comply with subsections (a) through (d) in delivering the record or part of the record that is not confidential under subdivision (1).

(g) This subsection applies to a medical record or part of a record concerning treatment for mental illness. The hospital employee with custody of the original medical records shall:

(1) Execute a verified affidavit:

(A) Identifying the record or part of a record that contains the confidential information concerning the treatment of mental illness; and

(B) Stating that the confidential record of part of the record will only be provided under a court order after *in camera* review; and

(2) Comply with subsections (a) through (d) in delivering the record or part of the record that is not confidential under subdivision (1).

(h) This subsection applies to a medical record or part of a record that contains information that is confidential under IC 16-41-8-1. The hospital employee with custody of the original medical records shall:

(1) Execute a verified affidavit:

(A) Identifying the record or part of a record that contains the confidential information concerning a dangerous communicable disease; and

(B) Stating that the confidential record or part of the record will only be provided under a court order after *in camera* review under IC 16-41-8-1; and

(2) Comply with subsection (a) through (d) in delivering the record or part of the record that is not confidential under subdivision (1).

(i) The hospital may charge the fee permitted under IC 16-39-9 to cover the costs of reproducing the hospital medical records.

Source: Indiana Rules Of Evidence

ARTICLE X. CONTENTS OF WRITINGS.

☞ **Rule 1001. Definitions.**

For purposes of this Article the following definitions are applicable:

(1) *Writings and recordings.* — "Writings" and "recordings" consist of letters, words, sounds, or numbers, or their equivalent, set down by handwriting, typewriting, printing, photostating, photographing, magnetic impulse, mechanical or

electronic recording, or other form of data compilation.

(2) *Photographs.* — "Photographs" include still photographs, x-rays films videotapes, and motion pictures.

(3) *Original.* — An "original" of a writing or recording is the writing or recording itself or any counterpart intended to have the same effect by a person executing or issuing it. An "original" of a photograph includes the negative or any print therefrom. If data are stored in a computer or similar device, any printout or other output readable by sight, shown to reflect the data accurately is an "original."

(4) *Duplicate.* — A "duplicate" is a counterpart produced by the same impression as the original, or from the same matrix, or by means of photography, including enlargements and miniatures, or by mechanical or electronic rerecording, or by chemical reproduction, or by facsimile transmission, or video tape or by other equivalent techniques which accurately reproduces the original.

☞ Rule 1003. Admissibility of duplicates.

A duplicate is admissible to the same extent as an original unless (1) a genuine question is raised as to the authenticity of the original or (2) in the circumstances it would be unfair to admit the duplicate in lieu of the original.

☞ Rule 1005. Public records.

The contents of an official record, or of a document authorized to be recorded or filed and

actually recorded or filed, including data compilation in any form, if otherwise admissible, may be proved by copy, certified as correct in accordance with Rule 902 or testified to be correct by a witness who has compared it with the original. If a copy complying with the foregoing cannot be obtained by the exercise of reasonable diligence, other evidence of the contents may be admnitted.

Source: Indiana Administrative Code

TITLE 60. OVERSIGHT COMMITTEE ON PUBLIC RECORDS.

ARTICLE 2. MICROFILMING STANDARDS FOR SOURCE DOCUMENTS WITH A RETENTION PERIOD OF MORE THAN FIFTEEN (15) YEARS.

Rule 1. General Provisions.

Citation: 60 IAC 2-1-1

✪ 60 IAC 2-1-1. Purpose.

Sec. 1. (a) The purposes of these microfilm standards is to create minimum legal, legibility, permanency standards for source document microfilm, with a retention period of more than fifteen (15) years, generated by agencies subject to IC 5-15-5.1-1. These microfilming standards are consistent with the microfilming standard approved by the Indiana State Supreme Court as Administrative Rule 6.

(b) This article does not apply to computer-output microforms nor does it apply to records filmed for administrative purposes with a retention schedule of fifteen (15) years or less.

Citation: 60 IAC 2-1-2

✪ 60 IAC 2-1-2. Fiscal impact.

Sec. 2. (a) Fiscal impact will affect both individual agencies currently microfilming and the Indiana commission on public records, which operates the state government's central microfilming micrographics facility. The rule is subdivided into three parts:

(1) legality, by creation of a documentation file;

(2) legibility, by use of certain targets and inspection procedures; and

(3) permanency, achieved through processing of camera-generated negatives according to American National Standards Institute (ANSI) standards and storing such in specially maintained vaults.

(b) For individual agencies currently microfilming, fiscal impact will result in labor and purchase of additional supplies. The legality aspect of the standards require [*sic.*] a documentation file in which the steps and procedures of the microfilming process are documented in writing. Both the microfilm and the documentation file must be capable of being produced as evidence in court as the official, legal record of agency action. A certain amount of labor generating such a file by record series is required. The extent of such labor will vary depending on the degree to which various agencies currently are generating such documentation. Additional labor is required for documenting each roll of microfilm, or microform, generated. Several hours per month, per record series, are required.

(c) Extensive labor may be required for the legibility section of these standards. Time to prepare source documents for microfilming, as well as inspecting each roll of microfilm, or each microform, for legibility and completeness, represents about seven (7) hours per every two thousand two hundred (2,200) images, which is equivalent to one (1) roll of microfilm. Since each agency currently should be preparing documents by microfilming, as well as checking each image for legibility and completeness, no additional fiscal impact should result. Secondly, labor is required to test microfilm for legibility. This requires the purchase and use of certain targets, especially resolution targets, at a cost generally not exceeding twenty-five dollars ($25) per agency. An inspection procedure using a microscope can be performed by the micrographics division of the commission on public records using existing equipment, on a regular basis, requiring no more than five (5) minutes per record series, per agency. Additional identification, information coding, and test charts are required but these are generated for each source document microfilm, or microform, as needed.

(d) Microfilm processing must meet ANSI standards. The fixing of the camera-generated negative is critical to generate permanent microfilm; excessive fixing chemical, thiosulfate, will continue the chemical process, destroying the image over time. An expensive test for such residual thiosulfate must be performed periodically for each microfilm processor. Conducting this test one (1) time a week is recommended. Each test costs about twenty-five dollars ($25) for supplies and equipment. As a maximum, five (5) tests per week, two hundred sixty (260) per year, may be required, costing approximately six thousand five hundred dollars ($6,500). Each test requires about fifteen (15) minutes or one and one-fourth (1 1/4) hours per week in staff labor.

(e) Microfilm storage must meet ANSI standards. The useful life of camera-generated negatives is directly related to humidity and temperature levels of storage environment. The approximate cost for proper storage is two dollars and twenty-five cents ($2.25) per cubic foot, per month.

(f) This article is designed to give uniformity to microfilming operations throughout state government, for the judicial (Administrative Rule 6), executive, and administrative branches of government. It clarifies certain minimum operating procedures which currently should be performed. Inspection and testing of microfilm provides [*sic*] the means to determine if equipment or operating procedures are sufficient to guarantee the integrity and readability of the microfilm image. Fiscal impact of implementation of this article is hard to measure since agencies currently are performing some or most of these standardized procedures. Fiscal impact includes labor and supplies.

Citation: 60 IAC 2-1-3

✪ 60 IAC 2-1-3. Permanency.

Sec. 3. (a) The American National Standards Institute (ANSI) has established industry-wide standards for microfilm permanency. To meet the ANSI standards for permanency, there are several major criteria to be met:

(1) Camera-generated negatives must be created according to ANSI PH1.25-1984;

(2) Camera-generated negatives must be processed according to ANSI PH4.8-1985; and

(3) Camera-generated negatives must be stored according to ANSI PH1.43-1985.

(b) These standards are explained in 60 IAC 2-2-5.

Citation: 60 IAC 2-2-1

✪ 60 IAC 2-2-1. Application of standards.

Sec. 1. All agencies, as defined by IC 5-15-5.1, shall meet the standards set forth under this article regarding the use of microfilm for the preservation of any record generated by that agency. Only those records or record series which have been approved by the oversight committee on public records, under IC 5-15-5.1-19, implementing IC 5-15-5.1-12, shall be eligible for microfilming.

Citation: 60 IAC 2-2-2

✪ 60 IAC 2-2-2. Definitions.

Sec. 2. The definitions in this section apply throughout this article.

(a) "AIIM" means Association for Information and Image Management.

(b) "ANSI" means American National Standards Institute.

(c) "MS" means microfilming standards.

(d) "Microfilm", when used as a noun, means a photographic film containing an image greatly reduced in size from the original, and when used as a verb, means the recording of microphotographs on film.

(e) "Microform" is a generic term for any form, usually film, which contains microimages.

(f) "NMS" means National Micrographics Standards.

(g) "PH" means photographics standards.

(h) "Target" means any document or chart containing identification information, coding, or test charts. A target is an aid to technical or bibliographical control which is photographed on the film proceeding [*sic*.] or following the document.

(i) "Standard" means a uniformly accepted set of compliances to a predefined norm.

(j) "Specifications" means a set of requirements to be satisfied, and whenever appropriate, the procedure which proves that the requirements given are satisfied.

(k) "Records series" means a group of related documents, either as to form or content, which are arranged under a single filing system, or kept together as a unit because they:

(1) consist of the same form;

(2) relate to the same subject;

(3) result in the same activity; and

(4) have certain physical characteristics (tapes, discs, microforms).

(l) "Record retention schedules" means a series of documents governing, on a continuing basis, the retention and disposition of recurring record series of an agency, court, or organization.

(m) "Reproduction" means the process of making an exact copy from an existing document

Citation: 60 IAC 2-2-3

✪ 60 IAC 2-2-3. Documentation.

Sec. 3. A formal written documentation file shall be crated and retained for the life of the microfilm based upon an approved retention schedule documenting the following:

(1) The authority to microfilm specifically enumerated records.

(2) The arrangement of originals to be microfilmed.

(3) Any weeding policy of documents to determine what papers from the file will be placed on microfilm.

(4) Any contracts with agents of record custodian, in-house or vendor, who will perform the actual microfilming.

(5) The reproduction process employed to assure accuracy.

(6) Verification of the microfilm for completeness and legibility.

(7) The justification for the microfilming of the originals, i.e., space reduction, security, and the written process for the destruction of originals as authorized by an approved retention schedule.

(8) The identity of persons who supervised the microfilming procedures who are capable of giving evidence of these procedures.

(9) The retention schedule for the documentation matching the length of time of the microform.

(10) Certification of compliance with this section to the director, Indiana commission on public records.

Citation: 60 IAC 2-2-4

✪ 60 IAC 2-2-4. Legibility.

Sec. 4. (a) Resolution in a microfilm system for documents shall be tested for resolution capability, upon installation, by use of a camera test chart such as the "Rotary Camera Test Chart", ANSI/AIIM MS112-1983 and ANSI/AIIM MS113-1983; "The Planetary Camera Test Chart", AIIM MS303-1980. Micrographics systems used for agency records must meet the following standards:

(1) A micrographics system for documents must produce a quality index level of not less than 5.0 for first-generation microfilm as measured according to ANSI/AIIM MS23-1983. In applying this ANSI standard, a lowercase letter "eá height of one and four-tenths (1.4) millimeters or less must be used.

(2) All pattern groups on the camera test chart must be read. The smallest line pattern, which corresponds to the highest number, in which both horizontal and vertical lines are clearly discernible is the resolving power of that pattern group.

(3) The film used in reading the camera test chart must be processed to the density standard in subsection (b).

(b) Density in microfilm systems used for agency records must meet the following standards:

(1) Background density in first-generation negative microfilm of documents must be maintained as nearly as practical in the range of 0.92 to 1.20. No density over 1.25 or under 0.87 is allowed.

(2) If a density in first-generation negative microfilm of documents occurs in the ranges 0.87 to 0.91 or 1.21 to 1.25, the records custodian shall determine by visual inspection that all such images satisfactorily reproduce all required record information.

(3) The density of microfilm in a clear area (base plus fog density or Dmin) must not be greater than 0.10.

(c) Reduction ration in microfilm systems for agency records must meet the following standards:

(1) For microfilming of documents, a ratio of 25:1 or 24:1 or less is required.

(2) A reduction ratio for microfilm of documents of greater than 25:1 may be used only if the micrographic system can maintain the required quality index at the higher reduction.

Citation: 60 IAC 2-2-5

✪ 60 IAC 2-2-5. Permanency.

Sec. 5. For records requiring permanent retention, based on an approved retention schedule, the following shall apply:

(1) Raw stock microfilm shall be of a safety-based permanent record film meeting specification of American National Standards Institute PH1.25-1984.

(2) The camera-generated master negative microfilm shall be silver-halide, silver-gelatin, meeting the permanency requirements of American National Standards Institute PH1.28-1984 and PH1.41-1984.

(3) Residual thiosulfate on the film must be measured using the methylene blue test and meet American National Standards Institute PH4.8-1985.

(4) The master microfilm record meeting the above criteria shall be stored at a site other than the producing agency's structure, in a fire-proof vault, meeting American National Standards Institute PH1.43-1985.

(5) In addition to the master microfilm record, which is a security copy, the agency may provide working copies of the microfilm. These may be on silver, diazo, vesicular, dry silver, or transparent electro-photograph film, on a safety base of cellulose or polyester material.

Citation: 60 IAC 2-2-6

✪ 60 IAC 2-2-6. Specifications.

Sec. 6. Specific brands of equipment, microfilm, and photographic chemicals are outside the nature of this article.

Citation: 60 IAC 2-2-7

☞ 60 IAC 2-2-7. Admissibility in courts.

Sec. 7. Source document microfilm produced under this article shall be admissible [*sic.*] in court according to IC 5-15-5.1-8.

State: Iowa
Source: Iowa Code

TITLE 6. HUMAN SERVICES.

SUBTITLE 2. HUMAN SERVICES — INSTITUTIONS.

CHAPTER 218. INSTITUTIONS GOVERNED BY HUMAN SERVICES DEPARTMENT.

Citation: IC 218.22

✪ § 218.22. Record privileged.

Except with the consent of the administrator in charge of an institution, or on an order of a court of record, the record provided in section 218.21 shall be accessible only to the administrator of the division of the department of human services in control of such institution, the director of the department of human services and to assistants and proper clerks authorized by such administrator or the administrator's director. The administrator of the division of such institution is authorized to permit the division of libraries and information services of the department of education and the historical division of the department of cultural affairs to copy or reproduce by any photographic, photostatic, microfilm, microcard or other process which accurately reproduces a durable medium for reproducing the original and to destroy in the manner described by law such records of residents designated in section 218.21.

TITLE 7. EDUCATION AND CULTURAL AFFAIRS.

SUBTITLE 7. CULTURAL AFFAIRS.

CHAPTER 304. STATE FORMS AND RECORDS.

Citation: IC 304.7

✪ 304.7 Rules.

The commission [state records commission] shall adopt rules in accordance with the provisions of Chapter 17A which are necessary for the exercise of the powers and duties granted by this chapter. The rules shall provide for:

* * * * *

6. Standards for the reproduction of records.

* * * * *

Citation: IC 304.13

✪ § 304.13. Duplicates.

The commission may make or cause to be made preservation duplicates of records and may designate as duplicates existing copies of initial state records. A preservation duplicate record shall be durable, accurate, complete and clear and shall be made by means designated by the commission.

A preservation duplicate record shall have the same force and effect for all purposes as the original record whether or not the original record is in existence. A transcript, exemplification or certified copy of a preservation duplicate record shall be deemed for all purposes to be a transcript, exemplification or certified copy of the original record.

The commission shall review all duplicating and microfilming systems and installations of agencies subject to this chapter and recommend any changes necessary to assure maximum efficiency and economic use of equipment and procedures, including but not necessarily limited to, the type of equipment, type of storage files, methods and procedures for keeping duplicate records and the location of equipment. The commission may establish centralized duplicating or microfilming facilities if it deems it in the best interest of the state. Agencies subject to this chapter shall consult with and receive approval of the commission prior to the purchase of any duplicating or microfilming equipment or files to be used for storage of records.

TITLE 8. TRANSPORTATION.

SUBTITLE 2. VEHICLES.

CHAPTER 321. MOTOR VEHICLES AND LAW OF THE ROAD.

Citation: IC 321.31

☞ ✪ **§ 321.31. Records system.**

A state and county record system shall be maintained in the following manner:

1. *State records system.* The department shall install and maintain a records system which shall contain the name and address of the vehicle owner, current and previous registration number, vehicle identification number, make, model, style, date of purchase, registration certificate number, maximum gross weight, weight, list price or value of the vehicle as fixed by the department, fees paid and date of payment. The records system shall also contain a record of the certificate of title including such information as the department deems necessary. The information to be kept in the records system shall be entered within forty-eight hours after receipt insofar as is practical. The records system shall constitute the permanent record of ownership of each vehicle titled under the laws of this state.

The department may make photostatic, microfilm, or other photographic copies of certificates of title, registration receipts, or other records, reports or documents which are required to be retained by the department. When copies have been made, the department may destroy the original records in such manner as prescribed by the director. The photostatic, microfilm, or other photographic copies, when no longer of use, may be destroyed in the manner prescribed by the director, subject to the approval of the state records commission. Photostatic, microfilm, or other photographic copies of records shall be admissible in evidence when duly certified and authenticated by the officer having custody and control of the copies of records. Records of vehicle certificates of title may be destroyed seven years after the date of issue.

The director shall maintain a records system of delinquent accounts owed to the state using information provided through the computerized data bank established in section 421.17. The department and county treasurers shall use the information maintained in the records system to determine if applicants for renewal of registration have delinquent accounts, charges, fees, loans, taxes, or other indebtedness owed to or being collected by the state as provided pursuant to section 421.17. The director and the director of revenue and finance shall establish procedures for updating the delinquent accounts records to add and remove accounts, as applicable.

2. *County records system.* Each county treasurer's office shall maintain a county records system for vehicle registration and certificate of title documents. The records system shall consist of information from the certificate of title including the notation and cancellation of security interests, and information from the registration receipt. The information shall be maintained in a manner approved by the department.

Records of vehicle certificates of title for vehicles that are delinquent for five or more consecutive years may be destroyed by the county treasurer. Automated files, optical disks, microfiche records, and photostatic, microfilm or other photographic copies of records shall be admissible in evidence when duly certified and authenticated by the officer having custody and control of the records.

TITLE 10. FINANCIAL RESOURCES.

SUBTITLE 1. REVENUES AND FINANCIAL MANAGEMENT.

CHAPTER 422. INCOME, SALES, SERVICES AND FRANCHISE TAXES.

Citation: IC 422.68

☞ ✪ **§ 422.68. Powers and duties.**

1. The director shall have the power and authority to prescribe all rules not inconsistent with the provisions of this chapter, necessary and advisable for its detailed administration and to effectuate its purposes.

2. The director may, for administrative purposes, divide the state into districts, provided that in no case shall a county be divided in forming a district.

3. The director may destroy useless records and returns, reports, and communications of any taxpayer filed with or kept by the department after those returns, records, reports, or communications have been in the custody of the department for a period of not less than three years or such time as the director prescribes by rule. However, after the accounts of a person have been examined by the director and the amount of tax and penalty due have been finally determined, the director may order the destruction of any records previously filed by that taxpayer, notwithstanding the fact that those records have been in the custody of the department for a period less than three years. These records and documents shall be destroyed in the manner prescribed by the director.

4. The department may make photostat, microfilm or other photographic copies of records, reports and other papers either filed by the taxpayer or prepared by the department. When such photostat or microfilm copies have been made, the department may destroy such original records in such manner as prescribed by the director. Such photostat or microfilm copies, when no longer of use, may be destroyed as provided in subsection 3. Such photostat, microfilm, or other photographic records shall be admissible in evidence when duly certified and authenticated by the officer having custody and control thereof.

SUBTITLE 4. EXCISE TAXES

CHAPTER 452A. MOTOR FUEL AND SPECIAL FUEL TAXES

Division 4. Provisions Common to Taxes Imposed Under Divisions 1 and 3.

Citation: IC 452A.80

✪ § 452A.80. Microfilm or photographic copies — originals destroyed.

The appropriate state agency shall have the power and authority to record, copy or reproduce by any photographic, photostatic, microfilm, microcard, miniature photographic or other process which accurately reproduces or forms a durable medium for so reproducing the original of any forms or records pertaining to motor fuel tax or undyed special fuel tax, or any paper or document with respect to refund of the tax. If the forms and records have been reproduced in accordance with this section, the state agency may destroy the originals and the reproductions shall be competent evidence in any court in accordance with the provision of section 622.30.

TITLE 15. JUDICIAL BRANCH AND JUDICIAL PROCEDURES.

SUBTITLE 3. CIVIL PROCEDURE.

CHAPTER 622. EVIDENCE.

Citation: IC 622.28

☞ § 622.28. Writing or record — when admissible — absence of record — effect.

Any writing or record, whether in the form of an entry in a book, or otherwise, including electronic means and interpretations thereof, offered as memoranda or records of acts, conditions or events to provide the facts stated therein, shall be admissible as evidence if the judge finds that they were made in the regular course of a business at or about the time of the act, condition or event recorded, and that the sources of information from which made and the method and circumstances of their preparation were such as to indicate their trustworthiness, and if the judge finds that they are not excludable as evidence because of any rule of admissibility of evidence other than the hearsay rule.

Evidence of the absence of a memorandum or record from the memoranda or records of a business of an asserted act, event or condition, shall be admissible as evidence to prove the nonoccurrence of the act or event, or the nonexistence of the condition, if the judge finds that it was in the regular course of that business to make such memoranda of all such acts, events or conditions at the time thereof or within a reasonable time thereafter, and to preserve them.

The term business, as used in this section, includes business profession, occupation, and calling of every kind.

Citation: IC 622.30

☞ § 622.30. Photographic copies — originals destroyed.

1. In all cases where depositions are taken by either method provided by law, outside of the county in which the case is for trial where books of account are competent evidence in the case, the party desiring to offer the entries of said books as evidence may cause the same to be photographed by or under the direction of the officer taking the deposition and such photographic copy when certified by such officer with his seal attached shall be attached to the deposition, and if the record shows affirmatively the preliminary proof required by section 622.28, such copy shall be admitted in evidence with the same force and effect as the original.

2. If any business, institution, member of a profession or calling, or any department or agency of government, in the regular course of business or activity has kept or recorded any memorandum, writing, entry print, representation or combination thereof, of any act, transaction, occurrence or event and in the regular course of business has caused any or all of the same to be recorded, copied or reproduced by any photographic, photostatic, microfilm, microcard, miniature photographic, or other process which accurately reproduces or forms a durable medium for so reproducing the original, the original may be destroyed in the regular course of business unless held in a custodial or fiduciary capacity or unless its preservation is required by law, except if the originals are records, reports or other papers of a county officer they shall not be destroyed until they have been preserved for ten years. Such reproduction, when satisfactorily identified, is as admissible in evidence as the original itself in any judicial or administrative proceeding whether the original is in existence or not and an enlargement or facsimile of such reproduction is likewise admissible in evidence if the original reproduction is in existence and available for inspection under direction of court. The introduction of a reproduced record, enlargement or facsimile, does not preclude admission of the original.

[Note: The following excerpts are from the "Uniform Rules of Evidence." See the "Uniform Laws Index" for additional provisions.]

Source: Iowa Rules of Evidence

ARTICLE X. CONTENTS OF WRITINGS, RECORDINGS.

☞ Rule 1001. Definitions

For purposes of this article the following definitions are applicable:

(1) *Writings and recordings.* — "Writings" and "recordings" consist of letters, words, or numbers, or their equivalent, set down by handwriting, typewriting, printing, photostating, photographing, magnetic impulse, mechanical or electronic recording, or other form of data compilation.

(2) *Photographs.* — "Photographs" include still photographs, X-ray films, video tapes, and motion pictures.

(3) *Original.* — An "original" of a writing or recording is the writing or recording itself or any counterpart intended to have the same effect by a person executing or issuing it. An "original" of a photograph includes the negative or any print therefrom. If data are stored in a computer or similar device, any printout or other output readable by sight, shown to reflect the data accurately, is an "original".

(4) *Duplicate.* — A "duplicate" is a counterpart produced by the same impression as the original, or from the same matrix, or by means of photography, including enlargements and miniatures, or by mechanical or electronic re-recording, or by chemical reproduction, or by other equivalent techniques which accurately reproduces the original.

☞ **Rule 1003. Admissibility of Duplicates.**

A duplicate is admissible to the same extent as an original unless (1) a genuine question is raised as to the authenticity of the original or (2) under the circumstances, admission of the duplicate would be unfair.

[See Appendix A. Uniform Rules of Evidence for additional provisions.]

Source: **Iowa Administrative Code**
Agency: **Department of Job Service**

EMPLOYMENT SECURITY

CHAPTER 2. EMPLOYER RECORDS AND REPORTS.

Citation: **IAC 345-2.1(96)**

✍ **§ 345-2.1(96). Records to be kept by the employer.**

2.1(1) Each employing unit having employment performed for it shall maintain records to show the information hereinafter indicated. Such records shall be kept in such form and manner that it will be possible from an inspection thereof to obtain the facts necessary to determine the eligibility of each employee when a claim has been filed. Such records shall be open to inspection and be subject to be copied by the department and its authorized representatives at any reasonable time. Such records shall be kept for a period of five years after the calendar year in which the remuneration to which they relate was paid, or if not paid was due.

2.1(2) Such records shall show with respect to each employee, unless the department has ruled that the particular service does not constitute employment:

a. Name of worker.

b. Social security account number.

c. Date on which employee was hired, rehired, or returned to work after a temporary layoff, and the date separated from work and the reason therefore.

d. Scheduled hours except for workers without a fixed schedule of hours, such as those working outside of the employer's establishment in such a manner that the employer has no definite knowledge of their working hours.

e. Total wages paid for employment in each period and the date of payment. For all pay periods ending in each quarter show separately: Money wages, the cash value of other remuneration such as any special payments for services such as wages in lieu of notice, bonuses, gifts, prizes, and the nature of payments such as accounts paid to employees as allowance or reimbursement for traveling and other business expenses, and the amounts of such expenditures actually incurred and accounted for by the employees.

f. The state or states in which the services are performed; and if any of such services are performed outside of this state and are not incidental to the service within the state, the base of operations (or if there is no base of operations then the place from which such services are directed or controlled) and the residence (by state), and the name of the county in Iowa in which services were performed.

g. When the pay period covers services performed both in covered employment and in excluded work, show the hours and wages for covered employment under this Act and also hours and wages for excluded work.

2.1(3) Such payroll records may be preserved by the employer in microfilm form, provided the employer:

a. Keeps a microfilm viewer available, and

b. Is willing to transcribe any information that may be required by the department.

2.1(4) Maintenance of records by out-of-state employing units.

Any employing unit having its principal place of business outside of Iowa shall maintain payroll records in this state with respect to wages paid to employees who perform some service in this state; provided, however, that an out-of-state employing unit may, with the approval of the department, maintain such payroll records outside the state upon its understanding that it will, when requested so to do, furnish the department with a true and correct copy of such payroll records. Failure to maintain said records in Iowa as required may result in estimated reports and payroll listings being made by the department. See rule 3.59(2).

Citation: **IAC 345-2.4(96)**

✍ **§ 345-2.4(96). Reporting of earnings data on magnetic tape.**

2.4(1) Employers may, in lieu of the individual wage item listing on 65-5300, employer's quarterly contribution and payroll report, submit a magnetic tape listing. Authorization for this reporting method will be given if the employer meets the specification requirements so as to be compatible with the division's computer capabilities. Such specifications will be furnished upon request.

2.4(2) A magnetic tape listing does not relieve the employer's responsibility to timely file Form 65-5300. If all wages are reported on magnetic tape, designate this on Form 65-5300 and enter the grand total of all wages on the 65-5300 grand total all pages line. If some wages are on magnetic tape and the balance individually listed on Form 65-5300, designate the total for each group on the form and enter the grand total of both groups on the 65-5300 grand total all pages line. All corrections to wages reported to the division must be listed and submitted in 68-0061, employer's wage adjustment report. Credit amounts must not be reported on tape. All reporting forms and contributions must be packaged and submitted separately from the tape.

This rule is intended to implement Iowa Code section 96.7.

TITLE 10. CIGARETTES AND TOBACCO.

CHAPTER 81. ADMINISTRATION.

Citation: **IAC 701-81.4(96)**

✍ **701-81.4(98). Records.**

Every taxpayer subject to the provisions of division 1 of Iowa Code chapter 98 (Cigarettes) shall keep, preserve, and make available to the department records for a period of two (2) years. Every taxpayer subject to the provisions of division II of Iowa Code chapter 98 (Cigars and Other Tobaccos) shall keep, preserve, and make available to the department records for a period of one (1) year. The following is a list of records subject to the provisions of this rule.

* * * * *

§ 81.4(11) Microfilm and related records system. Microfilm, microfiche, COM (computer on machine) and other related reduction in storage systems will be referred to as "microfilm" in this rule.

Microfilm reproductions of general books of account, such as a cash book, journals, voucher registers, ledgers, etc., are not acceptable other than those that have been approved by the

Internal Revenue Service under Revenue Procedure 76-43, Section 302. However, microfilm reproductions of supporting records of detail, such as sales invoices, purchase invoices, credit memoranda, etc., may be allowed providing all the following conditions are met and accepted by the taxpayer.

a. Appropriate facilities are provided to ensure the preservation and readability of the films.

b. Microfilm rolls are indexed, cross-referenced, labeled to show beginning and ending numbers or beginning and ending alphabetical listing of documents included, and are systematically filed.

c. The taxpayer agrees to provide transcripts of any information contained on microfilm which may be required for purposes of verification of tax liability.

d. Proper facilities are provided for the ready inspection and location of the particular record, including modern projectors for viewing and for the copying of records.

e. Any audit of "detail" on microfilm may be subject to sample audit procedures, to be determined at the discretion of the director or the director's designated representative.

f. A posting reference must be on each invoice.

g. Credit memoranda must carry a reference to the document evidencing the original transaction.

h. Documents necessary to support claimed exemptions from tax liability, such as bills of lading and purchase orders, must be maintained in an order by which they readily can be related to the transaction for which exemption is sought.

§ 81.4(12) Automatic data processing records. Automatic data processing is defined in this rule as including electronic data processing (EDP) and will be referred to as ADP.

a. An ADP tax accounting system must have built into its program a method of producing visible and legible records which will provide the necessary information for verification of the taxpayer's tax liability.

b. ADP records must provide an opportunity to trace any transaction back to the original source or forwarded to a final total. If detail printouts are not made of transactions at the time they are processed, then the system must have the ability to reconstruct these transactions.

c. A general ledger with source references, will be produced as hard copy to coincide with financial reports of tax reporting periods. In cases where subsidiary ledgers are used to support the general ledger accounts, the subsidiary ledgers should also be produced periodically.

d. Supporting documents and audit trail. The audit trail should be designed so that the details underlying the summary accounting data may be identified and made available to the director or the director's designated representative upon request. The system should be so designed that the supporting documents, such as sales invoices, purchase invoices, credit memoranda, etc., are readily available. (An audit trail is defined as the condition of having sufficient documentary evidence to trace an item from source (invoice, check, etc.) to a financial statement or tax return; or the reverse; that is, to have an auditable system).

e. *Program documentation.* A description of the ADP portion of the accounting program should be available. The statements and illustrations as to the scope of operations should be sufficiently detailed to indicate:

(1) The application being performed;

(2) The procedure employed in each application (which, for example, might be supported by flow charts, block diagrams or other satisfactory description of the input or output procedures); and

(3) The controls used to ensure accurate and reliable processing. Program and systems changes, together with their effective date should be noted in order to preserve an accurate chronological record.

f. Storage of ADP output will be in appropriate facilities to ensure preservation and readability of output.

State: Kansas
Source: Kansas Statutes Annotated

CHAPTER 12. CITIES AND MUNICIPALITIES.

Article 1. General Provisions

Citation: KSA 12-122

✪ **§ 12-122. Reproduction of records on film.**

The governing body may cause any or all records, documents or papers to be photographed, microphotographed or otherwise reproduced in a manner which accurately reproduces the original thereof in all details.

Citation: KSA 12-123

✪ **§ 12-123. Same; evidence in courts or administrative agencies.**

Photographs, microphotographs or reproductions shall be deemed to be an original record for all purposes, including introduction in evidence in all courts or administrative agencies. A transcript, exemplification or certified copy thereof, for all purposes recited herein, shall be deemed to be a transcript, exemplification, or certified copy of the original.

CHAPTER 17. CORPORATIONS.

Article 65. Meetings, Elections, Voting and Notices.

Citation: KSA 17-6514

✍ ☞ **§ 17-6514. Form of records.**

Any records maintained by a corporation in the regular course of its business, including its stock ledger, books of account and minute books, may be kept on, or be in the form of, punch cards, magnetic tape, photographs, microphotographs or any other information storage device, if the reports so kept can be converted into clearly legible written form within a reasonable time. Any corporation shall so convert any records so kept upon the request of any person entitled to inspect the same. Where records are kept in such manner, a clearly legible written form produced from the cards, tapes, photographs, microphotographs or other information storage device shall be admissible in evidence and shall be accepted for all other purposes, to the same extent as an original written record of the same information would have been, when said written form accurately portrays the record.

CHAPTER 19. COUNTIES AND COUNTY OFFICERS.

Article 2. County Commissioners.

Citation: KSA 19-250

✪ **§ 19-250. Reproduction and preservation of public records, other than court records; minimum standards.**

The board of county commissioners of any county in the state, may by resolution, provide for and authorize any officer of the county to photograph, microphotograph or reproduce or to have photographed, microphotographed or reproduced on film any of the records, papers or documents which are by law placed in the custody and control of such officer, except court records, and to acquire necessary facilities and equipment, and to acquire, maintain and use all such appropriate containers and files as shall be necessary to accommodate and preserve the photographs, microphotographs or films so obtained. Such photographing, microphotographing or filming may be so authorized for the reproducing of lists and records in the usual day by day official activities of any such officer, where to so will greatly promote efficiency in the office, or as a method of preserving old or worn records, papers and documents. The photographic film and prints or reproductions therefrom shall comply with federal standard No. 125a, dated April 24, 1958, or the latest revision thereof, issued pursuant to the federal property and administrative services act of 1949, and any amendments thereto, and the device used to reproduce such records on such film shall be one which accurately reproduces the original thereof in all details.

Citation: KSA 19-251

✪ **§ 19-251. Same; equipment and facilities; operation.**

Any such county may purchase, lease or acquire the equipment and facilities necessary to carry out the purposes and intent of this act and by contract and agreement arrange for the use thereof, and may employ such parties as are necessary to operate said equipment and facilities.

Citation: KSA 19-252

✪ **§ 19-252. Same; deemed original record; evidence; transcript.**

Such photographs, microphotographs or photographic film or prints or reproductions therefrom shall be deemed to be an original record for all purposes, and may be used as evidence in all courts or administrative agencies. A transcript, exemplification or certified copy thereof shall, for all purposes recited herein, be deemed to be a transcript, exemplification, or certified copy of the original.

CHAPTER 20. COURTS.

Article 1. Supreme Court

Citation: KSA 20-159

✪ **§ 20-159. Reproduction and preservation of court records; minimum standards.**

The supreme court may provide for and authorize any administrative judge of a judicial district, to photograph, microphotograph, or reproduce or to have photographed, microphotographed or reproduced on film any of the court records, papers or documents which are by law placed in the courts of that judicial district and to acquire necessary facilities and equipment and to acquire, maintain and use all such appropriate containers and files as shall be necessary to accommodate and preserve the photographs, microphotographs or films so obtained. The photographing, microphotographing or filming may be so authorized for the reproducing of court records, where to do so will promote efficiency in the office, or as a method of preserving old or worn records, papers or documents. The photographic films and prints or reproductions therefrom, shall comply with federal standard no. 125a, dated April 24, 1958, or the latest revision thereof, issued pursuant to the federal property and administrative services act of 1949, and any amendments thereto. The device used to produce such records on such film shall be one which accurately reproduces the original thereof in all details.

CHAPTER 44. LABOR AND INDUSTRIES.

Article 7. Employment Security Law.

Citation: KSA 44-714

✍ ☞ **§ 44-714. Administration of act; powers and duties of secretary; employees; political activities prohibited, penalties; advisory councils; reports andrecords, confidentiality; witnesses, oaths and subpoenas; state-federal cooperation; fees for document copies.**

* * * * *

(f) Records and reports. Each employing unit shall keep true and accurate work records, containing such information as the secretary may prescribe. Such records shall be open to inspection and subject to being copied by the secretary or the secretary's authorized representatives at any reasonable time and shall be preserved for a period of five years from the due date of the contributions or payments in lieu of contributions for the period to which they relate. Only one audit shall be made of any employer's records for any given period of time. Upon request the employing unit shall be furnished a copy of all findings by the secretary or the secretary's authorized representatives, resulting from such audit. A special inquiry or special examination made for a specific and limited purpose shall not be considered to be an audit for the purpose of this subsection. The secretary may require from any employing unit any sworn or unsworn reports, with respect to persons employed by it, which the secretary deems necessary for the effective administration of this act. Information thus obtained or obtained from any individual pursuant to the administration of this act shall be held confidential, except to the extent necessary for the proper presentation of a claim by an employer or employee under the employment security law, and shall not be published or be open to public inspection, other than to public employees in the performance of their public duties, in any manner revealing the individual's or employing unit's identity. Any claimant or employing unit or their representatives at a hearing before an appeal tribunal or the secretary shall be supplied with information from such records to the extent necessary for the proper presentation of the claim. The transcript made at any such benefits hearing shall not be discoverable or admissible in evidence in any other proceeding, hearing or determination of any kind or nature. In the event of any appeal of a benefits matter, the transcript shall be sealed by the hearing officer and shall be available only to any reviewing authority who shall reseal the transcript after making a review of it. In no event shall such transcript be deemed a public record. Nothing in this subsection (f) shall be construed to prohibit disclosure of any information obtained under the employment security law, including hearing transcripts, upon request of either of the parties, for the purpose of administering or adjudicating a claim for benefits under the provisions of any other state program, except that any party receiving such information shall be prohibited from further disclosure and shall be subject to the same duty of confidentiality otherwise imposed by this subsection (f) and shall be subject to the penalties imposed by this subsection (f) for violations of such duty of confidentiality. Nothing in this subsection (f) shall be construed to prohibit disclosure of any information obtained under the employment security law, including hearing transcripts, for use as evidence in open court in a criminal prosecution for perjury at an appeal hearing under the employment security law or for any criminal violation of the employment security law. If the secretary or any officer or employee of the secretary violates any provisions of this subsection (f), the secretary or such officer or employee shall be fined not less than $20 nor more than $200 or imprisoned for not longer than 90 days, or both. Original records of the agency and original paid benefit warrants of the state treasurer may be made available to the employment security agency of any other state or the federal government to be used as evidence in prosecution of violations of the employment security law of such state or federal government. Photostatic copies of such records shall be made and where possible shall be substituted for original records introduced in evidence and the originals returned to the agency.

* * * * *

CHAPTER 45. PUBLIC RECORDS, DOCUMENTS AND INFORMATION.

Article 4. Public Records Preservation.

Citation: KSA 45-412

✪ **§ 45-412. Microphotographic or optical disc copies of originals; original record destruction, when.**

(a) The state archivist shall prepare recommendations, to be approved by the state records board, based on the current standards of the federal government and the American national standards institute, for the quality of film or optical disc, proper arrangement of materials, suitable filming or other image reproduction techniques and equipment, quality of photographic or optical disc images, film processing results, and film or optical disc storage conditions which should be achieved or utilized by state and local agencies in making microphotographic or optical disc copies of government records with enduring value pursuant to K.S.A. 12-122, 19-250, or 75-3506, and amendments thereto. Whenever microphotographic or optical disc copies of records with enduring value fail to meet the standards recommended by the state archivist and approved by the state records board, the state archivist shall urge state and local agencies to retain the original records.

(b) Whenever photographs, microphotographs or other reproductions on film or optical disc have been prepared pursuant to K.S.A. 75-3506, and amendments thereto, and have been placed in conveniently accessible files and provisions made for preserving, examining and using the same, and when a negative copy of the film or a master copy of the optical disc has been deposited in a secure place where it will not be subject to use except in making additional positive copies, any state agency, with the approval of the state records board or as authorized by the retention and disposition schedules, may cause the original records from which the photographs, microphotographs or other reproductions on film or optical disc have been made, or any part thereof, to be destroyed. Such records shall not be destroyed and shall be retained by the agency or transferred to the state archives or temporarily to another suitable place designated by the board, if the board judges such materials to have been enduring value to their original form.

(c) Except as provided by subsection (b) of K.S.A. 12-120, and amendments thereto, whenever photographs, microphotographs or other reproductions on film have been prepared as provided in K.S.A. 12-122 or 19-250, and amendments thereto, and have been placed in conveniently accessible files and provisions made for preserving, examining and using the same, and when a negative copy of the film has been deposited in a secure place where it will not be subject to use except in making additional positive copies, a local agency may retain the original records in its custody at any suitable location, may deposit them in collections established pursuant to K.S.A. 12-1658 and 12-1660, and amendments thereto, or K.S.A. 19-2648 and 19-2649, and amendments thereto, or may dispose of the original records as provided in the retention and disposition schedules. If there are no relevant provisions in the retention and disposition schedules, the original records shall be offered to the state historical society prior to other disposition of them.

(d) The state historical society may prepare and deposit in the state archives a microfilm or other copy of any noncurrent government record which is retained by a state or local agency, unless public access to the record is restricted by statute or by administrative regulation authorized by statute.

Article 5. Miscellaneous Provisions

Citation: KSA 45-501

✪ **§ 45-501. Records made on electronically accessed media; authorization, conditions and procedures, application; notice to state records board.**

(a) Whenever any state agency or local agency is required by law to make a record or to record any transaction or any instrument, paper or document, the making of such record on computer disk, tape or other electronically accessed media, in accordance with this section, shall be deemed to be recording or the making of the record as required by law.

(b) When any such records are made on computer disks, tapes or other electronically accessed media under this section, such records shall be maintained and adequate provisions shall be made for their preservation, examination and availability for ready use by those persons lawfully entitled to view them through the use of computer terminal displays, computer printouts, other computer-generated displays or other suitable facilities which may be made available at one or more locations designated by the state agency or local agency therefore. The capability to produce a computer printout or other printed version of such records stored on computer disks, tapes or other electronically accessed media shall be maintained by the state agency or local agency at all times so that such a printed copy of such records may be made available to persons lawfully entitled to view the records, subject to any applicable fees for such printed copies, from one or more locations designated by the state agency or local agency therefore. Each computer or other electronically accessed media system used to make records under this section shall include adequate security procedures and other provisions for permanent record of all persons who have access to and make, amend or delete any records or other data in such system.

(c) No state agency or local agency which records or stores information on computer disks, tapes or other electronically accessed media shall be required to satisfy the standards and procedures imposed under this section, unless such records and information are records required by law and such records are not also made or maintained in another manner required or permitted by law. Each state agency or local agency which makes records or stores information on computer tapes, disks or other electronically accessed media in accordance with this section and which does not keep such records or information in another manner shall give written notice to the state records board thereof and shall identify all such records and information in such notice.

(d) As used in this section, the words and phrases set out in K.S.A. 45-402 and amendments thereto have the meanings ascribed to them in that section, unless the context requires a different meaning.

(e) This section shall be supplemental to existing statutes.

CHAPTER 60. PROCEDURE, CIVIL.

Article 4. Rules Of Evidence.

Authentication and Content of Writings.

Citation: KSA 60-465a

☞ **§ 60-465a. Reproductions of original court records deemed same as original record; certified copy as evidence.**

The photographs, microphotographs or photographic film or prints or reproductions of the original records as authorized in K.S.A. 20-159 shall be deemed to be an original record for all purposes, and may be used as evidence in all courts or administrative agencies. A copy thereof, certified in writing by the person designated by the administrative judge of the judicial district as having custody of such reproduction, may be used as evidence in all courts or administrative agencies.

Citation: KSA 60-469

☞ **§ 60-469. Proving content of business and public records.**

The content of any admissible writing made in the regular course of "a business" as defined by K.S.A. 60-459 and amendments thereto, or in the regular course of duty of any "public official" as defined by K.S.A. 60-459, and amendments thereto, may be proved by a nonerasable optical image reproduction provided that additions, deletions or changes to the original document are not permitted by the technology, or a photostatic, microfilm, microcard, miniature photographic or other photographic copy or reproduction or by an enlargement thereof, when duly authenticated, if it was in the regular course of such business, or official activity to make and preserve such copies or reproductions as a part of the records of such business or office. The introduction of such copy, reproduction or enlargement does not preclude admission of the original writing if it is still in existence.

CHAPTER 72. SCHOOLS.

Article 53. Miscellaneous Provisions.

Citation: KSA 72-5371

✪ **§ 72-5371. Reproduction of records on film.**

The governing body of any school district may cause any or all records, documents or papers to be photographed, microphotographed, or reproduced on film. Such photographic film shall comply with federal standard no. 125a, dated April 24, 1958, or the latest revision thereof, issued pursuant to the federal property and administrative services act of 1949, as amended, and the device used to reproduce such records on such film shall be one which accurately reproduces the original thereof in all details.

Citation: KSA 72-5372

✪ **§ 72-5372. Same; deemed original record; evidence; transcript.**

Such photographs, microphotographs or photographic film shall be deemed to be an original record for all purposes, including introduction in evidence in all courts or administrative agencies. A transcript, exemplification or certified copy thereof shall, for all purposes recited herein, be deemed to be a transcript, exemplification, or certified copy of the original.

Citation: KSA 72-5373

✪ **§ 72-5373. Same; preservation and destruction of original records, when.**

Whenever such photographs, microphotographs or reproductions on film shall be placed in conveniently accessible files and provisions made for preserving, examining and using the same, the custodial officer may, with the approval of the governing body cause the originals from which the photographs or microphotographs have been made or any part thereof to be deposited in a safe place if the same are of a permanent value or destroyed if not of permanent value.

CHAPTER 75. STATE DEPARTMENTS, PUBLIC OFFICERS AND EMPLOYEES.

Article 35. Public Records.

Citation: KSA 75-3506

✪ **§ 75-3506. Reproduction of records on film or disc.**

Any public officer of the state may cause any or all records, papers or documents kept by the public officer to be photographed, microphotographed, reproduced on film or optical disc. Such photographic film or optical disc shall comply with standards recommended by the state archivist and approved by the state records board pursuant to K.S.A. 45-412, and amendments thereto, and the device used to reproduce such records on such film or optical disc shall be one which accurately reproduces the original thereof in all details.

Citation: KSA 75-3507

✍ ✪ **§ 75-3507. Reproduction of records on film or disc; evidence in courts or administrative agencies.**

Such photographs, microphotographs, photographic film or reprinted images from an optical disc shall be deemed to be an original record for all purposes, including introduction in evidence in all courts or administrative agencies. A transcript, exemplification or certified copy thereof shall, for all purposes recited herein, be deemed to be a transcript, exemplification, or certified copy of the original.

Citation: KSA 75-3519

✍ ✪ **§ 75-3519. Agency statement deemed original record for image recognition and information storage system.**

For an image recognition and information storage system which is used by an agency to record and store information from records, papers or documents and which complies with standards recommended by the state archivist and approved by the state records board pursuant to K.S.A. 45-412, and amendments thereto, the agency's statement of the information shall be deemed to be an original record of the information for all purposes, including introduction into evidence in all courts or administrative agencies.

Source: **Kansas Administrative Regulations**

CHAPTER 92. DEPARTMENT OF REVENUE.

ARTICLE 19. KANSAS RETAILERS' SALES TAX.

Citation: **KAR 92-19-4a**

✍ § 92-19-4a. Record keeping sales and use tax transaction.

(a) Every person doing business in the state of Kansas, or storing, using, or otherwise consuming tangible personal property purchased from a retailer, and every lessor and lessee of tangible personal property for use in this state shall keep complete and adequate records as are necessary for the director to determine the liability of each retailer for sales and use tax pursuant to K.S.A. 79-3603, 79-3703 and amendments thereto. Unless the director authorizes an alternative method of record keeping in writing, these records shall show:

(1) Gross receipts from sales, or rental payments from leases, of tangible personal property in the state of Kansas, including any services that are a part of the sale or lease, regardless of whether the retailer believes the receipts to be taxable or non-taxable;

(2) all deductions allowed by law and claimed in filing returns;

(3) total purchase price of all tangible personal property purchased for sale, consumption, or lease in the state of Kansas;

(4) all exemption certificates; and

(5) a true and complete inventory taken at least once a year.

Each record shall consist of the normal books of account ordinarily maintained by the average prudent person engaged in the activity in question, including bills, receipts, invoices, cash register tapes, or other documents of original entry supporting the entries in the books of account, and all schedules or working papers used in connection with the preparation of tax returns.

(b) Each record may be microfilmed or microfiched, as long as the microfilmed or microfiched records are authentic, accessible, and readable, and the following requirements are fully satisfied:

(1) Each taxpayer shall provide transcriptions of any information concerning sales or use tax liability on microfilm or microfiche which may be required to verify liability. The taxpayer shall also provide appropriate facilities for preservation of the microfilm or microfiche for the periods required.

(2) All microfilmed and microfiched data shall be indexed, cross-referenced and labeled to show beginning and ending alphabetical listing of documents, and beginning and ending numbers. All microfilm and microfiched data shall be systematically filed to permit ready access.

(3) Each taxpayer shall make available upon request of the director or the director's authorized agent, a reader or printer in good working order, at the examination site, for reading, locating and reproducing any record concerning sales or use tax liability maintained on microfilm or microfiche.

(4) Each taxpayer shall set forth in writing the procedures governing the microfilm or microfiche system and the individual or individuals responsible for maintaining and operating the system.

(5) Each taxpayer shall maintain a complete microfilm or microfiche system and shall consistently use the system in the regular course of business.

(6) Each taxpayer shall establish appropriate documentation of procedures so that the original document can be followed through the microfilm or microfiche system.

(7) Each taxpayer shall establish internal procedures for microfilm or microfiche inspection and quality assurance.

(8) Each taxpayer shall be responsible for the effective identification, processing, storage, and preservation of microfilm or microfiche for a period of three years from the 1st day of the year to which they pertain.

(9) Each taxpayer shall keep a record identifying the persons or business entities that produced the microfilm or microfiche records.

(10) When displayed on a microfilm or microfiche reader or viewer, or reproduced on paper, the material shall exhibit a high degree of legibility. For this purpose, legibility is defined as the quality of a letter or numeral that enables the observer to identify it positively and quickly to the exclusion of all other letters or numerals being recognizable as words or complete numbers.

(11) All production of microfilm or microfiche and processing duplication, quality control, storage, identification, and inspection shall meet industry standards.

(c) An automated data processing tax accounting system may be used by the taxpayer to preserve sales and use tax records required for the verification of tax liability. An automated data processing system shall include a method of producing legible records which will provide the necessary information for verifying tax liability. Each taxpayer maintaining records on an automated data processing system shall satisfy the following requirements:

(1) Automated data processing records shall provide an opportunity to trace any transaction back to the original source or forward to a final total. If detailed printouts are not made of transactions at the time they are processed, the systems shall have the ability to reconstruct these transactions.

(2) A general ledger, with source references, shall be written out to coincide with financial reports for tax reporting periods. When subsidiary ledgers are used to support the general ledger accounts, the subsidiary ledgers shall also be written out periodically.

(3) An audit trail shall be designed so that the details underlying the summary accounting data may be identified and made available to the director or the director's authorized agent. The system shall be designed so that supporting documents, such as sales invoices, purchase invoices, and credit memoranda are readily available.

(4) Each taxpayer shall make available a description of the automated data processing portion of the accounting system. The statements and illustrations as to the scope of operations shall be sufficiently detailed to indicate:

(A) the application being performed;

(B) the procedures employed in each application, such as flow charts or block diagrams; and

(C) the controls used to insure accurate and reliable processing. Important changes, together with their effective dates, shall be noted in order to preserve an accurate chronological record.

(5) Adequate record retention facilities shall be available for storing tapes and printouts, as well as all supporting documents as may be required by this act.

(d) All records of a registered retailer or consumer pertaining to transactions involving sales or use tax liability shall be preserved for a period of not less than three years from the last day of the calendar year or of the fiscal year of the registered retailer or consumer, whichever comes later.

(e) All of the foregoing records shall be available for and subject to inspection by the director of taxation or the director's authorized agents and employees, at all times during business hours of the day.

(f) If any taxpayer fails to substantially comply with the requirements of this rule and regulation, the director shall impose penalties and interest pursuant to K.S.A. 79-3615 and 79-3706 and amendments thereto.

State: Kentucky
Source: Kentucky Revised Statutes Annotated

TITLE 14. LIBRARIES AND ARCHIVES.

CHAPTER 171. STATE LIBRARIES — LIBRARIANS — ARCHIVES AND RECORDS.

State Archives and Records

Citation: KRSA 171.410

✪ 171.410. Definitions for KRS 171.420 to 171.740.

As used in KRS 171.420 to 171.740:

(1) "Public record or record" means all books, papers, maps, photographs, cards, tapes, disks, diskettes, recordings, and other documentary materials, regardless of physical form or characteristics, which are prepared, owned, used, in the possession of or retained by a public agency. "Public record" shall not include any records owned by a private person or corporation that are not related to functions, activities, programs or operations funded by state or local authority;

* * * * *

Citation: KRSA 171.520

✪ § 171.520. Supervision of state and local agencies — Plan for comprehensive records management system for state government — Rules and regulations.

(1) The department shall, with due regard to the program activities of the state and local agencies concerned, prescribe the policies and principles to be followed by state and local agencies in the conduct of their records management programs, and to make provisions for the economical and efficient management of records by state and local agencies by analyzing, developing, promoting, and coordinating standards, procedures, and techniques designed to improve the management of records, to ensure the maintenance and security of records deemed appropriate for preservation, and to facilitate the segregation and disposal of records of temporary value and by promoting the efficient and economical utilization of space, equipment, and supplies needed for the purpose of creating, maintaining, storing, and servicing records. The department may accept, administer and grant any money appropriated or granted to it, in addition to appropriations from the general fund, for providing and improving records management programs of state and local agencies.

* * * * *

Citation: KRSA 171.660

✪ § 171.660. Authorized reproductions — Disposal of Originals.

Whenever the governor, lieutenant governor or any state agency or subdivision or the principal officer thereof, shall reproduce and preserve for record any records or papers by photographic, microphotographic, nonerasable optical image or other process which accurately reproduces the original records, which forms a durable medium, and which is performed in accordance with rules and regulations promulgated by the department, the original thereof may be disposed of or destroyed.

Citation: KRSA 171.670

✪ § 171.670. Destruction of records.

When there is a question whether a particular record or group of records should be destroyed, the commission shall have exclusive authority to decide whether or not the record or group of records are to be destroyed.

Source: Kentucky Rules of Evidence

ARTICLE X. CONTENTS OF WRITINGS, RECORDINGS, AND PHOTOGRAPHS.

☞ Rule 1001. Definitions.

For purposes of this article the following definitions are applicable:

(1) *Writings and recordings.* — "Writings" and "recordings" consist of letters, words, or numbers, or their equivalent, set down by handwriting, typewriting, printing, photostating, photographing, magnetic impulse, mechanical or electronic recording, or other form of data compilation.

(2) *Photographs.* — "Photographs" include still photographs, X-ray films, video tapes, and motion pictures.

(3) *Original.* — An "original" of a writing or recording is the writing or recording itself or any counterpart intended to have the same effect by a person executing or issuing it. An "original" of a photograph includes the negative or any print therefrom. If data are stored in a computer or similar device, any printout or other output readable by sight, shown to reflect the data accurately, is an "original."

(4) *Duplicate.* — A "duplicate" is a counterpart produced by the same impression as the original, or from the same matrix, or by means of photography, including enlargements and miniatures, or by mechanical or electronic rerecording, or by chemical reproduction, or by other equivalent technique which accurately reproduces the original.

☞ Rule 1003. Admissiblity of duplicates.

A duplicate is admissible to the same extent as an original unless:

(1) A genuine question is raised as to the authenticity of the original; or

(2) In the circumstances it would be unfair to admit the duplicate in lieu of the original.

☞ Rule 1005. Public records.

The contents of an official record, or of a document authorized to be recorded or filed and actually recorded or filed with a governmental agency, either federal, state, county, or municipal, in a place where official records or documents are ordinarily filed, including data compilations in any form, if otherwise admissible, may be proved by copy, certified as correct in accordance with KRE 902 or testified to be correct by a witness who has compared it with the original. If a copy which complies with the foregoing cannot be obtained by the exercise of reasonable diligence, then other evidence of the contents may be given.

Source: Kentucky Administrative Code
Agency: Department for Libraries and Archives

TITLE 725. EDUCATION, ARTS, AND HUMANITIES CABINET DEPARTMENT OF LIBRARIES AND ARCHIVES

CHAPTER 1. ARCHIVES

Citation: 725 KAR 1:020.

✪ § 1:020. Reproduction of public records.

RELATES TO: KRS 171.450(1)(c), 171.600, 171.670
STATUTORY AUTHORITY: KRS 171.450, 171.660, 171.670
NECESSITY AND FUNCTION: KRS 171.450(1)(c) requires the department to establish standards for the reproduction of public records by photographic or microphotographic process.

Section 1. Due to the rapid changes being brought about in technology, the Department for Libraries and Archives does not approve or disapprove of one method of recording by photographic or microphotographic process over another. In order to safeguard the present and future interests of the people of the Commonwealth, all agencies of state and local government should obtain advice from the Public Records Division prior to changing their methods of recording.

Section 2. Recording may be done on paper, photostats, electrostatic, thermographic or on film in accordance with KRS 171.660.

Section 3. If the recording is done on paper, it must be done on thirty-two (32) weight, 100 percent linen paper or its equivalent in accordance with specifications established by the National Bureau of Standards.

Section 4. If done on photostats, electrostatic or thermographic methods, it must be done on thirty-two (32) weight stock of proven permanency.

Section 5. If the recording is done on microfilm, miniprint, microcard, microfiche, or some other type of microform, the following safeguards must be observed to obtain approval of the Department for Libraries and Archives:

(1) A security copy (negative or positive in 16mm or 35mm) roll form must be provided the Public Records Division for security storage. This film shall be provided at no cost.

(2) Filming in a series should not be continued after the first roll until a test of the film has been completed. The Public Records Division shall be the principal microfilm advisory authority.

(3) The security and use copies of microfilm should be tested for resolution, density, and hypo-residue. The security film shall be physically inspected every five (5) years for mold, spots, or other evidences of deterioration.

(4) The security copy shall not be used or handled in any way to cause the film to be scratched or damaged.

(5) The Public Records Division shall be responsible, where necessary, for supervising appropriate tests of microfilm which shall follow the standards of the United States Government Bureau of Testing and National Microfilm Association.

Section 6. No original records may be destroyed by any state or local agency after being microfilmed or otherwise duplicated wihout written approval of the State Archives and Records Commission.

Section 7. The State Archives and Records Commission shall be the final authority in the executive branch of government for the disposition of all public records in Kentucky (state, county, and city) but shall not make any decisions without consultation with the agencies involved who shall participate in the decision making.

✪ POLICY MEMORANDUM ON OPTICAL STORAGE OF PUBLIC RECORDS

PM 96-1

Under the terms of KRS 171.660, the Department for Libraries and Archives is directed to establish rules and regulations governiing use of optically recorded images and the circumstance under which original, manual, eye-readable copies of imaged documents may be destroyed. As mandated by KRS 171.420, the State Archives and Records Commission is direccted to advise the department on matters relating to archives and records management. Because optical storage technologies are evolving so quickly and because the challenge of managing those recordkeeping technologies over time is substantial, the deparmtne is issuing the following poicy statements. The commission has reviewed and evaluated this memorandumd and fuly supports its provisions and implementation.

I. Public records which are either, (1) scheduled* as permanent or, (2) whose vital retention status is ten years or greater, must have manual, eye-readable counterparts.

Agencies desiring to maintain optically recorded public records in either of the above-named categories without manual, eye-readable backups may petition the Director, Public Records Division, for relief from this responsibility. The Director will ask the agency to demonstrate in writing the following elements in their imaging procedures:

A. Accuracy and Completeness of Records.

A process of inspection must be in place to confirm that imaged documents are legible and that no corners of the original documents were folded or obscured during scanning. This process should include systematic quality control and audit procedures, as well as operational oversight by staff with detailed knowledge of the process or system used to produce the records.

Resolution and use of gray scale should be appropriate to capture all needed detail within documents. Similarly, scanned images must capture all colors represented in the original documents which are needed to interpret or understand the meaning of the original. The accuracy of the indexing process must also be assured through procedures that visually verify indexes after they have been keyed or created through optical character recognition.

B. Maintenance and Retention of Documentaion.

Full and up-to-date process or system documentation should be maintained throughout the life of the records in question. Where processes or the system changes, documentation of processes must be retained until the retention periods have been met. Documentation should conform to standards established for documentation in the Commonwealth's published Systems Life Cycle Manual, which is available from the Kentucky Deparment of Information Systems.

C. Audit Trails and Security.

Audit trails documenting who accessed or used the system, when they used it, and what the results of use were must be maintained. Security measures consistent with guidelines and standards provided in the Kentucky Information Systems Architecture should be adopted and applied.

D. Access to Records.

Records maintained in imaging systems must meet all access requirements defined by Kentucky Revised Statutes or Administrative regulations.

E. Backup.

A backup copy of all image files and indexes must be created at intervals determined by the frequency of update and the criticality of the imaging system, as estabished by the creating agency. Kentucky Information Systems Architecture and Kentucky Department of Information Systems guidelines relating to backcups and disaster recovery should be used to determine the frequency and means of backing up imaged records. Agencies should contact DIS directly for copies of these guidelines. Off-site backups of permanent and vital records must be maintained.

F. Equipment Maintenance.

An effective maintenance program ensuring that scanner, optical disks, and magnetic storage devices are properly housed and regularly maintained must be in place. Equipment maintenance logs should be kept to document the occurrence of regular maintenance.

G. Training Programs.

Staff employing imaging systems must receive formal training in system use to ensure that standard procedures are routinely followed and that the record or official status of system contents is broadly accepted.

H. Compression Algorithms.

All images should be stored in or convertible to compression formats identified in the Kentucky Information Systems Architecture. Currently, the standard requires use of or an ability to convert to CCITT Group IV.

I. Migration of Data.

Migration paths for all records, including those stored offline, must be identified and employed to ensure usability of public records throughout their retention period.

If the above conditions are met, the Director, Public Records Division will provide written authorization for the petitioning agency to maintain records solely in optical format(s). Periodic review of compliance with these standards will be performed by, or on behalf of, Department for Libraries and Archives staff.

II. Transfer of optically stored public records to the State Archives may only be made when agencies have strictly adhered to the Statewide Information Systems Architecture and in those cases where agency recordkeeping systems allow relatively simple transference or export of usable records.

Both of these policies should make agencies consider the economies of maintaining records in manual formats for ultimate transfer to the archives or for creating microfilm copies of records early in their life-cycle.

III. Optically stored records whose retention period is less than permanent or without vital records retention status of ten years or greater may be maintained without hard copy, eye-readable originals.

Agencies are strongly advised, however, that meeting the criteria described above under policy statement I is critical to the acceptance of the records as valid documentation of agency transactions and is required for the legal admissibility of public records. Agencies should be further advised that records subject to audit are auditable regardless of format and that these criteria will be used by the State Auditor in evaluating the content of imaged records.

"Schedule" refers to a records schedule formally approved by the State Archives and Records Commission. This schedule provides the agency its only authority to legally destroy public records, in any fomat. Vital retention status is a designation given certain critical records whose loss would preclude an agency's immediate return to operation or which protect the rights of individuals or groups or document the obligations and transactions of public agencies.

State: **Louisiana**
Source: **Louisiana Revised Statutes Annotated**

TITLE 13. COURTS AND JUDICIAL PROCEDURE.

CHAPTER 17. WITNESSES AND EVIDENCE.

PART II. EVIDENCE IN GENERAL.

Citation: **13 LRSA 3733**

☞ **§ 3733. Business records; reproduction by photographic, photostatic or miniature photographic process, certification.**

A. Any business may cause any or all records kept by such business in regular course of its operation to be recorded, copied or reproduced by any photographic, photostatic or miniature photographic process which correctly, accurately and permanently copies, reproduces or forms a medium for copying or reproducing the original record on a film or other durable material, and such business may thereafter dispose of the original record, provided that every original record pertaining to any claim, tax, or report due the state of Louisiana or any of its agencies shall be preserved for five years from the 31st day of December of the year in which such claim arose, or such tax or report was due.

B. Any such photographic, photostatic or miniature photographic copy or reproduction shall be deemed to be an original record for all purposes and shall be treated as an original record in all courts or administrative agencies for the purpose of its admissibility in evidence. An enlargement or facsimile of such reproduction is likewise admissible in evidence if the original reproduction is in existence and available for inspection under the direction of the court.

C. For purposes of this Section "business" means and includes each business, industry, profession, occupation and calling of every kind.

D. Whenever any such photographic, photostatic, or miniature photographic copy or reproduction shall be certified with a certificate reading substantially as follows, it shall be deemed an original or authentic copy of the original record or document for purposes of its admissibility under Louisiana law, and specifically as authentic evidence for purposes of Code of Civil Procedure Art. 2636:

"STATE OF LOUISIANA
PARISH of______________________________,
Louisiana
I, ____________________ do hereby certify that this document is a true and correct copy of the original thereof, consisting of______page(s), being a reproduction thereof from the records on file with the undersigned, in accordance with Louisiana Revised Statutes, Title 13, Section 3733.

____
Date

TITLE 35. NOTARIES PUBLIC AND COMMISSIONERS.

CHAPTER 5. NOTARIES IN ORLEANS PARISH.

Part 3. Office and Custodian of Notarial Records.

Citation: **35 LRSA 323.1**

✪ **§ 323.1. Microfilm records; use; separate location.**

A. Permission is hereby granted to the custodian to install and use microfilm machinery and apparatus in the recordation, filing, preservation and reproduction of all records and documents filed or deposited with the custodian prior to July 29, 1970, and subsequent thereto.

B. Such microfilm records and documents may be used only in emergency situations arising from fire, storm, theft, loss or any other emergency circumstances which may render the original record or document useless. Such microfilm records and documents shall be kept at a separate location from the original records and documents filed with the custodian.

C. Such microfilm copy shall be deemed to be an original record for all purposes, and shall be admissible in evidence in all courts or administrative agencies. A facsimile, exemplification or certified copy thereof shall for all purposes be deemed to be a transcript, exemplification or certified copy of the original.

D. Nothing contained herein shall in any manner be construed to permit the destruction of any notarial records presently in the possession of, or which may hereafter come into the possession of the custodian of notarial records.

TITLE 44. PUBLIC RECORDS AND RECORDERS.

CHAPTER 1. PUBLIC RECORDS.

Part 2. General Provisions.

Citation: **44 LRSA 36**

✪ **§ 36. Preservation of records.**

A. All persons and public bodies having custody or control of any public record, other than conveyance, probate, mortgage, or other permanent records required by existing law to be kept for all time, shall exercise diligence and care in preserving the public record for the period or periods of time specified for such public records in formal records retention schedules developed and approved by the state archivist and director of the division of archives, records management, and history of the Department of State. However, in all instances in which a formal retention schedule has not been executed, such public records shall be preserved and maintained for a period of at least three years from the date on which the public record was made. However, where copies of an original record exist, only one copy of the duplicate copies shall be required to be kept. Where an appropriate form of the microphotographic process has been utilized to record, file, and otherwise preserve such public records with microforms produced in compliance with the provisions of R.S. 44:415, the microforms shall be deemed originals in themselves, as provided by R.S. 44:39(B), and disposition of original documents which have been microphotographically preserved and of duplicates and other copies thereof shall proceed as provided in R.S. 44:411.

* * * * *

Citation: **44 LRSA 39**

☞ ✪ **§ 39. Microfilm and electronic digitized records; use as evidence.**

A. All persons and public bodies having custody or control of any public records of the state of Louisiana or any of its subdivisions may utilize any appropriate form of the microphotographic process, or an electronic digitizing process capable of reproducing an unalterable image of the original source document, for the recordation, filing, and preservation of all existing public records, forms, and documents or records, forms, and documents hereafter accumulated which pertain to the their functions and operations in order to maintain efficient and economical records management programs and to conserve storage space, provided that the use of such microphotographic or electronic digitizing processes are not otherwise prohibited by law and that all microforms produced comply with standards established by the division of archives, records management, and history of the Department of State in accordance with the provisions of R.S. 44:415.

B. Any microfilm or electronically digitized copy, when satisfactorily identified, shall be deemed to be an original itself, and shall be admissible in evidence in all courts or administrative proceedings in any agency, whether the original document is in existence or not, and an enlargement or facsimile of a reproduction is likewise admissible in evidence, if the original reproduction is in existence and available for inspection under direction of the court or the administrative agency. Original records shall remain subject to subpoena.

CHAPTER 2. RECORDERS AND RECORDATION; PARISHES OTHER THAN PARISH OF ORLEANS.

Part 3. Recordation.

Citation: **44 LRSA 137**

✪ **§ 137. Photostatic, photographic, microfilm, or other photographic copies of records; indexes of conveyance and mortgage records.**

A. In all cases where the clerks of court and recorders of the various parishes throughout the state, Orleans Parish excepted, are required by law to make record of filings, documents, pleadings, and all other written instruments, except indexes, and register of the same, such records may be made by any method of photorecording, photocopying, microfilming, or other photographic method of reproduction. However, the film stock used in making photographic or microphotographic copies and the processing of the copies shall comply with the standards of the American National Institute for permanent record photographic microcopying film.

B. Whenever recordation by means of photorecording, photocopying, microfilming, or other photographic method of reproduction is used, any requirement expressed or implied in law for the above-mentioned records, other than indexes and registers of the same, to be maintained in a book or bound volume shall be satisfied by the appropriate storage unit of microfilm or other photographic method employed; provided that the originals of conveyances, probate, mortgage, and other permanent records required by existing law to be kept for all time shall continue to be maintained in a book or bound volume and shall remain subject to examination and copying under provisions of R.S. 44:31, et seq., and other applicable laws.

C. Notwithstanding the provisions of Subsections A and B of the Section or any other provision of law to the contrary, clerks of court and recorders may make indexes of conveyance and mortgage records by any method of photorecording, photocopying, microfilming, or other photographic method of reproduction; however, the standards described in Subsection A of this Section shall apply.

CHAPTER 3. RECORDERS AND RECORDATION; PARISH OF ORLEANS.

Part 1. Register of Conveyances.

Citation: 44 LRSA 205.1

✪ **§ 205.1. Methods of making and storing records.**

Notwithstanding any other provision of law to the contrary, the register may make records of filings, documents, all other written instruments, and indexes of conveyance records by any method of photo recording, photocopying, microfilming, or other photographic methods of reproduction. However, the film stock used in making photographic or microphotographic copies and the processing of the copies shall comply with the standards of the American National Standard Institute for permanent record photographic microcopying film. Further, the register may make records of filings, documents, all other written instruments, and indexes of conveyance records by electronically storing them on magnetic storage media.

Part 3. Books and Indexes.

Citation: 44 LRSA 261

✪ **§ 261. Recorder of mortgages to keep certain indexes; making of records.**

A. The recorder of mortgages shall provide and keep up to date:

(1) A general index of all conventional mortgages which have been inscribed in the records of his office.

(2) A general index of all judicial mortgages which have been inscribed in his office.

(3) A general index of all donations which have been inscribed in his office.

B. Notwithstanding the provisions of Subsection A of this Section, or any other provision of law to the contrary, the recorder may make records of filings, documents, and all other written instruments and indexes of mortgage records by any method of photorecording, photocopying, microfilming, or any other photographic methods of reproduction, in compliance with the standards set forth by the American National Standard Institute for permanent record photographic microcopying film; and/or may make records of filings, documents, and all other written instruments and indexes of mortgage records by electronically storing said records on magnetic storage media.

CHAPTER 5. STATE ARCHIVAL, HISTORICAL, AND PUBLIC RECORDS SERVICES.

Citation: 44 LRSA 405

✪ **§ 405. Powers and duties.**

A. The secretary shall enforce the provisions of this Chapter and pursuant thereof may promulgate, or authorize the state archivist to promulgate, policies not inconsistent with law and in accordance with the Administrative Procedure Act, establishing:

* * * * *

(3) Procedures for the reproduction of public records by photographic, microphotographic, or other appropriate process when necessary to assure the preservation thereof.

* * * * *

Citation: 44 LRSA 415

✪ **§ 415. Centralized microfilm service.**

The microfilm section of the records management program of the division shall be the centralized microfilm center for the state. All state agencies lacking existing internally established microfilming systems of their own, and those state agencies whose equipment or facilities are no longer adequate to meet the agency's need, shall contract with the division for microfilming services or shall obtain division approval for any such contract with any other vendor. All microfilming produced by state agency microfilming systems shall comply with standards established by the division in accordance with R.S. 44:405(A)(3). This provision shall not be applicable to any state agency where it can be demonstrated to be more economically feasible to continue the microfilming within the agency.

Citation: 44 LRSA 421

✪ **§ 421. Authorization to certify facts; evidentiary status of any reproductions.**

A. Any official who is authorized to certify to facts on the basis of records in his custody is authorized to certify to facts on the basis of records that have been transferred by him or his predecessors to the division; however, any fee due any official of the state or its subdivisions shall not be eliminated by this Chapter.

B. Whenever any officer of the state of Louisiana, any political subdivision, municipal corporation, or public corporation is required or authorized by law to record, copy, file, recopy, or replace any document, plat, paper, voucher, receipt, or book on file, or record in his office, he may do so by photostatic, microphotographic, microfilm, or other mechanical process which produces a clear, accurate, and permanent copy, reproduction, or facsimile of the original in accordance with standards not less than those established by the division for permanent records under the authority conveyed by R.S. 44:405(A)(3). Any document, when so reproduced and properly identified and certified, shall have full evidentiary value and force in law.

Source: **Louisiana Rules of Evidence**

ARTICLE X. CONTENTS OF WRITINGS, RECORDINGS, AND PHOTOGRAPHS.

☞ Rule 1001. Definitions.

For purposes of this article the following definitions are applicable:

(1) *Writings and recordings.* — "Writings" and "recordings" consist of letters, words, or numbers, or their equivalent, set down by handwriting, typewriting, printing, photostating, photographing, magnetic impulse, mechanical or electronic recording, or other form of data compilation.

(2) *Photographs.* — "Photographs" include still photographs, X-ray films, video tapes, and motion pictures.

(3) *Original.* — An "original" of a writing or recording is the writing or recording itself or any counterpart intended to have the same effect by a person executing or issuing it. An "original" of a photograph includes the negative or any print therefrom. If data are stored in a computer or similar device, any printout or other output readable by sight, shown to reflect the data accurately, is an "original."

(4) *Duplicate.* — A "duplicate" is a counterpart produced by the same impression as the original, or from the same matrix, or by means of photography, including enlargements and miniatures, or by mechanical or electronic rerecording, or by chemical reproduction, or by other equivalent technique which accurately reproduces the original.

☞ Rule 1003. Admissiblity of duplicates.

A duplicate is admissible to the same extent as an original unless:

(1) A genuine question is raised as to the authenticity of the original; or

(2) In the circumstances it would be unfair to admit the duplicate in lieu of the original.

Source: **Louisiana Administrative Code**
Agency: **Department of Revenue and Taxation**
State Tax Commission

Citation: **LAC Art. 1.4359**

✍ Article I.4359. Dealers required to keep records.

Every person required to collect or remit the tax imposed under this Chapter shall keep a permanent record of all transactions in sufficient detail to be of value in determining the correct tax liability under this Chapter. The records to be kept shall include all sales invoices, purchase orders, merchandise records, inventory records, credit memorandums, debit memorandums, bills of lading, shipping records, and all other records pertaining to any and all purchases, sales, or use of tangible personal property whether or not the person believes them to be taxable under this Chapter. Full detail must be kept of all property leased or rented from or to others and all services performed for or by others. They must also keep all summaries, recapitulations, totals, journal entries, ledger accounts, accounts receivable records, accounts payable records, statements, tax returns, and other documents, listing, summarizing, or pertaining to such sales, purchases, inventories, shipments, or other transactions dealing with tangible personal property.

Where such records are voluminous, they must be kept in chronological order or in some other systematic order compatible with the taxpayer's regular bookkeeping system which will enable the Collector to verify the accuracy of information contained in tax returns.

Records kept on punched cards, magnetic tape, or other mechanical or electronic record keeping devices are permissible provided the taxpayer makes available all necessary codes and equipment to enable the Collector to audit such records, or provides the Collector with written transcripts of those parts of the records which the Collector wishes to examine.

The books and records must contain complete information pertaining to both taxable and non-taxable items which are the subject of taxes imposed herein, and must be retained for a period of no less than three years from the date of the transaction. If a notice of assessment has been issued by the Collector of Revenue, the records for the period covered by the notice must be retained until such time as the issues involved in the assessment have been completely disposed of. Records required by this Section must be available at all times during the regular business hours of the day for inspection by the Collector of Revenue or his duly authorized agents.

Any person who fails to keep the records required herein or who refuses to make the records available for inspection by the Collector of Revenue or who keeps records which are insufficient for use by the Collector in determining the correct tax liability makes himself liable for a fine of up to $200.00 or imprisonment for up to sixty days, or both.

Agency: **Department of Revenue and Taxation**

TITLE 61. REVENUE AND TAXATION.

PART I. TAXES COLLECTED AND ADMINISTERED BY THE SECRETARY OF REVENUE AND TAXATION.

CHAPTER 43. SALES AND USE TAX.

Citation: **LAC Rule 4359**

✍ Rule 4359. Dealers required to keep records.

A. Every person required to collect or remit the tax imposed under this Chapter shall keep a permanent record of all transactions in sufficient detail to be of value in determining the correct tax liability under this Chapter. The records to be kept shall include all sales invoices, purchase orders, merchandise records, inventory records, credit memorandums, debit memorandums, bills of lading, shipping records, and all other records pertaining to any and all purchases, sales, or use of tangible personal property whether or not the person believes them to be taxable under this Chapter. Full detail must be kept of all property leased or rented from or to others and all services performed for or by others. They must also keep all summaries, recapitulations, totals, journal entries, ledger accounts, accounts receivable records, accounts payable records, statements, tax returns, and other documents, listing, summarizing, or pertaining to such sales, purchases, inventories, shipments, or other transactions dealing with tangible personal property.

B. Where such records are voluminous, they must be kept in chronological order or in some other systematic order compatible with the taxpayer's regular bookkeeping system which will enable the Secretary to verify the accuracy of information contained in tax returns.

C.1. Records kept on punched cards, magnetic tape, magnetic (floppy) diskettes or other mechanical or electronic record keeping equipment are permissible provided the taxpayer makes available all necessary codes, program specifications, and equipment to enable the secretary to audit such records, or provides the secretary with written transcripts of these parts of the records which the secretary wishes to examine.

2. If it is mutually agreed, the dealer may furnish the secretary with data in a machine readable form, such as on floppy disk or magnetic tape, in addition to the source documents necessary to verify the data in order to facilitate the examination.

D. The books and records must contain complete information pertaining to both taxable and non-taxable items which are the subject of taxes imposed herein, and must be retained until the taxes to which they relate have prescribed according to R.S. 47:1579. If a notice of assessment has been issued by the secretary, the records for the period covered by the notice must be retained until such time as the issues involved in the assessment have been completely disposed of. Records required by this Section must be available at all times during the regular business hours of the day for inspection by the secretary or his duly authorized agents.

E. Any person who fails to keep the records required herein or who refuses to make the records available for inspection by the secretary or who keeps records which are insufficient for use by the secretary in determining the correct tax liability makes himself liable for a fine of up to $500 for each reporting period or imprisonment for up to sixty days, or both.

State: Maine
Source: Maine Revised Statutes Annotated

TITLE 5. ADMINISTRATIVE PROCEDURES AND SERVICES.

CHAPTER 6. STATE ARCHIVIST.

Citation: 5 MRSA 95

✪ **§ 95. Powers and duties of State Archivist.**

The State Archivist shall have, upon consent of the Secretary of State, the duties and powers established under the following provisions governing the creation, use, maintenance, retention, preservation and disposal of state records:

* * * * *

12. Copies. To furnish copies of archival material upon the request of any person, on payment in advance of such fees as may be required. Copies of state records transferred in pursuance to law from the office of their origin to the custody of the State Archivist, when certified by the State Archivist, under the seal of that office, have the same legal force and effect as if certified by their original custodian. A facsimile of the signature of the State Archivist imprinted by or at thes direction of the State Archivist upon any certificate issued by the State Archivist has the same validity as the written signature;

* * * * *

CHAPTER 143. ACCOUNTS AND CONTROL.

Citation: 5 MRSA 1545

✪ **§ 1545. Reproduction of certain documents authorized.**

The State Controller is authorized to cause to be made, at the expense of the State, by any photostatic, photographic, microfilm or other mechanical process which produces a clear, accurate and permanent copy or reproduction thereof, copies of any part or all of the state canceled checks, vouchers and other documents on file in the Bureau of Accounts and Control.

TITLE 13-A. MAINE BUSINESS CORPORATION ACT.

CHAPTER 1. GENERAL PROVISIONS.

Citation: 13-A MRSA 106

✪ **§ 106. Filing of documents.**

* * * * *

3. If he so determines by rule, the Secretary of State may copy, on microfilm, any document filed by him under this Act or under any predecessor of this Act, and retain such microfilm copy in lieu of retaining the original as required by subsection 1, paragraph D; and he may thereafter destroy the original document or return it to the person who delivered the same to him for filing.

* * * * *

CHAPTER 6. BYLAWS, SHAREHOLDERS AND VOTING.

Citation: 13-A MRSA 625

☞ **§ 625. Books and records required to be kept by corporation; financial statements.**

1. Each corporation shall keep accurate books and records of account, which shall be in written form or in any other form capable of being converted into written form within a reasonable time; and shall keep written minutes of the proceedings of its shareholders, board of directors and committees of directors.

2. A. Each corporation shall keep, at its principal place of business or at the office of its clerk or of its transfer agent or registrar, a record of its shareholders, giving the name and address of each shareholder, and the number and class of the shares held by each; if the original record of its shareholders is maintained outside this State, the corporation shall maintain at one of the foregoing offices within this State a list of shareholders containing the information specified in this subsection.

B. Said list, if the original record of shareholders is not maintained in this State, shall be the most recent list prepared pursuant to section 607 or, at the corporation's option, a more recent list.

C. If the corporation maintains its stockholder records by means of electronic data processing equipment it may, at its option, in lieu of keeping the record or list in this State required by subsection 2, keep at the places mentioned in this State a written undertaking of its president and secretary to produce at those places a current list of shareholders, containing the information required by paragraph A, within 5 working days after demand therefore by any proper person.

3. Not later than 5 months after the close of each fiscal year, each corporation which is not a close corporation shall prepare, in accordance with good accounting practices, a balance sheet showing the financial condition of the corporation as of the close of its fiscal year, and a profit and loss statement respecting its operation for the fiscal year.

4. The books and records specified in subsection 1 shall be prima facie evidence of the facts stated therein, in favor of the plaintiff in any action or special proceedings against the corporation or any of its officers, directors or shareholders.

TITLE 13-B. MAINE NONPROFIT CORPORATION ACT.

CHAPTER 1. GENERAL PROVISIONS.

Citation:	13-B MRSA 106

✪ **§ 106. Filing of Documents.**

* * * * *

3. *Microfilmed.* If he so determines by rule, the Secretary of State may copy, on microfilm, any document filed by him under this Act or under any predecessor of this Act and retain such microfilm copy in lieu of retaining the original as required by subsection 1, paragraph D; and he may thereafter destroy the original document or return it to the person who delivered the same to him for filing.

* * * * *

TITLE 16. COURT PROCEDURE — EVIDENCE.

CHAPTER 3. RECORDS AND OTHER DOCUMENTS.

Subchapter III. Public Records.

Citation:	16 MRSA 456

✍ ☞ ✪ **§ 456. Photostatic and microfilm reproductions admissible.**

If, in the regular course of any business or governmental activity, there is kept or recorded any memorandum, writing, entry, print, representation or combination thereof, of any act, transaction, occurrence or event, and in the regular course of any such business or governmental activity, causes any or all of the same to be recorded, copied or reproduced by any photographic, photostatic, microfilm, micro-card, miniature photographic, optical disk that is not erasable or other process which accurately reproduces or forms a durable medium for so reproducing the original, such reproduction or copy, when satisfactorily identified, is as admissible in evidence as the original itself in any judicial or administrative proceeding whether the original is in existence or not and an enlargement or facsimile of such reproduction or copy is likewise admissible in evidence, if the original reproduction or copy is in existence and available for inspection under direction of court. The introduction of a reproduced record, enlargement or facsimile does not preclude admission of the original. This section shall not be construed to exclude from evidence any document or copy thereof which is otherwise admissible under the rules of evidence.

Source:	Maine Rules of Evidence

ARTICLE X. CONTENTS OF WRITINGS, RECORDINGS, AND PHOTOGRAPHS.

☞ **Rule 1001. Definitions.**

For purposes of this article the following definitions are applicable:

(1) *Writings and recordings.* — "Writings" and "recordings" consist of letters, words, or numbers, or their equivalent, set down by handwriting, typewriting, printing, photostating, photographing, magnetic impulse, mechanical or electronic recording, or other form of data compilation.

(2) *Photographs.* — "Photographs" include still photographs, X-ray films, video tapes, and motion pictures.

(3) *Original.* — An "original" of a writing or recording is the writing or recording itself or any counterpart intended to have the same effect by a person executing or issuing it. An "original" of a photograph includes the negative or any print therefrom. If data are stored in a computer or similar device, any printout or other output readable by sight, shown to reflect the data accurately, is an "original."

(4) *Duplicate.* — A "duplicate" is a counterpart produced by the same impression as the original, or from the same matrix, or by means of photography, including enlargements and miniatures, or by mechanical or electronic rerecording, or by chemical reproduction, or by other equivalent technique which accurately reproduces the original.

☞ **Rule 1003. Admissiblity of duplicates.**

A duplicate is admissible to the same extent as an original unless:

(1) A genuine question is raised as to the authenticity of the original; or

(2) In the circumstances it would be unfair to admit the duplicate in lieu of the original.

State:	Maryland
Source:	Maryland Code Annotated

TITLE 2. CORPORATIONS IN GENERAL — FORMATION, ORGANIZATION, AND OPERATION.

SUBTITLE 1. FORMATION AND POWERS.

Citation:	MCA 2-111

✍ **§ 2-111. Books and records.**

(a) *Records of accounts and minutes to be correct and complete.* — Each corporation shall keep correct and complete:

(1) Books and records of its accounts and transactions; and

(2) Minutes of the proceedings of its stockholders and board of directors and of any executive or other committee when exercising any of the powers of the board of directors.

(b) *Form of records and minutes.* — (1) The books and records of a corporation may be in written form or in any other form which can be converted within a reasonable time into written form for visual inspection.

(2) Minutes shall be recorded in written form but may be maintained in the form of a reproduction.

Source:	Courts And Judicial Proceedings

TITLE 10. EVIDENCE.

SUBTITLE 1. PROOF OF ACCOUNTS AND RECORDS.

Citation:	MCA 10-102

☞ **§ 10-102. Maryland Uniform Photographic Copies of Business and Public Records as Evidence Act.**

(a) *In general.* — If a business, institution, member of a profession or calling, or a department or agency of government, in the regular course of business or activity has kept or recorded a memorandum, writing, entry, print, representation, or a combination of them, of an act, transaction, occurrence, or event, and in the regular course of business has caused any or all of them to be recorded, copied, or reproduced by a photographic, photostatic, microfilm, microcard, miniature photographic, or other process which accurately reproduces or forms a durable medium for so reproducing the original, the original may be destroyed in the regular course of business unless its preservation is required by law. The reproduction, when satisfactorily identified, is as admissible in evidence as the original itself in a judicial or administrative proceeding whether the original is in existence or not and an enlargement or facsimile of the reproduction is likewise admissible in evidence if the original reproduction is in existence and available for inspection under direction of the court. The introduction of a reproduced record, enlargement, or facsimile does not preclude admission of the original.

(b) *Uniformity of interpretation.* — This section shall be interpreted and construed to effectuate its general purpose of making uniform the law of those states which enact it.

(c) *Short title.* — This section may be cited as the Maryland Uniform Photographic Copies of Business and Public Records as Evidence Act.

Source: State Government

TITLE 10. GOVERNMENTAL PROCEDURES.

SUBTITLE 6. RECORDS.

PART 3. ACCESS TO PUBLIC RECORDS.

Citation: MCA 10-642

✪ § 10-642. Reproductions.

(a) *Destruction authorized.* — With the written approval of the State Archivist, the head of a unit of the State government or of a unit of a county or municipal corporation may destroy original material that has been photographed, photocopied, or microphotographed is:

(1) the head offers the original material to the Archives, but the Archives declines to accept;

(2) the copy is made in a manner that meets the standard of quality of the Archives for permanent photographic records;

(3) the copy is placed in an adequately accessible container; and

(4) provisions are made:

(i) for the preservation, examination, and use of the copy in a manner that the Archives approves; and

(ii) as to the record that a statute otherwise expressly requires to be kept permanently, for the copy to be available, on request, in the same manner as the original material.

(b) *Conditions.* — (1) After materials are destroyed under this section, the head of the unit shall send to the Archives:

(i) a list of the materials that were destroyed; and

(ii) a certificate of destruction.

(2) The State Archivist shall keep each list of the materials destroyed under this section. This list shall be available for public inspection at reasonable times.

Source: Maryland Rules of Evidence

CHAPTER 1000. CONTENTS OF WRITINGS, RECORDINGS, AND PHOTOGRAPHS

☞ Rule 5-1001. Definitions.

In this chapter, the following definitions apply except as expressly otherwise provided or as necessary implication requires:

(a) *Writings and Recordings.*—"Writings" and "recordings" consist of letters, words, numbers, or their equivalent, set down by handwriting, typewriting, printing, photostating, photographing, magnetic or optical impulse, mechanical or electronic recording, or other form of data compilation.

Committee note: This is not intended to change the common law regarding the court's discretion to treat chattels inscribed with letters or numbers as writings.

(b) *Photographs.*—"Photographs" include still photographs, X-ray films, video tapes, and motion pictures.

(c) *Original.*— An "original" of a writing or recording is the writing or recording itself or any counterpart intended to have the same effect by a person executing or issuing it. An "original" of a photograph includes the negative or any print therefrom. If data are stored in a computer or similar device, any printout or other output readable by sight, shown to reflect the data accurately, is an "original".

(d) *Duplicate.*— A "duplicate" is a counterpart produced by the same impression as the original, or from the same matrix, or by means of photography, including enlargements and miniatures, or by mechanical or electronic re-recordings, or by chemical reproduction, or by other equivalent technique which accurately reproduces the original.

☞ § Rule 5-1003. Admissibility of Duplicates.

A duplicate is admissible to the same extent as an original unless (1) a genuine question is raised as to the authenticity of the original or (2) in the circumstances it would be unfair to admit the duplicate in lieu of the original.

☞ § Rule 5-1005. Public Records.

The contents of an official record, or of a document authorized to be recorded or filed and actually recorded or filed, including data compilations, if otherwise admissible, may be proved by copy, certified as correct in accordance with Rule 5-902 or testified to be correct by a witness who has compared it with the original. If a copy that complies with the foregoing cannot be obtained by the exercise of reasonable diligence, other evidence of the contents may be given.

Source: Code of Maryland Regulations

TITLE 14. INDEPENDENT AGENCIES

SUBTITLE 18. STATE ARCHIVES

Citation: CMR 14.18.04

✪ § 14.18.04 Electronic Records

.01 Purpose.

A. These regulations establish the minimum requirements to create, use, maintain, appraise, preserve, store, make accessible, and dispose of electronic records.

B. All electronic media are highly perishable. Electronic media do not last as long as traditional record keeping media such as paper or microfilm.

C. At at time when public records increasingly are created, maintained, and made accessible only in electronic form, it is vital that standards and procedures be established to identify and preserve these records in order to:

(1) Provide for the regular and timely appraisal of electronic public records to ensure that records of permanent historical,

administrative, fiscal, legal, or other archival value are identified and preserved;

(2) Make these records accessible to government and to the public in perpetuity;

(3) Safeguard government's legal and fiscal accountability through the preservation of important records; and

(4) Document the administrative history of government by preserving those records that illustrate agency goals and accomplishments.

.02 Scope.

These regulations apply to:

A. All agencies or offices of the State, county, or local governments, or any private vendor under contract with the agency or office to collect, maintain, disseminate public information in an electronic form;

B. All numeric, graphic, textual, and cartographic information recorded on machine readable media that includes, but is not limited to, magnetic media, such as tapes and disks (hard or floppy), and optical disks; and

C. All electronic records systems, including, but not limited to, microcomputers, minicomputers, main-frame computers, or optical image recording systems, regardless of storage media, in network or stand-along configuration.

.03 Definitions.

A. The following terms have the meanings indicated.

B. Terms Define:

(1) "Agency" means any unit of State, county, or local government.

(2) "Archives" means the State Archives.

(3) "Database" means a set of data, consisting of at least one file or a group of integrated files, usually maintained in one location and stored for security purposes in another and made available to several users for various applications.

(4) "Database management system" means a software system used to access and retrieve data stored in a database.

(5) "Datafile" means:

(a) An organized collection of related data that are stored together and treated as a unit by a computer or,

(b) Related numeric, textual, graphic, or cartographic information organized in a strictly required format.

(6) "Division" means the Records Management Division of the Maryland Department of General Services.

(7) "Electronic record" means any government information recorded in machine readable form.

(8) "Electronic records system" means any information system that produces, processes, or stores government records by using a computer.

(9) "Information system" means the organized collection, processing, transmission, and dissemination of information in accordance with defined procedures, whether automated or manual.

(10) "Life cycle" means the regular and systematic progression of an electronic record from one storage medium to another as necessary to ensure its preservation and accessibility from the time the record is created through to its ultimate disposition.

(11) "Nonpermanent electronic record" means any electronic record created or received by an agency or office in connection with the transaction of public business and appraised by the Archives as not having sufficient value to warrant preservation.

(12) "Office" means a part of an agency.

(13) "Periodic" means any time within the 5-year cycle established for the regular review of all agency recordkeeping practices (State Government Article § 10-634, Annotated Code of Maryland).

(14) "Permanent electronic record" means any electronic record created or received by an agency or office in connection with the transaction of public business and appraised by the Archives as having sufficient historical, administrative, legal, fiscal or other archival value to warrant preservation by the Archives beyond the item that the record is needed by the agency that created it.

(15) "Schedule" means a Records Retention and Disposition Schedule, an official document that lists and describes all records of an agency or office, authorizes the permanent retention by the Archives of those records considered by statute or by the Archives to be of permanent value, and authorizes the destruction of those records not essential to operations after the lapse of a stated period of time.

(16) "Security copy" means an exact duplicate copy of an electronic record stored off-site in a secure facility that can be used to replace lose or destroyed records.

(17) "System architecture" means the organizational structure of an electronic records system, including necessary application systems, computer equipment, a communications network, and related software which defines the nature, content, and interrelation of input, files, procedures, and output.

04. Agency Duties and Responsibilities.

A. Electronic Records to be covered by Records Retention and Disposition Schedules.

(1) All agencies are required to develop official records retention and disposition schedules according to COMAR 14.18.02. The unauthorized destruction or alienation of any public record is a criminal misdemeanor subject to penalties (Article 27, § 45A, Annotated Code of Maryland).

(2) All agencies shall identify and preserve permanently valuable records, safeguard their legal and fiscal accountability, document their administrative history, and ensure ongoing public access to the public records of government by adopting official schedules.

(3) The head of each agency or office shall ensure that all electronic records created by that agency or office are covered by an official schedule according to COMAR 14.18.02.

(4) The schedule clearly should outline regular agency procedures to recopy, reformat, and maintain electronic records to ensure the record's retention and usability throughout the record's authorized life cycle.

(5) As part of the scheduling process, the head of each agency or office shall submit to the Archives and the Division of electronic records inventory (DGS 550-6) to document each electronic records system.

(6) The electronic records inventory shall:

(a) Identify all inputs and outputs of the system;

(b) Define contents of files and records, policies on access and use, purpose and function of the system, and updating cycles or conditions and rules for revising information in the system;

(c) Provide for the ultimate disposition of the information, including periodic transfer of permanent electronic records to the Archives;

(d) Specify the location and media of which electronic records are maintained through the electronic records life cycle; and

(e) Provide current technical documentation for each electronic records system as it is modified or updated, which includes the following:

(i) Narrative description of the system,

(ii) Description of the physical and technical characteristics of the records with a record layout that defines each field giving its name, size, starting, or relative position, and description of the form of the data (such as alphabetic, decimal, or numeric), or a data dictionary or the equivalent information associated with a database management system, including a description of the relation between data elements in databases,

(iii) For geographic information systems, description of the physical and technical characteristics of the records, including a data dictionary, a quality and accuracy report, and a description of the graphic data structure, such as recommended by the "Spatial Data Transfer Standard (SDTS) (FIPS Pub 173, 1992 August 28)" and "Content Standards for Digital Spatial Metadata (March 31, 1994)" which are incorporated by reference, and

(iv) Description of the backup security plan by means of which permanent and nonpermanent electronic records shall be preserved and made accessible to government and the public throughout the electronic records life cycle, including any additional technical information, software, or platforms needed to read, copy, or process the records.

B. Electronic Records to be Appraised Regularly

(1) Given the highly perishable nature of all electronic media it is necessary that these records be appraised periodically in order to identify and preserve those records that require permanent preservation.

(2) This preservation safeguards the agency's legal and fiscal accountability and documents the agency's administrative history.

(3) To ensure the timely appraisal of all electronic records, the head of each agency or office shall:

(a) Provide for the periodic complete review of the agency's schedules; or

(b) Periodically submit to the Archives a copy of the Information Processing Plan prepared for the Department of Budget and Fiscal Planning, as part of the Division's Analysis of State Government Records conducted every 5 years according to COMAR 14.18.02.

C. Electronic Records to be Maintained Properly.

(1) To maintain the official record copy of electronic records systems for use by government and the public, the head of each agency or office shall:

(a) Provide a method for all authorized users of the system to retrieve desired documents;

(b) Provide an appropriate level of security to ensure the integrity of the documents;

(c) Identify the standard interchange format, when necessary, to permits the exchange of documents on electronic media between agency computers using different software or operating systems, and the conversion or migration of documents on electronic media from one system to another. and

(d) Provide for the disposition of the records, including a plan by means of which permanent electronic records will be preserved and made accessible to government and the public through periodic transfer to the Archives, including any additional technical information, software, or platforms needed to read, copy, or process the records.

(2) In the absence of conversation capabilities different from those in § C(1)(c) of this regulation, the following standards shall apply:

(a) A word processing or text creation system shall be able to import and export files in American Standard Code for Information Interchange (ASCII) format as required by the "Code for Information Interchange, Its Representations, Subsets, and Extensions (FIPS Pub 1-2, 1984 November 14)" which is incorporated by reference.

(b) Cartographic or graphic file systems shall be able to import and export files in Group III or Group IV compressed facsimile transmission format as specified in "Terminal Equipment and Protocols for Telematic Services (The International Telegraph and Telephone Consultative Committee, Blue Book Volume VII - Fascicle VII.3, 14-25 November 1988)" which is incorporated by reference.

D. Electronic Records to Bear Unique Identification.

(1) Before a record is created on electronic records systems, the head of each agency or office shall ensure that the record be uniquely identified to enable authorized personnel to retrieve, protect, and carry out the disposition of records in the system.

(2) Agencies shall ensure that records maintained in these systems can be correlated easily with related records on paper, microfilm, or other media.

(3) Electronic storage media shall be externally labeled in a manner that provides unique identification, including:

(a) Organizational unit responsible for the data;

(b) System title, including the version number of the application;

(c) Special security requirements or restrictions on access, if any;

(d) Software in use at the time or record creation;

(e) Date, place, and time of record creation; and

(f) Official schedule number that governs the retention of the records stored on that media.

E. Integrity of Electronic Records to be Maintained throughout Their Life Cycle. To ensure the legal admissibility of electronic records and to safeguard the legal and fiscal accountability of government the head of each agency or office shall:

(1) Document that similar kinds of records generated and stored electronically are created by the same processes each time and have a standardized retrieval routine;

(2) Substantiate that security procedures prevent unauthorized addition, modification, or deletion of a record and ensure systems protection against such problems as power interruptions;

(3) Identify the electronic media on which records are stored throughout their life cycle, the maximum time span for record to remain on each storage media, the official retention requirements mandated in the agency's schedule, and the plan by means of which permanent and nonpermanent electronic records will be preserved and made accessible to government and the public, including any additional technical information software, or platforms needed to read, copy, or process the records; and

(4) Maintain for each media storing electronic records:

(a) File title,

(b) Date, or dates of file creation,

(c) Inclusive dates of files,

(d) Recording density,

(e) Type of internal labels,

(f) Volumn serial number, if applicable,

(g) Number of tracks,

(h) Character code or software dependency,

(i) Block size, and

(j) Sequence number, if the file if part of a multi-media set.

F. Electronic Records to be Stored Properly and Made Accessible. For the storage of electronic records throughout their life cycle, the head of each agency or office shall select appropriate media and systems that:

(1) Permit easy and accurate retrieval in a timely fashion;

(2) Retain the records in a universally accessible format until authorized disposition, transfer to the Division or appropriate county records center, or periodic transfer of permanent electronic records to the Archives;

(3) Ensure that all authorized users can identify and retrieve information stored on various media by means of external labeling of the contents of diskettes, disks, tapes, or optical disks;

(4) Ensure that information is not lost due to changing technology or deterioration of storage media by developing a security plan by means of which permanent and nonpermanent records will be preserved and made accessible to government and the public throughout their life cycle, including any additional technical information, software, or platforms needed to

read, copy, or process the records; and

(5) Produce security copies of electronic records to be transferred to secure storage areas located in buildings separate from the location where the electronic records are maintained in order to safeguard against the loss of information due to equipment malfunctions or human error as outlined in the "Vital Records Protection Plan (Revised: January 1993)" which is incorporated by reference.

G. Electronic records to be Secured and Preserved.

(1) The head of each agency or office shall provide for the security and longevity of electronic records by implementing the procedures outlined in the "State Computerized Record System Security Requirements and Recommendations (Revised: June 2, 1993)", which is incorporated by reference.

(2) The head of each agency or office shall also:

(a) Read periodically a statistical sample of all electronic media containing records in order to identify any loss of information, and to discover and correct the cause of data loss;

(b) Establish regular procedures to copy all electronic media frequently onto tested and verified new media and the test will verify that the media are free of errors;

(c) Rewind stored electronic tapes only immediately before use to restore proper tension to the tape;

(d) Rewind electronic tapes with extreme cases of degradation when they are discovered to avoid more permanent damage;

(e) Prohibit smoking, eating, or drinking in electronic media storage, testing or evaluation areas;

(f) Establish a plan by means of which permanent electronic records are preserved and made accessible to government and the public through periodic transfer to the Archives; and

(g) Provide any additional technical information, software, or platforms needed to read, copy, or process the permanent electronic records so transferred.

H. Electronic Records on Compact Disk-Read Only Memory (CD-ROM) to Meet Certain Standards. If an agency or office head decides to transfer records on CD-ROM, which include fielded files or text files, the following standards shall apply, as recommended by "Read Only Memory (CD-ROM) Medium to Transfer Records to the National Archives (NARA Bulletin No. 94-4, 1994 July 20)".

(1) Files shall comply with "Information Processing — Volume and File Structure of CD-ROM for Information Interchange (ISO 9660, 1988 September)" which is incorporated by reference;

(2) Files shall comply with the American Standard Code for Information Interchange (ASCII) format as required by the "Code for Information Interchange, Its Representations, Subsets and Extensions (FIPS Pub 1-2, 1984 November 14)" which is incorporated by reference in § C(2)(a) of this regulation;

(3) Files may not depend on control characters or codes undefined in the ASCII character set;

(4) Files may not be compressed unless software to decompress the files is provided;

(5) Files shall be individually addressable; and

(6) Files shall comply with the documentation requirements of this chapter.

Citation: CMR 14.18.05

✪ § 14.18.05. Archival Standards for Records on Microfilm.

01. Purpose.

These regulations establish uniform methods for the microfilming of records. The standards in these regulations ensure the economical production and use of microfilm in record keeping to meet legal and archival requirements and preserve the integrity of the original records.

.02 Scope.

A. These regulations apply to the microfilming of record material by any agency of State, county or local governments.

B. With the written approval of the State Archivist, the head of an agency or office may destroy original material that has been photographed, photocopied, or microphotographed if:

(1) The head of the agency or office offers the original material to the Archives, but the Archives declines to accept;

(2) The copy is made in a manner that meets the standard of quality of the Archives for permanent photographic records;

(3) The copy is placed in an adequately accessible containers; and

(4) Provisions are made;

(a) For the preservation, examination, and use of the copy in a manner that the Archives approves, and

(b) For a record that a statute otherwise expressly requires to be kept permanently, for the copy to be available, upon request, in the same manner as the original material.

03. Definitions.

A. The following terms have the meanings indicated.

B. Terms Defined:

(1) "Agency" means any unit of State, county, or local government.

(2) "Archives" means the State Archives.

(3) "Division" means the Records Management Division of the Department of General Services.

(4) "Office" means a part of an agency.

(5) "Record" means documentary material in any form or format including paper, microform, electronic record, or other medium, that is:

(a) Created by an agency or office; or

(b) Received by an agency or office in connection with the transaction of public business.

04. Microfilm Standards.

A. Microfilm shall be of the type suitable for archival quality. Archival quality or permanent film is defined as any film that is equal to or better than silver gelatin film, as specified in the "American National Standard for Imaging Media (Film) - Silver-Gelatin Type - Specifications for Stability (ANSI/NAPM IT9.1-1992)" and in the "American National Standard for Photography - Determination of Regional Thiosulfate and Other Related Chemicals in Processed Photographic Materials - Methods Using Iodine - Amylose, Methylene Blue and Silver Sulfide (ANSI/NAPM IT9.17-1993)" which are incorporated by reference. Diazo or vesicular film are not acceptable as archival quality film.

B. If an agency is microfilming its own records, it shall be the responsibility of the head of each agency or office to ensure that microfilm equipment is cleaned and maintained according to manufacturer's specifications or accepted industry practice, or both.

C. For the production of archival quality or permanent film, microfilm shall be processed as follows:

(1) Permanent text records shall be microfilmed at a reduction ratio not greater than 24X;

(2) Permanent graphic records shall be microfilmed at a reduction ratio not greater than 36X;

(3) Each film roll shall contain not less than 18 inches of film leader, and 18 inches of film trailer;

(4) Microfilm Density.

(a) Optimum background densities of microfilm images are dependent upon the quality of the documents filmed;

(b) For permanent records, density or negative copies will be between .95 and 1.2;

(c) For nonpermanent records, the ultimate density criterion is that the microfilm be legible for its intended use (reading, copying, or production of a hard copy), and that all images on a roll can be printed, as much as is practicable, at the same printing exposure;

(d) The following classification indicates the maximum limits of density:

(i) Density not higher than 1.4 is required for high quality printed books, periodicals, and dense typing;

(ii) Density not higher than 1.3 is required for fine line originals, letters typed with a worn ribbon, pencil writing with a soft lead, and documents with small printing;

(iii) Density not lower than 1.0 is required for pencil drawings, faded printing, graph paper with pale fine colored lines, and very small printing such as footnotes;

(iv) Density not lower than 0.8 is required for very weak pencil manuscripts and drawings, and poorly printed, faint or faded documents; and

(v) Readings beyond these densities are unacceptable.

(5) Resolution of the completed microfilm may not be less than 100 lines per millimeter, as determined by inspection of a resolution test chart photographed on each roll of film.

(6) Residual thiosulfate concentration shall:

(a) Be less than 1 microgram per square centimeter as proved by subsequent testing of the processed film;

(b) At regular intervals agencies send samples of processed film to the Division's Microfilm Laboratory for methylene blue testing;

(c) Samples are to be processed within 1 week before testing if accurate results are to be obtained.

D. The following identification targets shall be used on each roll of film which are presented here in the order in which they are to appear:

(1) Resolution test target for rotary camera applications derived from the "Standards for Information and Image Management - Practice for Operational Procedures/Inspection and Quality Control of First Generation Silver Microfilm of Documents, Rotary Camera Test Chart (ANSI/AIIM MS 23-1991)" which is incorporated by reference, or for planetary camera applications "Photographic Microcopy Target (NBS 1010a)" which is incorporated by reference;

(2) A title target for each volume of records to be filmed shall include the agency name and the record title and volume identification, both identifiable without the use of a magnifier or viewer;

(3) A certification target signed by authorized agency personnel;

(4) Certificate of Camera Operator Target (RM-4); and

(5) The appropriate test chart.

E. During filming, if any document is suspected of not having been filmed correctly, follow that image with a correction target, followed by the document again.

F. After exposure, each roll of microfilm is developed and inspected to ensure completeness and legibility of every image. A light box inspection alone is not acceptable.

G. Illegible or missing records shall be microfilmed again as retakes, according to the following procedures:

(1) Allow 18 inches of blank leader at the beginning of the retakes for each individual volume;

(2) Photograph a start of retake section target;

(3) Microfilm the documents that were illegible or missing in the same order in which they would have appeared on the original roll if they had been available;

(4) Microfilm and end of retake section target;

(5) Allow 18 inches of blank trailer at the end of each section retakes; and

(6) After processing, inspection, and approval, splice retake images onto the beginning of the original roll of microfilm that bears the illegible images or lacks the documents contained on the retake roll.

H. Precautions shall be taken in the handling and storage of original camera microfilm. These precautions include, but are not limited to, the following:

(1) Always wear cotton gloves when handling film to prevent fingerprints or dirt on the microfilm images;

(2) Never use tape, paper clips, rubber bands, staples, etc. to splice or hold microfilm on rolls or any other microform;

(3) Do not place microfilm on reels that corrode or emit toxious elements that destroy microfilm; and

(4) Do not place microfilm on reels that corrode or emit toxious elements that destroy microfilm; and

(4) Do not store microfilm within 4 inches of the floor. Storage under improper conditions of temperature and humidity drastically shortens the useful life of microfilm;

(5) Recommended standards for temperature and humidity for the storage of microfilm are as follows:

(a) Short-term storage-temperature (under 10 years) may not exceed 75°F and relative humidity may not exceed 60 percent; and

(b) Permanent or archival storage temperature may not exceed 70° and relative humidity may not exceed 40 percent.

I. Archival microfilm of records scheduled for permanent retention shall be transferred periodically to the Archives. This microfilm shall be the silver-gelatin master negative.

.05 Agency Responsibility.

A. When paper records are to be microfilmed, and the microfilm is scheduled for permanent retention, the paper records not may be destroyed until the microfilming of those records, and the subsequent processing and inspection of the film has been completed in compliance with the standards in Regulation .04G and H of this chapter, nor until the State Archives has approved the destruction of those records. Permission to destroy record material shall be obtained by filing a Proposal and Certificate of Records Destruction (form DGS-550-9) with the Archives. This permission shall be received before any records destruction can take place.

B. It is the policy of the Division not to store paper records in the State Records Center after those records have been microfilmed. The State Records Center will hold the paper records until the microfilm has been inspected by agency personnel. Once the quality of the microfilm has been assured, the paper records shall be returned to the agency of record of disposed of in accordance with State Government Article, § 10-642, Annotated Code of Maryland.

C. The head of each agency shall ensure that the standards of this chapter are made a part of any contract for microfilming services into which an agency may enter.

State: Massachusetts
Source: Massachusetts General Laws

PART I. ADMINISTRATION OF THE GOVERNMENT.

TITLE 2. EXECUTIVE AND ADMINISTRATIVE OFFICERS OF THE COMMONWEATH.

CHAPTER 9. DEPARTMENT OF THE STATE SECRETARY.

Citation: 9 MGL 19

✪ § 19. Destruction or sale of documents of no value; reproduction of records of corporation, etc.

The state secretary, having first obtained authority from the governor and council, may destroy or sell such documents, records and papers as in his judgment are of no value; and if sold, the proceeds thereof shall be paid to the commonwealth.

Notwithstanding the foregoing or any provision of section forty-two of chapter thirty, if the secretary has caused any record relative to corporations, voluntary associations, limited partnerships or trusts which he is required to keep, to be recorded, copied or reproduced by any photographic, photostatic, microfilm, microcard, miniature photographic or other process which accurately reproduces or forms a durable medium for so reproducing the original, he may, at any time after two years from the date when the original was deposited with him, destroy such original. Such record, copy or reproduction shall be attested by the secretary, when required, as a true copy of the original.

TITLE 10. PUBLIC RECORDS.

CHAPTER 66. PUBLIC RECORDS.

Citation: 66 MGL 3

✪ § 3. "Record", defined; quality of paper and film; microfilm records.

The word "record" in this chapter shall mean any written or printed book or paper, or any photograph, microphotograph, map or plan. All written or printed public records shall be entered or recorded on paper made of linen rags and new cotton clippings, well sized with animal sizing and well finished or on one hundred percent bond paper sized with animal glue or gelatin, and preference shall be given to paper of American manufacture marked in water line with the name of the manufacturer. All photographs, microphotographs, maps and plans which are public records shall be made of materials approved by the supervisor or records. Public records may be made by handwriting, or by typewriting, or in print, or by the photographic process, or by the microphotographic process, or by any combination of the same. When the photographic or microphotographic process is used, the recording officer, in all instances where the photographic print or microphotographic film is illegible or indistinct, may make, in addition to said photographic or microphotographic record, a typewritten copy of the instrument, which copy shall be filed in a book kept for that purpose. In every such instance the recording officer shall cause cross references to be made between said photographic or microphotographic record and said typewritten record. If in the judgment of the recording officer an instrument offered for record is so illegible that a photographic or microphotographic record thereof would not be sufficiently legible, he may, in addition to the making of such record, retain the original in his custody, in which case a photographic or other attested copy thereof shall be given to the person offering the same for record, or to such person as he may designate.

Subject to the provisions of sections one and nine, a recording officer adopting a system which includes the photographic process or the microphotograph process shall thereafter cause all records made by either of said processes to be inspected at least once in every three years, correct any fading or otherwise faulty records and make report of such inspection and correction to the supervisor or records.

Citation: 66 MGL 4

✪ § 4. Regulation of recording materials and devices; mandamus.

No ink shall be used upon any permanent public record except ink of such a standard as established and approved by the supervisor of records, and no ribbon, pad or other device used for printing by typewriting machines, or stamping pad, or any ink contained in such ribbon, pad, device, stamping pad or carbon paper, shall be used upon any permanent public record, nor shall any photographic machine or device or chemical used in connection therewith be used in making any permanent public record, except such as has been approved by the supervisor or records, who may cancel his approval if he finds that any article so approved is inferior to the standards established by him. The supreme judicial or superior court shall have jurisdiction in mandamus, on petition of the supervisor of records and pursuant to section five of chapter two hundred and forty-nine, to order compliance with the provisions of this section.

Citation: 66 MGL 5

✪ § 5. Municipal records; copies.

County commissioners, city councils and selectmen may cause copies of records of counties, cities, or towns, of town proprietaries, of proprietors of plantations, townships or common lands, relative to land situated in their county, city or town or of easements relating thereto, to be made for their county, city or town, whether such records are within or without the commonwealth, and such records within the commonwealth may be delivered by their custodians to any county, city or town for such copying. City councils and selectmen may also cause copies to be made of the records of births, baptisms, marriages and deaths kept by a church or parish in their city or town.

Citation: 66 MGL 8

✪ § 8. Preservation and destruction of records, books and papers.

Every original paper belonging to the files of the commonwealth or of any county, city or town, bearing data earlier than the year eighteen hundred and seventy, every book of registry or record, except books which the supervisor of public records determines may be destroyed, every town warrant, every deed to the commonwealth or to any county, city or town, every report of an agent, officer or committee relative to bridges, public ways, sewers or other state, county or municipal interests not required to be recorded in a book and not so recorded, shall be preserved and safely kept; and every other paper belonging to such files shall be kept for seven years after the latest original entry therein or thereon, unless otherwise provided by law or unless such records are included in disposal schedules approved by the records conservation board for state records or by the supervisor of public records for county, city, or town records; and no such paper shall be destroyed without the written approval of the supervisor of records. Notwithstanding the foregoing, the register of deeds in any county may, without such written approval, destroy any papers pertaining to attachments or to the dissolution of discharge thereof in the files of his office following the expiration of twenty years after the latest original entry therein or thereon, unless otherwise specifically provided by law, and he may destroy all original instruments left for record and not called for within five years after the recording thereof.

Citation: 66 MGL 8A

✪ § 8A. Destruction of certain records by city and town clerks if microphotographed.

Any provision of general or special law to the contrary notwithstanding, the clerk of any city or town, with the written approval of the supervisor of records, may destroy any index of instruments made by any clerk of such city or town under the provision of law now embodied in section fifteen of chapter forty-one or any original record made by any such clerk under any of the provisions of law now embodied in section eleven of chapter two hundred and nine, section three of chapter two hundred and fifty-five, or any similar statute; provided, that such index or record, as the case may be, has been, or shall have been, micro-photographed, and that twenty years has, or shall have, expired after the making of such index or record. The microphotograph of any index or record so destroyed shall have the same force and effect as the original index or record from which such micro-photograph was made.

Citation: 66 MGL 9

✪ § 9. Preservation and copying of worn, etc., records.

Every person having custody of any public record books of the commonwealth, or of a county, city or town shall, at its expense, cause them to be properly and substantially bound. He shall have any such books, which may have been left incomplete, made up and completed from the files and usual memoranda, so far as practicable. He shall cause fair and legible copies to be seasonably made of any books which are worn, mutilated or are becoming illegible, and cause them to be repaired, rebound or renovated. He may cause any such books to be placed in the custody of the supervisor of records, who may have them repaired, renovated or rebound at the expense of the commonwealth, county city or town to which they belong. Whoever causes such books to be so completed or copied shall attest them, and shall certify, on oath, that they have been made from such files and memoranda or are copies of the original books. Such books shall then have the force of the original records.

PART 3. COURTS, JUDICIAL OFFICERS AND PROCEEDINGS IN CIVIL CASES.

TITLE 2. ACTIONS AND PROCEEDINGS THEREIN.

CHAPTER 233. WITNESSES AND EVIDENCE.

Citation: 233 MGL 79D

☞ § 79D. Photographic copies of newspaper in library; prints from photographic films.

Copies of any newspaper, or part thereof made by the photographic or microphotographic process deposited in any public library or a library of any college or university located in the commonwealth, shall, when duly certified by the person in charge thereof, be admitted in evidence equally with the originals.

A print, whether enlarged or not, from any photographic film, including any photographic plate, microphotographic film, photostatic negative or reproduction of any original record, document, instrument, plan, book or paper destroyed, lost or for any reason unavailable after such film was taken, shall be admissible in evidence in all instances that the original record, document, instrument, plan, book or paper might have been admitted in evidence, and shall have the full force and effect of said original if it is proved that (a) such reproduction was made in the regular course of any business and that it was the regular course of any such business to make such reproductions; (b) said photographic film, microphotographic, photostatic or similar reproduction was taken in order to keep a permanent record of the original; and (c) the said original was subsequently destroyed, lost or is unavailable.

Citation: 233 MGL 79E

☞ § 79E. Reproductions of public or business records.

If any business, institution, member of a profession or calling, or any department or agency of government, in the regular course of business or activity, has kept or recorded any memorandum, writing entry, print, representation or combination thereof of any act, transaction, occurrence or event, and in the regular course of business has caused any or all of the same to be recorded, copied or reproduced by any photographic, photostatic, microfilm, microcard, miniature photographic or other process which accurately reproduces or forms a durable medium for so reproducing the original, the original may be destroyed in the regular course of business unless its preservation is required by law. Such reproduction, when satisfactorily identified, shall be as admissible in evidence as the original itself in any judicial or administrative proceeding whether the original is in existence or not and an enlargement or facsimile of such reproduction shall be likewise admissible in evidence if the original reproduction is in existence and available for inspection under direction of the court. The introduction of a reproduced record, enlargement or facsimile, shall not preclude admission of the original.

Citation: 233 MGL 79J

☞ § 79J. Business records required to be produced in court; certification, admissibility and inspection; copies.

A record kept by any business which is required to be produced in court by any party shall be certified by the affidavit of the person in custody thereof to be a true and complete record and shall be delivered by such business to the clerk of such court who shall keep the same in his custody until its production is called for at the trial or hearing by the party requiring the said record. Such record, so certified and delivered shall be deemed to be sufficiently identified to be admissible in evidence if admissible in all other respects. The party requiring the production of said record and, in the discretion of the court, any other party may examine said record in the custody of the clerk at any time before it is produced in court. The clerk upon completion of such trial or hearing shall notify such business that said record is no longer required and will be returned by mail unless an authorized representative of the business calls for the same at the office of said clerk within seven days of said notice.

A copy of such record made by the photographic process may be delivered to the clerk of such court in place of the original and, if certified as hereinabove provided, shall be admitted in evidence equally with the original.

Source: **Code of Massachusetts Regulations**
Agency: **Department of Revenue**

CHAPTER 62C. ADMINISTRATIVE PROVISIONS RELATIVE TO STATE TAXATION.

Citation: **62C CMR 24**

✍ **§ 24: Record Retention.**

(1) *General Requirements.*

Every person subject to taxation under Chapters 62, 62B, 63, 63A, 64A, 64C, 64D, 64E, 64F, 64G, 64H, 64I, 65C, 121A, or 138, or liable for the collection of any such tax, or required by provisions of those Chapters or of Chapter 62C to file information with respect to any such tax, must preserve and maintain permanent books of account or records, sufficiently accurate and complete to establish the amount of gross income, deductions, credits or other matters required to be shown by such person in any return of such tax or information. The Commissioner may require any person to keep such specific records as he deems necessary to determine the amount of such person's tax liability under the aforementioned Chapters.

Every person required by statute, regulation, letter ruling, technical information release or by instructions applicable to a tax form, to keep a copy of a return, schedule, statement or other document, must keep such copy as part of his records.

Every person filing a claim for credit, refund, or abatement must retain records of sufficient detail to substantiate such claim.

(2) *Form of Records.*

The records required by this regulation must be in such form as to enable the Commissioner to ascertain whether liability for tax is incurred, and if so, the amount of liability.

(a) *Micrographic reproductions.* Microfiche/microfilm reproductions of general books of account, such as cash books, journals, vouchers, registers and ledgers, and microfiche/microfilm reproductions of supporting records of detail, such as payroll records and sales and purchase invoices and vouchers, are "suitable records" within the meaning of Chapter 62C, Section 25, and are also adequate for determining liability for other taxes, if the following conditions are met:

1. micrographic materials conform to the technical standards set forth in Federal Revenue Procedure 76-43 or any subsequent revenue procedure or regulation replacing 76-43;

2. micrographic materials are indexed, cross referenced, and labeled to show beginning and ending numbers or beginning and ending alphabetical listing of the documents included, and are systematically filed;

3. posting references appear on each invoice, and credit memoranda carry references to the documents evidencing the original transaction. Documents which are necessary to support claimed exemptions from tax liability, as bills of lading and purchasing orders, must be maintained in an order by which they can readily be related to the transactions for which exemptions are sought;

4. copies will be provided of any microfilmed records which the Commissioner requires for verifying tax liability;

5. appropriate facilities are provided for preserving and inspecting the micrographic records;

6. adequate projectors for viewing the records are provided;

7. the micrographic materials are readily available for inspection by the Commissioner at any reasonable time.

(b) *Automatic data processing (ADP) systems.* An ADP tax accounting system must produce legible and readily available records which will provide the necessary information for verification of the taxpayer's tax liability. The system must meet the following requirements:

1. ADP records must have the capacity to trace any transaction back to the original source or forward to a final total. If detailed printouts are not made of transactions at the time they are processed, then the system must have the ability to readily reconstruct these transactions;

2. general ledgers with source references must be written out to coincide with financial reports for tax reporting periods. Where subsidiary ledgers are used to support the general ledger accounts, the subsidiary ledgers must also be written out periodically;

3. audit trails must be designed so that the details underlying the summary accounting data may be identified and made available to the Commissioner upon request. The record keeping system must be capable of readily producing supporting documents such as sales invoices, purchase invoices, and credit memoranda;

4. written descriptions of the ADP portion of the accounting system must be available. The descriptions must be sufficiently detailed to indicate the operations being performed, the procedures employed in each application and the controls used to ensure accurate and reliable processing.

(3) *Period of Retention.*

The records required by this regulation must be kept so long as their contents are material in the administration of Massachusetts tax laws. At a minimum, unless the Commissioner consents in writing to an earlier destruction, the records must be preserved until the statute of limitations for making additional assessments for the period for which the return was due has expired; generally, this is three years after the due date of the return or the date the return is actually filed, whichever occurs later.

There are a number of situations, including but not limited to the following, where the three year limitation on assessments does not apply:

(a) in case of fraud or failure to file a required return the Commissioner may assess a tax and examine all records related to such return at any time;

(b) if an executor, as defined in Chapter 65C, omits from the gross estate, as reported in the estate tax return, items which should have been included in the return, and the sum of such items exceeds twenty-five per cent of the gross estate reported in the return, the Commissioner may assess the estate tax and examine all records related to such tax at any time within six years after the return was filed;

(c) where the taxpayer and the Commissioner have agreed to extend the time for assessing the tax, records are to be kept for such additional period;

(d) records related to a taxable event which will occur in the future, such as records of property for which a basis must be determined to compute gain or loss upon disposition, must be retained for three years after the return for the year in which the disposition occurred was due or was actually filed, whichever occurs later;

(e) any person claiming a refund, credit or abatement shall keep all records relating to the taxable period involved until final resolution of the claim.

Citation: 62C CMR 69

✪ **§ 69. Destruction of certain copies, returns, statements or documents.**

The commissioner may, after the lapse of three years from the date of their receipt, or three years after the end of the taxable period to which they relate, whichever occurs earlier, destroy copies, returns and statements made under section eighty-three and eighty-six of chapter fifty-nine and any returns and documents files with him for the purposes of taxation; provided however, that such copies, returns, statements or documents may be destroyed at any time if microfilm or other copies thereof are retained.

Agency: Division of Employment Security

✍ **§ 5.01. Work records.**

(1) Every employing unit shall keep sufficient records:

(a) To enable it to prepare accurate reports with respect to its employment as may be required by the Director; and

(b) To enable the Director to verify any report submitted by the employing unit; and

(c) To make it possible by an inspection thereof to determine with respect to each worker:

1. Wages earned by calendar weeks.

2. Whether any week was in fact a week of less than full-time work.

3. Time lost, if any, by such worker due to his unavailability for work, or inability to work.

(2) Any employing unit found to be in default with respect to the requirements of 430 CMR 5.01(1) will be duly notified in writing and failure to correct such default shall subject the employing unit to the penalties set forth under Section 47 of the Employment Security Law.

(3) payrolls, working sheets and other records from which information is assembled for the preparation of reports and the duplicate of reports filed with the Division shall be preserved for a period of for years from the date on which the report was filed.

Agency: Department of Public Utilities

§ 220 CMR 75.00. REGULATIONS TO GOVERN THE PRESERVATION OF RECORDS OF ELECTRIC, GAS, AND WATER UTILITIES

Citation: 220 CMR 75.01

✍ **§ 75.01. Applicability and Scope.**

(a) This section is prescribed and promulgated as the regulations governing the preservation of records by gas, electric, and water utility companies, and municipal gas and electric companies, subject to the jurisdiction of the Massachusetts Department of Public Utilities (hereinafter "Department"), to the extent and in the manner set forth therein.

(b) This section shall, as to all public utilities now subject to the jurisdiction of the Department, become effective as herein revised upon publication in the *Massachusetts Register.* As to any public utility that may hereafter become subject to the jurisdiction of the Department, this part shall become effective as of the date when such public utility becomes subject to the jurisdiction of the Department.

(c) The regulations in this section apply to all books of account and other records prepared by or on behalf of the public utility. See 220 CMR § 65.05(64) for those records that come into possession of the public utility in connection with the acquisition of property, such as purchase, consolidation, merger, or other business combination.

(d) The regulations in this section shall not be construed as excusing compliance with any other lawful requirement for the preservation of records for periods longer than those prescribed herein.

(e) The adoption of these regulations governing the preservation of records, being general in nature, shall not be construed to cancel, alter, modify, or amend Department orders, regulations, federal or state statutes or laws, customs, or precedents that have been established outside of the scope of the subject covered herein, unless otherwise changed by legislation, court decision, or order of the Department.

Citation: 220 CMR 75.02

✍ **§ 75:02. Definitions.**

When used in these regulations:

Affiliated companies (or affiliates) means companies or persons that directly, or indirectly through one or more intermediaries, control, or are controlled by, or are under common control with, the utility.

Continuing Plant Inventory Records shall be defined as it is in the Federal Energy Regulatory Commission regulations (18 CFR, Chapter 1, Part 101).

Department means the Massachusetts Department of Public Utilities, its Commissioners, and employees.

Destroy at option means to destroy at the discretion of the utility.

Image count indexing or *"blipping"* refers to a retrieval technique in which rectangular marks called blips or image count marks, that are encoded on microfilm, are counted by a reader to automatically advance the film to a specified frame.

Item means the categories or subcategories of § 75.05.

Public Utility means any electric, gas, or water company subject to the jurisdiction of the Department, and any municipal gas or electric company subject to the jurisdiction of the Department.

Regulatory Agency or agencies means federal or state entities with jurisdiction over the public utility.

Schedule means the Schedule of Records and Periods of Retention, set forth in these regulations at § 75.05.

Citation: 220 CMR 75.03

✍ **§ 75.03 General Instructions.**

(a) *Duplicate Copies and Non-Scheduled Records*

(1) Unless otherwise specified in these regulations, duplicate copies of records may be destroyed at any time, *provided, however,* that such duplicate copies contain no significant information not shown on the originals.

(2) Records other than those listed in the schedule may be destroyed at the option of the public utility, *provided, however,* that records that are used in lieu of those listed shall be preserved for the periods prescribed for the records used for substantially similar purposes. And, *provided further,* that retention

of records pertaining to added services, functions, plant, etc., the establishment of which cannot be presently foreseen, shall conform to the principles embodied herein.

(b) *Designation of supervisory official*

Each public utility subject to the regulations in this part shall designate one or more persons with official responsibility to supervise the utility's program for preservation and the authorized destruction of its records.

(c) *Protection and storage of records*

The public utility shall provide reasonable protection for records subject to the regulations in this part from damage by fire, floods, and other hazards and, in the selection of storage spaces, safeguard the records from unnecessary exposure to deterioration from excessive humidity, dryness, or lack of proper ventilation.

(d) *Definition of record media*

(1) For the purpose of these regulations, the data constituting the records listed in the Schedule of Records and Periods of Retention (§ 75.05) may be retained in any of the media forms in Table 1 of this section. However, records supporting plant cost shall be retained in their original form. (See general instructions 75.03(j), for periods of retention.)

(2) If the media form of the record retained is other than a readable paper copy, then reader and/or printer equipment and related printout programs, if required, shall be provided by the public utility for data reference.

(3) The media form initially selected for the record becomes the "original" for that particular record. If subsequent conditions (e.g., improved media life expectancy, increased utility resources, environmental factors) require and the remaining retention period permits a change in the media forms, the public utility may convert to another medium and dispose of its old equipment, provided the certification processes described in subsection (e) of this section, or other applicable certification processes, are observed and data referencing capability is maintained.

Table 1 — Record Media

Record media/form	Media expected life	Comments and standards
1. Paper and card stock (hardcopy).	Archival permanency.	For each document, paper stock should be selected with a life expectancy equal to or greater than the retention period specified for that document.
2. Magnetic storage:		
a. Computer Disk (i.e., hard disk and floppy disk).	5 years.	Assumes storage in a controlled environment with a temperature and humidity range of 60°-80° F. and 40-60% respectively. Assumes regular system of copying and regeneration is utilized.
b. Tape (e.g., computer and video tape).	5 years.	Same as above.
c. Punched tape or card.	Archival permanency.	For each record, tape media (paper, myler metallic base) should be selected with a life expectancy equal to or greater than the retention period specified for that record.
3. Microforms:		
a. Microfilm, including Computer Output Microfilm (COM), microfiche, jackets, and aperture cards.	Archival permanency.	Assumes processing to standards and storage in a controlled environment with a temperature and humidity range of 60°-80° degrees F. and 40-50% respectively. (Ref. American National Standards Institute (ANSI) standards PH 5.4-1970, PH 1.41-1976, PH 1.26-1979, PH 1.43-1961, or most current standards as accepted by the National Archives for use by Federal agencies. See 41 CFR 101-11.5)
b. Updatable type.	Dependent on use of media.	For temporary records not requiring archival permanency so long as the microfilm or film selected has a life expectancy equal to, or greater than, the retention period for that record. Same storage condition as for microfilm.
Metallic recording data strips.	Archival permanency.	Same storage conditions as for microfilm.
4. Optical Disk (including CD-ROM, WORM, and erasable types).	10-20 years.	Assumes regular system of copying and regeneration is available and utilized. Reference the following quality controls: (1) disk technology does not allow deletion or modification of record images, (2) image of each record is written onto two optical disks, (3) the legibility of each record image is verified to ensure that image is legible on both disks; if image is illegible, the hard copy record is maintained as a record, (4) one disk is stored in document imaging system for on-line retrieval, (5) second (backup) disk is stored in records storage facility meeting requirements of ANSI N45.2.9-1974 for single copy storage in separate remote location, (6) records stored on disk are acceptably copied (including verification) onto new disk before manufacturer's certified useful life of original disk is exceeded, (7) periodic random inspections of images stored on disks are performed to verify non-degradation of image quality, and (8) if replacing imaging system with incompatible system, records stored on old system's disks must be acceptably converted (including verification) into new system before old system is taken out of service.

(e) *Microform, tape, and computer output certification*

(1) As the initial recording media —

(i) Except as provided in paragraph (e)(1)(ii) of this subsection, each microform record series:

(A) shall contain, at the beginning, a microform introduction stating the title of the record series, the date prepared, the name of the official responsible for validating or confirming the data contained therein; and

(B) shall be closed with a clear and standard microform notation indicating the completion of the series and the date.

(ii) If an official, permanent record series is a computer output produce (i.e., output paper or microfilm, jacketed microfiche, or aperture cards), any certification that may otherwise be required under paragraph (e)(1)(i) of this subsection is not required if:

(A) The series is prepared in accordance with written standard procedures developed, or accepted general business practices followed, by the public utility that ensure the integrity of record series that are the product of computer output; and

(B) Such procedures or practices include the name or title of the official responsible for validating or confirming the data contained in the record series and confirming that a particular computer output record series was produced in accordance with the standard procedures or practices.

(iii) If, after validation, supplemental data and/or corrections (i.e., resulting from computer programming) are required, said microform may be produced separately or as a part of the series rerun, but shall be affixed to the original microform certificate as described in paragraph (e)(1)(i) of this subsection.

(iv) Each tape record series shall be labeled externally and shall include, as a basic part of the program, at the beginning of that series an introduction stating the record series title, date prepared, the name of the official responsible for validating or confirming the data contained therein, and an index where appropriate. Each record series shall be closed with a clear and standard notation indicating the completion of that series and the date.

(2) Conversion from other media —

(i) Each microform record series shall include, as an integral part, a certificate(s) stating that the microforms are direct and facsimile reproductions of the original records and that they have been made in accordance with prescribed instructions. Such certificate(s) shall be executed by a person(s) having personal knowledge of the facts covered thereby.

(ii) Each microform record series shall commence and end with a statement as to the nature and arrangement of the records reproduced, and the date. Rolls of film shall not be cut except to produce jacketed microfiche. Supplemental or retaken film, whether of misplaced or omitted documents or of portions of microform found to be defective, shall be attached to the beginning of the microform record series. However, if a retrieval system using such methods as, for example, image count indexing or "blipping" is used, the supplemental or retaken film may be attached at the end of the series, if provisions at the beginning of the series advise the viewer of the location of the problem frames and the location of the supplemental or retaken frames. If supplemental or retaken film of misplaced or omitted documents, or of portions of microform found to be defective, are attached to the microform record series, the certificate described in paragraph (e)(1)(i) of this subsection shall cover the supplemental or retaken film and shall state the reasons for the attachment.

(iii) If, in accordance with the provisions of paragraph (f) of this subsection, the public utility elects to convert records to a tape medium, the same certification provisions specified in paragraph (e)(1)(iii) of this subsection must be provided in the conversion program.

(f) *Change of media for existing record*

Those records prepared and maintained under previous regulations in a paper medium may be converted to a medium listed in Table 1 at the public utility's option, provided the applicable certification processes are observed and an audit referencing capability is maintained.

(g) *Media*

(1) All records created or maintained in a medium and a format other than readable entries on paper shall:

(i) Be prepared, arranged, classified, identified, and indexed so as to permit the subsequent location, examination, and reproduction of the record to a readable medium;

(ii) Be stored in such a manner as to provide reasonable protection from hazards such as fire, flood and, theft; and be maintained in a controlled environment; and

(iii) Be regenerated, including proper certification, when damaged. (Also see § 75.03(d)(1).)

(2) The public utility shall be prepared to furnish, at its own expense, standard facilities for reading media and additionally shall provide, if the Department so directs, copies of records in a readable form.

(3) All film stock shall be of approved operationally-permanent-record microcopying type, which meets the current specifications of the American National Standards Institute.

(h) *Destruction of records*

The destruction of the records permitted to be destroyed under the provisions of these regulations may be performed in any manner elected by the public utility concerned. Precautions should be taken, however, to macerate or otherwise destroy the legibility of records, the content of which is forbidden by law to be divulged to unauthorized persons.

(i) *Premature destruction or loss of records*

When records are destroyed or lost before the expiration of the prescribed period of retention, a certified statement listing, as far as may be determined, the records destroyed and describing the circumstances of accidental or other premature destruction or loss shall be filed with the Department within 90 days from the date of discovery of such destruction.

(j) *Schedule of records and periods of retention*

The Schedule of Records and Period of Retention (§ 75.05) shows the period of time that designed records shall be preserved. However, records related to plant shall be retained for a minimum of 25 years unless accounting adjustments resulting from reclassification and original cost studies have been approved by the Department and approved continuing plant inventory records are maintained. (Also see § 75.05.31.)

(k) *Retention periods designated "Destroy at option"*

Use of the retention period, "destroy at option," in these regulations constitutes authorization for such destruction under the conditions specified for the particular types of records, only if such optional destruction is appropriate to limited managerial interest in such records and if such optional destruction is not in conflict with other legal retention requirements or usefulness of such records in satisfying pending regulatory actions or directives.

(l) *Records of services performed by affiliated companies*

The public utility to which the regulations in this section apply shall assure the availability of records of services performed by affiliated companies for the periods indicated herein, as are necessary, to support the cost of services rendered to it by an affiliated company.

(m) *Index of records*

At each office of the public utility where records are kept or stored, such records as are herein required to be preserved shall be so arranged, filed, and currently indexed that they may be identified readily and made available to representatives of the Department.

Citation: **220 CMR 75.04**

✍ § 75.04: Application for Exceptions from Provision of These Regulations

Notwithstanding the provisions of the Schedule (§ 75.05), the Department may, upon the written request of a public utility, authorize a shorter period of retention for any record listed therein upon a showing by the public utility that preservation of such record for a longer period is not necessary or appropriate for the public interest or for the protection of investors or consumers.

In addition, notwithstanding the provisions of § 75.03(d)(1), the Department may, upon the written request of a public utility, authorize use of a record medium not included in the definition of record media in § 75.03(d)(1), Table 1 — Record Media, upon a showing by the public utility that the record medium ensures the preservation of records in a manner appropriate for the public interest as well as the protection of investors and consumers. Such a showing will include a demonstration that the medium meets acceptable industry standards for reliability and accuracy, and that appropriate safeguards are in place to prevent loss or destruction of records. The Department may seek comments from interested parties regarding such requests for exceptions. Petitioners are expected to provide the Department with a complete filing, including all necessary and relevant supporting documentation. Failure to make a complete filing may result in a dismissal of the petition for exception.§ 950 CMR 39.00: Regulations on Using Microfilm

§ 950 CMR 39.00: Regulations on Using Microfilm

Citation: 950 CMR 39.01

✪ § 39.01: Scope

950 CMR 39.00 shall apply to all records defined as public records by M.G.L. c. 4, s.7, clause 26, M.G.L. c. 66. The purpose of 950 CRM 39.00 is to ensure that microfilmed copies of public records have a life expectancy equal to or greater than the retention period assigned to the original record.

The minimum standards set out in 950 CMR 39.00 shall be adhered to in all microfilm applications for records the retention of which has been designated as more than 15 years by the Records Conservation Board for the records of the Commonwealth and by the Supervisor or Public Records for the records of counties, cities and towns, and to all records for which retention periods have not been assigned. No records shall be destroyed after microfilming without the written permission of the Records Conservation Board or the Supervisor of Public Records, as appropriate.

950 CMR 39.00 shall apply to all in-house preparations of such records, as well as to work contracted with microfilm service bureaus. It is the responsibility of the contracting agency to inform the microfilm service bureau of the requirements of 950 CMR 39.00.

It is recommended that records with a retention period of less than 15 years be microfilmed on base stock and processed in such a manner as required herein for long-term records. However, for economic reasons and for certain systems applications, other film types may be better suited for microforms containing short-term records; care should be taken that these film types are used and processed so as to provide a life expectancy equal to or greater than the retention period of the record. All filming and processing shall be in accordance with the manufacturers' specifications and all applicable ANSI and ISO standards. Microfilm of short-term records shall be stored under the conditions prescribed in the appendix to ANSI IT9.2.

Citation: 950 CMR 39.02

✪ § 39.02: Incorporation by Reference

The following standards of the American National Standards Institute (ANSI) and the International Organization for Standardization (ISO) contain provisions that, by reference in this text, constitute provisions of 950 CMR 39.00. These standards are subject to revision. Where a standard has been revised, the most current revision shall apply.

ANSI PH 1.25 Photography (Film) - Safety Photographic Film

ANSI/NAPM IT 9.1 Imaging Media (Film) - Silver Gelatin Type - Specifications for Stability

ANSI PH 1.43 Photography (Film) - Processed Safety Film - Storage

ANSI PH 1.51 Photographic Film - Micrographic Sheet and Roll Films - Dimensions

ANSI PH 2.51 American National Standard for Photography (Film) - Source Document Microfilms - Determination of ASA Speed and Average Gradient

ANSI IT 9.2 Photography (Processing) - Processed Films, Plates and Papers - Filing Enclosures and Containers for Storage

ANSI PH 4.8 Photograph (Chemicals) - Residual Thiosulfate and Other Chemicals in Films, Plates and Papers - Determination and Measurement

ANSI/ISO 3334 Microcopying - ISO Test Chart No. 2 - Description and Use in Photographic Documentary Reproduction

ANSI/AIIM MS 1 Recommended Practice for Alphanumeric Computer-Output Microforms - Operational Practices and Quality Control

ANSI/AIIM MS 5 Micrographics - Microfiche

ANSI/AIIM MS 14 Specifications for 16 and 35mm Microfilms in Roll Form

ANSI/AIIM MS 17 Test Chart for Rotary Microfilm Cameras

ANSI/AIIM MS 18 Splices for Imaged Film - Dimensions and Operational Constraints

ANSI/AIIM MS 19 Recommended Practice for Identification of Microforms

ANSI/AIIM MS 23 Practice for Operation Procedures/Inspection and Quality Control of First-Generation, Silver-Gelatin Microfilm of Documents

ANSI/AIIM MS 35 Recommended Practice for the Requirements and Characteristics of Original Documents to be Microfilmed

ANSI/AIIM MS 37 Recommended Practice for the Microphotography of Cartographic Materials

ANSI/AIIM MS 43 Recommended Practice for Operational Procedures/Inspection and Quality Control of Duplicate Microforms of Documents and from COM

ANSI/AIIM MS 45 Recommended Practice for Inspection of Stored Silver Gelatin Microforms for Evidence of Deterioration

ANSI Z 39.32 Information on Microfiche Headings

ANSI/NFPA 232 Protection of Records

Citation: 950 CMR 39.03

✪ § 39.03: Definitions

Definitions appropriate to 950 CMR 39.00 can be found in the Association of Information and Image Management publication, *Glossary of Micrographics*, TR-2-1992, or the latest revision thereof.

Citation: 950 CMR 39.04

✪ § 39.04: Film Base Materials

(1) *Original film.* All microfilm records regulated by 950 CMR 39.00 shall be generated on polyester-base silver gelatin-type film. All such film shall conform to the standards set forth in the American National Standards Institute publication, *Specifications for Safety Photographic Film*, ANSI PH 1.25. Such film

shall comply with the minimum standards of quality for film rated LE-500 described in *Imaging Media (Film) - Silver-Gelatin Type - Specifications for Stability*, ANSI/NAPM IT 9.1.

(2) *Duplicates*. The original, or "first generation" silver film shall be maintained for security purposes and not for reference. At least one duplicate copy of all records filmed shall be prepared for reference purposes. For records having a permanent retention period or for records which a retention period has not been assigned, a duplication master shall be produced from the master negative. Duplicate copies for reference or additional duplicate copies for security may be of the diazo, silver halide or vesicular composition. Duplicates shall be commensurate in quality with the original and shall comply with the minimum standards set forth in *Recommended Practice for Operational Procedures/Inspection and Quality Control of Duplicate Microforms of Documents and from COM*, ANSI/AIIM MS 43.

Citation: **950 CMR 39.05**

✪ § 39.05: Preparation of Film

(1) *Original Records*. Original source documents should be of sufficient legibility and high quality to ensure a microfilm of high quality. Should the source documents be of inferior legibility or of low quality, the microfilm output will be of similarly inferior legibility.

Proper care shall be taken in the preparation and arrangement of original records for filming to ensure that a true and accurate reproduction will be made. Insofar as is possible, preparation and arrangement shall be in accordance with *Practice for Operational Procedures/Inspection and Quality Control of First-generation, Silver Microfilm of Documents*, ANSI/AIIM MS 23. All staples, paper clips, folds, attachments, etc. shall be removed before document filming. Source documents shall be arranged and filmed in a manner consistent with their customary reference and usage.

(2) *Reduction Ratio*. Regardless of format, the guiding consideration in establishing a reduction ratio shall be the reproduction of readable records of film, which shall be system-compatible in usage. The reduction ratio employed shall be such as to ensure a Quality Index resolution level of 8 as described below.

It should be observed that reduction ratios of 24X are regarded as optimal in regular (16 mm) roll film production. Unitized microforms also are becoming standardized on the basis of 24X. Certain applications may require variations from this standard. For example, lower reduction may be beneficial where 35 mm film is used; higher reduction may be necessary where 105 mm film is used or where duplex filming is performed on a rotary camera, and 48X reduction is the norm for filming computer output pages. While such factors may necessitate variations, the 24X optimum shall be followed as closely as possible.

The reduction standards for computer output microfilm (COM) is 48X, as defined in *Recommended Practice for Alphanumeric Computer-Output Microforms - Operational Practices and Quality Control*, ANSI/AIIM MS 1.

(3) *Resolution*. The method for determining the minimum required resolution shall conform to the Quality Index Method of determining resolution as given in the *Practice for Operational Procedures/Inspection and Quality Control of First-Generation, Silver-Gelatin Microfilm of Documents*, ANSI/AIIM MS 23, and *Recommended Practice for Operational Procedures/Inspection and Quality Control of Duplicate Microforms of Documents and from COM*, ANSI/AIIM MS 43. Resolution shall be sufficient for the production of film producing fine detail and sharpness of image.

Resolution tests shall be performed using a NIST-SRM 1010a Microcopy Resolution Test Chart (a calibrated and certified photographic reproduction) as specified in *ISO Resolution Test Chart No. 2 - Description and Use*, ANSI/ISO 3334 (ANSI/AIIM MS 51) and the patterns will be read following the instructions of ANSI/ISO 3334. Rotary camera targets shall conform to the specifications and be used in accordance with *Test Chart for Rotary Microfilm Cameras*, ANSI/AIIM MS 17. A minimum Quality Index level of 8.0 (high quality) shall be maintained; i.e., a lower case "e" that is 2 mm high and will be reproduced to three generations shall be filmed on a system that will resolve the 5.0 pattern, regardless of the reduction ratio or the type of camera used.

Computer output microfilm shall meet the requirements of *Recommended Practice for Alphanumeric Computer Output Microforms - Operational Practices for Inspection and Quality Control*, ANSI/AIIM MS 1.

(4) *Density*. Throughout filming, density shall be monitored constantly. If density values are too low, the film will appear faded or "washed out." On the other hand, if the density is too high, fine or light lines from the original document will tend to fill in and bold black lines will tend to spread. Density values shall be such that exposed film shall have clear and open lines, as well as an absence of spread and/or widened letters (characters).

The most favorable background density values, in the case of first generation film, and when the base-plus-fog density of the film is less than or equal to 0.10, range from 0.80 to 1.50, depending on the original documents to be filmed. Optimum values for various original documents set forth in *Practice for Operational Procedures/Inspection and Quality Control of First-Generation Silver-Gelatin Microfilm of Documents*, ANSI/AIIM MS 23, are indicated below.

Classification
Description of Document
Background Density

Group 1
High-quality, high-contrast printed books, periodicals and black typing
1.30 - 1.50

Group 2
Fine-line originals, black opaque pencil writing, and documents with high contrast printing
1.15 - 1.40

Group 3
Pencil and ink drawings, faded printing, and very small printing, such as footnotes at the bottom of a printed page
1.0 - 1.20

Group 4
Low-contrast manuscripts and drawings, graph paper with pale, fine colored lines; letters typed with a worn ribbon; and poorly-printed, faint documents
0.80 - 1.0

Group 5
Poor-contrast documents (special exception)
0.70 - 0.85

Recommended visual diffuse transmission densities for computer-generated images are as follows:

Film Type	Process	Density Measurement Method	Min. DMax.*	Max. DMin.*	Minimum Density Difference
Silver gelatin (1P)	Conventional	Printing or diffuse	0.75	0.15 or 0.10 plus base^	0.60
Silver gelatin (1N)	Full reversal	Printing	1.50	0.20 plus base ^**	1.30

*Character or line density, measured with a microdensitometer or by comparing the film under a microscope with an image of a known density.
^Base equals the density of the uncoated base.
**Character or line density, measured with a microdensitometer or by comparing the film under a microscope with an image of a known density; the cut mark is useful for processing control only.

Targets and document samples shall be test filmed and density checked for the camera negative, each user generation to be used, and reader-printer blowbacks. The procedure for measurement of density is described in ANSI/AIIM MS 23.

(5) *Film Identification.* Specifications for film identification should be followed as given in the *Recommended Practice for the Identification of Microforms*, ANSI/AIIM MS 19.

At a minimum, identification targets shall display the following information: name of agency by which records are held; the declarations by the records custodian and camera operator; the title of the records (with identification of contents if not evident from series title); the microfilm reel number, camera number (where applicable); legal citation for access restriction (if any); the date of filming; and where possible, the inclusive dates, numbers, names or other data identifying the first and last records on the roll.

Unitized microforms (i.e., fiche, aperture cards, and jacketed film) shall contain records identification information in eye-readable headings in the appropriate places at the top (heading area) of the film material, or on the film jacket.

Any indexes, registers, or other finding aids shall be microfilmed and located in a readily identifiable place within the collection of microfilmed records.

(6) *Targets.* Standards targets shall be employed pursuant to ANSI/AIIM 19 and ANSI/AIIM MS 23. These shall include appropriate technical targets, restriction or classification targets, targeting for start/end of film record, camera operator's report, and records identification. Other targets, including retake, start file, or space targets, shall be used as necessary.

(7) *Film Processing.* As soon after the date of exposure as possible, (ideally within 24-48 hours), all film shall be processed in order that the film images be properly fixed.

Hypo-residue (sodium thiosulfate) shall meet the standards of *Imaging Media (Film) - Silver-Gelatin Type - Specifications for Stability*, ANSI/NAPM IT 9.1. In all such cases, film shall be washed to reduce the hypo residue to within allowable tolerances as defined in ANSI/NAPM IT 9.1. The amount of thiosulfate ion residue shall be greater than 0 and less than 0.014 gram/meter^2.

To confirm these tolerances, the chemical testing of processed film shall be required. The tests to be used in meeting this requirement are specified in *Photography (Chemicals) Residual Thiosulfate and Other Chemicals in Films, Plates and Papers - Determination and Measurement.* ANSI/ASC PH 4.8. If reversal processing will be used, it must be full photographic reversal and not the halide-type reversal.

The use of polysulfide or other treatment approved by the Image Permanence Institute to retard the deterioration of processed film is encouraged.

(8) *Post-filming Inspection.* It is the responsibility of the records custodian to ensure that, as soon after processing as possible, all film shall be inspected to determine if the material has been filmed in proper sequence, and to determine if photographic and physical requirements have been met. This shall include resolution, density, and residual thiosulfate ion checks, as well as visual inspections for the quality of the filmed product. Inspections shall be made as recommended by ANSI/AIIM MS 23 and reports shall be prepared detailing defects and errors, if any, and indicating any corrections which may be made. Said reports will be returned to the custodian of the records involved.

In regard to roll film, corrections and/or retakes are to be spliced in at the beginning of each reel in a retake section along with targets for retake certificates. Splices shall be made in accordance with *Splices for Imaged Film - Dimensions and Operational Constraints*, ANSI/AIIM MS 18. Equivalent procedures shall be applied in the correction of unitized microforms.

Citation: 950 CMR 39.06

✪ § 39.06: Storage

Standards for storing original or duplicate film shall comply with *Processed Safety Photographic Film - Storage*, ANSI IT 9.11. In regard to the original film, the following storage standards shall be met:

(1) *Film Enclosures.* Film enclosures shall be chemically stable and shall meet the requirements of ANSI IT 9.2.

Materials used for film enclosures shall be free of acids and peroxides that may be released over time and cause degradation of film. Paper and paperboard materials shall meet the requirements of the photographic activity test as outlines in ANSI IT 9.2.

Only enclosures of inert plastic or non-corroding metal such an anodized aluminum or stainless steel shall be used. Steel will be permitted only if such reels are well-protected by lacquer, enamel, tinning, or other corrosion-resistant finish.

Enclosure materials shall be sufficiently fire-resistive that they will not ignite or emit reactive fumes after heating for four hours at 150°F. Melting and distortion of the enclosure materials after such heating shall not damage or prevent the film from being removed from the enclosure.

Plastics and lacquers that might give off reactive fumes or emissions during storage shall not be used. Suitable plastic enclosure materials are photographic film support material such as uncoated polyester or cellulose acetate. Highly plasticized sheetings or coatings shall not be used. The plastics must be free of peroxides.

The use of rubber bands, tape, paper strips, etc. for fastening film onto reels or cores is prohibited. The materials used shall not ignite, decompose, or develop reactive fumes or vapors. Film on reels may be confined by tucking the film end between the roll and the flange. All adhesives shall meet the standards of ANSI IT 9.2.

(2) *Storage Containers.* The film shall be packaged either in chemically stable containers of metal or inert plastic of proven quality or paper-board boxes of low acidic composition. Plastics and lacquers that might give off reactive fumes or emissions during storage shall not be used. The plastics must be free of peroxides. All containers and adhesives shall meet the standards of ANSI IT 9.2. Containers shall be sealed when necessary to maintain prescribed humidity limits or to protect the film against gaseous impurities. If proper temperature and humidity are maintained as prescribed in 950 CMR 39.06(4), and if there is good ventilation and clean air in the storage area, the containers need not be sealed. Each containers shall be properly labeled with the series title, reel numbers, and number of documents

(where possible). All inks used for labeling shall pass the photographic activity test outlined in ANSI IT 9.2.

(3) *Storage Housings.* Microfilm shall be stored in closed housings such as drawers of shelving units equipped with doors, unless the film is in closed containers, in which case open racks and shelves may be used. Storage housings shall be noncorrosive and noncombustible. Air conditioning or ventilation shall be provided in accordance with ANSI IT 9.11.

(4) *Storage Facilities.* All original film shall be housed in clean, dust-free, environmentally controlled circumstances affording the maximum in security. All storage areas shall be constructed and maintained in accordance with *Processed Safety Film - Storage*, ANSI IT9.11.

Heat and Humidity can deform the film base and weaken the emulsion. Since the emulsion is an organic product, mold growth can also occur. The average relative humidity in areas in which first generation, master film is stored shall be between 20% and 30% with daily fluctuations not to exceed 5%. Temperature shall not exceed 70°F. with lower temperature providing better keeping characteristics.

Storage areas shall be equipped with air filters since air-entrained impurities, in the form of particulates, can cause abrasion of the film and certain fumes may react with the film to degrade the image.

First generation, master film shall be stored in fire resistant safes or vaults. Safes shall be UL Class 150 rated four hours. Vaults shall provide protection equivalent to ANSI/NFPA 232 except that provision for air-conditioning shall be made in accordance with ANSI IT9.11. Except in fire resistant buildings, all safes shall be on ground-supported flooring.

Citation: **950 CMR 39.07**

✪ § 39.07: Inspection

Regular procedures for the periodic inspection of film shall be followed. These procedures are the responsibility of the custodian of the records, except that the State Records Center will have the responsibility for inspecting the film stored in its vault.

(1) *Inspection Procedure.* At approximately two-year intervals, a randomly selected sample of one hundred microforms (i.e., rolls, fiche, aperture cards, etc.) or one tenth of one per cent of the collection, whichever is greater, shall be inspected. For any collection of less than 100 microforms of microfilm, the entire collection must be inspected. For each biennial inspection a different lot sample shall be chosen, allowing some overlapping to note any changes in previously inspected samples.

Sampling and inspection shall be as described in *Recommended Practice for Inspection of Stored Silver-Gelatin Microforms for Evidence of Deterioration*, ANSI/AIIM MS 45.

The film shall be inspected for microbial growths, residual processing chemicals, excessive brittleness, film curl or discoloration, evidence of separation of the emulsion from the base ("blocking or fused film"), adhesion of the emulsion, base shrinkage and the presence of redox blemishes. A re-reading of resolution test targets and a remeasurement of the film density shall be made. Cans, boxes or reels used to store the film shall also be inspected for evidence of rust, corrosion and other deterioration.

Additional samples of any lot of film rated as in fair condition shall be inspected and the entire lot of any film rated as poor or bad shall be inspected.

(2) *Inspection Reports.* On the basis of inspections, reports shall be prepared and filed regularly with the Supervisor of Public Records. Reports shall include:

(a) quantity and identity of microfilm on hand;

(b) quantity and identity of microfilm inspected;

(c) condition of the microfilm;

(d) corrective action required if necessary.

In the case of film stored at the State Records Center, the State Records Center shall report to the agency having custody, the condition of any of its film that has been inspected.

(3) *Deteriorating Film.* If deterioration is found among the microfilm of permanent records, a more extensive inspection shall be undertaken to locate all deteriorating film. A silver duplicate shall be prepared to replace all deteriorating film. A silver duplicate shall be prepared to replace all film rated as poor or bad.

(4) *Short-term Records.* Inspection of the microfilm of records having a retention period of less than 15 years is recommended but not required.

State: **Michigan**
Source: **Michigan Compiled Laws**

CHAPTER 600. REVISED JUDICATURE ACT OF 1961.

SUBCHAPTER 21. EVIDENCE.

Citation: **MCL 600.2137**

☞ § 600.2137. Photograph of public records; destruction of originals.

Requisites

(1) If a public officer reproduced court records kept by him or her pursuant to the records media act, the officer may offer the original records to the department of state for placement in the state archives. If the department of state accepts the offer within 30 days, the court shall transfer the records to that department. If the department of state does not accept the offer within 30 days, the court may dispose of or destroy the records in the manner provided for state agencies under accordance with sections 285 and 287 of the management and budget act, Act No. 431 of the Public Acts of 1984, being sections 18.1285 and 18.1287 of the Michigan Compiled Laws, and section 5 of Act No. 271 of the Public Acts of 1913, as amended, being section 399.5 of the Michigan Compiled Laws. The record of a court shall not be disposed of or destroyed until the record has been in the custody of the court for not less than six years.

Probate court

(2) In a county or probate court district in which the county board or boards of commissioners pass a resolution or resolutions for producing records pursuant to the records media act, the judge of probate may cause the records of the probate court to be so reproduced. The judge of probate shall cause a copy or a duplicate to be kept in a building outside of the probate office and shall keep a copy available in the probate office with any suitable equipment necessary for displaying the record at not less than its original size or for preparing copies for persons entitled to copies. The judge of probate then may order a record destroyed. A reproduction in a medium pursuant to the records media act or a reproduction consisting of a printout or other output readable by sight from such a medium is admissible as evidence before a court, commission, or administrative body the same as the original. The original file of an estate proceeding shall not be destroyed until 6 years have elapsed from the date of filing of the discharge of the fiduciary or 10 years have elapsed from the filing of the last document, whichever date occurs first.

Files and records of court of record other than district court

(3) A court of record other than the district court may order the destruction of a court reporter or recorder note, tape, or recording 15 years after the date that the note, tape, or recording was made for a felony case and 10 years after the date that the note, tape, or recording was made for any other case. One year after a transcript of a note, tape, or recording is filed with the court, the court may order the destruction of the note, tape, or recording. If a transcript of a trial or other proceeding in a court of record other than the district court is ordered other than for filing in the case file, the court stenographer also shall prepare and shall file a certified copy of the transcript in the case file at the expense of the person ordering the transcript unless a copy has been filed with the court or unless the chief judge of the court orders otherwise in an order filed in the case file. As used in this subsection, "felony case" does not include proceedings in a case that occurred before arraignment on information or indictment, or proceedings in a case in which the defendant is not convicted of a felony.

Files and records of judicial circuit

(4) Except as provided in subsection (3), a judicial circuit of the circuit court may order the destruction of its files and records in a case in which action has not been taken during the 25 years immediately preceding the order of destruction. All of the following procedures shall be followed before the issuance of an order of destruction of circuit court files and records:

(a) The judgment or decree, if any, shall be reproduced pursuant to the records media act, or separated and retained, and the original or reproduction shall be made available for public inspection.

(b) The circuit court shall offer the files and records subject to the order of destruction to the Michigan historical commission established by Act No. 271 of the Public Acts of 1913, as amended, being sections 399.1 to 399.9 of the Michigan Compiled Laws, or an historical commission created pursuant to Act No. 213 of the Public Acts of 1957, as amended, being sections 399.171 to 399.172 of the Michigan Compiled Laws. If the historical commission accepts the offer within 30 days, the circuit court shall transfer the files and records to the historical commission. If the historical commission does not accept the offer within 30 days, the circuit court shall issue an order of destruction.

Photographs or microphotographs as evidence

(5) A reproduction of a record in a medium pursuant to the records media act or a reproduction consisting of a printout or other output readable by sight from such a medium, made as provided by law, has the same force and effect as the original would have had and shall be treated as an original for the purpose of admissibility in evidence. A duly certified or authenticated copy of reproduction shall be admitted into evidence equally with the original reproduction.

Citation: MCL 600.2147

☞ **§ 600.2147. Same; use of photographic, photostatic or microphotographic reproduction as evidence.**

Sec. 2147. Notwithstanding any law of this state to the contrary, an individual, firm, association or corporation may introduce in evidence at a trial or hearing before a court, officer, arbiter, referee, board or tribunal, a reproduction of a business record of the individual or institution prepared or entered in the regular course of business, the original of which would be admissible in evidence, including an existing record and including, but not by way of limitation, a check, bill, note, acceptance or other type of commercial instrument, pass book, deposit slip, or statement furnished to depositors, whether or not the individual or institution regularly so reproduces any or all of such business records. The reproduction shall be in a medium pursuant to the records media act or consist of a printout or other output readable by sight from such a medium. The reproduction, if accompanied by the certificate of an individual or his or her employee or agent, or of the officer, agent or employee of the firm, association or corporation who supervised the making of the reproduction to the effect that the reproduction when made was a true, full and complete reproduction of the original, shall be received as evidence at the trial or hearing with the same force and effect as though the original document were produced. However, the court, officer, arbiter, referee, board or tribunal may in its discretion require that the original document be produced in evidence, and may also require the taking of testimony of the person who supervised the making the reproduction. The reproduction is admissible only if the party offering it delivers a copy of it or of so much of it as may relate to the controversy, to the adverse party a reasonable time before trial, unless in the opinion of the trial court, officer, arbiter, referee, board or tribunal the adverse party has not been unfairly surprised by the failure to deliver the copy. Nevertheless, such a reproduction need not be submitted to the adverse party as herein prescribed unless the original instrument would be required to be so submitted. If necessary, the reproduction may be offered in evidence by the use of a projector or other similar device. All circumstances surrounding the making of the reproduction may be shown upon the trial, hearing or proceeding for the purpose of affecting the weight but not the admissibility of the evidence.

Citation: MCL 600.2148

✍ ☞ **§ 600.2148. Preservation of reproduced records of business firms; destruction of originals; use as evidence.**

Sec. 2148. (1) A person, firm or corporation engaged in business may cause records kept by the business to be reproduced pursuant to the records media act, and the business may then dispose of the original record.

(2) A reproduction in a medium pursuant to the records media act under subsection (1) or a reproduction consisting of a printout or other output readable by sight from such a medium is considered to be an original record for all purposes and shall be treated as an original record in a court or administrative agency for the purpose of its admissibility in evidence. A facsimile, exemplification, enlargement or certified copy of such a reproduction for all purposes, is considered a facsimile, exemplification, or certified copy of the original record.

(3) For purposes of this section, "person" means an individual, association, firm, partnership, company or corporation.

CHAPTER 691. JUDICIARY.

REPRODUCTION OF PUBLIC RECORDS

Citation: MCL 691.1101

✪ **§ 691.1101. Public records, municipal court of record records; photograph; destruction.**

Sec. 1. If a department, commission, board or officer of the state, a political subdivision, or a municipal court of record reproduces pursuant to the records media act records kept by or in the department, commission, board, office or court, the department, commission, board officer or court may cause the original records to be disposed of or destroyed pursuant to sections 201, 285, 287, and 289 of the management and budget act, Act No. 431 of the Public Acts 1984, being section 18.1201, 18.1285, 18.1287, and 18.1289 of the Michigan Compiled Laws, if applicable, and section 5 of Act No. 271 of the Public Acts of 1913, as amended, being section 399.5 of the Michigan Compiled Laws. A record of a municipal court of record shall not be disposed of or destroyed unless the record has been in the custody of the court for at least 6 years.

Citation: MCL 691.1102

✪ **§ 691.1102. Register of deeds; microphotograph, duplicates; display equipment.**

Sec. 2. The register of deeds of a county, if so instructed by a resolution of the county board of commissioners, may reproduce pursuant to the records media act a deed, mortgage, map, instrument, or writing recorded in his or her office and a record or index required by law to be kept by him or her. The register of deeds shall make reproductions in duplicate and store 1 reproduction in a building separate from his or her office. The register of deeds shall retain the other reproduction in his or her office with suitable equipment for displaying the record at not less than its original size or for preparing copies for persons entitled to copies.

Citation: MCL 691.1103

☞ **§ 691.1103. Photographs, microphotographs, admissibility in evidence.**

Sec. 3. A reproduction of a record in a medium pursuant to the records media act or a reproduction consisting of a printout or other output readable by sight from such a medium prepared under any other law has the same force and effect as the original and shall be treated as an original for the purpose of admissibility in evidence. A duly certified or authenticated copy of the reproduction shall be admitted in evidence equally with the original reproduction.

Citation: MCL 691.1111

✪ **§ 691.1111. Public records; photostatic standards.**

Sec. 1. If an officer of a county or city is required or authorized by law to record, copy, recopy or replace a document, plat, paper, written instrument or book on file or of record in his or her office, the officer may do so pursuant to the records media act.

Citation: MCL 691.1112

✪ **§ 691.1112. Certification of replacement of original public records.**

Sec. 2. If an original document, plat, paper, written instrument, record or books of record filed or of record in the office of an officer described in section 1 is copied or replaced, and the officer is required by law to certify in or on the copy or replacement that it is a true and correct copy of the original, a copy of the certification by the officer, similarly made and included at the end of the copy or replacement, complies with the law.

Citation: MCL 691.1113

✪ **§ 691.1113. Public records; correction; alteration or endorsement, procedure.**

Sec. 3. When any record or replacement thereof in the office of any such officer is produced by such process, a correction, alteration, endorsement or entry, required or authorized to be made of or on any instrument or paper or on the record thereof, may be made by filing or inserting copies or recopies produced by the same process of the page or part of the page, so corrected, altered, or on which such endorsement or entry is made, next to the place wherein the copy or record of such instrument or paper is contained or in such other manner as such officer shall deem advisable or practicable. The uncorrected or unaltered record or copy shall also be preserved in its original condition and location and not destroyed or obliterated. The re-recording, re-filing or new instrument shall contain a statement that is given to correct, and shall state where the original record or file may be found.

Citation: MCL 691.1114

☞ ✪ **§ 691.1114. Transcripts.**

Sec. 4. Transcripts or certified copies of such copies, records, reproductions and replacements, shall be considered as transcripts or certified copies of the originals.

Citation: MCL 691.1115

☞ ✪ **§ 691.1115. Copies, reproductions; admissibility in evidence.**

Sec. 5. A reproduction in a medium pursuant to the records media act or a reproduction consisting of a printout or other output readable by sight from such a medium, which production is produced under this or any other law, shall be considered an original for all purposes, and is admissible in evidence in like manner as the original.

Source: Michigan Rules of Evidence

ARTICLE X. CONTENTS OF WRITINGS, RECORDINGS, AND PHOTOGRAPHS.

☞ **Rule 1001. Definitions**

For purposes of this article the following definitions are applicable:

(1) *Writings and recordings.* — "Writings" and "recordings" consist of letters, words, or numbers, or their equivalent, set down by handwriting, typewriting, printing, photostating, photographing, magnetic impulse, mechanical or electronic recording, or other form of data compilation.

(2) *Photographs.* — "Photographs" include still photographs, X-ray films, video tapes, and motion pictures.

(3) *Original.* — An "original" of a writing or recording is the writing or recording itself or any counterpart intended to have the same effect by a person executing or issuing it. An "original" of a photograph includes the negative or any print therefrom. If data are stored in a computer or similar device, any printout or other output readable by sight, shown to reflect the data accurately, is an "original".

(4) *Duplicate.* — A "duplicate" is a counterpart produced by the same impression as the original, or from the same matrix, or by means of photography, including enlargements and

miniatures, or by mechanical or electronic re-recording, or by chemical reproduction, or by other equivalent techniques which accurately reproduces the original.

☞ **Rule 1003. Admissibility of Duplicates.**

A duplicate is admissible to the same extent as an original unless (1) a genuine question is raised as to the authenticity of the original or (2) in the circumstances it would be unfair to admit the duplicate in lieu of the original.

[See Appendix A. Uniform Rules of Evidence for additional provisions.]

Source:	**Michigan Administrative Code**
Agency:	**Department of Public Health Division of Radiological Health**

Citation:	**MAC R325.5245**

✍ **§ R325.5245. Records of surveys, radiation monitoring, disposal and tests.**

Rule 245. (1) A licensee or registrant shall maintain records showing the radiation doses of all individuals for whom personnel monitoring is required under rule 222. These records shall be kept on department Form RH-102, in accordance with the instructions contained in that form, or on clear and legible records containing all the information required by Form RH-102. The doses entered on the forms or records shall be for periods of time not exceeding 1 calendar quarter.(2) A licensee or registrant shall maintain records in the same units used in this part, showing the results of surveys required in rule 221, disposals made under rules 238 to 240, and surveys required by other parts of these rules.

(3) Records of individual exposure to radiation and to radioactive material which shall be maintained pursuant to subrule (1) and records of bio-assays, including results of whole body counting examinations, made pursuant to rule 209 shall be preserved indefinitely or until the department authorizes their disposal.

(4) The discontinuance of or curtailment of activities, does not relieve the licensee or registrant of responsibility for retaining all records required by this rule. A licensee or registrant may, however, request the department to accept such records. The acceptance of the records by the department relieves the licensee or registrant of subsequent responsibility only in respect to their preservation as required by this rule.

(5) Records which shall be maintained pursuant to this part may be maintained in the form of microfilms.

Agency:	**Departments of Labor and Public Health Occupational Safety and Health**

PART 11. RECORDING AND REPORTING OF OCCUPATIONAL INJURIES AND ILLNESSES.

GENERAL PROVISIONS

Citation:	**MAC R408.22111**

✍ **§ R408.22111. Log and summary of recordable occupational injuries and illnesses; maintenance; location; recording injuries and illnesses; completing forms.**

Rule 1111. (1) An employer shall maintain, for each establishment, a log and summary of recordable occupational injuries and illnesses for that establishment. An employer may maintain the log and summary of recordable occupational injuries and illnesses at a central administrative office or at another location under the circumstances described in subrule (4).

(2) An employer shall enter each recordable occupational injury and illness in the log and summary as early as practicable, but not later than 6 working days after receiving information that a recordable case has occurred. For this purpose, form MIOSHA No. 200 or its equivalent shall be used.

(3) Form MIOSHA No. 200 or its equivalent shall be completed in the detail required by the form and the instruction contained in form MIOSHA No. 200. If a form equivalent to form MIOSHA No. 200 is used, such as a print-out from data processing equipment, the information shall be as readable and comprehensible to a person not familiar with the data processing equipment as the form MIOSHA No. 200 itself is readable and comprehensible.

(4) An employer may maintain the log and summary of recordable occupational injuries and illnesses at a place other than the establishment or by means of data processing equipment, or both, under the following circumstances:

(a) When there is available, at the place where the log and summary is maintained, sufficient information to complete the log and summary to a date within 6 working days after receiving information that a recordable case has occurred, as required by subrule (2).

(b) When there is available, at each of the employer's establishments, a copy of the log and summary that reflects separately any recordable occupational injury and illness experience of that establishment, complete and current to a date within 45 calendar days.

State:	**Minnesota**
Source:	**Minnesota Statutes**

STATE AGENCIES.

PART 1. PUBLIC RIGHTS.

CHAPTER 15. DEPARTMENTS OF STATE IN GENERAL.

Citation:	**MS 15.17**

✪ **§ 15.17. Official records.**

Subd. 1. *Must be kept.* All officers and agencies of the state, counties, cities, towns, school districts, municipal subdivisions or corporations, or other public authorities or political entities within the state, hereinafter "public officer," shall make and preserve all records necessary to a full and accurate knowledge of their official activities. All government records shall be made on a physical medium of a quality to ensure permanent records. Every public officer is empowered to reproduce records if the records are not deemed to be of permanent or archival value by the commissioner of administration and the records disposition panel under section 138.17. The public officer is empowered to reproduce these records by any photographic, photostatic, microphotographic, optical disk imaging system, microfilming, or other reproduction method that clearly and accurately reproduces the records. If a record is deemed to be of permanent or archival value, any reproduction of the record must meet archival standards specified by the Minnesota historical society provided, however, that this section does not prohibit the use of non-erasable optical imaging systems for the preservation of archival records without the preservation of paper or microfilm copies. Each public officer may order that those photographs, photostats, microphotographs, microfilms, optical images, or other reproductions, be substituted for the originals of them.

The public officer may direct the destruction or sale for salvage or other disposition of the originals from which they were made, in accordance with the disposition requirements of section 138.17. Photographs, photostats, microphotographs, microfilms, optical disk images, or other reproductions are for all purposes deemed the original recording of the papers, books, documents, and records reproduced when so ordered by any public officer and admissible as evidence in all courts and proceedings of every kind. A facsimile or exemplified or certified copy of a photograph, photostat, microphotograph, microfilm, optical disk image, or other reproduction, or an enlargement or reduction of it, has the same effect and weight as evidence as would a certified or exemplified copy of the original.

* * * * *

Citation: MS 15.171

✪ § 15.171. Official records; compilation, maintenance and storage of information.

Notwithstanding any other law, any public officer who has jurisdiction over a collection of official records may select and use, subject to the approval of the commissioner of administration, alternative methods for the compilation, maintenance and storage of the information contained in those records, subject to the following conditions:

(1) The methods selected must provide for access to the information contained in the records by those authorized by law to have access to that information; and

(2) The methods selected must provide for the preservationof the information contained in the records to the extent specified by law.

Citation: MS 15.172

✪ § 15.172. Approval of alternate method.

At least 90 days prior to the date upon which it is proposed to put into effect an alternate method of compilation, maintenance, and storage of records, the public official shall submit a description of the proposed method and the reasons for adopting it to the commissioner of administration. On finding that the proposed method complies with the conditions specified in section 15.171, the commissioner of administration shall approve its use; on finding otherwise, the commissioner shall disapprove its use. A failure of the commissioner of administration to act before the date upon which the public official proposes to put the alternative method into effect shall be deemed a disapproval of that method.

Citation: MS 15.173

✪ § 15.173. Notice of alternative method.

The commissioner of administration, on approving an alternative method of compilation, maintenance and storage, shall maintain a written notice of that approval, the date of taking effect of the alternate method, a description of the method and the reasons for its adoption in the commissioner's office as a public record. In the case of a record having less than statewide significance, the public official having jurisdiction over the records shall file a written notice containing the same information as the notice maintained by the commissioner of administration with the county auditor, clerk or other similar recording officer of the affected governmental subdivision and such notices shall also be maintained as public records.

Citation: MS 15.174

✪ § 15.174. Records now in use.

Notwithstanding section 15.171, any public official using an alternative method of compilation, maintenance and storage of a record on August 1, 1974, may continue to use that alternate method unless and until that method is expressly disapproved by the commissioner of administration. Such an official shall file a description of the method and the reasons for its use on or before August 1, 1974. Failure of the commission of administration to approve or disapprove such a method within 90 days shall be deemed an approval. Notice of such methods shall be filed as required in section 15.173.

STATE HISTORY

CHAPTER 138. HISTORICAL SOCIETIES; ARCHIVES; FIELD ARCHAEOLOGY; FOLKLIFE.

Citation: MS 138.17

✪ § 138.17. Government records; administration.

Subdivision 1. Destruction, preservation, reproduction of records; prima facie evidence.

(a) The attorney general, legislative auditor in the case of state records, state auditor in the case of local records, and director of the Minnesota historical society, hereinafter director, shall constitute the records disposition panel. The member of the panel shall have power by unanimous consent to direct the destruction or sale for salvage of government records determined to be no longer of any value, or to direct the disposition by gift to the Minnesota historical society or otherwise of government records determined to be valuable for preservation. The records disposition panel may by unanimous consent order any of those records to be reproduced by photographic or other means, and order that photographic or other reproductions be substituted for the originals of them. It may direct the destruction or sale for salvage or other disposition of the originals from which the same were made. Photographic or other reproductions shall for all purposes be deemed the originals of the records so reproduced when so ordered by the records disposition panel, and shall be admissible as evidence in all courts and in proceedings of every kind. A facsimile, exemplified or certified copy of a photographic, optical disk imaging, or other reproduction, or an enlargement or reduction of it, shall have the same effect and weight as evidence as would a certified or exemplified copy of the original. The records disposition panel, by majority vote, may direct the storage of government records, except as herein provided, and direct the storage of photographic or other reproductions. Photographic or other reproductions substituted for original records shall be disposed of in accordance with the procedures provided for the original records.

(b) For the purposes of this chapter:

(1) The term "government records" means state and local records, including all cards, correspondence, discs, maps, memoranda, microfilms, papers, photographs, recordings, reports, tapes, writings, optical disks, and other data, information or documentary material, regardless of physical form or characteristics, storage media or conditions of use, made or received by an officer or agency of the state and an officer or agency of a county, city, town, school district, municipal subdivision or corporation or other public authority or political entity

within the state pursuant to state law or in connection with the transaction of public business by an officer or agency;

(2) The term "state record" means a record of department, office, officer, commission, commissioner, board or any other agency, however styled or designated, of the executive branch of state government; a record of the state legislature; a record of any court, whether of statewide or local jurisdiction; and any other record designated or treated as a state record under state law;

(3) The term "local record" means a record of an agency of a county, city, town, school district, municipal subdivision or corporation or other public authority or political entity;

(4) The term "records" excludes data and information that does not become part of an official transaction, library and museum material made or acquired and kept solely for reference or exhibit purposes, extra copies of documents kept only for convenience of reference and stock of publications and processed documents, and bonds, coupons, or other obligations or evidence of indebtedness, the destruction or other disposition of which is governed by other laws;

(5) The term "state archives" means those records preserved or appropriate for preservation as evidence of the organization, functions, policies, decisions, procedures, operations or other activities of government or because of the value of the information contained in them, when determined to have sufficient historical or other value to warrant continued preservation by the state of Minnesota and accepted for inclusion in the collections of the Minnesota historical society.

* * * * *

Subd 10. Optical Image Storage.

(a) Any government record, including a record with archival value, may be transferred to and stored on a non-erasable optical imaging system and retained only in that format, if the requirements of this section are met.

(b) All documents preserved on non-erasable optical imaging systems must meet standards for permanent records specified in § 15.17, subdivision 1, and must be kept available for retrieval so long as any law requires. Standards under § 15.17, subdivision 1, may not be inconsistent with efficient use of optical imaging systems.

(c) A government entity storing a record on a optical imaging system shall create and store a backup copy of the record at a site other than the site where the original is kept. The government entity shall retain the backup copy and operable retrieval equipment so long as any law requires the original to be retained. The backup copy required by this paragraph must be preserved either

(1) on a non-erasable optical imaging system; or (2) by another reproduction method approved by the records disposition panel.

(d) All contracts for the purchase of optical imaging systems used pursuant to this chapter shall contain terms that insure continued retrievability of the optically stored images and conform to any guidelines that may be established by the information policy office of the department of administration for perpetuation of access to stored data.

VARIOUS STATE TAXES.

CHAPTER 290. INCOME AND FRANCHISE TAXES.

Citation: MS 290.91

✪ **§ 290.91. Destruction of returns.**

The commissioner of revenue is hereby authorized to destroy all tax returns, required under this chapter or chapter 290A, including audit reports, orders, and correspondence relating thereto, which have been on file in the commissioner's office for a period to be determined by the commissioner. The commissioner may make copies of such returns, orders, or correspondence by microfilm, photostat, or other similar means and may immediately destroy the original documents from which such copies have been made. Such copies, when certified to by the commissioner, shall be admissible in evidence in the same manner and be given the same effect as the original documents destroyed.

The commissioner may destroy correspondence and documents contained in the files of the division which do not relate specifically to any tax return.

Notwithstanding the above provisions the commissioner may, utilizing such safeguards as the commissioner in the commissioner's discretion deems necessary, (1) employ a commercial photographer for the purpose of developing microfilm or of documents, or (2) employ a vendor for the purpose of obtaining the vendor's services, an example of which is the preparation of income tax return labels.

CORPORATIONS

CHAPTER 302A. BUSINESS CORPORATIONS.

Citation: MS 302A.461

✍ ☞ **§ 302A.461. Books and records; inspection.**

Subdivision 1. Share register; dates of issuance. (a) A corporation shall keep at its principal executive office, or at another place or places within the United States determined by the board, a share register not more than one year old, containing the names and addresses of the shareholders and the number and classes of shares held by each shareholder.

(b) A corporation shall also keep, at its principal executive office, or at another place or places within the United States determined by the board, a record of the dates on which certificates or transaction statements representing shares were issued.

Subdivision 2. Other documents required. A corporation shall keep at its principal executive office, or, if its principal executive office is outside of this state, shall make available at its registered office within ten days after receipt by an officer of the corporation of a written demand for them made by a person described in subdivision 4, originals or copies of:

(a) Records of all proceedings of shareholders for the last three years;

(b) Records of all proceedings of the board for the last three years;

(c) Its articles and all amendments currently in effect;

(d) Its bylaws and all amendments currently in effect;

(e) Financial statements required by section 302A.463 and the financial statement for the most recent interim period prepared in the course of the operation of the corporation for distribution to the shareholders or to a governmental agency as a matter of public record;

(f) Reports made to shareholders generally within the last three years;

(g) A statement of the names and usual business addresses of its directors and principal officers;

(h) Voting trust agreements described in section 302A.453; and

(i) Shareholder control agreements described in section 302A.457.

(j) A copy of agreements, contracts, or other arrangements or portions of them incorporated by reference under § 302A.401, Subdivision 3.

Subdivision 3. Financial records. A corporation shall keep appropriate and complete financial records.

* * * * *

Subdivision 6. Computerized records. The records maintained by a corporation, including its share register, financial records, and minute books, may utilize any information storage technique, including, for example, punched holes, printed or magnetized spots, or micro-images, even though that makes them illegible visually, if the records can be converted accurately and within a reasonable time, into a form that is legible visually and whose contents are assembled by related subject matter to permit convenient use by people in the normal course of business. A corporation shall convert any of the records referred to in subdivision 4 upon the request of a person entitled to inspect them, and the expense of the conversion shall be borne by the person who bears the expense of copying pursuant to subdivision 5. A copy of the conversion is admissible in evidence, and shall be accepted for all other purposes, to the same extent as the existing or original records would be if they were legible visually.

CHAPTER 317A. NONPROFIT CORPORATIONS

Citation:	MS 317A.461

✍ § 317A.461. Books and Records; Financial Statement.

Subdivision 1. Articles and bylaws; minutes. A corporation shall keep at its registered office correct and complete copies of its articles and bylaws, accounting records, voting agreements, and minutes of meetings of members, board of directors, and committees having any of the authority of the board of directors for the last six years.

Subd. 2. Inspection. A member or a director, or the agent or attorney of a member or a director, may inspect all documents referred to in subdivision 1 or 3 for any proper purpose at any reasonable time. A proper purpose is one reasonably related to the person's interest as a member or director of the corporation.

Subd. 3 Financial statement. Upon request, a corporation shall give the member or the director a statement showing the financial result of all operations and transactions affecting income and surplus during its last annual accounting period and a balance sheet containing a summary of its assets and liabilities as of the closing date of the accounting period.

Subd. 4. Other use prohibited. A member or director who has gained access under this section to any corporate record may not use or furnish to another for use the corporate record or a portion of the contents for any purpose other than a proper purpose. Upon application of the corporation, a court may issue a protective order or order other relief as may be necessary to enforce the provisions of this subdivision.

Subd. 5. Cost of copies. The corporation may charge the requesting party a reasonable fee to cover the expenses of providing copies of documents under this section.

Subd. 6. Computerized records. The records maintained by a corporation may use any information storage technique, even though the technique makes them illegible visually, if the records can be converted accurately and within a reasonable time into a form that is legible visually and whose contents are assembled by related subject matter to permit convenient use by people in the normal course of business. A corporation shall convert any of the records referred to in subdivision 1 or 3 upon the request of the person who bears the expense of copying under subdivision 5. A copy of the conversion is admissible in evidence, and must be accepted for all other purposes, to the same extent as the existing or original records would be if they were legible visually.

Subd. 7. Remedies. A member or a director who is wrongfully denied access to or copies of documents under this section may bring an action for injunctive relief, damages, and costs and reasonable attorney fees.

PART 3. ESTATES OF DECEDENTS; GUARDIANSHIPS.

CHAPTER 525. PROBATE PROCEEDINGS.

Citation:	MS 525.091

✪ § 525.091. Destruction and reproduction of probate records.

Subdivision 1. The court administrator of any county upon order of the judge exercising probate jurisdiction may destroy all the original documents in any proceeding of record in his office five years after the file in such proceeding has been closed provided the original or a Minnesota state archives commission approved photographic, photostatic, microphotographic, microfilmed, or similarly reproduced copy of the original of the following enumerated documents in the proceeding are on file in the office.

Enumerated original documents:

(a) In estates, the jurisdictional petition and proof of publication of the notice of hearing thereof; will and certificate of probate; letters; inventory and appraisal; inheritance tax return or schedule of non-probate assets; inheritance tax return waiver or self assessed inheritance tax return; orders directing and confirming sale, mortgage, lease, or for conveyance of real estate; order setting apart statutory selection; receipts for federal estate taxes and state estate taxes; orders of distribution and general protection; decrees of distribution; federal estate tax closing letter, consent to discharge by commissioner of revenue and order discharging representative; and any amendment of the listed documents.

When an estate is deemed closed as provided in clause (d) of this subdivision, the enumerated documents shall include all claims of creditors.

(b) In guardianships or conservatorships, the jurisdictional petition and order for hearing thereof with proof of service; letters; orders directing and confirming sale, mortgage, lease or for conveyance of real estate; order for restoration to capacity and order discharging guardian; and any amendment of the listed documents.

(c) In mental, inebriety, and indigent matters, the jurisdictional petition, report of examination; warrant of commitment; notice of discharge from institution, or notice of death and order for restoration to capacity, and any amendment of the listed documents.

(d) Except for the enumerated documents described in this subdivision, the court administrator may destroy all other original documents in any probate proceeding without retaining any reproduction of the document. For the purpose of this subdivision, a proceeding in the probate court is deemed closed if no document has been filed in the proceeding for a period of 15 years, except in the cases of wills filed for safe-keeping and those containing wills of decedents not adjudicated upon.

Subd. 2. The court administrator of any county upon order of the probate court judge may destroy the original record books as enumerated in this subdivision provided a Minnesota state archives commission approved photographic, photostatic, microphotographic, microfilmed, or similarly reproduced copy of the original record book is on file in the office.

Enumerated original record books:

(a) All record books kept for recording in compliance with section 525.03, clauses (3), (4), (5), and (6).

(b) All record books kept for inheritance tax purposes in compliance with Minnesota Statutes, Section 291.29, Subdivisions 1 and 2, after the expiration of 15 years from the date of the last proceeding entered therein.

Subd. 3. A photographic, photostatic, microphotographic, microfilmed, or similarly reproduced record is of the same force and effect as the original and may be used as the original document or book of record in all proceedings.

Subd. 4. This section does not apply to the court of any county until the county board of the county adopts a resolution authorizing the destruction of probate records pursuant to the provisions of this section. When the county board has complied with this subdivision, section 525.092 and any act amendatory thereof shall no longer apply to the probate court of that county.

PART 4. REDRESS OF CIVIL INJURIES.

CHAPTER 600. DOCUMENTS AS EVIDENCE.

Citation: MS 600.135

☞ **§ 600.135. Photographic copies of business and public records.**

Subdivision 1. Records; destruction, photographic copies. If any business, institution, member of a profession or calling, or any department or agency of government, in the regular course of business or activity has kept or recorded any memorandum, writing, entry, print, representation or combination thereof, of any act, transaction, occurrence or event, and in the regular course of business has caused any or all of the same to be recorded, copied or reproduced by any photographic, photostatic, microfilm, microcard, miniature photographic, or other process which accurately reproduces or forms a durable medium for so reproducing the original, the original may be destroyed in the regular course of business unless held in a custodial or fiduciary capacity or unless its preservation is required by law. Such reproduction, when satisfactorily identified, is as admissible in evidence as the original itself in any judicial or administrative proceeding whether the original is in existence or not and an enlargement or facsimile of such reproduction is likewise admissible in evidence if the original reproduction is in existence and available for inspection under direction of court. The introduction of a reproduced record, enlargement or facsimile, does not preclude admission of the original.

Subd. 2. "In the regular course of business". The phrase "in the regular course of business" as used in subdivision 1 with reference to making reproductions of originals not held in a custodial or fiduciary capacity nor required by law to be preserved and also with reference to destroying such originals shall be construed to include reproducing at any time and destroying at any time, respectively, if done in good faith and without intent to defraud, and with reference to making reproductions of originals held in a custodial or fiduciary capacity shall be construed to mean reproducing at any time in good faith and without intent to defraud and whether or not made with the intention of thereafter destroying such originals. Neither the manner in which an original is destroyed, whether voluntarily or by casualty or otherwise, nor the fact that it was destroyed while it was held in a custodial or fiduciary capacity shall affect the admissibility of a reproduction. This subdivision shall not be construed to exclude from evidence any document or copy thereof which is otherwise admissible under the rules of evidence.

Subd. 3. Uniform. This section shall be so interpreted and construed as to effectuate its general purpose of making uniform the law of those states which enact it.

Subd. 4. Citation. This section may be cited as the uniform photographic copies of business and public records as evidence act.

Source: Minnesota Rules of Evidence

ARTICLE X. CONTENTS OF WRITINGS, RECORDINGS, AND PHOTOGRAPHS.

[Note: The following excerpts are from the "Uniform Rules of Evidence." See the "Uniform Laws Index" for additional provisions.]

☞ **Rule 1001. Definitions**

For purposes of this article the following definitions are applicable:

(1) *Writings and recordings.* — "Writings" and "recordings" consist of letters, words, or numbers, or their equivalent, set down by handwriting, typewriting, printing, photostating, photographing, magnetic impulse, mechanical or electronic recording, or other form of data compilation.

(2) *Photographs.* — "Photographs" include still photographs, X-ray films, video tapes, and motion pictures.

(3) *Original.* — An "original" of a writing or recording is the writing or recording itself or any counterpart intended to have the same effect by a person executing or issuing it. An "original" of a photograph includes the negative or any print therefrom. If data are stored in a computer or similar device, any printout or other output readable by sight, shown to reflect the data accurately, is an "original".

(4) *Duplicate.* — A "duplicate" is a counterpart produced by the same impression as the original, or from the same matrix, or by means of photography, including enlargements and miniatures, or by mechanical or electronic re-recording, or by chemical reproduction, or by other equivalent techniques which accurately reproduces the original.

☞ **Rule 1003. Admissibility of duplicates.**

A duplicate is admissible to the same extent as an original unless (1) a genuine question is raised as to the authenticity of the original or (2) in the circumstances it would be unfair to admit the duplicate in lieu of the original.

[See Appendix A. Uniform Rules of Evidence for additional provisions.]

Source: Minnesota Rules
Agency: Department of Labor and Industry
Occupational Safety and Health Division

CHAPTER 5210. DEPARTMENT OF LABOR AND INDUSTRY; SAFETY AND HEALTH ADMINISTRATION.

RECORDING AND REPORTING OCCUPATIONAL INJURIES AND ILLNESSES

Citation: MAR 5210.0630

✍ **§ 5210.0630. Log and summary of occupational injuries and illnesses.**

Subpart 1. Employer duty. Each employer shall maintain in

each establishment a log and summary of all recordable occupational injuries and illnesses for that establishment, except that under the circumstances described in subpart 2 an employer may maintain the log and summary of occupational injuries and illnesses at a place other than the establishment. Each employer shall enter each recordable occupational injury and illness on the log as early as practicable but no later than six working days after receiving information that a recordable case has occurred. For this purpose OSHA Form No. 200 or any private equivalent may be used. OSHA Form No. 200 or its equivalent shall be completed in the detail provided in the form and the instructions contained in OSHA Form No. 200. If an equivalent to OSHA Form No. 200 is used, such as a printout from data processing equipment, the information shall be as readable and comprehensible to a person not familiar with the data processing equipment as the OSHA Form No. 200 itself.

Subp. 2. Where log is kept. Any employer may maintain the log of occupational injuries and illnesses at a place other than the establishment or by means of data processing equipment, or both, under the following circumstances:

A. there is available at the place where the log is maintained sufficient information to complete the log to a date within six working days after receiving information that a recordable case has occurred, as required by subpart 1; and

B. at each of the employer's establishments, there is available a copy of the log which reflects separately the injury and illness experience of that establishment complete and current to a date within 45 calendar days.

Subp. 3. Period covered. Logs shall be established on a calendar year basis. The initial log shall include recordable occupational injuries and illnesses occurring on or after January 1, 1974.

Agency: **Department of Revenue**

CHAPTER 8130. SALES AND USE TAXATION.

Citation: **MAR 8130.7500**

✍ § 8130.7500. Returns and records.

* * * * *

Subpart 6. Records, general. Every seller, retailer, and person storing, using, or otherwise consuming in this state tangible personal property purchased from a retailer, and every lessor and lessee of tangible personal property for use in this state shall keep adequate and complete records showing:

A. gross receipts from sales or rental payments from leases of tangible personal property (including any services that are a part of the sale or lease) made within Minnesota irrespective of whether the seller or lessor regards the receipts as taxable or nontaxable;

B. all deductions allowed by law and claimed in filing returns; and

C. total purchase price of all tangible personal property purchased for sale or consumption or lease in Minnesota.

These records must include the normal books of account ordinarily maintained by the average prudent businessman engaged in the activity in question, together with all bills, receipts, invoices, cash register tapes, or other documents of original entry supporting the entries in the books of account as well as all schedules or working papers used in connection with the preparation of tax returns.

Subpart 7. Records; microfilm. Microfilm reproductions of general books of account, such as cash books, journals, voucher registers, ledgers, etc., are not acceptable in lieu of original records. However, microfilm reproductions of supporting records of details, such as sales invoices, purchase invoices, credit memoranda, etc., may be maintained providing the following conditions are met:

A. appropriate facilities are provided for preservation of the films for periods required;

B. microfilm rolls are indexed, cross-referenced , labeled to show beginning and ending numbers or beginning and ending alphabetical listing of documents included, and are systematically filed;

C. the taxpayer agrees to provide transcriptions of any information contained on microfilm which may be required for purposes of verification of tax liability; and

D. proper facilities are provided for the ready inspection and location of the particular records including modern projectors for viewing and copying the records.

A posting reference must be on each invoice. Credit memoranda must carry a reference to the documents evidencing the original transaction. Documents necessary to support claimed exemptions from tax liability, such as bills of lading and purchase orders, must be maintained in an order by which they readily can be related to the transactions for which exemption is sought.

Subpart 8. Records; EDP. "Records" are defined to include punched cards, magnetic tapes, magnetic disk packs, and other machine- sensible data media used for recording, consolidating, and summarizing accounting transactions and records within a taxpayer's electronic data processing system, and all such records are required to be retained so long as their contents may be material in the administration of any provision of the Sales and Use Tax Law. Any machine-sensible records which are clearly not material to the administration of this law need not be retained. The commissioner shall decide the materiality of any such records, and if the materiality of any record is questionable, then such record shall be retained. It shall not be required that taxpayers retain the same data on two or more machine-sensible media, i.e., if the same data is first punched into cards and then transferred to magnetic tape, then it is not necessary to retain the punched cards since the tape must be retained. If there is a duplication of data between punched cards and magnetic tapes, then the tapes shall always be retained rather than the cards.

Although EDP accounting systems will vary from one taxpayer to another, all systems must include a method of producing visible and legible records from the machine-sensible records which will provide the necessary information for the verification of the taxpayer's tax liability. Any records required under this subpart refer to printed "hard copy" records, and do not eliminate the necessity of maintaining the corresponding machine-sensible records as also required by the first paragraph of this subpart. These requirements apply to any taxpayer who maintains any records on EDP. The records to be maintained are as follows:

A. A general ledger, with source references, to coincide with financial reports for sales tax reporting periods. In cases where subsidiary ledgers are used to support the general ledger accounts, the subsidiary ledgers should be written out periodically.

B. The audit trail will be designed so that the details underlying the summary accounting data, such as invoices and vouchers, may be identified and made available to the department upon request.

C. The records must provide the opportunity to trace any transaction back to the original source or forward to a final total. If printouts are not made at the time of processing, then the system must have the ability to reconstruct these transactions.

D. Adequate record-retention facilities must be available for storing all machine-sensible records as well as supporting documents.

E. A general description of the EDP portion of the accounting system includes but is not limited to:

(1) standard programming conventions and procedures including flowcharting conventions, decisions table conventions, coding conventions, standard glossary and standard abbreviations, standard programming techniques, and debugging procedures and techniques;

(2) documentation of the system including a problem statement, system flowcharts, operator instructions, record layouts, program flowcharts and sense switches, program listings, test data, and approval and changes log; and

(3) standard operating procedures and control procedures, including the reconciliation of EDP controls to non-EDP controls, error listings and error logs, and any other controls, either EDP or manual, used to ensure accurate and reliable processing.

Any taxpayer retaining disbursement or revenue records on machine-sensible records for any individual original transactions, or any summary of such transactions subject to the tax under the provisions of the Sales and Use Tax Law shall separately show the amount of sales tax paid or the amount of sales tax collected. It shall be permissible, however, to group all taxable sales or all taxable purchases into various accounts, all of which are taxable, providing that if a nontaxable transaction is combined with a taxable transaction in the same account, then with respect to each individual transaction, the tax shall be separately shown in the machine-sensible record.

Agency:	**Minnesota Historical Society** **State Archives Department**
Source:	**Minnesota Historical Society Guidelines**

✪ REPRODUCTION OF GOVERNMENT RECORDS USING IMAGING SYSTEMS

Purpose

This guideline explains the standards to be used for the reproduction of government records using imaging systems. The standards related to this issues are:

1. ANSI/AIIM Standard S44-1988 - Recommended Practices for Quality Control of Image Scanners

2. ANSI/AIIM MS53 - File Format for Storage and Exchange of Images, or Bi-level File Format: Part 1

3. CCITT Group 3 or Group 4 Compression Techniques

This guideline explains when the standards are appropriate and required to be used. It also explains the management and technical aspects of reproducing government records using imaging systems related to the standards.

Minnesota Statutes 15.17 Subd. 1 requires the Minnesota Historical Society to specify standards for the reproduction of government records. This guideline and the standards they explain are in fulfillment of that law.

Other public policy specifically related to this issue are found in Minnesota Statues Chapter 13 (Minnesota Government Data Practices Act), Chapter 15.17 (Official Records Act), Chapter 138.17 (Government Records Act), and all other state and federal statutory requirements relating to data practices and records management.

Audience

This guideline is intended to be used by managers with general responsibility for the design, procurement, construction, installation, operation, and control of systems that will use imaging technology.

When Does This Guideline Apply?

This guideline for the reproduction of government records using imaging systems must be observed if *both* the following conditions exist:

- the records have been determined to be permanent or archivally valuable, and
- the record custodian is not retaining the original records permanently or reproducing them on microfilm as a security measure.

This guideline summarizes current industry consensus as to the best policies and practices for establishing and operating an image system. Observance of this guideline will help ensure an effective, legally acceptable, and cost-efficient program. Record custodians are urged to adopt it for *all* imaging applications, regardless of the retention requirements of the source documents.

How Do I Know If The Records Are Permanent Or Archival?

Records can be identified as permanent or archival in several ways.

- They are specifically required to be kept permanently by state statute.
- The public office responsible for the records designates them as permanent.
- They are designated as permanent by the state records disposition panel or identified as archival by the state archives as part of the process for submitting a request to dispose of original records. By statute, virtually no government record in Minnesota may be destroyed without prior authorization of the panel. Securing approval is a simple, one-time process that is described in a leaflet entitled *Procedures for the Proper Disposal of Government Records* which is available from the State Archives Department of the Minnesota Historical Society. The Archives staff provides assistance with this process. Determining the appropriate retention period of the source documents and securing the state records disposition panel's approval of the retention period selected should be completed before an imaging system becomes operational.

1.0 MANAGEMENT ISSUES

1.1 System Selection.

a. Government entities should conduct a feasibility study prior to implementation of an imaging system. This study should analyze conversion and ongoing costs of such a system and compare them to current costs of doing business. The study should identify and consider the needs of all users of the records, as well as future storage, equipment, and migration costs. (State government agencies are required to comply with related information resource development standards, policies, and guidelines promulgated by the Information Policy Office of the Department of Administration.)

b. Government entities should consider systems with open rather than proprietary designs to ensure maximum flexibility of equipment choice and to support interconnection, information systems integration, and information sharing.

c. Government entities shall ensure continued retrievability of records stored in imaging systems for as long as they are required by law to be retained. This statutory requirement is an important consideration. The hardware and software involved in electronic storage systems will inevitably become obsolete and need to be replaced many times over the lifetime of these records. The record custodian is required by law to continue to make the information accessible as the records migrate from one system to another. The data must be kept available. There are several strategies for achieving this requirement.

1. Select a new system that is 100% backwardly compatible with the previous one. This means that the new system will be able to "read" or reproduce any image "captured" by any previously used system. The initial selection of a system with an open, non-proprietary architecture will facilitate this option.

ii. Covert 100% of existing image and index data to the new system.

iii. Retain a copy of the data and maintain the obsolete retrieval equipment in working condition so long as the records are required to be kept by law. This is probably not a viable, long-term solution for records that must be kept permanently.

iv. Reproduce records and their indexes onto permanent microfilm as an alternative to migrating seldom used information to new systems.

1.2 Systems Administration

a. *Public access and privacy.* Government entities shall ensure that data in imaging systems is maintained in conformity with the Minnesota Government Data Practices Act. This law defines categories of records that are restricted or available to the public. Where information is restricted, procedures must ensure that it is protected from unauthorized access. Open record must be available as required by statute. Other laws, specific to governmental jurisdictions, functions, or records, also may require protection of certain data.

b. *Risk Management.* Government entities shall develop a comprehensive risk or disaster prevention and recovery plan.

c. *Legal Admissibility.* Government records stored in imaging systems that meet this guideline are "deemed for all purposes to be the original recording" and are" admissible as evidence in all courts and proceedings of every kind" according to Minnesota statute. As evidence that images in the system were produced in the regular course of business, the system administrator should prepare a policy statement that describes the mission of the office, the purpose and use of the imaging system, and the safeguards that are employed in its operations. The system documentation in section 2.6 of this guideline will provide an appropriate basis for such a policy statement.

2.0 TECHNICAL ISSUES

2.1 Storage Media

a. Only non-reusable media shall be used for imaging systems.

b. The storage media used shall have a certified pre-write shelf life of at least five years and post-write shelf life of at least 20 years, based on accelerated aging tests that apply to specific locations on the media surface.

2.2 Scanning

a. Scanner quality must be evaluated based on the standards procedures in *American National Standard for Information and Image Management — Recommended Practices for Quality Control of Image Scanners* (ANSI/AIIM Standard S44-1988 or latest version). Every image should be verified or test targets should be scanned at the start of each shift to determine the correctness of scanner settings.

b. Scanning density shall be no less than 200 dots per inch for textual documents containing no type font smaller than six point.

c. Scanning density shall be no less than 300 dots per inch for engineering drawings, maps, and other documents with background detail or small type.

d. Scanners shall receive periodic maintenance as specified by the manufacturer and shall be recalibrated at least annually.

2.3 Quality Assurance

a. Index entry verification shall be performed to ensure that all the images are retrievable.

b. The satisfactory quality of each image shall be visually verified to ensure that it is a legible representation of the original image.

c. A sample of recorded images should be retrieved from the storage media and displayed for inspection and comparison with the source documents to confirm that the optical drives, storage media, and other system components are working properly. Initially, this should be done on a daily basis and periodically thereafter.

2.4 Image File Headers

A standard image file header should be used. Since even some standard headers such as Tagged Image File Format (TIFF) are available in a variety of implementations, the vendor should supply a detailed definition of the image file header structure employed. If a proprietary header is used, the system must provide a bridge to a non-proprietary header label standard such as ANSI/AIIM MS53, File Format for Storage and Exchange of Images, or Bi-level File Format: Part 1.

2.5 Compression

Imaging systems shall utilize the Consultative Committee on International Telegraphy and Telephony (CCITT) Group 3 or Group 4 compression techniques without proprietary alterations to the algorithm. If the use of a proprietary compression algorithm is unavoidable, the system must provide a gateway to either Group 3 or Group 4 standards (or to a compression standard subsequently adopted by the American National Standards Institute).

2.6 Documentation

Government entities shall maintain full technical, operation, and security documentation of the system. This will include at least the following information:

a. *Hardware.* Types, brand names, model numbers, and dates of installation of all hardware components of the system.

b. *Software.* Version numbers, implementation dates, and backup copies of all systems software and applications programs. To ensure that data in the system can be migrated to new software in the future, system administrators should consider requiring the seller of the system to deposit a copy of the computer code with a bank or other storage facility for use by the administrator in case the vendor's business should fail.

c. *Operating procedures.* The description of methods for scanning or entering data and revising, updating, or expunging records; hardware and software operating manuals; indexing techniques; backup procedures for disks, tapes, microfilm, etc.; procedures for testing the readability of records; security safeguards to prevent tampering and unauthorized access to protected information; and the disposition of the source documents. The inclusion of appropriate logging and tracking procedures to provide necessary audit trails is very important. Such documentation is part of a legally acceptable records management program and vital to assuring the legal admissibility of records stored in imaging systems.

d. *System Security.* A description of physical security procedures, network and system security protocols, and password management.

2.7 Storage

a. Government entities shall adhere to the manufacturer's recommendations in the storage of working copies of indexes, images, and other system components used in imaging systems. Security copies of these documents and their indexes should be housed off-site, in an area with stable environmental conditions appropriate to the electronic media involved. Room temperatures between 65 and 75 degrees Fahrenheit and relative humidity between 40 and 45 percent are the current standard for magnetic media. These conditions should also be observed for security copies maintained on optical, compact disk, or other electronic media until formal national standards are published.

b. Government entities must ensure readability of electronically stored images. A sampling of images from both primary and security storage media must be read annually to verify continued accessibility. Imaging system data that is maintained on electronic media must be recopied onto new media at least once every 10 years.

c. Security copies shall be marked with appropriate external labels that identify the government entity, system and software used, and any access restrictions. The government entity shall maintain specific, detailed documentation of the contents of and the system specifications needed to access each security tape or disk.

2.8 Security Copies

a. Government entities shall establish a system for the regularly scheduled production of copies of system images and indexes as a security measure through batch copying onto disk or magnetic tape or simultaneous recording.

b. Security copies must be stored at another site.

c. Indexes stored on separate magnetic media should be copied to the optical media for additional security.

2.9 Media

Separately maintained indexes and system security backups shall be afforded the same level of security, quality control, preservation, and transferability to new systems described in this guideline regardless of the electronic media employed.

State: Mississippi
Source: Mississippi Code Annotated

TITLE 9. COURTS.

CHAPTER 7. CIRCUIT COURTS

Citation: MCA 9-7-128

✪ **§ 9-7-128. Disposal and destruction of certain case files and loose records; electronic storage of certain files, records and documents.**

(1) Where there is no requirement for a permanent record to be made, the clerk, upon order of the court, may dispose of and destroy all case files of the circuit or county court which have been in existence for ten (10) years or which have been reduced to judgment and that judgment satisfied and canceled. The clerk may also dispose of and destroy any loose records not required by law to be kept as permanent records after a period of ten (10) years. No records, however, may be destroyed without the approval of the Director of the Department of Archives and History.

(2) The files, records and other documents described herein may, upon order of the court in accordance with the provisions of this section, be electronically stored for convenience and efficiency in storage. The electronic storage of documents, for purposes of this section, shall have the same meaning as set forth in Section 9-1-51. In those counties electing to store files, records and documents by means of electronic storage, the following described case files shall be electronically stored after the time period described below have elapsed:

(a) Cases in county criminal or civil court which have been dismissed or in which a judgment has been entered at least three (3) years prior to the date upon which they are electronically stored; and

(b) Cases in circuit criminal or civil court which have been dismissed or in which a judgment has been entered at least five (5) years prior to the date upon which they are electronically stored.

(3) Nothing in this section shall serve as authority to destroy any docket book, minute book, issue docket, subpoena docket, witness docket book, execution docket book, voter registration book, marriage record book, trial order, abstract of judgment, judgment roll, criminal file where an indictment was returned and the defendant convicted if the file is not at least twenty (20) years old, habeas corpus docket, preliminary hearing docket or Supreme Court appeals docket.

TITLE 13. EVIDENCE, PROCESS AND JURIES.

CHAPTER 1. EVIDENCE.

Citation: MCA 13-1-151

✍ **§ 13-1-151. Reproduction of business records; disposal of originals.**

Any business may cause any or all records kept by such business in the regular course of its operation to be recorded, copied or reproduced by any photographic, photostatic or miniature photographic process which correctly, accurately and permanently copies, reproduces or forms a medium for copying or reproducing the original record on a film or other durable material, and such business may thereafter dispose of the original record, provided that every original record pertaining to any claim, tax or report due the State of Mississippi or any of its agencies shall be preserved for five (5) years from the thirty-first day of December of the year in which such claim arose, or such tax or report was due.

TITLE 19. COUNTIES AND COUNTY OFFICERS.

CHAPTER 15. RECORDS AND RECORDING.

Citation: MCA 19-15-1

✪ ✍ **§ 19-15-1. Preservation of essential public records of county governments.**

The legislature declares that records containing information essential to the operation of government and to the protection of the rights and interests of persons should be protected against the destructive effect of all forms of disaster whether fire, flood, storm, earthquake, explosion or other disaster, and whether such occurrence is caused by an act of nature or man, including an enemy of the United States. It is, therefore, necessary to adopt special provisions for the preservation of essential records of counties, and this section shall be liberally construed to effect its purposes. However, it is the express intention of this section that the provisions herein contained are not mandatory but are permissive only and shall authorize preservation of records as herein contemplated within the discretion of the governing authorities of the counties of the state.

The board of supervisors of any county is hereby authorized and empowered in its discretion to preserve essential records or any portion thereof, of such county deemed by the board of supervisors to be an essential record necessary to the operation of government in an emergency created by disaster or containing information necessary to protect the rights and interests of persons or to establish and affirm the powers and duties of governments in the resumption of operations after the destruction or damage of the original records.

The board of supervisors of any such county is authorized and empowered in its discretion to make and enter into contracts and agreements with any person, firm or corporation to make and prepare such copies or duplicates of records, and to provide for and enter into contracts concerning the safekeeping and preservation of such copies or duplicates at points of storage at a location within the state other than the legally designated or customary location and depository of the original of such records.

In the event that the original record or records shall have been destroyed, any such photographic or photostatic copy or reproduction shall be deemed to be an original record for all purposes and shall be treated as an original record in all courts or administrative agencies for the purpose of its admissibility in evidence. An enlargement or facsimile of such reproduction is likewise admissible in evidence if the original reproduction is in existence and available for inspection under direction of the court.

The board of supervisors of any such county is authorized and empowered, in its discretion, to appropriate and expend moneys out of the available funds of such county for the purposes of this section.

Citation: MCA 19-15-3

✪ **§ 19-15-3. Reproduction of certain county records; destruction of originals.**

Whenever any county records, documents, files or papers whatsoever which are required by law to be preserved and retained, or which are necessary or desirable to be preserved or retained, shall have been so retained and preserved for a period of six years, the board of supervisors of such county shall have the power and authority, in its discretion, to destroy or dispose of any such records, documents, files or papers after having reproductions made thereof as hereinafter provided.

Whenever the board of supervisors of any such county shall desire to destroy or dispose of any such records, documents, files or papers such board shall first cause the same to be electronically stored using microfilm, microfiche, data processing, computers, magnetic tape, optical disks, or other medium. If the county wherein such records and the like are to be destroyed or disposed of does not have or own the necessary equipment to reproduce same, the said board of supervisors shall be authorized and empowered to enter into a contract for the reproduction thereof, which contract may be for a period of not more than twelve (12) months from the date thereof. Said contract shall be awarded to the lowest and best bidder after said board of supervisors shall have advertised its intentions of awarding such contract by publication of a notice thereof once each week for at least three (3) consecutive weeks in some newspaper published or having a general circulation in such county.

After such reproduction of such records and the like shall have been made the said board of supervisors shall have the power and authority to destroy and dispose of the originals thereof and such reproductions shall thereafter be preserved, retained and stored by said board of supervisors as a permanent record of such county, and provision shall be made for preserving, examining and using the same. Any such reproductions or copy of any original record or other document shall be deemed to be the original record for all purposes and shall be admissible as evidence in all courts or administrative agencies. A facsimile, exemplification or certified copy thereof shall, for all purposes set forth herein be deemed to be a transcript, exemplification or certified copy of the original record.

The board of supervisors of any county is hereby authorized to pay all expenses incurred in reproducing such records and the like and in making provision for the preservation, retention, and storage of such reproductions from the general fund of such county.

When any of the records and the like of which reproductions are made under the provisions of this section, are declared by law, or are by their nature, confidential and privileged records, then the reproduction thereof shall likewise be deemed to be confidential and privileged to the same extent as the original records and the like.

Nothing herein shall be construed to require the keeping and preservation of any records and documents which are not required by law to be kept and preserved, or which it is not desirable or necessary to keep and preserve, and in all cases where records and the like are authorized by law to be destroyed or disposed of in a lesser period than six (6) years, such may be disposed of as authorized by the statute pertaining thereto.

Citation: MCA 19-15-5

✪ **§ 19-15-5. Equipment for electronic storage of documents for chancery clerks.**

The board of supervisors of any county is authorized and empowered, in its discretion, to purchase all the necessary equipment and supplies needed for the electronic storage of documents out of the general fund of said county. Before purchasing such equipment advertisement shall be made, as required by law for letting of bids, and the board shall purchase the equipment from the lowest and best bidder on the type machine desired to be purchased. Such machine shall be under the control and supervision of the chancery clerk and shall be part of the equipment of the chancery clerk's office.

TITLE 21. MUNICIPALITIES.

CHAPTER 15. OFFICERS AND RECORDS.

Citation: MCA 21-15-35

✪ **§ 21-15-35. Preservation of essential public records of municipal governments.**

The legislature declares that records containing information essential to the operation of government and to the protection of the rights and interests of persons should be protected against the destructive effect of all forms of disaster whether fire, flood, storm, earthquake, explosion or other disaster, and whether such occurrence is caused by an act of nature or man, including an enemy of the United States. It is, therefore, necessary to adopt special provisions for the preservation of essential records of municipalities, and this section shall be liberally construed to effect its purposes. However, it is the express intention of this section that the provisions herein contained are not mandatory but are permissive only and shall authorize preservation of records as herein contemplated within the discretion of the governing authorities of the municipalities of the state.

The governing authorities of any municipality within the state, regardless of the form of government under which they operate, are each hereby authorized and empowered in its discretion to make or cause to be made by means of photography, microphotography, photocopying, film or microfilm a copy or copies of the records, or any portion thereof, of such county, deemed by the board of supervisors to be an essential record necessary to the operation of government in an emergency created by disaster or containing information necessary to protect the rights and interests of persons or to establish and affirm the powers and duties of governments in the resumption of operations after the destruction or damage of the original records.

The governing authorities of such municipalities are authorized and empowered in its discretion to make and enter into contracts and agreements with any person, firm or corporation to make and prepare such copies or duplicates of records, and to provide for and enter into contracts concerning the safekeeping and preservation of such copies or duplicates at points of storage at a location within the state other than the legally designated or customary location and depository of the original of such records.

In the event that the original record or records shall have been destroyed, any such photographic or photostatic copy or reproduction shall be deemed to be an original record for all purposes and shall be treated as an original record in all courts or administrative agencies for the purpose of its admissibility in evidence. An enlargement or facsimile of such reproduction is likewise admissible in evidence if the original reproduction is in existence and available for inspection under direction of the court.

The governing authorities of any municipality within the state, regardless of the form of government under which they operate, are authorized and empowered, in its discretion, to appropriate and expend moneys out of the available funds of such municipality for the purposes of this section.

Citation: MCA 21-15-37

☞ ✪ § 21-15-37. Reproduction of municipal records; destruction of originals.

(1) The governing authority of a municipality shall have the power and authority, in its discretion, to destroy or dispose of any records, documents, files or papers which are required by law to be preserved and retained, or which are necessary or desirable to be preserved or retained, after having reproductions made thereof. However, nothing herein shall authorize the destruction or disposal of any books containing the minutes of the governing authority, dockets of any court, the minute books of any court, registration books or any other books or records which it is desirable or necessary to retain and preserve in their original form.

(2) Any reproductions or copy of any original record or other documents shall be deemed to be the original record for all purposes and shall be admissible as evidence in all courts or administrative agencies. A facsimile, exemplification or certified copy thereof shall, for all purposes set forth herein, be deemed to be a transcript, exemplification or certified copy of the original record.

(3) The governing authority of any municipality is hereby authorized to pay all expenses incurred in reproducing such records or other documents and in making provision for the preservation, retention and storage of such reproduction from the general support fund of such municipality.

(4) When any of the records or documents of which reproductions are made under the provisions of this section, are declared by law, or are by their nature, confidential and privileged records, then the reproduction thereof shall likewise be deemed to be confidential and privileged to the same extent as the original records or document.

(5) Nothing herein shall be construed to require the keeping and preservation of any records and documents which are not required by law to be kept and preserved, or which it is not desirable or necessary to keep and preserve, and in all cases where records and the like are authorized by law to be destroyed or disposed of in a lesser period than six years, which may be disposed of as authorized by the statute pertaining thereto.

(6) Municipalities may develop records control schedules as defined by Section 25-59-3(h) and destroy records in accordance with the retention schedules when approved by the Director of the Department of Archives and History.

TITLE 25. PUBLIC OFFICERS AND EMPLOYEES; PUBLIC RECORDS.

Citation: MCA 25-59-29

✪ § 25-59-29. Reproduction of records and storage of copies; destruction of originals.

Any custodian of public records as defined by this chapter is authorized to photocopy, microfilm or produce on film or by electronic method any part of the records kept by the office concerned unless otherwise prohibited by law or withheld from reproduction in the public interest. Such copies shall be produced by equipment and systems which shall accurately reproduce and preserve the original record in all details and in a durable form. Each agency shall preserve such photocopies, electrostatic copies or films in conveniently accessible files and provide for preserving, examining and using them. If the records are of enduring value to the agency concerned or are determined to be of archival value by the Mississippi Department of Archives and History, the reproduction and storage methods and procedures used must meet standards approved by the department. One (1) master copy of each record of enduring or archival value filmed shall be deposited with the department. Custodians of public records may destroy the original records from which the photographs, microphotographs, films or electrostatic copies have been made, or any part of them, provided that (a) the records are of no value to the agency concerned, (b) the Mississippi Department of Archives and History certified that the records may be destroyed through the provisions of retention schedules approved by the state records committee, and (c) the records microfilmed or reproduced and approved for destruction are reported to the Mississippi Department of Archives and History in such manner as it may direct. Any such reproduction or copy of any original record or other document shall be deemed to be the original record for all purposes and shall be admissible in evidence in all courts or administrative agencies. A facsimile, exemplified or certified copy thereof shall for all purposes be deemed to be a transcript or certified copy of the original record.

TITLE 27. TAXATION AND FINANCE.

CHAPTER 69. TOBACCO TAX.

Citation: MCA 27-69-35

✍ § 27-69-35. Records of dealers.

It shall be the duty of every person subject to the provisions of this chapter, to keep an accurate set of records, showing all transactions had with reference to the purchase, sale or gift of cigars, cigarettes, or smoking tobacco, and such person shall keep separately all invoices of cigars, cigarettes or smoking tobacco, and shall keep a record of all stamps purchased, and such records, and all stocks of cigars, cigarettes or smoking tobacco on hand, shall be open to inspection at all reasonable times to the commissioner; provided, however, that all retail dealers, transient vendors, distributing agents, or other dealers purchasing, or receiving cigars, cigarettes, or smoking tobacco from without the state, whether the same shall have been ordered through a wholesaler, or jobber in this state, or by drop shipment, or otherwise, shall within five (5) days after receipt of the same, mail a duplicate invoice of all such purchases, or receipts, to the commissioner, and failure to furnish such duplicate invoices shall be deemed a misdemeanor.

TITLE 79. CORPORATIONS, ASSOCIATIONS, AND PARTNERSHIPS.

CHAPTER 4. MISSISSIPPI BUSINESS CORPORATION ACT.

Article. 16. Records and Reports.

Subarticle A. Records.

Citation: **MCA 79-4-16.03**

✍ § 79-4-16.03. Scope of inspection right.

(a) A shareholder's agent or attorney has the same inspection and copying rights as the shareholder he represents.
(b) The right to copy records under Section 79-4-16.02 includes, if reasonable, the right to receive copies made by photographic, xerographic or other means.
(c) The corporation may impose a reasonable charge, covering the costs of labor and material, for copies of any documents provided to the shareholder. the charge may not exceed the estimated cost of production or reproduction of the records.
(d) The corporation may comply with a shareholder's demand to inspect the record of shareholders under Section 79-4-16.02(b)(3) by providing him with a list of its shareholders that was compiled no earlier than the date of the shareholder's demand.

TITLE 81. BANKS AND FINANCIAL INSTITUTIONS.

CHAPTER 12. SAVINGS ASSOCIATIONS.

Citation: **MCA 81-12-111**

✪ § 81-12-111. Records; reproduction by photostatic, photographic or microfilming process.

Any association may cause any or all records kept by such association to be copied or reproduced by any photostatic, photographic, or microfilming process which correctly and permanently copies, reproduces or forms a medium for copying or reproducing the original record on a film or other durable material, and such association may thereafter dispose of the original record. Any such copy or reproduction shall be deemed to be an original record for all purposes and shall be treated as an original record in all courts or administrative agencies for the purpose of its admissibility in evidence. A facsimile, exemplification or certified copy of any such copy or reproduction reproduced from a film record shall, for all purposes, be deemed a facsimile. exemplification or certified copy of the original record.

Source: **Mississippi Rules of Evidence**

ARTICLE X. CONTENTS OF WRITINGS, RECORDINGS AND PHOTOGRAPHS.

☞ Rule 1001. Definitions

For purposes of this article the following definitions are applicable:
(1) *Writings and recordings.* — "Writings" and "recordings" consist of letters, words, or numbers, or their equivalent, set down by handwriting, typewriting, printing, photostating, photographing, magnetic impulse, mechanical or electronic recording, or other form of data compilation.
(2) *Photographs.* — "Photographs" include still photographs, X-ray films, video tapes, and motion pictures.
(3) *Original.* — An "original" of a writing or recording is the writing or recording itself or any counterpart intended to have the same effect by a person executing or issuing it. An "original" of a photograph includes the negative or any print therefrom. If data are stored in a computer or similar device, any printout or other output readable by sight, shown to reflect the data accurately, is an "original".
(4) *Duplicate.* — A "duplicate" is a counterpart produced by the same impression as the original, or from the same matrix, or by means of photography, including enlargements and miniatures, or by mechanical or electronic re-recording, or by chemical reproduction, or by other equivalent techniques which accurately reproduces the original.

☞ Rule 1003. Admissibility of duplicates.

A duplicate is admissible to the same extent as an original unless (1) a genuine question is raised as to the authenticity of the original or (2) in the circumstances it would be unfair to admit the duplicate in lieu of the original.
[See Appendix A. Uniform Rules of Evidence for additional provisions.]

State: **Missouri**
Source: **Missouri Revised Statutes**

TITLE 8. PUBLIC OFFICERS, BONDS AND RECORDS.

CHAPTER 109. PUBLIC AND BUSINESS RECORDS.

Transcribing and Rebinding

Citation: **MRS 109.100**

✪ § 109.100. Photographic copies of records.

Wherever the statute authorizes books or records to be rebound, or their contents transcribed into new books, or new indexes to be made, the making of photographic copies of said books, records or indexes shall be deemed transcribing and the binding together of such photographic copies shall be deemed rebinding of such records within the meaning of this section.

Citation: **MRS 109.110**

☞ § 109.110. Transcript to be evidence, when.

After any book or record so transcribed is examined by the judge or justices of such courts, respectively, ordering the same to be transcribed, and he or they shall make an order on the records of the court that the same is correct, the same faith and credit shall be given to the transcript that the book or record transcribed was entitled.

Citation: **MRS 109.120**

☞ § 109.120. Records reproduced by photostatic process — cost— marginal releases prohibited.

1. The head of any business, industry, profession, occupation or calling, or the head of any state, county or municipal

department, commission, bureau or board may cause any and all records kept by such official, department, commission, bureau, board or business to be photographed, microphotographed, photostated or transferred to other material using photographic, video, or electronic processes and the judges and justices of the several courts of record within this state may cause all closed case files more than five years old to be photographed, microphotographed, photostated or transferred to other material using photographic, video, or electronic processes.

Such reproducing material shall be of durable material and the device used to reproduce the records shall be such as to accurately reproduce and perpetuate the original records in all details.

2. The cost of reproduction of closed files of the several courts of record as provided herein shall be chargeable to the county and paid out of the county treasury wherein that court is situated.

3. When any recorder of deeds in this state is required or authorized by law to record, copy, file, recopy, replace or index any document, plat, map or written instrument, he may do so by photostatic, photographic, microphotographic, microfilm, or similar mechanical process which produces a clear, accurate and permanent copy of the original. The reproductions so made may be used as permanent records of the original. When microfilm or a similar reproduction is used as a permanent record by recorder of deeds, duplicate reproductions of all recorded documents, indexes and files required by law to be kept by him shall be made and one copy of each document shall be stored in a fireproof vault and the other copy shall be readily available in his office together with suitable equipment for viewing the filmed record by projection to a size not smaller than the original and for reproducing copies of the recorded or filmed documents for any person entitled thereto. In all cases where instruments are recorded under the provisions of this section by microfilm, any release, assignment or other instrument affecting a previously recorded instrument by microfilm may not be made by marginal entry but shall be filed and recorded as a separate instrument and shall be in a separate book, cross-indexed to the document which it affects.

Citation: **MRS 109.130**

☞ **§ 109.130. Reproduced records deemed original, when.**

Such reproduction of the original records shall be deemed to be an original record for all purposes provided that the reproduction is equal in resolution to microfilm produced under those standards set forth in subsection 4 of section 109.241 and shall be admissible in evidence in all courts or administrative agencies. A facsimile, exemplification, or certified copy thereof shall, for all purposes recited in sections 109.120 and 109.140, be deemed to be a transcript, exemplification or certified copy of the original.

Citation: **MRS 109.140**

✪ **§ 109.140. Disposition of court records, how authorized — methods of disposition.**

The supreme court may authorize the disposition of its own closed court files and records more than five years old and such files and records of the several courts of record. Disposition may consist of destroying useless or duplicative files or records, or providing for archival storage of files or records, or the destruction of court files and records when photostatic copies, photographs, microphotographs or reproductions on film are made and placed in conveniently accessible files and provisions are made for preserving, examining and using them.

Citation: **MRS 109.156**

✪ **§ 109.156. Original may be destroyed after reproduction, exceptions.**

Following the reproduction of a record or records in the manner provided for in section 109.120, the head of any business may destroy the record or records from which such reproduction was made; provided, that this section shall not authorize the destruction of an original record of or relating to any asset or liability shown on the face of such record to be existing or outstanding.

TITLE 10. TAXATION AND REVENUE.

CHAPTER 144. SALES AND USE TAX.

Sales Tax

Citation: **MRS 144.190**

☞ **§ 144.190. Refund of overpayments — claim for refund — time for making claims — paid to whom — direct pay agreement for certain purchasers, collection fee deduction not permitted.**

1. If a tax has been incorrectly computed by reason of a clerical error or mistake on the part of the director of revenue, such fact shall be set forth in the records of the director of revenue, and the amount of the overpayment shall be credited on any taxes then due from the person legally obligated to remit the tax under sections 144.010 to 144.525, and the balance shall be refunded to the person legally obligated to remit the tax, his administrators or executors, as provided for in section 144.200.

2. If any tax, penalty or interest has been paid more than once, or has been erroneously or illegally collected, or has been erroneously or illegally computed, such sum shall be credited on any taxes then due from the person legally obligated to remit the tax under sections 144.010 to 144.525, and the balance, with interest as determined by section 32.065, RSMo, shall be refunded to the person, but no such credit or refund shall be allowed unless duplicate copies of a claim for refund are filed within three years from the date of overpayment.

* * * * *

TITLE 24. BUSINESS AND FINANCIAL INSTITUTIONS.

CHAPTER 369. SAVINGS AND LOAN ASSOCIATIONS.

Citation: **MRS 369.129**

✪ **§ 369.129. Association records, how kept.**

* * * * *

2. The director of the division of finance may by regulation permit accounting, bookkeeping, data processing or other recordkeeping services to be performed for an association by contract or otherwise, whether on or off its premises, but shall require assurances satisfactory to the director that the performance of such services will be subject to regulation and examination by the director of the division of finance to the same extent as if such service were being performed by the association itself

on its own premises.

3. In the absence of a regulation of the director of the division of finance establishing a different time, each association shall preserve all of its records of original or final entries for a period of ten years from the date of making the last entry thereon, but coupons accompanying deposits in a club account such as a Christmas club need not be retained for more than two years from the date of closing of such account.

4. In lieu of the original, film, photographic, photostatic or other copies which accurately reproduce all lines and markings on the original may be retained. Any copy of a record permitted to be kept in lieu of the original shall be admissible in evidence in any proceeding with the same effect as though it were the original.

Source: Supreme Court Rules

✪ Order of the Supreme Court — 1971

Courts of Appeals, August 21, 1971

Pursuant to authority contained in § 109.140(2), RSMo 1969, it is ordered:

That the disposal, archival storage or destruction of court files of the Courts of Appeals in all cases which have been closed and no action taken for more than ten years is hereby authorized, provided:

1. Such files are reproduced in accordance with § 109.120, RSMo 1969.
2. The reproductions are placed in conveniently accessible files, and provisions are made for preserving, examining and using them.
3. All action taken with respect thereto shall be under the authority and direction of the Judges of the Courts of Appeals, and any rules, or methods of preservation, and examination and use, or fees charged for reproducing shall be fixed by such Court of Appeals.

✪ Order of the Supreme Court — 1971 Probate Courts

It appearing to the Court that the disposal, archival storage or destruction of the Court files of the Probate Courts should be authorized in all cases which have been closed and no action taken for five years, instead of ten years as provided in order entered September 20, 1966, it is, therefore, ORDERED, pursuant to authority contained in § 109.140(2) RSMo 1969, V.A.M.S., that the disposal, archival storage or destruction of Court files of the Probate Courts in all cases which have been closed and no action taken for more than five years is hereby authorized, provided:

1. Such files are reproduced in accordance with § 109.120, RSMo 1969.
2. The reproductions are placed in conveniently accessible files, and provisions are made for preserving, examining and using them.
3. All action taken with respect thereto shall be under the authority and direction of the Judges of the Courts of Appeals, and any rules, or methods of preservation, and examination and use, or fees charged for reproducing shall be fixed by such Court of Appeals.

Source: Missouri Rules of Evidence

ARTICLE X. CONTENTS OF WRITINGS, RECORDINGS AND PHOTOGRAPHS.

☞ Rule 1001. Definitions

For purposes of this article the following definitions are applicable:

(1) *Writings and recordings.* — "Writings" and "recordings" consist of letters, words, or numbers, or their equivalent, set down by handwriting, typewriting, printing, photostating, photographing, magnetic impulse, mechanical or electronic recording, or other form of data compilation.

(2) *Photographs.* — "Photographs" include still photographs, X-ray films, video tapes, and motion pictures.

(3) *Original.* — An "original" of a writing or recording is the writing or recording itself or any counterpart intended to have the same effect by a person executing or issuing it. An "original" of a photograph includes the negative or any print therefrom. If data are stored in a computer or similar device, any printout or other output readable by sight, shown to reflect the data accurately, is an "original".

(4) *Duplicate.* — A "duplicate" is a counterpart produced by the same impression as the original, or from the same matrix, or by means of photography, including enlargements and miniatures, or by mechanical or electronic re-recording, or by chemical reproduction, or by other equivalent techniques which accurately reproduces the original.

☞ Rule 1003. Admissibility of duplicates.

A duplicate is admissible to the same extent as an original unless (1) a genuine question is raised as to the authenticity of the original or (2) in the circumstances it would be unfair to admit the duplicate in lieu of the original.

State: Montana
Source: Montana Code Annotated

TITLE 2. GOVERNMENT STRUCTURE AND ADMINISTRATION.

CHAPTER 6. PUBLIC RECORDS.

Part 1. Public Records Generally.

Citation: MCA 2-6-111

✪ § 2-6-111. Custody and reproduction of records by secretary of state.

(1) The secretary of state is charged with the custody of:
(a) the enrolled copy of the constitution;
(b) all the acts and resolutions passed by the legislature;
(c) the journals of the legislature;
(d) the great seal;
(e) all books, records, parchments, maps, and papers kept or deposited in his office pursuant to law.

(2) All records included in subsection (1) may be kept and reproduced in accordance with the rules adopted by the secretary of state in consultation with the state records committee provided for in 2-15-1013.

(3) The state records committee created by 2-15-1013 may approve the disposal of original records once those records are reproduced as provided for in subsection (2), unless disposal

takes the form of transfer of records; in that case, reproduction will not be necessary. The reproduction or certified copy of a record may be used in place of the original for all purposes, including as evidence in any court or proceeding, and has the same force and effect as the original record.

(4) The secretary of state shall prepare enlarged typed or photographic copies of the records whenever their production is required by law.

(5) At least two copies shall be made of all records reproduced as provided for in subsection (2). The secretary of state shall place one copy in a fireproof storage place and shall retain the other copy in his office with suitable equipment for displaying a record by projection to not less than its original size and for preparing, for persons entitled thereto, copies of the record.

(6) All duplicates of all records shall be identified and indexed.

Part 2. Public Record Management.

Citation: MCA 2-6-203

✪ § 2-6-203. Secretary of State's powers and duties.

(1) In order to insure the proper management and safeguarding of public records, the secretary of state shall undertake the following:

* * * * *

(e) operate a central microfilm unit which will microfilm, on a cost recovery basis, all records approved for filming by the office or origin and the secretary of state; and

(f) approve microfilming projects and microfilm equipment purchases undertaken by all state agencies.

* * * * *

Citation: MCA 2-6-206

✪ § 2-6-206. Protection of essential records.

(1) In order to provide for the continuity and preservation of civil government, each elected and appointed officer of the executive branch shall designate certain public records as essential records needed for an emergency or for the reestablishment of normal operations after any such emergency. A list of such records shall be forwarded to the secretary of state. The list shall be reviewed from time to time by the elected or appointed officers to ensure its accuracy. Any changes or revisions shall be forwarded to the secretary of state.

(2) Each elected and appointed officer of state government shall ensure that the security of essential records is accomplished by the most economical means possible. Protection of essential records may be by vaulting, planned or natural dispersal of copies, storage in the state archives, or any other method approved by the secretary of state.

(3) Reproductions of essential records may be by photocopy, magnetic tape, microfilm, or other methods approved by the secretary of state.

TITLE 26. EVIDENCE.

CHAPTER 10. MONTANA RULES OF EVIDENCE.

ARTICLE X. CONTENTS OF WRITINGS, RECORDINGS AND PHOTOGRAPHS

☞ Rule 1001. Definitions

For purposes of this article the following definitions are applicable:

(1) *Writings and recordings.* — "Writings" and "recordings" consist of letters, words, or numbers, or their equivalent, set down by handwriting, typewriting, printing, photostating, photographing, magnetic impulse, mechanical or electronic recording, or other form of data compilation.

(2) *Photographs.* — "Photographs" include still photographs, X-ray films, video tapes, and motion pictures.

(3) *Original.* — An "original" of a writing or recording is the writing or recording itself or any counterpart intended to have the same effect by a person executing or issuing it. An "original" of a photograph includes the negative or any print therefrom. If data are stored in a computer or similar device, any printout or other output readable by sight, shown to reflect the data accurately, is an "original".

(4) *Duplicate.* — A "duplicate" is a counterpart produced by the same impression as the original, or from the same matrix, or by means of photography, including enlargements and miniatures, or by mechanical or electronic re-recording, or by chemical reproduction, or by other equivalent techniques which accurately reproduces the original.

☞ § Rule 1003. Admissibility of duplicates, copies of certain entries.

A duplicate, or copy of an entry in the regular course of business as defined in Rule 1001(5), is admissible to the same extent as an original unless: (1) a genuine question is raised as to the authenticity of the original; or (2) in the circumstances it would be unfair to admit the duplicate or copy of an entry in the regular course of business in lieu of the original; or (3) otherwise provided by statute.

[See Appendix A. Uniform Rules of Evidence for additional provisions.]

Source: Montana Administrative Rules
Agency: Department of Health and Environmental Science
Occupational Health Bureau

Citation: MAR 16.40.421

✍ § 16.40.421. Records, Reports and Notification — Surveys, Radiation Monitoring, Disposal.

(1) Each licensee or registrant shall maintain records showing the radiation exposures of all individuals for whom personnel monitoring is required under ARM 16.40.410. Such records shall be kept on department form MRH-31, in accordance with the instructions contained in that form, or on clear and legible records containing all the information required by department form MRH-31. The doses entered on the forms or records shall be for periods of time not exceeding one calendar quarter.

(2) Each licensee or registrant shall maintain records in the same units used in this subchapter, showing the results of surveys required by ARM 16.40.409, monitoring required by

ARM 16.40.415(3), (4), and (5), and disposals made under ARM 16.40.417, 16.40.418, and 16.40.419.

(3) Records required by this subchapter shall be maintained for the following periods:

(a) Records of individual exposure to radiation and to radioactive material which must be maintained pursuant to the provisions of subsection (1) of this rule and records of bioassays, including results of whole body count examinations, made pursuant to ARM 16.40.408 shall be preserved until the department authorizes disposition.

(b) Records of the results of surveys and monitoring which must be maintained pursuant to subsection (2) of this rule shall be preserved for 2 years after completion of the survey except that the following records shall be maintained until the department authorizes their disposition:

(i) Records of the results of surveys to determine compliance with ARM 16.40.404(1).

(ii) In the absence of personnel monitoring data, records of the results of surveys to determine external radiation dose.

(iii) Records of the results of surveys used to evaluate the release of radioactive effluents to the environment.

(c) Records of disposal of licensed material made pursuant to ARM 16.40.417, 16.40.418 and 16.40.419 shall be maintained until the department authorizes their disposition.

(d) Records which must be maintained pursuant to this subchapter may be the original or a reproduced copy or microform if such reproduced copy or microform is duly authenticated by authorized personnel and the microform is capable of producing a clear and legible copy after storage for the period specified by department rules.

(e) If there is a conflict pertaining to the retention period for the same type of record, the retention period specified in this subchapter for such records shall apply unless the department, pursuant to ARM 16.40.103(1) has granted a specific exemption from the record retention requirements specified in this subchapter.

(4) The discontinuance of or curtailment of activities, does not relieve the licensee or registrant of responsibility for retaining all records required by this rule. A licensee or registrant may, however, request the department to accept such records. The acceptance of the records by the department relieves the licensee or registrant of subsequent responsibility only in respect to their preservation as required by this rule.

State: Nebraska
Source: Revised Statutes of Nebraska

CHAPTER 23. COUNTY GOVERNMENT AND OFFICERS.

Article 15. Register of Deeds.

Citation: RSN 23-1517.01

✪ § 23-1517.01. Records; microfilm; requirements.

The recording of all instruments by the roll form of microfilm may be substituted for the method of recording instruments in books, and the filing of all documents by the roll form of microfilm may be substituted for the method of filing original documents. If this method of recording instruments on microfilm or filing documents on microfilm is used, the original instruments so recorded and the original documents so filed need not be retained after the microfilm has been verified for accuracy and quality, and a security copy on silver negative microfilm in roll form must be maintained and filed off premises under safe conditions to ensure the protection of the records and shall meet the microfilm standards as prescribed by the State Records Administrator as provided in section 84-1201 to 84-1220. The fee books shall provide the proper index information as to the microfilm roll and numerical sequence of all such recorded instruments and of all such filed documents. The internal reference copies or work copies of the instruments recorded on microfilm and of documents filed on microfilm may be in any photographic form to provide the necessary information as may be determined by the official in charge.

CHAPTER 24. COURTS.

Article 10. Courts — General Provisions.

Citation: RSN 24-1005

☞✪ § 24-1005. Records; microfilm; admissible in evidence; destruction of original record.

The clerk of any district court of any other court of record may microfilm any court record. The original record may be destroyed only with the approval of the State Records Administrator pursuant to section 84-1201 to 84-1220. The reproduction of the microfilm shall be admissible in evidence in any court of record in the State of Nebraska.

CHAPTER 25. COURTS; CIVIL PROCEDURE.

Article 12. Evidence.

Citation: RSN 25.1281

☞✪ § 25.1281. Official records; photographic copies; admissibility; destruction of original records.

In all cases in which any instrument or document is required by law to be copied or recorded in any public record in any public office within the state of Nebraska, the officials having charge of the making of such records may employ the use of photographic processes for the reproduction of such instrument or document. This shall be done for the public records and shall be a true copy of the original instrument or document to be so recorded, and may likewise use any such photographic process for the making of certified copies of such public records; *Provided*, no such photographic processes shall be used for making of permanent records until it shall have been demonstrated to the satisfaction of the officials having charge of such records and the State Records Administrator, that the processes to be used will produce an accurate and permanent record of the instrument or document to be recorded. Any such existing records when reproduced by such photographic processes may be destroyed by the official having charge of the same when approval is given by the State Records Administrator.

UNIFORM PHOTOGRAPHIC COPIES OF BUSINESS AND PUBLIC RECORDS AS EVIDENCE ACT

Citation: RSN 25-12,112

☞ § 25-12,112. Admissibility of reproduced records in evidence; destruction of records; approval.

If any business, institution, member of a profession or calling, or any department or agency of government, in the regular course of business or activity has kept or recorded any memorandum, writing, entry, print, representation or combination thereof, of any act, transaction, occurrence, or event, and in the regular course of business has caused any or all of the same to be recorded, copied, or reproduced by any photographic, photostatic, optical imagery, microfilm, microcard, miniature photographic, optical disk, or other process which accurately reproduces or forms a durable medium for so reproducing the original, the original may be destroyed in the regular course of business unless held in a custodial or fiduciary capacity or unless its preservation is required by law and, with respect to agencies or departments of government, if the State Records Administrator approves such destruction. Such reproduction, when satisfactorily identified, is as admissible in evidence as the original itself in any judicial or administrative proceeding whether the original is in existence or not and an enlargement or facsimile of such reproduction is likewise admissible in evidence if the original reproduction is in existence and available for inspection under direction of the court. The introduction of a reproduced record, enlargement, or facsimile, does not preclude admission of the original.

Article 22. General Provisions.

Citation: RSN 25-2209

✪ § 25-2209. Clerk of district court; required record books enumerated; compilation and filing; methods authorized.

The clerk of the district court shall keep records to be called the appearance docket, the trial docket, the journal, the complete record, the execution docket, the fee book, the general index, and the judgment record. Such records may be compiled, filed, and maintained on a computer system. Effective not later than October 1, 1992, provision for dockets and records of the district courts shall be established by rule of the Supreme Court. The journal and complete record may be compiled and filed on microfilm. The recording of all instruments by the roll form of microfilm may be substituted for the method of recording instruments in books. If this method of recording instruments on microfilm is used, a security copy on silver negative microfilm in roll form must be maintained and filed off premises under safe conditions to ensure the protection of the records. The internal reference copies or work copies of the instruments recorded on microfilm may be in any photographic form to provide the necessary information as may be determined by the official in charge, and shall meet the microfilm standards as prescribed by the State Records Administrator.

CHAPTER 27. COURTS; RULES OF EVIDENCE.

ARTICLE 10. CONTENTS, OF WRITINGS, RECORDINGS AND PHOTOGRAPHS

Citation: RSN 27-1001

☞ § 27-1001. Rule 1001. Definitions

For purposes of this article the following definitions are applicable:

(1) *Writings and recordings.* — "Writings" and "recordings" consist of letters, words, or numbers, or their equivalent, set down by handwriting, typewriting, printing, photostating, photographing, magnetic impulse, mechanical or electronic recording, or other form of data compilation.

(2) *Photographs.* — "Photographs" include still photographs, X-ray films, video tapes, and motion pictures.

(3) *Original.* — An "original" of a writing or recording is the writing or recording itself or any counterpart intended to have the same effect by a person executing or issuing it. An "original" of a photograph includes the negative or any print therefrom. If data are stored in a computer or similar device, any printout or other output readable by sight, shown to reflect the data accurately, is an "original".

(4) *Duplicate.* — A "duplicate" is a counterpart produced by the same impression as the original, or from the same matrix, or by means of photography, including enlargements and miniatures, or by mechanical or electronic re-recording, or by chemical reproduction, or by other equivalent techniques which accurately reproduces the original.

Citation: RSN 27-1003

☞ § 27-1003. Rule 1003. Admissibility of duplicate.

A duplicate is admissible to the same extent as an original unless (1) a genuine question is raised as to the authenticity of the original or (2) in the circumstances it would be unfair to admit the duplicate in lieu of the original.

[See Appendix A. Uniform Rules of Evidence for additional provisions.]

CHAPTER 81. STATE ADMINISTRATIVE DEPARTMENTS.

Article 11. Department of Administrative Services

Citation: RSN 81-1117.04

✪ § 81-1117.04. Computer file data; public records defined.

Except as otherwise provided by law, public records shall mean all papers, correspondence, memoranda, accounts, reports, maps, plans, photographs, sound recordings, or other documents, regardless of physical form, including records produced by or for use with electronic or mechanical data processing devices, and which have been or shall be created or received by any agency or its lawful successor or official thereof in the exercise of his office or in the conduct, transaction, or performance of any business, duty, or function pursued in accordance with law, but shall not include library or museum material made or acquired and preserved solely for reference purposes, extra copies of documents preserved only for convenience or reference, and stock of publications and reproduced documents.

CHAPTER 84. STATE OFFICERS.

Article 12. Records Management Act.

Citation: RSN 84-1208

✪ § 84-1208. Administrator [State Records Administrator]; preservation duplicates of essential records; process used; exception.

(1) The administrator may make or cause to be made preservation duplicates of essential records, or may designate as preservation duplicates existing copies thereof. A preservation duplicate shall be durable, accurate, complete and clear, and if made by means of photography, microphotography, photocopying, film, microfilm, or similar processes, shall be prepared in conformity to standards prescribed and approved by the board.

(2) A preservation duplicate made by a photographic, photostatic, microfilm, microcard, miniature photographic or similar process, which accurately reproduced or forms a durable

medium for so reproducing the original, shall have the same force and effect for all purposes as the original record, whether the original is in existence or not. A transcript, exemplification, or certified copy of such preservation duplicate shall for all purposes be deemed a transcript, exemplification or certified copy of the original record.

(3) No copy of an essential record shall be used as a preservation duplicate unless, under the general laws of the state, the copy has the same force and effect for all purposes as the original record.

Citation: RSN 84-1214.01

✪ **§ 84-1214.01. State Archives; authority; duties.**

The State Archives of the Nebraska State Historical Society has the authority to acquire, in total or in part, any document, record, or material which has been submitted to the board for disposition or transfer when such material is determined to be of archival or historical significance by the State Archivist or the board. The head of any agency shall certify in writing to the society the transfer of the custody of such material to the State Archives. No agency shall dispose of, in any other manner except by transfer to the State Archives, that material which has been appraised as archival or historical without the written consent of the State Archivist and the administrator. If such material is determined to be in jeopardy of destruction or deterioration and such material is not necessary to the conduct of daily business in the agency of origin, it shall be the prerogative of the State Archivist to petition the administrator and the agency of origin for the right to transfer such material into the safekeeping of the State Archives. It shall be the responsibility of the administrator to hear arguments for or against such petition and to determine the results of such petition. The State Archivist shall prepare invoices and receipts in triplicate for materials acquired under this section, shall retain one copy, and shall deliver one copy to the administrator and one copy to the agency head from whom the records are obtained.

Citation: RSN 84-1222

✪ **§ 84-1222. Purchase of microfilm system or equipment; approval; property of State Records Administrator.**

After May 18, 1977, no state agency shall purchase any microfilm system or equipment prior to the approval of the State Records Administrator. The administrator shall not approve internal microfilm activities of any state agency unless such activities may not be feasibly provided by the central microfilming agency and are necessary to a particular operation within the state agency. Any equipment purchased under this section shall become the property of the State Records Administrator and shall be subject to the provisions of section 84-1223.

Citation: RSN 84-1223

✪ **§ 84-1223. Micrographic production, processing, and viewing equipment; property of administrator; exception; credit.**

On May 19, 1979, all micrographic production, processing, and viewing equipment currently owned or subsequently acquired under the provisions of section 84-1222 by any state executive, judicial, or legislative agency, except the University of Nebraska or the state colleges, shall become the property of the State Records Administrator, regardless of the fund source from which the equipment was originally purchased. Appropriate credit, against future charges, shall be given to all agencies for the fair market value of all equipment accepted which had been purchased with federal funds or trust funds. Equipment purchased with funds from the Highway Cash Fund shall not be deemed to have been purchased with federal funds or trust funds.

Citation: RSN 84-1224

✪ **§ 84-1224. State Records Administrator; microfilm; micrographic equipment; powers.**

The State Records Administrator shall:

(1) Be empowered to review the microfilm systems within every agency of the state;

(2) Be empowered to cause such systems to be merged with a central microfilm agency in the event that a cost analysis shows that economic advantage may be achieved.

(3) Be empowered to permit the establishment of microfilming services within any agency or department of the state if a potential economy or a substantial convenience for the state would result; and

(4) After July 1, 1978, be empowered to determine the operating locations of all micrographic equipment in his possession.

Citation: RSN 84-1225

✪ **§ 84-1225. State Record Administrator; micropublishing and computer output microfilm services; charges.**

The State Records Administrator shall provide for a system of charges for micropublishing services and computer output microfilm services rendered by the central microfilming agency to any other department or agency of the state when these charges are allocable to a particular project carried on by such microfilming agency. Such charges shall, as nearly as may be practical, reflect the actual cost of services provided by the central microfilming agency. On July 1, 1978, and thereafter the State Records Administrator shall extend this system of charges to include source document microfilming. The State Records Administrator shall extend this system of charges and user fees for all micrographic equipment which is the property of the administrator and which is used by any other state agency or department.

Source: Nebraska Administrative Rules and Regulations
Agency: Department of Revenue

TITLE 36. DEPARTMENT OF REVENUE.

CHAPTER 81. MOTOR VEHICLE FUELS TAX REGULATIONS.

Citation: NAR 81-007

✍ **§ 81-007. Records.**

* * * * *

007.02 Invoices, meter readings, pipeline terminal and refinery bills of lading, inventory records, including inventory control records maintained for the State Fire Marshal, and other memorandum must be retained in addition to the information required above. The maintenance of this information in a provable computer format or on microfilm is acceptable in lieu of retention of the original documents.

* * * * *

CHAPTER 85. AIRCRAFT FUELS TAX REGULATION.

Citation:	NAR 85-007

✍ **§ 85-007. Records.**

* * * * *

007.02 Invoices, meter readings, pipeline terminal and refinery bills of lading, inventory records, including inventory control records maintained for the State Fire Marshal, and other memoranda must be retained in addition to the information required above. The maintenance of this information in a provable computer format or on microfilm is acceptable in lieu of retention of the original documents.

* * * * *

State:	Nevada
Source:	Nevada Revised Statutes

TITLE 4. WITNESSES AND EVIDENCE.

CHAPTER 51. HEARSAY.

Citation:	NRS 51.135

☞ **§ 51.135. Hearsay exceptions: Records of regularly conducted activity; affidavit of custodian of medical records.**

1. A memorandum, report, record or data compilation, in any form, of acts, events, conditions, opinions or diagnoses, made at or near the time by, or from information transmitted by, a person with knowledge, all in the course of a regularly conducted activity, as shown by the testimony of the custodian or other qualified witness, is not inadmissible under the hearsay rule unless the source of information or the method or circumstances of preparation indicate lack of trustworthiness.
2. An affidavit signed by a custodian of medical records verifying that the copy of medical records is a true and complete reproduction of the original medical records is not inadmissible under the hearsay rule and shall be accepted by the court in lieu of testimony.

CHAPTER 52. DOCUMENTARY AND OTHER PHYSICAL EVIDENCE.

CONTENTS OF WRITINGS, RECORDINGS AND PHOTOGRAPHS

Citation:	NRS 52.195

☞ **§ 52.195. "Duplicate" defined.**

"Duplicate" means a counterpart produced:
1. By the same impression as the original;
2. From the same matrix;
3. By means of photography, including enlargements and miniatures;
4. By mechanical or electronic rerecording, including a counterpart produced by an optical imaging system;
5. By chemical reproduction;
6. By any other equivalent technique designed to ensure an accurate reproduction of the original.

Citation:	NRS 52.205

☞ **§ 52.205. "Original" defined.**

1. An "original" of a writing or recording is the writing or recording itself or any counterpart intended to have the same effect by a person executing or issuing it.
2. An "original" of a photograph includes the negative or any print therefrom. 3. If data are stored in a computer or similar device, any printout or other output readable by sight, shown accurately to reflect the data, is an "original".

Citation:	NRS 52.215

☞ **§ 52.215. "Photographs" defined.**

"Photographs" include still photographs, X-ray films, video tapes and motion pictures.

Citation:	NRS 52.225

☞ **§ 52.225. "Writings," "recordings" defined.**

"Writings" and "recordings" consist of letters, words, or numbers, or their equivalent, set down by handwriting, typewriting, printing, photostating, photographing, magnetic impulse, mechanical or electronic recording, or other form of data compilation.

Citation:	NRS 52.245

☞ **§ 52.245. Admissibility of duplicates.**

1. In addition to the situations governed by subsection 2, a duplicate is admissible to the same extent as an original unless:
(a) A genuine question is raised as to the authenticity of the original; or
(b) In the circumstances it would be unfair to admit the duplicate in lieu of the original.
2. Except as otherwise provided in N.R.S. 52.247, a duplicate is admissible to the same extent as an original if the person or office having custody of the original was authorized to destroy the original after preparing a duplicate, and in fact did so.

Citation:	NRS 52.247

☞ **§ 52.247 Admissibility of rerecorded, copied or reproduced records; certain records of governmental agency deemed public records.**

1. Unless held in a fiduciary or custodial capacity or unless specifically prohibited by a federal or state statute or regulation, by a local ordinance or by an order or judgment of a court of competent jurisdiction, if any business or governmental agency has, in the regular course of its business:
(a) Produced, kept or maintained any document, memorandum, writing, entry, print or other record of any act, transaction, occurrence or event relating to the conduct of its business; and
(b) Has caused any of those records to be rerecorded, copied or reproduced by any photographic, photostatic or other process which ensures an accurate reproduction or creates a reliable medium for reproducing the original of any of those records, the business or governmental agency may, in the regular course of its business, destroy any of those records.
2. Any rerecorded, copied or reproduced record specified in subsection 1 is admissible to the same extent as an original,

regardless of whether the original is available for inspection or has been lost or destroyed, if the rerecorded, copied or reproduced record is sufficiently authenticated.

3. An enlargement or facsimile of a rerecorded, copied or reproduced record specified in subsection 2 is admissible to the same extent as an original if:

(a) The record has not been lost or destroyed; and

(b) It is available for inspection by the court.

The introduction of an enlargement or facsimile of a record pursuant to the provisions of this subsection does not prohibit the admission of the original of that record.

4. If a governmental agency destroys any of its records and causes those records to be recorded, copied or reproduced pursuant to subsection 1:

(a) The recorded, copied or reproduced record shall be deemed a public record for the purposes of chapter 239 or NRS; and

(b) The governmental agency shall render such assistance as is necessary to allow any member of the public access to the recorded, copied or reproduced record if the record is not otherwise declared by law to be confidential.

5. As used in this section, "business" means any proprietorship, including any member of a profession licensed pursuant to Title 54 of NRS, corporation, partnership, association, trust, unincorporated organization or other enterprise doing business in this state.

Citation: NRS 52.265

☞ **§ 52.265. Public records.**
✪

1. Except as otherwise provided in N.R.S. 52.247, the contents of an official record, or of a document authorized to be recorded or filed and actually recorded or filed, including data compilations in any form, if otherwise admissible, may be proved by copy, certified as correct by the custodian or other person authorized to make the certification or testified to be correct by a witness who has compared it with the original.

2. If a copy which complies with the foregoing cannot be obtained by the exercise of reasonable diligence, then other evidence of the contents may be given.

Citation: NRS 52.295

☞ **§ 52.295. Functions of judge, jury.**

1. Except as otherwise provided in subsection 2, when the admissibility of other evidence of contents under these rules depends upon the fulfillment of a condition of fact, the question whether the condition has been fulfilled is for the judge to determine.

2. When an issue is raised:

(a) Whether the asserted writing ever existed;

(b) Whether another writing, recording or photograph produced at the trial is the original; or

(c) Whether other evidence of contents correctly reflects the contents, the issue is for the trier of fact to determine as in the case of other issues of fact.

Citation: NRS 52.320

☞ **§ 52.320. Definitions.**

As used in NRS 52.320 to 52.375, inclusive, unless the context otherwise requires:

1. "Custodian of medical records" means a chiropractor, physician, registered physical therapist or licensed nurse who prepares and maintains medical records, or any employee or agent of such a person or a facility for convalescent care, medical laboratory or hospital who has care, custody and control of medical records for such a person or institution.

2. "Medical records" includes bills, ledgers, statements and other accounts which show the cost of medical services or care provided to a patient.

MEDICAL RECORDS

Citation: NRS 52.325

☞ **§ 52.325. Subpoenaed records: Delivery of authenticated copy by custodian; order for return of record; form of affidavit of authentication.**

1. A custodian of medical records sufficiently complies with a subpoena calling for the production of medical records in his custody if he delivers, at or before the time set for the return of the subpoena, either personally or by mail, to the clerk of the court issuing the subpoena a true and exact photographic, electrostatic or other acceptable copy of the original record authenticated as provided in this section. This section does not apply to X-ray films or to any other portion of a medical record which is not susceptible to photostatic reproduction.

2. The copy must be authenticated by an affidavit signed by the custodian of the medical records verifying that it is a true and complete reproduction of the original medical record and that the original record was made at or near the time of the act, event, condition, opinion or diagnosis by or from information transmitted by a person with knowledge in the course of a regularly conducted activity.

3. If the court quashes or suppresses a subpoena for medical records, it may order the subpoenaed record to be returned to the submitting custodian.

4. The affidavit required by subsection 2 must be substantially in the form prescribed in subsection 3 of NRS 52.260.

* * * * *

TITLE 7. CORPORATIONS; ASSOCIATIONS; PARTNERSHIPS.

CHAPTER 78. PRIVATE CORPORATIONS.

Citation: NRS 78.105

☞ **§ 78.105. Copies of articles, bylaws, duplicate stock ledgers or statements to be kept at principal office; rights of judgment creditors, stockholders; penalties.**

1. Every corporation shall keep and maintain at its principal office in this state:

(a) A certified copy of its certificate of incorporation or articles of incorporation, and all amendments thereto; and

(b) A certified copy of its bylaws and all amendments thereto; and

(c) A stock ledger or a duplicate stock ledger, revised annually, containing the names, alphabetically arranged, of all persons who are stockholders of the corporation, showing their places of residence, if known, and the number of shares held by them respectively; or

(d) In lieu of the stock ledger or duplicate stock ledger specified in paragraph (c), a statement setting out the name of the custodian of the stock ledger or duplicate stock ledger, and the present and complete post office address, including street and number, if any, where such stock ledger or duplicate stock ledger specified in this section is kept.

* * * * *

TITLE 19. MISCELLANEOUS MATTERS RELATED TO GOVERNMENT AND PUBLIC AFFAIRS.

CHAPTER 239. PUBLIC RECORDS.

Reproduction of Records

Citation: **NRS 239.051**

✪ **§ 239.051. Reproduction of public records before destruction: Requirements.**

1. Unless destruction of a particular record without reproduction is authorized by a schedule adopted pursuant to NRS 239.080 or 239.125, any custodian of public records in this state may destroy documents, instruments, papers, books and any other records or writings in his custody only if those records or writings have been placed on microphotographic film or if the information they contain has been entered into a computer system which permits the retrieval and reproduction of that information. A reproduction of that film or that information shall be deemed to be the original.

2. Microphotographs made pursuant to this section must be made on film which complies with minimum standards of quality approved by the American National Standards Institute.

3. The custodian of the records or writings shall:

(a) Promptly store at least one copy of the microphotographic film or the tape, disk or other medium used for the storage of that information by the computer in such a manner and place as to protect it reasonably from loss or damage; and

(b) Maintain for the use of authorized persons a copy of a reproduction of the film or the information stored by the computer.

Citation: **NRS 239.070**

✪ **§ 239.070. Use of microfilm by county recorder for recording; division to provide microfilming or similar service; requirements; sale of duplicate.**

1. In lieu of or in addition to the method of recording required or allowed by statute, the county recorder may use microfilm for such recording.

2. The division, in cooperation with the state printing and micrographics division of the department of general services, shall provide microfilming service to any local government. The charge for the service must not exceed the actual cost.

3. If microfilming is used:

(a) The microphotographs or micronegative films must be properly indexed and placed in conveniently accessible files.

(b) Each film must be designated and numbered.

(c) Provision must be made for preserving, examining, and using the films.

4. A duplicate of each such film must be made and kept safely in a separate place.

5. Duplicates of each such film must be made available by the county recorder for sale at a price not exceeding cost upon the request of any person, firm or organization. Subject to the approval of the board of county commissioners, the county recorder may, at any time, make additional duplicates of each such film available for sale to the public at a price not exceeding cost.

6. The division shall provide services for recording other than microfilming to any local government if the division has the equipment necessary to provide the services. The services provided are subject to the requirements of this section relating to microfilming.

Disposal of Obsolete Records

Citation: **NRS 239.080**

✪ **§ 239.080 State Records: Schedules for retention and disposition.**

1. An official state record may be disposed of only in accordance with a schedule for retention and disposition of each type of official state record.

2. In cooperation with the division, each agency, board and commission shall develop a schedule for the retention and disposition of each type of official state record.

3. The division shall submit the schedules described in subsection 2 to the committee for final approval.

4. As used in this section, "official state record" includes without limitation, any:

(a) Papers, unpublished books, maps and photographs;

(b) Information stored on magnetic tape or computer, laser or optical disc;

(c) Materials which are capable of being read by a machine, including microforms and audio and visual materials; and

(d) Materials which are made or received by a state agency and preserved by that agency or its successor as evidence of the organization, operation, policy or any other activity of that agency or because of the information contained in the material.

Citation: **NRS 239.110**

✪ **§ 239.110. Judicial records: Destruction; microphotographic copies.**

1. The clerk of the supreme court, a county clerk, deputy clerk of a justice's court or clerk of a municipal court may destroy all documents, records, instruments, books, papers, depositions and transcripts of in any action or proceeding in the supreme court, district court, justice's court or municipal court, respectively, or otherwise filed in his office pursuant to law, including transcripts of coroners' inquests and depositions, if the records of the clerk do not show that the action or proceeding is pending on appeal or review in any court, except that:

(a) If the written consent of the district attorney is first obtained, transcripts of preliminary hearings may be destroyed as provided in this section; and

(b) Minutes of the supreme court, district court, justice's court or municipal court, affidavits supporting applications for marriage licenses, after those licenses have been issued, and certificates of fictitious names of businesses may be destroyed immediately subject to the provisions of subsections 2 and 3.

2. The clerk shall maintain for the use of the public a micrographic film print or copy of each document, record, instrument, book, paper, deposition or transcript so destroyed, if the print or copy is placed and kept in a sealed container under certificate of the clerk and properly indexed. This print or copy shall be deemed to be the original.

3. The clerk shall promptly seal and store at least one original negative of each microphotographic film in such manner and place as may reasonably ensure its preservation indefinitely

against loss, theft, defacement, or destruction.

4. The supreme court may provide by rule for the destruction, without prior microfilming, of such other documents of the several courts of this state as are held in the offices of the clerks but which:

(a) No longer serve any legal, financial or administrative purpose; and

(b) Do not have any historical value.

5. The court administrator may request the division to advise and assist the supreme court in its establishment of the rules.

Citation: NRS 239.125

✪ § 239.125. Local Government Records: Program for Management; Regulations of State Librarian.

1. A local governmental entity may establish a program for the management of records, including the adoption of schedules for the retention of records and procedures for microfilming, which must be approved by the governing body and comply with the applicable provisions of this chapter and any regulations adopted pursuant thereto.

2. The state librarian shall adopt regulations to carry out a program to establish and approve minimum periods of retention for records of local governments. The proposed regulations or any amendment thereto must be submitted to the local government advisory committee, established pursuant to NRS 354.594, for its advice and recommendations.

Citation: NRS 239.590

✪ § 239.590. "Duplicate" defined.

"Duplicate" means a counterpart produced:

1. By the same impression as the original;

2. From the same matrix;

3. By means of photography, including enlargements and miniatures;

4. By mechanical or electronic rerecording;

5. By chemical reproduction; or

6. By other equivalent technique designed to ensure an accurate reproduction of the original.

The term includes an accurate an unabridged copy of a record or series of records that is not an original.

Citation: NRS 239.605

✪ § 239.605. "Image" defined.

"Image" means an exact duplicate of an original document.

Citation: NRS 239.640

✪ § 239.640. "Optical imaging system" defined.

"Optical imaging system" means hardware and software for computer which record complete images by:

1. Scanning the images with a source of light, such as a laser;

2. Converting the images into a digital electronic format, and

3. Storing the converted images on an optical media which allows for the rapid retrieval of the stored images through indexing and the reproduction of the entire original image.

Citation: NRS 239.645

✪ § 239.645. "Optical media" defined.

"Optical media" means a special disk, computer hard disk or magnetic tape on which images are stored.

Citation: NRS 239.650

✪ § 239.650. "Original" Defined.

1. An "original" of a writing or recording is the writing or recording itself or any counterpart intended to have the same effect by a person executing or issuing it.

2. An "original" of a photograph includes the negative or any print therefrom.

3. If data are stored in a computer or similar device, any printout or other output readable by sight, shown accurately to reflect the data, is an "original".

4. A reproduction made pursuant to the provisions of NRS 239.051, or any record designated by the state board of examiners to be an original, including the stored security copy and the copy maintained for the use of authorized persons is an "original".

Citation: NRS 239.655

✪ § 239.655. "Preserved" defined.

"Preserved" means the filing, storage or other method of systematically maintaining documentary materials by an agency. The terms also applies to materials while they are temporarily removed from established filing systems.

Citation: NRS 239.660

✪ § 239.660. "Received" defined.

"Received" means the receipt of documentary materials by personnel of a state agency, whether in person, by messenger, mail, electronic transmission or by any other method. The term does not refer to misdirected materials.

Citation: NRS 239.755

✪ § 239.755. Priority for microfilming and protection of vital records.

Each state agency shall give priority to the microfilming and protection of its vital records within the limits of the agency's budget. If money has been appropriated for the microfilming or storage of records, the microfilming of vital records must be given priority.

Citation: NRS 239.760

✪ § 239.760. Treatment of electronic records.

1. A state agency; which produces an electronic record must include the entire record or image. Each electronic record must include:

(a) The date the record was produced;

(b) The date any alteration was produced; and

(c) Evidence that the record was authorized for issue or signature.

2. The temperature in the area used to store electronic records must be maintained at or above 50 degrees Fahrenheit, but not

more than 75 degrees Fahrenheit.

3. The agency's personnel shall transfer electronic mail records to a medium which will ensure retention until the minimum period for retention has passed.

4. After the minimum period for retention has passed, the agency may destroy the electronic records by erasing or destroying the disk or tape.

5. Except as otherwise provided in this subsection, electronic records that have been appraised and scheduled to be transferred to the division must not be sent in computer disk or tape format. The agency shall transfer the electronic record onto bond paper, microfilm or microfiche before transferring it to the division. Audio and audio-visual tapes and cassettes may be transferred in their original form.

6. As used in this section, "electronic records" mean official state records which are stored, accessed and retrieved through a machine readable system, whether by magnetic impulse, mechanical or electronic recording, or other form of data compilation, including all computer systems, floppy disks, optical disks, magnetic tape, hard disks and audio-visual systems.

USE OF OPTICAL IMAGING SYSTEM

Citation: NRS 239.765

✪ § 239.765. Applicability.

The provisions of NAC 239.770 to 239.845, inclusive, apply to any state agency that uses an optical imaging system to use, maintain, retain, or preserve its records.

Citation: NRS 239.770

✪ § 239.770. Maintenance of access to digital information stored on optical media.

To ensure that access to digital information stored on optical media is maintained, a state agency shall:

1. Use an optical imaging system that is built from hardware and software for computers that conform to nonproprietary standards or generally accepted standards within the industry; and

2. Require the seller of the system to deposit a copy of the computer code with a bank, the state archives or a facility for the storage of records for use by the agency if the seller's business fails.

Citation: NRS 239.775

✪ § 239.775. Preservation of records stored on optical media; media for storage of images.

1. To ensure that records stored on optical media are preserved, a state agency shall:

(a) Adopt and enforce written procedures for the proper care and handling of that part of the optical imaging system where images are stored. The procedures must:

(1) Include standards for keeping the equipment in an area that is clean and free from dust;

(2) Prohibit eating, drinking and smoking in the area in which the equipment is stored or operated; and

(3) Require the use of devices that protect against the sudden loss or increase of electricity, such as surge protectors and, if needed, line conditioners.

(b) Maintain stable environmental conditions in the areas where the equipment and optical media are stored.

2. Images may be stored on a special disk, computer hard disk or magnetic tape.

Citation: NRS 239.780

✪ § 239.780. Maintenance of access to long-term records.

To ensure that access to long-term records is maintained, a state agency shall:

1. Improve its equipment as technology advances, within budgetary constraints, and recopy optical media as required;

2. Recopy optical media at least every 10 years, based upon the projected longevity of the optical disc; or

3. Transfer data from an obsolete method of generating optical technology to an improved method and, if appropriate, reject accepted methods which are at risk of becoming obsolete.

Citation: NRS 239.785

✪ § 239.785. Options regarding file headers.

A state agency shall:

1. Require the use of nonproprietary file headers to label digital images, such as "Tagged Image File Format (TIFF)";

2. Require the developer of the optical imaging system to provide a bridge to nonproprietary file headers; or

3. Require the developer of the optical imaging system to supply a detailed definition of the structure of the file headers used to label digital images.

Citation: NRS 239.790

✪ § 239.790. Maintenance of readability of digital images.

The written procedures used by a state agency for the operation of an optical imaging system must ensure that the readability of the digital images is maintained by copying the optical media periodically when the relocation table reaches a 70-percent capacity.

Citation: NRS 239.795

✪ § 239.795. Protection of quality of digital images.

A state agency shall protect the quality of digital images recorded and stored by an optical imaging system. To carry out this duty, a state agency shall:

1. Provide periodic maintenance for the optical imaging system.

2. Ensure the optical drives are recalibrated annually.

3. Periodically evaluate the quality of a sampling of scanned images and related index data.

4. Ensure that the data for each scanned image is written to optical media after the scanning.

5. Use a scanning density of at least 200 dots per inch for office documents.

6. Use a scanning density of at least 300 dots per inch for engineering drawings, maps and documents with detailed backgrounds.

7. Periodically validate the scanning density selected by testing documents.

8. Test selected documents to verify the capability of the scanner and the requirements for modifying the hardware used before initiating a project to convert to an optical imaging system that captures the full spectrum of color.

9. Restrict the use of the gray scale to photographs with a continuous tone, except in unusual circumstances.

10. Organize a committee within the agency to determine the best quality of the image required for different formats of

records before and after the records are scanned. The decisions made by this committee must be kept in a written log.

11. If possible, ensure that its optical imaging system has the capacity to comply with the standards of the Consultative Committee on International Telegraphy and Telephony relating to the use of standard compression techniques to reduce the volume of digital information that comprises a scanned image for long-term records.

12. If the optical imaging system does not have the capacity to use standard compression techniques, require the seller to provide a bridge between proprietary compression techniques and standard compression techniques which comply with the standards established by the Consultative Committee on International Telegraphy and Telephony.

Citation: NRS 239.800

✪ § 239.800. Duties of state agency acquiring new optical imaging system.

If a state agency is acquiring a new optical imaging system, the agency shall:

1. Acquire a system that is designed to permit the users to interchange hardware with minimal impact on the primary operating software and is capable of being improved without the loss of data; or

2. Require the seller to provide a bridge to an optical imaging system with nonproprietary configurations.

Citation: NRS 239.805

✪ § 239.805. Minimizing obsolescence of system.

A state agency shall ensure that the obsolescence of its optical imaging system if minimized by:

1. Improving its system so that it has the capability of reading and converting information written by systems with older technology;

2. Acquiring a new optical imaging system that is capable of reading and converting information written by its existing system; or

3. Requiring the seller to guarantee the conversion of 100 percent of the stored images and index data in lieu of having the capability to use hardware.

Citation: NRS 239.810

✪ § 239.810. Documentation of method used to enable communication of peripheral devices from different manufacturers.

A state agency shall obtain from the manufacturer of its optical imaging system or from the person who integrated its system, complete documentation of the hardware and software used by its system to enable optical drives and other peripheral devices obtained from different manufacturers to communicate with each other.

Citation: NRS 239.815

✪ § 239.815. Protection of indexing data.

A state agency shall ensure that the indexing data of its optical imaging system will not be lost by:

1. Storing the indexing data in the computer memory or on magnetic tape; or

2. Writing the indexing data for each optical platter at various locations on that disk.

Citation: NRS 239.820

✪ § 239.820. Procedures to ensure availability of technical information.

To ensure that all technical information relating to its optical imaging system will be available, a state agency shall:

1. Require the delivery of a complete set of technical information to the organization responsible for the operation of the application system for the optical imaging system;

2. Maintain records relating to all aspects of:

(a) The design and use of the optical imaging system, including the administrative procedures for digital imaging and the retrieval and storage of information;

(b) The specifications for the technical system; and

(c) Any problems encountered from the use of the system and the measures used to solve those problems, including any manner in which the hardware or software was modified; and

3. Maintain records of all information describing the indexing system used.

Citation: NRS 239.825

✪ § 239.825. Use of rewritable recording system or system capable of writing information once and reading it many times.

1. A state agency shall:

(a) Use an optical imaging system that is capable of writing information once and reading it many times (WORM) for long-term records with legal or research or archival value;

(b) Establish written security procedures to be followed by persons who are allowed to use such and system; and

(c) Maintain a record of all rewrites and deletions that are made on an optical imaging system.

2. Before selecting an optical imaging system that is capable of writing information once and reading it many times or when selecting a rewritable recording system, a state agency shall consider:

(a) Whether the functions and duties of the agency will best be carried out by the use of such a system;

(b) The available resources; and

(c) The level of standardization that can be achieved by the use of an optical imaging system.

Citation: NRS 239.830

✪ § 239.830. Composition of optical disk media.

A state agency shall use an optical disk media composed of polycarbonate or tempered glass substrates, or a material of equal or greater quality.

Citation: NRS 239.835

✪ § 239.835. Use of jukebox to store optical media.

A state agency may use a jukebox to store optical media if:

1. Rapid access to the optical media is required;

2. Physical control of the optical media is required; or

3. It is storing a large number of records.

Citation: NRS 239.840

✪ **§ 239.840. Minimum expected longevity of optical media; storage and cleaning of optical media; avoidance of electrical interference.**

A state agency shall:

1. Use optical media with an expected longevity of at least 20 years after information is entered on the disk, as determined by accelerated aging tests that are applied to specific locations on the surface of the media.
2. If possible, store optical media in an area with stable temperatures of not less than 65 degrees Fahrenheit and not more than 75 degrees Fahrenheit.
3. Not use an optical imaging system in the same physical proximity with an electrostatic copier or other electronic device that may cause electrical interference.
4. Periodically clean optical media and equipment to remove dust and other particulates.

Citation: NRS 239.845

✪ **§ 239.845. Retention of certain original records required; copies of stored images.**

1. A state agency shall:

(a) Retain the original of any long-term record with legal or research or archival value that is stored by an optical imaging system; and

(b) Provide for a copy of all images stored by an optical imaging system, as prescribed by paragraph (a) of subsection 3 of NRS 239.051.

2. An original of any record stored by an optical imaging system shall be deemed to include any copy produced by the stored image on the optical media and the copy provided for pursuant to subsection 1.

TITLE 23. PUBLIC OFFICERS AND EMPLOYEES.

CHAPTER 281. GENERAL PROVISIONS.

Citation: NRS 281.380

☞ ✍ ✪ **§ 281.380. Public officers and employees required to accept reproductions of business records for examination and other purposes.**

If any business, institution or member of a profession or calling has kept or recorded any memorandum, writing, entry, print, representation or combination thereof, of any act, transaction, occurrence or event and has caused any of all of such records to be recorded, copied or reproduced by any photographic, photostatic, microfilm, microcard, miniature photographic, or other process which accurately reproduces or forms a durable medium to so reproducing the original, such reproduction shall be accepted by all public officers and employees for examination, filing, copying or any other purpose as if it were the original, whether or not the original is then in existence.

TITLE 32. REVENUE AND TAXATION.

CHAPTER 365. TAXES ON FUELS.

Credits, Overpayments and Refunds

✍ **§ 365.400. Payment of refund based on duplicate invoice.**

In the event of the loss of an original invoice, the person claiming a refund may submit in lieu thereof a duplicate copy of the invoice, which shall be retained by the department until the expiration of the period specified for filing of refund applications. No payment of refund based upon a duplicate invoice shall be made until after the expiration of such statutory period.

TITLE 53. LABOR AND INDUSTRIAL RELATIONS.

CHAPTER 612. UNEMPLOYMENT COMPENSATION.

Citation: NRS 612.260

✍ **§ 612.260. Records and reports of employing units: Inspection; destruction.**

1. Each employing unit shall keep true and accurate work records, containing such information as the administrator may prescribe. Such records must be open to inspection and may be copied by the administrator or his authorized representatives at any reasonable time and as often as may be necessary.
2. The administrator, the board of review, or any appeal tribunal may require from any employing unit any sworn or unsworn reports, with respect to persons employed by it, which he or the board of review deems necessary for the effective administration of this chapter.
3. Except as limited by this subsection, the administrator may:

(a) Destroy any letter of the unemployment compensation service or employment service and any form, benefit determination or redetermination, ruling, employer's status or contribution report, wage slip report, claim record, wage list or any auxiliary computer file related thereto at the expiration of 4 years after the record was originated or filed with the service; or

(b) Destroy such records at any time after having microphotographed them in the manner and on film or paper that complies with the minimum standards of quality approved for such photographic records by the American National Standards Institute. The microphotographed records must be retained for not less than 4 years.

This subsection does not apply to records pertaining to grants, accounts or expenditures for administration, or to the records of the unemployment compensation administration fund.

CHAPTER 616. INDUSTRIAL INSURANCE.

GENERAL PROVISIONS

Citation: NRS 616.193

✍ **§ 616.193. Files of claims: Inspection; copying; filming.**

1. The insurer must provide access to the files of claims in its offices.
2. A file is available for inspection during regular business hours by the employee or his designated agent, the employer or his designated agent and the administrator or his designated agent.
3. Upon request, the insurer must make copies of anything in

the file and may charge a reasonable fee for this service. Copies of materials in the file which are requested by the administrator or his designated agent, or the Nevada attorney for injured workers or his designated agent must be provided free of charge.

4. Until a claim is closed the file must be kept in the office nearest to the place where the injury occurred.

5. If a claim has been closed for at least 1 year, the insurer may microphotograph or film any of its records relating to that claim. The microphotographs or films must be placed inconvenient and accessible files, and provision must be made for preserving, examining and using the words.

6. Nothing in this section requires the insurer to allow inspection or reproduction of material regarding which a legal privilege against disclosure has been conferred.

CHAPTER 616B. INDUSTRIAL INSURANCE: INSURERS; LIABILITY FOR PROVISION OF COVERAGE.

Citation: NRS 616B.021

✍ **§ 616B.021. Files of claims: Inspection; copying; filming.**

1. The insurer must provide access to the files of claims in its offices.

2. A file is available for inspection during regular business hours by the employee or his designated agent, the employer or his designated agent and the administrator or his designated agent.

3. Upon request, the insurer must make copies of anything in the file and may charge a reasonable fee for this service. Copies of materials in the file which are requested by the administrator or his designated agent, or the Nevada attorney for injured workers or his designated agent must be provided free of charge.

4. If a claim has been closed for at least 1 year, the insurer may microphotograph or film any of its records relating to that claim. The microphotographs or films must be placed in convenient and accessible files, and provision must be made for preserving, examining and using the records.

5. Nothing in this section requires the insurer to allow inspection or reproduction of material regarding which a legal privilege against disclosure has been conferred.

Citation: NRS 616B.024

✍ **§ 616B.024. Destruction of records.**

1. Upon written approval of the administrator, the insurer may destroy accumulated and noncurrent detail records such as payroll reports, checks, claims, and other records of similar importance for the period July 1, 1913, to January 1, 1947, if:

(a) Claims from January 1, 1940, and after are first microphotographed; and

(b) A brief inventory of the destroyed records is retained.

2. The insurer may dispose of or destroy any record which has been microphotographed or filmed if the procedure required by NRS 239.051 has been followed.

3. The principal records, such as the general and regular journals and the general ledgers, must be retained intact until audited and then must be microfilmed for retention until their destruction pursuant to NRS 239.051.

CHAPTER 629. HEALING ARTS GENERALLY.

Citation: NRS 629.021

✍ **§ 629.021. "Health care records" defined.**

"Health Care Records" means any reports, notes, orders, photographs, X-rays or other recorded data or information whether maintained in written, electronic or other form which is received or produced by a provider of health care, or any person employed by him, and contains information relating to the medical history, examination, diagnosis or treatment of the patient.

✍ **§ 629.051 Health care records: Retention.**

Each provider of health care shall retain the health care records of his patients as part of his regularly maintained records for 5 years after their receipt or production. Health care records may be retained in written form, or by microfilm or any other recognized form of size reduction, including, without limitation, microfiche, computer disc, magnetic tape and optical disk, which does not adversely affect their use for the purposes of NRS 629.061. Health care records may be created, authenticated and stored in a computer system which limits access to those records.

TITLE 55. BANKS AND RELATED ORGANIZATIONS

CHAPTER 665. EXAMINATIONS AND REPORTS

Citation: NRS 665.165

✍ **§ 665.165. Preservation of records.**

1. Every state bank shall retain its business records for such periods as are or may be prescribed by or in accordance with the terms of the section.

2. Each state bank shall retain permanently the minute books of meetings of its stockholders and directors, its capital stock ledger and capital stock certificate ledger or stubs, its general ledger, its investment ledger, its copies of bank examination reports, and all records which the commissioner in accordance with this section requires to be retained permanently.

3. All other bank records must be retained for such periods as the commissioner may in accordance with this section prescribe.

4. The commissioner shall, from time to time, issue regulations classifying all records kept by state banks and prescribe the period for which records in each class must be retained. Such periods may be permanent or for a lesser term of years. The commissioner shall keep such regulations current and shall revise them at least once every 3 years. In issuing and revising such regulations, the commissioner shall consider:

(a) Actions at law and administrative proceedings in which the production of bank records might be necessary or desirable.

(b) State and federal statutes of limitation applicable to such actions or proceedings.

(c) The availability of information contained in bank records from other sources.

(d) Such other matters as the commissioner considers pertinent in order that his regulations will require banks to retain their records for as short a period as is commensurate with the interests of bank customers and shareholders and of the people of this state in having bank records available.

5. Any state bank may dispose of any record which has been retained for the period prescribed by or in accordance with the

terms of this section for retention of records of its class, and shall thereafter be under no duty to produce such record in any action or proceeding.

6. Any state bank may cause any or all records required to be kept pursuant to this section to be reproduced by the microphotographic process, optical disk imaging or any other equivalent technique designed to ensure an accurate reproduction of the original. Any such reproduction has the same effect as the original. Any such reproduction has the same effect as the original. Upon completion of such a duplication, the original of any record may be destroyed.

7. To the extent that they are not in contravention of any law of the United States, the provisions of this section apply to all banks doing business in this state.

Source: Nevada Administrative Code

Citation: NAC 239.590

✪ § 239.590. "Duplicate" defined.

"Duplicate" means a counterpart produced:

1. By the same impression as the original;
2. From the same matrix;
3. By means of photography, including enlargements and miniatures;
4. By mechanical or electronic rerecording;
5. By chemical reproduction; or
6. By other equivalent technique designed to ensure an accurate reproduction of the original.

The term includes an accurate an unabridged copy of a record or series of records that is not an original.

Citation: NAC 239.605

✪ § 239.605. "Image" defined.

"Image" means an exact duplicate of an original document.

Citation: NAC 239.640

✪ § 239.640. "Optical imaging system" defined.

"Optical imaging system" means hardware and software for computer which record complete images by:

1. Scanning the images with a source of light, such as a laser;
2. Converting the images into a digital electronic format, and
3. Storing the converted images on an optical media which allows for the rapid retrieval of the stored images through indexing and the reproduction of the entire original image.

Citation: NAC 239.645

✪ § 239.645. "Optical media" defined.

"Optical media" means a special disk, computer hard disk or magnetic tape on which images are stored.

Citation: NAC 239.650

✪ § 239.650. "Original" Defined.

1. An "original" of a writing or recording is the writing or recording itself or any counterpart intended to have the same effect by a person executing or issuing it.
2. An "original" of a photograph includes the negative or any print therefrom.
3. If data are stored in a computer or similar device, any printout or other output readable by sight, shown accurately to reflect the data, is an "original".
4. A reproduction made pursuant to the provisions of NRS 239.051, or any record designated by the state board of examiners to be an original, including the stored security copy and the copy maintained for the use of authorized persons is an "original".

Citation: NAC 239.655

✪ § 239.655. "Preserved" defined.

"Preserved" means the filing, storage or other method of systematically maintaining documentary materials by an agency. The terms also applies to materials while they are temporarily removed from established filing systems.

Citation: NAC 239.660

✪ § 239.660. "Received" defined.

"Received" means the receipt of documentary materials by personnel of a state agency, whether in person, by messenger, mail, electronic transmission or by any other method. The term does not refer to misdirected materials.

Citation: NAC 239.755

✪ § 239.755. Priority for microfilming and protection of vital records.

Each state agency shall give priority to the microfilming and protection of its vital records within the limits of the agency's budget. If money has been appropriated for the microfilming or storage of records, the microfilming of vital records must be given priority.

Citation: NAC 239.760

✪ § 239.760. Treatment of electronic records.

1. A state agency; which produces an electronic record must include the entire record or image. Each electronic record must include:
   (a) The date the record was produced;
   (b) The date any alteration was produced; and
   (c) Evidence that the record was authorized for issue or signature.
2. The temperature in the area used to store electronic records must be maintained at or above 50 degrees Fahrenheit, but not more than 75 degrees Fahrenheit.
3. The agency's personnel shall transfer electronic mail records to a medium which will ensure retention until the minimum period for retention has passed.
4. After the minimum period for retention has passed, the agency may destroy the electronic records by erasing or destroying the disk or tape.
5. Except as otherwise provided in this subsection, electronic records that have been appraised and scheduled to be transferred to the division must not be sent in computer disk or tape format. The agency shall transfer the electronic record onto bond paper, microfilm or microfiche before transferring it to the division. Audio and audio-visual tapes and cassettes may be transferred in their original form.
6. As used in this section, "electronic records" mean official

state records which are stored, accessed and retrieved through a machine readable system, whether by magnetic impulse, mechanical or electronic recording, or other form of data compilation, including all computer systems, floppy disks, optical disks, magnetic tape, hard disks and audio-visual systems.

USE OF OPTICAL IMAGING SYSTEM

Citation: NAC 239.765

✪ § 239.765. Applicability.

The provisions of NAC 239.770 to 239.845, inclusive, apply to any state agency that uses an optical imaging system to use, maintain, retain, or preserve its records.

Citation: NAC 239.770

✪ § 239.770. Maintenance of access to digital information stored on optical media.

To ensure that access to digital information stored on optical media is maintained, a state agency shall:

1. Use an optical imaging system that is built from hardware and software for computers that conform to nonproprietary standards or generally accepted standards within the industry; and
2. Require the seller of the system to deposit a copy of the computer code with a bank, the state archives or a facility for the storage of records for use by the agency if the seller's business fails.

Citation: NAC 239.775

✪ § 239.775. Preservation of records stored on optical media; media for storage of images.

1. To ensure that records stored on optical media are preserved, a state agency shall:

(a) Adopt and enforce written procedures for the proper care and handling of that part of the optical imaging system where images are stored. The procedures must:

(1) Include standards for keeping the equipment in an area that is clean and free from dust;

(2) Prohibit eating, drinking and smoking in the area in which the equipment is stored or operated; and

(3) Require the use of devices that protect against the sudden loss or increase of electricity, such as surge protectors and, if needed, line conditioners.

(b) Maintain stable environmental conditions in the areas where the equipment and optical media are stored.

2. Images may be stored on a special disk, computer hard disk or magnetic tape.

Citation: NAC 239.780

✪ § 239.780. Maintenance of access to long-term records.

To ensure that access to long-term records is maintained, a state agency shall:

1. Improve its equipment as technology advances, within budgetary constraints, and recopy optical media as required;
2. Recopy optical media at least every 10 years, based upon the projected longevity of the optical disc; or
3. Transfer data from an obsolete method of generating optical technology to an improved method and, if appropriate, reject accepted methods which are at risk of becoming obsolete.

Citation: NAC 239.785

✪ § 239.785. Options regarding file headers.

A state agency shall:

1. Require the use of nonproprietary file headers to label digital images, such as "Tagged Image File Format (TIFF)";
2. Require the developer of the optical imaging system to provide a bridge to nonproprietary file headers; or
3. Require the developer of the optical imaging system to supply a detailed definition of the structure of the file headers used to label digital images.

Citation: NAC 239.790

✪ § 239.790. Maintenance of readability of digital images.

The written procedures used by a state agency for the operation of an optical imaging system must ensure that the readability of the digital images is maintained by copying the optical media periodically when the relocation table reaches a 70-percent capacity.

Citation: NAC 239.795

✪ § 239.795. Protection of quality of digital images.

A state agency shall protect the quality of digital images recorded and stored by an optical imaging system. To carry out this duty, a state agency shall:

1. Provide periodic maintenance for the optical imaging system.
2. Ensure the optical drives are recalibrated annually.
3. Periodically evaluate the quality of a sampling of scanned images and related index data.
4. Ensure that the data for each scanned image is written to optical media after the scanning.
5. Use a scanning density of at least 200 dots per inch for office documents.
6. Use a scanning density of at least 300 dots per inch for engineering drawings, maps and documents with detailed backgrounds.
7. Periodically validate the scanning density selected by testing documents.
8. Test selected documents to verify the capability of the scanner and the requirements for modifying the hardware used before initiating a project to convert to an optical imaging system that captures the full spectrum of color.
9. Restrict the use of the gray scale to photographs with a continuous tone, except in unusual circumstances.
10. Organize a committee within the agency to determine the best quality of the image required for different formats of records before and after the records are scanned. The decisions made by this committee must be kept in a written log.
11. If possible, ensure that its optical imaging system has the capacity to comply with the standards of the Consultative Committee on International Telegraphy and Telephony relating to the use of standard compression techniques to reduce the volume of digital information that comprises a scanned image for long-term records.
12. If the optical imaging system does not have the capacity to use standard compression techniques, require the seller to provide a bridge between proprietary compression techniques and standard compression techniques which comply with the standards established by the Consultative Committee on International Telegraphy and Telephony.

Citation: NAC 239.800

✪ § 239.800. Duties of state agency acquiring new optical imaging system.

If a state agency is acquiring a new optical imaging system, the agency shall:

1. Acquire a system that is designed to permit the users to interchange hardware with minimal impact on the primary operating software and is capable of being improved without the loss of data; or
2. Require the seller to provide a bridge to an optical imaging system with nonproprietary configurations.

Citation: NAC 239.805

✪ § 239.805. Minimizing obsolescence of system.

A state agency shall ensure that the obsolescence of its optical imaging system if minimized by:

1. Improving its system so that it has the capability of reading and converting information written by systems with older technology;
2. Acquiring a new optical imaging system that is capable of reading and converting information written by its existing system; or
3. Requiring the seller to guarantee the conversion of 100 percent of the stored images and index data in lieu of having the capability to use hardware.

Citation: 239.810

✪ § 239.810. Documentation of method used to enable communication of peripheral devices from different manufacturers.

A state agency shall obtain from the manufacturer of its optical imaging system or from the person who integrated its system, complete documentation of the hardware and software used by its system to enable optical drives and other peripheral devices obtained from different manufacturers to communicate with each other.

Citation: NAC 239.815

✪ § 239.815. Protection of indexing data.

A state agency shall ensure that the indexing data of its optical imaging system will not be lost by:

1. Storing the indexing data in the computer memory or on magnetic tape; or
2. Writing the indexing data for each optical platter at various locations on that disk.

Citation: NAC 239.820

✪ § 239.820. Procedures to ensure availability of technical information.

To ensure that all technical information relating to its optical imaging system will be available, a state agency shall:

1. Require the delivery of a complete set of technical information to the organization responsible for the operation of the application system for the optical imaging system;
2. Maintain records relating to all aspects of:

(a) The design and use of the optical imaging system, including the administrative procedures for digital imaging and the retrieval and storage of information;

(b) The specifications for the technical system; and

(c) Any problems encountered from the use of the system and the measures used to solve those problems, including any manner in which the hardware or software was modified; and

3. Maintain records of all information describing the indexing system used.

Citation: NAC 239.825

✪ § 239.825. Use of rewritable recording system or system capable of writing information once and reading it many times.

1. A state agency shall:

(a) Use an optical imaging system that is capable of writing information once and reading it many times (WORM) for long-term records with legal or research or archival value;

(b) Establish written security procedures to be followed by persons who are allowed to use such and system; and

(c) Maintain a record of all rewrites and deletions that are made on an optical imaging system.

2. Before selecting an optical imaging system that is capable of writing information once and reading it many times or when selecting a rewritable recording system, a state agency shall consider:

(a) Whether the functions and duties of the agency will best be carried out by the use of such a system;

(b) The available resources; and

(c) The level of standardization that can be achieved by the use of an optical imaging system.

Citation: NAC 239.830

✪ § 239.830. Composition of optical disk media.

A state agency shall use an optical disk media composed of polycarbonate or tempered glass substrates, or a material of equal or greater quality.

Citation: NAC 239.835

✪ § 239.835. Use of jukebox to store optical media.

A state agency may use a jukebox to store optical media if:

1. Rapid access to the optical media is required;
2. Physical control of the optical media is required; or
3. It is storing a large number of records.

Citation: NAC 239.840

✪ § 239.840. Minimum expected longevity of optical media; storage and cleaning of optical media; avoidance of electrical interference.

A state agency shall:

1. Use optical media with an expected longevity of at least 20 years after information is entered on the disk, as determined by accelerated aging tests that are applied to specific locations on the surface of the media.
2. If possible, store optical media in an area with stable temperatures of not less than 65 degrees Fahrenheit and not more than 75 degrees Fahrenheit.
3. Not use an optical imaging system in the same physical proximity with an electrostatic copier or other electronic device

that may cause electrical interference.

4. Periodically clean optical media and equipment to remove dust and other particulates.

Citation:	NAC 239.845

✪ **§ 239.845. Retention of certain original records required; copies of stored images.**

1. A state agency shall:

(a) Retain the original of any long-term record with legal or research or archival value that is stored by an optical imaging system; and

(b) Provide for a copy of all images stored by an optical imaging system, as prescribed by paragraph (a) of subsection 3 of NRS 239.051.

2. An original of any record stored by an optical imaging system shall be deemed to include any copy produced by the stored image on the optical media and the copy provided for pursuant to subsection 1.

Citation:	NAC 449.379

✪ **§ 449.379. Hospitals: Medical records.**

1. A medical record must be maintained for every patient admitted to a hospital.

2. Records must be permanent, either printed, typewritten or legibly written. All records must be kept in conformity with recognized standards. Medical histories must be retained for 25 years and may be microfilmed after 3 years if stored on rolls. Emergency room and outpatient records may be microfilmed after 1 year. If unitized jackets or cards are used, microfilming may be done at the time of discharge. Evidence of compliance with these requirements must be demonstrated to the health division.

3. If applicable, records must include the following:

(a) Patient's name.

(b) Address at time of admission.

(c) Date of birth.

(d) Sex.

(e) Social security number.

(f) Marital status.

(g) Date of admission.

(h) Name, address and telephone number of person or agency responsible for patient.

(i) Name of attending physician.

(j) If patient is a minor, name and address of parents or guardian.

(k) Diagnosis upon admission.

(l) Race.

(m) Religion.

(n) State and county of birth.

(o) Progress notes by physician.

(p) Chief complaint.

(q) Consultations.

(r) Nurse's notes which must conform with statute of limitations.

(s) Citizenship.

(t) Orders for medication and treatment.

(u) Orders for diet.

(v) History and physical examination.

(w) Condition and diagnosis of patient at time of discharge.

(x) Place where discharged.

(y) Laboratory reports of all tests completed.

(z) Reprots of all X-rays completed.

(aa) Complete surgical record, including anesthesia record, preoperative diagnosis, operative procedure and findings, postoperative diagnosis and tissue diagnosis on all specimens surgically removed.

(bb) Complete obstetrical record, including prenatal, labor, delivery, and complete newborn record including birth certificate, test results and the general condition of the baby on discharge.

(cc) Copy of death certificate.

4. Records must contain sufficient information to justify the diagnosis, warrant treatment and vindicate the end results. Only members of the medical and house staff may write or dictate medical histories and physical examinations. Records must be authenticated and signed by a licensed physician.

Agency:	Department of Industrial Relations Division of Occupational Safety and Health

REGULATIONS FOR THE NEVADA OCCUPATIONAL SAFETY AND HEALTH ENFORCEMENT PROGRAM

RECORDS AND REPORTS

Citation:	NAC 618.556

✍ **§ 618.556. Employer's log and summary.**

1. Except as otherwise provided in subsection 2 and NAC 618.589, each employer shall maintain in each of his establishments a log and summary of all recordable occupational injuries and illnesses for that establishment. Each employer shall enter each recordable occupational injury and illness on the log and summary as early as practicable, but no later than 6 working days after receiving information that a recordable case has occurred. For this purpose, Occupational Safety and Health Administration Form No. 200 or any state or private form which is equivalent may be used. Form No. 200 or its equivalent must be completed in detail as provided in the form and the instruction contained in it. If an equivalent form is used, such as a printout from data processing equipment, the information must be as readable and comprehensible as Form No. 200 to a person not familiar with the data processing equipment.

2. Any employer may maintain the log and summary of occupational injuries and illnesses at a place other than the establishment or by means of data processing equipment, or both, if:

(a) There is available at the place where the log and summary are maintained sufficient information to complete the log and summary within 6 working days after receiving information that a recordable case has occurred; and

(b) At the particular establishment, there is available a copy of the log and summary which reflects separately the occupational injuries and illnesses which have occurred at that establishment and is complete and current to a date within 45 calendar days after the date of occurrence.

State: New Hampshire
Source: New Hampshire Revised Statutes

TITLE 1. THE STATE AND ITS GOVERNMENT.

CHAPTER 5. DEPARTMENT OF STATE.

Citation: NHRS 5:38

✪ **§ 5:38. Disposal of Records.**

Unless otherwise provided by law with respect to particular departments or particular records, records not having a permanent or historical value may be destroyed at the end of 4 years from their making, provided that the rules of the director, as adopted under RSA 5:40, may provide that designated records may be destroyed at an earlier period or require their retention for a longer period.

CHAPTER 6. STATE TREASURER AND STATE ACCOUNTS.

Citation: NHRS 6:6

✪ **§ 6:6. Destruction of Documents.**

The state treasurer may destroy documents, canceled checks, and papers filed in his office at the end of 7 years from the time of filing as herein provided. All checks issued prior to July 1, 1945 may be destroyed without microfilming or photostating or other process of reproduction. All checks of which a microfilm or photostat record has been made or which have been accurately reproduced by some other process may be destroyed at the end of 2 years from the time of filing. He shall submit to the governor and council a statement describing documents, checks and papers that he desires to remove from the files and a committee of the council shall examine the same. If the committee approves such destruction a record shall be made of all such documents, checks and papers, and they shall then be destroyed by the state treasurer in the presence of the committee.

CHAPTER 33-A. DISPOSITION OF MUNICIPAL RECORDS.

Citation: NHRS 33-A:5

✪ **§ 33-A:5. Microfilming.**

If municipal records are disposed of by microfilming, 2 films shall be produced. One film shall be retained by the municipality in a fireproof container and properly labeled. One shall be transferred to a suitable location for permanent storage.

TITLE 28. PARTNERSHIPS.

CHAPTER 304-B. UNIFORM LIMITED PARTNERSHIP ACT.

Citation: NHRS 304-B:5

✍ **§ 304-B:5. Records to be kept.**

I. Each limited partnership shall keep at the office referred to in RSA 304-B:4,I the following:
(a) A current list of the full name and last known business address of each partner, separately identifying the general partners (in alphabetical order) and the limited partners (in alphabetical order);
(b) A copy of the certificate of limited partnership and all certificates of amendment thereto, together with executed copies of any powers of attorney pursuant to which any certificate has been executed;
(c) Copies of the limited partnership's federal, state and local income tax returns and reports, if any, for the 3 most recent years;
(d) Copies of any then effective written partnership agreements and of any financial statements of the limited partnership for the 3 most recent years; and
(e) Unless contained in a written partnership agreement, a writing setting out:
(1) The amount of cash and a description and statement of the agreed value of the other property or services contributed by each partner and which each partner has agreed to contribute;
(2) The times at which or events on the happening of which any additional contributions agreed to be made by each partner are to be made;
(3) Any right of a partner to receive, or of a general partner to make, distributions to a partner which include a return of all or any part of the partner's contribution; and
(4) Any events upon the happening of which the limited partnership is to be dissolved and its affairs wound up.
II. Records kept under this section are subject to inspection and copying at the reasonable request and at the expense of any partner during ordinary business hours.

CHAPTER 304-C. LIMITED LIABILITY COMPANIES.

MEMBERS AND MANAGERS

Citation: NHRS 304-C:28

✍ **§ 304-C:28 Access to and Confidentiality of Information; Records.**

I. Each member of a limited liability company has the right to obtain from the limited liability company from time to time upon reasonable demand for any purpose reasonably related to the member's interest as a member of the limited liability company:
(a) True and full information regarding the status of the business and financial condition of the limited liability company as may be set forth in information required to be documented or filed by law;
(b) Promptly after becoming available, a copy of the limited liability company's federal, state and local income tax returns for each year;
(c) A current list of the name and last known business, residence or mailing address of each member and manager;
(d) A copy of the limited liability company agreement and the certificate of formation and all amendments, together with executed copies of any written powers of attorney pursuant to which the limited liability company agreement and any certificate and al amendments have been executed;
(e) True and full information regarding the amount of cash and a description and statement of the agreed value of any other property or services contributed by each member and which each member has agreed to contribute in the future, and the date on which each became a member; and
(f) Other information regarding the affairs of the limited liability company as is just and reasonable.
II. Each manager shall have the right to examine all of the information described in paragraph I for a purpose reasonably related to his position as a manager.
III. The manager of a limited liability company shall have the right to keep confidential from the members, for such period of time as the manager deems reasonable, any information which the

manager reasonably believes to be in the nature of trade secrets or other information the disclosure of which the manager in good faith believes is not in the best interest of the limited liability company or could damage the limited liability company or its business or which the limited liability company is required by law or by agreement with a third party to keep confidential.

IV. A limited liability company may maintain its records in other than a written form is such form is capable of conversion into written form within a reasonable time.

V. Any demand by a member under this section shall be in writing and shall state the purpose of such demand.

VI. Access to information and records provided by this section may be conditioned upon and provided subject to such reasonable standards as may be set forth in a limited liability company agreement or otherwise established by a manager or, if there is not manager, the members, as to:

(a) The location of the documents;

(b) The time and days of the week during which the information will be available;

(c) If the records are not those maintained in the ordinary course of business, the expense of providing the information requested.

VII. Any action to enforce any right arising under this section shall be brought in the superior court.

TITLE 31. TRADE AND COMMERCE.

CHAPTER 337-A. PRESERVATION OF PRIVATE BUSINESS RECORDS.

Citation: **NHRS 337-A:1**

✍ § 337-A:1. Definitions.

As used in this chapter:

I. "Business" includes every kind of private business, profession, occupation, calling or operation of private institutions, whether carried on for profit or not.

II. "Person" means an individual, partnership, corporation, or any other association.

III. "Records" or "business records" include books of account, vouchers, documents, canceled checks, payrolls, correspondence, records of sales, personnel, equipment and production, reports relating to any or all such records, and other business papers.

IV. "Reproduction" means a reproduction or durable medium for making a reproduction obtained by any photographic, photostatic, microfilm, microcard, miniature photographic or other process which accurately reproduces or forms a durable medium for so reproducing the original.

Citation: **NHRS 337-A:3**

✍ § 337-A:3. Reproductions.

If in the regular course of business a person makes reproductions of original business records, the preservation of such reproductions constitutes compliance with any laws of this state requiring that business records be kept or preserved.

Source: **New Hampshire Rules of Evidence**

☞ Rule 1001. Definitions

For purposes of this article the following definitions are applicable:

(1) *Writings and recordings.* — "Writings" and "recordings" consist of letters, words, or numbers, or their equivalent, set down by handwriting, typewriting, printing, photostating, photographing, magnetic impulse, mechanical or electronic recording, or other form of data compilation.

(2) *Photographs.* — "Photographs" include still photographs, X-ray films, video tapes, and motion pictures.

(3) *Original.* — An "original" of a writing or recording is the writing or recording itself or any counterpart intended to have the same effect by a person executing or issuing it. An "original" of a photograph includes the negative or any print therefrom. If data are stored in a computer or similar device, any printout or other output readable by sight, shown to reflect the data accurately, is an "original".

(4) *Duplicate.* — A "duplicate" is a counterpart produced by the same impression as the original, or from the same matrix, or by means of photography, including enlargements and miniatures, or by mechanical or electronic re-recording, or by chemical reproduction, or by other equivalent techniques which accurately reproduces the original.

☞ Rule 1003. Admissibility of duplicates.

A duplicate is admissible to the same extent as an original unless (1) a genuine question is raised as to the authenticity of the original or (2) in the circumstances it would be unfair to admit the duplicate in lieu of the original.

[See Appendix A. Uniform Rules of Evidence for additional provisions.]

State: **New Jersey**
Source: **New Jersey Statutes Annotated**

TITLE 2A. ADMINISTRATION OF CIVIL AND CRIMINAL JUSTICE

SUBTITLE 9. EVIDENCE, WITNESS AND PUBLIC HEARINGS.

CHAPTER 82. DOCUMENTS, RECORDS AND OTHER WRITTEN INSTRUMENTS.

Article 8. Photographic Copies.

Photographic Copies of Business and Public Records As Evidence Act

Citation: **NJSA 2A:82-38**

☞ § 2A:82-38. Photographic, photostatic, etc., copies as competent evidence.

If any business, institution, member of a profession or calling, or any department or agency of government, in the regular course of business or activity has kept or recorded any memorandum, writing, entry, print, representation or combination thereof, of any act, transaction, occurrence or event, and in the regular course of business has caused any or all of the same to be recorded, copied or reproduced by any photographic, photostatic, microfilm, microcard, miniature photographic, or other process which accurately produces or forms a durable medium for so reproducing the original, the original may be destroyed in the regular course of business unless its preservation is required by law. Such reproduction, when satisfactorily identified, is as admissible in evidence as the original itself in any judicial or administrative proceeding whether the original is in existence or not and an enlargement or facsimile of such reproduction is likewise admissible in evidence if the original reproduction is in existence and available for inspection under direction of court. The introduction of a reproduced record, enlargement or facsimile, does not preclude admission of the original.

TITLE 26. HEALTH AND VITAL STATISTICS.

CHAPTER 8. REGISTRATION OF VITAL STATISTICS.

Citation: NJSA 26:8-5

✍ ✪ **§ 26:8-5. Institutional Records.**

The person in charge of a hospital, almshouse, lying-in, penal, or other institution, public or private, to which any person resorts for treatment of disease or confinement, or is committed by process of law, shall make a record of all the personal and statistical particulars relative to each inmate in such institution, at the time of admission, and shall make a complete medical record covering the period of such person's confinement in such institution.

The medical records provided for herein or photographic reproductions thereof shall be retained by the custodian of records of such institution for a period of 10 years following the most recent discharge of the patient, or until the person confined therein reaches the age of 23 years, whichever is the longer period of time. In addition, a discharge summary sheet shall be retained by such custodian of records for a period of 20 years following the most recent discharge of the patient. The discharge summary sheet shall contain the patient's name, address, dates of admission and discharge and a summary of the treatment and the medication rendered during the patient's stay. Any X-ray films related to such confinement, or any size reproductions thereof which maintain the clarity of the original shall be retained by such custodian of records for a period of 5 years.

In case of any person admitted or committed for treatment of disease, the physician in charge shall specify, for entry in the record, the nature of the disease and where, in his opinion, it was contracted.

The personal particulars and information required by this section shall be obtained from the individual himself if practicable; and when not, they shall be obtained in as complete a manner as possible from relatives, friends, or other persons acquainted with the facts.

TITLE 34. LABOR AND WORKMEN'S COMPENSATION.

CHAPTER 15. WORKMEN'S COMPENSATION.

Citation: NJSA 34:15-41

☞ **§ 34:15-41. Claims barred after two years.**

In case of personal injury or death all claims for compensation on account thereof shall be forever barred unless a petition is filed in duplicate with the secretary of the workmen's compensation bureau, as prescribed by section 34:15-51 of this title.

Article 6. Reports by Employer and Insurer.

Citation: NJSA 34:15-97

☞ **§ 34:15-97. Report by employer not carrying insurance.**

An employer not carrying compensation insurance shall make report of any accident or compensable occupation disease causing a disability extending beyond the waiting period or causing any permanent injury. The report shall be prepared and sent immediately upon the employer's having knowledge of the disability or injury named above, and shall be made out in duplicate upon forms to be secured from the workers' compensation bureau. One copy shall be mailed to the bureau and one copy kept on file by the employer. Within three weeks after the accident, or the obtaining of knowledge of compensable occupational disease, the employer operating under article 2 of this chapter (34:15-7 et seq.), shall send to the bureau a second report, containing a statement of wages and an agreement to care for the case according to the terms of the compensation law. This form shall be signed by the employee as provided thereon and by the employer. Immediately upon the employee's recovering so as to be able to resume work, the employer shall file with the bureau a final report setting forth the length of disability, the nature and extent of permanent injury, if any, and the compensation payable for each. This form shall also be signed by the employer and the employee.

Article 8. Destruction of Records

Citation: NJSA 34:15-126

☞ ✪ **§ 34:15-126. Microfilm, force and effect of.**

Any microfilm made by the Division of Workmen's Compensation pursuant to law, or a certified copy of such microfilm, shall have the same force and effect as the original in any court or public proceeding and shall be evidential in like manner and to the same effect as though the original record had been there produced and proved.

TITLE 39. MOTOR VEHICLES AND TRAFFIC REGULATION.

CHAPTER 3. MOTOR VEHICLES.

Citation: NJSA 39:3-28

☞ ✪ **§ 39:3-28. Licenses and registrations indexed; certified copies of applications as evidence; destruction of applications and copies.**

The director shall cause all applications for registration and drivers' licenses to be alphabetically indexed, and any original application or copy thereof, whether made by photography, micrograph or otherwise, certified to be a true copy under the hand of the director shall be received as evidence in any court to prove the facts contained therein. For each uncertified copy so issued the director shall collect a fee of $8 and for each certified copy so issued the director shall collect a fee of $10.

The director may destroy all records of registration certificates or drivers' licenses and their alphabetical indices when such registration or drivers' licenses applicable thereto have expired, after having made copies of such records by means of photography, microphotograph or otherwise. Such copies made by photography, micrograph or otherwise may be destroyed when they have been on file in the office of the director for a period of 3 years, or more.

TITLE 47. PUBLIC RECORDS.

CHAPTER 1. RECORDS AND RECORDING OFFICES GENERALLY.

Citation: NJSA 47:1-5

☞ ✪ **§ 47:1-5. Photographic, data records in certain offices.**

All papers, documents and instruments in writing authorized or required by law to be recorded, filed, registered, or indexed in the office of the Secretary of State, clerk, register of deeds and mortgages and surrogate of any county of this State, as well as the record and index of any such papers, documents or instruments in writing, which may be recopied, recorded or transcribed pursuant to any law of this State, may be recopied, rerecorded, reindexed or transcribed in such offices by means of photography, data processing or image processing, and such rerecord or transcribing, made by means of photography, data processing or image processing, shall have the same legal force, meaning and effect as if made in handwriting or in typewriting.

The Secretary of State, clerk, register of deeds and mortgages end surrogate of any county of this State may make a copy by means of photography, data processing or image processing of any document or instrument and such photographic, data processed or image processed copy, if made, shall have the same legal force, meaning and effect as if made in handwriting or in typewriting.

CHAPTER 2. PUBLIC RECORDS OFFICE.

Citation: NJSA 47:2-6

✪ **§ 47:2-6. Copies of record as evidence; certification; originals preserved.**

Whenever a copy of any record is made in accordance with the provisions of section 47:2-5 of this title, and after it has been compared with the original, it shall be certified by the public official or board having the legal custody and control of the original. Thereafter, the copy shall be considered and accepted as evidence, and treated for all other purposes, as though it were the original.

The original shall be cared for and preserved, as if no copy had been made, for such examination as may be directed by an order of court in any action or proceeding in which the accuracy of the copy is questioned.

Citation: NJSA 47:3-26

✪ **§ 47:3-26. Photographing, microphotographing and microfilming of public records; destruction of originals; evidence.**

The Bureau of Archives and History in the Department of Education, with the approval of the State Records Committee, established by section six hereof, shall formulate standards and procedures for the photographing, microphotographing and microfilming of public records and for the preservation, examination and use of such records, including the indexing and arrangement thereof, for convenient reference purposes.

Whenever any officer, commission, agency or authority of the State or of any political subdivision thereof, including subordinate boards thereof, shall have photographed, microphotographed or microfilmed all or any part of the public records, kept or required by law to be received and indexed in such manner as to conform with the standards and procedures, and such photographs, microphotographs or microfilms have been placed in conveniently accessible files and provision shall have been made for the preservation, examination and use of the same in conformity with the said standards and procedures, the original records from which the photographs, microphotographs or microfilms have been made, or any part thereof, may be destroyed or the records therein otherwise effectively obliterated; *provided*, the said bureau shall first have given its written consent to such destruction or other disposition.

In the event of any such destruction or other disposition of any public records under the provisions of this section, the photograph, microphotograph or microfilm, or a certified copy of said photograph, microphotograph or microfilm, shall be receivable in evidence in any court or proceeding and shall have the same force and effect as though the original public record had been there produced and proved.

Citation: NJSA 47:11-12

✪ **§ 47:11-12 Rules, regulations, systems of recording.**

6.a. The Division of Archives and Records Management in the Department of State, with the approval of the State Records Committee established pursuant to section 8 of P.L. 1953, c. 410 (C.47:3-20), shall promulgate such rules and regulations as may be necessary to effectuate the purposes of this act and to safeguard the State's documentary heritage.

b. No public agency, County Clerk or Register shall adopt, use or employ any system for recording, filing, registration or indexing as authorized by R.S.47:1-5, as amended by this act, unless the same shall conform to the rules and regulations to be promulgated by the Division of Archives and Records Management in the Department of State pursuant to subsection a of this section, and shall first be approved by the Division of Archives and Records Management. No such system shall be approved until the Division of Archives and Records Management shall have fully promulgated those rules and regulations.

c. Any system for recording, filing, registration or indexing as authorized by R.S. 47:1-5, as amended by this act, which employs data processing or image processing, and which was adopted, used or employed prior to the effective date of this act, shall nevertheless be subject to the rules and regulations to be promulgated by the Division of Archives and Records Management pursuant to subsection a. of this section. The approval of the Division of Archives and Records Management shall be necessary to bring about the compliance of such system, in a prompt and orderly fashion, with the standards set forth in the rules and regulations.

Source: New Jersey Rules of Evidence

ARTICLE X. CONTENTS OF WRITINGS, RECORDINGS AND PHOTOGRAPHS.

☞ **Rule 1001. Definitions**

For purposes of this article the following definitions are applicable:

(1) *Writings and recordings.* — "Writings" and "recordings" consist of letters, words, or numbers, or their equivalent, set down by handwriting, typewriting, printing, photostating, photographing, magnetic impulse, mechanical or electronic recording, or other form of data compilation.

(2) *Photographs.* — "Photographs" include still photographs, X-ray films, video tapes, and motion pictures.

(3) *Original.* — An "original" of a writing or recording is the

writing or recording itself or any counterpart intended to have the same effect by a person executing or issuing it. An "original" of a photograph includes the negative or any print therefrom. If data are stored in a computer or similar device, any printout or other output readable by sight, shown to reflect the data accurately, is an "original".

(4) *Duplicate.* — A "duplicate" is a counterpart produced by the same impression as the original, or from the same matrix, or by means of photography, including enlargements and miniatures, or by mechanical or electronic re-recording, or by chemical reproduction, or by other equivalent techniques which accurately reproduces the original.

☞ Rule 1003. Admissibility of duplicates.

A duplicate is admissible to the same extent as an original unless (1) a genuine question is raised as to the authenticity of the original or (2) in the circumstances it would be unfair to admit the duplicate in lieu of the original.

Source: New Jersey Administrative Code
Agency: Department of Labor and Industry, Division of Employment Security

TITLE 12. DEPARTMENT OF LABOR AND INDUSTRY.

CHAPTER 16. CONTRIBUTIONS, RECORDS & REPORTS.

SUBCHAPTER 2. RECORDS.

Citation: NJAC 12:16-2.3

✍ § 12:16-2.3. Records defined.

Records are defined as all books of original entry plus any summarizations of other media used to post to a general ledger or its equivalent as well as all Federal and State tax returns. Records shall also include machine sensible data media used for recording, consolidating, and summarizing accounting transactions within an employing unit's automatic data processing system.

Citation: NJAC 12:16-13.7

✍ § 12:16-13.7. Wage reporting.

* * * * *

(c) The following pertains to magnetic media reporting:

1. For all calendar quarters subsequent to the quarter ending December 31, 1994 all employers who would report in excess of 250 employees on Form WR-30, "Employer Report of Wages Paid," in any calendar quarter shall file such report via magnetic media in a form and manner specified by the Controller or his or her designee.
2. For all calendar quarters subsequent to the quarter ending December 31, 1995 all employers who would report in excess of 100 employees on Form WR-30, "Employer Report of Wages Paid," in any calendar quarter shall file such report via magnetic media in a form and manner specified by the Controller or his or her designee.
3. For all calendar quarters subsequent to the quarter ending December 31, 1994, all third party payroll processors who on a quarterly basis generate and file with the New Jersey Department of Labor Form WR-30 "Employer Report of Wages Paid," and Form UC-27, "Quarterly Contributions Report," together with payment of contributions liability shall file the WR-30 reports for all such clients via magnetic media directly to the Division of Unemployment Insurance/Disability Financing in a form and manner specified by the Controller or his or her designee, if the aggregate number of employees for all clients processed and so reported by the third party exceeds 100 in any calendar quarter.
4. Employers or third-party payroll processors may have the requirements in (c)1 through 3 above waived or extended for good cause as defined in N.J.A.C. 12:19-1.2 upon written application for waiver or extension to the Controller or his or her designee.
5. If an employer or third-party payroll processor fails to comply with the provisions of this subsection the penalties specified in N.J.A.C. 12:16-13.7(b) shall apply.

Agency: Department of the Treasury

TITLE 18. DEPARTMENT OF TREASURY — TAXATION.

CHAPTER 24. SALES AND USE TAX ACT.

Citation: NJAC 18:24-2.3

✍ § 18:24-2.3. General requirements.

(a) A true copy of all sales slips, invoices, receipts, statements, memoranda of price, or cash register tapes, issued to any customer by a vendor who is required to be registered pursuant to the provisions of the Sales and Use Tax Act (N.J.S.A. 54:32B-1 et seq.) must be available for inspection and examination at any time upon demand by the Director, Division of Taxation, or his duly authorized agent or employee and shall be preserved for a period of three years from the filing date of the quarterly period for the filing of sales tax returns to which such records pertain.

(b) Microfilm reproductions of general books of account, such as cash books, journals, voucher registers, ledgers, etc., are not acceptable in lieu of original records. However, microfilm reproductions of supporting records of details, such as sales invoices, purchase invoices, credit memoranda, etc., may be maintained providing the following conditions are met:

1. Appropriate facilities are provided for preservation of the films for periods required.
2. Microfilm rolls are indexed, cross referenced, labeled to show beginning and ending numbers or beginning and ending alphabetical listing of documents included, and are systematically filed.
3. The taxpayer agrees to provide transcriptions of any information contained on microfilm which may be required for purposes of verification of tax liability.
4. Proper facilities are provided for the ready inspection and location of the particular records, including modern projectors for viewing and copying the records.

(c) A posting reference must be on each invoice. Credit memoranda must carry a reference to the document evidencing the original transaction. Documents necessary to support claimed exemptions from tax liability, such as bills of lading and purchase orders, must be maintained in an order by which they readily can be related to the transactions for which exemption is sought.

(d) An automatic data processing tax accounting system must have built into its program a method of producing visible and legible records which will provide the necessary information for verification of the taxpayer's tax liability.

1. Machine-sensible data media, records such as punched cards, magnetic tape and disks are deemed to be within the meaning of N.J.S.A. 54:32B-16 and must be retained in accordance with said statute.
2. Automatic data processing records must provide an

opportunity to trace any transaction back to the original source or forward to a final total. If detail printouts are not made of transactions at the time they are processed, then the system must have the ability to reconstruct these transactions.

3. A general ledger with source references will be written out to coincide with financial reports for tax reporting periods. In cases where subsidiary ledgers are used to support the general ledger accounts, the subsidiary ledgers should also be written out periodically.

4. The audit trail should be designed so that the details underlying the summary accounting data may be identified and made available on request. The system should be so designed that supporting documents, such as sales invoices, purchase invoices, credit memoranda, etc., are readily available.

5. A description of the automatic data processing portion of the accounting system should be available. The statements and illustrations as to the scope of operations should be sufficiently detailed to indicate the following:

i. The application being performed;

ii. The procedures employed in each application (which, for example, might be supported by flow charts, block diagrams or other satisfactory description of the input or output procedures); and

iii. The controls used to insure accurate and reliable processing.

6. Important changes, together with their effective dates, should be noted in order to preserve an accurate chronological record.

State: New Mexico
Source: New Mexico Statutes

CHAPTER 14. RECORDS, LEGAL NOTICES AND OATHS.

Article 1. Preservation, Restoration and Destruction of Records.

Citation: NMS 14-1-3

✪ § 14-1-3. Method of copying.

That copies of such maps, plats or other documents may be made in any manner which the county clerk shall determine to be best to correctly and completely exemplify the original, including the making of copies of photographic, photostatic or any other mechanical process.

Citation: NMS 14-1-4

✪ § 14-1-4. "Public officer" defined for purpose of microfilming records.

The term public officer means any officer of the legislative, executive and judicial departments of the state whether elected or appointed, including officers of the boards, commissions, bureaus and all other agencies of this state and the departments thereof, and including officers of the state legislature and the officers and clerks of the courts of this state and, in like manner, the county and municipal officers of the counties, cities, towns, and villages of this state.

Citation: NMS 14-1-5

✪ § 14-1-5. Authorization for photographing and microfilming public records.

Any public officer of the state may cause any or all records, papers or documents kept by him to be photographed, microfilmed, microphotographed or reproduced on film. Such photographic film and the device used to reproduce such records on such film shall be one which accurately reproduces the original thereof in details.

Citation: NMS 14-1-6

✪ § 14-1-6. Photographed or microfilmed copies deemed original records.

Such photographs, microfilms, photographic film or microphotographs shall be deemed to be an original record for all purposes, including introduction in evidence in all courts or administrative agencies. A transcript, exemplification, or certified copy thereof shall, for all purposes recited herein, be deemed to be a transcript, exemplification or certified copy of the original.

Article 3. Public Records.

Citation: NMS 14-3-15

✪ § 14-3-15. Reproduction on film; evidence; review, inventory and approval of systems.

A. Any public officer of the state or of any district or political subdivision may cause any public records, papers or documents kept by him to be photographed, microphotographed, or reproduced on film.

B. The state records administrator shall review any proposed state agency microphotography system and shall advise and consult with the agency. The administrator has the authority to approve or disapprove the system of any state agency.

C. The microphotography system used pursuant to this section shall comply with the minimum standards approved by the New Mexico commission of public records. The microphotography system used to reproduce such records shall be one which accurately reproduces the original in all details.

D. The administrator shall establish and maintain an inventory of all microfilm equipment owned or leased by state agencies. The administrator is authorized to arrange the transfer of microphotography equipment from a state agency which does not use it, and which has released it, to a state agency needing such equipment for a current microphotography system.

E. Photographs, microphotographs or photographic film made pursuant to this section shall be deemed to be original records for all purposes, including introduction in evidence in all courts and administrative agencies. A transcript, exemplification or certified copy, for all purposes, shall be deemed to be a transcript, exemplification or certified copy of the original.

F. Whenever such photographs, microphotographs or reproductions on film are properly certified and are placed in conveniently accessible files, and provisions are made for preserving, examining and using them, any public officer may cause the original records from which the photographs or microphotographs have been made, or any part thereof, to be disposed of according to methods prescribed by Sections 14-3-9 through 14-3-11 NMSA 1978. Copies shall be certified by their custodian as true copies of the originals before the originals are destroyed or lost, and the certified copies shall have the same effect as the originals. Copies of public records transferred from the office of origin to the administrator, when certified by the administrator or his deputy, shall have the same legal effect as if certified by the original custodian of the records.

G. For the purposes of this section, "state agency" shall include the district courts.

Source: New Mexico Rules of Evidence

ARTICLE X. CONTENTS OF WRITINGS, RECORDINGS AND PHOTOGRAPHS

☞ Rule 1001. Definitions

For purposes of this article the following definitions are applicable:

(1) *Writings and recordings.* — "Writings" and "recordings" consist of letters, words, or numbers, or their equivalent, set down by handwriting, typewriting, printing, photostating, photographing, magnetic impulse, mechanical or electronic recording, or other form of data compilation.

(2) *Photographs.* — "Photographs" include still photographs, X-ray films, video tapes, and motion pictures.

(3) *Original.* — An "original" of a writing or recording is the writing or recording itself or any counterpart intended to have the same effect by a person executing or issuing it. An "original" of a photograph includes the negative or any print therefrom. If data are stored in a computer or similar device, any printout or other output readable by sight, shown to reflect the data accurately, is an "original".

(4) *Duplicate.* — A "duplicate" is a counterpart produced by the same impression as the original, or from the same matrix, or by means of photography, including enlargements and miniatures, or by mechanical or electronic re-recording, or by chemical reproduction, or by other equivalent techniques which accurately reproduces the original.

☞ Rule 1003. Admissibility of duplicates.

A duplicate is admissible to the same extent as an original unless

(1) a genuine question is raised as to the authenticity of the original or (2) in the circumstances it would be unfair to admit the duplicate in lieu of the original.

[See Appendix A. Uniform Rules of Evidence for additional provisions.]

Source: New Mexico State Records Center and Archives

PERFORMANCE GUIDELINES FOR THE LEGAL ACCEPTANCE OF PUBLIC RECORDS PRODUCED BY INFORMATION TECHNOLOGY SYSTEMS

1. Rule History: This is a new rule.
2. Scope: All State Agencies.
3. Authority: Public Records Act 14-3-4 NMSA 1978.
4. Purpose:

Admissibility into evidence of records produced by information technology systems employing media such as magnetic tapes or magnetic disk (and, by implication optical disk) has been addressed at the federal level by statutes and by the rules of evidence as adopted by the New Mexico Supreme Court.

Reported decisions indicate that the courts are quite lenient in interpreting these statutes and rules as applicable to records produced by information technology systems (analog or digital). However, problems arise if appropriate procedures are not followed in creating and maintaining such records, making it difficult to lay a proper foundation for admissibility. The court must be convinced that the process or system used is trustworthy in producing accurate records, i.e., the records reflect the source data used to create them. (Whether the source data are correct is a separate issue.)

The purpose of these guidelines is to provide direction for state agencies in the design, management, and operation of their information technology systems to improve the possibility of the admissibility into evidence of their records. The guidelines have been adapted for New Mexico by the Commission of Public Records' Legality of Electronic Records Advisory Committee composed of representatives from the Supreme Court Law Library, the Office of the Attorney Genera, the State Bar of New Mexico, the General Service Department, and the State Records Center and Archives. The Guidelines were adapted from the Association for Information and Image Management's (AIIM) Technical Report: *Performance Guideline for the Legal Acceptance of Records Produced by Information Technology Systems* (AIIM TR31-1992).

5 Evidence — Background:

5.1 *Traditional rules of evidence*:

5.1.1 *Hearsay*:

Courts have traditionally classified records as "hearsay". Hearsay is a statement offered to show the truth of the matter asserted when the person who made the statement is not available for cross-examination. SCRA 11-801(C). Such records were initially excluded from evidence because they depended upon the veracity and competence of the out-of-court declarant. Later, through exceptions to the hearsay rule, courts admitted these records into evidence, when the records met the other established criteria for admissibility. These exceptions to the hearsay rule were based on the presumption that the public records reflected accurate information produced by trustworthy procedures. These exceptions were at first restricted to "original writing" but were later modified to accommodate impact printing and other duplication technologies (e.g., micrographics and photocopying machines) as they became common tools.

5.1.2 *The best evidence rule*:

The courts also developed the "best evidence rule". The rule generally states that only the best form of the evidence is admissible. Initially, only original documents were admissible. As the rule evolved, the courts allowed secondary evidence if it was shown that the original was unavailable without fault of the offering party. Early duplicate records were probably not admissible since they were made using the transcription process — the copying of records by hand involving human intervention. Due to the high likelihood of error, transcription could not produce trustworthy results.

Over time, courts allowed true duplicate records — duplicates produced by mechanical or other non-human processes — to be admitted in evidence in limited circumstances when the originals were not available because: (1) they were public records; (2) the originals had been destroyed; (3) the originals were in the possession of an adverse party who refused to cooperate; or (4) the originals simply could not be found with reasonable effort. Once these situations were adequately proven to the court, reproductions could then be admitted.

Besides the historical basis for the best evidence rule, the preference for original records serves to reduce forgeries or other fraud in duplicates. Alternations can readily be detected in original documents while similar detection is difficult if not impossible in duplicates. Handwriting analysts can more accurately analyze signatures from originals records than from duplicates.

In New Mexico case law the relation between computer printouts and the best evidence rule is discussed in *Sierra Life Ins. Co. v. First National Life Ins. Co.* 85 NM 409, 412, 512, P.2d 1245, 1248 (1973).

5.2 *Modern rules of evidence*:

The federal government follows the Federal Rules of Evidence while most states have adopted one or more uniform laws that establish the admissibility of records in evidence. New Mexico has adopted the *Uniform Rules of Evidence* with few changes. New Mexico's rules of evidence permit original and duplicate records to be admitted into evidence provided that a proper foundation is laid. For example, visible records produced with a computer in the form of computer printouts or computer output microfilm (COM) are considered originals if an appropriate witness can convince the court that they accurately reflect the information in the computer files. Information processing methods commonly employed in the business world are more readily accepted as reliable, while new information system technologies are subject to greater scrutiny.

5.3 *Problems with rules of evidence*:

Based upon the traditional position of courts and regulatory agencies, original, paper records are the best evidence, and duplicate records are considered secondary evidence. Modern rules of evidence perpetuate this concept but provide exceptions for properly made duplicate records.

The basic legal principle behind the Best Evidence Rule is seldom applicable in the world of information technology. Paper records systems are often inferior to automated systems in terms of preserving evidence for the following reasons:

> *Paper records systems generally result in the preparation of one copy of the record.* In case of fire, flood, or other natural disaster, the single version of the records will be destroyed and no longer available for any evidence, regulatory or other purpose.

> *Documents can be removed from paper records systems without detection.* While erasures can be detected on originals, most other forms of fraud cannot. For example, when records are subpoenaed by the court or requested by government agencies, certain documents can be provided while others destroyed or hidden. The fraud resulting from the selective withholding of records can rarely be detected.

Alternatively, original paper records can inappropriately be destroyed. These records may than be unavailable for any purpose including evidence and regulation. Unless the fraud related to the destruction is detected, the omission as well as the contents of the records will effectively be excluded from consideration.

> *Original paper records may not have a very long life expectancy.* This is especially true today because original paper records are often produced using poor quality paper, poor quality ink, lift-off typewriter ribbons, or other inexpensive, short-term methods. Even records properly organized and stored may not be usable by the time they are needed for a court proceeding.

> *Paper records are rarely created as part of a rigorous process or system.* Many agencies do not have a records management program. Even those that do, rarely establish rigorous procedures related to records creation, maintenance and disposition. Many records created in each agency reflect individual whims rather than systematic policy. The accuracy of records will therefore vary based upon the integrity, accuracy and capabilities of the individuals involved.

> *Paper records are rarely audited for accuracy.* Few agencies audit paper records systems to determine the accuracy of the information recorded.

> *Paper records are rarely subjected to adequate security.* Any individual, including the janitor, may get access to paper records. The types of fraud discussed above can be accomplished without detection.

Modern information technology systems often differ from paper-based systems through the establishment of processes or systems that reliably produce accurate results. Modern reproduction systems such as microfilm or optical disk, and even data processing systems, offer the following characteristics that generally provide for more accurate and trustworthy records than are possible with paper records systems:

> *Modern information technology systems by their nature produce records as part of a process or systems that requires a disciplined operation based on standard procedures, written documentation, adequate training, and thoroughly tested equipment and software components.*

> *Modern information technology systems can provide an audit trail that identifies not only what actions were taken related to records but also the individuals involved.*

> *Modern information technology systems can prohibit or detect alterations and attempted alterations to records.* Most optical disk systems, for example, inherently preclude alteration of images. Bypass of alteration safeguards can be very difficult, requiring special knowledge and technical capabilities.

> *Modern information technology systems can provide for routine security backup for records produced.* Typically, microfilm, magnetic tape or disk, and optical disk systems will produce backup records at appropriate intervals as required. These records are generally stored in properly maintained remote locations where they can be retrieved if the original information is damaged or destroyed.

In sum, properly designed, implemented and maintained information technology systems are capable of producing records that are more reliable and accurate than paper-based systems.

It should be noted, however, that although paper-based systems are more susceptible to irretrievable loss or destruction of records and undetectable omissions, without the safeguards stated above, disasters and fraud can be much more costly and damaging to an agency dependent on an information technology system.

5.4 *Further challenges*:

With the safeguards that can be built into today's modern information technology systems, the best evidence of a record should not be dependent on a specifically sanctioned technology, but on a showing that the records was the result of a process or system that accurately reproduced it.

Rule 901(b) of the New Mexico Rules of Evidence lists examples that conform with the requirement of authentication or identification as a condition precedent to admissibility of evidence, i.e., "evidence sufficient to support a finding that the matter in question is what its proponent claims." Example (9) of Rule 901(b) reflects what should be the criteria for introducing records produced by information technology systems into evidence in all jurisdictions.

Example (9) of Rule 901(b) provides for authentication or identification by "evidence describing a process or system used to produce a result and showing that the process or system produces an accurate result." This example was designed for evidence such as X-rays and computer printouts where accuracy of the evidence is dependent upon the process or system that produces it.

When applied to records produced by information technology systems, this provision has no bias towards originals, duplicates, or any particular technology. The accuracy of the process or system used to produce the result will determine the authenticity or identification, and hence the admissibility of the evidence.

As new information technologies evolve, such as electronic imaging and optical disk systems, some jurisdictions feel compelled to modify existing laws or establish additional criteria for legal acceptance in evidence. It is important that New Mexico develop realistic and non-conflicting requirements.

The performance guidelines represent reasonable criteria to provide for designing and operating information technology systems that insure accuracy, reliability, and ultimately, the trustworthiness of information. Once implemented, the guidelines can apply to future technologies.

The guidelines relate to the functional or performance criteria for the system used to produce the records rather than to the media or specific technology involved. The trustworthiness of the process or system determines the legal admissibility of records in evidence, not the type of media or technology utilized.

6 *Definitions*:

The following definitions apply to the process or system assessment criteria set forth below:

6.1 *Records*:

Information preserved by any technique in any medium, now known, or later developed, that can be recognized by ordinary human sensory capabilities either directly or with the aid of technology.

6.2 *Original record*:

A record prepared in the first instance or any counterpart intended to have the same effect by a person executing or issuing it. If data are stored in a computer or similar device, any printout or other output readable by sight shown to reflect the data accurately is an "original."

6.3 *Duplicate records*:

A record that is produced by the same impression as the original, or from the same matrix, or by any other technological device for producing or reproducing records.

6.4 *Information technology system*:

Any process or system that employs a mechanical, photo-optical, magnetic, electronic or other technological device for producing or reproducing records.

6.5 *Records custodian*:

The statutory head of an agency utilizing or maintaining the information system, or their designate.

7 *Applicability*:

The guidelines apply to records produced by information technology systems regardless of the physical characteristics of the record media or technology employed. This includes records produced by any technique employing an information technology system as defined above.

8 *Information technology system assessment criteria*:

Following are criteria for designing and operating an information technology system to improve the admissibility of records into evidence.

8.1 *Quality*:

Quality relates to ability of the information technology system to reliably produce and preserve records so that they can be used or recognized by the intended audience.

8.1.1 *General requirements*:

The following should appear with sufficient clarity so that each can be recognized:

* Individual letters, number and symbols

* Combinations of letters, numbers and symbols forming words or sentences

* Graphics such as signatures, logos, pictures, etc.

* Sounds

* Other features of records such as color, shape, texture, etc., that relate to the content of the information

8.1.2 *Original records*:

Original records preserve information over time in the identical or functionally equivalent form to the original information.

Original records may present information in a form different from the original information without affecting its quality. For example, information preserved in digital format may be printed on paper using different fonts at different times.

8.1.3 *Duplicate records*:

Duplicate records accurately reproduce original records. Information that is readable or recognizable on originals should be readable or recognizable on duplicates. Similarly, information that is readable or recognizable on duplicates must be readable or recognizable on originals, except that duplicates may contain production, control, indexing, certification or other data not related to informational content of the records.

The exception allows additional data to be included on duplicates for administration of the reproduction process if it does not adversely affect the informational content of the record. For example, control and indexing data stored with digital images may be necessary to retrieve the images, does not affect the content of the record themselves.

Image enhancement techniques may be used provided that they do not change the information content of the records.

When duplications processes change information content of the records, the resulting records will be new originals.

8.2 *Records retention versus life expectancy of data on media*:

Records should be retained, regardless of media, for the period required by the agency's records retention program for any legal, user, historical or other purpose. The life expectancy of the media per se has not bearing on the admissibility of the records.

The information maintained on the media and the admissibility of the system to produce records from the information must achieve the required retention period. This means that for some technologies it may be necessary to periodically convert, regenerate, copy or transfer the information from one medium or technology to another to preserve the information for the required period.

Regardless of the retention period or life expectancy of the media, records must continue to exist when litigation, government investigation or audit is pending, imminent or, in some cases, merely foreseeable. In some instances, a court order will issue prohibiting specified records from being destroyed or otherwise rendered unavailable.

The life expectancy of the data on the media must be at least as long as the retention period established for the original record by the Commission of Public Records, or there needs to be a provision in the system for the periodic reproduction of the data, or the periodic revitalization of the data on the media. (also see § 8.5.3 b.)

8.3 *Conversion of records*:

Procedures followed to convert records from one media or technology to another should be carefully documented. Conversion of the records should not affect their legal status provided that quality and accuracy does not functionally change during conversion.

8.4 *Form of evidence*:

8.4.1 Records should be presented in a readable or recognizable form acceptable to the court. For written records, the records may be readable without any equipment or readable using equipment available to the court. The court may also accept records in other forms when equipment for their retrieval and use is also provided.

8.4.2 The form of records acceptable in evidence will vary based upon the nature of the information. For example, digitized voice information must be presented in an audible, understandable form while digitized video information must be presented in a readable or recognizable form. Records that contain information that relates to multiple human senses such as video records that must be both seen and heard to be complete must be presented in a form that provides all the necessary sensory information to the court.

8.4.3 Records systems should be able to produce readable (by either visual or tactile means) or audible records regardless of the technology used.

8.5 *Process or system used to produce records*:

8.5.1 *Characteristics of a process or system*:

Characteristics of the process or system used to produce the information facilitate the accuracy of the information. A description of these characteristics in simple terms facilitates the showing that the process or system is reliable and accurate, and hence capable of producing trustworthy records. Each records systems should regularly maintain and update complete documentation of both the collection (input) process and the output process.

Records produced as part of a regularly conducted activity such as those produced in the regular course of operations are more inherently reliable than those produced for a special purpose or for litigation. A regularly conducted activity may include a regular pattern of activity to produce the records on a daily, weekly, monthly, yearly or other cyclical schedule.

A regularly conducted activity may also include records created as part of a regular program of the agency, but at irregular times. For example, records created as part of a retro-conversion project may still, in appropriate circumstances, be regarded as converted in the regular course of operations, even though it only occurred once.

(b) *Accuracy*:

Accuracy may be increased by systematic quality control and audit procedures, as well as operational oversight by persons with detailed knowledge or the process or system used to produce the records.

(c) *Timeliness*:

Records produced within a short period after the event or activity occurs tend to be more readily acceptable as accurate than records produced long after the event or activity. However, a challenge to admissibility of a later-produced record can be overcome by showing that the time lapse had no effect on the record's content. For example, a computer printout of a statistical report produced annually in the regular course of operations can be shown to accurately consolidate data complied over the course of a year.

8.5.2 *Components of a process or system*:

The records program depends upon both the system's components and the processes used in preparing them. The records are more trustworthy if the program under which they were produced include adequate procedures, training programs, audit trails and audits.

(a) *Procedures*:

Procedures reflect the detailed steps to be followed when creating, modifying, duplicating, destroying or otherwise managing records. They provide for consistent quality control, problem resolution and other activities that might otherwise be subject to inconsistent action, multiple interpretation or misinterpretation.

Established procedures only show what an agency intended to do in managing and controlling the process or system. The trustworthiness of an agency's records depends not only upon established procedures but depend also on how closely they are followed. Deviations from established procedures will be scrutinized, and such deviations might result in the records being inadmissible.

(b) *Training programs*:

Formal training programs for staff on details of the system procedures help insure that the procedures were correctly followed. When an agency can demonstrate that staff understood the required procedures, the court will tend to find that the procedures were in fact followed. It may be advisable to provide certification of training for certain staff members prior to the staff members' assumption of responsibility for those procedures, especially for those who are likely to testify in court.

(c) *Access and audit trails*:

Audit trails document who used the system, when they used it, what they did while using the system, and what were the results. Properly implemented audit trails can automatically detect who had access to the system, whether staff followed standard procedures or whether fraud or other unauthorized acts occurred or might be suspected. They provide independent confirmation that proper procedures were in fact followed. It may be advisable to provide various levels of access security.

(d) *Audits*:

The term "audits" as used in this section is different than quality control specified in most system procedures. Audits performed periodically can confirm that the process or system produces accurate results. Audits should compare the procedures stated in the procedure's documentation with procedures actually followed. They provide verification that the system adheres to these guidelines.

For purposes of establishing the credibility of the records, audits should be performed by an independent source, i.e., persons other than those who created the records or person without an interest in the content of the records. Trained auditors with agency-wide audit responsibilities provide an acceptable level of independence.

No particular method of auditing is required. For purposes of original records, audits should focus on whether the records accurately incorporate information of the acts, events, or activities leading to the record. For duplicates and other forms of information transfer, audits should confirm that the duplicates accurately reproduce the original information. Such audits must be accomplished prior to destruction of the originals. The destruction must be conducted in accordance with existing agency retention and disposition schedules.

8.5.3 *Documentation of a process or system*:

Documentation of the process or systems provides verification of the process or system followed to produce the records. Without documentation, witnesses must rely solely on memory — which over time becomes less trustworthy and more susceptible to contradiction. Documentation preserves the information about the process or system independent of the individuals involved. The documentation should always be reviewed by the agency witness prior to giving testimony. In a proper case, the documentation can be introduced into evidence.

(a) *Content*:

A knowledgeable person should prepare and maintain documentation for the process or system used to produce the records.

Documentation should be prepared during the design of the system. If the system was implemented without documentation, documentation should be prepared immediately. Documentation should be kept of all changes in the system. All documentation of changes should be kept for the full retention period of the data. Documentation should be complete and up-to-date. This enables staff to know and follow the most current procedures. It also ensures that reliable system documentation is immediately available if needed for court proceedings. Documentation of a system prepared for purposes of litigation is subject to greater challenge.

No particular form or level of detail is required for describing the process or system, although visual aids outlining the documentation can be helpful. Documentation should be sufficient to demonstrate the steps required to get from the beginning to the end of the process. Documentation should be understandable to non-technical personnel. An agency may be required to introduce evidence that any equipment or software involved operated properly at the time the records were produced.

Program documentation should state the control methods in force and how they are to be applied and should also state the times at which each part of a process is to be completed.

Training documentation should record the distribution of written procedures, course materials, attendance of individuals at training sessions, remedial or refresher training programs, certifications of training completion and other relevant information.

The actual audit trail records demonstrate what activities actually took place as part of the process or system. The actual audit reports indicate whether the records were actually produced. Where audit reports have revealed inaccuracies, the documentation should reflect what remedial procedures were applied. The documentation should state who (by individual or job class) has access to the system at each level of access and should indicate how audit trails are maintained.

Evidence of the actual system procedures followed during the period the records in question were produced should be maintained in sufficient detail to enable the records custodian to describe the process or system to the court.

(b) *Retention*:

When the documentation changes, the old versions should continue to be maintained for the requisite period. The agency should establish procedures to insure that the Records Custodian is notified whenever a record needs to be maintained longer than its retention period.

9 *Availability of process or system for outside inspection*:

The courts encourage pretrial discovery of computer programs and related materials in order to facilitate effective cross examination when computer produced data are introduced into evidence. These guidelines apply this principle to records produced by any information systems technology.

9.1 *Inspection*:

The process or system used to produce records introduced into evidence is subject to outside inspection by opposing parties and the court. Outside inspection my include reviews of procedures documentation, review of system operation, independent audits and quality control tests, independent audit, testing of process or system operation, review of equipment design and software documentation, review of training programs or any other matter related to the operation of the process or system.

If the records were produced on the current or substantially similar system, access to the system may be required. Outside parties may request to process their own test data on the agency's system. If the system used to produce the records no longer exists, the court may require that all existing documentation be made available. Lack of pertinent documentation because it no longer exists may jeopardize admissibility of the records if their trustworthiness cannot otherwise be established.

In sum, any relevant step of the process or system can be reviewed by the outside party.

10 *Legal status of public records offered as evidence*:

The destruction of the original copy of a public record, after production, will not affect the legal status of such reproduction as a public record.

An agency's ability to show that the process or system used to store and reproduce a public record is trustworthy in terms of producing an accurate result, will normally be sufficient to insure reliability.

11 *Testimony of Records Custodian*:

The record custodian is the statutory head of the agency that utilizes or maintains the information system. This responsibility may be delegated in appropriate circumstances down to the level of clerk. However, it is customary to have the individual who is responsible for the management of the information system documentation and operation provide testimony about the system. In some circumstances, it might be necessary to have the testimony of the individual who actually prepared to record.

11.1 *Appearing in court*:

When records from an information system are required to be introduced in court, the level of proof may vary from simply certifying a record produced by the system to providing expert testimony about the operations of the system. When confronted with testifying in court, it is usually sufficient for a records custodian to provide for the following:

* copy of the record

* documentation of the system

* documentation of any variance of standard operating procedure in the production of the record, especially variations with respect to time and format.

11.2 *Certification of records*

11.2.1 *Recommended form of certification*

The following is a recommended form of certification:

As a custodian of this record, I certify that it is a copy accurately produced, maintained, and reproduced by this agency in accordance with the procedures attached hereto. This is page ___ of ___ pages of certified document. This is certified on this ___ day of __________.

____

Records Custodian

11.2.2 *Sample certification procedure*

The following is a sample certification procedure, it is meant to be suggestive only. An agency's certification procedure will vary according to the type and complexity of the system.

The ____(agency name)______ of the State of New Mexico has produced the attached document using the following procedures:

1. The original document containing the information requested was received in this office in the normal course of operations of the ___(agency name)____ carrying out its duties pursuant to the laws of the State of New Mexico. It was then ___(method of conversion/input____ and placed onto ___(method of storage)___.

2. The accuracy of this production was verified at the time of conversion/input by comparison. The storage procedure allows the agency to determine whether the stored data was altered from the time of this document's conversion/input to the production of the attached (printout).

3. Documents are converted /input from the original within ___ days after the original is received for official recordation or filing.

4. Specificallyi as to·the attached (printout), the following deviations from the above procedure are noted as follows: (none)

____

Signature by Records Custodian of agency

11.3 *Challenges to testimony*:

The testimony offered by the records custodian will vary based upon their own expertise, level of responsibility, and most especially any challenge offered to the introduction of the record. In appropriate cases and based on the nature of the challenge, it may be necessary to introduce expert witnesses. Information system records can be challenged on many grounds, a discussion of the most common grounds follow:

11.3.1 *Challenges to hardware*:

Because equipment which is not functioning properly can alter the content of computerized information, the reliability of the data processing equipment used to store and produce the records may be challenged. The information contained in the systems documentation should be sufficient to overcome this. However, if the hardware is challenged, it may be necessary to present evidence that the equipment operated reliably the day the data were initially entered and on the day the computer record was produced. A log of computer operations indicating the absence, or presence, of any malfunction that did or did not affect the data is generally adequate. The agency may also be required to produce a person who has actually tested the equipment.

11.3.2 *Challenges to software*:

(a) Errors in computer records can result form errors in the computer programs. Consequently, the reliability of the computer programs and formulas used to process the data may be challenged. Normally, introduction of the systems documentation will be sufficient to demonstrate the reliability of the programs and formulas. However, evidence about the development and testing of the programs may also be required, as well as expert testimony from the creator or the software or from individuals who have run validation tests on the software.

(b) A records custodian may also be required to present the specific version of the computer program used to process the data on the date the information entered into evidence was created. A different version of the program may be considered, if it is the only one available, but the absence of the exact version of the program may raise some serious questions about the trustworthiness of the computer records.

(c) The measures taken to verify the proper operation and accuracy of these programs and formulas may be challenged. Normally, introduction of the systems documentation will be sufficient to demonstrate the verification of the programs and formulas. However, expert testimony from the creator of the software or from individuals who have run validation tests on the software may be required.

11.3.3 *Challenges to input*:

(a) The manner in which the basic data were initially entered into the system may be challenged. The information contained in the systems documentation should be sufficient to demonstrate how the data were entered. However, if it is challenged, it may be necessary to produce a person who actually does data entry.

(b) There the data were entered in the regular course of operations may be challenged. The information contained in the systems documentation should be sufficient to overcome this. However, if it is challenged, it may be necessary to produce a person who actually does data entry, or who has audited the system.

(c) Whether the data were entered within a reasonable time after the events recorded by the persons having knowledge of the events may be challenged. The procedures outlined in paragraphs a. and b. above should be sufficient to overcome this. However, where the data are entered at a different time, then the agency's records should not only reflect the data the original data were created, but also the data they were entered.

(d) The measures taken to insure the accuracy of the data entered may be challenged. Normally, introduction of the systems documentation will be sufficient to demonstrate the accuracy of the data. However, it may be necessary to have expert testimony on verification, proof reading, internal audit trails, or computer security in general. It may be necessary as well to introduce the training records of the data entry staff.

11.3.4 *Challenges to output*:

Computer printouts prepared in the regular course of operations are considered more trustworthy than similar computer printouts prepared for trial. Consequently, the time and mode of preparation of printouts may be challenged. Normally, introduction of the systems documentation will be sufficient. However, where the printout is not created in the normal course of operations, an audit trail leading to the creation of the data may be required. If a specially written search or program was used to extract the data (as, for example, from a screen) the search or program should be included as well.

11.3.5 *Challenges to security*:

The method of storing the data (for example, magnetic tape) and the safety precautions taken to

prevent loss of the data while in storage may be challenged. Backup only becomes an issue if it was used to generate the record. Where an agency is certifying that it does not have any record with regard to a transaction, it will usually be required to search not only the current systems but also the oldest backup that would be likely to contain such a record. Normally, introduction of the systems documentation will be sufficient to demonstrate the method of backup and storage. However, it may be necessary to obtain testimony concerning access to the system, what procedures were in place to prevent unauthorized access, and whether these procedures were carried out with respect to the records in question.

TITLE. ADMINISTRATION.

CHAPTER 3. PUBLIC RECORDS.

Citation:	**State Records Center and Archives Guidelines**

✪ PART 50. PERFORMANCE GUIDELINES FOR THE LEGAL ACCEPTANCE OF PUBLIC RECORDS PRODUCED BY INFORMATION TECHNOLOGY SYSTEMS

1 *Issuing Agency:* State Records Center and Archives [10-1-94]

2 *Scope:* All State Agencies [9-2-93]

3 *Statutory Authority:* Public Records Act 14-3-4 NMSA

1978 [9-2-93]

4 *Duration:* Permanent [10-1-94]

5 *Effective date* October 1, 1994 [10-1-04]

6 *Objective:*

Admissibility into evidence of records produced by information technology systems employing media such as magnetic tapes or magnetic disk (and, by implication optical disk) has been addressed at the federal level by statutes and by the rules of evidence as adopted by the New Mexico Supreme Court.

Reported decisions indicate that the courts are quite lenient in interpreting these statutes and rules as applicable to records produced by information technology systems (analog or digital). However, problems arise if appropriate procedures are not followed in creating and maintaining such records, making it difficult to lay a proper foundation for admissibility. The court must be convinced that the process or system used is trustworthy in producing accurate records, i.e., the records reflect the source data used to create them. (Whether the source data are correct is a separate issue.)

The purpose of these guidelines is to provide direction for state agencies in the design, management, and operation of their information technology systems to improve the possibility of the admissibility into evidence of their records. The guidelines have been adapted for New Mexico by the Commission of Public Records' Legality of Electronic Records Advisory Committee composed of representatives from the Supreme Court Law Library, the Office of the Attorney Genera, the State Bar of New Mexico, the General Service Department, and the State Records Center and Archives. The Guidelines were adapted from the Association for Information and Image Management's (AIIM) Technical Report: *Performance Guideline for the Legal Acceptance of Records Produced by Information Technology Systems* (AIIM TR31-1992). [9-2-93]

7 Evidence — Background:

7.1 *Traditional rules of evidence:*

7.1.1 *Hearsay:*

Courts have traditionally classified records as "hearsay". Hearsay is a statement offered to show the truth of the matter asserted when the person who made the statement is not available for cross-examination. SCRA 11-801(C). Such records were initially excluded from evidence because they depended upon the veracity and competence of the out-of-court declarant. Later, through exceptions to the hearsay rule, courts admitted these records into evidence, when the records met the other established criteria for admissibility. These exceptions to the hearsay rule were based on the presumption that the public records reflected accurate information produced by trustworthy procedures. These exceptions were at first restricted to "original writing" but were later modified to accommodate impact printing and other duplication technologies (e.g., micrographics and photocopying machines) as they became common tools. [9-2-93]

7.1.2 *The best evidence rule:*

The courts also developed the "best evidence rule". The rule generally states that only the best form of the evidence is admissible. Initially, only original documents were admissible. As the rule evolved, the courts allowed secondary evidence if it was shown that the original was unavailable without fault of the offering party. Early duplicate records were probably not admissible since they were made using the transcription process — the copying of records by hand involving human intervention. Due to the high likelihood of error, transcription could not produce trustworthy results.

Over time, courts allowed true duplicate records — duplicates produced by mechanical or other non-human processes — to be admitted in evidence in limited circumstances when the originals were not available because: (1) they were public records; (2) the originals had been destroyed; (3) the originals were in the possession of an adverse party who refused to cooperate; or (4) the originals simply could not be found with reasonable effort. Once these situations were adequately proven to the court, reproductions could then be admitted.

Besides the historical basis for the best evidence rule, the preference for original records serves to reduce forgeries or other fraud in duplicates. Alternations can readily be detected in original documents while similar detection is difficult if not impossible in duplicates. Handwriting analysts can more accurately analyze signatures from originals records than from duplicates.

In New Mexico case law the relation between computer printouts and the best evidence rule is discussed in *Sierra Life Ins. Co. v. First National Life Ins. Co.* 85 NM 409, 412, 512, P.2d 1245, 1248 (1973). [9-2-93]

7.2 *Modern rules of evidence*:

The federal government follows the Federal Rules of Evidence while most states have adopted one or more uniform laws that establish the admissibility of records in evidence. New Mexico has adopted the *Uniform Rules of Evidence* with few changes. New Mexico's rules of evidence permit original and duplicate records to be admitted into evidence provided that a proper foundation is laid. For example, visible records produced with a computer in the form of computer printouts or computer output microfilm (COM) are considered originals if an appropriate witness can convince the court that they accurately reflect the information in the computer files. Information processing methods commonly employed in the business world are more readily accepted as reliable, while new information system technologies are subject to greater scrutiny. [9-2-93]

7.3 *Problems with rules of evidence*:

Based upon the traditional position of courts and regulatory agencies, original, paper records are the best evidence, and duplicate records are considered secondary evidence. Modern rules of evidence perpetuate this concept but provide exceptions for properly made duplicate records.

The basic legal principle behind the Best Evidence Rule is seldom applicable in the world of information technology. Paper records systems are often inferior to automated systems in terms of preserving evidence for the following reasons:

> *Paper records systems generally result in the preparation of one copy of the record.* In case of fire, flood, or other natural disaster, the single version of the records will be destroyed and no longer available for any evidence, regulatory or other purpose.

> *Documents can be removed from paper records systems without detection.* While erasures can be detected on originals, most other forms of fraud cannot. For example, when records are subpoenaed by the court or requested by government agencies, certain documents can be provided while others destroyed or hidden. The fraud resulting from the selective withholding of records can rarely be detected.

Alternatively, original paper records can inappropriately be destroyed. These records may than be unavailable for any purpose including evidence and regulation. Unless the fraud related to the destruction is detected, the omission as well as the contents of the records will effectively be excluded from consideration.

> *Original paper records may not have a very long life expectancy.* This is especially true today because original paper records are often produced using poor quality paper, poor

quality ink, lift-off typewriter ribbons, or other inexpensive, short-term methods. Even records properly organized and stored may not be usable by the time they are needed for a court proceeding.

Paper records are rarely created as part of a rigorous process or system. Many agencies do not have a records management program. Even those that do, rarely establish rigorous procedures related to records creation, maintenance and disposition. Many records created in each agency reflect individual whims rather than systematic policy. The accuracy of records will therefore vary based upon the integrity, accuracy and capabilities of the individuals involved.

Paper records are rarely audited for accuracy. Few agencies audit paper records systems to determine the accuracy of the information recorded.

Paper records are rarely subjected to adequate security. Any individual, including the janitor, may get access to paper records. The types of fraud discussed above can be accomplished without detection.

Modern information technology systems often differ from paper-based systems through the establishment of processes or systems that reliably produce accurate results. Modern reproduction systems such as microfilm or optical disk, and even data processing systems, offer the following characteristics that generally provide for more accurate and trustworthy records than are possible with paper records systems:

Modern information technology systems by their nature produce records as part of a process or systems that requires a disciplined operation based on standard procedures, written documentation, adequate training, and thoroughly tested equipment and software components.

Modern information technology systems can provide an audit trail that identifies not only what actions were taken related to records but also the individuals involved.

Modern information technology systems can prohibit or detect alterations and attempted alterations to records. Most optical disk systems, for example, inherently preclude alteration of images. Bypass of alteration safeguards can be very difficult, requiring special knowledge and technical capabilities.

Modern information technology systems can provide for routine security backup for records produced. Typically, microfilm, magnetic tape or disk, and optical disk systems will produce backup records at appropriate intervals as required. These records are generally stored in properly maintained remote locations where they can be retrieved if the original information is damaged or destroyed.

In sum, properly designed, implemented and maintained information technology systems are capable of producing records that are more reliable and accurate than paper-based systems.

It should be noted, however, that although paper-based systems are more susceptible to irretrievable loss or destruction of records and undetectable omissions, without the safeguards stated above, disasters and fraud can be much more costly and damaging to an agency dependent on an information technology system. [9-2-93]

7.4 *Further challenges*:

With the safeguards that can be built into today's modern information technology systems, the best evidence of a record should not be dependent on a specifically sanctioned technology, but on a showing that the records was the result of a process or system that accurately reproduced it.

Rule 901(b) of the New Mexico Rules of Evidence lists examples that conform with the requirement of authentication or identification as a condition precedent to admissibility of evidence, i.e., "evidence sufficient to support a finding that the matter in question is what its proponent claims." Example (9) of Rule 901(b) reflects what should be the criteria for introducing records produced by information technology systems into evidence in all jurisdictions.

Example (9) of Rule 901(b) provides for authentication or identification by "evidence describing a process or system used to produce a result and showing that the process or system produces an accurate result." This example was designed for evidence such as X-rays and computer printouts where accuracy of the evidence is dependent upon the process or system that produces it.

When applied to records produced by information technology systems, this provision has no bias towards originals, duplicates, or any particular technology. The accuracy of the process or system used to produce the result will determine the authenticity or identification, and hence the admissibility of the evidence.

As new information technologies evolve, such as electronic imaging and optical disk systems, some jurisdictions feel compelled to modify existing laws or establish additional criteria for legal acceptance in evidence. It is important that New Mexico develop realistic and non-conflicting requirements.

The performance guidelines represent reasonable criteria to provide for designing and operating information technology systems that insure accuracy, reliability, and ultimately, the trustworthiness of information. Once implemented, the guidelines can apply to future technologies.

The guidelines relate to the functional or performance criteria for the system used to produce the records rather than to the media or specific technology involved. The trustworthiness of the process or system determines the legal admissibility of records in evidence, not the type of media or technology utilized. [9-2-93]

8 *Definitions*:

The following definitions apply to the process or system assessment criteria set forth below: [9-2-93]

8.1 *Records*:

Information preserved by any technique in any medium, now known, or later developed, that can be recognized by ordinary human sensory capabilities either directly or with the aid of technology. [9-2-93]

8.2 *Original record*:

A record prepared in the first instance or any counterpart intended to have the same effect by a person executing or issuing it. If data are stored in a computer or similar device, any printout or other output readable by sight shown to reflect the data accurately is an "original." [9-2-93]

8.3 *Duplicate records*:

A record that is produced by the same impression as the original, or from the same matrix, or by any other technological device for producing or reproducing records. [9-2-93]

8.4 *Information technology system*:

Any process or system that employs a mechanical, photo-optical, magnetic, electronic or other technological device for producing or reproducing records. [9-2-93]

8.5 *Records custodian*:

The statutory head of an agency utilizing or maintaining the information system, or their designate. [9-2-93]

9 *Applicability*:

The guidelines apply to records produced by information technology systems regardless of the physical characteristics of the record media or technology employed. This includes records produced by any technique employing an information technology system as defined above. [9-2-93]

10 *Information technology system assessment criteria*:

Following are criteria for designing and operating an information technology system to improve the admissibility of records into evidence. [9-2-93]

10.1 *The issue of accuracy:*

These guidelines provide an analytical structure for validating electronic record systems with respect to the preservation of accuracy from the time of original source data capture until the time of record output. While the accuracy of the data that is passed to the system needs to be of concern to agencies, that issue can only be addressed after the reliability of the record management system is established. As such, the guidelines are only concerned with the integrity of record management processes as implemented within automation systems.

While the guidelines do need to be applied to the entire record management process from the agency's receipt/creation of data until the eventual destruction of agency records, they are designed to be applied to individual subsystems which can be independently validated. This block structured approach allows a single subsystem to be changed without having to reexamine the entire process. It also facilitates the separation of original data accuracy manipulation and storage. Compliance with the guidelines will thereby ensure that the processes that agencies use to manage data do not jeopardize the legal admissibility of records, regardless of the accuracy of the original source material. [10-1-94]

10.2 *Quality*:

Quality relates to ability of the information technology system to reliably produce and preserve records so that they can be used or recognized by the intended audience. [9-2-93]

10.2.1 *General requirements*:

The following should appear with sufficient clarity so that each can be recognized:

- Individual letters, number and symbols
- Combinations of letters, numbers and symbols forming words or sentences
- Graphics such as signatures, logos, pictures, etc.
- Sounds
- Other features of records such as color, shape, texture, etc., that relate to the content of the information [9-2-93]

10.2.2 *Original records*:

Original records preserve information over time in the identical or functionally equivalent form to the original information.

Original records may present information in a form different from the original information without affecting its quality. For example, information preserved in digital format may be printed on paper using different fonts at different times. [9-2-93]

10.2.3 *Duplicate records*:

Duplicate records accurately reproduce original records. Information that is readable or recognizable on originals should be readable or recognizable on duplicates. Similarly, information that is readable or recognizable on duplicates must be readable or recognizable on originals, except that duplicates may contain production, control, indexing, certification or other data not related to informational content of the records.

The exception allows additional data to be included on duplicates for administration of the reproduction process if it does not adversely affect the informational content of the record. For example, control and indexing data stored with digital images may be necessary to retrieve the images, does not affect the content of the record themselves.

Image enhancement techniques may be used provided that they do not change the information content of the records.

When duplications processes change information content of the records, the resulting records will be new originals. [9-2-93]

10.3 *Records retention versus life expectancy of data on media*:

Records should be retained, regardless of media, for the period required by the agency's records retention program for any legal, user, historical or other purpose. The life expectancy of the media per se has not bearing on the admissibility of the records.

The information maintained on the media and the admissibility of the system to produce records from the information must achieve the required retention period. This means that for some technologies it may be necessary to periodically convert, regenerate, copy or transfer the information from one medium or technology to another to preserve the information for the required period.

Regardless of the retention period or life expectancy of the media, records must continue to exist when litigation, government investigation or audit is pending, imminent or, in some cases, merely foreseeable. In some instances, a court order will issue prohibiting specified records from being destroyed or otherwise rendered unavailable.

The life expectancy of the data on the media must be at least as long as the retention period established for the original record by the Commission of Public Records, or there needs to be a provision in the system for the periodic reproduction of the data, or the periodic revitalization of the data on the media. (also see § 10.6.3 b.) [9-2-93]

10.4 *Conversion of records*:

Procedures followed to convert records from one media or technology to another should be carefully documented. Conversion of the records should not affect their legal status provided that quality and accuracy does not functionally change during conversion. [9-2-93]

10.5 *Form of evidence*:

10.5.1 *Records should be presented in a readable or recognizable form acceptable to the court.* For written records, the records may be readable without any equipment or readable using equipment available to the court. The court may also accept records in other forms when equipment for their retrieval and use is also provided. [9-2-93]

10.5.2 *The form of records acceptable in evidence will vary based upon the nature of the information.* For example, digitized voice information must be presented in an audible, understandable form while digitized video information must be presented in a readable or recognizable form. Records that contain information that relates to multiple human senses such as video records that must be both seen and heard to be complete must be presented in a form that provides all the necessary sensory information to the court. [9-2-93]

10.5.3 *Records systems should be able to produce readable (by either visual or tactile means) or audible records regardless of the technology used.* [9-2-93]

10.6 *Process or system used to produce records*:

10.6.1 *Characteristics of a process or system*:

Characteristics of the process or system used to produce the information facilitate the accuracy of the information. A description of these characteristics in simple terms facilitates the showing that the process or system is reliable and accurate, and hence capable of producing trustworthy records. Each records systems should regularly maintain and update complete documentation of both the collection (input) process and the output process. [9-2-93]

(a) *Records produced as part of a regularly conducted activity:*
Records produced as part of a regularly conducted activity such as those produced in the regular course of operations are more inherently reliable than those produced for a special purpose or for litigation. A regularly conducted activity may include a regular pattern of activity to produce the records on a daily, weekly, monthly, yearly or other cyclical schedule.

A regularly conducted activity may also include records created as part of a regular program of the agency, but at irregular times. For example, records created as part of a retro-conversion project may still, in appropriate circumstances, be regarded as converted in the regular course of operations, even though it only occurred once. [9-2-93]

(b) *Accuracy*:
Accuracy may be increased by systematic quality control and audit procedures, as well as operational oversight by persons with detailed knowledge or the process or system used to produce the records. [9-2-93]

(c) *Timeliness*:
Records produced within a short period after the event or activity occurs tend to be more readily acceptable as accurate than records produced long after the event or activity. However, a challenge to admissibility of a later-produced record can be overcome by showing that the time lapse had no effect on the record's content. For example, a computer printout of a statistical report produced annually in the regular course of operations can be shown to accurately consolidate data complied over the course of a year. [9-2-93]

10.6.2 *Components of a process or system*:
The records program depends upon both the system's components and the processes used in preparing them. The records are more trustworthy if the program under which they were produced include adequate procedures, training programs, audit trails and audits.

(a) *Procedures*:
Procedures reflect the detailed steps to be followed when creating, modifying, duplicating, destroying or otherwise managing records. They provide for consistent quality control, problem resolution and other activities that might otherwise be subject to inconsistent action, multiple interpretation or misinterpretation.

Established procedures only show what an agency intended to do in managing and controlling the process or system. The trustworthiness of an agency's records depends not only upon established procedures but depend also on how closely they are followed. Deviations from established procedures will be scrutinized, and such deviations might result in the records being inadmissible. [9-2-93]

(b) *Training programs*:
Formal training programs for staff on details of the system procedures help insure that the procedures were correctly followed. When an agency can demonstrate that staff understood the required procedures, the court will tend to find that the procedures were in fact followed. It may be advisable to provide certification of training for certain staff members prior to the staff members' assumption of responsibility for those procedures, especially for those who are likely to testify in court. [9-2-93]

(c) *Security Controls:*
Effective security controls are essential for maintaining tamper free systems. An agency must be able to demonstrate to the court that security appropriate to the value and importance of the information was in place.

Typical security controls would include varying levels of access secured by passwords, restricted terminal locations, physical security of processing equipment, and time use restrictions. [10-1-94]

(d) *Access and audit trails*:
Audit trails document who used the system, when they used it, what they did while using the system, and what were the results. Properly implemented audit trails can automatically detect who had access to the system, whether staff followed standard procedures or whether fraud or other unauthorized acts occurred or might be suspected. They provide independent confirmation that proper procedures were in fact followed. It may be advisable to provide various levels of access security. [9-2-93]

(e) *Audits*:
The term "audits" as used in this section is different than quality control specified in most system procedures. Audits performed periodically can confirm that the process or system produces accurate results. Audits should compare the procedures stated in the procedure's documentation with procedures actually followed. They provide verification that the system adheres to these guidelines.

For purposes of establishing the credibility of the records, audits should be performed by an independent source, i.e., persons other than those who created the records or person without an interest in the content of the records. Trained auditors with agency-wide audit responsibilities provide an acceptable level of independence.

No particular method of auditing is required. For purposes of original records, audits should focus on whether the records accurately incorporate information of the acts, events, or activities leading to the record. For duplicates and other forms of information transfer, audits should confirm that the duplicates accurately reproduce the original information. Such audits must be accomplished prior to destruction of the originals. The destruction must be conducted in accordance with existing agency retention and disposition schedules. [9-2-93]

10.6.3 *Documentation of a process or system*:
Documentation of the process or systems provides verification of the process or system followed to produce the records. Without documentation, witnesses must rely solely on memory — which over time becomes less trustworthy and more susceptible to contradiction. Documentation preserves the information about the process or system independent of the individuals involved. The documentation should always be reviewed by the agency witness prior to giving testimony. In a proper case, the documentation can be introduced into evidence. [9-2-93]

(a) *Content*:
A knowledgeable person should prepare and maintain documentation for the process or system used to produce the records. Documentation should be prepared during the design of the system. If the system was implemented without documentation, documentation should be prepared immediately. Documentation should be kept of all changes in the system. All documentation of changes should be kept for the full retention period of the data. Documentation should be complete and up-to-date. This enables staff to know and follow the most current procedures. It also ensures that reliable system documentation is immediately available if needed for court proceedings. Documentation of a system prepared for purposes of litigation is subject to greater challenge.

No particular form or level of detail is required for describing the process or system, although visual aids outlining the documentation can be helpful. Documentation should be sufficient to demonstrate the steps required to get from the beginning to the end of the process. Documentation should be understandable to non-technical personnel. An agency may be required to introduce evidence that any equipment or software involved operated properly at the time the records were produced.

Program documentation should state the control methods in force and how they are to be applied and should also state the times at which each part of a process is to be completed.

Training documentation should record the distribution of written procedures, course materials, attendance of individuals at training sessions, remedial or refresher training programs, certifications of training completion and other relevant information.

The actual audit trail records demonstrate what activities actually took place as part of the process or system. The actual audit reports indicate whether the records were actually produced. Where audit reports have revealed inaccuracies, the documentation should reflect what remedial procedures were applied. The documentation should state who (by individual or job class) has access to the system at each level of access and should indicate how audit trails are maintained.

Evidence of the actual system procedures followed during the period the records in question were produced should be maintained in sufficient detail to enable the records custodian to describe the process or system to the court. [9-2-93, 10-2-94]

(b) *Retention*:

When the documentation changes, the old versions should continue to be maintained for the requisite period. The agency should establish procedures to insure that the Records Custodian is notified whenever a record needs to be maintained longer than its retention period. [9-2-93]

11 *Availability of process or system for outside inspection*:

The courts encourage pretrial discovery of computer programs and related materials in order to facilitate effective cross examination when computer produced data are introduced into evidence. These guidelines apply this principle to records produced by any information systems technology. [9-2-93]

11.1 *Inspection*:

The process or system used to produce records introduced into evidence is subject to outside inspection by opposing parties and the court. Outside inspection my include reviews of procedures documentation, review of system operation, independent audits and quality control tests, independent audit, testing of process or system operation, review of equipment design and software documentation, review of training programs or any other matter related to the operation of the process or system.

If the records were produced on the current or substantially similar system, access to the system may be required. Outside parties may request to process their own test data on the agency's system. If the system used to produce the records no longer exists, the court may require that all existing documentation be made available. Lack of pertinent documentation because it no longer exists may jeopardize admissibility of the records if their trustworthiness cannot otherwise be established.

In sum, any relevant step of the process or system can be reviewed by the outside party. [9-2-93]

12 *Legal status of public records offered as evidence*:

The destruction of the original copy of a public record, after production, will not affect the legal status of such reproduction as a public record.

An agency's ability to show that the process or system used to store and reproduce a public record is trustworthy in terms of producing an accurate result, will normally be sufficient to insure reliability. [9-2-93]

13 *Testimony of Records Custodian*:

The record custodian is the statutory head of the agency that utilizes or maintains the information system. This responsibility may be delegated in appropriate circumstances down to the level of clerk. However, it is customary to have the individual who is responsible for the management of the information system documentation and operation provide testimony about the system. In some circumstances, it might be necessary to have the testimony of the individual who actually prepared to record. [9-2-93]

13.1 *Appearing in court*:

When records from an information system are required to be introduced in court, the level of proof may vary from simply certifying a record produced by the system to providing expert testimony about the operations of the system. When confronted with testifying in court, it is usually sufficient for a records custodian to provide for the following:

* copy of the record

* documentation of the system

* documentation of any variance of standard operating procedure in the production of the record, especially variations with respect to time and format. [9-2-93]

13.2 *Certification of records*

13.2.1 *Recommended form of certification*

The following is a recommended form of certification:

As a custodian of this record, I certify that it is a copy accurately produced, maintained, and reproduced by this agency in accordance with the procedures attached hereto. This is page ___ of ___ pages of certified document. This is certified on this ___ day of __________.

____

Records Custodian [9-2-93, 10-1-94]

13.2.2 *Sample certification procedure*

The following is a sample certification procedure, it is meant to be suggestive only. An agency's certification procedure will vary according to the type and complexity of the system.

The ___(agency name)_____ of the State of New Mexico has produced the attached document using the following procedures:

1. The original document containing the information requested was received in this office in the normal course of operations of the ___(agency name)____ carrying out its duties pursuant to the laws of the State of New Mexico. It was then ___(method of conversion/input____ and placed onto ___(method of storage)___.

2. The accuracy of this production was verified at the time of conversion/input by comparison. The storage procedure allows the agency to determine whether the stored data was altered from the time of this document's conversion/input to the production of the attached (printout).

3. Documents are converted /input from the original within ___ days after the original is received for official recordation or filing.

4. Specificallyi as to the attached (printout), the following deviations from the above procedure are noted as follows: (none)

____

Signature by Records Custodian of agency [9-2-93, 10-1-94]

13.2.3 *Sample certification procedure for data output:*

The ____*(agency name)*____ has examined all records pertaining to data storage including audit trails, operations logs, and maintenance logs and has determined that there has been no purposeful alterations of the stored data and that there has been no hardware malfunctions that would compromise the integrity of the data.

Any variations from standard operating procedure are noted as follows:

____

Signature by Records Custodian of agency [9-2-93, 10-1-94]

13.3 Challenges to testimony:

The testimony offered by the records custodian will vary based upon their own expertise, level of responsibility, and most especially any challenge offered to the introduction of the record. In appropriate cases and based on the nature of the challenge, it may be necessary to introduce expert witnesses. Information system records can be challenged on many grounds, a discussion of the most common grounds follow. [9-2-93]

13.3.1 *Challenges to hardware*:

Because equipment which is not functioning properly can alter the content of computerized information, the reliability of the data processing equipment used to store and produce the records may be challenged. The information contained in the systems documentation should be sufficient to overcome this. However, if the hardware is challenged, it may be necessary to present evidence that the equipment operated reliably the day the data were initially entered and on the day the computer record was produced. A log of computer operations indicating the absence, or presence, of any malfunction that did or did not affect the data is generally adequate. The agency may also be required to produce a person who has actually tested the equipment. [9-2-93]

13.3.2 *Challenges to software*:

(a) Errors in computer records can result form errors in the computer programs. Consequently, the reliability of the computer programs and formulas used to process the data may be challenged. Normally, introduction of the systems documentation will be sufficient to demonstrate the reliability of the programs and formulas. However, evidence about the development and testing of the programs may also be required, as well as expert testimony from the creator or the software or from individuals who have run validation tests on the software. [9-2-93]

(b) A records custodian may also be required to present the specific version of the computer program used to process the data on the date the information entered into evidence was created. A different version of the program may be considered, if it is the only one available, but the absence of the exact version of the program may raise some serious questions about the trustworthiness of the computer records. [9-2-93]

(c) The measures taken to verify the proper operation and accuracy of these programs and formulas may be challenged. Normally, introduction of the systems documentation will be sufficient to demonstrate the verification of the programs and formulas. However, expert testimony from the creator of the software or from individuals who have run validation tests on the software may be required. [9-2-93]

13.3.3 *Challenges to input*:

(a) The manner in which the basic data were initially entered into the system may be challenged. The information contained in the systems documentation should be sufficient to demonstrate how the data were entered. However, if it is challenged, it may be necessary to produce a person who actually does data entry. [9-2-93]

(b) There the data were entered in the regular course of operations may be challenged. The information contained in the systems documentation should be sufficient to overcome this. However, if it is challenged, it may be necessary to produce a person who actually does data entry, or who has audited the system. [9-2-93]

(c) Whether the data were entered within a reasonable time after the events recorded by the persons having knowledge of the events may be challenged. The procedures outlined in paragraphs a. and b. above should be sufficient to overcome this. However, where the data are entered at a different time, then the agency's records should not only reflect the data the original data were created, but also the data they were entered. [9-2-93]

(d) The measures taken to insure the accuracy of the data entered may be challenged. Normally, introduction of the systems documentation will be sufficient to demonstrate the accuracy of the data. However, it may be necessary to have expert testimony on verification, proof reading, internal audit trails, or computer security in general. It may be necessary as well to introduce the training records of the data entry staff. [9-2-93]

13.3.4 *Challenges to output*:

Computer printouts prepared in the regular course of operations are considered more trustworthy than similar computer printouts prepared for trial. Consequently, the time and mode of preparation of printouts may be challenged. Normally, introduction of the systems documentation will be sufficient. However, where the printout is not created in the normal course of operations, an audit trail leading to the creation of the data may be required. If a specially written search or program was used to extract the data (as, for example, from a screen) the search or program should be included as well. [9-2-93]

13.3.5 *Challenges to security*:

The method of storing the data (for example, magnetic tape) and the safety precautions taken to

prevent loss of the data while in storage may be challenged. Backup only becomes an issue if it was used to generate the record. Where an agency is certifying that it does not have any record with regard to a transaction, it will usually be required to search not only the current systems but also the oldest backup that would be likely to contain such a record. Normally, introduction of the systems documentation will be sufficient to demonstrate the method of backup and storage. However, it may be necessary to obtain testimony concerning access to the system, what procedures were in place to prevent unauthorized access, and whether these procedures were carried out with respect to the records in question. [9-2-93]

Citation: **State Records Center and Archives Rule 92-04**

✪ SRC Rule No. 92-04. Microphotography Standard Forms and Operating Procedures

1. This rule supersedes SRC Rule No. 80-12, dated December 8, 1980 and amendment No. 1 dated December 14, 1981.

2. *Authority.* Section 14-3-6, NMSA 1978, directs that the State Records Administrator adopt regulations to carry out the purposes of the Public Records Act (Sections 14-3-1 to 14-3-25, NMSA 1978).

3. *Applicability and Definitions.* The rule applies to "agencies" as defined in Sections 14-3-2, paragraph D, and 14-3-15, paragraph G, NMSA, 1978; to "public officer" as defined in

Section 14-1-4, NMSA, 1978; to "public records" as defined in section 14-3-2, paragraph C, NMSA, 1978; and "to microphotography system" as defined in Section 14-3-2, paragraph F, NMSA, 1978. For purposes of this rule "archival" shall be defined as permanent.

4. *Microphotography Standards Forms and Operating Procedures*:

To ensure uniformity, legal acceptance, and to facilitate the microfilming of public records by government entities the following standards forms and operating procedures shall be adopted for source document microfilming in addition to the requirements set forth in SRC Rule No. 92-03, Microphotography Standards.

(a) The following national standards are incorporated into this rule as requirements of the standard forms and operating procedures for any microphotography system as defined in Section 3 above. The required national standards are available for reference at the New Mexico State Records Center & Archives, Santa Fe, NM.

ANSI/AIIM MS47 Rotary Cameras for 16mm Microfilm - Mechanical & Optical Characteristics

ANSI/AIIM MS14 Specifications for 16mm and 35mm Microfilms in Roll Form

ANSI/AIIM MS111 Microfilming Newspapers

ANSI/AIIM MS 48 Recommended Practice for Microfilming Public Records on Silver Gelatin Film

(b) The requirements of the most current revision of the standards listed in subsection (a) shall prevail, unless otherwise specified in this rule.

(c) The State Records Center shall inspect master negative microfilm submitted by state agencies as defined in section 2 above. The inspection shall consist of verifying the inclusion of required targets and indexing, measuring density and resolution, and visual observation of the film on a light box for the identification of major defects or errors. Agencies/offices which produce microforms not inspected by the NM State Records Center must make film inspection provisions which meet all requirements of SRC Rule No. 92-03 and SRC Rule No. 92-04. The agencies/offices must notify the NM State Records Center of the inspection provisions made, and must maintain a file of all inspection results.

(1) All agencies/offices should inspect all master negative film and any microfilm copies of the agency/office records. This inspection must include the verification of required targets and indexing, density and resolution measurements, visual observation of the film on a light box for the identification of major defects or errors, indexing accuracy, and inspection of all images for accuracy, legibility and photographic quality.

(2) Prior to the final disposition of any microfilmed paper records, all requirements of the Public Records Act must be met. In addition, the following verification requirements must be met.

(i) Agencies/offices required to submit a Request for Destruction must include the following statement on the Request for Destruction, and the statement must be signed by the agency/office records custodian.

"The records listed on this request meet all requirements of SRC Rule No. 93-03 and SRC Rule No. 93-04. All microfilms of these records have been verified, and are complete and contain all information shown on the originals."

(ii) Agencies/offices not required to submit a Request for Destruction to the NM State Records Center must maintain a record of record destruction which meets the requirements of the Public Records Act. This record must include the above statement identifiable with specific records and microforms, and the statement must be signed by the agency/office records custodian.

(d) *Indexing of Master Microfilm.* This is to be used in accordance with SRC Rule No. 92-03, paragraph (k). All master microfilm rolls shall be indexed to include the following information: (see figure 1)

(1) *Roll Number.* This number must also appear on the "Start of Roll" and "End of Roll" targets.

(2) Date the roll of film is removed from the camera.

(3) The first and last document on the roll of film.

(4) A breakdown of the contents of the film and the indexing information by which the images can be retrieved.

(5) The inclusive dates of the records contained on the roll of film.

(6) The name and address of the agency producing the roll of film.

(e) *Statement of Intent and Purpose.* This form must be used in compliance with SRC Rule No. 92-03, paragraph (m). It contains the following information: (see figure 2)

(1) Authority under which Microfilming is being done.

(2) Name of the agency/office for which the microfilming is being done.

(3) Statement to the effect that the records microfilmed are the actual records of the agency, and that the records were created as part of the normal course of business.

(4) Statement to the effect that it is the policy of the agency/office to microfilm specified records as part of the normal course of business, and (when applicable) that the backlog will be microfilmed as part of a conversion process to maintain a valid and cost efficient record keeping program.

(5) Statement to the effect that it is the policy of the agency/office to microfilm specified record to maintain as the legal copy of record in lieu of paper, and that the paper records are destroyed after microfilming in accordance with all requirements of the Public Records Act.

(6) Name, title and signature of the records custodian authorizing the microfilm policy as stated.

(f) *Certification Plaque.* This form must be used in compliance with SRC Rule No. 92-03, paragraph (m). (See figure 3)

(1) Certification Plaque A will be filmed on the first and last image of a film strip.

(2) Certification Plaque B will be filmed on single image film strips, such as aperture cards.

(g) *Resolution Target.* An original chart must be used in compliance with SRC Rule No. 92-03, paragraph (e). (see figure 5)

(h) *Density Target.* This form must be used in compliance with SRC Rule No. 92-03, paragraph (f). (see figure 4)

(i) *Start of Roll Target.* This form must be used in compliance with SRC Rule No. 92-03, paragraph (n), and must contain the following information: (see figure 6)

(1) roll number

(2) name of agency/office to which the records belong

(3) record(s) or file(s) being microfilmed

(4) date of filming and name of camera operator

(5) description of first record image on the roll of film

(j) *End of Roll Target.* This form must be used in compliance with SRC Rule No. 92-03, paragraph (n), and must contain the following information: (see figure 7)

(1) roll number

(2) name of agency/office to which the records belong

(3) record(s) or file(s) being microfilmed

(4) date of filming and name of camera operator

(5) description of last record image on the roll of film

(k) *Microfilm Image Sequence and Spacing.* Starting with a new roll of film in the camera, the following image sequence and spacing is required.

(Start of Roll)

1. Film Leader
2. Statement of Intent and Purpose
3. Resolution Target
4. Density Target
5. Start of Roll
6. Four (4) Spaces
7. Records images for the roll
(End of Roll)
8. Four (4) Spaces
9. End of Roll
10. Density Target
11. Resolution Target
12. Statement of Intent and Purpose
13. Film Trailer

Citation: **REGULATION 401**

✍ § 401. Records of employing units.

A. Each employing unit shall keep true and accurate employment and payroll records which shall include, with reference to the employing unit the name and correct address of such employing unit, and the name and address of each branch or division or establishment operated, owned or maintained by such employing unit at different locations in New Mexico, all disbursement for services rendered to the employing unit; and with reference to each and every individual performing services for it, the following information:

(1) The individual's name, address and Social Security number;

(2) The dates on which the individual performed services for such employing unit, including beginning and ending dates, and the State or States in which such services were performed;

(3) The total amount of wages paid to the individual for each separate payroll period, date of payment of said wages, and amounts or remuneration paid to the individual for each separate payroll period other than "wages", as defined in the Unemployment Compensation Law;

(4) Whether, during any payroll period the individual worked less than full time, and if so, the hours and dates worked;

(5) The reasons for separation of the individual.

B. Each employment unit shall keep, in addition to the records required by subsection (A) of this regulation, such records as will establish the ownership and any changes of ownership of such employing unit and the address at which such records are available for inspection or audit by representatives of the division. Such records shall show the addresses of the owners of the employing unit or, in the event the employing unit is a corporation or unincorporated organization, such records shall show the addresses of directors, officers and any person on whom subpoenas or legal process may be served in New Mexico. In the event the employing unit is a group account, such records shall show the address of the group representative.

C. If any remuneration other than money wages is paid to or received by an individual with respect to services performed by his employer, the records shall show the total amount of cash wages and the cash value of any other remuneration.

D. All records shall be kept and maintained as to establish clearly the correctness of all reports which the employing unit is required to file with the division and shall be readily accessible to authorized representatives of the tax section of the division within the geographical boundaries of New Mexico; and in the even such records are not maintained or are not available in New Mexico, the employing unit shall pay to the division the expenses and costs incurred when a representative of the tax section of the division is required to go outside the State of New Mexico to inspect or audit such records.

E. For purposes of compliance with this regulation, magnetic media shall be considered a process for accurately producing an original record of durable medium. However, if an employing unit elects to maintain its payroll records on magnetic media, it shall be the obligation of such employing unit to reproduce such records on a media, readable by the human eye, if requested to do so by the division, for the purpose of an audit.

F. The records prescribed by this regulation shall be preserved for a period of at least four years in addition to the current calendar year.

State: **New York**
Source: **Arts and Cultural Affairs Law**

TITLE U. DIVISIONS OF HISTORY AND PUBLIC RECORDS.

Article 57. Divisions of History and Public Records.

Citation: **CLNY-CA 57.05**

✪ § 57.05. State archives.

1. There shall be continued within the education department the state archives. The state archives shall acquire, appraise, preserve either in original or duplicate form, catalog, display, duplicate and make available for reference and use by state officials and others those official records that have been determined to have sufficient historical value or other value to warrant their continued preservation by the state.

2. For the purposes of this section, official records shall include all books, papers, maps, photographs, or other documentary materials, regardless of physical form or characteristics, made or received by any agency of the state or by the legislature or the judiciary in pursuant of law or in connection with the transaction of public business and preserved or appropriate for preservation by that agency or its legitimate successor as evidence of the organization, functions, policies, decisions, procedures, operations, or other activities, or because of the information contained therein.

3. Library or museum material made or acquired and preserved solely for reference or exhibition purposes, extra copies of documents preserved only for convenience of reference, and stocks of publications and of processed documents shall not be deemed to constitute official records for the purposes of this section.

* * * * *

Source: **Civil Practice Law And Rules**

ARTICLE 45. EVIDENCE.

Uniform Photographic Copies of Business and Public Records As Evidence Act

Citation: **CPLR Rule 4539**

☞ ✍ Rule 4539. Uniform Photographic Copies of Business and Public Records as Evidence Act.

If any business, institution, or member of a profession or calling, in the regular course of business or activity has made, kept or recorded any writing, entry, print or representation and in the regular course of business has recorded, copied, or reproduced it by any process which accurately reproduces or forms a durable medium for reproducing the original, such reproduction, when satisfactorily identified, is as admissible in evidence as the original, whether the original is in existence or not, and an enlargement or facsimile of such reproduction is admissible in evidence if the original reproduction is in existence and available for inspection under direction of the court. The introduction of a reproduction does not preclude admission of the original.

Source: Legislative Law

CHAPTER 32 OF THE CONSOLIDATED LAWS.

Article 2. Members, Officers and Employees of the Legislature.

✪ § 22-a. Reproduction and destruction of certain records, books and papers of the senate.

1. Notwithstanding any other provision of law, the officers or employees of the senate designated by the temporary president of the senate may cause any of the following described records, books and papers on file with or in the custody of such officers or employees to be photographed, microphotographed or reproduced on film or otherwise and may destroy or otherwise dispose of such original records, books and papers, after such reproductions have been made. Such reproductions may be destroyed or otherwise disposed of by such officers or employees after the lapse of the following periods of time from the dates upon which the originals thereof were filed in their offices or placed in their custody:

AFTER TWENTY-FIVE YEARS

Senate committee books of standing committees and home rule record books in the office of the journal clerk,

AFTER FIFTEEN YEARS

Record books of printed bills and index to documents,

AFTER TEN YEARS

Miscellaneous reports from other than state agencies, submitted pursuant to special acts,

Records in the financial clerk's office, except those relating to retirement matters and senators' and employees' pay account books,

Material relating to specifications, bids, awards and correspondence relating thereto, in connection with alterations, improvement, purchase of material,

Record books used at the senate desk and engrossing room,

Senators' receipts,

Senators' warrants,

Social security information and records,

AFTER SEVEN YEARS

General correspondence,

Duplicate copies of payroll schedules, the originals having been transmitted to the office of the state comptroller,

Duplicate copies of maintenance and operation schedules with duplicate copy of each bill, the original schedules and original bills having been transmitted to the office of the state comptroller,

Duplicate copies of purchase orders,

Personnel applications,

Personal service certification forms of employees,

Lists of personnel prepared pursuant to joint rules for members of the press,

Copies of certification lists of employees transmitted to the office of the state comptroller.

2. Such photographic film or other material shall be of durable quality and the device used to produce such records, books or papers shall be one which accurately reproduces the originals in all details. Such photographing film or other material shall be deemed to be an original record, book or paper for all purposes, including introduction in evidence in all courts and administrative agencies. A transcript, exemplification or certified copy thereof shall be deemed to be a transcript, exemplification or certified copy of the original for all purposes.

3. At least thirty days previous to the destruction or other disposition of any of such original records, books or papers, or any reproductions thereof, such officers or employees shall notify the commissioner of education of their intention to destroy or otherwise dispose thereof and afford the commission of education reasonable opportunity to examine the same to enable him to ascertain whether any of such original or reproduced records, books or papers are of historical value. Any such original or reproduced records, books and papers so ascertained to be of historical value shall not be destroyed and shall be transferred to depositories designated by the temporary president of the senate.

✪ § 22-b. Destruction and reproductions of assembly books and records.

1. Notwithstanding any other provision of law, the officers or employees of the assembly designated by the speaker of the assembly may cause any of the following described records, books and papers on file with or in the custody of such officers or employees to be photographed, microphotographed or reproduced on film or otherwise and may destroy or otherwise dispose of such original records, books and papers after such reproductions have been made. Such reproductions may be destroyed or otherwise disposed of by officers or employees after the lapse of the following periods of time from the date upon which the originals thereof were filed in their offices or placed in their custody:

AFTER TWENTY-FIVE YEARS

Assembly committee books of standing committees and home rule record books in the office of the journal clerk.

AFTER FIFTEEN YEARS

Record books of printed bills and index to documents.

AFTER TEN YEARS

Miscellaneous reports from other than state agencies, submitted pursuant to special acts.

Material relating to specifications, bids, awards and correspondence relating thereto, in connection with alterations, improvements and purchase of materials.

Records books used at the assembly desk and engrossing clerk's office,

Social security information and records.

AFTER SEVEN YEARS

General correspondence.

Duplicate copies of payroll forms, the originals having been transmitted to the officer of the state comptroller.

Duplicate copies of maintenance and operation schedules with duplicate copy of each bill, the original schedule and bills having been transmitted to the office of the state comptroller.

Duplicate copies of purchase orders.

Personnel records and lists.

Personal services voucher certification forms of employees.

Duplicate copies of certification lists of employees, the originals having been transmitted to the office of the state comptroller.

2. Such photographic film or other material shall be of durable quality and the device used to produce such records, books or papers shall be one which accurately reproduces the originals in all details. Such photographing film or other material shall be deemed to be an original record, book or paper for all purposes, including introduction in evidence in all courts and administrative agencies. A transcript, exemplification or certified copy

thereof shall be deemed to be a transcript exemplification or certified copy of the original for all purposes.

3. At least thirty days prior to the destruction or other disposition of any records, books or papers of any assembly standing committee, or of the journal clerk's office, or of the assembly desk, or of the engrossing clerk's office, such officers or employees shall notify the commissioner of education of his intention to destroy or otherwise dispose thereof and afford the commissioner of education reasonable opportunity to examine the same to ascertain whether any of such records, books or papers are of historical value. Any such records, books or papers so ascertained to be of historical value shall not be destroyed and shall be transferred to depositories designated by the speaker of the assembly.

Source: New York Compiled Code of Rules and Regulations

Agency: State Archives and Records Administration

TITLE 8. REGULATIONS OF THE COMMISSIONER OF EDUCATION

PART 188. STATE GOVERNMENT ARCHIVES AND RECORDS MANAGEMENT

Citation: 8 NYCCRR 188.1

✪ § 188.1 Purpose.

This Part establishes a framework of policies and procedures for the creation, maintenance, disposition, and selective preservation of State government records. Based on this framework, the State Archives and Records Administration will work in partnership with state agencies, and where applicable with the judiciary, to carry out records management programs that support effective program management and public services delivery, promote economical and efficient management of information resources, and ensure that records of archival value are identified, protected, and when appropriate, transferred to the State Archives for preservation.

Citation: 8 NYCCRR 188.18

✪ § 188.18. Duplicating and/or Replacing Agency Records by Microfilming.

(a) For the purposes of this section, "microfilming" means the photographic process of creating miniaturized copies of human-readable records on film and "source records" means the records that are copied. The provisions of this section apply only to the duplication of source records by microfilming, which is commonly known as "source document microfilming", and do not apply to computer-generated microfilm.

(b) An agency shall obtain records disposition authorization for source records that are microfilmed and for the microform copy.

(c) When source records are duplicated on microform, with the intent of destroying the source records and retaining only the microfilm copy, an agency shall establish procedures to ensure that microfilm is an authentic copy of the original records.

(d) In addition to the provisions of this section, an agency may destroy source records and retain only the microfilm copy provided that the film images are clear and legible; the master camera negative is used only to produce a printing master from which all additional copies are made; the master camera negative is stored in a records center facility vault or a comparable secure storage facility; and the agency records management officer certifies that microfilm production and processing techniques were selected to ensure that the microfilm will remain usable for the required retention period.

(e) If archival source records are duplicated on microfilm, an agency must comply with all other provisions of this section and the following:

(1) Only a safety-base silver gelatin microform shall be used as the original camera negative film.

(2) Each batch of processed film shall be tested to ensure that processing chemicals which could cause image deterioration are washed from the film.

(f) Prior to the destruction of any source records that are to be replaced by microfilm, the director or a designee may inspect the agency microfilm procedures and products to verify compliance with the applicable provisions of this section.

Citation: 8 NYCCRR 188.19

✪ § 188.19. Computer-generated Recording of Information on Microfilm.

(a) The provisions of this section apply only to original records produced by computer-generated recording of information on microfilm, the resulting product of which is commonly known as computer-output microfilm (COM).

(b) When COM records are identified as archival records, the following shall apply to the production and maintenance of the COM:

(1) Only a safety-base silver gelatin microform shall be used as the original film copy, which shall be used only to produce a printing master from which all additional copies will be made. The original film copy shall be stored in a records center facility fault or a comparable storage facility.

(2) Each batch of processed film shall be tested to ensure that processing chemicals which could cause image deterioration are washed from the film.

Citation: 8 NYCCRR 188.20

✪ § 188.20. Retention and Preservation of Electronic Records.

(a) An agency shall ensure that records retention requirements are incorporated into any plan and process for design, redesign, or substantial enhancement of an agency information system that uses electronic date processing or electronic optical imaging technologies to maintain or store electronic records.

(b) An agency shall ensure that electronic records are not rendered unusable because of changing technology before their retention and preservation requirements are met. In the case of archival electronic records, an agency, in consultation with SARA, must determine that the records will remain usable and accessible through conversion of the records to a new system hardware and software and through the creation of adequate documentation as defined in subdivision (c) of this section. If an agency cannot accomplish such a conversion, it shall transfer the archival electronic records to the State Archives in a usable and accessible format.

(c) An agency shall develop and maintain up-to-date documentation about all archival electronic records sufficient to:

(1) specify all technical characteristics necessary for reading and processing the records;

(2) identify all defined inputs and outputs from the system;

(3) define the contents of the files and records;

(4) determine restrictions on access and use;

(5) understand the purposes and functions of the system;

(6) describe update cycles or conditions and rules for adding information to the system, or deleting information; and

(7) ensure the ongoing retention of records by the agency or the authorized transfer of records to an archives facility.

(d) An agency shall prepare and store in a records center facility backup copies of archival electronic records in order to safeguard against loss.

(e) For magnetic computer media that contain archival electronic records, an agency shall institute maintenance procedures to:

(1) verify no more than 6 months prior to use that the magnetic media used to store archival electronic records is free of permanent errors;

(2) rewind under constant tension all tapes and cartridges at least every 2 years;

(3) annually test a 3 percent statistical sample of all volumes, or 10 volumes of each type, of magnetic media, whichever is larger, to identify any loss of data and to discover and correct the causes of data loss;

(4) copy immediately onto new media any archival electric records stored on media with 10 or more permanent errors per volume;

(5) copy all archival electronic records onto new media before the media is 10 years old;

(6) prepare external labels which provide a unique identifier for each volume, the name of the organizational unit responsible, and the archival electronic records title.

Agency: **Department of Taxation and Finance**

TITLE 20. TAXATION AND REVENUE.

CHAPTER 2. INCOME TAXES.

PART 152. REQUIREMENTS CONCERNING NEW YORK STATE INCOME TAX RETURNS, NOTICES, RECORDS AND STATEMENTS.

Citation: **20 NYCCRR 152.2**

✍ § 152.2. Records to be kept by farmers and wage earners.

Individuals deriving gross income from the business of farming, and individuals whose gross income includes salaries, wages or similar compensation for personal services rendered, are required, with respect to such income, to keep such records (including duplicate copies of the wage and tax statements furnished by their employers) as will enable the Tax Commission to determine the correct amount of New York State income subject to tax. It is not necessary, however, that with respect to such income individuals keep the books of account and records required by section 152.1 of this Part.

Agency: **Department of Taxation and Finance**

PART 152. REQUIREMENTS CONCERNING NEW YORK STATE INCOME TAX RETURNS, NOTICES, RECORDS AND STATEMENTS.

Citation: **20 NYCCRR 152.15**

✍ § 152.15. Required or elective use of magnetic media for filing information returns.

(a) *Definitions*. For purposes of this section:

(1) the term "Commissioner" means the Commissioner of Taxation and Finance or his delegates;

(2) the term "Department" means the Department of Taxation and Finance;

(3) the term "machine-readable paper form" means any machine- readable paper form, including optical scan paper form, as described by the Department in instructions for use in complying with the requirements of this section;

(4) the term "magnetic media" means media, including magnetic tape, diskette, cassette and mini-disk, as described by the Department in instructions for use in complying with the requirements of this section; and

(5) the term "person" means any individual, trust, estate, partnership, association, company, corporation, governmental entity, or any other entity required to file a return described in this section.

(b) *Returns required on magnetic media.*

(1) *Form IT-2102 (or Federal equivalent).*

(i) *General rule*. For calendar years beginning after December 31, 1988, any person having two hundred fifty or more employees in New York State shall be required to file returns utilizing Form IT-2102, Wage and Tax Statement (or its Federal equivalent, Form W-2), with the Department on magnetic media.

(ii) *Employees in the State*. For purposes of this paragraph, the term "employees in New York State" shall have the meaning prescribed in Subpart 4-5 of this Title, except that such term shall include general executive officers or directors otherwise meeting the requirements contained in such Subpart.

(iii) *250 employee requirements not based on average number of employees*. If a person has an aggregate of two hundred fifty or more employees in New York State during the calendar year for which Form IT-2102 is required to be filed, such person shall furnish such forms to the Department on magnetic media, even if such person employs less than two hundred fifty employees in New York State, on average, during such year.

(iv) *Examples*. The provisions of this paragraph can be illustrated by the following examples:

Example 1. Corporation M is a seasonal employer. During calendar year 1989, M employees, on average, 150 employees in New York State. However, in December, its peak season, M has 300 employees in New York State. M will be required to file with the Department all of its 1989 Forms IT-2102 (or Federal equivalent Forms W-2), on magnetic media by February 28, 1990.

Example 2. Corporation N employs an average of 200 employees in New York State during calendar year 1989. However, due to a high turnover rate, N employs a total of 450 employees in New York State during such year. N will be required to file with the Department all of its Forms IT-2102 (or Federal equivalent Forms W-2) on magnetic media by February 28, 1990.

(2) *Form IT-2102G (or Federal equivalent) and Form IT-2102P (or Federal equivalent)*. For calendar years beginning after December 31, 1988, any person required to file two hundred fifty or more returns for a calendar year utilizing Form IT-2102G, Statement for Recipients of Certain Gambling

Winnings, (or its Federal equivalent Form W-2G), or Form IT 2102P, Statement for Recipients of Annuities, Pensions, Retirement Pay or IRA Payments, (or its Federal equivalent Form W-2P), shall file such returns with the Department on magnetic media.

(3) *Federal-State conformity.*

(i) *Rule.* Any person filing a return utilizing Form W-2, W-2G, or W-2P on magnetic media for Federal purposes, whether or not required to do so pursuant to section 6011 of the Internal Revenue Code and regulations promulgated thereunder, shall, if otherwise required to file one or more of the returns specified in this subdivision with the Department, file such return or returns on magnetic media for New York State purposes.

(ii) *Example.* The provisions of subparagraph (i) of this paragraph can be illustrated by the following example:

Corporation Y employs an average of 200 employees nationwide during calendar year 1989. However, due to a high turnover rate, Y employees a total of 400 employees nationwide during such year. Fifty of such employees are located in New York State. In accordance with applicable Federal regulations (26 CFR 301.6011-2(c)), Y must file its Forms W-2 with the Federal government on magnetic media. Thus, Y will be required to file its Forms IT-2102 (or Forms W-2) for New York State purposes on magnetic media.

(4) Election to file using magnetic media. Any person not required to file one or more of the returns referred to in this subdivision with the Department on magnetic media may nevertheless elect to file such return or returns utilizing magnetic media.

(5) *Instructions.* Returns submitted on magnetic media pursuant to the provisions of this subdivision shall be filed in accordance with instructions promulgated by the Department, and shall contain such information as the Department shall specify in such instructions.

* * * * *

(e) *Failure to file.*

(1) *Magnetic media.* A person required to file a return on magnetic media pursuant to section 658 of the Tax Law and this section is deemed to have failed to file the return if such person:

(i) fails to file such return on magnetic media, or

(ii) files such return using a magnetic media format not described by the Department in instructions.

(2) *Prescribed New York State paper format.* If a person making a return on a paper form under subdivision (c) of this section for calendar year 1989 fails to file such return on the prescribed New York State paper format when required to do so by section 658 of the Tax Law and this section, such person is deemed to have failed to file the return.

(3) *Machine-readable paper form.* If a person making a return on a paper form under subdivision (c) of this section for a calendar year beginning after December 31, 1989 fails to file such return on a machine-readable paper form when required to do so by section 658 of the Tax Law and this section, such person is deemed to have failed to file the return.

(4) *Cross-reference.* See subsection (h) of section 685 of the Tax Law for penalties for failure to file certain returns.

(f) *Use of magnetic media when filing information returns not referred to in this section.* The Department may grant authorization to file information returns other than the IT-2102/W-2, IT-2102P/W-2P, and IT-2102G/W-2G on magnetic media. Persons granted such authorization must comply with the instructions referred to in subdivision (b) of this section covering filing of information returns on magnetic media.

State: North Carolina
Source: North Carolina General Statutes

CHAPTER 8. EVIDENCE.

ARTICLE 4A. PHOTOGRAPHIC COPIES OF BUSINESS AND PUBLIC RECORDS.

Citation: NCGS 8-45.1

☞ § 8-45.1. Photographic reproductions admissible; destruction of originals.

If any business, institution, member of a profession or calling, or any department or agency of government, in the regular course of business or activity has kept or recorded any memorandum, writing, entry, print, representation, X ray or combination thereof, of any act, transaction, occurrence or event, and in the regular course of business has caused any or all of the same to be recorded, copied or reproduced by any photographic, photostatic, microfilm, microcard, miniature photographic, or other process which accurately reproduces or forms a durable medium for so reproducing the original, the original may be destroyed in the regular course of business unless held in a custodial or fiduciary capacity or unless its preservation is required by law. Such reproduction, when satisfactorily identified, is as admissible in evidence as the original itself in any judicial or administrative proceeding whether the original is in existence or not and an enlargement or facsimile of such reproduction is likewise admissible in evidence if the original reproduction is in existence and available for inspection under direction of court. The introduction of a reproduced record, enlargement or facsimile, does not preclude admission of the original.

CHAPTER 8C. EVIDENCE CODE.

Article 10. Contents of Writings, Recordings and Photographs.

☞ Rule 1001. Definitions

For purposes of this article the following definitions are applicable:

(1) *Writings and recordings.* — "Writings" and "recordings" consist of letters, words, or numbers, or their equivalent, set down by handwriting, typewriting, printing, photostating, photographing, magnetic impulse, mechanical or electronic recording, or other form of data compilation.

(2) *Photographs.* — "Photographs" include still photographs, X-ray films, video tapes, and motion pictures.

(3) *Original.* — An "original" of a writing or recording is the writing or recording itself or any counterpart intended to have the same effect by a person executing or issuing it. An "original" of a photograph includes the negative or any print therefrom. If data are stored in a computer or similar device, any printout or other output readable by sight, shown to reflect the data accurately, is an "original".

(4) *Duplicate.* — A "duplicate" is a counterpart produced by the same impression as the original, or from the same matrix, or by means of photography, including enlargements and miniatures, or by mechanical or electronic re-recording, or by chemical reproduction, or by other equivalent techniques which accurately reproduces the original.

☞ **Rule 1003. Admissibility of duplicates.**

A duplicate is admissible to the same extent as an original unless

(1) a genuine question is raised as to the authenticity of the original or (2) in the circumstances it would be unfair to admit the duplicate in lieu of the original.

[See Appendix A. Uniform Rules of Evidence for additional provisions.]

CHAPTER 53. BANKS.

Citation: NCGS 53-110

✍ **§ 53-110. Banking Commission to prescribe books, records, etc., retention, reproduction and disposition of records.**

(a) Whenever in its judgment it may appear to be advisable, the State Banking Commission may issue such rules, instructions, and regulations prescribing the manner of keeping books, accounts, and records of banks as will tend to produce uniformity in the books, accounts, and records of banks of the same class.

(b) The following provisions shall be applicable to banks and trust companies operating under Chapter 53 of the General Statutes and amendments thereto, and to national banking associations insofar as this section does not contravene paramount federal law:

(1) Each bank shall retain permanently the minute books of meetings of its stockholders and directors, its capital stock ledger and capital stock certificate ledger or stubs, and all records which the Banking Commission shall in accordance with the terms of this section require to be retained permanently.

(2) All other bank records shall be retained for such periods as the Banking Commission shall in accordance with the terms of this section prescribe.

(3) The Banking Commission shall from time to time issue regulations classifying all records kept by banks and prescribing the period for which records of each class shall be retained. Such periods may be permanent or for a lesser term of years. Such regulations may from time to time be amended or repealed, but any amendment or repeal shall not affect any action taken prior to such amendment or repeal. Prior to issuing any such regulations the Commission shall consider:

a. Actions at law and administrative proceedings in which the production of bank records might be necessary or desirable;

b. State and federal statutes of limitation applicable to such actions or proceedings.

c. The availability of information contained in bank records from other sources; and

d. Such other matters as the Banking Commission shall deem pertinent in order that its regulation will require banks to retain their records for as short a period as is commensurate with the interest of bank customers and stockholders and of the people of this State in having bank records available.

(4) Any bank may cause any or all records kept by it to be recorded, copied or reproduced by any photographic, photostatic, or miniature photographic process which correctly, accurately, and permanently copies, reproduces or forms a medium for copying or reproducing the original record on a film or other durable material.

(5) Any such photographic, photostatic or miniature photographic copy or reproduction shall be deemed to be an original record for all purposes and shall be treated as an original record in all courts and administrative agencies for the purpose of its admissibility in evidence. A facsimile, exemplification or certified copy of any such photographic copy or reproduction shall, for all purposes, be deemed a facsimile, exemplification or certified copy of the original record.

(6) Any bank may dispose of any record which has been retained for the periods prescribed by the Banking Commission or in accordance with the terms of this section for retention of records for its class.

CHAPTER 55A. NONPROFIT CORPORATION ACT.

Citation: NCGS 55A-27.1

☞ ✍ **§ 55A-27.1. Form of records.**

Any records maintained by a corporation in the regular course of its business, including its books of account and minute books, may be kept on, or be in the form of, punch cards, magnetic tape, photographs, microphotographs, or any other information storage device; provided that the records so kept can be converted into clearly legible form within a reasonable time. Any corporation shall so convert any records so kept upon the request of any person entitled to inspect the same. Where records are kept in such manner, the cards, tapes, photographs, microphotographs or other information storage device together with a duly authenticated readout or translation shall be admissible in evidence, and shall be accepted for all other purposes, to the same extent as an original written record of the same information would have been.

CHAPTER 121. ARCHIVES AND HISTORY.

Citation: NCGS 121-5

✪ **§ 121-5. Public records and archives.**

* * * * *

(b) *Destruction of Records Regulated.* — No person may destroy, sell, loan, or otherwise dispose of any public record without the consent of the Department of Cultural Resources. Whoever unlawfully removes a public record from the office where it is usually kept, or alters, mutilates, or destroys it shall be guilty of a misdemeanor and upon conviction fined at the discretion of the court.

* * * * *

(d) *Preservation of Permanently Valuable Records.* —

Public records certified by the Department of Cultural Resource as being of permanent value shall be preserved in the custody of the agency in which the records are normally kept or of the North Carolina State Archives. Any State, county, municipal, or other public official is hereby authorized and empowered to turn over to the Department of Cultural Resources any State, county, municipal, or other public records no longer in current official use. and the Department of Cultural Resources is authorized in its discretion to accept such records, and having done so shall provide for their administration and preservation in the North Carolina State Archives. When such records have been thus surrendered, photocopies, microfilms, typescripts, or other copies of them shall be made and certified under seal of the Department, upon application of any person, which certification shall have the same force and effect as if made by the official or agency by which the records were transferred to the Department of Cultural Resources; and the Department may charge reasonable fees for such copies. The Department may answer written inquiries for nonresidents of North Carolina and for such service charge a search and handling fee not to exceed ten dollars ($10.00), the receipts from which fee shall be used to defray the cost of providing such service.

CHAPTER 132. PUBLIC RECORDS.

Citation: NCGS 132-3

✪ § 132-3. Destruction of records regulated.

(a) *Prohibition.* No public official may destroy, sell, loan, or otherwise dispose of any public record, except in accordance with G.S. 121-5, without the consent of the Department of Cultural Resources. Whoever unlawfully removes a public records from the office where it is usually kept, or alters, defaces, mutilates or destroys it shall be guilty of a Class 3 misdemeanor and upon conviction fined not less than ten dollars ($10.00) nor more than five hundred dollars ($500.00).

(b) *Revenue Records.* Notwithstanding subsection (a) of this section and G.S. 121-5, when a record of the Department of Revenue has been copied in any manner, the original record may be destroyed upon the order of the Secretary of Revenue. If a record of the Department of Revenue has not been copied, the original record shall be preserved for at least three years. After three years the original record may be destroyed upon the order of the Secretary of Revenue.

✪ § 132-7. Keeping records in safe places; copying or repairing; certified copies.

Insofar as possible, custodians of public records shall keep them in fireproof safes, vaults, or rooms fitted with noncombustible materials and in such arrangement as to be easily accessible for convenient use. All public records should be kept in the buildings in which they are ordinarily used. Record books should be copies or repaired, renovated or rebound if worn, mutilated, damaged or difficult to read. Whenever any State, county, or municipal records are in need of repair, restoration, or rebinding, the head of such State agency, department, board, or commission, the board of county commissioners of such county, or the governing body of such municipality may authorize that the records in need of repair, restoration, or rebinding be removed from the building or office in which such records are ordinarily kept, for the length of time required to repair, restore, or rebind them. Any public official who causes a record book to be copied shall attest it and shall certify on oath that it is an accurate copy of the original book. The copy shall then have the force of the original.

Citation: NCGS 132-8.2

✪ § 132-8.2. Selection and preservation of records considered essential; making or designation of preservation duplicates; force and effect of duplicates or copies thereof.

In cooperation with the head of each State agency and the governing body of each county, municipality, and other subdivision of the government, the Department of Cultural Resources shall establish and maintain a program for the selection and preservation of public records considered essential to the operation of government and to the protection of the rights and interests of persons, and, within the limitations of funds available for the purpose, shall make or cause to be made preservation duplicates or designate as preservation duplicates existing copies of such essential public records. Preservation duplicates shall be durable, accurate, complete and clear, and such duplicates made by a photographic, photostatic, microfilm, micro card, miniature photographic, or other process which accurately reproduces and forms a durable medium for so reproducing the original shall have the same force and effect for all purposes as the original record whether the original record is in existence or not. A transcript, exemplification, or certified copy of such preservation duplicate shall be deemed for all purposes to be a transcript, exemplification, or certified copy of the original record. Such preservation duplicates shall be preserved in the place and manner of safekeeping prescribed by the Department of Cultural Resources.

CHAPTER 153A.

Citation: NCGS 153A-436

☞ ✪ § 153A-436. Photographic reproduction of county records.

(a) A county may provide for the reproduction, by photocopy, photograph, microphotograph, or any other method of reproduction that gives legible and permanent copies, of instruments, documents, and other papers filed with the register of deeds and of any other county records. The county shall keep each reproduction of an instrument, document, paper, or other record in a fire-resistant file, vault, or similar container. If a duplicate reproduction is made to provide a security-copy, the county shall keep the duplicate in a fire-resistant file, vault, or similar container separate from those housing the principal reproduction.

If a county has provided for reproducing records, any custodian of public records of the county may cause to be reproduced any of the records under, or coming under, his custody.

(b) If the county has provided for reproducing some or all county records, the custodian of any instrument, document, paper, or other record may permit it to be removed from its regular repository for up to 24 hours in order to be reproduced. An instrument, document, paper or other record may be removed from the county in order to be reproduced. The board of commissioners may permit an instrument, document, paper, or other record to be removed for longer than 24 hours if a longer period is necessary to complete the process of reproduction.(c) The original of any instrument, document, or other paper received by the register of deeds and reproduced pursuant to this Article shall be filed, maintained, and disposed of in accordance with G.S. 161-17 and G.S. 121-5. The original of any other county record that is reproduced pursuant to this Article may be kept by the county or disposed of pursuant to G.S. 121-5.

(d) If an instrument, document, or other paper received by the register of deeds is reproduced pursuant to this Article, the recording of the reproduction is a sufficient recording for all purposes.(e) A reproduction, made pursuant to this Article, of an instrument, document, paper, or other record is as admissible in evidence in any judicial or administrative proceeding as the original itself, whether the original is extant or not. An enlargement or other facsimile of the reproduction is also admissible in evidence if the original reproduction is extant and available for inspection under the direction of the court or administrative agency.

Source: North Carolina Administrative Code
Agency: Employment Security Commission

✍ REGULATION NO. 4. EMPLOYING UNIT RECORDS.

4.10 Each employing unit shall maintain records required by the Commission for each worker in employment who is paid wages for services rendered. These records shall be maintained by the employing unit for at least five (5) years after the calendar year in which wages for such services are paid.

4.11 For each worker in employment, the employing unit shall maintain records containing the following:

(A) The worker's name.

(B) The worker's social security number. If an employing unit has a worker in employment who does not have a social security number, the employing unit shall request the worker to produce a receipt issued by an officer of the Social Security Administration indicating that the worker has filed an application for a number. The receipt shall be retained by the worker.

(C) The state or states in which the worker's services are performed; and, if any of the services are performed outside North Carolina and are not incidental to the services performed in North Carolina, the base of operations with respect to such services, or if there is no base of operations then the place from which the services are directed or controlled, and the worker's state of residence.

(D) The dates which the worker was hired, rehired, returned to work after temporary layoff, and separated from work.

(E) The reasons for the worker's separation from work.

(F) The wages paid for the worker's services and dates of such payments.

(G) Amounts paid to the worker as allowances or reimbursements for traveling or other business expenses, dates of such payments, and the amounts of such expenditures actually incurred and accounted for by the worker.

(H) The number of hours the worker spends in employment.

4.12 Records shall be maintained by employing units from which the following can be determined regarding each worker:

(A) Earnings by pay period weeks, if paid on a weekly basis, or if not so paid, then by calendar weeks.

(B) Whether any week was a week during which the worker worked less than the equivalent of three (3) customary scheduled full-time days for the employing unit because of lack or work.

(C) Actual number of hours worked each day and total number of hours worked each week.

(D) Time worked for reasons other than lack of work.

4.13 Where part or all of the employing unit's accounting records are maintained by an automatic data processing system, the following must be provided by or with the system:

(A) Audit trails with supporting documents.

(B) General books of account containing a general ledger with source references which coincide with financial reports for reporting periods.

(C) A description of the automatic data processing portion of the employing unit's accounting system.

Source:	**North Carolina Department of Cultural Resources**

Citation:	**North Carolina Department of Cultural Resources Guidelines**

✪ Destruction of Public Records

* * * * *

2. *Destruction of original records that have been duplicated.* Original records that have been duplicated on microfilm, microfiche, data processing or word processing equipment, or other form may be destroyed prior to the retention period specified in the records schedule without further approval from the Division of Archives and History provided the following three conditions are met:

a. The duplicate copy of the information contained in the original record is maintained for the specified time.

b. The original record has not been scheduled for permanent preservation.

c. The governing body has agreed to the destruction of the original paper records and the destruction is recorded in a permanent record, such as the minutes of the governing body.

3. *Destruction of data processing records.* Computer printouts and other data processing input/output may be destroyed without specific authorization and recording, provided the following conditions apply:

a. The information is retained on magnetic media (e.g., magnetic tape, diskettes, etc.) and the media is scheduled in a records retention and disposition schedule.

b. The output copy is not specifically listed and scheduled in this records retention and disposition schedule.

4. *Methods of destruction.* Public records scheduled to be destroyed must not be permitted to fall into unauthorized hands. Where authorized, records scheduled for destruction shall be burned; otherwise, shredding, pulping, or burial under dirt rather than merely dropping the records into a hole should be used.

5. [inoperative]

6. *Disposition of records not authorized for destruction by this schedule.* Custodians with records not authorized for destruction or other disposition by this schedule may dispose of records series in this category by:

a. *Complying with paragraph 1c.* Address correspondence to the Assistant Records Administrator, State Records Center, 109 E. Jones Street, Raleigh, North Carolina 27611. List title of records, inclusive dates, and records volume. Include a statement to the effect that these records have no further use or value for official or administrative purposes. Concurrence or instructions will be sent by return mail.

b. *Custodians with records series no longer in current use which are identified as permanent and not authorized for destruction by this schedule, or with paper records that have been microfilmed are authorized and empowered to turn over such records to the Department of Cultural Resources.* The Department of Cultural Resources is authorized, at its discretion, to accept custody of these records providing they have adequate space and staff in the State Archives. A written offer of the records should be made to the address, and with the information listed in 6a, above.

State:	**North Dakota**
Source:	**North Dakota Century Code**

TITLE 7. BUILDING AND LOAN ASSOCIATIONS.

CHAPTER 7-04. OPERATION OF ASSOCIATIONS.

Citation:	**NDCC 7-04-23**

✍ § 7-04-23. Retention of records — Actions for unpaid balances.

No association may be required to preserve its records of account or files for a longer period than six years next after the first day of January of the year following the date of such record or files. Ledger sheets showing unpaid balances in favor of depositors or investors may not be destroyed unless a photostatic copy is retained under § 31-08-01.1, and this section does not limit the time when actions may be brought to recover such balances.

TITLE 10. CORPORATIONS.

CHAPTER 10-19.1. NORTH DAKOTA BUSINESS CORPORATION ACT — GENERAL PROVISIONS.

Citation: NDCC 10-19.1-84

✍ § 10-19.1-84. Books and records — Inspection.

1. A corporation shall keep at its principal executive office, or at another place or places within the United States determined by the board, a share register not more than one year old, containing the names and addresses of the shareholders and the number and classes of shares held by each shareholder. A corporation shall also keep, at its principal executive office, or at another place or places within the United States determined by the board, a record of the dates on which certificates were issued.

2. A corporation shall keep at its principal executive office, or, if its principal executive office is outside of this state, shall make available at its registered office within ten days after receipt by an officer of the corporation of a written demand for them made by a person described in subsection 4 or 5 originals or copies of:

a. Records of all proceedings of shareholders for the last three years;

b. Records of all proceedings of the board for the last three years;

c. Its articles and all amendments currently in effect;

d. Its bylaws and all amendments currently in effect;

e. Financial statements required by section 10-19.1-85 and the financial statement for the most recent interim period prepared in the course of the operation of the corporation for distribution to the shareholders or to a governmental agency as a matter of public record;

f. Reports made to shareholders generally within the last three years;

g. A statement of the names and the usual business addresses of its directors and principal officers;

h. Voting trust agreements described in section 10-19.1-81;

i. Shareholder control agreements described in section 10-19.1-83; and

j. A copy of agreements, contracts, or other arrangements or portions of them incorporated by reference under subsection 3 of section 10-19.1-61.

3. A corporation shall keep appropriate and complete financial records.

4. A shareholder or a holder of a voting trust certificate has an absolute right, upon written demand, to examine and copy, in person or by a legal representative, at any reasonable time, and the corporation shall make available within ten days after receipt by an officer of the corporation of the written demand:

a. The share register; and

b. All documents referred to in subsection 2.

* * * * *

11. The records maintained by a corporation, including its share register, financial records, and minute books, may utilize any information storage technique, including, for example, punched holes, printed or magnetized spots, or microimages, even though that makes them illegible visually, if the records can be converted accurately and within a reasonable time, into a form that is legible visually and whose contents are assembled by related subject matter to permit convenient use by people in the normal course of business. A corporation shall convert any of the records referred to in subsection 4 upon the request of a person entitled to inspect them, and the expense of the conversion shall be borne by the person who bears the expense of copying pursuant to subsection 10. A copy of the conversion if admissible in evidence, and must be accepted for all other purposes, to the same extent as the existing or original records would be if they were legible visually.

TITLE 31. JUDICIAL PROOF.

CHAPTER 31-08. PRIVATE RECORDS AND WRITINGS.

Citation: NDCC 31-08-01.1

☞ § 31-08-01.1. Certain copies of business and public records admissible in evidence.

If any business, institution, member of a profession or calling, or any department or agency of government in the regular course of business or activity has kept or recorded any memorandum, writing, entry, print, representation, or combination thereof, of any act, transaction, occurrence, or event, and in the regular course of business has caused any or all of the same to be recorded, copied, or reproduced by any photographic, photostatic, microfilm, micro-card, miniature photographic, optical disk, or other process which accurately reproduces or forms a durable medium for so reproducing the original, the original may be destroyed in the regular course of business unless its preservation is required by law.

Such reproduction, when satisfactorily identified, is as admissible in evidence as the original itself in any judicial or administrative proceeding whether the original is in existence or not and an enlargement or facsimile of such reproduction is likewise admissible in evidence if the original reproduction is in existence and available for inspection under direction of court. The introduction of a reproduced record, enlargement, or facsimile does not preclude admission of the original.

Citation: NDCC 31-08-01.3

☞ ✍ § 31-08-01.3. Medical records recording.

The recording of hospital medical records by an electronic image system or reproduction process is considered a photographic process. The making or recording of hospital medical records by electronic data processing systems is considered an original written record, and printout or other types of retrieved information in written or printed form must be treated as original records in all courts or administrative agencies for the purpose of its admissibility into evidence.

TITLE 54. STATE GOVERNMENT.

CHAPTER 54-46.1. CENTRAL MICROFILM UNIT.

Citation: NDCC 54-46.1-02.1

✪ § 54-46.1-02.1. Optical data storage authorized.

Any public entity may adopt and use an optical data storage process for the storage of records by optical disk mediums when the use of the process is consistent with good records management practices. The state records administrator may prescribe such practices, except for specialized commercial data bases such as those used in libraries. As used in this chapter, an optical data storage process includes the optical disk software and hardware used in that process and the records stored by that process after the entity involved has established a records management program with respect to optical data storage.

Citation: NDCC 54-46.1-03

☞ § 54-46.1-03. Reproductions admissible in evidence — Preparation of copies.

A photographic, microphotographic, or microfilm copy of any record, a paper or microfilm reproduction of any record stored by optical disk, or a certified copy thereof, is admissible as evidence in any court or proceeding and has the same force and effect as though the original record has been produced and proved. The custodian of such records shall prepare enlarged copies of microphotographic or microfilm copies of the records and paper copies of records stored by optical disk and shall document the accuracy of the processes whenever their production is required by law.

Citation: NDCC 54-46.1-04

✪ § 54-46.1-04. Duplicate storage of microfilm records.

Whenever any record or document is copied or reproduced as provided in this chapter, the state records administrator shall provide for duplicate storage of the photographic reproductions. The administrator may enter into contracts for duplicate storage services if, in the administrator's judgment, such contracts are necessary for the safekeeping of photographic reproductions.

Source: North Dakota Rules of Evidence

☞ Rule 1001. Definitions

For purposes of this article the following definitions are applicable:

(1) *Writings and recordings.* — "Writings" and "recordings" consist of letters, words, or numbers, or their equivalent, set down by handwriting, typewriting, printing, photostating, photographing, magnetic impulse, mechanical or electronic recording, or other form of data compilation.

(2) *Photographs.* — "Photographs" include still photographs, X-ray films, video tapes, and motion pictures.

(3) *Original.* — An "original" of a writing or recording is the writing or recording itself or any counterpart intended to have the same effect by a person executing or issuing it. An "original" of a photograph includes the negative or any print therefrom. If data are stored in a computer or similar device, any printout or other output readable by sight, shown to reflect the data accurately, is an "original".

(4) *Duplicate.* — A "duplicate" is a counterpart produced by the same impression as the original, or from the same matrix, or by means of photography, including enlargements and miniatures, or by mechanical or electronic re-recording, or by chemical reproduction, or by other equivalent techniques which accurately reproduces the original.

☞ Rule 1003. Admissibility of Duplicates.

A duplicate is admissible to the same extent as an original unless (1) a genuine question is raised as to the authenticity or continuing effectiveness of the original or (2) in the circumstances it would be unfair to admit the duplicate in lieu of the original.

[See Appendix A. Uniform Rules of Evidence for additional provisions.]

State: Ohio
Source: Ohio Revised Code Annotated

TITLE 1. STATE GOVERNMENT.

CHAPTER 9.

Citation: ORCA 9.01

✪ §9.01. Photostat, microfilm or other recording.

When any officer, office, court, commission, board, institution, department, agent, or employee of the state, or of a county, or any political subdivision, who is charged with the duty or authorized or required by law to record, preserve, keep, maintain, or file any record, document, plat, court file, paper, or instrument in writing, or to make or furnish copies of any thereof, deems it necessary or advisable, when recording any such document, plat, court file, paper, or instrument in writing, or when making a copy or reproduction of any thereof or of any such record, for the purpose of recording or copying, preserving, and protecting the same, reducing space required for storage, or any similar purpose, to do so by means of any photostatic, photographic, miniature photographic, film, microfilm, or microphotographic process, or perforated tape, magnetic tape, other magnetic means, electronic data processing, machine readable means, graphic or video display, or any combination thereof, which correctly and accurately copies, records, or reproduces, or provides a medium of copying, recording, or reproducing, the original record, document, plat, court file, paper, or instrument in writing, such use of any such photographic or electromagnetic processes, for any such purpose, is hereby authorized. Any such records, copies, or reproductions may be made in duplicate, and such duplicates shall be stored in different buildings. The film or paper used for this process shall comply with the minimum standards of quality approved for permanent photographic records by the national bureau of standards. All such records, copies, or reproductions shall carry a certificate of authenticity and completeness, on a form specified by the state records administrator.

Any such officer, office, court, commission, board, institution, department, agent, or employee of the state, a county, or any political subdivision may purchase or rent required equipment for any such photographic process and may enter into contracts with private concerns or other governmental agencies for the development of film and the making of reproductions thereof as a part of any such photographic process.

When so recorded, or copied or reproduced to reduce space required for storage or filing of such records, said photographs, microphotographs, microfilms, perforated tape, magnetic tape, other magnetic means, electronic data processing, machine readable means, graphic or video display, or any combination thereof, or films, or prints made therefrom, when properly identified by the officer by whom or under whose supervision the same were made, or who has the custody thereof, have the same effect at law as the original record or of a record made by any other legally authorized means, and may be offered in like manner and shall be received in evidence in any court where such original record, or record made by other legally authorized means, could have been so introduced and received. Certified or authenticated copies or prints of such photographs, microphotographs, films, microfilms, perforated tape, magnetic tape, other magnetic means, electronic data processing, machine readable means, graphic or video display, or any combination thereof, shall be admitted in evidence equally with the original photographs, microphotographs, films, or microfilms.

Such photographs, microphotographs, microfilms, or films

shall be placed and kept in conveniently accessible, fireproof, and insulated files, cabinets, or containers, and provisions shall be made for preserving, safekeeping, using, examining, exhibiting, projecting, and enlarging the same whenever requested, during office hours.

All persons utilizing the methods described in this section for keeping records and information shall keep and make readily available to the public the machines and equipment necessary to reproduce the records and information in a readable form.

CHAPTER 149. DOCUMENTS, REPORTS, AND RECORDS.

[State Records Commission]

Citation: ORCA 149.32

✪ **§ 149.32. State records commission.**

[This section will be repealed effective January 1, 2005.]

There is hereby created a "state records commission," to be composed of the superintendent of public instruction, the auditor of state, the attorney general, the secretary of state, the director of administrative services, and the director of the Ohio historical society, or their designated representatives. The archivist of the Ohio historical society shall be the secretary of the commission and shall advise the commission on the archival value of state records. The commission shall elect a chairman from its members and prescribe procedures for the compiling and submitting to the state records administrator of lists and schedules of records proposed for retention and disposal, procedures for the disposal of records authorized for disposal, and standards for the reproduction of records by photographic or microphotographic processes with a view to the disposal of the original records.

The functions of the said commission shall be to review all applications for records disposal or transfer and all schedules of records retention and destruction as submitted by the state records administrator. The decision of the commission to approve, reject, or modify the applications of schedules shall be based upon the continuing administrative, legal, fiscal, or historical value of the records to the state or to its citizens.

The Ohio historical society shall be given a period of thirty days after the date of such review and before such records are otherwise disposed of to select for its custody such records as it may deem to be of continuing historical value. Records not so selected shall be disposed of in accordance with the procedures established by the state records commission.

The commission may revise, alter, approve, or reject any schedule and application or portion thereof and may designate transfer and disposal dates and methods of disposal of records when such are not specifically provided for by law. No records shall be retained, destroyed, or otherwise transferred in violation of any records schedule or application approved as provided in this section.

The commission shall make an annual report to the governor as prescribed by section 149.01 of the Revised Code.

TITLE 17. CORPORATIONS — PARTNERSHIPS

CHAPTER 1705. LIMITED LIABILITY COMPANIES.

Citation: ORCA 1705.22

✍ **§ 1705.22. Right of member to obtain information and copies of documents.**

* * * * *

(C) A limited liability company may maintain its records in a form other than a written form if the form used is capable of conversion into written form within a reasonable time.

* * * * *

CHAPTER 1782. LIMITED PARTNERSHIPS.

Citation: ORCA 1782.21

✍ **§ 1782.21. Rights of limited partner to information and copies of documents.**

* * * * *

(C) A limited partnership may maintain its records in a form other than a written form if the form used is capable of conversion, within a reasonable time, into written form.

* * * * *

TITLE 23. COURTS — COMMON PLEAS.

CHAPTER 2303. CLERK OF THE COURT OF COMMON PLEAS.

Citation: ORCA 2303.12

✪ **§ 2303.12. Books to be kept by clerk.**

The clerk of the court of common pleas shall keep at least four books. They shall be called the appearance docket, trial docket and printed duplicates of the trial docket for the use of the court and the officers thereof, journal, and execution docket. He shall also keep a record in book form or he may prepare a record by using any photostatic, photographic, miniature photographic, film, microfilm, or microphotographic process, electrostatic process, perforated tape, magnetic tape, or other electromagnetic means, electronic data processing, machine readable media, graphic or video display, or any combination thereof, which correctly and accurately copies or reproduces the original document, paper, or instrument in writing. He shall use materials that comply with the minimum standards of quality for the permanent photographic records prescribed by the National Bureau of Standards. He shall keep an index to the trial docket and of the journal direct, and to the appearance docket, record, and execution docket, direct and reverse.

All clerks keeping records and information by the methods described in this section shall keep and make readily available to the public the machine and equipment necessary to reproduce the records and information in a readable form.

CHAPTER 2317. EVIDENCE.

Citation: ORCA 2317.41

☞ **§ 2317.41. Photographic copies of records admissible as competent evidence.**

"Photograph" as used in this section includes but is not limited to microphotograph, a roll or strip of film, a roll or strip of microfilm, or a photostatic copy.

To the extent that a record would be competent evidence under section 2317.40 of the Revised Code, a photograph of such record shall be competent evidence if the custodian of the photograph or the person who made such photograph or under whose supervision such photograph was made testifies to the identity of and the mode of making such photograph, and if, in the opinion of the trial court, the record has been destroyed or otherwise disposed of in good faith in the regular course of business, and the mode of making such photograph was such as to justify its admission. If a photograph is admissible under this section, the court may admit the whole or a part thereof.

Such photograph shall be admissible only if the party offering it has delivered a copy of it, or so much thereof as relates to the controversy, to the adverse party a reasonable time before trial, unless in the opinion of the court the adverse party has not been unfairly surprised by the failure to deliver such copy. No such photograph need be submitted to the adverse party as prescribed in this section unless the original instrument would be required to be so submitted.

Source: Ohio Rules of Evidence

☞ **Rule 1001. Definitions**

For purposes of this article the following definitions are applicable:

(1) *Writings and recordings.* — "Writings" and "recordings" consist of letters, words, or numbers, or their equivalent, set down by handwriting, typewriting, printing, photostating, photographing, magnetic impulse, mechanical or electronic recording, or other form of data compilation.

(2) *Photographs.* — "Photographs" include still photographs, X-ray films, video tapes, and motion pictures.

(3) *Original.* — An "original" of a writing or recording is the writing or recording itself or any counterpart intended to have the same effect by a person executing or issuing it. An "original" of a photograph includes the negative or any print therefrom. If data are stored in a computer or similar device, any printout or other output readable by sight, shown to reflect the data accurately, is an "original".

(4) *Duplicate.* — A "duplicate" is a counterpart produced by the same impression as the original, or from the same matrix, or by means of photography, including enlargements and miniatures, or by mechanical or electronic re-recording, or by chemical reproduction, or by other equivalent techniques which accurately reproduces the original.

☞ **Rule 1003. Admissibility of Duplicates.**

A duplicate is admissible to the same extent as an original unless (1) a genuine question is raised as to the authenticity of the original or (2) in the circumstances it would be unfair to admit the duplicate in lieu of the original.

[See Appendix A. Uniform Rules of Evidence for additional provisions.]

Source: Attorney General Opinion

✪

1. (1989) The optical disk process of recording records is a "machine readable means" of information recording authorized by RC § 9.01, and the Department of Highway Safety may store records of the Administration Division and the Bureau of Motor Vehicles Division of the department by such method: OAG No. 89-042.

2. (1989) Revised Code § 9.01 permits the admission into Ohio state courts of a print or other reproduction of information in a public record stored by the optical disk process: OAG No. 89-042.

3. (1989) A county auditor is required only to have machines available to reproduce public records stored on magnetic tape. There is no requirement to provide records in the form of magnetic computer tapes and the software to access them: *State ex re. Recodat Co. v. Buchanan,* 46 OS3d 163, 546 NE2d 203.

State: Oklahoma
Source: Oklahoma Statutes

TITLE 12. CIVIL PROCEDURE.

CHAPTER 2. GENERAL PROVISIONS.

CLERK; RECORDS.

Citation: 12 OS 24

✪ **§ 24. Journal record — Instruments to be entered — Microfilm**

Upon the journal record required to be kept by the clerk of the district court in civil cases exclusive of the small claims docket and juvenile proceedings docket shall be entered copies of the following instruments on file:

1. All items of process by which the court acquired jurisdiction of the person of each defendant in the case; and

2. All instruments filed in the case that bear the signature of the judge and specify clearly the relief granted or order made.

The journal may be kept entirely in microfilm record. Existing journal records in custody of court clerk may be destroyed after being microfilmed.

The microfilm record shall consist of two films, one of which shall be placed by the court clerk with the Archives and Records Division of the Oklahoma Department of Libraries, or in a bank or other appropriate local depository, and one shall be available for public use in the court clerk's office. In case of functional failure of the film in the court clerk's office the copy in storage shall be made available to anyone requesting access to it. The cost of microfilm, microfilm equipment and view-scopes shall be paid out of the court fund upon approval by the Chief Justice of the Supreme Court. Copies of the journal record on microfilm and copies of the original instruments that are part of the journal records, when certified by the court clerk having the custody of the original, may be received in evidence with the same effect as the original would have had and without further identification by the party desiring to offer them.

Citation: 12 OS 24.1

✪ **§ 24.1. Disposal of record.**

Any clerk, upon microfilming the record as above set forth, is directed to destroy the record, provided that such record shall first be offered to the county and State Historical Society.

CHAPTER 40. EVIDENCE CODE.

ARTICLE X. CONTENTS OF WRITINGS, RECORDINGS AND PHOTOGRAPHS

Citation: 12 OS 3001

☞ **§ 3001. Definitions.**

1. "Writings" and "recordings" consist of letters, words, or numbers, or their equivalent, set down by handwriting, typewriting, printing, photostating, photographing, magnetic impulse, mechanical or electronic recording, or other form of data compilation;
2. "Photographs" include still photographs, x-ray films, video tapes, and motion pictures;
3. An "original" of a writing or recording is the writing or recording itself or any counterpart intended to have the same effect by a person executing it. An "original" of a photograph includes the negative or any print therefrom. If data are stored in a computer or similar device, any print out or other output readable by sight, shown to reflect the data accurately, is an "original"; and
4. A "duplicate" is a counterpart produced by the same impression as the original, or from the same matrix, or by means of photography, including enlargement and miniatures, or by mechanical or electronic rerecording, or by chemical reproduction, or by other equivalent technique including, but not limited to, storage and reproduction by means of an optical disk, or other forms of mass storage, electronic imaging, or electronic data processing, or a facsimile machine or similar device which reproduces documents transmitted over telephone lines, or similar devices or processes and which accurately reproduce the original.

Citation: 12 OS 3003

☞ **§ 3003. Admissibility of Duplicates.**

A duplicate is admissible to the same extent as an original under this rule or as may otherwise be provided by statute unless:
1. A question is raised as to the authenticity of the original; or
2. In the circumstances it would be unfair to admit the duplicate in lieu of the original.

Citation: 12 OS 3004

☞ **§ 3004. Admissibility of other evidence of contents.**

The original is not required, and a duplicate or other evidence of the contents of a writing, recording, or photographic is admissible if:
1. All originals are lost or have been destroyed unless the proponent loses or destroyed them in bad faith;
2. No original can be obtained by any available judicial process or procedure;
3. At a time when an original was under the control of the party against whom offered, the party was put on notice, by the pleadings or otherwise, that the contents would be subject of proof at the hearings and the party does not produce the original at the hearing; or
4. The writing, recording, or photograph is not closely related to a controlling issue.

TITLE 18. CORPORATIONS.

CHAPTER 22. GENERAL CORPORATION ACT.

Citation: 18 OS 1069

✍ ☞ **§ 1069. Form of records.**

Any records maintained by a corporation in the regular course of its business, including its stock ledger, books of account, and minute books, may be kept in, or be in the form of, punch cards, magnetic tape, photographs, microphotographs, or any other information storage device, provided that the records so kept can be converted into clearly legible written form within a reasonable time. Any corporation shall so convert any records so kept upon the request of any person entitled to inspect the same. Where records are kept in such manner, a clearly legible written form produced from the cards, tapes, photographs, microphotographs or other information storage device shall be admissible in evidence and shall be accepted for all other purposes, to the same extent as an original written record of the same information would have been, when said written form accurately portrays the record.

TITLE 20. COURTS.

CHAPTER 15. DESTRUCTION OF COURT RECORDS.

Citation: 20 OS 1004

✪ **§ 1004. Destruction of court records — Method — Microfilm**

A. The chief judge of a district court may authorize the court clerk to dispose of the judicial records enumerated in this subsection by first offering all or part of said records to the Archives and Records Division of the Oklahoma Department of Libraries for preservation as historical research materials, and by destroying all those which are not accepted by the Division. The judicial records subject to disposal or destruction shall be:
1. All divorce cases in which there has been no activity for more than twenty (20) years.
2. Divorce cases that have been dismissed for more than one (1) year.
3. Actions brought forth for money judgment only in which a dismissal or release and satisfaction has been filed for more than five (5) years; and
4. Civil and criminal records of cases which have been finally adjudicated for more than ten (10) years.

The judicial records and the appearance docket books or sheets on which they are entered, prior to their disposal or destruction, shall be microfilmed on at least two microfilm records, one of which shall be placed in the Archives and Records Division of the Oklahoma Department of Libraries or in a bank or other appropriate local depository and the other shall be available for public use in the court clerk's office.

The copy in the Department of Libraries or other depository shall be available for replacement in case of functional failure of the one available for public use. The cost of microfilm, microfilm equipment, and viewerscopes shall be paid out of the court fund, upon approval by the Chief Justice of the Supreme Court. Microfilm records of the court files disposed of pursuant to provisions of this section shall be received in evidence and have the same legal efficacy as the original would have had.

* * * * *

Citation: 20 OS 1005

✪ **§ 1005. Destruction of court records — Storage on microfilm, optical disk or other medium.**

A.Unless there is an objection by the chief judge of a district court, the court clerk is authorized to dispose of the judicial records enumerated in this subsection by first offering all or part of said records to the Archives and Records Division of the Oklahoma Department of Libraries for preservation as historical research materials, and by destroying all those which are not accepted by the Division. The judicial records subject to disposal or destruction shall be:

1. All domestic relations cases after a twenty-year period had elapsed since any pleading has been filed or any action taken in the case. Domestic relations cases shall include, but not be limited to, cases filed concerning divorce, separate maintenance, annulment, reciprocal actions for enforcement of support, child custody, domestic abuse, foreign judgments in domestic relations cases, income assignments relating to an order of support, paternity, appeal on administrative order relating to support or paternity, habeas corpus relating to children, and other domestic-related filings;

2. Domestic relations cases that have been dismissed and no pleading has been filed or any action taken in the case for more than one (1) year.

3. Actions brought forth for money judgment only in which a dismissal or release and satisfaction has been filed for more than five (5) years; and

4. Civil and criminal records of adjudicated cases after a ten-year period has elapsed since any pleading has been filed or any action taken in the case.

B. The judicial records and the appearance docket books or sheets on which they are entered, prior to their disposal or destruction, shall be stored on at least two microfilm records, optical disks or other appropriate medium, one of which shall be placed in the Archives and Records Division of the Oklahoma Department of Libraries or in a bank or other appropriate local depository and the other shall be available for public use in the court clerk's office. The copy in the Department of Libraries or other depository shall be available for replacement in case of functional failure of the one available for public use. The cost of the storage medium and equipment for viewing and copying shall be paid out of the court fund, upon approval by the Chief Justice of the Supreme Court. Records reproduced from microfilm, optical disk, and other media produced pursuant to the provisions of this section shall be received in evidence and have the same legal efficacy as the original.

C. The court clerk of each district court shall destroy the judicial records of traffic cases and the appearance docket books or sheets on which they are entered after a five-year period has elapsed since any pleading has been filed or any action taken in the case, except in the case of a conviction for driving under the influence of intoxicating liquor or any narcotic drug.

D. The court clerk of each district court shall destroy the judicial records of justice of the peace courts including docket books on which they are entered; small claims cases including the docket books and sheets on which they are entered after a five-year period has elapsed since any pleading has been filed or any action taken in the case.

Citation: 20 OS 1005.1

✪ **§ 1005.1. Disposal of paper records after recording on other medium or passage of 22 years.**

All paper records which have been recorded on microfilm, microfiche, or compact disc may be destroyed after the respective case has been adjudicated. With the exception of felony conviction records, probate, adoption, quiet title, ejectment, partition, marriage and divorce records, and Indian deed approval records, all court records which have not been recorded on microfilm, microfiche, or compact disc and in which no activity has occurred for twenty-two (22) years, may be destroyed or may be given as historical research materials to an appropriate organization as determined by the court clerk of the district court.

* * * * *

TITLE 54. PARTNERSHIP.

CHAPTER 6. OKLAHOMA REVISED UNIFORM LIMITED PARTNERSHIP ACT.

Citation: 54 OS 306

✍ **§ 306. Records to be kept.**

A. Each limited partnership shall keep the following at the office required pursuant to Section 305 of this title.

1. A current list of the full name and last-known business address of each partner, separately identifying the general partners in alphabetical order and the limited partners in alphabetical order,

2. A copy of the certificate of limited partnership and all certificates of amendment thereto together with executed copies of any powers of attorney pursuant to which any certificate has been executed;

3. Copies of the limited partnership's federal and state income tax returns and reports, if any, for the three (3) most recent years; and

4. Copies of any then effective written partnership agreements and of any financial statements of the limited partnership for the three (3) most recent years.

5. Unless contained in a written partnership agreement, a writing setting out:

a. the amount of cash and a description and statement of the agreed value of the other property or services contributed by each partner and which each partner has agreed to contribute;

b. the times at which or events on the happening of which any additonal contributions agreed to be made by each partner are to be made;

c. any right of a partner to receive, or of a general partner to make, distributions to a partner which include a return of all or any part of the partner's contribution, and

d. any events upon the happening of which the limited partnership is to be dissolved and its affairs wound up.

B. Records kept under this section are subject to inspection and copying at the reasonable request, and at the expense, of any partner during ordinary business hours.

TITLE 62 PUBLIC FINANCE.

CHAPTER 1. STATE FISCAL AFFAIRS.

Records of Warrants

Citation: 62 OS 275.1

✪ **§ 275.1. Microfilming of public welfare warrants — Destruction of originals after microfilming — Permanent copies maintained.**

All warrants issued by the Oklahoma Public Welfare Commission and the State Treasurer, in payment of assistance to the needy, aged persons, blind or dependent children, shall be microfilmed by the Department of Institutions, Social and Rehabilitative Services, starting with the fiscal year beginning July 1, 1947, and thereafter, provided further that the Department of Institutions, Social and Rehabilitative Services is hereby authorized and directed to destroy said warrants, by burning, shredding, chemical process or any other method which will ensure the complete destruction thereof, after microfilm copies are made thereof. Permanent microfilm copies of said warrants shall be maintained by the Department of Institutions, Social and Rehabilitative Services.

Citation: 62 OS 275.2

✪ **§ 275.2. Destruction of warrant registers after warrants microfilmed.**

Warrant registers maintained by the State Treasurer, listing warrants issued in payment to the needy persons referred to in Section 275.1, shall be destroyed in the manner hereinabove provided by said officers upon receipt of notice from the Department of Institutions, Social and Rehabilitative Services that warrants listed thereon have been microfilmed.

TITLE 67. RECORDS.

CHAPTER 3. PHOTOGRAPHIC COUNTY RECORDS.

Citation: 67 OS 91

✪ **§ 91. Adoption of system of recording — Equipment, supplies and operators — Contracts for recording work.**

The board of county commissioners of any county in this state may by resolution adopt the system of photographic recording for any or all offices of the respective counties where instruments are filed which are required to be recorded in books to be kept for that purpose. Said board of county commissioners in such counties where such system of recording is adopted may purchase such machines, equipment, and supplies as may be necessary and proper to do said work and also employ a competent operator or operators to be fixed by the board of county commissioners in such amount as they shall deem advisable. In lieu of the purchase of said machines, equipment, and supplies by the county, the board of county commissioners may, if they deem it advisable, contract with some suitable person or persons, firm, or corporation having proper machines and equipment therefore to do all recording work required to be done in any office in their respective counties and fix the compensation therefore. No contract shall be made wherein the county shall be required to pay for such work a greater price than sixty percent (60%) of the total fees charged for such recording, as fixed by law at the time said contract is entered into. The adoption of this system by any county prior to the passage of this act, and the record heretofore made by such system, are hereby validated.

Citation: 67 OS 93

✪ **§ 93. Procedure in making photographic record — Place of doing work — Liability for instruments.**

When said work is done by contract, each instrument sought to be recorded shall be first filed with the officer having charge of the records of the office in which such instrument is sought to be recorded, and by him entered in a receiving book, kept for that purpose, and with reasonable dispatch thereafter delivered to such person, firm or corporation designated in said contract, for the purpose of recording, who shall with equal dispatch, make one photographic copy thereof on loose-leaf duplex (sheets coated with sensitized photographic emulsion on both sides) sheets, capable of being bound in permanent volume, as a part of the official records of such county, and immediately thereafter, deliver the original of such instrument together with said photographic copy to the office in which the same was received, and shall make, preserve and maintain an additional photographic copy of said record in some suitable and safe place, so that in the event of destruction or mutilation of the official record, the same can be replaced or substituted from the additional copy so preserved and maintained; Provided, further, that no record shall be removed from the county for the purpose of photographing and when the work is done by contract, if not done at the courthouse, the place of doing said work shall be definitely fixed and subscribed in said contract with reasonable accuracy and certainty; Provided, further, that the board of county commissioners shall have the right and privilege to fix the size of the sheet upon which such instrument is being photographed for record at the time of making said contract; Provided, further, that when any instrument is delivered to the contractor for recording, the official bond of such contractor shall be liable for the prompt and safe return of such instrument to the office in which it belongs and during such interval of time between delivery to the contractor and return to the proper officer, such officer having the permanent custody and control of said record shall not be liable on his official bond for the preservation of such instrument; Provided, further, that the contractor shall give his receipt for every instrument at time of receiving same and may require the officer to give receipt upon return of such instrument.

CHAPTER 7. UNIFORM PRESERVATION OF PRIVATE BUSINESS RECORDS ACT.

Citation: 67 OS 251

✍ **§ 251. Definitions.**

As used in this act, "business" includes every kind of private business, profession, occupation, calling or operation of private institutions, whether carried on for profit or not. "Persons" means an individual, partnership, corporation, or any other association. "Record" or "business records" include books of account, vouchers, documents, canceled checks, payroll, correspon dence, records of sales, personnel, equipment and production, reports relating to any or all of such records, and other business papers. "Reproduction" means a reproduction or durable medium for making a reproduction obtained by any phot ographic, photostatic, microfilm, microcard, miniature photographic or other process which accurately reproduces or forms a durable medium for so reproducing the original.

✍ § 253. Reproductions.

If in regular course of business a person makes reproductions of original business records, the preservation of such reproductions constitutes compliance with any laws of this state requiring that business records be kept or preserved.

CHAPTER 8. REPRODUCTION OF PUBLIC RECORDS.

Citation: 67 OS 301

✪ § 301. Photographing, microphotographing or filming of records — Standards — Preservation of original negatives.

A.1. Any public officer of the state or any county, public trust, authority or agency, city, municipality, district or legal subdivision thereof, may cause any or all records, papers or documents kept by him to be photographed, microphotographed or reproduced on film. The custodian of the record may permit any record to be removed from his office for the purpose of photographic filming, and his responsibility for their care and return shall continue during the times of their removal from the area controlled by the custodian of the records during photographic sessions. The custodian of the records shall, before delivering any records for photographing or microphotographing make a complete catalog list of the records to be filmed and retain the same until the records are returned. He may require a bond, and shall require written receipt identifying each record removed from his custody. Such photographic film shall comply with the minimum standards of quality for film, processing, and storage of permanent photographic records promulgated by the Archives and Records Commission. The device used to reproduce such records on such film shall accurately reproduce the original thereof in all details. Such photographs, microphotographs or photographic film shall be deemed to be original records for all purposes, including introduction in evidence in all courts or administrative agencies. A transcript, exemplification, or certified copy thereof, for all purposes recited herein, shall be deemed to be a transcript, exemplification, or certified copy of the original.

2. The original photographs, microphotographs, or film shall be stored in a maximum security vault and only be removed therefrom for the purpose of making copies thereof as the custodian of the records may require. At the election of the custodian of the records, however, the master negative may, immediately upon being made, be deposited with the Oklahoma Department of Libraries which shall retain it in a maximum security vault and furnish such copies thereof as may be required for the purposes of the custodian of the records. The cost of any photographic, microphotographic, or filming services requested by and furnished to a state agency or subdivision of government shall be paid to the Department of Libraries rendered on the basis of fee schedu les established by the Archives and Records Commission.

3. A copy of such photographs, microphotographs or reproductions on film properly certified and cataloged shall be placed in conveniently accessible files and provisions made for preserving, examining and using the same, including reproduction of same. There shall be available for use by the public at least two devices for viewing, and at least one of said devices shall provide for reproducing the photographic records. Such copies shall be certified by their custodian as true copies of the originals, and the copies so certified shall have the same force and effect as the originals. A statement in writing describing the record and certifying it to be a true copy, and attached securely to the reproduction, will be deemed a sufficient certification. Any viewing devices in use at the time of the passage of this act may continue to be used, although such device does not provide a reproducing system.

B. The provisions of this section shall not affect and are cumulative to the provisions of the Records Management Act, Section 201 et seq. of this title and Sections 564 through 576 of Title 74 of the Oklahoma Statutes.

Citation: 67 OS 302

✪ § 302. Instruments filed for record — Microfilming — copies — Sale of copies.

The county clerk and ex officio registrar of deeds may record the instruments lawfully filed for record in his office by making and preserving microfilm thereof.

Whenever a system of microfilming is established at least two (2) microfilms shall be made of each recorded instrument which shall be kept separate, in order that they may not be subject to the same hazards. Additional copies of such microfilmed records may be produced by the public officer for sale to bonded abstractors of the county at a price not to exceed the cost of production plus twenty percent (20%).

The security copy of the microfilm may be deposited in a bank or other safe place.

Citation: 67 OS 303

✪ § 303. Court or judicial records.

This act [Title 67, § 301 et seq.] shall not apply to any court or judicial records.

CHAPTER 10A. ARCHIVES AND RECORDS COMMISSION

Citation: 67 OS 309

✪ § 309. Microfilm or microphotograph film deemed original record — Exemplification or certified copy.

Any microfilm or microphotograph film of any original record or archives shall be deemed to be an original record or archive for all purposes and shall be admissible in evidence in all courts or administrative agencies the same as the originals. A facsimile exemplification or certified copy thereof shall for all purposes recited herein be deemed to be a description exemplification or certified copy of the original.

Source: Oklahoma Administrative Regulations

TITLE 60. ARCHIVES AND RECORDS COMMISSION.

CHAPTER 10. ARCHIVES AND RECORDS.

Subchapter 7. Microfilm.

Citation: 60 OAR 10-7-1

✪ § 60:10-7-1. Authenticity and photographic quality.

The Archives and Records Commission requires, prior to authorization for destruction of original records previously microfilmed, that state agencies seeking such destruction must first obtain certification of the identity and photographic quality of such film from the Micrographics Section of the Records Management Division of the Oklahoma Department of Libraries or personnel in their micrographics laboratories certified by the State Records Administrator. The Commission suggests

ANSI/AIIM MS 23-1991, "Practice for Operational Procedures/Inspection and Quality Control of First-Generation Silver-Gelatin Microfilm of Documents," as a guide for agency microfilming programs.

Citation: 60 OAR 10-7-2

✪ § 60:10-7-2. Quality control standards.

The following are quality control standards for microfilm of state records:

(1) Records and Microfilm Identification Declarations must be completed and signed by the official who has legal custody of the original records and by the camera operator, and filmed at the beginning and end of each roll of film thus identifying the records on that particular roll. The Commission suggests ANSI/AIIM MS 19-1993, "Recommended Practice for Identification of Microforms," as a guide for completing Microform Identification Declarations.

(2) Documents in a condition making it impossible to reproduce them in a legible and readable condition, as displayed on a microfilm reader or reproduced in paper copy, should be marked with a target to that effect, such as "The following document is below standards for microfilm." After being filmed, such documents must be withdrawn from the sequence and retained in the original for the same length of time as the applicable microfilm. Legibility is defined as the quality of a letter or numeral which enables the observer to identify it positively and quickly to the exclusion of all other letters and numerals. Readability is defined as the quality of a group of letters or numerals which makes them recognizable as words or whole numbers.

(3) Microfilm stock used for preservation of documents shall be safety base permanent record film, as specified in ANSI IT9.6-1991, "Photography — Photographic Films — Specifications for Safety Film (revision and redesignation of ANSI PH 1.25-1984)."

(A) The required master record on microfilm (camera negative) shall be permanent record film as specified in ANSI/NAPM IT9.1-1992, "Imaging Media (Film) — Silver-Gelatin Type — Specifications for Stability (revision and redesignation of ANSI PH9.1-1989)."

(B) In addition to the master record, a working copy of the microfilm may be provided.

The working copy may be silver, diazo or vesicular type on a safety base of cellulose estar or polyester materials.

(4) In clear-base, negative-appearing microfilm of paper documents, the gross background density shall be between 0.8 and 1.50, depending on the type of original document and the reduction ratio. The base-plus-fog density of unexposed, processed, clear-base film must not exceed 0.1Q. When a tinted-base film is used, the density will increase by 0.1 or 0.2 which must be added to the 0.10 value. The Procedures for density measurement are described in ANSI/AIIM MS 23-1991, "Practice for Operational Procedures/Inspection and Quality Control of First-Generation Silver-Gelatin Microfilm of Documents." On negative microfilm produced by Computer Output Microfilm (COM), the background density shall be a minimum 1.1. These requirements apply only to the master records.

(5) Every master record shall have density measurements taken at five (5) separate locations listed in (a) through (e) o this paragraph. Whenever possible, the areas selected for recording density measurements shall be free of information. The locations for density measurement are:

(A) at the beginning of the reel (within the first ten (10) frames);

(B) one/quarter (1/4) of the way through the reel;

(C) one/half (1/2) of the way through the reel;

(D) three/quarters (3/4) of the way through the reel; and

(E) at the end of the reel (within the last ten (10) frames).

(6) The maximum residual thiosulfate ion concentration for the master record shall not exceed 0.014 grams per square meter for records of permanent value or 0.030 grams per square meter for microfilm that the Archives and Records Commission has authorized for destruction within fifty years as determined by the methylene blue method for measuring thiosulfate as specified in ANSI/NAPM IT 9.1-1992, "Imaging Media (Film) — Silver-Gelatin Type — Specifications for Stability (revision and redesignation of ANSI PH9.1-1989)." The residual thiosulfate ion test shall be performed in accordance with procedures outlined in ANSI/ISO 417-1993; ANSI/NAPM IT9.17-1993, "Determination of Residual Thiosulfate and other Related Chemicals in Processed Photographic Materials — Methods Using Iodine-Amylose, Methylene Blue and Silver Sulfide" (revision and redesignation of ANSI PH 4.8-1985), whenever any change in film, chemicals, or processing is made. Regular test periods should be observed, and if any reading of more than 0.014 grams per square meter occurred, the test shall be performed on a daily basis until the condition is corrected. The silver densitometric method, as outlined in ANSI/ISO 417-1993; ANSI/NAPM IT9.17-1993, "Determination of Residual Thiosulfate and other Related Chemicals in Processed Photographic Materials — Methods using Iodine-Amylose, Methylene Blue and Silver Sulfide" (revision and redesignation of ANSI 4.8-1985), may be used for routine daily analysis providing the density stain differential produced in this method is no greater than 0.02, but this test is not a sufficiently reliable substitute for the methylene blue method required by this section.

(7) Archival quality as defined in ANSI/NAPM IT9.1-1992, "Imaging Media (Film) — Silver-Gelatin Type — Specifications for Stability (revision and redesignation of ANSI PH9.1-1989)" is required for records with a retention requirement greater than ten (10) years except that thermally processed silver film (TPS) is acceptable as the master negative for microfilm that the Archives and Records Commission has authorized as permanent. The master record must be stored in accordance with ANSI IT9.11, "Imaging Media — Processed Safety Photographic Film — Storage (revision and redesignation of ANSI PH1.43-1985)."

(8) Retakes, properly identified, may be spliced to either the beginning or end of the reel containing the images for which the retakes are necessary. Splices shall be butt welded or by use of photographic splicing tape or ultrasonic splicer. Retakes, properly identified, may be produced as a separate reel. Splices within the sequence of filmed documents are not acceptable.

(9) Requests for destruction of records that have been microfilmed must include quality evaluation forms from the Micrographics Section of the Records Management Division of the Oklahoma Department of Libraries or authorized personnel in other micrographics laboratories certified by the State Records Administrator certifying that the microfilm meets the above standards for identification, photographic quality, and storage.

Citation: 60 OAR 10-7-3

✪ § 60:10-7-3. Computer output microfilm (COM)

The master records produced by computer output microfilm (COM) technology shall meet the same standards for storage delineated in 60:10-7-2(7). For microfilm that the Archives and Records Commission has authorized as permanent, either wet processed silver film or thermally processed silver film (TPS) is acceptable COM output.

Citation: 60 OAR 10-7-4

✪ § 60:10-7-4. Microfilm laboratory certification.

The State Records Administrator, in conjunction with the Archives and Records Commission, shall establish criteria for, and certify, agency and other micrographics programs that provide microfilming services for state records, in accordance with approved records disposition schedules. Film produced by programs that are not certified shall be quality evaluated by the Micrographics Section of the Records Management Division. Program certification shall be for one (1) year, and may be revoked at any time by the State Records Administrator, on written notice to the agency head or applicable private firm official stating the reason for certification revocation.

Subchapter 8. Optical Imaging.

Citation: 60 OAR 10-8-1

✪ § 60:10-8-1. Purpose.

The purpose of this subchapter is to establish rules for state government records which have an approved retention period of ten (10) years or longer which will be maintained on optical imaging systems.

Citation: 60 OAR 10-8-2

✪ § 60:10-8-2. Scope.

This subchapter establishes rules for the maintenance, use, retention, and disposition of state government records which have an approved retention period of ten (10) years or longer which will be maintained on optical imaging systems. These rules do not apply to state government records which have an approved retention period of less than ten (10) years which will be maintained on optical imaging systems. State Government records which have an approved retention period of less than ten (10) years which will be maintained on optical imaging systems are subject to the disposition authority of the Commission and shall be scheduled in the same manner as any other record.

Citation: 60 OAR 10-8-3

✪ § 60:10-8-3. Definitions.

The following words and terms, when used in this subchapter, shall have the following meaning, unless the context clearly indicates otherwise.

"*AIIM*" means the Association for Information and Image Management.

"*ANSI*" means the American National Standards Institute.

"*CCITT*" means the Consultative Committee on International Telegraph and Telephone.

"*CD-ROM*" means Compact Disk Read Only Memory. A type of optical disk which, like WORM optical disks, cannot be erased or altered.

"*Compression*" means the method by which redundant digital image data streams are reduced to much smaller sizes, resulting in lower digital storage and data transmission requirements.

"*Optical Imaging System*" means a system that consists of hardware and software for computers which records complete images by:

(A) scanning the images with a source of light such as a laser;

(B) converting the images to a digital electronic format; and

(C) storing the converted images on an optical media which allows for the rapid retrieval of the stored images through indexing and the reproduction of the entire original image.

"*Rewritable Disk*" means an optical platter that, unlike WORM disks, can be erased, written over, or otherwise reused or altered. These are sometimes referred to as Erasable optical Disks (EOD).

"*WORM*" optical Write Once Read Many means a type of optical disk, which cannot be erased or altered.

Citation: 60 OAR 10-8-4

✪ § 60:10-8-4. Documentation standards.

The following are the minimum documentation standards for maintaining state government records on optical imaging systems. All agencies using optical imaging systems for maintaining state government records shall maintain complete, up to date technical, operation, and security documentation that includes at least:

(1) The brand names; version numbers; serial numbers; and dates of installation, upgrades, replacements, and conversions for all hardware and software.

(2) A narrative description of the system.

(3) The physical and technical characteristics of the records, including a record layout that describes each field including its name, size, starting or relative position, and a description of the form of the data (such as alphabetic, decimal, or numeric), or a data dictionary, or the equivalent information associated with a data base management system including a description of the relationship between data elements and data bases.

(4) Operating procedures, including methods for scanning, editing, revising, updating, indexing, or expunging records, and for backing up disks;

(5 All hardware and software operating manuals;

(6) Any other technical information needed to read or process the records.

Citation: 60 OAR 10-8-5

✪ § 60:10-8-5. Standards for the creation, use, and storage of records maintained on optical imaging systems.

(a) Optical imaging systems that maintain the state office of record copy of any state government records shall meet the following minimum requirements:

(1) All records stored in optical imaging systems shall be identified in such a manner as to enable authorized personnel to retrieve, protect, and implement approved dispositions for all records in the system.

(2) Provide a standard interchange format when necessary to permit the exchange of records and information stored in optical imaging systems in the agency that utilize different software and/or hardware.

(3) Provide for an approved disposition of the records, including, when appropriate, transfer to the State Archives for permanent preservation.

(b) Agencies shall insure that no information is lost prior to the expiration of the stipulated retention periods because of changing technology or deterioration of the storage media by converting storage media and taking other actions as required to provide compatibility with the agency's existing hardware and software. The migration strategy used for upgrading equipment as technology changes shall be documented and include provisions for:

(1) Periodically recopying to the same electronic media as required and/or transferring all records to new media. Data

maintained on optical disks shall be recopied a minimum of once every ten (10) years onto tested and verified new media. The State Records Administrator may waive this requirement to recopy once every ten (10) years onto tested and verified new media if the following two conditions are satisfied:

(A) The agency demonstrates that such recopying will pose an undue cost burden.

(B) The agency and the State Records Administrator both certify in writing that all original images copied to the optical disk can still be retrieved and reproduced in their original form.

(2) When systems are upgraded or replaced, the new system shall be backward compatible with the existing system and all records and applicable indexes in the existing system shall be transferred to the new system or converted to permanent microfilm that meets all standards for authenticity, photographic quality, and bibliographic integrity required by Commission Rule 60:10-7-2.

(c) WORM, CD-ROM, and rewritable optical disks may be utilized for maintaining state government records in optical imaging format. If rewritable optical disks are utilized, agencies shall maintain and regularly audit a lit of all users of the system and their authorized access privileges and maintain a written record of all rewrites and deletions.

(d) Optical disks used for the storage of state government records shall have a guaranteed minimum pre-write shelf life of at least five (5) years and a guaranteed post-write shelf life of at least twenty (20) years.

(e) Agencies shall maintain back up/security copies of all optical disks. All back up/securities copies shall be maintained in an off site storage facility that meets the manufacturer's recommendations for temperature and humidity controls. If no recommendations are provided by the manufacturer, back up/security disks shall be stored in an area whose temperature is between 65° and 75° Fahrenheit and whose relative humidity is between 30% and 50%. As an alternative back up/security procedure, agencies may use permanent microfilm that meets all standards for authenticity, photographic quality, and bibliographic integrity required by Commission Rule 60:10-7-2.

(f) Optical disks shall be inspected at least annually. Inspections shall include a visual examination of the medium and its housing and a reading of statistical sample of all data to identify any loss of information and to discover and correct the cause of any data loss.

(g) Scanning densities shall be evaluated on standard procedures enumerated in ANSI/AIIM MS 44-1988, "Recommended Practice for Quality Control of Image Scanners." The following scanning densities shall be used for state government records.

(1) A minimum of 200 dots per inch (dpi) for records with no type fonts smaller than six point.

(2) A minimum of 300 dots per inch (dpi) for engineering drawings, maps, and other records with background detail.

(h) Visual quality control shall be performed for each scanned image and related index data.

(i) Scanners and optical drives shall receive periodic maintenance as specified by manufacturers and optical drives shall be recalibrated at least annually.

(j) Optical imaging systems shall either use CCITT Group 3 or Group 4 compression techniques without proprietary alterations to the algorithm or provide a gateway to either Group 3 or Group 4 compression techniques when proprietary compression techniques are utilized.

(k) Nonproprietary file header labels shall be used or the system developer shall either provide a bridge to nonproprietary file header labels or provide a detailed definition of image file header label instructions.

Citation: **60 OS 10-8-6**

✪ § 60:10-8-6. Annual Compliance Report.

(a) Every agency, board, commission, or institution maintaining records in optical imaging format with an approved retention period of ten (10) years or more in accordance with approved records disposition schedules shall file annually each July with the State Records Administrator a report stating that it is in compliance with all statutory provisions and Archives and Records Commission Rules pertaining to maintaining records in optical imaging format. Upon receipt and acknowledgement of the report, the State Records Administrator or his/her designee shall transmit a copy of the report to the submitting agency, board, commission, or institution. The report shall be on a reporting form provided by the Records Management Division that contains the following information:

(1) The name of the agency, board, commission, or institution filing the report.

(2) The year covered by the report.

(3) The name and signature of the person who compiled the report.

(4) The date the report was compiled.

(5) The name of the optical imaging system administrator.

(6) The schedules, records series numbers, and records series titles of all records with a retention period of ten (10) years or more maintained in optical imaging format.

(7) The name and signature of the person submitting the compliance report.

(8) The date the report was received by the State Records Administrator and the name of the person acknowledging receipt.

(b) The State Records Administrator shall notify the Archives and Records Commission of any agency, board, commission, or institution that fails to file an annual report.

State: **Oregon**
Source: **Oregon Revised Statutes**

TITLE 4. EVIDENCE AND WITNESSES

CHAPTER 40. EVIDENCE CODE.

CONTENTS OF WRITINGS, RECORDINGS, AND PHOTOGRAPHS

Citation: **ORS 40.550**

☞ § 40.550. Rule 1001. Definitions for ORS 40.550 to 40.585.

As used in ORS 40.550 to 40.585, unless the context requires otherwise:

(1) "Duplicate" means a counterpart produced by the same impression as the original, or from the same matrix, or by means of photography, including enlargements and miniatures, by mechanical or electronic re-recording, by chemical reproduction or by other equivalent techniques which accurately reproduce the original, including reproduction by facsimile machines if the reproduction is identified as a facsimile and printed on nonthermal paper.

(2) "Original" of a writing or recording is the writing or recording itself or any counterpart intended to have the same effect by a person executing or issuing it. An "original" of a photograph includes the negative or any print therefrom. If data are stored in a computer or similar device, any printout or other output readable by sight, shown to reflect the data accurately, is

an "original".

(3) "Photographs" include still photographs, X-ray films, video tapes, and motion pictures.

(4) "Writings" and "recordings" mean letters, words, or numbers, or their equivalent, set down by handwriting, typewriting, printing, photostating, photographing, magnetic impulse, mechanical or electronic recording or other form of data compilation.

Citation: ORS 40.560

☞ § 40.560. Rule 1003, Admissibility of duplicates.

A duplicate is admissible to the same extent as an original unless: (1) A genuine question is raised as to the authenticity of the original; or (2) In the circumstances it would be unfair to admit the duplicate in lieu of the original.

[See Appendix A. Uniform Rules of Evidence for additional provisions.]

CHAPTER 192. PUBLIC AND PRIVATE RECORDS; PUBLIC REPORTS AND MEETINGS.

CUSTODY AND MAINTENANCE OF PUBLIC RECORDS

Citation: ORS 192.040

✪ § 192.040. Making, filing and recording records by photocopying.

A state agency or political subdivision making public records or receiving and filing or recording public records, may do such making or receiving and filing or recording by means of photocopying. Such photocopying shall, except for records which are treated as confidential pursuant to law, be made, assembled and indexed, in lieu of any other method provided by law, in such manner as the governing body of the state agency or political subdivision considers appropriate.

Citation: ORS 192.050

✪ § 192.050. Photocopying records; evidentiary effect.

A state agency or political subdivision may, with the approval of the proper budgetary authority, cause any public records in its official custody to be photocopied or captured by digital imaging system as in the case of original filings or recordings or recorded by means of analog or digital audio and video tape technology. Each photocopy, digital image and analog or digital audio and video tape shall be made in accordance with the appropriate standard as determined by the State Archivist. Every such reproduction shall be deemed an original; and a transcript, exemplification or certified copy of any such reproduction shall be deemed a transcript, exemplification or certified copy, as the case may be, of the original.

Citation: ORS 192.060

✪ § 192.060. Indexing and filing photocopied records.

All photocopies, digital images and analog or digital audio and video tapes made under ORS 192.040 and 192.050 shall be properly indexed and placed in conveniently accessible files. Each roll of microfilm shall be deemed a book or volume and shall be designated and numbered and provision shall be made for preserving, examining and using the same.

Citation: ORS 192.070

✪ § 192.070. Duplicate rolls of microfilm required; delivery to State Archivist.

A duplicate of every roll of microfilm of documents recorded pursuant to law and the indexes therefore shall be made and kept safely. The State Archivist upon request may, pursuant to ORS 357.865, accept for safekeeping the duplicate microfilm.

CHAPTER 241. CIVIL SERVICE FOR COUNTY EMPLOYEES.

GENERAL PROVISIONS

Citation: ORS 241.105

✪ § 241.105. Preservation and destruction of records and examinations; public records.

(1) The commission shall keep on file all examination papers and their markings and all other papers, documents and communications received by it. All such reports and files of the commission shall be public records and accessible at convenient times in like manner as other public records.

(2) The commission may destroy any reports and files of the commission which are:

(a) Not less than four years old.

(b) Less than four years old, provided they have been recorded by means of photography, microphotography, photocopying or filing and the commission determines that they have no further evidential value.

Source: Oregon Administrative Rules
Agency: Department of Insurance and Finance
Accident Prevention Division

CHAPTER 437. ACCIDENT PREVENTION.

DIVISION 01. RULES FOR THE ADMINISTRATION OF THE OREGON SAFE EMPLOYMENT ACT.

RECORDKEEPING AND REPORTING.

✍ § 437-01-705. Log and Summary of Occupational Injuries and Illnesses.

(1) Except as provided in subsection (2) of this section, each employer shall maintain in each establishment a log and summary of all recordable occupational injuries and illnesses for that establishment, and enter each recordable injury or illness on the log and summary as early as practicable but no later than six working days after receiving information that a recordable case has occurred. For this purpose, OSHA Form No. 200, or an equivalent which is as readable and comprehensible to a person not familiar with it shall be used. The log and summary shall be completed in the detail provided in the form and instructions of OSHA Form No. 200.

(2) Any employer may maintain the log and summary of all recordable occupational injuries and illnesses at a place other than the establishment or by means of data processing equipment, or both, if there is available at the place where the log and summary are maintained sufficient information to complete the log and summary to a date within six working days after receiving information that a recordable case has occurred, and at each of the employer's establishments there is available a copy of the

log and summary which reflects separately the injury and illness experience of that establishment complete and current to within 45 calendar days.

State:	**Pennsylvania**
Source:	**Pennsylvania Consolidated Statutes**

TITLE 15 CORPORATIONS AND UNINCORPORATED ASSOCIATIONS

PART II. CORPORATIONS

SUBPART B. BUSINESS CORPORATIONS

ARTICLE B. DOMESTIC BUSINESS CORPORATIONS GENERALLY

CHAPTER 15. CORPORATE POWERS, DUTIES AND SAFEGUARDS

Subchapter A. General Provisions.

Citation: **15 PCS 1508**

✍ **§ 1508. Corporate records; inspection.**

(a) *Required records.* — Every business corporation shall keep complete and accurate books and records of account, minutes of the proceedings of the incorporators, shareholders and directors and a share register giving the names and addresses of all shareholders and the number and class of shares held by each. The share register shall be kept at either the registered office of the corporation in this Commonwealth or at its principal place of business wherever situated or at the office of its registrar or transfer agent. Any books, minutes or other records may be in written form or any other form capable of being converted into written form within a reasonable time.

* * * * *

TITLE 24. EDUCATION.

Citation: **24 PCS 5-518**

✪ **§ 5-518. Retention of records.**

Every board of school directors shall retain as a permanent record of the district, the minute book, each annual auditor's report, and each annual financial report. All other financial records of the district, including financial account books, orders, bills, contracts, invoices, receipts, and purchase orders shall be retained by the district for a period of not less than six years. Records may be retained as photographed, microphotographed or microfilmed copies in accordance with the act of January 18, 1968, known as the "Municipal Records Act.".

TITLE 42. JUDICIARY AND JUDICIAL PROCEDURE.

PART VI. ACTIONS, PROCEEDINGS AND OTHER MATTERS GENERALLY.

CHAPTER 43. DOCKETS, INDICES AND OTHER RECORDS.

Subchapter B. Disposition of Obsolete Records.

Citation: **42 PCS**

CHAPTER 61. RULES OF EVIDENCE.

Subchapter A. Documentary Evidence.

Citation: **42 PCS 6109**

☞ **§ 6109. Photographic copies of business and public records.**

(a) Short title of section. — This section shall be known and may be cited as the "Uniform Photographic Copies of Business and Public Records as Evidence Act."

(b) General rule. — If any business institution, member of a profession or calling, or any department or agency of government, in the regular course of business or activity, has kept or recorded any memorandum, writing, entry, print, representation, or combination thereof, of any act, transaction, occurrence or event, and in the regular course of business has caused any or all of the same to be recorded, copied or reproduced by any photographic, photostatic, microfilm, microcard, miniature photographic, or other process which accurately reproduces or forms a durable medium for so reproducing the original, the original may be destroyed, in the regular course of business, unless its preservation is required by law. Any such reproduction in order to comply with this section must accurately reproduce all lines and markings which appear on the original. Such reproduction, when satisfactorily identified, is as admissible in evidence as the original itself in any judicial or administrative proceeding, whether the original is in existence or not, and an enlargement or facsimile of such reproduction is likewise admissible in evidence if the original reproduction is in existence and available for inspection under direction of the tribunal. The introduction of a reproduced record, enlargement or facsimile does not preclude admission of the original.

TITLE 43. LABOR.

CHAPTER 4. FEMALE LABOR.

Citation: **43 PCS 113**

✍ **§ 113. Posting abstract of act; records of hours of work; microfilm.**

* * * * *

(b) Every person employing or permitting any female to work in any establishment shall maintain a true and accurate record of the hours worked by each such female. Such record shall contain the name of the female employee, the hours of commencing and stopping work, the hours when the time allowed for meal or rest periods shall begin and end for each day of the week, and the total daily hours and total weekly hours for each such female employee.

Where records are maintained at a central, recordkeeping office, other than in the place of employment such records shall be made available for inspection at the place of employment within seven calendar days following verbal or written notice from the Secretary of Labor and Industry or his authorized representative. Such records shall be maintained for a period of three years.

The use of microfilm for recordkeeping purposes is permitted: Provided, however, That employers who use such microfilm shall make available to authorized representatives of the Department of Labor and Industry the equipment which is necessary to facilitate review of the records.

CHAPTER 8. WAGES.

WAGE PAYMENT AND COLLECTION LAW

Citation: 43 PCS 260.8

✍ **§ 260.8. Enforcement.**

* * * * *

Every employer shall keep open to inspection by the secretary or his authorized representative, all payroll records or other records or documents relative to the enforcement of this act. Such inspection may be made by the secretary or his authorized representative at any reasonable time. Every employer shall permit the secretary or any authorized representative to interrogate any employee in the place of employment and during work hours with respect to such records or documents. Where such records are maintained at a central recordkeeping office outside of the Commonwealth, such records shall be made available for inspection at the place of employment within seven calendar days following verbal or written notice from the secretary or his authorized representative. Where a microfilm or any other method is authorized for recordkeeping purposes, the employer shall make available to the secretary or his authorized representative, the equipment which is necessary to facilitate review of the records.

TITLE 53. MUNICIPAL AND QUASI-MUNICIPAL CORPORATIONS.

CHAPTER 28. MUNICIPAL RECORDS ACT.

Citation: 53 PCS 9008

✪ **§ 9008. Photocopies, etc. of records; destruction of originals; copies as evidence.**

Whenever any officer, commission or agency of the municipality shall have photographed, microphotographed or microfilmed any public record with the approval of and in conformance with standards established by the Local Government Records Committee, the original record may be destroyed, provided the department shall first have given its written consent to such destruction or other disposition.

In the event of any such destruction or other disposition of any public records under the provisions of this section, the photograph, microphotograph or microfilm or a certified copy of said photograph, microphotograph or microfilm shall be receivable in evidence in any court or proceeding, and shall have the same force and effect as though the original public record had been there produced and proved.

TITLE 71. STATE GOVERNMENT.

CHAPTER 2. THE ADMINISTRATIVE CODE OF 1929.

Article 5. Powers and Duties in General.

Citation: 71 PCS 205

✪ **§ 205. (Adm. Code § 525). Microfilm records.**

Any administrative department, board or commission may, with the approval of the Executive Board, have microfilm records made of any correspondence, records or other papers for the purpose of protecting and safeguarding the original correspondence, records or other papers, or for the purpose of conserving filing space, and such microfilm reproduction shall, when properly identified, be admitted in evidence in any proceedings in place of the original correspondence, records or other papers. In any case where original correspondence, records or other papers are microfilmed under the provisions of this section for the purpose of conserving filing space, the administrative department, board or commission concerned, may, with the approval of the Executive Board, destroy such original correspondence, records or other papers.

The provisions of this section expressly include, but are not limited to, any returns, reports, claims or other papers pertaining to the administration, settlement, payment or collection of taxes, license fees, and other moneys or property due the Commonwealth or rebates payable. Microfilm reproductions of such papers shall be admitted into evidence in any proceedings in place of the original papers in accordance with the "Uniform Photographic Copies of Business and Public Records as Evidence Act."[See 42 Pa.C.S.A. § 6109.]

Source: Pennsylvania Code

TITLE 34. LABOR AND INDUSTRY.

PART 12. BUREAU OR LABOR STANDARDS.

CHAPTER 231. MINIMUM WAGE.

Citation: 34 PC 231.31

✍ **§ 231.31. Contents of record.**

(a) Every employer shall keep a true, accurate and legible record for each employee. The records shall be preserved for a period of 3 years from date of last entry and shall contain the following information:

(1) Name in full, and on the same record, the identifying symbol of the employee or number, if such is used in place of name on time work or payroll records.

(2) Home address including zip code.

(3) Regular hourly rate of pay.

(4) Occupation.

(5) Time and day that the workweek begins. If the employee is part of a work force or employed in or by an establishment where all workers have a work week beginning at the same time on the same day, a single notation of the time of the day and beginning day of the workweek for all workers shall suffice.

(6) The number of hours worked daily and weekly.

(7) Total daily or weekly straight time wages, that is, the total wages due for hours worked during the workweek, including all wages due during any overtime worked by exclusive of overtime excess compensation.

(8) Total overtime excess compensation for the workweek, that is, the excess compensation for overtime worked, which amount is over and above all straight time earnings or wages also earned during overtime worked.

(9) Total additions to or deductions from wages paid each pay period. Every employer making additions to or deductions from wages shall also maintain, in individual employee's accounts, a record of the dates, amounts and nature of the items which make up the total additions and deductions.

(10) Allowances, if any, claimed as part of the minimum wage.

(11) Total wages paid each pay period.

(12) Date of payment and the pay period covered by payment.

(13) Special certificates for students and learners as set forth in section 4(b) of the act (43 P.S. § 333.104(b)).

(b) Where microfilm or another method is used for recordkeeping purposes, employers who use the microfilm or another method shall make available to authorized representatives of the Department the equipment which is necessary to facilitate review of the record.

(c) Where records are maintained at a central recordkeeping office other than in the place of employment, the records shall be made available for inspection at the place of employment within 7 calendar days following verbal or written notice from the Secretary or the authorized representative of the Secretary. The records shall be maintained for a period of 3 years from the date of last entry.

Agency: **Department of Revenue**

TITLE 61. TAXATION.

SALES AND USE TAX REGULATION 401

Citation: **61 PC 34.2**

✍ § 34.2. Keeping of Records.

(a) *General Requirements.* The act provides that every sale of tangible personal property or services thereon shall be presumed to be at retail and to be subject to sales tax. Therefore, every person who sells or uses personal property or services shall be required to keep the following basic records:

(1) For purposes of accountability for use tax, taxpayers shall be required to retain all purchase invoices, requisitions, documents, and other records relating to their acquisition of tangible personal property and services. The purchaser shall maintain records showing that the tax was paid where the purchaser has paid the tax to his vendor, and where the purchaser has not paid tax to his vendor but has paid use tax directly to the Commonwealth. Where the purchaser has not paid tax in the above cited instances, he shall create and maintain records showing the reason he considered the purchase as nontaxable, and information concerning the nature, use, price and dates of purchases and use of the property, from which it can be ascertained by the Department, with reasonable facility, whether or not use tax is due thereon and, if due, the amount of tax.

(2) As a minimum for practicable enforcement, the act required the following sales tax records which are amenable to a three-point audit:

(i) With respect to sales, records shall be maintained for each store or other outlet showing the total amount of taxable and nontaxable sales, that is, gross sales, made on each day and during each tax reporting period. Total sales should also be divided as to cash sales and credit sales.

(A) Sales tax records shall be maintained from which it is possible to ascertain the vendor's compliance with the taxing and exemption features of the act, that is, whether sales made without collection of tax were in fact nontaxable. The records shall describe items sold without tax, and show those sales which were made tax free because the purchase price was less than the amount at which the statute begins to impose tax. This is the first essential for determining the amount of tax incurred in the vendor's business.

(B) The vendor shall obtain from purchaser and also retain certificates of exemption with respect to sales of a taxable character which are sold tax free on the claim that they are exempt because of the nature of the purchaser's activity and the use for which they are purchased. In such cases, the identification of items sold as well as the purchaser is necessary because the use of property in many instances is clearly determined by such identification. For example, stationery may not be validly exempt under a certificate stating that it is to be used directly in the production, rendition or delivery of a public utility service.

(ii) The second essential is that sales tax records shall show the tax incurred on each taxable sale so that a so-called effective rate may be determined. Under the bracket schedule established by the act the rate of tax incurred varies according to the purchase price of the sale. The overall effective rate of the vendor's tax incurred cannot be determined unless there are reliable sales records showing taxable sales price of individual sales.

* * * * *

(e) *Accessibility of Information and Records.* All records, including sales memoranda and records created at the time of sale and any other documents, books or records pertaining to tax liability and tax collections shall be dated, legible, written in the English language and maintained and preserved in such manner as to disclose in readily accessible and verifiable detail the basis for and accuracy of the vendor's or user's entries on his sales and use tax returns.

(1) Persons Engaged in Separate Businesses. Any person engaged in business as a retail dealer in taxable items who, at the same time, is engaged in another business or businesses which do not involve the making of taxable sales, shall keep separate books and records of his businesses. For example, a person engaged in business as a retail dealer who is also engaged in business as a construction contractor, shall keep separate records and accounts of his retail business and his construction business. Reference should be made to section 271(d) of the act.

(2) Audit Requirement. Upon audit by the Department, or at such other times as the Department requests, the vendor or user shall present his records in an orderly manner, together with such summaries and schedules as the Department may request. Such vendor or user shall provide the auditors or examiners of the Department with suitable facilities for conducting their audit or examination.

(3) *Retention of Records.* Records required to be maintained pursuant to the act or this section shall be retained for a period of at least three years from the end of the calendar year to which the records relate. Reference should be made to section 272 of the act.

* * * * *

(g) *Microfilm Reproduction of General Books of Account and Supporting Records of Detail.* The Department of Revenue will consider the microfilm, including microfiche, reproduction of general books of account and their supporting records of detail as acceptable books and records when such reproduction satisfactorily complies with the standards and procedures established by the United States Internal Revenue Service and approval of such reproduction is granted by the same. In addition, the taxpayer shall make available all necessary codes and equipment to enable the Department to audit such books and records.

Source: **Historical and Museum Commission Division of Archival and Records Management Services**

✪ § 6. Standards for Microfilming County Records.

(a) *Authority*

The standards were adopted by the County Records Committee in accordance with the County Records Act (16 P. S. § 13001-13006).

(b) *Purpose*

The standards are designed to help ensure the accuracy, usability, longevity and legal acceptance of microforms generated by county offices.

(c) *Scope*

The standards relate to the filming, processing, inspection, handling and storage of microform copies of county records. They must be included as part of the requirements in all microfilm service contracts. With minor exceptions, these standards are in strict conformance with American National Standards Institute (ANSI) and Association for Information and Image Management (AIIM) standards and practices. Color films are not covered by the standards.

(d) *General Provisions*

When a microform copy is to serve as or in place of the original record or is to serve as a security copy of the original record, the following general standards shall apply:

(i) Microimages, including the generation intended for use by office staff or the general public, shall contain all of the recorded information shown on the originals and shall be able to serve the purpose for which the original records were created or obstructions, shadows or glare which impair the legibility of a document.

(ii) Microimages of the records shall be arranged, identified and indexed so that any individual document or component of the records can be located with reasonable ease.

(e) Creation of Archival Security Microfilm Copies of Permanent Records.

(i) All county records custodians engaged in, or contracting for, the microfilming or permanent records shall provide for the creation of an archival security microfilm copy of such records.

(ii) Permanent records are those records which have been scheduled for permanent retention either in the original or microfilm copy by the County Records Committee or by applicable statute and regulation.

(iii) An archival security microfilm copy is a copy which is created, used, inspected and stored in conformance with standards for archival security microfilm.

(iv) The original camera film (Master Negative) of records scheduled for permanent retention shall never be used for reference purposes and should normally be designated as the archival security microfilm copy. Silver-gelatin duplicate negatives or silver-gelatin duplicate positives that meet appropriate standards may serve as the security copy if necessary. If the original camera film is to be jacketed or cut for aperture cards, and uncut duplicate roll of silver halide film that meets the appropriate standards for security film shall be made and designated as the official security copy. Records custodians employing systems that do not produce an original silver-gelatin microfilm which meets permanency standards shall make a silver-gelatin duplicate negative or silver-gelatin duplicate positive which does meet these standards.

(f) *Film Stock, Processing and Quality Standards for Archival Security Microfilm Copies of Permanent Records.*

(i) *Film Stock*

Safety Photographic film as specified in ANSI/NAPM IT9.1-1992 (revision of ANSI IT9.1-1989) and ANSI IT9.6-1991 (revision of ANSI PH1.25-1984).

(ii) *Density*

Background densities of negative-appearing archival security microfilm copies shall, where possible, be between .9 and 1.2. In certain instances, some poor-contrast documents may require lower densities in order to make the entire image legible and reproducible as mentioned in ANSI/AIIM MS23-1991. Background density on positive appearing negative camera film shall not exceed 0.35. The density of silver duplicate positives designated as the security copy shall be between 0.04 and 0.20 where possible. Background density of Computer Output Silver Gelatin (1N) Microfilm (full reversal processing) shall, where possible, be between 1.5-1.8 (1.8 preferred).

(iii) *Base-plus-Fog Density*

The base-plus-fog density of unexposed, processed, clear-based film shall not exceed 0.10. When a tinted-base film is used, the density will increase by 0.10 or 0.20 which must be added to the 0.10 value. The use of tinted, high fog base films is not recommended.

(iv) *Resolution*

A minimum resolution of 90 lines per millimeter shall be obtained regardless of reduction ratio used or the type of camera used, and the 4.0 pattern shall be resolved. A paper print made from the third generation microfilm copy should be able to serve the same purpose for which the original records were created.

(v) *Residual Thiosulfate*

Residual Thiosulfate ion concentration must be greater than zero but not exceed 0.014 grams per square meter in a clear area in accordance with ANSI/NAPM IT9.1-1992.

(g) *Identification, Technical, and Declaratory Targets for Roll Microfilm (See Appendix III).*

All roll microfilm shall include targets which adequately identify the records and targets needed to check for compliance with resolution requirements. A blank, white sheet of paper shall be photographed at the beginning of each roll to test the uniformity of the illumination and the cleanliness of the camera's optical system. Resolution test targets shall be filmed near the beginning and end of each roll. Targets used shall be either the NIST SRM 1010A Microcopy Resolution Test Chart or an equivalent for planetary cameras such as the AIIM X303 test chart and the AIIM X112-1992 (plastic target) or AIIM X113-1992 (paper target) or their equivalents for rotary cameras. Do not use photostatic or electrostatic copies of resolution charts. Identification targets shall state the name of the county and office; name and title of the records custodian responsible for the records at the time of filming; reduction ratio; and record series title, dates, and such volumes or serial numbers needed to clearly identify the records. Each roll shall end with a declaration by the camera operator. The declaration shall include the operator's signature, date the declaration was filmed, and restatement of records filmed. Retakes and retake targets should normally be spliced onto the beginning of the roll in which the errors occurred, preceding the start target. The use of intelligent/blip encoded microfilm may necessitate the use of different retake procedures.

Filming sequence should be:

1) blank white sheet of paper
2) start target
3) roll number target
4) resolution test target
5) reduction ratio target
6) agency and record series identification target(s)
7) if applicable, "continued from preceding roll" target — instances where volume is filmed on more than one roll
8) the text

9) if end of book, film "end of volume" target — if not end of volume, but end of roll coming, film "continued on next roll" target

10) if end of roll, film the declaration by the camera operator, the resolution target, and the "end of roll" target

11) retakes and retake targets should usually be spliced onto the beginning of the roll as explained earlier

(h) Splices

Splicing of archival security microfilm rolls should be avoided, but if splicing is necessary, care should be taken to keep the number of splices to a maximum four per roll. Ultrasonic splicing meets standards for polyester base film.

(i) *Quality Control Practices and Procedures*

(i) Procedures to be followed in establishing and operating a microfilm program should conform to appropriate recommendations contained in ANSI/AIIM MS23-1991 *Practice for Operational Procedures/Inspection and Quality Control of First-generation, Silver Microfilm of Documents.* Each camera negative shall be checked for proper identification targets, density, resolution and visual defects.

(ii) The ability of archival security microfilm copies of permanent records to serve as a substitute for the original records shall be adequately confirmed and documented. Quality control logs for such film shall be maintained to document adherence to standards (see Appendix IV). At a minimum, such logs should verify the following:

A. The images were legible and can serve the purposes for which the original records were created or maintained.

B. Roll film contains all required identification, technical and declaratory targets.

C. Density readings were taken on a blank white sheet of paper at the beginning of the roll, and, at a minimum, on the background of document images at the beginning, middle, and end of each roll.

D. A Base-plus-Fog Density Reading (Dmin) for each roll.

E. The number of the pattern resolved from a reading of the resolution test chart and the reduction ratio on each roll.

F. Methylene Blue tests are being done on a regular basis. Testing should be done by an outside laboratory at a minimum on a monthly basis. Appropriate sample strips must be inspected within fourteen days after processing. Certificates from the laboratory, documenting that the microfilm passed the methylene blue test, should be maintained along with the logs. The certificates should include the name of the agency whose film was processed, processing date, date of methylene blue test, test results, processor used and the signature of the person who did the test.

(j) *Formats and Headings for Unitized Microfilm Systems (aperture cards, microfiche and jacketed film)*

Unitized microfilm systems records should be designed and administered so that the resulting microfilm file is an accurate representation of the original records. Any indexes, registers, or other finding aids should be microfilmed and located in a readily identifiable place within the collection of microfilmed records. Formats for microfiche should conform to ANSI/AIIM MS5-1991. The data on heading or title areas on all microforms should be legible without magnification. The data should conform to ANSI/AIIM MS19-1987.

(k) *Computer Output Silver Gelatin (1N) Microfilm Procedures*

COM programs should conform to standards set down in ANSI/AIIM MS1-1988. Density of Computer-Output Microfilm should be between 1.5 and 1.8 (Full Reversal).

(l) *Storage Conditions for Archival Security Microfilm Copies of Permanent Records.*

The security copy shall be stored and inspected in conformance with ANSI IT9.11-1991 (revision and redesignation of ANSI PH1.43-1985), ANSI IT9.2-1991 and ANSI/AIIM MS45-1990.

(i) Temperature/humidity shall not exceed 70 degrees/40 percent. Fluctuations shall not exceed 5 degrees/5 percent over a 24-hour period.

(ii) Air-conditioning with filtration system shall be utilized to remove gaseous impurities.

(iii) Facility shall provide protection from fire, theft and natural disaster.

(iv) The security microfilm copy shall be maintained in a separate building from the user copy.

(v) Film shall be stored in closed containers made of an inert material such as plastic, acid-free paper, or nonferrous metals. Cores or reels shall be noncorroding such as plastic compounds or nonferrous metals. Rubber bands shall not be used to fasten film onto reels or cores.

(vi) Security copy shall not be stored with non-silver film

(vii) As appropriate, a sampling of randomly selected microforms shall be inspected in conformance with ANSI/AIIM MS45-1990. For each inspection period, a different lot shall be chosen allowing some overlap to note changes in previously inspected film.

(m) *Security Copies of Vital and Long-Term Records*

The security microfilm copy of long-term records shall be created and stored in conformance with standards for archival security microfilm copies of permanent records. The following sections are applicable to long-term records: Sections (d); (e); (f); (g); (h); Section (i), subsection (i); and Sections (j); (k); and (l). Long-term records are any records that need to be maintained for more than ten years either in the original or microfilm copy. Security microfilm copies of vital records should be stored where appropriate in conformance with standards for long-term and permanent records. All security microfilm copies of vital records, regardless of retention periods, should be stored in a separate building from the user copy.

(n) *Short-Term Records*

Short-term records are defined as records that require retention for ten years or less as indicated in the County Records Manual. Silver halide or other films are acceptable as the camera film. Film shall be processed in accordance with applicable ANSI/AIIM standards for the particular film types. The following sections are applicable to short-term records: Section (d); Section (f); subsection (ii), (iii), (iv); Section (g); and Section (i), subsection (i).

(o) *Reference Copies of Microforms*

The standards relating to the film stock, processing, use and storage of archival security microfilm copies of permanent records do not apply to reference, user or additional duplicate copies These copies may be on film types other than silver-halide, safety base film and should be processed in accordance with applicable ANSI/AIIM standards for their particular film types.

For additional information, contact:
Pennsylvania Historical and Museum Commission
Division of Archival and Records Management Services
P. O. Box 1026
Harrisburg, PA 17108-1026
(717) 783-9874 or (717) 787-3913

✪ § 7. Audit Requirements, Federal and State Statutes and Administrative Regulations

(a) Records subject to audit must be retained for the periods listed in the schedule and must be audited and all findings resolved before such records may be destroyed. Applicable Federal and State statutes and administrative regulations may necessitate retaining records for a longer period of time than indicated in the schedule. Information on specific program regulations should be obtained from the appropriate administering/funding/licensing agency.

(b) Records involved in any litigation must be retained until final disposition of the case even if they have met the minimum retention requirements.

✪ § 8. Policy and Guidelines for the Retention and Disposition of Original County Records Copied onto Optical Image Systems and County Records Stored on Optical Disks

(a) *Purpose*

Establish and clarify a records management policy for county officers with respect to the retention and ultimate disposition of original records copied onto optical imaging systems and to records stored on optical disks in order to enable officers to incorporate information retention and retrieval considerations at the earliest possible time into their plans to acquire optical imaging systems. Electronic Data Interchange, Optical Character Recognition data, or static electronic database information that an officer may wish to store on optical media are not addressed in this policy.

(b) *Objectives*

(i) To integrate records maintained on optical disks into county records management programs.

(ii) To provide information needed by county officers to properly evaluate the effect of optical imaging systems on their operations.

(iii) To ensure that information stored on optical imaging systems will be accessible in conformance with records retention and disposition schedules and procedures approved by the County Records Committee.

(iv) To reduce the risks associated with optical imaging system hardware and software obsolescence.

(c) *Scope*

Applies to all county officers covered by the County Records Act and by Supreme Court Rule of Judicial Administration 507(a).

(d) *Policy*

(i) Records relating to optical imaging systems, including systems documentation, may be disposed of only in accordance with schedules approved by the County Records Committee.

(ii) Permanent records are those records which have been scheduled for permanent retention either in the original or microform copy by the County Records Committee or by applicable statute and regulation. Long-term records are any records that need to be retained for more than ten years either in the original or microfilm copy.

(iii) County officers are responsible for making provisions to retain either the original copies of permanently valuable records or making archival security microform copies to serve as a substitute. Archival security microform copies must be created and maintained in conformance with applicable standards approved by the County.

(iv) In those instances where the optical disk is the original medium for records scheduled for permanent retention, such as the procedural or transactional recording of deeds, provisions must be made to retain paper copies of such records or to create archival security microfilm copies of the records. The preferred strategy for ensuring the creation of an archival security microfilm copy would require the retention of the original instrument or a paper copy made from the original instrument, until the film copy has been verified.

(v) With certain exceptions, county officers will not have to make provisions to retain non-permanent records copied onto optical disks in a human-readable format. There are substitutions which, due to the unusually vital nature of the records or their relatively long retention period, will make it necessary to requite the retention of a human readable copy.

(e) *Optical Imaging Guidelines*

(i) A county officer who purchases and operates an optical imaging system must provide for the usability of image and index data over time by:

A. *Management*

In order to maintain access to digital information stored on optical media, a county officer must ensure that:

(1) All information retention requirements and procedures established by the County Records Committee are addressed during the system planning

(2) Where possible, systems should be built from hardware and software components that conform to non-proprietary and/or commonly accepted standards, and

(3) Vendors should deposit a copy of computer source code and associated documentation with the county for use in the event of the vendor's business failure.

B. *Preservation Strategy*

To ensure that records stored on optical media are preserved, a county officer must:

(1) Maintain proper care and handling procedures for optical media by keeping a clean, dust-free environment for all equipment and prohibit eating, drinking or smoking in the area.

C. *Migration Strategy*

To ensure access to long-term records, a county officer must provide a means to:

(1) Upgrade equipment as technology evolves and periodically recopy optical media as required, or

(2) Recopy optical media (based upon projected longevity of the optical disk) every ten years, or

(3) Transfer data from an obsolete generation of optical technology to a newly emerging generation, in some cases bypassing the generation that is mature, but at risk of becoming obsolete.

D. *Image File Headers*

The use of proprietary image file headers will make it difficult to ensure the long-term intelligibility of digital images when system upgrades or modifications occur, therefore a county officer must:

(1) Require use of a non-proprietary image file header label, or

(2) Require the system developer to provide a bridge to a non-proprietary image file header label, or

(3) Require the system developer to supply a detailed definition of image file header label structure.

E. *Error Detection and Correction*

The ability to predict the point at which optical media is no longer readable is critical so that media recopying can take place. A county officer must:

(1) Specify that the SCSI (Small Computer System Interface - the primary communications interface used in optical systems) command "Write and Verify" is used when writing data to optical media.

(2) Acquire a utility program that monitors the amount of disk space used to relocate data sectors as errors are detected, and

(3) Ensure through systems operations procedures that current readability is maintained through periodic recopying when the relocation table reaches 70% capacity.

(ii) County officers must protect the quality of digital images captured and stored by an optical imaging system by providing for:

A. *Input Quality Control*

Regular equipment maintenance is a necessary process

control procedure under which optical imaging systems should operate. A county officer must:

(1) Ensure that the optical system receives periodic maintenance,

(2) Ensure that the optical disk drives are recalibrated annually or more frequently based upon on "hours in use" formula,

(3) Ensure that quality control evaluation of each scanned image and related index data is performed prior to writing image data to optical media,

(4) Evaluate the scanner quality based on standards procedures recommended in ANSI/AIIM MS44-1988, *Recommended Practice for Quality Control of Image Scanners* (ANSI - American National Standards Institute). ANSI is composed of representatives from industry, technical societies, consumer organizations and government agencies. AIIM - Association for Information and Image Management (formerly National Micrographics Association - NMA).

B. *Scanning Density*

Scanning density is vital to ensure image legibility. A county officer must:

(1) Employ a scanning density of 200 dpi for office documents that contain no type fonts smaller than six (6) point,

(2) Employ a higher scanning density (300 dpi or 600 dpi) as needed for engineering drawings, maps, and six (6) point or significant background detail, and

(3) Validate the selected scanning density with actual document tests.

C. *Scanner Color Spectrum*

Because some digital scanners may not capture the full color spectrum - especially yellow and sepia tones - it is possible to lose significant detail in scanning a document containing certain colors. Therefore, before launching a document conversion project a county officer must:

(1) Verify scanner capability and hardware modification requirements by conducting a test of selected documents.

D. *Gray Scale*

Use of the scale is necessary when scanning continuous tone photographs. A low scanning density is used in this process, which would reduce the quality of other images scanned. Except in circumstances where the characteristics of the original document (i.e., shading, color) are beyond the receiving office's control, a county officer must:

(1) Restrict the use of the gray scale to continuous tone photographs except in those instances where the use of the gray scale promotes readability of text documents.

E. *Image Input Quality*

At this time, there are no objective, empirical indicators of acceptable image quality for digitally scanned images. Therefore a county officer must:

(1) Select sample documents based upon levels of legibility (poor to excellent), organize a panel within the office to establish consensus on what settings produce the "best" image for different categories of documents, and use the settings as the operational criteria for acceptable image quality.

F. *Compression Techniques*

There are two broad categories of compression techniques - proprietary and standards. Proprietary compression techniques tend to be fast and offer higher compression capabilities but the stored images might not be transportable between different systems. Standardized compression techniques, although they may not be as powerful, support image data transfer between systems that otherwise might be incompatible. There are two international standard compression techniques currently available - CCITT Group 3 and Group 4. Therefore a county officer must:

(1) Require that digital imaging systems support the prevailing CCITT standards, but

(2) If a proprietary compression technique is unavoidable, require the vendor to specify compression/decompression algorithms that ensure that no information is "lost" during the transmission.

(iii) County officers must provide for the continuing functionality of system components over time by:

A. *Open Systems*

Open systems architecture is defined as a systems design approach that permits users to interchange system hardware components with minimal impact on the primary operating software and to upgrade the system over time without risk of data loss. A county officer must:

(1) Require an open systems architecture for new optical disk media applications, or

(2) Require vendors to provide a bridge to systems with non-proprietary configurations.

B. *Backward Compatibility*

Obsolescence of the technology is a major consideration of any imaging system design. Its impact can be minimized by requiring a backward compatibility - that the optical imaging system is able to read and convert information written by an older generation of technology to a newer one. Therefore a county officer must:

(1) Require system upgrades or new systems to provide backward compatibility to the existing system, or

(2) When necessary, require vendors to guarantee conversion of 100 percent of extant image and index data to the new system if such a system cannot provide hardware compatibility.

C. *Small Computer System Interface*

The Small Computer System Interface (SCSI) is the communications interface used in many optical media systems. It is the primary mechanism that enables drives and other peripheral devices from different manufacturers to communicate with each other. However, since differences between interface standards restrict compatibility, a county officer must:

(1) Require system manufacturers and integrators to provide complete documentation about the specific hardware and software SCSI interface used.

D. *Location of Index Database*

To ensure that the index information will not be lose, a county officer must:

(1) For processing purposes, store index data on the system's mass storage device (i.e., hard drive), or

(2) For fail-safe indexing, write index data for each optical disk at multiple locations on that disk.

E. *Technical Documentation*

To ensure that all technical information will be available, a county officer must:

(1) Require delivery of a complete set of documentation (including source code, object code, and maintenance documentation) to the organization responsible for operation of an optical media application system, and

(2) Document all aspects of the design and use, including administrative procedures for digital imaging, retrieval, and storage; technical system specifications; problems encountered over time; and measures taken to address them, including hardware and software modifications.

(iv) County officers must provide for the stability of optical media by:

A. *Recording Performance*

Write once, read many times (WORM) and rewritable optical media recording technologies each offer advantages and disadvantages. The selection of WORM or rewritable recording must be linked to the user's application requirements, available resources, and the level of standardization achieved by the optical media technologies. It is possible that accidental or intentional erasure of data stored on rewritable media could occur and this must be taken into account, particularly when the records have substantial legal, financial, and other long-term value. A county officer must:

(1) Require the use of WORM technology for records of long-term legal, financial or archival research value, and

(2) Ensure that read/write privileges are carefully controlled and that an audit trail of rewrites is maintained when rewritable technology is used.

B. *Disk Substrate Composition*

Optical disks are manufactured from a variety of materials. Each substrate offers advantages and disadvantages. Since all three types are likely to outlast the hardware and software components of the full system when they are properly stored, county officers may:

(1) Use polycarbonate, tempered glass or aluminum substrates.

C. *Jukebox System*

A jukebox storage system is not appropriate when simultaneous, on-line access to information is required. Neither is a jukebox storage system required when the access delays and risks inherent in the manual selection, insertion, and refiling of optical disks are acceptable to managers and users. Where it is important to maintain physical control of optical disks during use, a jukebox storage system may be appropriate. Therefore a county officer should use a jukebox only:

(1) When rapid access or physical control of numerous optical disks is required, or

(2) When a large volume of records is to be stored, or

(3) When multiple users or networking to various offices may dictate its use.

D. *Durability*

Durability is defined as the shelf life before writing plus the post-write life of the optical disk. To ensure maximum usability, the county officer must:

(1) Require the acquisition and use of optical media with a pre-write shelf life of at least five years, and

(2) Require the use of optical media with a minimum post-write life of twenty years based upon accelerated aging tests that apply to specific locations of the media surface.

E. *Storage Environment*

Optical media should be stored in a protected environment. Therefore a county officer must:

(1) Store optical media in areas with stable room temperatures (65 to 75 degrees Fahrenheit) where the relative humidity does not exceed 50 percent and does not fall below 30 percent.

(2) Not locate optical systems near areas of electromagnetic radiation, such as transformers, or areas of high radio frequency radiation,

(3) Periodically clean optical media to remove dust and other particulates (e.g., fingerprints if media are handled).

✪ § 250. An Act.

Section 1. When any public officer of any county, other than counties of the first class, city, other than cities of the first class, borough, town, township, school, poor or institution district, or agency thereof, is required or authorized by law or otherwise to record, copy or recopy any document, plat, paper or instrument of writing, he may do so by any photostatic, photographic, microphotographic, microfilm or other mechanical process which produces a clear, accurate and permanent copy, microcopy or reproduction of the original in accordance with standards not less than those approved for permanent records by the National Bureau of Standards. Any such office may also reproduce by such processes any document, plat, paper or instrument of writing which has previously been recorded, copied or recopied.

Section 2. Copies of records thus produced, or enlarged reproductions of copies of records thus produced, shall have the same effect, and be admissible in evidence in like manner and under the same conditions, as copies of original records produced in accordance with the law in effect immediately prior to the passage of this act.

Section 3. Each roll of microfilm bearing official copies of records shall begin with a separate photographic image showing on a title target the name and location of the office holding the records copied, the name and title of the officer having custody of the records at the date of copying, a brief, but clear, title for the particular series of records copied, and such volume, numbers, inclusive dates and serial numbers as shall make identification of the records filmed clear and positive. Each roll shall end with a separate photographic image repeating in substance the information given on the title target, together with the signature of the camera operator, appended to a certificate which shall state the day month and year on which the records were copied and affirm that the copying was performed in accordance with procedures prescribed by the custodian. It shall be the responsibility of the custodian of the records copied to regulate and supervise the copying process and to inspect the resulting microcopies so as to satisfy himself that all copies are complete, accurate and clearly legible. When any enlarged reproduction of a negative or positive film is to be used as evidence, the reproduction shall contain, or have attached thereto, the signed and sealed attestation of the officer having the official custody of the negative or positive film that the same is a true and correct copy thereof.

Section 4. In order to provide insurance for the more actively used film copies against damage or loss through wear or disaster, duplicate rolls of all microfilmed records shall be maintained at such locations as shall be approved by the court of common pleas of the proper county.

Section 5. Reproductions from the master microfilm negative of records copied under the provisions of this set may be sold with the approval of the court of common pleas of the proper county, except as hereinafter noted, to title companies, historical societies and other agencies or individuals, and the proceeds from such sale deposited as miscellaneous revenue in the treasury of the governmental unit in which the records originated. Microcopies of the records of the register of wills or of the clerk of the orphans' court may be sold with the approval of the orphans' court of the proper county, under the same conditions.

Section 6. Records which have been reproduced or copied in accordance with section one of this act or other records which are deemed valueless may be destroyed or otherwise disposed of, subject to the approval of the court of common please of the proper county. The records of the register of wills and of the clerk of the orphans' court which have been so reproduced or which are deemed valueless may be destroyed or disposed of, subject to the approval of the orphans' court of the proper county.

Section 7. Whenever an original record received by or resting in the custody of, any public officer shall, in the opinion of the custodian, possess such value that it merits special care, a photographic or microphotographic copy of the record shall be made, officially certified and place on file in lieu of the original record and the original shall be transferred to the custody of the county commissioners of the proper county for permanent preservation, such transfer being subject to the approval of the court of proper jurisdiction, as provided in section 6 of this act.

* * * * *

✪ § 311. An Act.

Section 1. Whenever any officer of any county of the first class or of any city of the first class is required or authorized by law to record, copy, recopy, or replace, any document, plat, paper, written instrument, or book, on file or of record in his office, he may do so by photostatic, photographic, microphotographic, microfilm, or other mechanical process which produces a clear, accurate, and permanent, copy or reproduction of the original document, plat, paper, written instrument, or record, in accordance with standards not less than those approved for permanent records by the National Bureau of Standards.

Section 2. In any case where an original document, plat, paper, written instrument, record, or book of record, previously filed or of record in the office of such officer is, whether because of the worn or injured condition thereof or for any other reason, copied and replaced by such process, and where such officer is required by law to certify in or on the paper or book replacing the original so copied that the replacement is a true and correct copy of the original, a copy of such certification by such officer, similarly made and produced and included at the end of the replacement, shall be sufficient compliance with such law.

Section 3. Copies, records, reproductions and replacements, or enlarged reproductions thereof, thus produced, shall be considered as original copies, records, papers, or books of record, for all purposes, shall have the same effect in law and equity, and shall be admissible in evidence in like manner and under the same conditions as original copies, records, papers, or books of record, produced or copied in any other manner authorized by law.

Section 4. Transcripts or certified copies of such copies, records, reproductions, and replacements, shall be considered as transcripts or certified copies of the originals.

Section 5. In any case where any record or replacement thereof in the office of any such officer is produced by such process, any correction, alteration, endorsements, or entry, required or authorized to be made of or on any instrument or paper or on the record thereof, may be made by filing or inserting copies or recopies produced by the same process, of the pages, page, or part of the page, so corrected, altered, or on which such endorsement or entry is made, next to the place wherein the copy or record of such instrument or paper is contained or in such other manner as such officer shall deem advisable or practicable.

*****

Citation: **HISTORICAL AND MUSEUM COMMISSION GUIDELINES**

✪ STANDARDS FOR MICROFILMING MUNICIPAL RECORDS

(a) Authority

The standards were adopted by the Local Government Records Committee in accordance with the Municipal Records Act (53 P. S. § 9001-9010).

(b) Purpose

The standards are designed to help ensure the accuracy, usability, longevity and legal acceptance of microforms generated by municipal offices.

(c) Scope

The standards relate to the filming, processing, inspection, handling and storage of microform copies of municipal records. They must be included as part of the requirements in all microfilm service contracts. With minor exceptions, these standards are in strict conformance with American National Standards Institute (ANSI) and Association for Information and Image Management (AIIM) standards and practices. Color films are not covered by the standards.

(d) General Provisions

When a microform copy is to serve as or in place of the original record or is to serve as a security copy of the original record, the following general standards shall apply:

(i) Microimages, including the generation intended for use by office staff or the general public, shall contain all of the recorded information shown on the originals and shall be able to serve the purpose for which the original records were created or maintained. Microimages shall be free of obstructions, shadows or glare which impair the legibility of a document.

(ii) Microimages of the records shall be arranged, identified and indexed so that any individual document or component of the records can be located with reasonable ease.

(e) Creation of Archival Security Microfilm Copies of Permanent Records.

(i) All municipal records custodians engaged in, or contracting for, the microfilming of permanent records shall provide for the creation of an archival security microfilm copy of such records.

(ii) Permanent records are those records which have been scheduled for permanent retention either in the original or microfilm copy by the Local Government Records Committee or by applicable statute and regulation.

(iii) An archival security microfilm copy is a copy which is created, used, inspected and stored in conformance with standards for archival security microfilm.

(iv) The original camera film (Master Negative) of records scheduled for permanent retention shall never be used for reference purposes and should normally be designated as the archival security microfilm copy. Silver-gelatin duplicate negatives or silver-gelatin duplicate positives that meet appropriate standards may serve as the security copy if necessary. If the original camera film is to be jacketed or cut for aperture cards, and uncut duplicate roll of silver halide film that meets the appropriate standards for security film shall be made and designated as the official security copy. Records custodians employing systems that do not produce an original silver-gelatin microfilm which meets permanency standards shall make a silver-gelatin duplicate negative or silver-gelatin duplicate positive which does meet these standards.

(f) Film Stock, Processing and Quality Standards for Archival Security Microfilm Copies of Permanent Records.

(i) *Film Stock*

Safety photographic film as specified in ANSI/NAPM IT9.1-1992 (revision of ANSI IT9.1-1989) and ANSI IT9.6-1991 (revision of ANSI PH1.25-1984).

(ii) *Density*

Background densities of negative-appearing archival security microfilm copies shall, where possible, be between .9 and 1.2. In certain instances, some poor-contrast documents may require lower densities in order to make the entire image legible and reproducible as mentioned in ANSI/AIIM MS23-1991. Background density on positive appearing negative camera film shall not exceed 0.35. The density of silver duplicate positives designated as the security copy shall be between 0.04 and 0.20 where possible. Background density of Computer Output Silver Gelatin (1N) Microfilm (full reversal processing) shall, where possible, be between 1.5-1.8 (1.8 preferred).

(iii) *Base-plus-Fog Density*

The base-plus-fog density of unexposed, processed, clear-based film shall not exceed 0.10. When a tinted-base film is used, the density will increase by 0.10 or 0.20 which must be added to the 0.10 value. The use of tinted, high fog base films is not recommended.

(iv) *Resolution*

A minimum resolution of 90 lines per millimeter shall be obtained regardless of reduction ratio used or the type of camera used, and the 4.0 pattern shall be resolved. A paper print made from the third generation microfilm copy should be able to serve the same purpose for which the original records were created.

(v) *Residual Thiosulfate*

Residual Thiosulfate ion concentration must be greater than zero but not exceed 0.014 grams per square meter in a clear area in accordance with ANSI/NAPM IT9.1-1992.

(g) Identification, Technical, and Declaratory Targets for Roll Microfilm (See Appendix E).

All roll microfilm shall include targets which adequately identify the records and targets needed to check for compliance with resolution requirements. A blank, white sheet of paper shall be photographed at the beginning of each roll to test the uniformity of the illumination and the cleanliness of the camera's optical system. Resolution test targets shall be filmed near the beginning and end of each roll. Targets used shall be either the NIST SRM 1010A Microcopy Resolution Test Chart or an equivalent for planetary cameras such as the AIIM X303 test chart and the AIIM X112-1992 (plastic target) or AIIM X113-1992 (paper target) or their equivalents for rotary cameras. Do not use photostatic or electrostatic copies of resolution charts. Identification targets shall state the name of the municipality and office; name and title of the records custodian responsible for the records at the time of filming; reduction ratio; and record series title, dates, and such volumes or serial numbers needed to clearly identify the records. Each roll shall end with a declaration by the camera operator. The declaration shall include the operator's signature, date the declaration was filmed, and restatement of records filmed. Retakes and retake targets should normally be spliced onto the beginning of the roll in which the errors occurred, preceding the start target. The use of intelligent/blip encoded microfilm may necessitate the use of different retake procedures.

Filming sequence should be:

1) blank white sheet of paper
2) start target
3) roll number target
4) resolution test target
5) reduction ratio target
6) agency and record series identification target(s)
7) if applicable, "continued from preceding roll" target — instances where volume is filmed on more than one roll
8) the text
9) if end of book, film "end of volume" target — if not end of volume, but end of roll coming, film "continued on next roll" target
10) if end of roll, film the declaration by the camera operator, the resolution target, and the "end of roll" target
11) retakes and retake targets should usually be spliced onto the beginning of the roll as explained earlier.

(h) Splices

Splicing of archival security microfilm rolls should be avoided, but if splicing is necessary, care should be taken to keep the number of splices to a maximum four per roll. Ultrasonic splicing meets standards for polyester base film.

(i) Quality Control Practices and Procedures

(i) Procedures to be followed in establishing and operating a microfilm program should conform to appropriate recommendations contained in ANSI/AIIM MS23-1991 *Practice for Operational Procedures/Inspection and Quality Control of First-Generation, Silver-Gelatin Microfilm of Documents.* Each camera negative shall be checked for proper identification targets, density, resolution and visual defects.

(ii) The ability of archival security microfilm copies of permanent records to serve as a substitute for the original records shall be adequately confirmed and documented. Quality control logs for such film shall be maintained to document adherence to standards (see Appendix F). At a minimum, such logs should verify the following:

A. The images are legible and can serve the purposes for which the original records were created or maintained.

B. Roll film contains all required informational and certification targets.

C. Density readings were taken on a blank white sheet of paper at the beginning of the roll, and, at a minimum, on the background of document images at the beginning, middle, and end of each roll.

D. A Base-plus-Fog Density Reading (Dmin) for each roll.

E. The number of the pattern resolved from a reading of the resolution test chart and the reduction ratio on each roll.

F. Methylene Blue tests are being done on a regular basis. Testing should be done by an outside laboratory at a minimum on a monthly basis. Appropriate sample strips must be inspected within fourteen days after processing. Certificates from the laboratory, documenting that the microfilm passed the methylene blue test, should be maintained along with the logs. The certificates should include the name of the agency whose film was processed, processing date, date of methylene blue test, test results, processor used and the signature of the person who did the test.

(j) Formats and Headings for Unitized Microfilm Systems (aperture cards, microfiche and jacketed film)

Unitized microfilm systems records should be designed and administered so that the resulting microfilm file is an accurate representation of the original records. Any indexes, registers, or other finding aids should be microfilmed and located in a readily identifiable place within the collection of microfilmed records. Formats for microfiche should conform to ANSI/AIIM MS5-1991. The data on heading or title areas on all microforms should be legible without magnification. The data should conform to ANSI/AIIM MS19-1987.

(k) Computer Output Silver Gelatin (1N) Microfilm Procedures

COM programs should conform to standards set down in ANSI/AIIM MS1-1988. Density of Computer-Output Microfilm should be between 1.5 and 1.8 (Full Reversal).

(l) Storage Conditions for Archival Security Microfilm Copies of Permanent Records

The security copy shall be stored and inspected in conformance with ANSI IT9.11-1991 (revision and redesignation of ANSI PH1.43-1985), ANSI IT9.2-1991 and ANSI/AIIM MS45-1990.

(i) Temperature/humidity shall not exceed 70 degrees/40 percent. Fluctuations shall not exceed 5 degrees/5 percent over a 24-hour period.

(ii) Air-conditioning with filtration system shall be utilized to remove gaseous impurities.

(iii) Facility shall provide protection from fire, theft and natural disaster.

(iv) The security microfilm copy shall be maintained in a separate building from the user copy.

(v) Film shall be stored in closed containers made of an inert material such as plastic, acid-free paper, or nonferrous metals. Cores or reels shall be noncorroding such as plastic compounds or nonferrous metals. Rubber bands shall not be used to fasten film onto reels or cores.

(vi) Security copy shall not be stored with non-silver film.

(vii) As appropriate, a sampling of randomly selected microforms shall be inspected in conformance with ANSI/AIIM MS45-1990. For each inspection period, a different lot shall be chosen allowing some overlap to note changes in previously inspected film.

(m) Security Copies of Vital and Long-Term Records

The security microfilm copy of long-term records shall be created and stored in conformance with standards for archival security microfilm copies of permanent records. The following sections are applicable to long-term records: Sections (d); (e); (f); (g); (h); Section (i), subsection (i); and Sections (j); (k); and (l). Long-term records are any records that need to be maintained for more than ten years either in the original or microfilm copy. Security microfilm copies of vital records should be stored where appropriate in conformance with standards for long-term and permanent records. All security microfilm copies of vital records, regardless of retention periods, should be stored in a separate building from the user copy.

(n) Short-Term Records

Short-term records are defined as records that require retention for ten years or less as indicated in the Municipal Records Schedule. Silver halide or other films are acceptable as the camera film. Film shall be processed in accordance with applicable ANSI/AIIM standards for the particular film types. The following sections are applicable to short-term records: Section (d); Section (f); subsection (ii), (iii), (iv); Section (g); and Section (i), subsection (i).

(o) Reference Copies of Microforms

The standards relating to the film stock, processing, use and storage of archival security microfilm copies of permanent records do not apply to reference, user or additional duplicate copies These copies may be on film types other than silver-halide, safety base film and should be processed in accordance with applicable ANSI/AIIM standards for their particular film types.

Citation: **HISTORICAL AND MUSEUM COMMISSION GUIDELINES**

✪ POLICY AND GUIDELINES FOR THE RETENTION AND DISPOSITION OF ORIGINAL MUNICIPAL RECORDS COPIED ONTO OPTICAL IMAGE SYSTEMS AND MUNICIPAL RECORDS STORED ON OPTICAL DISKS

(a) Purpose

Establish and clarify a records management policy for municipal officers with respect to the retention and ultimate disposition of original records copied onto optical imaging systems and to records stored on optical disks in order to enable officers to incorporate information retention and retrieval considerations at the earliest possible time into their plans to acquire optical imaging systems. Electronic Data Interchange, Optical Character Recognition data, or static electronic database information that an officer may wish to store on optical media are not addressed in this policy.

(b) Objectives

(i) To integrate records maintained on optical disks into municipal records management programs.

(ii) To provide information needed by county officers to properly evaluate the effect of optical imaging systems on their operations.

(iii) To ensure that information stored on optical imaging systems will be accessible in conformance with records retention and disposition schedules and procedures approved by the Local Records Committee.

(iv) To reduce the risks associated with optical imaging system hardware and software obsolescence.

(c) Scope

Applies to all county officers covered by the Municipal Records Act.

(d) Policy

(i) Records relating to optical imaging systems, including systems documentation, may be disposed of only in accordance with schedules approved by the Local Government Records Committee.

(ii) Permanent records are those records which have been scheduled for permanent retention either in the original or microform copy by the Local Government Records Committee or by applicable statute and regulation. Long-term records are any records that need to be retained for more than ten years either in the original or microfilm copy.

(iii) Municipal officers are responsible for making provisions to retain either the original copies of permanently valuable records or making archival security microform copies to serve as a substitute. Archival security microform copies must be created and maintained in conformance with applicable standards approved by the Local Government Records Committee.

(iv) In those instances where the optical disk is the original medium for records scheduled for permanent retention, such as the procedural or transactional recording of deeds, provisions must be made to retain paper copies of such records or to create archival security microfilm copies of the records. The preferred strategy for ensuring the creation of an archival security microfilm copy would require the retention of the original instrument or a paper copy made from the original instrument, until the film copy has been verified.

(v) With certain exceptions, county officers will not have to make provisions to retain non-permanent records copied onto optical disks in a human-readable format. There are substitutions which, due to the unusually vital nature of the records or their relatively long retention period, will make it necessary to requite the retention of a human readable copy.

(e) Optical Imaging Guidelines

(i) A municipal officer who purchases and operates an optical imaging system must provide for the usability of image and index data over time by:

A. Management

In order to maintain access to digital information stored on optical media, a municipal officer must ensure that:

(1) All information retention requirements and procedures established by the Local Government Records Committee are addressed during the system planning

(2) Where possible, systems should be built from hardware and software components that conform to non-proprietary and/or commonly accepted standards, and

(3) Vendors should deposit a copy of computer source code and associated documentation with the county for use in the event of the vendor's business failure.

B. Preservation Strategy

To ensure that records stored on optical media are preserved, a municipal officer must:

(1) Maintain proper care and handling procedures for optical media by keeping a clean, dust-free environment for all equipment and prohibit eating, drinking or smoking in the area.

C. Migration Strategy

To ensure access to long-term records, a municipal officer must provide a means to:

(1) Upgrade equipment as technology evolves and periodically recopy optical media as required, or

(2) Recopy optical media (based upon projected longevity of the optical disk) every ten years, or

(3) Transfer data from an obsolete generation of optical technology to a newly emerging generation, in some cases bypassing the generation that is mature, but at risk of becoming obsolete.

D. Image File Headers

The use of proprietary image file headers will make it difficult to ensure the long-term intelligibility of digital images when system upgrades or modifications occur, therefore a municipal officer must:

(1) Require use of a non-proprietary image file header label, or

(2) Require the system developer to provide a bridge to a non-proprietary image file header label, or

(3) Require the system developer to supply a detailed definition of image file header label structure.

E. Error Detection and Correction

The ability to predict the point at which optical media is no longer readable is critical so that media recopying can take place. A municipal officer must:

(1) Specify that the SCSI (Small Computer System Interface - the primary communications interface used in optical systems) command "Write and Verify" is used when writing data to optical media.

(2) Acquire a utility program that monitors the amount of disk space used to relocate data sectors as errors are detected, and

(3) Ensure through systems operations procedures that current readability is maintained through periodic recopying when the relocation table reaches 70% capacity.

(ii) Municipal officers must protect the quality of digital images captured and stored by an optical imaging system by providing for:

A. *Input Quality Control*

Regular equipment maintenance is a necessary process control procedure under which optical imaging systems should operate. A municipal officer must:

(1) Ensure that the optical system receives periodic maintenance,

(2) Ensure that the optical disk drives are recalibrated annually or more frequently based upon on "hours in use" formula,

(3) Ensure that quality control evaluation of each scanned image and related index data is performed prior to writing image data to optical media,

(4) Evaluate the scanner quality based on standards procedures recommended in ANSI/AIIM MS44-1988, *Recommended Practice for Quality Control of Image Scanners* (ANSI - American National Standards Institute). ANSI is composed of representatives from industry, technical societies, consumer organizations and government agencies. AIIM - Association for Information and Image Management (formerly National Micrographics Association - NMA).

B. *Scanning Density*

Scanning density is vital to ensure image legibility. A municipal officer must:

(1) Employ a scanning density of 200 dpi for office documents that contain no type fonts smaller than six (6) point,

(2) Employ a higher scanning density (300 dpi or 600 dpi) as needed for engineering drawings, maps, and six (6) point or significant background detail, and

(3) Validate the selected scanning density with actual document tests.

C. *Scanner Color Spectrum*

Because some digital scanners may not capture the full color spectrum - especially yellow and sepia tones - it is possible to lose significant detail in scanning a document containing certain colors. Therefore, before launching a document conversion project a municipal officer must:

(1) Verify scanner capability and hardware modification requirements by conducting a test of selected documents.

D. *Gray Scale*

Use of the scale is necessary when scanning continuous tone photographs. A low scanning density is used in this process, which would reduce the quality of other images scanned. Except in circumstances where the characteristics of the original document (i.e., shading, color) are beyond the receiving office's control, a municipal officer must:

(1) Restrict the use of the gray scale to continuous tone photographs except in those instances where the use of the gray scale promotes readability of text documents.

E. *Image Input Quality*

At this time, there are no objective, empirical indicators of acceptable image quality for digitally scanned images. Therefore a municipal officer must:

(1) Select sample documents based upon levels of legibility (poor to excellent), organize a panel within the office to establish consensus on what settings produce the "best" image for different categories of documents, and use the settings as the operational criteria for acceptable image quality.

F. *Compression Techniques*

There are two broad categories of compression techniques - proprietary and standards. Proprietary compression techniques tend to be fast and offer higher compression capabilities but the stored images might not be transportable between different systems. Standardized compression techniques, although they may not be as powerful, support image data transfer between systems that otherwise might be incompatible. There are two international standard compression techniques currently available - CCITT Group 3 and Group 4. A municipal officer must:

(1) Require that digital imaging systems support the prevailing CCITT standards, but

(2) If a proprietary compression technique is unavoidable, require the vendor to specify compression/decompression algorithms that ensure that no information is "lost" during the transmission.

(iii) Municipal officers must provide for the continuing functionality of system components over time by:

A. *Open Systems*

Open systems architecture is defined as a systems design approach that permits users to interchange system hardware components with minimal impact on the primary operating software and to upgrade the system over time without risk of data loss. A municipal officer must:

(1) Require an open systems architecture for new optical disk media applications, or

(2) Require vendors to provide a bridge to systems with non-proprietary configurations.

B. *Backward Compatibility*

Obsolescence of the technology is a major consideration of any imaging system design. Its impact can be minimized by requiring a backward compatibility - that the optical imaging system is able to read and convert information written by an older generation of technology to a newer one. Therefore a municipal officer must:

(1) Require system upgrades or new systems to provide backward compatibility to the existing system, or

(2) When necessary, require vendors to guarantee conversion of 100 percent of extant image and index data to the new system if such a system cannot provide hardware compatibility.

C. *Small Computer System Interface*

The Small Computer System Interface (SCSI) is the communications interface used in many optical media systems. It is the primary mechanism that enables drives and other peripheral devices from different manufacturers to communicate with each other. However, since differences between interface standards restrict compatibility, a municipal officer must:

(1) Require system manufacturers and integrators to provide complete documentation about the specific hardware and software SCSI interface used.

D. *Location of Index Database*

To ensure that the index information will not be lost, a municipal officer must:

(1) For processing purposes, store index data on the system's mass storage device (i.e., hard drive), or

(2) For fail-safe indexing, write index data for each optical disk at multiple locations on that disk.

E. *Technical Documentation*

To ensure that all technical information will be available, a municipal officer must:

(1) Require delivery of a complete set of documentation (including source code, object code, and maintenance documentation) to the organization responsible for operation of an optical media application system, and

(2) Document all aspects of the design and use, including administrative procedures for digital imaging, retrieval, and storage; technical system specifications; problems encountered over time; and measures taken to address them, including hardware and software modifications.

(iv) Municipal officers must provide for the stability of optical media by:

A. *Recording Performance*

Write once, read many times (WORM) and rewritable optical media recording technologies each offer advantages and disadvantages. The selection of WORM or rewritable recording must be linked to the user's application requirements, available resources, and the level of standardization achieved by the optical media technologies. It is possible that accidental or intentional erasure of data stored on rewritable media could occur and this must be taken into account, particularly when the records have substantial legal, financial, and other long-term value. A municipal officer must:

(1) Require the use of WORM technology for records of long-term legal, financial or archival research value, and

(2) Ensure that read/write privileges are carefully controlled and that an audit trail of rewrites is maintained when rewritable technology is used.

B. *Disk Substrate Composition*

Optical disks are manufactured from a variety of materials. Each substrate offers advantages and disadvantages. Since all three types are likely to outlast the hardware and software components of the full system when they are properly stored, municipal officers may:

(1) Use polycarbonate, tempered glass or aluminum substrates.

C. *Jukebox System*

A jukebox storage system is not appropriate when simultaneous, on-line access to information is required. Neither is a jukebox storage system required when the access delays and risks inherent in the manual selection, insertion, and refiling of optical disks are acceptable to managers and users. Where it is important to maintain physical control of optical disks during use, a jukebox storage system may be appropriate. Therefore a municipal officer should use a jukebox only:

(1) When rapid access or physical control of numerous optical disks is required, or

(2) When a large volume of records is to be stored, or

(3) When multiple users or networking to various offices may dictate its use.

D. *Durability*

Durability is defined as the shelf life before writing plus the post-write life of the optical disk. To ensure maximum usability, the municipal officer must:

(1) Require the acquisition and use of optical media with a pre-write shelf life of at least five years, and

(2) Require the use of optical media with a minimum post-write life of twenty years based upon accelerated aging tests that apply to specific locations of the media surface.

E. *Storage Environment*

Optical media should be stored in a protected environment. Therefore a municipal officer must:

(1) Store optical media in areas with stable room temperatures (65 to 75 degrees Fahrenheit) where the relative humidity does not exceed 50 percent and does not fall below 30 percent.

(2) Not locate optical systems near areas of electromagnetic radiation, such as transformers, or areas of high radio frequency radiation,

(3) Periodically clean optical media to remove dust and other particulates (e.g., fingerprints if media are handled).

GOVERNOR'S OFFICE

MANAGEMENT DIRECTIVE

Citation: **MANAGEMENT DIRECTIVE 210.8**

✪ **Management Directive 210.8. Micrographics Procedures to be Used in Conjunctions With Central Microfilm Management**

1. *Purpose.* To establish procedures to ensure the accuracy, usability, longevity, and legal acceptance of the microforms generated by agencies subject to *The Administrative Code of 1929.*

2. *Scope.* The standards apply to all agencies covered by *The Administrative Code of 1929.* Legislative and judicial agencies and other executive branch agencies are invited to use the same policies and procedures. The standards relate to the filming, processing, inspection, handling, and storage of microform copies of records of executive branch departments, boards and commissions. They must be included as part of the requirements in all microfilm service contracts. With minor exceptions, these standards are in strict conformance with the American National Standards Institute (ANSI) and the Association for Information and Image Management (AIIM) standards and practices. Color films are not covered by the standards.

3. *Definitions*

a. AIIM. Association for Information and Image Management. Trade association and professional society for the micrographics, optical disk, and electronic image management markets.

b. ANSI. American National Standards Institute. ANSI is a voluntary nonprofit consensus standards organization which coordinates private sector standards activities and serves all industries and users in the United States. ANSI is the primary interface with the U.S. Government on matters relating to standards and is the recognized representative to the International Organization for Standardization (ISO).

c. Aperture card.

(1) A card with a rectangular opening(s) specifically prepared for the mounting or insertion of microfilm.

(2) A processable card of standard dimensions into which microfilm frames can be inserted.

d. Archival quality. The ability of a processed print or film to permanently retain its original characteristics. The ability to resist deterioration.

e. Base. Transparent plastic material, usually of cellulose triacetate or polyester, upon which a photographic emulsion or other material may be coated.

f. Book cradle. A device which holds a large bound book open and flat during filming with a planetary camera.

g. Camera microfilm. First generation microfilm; also called the master film.

h. Camera-processor. A device which performs both filming and processing within one unit.

i. Cartridge. A container enclosing processed microforms, designed to be inserted into readers, reader-printers, and retrieval devices. When applied to roll microfilm, it describes a single-core device.

(j) Cassette.

(1) A double core containers enclosing processed roll microfilm, designed to be inserted into readers, reader-printers, and retrieval devices.

(2) A lightproof containers of rigid metal or plastic containing film for daylight loading in cameras.

(3) A container for magnetic tape.

(k) Cellulose ester. A film base composed mainly of cellulose esters of acetic, prionic or butyric acids or mixtures thereof.

(l) Cine mode. Vertical mode.

(1) The arrangement of images on roll microfilm in which the lines of print or writing are perpendicular to the length of the film for horizontal script and parallel for vertical script.

(2) The arrangement of images on a microfiche in which the first microimage is in the top left-hand corner of the grid pattern and succeeding microimages appear in sequence from top to bottom and in columns from left to right.

(m) Cosmic mode. Horizontal mode.

(1) The arrangement of images on roll microfilm in which the lines of print or writing are parallel to the length of the film for horizontal script and perpendicular for vertical script.

(2) The arrangement of images on a microfiche in which the first microimage is in the top left-hand corner of the grid pattern and succeeding microimages appear in sequence from left to right and in rows from top to bottom.

n. Computer-output microfilm (COM). Microforms containing data produced by a recorder from computer-generated electrical signals.

o. Densitometer. A device used to measure the optical density of an image or base by measuring the amount of light reflected or transmitted.

p. Density. The light-absorbing or light-reflecting characteristics of a photographic image.

q. Diazo film. A slow print film, sensitized by a coating of diazonium salts which, subsequent to exposure to light and development, forms an image. Diazo film generally produces nonreversed images; i.e., a positive image will produce a positive image and a negative image will produce a negative image.

r. Dry-process silver film. A nongelatin silver film that is developed by application of heat.

s. Duplicate.

(1) A copy of a microform made by contact printing or by optical means.

(2) To make multiple copies of a document or microfilm, usually with the aid of the master film or intermediate copies.

t. Emulsion. A single-or multilayered coating consisting of light-sensitive materials in a medium carried as a thin layer on a film base.

u. Exposure.

(1) The act of exposing a sensitive material to light/radiant energy.

(2) The time during which a sensitized material is subjected to the action of radiation.

(3) The product of radiation intensity and the time during which it acts on the photo-sensitive material.

v. Eye loupe (measuring magnifier). A hand-held magnifying glass with a power of 6 to 15x.

w. Generation. One of the successive stages of photographic reproduction. The first generation is the camera film. Copies made from this first generation are second generation, etc.

x. Hardcopy.

(1) An enlarged reproduction from a microform usually on paper.

(2) A printed copy of machine output in a readable form, for example, output from a computer printer.

y. Image. A representation of information produced by light/radiant energy.

z. International Organization for Standardization (ISO). Produces standards or recommendations, including those that impact the information technology field, which are the result of free and open agreement among nations. Its purpose is to coordinate standardization efforts and encourage cooperation in economic, intellectual, technological, and scientific endeavors.

aa. Jacket. A flat, transparent, plastic carrier with single or multiple film channels made to hold single or multiple microfilm images.

bb. Life expectancy rating (LE rating). The life expectancy of film when stored under specified storage conditions. For example, film with an LE rating of 100 would have an estimated life expectancy of 100 years when stored under recommended storage conditions.

cc. Light box. A device for inspecting film that provides diffused illumination evenly dispersed over the viewing area.

dd. Master film. Any film, but generally the camera microfilm, used to produce further reproductions, such as intermediates or distribution copies.

ee. Methylene blue. A chemical dye formed during the testing of archival permanence of processed microimages using the methylene blue method.

ff. Microfiche. A transparent sheet of film with microimages arranged in a grid pattern.

gg. Microfilm.

(1) A fine-grain, high-resolution film used to record images reduced in size from the original.

(2) A microform consisting of strips of film on rolls that contain multiple microimages.

(3) To record microphotographs on film.

hh. Microform. A form, usually film, which contains microimages.

ii. Micrographics. Refers to the techniques associated with the production and handling of microfilm. microfiche, and related storage technologies based on retaining a photographic representation on film.

jj. Negative-appearing image. An image in which the lines and characteristics appear light against a dark background.

kk. Planetary camera. A type of microfilm camera in which the document being photographed and the film remain in a stationary position during the exposure. The document is on a plane surface at the time of filming. Also known as a flatbed camera.

ll. Polarity. The change or retention of the dark to light relationship of an image, i.e., a first-generation negative to a second-generation positive indicates a polarity change, while a first-generation negative to a second-generation negative indicates the polarity is retained.

mm. Polyester. A transparent plastic made from polyesters and used as a film base because of its dimensional stability, strength, resistance to tearing, and relative noninflammibility.

nn. Positive-appearing image. An image in which the lines and characters appear dark against a light background.

oo. Processing. A series of steps involved in the treatment of exposed photographic material to make the latent image visible and ultimately usable, e.g., development, fixing, washing, and drying.

pp. Redox blemish. A microspot formation on silver-gelatin type films caused by air pollution, improper packaging or storage conditions. Synonymous with aging blemishes, measles, microspots and red spots.

qq. Reduction ratio. The relationship (ratio) between the dimensions of the original or master and the corresponding dimensions of the microimage; e.g., reduction ration is expressed as 1:24.

rr. Residual thiosulfate ion. Ammonium or sodium thiosulfate (hypo) remaining in film or paper after washing. Synonymous with residual hypo.

ss. Resolution. The ability of a photographic system to record fine detail.

tt. Resolving power. The numeric expression of the ability of an optical or photographic system to distinguish or separate two entities spaced closely together. In micrographics, it is the product of the number of the resolution test pattern resolved in the image multiplied by the reduction and is expressed in line pairs per millimeter.

uu. Roll microfilm. Microfilm that is or can be put on a reel, spool, or core.

vv. Rotary camera. A type of microfilm camera that photographs documents while they are being moved by some form of transport mechanism. The document transport mechanism is connected to a film-transport mechanism, and the film also moves during exposure so there is no difference in the rate of relative movement between the film and the image of the document.

ww. Safety film. A comparatively nonflammable film support (base) that meets ANSI requirements for safety film.

xx. Silver film. A photographic film containing photosensitive silver compounds suspended in a suitable material. When developed, the image consists of metallic silver.

yy. Silver halide. A compound of silver and one of the following elements known as halogens: chlorine bromine, iodine, and fluorine.

zz. Splice. A joint made by cementing, taping, or welding (heat splice) two pieces of film or paper together so they will function as a single piece when passing through a camera, processing machine, viewer, or other apparatus.

aaa. Step-and-repeat camera. A type of microfilm camera that can expose a series of separate images on an area of film according to a predetermined format, usually in orderly rows and columns, e.g., microfiche.

bbb. Target.

(1) Any document or chart containing identification information, coding, or test charts.

(2) An aid to technical or bibliographic control that is photographed on the film preceding or following the document.

ccc. Vesicular film. A film in which the light-sensitive component is suspended in a plastic layer. On exposure, the component creates optical vesicles (bubbles) in the layers. These imperfections form the latent image which becomes visible and permanent by heating the plastic layers and then allowing it to cool.

4. *Responsibilities.*

a. *Heads of agencies* are to ensure compliance with all micrographics standards.

b. *Division of Archival and Records Management Services (DARMS), Historical and Museum Commission (HMC),* is to provide technical advice and assistance to agencies engaged in, or contracting for, the microfilming of government records.

5. *Procedures.*

a. *When a microform copy is to serve as, or in place of, the original record or to serve as a security copy of the original record, the following procedures shall apply:*

(1) Microimages, including the generation intended for use by office staff or the general public, shall contain all of the recorded information shown on the originals and shall be able to serve the purpose for which the original records were created or maintained. Microimages shall be free of obstructions, shadows, or glare which impair the legibility of a document.

(2) Microimages of the records shall be arranged, identified, and indexed so that any individual document or component of the records can be located with reasonable ease.

b. *Creation of archival security microfilm copies of permanent records.*

(1) All state agencies, boards, or commissions covered by the *Administrative Code of 1929*, engaged in, or contracting for, the microfilming of permanent records shall provide for the creation of an archival security microfilm copy of such records.

(2) Permanent records are those scheduled for permanent retention by the creating/administering agency or appraisal as being permanently valuable by the Historical and Museum Commission's Division of Archival and Records Management Services.

(3) An archival security microfilm copy is a copy which is created, used, inspected, and stored in conformance with standards for archival security microfilm.

(4) The original camera film (Master Negative) of records scheduled for permanent retention shall never be used for reference purposes and should normally be designated as the archival security microfilm copy. Silver-gelatin duplicate negatives or silver-gelatin duplicate positives that meet appropriate standards may serve as the security copy, if necessary. If the original camera film is to be jacketed or cut for aperture cards, an uncut publicate roll of silver halide film that meets the appropriate standards for security film shall be made and designated as the official security copy. State agencies employing systems that do not produce an original silver-gelatin microfilm which meets permanent agency standards shall make a silver-gelatin duplicate negative or silver-gelatin duplicate positive which meets these standards.

c. *Film stock, processing, and quality standards for archival security microfilm copies.*

(1) *Film stock.* Safety photographic film as specified in *ANSI PH1.25-1984 (R1989* and *ANSI IT9.1-1989.*

(2) *Density.* Background densities of negative-appearing archival security microfilm copies shall, where possible, be between 0.9 and 1.2. In certain instances, some poor-contrast documents may require lower densities in order to make the entire image legible and reproducible as mentioned in *ANSI/AIIM MS23-1991*. Background density on positive-appearing negative camera film shall not exceed 0.35. The density of silver duplicate positives designated as the security copy shall be between 0.04 and 0.20 where possible. Background density of Computer Output Silver Gelatin (1N) Microfilm (full reversal) shall, where possible, be between 1.5 and 1.8 (1.8 preferred).

(3) *Base-plus-fog density.* The base-plus-fog density of unexposed, processed, clear-based film shall not exceed 0.10. When a tinted-base film is used, the density shall increase by 0.10 or 0.20 which must be added to the 0.10 value, The use of tinted, high fog base films is not recommended.

(4) *Resolution.* A minimum resolution of 90 lines per millimeter shall be obtained regardless of reduction ratio used or the type of camera used, and the 4.0 pattern shall be resolved. A paper print made from the third generation microfilm copy should be able to serve the same purpose for which the original records were created.

(5) *Residual thiosulfate.* Residual Thiosulfate ion concentration must be greater than zero but shall not exceed 0.014 grams per square meter in a clear area in accordance with *ANSI IT9.1-1989.*

d. *Identification and technical targets for roll microfilm.*

(1) All roll microfilm shall include targets which adequately identify the records and targets needed to check for compliance with resolution requirements. A blank, white sheet of paper

shall be photographed at the beginning of each roll to test the uniformity of the illumination and the cleanliness of the camera's optical system. Resolution test targets shall be filmed near the beginning and end of each roll. Targets used shall be either the *NIST SRM 1010A Microcopy Resolution Test Chart* or an equivalent for planetary cameras such as the *AIIM X303 test charge* and the *AIIM X-113-1992 (paper target) or their equivalents for rotary cameras*. Do not use photostatic or electrostatic copies of resolution charts.

(2) Identification charts shall state the name of the executive branch department, board, commission, or agency; title of the records custodian responsible for the records at the time of filming, reduction ratio; and record series title, dates, and such volumes as serial numbers needed to clearly identify the records. Each roll shall end with a declaration by the camera operator. The declaration shall include the operator's signature, date the declaration was filmed, and restatement of records filmed. Retakes and retake targets should normally be spliced onto the beginning of the roll in which the errors occurred, preceding the start target. The use of intelligent/blip encoded microfilm may necessitate the use of different retake procedures.

(3) Filming sequence should be:

(a) blank white sheet of paper;

(b) start target;

(c) roll number target;

(d) resolution test target;

(e) reduction ratio target;

(f) state agency and record series identification target(s);

(g) if applicable, "continued from preceding roll" target - instances where volume is filmed on more than one roll;

(h) the text;

(i) if end of book, film "end of volume" target - if not end of volume, but end of roll coming, film "continued on next roll" target;

(j) if end of roll, film the declaration by the camera operator, the resolution target, and the "end of roll" target; and

(k) retakes and retake targets should usually be spliced onto the beginning of the roll as explained earlier.

e. *Splices*. Splicing of archival security microfilm rolls should be avoided, but if splicing is necessary, care should be taken to keep the number of splices to a maximum of four per roll. Ultrasonic splicing meets standards for polyester base film.

f. *Quality control practices and procedures*.

(1) Procedures to be followed in establishing and operating a microfilm quality control program should conform to appropriate recommendations contained in *ANSI/AIIM MS23-1991, Practice for Operational Procedures/Inspection and Quality Control of First-Generation Silver-Gelatin Microfilm of Documents*. Each camera negative shall be checked for proper identification targets, density, resolution, and visual defects.

(2) The ability of archival security microfilm copies of permanent records to serve as a substitute for the original records shall be adequately confirmed and documented. Quality control logs for such film shall be maintained to document adherence to standards. At a minimum, quality control logs shall verify the following:

(a) The images are legible and can serve the purposes for which the original records were created or maintained.

(b) Roll film contains all required informational and declaratory targets.

(c) Density readings were taken on a blank white sheet of paper at the beginning of the roll, and, at a minimum, on the background of document images at the beginning, middle, and end of each roll.

(d) A Base-plus-Fog Density Reading (Dmin) for each roll.

(e) The number of the pattern resolved from a reading of the resolution test chart.

(f) The reduction ratio on each roll.

(g) Methylene blue tests are being done on a regular basis. Testing should be done by an outside laboratory at least once a month. Appropriate sample strips must be inspected within fourteen days after processing. Certificates from the laboratory, documenting that the microfilm passed the methylene blue test, should be maintained along with the quality control logs. The certificates should include the name of the agency whose film was processed, processing date, date of methylene blue test, test results, processor used, and the signature of the person who did the test.

Standards quality control log forms are available through the Historical and Museum Commission's Division of Archival and Records Management Services. Logs in any other format must be pre-approved by that division.

g. *Formats and headings for unitized microfilm systems (aperture cards, microfiche, and jacketed film)*. Unitized microfilm system records should be designed and administered so that the resulting microfilm file is an accurate representation of the original records. Any indexes, registers, or other finding aids should be microfilmed and located in a readily identifiable place within the collection of microfilmed records. Formats for microfiche should conform to *ANSI/AIIM MS5-1985*. The data on heading or title areas on all microforms should be legible without magnification. The data should conform to *ANSI/AIIM MS19-1987*.

h. *Computer output silver-gelatin (1N) microfilm procedures*. COM programs should conform to standards set down in *ANSI/AIIM MS1-1988*. Density of computer output microfilm should be between 1.5 and 1.8 (Full Reversal).

i. *Storage conditions for archival security microfilm copies of permanent records*. The security copy shall be stored and inspected in conformance with *ANSI PH1.43-1985, ANSI IT9.11-1991, ANSI IT9.2-1991*, and *ANSI/AIIM MS45-1990*.

(1) Temperature/humidity shall not exceed 70 degrees/40 percent. Fluctuations shall not exceed five degrees/five percent over a 24-hour period.

(2) Air-conditioning with a filtration system shall be utilized to remove gaseous impurities.

(3) Facility shall provide protection from fire, theft, and natural disaster.

(4) The security microfilm copy shall be maintained in a separate building from the user copy.

(5) Film shall be stored in closed containers made of an inert material such as plastic, acid-free paper, or nonferrous metals. Cores or reels shall be noncorroding such as plastic compounds or nonferrous metals. Rubber bands shall not be used to fasten film onto reels or cores.

(6) Security copy shall not be stored with non-silver film.

(7) As appropriate, a sampling of randomly selected microforms shall be inspected in conformance with *ANSI/AIIM MS45-1990*. For each inspection period, a different lot shall be chosen allowing some overlap to note changes in previously inspected microforms.

j. *Security copies of vital and long-term records*. The security microfilm of long-term records shall be created and stored in conformance with standards for archival security microfilm copies of permanent records.

(1) The following sections under 5., Procedures, are applicable to long-term records: Sections a, b, c, d, e; Section f(1), and Sections g, h, and i.

(2) Long-term records are any records that need to be maintained for more than ten years either in the original or microfilm copy. Security microfilm copies of vital records shall be stored, when appropriate, in conformance with standards for long term and permanent records.

(3) All security microfilm copies of vital records, regardless

of retention periods, should be stored in a separate building from the user copy.

k. *Security copies of short-term records.* Short-term records are defined as records that require retention for less than ten years as determined by an approved agency records retention and disposition schedule. Silver halide or other films are acceptable as the camera film. Film shall be processed in accordance with applicable AIIM/ANSI standards for their particular film types.

The following Sections under 5., Procedures, are applicable to short-term records: Section a.; Section c.(2), (3), and (4); Section d.; and Section f(1).

l. *Reference copies of microforms.* The standards relating to the film stock, processing, use and storage of archival security microfilm copies of permanent records do not apply to reference, user or additional duplicate copies. These copies may be on film types other than silver-halide, safety base film but shall be processed in accordance with applicable ANSI/AIIM standards for their particular film types.

Sample targets, the standard quality control log form, a suggested sequence for roll microfilm, and information on obtaining appropriate copies of government and industry standards can be obtained by contacting the:

Historical and Museum Commission
Division of Archival and Records Management Services
State Archives Building
Telephone, 717-787-8953
OR; for U.S. Mail:
P.O. Box 1026
Harrisburg, PA 17108-1026

Citation: MANAGEMENT DIRECTIVE 210.9

✪ Management Directive 210.9. Optical Imaging System Procedures Relating to the Retention and Disposition of Records.

1. *Purpose.* Establish and clarify state records management policy with respect to the scheduling and ultimate disposition of original records copied onto optical imaging systems and to records stored on optical disks, to enable program managers to incorporate information retention and retrieval considerations at the earliest possible time into their plans to acquire optical imaging systems. Electronic Data Interchange, Optical Character Recognition data, or static electronic database information that an agency may wish to store on optical media are not addressed in this directive.

2. *Scope.* Applies to all agencies subject to The Administrative Code of 1929.

3. *Objectives.*

a. To integrate records maintained on optical disks into the State Records Management Program.

b. To provide information needed by agencies to properly evaluate the effect of optical imaging systems on their operations.

c. To ensure that information stored on optical imaging systems will be accessible in conformance with agency records retention and disposition schedules.

d. Reduce the risks associated with optical imaging system hardware and software obsolescence.

4. *Policy.* Records relating to any aspect of an optical imaging system may be disposed of only in accordance with schedules approved by the Executive Board. Each agency shall schedule all records relating to an optical disk imaging system before the system goes into operation. All records including input documents, additional paper or microform copies, and disk copies must be scheduled at this time in compliance with Management Directive 210.5. Schedules shall be prepared and submitted in compliance with the following:

a. Provisions must be made for the continued retention of permanently valuable records in a human-readable format even though they are copied onto optical disk.

b. Permanent records are those schedule for permanent retention by the creating/administering agency or appraised as being permanently valuable by the Historical and Museum Commission (HMC), Division of Archival and Records Management Services (DARMS).

c. Agencies are responsible for making provisions to retain the original copy of a permanently valuable record or for making an archival security microform copy to service as a substitute. Archival security microform copies must be created and maintained in conformance with applicable state standards.

d. In those instances where optical disk is the original medium for records scheduled for permanent retention, such as the procedural or transactional recording of deeds, provisions must be made to retain paper copies of such records or to create archival security microfilm copies of the records. The preferred strategy for ensuring the creation of an archival security microfilm copy would require the retention of the original instrument or a paper copy made from the original instrument, until the film copy has been verified.

e. Normally, agencies will not have to make provisions to retain nonpermanent records copied onto optical disks in a human-readable format. In some instances, it may be necessary to require the retention of a human-readable copy due to the vital nature of the records or their relative long retention period.

5. *Definitions.*

a. *Algorithm.* A formula used by a computer to solve a problem.

b. *Baud.* A measure of data flow in bits per second.

c. *Binary.* A method of processing information in electronic systems. The information is encoded using two characters, such as 0 and 1.

d.*Bit.* Abbreviation for binary digit. The smallest unit of digital information, either the digit 0 or 1.

e. *Bit-Map.* Divides an image into points or dots which are represented by bits. Digital representation of an image.

F. .*Byte.* A unit of digital data consisting of eight bits. The representation of a character.

g. *Compact Disk-Read Only Memory (CD-ROM).* A compact disk that is premastered for storage or digital data, used for publishing.

h. *Compression.* The processing of reducing the number of bytes required for digitized image storage and transmission by "removing" unused white space from an image of a document.

i. *Consultative Committee for International Telephone and Telegraph (CCITT).* This group establishes international standards for telecommunications including the Group III and Group IV digital standards that cover data compression and decompression.

j. *Digital.* Information in the form of on/off or zero/one electrical impulses. The opposite of analog transmission.

k. *Digitize.* The process of representing images as a matrix of binary code, with zero representing white space and one representing non-white space.

l. *Disk Drive.* A device that spins the disk and writes/reads information on/off disks.

m. *Dots Per Inch (DPI).* A method of measuring the resolution of a scanning device, display, or printer/plotter.

n. *Gray Scale.* The representation of shades of gray from white to black.

o. *Head.* A device within the disk drive that writes/reads information on/off disks.

p. *Head Crash.* With magnetic disks, the read/write head physically touches the disk and destroys the information on the disk.

q. *Image.* For the purpose of this directive, "image" means an exact duplicate of the original input/source document. Images must contain all the recorded information that appears on the original document and be able to serve the purpose for which the original was created or maintained.

r. *Image Enhancement.* The process of cleaning up or intensifying a digital image using algorithms to improve legibility.

s. *Image File Headers.* Analogous to a "table of contents" describing a set of scanned images stored on a disk. Data may include such items as the film size, compression formula, and image density and is used to link a user's request for an image to a specific location on the storage device.

t. *Integration.* To make into a whole by bringing all parts together, to unify.

u. *Jukebox.* An automated optical disk library. This devices stores disks, uses robotic technology to retrieve a disk, and has one or more read/write drives.

v. *Local Area Network (LAN).* A shared network of interconnected computers and peripherals, usually located within a small area such as a single office, group of offices, or a building.

w. *Laser.* A device emitting a highly coherent beam of light for burning information onto optical disks. Using less power, a laser can "read" information from an optical disk.

x. *Optical Character Recognition (OCR).* The identification of characters (alphanumeric) by their shape.

y. *Optical Disk.* A disk coated with a recording alloy into which binary information is burned using a laser.

z. *Optical Imaging System.* For the purpose of this directive, an optical imaging system is an amalgam of technological processes that includes, at a minimum, digital imaging, optical storage, and computer retrieval of document images.

aa. *Packing Density.* The determination of the amount of information contained with defined dimensions.

bb. *Peripheral.* Any device that connects to a computer: for example, CRT terminal, printer, disk drive.

cc. *Pixel.* Abbreviation for picture element. The smallest element in an image. The more pixels, the higher the resolution. Measured in dots per inch (DPI).

dd. *Scanner.* A device that uses a narrow beam of light to resolve a document into a stream of bits.

ee. *Small Computer Systems Interface (SCSI).* Pronounced "scuzzy." The Small Computer Systems Interface (SCSI) is the communications interface used in many optical media systems. It is the primary mechanism that enables drives and other peripheral devices from different manufacturers to communicate with each other.

ff. *System.* A group of interacting and inter-related elements forming a collective entity.

gg. *Write-Once-Read-Many (WORM).* An optical disk that is user written (once) and read many times thereafter.

hh. *Write Once.* Capable of being written but not erased.

5. *Procedures.*

a. *Agencies which purchase and operate an optical imaging system must provide for the usability of image and index data over time by:*

(1) *Management.* In order to maintain access to digital information stored on optical media, agencies must ensure that:

(a) All information retention requirements are addressed during the system planning phrase. Agencies must prepare and receive tentative approval of a comprehensive retention schedule for all system related records regardless of format from the Historical and Museum Commission (HMC), Division of Archival and Records Management Services (DARMS).

b. Where possible, systems should be built from hardware and software components that conform to nonproprietary and/or commonly accepted standards.

c. Vendors should deposit a copy of computer source code and associated documentation with the State Archives for use in the event of the vendor's business failure.

(2) *Preservation Strategy.* To ensure that records stored on optical media are preserved, agencies must:

(a) Maintain proper care and handling procedures for optical media by keeping a clean, dust-free environment for all equipment.

(b) Prohibit eating, drinking, or smoking in the same area.

(3) *Migration Strategy.* To ensure access to long-term records, agencies must provide a means to:

(a) Upgrade equipment as technology evolves and periodically recopy optical media as required, or

(b) Recopy optical media (based upon projected longevity of the optical disk) every ten years, or

(c) Transfer data from an obsolete generation of optical technology to a newly emerging generation, in some cases bypassing the generation that is mature, but at risk of becoming obsolete.

(4) *Image File Headers.* The use of proprietary image file headers will make it difficult to ensure the long-term intelligibility of digital images when system upgrades or modifications occur. Therefore, agencies must:

(a) Require use of a nonproprietary image file header label, or

(b) Require the system developer to provide a bridge to nonproprietary image file header label, or

(c) Require the system developer to supply a detailed definition of image file header label structure.

(5) *Error Detection and Correction.* The ability to predict the point a which optical media is no longer readable is critical so that media recopying can take place. Agencies must:

(a) Specify that the SCSI (the primary communications interface used in optical systems) command "Write and Verify" is used when writing data to optical media.

(b) Acquire a utility program that monitors the amount of disk space used to relocate data sectors as errors are detected.

(c) Ensure through systems operations procedures that current readability is maintained through periodic recopying when the relocation table reaches 70 percent capacity.

b. Agencies must protect the quality of digital images captured and stored by an optical imaging system by providing for:

(1) *Input Quality Control.* Regular equipment maintenance is a necessary process control procedure under which optical imaging systems should operate. Agencies must:

(a) Ensure that the optical system receives periodic maintenance.

(b) Ensure that the optical drives are recalibrated annually or more frequently based upon an "hours in use" formula.

(c) Ensure that quality control evaluation of each scanning image and related index data is performed prior to writing image data to optical media.

(d) Evaluate the scanner quality based on standard procedures recommended in ANSI/AIIM MS44-1988, "Recommended Practice for Quality Control of Image Scanners" (ANSI-American National Standards Institute. ANSI is composed of representative from industry, technical societies, consumer organizations, and government agencies. AIIM-Association for Information and Image Management (formerly National Micrographic Association (NMA)).

(2) *Scanning Density.* Scanning density is vital to ensure image legibility. Agencies must:

(a) Employ a scanning density of 200 dpi for office documents that contain no type fonts smaller than six points.

(b) Employ a higher scanning density (300 dpi or 600 dpi) as needed for engineering drawings, maps, and documents with type fonts smaller than six points or significant background detail.

(c) Validate the selected scanning density with actual document tests.

(3) *Scanner Color Spectrum.* Because some digital scanners may not capture the full color spectrum, especially yellow and sepiatones, its is possible to lose significant detail in scanning a document containing certain colors. Therefore, before launching a document conversion project, agencies must verify scanner capability and hardware modification requirements by conducting a test of selected documents.

(4) *Gray Scale.* Use of the scale is necessary when scanning continuous tone photographs. A low scanning density is used in this process, which would reduce the quality of other images scanned. Except in circumstances where the characteristics of the original document (i.e., shading, color) are beyond the receiving agencies' control, agencies must restrict the use of the gray scale to continuous stone photographs except in instances where the use of the gray scale promotes readability of text documents.

(5) *Image Input Quality.* At this time, there are no objective, empirical indicators of acceptable image quality for digitally scanned images. Therefore, agencies must:

(a) Select sample documents based upon levels of legibility (poor to excellent).

(b) Organize a panel within the agency to establish consensus on what settings produce the "best" image for different categories of documents.

(c) Use the settings as the operational criteria for acceptable image quality.

(6) *Compression Techniques.* There are two broad categories of compression techniques - proprietary and standard. Proprietary compression techniques tend to be last and offer higher compression capabilities, but the stored images might not be transportable between different systems. Standardized compression techniques, although they may not be as powerful, support image data transfer between systems that otherwise might be incompatible. There are two international standard compression techniques currently available - CCITT Group 3 and Group 4. Agencies must:

(a) Require that digital imaging systems support the prevailing CCITT standards, but

(b) If a proprietary compression technique is unavoidable, require the vendor to specify compression/decompression algorithms that ensure that no information is "lost" during the transmission.

c. Agencies must provide for the continuing functionality of system components over time by:

(1) *Open Systems.* Open systems architecture is defined as a systems design approach that permits users to interchange system hardware components with minimal impact on the primary operating software and to upgrade the system over time without risk of data loss.

Agencies must:

(a) Require an open systems architecture for new optical media applications, or

(b) Require vendors to provide a bridge to systems with nonproprietary configurations.

(2) *Backward Compatibility.* Obsolescence of the technology is a major consideration of any imaging system design. Its impact can be minimized by requiring a backward compatibility - that the optical imaging system is able to read and convert information written by an older generation of technology to a newer one. Therefore, agencies must:

(a) Require system upgrades or new systems to provide backward compatibility to existing system, or

(b) When necessary, require vendors to guarantee conversion to 100 percent of extant image and index data to the new system if such a system cannot provide hardware compatibility.

(3) *Small Computer Systems Interface (SCSI).* Since difference between interface standards restrict compatibility, agencies must require system manufacturers and integrators to provide complete documentation about the specific hardware and software SCSI interface used.

(4) *Location of Index Database.* To ensure that the index information will not be lost, agencies must:

(a) For processing purposes, store index data on the system's mass storage device (i.e., hard drive), or

(b) For fail-safe indexing, write index data for each optical disk at multiple locations on that disk.

(5) *Technical Documentation.* To ensure that all technical information will be available, agencies must:

(a) Require delivery of a complete set of documentation (including source code, object code, and maintenance documentation) to the organization responsible for operation of an optical media application system.

(b) Document all aspects of the design and use including administrative procedures for digital imaging, retrieval, and storage; technical system specification, problems encountered over time, and measures taken to address them including hardware and software modifications.

d. Agencies must provide for the stability of optical media by:

(1) *Recording Performance.* Write once, read many times (WORM) and rewritable optical media recording technologies each offer advantages and disadvantages. The selection of WORM or rewritable recording must be linked to the user's application requirements, available resources, and the level of standardization achieved by the optical media technologies. It is possible that accidental or intentional erasure of data stored on rewritable media could occur and this must be taken into account, particularly when the records have substantial legal, financial, or other long-term value. Agencies must:

(a) Require the use of WORM technology for records of long-term legal or archival research value.

(b) Ensure that read/write privileges are carefully controlled and that an audit trail of rewrites is maintained when rewritable technology is used.

(2) *Disk Substrate Composition.* Optical disks are manufactured from a variety of materials. Each substrate offers advantages and disadvantages. Since all three types are likely to outlast the hardware and software components of the full system when they are properly stored, agencies may use polycarbonate, tempered glass, or aluminum substrates.

(3) *Jukebox System.* A jukebox storage system is not appropriate when simultaneous on-line access to information is required. Neither is a jukebox storage system required when the access delays and risks inherent in the manual selection, insertion, and refilling of optical disks are acceptable to managers and users. Where it is important to maintain physical control of optical disks during use, a jukebox storage system may be appropriate. Therefore, agencies should:

(a) Use a jukebox only when rapid access or physical control of numerous optical disks is required, or

(b) When a large volume of records is to be stored, or

(c) When multiple users or networking to various offices may dictate its use.

(4) *Durability.* Durability is defined as the shelf life before writing plus the post-write life of the optical disk. To ensure maximum usability, agencies must:

(a) Require the acquisition and use of optical media with prewrite shelf life of at least five years, or

(b) Require the use of optical media with a minimum of post-write life of 20 years based upon accelerated aging tests that apply to specific locations of the media surface.

(5) *Storage Environment.* Optical media should be stored in a protected environment. Therefore, agencies must:

(a) Store optical media in areas with stable room temperatures (65 to 75 degrees Fahrenheit) where the relative humidity does not exceed 50 percent and does not fall below 30 percent.

(b) Not locate optical systems near areas of electromagnetic radiation, such as transformers, electrical equipment storage rooms, or areas of high radio frequency radiation.

(c) Periodically clean optical media to remove dust and other particulates (e.g., fingerprints if media are handled).

Citation: MANAGEMENT DIRECTIVE 210.10

✪ Management Directive 210.10. Electronic Records Management

1. *Purpose.* To establish and clarify state records management policy with respect to the creation, use, maintenance, scheduling and disposition of electronic records and information systems.

2. *Scope.* Applies to all agencies subject to *The Administrative Code of 1929.*

3. *Objectives.*

a. To ensure the efficient administration and management of electronic records and the preservation of those having long term and historical value.

b. To identify and protect vital electronic records.

c. To ensure the accessibility of electronically-stored information in conformance with agency needs and records retention and disposition schedules.

4. *Policy.*

a. Electronic records may be disposed of only in accordance with records schedules approved by the Executive Board.

b. Electronic records may be destroyed only if they have exhausted their administrative, fiscal, and legal value to the Commonwealth, have met all relevant state or federal auditing and retention requirements, and the Pennsylvania Historical and Museum Commission has determined that they do not have sufficient historical value to warrant their continued preservation.

c. Paper or microfilm records that serve as input or output documents for electronic information systems must be scheduled and disposed of in accordance with procedures in *Management Directive 210.5, Records Management.*

d. The scheduling and ultimate disposition of original records copied onto optical imaging systems and to records stored on optical disks is covered by *Management Directive 210.9, Optical Imaging System Procedures Relating to the Retention and Disposition of Records.*

e. This directive should be used in conjunction with *Management Directives 210.5, Records Management, 245.1, Management of Automated Technology,* and *245.8, Development of Automated Technology Contingency/Disaster Recovery Plans.*

5. *Responsibilities. Agencies* are responsible for:

a. Creating, using, maintaining, and disposing of electronic records in accordance with policy and procedures in this directive.

b. Maintaining electronic records needed to transact government business.

c. Maintaining a current inventory of all electronic information systems covered under the *Records Schedule for Electronic Records.* The compilation and maintenance of the inventory is primarily the responsibility of agency program managers and staff end users. However, in the case of mainframe applications, input from Management Information Systems (MIS) staff will be needed. Such inventories shall:

(1) List system title and responsible program unit.

(2) Describe the system in terms of purpose and function.

(3) Identify all inputs and outputs of the system.

(4) Define the contents of the system, including record formats and data base tables.

(5) Identify vital records and information.

(6) Describe policies and restrictions on access and use, data retention periods, and rules for updating or revising the system.

5. *Definitions.*

a. *Data.* Symbols or representations of facts or ideas that can be communicated, interpreted, or processed by manual or automated means. Often associated with electronic data or with statistics or measurements.

b. *Data Base.* A set of data, consisting of at least one file or a group of integrated files, usually stored in one location and made available to several users at the same time for various applications.

c. *Data Base Management System.* A software system used to access and retrieve data stored in a data base.

d. *Data File.* An organized collection of related data, usually arranged into logical records that are stored together and treated as a unit.

e. *Electronic Records.* Records stored in a form that only a computer can process. Also called machine-readable records or EDP records.

f. *Electronic Records System.* Information system that produces, manipulates, or stores auditable records of an agency's transactions by using a computer.

g. *Information System.* The organized collection, processing, transmission, and dissemination of information in accordance with defined procedures, whether automated or manual. May also be a record system.

h. *Permanent Records.* Those records scheduled for permanent retention by the creating/administering agency or appraised as being permanently valuable by the Pennsylvania Historical and Museum Commission.

i. *Record.* Any books, papers, maps, photographs, microphotographs, machine-readable materials, or other documentary materials, regardless of physical form or characteristics, made or received by an executive branch agency under state law or in connection with the transaction of public business in the exercise of its legitimate functions and the discharge of its responsibilities.

j. *Record-Keeping System.* A set of policies and procedures for organizing and identifying files or documents to speed their retrieval, use and disposition and to provide adequate documentation of the agency's functions and transactions.

k. *Text Documents.* Narrative or tabular documents, such as letters, memorandums, and reports, in loosely prescribed form and format.

6. *Procedures.*

a. *Creation and use of data files.*

(1) For electronic records systems that produce, use, or store data files, disposition instructions for the data must be incorporated into a system's design and updated as necessary.

(2) Agencies must maintain proper, up-to-date technical and system documentation for each electronic records system that produces, uses, or stores data files. Minimum documentation required is a narrative description of the system; physical and technical characteristics of the records, including a record layout that describes each field including its name, size, starting or relative position and a description of the form of the data (such as alphabetic, zoned, decimal, packed decimal or numeric), or a data dictionary or the equivalent information associated with a data base management system including a description of the relations between data elements in data bases; and any other technical information needed to read or process

the records.

b. *Creation and use of text documents.*

(1) Electronic records systems that maintain the official file copy of text documents on electronic media must meet the following minimum requirements:

(a) Provide a method for all authorized users of the system to retrieve desired documents, such as an indexing or text search system.

(b) Provide an appropriate level of security to ensure integrity of the documents.

(c) Provide a standard interchange format, when necessary, to permit the exchange of documents on electronic media using different software/operating systems and allow or the conversion or migration of documents on electronic media from one system to another.

(d) Provide for the disposition of the documents including, when necessary, transferring permanent records to the State Archives.

(2) Before a document that will serve as the official file copy is created and maintained on electronic records systems, documents must be identified sufficiently to enable authorized personnel to retrieve, protect, and carry out the disposition of documents in the system. Appropriate identifying information for each document maintained on the electronic media may include: office of origin, file code, key words for retrieval, addressee (if any), signature, author, date, authorized disposition (coded or otherwise), and security classification (if applicable). Agencies should ensure that records maintained in such systems can be correlated with related records on paper, microform, or other media.

d. *Legal admissibility of electronic records.* To enhance legal admissibility of records in an electronic format and help ensure state records may be used as evidence in court proceedings, trustworthiness must be established by thoroughly documenting the information system's operation and the controls imposed upon it. To implement procedures to enhance the legal admissibility of electronic records, agencies should:

(1) Document that similar kinds of records generated and stored electronically are created by the same processes each time and have a standardized retrieval approach.

(2) Substantiate that security procedures prevent unauthorized addition, modification or deletion of a record and ensure system protection against such problems as power interruptions.

(3) Identify the electronic media on which records are stored throughout their life cycle and the maximum time span that records remain on each storage medium in order to comply with minimum retention periods.

(4) Coordinate all of the above with legal counsel, information managers, and records management staff.

d. *Security of electronic records.* Agencies must implement and maintain an effective records security program that incorporates the following to:

(1) Ensure that only authorized personnel have access to electronic records.

(2) Provide for backup and recovery of records to protect against information loss.

(3) Ensure that appropriate agency personnel are trained to safeguard sensitive or classified electronic information.

(4) Minimize the risk of unauthorized alteration or erasure of electronic records.

(5) Ensure that electronic records security is included in a computer systems security plan.

e. *Selection and maintenance of electronic records storage media.*

(1) Agencies must select appropriate media and systems for storing agency records throughout their life which meet the following requirements:

(a) Permit easy retrieval in a timely fashion.

(b) Facilitate the distinction between records and non-records as defined in *Management Directive 210.5, Records Management.*

(c) Retain the records in a usable format for the length of their authorized retention period.

(d) When appropriate, meet requirements for transferring electronic records to the State Archives.

(2) The following factors must be considered before selecting a storage media or when converting from one medium to another:

(a) The required retention period of the records.

(b) The maintenance necessary to retain the records in that format.

(c) The costs of storing and retrieving the records stored in that format.

(d) The density of the record.

(e) The access time necessary to retrieve stored records.

(f) The portability of the medium (selecting a medium that will run on equipment produced by multiple manufacturers) and the ability to transfer information from one medium to another as well as the flexibility of the software to be migrated into a different medium if desirable or necessary.

(g) Compliance of the storage medium with current industry standards.

(3) Agencies must avoid the use of floppy disks for the exclusive long-term storage of permanent electronic records.

(4) Agencies must ensure that all authorized users can identify and retrieve information stored on removable disks, or tapes by establishing or by adopting procedures for external labeling as well as procedures for computer tape library subsystems for storage media identification.

(5) Agencies must ensure that information is not lost because of changing technology or deterioration by converting storage media to provide compatibility with the agency's current hardware and software. Before conversion to a different medium, an agency must determine that the authorized dispositions of the electronic records can be implemented after conversion.

(6) Agencies should back up electronic records on a regular basis to safeguard against the loss of information due to equipment malfunctions or human error. Duplicate copies of permanent records should be maintained in separate buildings. All security copies of vital electronic records, regardless of retention period, should be stored in a separate building.

(7) For the maintenance of magnetic computer medium, agencies must follow industry and national standards for safeguarding information.

(8) Maintenance of magnetic computer tape and cartridges containing permanent records.

(a) Agencies must provide for the testing of magnetic computer tapes/cartridges no more than six months prior to using them to store electronic records that are scheduled for permanent retention. This test should verify that the tape/cartridge is free of permanent errors and in compliance with National Institute of Standards and Technology or industry standards.

(b) Agencies must maintain the storage and test areas for computer magnetic tapes/cartridges containing permanent records at the following temperature and relative humidities:

Constant temperature - 62 to 68 degrees Fahrenheit.

Constant relative humidity - 35 to 45 percent.

(c) Agencies should rewind according to tape specifications all tapes containing permanent records every 3-1/2 years.

(d) Agencies must annually read a statistical sample of all reels or cartridges of magnetic computer tape containing permanent records to identify any loss of data and to discover and correct the causes of data loss. In magnetic medium storage libraries with 1,800 or fewer reels/cartridges, a 20 percent sample or a sample size of 50 reels/cartridges, whichever is larger, should be read. In magnetic medium storage libraries with more than 1,800 reels/cartridges, a sample of 384 reels/cartridges should be read. Tapes/cartridges with many errors must be replaced and, when possible, lost data must be restored. All other tapes/cartridges which might have been affected by the same cause (i.e., poor quality tape/cartridges, high usage, poor environment, improper handling) must be read and corrected, as appropriate.

(e) Agencies must copy permanent data on magnetic tapes/cartridges before they are 10 years old onto tested and verified new tapes/cartridges.

(f) Agencies must ensure that external labels (or the equivalent automated tape management system) for magnetic tapes/cartridges used to store permanent electronic records must provide unique identification for each reel/cartridge, including the name of the office responsible for the data, system title, and security classification, if applicable. Additionally, the following information must be maintained for (but not necessarily attached to) each reel/cartridge used to store permanent electronic records: file title(s); dates of creation; dates of coverage; the recording density; type of internal labels; volume serial number, if applicable; number of tracks; character code/software dependency; information about block size; and reel/cartridge sequence number, if the file is part of a multi-reel/cartridge set. For numeric data files, include record format and logical record length, if applicable; data set name(s) and sequence, if applicable; and number of record for each data set.

(g) Agencies must maintain proper care and handling procedures for electronic media by keeping a clean, dust-free environment for all equipment and prohibit eating, drinking or smoking in magnetic computer medium storage libraries and test or evaluation areas that contain permanent records.

(9) Maintenance of direct access media.

(a) Agencies must issue written procedures which draw upon the recommendations of the manufacturers for the care and handling of direct access storage media.

(b) External labels for diskettes or removable disks used when processing or temporarily storing permanent records must include the following information: name of the office responsible for the records, descriptive title of the contents, dates of creation, security classification, if applicable and identification of the software and hardware used.

f. *Appraisal of electronic systems.*

(1) Each agency's records management program must provide for the appraisal of its electronic systems by the PHMC.

(2) Appraisals to determine the historical value of electronic records systems are to be obtained as follows:

Action By	Step	Action
Agency.	1.	Prepares Form STD-57A, Electronic Records Inventory and Analysis, for each agency electronic system.
	2.	Forwards Form STD-57A to the Division of Archival and Records Management Services (DARMS), PHMC.
DARMS, PHMC	3.	Reviews requests for adequacy of description and identification.
	4.	Returns to agency if corrections or clarifications are needed.
	5.	Indicates if system may be destroyed/deleted in accordance with agency retention policy, or if it needs further archival review.
	6.	If necessary, conducts further archival review to determine if it has sufficient historical value to warrant its permanent retention.
Executive Director/PHMC	7.	Completes review by signing Form STD-57A.

State: **Puerto Rico**
Source: **Laws of Puerto Rico**

TITLE 3. EXECUTIVE.

CHAPTER 41. PUBLIC DOCUMENTS, ADMINISTRATION OF; GENERAL ARCHIVES.

Citation: **3 PRL 1001**

✪ § 1001. Definitions.

(a) "Document" — The word document shall include any paper, book, pamphlet, photograph, photostatic copy, film, microfilm, recording tape, map, drawing, plan, magnetic tape, record, video tape or any other material read by machine or any other informative material, regardless of its form or characteristics. Publications and bibliographical or museum material acquired for public viewing, consultation, or other related purposes, are not included in the definition of the word document.

(b) "Public document" — Any document which originates, or is kept or received, in any dependency of the Commonwealth, according to law or in relation to the management of public affairs, and which is to be permanently or temporarily preserved as evidence of transactions, or because of its administrative usefulness, or legal, fiscal, cultural or informative value, as the case may be, or which is to be destroyed because of its lack of permanent value or administrative, legal, fiscal, cultural or informative usefulness, and a copy of every publication issued by government dependencies. It shall also be understood that a public document is any document which is specifically declared as such by any law in effect or which is enacted in the future.

* * * * *

Citation: **3 PRL 1002a**

✪ § 1002a. Photographic reproduction of documents.

(1) Program Administrators may authorize the heads of dependencies under their respective jurisdiction to reproduce through the process of microphotography, photography, miniature photographic reproduction or photographic copy, or any other method of electronic reproduction, any public documents under their custody which merit conservation because of their legal, fiscal, administrative, informational or historical value.

(2) The originals of the documents reproduced in accordance with the preceding paragraph may be destroyed pursuant to the provisions of this chapter and the regulations promulgated hereunder.

(3) Reproductions by microphotography, photocopy, miniature photographic reproduction or other photographic copy, or any other method of electronic reproduction of said documents, shall be admitted as evidence and shall have the same value and

effect as the originals, provided they are certified by the respective dependency heads in charge of their custody, or their authorized representatives, or by the General Archivist of Puerto Rico in those cases in which the documents have already been transferred to the General Archives of Puerto Rico.

TITLE 24. HEALTH AND SANITATION.

CHAPTER 95. ADMINISTRATIVE PROVISIONS.

Citation: 24 PRL 1239

✪ **§ 1239. Photographic reproductions — Microfilming and old Civil Registers.**

The Secretary of Health of Puerto Rico is hereby authorized to copy in photographic film, by means of the process known as "microfilm" and/or any other adequate process, all birth, marriage, and death certificates or registrations entered in the books of the old Civil Registry of Puerto Rico, as organized in the Island from January 1, 1885 to July 21, 1931. To ensure greater efficiency in this task, the Secretary may direct the temporary removal to the Department, for the purpose of copying them, of such books of the old Civil Registry as in his judgment may be necessary; Provided, That the Secretary of Health or any other official or person in charge of the Registry of Vital Statistics shall be under obligation to conserve the original documents.

✪ **§ 1240. Microfilming General Registry of Vital Statistics.**

In the same manner as stated in the preceding section, he may make copies of all birth, marriage, and death certificates or registrations entered in the General Registry of Vital Statistics of Puerto Rico, as well as of the affidavits and other documents which may have been presented for making such registrations.

Citation: 24 PRL 1241

✪ **§ 1241. Preservation of microfilms.**

A copy of such records, as obtained in the manner indicated, shall be filed permanently in the Division of Demographic Registry and Vital Statistics of the Department of Health; and another copy shall be deposited with the agency of the Commonwealth or federal governments which, in the judgment of the Secretary of Health, offer the best conditions of safety for its preservation.

TITLE 32. CODE OF CIVIL PROCEDURE.

APPENDIX IV. RULES OF EVIDENCE FOR THE GENERAL COURT OF JUSTICE, 1979.

CHAPTER IX: CONTENTS OF WRITINGS, RECORDINGS AND PHOTOGRAPHS.

☞ **Rule 73. Duplicates.**

A duplicate is admissible to the same extent as an original unless a genuine question is raised as to the authenticity of the original, or if the circumstances of the case it would be unfair to admit the duplicate in lieu of the original.

State: Rhode Island
Source: General Laws of Rhode Island.

TITLE 31. MOTOR AND OTHER VEHICLES.

CHAPTER 36. GASOLINE TAX.

Citation: RIGL 31-31-6

✍ **§ 31-36-6. Distributors' sales records.**

Every distributor shall keep a complete and accurate record of the number of gallons of fuels sold by him and of the number of gallons of fuels used by him, the date of such sales and of such use and, except in the case of retail sales through filling stations operated by such distributor, the names and addresses of the purchasers. Such record shall be in such form and contain such information as the said administrator may prescribe. Every distributor shall make for every sale of fuels, except retail sales through filling stations operated by such distributor, a written statement in duplicate containing the names and addresses of the distributor and the purchaser, and number of gallons sold and the date of sale and delivery, one of which shall be delivered to the purchaser and the other retained by the distributor.

Each such record and such statement shall be preserved by the distributor and purchaser for a period of three (3) years, and shall be open to inspection upon demand of the tax administrator or his authorized agents.

TITLE 38. PUBLIC RECORDS.

CHAPTER 1. GENERAL PROVISIONS

Citation: RIGL 38-1-11

✪ **§ 38-1-11. Assistance of the public records administration program.**

The public records administration program of the department of administration shall have the right to examine the condition of public records and shall give advice and assistance to public officials in the solution of their problems of preserving, creating, filing and making available the public records in their custody. When requested by the program, public officials shall assist the program in the preparation of records control schedules of public records in their custody approved by the head of the agency having custody of the records. Upon review and approval of the schedules by the program, the program shall, subject to the availability of necessary space, staff and other facilities for such purposes, make available space in its record center for the filing of semi-current records so scheduled and in its public records repository for noncurrent records of permanent value and shall render such other assistance as needed, including the microfilming of records so scheduled.

CHAPTER 3. PUBLIC RECORDS ADMINISTRATION.

Citation: RIGL 38-3-5.1

☞ ✪ **§ 38-3-5.1. Reproduction of public records — Destruction of original records.**

If any department or agency of government, in the regular course of business or activity, has kept or recorded any memorandum, writing, state tax returns, report, application, payment, entry, print, representation or combination thereof, or any act, transaction, occurrence, or event, and, in the regular course of business, has caused any or all of the same to be recorded, copied, or reproduced by a photographic, photostatic, microfilm, micro-card, optical disk, miniature photographic, or other process which accurately reproduces or forms a durable medium for reproducing the original, the original may be destroyed in the regular course of business, provided the process meets standards established by the public records administration, and provided all provisions of § 38-3-6 concerning disposal of public records are fulfilled. The reproduction, when satisfactorily identified, shall be admissible in evidence as the original in any judicial or administrative proceeding whether or not the original exists or is available, and an enlargement or facsimile of the reproduction shall be likewise admissible in evidence if the original is in existence and available for inspection under the direction of the court. The introduction of a reproduced record, enlargement, or facsimile into evidence shall not preclude the admission into evidence of the original. This section shall not be construed to exclude from introduction into evidence any document or copy thereof which is otherwise admissible under the Rhode Island general laws as amended.

Source: **Rhode Island Rules of Evidence**

ARTICLE X. CONTENTS OF WRITINGS, RECORDINGS AND PHOTOGRAPHS.

☞ Rule 1001. Definitions

For purposes of this article the following definitions are applicable:

(1) *Writings and recordings.* — "Writings" and "recordings" consist of letters, words, or numbers, or their equivalent, set down by handwriting, typewriting, printing, photostating, photographing, magnetic impulse, mechanical or electronic recording, or other form of data compilation.

(2) *Photographs.* — "Photographs" include still photographs, X-ray films, video tapes, and motion pictures.

(3) *Original.* — An "original" of a writing or recording is the writing or recording itself or any counterpart intended to have the same effect by a person executing or issuing it. An "original" of a photograph includes the negative or any print therefrom. If data are stored in a computer or similar device, any printout or other output readable by sight, shown to reflect the data accurately, is an "original".

(4) *Duplicate.* — A "duplicate" is a counterpart produced by the same impression as the original, or from the same matrix, or by means of photography, including enlargements and miniatures, or by mechanical or electronic re-recording, or by chemical reproduction, or by other equivalent techniques which accurately reproduces the original.

☞ Rule 1003. Admissibility of duplicates.

A duplicate is admissible to the same extent as an original unless (1) a genuine question is raised as to the authenticity of the original or (2) in the circumstances it would be unfair to admit the duplicate in lieu of the original.

[See Appendix A. Uniform Rules of Evidence for additional provisions.]

Source: **Rhode Island Regulations**
Agency: **Department of Administration**
Division of Taxation

✍ Records:

Each retailer as defined in the act shall keep adequate and complete records of his business in this state showing:

(1) The gross receipts from the sales of tangible personal property including both taxable and nontaxable items and any services that are part of a sale.

(2) All deductions allowed by law and claimed in filing returns.

(3) Total purchase price of all tangible personal property purchased for resale and the total purchase price of all such property purchased for use or consumption in this state.

These records must include the normal books of account ordinarily maintained by the average prudent businessman engaged in the activity in question, together with all bills, receipts, invoices, cash register tapes, or other documents of original entry supporting the entries in the books of account as well as all schedules or working papers used in connection with the preparation of tax returns.

Failure to maintain such records will be considered evidence of negligence or intent to evade the tax, and will result in the imposition of appropriate penalties.

All such records must be maintained for state tax division audits for a period of at least three years unless the destruction or other disposal of the same shall be authorized by the Tax Administrator or his authorized representative in writing.

Microfilm records. Microfilm reproduction of general books of account, such as cash books, journals, voucher registers, ledgers, etc., are not acceptable in lieu of original records. However, microfilm reproductions of supporting records of details, such as sales invoices, purchase invoices, credit memoranda, etc., may be maintained providing the following conditions are met:

(1) Appropriate facilities are provided for preservation of the films for periods required.

(2) Microfilm rolls are indexed, cross referenced, labeled to show beginning and ending numbers or beginning and ending alphabetical listing of documents included, and are systematically filed.

(3) The taxpayer agrees to provide transcriptions of any information contained on microfilm which may be required for purposes of verification of tax liability.

(4) Proper facilities are provided for the ready inspection and location of the particular records, including modern projectors for viewing and copying the records.

A posting reference must be on each invoice. Credit memoranda must carry a reference to the document evidencing the original transaction. Documents necessary to support claimed exemptions from tax liability, such as bills of lading and purchase orders, must be maintained in an order by which they readily can be related to the transactions for which exemption is sought.

Repairmen are retailers of parts and materials furnished in connection with repair work in which the value of the parts and materials is substantial in relation to the total charge. This applies, for example, to repairers of motor vehicles, airplanes, bicycles, machinery, refrigerators, farm implements, musical instruments, radios, boats and furniture. The repairmen should segregate on the invoices to their customers and in their records the fair retail selling price of the parts and materials from the charges for labor of repair and installation and other services. If the labor and other services are not thus shown separately from the selling price of the property furnished, it will be presumed that the entire charge represents the sale price of the property.

Source:	**Rhode Island Department of Administration Public Records Administration Public Records Advisory Council**
Citation:	**PUBLIC RECORDS ADVISORY COUNCIL MICROFILM STANDARDS**

✪ MICROFILM STANDARDS

Introduction

On December 9, 1987, the Public Records Advisory Council approved the enclosed revisions to section REC-1-87 of the Rhode Island Administrative Code. Microfilm quality-control standards have thus been brought into conformity with national standards. This pamphlet contains those standards and requirements.

The regulations establish standards and guidelines for: 1) the selection of records to be microfilmed, 2) the selection of equipment and vendors, 3) the security duplication of microfilm records, and 4) the quality of the microfilming, processing, duplication, and storage processes.

These regulations take effect on January 1, 1988. After January 1, 1988, authorization will not be given to dispose of records that have been microfilmed unless the state standards have been met and certification of this is attached to the "Certificate of Records Destruction" (form RI/PRA 003). A sample of the required certificate is included.

In summary, the major points included in the new standards are:

A. All roll microfilm must have the required targets at the beginning and end of each roll.

B. A minimum and maximum allowable density is established. A transmission densitometer must be used to determine density.

C. Minimum allowable resolution standards are established. A microscope must be used to determine resolution.

D. The methylene blue test must be performed once each month to determine if residual thiosulfate concentration falls within acceptable limits.

E. The master negative roll of microfilm must be stored under archival conditions. It is not to be used except for producing copy rolls.

F. PRA 003 forms listing microfilmed records must be accompanied with a signed certificate of compliance with these standards.

G. An updatable microfiche system is to be used only under special circumstances. The system must meet all microfilm specifications. Each time the microfiche is updated, a new certificate of authenticity must be added, the microfiche copy must be reproduced on silver halide film, and the expunging equipment must be rendered inoperative.

Also included herewith are samples of the targets required to be placed on all microfilm. Resolution charts may be obtained from:

AIIM
1100 Wayne Avenue, Suit
e 1100
Silver Spring, MD 20910

Any questions concerning these standards and requirements, or the development of microfilm projects should be directed to:

Supervisor, Central Microfilm Services
State Records Center
83 Park Street
Providence, RI 02903

MICROFILM STANDARDS

Administrative Code REC-1-87

1a. Standards for Microfilming Public Records: Purpose

These microfilm standards have been designed to promote uniformity and quality in the production of microfilm for state and municipal governments in Rhode Island. All agencies engaged in microfilming government records must meet these standards to ensure the following:

i. that microfilm copies contain all significant detail shown on the original record;

ii. that microfilm copies are useable and legible reproductions of the original record;

iii. that the microfilm reproduction will have the same acceptability and legal status as the original;

iv. that the microfilm reproduction will meet standards of archival quality.

b. Authority to Establish Microfilm Standards

Concerning the photographic reproduction of public records, G.L. 38-3-6 (11.c) provides that the Public Records Administration shall adopt reasonable rules and regulations relating to public records including "standards for the reproduction of records for security or with the view to disposal of the original record."

2. Notice of Intention to Microfilm Public Records

If, a record series is selected to be microfilmed, notice should be given to the Public Records Administration (PRA) of such intention specifying the record series involved. Such notification will give the PRA's technical staff an opportunity to make constructive recommendations should such be necessary. This will also ensure proper conformance with the statute.

c. Microfilm Standards

The following standards must be met before permission to destroy the originals is granted:

a. Since many factors are involved in the use of microphotography for records management, a careful analysis of each record group should be made before microfilming. Following are some of the most important factors in determining which records are to be filmed.

i. *Retention period and volume:* since microfilming is not inexpensive, only records in large volume or with long retention periods should normally be considered. Microfilming records of shorter retention or smaller volumes may be justified due to the need for security copies or distribution of duplicate copies of record.

ii. *Rate and reference to records:* records with high reference rates or unusual methods of indexing may be poor subjects for microfilming.

iii. *Physical make-up of the records series:* size, color, legibility and condition can affect the cost and quality of the microfilm.

b. When converting documents to microfilm, certain measures must be followed to ensure quality, legality and access to information contained on the microfilm.

i. The records to be filmed must be arranged, identified and indexed to ensure reasonable ease in locating individual documents.

ii. All roll film must have the following targets at the beginning of the reel: National Bureau of Standards' resolution target; density target, certificate of authenticity; camera operations certificate containing title of records filmed, filmed start file and end file (if known), reduction ratio, camera type, film type, and department or agency having custody of the records; and title target.

iii. All roll film will have the following targets at the end of each reel: camera operator's certificate, certificate of authenticity, and end of roll flasher.

iv. Where applicable, roll film should contain retake and correction targets at the beginning and end of a series of refilmed records.

v. Examples of the above targets are available from the Public Records Administration.

c. The master negative is the original reel of the film produced.

i. Only a safety-base, permanent record film with a gelatin-silver halide emulsion, developed to a black and white image and meeting the standards of the American National Standards Institute: PH 1.28, PH 1.29 and PH 1.41, will be used for copies of records.

ii. For most documents, optimum density should read 1.0 and 1.20 for original first generation camera film. Acceptable standards will fall between a minimum of 0.80 and 1.35. The supervisor must use judgment to determine the most suitable density within this range for the documents being filmed. To permit a more accurate reproduction of the original roll, each image should maintain, as far a possible, a special density throughout the roll. Since the color of the original documents will affect the density of the image, and not all documents in a particular record series may have the same color, an average density aim point should be chosen.

iii. A density minimum reading taken from the non-image or clear area of the film will not exceed a reading of 0.12 or manufacturer's specifications using automatic retrieval systems. Readings should be made close to the center of the film strip to avoid edge fog interference. (NOTE) Both background density and D-min density must be taken with a transmission densitometer.

iv. A microscope having a magnification of 50X to 150X with achromatic objectives must be used to read the resolution from the National Archives Bureau of Standards' microcopy resolution test chart. The line direction method will be used in making the determination of resolution. A minimum resolution of 80 lines per millimeter on rotary cameras and 110 lines per millimeter on planetary cameras must be obtained on first generation camera film.

v. Thiosulfate residual content should be tested at least once a month. Only the methylene blue test will be considered sufficiently reliable to determine archival quality. American National Standards Institute: PH 1.28 of 1973 states the following levels of thiosulfate concentration that must be observed for archival microfilm.

Limits for Thiosulfate Concentration

Classification of Films according to graininess of developed image	Maximum permissible concentration of Thiosulfate Ion ($_2O_3$) in micrograms per square centimeter
Class 1 Fine-grain copying, duplication and printing films (include ordinary microfilms)	0.7
Class 2 Medium-grain continuous-tone camera films (negative and reversal) and coarse-grain x-ray films	2

vi. A target indicating the beginning and end of retakes must be used. Retakes may be placed at the beginning or end of a roll of film and, when possible, in sequence. When computer-assisted or random retrieval methods are used, retakes may be placed on the following roll without retake targets. Placement of retakes should be decided before the start of filming and remain consistent.

vii. Splices should not be used except for adding corrections or retakes to the beginning or end of a roll. When splicing images in proper sequence within the roll, only heat-weld splicing should be considered archival. Any splices within a roll may jeopardize the legal status of the microfilm and its admissibility in court.

viii. All film will be processed to meet National Bureau of Standards PH 4.8. Dry chemical processing will not be acceptable. Film failing to meet the specified limits for thiosulfate concentration will not be acceptable.

ix. All film must be inspected for proper indexing, density, resolution and, for residual thiosulfate. Film should be free of scratches, abrasions, blemishes or other defects.

d. The original roll of film must be maintained in archival storage when the records contain information essential to the continuity of governmental operations and the protection of the rights of individuals. Any irreplaceable records having a retention period classified as permanent should be included in this category. When film is to be cut for jackets or aperture cards, the original roll may be used provided an uncut duplicate roll of silver halide film has been prepared for storage. American National Standards Institute requires film specifications for archival storage PH 1.28, PH 1.25 and PH 1.41. The following specifications must be followed for archival storage:

i. The relative humidity of the storage vault or room must not exceed 40 percent.

ii. Temperatures must not exceed 70 degrees F.

iii. Rapid and wide-range cycling of humidity or temperature must be avoided and in no instance exceed +/-5 percent in a 24-hour period.

iv. No rubber bands, tape or other foreign objects may be used to hold film on the reels.

v. The materials used for storage should not ignite, decompose, or develop reactive fumes or vapors.

vi. Film must be stored in a closed container of such inert material as metal or plastic.

vii. At every two-year interval, a one percent random sample should be inspected. For each biennial inspection, a different lot sample should be chosen with some samples of the previous lot reinspected. Any signs of deterioration, including signs of peeling emulsion, brittleness, molding and blemishes, may require special treatment of the microfilm to prevent loss of the record.

e. Methods of duplication include the use of silver halide, diazo and vesicular film.

i. Silver halide duplication film is the only duplicating film considered suitable for producing microfilm of archival quality. Silver halide film must be used when producing copies of the original master negative intended for archival storage. Although the cost is high compared to other types of duplicating film, both negative and positive copies can be produced.

ii. Diazo duplication film is not considered archival in quality and must not be used to produce master-negative copies of originals. A diazo copy will remain the same polarity as the original master (negative to negative; positive to positive). Unexposed diazo film has a very short shelf life unless refrigerated. After exposure and processing, diazo film has an estimated usability of twenty years under ideal storage conditions. Diazo film is less expensive than silver halide film and very durable. Due to ammonia use in processing most diazo film, this type of film should not be stored with silver halide microfilm to avoid damage to archival film.

iii. Vesicular duplication film is not archival in quality and must not be used to produce master-negative film. Vesicular film is a reversing process film - the polarity of the copy will be reversed to that of the original master (positive to negative, negative to positive) through exposure and processing by heat. Vesicular film should only be used for short-term storage applications. However, when not fully exposed, vesicular film may develop eye-legible cosmetic blemishes. Vesicular duplication film may also be considered suitable for distribution or working copies when archival quality is not a factor.

4. Service Contract Specifications and Technical Assistance

A sate or municipal agency may wish to have its microfilming done by a private company on a service contract basis.

In considering any such arrangement, the contracting agency should be cognizant of the following points:

1. All contracts must meet the microfilm specifications established by the Public Records Administration.

2. The Public Records Administration will serve as a consultant to any state or municipal agency requesting such consultation, and will, upon request, review the microfilm service contracts prepared by state or local agencies.

5. Disposal of Original Public Records After Microfilming

a. No original records may be destroyed after microfilming unless the agency obtains permission to do so from the Public Records Administration per R.I.G.L. 38-3-6(10).

b. Form RI/PRA 003, "Certificate of Records Destruction", may be used for this purpose. Signed certification shall accompany the form stating that the listed records have been microfilmed in accordance with the rules and regulations of this subchapter and that with the creation of these microfilm copies, the original records have ceased to have sufficient value to warrant their retention.

6. Updatable Microfiche Systems

Updatable microfiche does not meet archival standards and should be used only in special applications. Any agency considering using such a system should first contact the Public Records Administration to review the proposed application.

a. If permanent records are to be microfilmed and the hard copy records destroyed, a security copy must be on silver halide film and stored under archival conditions.

State: South Carolina
Source: South Carolina Code Annotated

TITLE 19. EVIDENCE.

CHAPTER 5. PUBLIC DOCUMENTS, RECORDS AND BOOKS.

Article 11. Photographic Copies.

Citation: SCCA 19-5-610

☞ § 19-5-610. Uniform Photographic Copies of Business and Public Records as Evidence Act.

If any business, institution, member of a profession or calling, or any department or agency of government, in the regular course of business or activity has kept or recorded any memorandum, writing, entry, print, representation or combination thereof, of any act, transaction, occurrence or event, and in the regular course of business has caused any or all of the same to be recorded, copied or reproduced by any photographic, photostatic, microfilm, microcard, miniature photographic or other process which accurately reproduces or forms a durable medium for so reproducing the original, the original may be destroyed in the regular course of business unless held in a custodial or fiduciary capacity or unless its preservation is required by law. Such reproduction, when satisfactorily identified is as admissible in evidence as the original itself in any judicial or administrative proceeding whether the original is in existence or not and an enlargement or facsimile of such reproduction is in existence and available for inspection under direction of court. The introduction of a reproduced record, enlargement or facsimile does not preclude admission of the original.

This section shall be so interpreted and construed as to effectuate its general purpose of making uniform the law of those states which enact or adopt it.

This section may be cited as the Uniform Photographic Copies of Business and Public Records as Evidence Act.

TITLE 30. PUBLIC RECORDS.

CHAPTER 1. PUBLIC RECORDS, REPORTS AND OFFICIAL DOCUMENTS.

Citation: SCCA 30-1-90

✪ § 30-1-90. Archives shall assist in creating, filing and preserving records, inventories, and schedules.

* * * * *

(D) No records of long term or enduring value created, including those filed, kept, or stored electronically, or those records converted from paper to magnetic, optical, film, or other media in the transaction of public business may be disposed of, destroyed, or erased without an approved records schedule. All records disposals that are carried out in accordance with duly approved records schedules must be documented and reported in accordance with procedures developed by the Archives.

Citation: SCCA 30-1-100

✪ § 30-1-100. Additional powers and duties of Archives.

(A) In cooperation with the executive officer of each public agency or body and the governing body of each subdivision, the Archives shall establish and maintain a program for the selection and preservation of public records considered essential to the operation of government, for the protection of the interests of the public and for the preservation of the state's documentary heritage. The Archives has the authority to determine in what medium records of archival value must be retained and transferred to the department. Within the limits of available funds, the Archives shall require preservation duplicates to be made of essential or historical records including those retained on electronic or optical disc systems or designate as preservation duplicates existing copies of these records including security copies on microfilm, computer output microfilm, or other media acceptable by the department or select certain original records for permanent preservation.

* * * * *

Citation: SCCA 30-1-110

✪ § 30-1-110. Destruction or other disposition of records.

The director may approve the destruction or other disposition of accessioned records of any agency or subdivision which are in the custody of the department and which, after due appraisal according to archival principles, are determined not to be of archival or continuing administrative, legal, or fiscal value.

Citation:	**SCCA 30-1-120**

✪ **§ 30-1-120. Inventorying, repairing and microfilming records.**

The Archives may execute a program of inventorying, repairing, and microfilming for security purposes the public records of the agencies and subdivisions which it determines have permanent value, and of providing safe storage of microfilm copies of such records.

Citation:	**SCCA 30-1-130**

✪ **§ 30-1-130. Custodians may microfilm or photocopy records; preservation or disposition of such copies.**

Any custodian of public records as defined by § § 30-1-10 to 30-1-140 is authorized to photocopy, microfilm or reproduce on film or by electrostatic method any part of the records kept by the office concerned unless otherwise prohibited by law or withheld from reproduction in the public interest. These copies shall be used only in equipment or systems which shall accurately reproduce and preserve the original record in all details in a durable form. Each agency or subdivision shall preserve such photocopies, electrostatic copies, or films in conveniently accessible files and shall provide for preserving, examining and using them. If the records are of permanent value to the agency or subdivision concerned or are determined to be of archival value by the Archives, one master copy of each record filmed shall meet standards approved by the Archives and be deposited there. Custodians of public records may destroy the original records from which the photographs, microphotographs, films or electrostatic copies have been made, or any part of them if the records are of no value to the agency concerned, and the Archives certifies that the records may be destroyed through this procedure or retention schedules approved by the Archives. The records microfilmed or reproduced and approved for destruction must be reported to the Archives in such manner as it may direct.

Source:	**South Carolina Department of Archives and History Archives and Records Management Division**

Citation:	**ARCHIVES AND RECORDS MANAGEMENT DIVISION POLICY STATEMENT**

✪ **Policy Statement**

The South Carolina Department of Archives and History placed this policy into effect on 10 March 1995. It supersedes the policy placed into effect on 3 February 1992.

Purpose: This policy clarifies the position of the South Carolina Department of Archives and History regarding the use of optical disk technology for the maintenance of public records, as defined by § 30-4-20(C) of the *Code of Laws of South Carolina, 1976,* as amended.

Authority: § 30-1-80 through 30-1-100 of the *Code of Laws of South Carolina, 1976,* as amended, provide the authority for the establishment of this policy.

Scope: This policy statement applies to the records of all public bodies as defined by § 30-1-10 of the *Code of Laws of South Carolina, 1976*, as amended.

Statement: To ensure accessibility, reduce the risk of premature disposition, and preserve records of permanent (archival) value, the following policy is established for the disposition of public records stored on optical disk:

[**Special note:** This policy does not supersede existing laws and regulations (federal, state, or local) that require the maintenance of public records and documents in a prescribed format.]

Records with an established retention of ten years or less

State and local government officials can maintain public records with an established retention value of ten years or less in an optical disk system and can dispose of the originals after receiving an authorization for disposal from the South Carolina Department of Archives and History. If the records are vital records, a security copy should be stored off-site in a secure location.

Non-permanent records with an established retention of more than ten years

State and local government officials can maintain non-permanent public records with an established retention of more than ten years in an optical disk system and dispose of the originals *provided* they:

1. maintain security copies of the disks and indexes in off-site storage.
2. *either* migrate and convert both the working and security copies of the disks and indexes if optical systems are upgraded or changed in a way that prevents access to the contents of the disks created by the old system *or* recopy to new disks every ten years, whichever comes first.
3. sample both the working and security copies of the disks and indexes at least once a year to make sure the data is readable and recopy to new disk immediately if any loss of information is detected.
4. obtain an authorization for disposal in advance from the South Carolina Department of Archives and History.

[Those not able to ensure compliance with 1-4 above must retain a paper record or a microform that meets state standards for the established retention period.]

Records of permanent value

Transfers to Archives. Records of permanent value that are scheduled for transfer to the South Carolina Department of Archives and History and are maintained in optical disk systems will be authorized for disposal *only after* a paper record or a microform that meets state standards has been transferred to the South Carolina Department of Archives and History. To provide access to the information in all paper and microform records transferred to the Department, the records must include appropriate indexes or other finding aids.

Non-transfers. Public records of permanent value* that are maintained in an optical disk system but not scheduled for transfer to the Department can be disposed of *provided* state and local government officials comply with 1-4 above. If the optical disk is the original medium for the records — as it is with the procedural or transactional recording of deeds, for example — we highly recommend the generation and permanent retention of either paper copies or microforms that meet state standards.** If paper or microform copies are not to be generated and retained, state and local government officials must certify in writing their intention to comply with 1-4 above before using the optical disk system.

[Those not able to ensure compliance with 1-4 above must

retain permanently a paper record or a microform that meets state standards.]

*Retention values must be established through approved records retention schedules developed in accordance with section 30-1-90 of the *Code of Laws of South Carolina, 1976*, as amended.

**Quality Standards and Practices for the Microfilming of Public Records (Regulations 12-200 through 12-203, *Code of Laws of South Carolina, 1976* as amended.)

Recommendations for the selection and use of optical systems

The Department recommends the use of the following guidelines for the design, selection, and operation of optical disk systems. These guidelines and practices will help you produce records and copies that will be acceptable in legal proceedings; they will enable you to maintain and retrieve information in ways that will meet your statutory obligations and operational needs as a record custodian; and they will help you to fulfill public requests. These considerations are particularly important for records that must be kept for a long time or permanently.

Legally-acceptable records management program

To ensure the acceptance of government records as legal documents, you should maintain and dispose of those records — including records stored in optical systems — as part of a legally-acceptable records management program. To conduct such a records management program, you should:

Include every record and all reproductions on records retention schedules that adequately describe the records and define the period for their retention and manner of disposition. These schedules, which must be approved by the Department, are of two types:

Specific Schedules: These schedules are written for records that are unique to a particular agency, office, or jurisdiction. They list the different physical forms of each record separately (e.g., paper, magnetic tape or disk, microfilm, optical disk) because each form may have a unique use, value, and retention period.

General Schedules: These schedules cover categories of records that many offices and agencies have in common: they typically do not specify particular physical forms. When you implement general schedules, however, you must take into account the various reproduction and storage requirements of these physical forms.

Carry out records retention and disposition procedures systematically as part of the regular course of business.

Maintain the documentation that supports the development and implementation of retention schedules.

Regularly dispose of records when their retention period has expired, either through destruction or transfer to an archival repository, as the schedule specifies.

Other legal considerations

Government offices and agencies must maintain data in optical storage systems according to the terms of the South Carolina Freedom of Information Act (§ § 30-4-10 through 30-4-110 of the *Code of Laws of South Carolina, 1976*, as amended). This act categorizes records as either restricted from or open to the public. You must adopt procedures that protect restricted records from unauthorized access and allow access to open records. Other laws applicable to particular governmental jurisdictions, functions, or records may require you to restrict specific records or information within certain records. Your procedures should cover these records as well.

Selection and use of optical storage systems

Optical storage systems require hardware (equipment) and software (computer programs) to retrieve and translate information into an eye-readable form. Because the storage medium itself is not permanent, you must select an appropriate system and operate it in a way that will let you retain and retrieve information over time as hardware and software change and the optical disks deteriorate physically.

Since few nationally-accepted standards have been set for optical systems, the Division of Archives and Records Management offers the following suggestions to help you use this technology. These recommendations represent generally accepted principles and practices and address issues of concern. In this changing technical environment, these recommendations will help you to keep your records accessible and your programs in conformity with national standards as they are developed. This subject is discussed in detail in a technical report issued by the Association of Information and Image Management, *The Use of Optical Disks for Public Records.*[1]

System documentation: If you wish to maintain an effective operation and continue to retrieve data as your operating environment changes over time, you must keep full documentation of:

Hardware and software, including brand names, version numbers and dates of installation, upgrades, replacements, and conversions.

Data structure and content, including the file layout and data dictionaries.

"Enhancement" algorithms.

Operating procedures, including methods for scanning or entering data: revising, updating, or expunging records; indexing; backing up disks, tapes, microfilm, etc.; testing the readability of records; applying safeguards to prevent tampering and unauthorized access to protected information; and carrying out the disposition of original records. In addition, to provide audit trails, you should document procedures for logging and tracking. Full documentation of your operating procedures will contribute to the legal acceptability of your records management program and will help to make the data you produce from optical disks admissible as evidence in legal proceedings.

Hardware and software:

When you are selecting a system, strongly consider those with open rather than proprietary designs; open systems will give you most flexibility when you are choosing equipment and will support interconnection, information system integration, and information sharing.

Prepare specifications for hardware and software that will require your vendors to continue to support and maintain their products.

Establish performance standards, incorporate them into your specifications for hardware and software, and require vendors to support them with a substantial performance bond.

Select systems that provide enough scanning resolution to produce a high-quality image. Validate the quality of the image by testing the actual documents.

Seek vendors who use standard rather than proprietary compression algorithms and file headers to make future migrations of data more certain and reliable. If vendors use proprietary algorithms, they must be able to demonstrate their capacity to bridge to standard compressions and file headers.

Seek vendors who use standard rather than proprietary compression algorithms and file headers to make future migrations of data more certain and reliable. If vendors us proprietary algorithms, they must be able to demonstrate their capacity to bridge to standards compressions and file headers.

Require vendors to supply programs or provide services to test the readability of your disks periodically.

Consider systems that will allow you to index or incorporate other retrieval information directly onto both the optical disk and the computer hard disk.

Verification and inspection: Include visual inspection in your operational procedures to verify the completeness and accuracy of the scanning process once documents have been transferred to a disk.

Indexing: When information is stored in a medium that is not eye-readable, complete and accurate indexes are essential. Your system design, therefore, must include provisions for appropriate indexing. When information will be retrieved for many years — from records that will be retained and used over a long period, for example — you must develop and document indexes with future users in mind and include in your operational procedures an index check for accuracy at the time the index is created.

Labeling. Label disks, tapes, and other storage containers with particular care since it is impossible to determine content merely by looking at a disk or tape.

Back-up and storage: It is vital to make full, frequent, and regular backups of optical records and magnetic indexes. Store your security copies in secure and suitable facilities, preferably off-site, and since environmental conditions for the storage of optical disks have not been established, follow the manufacturers' specifications. If you transfer images stored on magnetic media to optical disk, you should back up the magnetic media before the transfer and then back up the optical disk after it.

Refreshment, migration, and conversion plans: Prepare an appropriate plan for "refreshing" data and for migrating and converting images and corollary indexes to new storage media as needed to preserve the records in an accessible form.

Risk management. Develop a comprehensive risk or disaster prevention and recovery plan.

[1] Association for Information and Image Management. *Technical Report for Information and Image Management — The Use of Optical Disks for Public Records [AIIM TR25-1990]* (Silver Spring, MD: AIIM, 1990).

State: South Dakota
Source: South Dakota Codified Laws Annotated

TITLE 1. STATE AFFAIRS AND GOVERNMENT.

CHAPTER 1-27. PUBLIC RECORDS AND FILES.

Citation: SDCL 1-27-4

✪ **§ 1-27-4. Photographic and mechanical processes authorized for copying and recording.**

Whenever any officer of the state of South Dakota, any political subdivision, municipal corporation, or public corporation is required or authorized by law to record, copy, file, recopy, or replace any document, plat, paper, voucher, receipt, or book on file or of record in his office, he may do so by photostatic, microphotographic, microfilm, or other mechanical process which reproduces a clear, accurate, and permanent copy or reproduction of the original in accordance with the standards not less than those approved for permanent records by the national bureau of standards or the American National Standards Association.

Citation: SDCL 1-27-6

✪ **§ 1-27-6. Retention of reproduced records.**

Whenever any record or document is copied or reproduced in a method described in § 1-27-4, the officer shall retain a copy or reproduction in his office.

Citation: SDCL 1-27-7

✪ **§ 1-27-7. Viewing and reproduction equipment to be provided.**

If the original records or documents are disposed of or destroyed, the officer shall, unless viewing equipment is otherwise available within the corporate limits of the town or city wherein the records or documents are kept, provide suitable equipment for displaying such record or document in whole or in part by projection to no less than its original size, or for preparing persons entitled thereto copies of the record or document, but which shall not be required to be in its original size.

Citation: SDCL 1-27-8

✪ **§ 1-27-8. Reproductions admissible in evidence — Preparation of enlarged copies.**

A photographic, microphotographic, or microfilm copy of any such record, or a certified copy thereof, shall be admissible as evidence in any court or proceeding and it shall have the same force and effect as though the original record has been produced and proved. It shall be the duty of the custodian of such records to prepare enlarged typed or photographic copies of the records whenever their production is required by law.

TITLE 6. LOCAL GOVERNMENT GENERALLY.

CHAPTER 6-1. ACTS AND RECORDS OF LOCAL OFFICERS.

Citation: SDCL 6-1-11

✪ **§ 6-1-11. Form of certain public records — Duplicate —Computerization.**

Whenever the creation, maintenance or storage of any public record is specified by state law for political subdivisions, such record may be in the form of punched cards, magnetic tapes, disks and other machine-sensible data media within a data processing system. Such records shall be backed up by a duplicate, be accessible to viewing members of the public, and be retained in accordance with all applicable requirements for the retention of manual records. To the extent an office is computerized, the office need not keep a hard, paper copy. If current public records are converted to a computerized format, the political subdivision may destroy those records which the state records destruction board has pursuant to § 1-27-19, declared to be of no further administrative, legal, fiscal, research or historical value.

TITLE 7. COUNTIES.

CHAPTER 7-9. REGISTER OF DEEDS.

Citation: SDCL 7-9-1.1

✪ **§ 7-9-1.1. Recording, filing, and indexing of records by microfilming or computerization.**

The functions of the register of deeds, including but not limited to, the recording of instruments, liens, satisfactions and releases and the filing of records, as well as the index to any such record, may be accomplished by means of microfilming or computerization, as provided in § 6-1-11.

TITLE 19. EVIDENCE.

CHAPTER 19-7. DOCUMENTS, RECORDS AND JUDICIAL PROCEEDINGS.

Citation: SDCL 19-7-12

☞ **§ 19-7-12. Photographic copies of business and public records.**

If any business, institution, member of a profession or calling, or any department or agency of government, in the regular course of business or activity has kept or recorded any memorandum, writing, entry, print, representation or combination thereof, of any act, transaction, occurrence or event, and in the regular course of business has caused any or all of the same to be recorded, copied or reproduced by any photographic, photostatic, microfilm, microcard, miniature photographic, or other process which accurately reproduces or forms a durable medium for so reproducing the original, the original may be destroyed in the regular course of business unless held in a custodial or fiduciary capacity or unless its preservation is required by law. Such reproduction, when satisfactorily identified is as admissible in evidence as the original itself in any judicial or administrative proceeding whether the original is in existence or not and an enlargement or facsimile of such reproduction is likewise admissible in evidence if the original reproduction is in existence and available for inspection under direction of court. The introduction of a reproduced record, enlargement or facsimile, does not preclude admission of the original.

This section shall be so interpreted and construed as to effectuate its general purpose of making uniform the law of those states which enact or adopt it.

This section may be cited as the Uniform Photographic Copies of Business and Public Records as Evidence Act.

CHAPTER 19-18. CONTENTS OF WRITINGS, RECORDINGS AND PHOTOGRAPHS.

Citation: SDCL 19-18-1

☞ **§ 19-18-1. (Rule 1001) Definition of terms.**

Terms used in this chapter mean:

(1) "Duplicate," is a counterpart produced by the same impression as the original, or from the same matrix, or by means of photography, including enlargements and miniatures, or by mechanical or electronic re-recording, or by chemical reproduction, or by other equivalent techniques which accurately reproduce the original.

(2) "Original," a writing or recording or any counterpart of the writing or recording intended to have the same effect by a person executing or issuing it. An "original" of a photograph includes the negative or any print therefrom. If data are stored in a computer or similar device, any printout or other output readable by sight, shown to reflect the data accurately, is an "original"

(3) "Photographs," still photographs, X-ray films, video tapes, and motion pictures.

(4) "TDD," or "TTY," any auxiliary aids or services consisting of assistive listening or transcription systems which allow the reception or transmission of aurally delivered communication and materials for the benefit of individuals with hearing, speech or physical impairments; and

(5) "Writings" and "recordings," letters, words, or numbers, or their equivalent, set down by handwriting, typewriting, printing, photostating, photographing, magnetic impulse, mechanical or electronic recording, or other form of data compilation.

Citation: SDCL 19-18-3

☞ **§ 19-18-3. (Rule 1003) Duplicate admissible as original — Exceptions.**

A duplicate is admissible to the same extent as an original unless (1) a genuine question is raised as to the authenticity of the original or (2) in the circumstances it would be unfair to admit the duplicate in lieu of the original.

Citation: SDCL 19-18-5

☞ **§ 19-18-5. (Rule 1005) Certified copy of official record — Other evidence.**

The contents of an official record, or of a document authorized to be recorded or filed and actually recorded or filed, including data compilations in any form, if otherwise admissible, may be proved by copy, certified as correct in accordance with § 19-17-5 or testified to be correct by a witness who has compared it with the original. If a copy which complies with the foregoing cannot be obtained by the exercise of reasonable diligence, then other evidence of the contents may be given.

Source: **South Dakota Administrative Rules**

CHAPTER 4:04:09. MEDICAL RECORD SERVICES.

Citation: **SDAR 44:04:09:07**

✍ **§ 44:04:09:07. Authentication.**

A health care facility must ensure that entries to the medical record are signed or electronically authenticated. If the facility permits any portion of the medical record to be generated by electronic or optical means, policies and procedures must exist to effectively limit the use of authentication by unauthorized users.

Citation: **SDAR 44:04:09:09**

✍ **§ 44:04:09:09. Storage of medical records.**

A health care facility must provide for filing, safe storage, and easy accessibility of medical records. The medical records must be preserved as original records, on microfilm, or in other readily retrievable form. Medical records must be protected against access by unauthorized individuals. All medical records must be retained by the health care facility upon change of ownership.

Agency: **Department of Revenue**

Citation: **SDAR 64:06:01:35.01**

✍ **§ 64:06:01:35.01. Microfilm records.**

The department will not accept microfilm reproductions in lieu of original records of general books of account, such as cash books, journals, voucher registers, and ledgers. However, supporting records of details, such as sales invoices, purchase invoices, and credit memoranda may be maintained by microfilm, computer imaging, or other preapproved reproductions if the following conditions are met:

(1) Facilities are provided for preservation of the films or media for the periods required;

(2) Microfilm rolls or other types of preapproved media are indexed, cross-referenced, labeled to show beginning and ending numbers or beginning and ending alphabetical listing of the documents included, and are systematically filed;

(3) The taxpayer agrees to provide transcriptions of any information contained on microfilm or other media which may be required for purposes of verification of tax liability;

(4) Facilities are provided for the ready inspection and location of the particular records, including modern projectors or terminals for viewing and copying the records.

Posting references must be on each invoice. Credit memoranda must carry a reference to the document evidencing the original transaction. Documents necessary to support claimed exemptions from tax liability, such as bills of lading and purchase orders, must be maintained in an order by which they readily can be related to the transactions for which exemption is sought.

Citation: **SDAR 64:06:01:35.02**

✍ **§ 64:06:01:35.02. Records prepared by automated data processing systems.**

An automated data processing (ADP) tax accounting system must have built into its program a method of producing visible and legible records which will provide the necessary information for verification of the taxpayer's tax liability. Requirements are as follows:

(1) Recorded or reconstructible data: ADP records must provide an opportunity to trace any transaction back to the original source or forward to a final total. If detailed printouts are not made of transactions at the time they are processed, the system must have the ability to reconstruct these transactions;

(2) General and subsidiary books of account: A general ledger with source references shall be written out to coincide with financial reports for tax reporting periods. Where subsidiary ledgers are used to support the general ledger accounts, the subsidiary ledgers shall also be written out;

(3) Supporting documents and audit trail: The audit trail shall be designed to identify the details underlying the summary accounting data and shall be made available to the department upon request. The system shall be designed so that supporting documents, such as sales invoices, purchase invoices, and credit memoranda are readily available;

(4) Program documentation: A description of the ADP portion of the accounting system shall be available. The statements and illustrations of the scope of operations shall be sufficiently detailed to indicate the following:

(a) The application being performed;

(b) The procedures employed in each application, which may be supported by flow charts, block diagrams, or other satisfactory description of the input or output procedures; and

(c) The controls used to insure accurate and reliable processing.

Source: **Office of the Attorney General**

OFFICIAL OPINION NO. 74-2

January 11, 1974
Gene Paul Kean
States Attorney
Minnehaha County
Sioux Falls, South Dakota 57102
Official Opinion No. 74-2

The clerk of courts of a county may microfilm all public records in his charge and may destroy the original with the permission of the State Records Destruction Board.

Dear Mr. Kean:

In your request for an opinion, you have set forth the following factual situation:

> The clerk of courts in Minnehaha County plans to commence microfilming records of files in January, 1974. In conformance with SDCL 1-27-4, all records so microfilmed will be destroyed. A prior section of the South Dakota Code, SDCL 1-27-5 required (a) that no records could be destroyed unless microfilmed and more than ten (10) years old, and (b) only upon order of the Circuit Court. SDCL 1-27-5 was repealed in 1970 leaving no provision directing how long records must be kept or whether an order to the Circuit Court is needed.

In connection with this factual situation, you have posed the following questions:

1. May the clerk of courts destroy court records once they have been microfilmed according to SDCL 1-27-4?

2. Does the clerk of courts need an order of the Circuit Court of appropriate jurisdiction before he may destroy any records which have been properly microfilmed according to SDCL 1-27-4?

3. How long must the clerk of courts retain the original records before these records may be destroyed?

SDCL 1-27-4 reads as follows:

> Whenever any officer of the state of South Dakota, any political subdivision, municipal corporation, or public corporation is required or authorized by law to record, copy, file, recopy, or replace any document, plat, paper, voucher, receipt, or book on file or of record in his office, he may do so by photostatic, microphotographic, microfilm, or other mechanical process which produces a clear, accurate and permanent copy or reproduction of the original in accordance with the standards not less than those approved for permanent records by the National Bureau of Standards or the American National Standards Association.

This statute permits the microfilming of all public records a clerk of court is required to keep. SDCL 1-27-10 reads as follows:

> All records made or received by, or under the authority of, or coming into the custody, control, or possession of public officials of this state in the course of their public duties, are the property of the state and shall not be mutilated, destroyed, transferred, removed, or otherwise damaged or disposed of, in whole or in part, except as provided by law.

This indicates for all purposes that the clerk of courts may not destroy public records except as provided by law.

SDCL 1-27-11 created the State Record Destruction Board, which board possesses the exclusive authority to permit the destruction of public records and the exclusive authority to promulgate rules, regulations, standards and procedures relating to the disposal of records.

SDCL 1-27-19 reads as follows:

> The state record destruction board shall meet at least once each year and consider requests of all political subdivisions for the destruction of records and to authorize their destruction as in the case of state records.

It is obvious from a reading of this statute and those cited above that the Legislature has authorized the destruction of public records when the proper procedure is followed.

Therefore, the answer to your first question is, YES, the clerk of courts may destroy court records once they have been microfilmed pursuant to SDCL 1-27-4, however, he must receive permission from the State Record Destruction Board.

The foregoing provides the sole statutory procedure for the destruction of public records. An order of the circuit court permitting the destruction of public records is no longer necessary since SDCL 1-27-5 which made such an order a requirement has been repealed by the 1970 State Legislature. Therefore, the answer to your second question is, NO.

Concerning your third question on the length of time the clerk of courts must retain the original records after they have been microfilmed, I would inform you that the South Dakota Compiled Laws are silent. Further, there have been no rules promulgated by the State Record Destruction Board which would require the clerk of courts to retain the originals for any length of time after microfilming is completed. Therefore, in answer to your third question, the clerk of courts may destroy original records which have been microfilmed pursuant to SDCL 1-27-4 as soon as the State Record Destruction Board authorizes the destruction of the records, pursuant to SDCL 1-27-19.

Respectfully submitted,
KERMIT A. SANDE
ATTORNEY GENERAL

OFFICIAL OPINION NO. 76-42

Microfilming of records under SDCL 1-27-4
Dear Mr. Duxbury:
You have requested an official opinion from this office based upon the following facts:

> Records of public hearings held by the Dairy Marketing Commission, a Division of the South Dakota Department of Agriculture for the period of 1967 through 1973, are at this time stored by Records Management. Records Management has requested permission to microfilm these records and destroy the originals. As the hearings have been held for the purpose of amending rules, and as Section 11 of the check list for passing rules indicated that the original copy of all documents be retained by the agency, it appears that there is some question about whether the requirements of SDCL 1-26 would be met if the original copies were microfilmed pursuant to SDCL 1-27.

Based on the above facts, you ask:

> In the case of public hearings under SDCL 1-26, do the microfilmed copies of the original records have the same legal standing as the original, and if so, may the original records be destroyed?

SDCL 1-26-7 provides:

> Each agency shall keep the original records, documents and instruments required by this chapter. Agencies shall make copies of all records, documents and exhibits available to members of the Legislature upon request. The secretary of state shall keep a copy of the agency's current rules and certificates pertaining thereto, which shall be open to public inspection.

SDCL 1-27-4 provides:

> Whenever any office of the state of South Dakota, any political subdivision, municipal corporation, or public corporation is required or authorized by law to record,, copy, file, recopy, or replace any document, plat, paper, voucher, receipt, or book on file or of record in his office, he may do so by photostatic, microphotographic, microfilm, or other mechanical process which produces a clear, accurate, and permanent copy or reproduction of the original in accordance with the standards not less than those approved for permanent records by the national bureau of standards or the American National Standards Association.

In my opinion, the requirement in SDCL 1-26-7 relating to the agency keeping the original records, documents, and instruments required by the chapter, would be satisfied if the agency followed the procedures of SDCL 1-27 relating to the mechanical reproducing and recording of public documents. Presuming that accurate copies are made pursuant to SDCL 1-27, and that the Records Destruction Board would approve of the physical destruction of the original records you refer to, I believe such destruction would be lawful and the department would be in compliance with the requirements of SDCL 1-26.

Respectfully submitted,
WILLIAM J. JANKLOW
ATTORNEY GENERAL

State: Tennessee
Source: Tennessee Code Annotated

TITLE 10. PUBLIC LIBRARIES, ARCHIVES AND RECORDS.

CHAPTER 7. PUBLIC RECORDS.

Part 3. Public Records Commission.

Citation: TCA 10-7-303

✪ § 10-7-303. Records management division — Creation, disposition and reservation of records — Land, legislative and judicial records.

(a) The records management division of the department of general services shall be the primary records management agency for state government, and as such shall direct the disposition of all records including electronic processed records and computer output microfilm records.

* * * * *

(d) No record or records shall be scheduled for destruction without the unanimous approval of the voting members of the public records commission.

* * * * *

Citation: TCA 10-7-306

✪ § 10-7-306. Rules and regulations of commission.

(a) The commission shall issue rules and regulations which shall include such procedures as may be necessary to carry out the purposes of this chapter. Such rules and regulations shall provide but not be limited to:

* * * * *

(2) Standards and procedures for the reproduction of records for security or for disposal of original records;

* * * * *

Part 4. County Public Records Commission.

Citation: TCA 10-7-406

✪ § 10-7-406. Original records photographed in duplicate before destruction — Stored for safekeeping — Accessible to public.

(a)(1) Whenever the county records commission with the consent and concurrence of the officers and bodies, if any, as prescribed in § § 10-7-404 and 10-7-405 shall decide to destroy the originals of any records required by law to be permanently kept, the commission shall cause the records to be photographed, microphotographed, filmed or microfilmed in duplicate. This duplication process shall result in permanent records of a quality at least as good as is prescribed by the minimum standards of quality for permanent photographic records made and established by the bureau of standards of the United States government. If a marginal release or other information on an old record has failed or has been obliterated to a degree that it is impossible to photograph, the same may be verified on the margin by the register before microfilming. One (1) copy of such reproduction shall be stored for safekeeping in a place selected by the commission and concurred in by the county legislative body.

(2) Such place shall be in the state if proper facilities are available, but, if not, then in a place outside the state.

(3) Such location shall be selected with a view of protection of the records from fire and all other hazards. The other copy of each document shall be kept in an office in the county accessible to the public and to the several county officers and the county clerks, together with the proper equipment for using, examining, exhibiting, projecting and enlarging the same whenever required and requested by the public during reasonable office hours. The records of each office may be kept in that office, or if the commission shall so determines, all the reproduced records may be kept in one (1) central records office.

(b) Any public record defined as "temporary record" and/or "working papers" as defined in § § 10-7-301 and 10-7-403 may be destroyed in accordance with the rules and regulations adopted by the commission without retaining the originals of such records.

(c) The purpose and intent of this chapter is to provide for the original recording of any and all instruments by photograph, photostat, film, microfilm or other microphotographic process. If any laws or parts of laws as set forth in this chapter are in conflict with such purpose, such laws or parts of laws to that extent are hereby repealed.

Citation: TCA 10-7-410

✪ § 10-7-410. Reproductions admissible in evidence.

Any reproduction of any record herein authorized to be made shall be deemed to be the original of the record so reproduced for all purposes and any facsimile of such record duly certified to be such by the officer or clerk charged by law with the custody thereof shall be admissible in evidence in any court or proceeding in this state and shall have the same force and effect as would the original of the document or a certified copy thereof if made from the original record, document or paper.

Part 5. Miscellaneous Provisions

Citation: TCA 10-7-501

✪ § 10-7-501. Reproduction of state records on film.

The head of any department, commission, board, or agency of the state government may cause any or all records kept by him or it to be photographed, microphotographed or reproduced on film, provided that the microfilm project has been evaluated and approved by the records management division of the department of general services. Such photographic film shall comply with the minimum standards of quality approved for permanent photographic records by the national bureau of standards and the device used to reproduce such records on film shall be one which accurately reproduces the original thereof in all details.

Citation: TCA 10-7-502

✪ § 10-7-502. Photographic copy deemed original record.

(a) Any photograph, microphotograph or photographic film of any state, county, or municipal public record are deemed to be original records for all purposes, including introduction in evidence in all courts or administrative agencies.

(b) A transcript, exemplification, or certified copy thereof shall, for all purposes recited therein, be deemed to be a transcript, exemplification or certified copy of the original.

Source: Tennessee Rules of Evidence

ARTICLE X. CONTENTS OF WRITINGS, RECORDINGS AND PHOTOGRAPHS.

☞ Rule 1001. Definitions

For purposes of this article the following definitions are applicable:

(1) *Writings and recordings.* — "Writings" and "recordings" consist of letters, words, or numbers, or their equivalent, set down by handwriting, typewriting, printing, photostating, photographing, magnetic impulse, mechanical or electronic recording, or other form of data compilation.

(2) *Photographs.* — "Photographs" include still photographs, X-ray films, video tapes, and motion pictures.

(3) *Original.* — An "original" of a writing or recording is the writing or recording itself or any counterpart intended to have the same effect by a person executing or issuing it. An "original" of a photograph includes the negative or any print therefrom. If data are stored in a computer or similar device, any printout or other output readable by sight, shown to reflect the data accurately, is an "original".

(4) *Duplicate.* — A "duplicate" is a counterpart produced by the same impression as the original, or from the same matrix, or by means of photography, including enlargements and miniatures, or by mechanical or electronic re-recording, or by chemical reproduction, or by other equivalent techniques which accurately reproduces the original.

☞ Rule 1003. Admissibility of duplicates.

A duplicate is admissible to the same extent as an original unless a genuine question is raised as to the authenticity of the original.

[See Appendix A. Uniform Rules of Evidence for additional provisions.]

Source: Tennessee Compilation of Rules and Regulations
Agency: Department of Revenue

CHAPTER 1320-4-3. UNFAIR CIGARETTE SALES LAW AND TOBACCO TAX RULES.

Citation: TCRR 1320-4-3-.05

☞ § 1320-4-3-.05. Records and reports.

* * * * *

(5) It shall be the duty of every wholesaler and retailer, as those terms are defined in TCA 47-25-302, to keep and preserve for a period of three (3) years suitable records of all sales and purchases and such other books of account as may be necessary to determine compliance with the Unfair Cigarette Sales Law, TCA 47-25-301 et seq. Such records and other books of account shall include by not be limited to all invoices, bills of lading, pertinent records whether stored electronically or otherwise, papers and memoranda reflecting sales and purchases, operating and proprietary ledgers, and any other document of information that may be required by the Commissioner, and all such books and records shall be open to examination at all reasonable hours to the Commissioner or any of his authorized agents.

CHAPTER 1320-7-8. FUEL USE TAX.

Citation: TCRR 1320-7-8-.05

✍ § 1320-7-8-.05. Records.

The permittee shall maintain a complete and accurate record of miles traveled in the State of Tennessee by each qualified vehicle. Additionally, each permittee shall maintain a complete record of all fuel purchased, received, and used in the conduct of its business. These records shall be maintained for at least four (4) years, except the ICC logs which shall be retained a minimum of two (2) tax quarters, plus the current tax quarter.

(1) Mileage records shall be compiled by tax periods.

(2) Mileage records shall show the date and route traveled in Tennessee and the mileage recaps for each vehicle.

(3) Records of fuel purchased, received or used, shall contain, but not be limited to:

(a) The date of each receipt of fuel;

(b) The name and address of the person from whom purchased or received;

(c) The number of gallons received;

(d) The fuel type, and;

(e) The qualified vehicle or equipment into which the fuel was placed.

(f) In the case of bulk fuel storage facilities the above requirements shall apply, and additional records shall be provided showing the date of dispensing the fuel and the unit identification into which the fuel was placed.

(4) Receipt Documentation

(a) Acceptable receipt documentation may include, but not be limited to, a receipt or invoice, a credit care receipt or invoice, computer generated listings of fuel purchases originated by fuel vendors or transportation service companies, or microfilm/microfiche of the receipt or invoice.

(b) An acceptable receipt or invoice for tax paid purchases must include, but not be limited to, the following:

1. Date of Purchase;
2. Seller's name and address;
3. Number of gallons purchased;

4. Fuel type;
5. Price per gallon or total amount of sale;
6. Unit numbers, and;
7. Purchaser's name. In the case of a lease agreement, receipts will be accepted in either the name of the lessor or lessee, provided a written contract is furnished to the department that clearly establishes this relationship between the parties.

(c) Photocopies other than microfilm/microfiche, of receipts or invoices will not be accepted as suitable substitutes for the documents required herein.

(5) Audit Authority — Records supporting the Tennessee Highway Fuel Tax reports shall be subject to inspection and audit by authorized agents of the Tennessee Department of Revenue. The commissioner may also require that fuel purchase records be submitted to the department for review on a selective basis. All requests for submission of fuel purchase records shall be in writing. The permittee shall be allowed a minimum of thirty (30) days to comply.

(6) Unavailability of Records — In the event any records required to be maintained by the permittee are not available due to fire, theft, flood or any other cause, the permittee shall notify the department in writing within sixty (60) days of becoming aware of such loss.

(7) Upon the presentation of substitute records to the department by the permittee the commissioner will determine the acceptability of such substitute records.

State: Texas
Source: Texas Codes Annotated – Alcoholic Beverage Code

TITLE 2. ADMINISTRATION OF CODE.

CHAPTER 5. ALCOHOLIC BEVERAGE COMMISSION.

SUBCHAPTER B. POWERS ANDS DUTIES

Citation: TABC 5.51

✍ § 5.51 Bookkeeping Records.

A permittee who holds a permit issued under Chapters 28 through 33 of this code may elect to keep all records required under this code on a machine bookkeeping system. A permittee who desires to use such a system must submit a written application for commission approval of the system before implementing the system. The commission may authorize a permittee to centralize the permittee's records.

Source: Texas Business and Commerce Code

TITLE 4. MISCELLANEOUS COMMERICAL PROVISIONS

CHAPTER 35. MISCELLANEOUS

Subchapter D. Miscellaneous

Citation: TBCC 35.48

✍ § 35.48. Retention of Business Records.

(a) In this section:

(1) "Business record" means letters, words, sounds, or numbers, or the equivalent of letters, words, sounds, or numbers, recorded in the operation of a business by:
(A) handwriting;
(B) typewriting;
(C) printing;
(D) photostat;
(E) photograph;
(F) magnetic impulse;
(G) mechanical or electronic recording;
(H) digitized optical image; or
(I) another form of data compilation.

(2) "Reproduction" means a counterpart of an original business record produced by:
(A) production from the same impression or the same matrix as the original;
(B) photograph, including an enlargement or miniature;
(C) mechanical or electronic rerecording;
(D) chemical reproduction;
(E) digitized optical image; or
(F) another technique that accurately reproduces the original.

(b) A business record required to be kept by state law may be destroyed at any time after the third anniversary of the date the record was created unless a law or regulation applicable to the business record prescribes a different retention period or procedure for disposal.

(c) A state law requiring retention of a business record is satisfied by retention of a reproduction of the business record.

Source: Texas Government Code

TITLE 4. EXECUTIVE BRANCH.

SUBTITLE D. HISTORY, CULTURE, AND EDUCATION.

CHAPTER 441. LIBRARIES AND ARCHIVES.

Subchapter C. Records Management Division of Texas State Library.

Citation: TGC 441.035

✪ § 441.035. Destruction of records.

(a) The director and librarian may transfer, destroy, or otherwise dispose of any state record that has been consigned by law to the custody of the director or librarian, that is more than 10 years old, and that the director and librarian determines to be valueless or of no further use to the state as an historical record if the comptroller, state auditor, and attorney general agree with the director and librarian that the preservation of the record is not necessary as evidence and will serve no useful purpose in the future efficient to the operation of state government. Any record disposed of as agreed must be generally listed and referred to, and each official shall consent to the disposition by subscribing to the list.

(b) The director and librarian may destroy a record of a local government that has been transferred or consigned by law to the custody of the director or librarian if the retention period for the record has expired in a records retention schedule approved according to law. If the record does not appear on a records retention schedule, it may be destroyed if in the judgment of the director and librarian it does not have sufficient historical value to merit retention. An original record of a local government in the custody of the director and librarian may be destroyed before the expiration of its retention period if it is microfilmed or duplicated on electronic media and the microfilm or electronic media meets standards established by the Texas State Library and Archives Commission under Section 204.004 or 205.003, Local Government Code. A notice of the destruction of the records shall be filed among the records of the state library.

(c) Any state record that the director and librarian, comptroller, state auditor, or attorney general considers necessary to preserve may be preserved by microfilming the record if funds are appropriated by the legislature to cover the cost of microfilming for the state or are otherwise available for that purpose. Once microfilmed, an original records may be disposed of in a manner agreed on by the officials. A microfilm copy constitutes an original for all legal purposes.

(d) A state record determined to be no longer needed for the operations of state government or replaced by microfilm copy may be transferred to the archives division of the state library if the director and librarian considers the record to be of historical value.

(e) With the approval of the director and librarian, in accordance with this section, the head of any department or institution may destroy any state record in the custody of the head of the department or institution that, in the opinion of the head of the department or institution, does not have any further legal, administration, or historical value.

Before destroying the state record, the head of the department or institution must file an application to do so with the director and librarian that describes the original purpose and the contents of the state record. In addition, the approval of the state auditor is required in the case of the destruction of a state record of a fiscal or financial nature before the expiration of the retention period recommended for that class of records by the director and librarian in consultation with the state auditor.

Citation: TGC 441.038

✪ § 441.038. Photographic Reproductions.

(a) On request of the head of a department or institution, or on the director and librarian's own initiative with the consent of the head of the department or institution, the director and librarian may provide for making photographic reproductions of the public records of the department or institution. Public records are open to the director and librarian for that purpose.

(b) Any photographic reproduction of a public record made by microprint or by microphotography on film must comply with the minimum standards of quality approved for permanent photographic records by the National Bureau of Standards.

(c) Any device used to produce a public record must accurately reproduce the original record in detail.

(d) The director and librarian may make photographic reproductions for public use as follows:

(1) free of charge for official use of a department or institution;

(2) for a fee to cover costs for official use of a local unit of government; or

(3) for standard commercial rates fixed by the director and librarian for private use.

(e) Any money the state library receives in payment for charges for photographic reproduction shall be deposited in the state treasury.

(f) A state official may designate a photographic reproduction of a state record in the officer's office as an original record for all legal purposes, even though the record is current. The officer may transfer the replaced record to the director and librarian, who shall issue a receipt for the record. The director and librarian may further transfer or destroy the transferred record. Copies, in any form, of a photographic reproduction that has been designated as an original record and certified or authenticated according to law may be introduced in evidence.

SUBCHAPTER D. PRESERVATION OF ESSENTIAL RECORDS

Citation: TGC 441.058

✪ § 441.058. Preservation duplicates.

(a) The records preservation officer shall make preservation duplicates or shall designate as preservation duplicates existing copies of essential state records. A preservation duplicate made by means of photography, microphotography, photocopying, or microfilm must be made according to standards that the records preservation officer prescribes in conformity with the rules of the United States Bureau of Standards.

(b) A preservation duplicate made by a process that accurately reproduces or forms a durable medium for accurately reproducing the original record has the same force and effect for all purposes as the original record, regardless of whether the original record exists. A transcript, exemplification, or certified copy of such a preservation duplicate is for all purposes a transcript, exemplification, or certified copy of the original record.

Citation: TGC 441.059

✪ § 441.059. Storage.

(a) The records preservation officer shall prescribe the place and manner of safekeeping of essential records or preservation duplicates and shall establish storage facilities for the records and duplicates. At least one copy of each essential record and a duplicate seal of the state shall be stored in the safest possible location in facilities constructed to withstand blast, fire, water, and other destructive forces. The facilities must be in a place other than the legally designated or customary storage location for the records or duplicates. The records preservation officer shall properly maintain essential records and preservation duplicates that the records preservation officer stores.

(b) The regularly designated custodian of an agency record or preservation duplicate stored by the records preservation officer may recall the record or duplicate for temporary use as necessary for the proper conduct of an agency. The custodian shall return the record or duplicate to the records preservation officer immediately after the use.

(c) On request of the regularly designated custodian of an essential record stored by the records preservation officer, the records preservation officer shall provide the record for inspection or the making of certified copies. Copies certified by the records preservation officer have the same force and effect as if certified by the regularly designated custodian.

LOCAL GOVERNMENT.

TITLE 6. RECORDS.

SUBTITLE B. COUNTY RECORDS.

CHAPTER 194. MICROFILMING OF COUNTY RECORDS.

Citation: TGC 194.0025

✪ § 194.0025. Authorization of Optical Data Storage Process.

(a) For the purposes described by Section 194.002(a), a county clerk or clerk of the county court may adopt and use an optical data storage process for the storage of records by optical disk.

(b) This chapter applies, to the extent feasible, to the optical data storage process, the optical disk used in that process, and the records stored by that process in a manner equivalent to the manner in which this chapter applies to a microfilm process, the film used in that process, and the records stored by that process.

Citation: TGC 194.0065

✪ § 194.0065. Computerized Index for Official Public Records.

An index for an official public record may be stored or maintained by computer, provided that a security or backup copy of such index be created on a daily basis and stored in a climate-controlled location, equipped with fire alarms and sprinklers, which must be separate and apart from the building in which the computer is located.

Citation: TGC 194.010

✪ § 194.010. Standards for Filming.

(a) If a state public records commission is created, an original negative roll and an original ne
gative discrete image of a microfilm record must meet the requirements of that commission relating to archival quality, density, resolution, and definition. If that commission is not created, a microfilm record must meet such requirements of the American National Standards Institute.

(b) A camera used for microfilming must meet or exceed the then current requirements of the American National Standards Institute for the documentation of permanent records.

* * * * *

SUBTITLE C. RECORDS PROVISIONS APPLYING TO MORE THAN ONE TYPE OF LOCAL GOVERNMENT.

CHAPTER 204. MICROFILMING OF RECORDS [NEW].

Citation: TGC 204.001

✪ § 204.001. Definitions.

In this chapter:

(1) "Microfilm" means roll microfilm, microfiche, and all other formats produced by any method of microphotography or other means if miniaturization on film.

(2) "Microfilming" means the methods, procedures, and processes used to produce roll microfilm, microfiche, or other microphotographic formats.

Citation: TGC 204.002

✪ § 204.002. Authorization.

Any local government record may be maintained on microfilm in addition to or instead of paper or other media, subject to the requirements of this chapter and rules adopted under it.

Citation: TGC 204.003

✪ § 204.003. Microfilm Produced Under Prior Law.

(a) All microfilm produced before June 1, 1990, under prior law is validated to the extent the microfilm was produced in the manner and according to the standards prescribed by prior law.

(b) In rules adopted under Section 204.004, the commission may establish procedures for the retrospective certification of uncertified or improperly certified microfilm produced before April 1, 1990, that otherwise meets the standards prescribed by prior law.

Citation: TGC 204.004

✪ § 204.004. Standards and Procedures.

(a) The commission shall adopt rules on or before April 1, 1990, establishing standards and procedures for the microfilming of local government records. The rules must be approved as required by Section 441.165, Government Code.

(b) The rules must prescribe:

(1) standards for film quality, resolution, density, definition, and chemical stability;

(2) tests and other methods of inspection required to establish that prescribed standards have been met;

(3) procedures for verifying that records have been filmed accurately;

(4) procedures for the certification of microfilmed records;

(5) standards for the use of editorial and technical targets on microfilm;

(6) standards for the production of use copies from and the storage of master microfilm negatives;

(7) procedures for the labeling and indexing of microfilmed records;

(8) procedures establishing the manner in which court case papers must be filmed;

(9) procedures for the expungement of criminal records on microfilm pursuant to court order;

(10) standards for computer-output microfilm; and

(11) standards for providing access by the members of the public to records on microfilm to which they are entitled under law.

(c) In rules adopted under this section, the commission may establish differing standards and procedures for the microfilming of:

(1) any permanent record;

(2) any record of a municipal, justice, county, or district court; or

(3) any record to which access is restricted under Chapter 552, Government Code, or other state law.

Citation: TGC 204.005

✪ § 204.005. Rules to be Updated.

The director and librarian shall monitor standards relating to microfilming developed for use by federal agencies or adopted by national organizations that develop and set standards in the fields of information and records management in order to recommend to the commission any needed amendments to rules.

Citation: TGC 204.006

✪ § 204.006. Indexing.

An index to a microfilm record must show the same information that may be required by state law for an index to the same record if it is not microfilmed.

Citation: TGC 204.007

✪ § 204.007. Destruction of Original Records.

(a) Except as provided by Section 204.008, the original of a record that has been microfilmed pursuant to this chapter and rules adopted under it may be destroyed before the expiration of its retention period on a records retention schedule issued by the commission.

(b) A list of the originals of microfilmed records destroyed shall be filed with the records management officer.

(c) The microfilm record must be retained until the expiration of the retention period for the original record.

Citation: TGC 204.008

✪ § 204.008. Destruction of Permanent Records.

(a) The original of a permanent record may not be destroyed until a destruction authorization request is submitted to the director and librarian certifying that the microfilm of the record meets the standards of this chapter and rules adopted under it.

(b) Requests shall be submitted by the records management officer or under the officer's direction or, if a records management officer has not yet been designated under Section 203.025, by the custodian of the microfilm records.

(c) If the director and librarian or the designee of the director and librarian approves the request, the original record may be destroyed.

(d) In lieu of destruction, the director and librarian may require that the original record be transferred to the custody of the commission.

(e) If the director and librarian or the designee of the director and librarian disapproves the request, the reasons for the disapproval shall be stated in writing within a reasonable time to the records management officer or custodian. The original records may not be destroyed until the microfilm of the records is brought into compliance with this chapter and the rules adopted under it as evidenced by the submission of a new destruction authorization request.

(f) The director and librarian shall determine the form and manner of submission of destruction authorization requests required by this section.

Citation: TGC 204.009

✪ § 204.009. Microfilm of Permanent Records to be Supplied.

(a) A local government or elected county officer, at the request of the director and librarian, shall supply to the commission a copy of the microfilm of any permanent record to which access is not restricted by law.

(b) The commission shall reimburse the local government or elected county officer for the cost of the copy. If the film duplication is performed by the local government or elected county officer, the cost must be the same as that paid by state agencies to the Texas State Library for a similar microfilm copy. If the film duplication is done by a commercial microfilming service under contract with the local government or elected county officer, the cost of the copy may not exceed the cost paid by the local government or elected county officer for a copy under the contract.

(c) The director and librarian or an employee of the commission may not provide certified copies of a record on microfilm obtained under this section without the consent of the original local custodian of the record.

Citation: TGC 204.010

✪ § 204.010. Commercial Microfilm Storage Facilities.

(a) The commission may establish a program for the certification of commercial microfilm storage facilities for the storage of the master microfilm negatives of local government records.

(b) If the commission establishes a certification program, the procedures of this subsection apply. On request by the commercial storage facility, the director and librarian or the representative of the director and librarian shall inspect the facility to determine if the facility meets the minimum standards established by the commission under Section 204.004 for the storage of the microfilm of local government records.

If the commercial storage facility meets the minimum standards established by the commission, the name of the facility shall be added to a list of certified storage facilities to be prepared by the director and librarian and made available on request to a local government, elected county officer, or other interested party. The inspection and certification of commercial storage facilities shall be on a fee basis to be determined by the commission.

(c) The commissioner shall determine the period a certification made under this section is effective.

Citation: TGC 204.011

✍ ✪ § 204.011. Effective as Original Record.

(a) A microfilmed record created in compliance with this chapter and rules adopted under it, including microfilm validated by Section 204.003, is an original record and shall be accepted by any court or administrative agency of this state.

(b) If issued and certified by a local government recordkeeper, a copy on paper or film of a microfilmed record shall be accepted by a court or administrative agency of this state as a certified copy of an original record.

CHAPTER 205. ELECTRONIC STORAGE OF RECORDS.

Citation: TGC 205.001

✪ § 205.001. Definitions.

In this chapter:

(1) "Electronic storage" means the maintenance of local government record data in the form of digital electronic signals on a computer hard disk, magnetic tape, optical disk, or similar machine-readable medium.

(2) "Local government record data" means the information that by law, regulation, rule of court, ordinance, or administrative procedure in a local government comprises a local government record as defined by Section 201.003.

(3) "Source document" means the local government record from which local government record data is obtained for electronic storage. The term does not include backup copies of the data in any media generated from electronic storage.

Citation: TGC 205.002

✪ § 205.002. Authorization.

Any local government record data may be stored electronically in addition to or instead of source documents in paper or other media, subject to the requirements of this chapter and rules adopted under it.

Citation: TGC 205.003

✪ § 205.003. Standards and Procedures to be Adopted.

(a) The commission shall adopt rules establishing standards and procedures for the electronic storage of any local government record data of permanent value and may adopt rules establishing standards and procedures for the electronic storage of any local government record data whose retention period is at least 10 years on a records retention schedule issued by the commission. The rules must be approved as required by Section 441.165, Government Code.

(b) With regard to the types of local government record data covered by Subsection (a), the rules may require or prescribe:

(1) standards and procedures for the generation of backup or preservation copies of the local government record data on paper, microfilm, electronic, or other approved media;

(2) standards and procedures for the recopying or duplication of the magnetic tape, optical disk, or similar machine-readable medium on which the local government record data are stored;

(3) standards and procedures for the physical storage and maintenance of magnetic tapes, optical disks, or similar machine-readable media;

(4) standards and procedures for providing access by members of the public to electronically stored local government record data to which they are entitled under law; and

(5) other standards and procedures that the commission considers necessary to ensure the availability, readability, or integrity of the local government record data.

Citation: TGC 205.004

✪ § 205.004. Rules to be Updated.

The director and librarian shall monitor standards and procedures relating to electronic storage developed for use by federal agencies or adopted by national organizations that develop and set standards in the fields of records and information management in order to recommend to the commission any needed amendments to rules.

Citation: TGC 205.005

✪ § 205.005. Supreme Court Rules.

This chapter is not intended to conflict with Subchapter 1, Chapter 51, Government Code, relating to the electronic filing of certain documents in district and county courts. The commission shall incorporate any rules adopted under that subchapter into its own.

Citation: TGC 205.006

✪ § 205.006. Index.

An index to local government record data stored electronically must provide the same information that may be required by state law for an index to the source document, if applicable.

Citation: TGC 205.007

✪ § 205.007. Electronic Storage Authorization Requests.

(a) Before the electronic storage of any local government record data of permanent value or, if stipulated in commission rules, any local government record data whose retention period is at least 10 years on a records retention schedule issued by the commission, an electronic storage authorization request shall be submitted to the director and librarian for approval.

(b) Electronic storage authorization requests shall be submitted by the records management officer or under the officer's direction or, if a records management officer has not yet been designated under Section 203.025, by the custodian of the local government record data
to be stored electronically.

(c) If the director and librarian or the designee of the director and librarian approved the request, the local government data record may be stored electronically.

(d) If the director and librarian or the designee of the director and librarian disapprove the request, the reasons for the disapproval shall be stated in writing within a reasonable time to the records management officer or custodian. Electronic storage of the local government record data may not take place until an electronic storage authorization request receives the approval of the director and librarian or the designee of the director and librarian.

(e) The director and librarian or the designee of the director and librarian may disapprove an electronic storage authorization request only if the standards and procedures proposed for the electronic storage of the local government record data are violation of this chapter or rules adopted under it.

(f) The director and librarian shall determine the form and manner of submission authorization requests required by this chapter.

Citation: TGC 205.008

✪ § 205.008. Destruction of Source Documents.

(a) The source document, if any, for electronically stored local government record data covered by section 205.007(a) may be destroyed or returned to the person who filed it for record if the electronic storage authorization request is approved.

(b) The magnetic tape, optical disk, or similar medium containing the local government record data and the hardware and software necessary to provide access to it must be retained by the local government or be available to the local government until expiration of the retention period for all source documents, subject to the rules adopted in this chapter.

(c) The source document, if any, for electronically stored local government record data not covered by Section 205.007(a) may be destroyed before the expiration of the retention period for the source document in a records retention schedule issued by the commission if the magnetic tape, optical, disk, or similar medium and hardware and software necessary to provide access to local government record data on the media are retained for the retention period in the schedule. Conversely, the magnetic tape, optical disk, or similar medium may be erased, written over, or destroyed before the expiration of the retention period for a source document for local government record data not covered in Section 205.007(a), if the source document, if any, is retained until the expiration of the retention period or, if the source document has already been destroyed, paper or microfilm copies are generated from the magnetic tape, optical disk, or similar medium before destruction or erasure and retained until the expiration of the retention period for the source document.

Citation: TGC 205.009

✪ § 205.009. Denial of Access Prohibited.

A person under contract or agreement with a local government or elected county officer to create, file, or store local government record data electronically or to provide services, equipment, or the means for creation, filing, or storage, may not, under any circumstances, refuse to provide local government record data to the local government in a timely manner in a format accessible and usable by the local government.

Source: **Texas Revised Civil Statutes Annotated**

BUSINESS CORPORATION ACT

PART 2

Citation: **TRCSA 2.44**

✍ Article 2.44. Books and Records.

A. Each corporation shall keep books and records of account and shall keep minutes of the proceedings of its shareholders, its board of directors, and each committee of its board of directors. Each corporation shall keep at its registered office or principal place of business, or at the office of its transfer agent or registrar, a record of the original issuance of shares issued by the corporation and a record of each transfer of those shares that have been presented to the corporation for registration or transfer. Such records shall contain the names and addresses of all past and current shareholders of the corporation and the number and class or series of shares issued by the corporation held by each of them. Any books, records, minutes, and share transfer records may be in written form or in any other form capable of being converted into written form within a reasonable time. The principal place of business of a corporation, or the office of its transfer agent or registrar, may be located outside the State of Texas.

* * * * *

LOCAL GOVERNMENT

TITLE 6. RECORDS.

SUBTITLE B. COUNTY RECORDS.

CHAPTER 194. MICROFILMING COUNTY RECORDS.

Citation: **TRCSA 194.017**

✪ § 194.017. Disposal of Originals.

The commissioners court of a county may authorize by order the disposal of an original paper record from which a microfilm or an optical image record is made if the county clerk certifies to the court that:

(1) the original negative microfilm of the record fully meets the requirements of the American National Standards Institute for archival quality, density, resolution, and definition; or

(2) the optical image of the record meets the standards approved by the Texas State Library and Archives Commission.

Source: **Texas Rules Annotated—Rules of Evidence**

ARTICLE IX. AUTHENTICATION AND IDENTIFICATION.

☞ Rule 902. Self-Authentication.

Extrinsic evidence of authenticity as a condition precedent to admissibility is not required with respect to the following:

* * * * *

(10) Business records accompanied by affidavit.

a. Records or photocopies; admissibility; affidavit; filing. Any record or set of records or photographically reproduced copies of such records, which would be admissible under Rule 803(6) or (7) shall be admissible in evidence in any court in this state upon the affidavit of the person who would otherwise provide the prerequisites of Rule 803(6) or (7), that such records attached to such affidavit were in fact so kept as required by Rule 803(6) or (7), provide further, that such record or records along with such affidavit are filed with the clerk of the court for inclusion with the papers in the cause in which the record or records are sought to be used as evidence at least fourteen (14) days prior to the day upon which trial of said cause commences, and provided the other parties to said cause are given prompt notice by the party filing same of the filing of such record or records and affidavit, which notice shall identify the name and employer, if any, of the person making the affidavit and such records shall be made available to the counsel for other parties to the action or litigation for inspection and copying. The expense for copying shall be borne by the party, parties or persons who desire copies and not by the party or parties who file the records and serve notice of said filing, in compliance with this rule. Notice shall be deemed to have been promptly given if it is served in the manner contemplated by Rule 21a, Texas Rules of Civil Procedure, fourteen (14) days prior to commencement of trial in said cause.

b. Form of affidavit. A form for the affidavit of such person as shall make such affidavit as is permitted in paragraph (a) above shall be sufficient if it follows this form, though this form shall not be exclusive, and an affidavit which substantially complies with the provisions of this rule shall suffice, to-wit:

No. ________________
(Name of Plaintiff)
John Doe
IN THE ______________
(Name of Plaintiff)
v.
COURT IN AND FOR
Joe Roe
(Name of Defendant)
COUNTY, TEXAS
AFFIDAVIT

Before me, the undersigned authority, personally appeared, who, being by me duly sworn, deposed as follows:

My name is ____________, I am of sound mind, capable of making this affidavit, and personally acquainted with the facts herein stated:

I am the custodian of the records of ____________. Attached hereto are ___________ pages of records from ___________. These said ______________ pages of records are kept by ___________ in the regular course of business, and it was the regular course of business of ___________ for an employee or representative of ___________, with knowledge of the act, event, condition, opinion, or diagnosis, recorded to make the record or to transmit information thereof to be included in such record; and the record was made at or near the time or reasonably soon thereafter. The records attached hereto are the original or exact duplicates of the original.

Affiant

SWORN TO AND SUBSCRIBED before me on the ________ day of ____________, 19 ___________.

____
Notary Public in and for ______________ County, Texas.

ARTICLE X. CONTENTS OF WRITINGS, RECORDINGS, AND PHOTOGRAPHS.

☞ Rule 1001. Definitions

For purposes of this article the following definitions are applicable:

(1) *Writings and recordings.* — "Writings" and "recordings" consist of letters, words, or numbers, or their equivalent, set down by handwriting, typewriting, printing, photostating, photographing, magnetic impulse, mechanical or electronic recording, or other form of data compilation.

(2) *Photographs.* — "Photographs" include still photographs, X-ray films, video tapes, and motion pictures.

(3) *Original.* — An "original" of a writing or recording is the writing or recording itself or any counterpart intended to have the same effect by a person executing or issuing it. An "original" of a photograph includes the negative or any print therefrom. If data are stored in a computer or similar device, any printout or other output readable by sight, shown to reflect the data accurately, is an "original".

(4) *Duplicate.* — A "duplicate" is a counterpart produced by the same impression as the original, or from the same matrix, or by means of photography, including enlargements and miniatures, or by mechanical or electronic re-recording, or by chemical reproduction, or by other equivalent techniques which accurately reproduces the original.

☞ Rule 1003. Admissibility of Duplicates.

A duplicate is admissible to the same extent as an original unless (1) a genuine question is raised as to the authenticity of the original or (2) in the circumstances it would be unfair to admit the duplicate in lieu of the original.

[See Appendix A. Uniform Rules of Evidence for additional provisions.]

Source: **Texas Administrative Code**
Agency: **Comptroller of Public Accounts**

LIMITED SALES AND USE TAX RULE.

✍ Rule 3.281. Records required and information required.

(a) *Records required.*

(1) Every person engaged in:

(A) Making sales, leases or rentals of tangible personal property;

(B) Performing taxable labor, such as fabricating, processing, and producing tangible personal property; or

(C) Performing taxable services, such as amusement services, cable television services, personal services, motor vehicle parking and storage services, and the repair, remodeling, maintenance, and restoration of certain tangible personal property; or

(D) Purchasing taxable items must keep records in such form as may readily be examined by the Comptroller or his authorized agents or employees.

(2) The records must reflect the total gross receipts from sales, rentals, leases, taxable services, and taxable labor. Purchasers' records must reflect the total purchases of taxable items. Additional records must be kept to substantiate any claimed deductions or exclusions authorized by law. When records regarding the amount and applicability of any deductions or exclusions from the measure of the tax, or evidence of compliance with optional reporting methods, are insufficient, the Comptroller may estimate deductions or exclusions based on any records available or disallow all deductions and exclusions.

(b) *Failure to keep accurate records.* If any person fails to keep accurate records of gross receipts and gross purchases the Comptroller will estimate the tax liability based on any information available, including, but not limited to, records of suppliers. In addition, the Comptroller may suspend the permit of the taxpayer, file misdemeanor charges, or take other action as authorized by statute to enforce compliance. Records may be written, kept on microfilm, or stored on data processing equipment.

(c) *Information required.*

(1) The Comptroller may require any person subject to the Limited Sales and Use Tax Act to furnish information necessary to:

(A) Identify any person applying for a permit or any person required to file a return;

(B) Determine the amount of bond required to commence or continue business;

(C) Determine possible successor liability; and

(D) Determine the amount of tax the person is required to remit.

(2) The information required may include, but is not limited to the following:

(A) Name of the actual owner of the business.

(B) Name of each partner in a partnership.

(C) Names of officers and directors of corporations and other organizations.

(D) All trade names under which the owner operates.

(E) Mailing address and actual locations of all business outlets.

(F) License numbers, title numbers, and other identification of business vehicles.

(G) Identification numbers assigned by other governmental agencies, including social security numbers, federal employers identification numbers, and drivers license numbers.

(H) Names of suppliers, banks, and other persons with whom the taxpayer transacts business.

(I) Names and last known addresses of former owners of the business.

ADMINISTRATIVE RULES OF TEXAS STATE LIBRARY AND ARCHIVES COMMISSION

STANDARDS AND PROCEDURES FOR ELECTRONIC RECORDS OF STATE AGENCIES

TITLE 13, CHAPTER 6

✪ § 6.91. Definitions.

The following words and terms, when used in this chapter, shall have the following meanings, unless the contest clearly indicates otherwise. For local governments, terms not defined in these rules shall have the meanings defined in the Local Government Code, Title 6, Subtitle C, Chapter 201. For state agencies, terms not defined in these rules shall have the meanings defined in the Government Code, § § 441.031-441.039 and § § 441.051-441.062.

AIIM - The Association for Information and Image Management.

ANSI - The American National Standards Institute.

Archival record - A record of a state agency scheduled to be reviewed by or that has been approved by an archives for permanent preservation.

Database - (A) collection of digitally stored data records; (B) collection of data elements within records within files that have relationships with other records within other files.

Database Management System (DBMS) - Set of programs designed to organize, store, and retrieve machine-readable information from a computer-maintained database or data bank.

Data file - Related numeric, textual, or graphic information that is organized in a strictly prescribed form and format.

Electronic media - All media capable of being read by a computer including computer hard disks, magnetic tapes, optical disks, or similar machine-readable media.

Electronic record - Any information that is recorded in a form for computer processing and that satisfies the definition of a state record in the Government Code, — 441.031(5), or the definition of local government record data in the Local Government Code, § 205.001.

Electronic records system - Any information system that produces manipulates, and stores state or local government records by using a computer.

IEC - International Electrotechnical Commission.

ISO - International Organization for Standardization.

Long-term record - A record for which the retention periods on a records retention schedule is 100 years or more but less than permanent.

Medium-term record - A record for which the retention period on a records retention schedule is 10 years or more but less than 100 years.

Records administrators - The person appointed by the head of each agency to act as the agency's representative in all issues of records management policy, responsibility, and statutory compliance.

Records custodian - The appointed or elected pubic officer who by the state constitution, state law, ordinance, or administrative policy is in charge of an office that creates or receives local government records.

Records management officer - Each elected county officer or the person designated by the governing body of each local government pursuant to the Local Government Code, § 203.025.

Short-term record - A record for which the retention period on a records retention schedule is less than 10 years.

Permanent record - A record for which the retention period on a records retention schedule is permanent.

Text documents - Narrative or tabular documents, such as letters, memorandums, and reports, in loosely prescribed form and format.

✪ § 6.92. General.

(a) These rules establish the minimum requirements for the maintenance, use, retention, and storage of all medium-term, long-term, and permanent electronic records of state agencies and local governments, and archival electronic records of state agencies. These rules do not apply to short-term electronic records, but the short-term electronic records of local government are subject to the applicable provisions of the Local Government Code, Chapter 205.

(b) Unless otherwise noted, these requirements apply to all electronic records storage systems, whether on microcomputers, minicomputers, or main-frame computers, regardless of storage media.

(c) An electronic storage authorization request certifying that these rules will be followed must be submitted to and approved by the director and librarian for all existing electronic storage of medium-term, long-term, and permanent state and local government records and state archival records, and before any new electronic storage of medium-term, long-term, and permanent state or local government records and state archival records. The authorization request must be submitted in a form and manner to be determined by the director and librarian and must be signed by the agency head or designated records administrator (for state agencies), or the records management officer (for local governments).

(d) The agency head or designated records administrator (for state agencies), and the governing body or records management officer in cooperation with records custodians (for local governments) must:

(1) administer a program for the management of records created, received, and maintained, used, or stored on electronic media,

(2) integrate the management of electronic records with other records and information resources management programs of the agency;

(3) incorporate electronic records management objectives, responsibilities, and authorities in pertinent agency directives;

(4) establish procedures for addressing records management requirements, including recordkeeping requirements and disposition;

(5) ensure that training is provided for users of electronic records systems in the operation, care, and handling of the equipment, software, and media used in the system;

(6) ensure the development and maintenance of up-to-date documentation abut all electronic records systems that is adequate to specify all technical characteristics necessary for reading or processing the records and the timely, authorized disposition of records; and

(7) specify the location and media on which electronic records are maintained to meet retention requirements and maintain inventories of electronic records systems to facilitate disposition.

(e) With the exception of subsections (c) and (f) of this section, which are effective immediately, state agencies and local government must be in compliance with the Standards and Procedures for Electronic Records on or before January 2, 1995.

(f) Any electronic recordkeeping system not meeting the provisions of these rules may be utilized for medium-term, long-term, or permanent state or local government records and state archival records provided the source document, if any, or a paper copy is maintained, or the record is microfilmed in accordance with the specifications in *American National Standards for Imaging Media (Film) — Silver-Gelatin Type — Specifications for Stability* (ANSI IT9.1-1989 or latest revision) for state records or in accordance with the provisions of Local Government Code, Chapter 204, and the rules adopted under it for local government records.

✪ § 6.93. Creation and Use of Data Files.

(a) Disposition instruction for the data must be incorporated into electronic records systems that produce, use, and store data files.

(b) State agencies and local governments must maintain up-to-date technical documentation for each electronic records system that produces, uses, and stores data files. Minimum documentation required is:

(1) a narrative description of the description;

(2) the physical and technical characteristics of the records, including a record layout that describes each field including its

name, size, starting or relative position, and a description of the form of the data (such as alphabetic, zoned decimal, packed decimal, (or numeric), or a data dictionary, or the equivalent information associated with a database management system including a description of the relationship between data elements and databases; and

(3) any other technical information needed to read or process the records.

✪ § 6.94. Creation and Use of Text Documents.

(a) Electronic records systems that maintain the official file copy of text documents or data used to generate the official file copy of text documents on electronic media must meet the following minimum requirements:

(1) provide a method for all authorized users of the system to retrieve desired documents, such as an indexing or text search system;

(2) provide security to ensure integrity of the documents;

(3) provide a standard interchange format when determined to be necessary by the agency or local government to permit the exchange of documents on electronic media among the components of the agency or local government using different software/operating systems; and

(4) provide for the disposition of the documents including, when necessary, the requirements for transferring archival records to the State Archives as detailed in § 6.97 of this title (relating to Retention of Electronic Records).

(b) A document created on an electronic records system must be identified sufficiently to enable authorized personnel to retrieve, protect, and carry out the disposition of documents in the system. Agencies must ensure that records maintained in such systems can be correlated with related records on paper, microform, or other media.

✪ § 6.95. Security of Electronic Records.

(a) State agencies and local governments must implement and maintain an electronic records security program for office and storage areas that:

(1) ensures that only authorized personnel have access to electronic records;

(2) provides for backup and recovery of records to protect against information loss;

(3) ensures that personnel are trained to safeguard confidential electronic records;

(4) minimizes the risk of unauthorized alteration or erasure of electronic records; and

(5) documents that similar kinds of records generated and stored electronically are created by the same processes each time and have a standardized retrieval approach.

(b) A duplicate copy of essential records and any software or documentation required to retrieve and read the records must be maintained in a storage area located in a separate building from the building where the records that have been copied are maintained.

(c) For all permanent records stored on rewritable electronic media, the system must ensure that read/write privileges are controlled and that an audit trail of rewrites is maintained.

✪ § 6.96. Maintenance of Electronic Records Storage Media.

(a) State agencies and local governments must ensure that the accuracy, completeness, and accessibility of information are not lost prior to its authorized destruction date because of changing technology or media deterioration, by converting electronic storage media and taking other action as required to provide compatibility with current hardware and software. The migration strategy for upgrading equipment as technology evolves must be documented and include:

(1) periodically recopying to the same electronic media as required, and/or transferring of data from an obsolete technology to a supportable technology; and

(2) providing backward system compatibility to the data in the old system, and/or converting data to media that the systems upgrade and/or replacement can support.

(b) Paragraphs (1)-(3) of this section outline the maintenance of backup electronic media stored offsite.

(1) Magnetic computer tapes must be tested and verified no more than 6 months prior to using them to store electronic records. Pretesting of tapes is not required if an automated system is used that monitors read/write errors and there is a procedure in place for correcting errors.

(2) The storage areas for electronic media must be maintained within the following temperatures and relative humidities:

(A) for magnetic media-65 degrees Fahrenheit to 75 degrees Fahrenheit, and 30% to 50% relative humidity;

(B) for optical disks-storage environmental conditions as specified in *Information technology — 130 mm optical disk cartridge, write once, for information interchange* (ISO/IEC 9171-1, 1990 or latest revision).

(3) A random sample of all magnetic computer tapes must be read annually to identify any loss of data and to discover and correct causes of data loss. At least a 10% sample or a sample size of 50 magnetic tapes, whichever is less, must be read. Tapes with recoverable errors must be replaced and, when possible, lost data must be restored. All other tapes which might have been affected by the same cause (i.e. poor quality tape, high usage, poor environment, improper handling) must be read and corrected.

(c) State agencies and local governments must recopy data maintained on electronic media according to the following schedule.

(1) Data maintained on magnetic tape must be recopied into new or used tape a minimum of once every three years.

(2) An alternative option for recopying magnetic tape is for the data to be recopied onto new tape a minimum of once every ten years, provided the tape is rewound under controlled tension every three and one-half years. The requirement for rewinding does not apply to 3480-type tape cartridges.

(3) Data maintained on optical disks must be recopied a minimum of once every 10 years.

(d) Floppy disks (diskettes) or any type of flexible disk system may not be used for the exclusive storage of medium-term, long-term, or permanent records and state archival records.

(e) External labels, or an eye-readable index relating to unique identifiers, for electronic media used to process or store electronic records must include the following information:

(1) name or other identifier of the organizational unit responsible for the records;

(2) descriptive title of the contents;

(3) dates of creation and authorized disposition data;

(4) security classification;

(5) identification of the software (to include specific application if appropriate) and hardware used; and

(6) system title, including the version number of the application.

(f) Additionally, the following information must be maintained for electronic media used to store permanent electronic records:

(1) file title(s);

(2) dates of coverage;

(3) the recording density;
(4) type of internal labels;
(5) volume serial number, if applicable;
(6) the number of tracks;
(7) character code/software dependency;
(8) information about block size;
(9) sequence number, if the file is part of a multi-media set; and
(10) relative starting position of data, if applicable.

(g) The following standards must be met for electronic records stored as digital images on optical media.

(1) A non-proprietary image file header label must be used, or the system developer must provide a bridge to a non-proprietary image file header label, or the system developer must supply a detailed definition of image file header label structure.

(2) The system hardware and/or software must provide a quality assurance capability that verifies information that is written to the optical media.

(3) Periodic maintenance of optical data storage systems is required, including an annual recalibration of the optical drives.

(4) Scanner quality must be evaluated based on the standard procedures in *American National Standard for Information and Image Management — Recommended Practice for Quality Control of Image Scanners* (ANSI/AIIM MS44-1988 or latest revision).

(5) A visual quality control evaluation must be performed for each scanned image and related index data.

(6) A scanning density with a minimum of 200 dots per inch is required for recording documents that contain no type font smaller than six point.

(7) A scanning density with a minimum of 300 dots per inch is required for engineering drawings, maps, and other documents with background detail.

(8) The selected scanning density must be validated with tests on actual documents.

(9) The use of the Consultative Committee on International Telegraphy and Telephony (CCITT) Group 3 or Group 4 compression techniques is required for document images without continuous tonal qualities. If use of a proprietary compression technique is unavoidable, the vendor must provide a gateway to either Group 3 or Group 4 compression techniques.

(10) Optical drive systems must not be operated in environments with high levels of airborne particulates.

(11) All aspects of the design and use of the imaging system must be documented, including administrative procedures for digital imaging, retrieval, and storage, technical system specifications; problems encountered; and measures taken to address them, including hardware and software modifications.

(h) Smoking, drinking, and eating must be prohibited in electronic media storage areas.

✪ § 6.97. Retention of Electronic Records.

(a) State agencies and local governments must establish policies and procedures to ensure that electronic records and any software, hardware, and/or documentation, including maintenance documentation, required to retrieve and read the electronic records are retained as long as the approved retention period for the electronic records.

(b) The retention procedures must include provisions for:

(1) scheduling the disposition of all electronic records, according to statutory requirements, as well as related software, documentation, and indexes; and

(2) establishing procedures for regular recopying, reformatting, and other necessary maintenance to ensure the retention and usability of electronic records until the expiration of their retention periods.

(c) State records having archival value and scheduled to be preserved at the State Archives must be transferred to the State Archives as the source document, or printed out on alkaline paper for computer generated information, or on microforms that meet the specifications in *American National Standard for Imaging Media (Film) — Silver-Gelatin Type — Specifications for Stability* (ANSI IT9.1-1989 or latest revision).

✪ § Destruction of Electronic Records.

(a) Electronic records may be destroyed only in accordance with a records schedule approved by the director and librarian or designee, in lieu of an approved records schedule, an approved records disposition authorization request.

(b) Each state agency and local government must ensure that:

(1) electronic records scheduled for destruction are disposed of in a manner that ensures protection of any confidential information; and

(2) magnetic storage media previously used for electronic records containing confidential information are not reused if the previously recorded information can be compromised by reuse in any way.

(c) The court ordered expungement of information recorded on an optical Write-Once-Read-Many (WORM) system must be implemented according to the recommendations provided in *Technical Report for Information and Image Management — The Expungement of Information Recorded on Optical Write-Once-Read-Many (WORM Systems* (AIIM TR28-1991 or latest revision).

✪ § 6.99. Public Access to Electronic Records.

An electronic recordkeeping system must not provide an impediment to access to public records.

TITLE 13, CHAPTER 7.

✪ § 7.21. Definitions.

The following words and terms, when used in this chapter, shall have the following meanings, unless the context clearly indicates otherwise. Terms not defined in these rules shall have the meanings defined in the Local Government Code, Title 6, Chapter 201, or the standards of the Association for Information and Image Management according to *Technical Report for Glossary of Imaging Technology* (TR2-1002 or latest revision)

AIIM - The Association for Information and Image Management.

ANSI - The American National Standards Institute.

Archival record - A record having a permanent retention period.

Aperture card - A card with a rectangular opening(s) into which 16mm microfilm frames can be inserted, mounted, or pre-mounted.

Archival storage conditions - Environmental conditions suitable for preserving photographic film that is to be retained permanently.

Batch - A quantity of chemicals or film which has been prepared at one time, and which has been identified through labeling or through other means by the manufacturer as a batch or lot.

Cad (computer assisted design) - A method of creating microimages by computer-driven laser.

Convenience film - Microfilm copies of records created only for convenience of use and considered nonrecords under the Local Government Code, § 201.003(8)(A).

Custodian - The appointed or elected public officer who by the state constitution, state law, ordinance, or administrative policy is in charged of an office that creates or receives local government records.

Diazo - Coated film containing sensitized layers composed of diazonium salts that react with couplers to form azo dye images.

Dmax - Measurement of maximum obtainable density taken from a completely exposed area of conventionally processed silver-gelatin film (i.e. leader or trailer).

Essential record - Any local government record necessary to the resumption or continuation of government operations in an emergency or disaster, to the re-creation of the legal and financial status of the government, or to the protection and fulfillment of obligations to the people of the state.

Film - Microfilm.

First-generation film - Film produced directly from a subject.

Legible - The quality of a letter or numeral which enables the observer to identify it positively and quickly to the exclusion of all other letters and numerals.

Local government record - Any document, paper, letter, book, map, photograph, sound or video recording, microfilm, magnetic tape, electronic medium, or other information recording medium, regardless of physical form or characteristic and regardless of whether public access to it is open or restricted under the laws of the state, created or received by a local government of any of its officers or employees pursuant to law, including an ordinance, or in the transaction of public business, except for materials excluded under the Local Government Code, Chapter 201.

Long-term film - Film suitable for the preservation of records for a minimum of 100 years when stored under proper conditions, providing the original film was processed correctly.

Long-term record - A record for which the retention period on a records retention schedule is 100 years but less than permanent.

Master negative - The copy of microfilm stored offsite for security and used only for generating use copies.

Medium-term film - Film suitable for the preservation of records for 10 years or more but less than 100 years when stored under proper conditions, providing the original film was processed correctly.

Medium-term record - A record for which the retention period on a records retention schedule is 10 years or more but less than 100 years.

Medium-term storage conditions - Storage conditions meeting ANSI/AIIM standards to ensure a life of 100 years for medium-term film.

Microfilm - Roll microfilm, microfiche, computer output microfilm (COM), and all other formats produced by any method of microphotography or other means of miniaturization on film.

Microfilming - The methods, procedures, and processes used to produce microfilm.

Permanent film - Film that is suitable for the preservation of records having permanent value when the film is properly processed and stored under archival storage conditions, provided that the original images are of suitable quality.

Permanent record - A record for which the retention period on a records retention schedule is permanent.

Readable - The quality of a group of letters or numerals which makes them recognizable as words or whole numbers.

Records management officer - The person identified under the Local Government Code, § 203.001 or designated under the Local Government Code, § 203.025 as the records management officer.

Records retention schedule - A document issued by the Texas State Library and Archives Commission under authority of the Government Code, § 441.158, establishing mandatory retention periods for local government records.

Records series - File unit(s) or document(s) arranged in accordance with a filing system or maintained as a unit because they relate to a particular subject or function, result from the same activity, have a particular form, or because of some other relationship arising out of their creation, receipt, or use.

Retention period - The minimum time that must pass after the creation, recording, receipt of a record, or the fulfillment of certain actions associated with a record before it is eligible for destruction.

Second-generation microfilm - A microfilm copy made from the master negative.

Short-term film - Film suitable for the preservation of records for less than 10 years when stored under proper conditions, providing the original film was processed correctly.

Short-term record - A record for which the retention period on a records retention schedule is less than 10 years.

Step-and-repeat system - A method of microfilming by which images are directly placed on an area of film according to a predetermined format, usually in orderly rows and columns.

Vesicular - Film in which the light-sensitive component is suspended in a plastic layer in which optical vesicles are created on exposure to form the image.

✪ § 7.22. General.

(a) Where these rules to not specify a standard or procedure, ANSI/AIIM standards are the minimum requirements for all microfilming of local government records.

(b) The originals of records that have been microfilmed may not be destroyed prior to the expiration of their retention periods unless the microfilm has met minimum standards of the tests required under these rules.

(c) These rules apply to the microfilming of any local government record, including court case papers, which is to be maintained solely in microfilm format and to all microfilm which is crated or maintained as a backup or security copy of short-term, medium-term, long-term, or permanent records. These rules do not apply to convenience filming.

(d) Custodians must maintain, or require to be maintained, documentation identifying titles of records filmed, quality control tests conducted, the results of quality controls tests, dates records filmed, disposition of records after filming, dates film processed, disposition of film, reduction ration used, records series contained on each microfilm, and equipment on which each microfilm was filmed and processed. The documentation must be retained until final disposition of all microfilm documented in the log or equivalent.

(e) Chemicals, film, and processor used in processing must be compatible.

(f) The records custodian, records management officer, or other authorized representative of the governing body of a local government may make unannounced inspections of the microfilm facilities in which the master microfilm of the local government is filmed, processed, and/or stored.

(g) Master microfilm produced for a local government shall be the property of the local government and the local government shall have the same responsibilities for ensuring its management and preservation as it would have for the records under the Local Government Code, Title 6, Subtitle C, if they were not microfilmed. If the master microfilm is to be stored by a service provider, the local government may demand and receive delivery of the master microfilm upon five working days' notice.

(h) If microfilmed records contain information to which access by the public is restricted or confidential, such information must be expunged from any microfilm copies or hard copies made available to the public.

✪ § 7.23. Standards for Film Quality, Resolution, Density, Definition, and Chemical Stability.

(a) Master microfilm must meet *American National Standard for Imaging Media (Film) — Silver-Gelatin Type — Specifications for Stability* (ANSI IT9.1-1989 or latest revision), except where these standards specifically state otherwise. Polyester film must be used for permanent and long-term film.

(b) Duplicate film must be diazo film conforming to *American National Standard for Imaging Media (Film) — Ammonia-Processed Diazo Films — Specifications for Stability* (ANSI IT9.5-1988 or latest revision), vesicular film conforming to *American National Standards for Photography (film) — Processed Vesicular Film — Specifications for Stability* (ANSI PH1.67-1985 or latest revision), or silver film conforming to *American National Standard for Imaging Media (Film) — Silver-Gelatin Type — Specifications for Stability* (ANSI IT9.1-1989 or latest revision). Duplicate film must meet *Standard for Information and Image Management — Recommended Practice for Operational Procedures/Inspection and Quality Control of Duplicate Microforms of Documents and From COM* (ANSI/AIIM MS43-1988 with 1991 supplement or latest revision).

(c) Any film type may be used for short-term film, provided a duplicate is made immediately after filming that will last for the designated retention period. The original and duplicate film must be maintained for the retention of the film.

(d) All microfilm must comply with *American National Standard for Photography (Film) — Micrographic Sheets and Roll Films — Dimensions* (ANSI PH1.51-1083 or latest revision).

(e) The following ANSI standards must be complied with in the processing and filming of records: *Standards for Information and Image Management-Specifications for 16 mm and 35 mm Roll Microfilm* (ANSI/AIIM MS14-1988 or latest revision), *American National Standard for Information and Image Management-Microfiche* (ANSI/AIIM MS5-1991 or latest revision), *American National Standards for Information on Microfiche Headings* (ANSI Z39.32-1981 or latest revision), *Standard for Information and Image Management-Method for Measuring Thickness of Buildup Area on Unitized Microfilm Carriers (Aperture, Camera, Copy, and Image Cards)* (ANSI/AIIM MS9-1987 or latest revision), and *Standard for Information and Image Management-Method for Determining Adhesion of Protection Sheet to Aperture Adhesive of Unitized Microfilm Carrier (Aperture Card)* (ANSI/AIIM MS10-1987 or latest revision).

(f) Images of documents must be uniformly placed on the film and must be free of any obstructions, shadows, glare, fog, overlap of records, scratches, overexposure, underexposure, water spots, or foreign objects in filming area that would interfere with the documents being read.

(g) All silver-gelatin film tested must have a residual thiosulphate content greater than zero but not exceeding 0.014 gram per meter squared.

(h) The quality-index graph in *American National Standards Institute Practice for Operational Procedures/Inspection and Quality Control of First Generation, Silver-Gelatin Microfilm of Documents* (ANSI/AIIM MS23-1991 or latest revision) must be followed as the minimum acceptable range of performance readings for all essential and permanent film and 10% of the total volume of short-term, medium-term, and long-term film. All microfilm of essential and permanent records must meet a minimum quality index level of 5.0. Microfilm of short-term, medium-term, and long-term records must meet a minimum quality index level of 3.6.

(i) Densitometer used must be calibrated daily, when in use.

✪ § 7.24. Tests and Other Methods of Inspection and Verification.

(a) General.

(1) With the exception of retakes, if a defect is found on any microfilm, the microfilm immediately preceding and following the sample of microfilm on which the defect was found must be inspected. If a defect is found on those microfilms, the uninspected microfilm preceding and/or following those microfilms must be inspected by image until all defective film has been identified.

(2) Water used in microfilm processing must meet the requirements in *American National Standards Institute Practice for Operational Procedures/Inspection and Quality Control of First Generation, Silver-Gelatin Microfilm of Documents* (ANSI/AIIM MS23-1991 or latest revision).

(b) The following tests must be utilized in the production of all film:

(1) Methylene blue test.

(A) Methylene blue test for conventionally processed silver-gelatin film as specified in *American National Standard for Photography (chemicals)* — Residual Thiosulfate and Other Chemicals in Films, Plates, and Papers — Determination and

Measurement (ANSI/ASC PH4.8-1985 or latest revision) must be followed.

(B) A test must be performed at least once each week during which processing is done on a test strip of approximately six inches from a master microfilm or on a process control strip. If processing is performed by a service bureau a test performed for one local government agency may satisfy this requirement for more than one local government.

(C) A test must also be performed whenever a batch of fixer or developer is changed, or when changes in processing such as replacement or addition of filter, water softener, or replenishing system are made, or when water is changed.

(D) The test results must be obtained on a scheduled basis within 10 days of processing. IF film fails to meet the standards established by these rules, it must be rewashed and retested within the 14 days of initial processing.

(E) Once a year, two test strips must be taken from the same microfilm; one must be sent to an independent testing laboratory and the other to the laboratory which performs the weekly test, for verification of test results.

(F) If either test result is greater than 0.014 gram per meter squared, the records custodian must identify and remedy the cause of the deviation from the required standard.

(2) Density test.

(A) The density test must be performed on all master microfilm.

(B) Testing procedures as specified in *American National Standards Institute Practice for Operational Procedures/Inspection and Quality Control of First Generation, Silver-Gelatin Microfilm of Documents* (ANSI/AIIM MS23-1991 or latest revision) must be performed.

(C) Background density must be in accordance with *American National Standards Institute Practice for Operational Procedures/Inspection and Quality Control of First Generation, Silver-Gelatin Microfilm of Documents* (ANSI/AIIM MS32-1991 or latest revision).

(3) Resolution test.

(A) The resolution test must be performed on all master microfilm.

(B) The resolution test must be conducted in accordance with *American National Standards Institute Practice for Operational Procedure/Inspection and Quality Control of First Generation, Silver-Gelatin Microfilm of Documents* (ANSI/AIIM MS23-1991 or latest revision).

(C) The resolution target must meet the *American National Standard Microcopying — ISO Test Chart No. 2 — Description and Use in Photographic Documentary Reproduction* (ANSI/AIIM MS51-1991 or latest revision) and/or *American National Standard Test Chart for Rotary Microfilm Cameras* (ANSI/AIIM MS17-1983 or latest revision)) and/or *Standard for Information and Image Management — Recommended Practice for Identification of Microforms* (ANSI/AIIM MS19-1987 or latest revision). Photocopies may not be used.

(4) Visual inspection.

(A) Inspection must be completed within two weeks of completion of the methylene blue test.

(B) All film of records having medium-term, long-term, or permanent retention periods, or which are designated as essential records must be inspected image by image, by the records custodian or records management officer, or local government office, or independent testing facility under contract with the local government or custodian.

(C) Short-term film of non-essential records must be inspected at least every three meters (10 feet) of each third roll or every third fiche.

(c) If film processing is done by a service bureau, the local government must obtain a certified statement of the results of density, resolution, methylene blue, and visual inspection tests from the service bureau attesting to the accurate reproduction of records filmed.

(d) If microfilm is not to be stored by the service bureau which processed the film, the local government must obtain test results at the same time it obtains the microfilm. If the microfilm is stored by the service bureau which processed the film, the local government must receive the test results within ten days of completion of the test(s). The custodian, records management officer, local government office, or independent testing facility under contract with the local government or custodian, must inspect the film to verify the results reported by the processor.

(e) An inspection of stored master microfilm must be conducted in accordance with *American National Standard for Photography (Film) — Processed Safety Film — Storage* (ANSI IT9.11-1991 or latest revision).

(1) A minimum of 1.0% of the total volume of microfilm of each local government office comprising a cross section of all microfilm (roll, jacket, microfiche, aperture card, COM, etc.) must be inspected for deterioration such as peeling emulsion, brittleness, film curl, discoloration, molding, and blemishes on the film.

(2) Of the microfilm selected, 70% shall never before have been inspected, 20% shall have been inspected during the immediately previous inspection, and 10% shall be samples of the oldest and newest film.

(3) An inspection of stored master microfilm must be conducted every two years, except if the microfilm has been stored under temperature and/or humidity conditions other than those required under these rules, it must be inspected yearly.

(4) Cans, boxes, and reels used to store the film must be inspected for evidence of rust, corrosion, and other deterioration.

(5) Master microfilm must not be inspected on a reader printer. Master microfilm must be inspected on a light box with rewinds or comparable equipment which will not scratch the film.

(6) The following information must be recorded for each inspection.

(A) the quantity and identification of microfilm inspected;

(B) the condition of the microfilm, including description of any deterioration such as peeling emulsion, brittleness, film curl, discoloration, molding, and blemishes on the film;

(C) the corrective action required (if necessary);

(D) the date(s) of inspection and signed certification of inspector;

(E) the date corrective action was completed.

(7) The inspection log must be maintained by year and within each year numerically according to microfilm identifier or number.

(8) If deterioration is found, a more extensive inspection must be conducted to locate all deteriorating film.

(9) Any deteriorating film must immediately be removed from the storage area and a new master microfilm created.

✪ § 7.25. Certification and Documentation.

(a) After the microfilm has been prepared, processed, and inspected the records custodian must complete and maintain a certificate of authenticity stating: "I (name of records custodian) acting for the (name of agency), a local government in the state of Texas, do hereby declare that I am the (RM) or custodian) of the (name of department) records. The official records appearing on (identifier) microfilm are accurate reproductions of the records series entitled (record series title). These records were created in the regular course of business and microfilmed as part of a planned records management program adopted by (name of governing body), under provisions of the Local Government Code, § 203.005 or § 203.026."

(b) The certificate of authenticity must contain the printed or typed name of government, name of office, the name and title of the records custodian, RMO, or deputy, and the date and place certified, and must be signed by the records custodian, RMO, or, if the inspector is a deputy of the custodian, it may be signed by the deputy.

(c) A procedure and operational manual must be prepared for the microfilm program and periodically updated so as to reflect current practice and at a minimum must include a description of:

(1) purpose of microfilm program;
(2) documentation maintained;
(3) prepping;
(4) camera/filming;
(5) processing;
(6) quality controls;
(7) duplication;
(8) storage; and
(9) inspection of stored microfilm.

(d) Training manuals must be created and maintained for all staff in the microfilm program and periodically updated so as to reflect current practice. Proof of appropriate training and satisfactory completion of required training must be documented for all staff.

(e) The microfilm program must be reviewed yearly for compliance with the Local Government Code, Chapter 204 and the rules adopted under it.

✪ § 7.26. Use of Editorial and Technical Targets.

(a) A title page target must identify the local government and subordinate organizational unit(s), the records which are included on the microfilm, title of the records (with identification of contents of the obvious from series titles), restriction or classification (if necessary), bibliography information (if any), unique identifier, and date(s) of records being filmed.

(b) Restriction or classification targets, if used, must identify the office or agency authorizing the classification or restriction, the statutory or administrative authorization for the restriction or classification, the beginning record and ending record of the record series of which the classified or restricted items are a part, the date of filming, and the nature of the restriction or classification.

(c) A declaration of camera operator must state where, when, and by whom records were filmed, name and title of camera operator, the camera and the reduction ration used.

(d) Whenever possible, targets must all face the same direction as the records being microfilmed. Whenever possible the letters on the target title must be readable to the naked eye without magnification and the image on the film must be at least 2 millimeters (0.08 inch) high.

(e) If the condition of the original record is of poor quality and it is anticipated the images will not be legible and readable when displayed on a microfilm reader or when reproduced in paper copy, a target or stamp stating the reason for the poor image quality must be placed before or directly on the image(s).

✪ § 7.27. Image Sequence.

(a) The image sequence on roll microfilm must be:

(1) leader (minimum of 700 millimeters (28 inches) of blank film);
(2) retakes according to required sequence of subsection (d) of this section (if any);
(3) density target and resolution target, in any order or combination;
(4) title page;
(5) records being microfilmed;
(6) certificate of authenticity (if used on microfilm);
(7) density target and resolution target, in any order or combination;
(8) retakes according to required sequence of subsection (d) of this section (if any);
(9) trailer (minimum of 700 millimeters (28 inches) of blank film).

(b) For non-essential and short-term microfilm, if the image sequence required in subsection (a) of this section is not used the following must be used:

(1) density and resolution target, in any order or combination, must be on the microfilm or a test strip of the microfilm;
(2) title page target;
(3) if the film is updated, the title page target must be prior to the first image of the records being microfilmed.

(c) All microfilm produced for a local government must bear a unique number within the generating department.

(d) The filming sequence for retakes on all microfilm must be:

(1) title target identifying the retake records;
(2) the retake records;
(3) certificate of authenticity (if used on all microfilm.

✪ § 7.28. Master Microfilms.

(a) Master microfilm, containing essential, short-term, medium-term, long-term, or permanent records, must be stored in a separate building from that in which duplicate copies, if any, or the original records are housed, and under conditions that meet the requirements of this section.

(b) For master microfilm containing short-term records and not meeting the specifications in *American National Standard for Imaging Media (Film) — Silver-Gelatin Type — Specifications for Stability* (ANSI IT9.1-1989 or latest version) and silver film that is not included in the testing program required by § 7.24(b)(1) of this title (relating to Tests and Other Methods of Inspection and Verification) a duplicate security copy must be made in accordance with *Standard for Information and Image Management — Recommended Practice for Operational Procedures/Inspection and Quality Control of Duplicate Microforms of Documents and From COM* (ANSI/AIIM MS43-1988 with 1991 supplement or latest revision).

(1) The master microfilm and security copy must not be used for route reference.
(2) If film is needed for reference, a use copy must be made from the master microfilm or security copy.
(3) Cameras and ancillary equipment must be calibrated, tested, or otherwise inspected and adjusted at least twice annually or more often if required to comply with manufacturer's specifications or recommended operating and maintenance procedures.
(4) If short-term film is updated or changed in any way, a new security copy must be made. The destruction of any security copy previously produced must comply with the statutes and rules which govern destruction of documents.

(c) Clean, lint-free cotton or nylon gloves must be used to handle silver-gelatin film.

(d) Storage requirements.

(1) Storage containers and reels must be made from a noncombustible and noncorrosive material such as anodized aluminum or plastic and must conform to *American National Standard for Photography (film) — 16-mm 100-foot, 16-mm*

200-foot, 35-mm 100-foot, and 70-mm 100-foot Spools for Recording Instruments, Microfilms, and Still-Picture Cameras — Dimensions (ANSI PH1.33-1990 or latest revision) and *American National Standard for Imaging Media — Photographic Processed Films, Plates, and Papers — Filing Enclosures and Storage Containers* (ANSI IT9.2-1991 or latest revision).

(2) Containers must be labeled to indicate that they contain master negatives (specifying whether first-generation, second-generation, etc.) and the identifying information or number, records series, and office of origin.

(3) Containers must be fully enclosed and composed of inert material such as metal, plastic, or acid-free paper.

(4) No printed material, except information on the label, may be inside a microfilm storage container.

(5) Inks used on the outside of the containers and on the label must not bleed, spread, or transfer, nor be a source of products that may damage the photograph or the enclosure itself.

(6) Containers must be stored in a closed housing such as a drawer, or on shelves and racks that are enclosed by a door and free from all contaminates that may harm the film.

(7) Film must be wound firmly, but not tightly, and must allow room for proper operation when installed in a reader and/or a reader/printer.

(8) Rubber bands, paper clips, tape, and other foreign objects harmful to film may not be used to secure film.

(9)Adhesives that may have a harmful effect on microfilm must not be used. Adhesives used to secure microfilm must pass the photographic activity test as outlined in *American National Standard for Imaging Media — Photographic Processed Films, Plates, and Papers — Filing Enclosures and Storage Containers* (ANSI (IT9.2-1991 or latest revision).

(10) Paper may be used to secure rolls, if it conforms to the specifications contained in *American Standard for Imaging Media — Photographic Processed Films, Plates, and Papers — Filing Enclosures and Storage Containers* (ANSI IT9.2-1991 or latest revision).

(A) Paper in direct contact with film must have a pH of 7.5 to 9.5, over 87% alpha cellulose content, over 2.0% alkali reserve, and matte surface for the paper in accordance with *American National Standard for Imaging Media — Photographic Processed Films, Plates, and Papers — Filing Enclosures and Storage Containers* (ANSI IT9.2-119 or latest revision).

(B) Paper not in direct contact with film must have a pH between 7.2 and 9.5 and alkali reserve must be the molar equivalent to at least 2.0% calcium carbonate.

(11) Films of different generic types must not be interfiled or be in physical contact with each other.

(12) Short-term microfilm, not meeting the specifications in *American National Standard for Imaging Media (Film) — Silver-Gelatin Type — Specifications for Stability* (ANSI IT9.1-1989 or latest revision), must not be stored in the same room or a room sharing common ventilation with that in which essential, long-term, and permanent microfilm is stored.

(13) Film must be handled by the edges.

(14) Microfilm must be enclosed in a way that does not cause abrasion.

(15) COM and microfiche of permanent records must be in acid-free envelopes.

(16) Film must be stored above the floor of the storage area to avoid water damage.

(17) Film must be stored out of direct exposure to fluorescent light, sunlight, and other strong lights.

(18) Routine housekeeping procedures must be maintained to minimize mold, dust, dirt, rodents, insects, and chemical vapors.

(19) No flammable materials, or materials that develop reactive fumes or vapors, or chemicals may be stored near microfilm.

(20) Temperature and humidity must be checked frequently with a reliable hygrometer, such as a sling psychrometer.

(21) Smoking, food, and drink must be kept away from the microfilm equipment and microfilm.

(22) Microfilm must be stored in storage rooms and vaults meeting the following:

(A) be separate from temporary storage facilities, offices, or work areas and must offer protection from unauthorized access, fire, water steam, structural collapse, and other potential hazards;

(B) be equipped with a fire alarm system and be capable of preventing temperatures inside the vault from exceeding 150 degrees Fahrenheit (66 degrees Celsius), and a relative humidity not exceeding 85% for up to two hours, and if constructed or readapted after 1991 to serve as a microfilm storage facility, be equipped with a fire suppression system and with automatic fire control dampers in ducts carrying air to or from the vault or storage room;

(C) be equipped with a system capable of removing those gaseous impurities in the surrounding environment such as sulfur dioxide, nitrous oxide, ammonia, peroxide, and hydrogen sulfide as specified in *American National Standard for Photography (Film) — Processed Safety Film — Storage* (ANSI IT9.11-1991 or latest revision);

(D) if subject to invasion of solid particles that can abrade film or react on the images, have mechanical filters or electrostatic precipitators installed having a cleaning efficiency of at least 80% when tested with atmospheric air in accordance with *American National Standard for Photograph (Film) — Processed Safety Film — Storage* (ANSI (IT9.11-1991 or latest revision);

(E) have approximately 0.05 inch of pressure above atmospheric pressure;

(F) for the microfilm of essential, medium-term, long-term, and permanent records, maintain a temperature of 65 to 75 degrees Fahrenheit (18 to 21 degrees Celsius), and a relative humidity of 20% to 30% with a maximum variance of plus/minus 5.0% relative humidity in a 24-hour period;

(G) for storage of the microfilm of short-term records maintain a temperature of 68 to 77 degrees Fahrenheit (20 to 25 degrees Celsius), and constant relative humidity range between 30% and 60% and maximum variation of plus/minus 5.0% relative humidity in a 24-hour period.

(e) All cuts must be made on clear portions of film and splicing must not distort the image. All images must remain legible and readable.

(f) All splices must be in accordance with *Standard for Information and Image Management — Splices for Imaged Film — Dimensions and Operational Constraints* (ANSI/AIIM MS18-1987 or latest revision).

✪ § 7.29. Labeling and Indexing.

(a) All container information must be legible and on a self-adhesive label.

(b) Container label information must include the roll number, name of government, office of origin, record series, volume number (if any), and retakes (if any).

(c) Microfiche and jacket labeling must comply with *American National Standard for Information on Microfiche Headings* (ANSI Z39.32-1981 or latest revision) and *Technical Report for Information and Image Management — Microfilm Jacket Formatting and Loading Techniques* (AIIM TR11-1987 or latest revision) and must have the following information on the heading of each fiche: name of government, office or origin, records series, and description of content if less than full records series.

(d) Aperture cards must have the following label heading information: name of government, office of origin, records series, and/or record locator number.

(e) Location aids must be employed to ensure that microfilmed images can be readily located. Such location aids may include: detailed container labeling, an external index of the documents on microfilm, flash targets placed on the microfilm, an index placed upon the microfilm, image marking on the microfilm, or sequential number on the microfilm. In those instances where records are not self-indexing, (i.e., not in a readily identifiable numeric or alphabetic sequence) an index must be maintained. Any use of image marking must comply with *Standard for Information and Image Management — Image Mark (Blip) Used in Image Mark Retrieval Systems* (ANSI/AIIM MS8-1988 or latest revision).

(f) If bar coding is used it must meet standards of *Technical Report for Information and Image Management — Bar Coding on Microfiche Production and Dynamic Distribution Control* (AIIM TR12-1988 or latest revision).

✪ § 7.30. Computer Output Microfilm (COM).

(a) Standards for production, processing, testing, and storage of computer output microfilm are the same as those established in these rules for other microfilm formats, except as stated in this section.

(b) COM master microfilms must be wet processed silver-gelatin film for essential, medium-term, long-term, and permanent records. If silver-gelatin film is not used for the master of non-essential and short-term records, thermally processed silver film must be produced in accordance with *Technical Report for Thermally Processed Silver Microfilm* (AIIM TR3-1981 with 1991 addendum or latest revision) and a duplicate must be made on diazo, vesicular, or silver-gelatin film.

(c) Off-film certification must be maintained by the records custodian and must contain the following:

(1) "This is to certify that the official records appearing on (identifier) microfilm are accurate and complete reproductions in strict accordance with the Local Government Code, Chapter 204; of the records series entitled (records series title), for the (name of department). These records were created in the normal course of business and microfilmed as part of a planned records management program; no addition, deletion, or alteration has been made."

(2) The off-film certificate of legality and authenticity must contain the printed or typed name of government, name of office, the name and title of the records custodian or deputy, and the date and place certified, and must be signed by the custodian or, if the camera operator is a deputy of the custodian, it may be signed by the deputy, and the authorized representative and printed name of the service bureau (if any).

(d) The following standards must be met:

(1) *Standard for Information and Image Management — Recommended Practice for Alphanumeric Computer-Output Microforms — Operational Practices for Inspection and Quality Control* (ANSI/AIIM MS1-1988 or latest revision),

(2) *Standard for Information and Image Management — Alphanumeric COM Quality Test Slide* (ANSI/AIIM MS28-1987 or latest revision),

(3) *Standard for Information and Image Management — Recommended Practice for Operational Procedures/Inspection and Quality Control of Duplicate Microforms of Documents and From COM* (ANSI/AIIM MS43-1988 with 1991 supplement or latest revision).

(e) The following eye-legible titling information must appear:

(1) name of organization or custodian of the records;

(2) name of report or record;

(3) date; and

(4) starting and/or ending indexing information.

(f) A reduction ration not exceeding 48:1 must be used.

(g) Required testing and methods of inspection are as follows:

(1) COM must use the alphanumeric COM quality test form slide as specified in *Standard for Information and Image Management — Alphanumeric COM Quality Test Slide* (ANSI/AIIM MS28-1987 or latest revision).

(2) Methylene blue tests must be performed according to 7.24 of this title (relating to Tests and Other Methods of Inspection and Verification).

(3) Density must be in accordance with *Standards for Information and Image Management — Recommended Practice for Alphanumeric Computer-Output Microforms — Operational Practices for Inspection and Quality Control* (ANSI/AIIM MS1-1988 or latest revision).

(4) Resolution must be in accordance with *Standard for Information and Image Management — Alphanumeric COM Quality Test Slide* (ANSI/AIIM MS28-1987 or latest revision).

(5) Resolution target images must be evaluated under a microscope to determine if resolution loss from duplicating is acceptable. A maximum acceptable loss is one pattern per generation.

(6) A visual inspection must be conducted on all film to verify legibility and readability. COM of permanent records must be visually inspected every 10 feet.

(7) Offline processors must be monitored on a scheduled basis with process control strips (sensitometric strips) at a minimum at the start of processing each day and whenever a batch of film, fixer, or developer is changed, or when changes in processing such as replacement or addition of filter, water softener, or replenishing system are made, or when water is changed.

(h) § 7.26 of this title (relating to Use of Editorial and Technical Targets) and § 7.27 of this title (relating to Image Sequence) do not apply to COM.

✪ § 7.31. Jacketing.

(a) Standards for production, processing, testing, and storage of jackets are the same as those established in these rules for other microfilm formats, except as stated in this section.

(b) If master microfilm is placed in a jacket, the jacket must be made completely from ultrasonically welded Mylar (polyester) sheets. Jackets made from Mylar M (a polyester coated with a layer of PVDC, a polymer related to PVC) must not be used for storing master microfilm.

(c) A duplicate of first-generation film must have a resolution loss of no more than one test pattern of the test objects as described in *American National Standard Microcopying — ISO Test Chart No. 2 — Description and Use in Photographic Documentary Reproduction* (ANSI/ISO 3334-1991 (ANSI/AIIM MS51-1991) or latest revision).

(d) The jacket heading must be right reading and upright and the microimages must be right reading.

(e) Heading information must be created with a black carbon-type ribbon or other ink that will not bleed, spread, or transfer.

(f) All jacketed film must comply with *Technical Report for Information and Image Management — Microfilm Jacket Formatting and Loading Techniques* (AIIM TR11-1987 or latest revision), and *Standard for Information and Image Management — Microfilm Jackets* (ANSI/AIIM MS11-1987 or latest revision).

(h) A resolution test must be conducted at the beginning of each day of filming and at a minimum of once every roll, or in using strip film processors cameras, at a minimum of once every roll or every 3,000 images.

(i) Density and resolution targets must be on the microfilm or a sample of the microfilm.

(j) The following image sequence must be followed:

(1) title page target;

(2) records being microfilmed; and

(3) certificate of authenticity (if used on microfilm).

(k) Adherence to the provisions of § 7.27 of this title (relating to Image Sequence) is not required.

(l) The jackets must not be stored under pressure; e.g., packed too tightly in drawers.

✪ § 7.32. Expungement of Records.

(a) Expungement of records must comply with statutory law and *Standard for Information and Image Management — Recommended Practice for the Expungement, Deletion, Correction, or Amendment of Records on Microforms* (ANSI/AIIM MS42-1989 or latest revision).

(b) If the film is spliced the following information must be inserted in place of the expunged record(s):

(1) a start of expungement target;

(2) replacement documents for documents that were expunged (if necessary);

(3) an expungement certificate containing the following information:

(A) order of the district court or other authorizing agency or, if the order shows information to be expunged, the number of the order;

(B) the image location that has been expunged;

(C) the signature, printed name, and title of the custodian of expunged records;

(D) the date of expungement.

(c) If the abrasion method is used, an expungement certificate containing the following information must be maintained and preserved until the microfilm's final disposition:

(1) order of the district court or other authorizing agency or, if the order shows information to be expunged, the number of the order;

(2) the image location that has been expunged;

(3) the signature, printed name, and title of the custodian of expunged records;

(4) the date of expungement.

(d) Images on film may not be expunged by punching holes through film, by using opaque, by blotting with ink-type pen, or by using chemical means such as potassium dichromate (bleach) on film emulsion.

(e) Expungement certificates may not be used when an amended certificate of birth is prepared and filed based on adoption, legitimation, or paternity determination. No evidence may be retained in the microfilm, index, or cross-referenced through which the confidentiality of adoption, legitimation, or paternity actions may be directly or indirectly violated.

✪ § 7.33. Public Access to Information.

Local governments must adopt procedures to ensure that the public has the same access to information on microfilm as they would be entitled to if the information were recorded in another medium. Where microfilm is the only storage medium for a record, a microfilm, paper, or other type of copy other than the master microfilm must be available for public use; the custodian shall not be required to make available for public access the master microfilm.

✪ § 7.34. Aperture Card/CAD Systems.

(a) Standards for production, processing, testing, and storage of aperture cards are the same as those established in these rules for other microfilm formats, except as stated in this section.

(b) The microfilm and enclosure must pass the photographic activity test criteria outlined in the *American National Standards for Imaging Media — Photographic Processed Films, Plates, and Papers — Filing Enclosures and Storage Containers* (IT9.2-1991 or latest revision).

(c) A density test must be conducted on a sample at a minimum of once every 250 cards or every 1,000 images, whichever is greater.

(d) A resolution test must be conducted on a sample at a minimum of once every 250 cards or every 1,000 images, whichever is greater.

(e) Density and resolution targets must be on the microfilm or a test sample of the microfilm.

(f) Aperture cards must have the following information on label headings: name of government, office of origin, record series, and unique identifier.

(g) The following target and certificate must be maintained on or off film:

(1) title page; and

(2) certificate of authenticity.

(h) Adherence to the provisions of § 7.27 of this title (relating to Image Sequence) is not required.

(i) The aperture cards must not be stored under pressure; e.g., packed too tightly in drawers.

✪ § 7.35. Step-and-Repeat Systems.

(a) Standards for production, processing, testing, and storage of microfilm from a step-and-repeat system are the same as those established in these rules for other microfilm formats, except as stated in this section.

(b) Silver-gelatin microfilm in roll or microfiche form must be used for master negatives.

(c) A density test must be conducted at the beginning of each day of filming and at a minimum of once every roll, or in using pre-cut film, every 3,000 images.

(d) A resolution test must be conducted at the beginning of each day of filming and at a minimum of once every roll, or in using pre-cut film, every 3,000 images.

(e) Density and resolution targets must be on the microfilm or a sample of the microfilm.

(f) The following image sequence must be followed:

(1) title page target;

(2) records being microfilmed;

(3) certificate of authenticity (if used on microfilm).

(g) Master negatives in microfiche form must not be stored under pressure; e.g., packed too tightly in drawers.

✪ § 7.71. Definitions.

The following words and terms, when used in this chapter, shall have the following meanings, unless the context clearly indicates otherwise. For local governments, terms not defined in these rules shall have the meanings defined in the Local Government Code, Title 6, Subtitle C, Chapter 201. For state agencies, terms not defined in these rules shall have the meanings defined in the Government Code, § § 441.031-441.039 and SS441.051-441.062.

AIIM - The Association for Information and Image Management.

ANSI - The American National Standards Institute.

Archival record - A record of a state agency scheduled to be reviewed by or that has been approved by an archives for permanent preservation.

Database - (A) collection of digitally stored data records, (B) collection of data elements within records within files that have relationships with other records within other files.

Database Management System (DBMS) - Set of programs designed to organize, store, and retrieve machine-readable information from a computer maintained database or data bank.

Data file - Related numeric, textual, sound, or graphic information that is organized in a strictly prescribed form and format.

Electronic media - All media capable of being read by a computer including computer hard disks, magnetic tapes, optical disks, or similar machine-readable media.

Electronic record - Any information that is recorded in a form for computer processing and that satisfied the definition of a state record in the Government Code, § 441.031(5), or the definition of local government record data in the Local Government Code, § 205.001.

Electronic records systems - Any information system that produces, manipulates, and stores state or local government records by using a computer.

IEC - International Electrotechnical Commission.

ISO - International Organization for Standardization.

Long-term record - A record for which the retention period on a records retention schedule is 100 years or more but less than permanent.

Medium-term record - A record for which the retention period on a records retention schedule is 10 years or more but less than 100 years.

Records administrator - The person appointed by the head of each agency to act as the agency's representative in all issues of records management policy, responsibility, and statutory compliance.

Records custodian - The appointed or elected office who by the state constitution, state law, ordinance, or administrative policy is in charge of an office that creates or receives local government records.

Records management officer - Each elected county officer or the person designated by the governing body of each local government pursuant to the Local Government Code, § 203.025.

Short-term record - A record for which the retention period on a records retention schedule is less than 10 years.

Permanent record - A record for which the retention period on a records retention schedule is permanent.

Text documents - Narrative or tabular documents, such as letters, memorandums, and reports, in loosely prescribed form and format.

✪ § 7.72. General.

(a) These rules establish the minimum requirements for the maintenance, use, retention, and storage of all medium-term, long-term, and permanent electronic records of state agencies and local governments, and archival electronic records of state agencies. These rules do not apply to short-term electronic records, but the short-term electronic records of local governments are subject to the applicable provisions of the Local Government Code, Chapter 205.

(b) Unless otherwise noted, these requirements apply to all electronic records storage systems, whether on microcomputers, minicomputers, or main-frame computers, regardless of storage media.

(c) An electronic storage authorization request certifying that these rules will be followed must be submitted to and approved by the director and librarian for all existing electronic storage of medium-term, long-term, and permanent state or local government records and state archival records, and before any new electronic storage of medium-term, long-term, and permanent state or local government records and state archival records. The authorization request must be submitted in a form and manner to be determined by the director and librarian and must be signed by the agency head or designated records administrator (for state agencies), or the record management officer (for local governments).

(d) The agency head or designated records administrator (for state agencies), and the governing body or records management officer in cooperation with records custodians (for local governments) must:

(1) administer a program for the management of records created, received, maintained, used, or stored on electronic media;

(2) integrate the management of electronic records with other records and information resources management programs of the agency;

(3) incorporate electronic records management objectives, responsibilities, and authorities in pertinent agency directives;

(4) establish procedures for addressing records management requirements, including recordkeeping requirements and disposition;

(5) ensure that training is provided for users of electronic records systems in the operation, care, and handling of the equipment, software, and media used in the system;

(6) ensure the development and maintenance of up-to-date documentation about all electronic records systems that is adequate to specify all technical characteristics necessary for reading or processing the records and the timely, authorized disposition of records; and

(7) specify the location and media on which electronic records are maintained to meet retention requirements and maintain inventories of electronic records systems to facilitate disposition.

(e) With the exception of subsections (c) and (f) of this section, which are effective immediately, state agencies and local governments must be in compliance with the Standards and Procedures for Electronic Records on or before January 2, 1995.

(f) Any electronic recordkeeping system not meeting the provisions of these rules may be utilized for medium-term, long-term, or permanent state or local government records and state archival records provided the source document, if any, or a paper copy of maintained, or the record is microfilmed in accordance with the specifications in *American National Standard for Imaging Media (Film) — Silver-Gelatin Type — Specifications for Stability* (ANSI IT9.1-1989 or latest revision) for state records or in accordance with the provisions of Local Government Code, Chapter 204, and the rules adopted under it for local government records.

✪ § 7.73. Creation and Use of Data Files.

(a) Disposition instructions for the data must be incorporated into electronic records systems that produce, use, and store data files.

(b) State agencies and local governments must maintain up-to-date technical documentation for each electronic records system that produces, uses, and stores data files. Minimum documentation required is:

(1) a narrative description of the system;

(2) the physical and technical characteristics of the records, including a record layout that describes each field including its name, size, starting or relative position, and a description of the form of the data (such as alphabetic, zoned decimal, packed decimal, or numeric), or a data dictionary, or the equivalent

information associated with a database management system including a description of the relationship between data elements in databases; and

(3) any other technical information needed to read or process the records.

✪ § 7.74. Creation and Use of Text Documents.

(a) Electronic records systems that maintain the official file copy of text documents or data used to generate the official file copy of text documents on electronic media must meet the following minimum requirements.

(1) provide a method for all authorized users of the system to retrieve desired documents, such as an indexing or text search system;

(2) provide security to ensure integrity of the documents;

(3) provide a standard interchange format when determined to be necessary by the agency or local government to permit the exchange of documents on electronic media among the components of the agency or local government using different software/operating systems; and

(4) provide for the disposition of the documents including, when necessary, the requirements for transferring archival records to the State Archives as detailed in § 7.77 of this title (relating to Retention of Electronic Records).

(b) A document created on an electronic records system must be identified sufficiently to enable authorized personnel to retrieve, protect, and carry out the disposition of documents in the system. Agencies must ensure that records maintained in such systems can be correlated with related records on paper, microform, or other media.

✪ § 7.75. Security of Electronic Records.

(a) State agencies and local governments must implement and maintain an electronic records security program for office and storage areas that:

(1) ensures that only authorized personnel have access to electronic records;

(2) provides for backup and recovery of records to protect against information loss;

(3) ensures that personnel are trained to safeguard confidential electronic records;

(4) minimizes the risk of unauthorized alteration or erasure of electronic records; and

(5) documents that similar kinds of records generated and stored electronically are created by the same processes each time and have a standardized retrieval approach.

(b) A duplicate copy of essential records and any software or documentation required to retrieve and read the records must be maintained in a storage area located in a separate building from the building where the records that have been copies are maintained.

(c) For all permanent records stored on rewritable electronic media, the system must ensure that read/write privileges are controlled and that an audit trail of rewrites is maintained.

✪ § 7.76. Maintenance of Electronic Records Storage Media.

(a) State agencies and local governments that ensure that the accuracy, completeness, and accessibility of information are not lost prior to its authorized destruction data because of changing technology or media deterioration, by converting electronic storage media and taking other action as required to provide compatibility with current hardware and software. The migration strategy for upgrading equipment as technology evolves must be documented and include:

(1) periodically recopying to the same electronic media as required, and/or transferring of data from an obsolete technology to a supportable technology; and

(2) providing background system compatibility to the data in the old system, and/or converting data to media that the system upgrade and/or replacement can support.

(b) Paragraphs (1) - (3) of this subsection outline the maintenance of backup electronic media stored offsite.

(1) Magnetic computer tapes must be tested and verified no more than 6 months prior to using them to store electronic records. Pretesting of tapes is not required if an automated system is used that monitors read/write errors and there is a procedure in place for correcting errors.

(2) The storage areas for electronic media must be maintained within the following temperatures and relative humidities:

(A) for magnetic media — 65 degrees Fahrenheit to 75 degrees Fahrenheit, and 30% to 50% relative humidity;

(B) for optical disks — storage environmental conditions as specified in *Information technology — 130 mm optical disk cartridge, write once, for information interchange* (ISO/IEC 9171-1, 1990 or latest revision).

(3) A random sample of all magnetic computer tapes must be read annually to identify any loss of data and to discover and correct the causes of data loss. At least a 10% sample or a sample size of 50 magnetic tapes, whichever is less, must be read. Tapes with unrecoverable errors must be replaced and, when possible, lost data must be restored. All other tapes which might have been affected by the same cause (i.e., poor quality tape, high usage, poor environment, improper handling) must be read and corrected.

(c) State agencies and local government must recopy data maintained on electronic medial according to the following schedule.

(1) Data maintained on magnetic tape must be recopied onto new or used tape a minimum of once every three years.

(2) An alternative option for recopying magnetic tape is for the data to be recopied onto new tape a minimum of once every ten years, provided the tape is rewound under controlled tension every three and one-half years. The requirement for rewinding does not apply to 3480-type tape cartridges.

(3) Data maintained on optical disks must be recopied a minimum of once every 10 years.

(d) Floppy disks (diskettes) or any type of flexible disk system may not be used for the exclusive storage of medium-term, long-term, or permanent records and state archival records.

(e) External labels, or an eye-readable index relating to unique identifiers, for electronic media used to process or store electronic records must include the following information:

(1) name of other identifier of the organizational unit responsible for the records;

(2) descriptive title of the contents;

(3) dates of creation and authorized disposition date;

(4) security classification;

(5) identification of the software (to include specific application if appropriate) and hardware used; and

(6) system title, including the version number of the application.

(f) Additionally, the following information must be maintained for electronic media used to store permanent electronic records:

(1) file title(s);

(2) dates of coverage;

(3) the recording density;

(4) type of internal labels;

(5) volume serial number, if applicable;
(6) the number of tracks;
(7) character code/software dependency;
(8) information about block size;
(9) sequence number, if the file is part of a multi-media set; and
(10) relating starting position of data, if applicable.

(g) The following standards must be met for electronic records stored as digital images on optical media.

(1) A non-proprietary image file header label must be used, or the system developer must provide a bridge to a non-proprietary image file header label, or the system developer must supply a detailed definition of image file header label structure.

(2) The system hardware and/or software must provide a quality assurance capability that verifies information that is written to the optical media.

(3) Periodic maintenance of optical data storage systems is required, including an annual recalibration of the optical drives.

(4) Scanner quality must be evaluated based on the standard procedures in *American National Standards for Information and Image Management — Recommended Practice for Quality Control of Image Scanners* (ANSI/AIIM MS44-1988 or latest revision).

(5) A visual quality control evaluation must be performed for each scanned image and related index data.

(6) A scanning density with a minimum of 200 dots per inch is required for recording documents that contain no type font smaller than six point.

(7) A scanning density with a minimum of 300 dots per inch is required for engineering drawings, maps, and other documents with background detail.

(8) The selected scanning density must be validated with tests on actual documents.

(9) The use of the Consultative Committee on International Telegraphy and Telephony (CCITT)

Group 3 or Group 4 compression techniques is required for document images without continuous tonal qualities. If use of a proprietary compression technique is unavoidable, the vendor must provide a gateway to either Group 3 or Group 4 compression techniques.

(10) Optical drive systems must not be operated in environments with high levels of airborne particulates.

(11) All aspects of the design and use of the imaging system must be documented, including administrative procedures for digital imaging, retrieval, and storage; technical system specifications; problems encountered; and measures taken to address them, including hardware and software modifications.

(h) Smoking, drinking, and eating must be prohibited in electronic media storage areas.

✪ § 7.77. Retention of Electronic Records.

(a) State agencies and local governments must establish policies and procedures to ensure that electronic records and any software, hardware, and/or documentation, including maintenance documentation, required to retrieve and read the electronic records are retained as long as the approved retention period for the electronic records.

(b) The retention procedures must include provisions for:

(1) scheduling the disposition of all electronic records, according to statutory requirements, as well as related software, documentation, and indexes; and

(2) establishing procedures for regular recopying, reformatting, and other necessary maintenance to ensure the retention and usability of electronic records until the expiration of their retention periods.

(c) State records having archival value and scheduled to be preserved at the State Archives must be transferred to the State Archives as the source document, or printed out on alkaline paper for computer generated information, or on microforms that meet the specifications in *American National Standard for Imaging Media (Film) — Silver-Gelatin Type — Specifications for Stability* (ANSI IT9.1-1989 or latest revision).

✪ § 7.78. Destruction of Electronic Records.

(a) Electronic records may be destroyed only in accordance with a records schedule approved by the director and librarian or designee or, in lieu of an approved records schedule, an approved records disposition authorization request.

(b) Each state agency and local government must ensure that:

(1) Electronic records scheduled for destruction are disposed of in a manner that ensures protection of any confidential information; and

(2) magnetic storage media previously used for electronic records containing confidential information are not reused if the previously recorded information can be compromised by reuse in any way.

(c) The court ordered expungement of information recorded on an optical Write-Once-Read-Many (WORM) system must be implemented according to the recommendations provided in *Technical Report for Information and Image Management — The Expungement of Information Recorded on Optical Write-Once-Read-Many (WORM) Systems* (AIIM TR28-1991 or latest revision).

✪ § 7.79. Public Access to Electronic Records.

An electronic recordkeeping system must not provide an impediment to access to public records.

State: Utah
Source: Utah Code Annotated

TITLE 59. REVENUE AND TAXATION.

CHAPTER 13. MOTOR AND SPECIAL FUEL TAX ACT.

Part 3. Special Fuel.

Citation: UCA 59-13-312

✍ § 59-13-312. User and user-dealer reports on special fuel — Commission examination of reports — Auditing requirements — Deposit of funds with treasurer as dedicated credits.

(1) Each user, user-dealer, and any other person importing, manufacturing, refining, dealing in, transporting, or storing fuel shall keep a record, in the form prescribed by the commission, of all purchases, receipts, sales, meter, readings, inventories, and distribution of special fuel. The records shall include copies of all invoices or bills of all sales, and are subject to inspection by the commission or its authorized representative during regular business hours. All records shall be preserved for a period of three years.

(2) Any user claiming a refund for taxes paid to a user-dealer shall retain on file a receipt or invoice, or a microfilm or microfiche of the receipt or invoice, evidencing the purchase of special fuel and the payment of the tax. The commission may require the user to furnish summaries or copies of original documentation substantiating the amount of refund claimed.

(3) The commission or its authorized representative may examine the books, papers, records, and equipment of any

user-dealer, user, or person dealing in, transporting, or storing special fuel and may investigate the character of the disposition which any person makes of special fuel in order to determine whether all taxes due are being properly reported and paid. The fact that the books, papers, records, and equipment are not maintained in this state at the time of demand does not cause the commission to lose any right of examination under this part when and where the records become available.

(4) If the payer of this tax or the person dealing in special fuel does not maintain records in this state so that an audit of the records may be made by the commission or its representative, that person may be required to:

(a) forward the necessary records to the commission for examination; or

(b) pay the necessary expenses for an auditor of the commission to travel to the location of the records outside of this state to make an examination.

(5) Any funds collected under this section shall be deposited with the state treasurer and are dedicated credits for the commission.

TITLE 63. STATE AFFAIRS IN GENERAL.

CHAPTER 2. GOVERNMENT RECORDS ACCESS AND MANAGEMENT ACT

RECORDS RETENTION POLICY

Records retention and disposition will be provided for by one of the following alternatives. Each court location will select that process which meets its specific needs.

Records that are classified as permanent in accordance with this schedule shall be preserved and retained by the clerk of the court permanently in the form of the original record or a microfilm or other permanent copy thereof.

Courts using any type of microfilm process shall follow standards to ensure that the film is of archival quality and will be stored properly. Courts retaining the original records must provide proper storage to prevent damage or destruction to the original record.

If the microfilm process is selected to create the permanent record, the record may be taken to the Utah State Archives for filming or may be microfilmed at the local court. The microfilm copy will then be retained by the clerk of the court in place of the original record. If the original record is microfilmed at the local court level, the original record will be transferred to the Utah State Archives. All records sent to the Utah State Archives for microfilming will be returned to the local court for permanent storage or destruction, at the option of the local court.

No document which has been filed or placed with the court that is a permanent record shall be destroyed or disposed of, unless done so pursuant to this policy and the following retention schedule.

Records that are not classified as permanent may be destroyed or disposed of at the end of the minimum retention period as shown on the retention schedule.

RECORDS RETENTION SCHEDULE

The Records Retention Schedule is a working guide for the retention and disposition of court records. The primary purpose is to help court administrators and clerks manage the ever increasing volume of paper and records moving through the court system. This assistance includes provisions for the outright destruction of records, the microfilming and destruction of records, or the transfer of records.

The provisions of this schedule relating to disposal of court records are not mandatory in nature. A local court may retain its records as long as it has adequate storage space. For courts plagued by storage space and storage rental charges, the schedule provides a timetable for the destruction of court records.

DISTRICT COURTS

Record Title	Retention Period	Years to retain before microfilm and destroying	Destroy after microfilming	De-stroy
Adoption files	Permanent	9*	X*	
Civil files	Permanent	9	X	
Court Calendars				X
Court Minutes	Permanent	9	X	
Court Reporter's notes	10 years			X
Criminal files	Permanent	9	X	
Exhibits	3 months			
Fee Books	3 years			X
Guardianship files	Permanent	9	X	
Indexes	Permanent	9	X	
Judgment Dockets	Permanent	9	X	
Jury lists & Certificates	2 years			X
Mental health files & Taped hearings	Permanent	9	X	
Naturalization records	Permanent			
Probate files	Permanent	9	X	
Registers of Action	Permanent	9	X	
Witness certificates	2 years	9		X

*Note: Adoption records may be microfilmed and originals destroyed after 9 years if the records are filmed separately, marked "confidential" and sealed. Adoption records filed with the Court shall be sealed and are subject to inspection only upon written court order after good cause has been shown.

* * * * *

TITLE 78. JUDICIAL CODE.

PART 3. PROCEDURE

CHAPTER 25. EVIDENCE.

Citation: UCA 78-25-16

☞ § 78-25-16. Parole evidence of contents of writings—When admissible.

There can be no evidence of the contents of a writing, other than the writing itself, except in the following cases:

(1) When the original has been lost or destroyed, in which case proof of the loss or destruction must first be made.

(2) When the original is in the possession of the party against whom the evidence is offered and he fails to produce it after reasonable notice.

(3) When the original is a record or other document in the custody of a public officer.

(4) When the original has been recorded, and the record or a certified copy thereof is made evidence by this code or other statute.

(5) When the original consists of numerous accounts or other documents which cannot be examined in court without great loss of time, and the evidence sought from them is only the general result of the whole.

Provided, however, if any business, institution, member of a profession or calling, or any department or agency of government, in the regular course of business or activity has kept or recorded any memorandum, writing, entry, print, representation or combination thereof, of any act, transaction, occurrence or event, and in the regular course of business has caused any or all of the same to be recorded, copied or reproduced by any photographic, photostatic, microfilm, micro-card, miniature photographic, or other process which accurately reproduces or forms a durable medium for so reproducing the original, the original may be destroyed in the regular course of business unless its preservation is required by law, and such reproduction, when satisfactorily identified, is as admissible in evidence as the original itself in any judicial or administrative proceeding whether the original is in existence or not, an enlargement or facsimile of such reproduction is likewise admissible in evidence if the original reproduction is in existence and available for inspection under direction of court. The introduction of a reproduced record, enlargement of facsimile, does not preclude admission of the original.

In the cases mentioned in subdivisions (3) and (4), a copy of the original, or of the record, must be produced; in those mentioned in subdivisions (1) and (2), either a copy or oral evidence of the contents.

Source: **Rules of Evidence**

ARTICLE 10.Contents of Writings, Recordings, and Photographs.

☞ Rule 1001. Definitions

For purposes of this article the following definitions are applicable:

(1) *Writings and recordings.* — "Writings" and "recordings" consist of letters, words, or numbers, or their equivalent, set down by handwriting, typewriting, printing, photostating, photographing, magnetic impulse, mechanical or electronic recording, or other form of data compilation.

(2) *Photographs.* — "Photographs" include still photographs, X-ray films, video tapes, and motion pictures.

(3) *Original.* — An "original" of a writing or recording is the writing or recording itself or any counterpart intended to have the same effect by a person executing or issuing it. An "original" of a photograph includes the negative or any print therefrom. If data are stored in a computer or similar device, any printout or other output readable by sight, shown to reflect the data accurately, is an "original".

(4) *Duplicate.* — A "duplicate" is a counterpart produced by the same impression as the original, or from the same matrix, or by means of photography, including enlargements and miniatures, or by mechanical or electronic re-recording, or by chemical reproduction, or by other equivalent techniques which accurately reproduces the original.

☞ Rule 1003. Admissibility of duplicates.

A duplicate is admissible to the same extent as an original unless (1) a genuine question is raised as to the authenticity of the original or (2) in the circumstances it would be unfair to admit the duplicate in lieu of the original.

[See Appendix A. Uniform Rules of Evidence for additional provisions.]

State: **Vermont**
Source: **Vermont Statutes Annotated**

TITLE 3. EXECUTIVE.

CHAPTER 1. GOVERNOR.

Citation: **3 VCA 4**

✪ § 4. Correspondence.

(a) The official correspondence of the governor is the property of the state. Upon retiring from office he shall cause such correspondence to be bound or cause an itemized list thereof to be made and deposit such correspondence and list with the secretary of state.

(b) In the discretion of the secretary of state, such correspondence and list, in whole or in part, may be microfilmed by the public records division and the originals destroyed of those papers that are actually microfilmed. The microfilmed copies so made shall have the same force and effect for all purposes as the original record. The portion of such itemized list or correspondence that is not microfilmed shall be preserved in the office of the secretary of state, and the microfilmed copies shall be preserved by the public records division but shall remain subject to the order of the secretary of state.

CHAPTER 5. SECRETARY OF STATE.

SUBCHAPTER 1. GENERAL PROVISIONS.

Citation: **3 VCA 106**

✪ § 106. Acts and resolutions of the general assembly.

After the original acts and resolutions of the general assembly are delivered to the secretary pursuant to section 104 of Title 3 he shall cause them to be microfilmed in cooperation with the public records director. He shall then keep the originals on permanent file in his office.

CHAPTER 9. ADMINISTRATIVE DEPARTMENTS.

Citation: **3 VCA 219**

✪ § 219. Records and file equipment.

The following requests, for additional equipment shall require prior approval by the director of public records for the purpose of determining whether or not the requesting agency is making sufficient effort to improve records management:

(1) file cabinets;
(2) open files and shelving;
(3) vaults and safes;
(4) microfilm equipment;
(5) electronic or mechanical files.

TITLE 4. JUDICIARY.

CHAPTER 17. CLERKS OF COURT; COURT AND OTHER RECORDS AND ACCOUNTS.

SUBCHAPTER 1. SUPREME COURT AND SUPERIOR COURT

Citation: 4 VCA 652

✪ § 652. Records of judgments and other proceedings; dockets; certified copies.

The clerk shall:

(1) At the close of each stated, special or adjourned term of the court enter of record in due form the judgments rendered by the court in a book kept for that purpose and submit the same to the inspection of the judges of the court;

(2) Make and keep dockets of the causes pending at each term of the court;

(3) Record any other proceedings that the court may direct, and make and sign all process regularly issuing from the court; and

(4) Except as provided in section 454 of Title 22, he shall keep on file and preserve all process, pleadings and papers relating to causes in superior court which together with the records of the court, he shall give to any person, on demand and tender of the legal fees, certified copies of any of the records, proceedings or minutes in his office, and all proper certificates, under the seal of the court. However, the clerk shall not disclose the filing of an action or release any records, proceedings, or minutes pertaining to it until service of process has been completed; nor shall he disclose any materials or information required by law to be kept confidential. Original court records shall be maintained for two years after final court action and thereafter may be maintained on microfilm.

Citation: 4 VCA 658

✪ § 658. Supreme court records.

Whenever the records of the supreme court are transcribed by the county clerk, he shall forthwith transmit the original of such record to the court administrator for safekeeping, together with a certified copy thereof. The county clerk shall keep on file an additional certified copy of such transcription in place of the original so transmitted. A copy of such original record certified by the court administrator from the original or a copy certified by the county clerk from the transcript retained on file by him shall be entitled to the same faith and credit and have the same force as the original record. The expense of making such transcript and of transmittal of the original record shall be paid by the state.

Citation: 4 VCA 659

✪ § 659. Microfilming of court records.

(a) The supreme court by administrative order may provide for permanent preservation of all court records by microfilming, or by any other photographic process which will provide compact records in reduced size, in accordance with standards established by the department of general services of the Vermont agency of administration which take into account the quality and security of the microphotographed records, and ready access to the micrographic record of any cause so recorded.

(b) After microfilming, the supreme court by administrative order may provide for the disposition of original court records by destruction or in cases where the original court record may have historical or intrinsic value by transfer to an appropriate institutional facility such as the archives of the secretary of state, the department of general services of the agency of administration, the Vermont historical society, or the university of Vermont.

Citation: 4 VCA 693

✪ § 693. Docket and records.

The clerk shall keep a docket, to be furnished by the state, of all causes pending in the court. Except as provided in section 454 of Title 22, he shall keep on file and preserve all process, pleadings and papers relating to causes in the district court which, together with the records of the court, shall be subject inspection and examination by parties interested in those causes and, upon tender of the legal fees, he shall furnish, or cause to be furnished, duly certified copies of any records, pleadings, process or papers; except that he shall not disclose any materials or information required by law to be kept confidential. In a book kept for that purpose, he shall also make a record of all causes determined, but he need not spread at length upon the record, the process or the pleadings. Original court records shall be maintained for two years after final court action and thereafter may be maintained on microfilm.

TITLE 8. BANKING AND INSURANCE.

PART 2. BANKS AND OTHER FINANCIAL INSTITUTIONS

CHAPTER 51. SUPERVISION AND REGULATION.

Citation: 8 VCA 502

✍ § 502. Preservation of records.

* * * * *

(d) Any state bank may cause records at any time in its custody to be reproduced by the microphotographic or other process approved by the commissioner and any reproduction so made shall have the same force and effect as the original thereof and be admitted in evidence equally with the original.

TITLE 12. COURT PROCEDURE.

CHAPTER 63. RECORDS AND OTHER DOCUMENTS.

Citation: 12 VCA 1701

☞ § 1701. Uniform photographic copies of business and public records as evidence act.

(a) If any business, institution, member of a profession or calling, or any department or agency of government, in the regular course of business or activity has kept or recorded any memorandum, writing, entry, print, representation or combination thereof, of any act, transaction, occurrence or event, and in the regular course of business has caused any or all of the same to be recorded, copied or reproduced by any photographic, photostatic, microfilm, micro-card, miniature photographic, or other process which accurately reproduces or forms a durable medium for so reproducing the original, the original may be destroyed in the regular course of business unless held in a custodial or fiduciary capacity or unless its preservation is required by law. Such reproduction, when satisfactorily identified, is as admissible in evidence as the original itself in any judicial or administrative proceeding whether the original is in existence or not and an enlargement or facsimile of such reproduction is likewise admissible in evidence if the original reproduction is in existence and available for inspection under direction of court. The introduction of a reproduced record, enlargement or facsimile, does not preclude admission of the original.

(b) This section shall be so interpreted and construed as to effectuate its general purpose of making uniform the law of those states which enact it.

TITLE 22. LIBRARIES AND HISTORY.

CHAPTER 11. PUBLIC RECORDS.

Citation: 22 VCA 453

✪ § 453. Duties of commissioner of general services and chief of administration.

In addition to the duties otherwise assigned to him or her by law the commissioner of general services and chief of administration may:

* * * * *

(12) Administer a central microfilm program for public records, including land records in the possession of town or county officers. Public records which are preserved on microfilm shall be taken and received in all courts, public offices, and official bodies as prima facie evidence.

(13) The commissioner shall accept for filing copies of land records submitted in microfilm or similar compressed form by town or county clerks.

Citation: 22 VCA 454

✪ § 454. Disposition of public records.

(a) A custodian of public records shall not destroy, give away, sell, discard or damage any record or records in his or her charge, unless specifically so authorized by law, without having first submitted to the commissioner of general services a list thereof, with accurate description.

(b) Within sixty days after receipt of the list and description, with an application for permission to destroy, cancel or dispose of the records, the commissioner of general services with the prior advice of the public records advisory board shall order the preservation, destruction, cancellation, or disposal thereof, in whole or in part, which order shall be duly recorded by the custodian, and shall be binding on him or her and his or her successors.

(c) Before approving a request for the destruction of any public record, the commissioner of general services, or the custodian of the record if the commissioner approves, may make photographic copies of it and copies so made shall have the same force and effect for all purposes as the original record. Statutes concerning the retention of original materials shall be considered satisfied and no violation incurred when public records are officially microfilmed and stored and the original material destroyed pursuant to sections 453 and 457 of this title.

(d) For the purpose of this chapter, "disposal" of public records includes transferal of records to the custody of the secretary of state for archival purposes.

TITLE 23. MOTOR VEHICLES.

CHAPTER 3. MOTOR VEHICLE DEPARTMENT

Citation: 23 VCA 104

✪ § 104. Public records.

The records of the registration of motor vehicles, snowmobiles and motorboats, licensing of operators and registration of dealers, all original accident reports, and the records showing suspension and revocation of licenses and registration and the records regarding revocation of licenses and registration and the records regarding diesel, fuel, gasoline and rental vehicle taxes shall be deemed official and public records, and shall be open to public inspection at all reasonable hours. The commissioner shall furnish certified copies of the records to any interested person of such fee as established by § 114(a)(21) of this title. Notwithstanding section 114 of this title information from the records of the department may be made available to government agencies in the manner determined by the commissioner and at the actual cost of furnishing the same. The records may be maintained on microfilm or electronic imaging.

Source: Rules of Evidence

ARTICLE 10. Contents of Writings, Recordings, and Photographs.

☞ Rule 1001. Definitions

For purposes of this article the following definitions are applicable:

(1) *Writings and recordings.* — "Writings" and "recordings" consist of letters, words, or numbers, or their equivalent, set down by handwriting, typewriting, printing, photostating, photographing, magnetic impulse, mechanical or electronic recording, or other form of data compilation.

(2) *Photographs.* — "Photographs" include still photographs, X-ray films, video tapes, and motion pictures.

(3) *Original.* — An "original" of a writing or recording is the writing or recording itself or any counterpart intended to have the same effect by a person executing or issuing it. An "original" of a photograph includes the negative or any print therefrom. If data are stored in a computer or similar device, any printout or other output readable by sight, shown to reflect the data accurately, is an "original".

(4) *Duplicate.* — A "duplicate" is a counterpart produced by the same impression as the original, or from the same matrix, or by means of photography, including enlargements and miniatures, or by mechanical or electronic re-recording, or by chemical reproduction, or by other equivalent techniques which accurately reproduces the original.

☞ Rule 1003. Admissibility of Duplicates.

A duplicate is admissible to the same extent as an original unless

(1) a genuine question is raised as to the authenticity of the original or (2) in the circumstances it would be unfair to admit the duplicate in lieu of the original.

[See Appendix A. Uniform Rules of Evidence for additional provisions.]

State: Virgin Islands
Source: Virgin Islands Code Annotated

TITLE 3. EXECUTIVE.

CHAPTER 2. OFFICE OF LIBRARIES AND ARCHIVES.

Citation: 3 VICA 28f

✪ **§ 28f. Archivist; appointment; duties.**

* * * * *

(5) establish standards for the reproduction of records by photographic, microphotographic or other processes with a view to the disposal of the original records. Reproduction made in compliance with such standards shall have the same force and effect as the originals thereof would have and shall be treated as originals for the purpose of their admissibility in evidence;

* * * * *

TITLE 4. JUDICIARY.

CHAPTER 5. TERRITORIAL COURT.

Citation: 4 VICA 87

✪ **§ 87. Microfilming; preservation; destruction of original records.**

(a) The Territorial Court is hereby authorized to microfilm in duplicate all original records, files and documents, with the exception of traffic tickets, maintained pursuant to its judicial function.

All such original records, files and documents shall be retained until reproduced by microphotographic process, and thereafter may be destroyed, provided that no records, files or documents less than one year old shall be subject to destruction. Traffic tickets which have either been paid or dismissed may also be destroyed by order of the Presiding Judge, notwithstanding the fact that the microfilming of same is not authorized by law.

(b) One duplicate original of each of the aforesaid microphotographed writings shall be retained by the Court in the Judicial Division where such writings were originally filed and the other duplicate original shall be forwarded to the archives of the Government of the Virgin Islands for preservation and safekeeping. Upon transmission to the archives, the microphotographed writings of the Territorial Court shall be subject to the same restrictions and prohibitions as they would have been if custody was retained in the Territorial Court.

(c) Microphotographs of records made in compliance with this section shall have the same effect as the original and shall be treated as originals for the purpose of their admissibility in evidence. Certified or authenticated reproductions of the microphotographs shall be admitted in evidence equally with the original microphotographs.

TITLE 5. JUDICIAL PROCEDURE.

SUBTITLE 1. CIVIL PROCEDURE.

PART 5. EVIDENCE.

CHAPTER 67. ADMISSIBILITY OF EVIDENCE; UNIFORM RULES OF EVIDENCE.

SUBCHAPTER 9. AUTHENTICATION AND CONTENT OF WRITINGS.

Citation: 5 VICA 956

✍ **§ 956. Photographic copies to prove content of business and public records.**

The content of any admissible writing made in the regular course of "a business" as defined by section 931 of this title or in the regular course of duty of any "public official" as defined by said section, may be proved by a photostatic, microfilm, microcard, miniature photographic or other photographic copy or reproduction or by an enlargement thereof, when duly authenticated, if it was in the regular course of such business or official activity to make and preserve such copies or reproductions as a part of the records of such business or office. The introduction of such copy, reproduction or enlargement does not preclude admission of the original writing if it is still in existence.

State: Virginia
Source: Virginia Code Annotated

TITLE 8.01. CIVIL REMEDIES AND PROCEDURE.

CHAPTER 3. ACTIONS.

Article 3. Injury to Person or Property.

Citation: VCA 8.01-40.1

✍ **§ 8.01-40.1. Action for injury resulting from violation of Computer Crimes Act; limitations.**

Any person whose property or person is injured by reason of a violation of the provisions of the Virginia Computer Crimes Act (18.2-152.1 et seq.) may sue and recover damages as provided in 18.2-152.12. An action shall be commenced before the earlier of (i) five years after the last act in the course of conduct constituting a violation of the Computer Crimes Act or (ii) two years after the plaintiff discovers or reasonably should have discovered the last act in the course of conduct constituting a violation of the Computer Crimes Act.

CHAPTER 14. EVIDENCE.

ARTICLE 2. LAWS, PUBLIC RECORDS, AND COPIES OF ORIGINAL RECORDS AS EVIDENCE.

Citation: VCA 8.01-391

☞ **§ 8.01-391. Copies of originals as evidence.**

* * * * *

C. If any business or member of a profession or calling in the regular course of business or activity has made any record, and again in the regular course of business has caused any or all of such record to be copied, the copy shall be as admissible in evidence as the original, whether the original exists or not, provided that such copy is satisfactorily identified and authenticated as a true copy both by the custodian of such record and by the person to whom said custodian reports, if they be different, and is accompanied by a certificate that said person does in fact have the custody. Copies in the regular course of business shall be deemed to include reproduction at a later time, if done in good faith and without intent to defraud.

The original of which a copy has been made may be destroyed in the regular course of business unless its preservation is required by law, or its validity has been questioned.

D. The introduction in an action of a copy under this section neither precludes the introduction or admission of the original nor the introduction of a copy or the original in another action.

E. Copy, as used in this section, shall be deemed to include photographs, microphotographs, photostats, microfilm, microcard, printouts or other reproductions of electronically stored data, or copies from optical disks or any other reproduction of an original from a process which forms a durable medium for its recording, storing, and reproducing.

TITLE 15.1. COUNTIES, CITIES AND TOWNS.

CHAPTER 1. GENERAL.

ARTICLE 2. GENERAL PROVISIONS; CERTAIN POWERS.

Citation: VCA 15.1-8

☞ ✪ § 15.1-8. Reproductions of records and documents and legal status thereof; destruction of originals.

The governing body of any county, city or town is authorized to provide for the photographing or microphotographing, or the recording by any other process which accurately reproduces or forms a durable medium for reproducing the original of all or any part of the papers, records, documents or other materials kept by or in charge of any department, agency or institution of such county, city or town in accordance with such standards and retention schedules as may be issued in pursuance of § 42.1-82.

A reproduction thereof if substantially the same size as the original, when satisfactorily identified, is as admissible in evidence as the original itself in any judicial or administrative proceeding whether the original is in existence or not and an enlargement or facsimile of such reproduction is likewise admissible in evidence if the original reproduction is in existence and available for inspection under direction of the court. The introduction of a reproduced record, enlargement or facsimile, does not preclude admission of the original.

Whenever photographs or microphotographs shall have been made and put in conveniently accessible files, and provision has been made for preserving, examining and using the same, the governing body of the county, city or town may notify the State Librarian that it intends to destroy the records and papers so photographed or microphotographed, or any part thereof. If within sixty days the State Librarian has not notified the governing body that such records or papers should be retained, the governing body may cause them to be destroyed. Such governing body may also, in its discretion, consult with the county, city or town librarian with reference to the advisability of destroying any such records, papers, documents or other material because of any historical significance or value.

With the approval of the judge of the circuit court of the county entered of record, the clerk, and the clerk of the county court may, if directed to do so by the county governing body, microphotograph records in their respective offices which are not required for current use. No record so microphotographed shall be destroyed but may be stored in a safe place. The microphotograph or a certified copy thereof shall be of the same force and effect as the original record.

TITLE 17. COURTS OF RECORD.

CHAPTER 2. CLERKS, CLERKS' OFFICES AND RECORDS.

Article 3. Records, Recordation and Indexing Generally

Citation: VCA 17-60

✪ § 17-60. Documents to be recorded in deed books.

All deeds, deeds of trust, deeds of release, certificates of satisfaction or certificates of partial satisfaction, quitclaim deeds, homestead deeds, grants, transfers and mortgages of real estate, releases of such mortgages, powers of attorney to convey real estate, leases of real estate, notices of lis pendens and all contracts in reference to real estate, which have been acknowledged as required by law, and certified copies of final judgments or decrees of partition affecting the title or possession of real estate, any part of which is situated in the county or city in which it is sought to be recorded, and all other writings relating to or affecting real estate which are authorized to be recorded, shall, unless otherwise provided, be recorded in a book to be known as the deed book. All deeds, deeds of trust, deeds of release, quitclaim deeds, grants, transfers, and mortgages of real estate or any addendum or memorandum relating to any of these instruments susbmitted for recordation in the deed books of the appropriate office of the clerk of court shall be prepared according to the requirements for deeds as set forth in § § 55-48 and 55-58 and shall include the names of all grantors and grantees in the first clause of each such instrument. Each instrument shall be indexed under all such names in accordance with the provisions of § 17-79. With the approval of the judges of a circuit court of any county or city, recording may be accomplished by procedural microphotographic process which meets archival standards as recommended by the Archives Division of the State Library and Archives.

Citation: VCA 17-60.1

✪ § 17-60.1. Recording releases of deeds of trust, partial releases of deeds of trust, court ordered releases, or other liens or assignments in cities and counties using microfilm.

Notwithstanding any other provision of law, whenever the writings required by law to be recorded in the deed book in the office of the clerk of the circuit court of any city or county are recorded by a microphotographic process or by any other method or process which renders impractical or impossible the subsequent entering of marginal notations upon a recorded instrument, an appropriate certificate, certificate of satisfaction, certificate of partial satisfaction, certified copy of order, or other separate instrument setting forth the necessary information shall be recorded and indexed according to law.

When existing deed books in the office of the clerk of the circuit court of any county or city are to be microfilmed for security purposes, the court, by order entered of record, may provide that marginal notations to accomplish the release of deeds of trust or other liens shall not be made in such deed book so microfilmed.

TITLE 42.1. LIBRARIES.

CHAPTER 7. VIRGINIA PUBLIC RECORDS ACT.

Citation: VCA 42.1-83

✪ **§ 42.1-83. Program for inventorying, scheduling, microfilming records; records of counties and cities; storage of records.**

The State Library Board shall formulate and execute a program to inventory, schedule, and microfilm official records of counties, cities and towns which it determines have permanent value and to provide safe storage for microfilm copies of such records, and to give advice and assistance to local officials in their programs for creating, preserving, filing and making available public records in their custody.

Original archival public records shall be either stored in the The Library of Virginia or in the locality at the decision of the local official responsible for maintaining public records. Original archival public records shall be returned to the locality upon the written request of the local officials responsible for maintaining local public records. Microfilm shall be stored in the The Library of Virginia but the use thereof shall be subject to the control of the local officials responsible for maintaining local public records.

Citation: VCA 42.1-84

✪ **§ 42.1-84. Same; records of agencies and subdivisions not covered under § 42.1-83.**

The State Library Board may formulate and execute a program of inventorying, repairing, and microfilming for security purposes the public records of the agencies and subdivisions not covered under the program established under § 42.1-83 which it determines have permanent value, and of providing safe storage of microfilm copies of such records.

Source: Virginia Register of Regulations
Agency: Department of Taxation and Finance

SALES AND USE TAX REGULATION 401

Citation: VRR 630-10-30

✍ **§ 630-10-30. Dealer's records.**

Every person who is liable for collection of sales tax and/or remittance of use tax is required to keep and preserve for three years adequate and complete records necessary to determine the amount of tax liability. Such records must include:

a. A daily record of all cash and credit sales, including sales under any type of financing or installment plan in use;

b. A record of the amount of all merchandise purchased, including a bill of lading, invoice, purchase order or other evidence to substantiate each purchase;

c. A record of all deductions and exemptions claimed in filing sales or use tax returns, including exemption and resale certificates, returned or repossessed goods, and bad debts;

d. A record of all tangible personal property used or consumed in the conduct of the business;

e. A true and complete inventory of the stock on hand and its value, taken at least once per each year.

Records must be open for inspection and examination at all reasonable hours of the business day by the Department of Taxation. The dealer may maintain such records on microfilm.

If an assessment has been made and an appeal to the Commissioner or to court is pending, all records relating to the period covered by such assessment must be preserved until the final disposition of the appeal.

MOTOR VEHICLE FUEL SALES

Citation: VRR 32

✍ **§ 32. Records and their preservation.**

Every dealer is required to keep and preserve for three years adequate and complete records necessary to determine the amount of tax liability. Such records must include:

(a) A daily record of all cash and credit sales;

(b) A record of the amount of all fuel purchased, including a bill of lading, invoice, purchase order or other evidence to substantiate each purchase;

(c) A record of all deductions and exemptions claimed in filing tax returns, including exemption and resale certificates and bad debts;

(d) A true and complete inventory of the stock on hand and its value, taken at least once each year.

Records must be open for inspection and examination at all reasonable hours of the business day by the Department of Taxation. The dealer may maintain such records on microfilm.

If an assessment has been made and an appeal to the Commissioner or to a court is pending, all records relating to the period covered by such assessment must be preserved until the final disposition of the appeal.

State: Washington
Source: Revised Code of Washington

TITLE 5. EVIDENCE.

CHAPTER 5.46. UNIFORM PHOTOGRAPHIC COPIES OF BUSINESS AND PUBLIC RECORDS AS EVIDENCE ACT.

Citation: RCW 5.46.010

☞ ✍ ✪ **§ 5.46.010. Copies of business and public records as evidence.**

If any business, institution, member of a profession or calling or any department or agency of government, in the regular course of business or activity has kept or recorded any memorandum, writing, entry, print, representation or combination thereof, of any act, transaction, occurrence or event, and in the regular course of business has caused any or all of the same to be recorded, copied or reproduced by any photographic, photostatic, microfilm, microcard, miniature photographic, optical imaging, or other process which accurately reproduces or forms a durable medium for so reproducing the original, the original may be destroyed in the regular course of business unless the same is an asset or is representative of title to an asset held in a custodial or fiduciary capacity or unless its preservation is required by law. Such reproduction, when satisfactorily identified, is as admissible in evidence as the original itself in any judicial or administrative proceeding whether the original is in existence or not and an enlargement or facsimile of such reproduction is likewise admissible in evidence if the original reproduction is in existence and available for inspection under direction of court. The introduction of a reproduced record, enlargement or facsimile, does not preclude admission of the original.

TITLE 25. PARTNERSHIPS.

CHAPTER 25.15. LIMITED LIABILITY COMPANIES.

ARTICLE 3.

Citation: RCW 25.15.135

✍ § 25.15.135. Records and information.

(1) A limited liability company shall keep at its principal place of business the following:

(a) A current and a past list, setting forth the full name and last known mailing address of each member and manager, if any;

(b) A copy of its certificate of formation and all amendments thereto;

(c) A copy of its current limited liability company agreement and all amendments thereto, and a copy of any prior agreements no longer in effect;

(d) Unless contained in its certificate of formation or limited liability company agreement, a written statement of:

(i) The amount of cash and a description of agreed value of the other property or services contributed by each member (including that member's predecessors in interest), and which each member has agreed to contribute;

(ii) The times at which or events on the happening of which any additional contributions agreed to be made by each member are to be made; and

(iii) Any right of any member to receive distributions which include a return of all or any part of the member's contribution.

(e) A copy of the limited liability company's federal, state, and local tax returns and reports, if any, for the three most recent years; and

(f) A copy of any financial statements of the limited liability company for the three most recent years.

(2) The records required by subsection (1) of this section to be kept by a limited liability company are subject to inspection and copying at the reasonable request, and at the expense, of any member during ordinary business hours. A member's agent or attorney has the same inspection and copying rights as the member.

(3) Each manager shall have the right to examine all of the information described in subsection (1) of this section for a purpose reasonably related to his or her position as a manager.

(4) A limited liability company may maintain its records in other than a written form if such form is capable of conversion into written form within a reasonable time.

(5) Any action to enforce any right arising under this section shall be brought in the superior courts.

TITLE 40. PUBLIC DOCUMENTS, RECORDS AND PUBLICATIONS.

CHAPTER 40.10. MICROFILMING OF RECORDS TO PROVIDE CONTINUITY OF CIVIL GOVERNMENT.

Citation: RCW 40.10.010

✪ § 40.10.010. Essential records — Designation — List and protection — Reproduction.

In order to provide for the continuity and preservation of civil government, each elected and appointed officer of the state shall designate those public documents which are essential records of his office and needed in an emergency for the reestablishment of normal operations after any such emergency. A list of such records shall be forwarded to the state archivist on forms prescribed by the state archivist. This list shall be reviewed at least annually by the elected or appointed officer to ensure its completeness. Any changes or revisions following this review shall be forwarded to the state archivist. Each such elected and appointed officer of state government shall ensure that the security of essential records of his office is by the most economical means commensurate with adequate protection. Protection of essential records may be by vaulting, planned or natural dispersal of copies, or any other method approved by the state archivist. Reproductions of essential records may be by photo copy, magnetic tape, microfilm or other method approved by the state archivist. Local government offices may coordinate the protection of their essential records with the state archivist as necessary to provide continuity of local government under emergency conditions.

Citation: RCW 40.10.020

✪ § 40.10.020. Essential records — Reproduction and storage — Coordination of protection program — Fees.

The state archivist is authorized to reproduce those documents designated as essential records by the several elected and appointed officials of the state and local government by microfilm or other miniature photographic process and to assist and cooperate in the storage and safeguarding of such reproductions in such place as is recommended by the state archivist with the advice of the director of community development. The state archivist shall coordinate the essential records protection program and shall carry out the provisions of the state emergency plan as they relate to the preservation of essential records. The state archivist is authorized to charge the several departments of the state and local government the actual cost incurred in reproducing, storing and safeguarding such documents: *Provided,* That nothing herein shall authorize the destruction of the originals of such documents after reproduction thereof.

CHAPTER 40.14. PRESERVATION AND DESTRUCTION OF PUBLIC RECORDS.

Citation: RCW 40.14.020

✪ § 40.14.020. Divison of archives and records management — State archivist — Powers and duties — Duties of public officials.

All public records shall be and remain the property of the state of Washington. They shall be delivered by outgoing officials and employees to their successors and shall be preserved, stored, transferred, destroyed or disposed of, and otherwise managed, only in accordance with the provisions of this chapter. In order to insure the proper management and safeguarding of public records, the division of archives and records management is established in the office of the secretary of state. The state archivist, who shall administer the division and have reasonable access to all public records, wherever kept, for purposes of information, surveying, or cataloguing, shall undertake the following functions, duties, and responsibilities:

(1) To manage the archives of the state of Washington;

(2) To centralize the archives of the state of Washington, to make them available for reference and scholarship, and to insure their proper preservation;

(3) To inspect, inventory, catalog, and arrange retention and transfer schedules on all record files of all state department and

other agencies of state government;

(4) To insure the maintenance and security of all state public records and to establish safeguards against unauthorized removal or destruction;

(5) To establish and operate such state record centers as may from time to time be authorized by appropriation, for the purpose of preserving, servicing, screening and protecting all state public records which must be preserved temporarily or permanently, but which need not be retained in office space and equipment;

(6) To adopt rules under chapter 34.05 RCW:

(a) Setting standards for the durability and permanence of public records maintained by state and local agencies:

(b) Governing procedures for the creation, maintenance, transmission, cataloging, indexing, storage, or reproduction of photographic, optical, electronic, or other images of public documents or records in a manner consistent with current standards, policies, and procedures of the department of information services for the acquisition of information technology;

(c) Governing the accuracy and durability of, and facilitating access to photographic, optical, electronic, or other images used as public records; or

(d) To carry out any other provision of this chapter;

(7) To gather and disseminate to interested agencies information on all phases of records management and current practices, methods, procedures, techniques, and devices for efficient and economical management and preservation of records;

(8) To operate a central microfilming bureau which will microfilm, at cost, records approved for filming by the head of the office of origin and the archivist; to approve microfilming projects undertaken by state departments and all other agencies of state government; and to maintain proper standards for this work;

(9) To maintain necessary facilities for the review of records approved for destruction and for their economical disposition by sale or burning; directly to supervise such destruction of public records as shall be authorized by the terms of this chapter; [and]

(10) To assist and train state and local agencies in the proper methods of creating, maintaining, cataloging, indexing, transmitting, storing, and reproducing photographic, optical, electronic, or other images used as public records.

(11) To adopt rules under chapter 34.05 RCW to carry out the state archivist's duties under this chapter.

Citation: RCW 40.14.070

✪ **§ 40.14.070. Destruction, disposal of local government records — Preservation for historical interest — Local records committee, duties — Record retention schedules.**

County, municipal, and other local government agencies may request authority to destroy noncurrent public records having no further administrative or legal value by submitting to the division of archives and records management lists of such records on forms prepared by the division. The archivist ,a representative appointed by the state auditor, and a representative appointed by the attorney general shall constitute a committee, known as the local records committee, which shall review such lists and which may veto the destruction of any or all items contained therein.

A local government agency, as an alternative to submitting lists, may elect to establish a records control program based on recurring disposition schedules recommended by the agency to the local records committee. The schedules to be submitted on forms provided by the division of archives and records management to the local records committee, which may either veto, approve, or amend the schedule. Approval of such schedule or amended schedule shall be by unanimous vote of the local records committee. Upon such approval, the schedule shall constitute authority for the local government agency to destroy the records listed thereon, after the required retention period, on a recurring basis until the schedule is either amended or revised by the committee.

Except as otherwise provided by law, no public records shall be destroyed until approved for destruction by the local records committee. Official public records shall not be destroyed unless:

(1) The records are six or more years old;

(2) The department of origin of the records has made a satisfactory showing to the state records committee that the retention of the records for a minimum of six years is both unnecessary and uneconomical, particularly where lesser federal retention periods for records generated by the state under federal programs have been established; or

(3) The originals of official public records less than six years old have been copies or reproduced by any photographic, photostatic, microfilm, miniature photographic, or other process approved by the state archivist which accurately reproduced the or forms a durable medium for so reproducing the original.

An automatic reduction of retention periods from seven to six years for official public records on record retention schedules existing on June 10, 1982, shall not be made, but the same shall be reviewed individually by the local records committee for approval or disapproval of the change to a retention period of six years.

The state archivist may furnish appropriate information, suggestions, and guidelines to local government agencies for their assistance in the preparation of lists and schedules or any other matter relating to the retention, preservation, or destruction of records under this chapter. The local records committee may adopt appropriate regulations establishing procedures to be followed in such matters.

Records of county, municipal, or other local government agencies, designated by the archivist as of primarily historical interest, may be transferred to a recognized depository agency.

CHAPTER 40.20. REPRODUCED RECORDS FOR GOVERNMENTS AND BUSINESS.

Citation: RCW 40.20.020

✍ ☞ **§ 40.20.020. Reproduction by film or photograph.**

The head of any business or the head of any state, county or municipal department, commission, bureau or board may cause any or all records required or authorized by law to be made or kept by such official, department, commission, bureau, board or business to be photographed, microphotographed, photostated or reproduced on film for all purposes of recording documents, plats, files or papers, or copying or reproducing such records. Such film or reproducing material shall be of permanent material and the device used to reproduce such records on such film or material shall be such as to accurately reproduce and perpetuate the original records in all details, and shall be approved for the intended purpose; *Provided,* That the state archivist shall approve such material for state records use: *Provided, further,* That the state auditor shall approve such material for use by local government subdivisions.

Citation: RCW 40.20.030

☞ ✪ **§ 40.20.030. Use as original.**

Such photostatic copy, photograph, microphotograph, or photographic film record, or copy of the original records shall be deemed to be an original record for all purposes, and shall be admissible in evidence in all courts or administrative agencies. A facsimile, exemplification or certified copy thereof shall, for all purposes recited herein, be deemed to be a transcript, exemplification or certified copy of the original.

Source: Rules of Evidence

ARTICLE 10. Contents of Writings, Recordings, and Photographs.

☞ Rule 1001. Definitions

For purposes of this article the following definitions are applicable:

(1) *Writings and recordings.* — "Writings" and "recordings" consist of letters, words, or numbers, or their equivalent, set down by handwriting, typewriting, printing, photostating, photographing, magnetic impulse, mechanical or electronic recording, or other form of data compilation.

(2) *Photographs.* — "Photographs" include still photographs, X-ray films, video tapes, and motion pictures.

(3) *Original.* — An "original" of a writing or recording is the writing or recording itself or any counterpart intended to have the same effect by a person executing or issuing it. An "original" of a photograph includes the negative or any print therefrom. If data are stored in a computer or similar device, any printout or other output readable by sight, shown to reflect the data accurately, is an "original".

(4) *Duplicate.* — A "duplicate" is a counterpart produced by the same impression as the original, or from the same matrix, or by means of photography, including enlargements and miniatures, or by mechanical or electronic re-recording, or by chemical reproduction, or by other equivalent techniques which accurately reproduces the original.

✍ Rule 1003. Admissibility of duplicates.

A duplicate is admissible to the same extent as an original unless (1) a genuine question is raised as to the authenticity of the original or (2) in these circumstances it would be unfair to admit the duplicate in lieu of the original.

[See Appendix A. Uniform Rules of Evidence for additional provisions.]

Source: Washington Administrative Code
Agency: Department of Labor and Industries
Division of Industrial Safety and Health

WASHINGTON INDUSTRIAL SAFETY AND HEALTH ACT

CHAPTER 296-27. RECORDKEEPING AND REPORTING.

Citation: WAC 296-27-030

✍ § 296-27-030. Log and summary of occupational injuries and illnesses.

(1) Except as provided in subsection (2) of this section, each employer shall:

(a) Maintain in each establishment a log and summary of all recordable occupational injuries and illnesses for that establishment; and

(b) Enter each recordable injury and illness on the log as early as practicable, but no later than six working days after receiving information that a recordable case has occurred. For this purpose Form OSHA NO. 200 or an equivalent which is as readable and comprehensible to a person not familiar with it shall be used. The log and summary shall be completed in the detail provided in instructions on Form OSHA No. 200.

(2) Any employer may maintain the log and summary of all recordable occupational injuries and illnesses at a place other than the establishment or by means of data processing equipment, or both, if at each of the employer's establishments there is available a copy of the log and summary which reflects separately the injury and illness experience of that establishment complete and current to a date within forty-five calendar days.

Agency: Department of Revenue

Citation: WAC 458-20-254

✍ § 458-20-254 Recordkeeping.

(1) Every person liable for an excise tax imposed by the laws of the state of Washington for which the department of revenue has primary or secondary administrative responsibility, i.e., Title 82 RCW, and, chapters 67.28 RCW (hotel/motel tax), 70.93 RCW (litter tax), 70.95 RCW (tax on tires), and 84.33 RCW (forest excise tax), shall keep complete and adequate records from which the department may determine any tax for which such person may be liable,.

(2) *General Requirements.*

(a) It is the duty of each taxpayer to prepare and preserve all books of record in a systematic manner conforming to accepted accounting methods and procedures. Records are to be kept, preserved, and presented upon request of the department which will demonstrate:

(i) The amounts of gross receipts and sales from all sources, however, derived, including barter or exchange transactions, whether or not such receipts or sales are taxable. These amounts must be supported by original source documents including but no limited to all purchase and sales invoices and contracts or such other documents as may be necessary to substantiate gross receipts and sales;

(ii) The amounts of all deductions, exemptions, or credits claimed through supporting documentation required by statute or administrative rule, or such other supporting documentation necessary to substantiate the deduction, exemption, or credit.

(b) The records kept, preserved and presented must include the normal books of account maintained by an ordinary prudent business person. Such records may include general ledgers, sales journals, cash receipts journals, check registers, and purchase journals, together with all bills, invoices, cash register tapes, or other documents of original entry supporting the books of account entries. The records shall include all federal and state tax returns and reports and all schedules or work papers used in the preparation of tax reports or returns.

(c) All such records shall be open for inspection and examination at any time by the department, upon reasonable notice, and shall be kept and preserved for a period of five years. RCW 82.32.070

(3) *Microfilm and/or Microfiche.* Records may be microfilmed or microfiched, such as general books of accounts including cash books, journals, voucher registers, ledgers and like documents provided the microfilmed and/or microfiched records are authentic, accessible, and readable, and all of the following requirements are fully satisfied:

(a) Appropriate facilities are provided to preserve the films or fiche for the periods such records are required to be open to examination and to provide transcriptions of any information on film or fiche required to verify tax liability.

(b) All microfilmed or microfiched data must be indexed, cross referenced, and labeled to show beginning and ending numbers and beginning and ending alphabetical listings of all documents included.

(c) Taxpayers must make available upon request of the department, a reader/printer in good working order at the examination site for reading, locating, and reproducing any record that is maintained on microfilm or microfiche.

(d) Taxpayers must set forth in writing the procedures governing the establishment of a microfilm or microfiche system and the names of persons who are responsible for maintaining and operating the system with appropriate authorization from the boards of directors, general partner(s), or owner(s), whichever is applicable.

(e) The microfilm or microfiche system must be complete and must be used consistently in the regular conducted activity of the business.

(f) Taxpayers must establish procedures with the appropriate documentation so that an original document can be traced through the microfilm or microfiche system.

(g) Taxpayers must establish internal procedures for microfilm or microfiche inspection and quality assurance.

(h) Taxpayers must keep a record identifying where, when, by whom, and on what equipment the microfilm or microfiche was produced.

(i) When displayed on a microfilm or microfiche reader (viewer) or reproduced on paper, the material must be legible and readable. For this purpose, legible means the quality of a letter or numeral which enables the reader to identify it positively and quickly to the exclusion of all other letters or numerals. Readable means the quality of a group of letters or numerals recognizable as words or complete number.

(j) All production of microfilm or microfiche and the processing duplication, quality control, storage, identifications, and inspection thereof must meet industry standards as set forth by the American National Standards Institute, National Micrographics Association, or National Bureau of Standards.

(4) *Automated Data Processing System.* An automated data processing (ADP) accounting system may be used to provide the records required to verify tax liability. All ADP systems used for this purpose must include a method for producing legible and readable records to verify tax liability, reporting, and payment. The following requirements apply to any taxpayer who maintains records on an ADP system:

(a) ADP records shall provide an opportunity to trace any transaction back to the original source or forward to a final total. If detailed printouts are not made of transactions at the time they are done, the system must have the capability to reconstruct these transactions.

(b) A general ledger, with source references, shall be written out to coincide with financial reports for tax reporting periods. In the cases where subsidiary ledgers are used to support the general ledger accounts, the subsidiary ledgers shall be written out periodically.

(c) The audit trail shall be so designed that the details underlying the summary accounting data may be identified and made available to the department and that supporting documents, such as sales invoices, purchase invoices, credit memoranda, and like documents are readily available.

(i) The application being performed;

(ii) The procedures employed in each application (which, for example, might be supported by flow charts, block diagrams or other satisfactory description of the input or output procedures); and

(iii) The controls used to insure accurate and reliable processing.

(e) Important changes in an ADP accounting system or any part thereof, together with their effective dates, shall be noted to preserve an accurate chronological record of such changes.

(f) Adequate record retention facilities shall be available for the storage of such information, printouts and all supporting documents.

(5) *Out-of-State Businesses.* An out-of-state business which does not keep the necessary records within this state may either produce within this state such records as are required for examination by the department, or, permit the examination of the records by the department at the place where the records are kept. RCW 82.32.070, see also, WAC 458-20-215.

(6) *Failure of Taxpayer to Maintain and Disclose Complete and Adequate Records.* Any person who fails to comply with the requirements of RCW 82.32.070 or this section shall be forever barred from questioning, in any court action or proceedings, the correctness of any assessment of taxes made by the department based upon any period for which such books, record, and invoices have not been so kept and preserved. RCW 82-32.070

Agency: **Office of the Secretary of State Division of Archives and Records Management**

CHAPTER 434-663. IMAGING SYSTEMS, STANDARDS FOR ACCURACY AND DURABILITY.

LEGALITY OF ELECTRONIC IMAGING SYSTEMS USED FOR MANAGING AND STORING PUBLIC RECORDS

Citation: **WAC 434-663-001**

✪ **§ 434-663-001. Legality.**

Electronic imaging systems may be legally used for recording, producing, reproducing, maintaining, and storing public records provided that they meet the standards set forth in this regulation; and the retention and disposition of the original and copies are scheduled in accord with Chapter 40.14 RCW.

DEFINITIONS

Citation: **WAC 434-663-005**

✪ **§ 434-663-005. Electronic Document Imaging System.**

An electronic document imaging system is a computer-based configuration of equipment and software that stores machine-readable document images and their associated character-coded index data for on-demand retrieval. Electronic images can be computer generated, or created through document scanning.

Citation: **WAC 434-663-006**

✪ **§ 434-663-0006. Digital.**

The representation of information as discrete pulses that correspond to the binary digits (bits) 0 and 1. The process of digitation converts human-readable information into a form that machines can process.

Citation: **WAC 434-663-007**

✪ **§ 434-663-007. Pixel.**

PIX (picture)EL(ement) is the smallest display element on a video screen or the smallest element in a grid that is placed over a page of text or graphics, also known as PEL (Picture Element).

Citation: WAC 434-663-008

✪ **§ 434-663-008. Resolution.**

The number of picture elements (pixels) that resides horizontally and vertically in one square inch of the document page image. Resolution can be expressed in dpi (dots per inch), ppi (pixels per inch), or bpi (bits per inch). For example, 200 dpi means 200 dots by 200 dots, or 40,000 dots per square inch. The higher the resolution value, the clearer and more detailed the image is.

Citation: WAC 434-663-009

✪ **§ 434-663-009. Contrast.**

Contrast is the difference in reflected light between the light and dark areas of the document. The parts of the document that reflects light in excess of some specified amount are considered white and are encoded as a one or a zero bit. Where the amount of reflected light is lower than the predetermined threshold amount, those parts are considered black and are represented by the opposite bit value.

Citation: WAC 434-663-010

✪ **§ 434-663-010. Compression.**

The process used to reduce the space required for the storage or transfer of an image. There are various techniques including CCITT Group 3 and 4, JPEG, MPEG, and fractals.

Citation: WAC 434-663-011

✪ **§ 434-663-011. Document scanning.**

A specially designed input workstation is required to convert documents or images to machine-readable form for computer processing and storage. At a minimum, the input workstation includes a document scanner, an image processor unit, a video display unit with keyboard, and access to storage. Using a solid-state array or other photo sensitive components, the document scanner measures the amount of light associated with successively encountered PELs and transmits a corresponding electrical signal that is converted to computer compatible digital codes.

Citation: WAC 434-663-012

✪ **§ 434-663-012. Image.**

An image can be a document, picture, or graphic. An image can be produced either by scanning paper or film documents, producing images through a computer program, or receiving an image by means of a fax.

Citation: WAC 434-663-013

✪ **§ 434-663-013. Enhancement.**

Any method including adjusting brightness and contrast, or algorithm employed with the objective of producing an accurate and legible copy.

Citation: WAC 434-663-014

✪ **§ 434-663-014. Archival Records.**

Archival records are records that have permanent and/or historical value. Long term records are records having value for a period in excess of 10 years.

Citation: WAC 434-663-015

✪ **§ 434-663-015. Open System.**

Open system is defined to be a system that implements sufficient public specifications for interfaces, services and supporting formats to enable applications software to be ported across a wide range of systems, to inter operate with other applications on local and remote systems, and to interact with users in a style that facilitates user portability. Public specifications are maintained by open, public consensus process to accommodate new technology over time, and which is consistent with international standards.

Citation: WAC 434-663-016

✪ **§ 434-663-016. De Facto Standard.**

A de facto standard is a widely accepted industry standard without official recognition by a standards group.

Citation: WAC 434-663-020

✪ **§ 434-663-020. Quality of Digital Images.**

Ensuring the quality of digital images requires exercising control over six processes: conversion of the original image to digital data, enhancement of the digital image if necessary, compression of the digital data for storage, decompression of digital data for retrieval, displaying the image, and printing.

Citation: WAC 434-663-021

✪ **§ 434-663-021. Conversion of Documents to Digital Data.**

A minimum scanning density of 200 dpi is required for office documents, maps, graphics, and images. Employ a scanning density of 300 dpi or greater for documents having very detailed information such as engineering drawings, and detailed maps. Before commencing a document conversion project, conduct tests using samples of actual documents to be converted to digital data and resolution targets. The purpose of the test is to verify the color spectrum capability of the scanner and the scanning density required. Except in unusual circumstances, restrict use of gray scale to continuous tone photographs.

Citation: WAC 434-663-022

✪ **§ 434-663-022. Enhancement of Original Image.**

Enhancement should be used only to ensure readability of the document and to improve the accuracy of the copy. Select samples of original documents to be scanned based upon levels of legibility (poor to excellent), scan these documents using varying enhancements algorithm settings. Compare original documents with test images. Use the best scanned images as the operation criteria for acceptable image quality.

Citation: WAC 434-663-023

✪ § 434-663-023. Compressing Image Data for Storage.

Imaging systems must use a compression technique that meets either a published or de facto standard such as CCITT Group 3 or Group 4, JPEG, or MPEG. If such a technique cannot be used, the software vendor must provide a bridge to the prevailing CCITT standard.

Citation: WAC 434-663-030

✪ § 434-663-030. Usability of Image and Index Data Over Time.

Maintaining access to an usability of electronic records requires ensuring continuous readability and intelligibility. Readability means the ability to process images both on the computer system on which they were created and on different computer systems without appreciable errors. Intelligibility means that humans can comprehend the information the computer reads. Ensuring readability and intelligibility of electronic records over time entails maintenance of environmental conditions, periodic recopying, and strategies to preserve data by migration from one generation of technology to another through a commitment to open architecture. Fax transmissions can be used as a gateway.

Citation: WAC 434-663-031

✪ § 434-663-031. Defining Indexing Requirements.

The selection of indexing parameters is based on analysis of retrieval requirements associated with a particular application, and must ensure rapid and accurate retrieval of information. For systems containing records with archival or long term value, index design should take into account the retrieval requirements of both current and future users of the records, including government agency personnel as well as researchers and the general public.

Citation: WAC 434-663-032

✪ § 434-663-032. Index Search Specifications.

For new systems containing records with archival or long term value, index design should include the following functions. For numeric fields, the retrieval software should permit index searches based on ranges of field values specified by the following relational expressions: greater than, less than, greater than or equal to, and less than or equal to. For textual fields, the retrieval software should permit index searches based on root word matches (term truncation). The retrieval software should permit the logical Boolean AND operator. The retrieval software's initial response to an index search command should be an indication of the number of database records that satisfy the seat specifications. The user can then decide whether to view the indicated database records or modify the search specification to retrieve more or fewer items.

Citation: WAC 434-663-033

✪ § 334-663-033. Preservation Strategy.

A preservation strategy must be developed and implemented for each image system containing long term or archival information. Four preservation strategy options are acceptable.
(1) retain the original paper documents, or
(2) microfilm the original documents, or
(3) recopy optical and magnetic media every 10 years, or
(4) print images on microfilm.

Citation: WAC 434-663-034

✪ § 434-663-034. Header Files.

A non-proprietary header label on files or a gateway to a non-proprietary header label is required for imaging systems that contain long term or archival information.

Citation: WAC 434-663-035

✪ § 434-663-035. Backup for Recovery.

In order to facilitate a recovery of lost information and the restoration of system operations in the event of a malfunction or other disaster, properly implemented backup procedures must be in place. Produce security copies of document images and indexes through either simultaneous recording, or periodic batch mode backed up.

Citation: WAC 434-663-036

✪ § 434-663-036. Ensuring Usability.

At a minimum, the system must include an electronic error checking utility that will check for bad sectors in order to ensure the integrity of the data over time.

Citation: WAC 434-663-037

✪ § 434-663-037. Stability of Media.

Records and their indexes having a permanent or archival retention or a retention of over 10 years require long-term stability of the media used. Three inter-related issues impact long-term stability: 1. media selection, including storage and recording technology; 2. quality of data stored; 3. media protection.

Citation: WAC 434-663-038

✪ § 434-663-038. Storage Media.

Write once read many (WORM) media should be used for records having a permanent or archival retention or a retention of over 10 years. If WORM technology is not practical for an application, and rewritable media is used, ensure that read/write privileges are carefully controlled and that an audit trail of rewrites is maintained.

Citation: WAC 434-663-039

✪ § 434-663-039. Optical Platters.

Bi-metallic recording technology is required for records of long term or archival value using optical media.

Citation: WAC 434-663-040

✪ § 434-663-040. Optical Media Durability.

Durability for optical media is defined as shelf life before writing and post-writing life. For records having permanent or archival retention or a retention of over 10 years, use media with a pre-write shelf life of five years. Use media with a minimum 20 year post-writ life, guaranteed by the vendor based on accelerated aging tests linked to specific locations on the surface of the media. Vendors must document that aging tests have been conducted by an independent testing laboratory.

Citation: WAC 434-663-041

✪ **§ 434-663-041. Long-Term Off Line Storage Environment.**

Store media in a dust free area with a stable temperature between 65 and 75 degrees Fahrenheit (plus or minus 2 degrees) and relative humidity between 40 and 45 percent. Optical disks and magnetic tapes should be stored vertically. Optical disks should be cleaned at least every 6 months to remove particulate and fingerprints. Blank magnetic tape should be tested prior to being used for the storage of information. Magnetic tape should be stored in a suitable container. Magnetic tape should be precision rewound every five years and before each use. Every ten years, the reliability of the data should be tested, with the information being transferred to pretested fresh stock.

FUNCTIONALITY OF SYSTEM COMPONENTS

Citation: WAC 434-663-050

✪ **§ 434-663-050. Open Systems Architecture.**

Ensuring the usability of digital images to serve the functions for which they were designed involves long-term commitment to an open systems architecture and an approach to component upgrading, data transfer, and migration path that guarantees the portability of current data to be used with future technologies. Open systems architecture is required for records having long term or archival value.

Citation: WAC 434-663-051

✪ **§ 434-663-051. Backward Compatibility.**

System upgrades or new systems acquired after the effective date of this regulation must provide backward compatibility to any existing systems containing the same records series.

Citation: WAC 434-663-052

✪ **§ 434-663-052. Location of Index Database on Off Line Media.**

The index data pertaining to the contents of each disk or tape shall be written to that disk or tape in addition to a peripheral device of the operating computer whenever possible. This assures that the index data will be secure for as long as the media is readable and there is a software available to interpret what is read. If this is not possible, then the index must be preserved either through being written to off line storage and linked through labeling to the file it relates to, or if the index is on-line the location of the index is well documented on the label of the container of the file, so that in either case the index can be used to access the images.

Citation: WAC 434-663-053

✪ **§ 434-663-053. Technical Documentation.**

Technical documentation on system components, application software and operating systems is essential to facilitate long-term access to records stored on optical media. The system's hardware and software characteristics must be fully documented, indicating the types, brand names, and model numbers of all hardware components including recording media with the dates that specific pieces of equipment were put into and taken out of service. Documentation must also include all system software including version numbers and implementation dates of all upgrade. Vendors are required to place a complete set of documentation with the agency responsible for operating the optical media system. Documentation includes a hardware systems administrator's manual detailing configuration, software applications documentation, and application specific operational procedures. If customized application software was developed, flow charts, source code, and other developmental documentation must be included.

RETENTION AND DISPOSITION OF RECORDS

Citation: WAC 434-663-061

✪ **§ 434-663-061. Retention and Disposition of Public Records.**

Conversion to an imaging systems does not automatically authorize the destruction of the original records. Destruction of, or changes to the retention of any public records due to conversion to or the use of a new media requires legal approval of the State or Local Records Committee of the State of Washington through the retention and disposition scheduling process in accord with Chapter 40.14 RCW, and WAC 434-628 and WAC 434-635.

Citation: WAC 434-663-062

✪ **§ 434-663-062. Records Retention Scheduling-Records on Imaging System.**

The retention scheduling of information to be placed on an imaging system must be done prior to the creation or copying of the records, and may require a cost benefit analysis. Decisions about the retention value of information stored on an imaging system are related to the value of the original information included in the system.

Citation: WAC 434-663-063

✪ **§ 434-663-063. Security Copies.**

Records with enduring or permanent legal value, such as land record and deeds, stored on electronic media should have a security backup copy on another type of media. If this is impractical, the user must obtain permission to retain electronic copies as the sole media from the State Records Commission or the Local Records Commission on a case by case basis as part of the records scheduling process. Such permission will be granted only if there are strong back up systems in place and procedures in place for periodic recopying.

Citation: WAC 434-663-064

✪ **§ 434-663-064. Agency Automation Plans-DIS Approval.**

State agencies intending to utilize an imaging system for the storage or conversion of public records must include such plans in their annual automation plan submitted to the Department of Information and comply with other requirements of DIS as may apply.

SYSTEM OPERATION

Citation: WAC 434-663-070

✪ § 434-663-070. Systems Administrators.

Each imaging system shall have a system administrator who will be responsible for the operation of the system, and will be able to provide legal verifications of the authenticity of copies. Other legal duties of the administrator are control of release and expungement of document images, and periodic systems performance audits.

Citation: WAC 434-663-071

✪ § 434-663-071. Written Policy Statement.

A written policy statement, approved by the appropriate officials, must formalize the use of imaging as part of a government agency's regular business practices. The statement must enumerate the specific record series to be imaged, whether the backfile will be converted, and final disposition of the originals. Possible destruction of the original must be indicated in the retention schedule for the specific record series. The retention schedules must be approved by the Agency Records Manager, and the State or Local Records Committee in accord with Chapter 40.14 RCW, WAC 434-628, and WAC 434-635. Original documents must be retained in accord with approved records retention schedules and until the quality assurance check has been completed.

Citation: WAC 434-663-072

✪ § 434-663-072. Operating Procedures.

Document scanning, data entry, and quality control procedures shall be fully documented for each imaging application. There must be scheduled periodic formal documented training for all workers. Written instructions must be prepared for operators of all equipment used in document scanning, index data entry, and image inspection. The instruction shall indicate the scanning resolution, and image compression algorithm to be used in a given application. A log must be kept which indicates the names of the people operating the equipment on specific dates. Quality control procedures must be specified in writing, and a record must be kept of inspections, scanner tests, and other quality control procedures performed on specific dates. Identification certificates should be included with documents imaged, indicating the documents recorded on specific dates, the identify of the persons performing the scanning, indexing, and quality control procedures. Periodic performance audits must be conducted on the functioning of the system.

Citation: WAC 434-663-073

✪ § 434-663-073. Quality Assurance.

At a minimum, such procedures involve the visual inspection of digitized images, scanner testing, and verification of index data. Image inspection involves confirmation of proper scanning. The operator must determine that no parts of the digitized images were obscured, that the displayed image is legible, and that all information (small fonts, pencil marks, etc.) is adequately reproduced. To be considered a true copy, a digitized image must contain all specific details from the original document and must be an adequate substitute for the original document for all purposes for which the document was created or maintained. If the image does not satisfy quality requirements, the document can be rescanned and enhanced for readability, or if that proves fruitless the document can be declared unscannable.

Citation: WAC 434-663-074

✪ § 434-663-074. Scanner Testing and Adjustment.

Scanner testing and adjustment are an important facet of quality control. ANSI/AIIM MS 44-1988 outlines procedures and describes specially designed targets to facilitate such testing and adjustments. These procedures are adopted in this rule by reference. The quality control procedures involve scanning a test target, examining its displayed image for legibility, printing the image and examining the hard copy. These procedures are repeated, as necessary to establish reference images and hard copies for quality control purposes. Like microfilm test steps, these procedures must be performed to establish quality references and appropriate scanner settings for documents with various characteristics. Frequent, periodic testing is recommended to ensure image quality. At a minimum, test targets shall be scanned to determine the correctness of the scanner settings at the start of each shift, and whenever the scanner is repaired or adjusted.

Citation: WAC 434-663-075

✪ § 434-663-075. Verification of Image Recording.

In order to confirm that system components are recording information properly, a sample of recorded images shall be retrieved and displayed and printed for operator inspection and comparison with the source documents from which the images were produced.

Citation: WAC 434-663-076

✪ § 434-663-076. Container Labeling.

Media storage containers must be clearly labeled with enough information to uniquely identify the contents. At the minimum the labels shall include: 1) the name of the agency, office, or other organizational unit that created the disk or tape, 2) name of the system on which media is used, including version number of software used when the disk or tape was created, 3) physical characteristics of the media, including size, storage capacity, number of recording surfaces, 4) a brief description of the data set(s) and/or application(s) to which the contents of the disk or tape pertains, 5) unique identification to distinguish the disk or tape from others used with the same application, 6) date of manufacture of the disk or tape, 7) span of dates during which the media was used for image or other information recording, 8) special security requirements or restrictions on access if any, and 9) an indication of whether the media is a working copy or a storage copy.

Citation: WAC 434-663-077

✪ § 434-663-077. Expungement.

Records may be subject to court ordered expungement. Expungement orders may require the deletion, obliteration, correction, or amendment of records. Expungement of document images or information recorded on optical disks or magnetic tape may involve deletion of index records and deletion of the docent image from both working and security copies.

Deletion of index records, known as virtual purging, alone may not be acceptable for court ordered expungements. WORM optical disks can be expunged by the process of transferring document images to a new disk, omitting the document images to be expunged. The old disk is then destroyed. This can be an expensive process. Rewritable optical disks and magnetic media permit erasure of or writing of document images. Court ordered expungement requirements should be determined as part of the system design especially for those types of records containing personally identifying information that is most likely subject to expungement orders. Expungements must be performed according to well-defined and fully documented procedures that include certifying the copying process and thoroughly testing the new copy disk so that nothing other than records ordered expunged are deleted.

Citation: WAC 434-663-078

✪ § 434-663-078. Security Provisions.

Access control procedures, such as password protection and privilege controls, must be fully documented. A list of all users and their access privileges, ability to add images, or edit index, shall be maintained and audited regularly.

Citation: WAC 434-663-079

✪ § 434-663-079. Controlling Access.

Access to public records that contain private personal information or classified information shall be restricted to authorized persons. In such cases, an electronic document imaging system must include software controls that prevent the unauthorized access to index information or document images. Access can be controlled through the use of passwords and by restricting the types of operations allowed to groups and users.

State: West Virginia
Source: West Virginia Code

CHAPTER 5A. DEPARTMENT OF ADMINISTRATION

Article 8. Public Records Management and Administration Act

Citation: WVC 5A-8-3

✪ § 5A-8-3. Definitions.

As used in this article:

(a) "Disaster" means any occurrence of fire, flood, storm, earthquake, explosion, epidemic, riot, sabotage or other condition of extreme peril resulting in substantial damage or injury to persons or property within this state, whether such occurrence is caused by an act of God, nature or man, including an enemy of the United States.

(b) "Record" means document, book, paper, photograph, sound recording or other material, regardless of physical form or characteristics, made or received pursuant to law or ordinance or in connection with the transaction of official business. Library and museum material made or acquired and preserved solely for reference of exhibition purposes, extra copies of documents preserved only for convenience of reference, and stocks of publications and of processed documents are not included within the definition of records as used in this article.

(c) "State record" means:

(1) A record of a department, office, commission, board or other agency, however designated, of the state government.

(2) A records of the state Legislature.

(3) A record of any court of record, whether of statewide or local jurisdiction.

(4) Any record designated or treated as a state record under state law.

(d) "Local record" means a record of a county, city, town, authority or any public corporation or political entity whether organized and existing under charter or under general law unless the record is designated or treated as a state record under state law.

(e) "Agency" means any department, office, commission, board or other unit, however designated, of the executive branch of state government.

(f) "Preservation duplicate" means a copy of an essential state record which is used for the purpose of preserving such state record pursuant to this article.

Citation: WVC 5A-8-10

✪ § 5A-8-10. Essential state records — Preservation duplicates.

(a) The administrator may make or cause to be made preservation duplicates or may designate as preservation duplicates existing copies of essential state records. A preservation duplicate shall be durable, accurate, complete and clear, and a preservation duplicate made by means of photography, microphotography, photocopying, film or microfilm shall be made in conformity with the standards prescribed therefor by the administrator.

(b) A preservation duplicate made by a photographic, photostatic, microfilm, microcard, miniature photographic, or other process which accurately reproduces or forms a durable medium for so reproducing the original, shall have the same force and affect for all purposes as the original record whether the original record is in existence or not. A transcript, exemplification or certified copy of such preservation duplicate shall be deemed for all purposes to be a transcript, exemplification or certified copy of the original record.

CHAPTER 51. COURTS AND THEIR OFFICERS

Article 4. General Provisions Relating to Clerks of Courts

Citation: WVC 51-4-3

✪ § 51-4-3. Preservation and destruction of papers; microphotography and electronic storage.

All papers lawfully returned to or filed in the clerk's office shall be preserved therein, subject to the conditions set out herein, until legally delivered out.

Notwithstanding any other provisions of this code to the contrary, the clerk may destroy all documents, records, instruments, books, papers, depositions and transcripts in any; action or proceeding in the circuit court or other court of record, or otherwise filed in his office pursuant to law, provided that:

(a) Destruction is done in accordance with a "Record Retention Schedule" to be adopted, promulgated and amended, from time to time, by the Supreme Court of Appeals; and

(b) The clerk maintains for the use of the public a microphotographic film or electronic storage media record of all documents required to be permanently preserved under the "Record Retention Schedule," together with an index and a mechanical or electronic device by which such microphotographic film or electronic storage media record may be conveniently examined. The clerk shall promptly seal and store at least one original of each microphotographic film or electronic storage media record in such manner and place as will reasonably assure its preservation indefinitely against loss, theft, defacement, intentional alteration, fire or other destruction. Any electronic method used must provide an exact copy of each document so stored and must be secure to the point that an attempt to alter a document is readily recognized.

A photographic reproduction or electronic media reproduction of any of the records described in this section, the negative or film or electronic record of which has been certified by the clerk in charge of such reproduction as being an exact replica of the original, shall be received in evidence in all courts, and in hearings before any officer, board or commission having jurisdiction or authority to conduct such hearings, in like manner as the original.

CHAPTER 57. EVIDENCE AND WITNESSES.

Article 1. Legislative Acts and Resolutions; Public Records.

Citation: WVC 57-1-7a

☞ ✪ **§ 57-1-7a. Use of photographic copies in evidence; state records, papers or documents; destruction or transfer to archives of originals; destruction of canceled checks and paid and canceled bonds and coupons.**

Any public officer of the State may, with the approval of the state records administrator, cause any or all records, papers or documents kept by him to be photographed, microphotographed or reproduced on film. Such photographic film shall be of durable material and the device used to reproduce such records on such film shall be one which accurately reproduces the original thereof in all details.

Such photographs, microphotographs, microfilms or photographic film shall be deemed to be an original record for all purposes, including introduction in evidence in all courts or administrative agencies. A transcript, exemplification or certified copy thereof shall, for all purposes recited herein, be deemed to be a transcript, exemplification, or certified copy of the original. Whenever photographs, microphotographs, microfilms or reproductions on film have been made and put in conveniently accessible fireproof files, and provision has been made for preserving, examining and using the same, the respective heads of the departments, divisions, institutions and agencies of the State may, with the approval of the state records administrator, cause the records and papers so photographed, microphotographed or reproduced on film, or any part thereof, to be destroyed; but before any such records, papers or documents are authorized to be destroyed, the state records administrator shall obtain the advice and counsel of the state historian and archivist, or his designated representative, as to the desirability of placing the said records, papers and documents in the archives of that department. In the event the administrator is of the opinion that the record has no further administrative, legal, fiscal, research or historical value, the administrator may destroy or otherwise dispose of the record, paper or document if otherwise permitted to do so after complying with the provisions of section seventeen [§ 5A-8-17], article eight, chapter five-a of this code. Not withstanding any other provisions of this code to the contrary, the state treasurer may at his discretion destroy any canceled checks of the state after ten years have elapsed since the date of the check, whether or not such checks have been photographed, microphotographed or reproduced on film; Provided, however, that any canceled bonds or interest coupons of any bond issues of this State in the custody of the treasurer, or for which the treasurer acts as fiscal agent or paying agent, may at his discretion be destroyed by one of the first two methods described below:

Method I — The treasurer shall maintain a permanent record for the purposes of recording the destruction of bonds and coupons, showing the following:

(1) With respect to bonds, the purpose of issuance, the date of issue, denomination, maturity date, and total principal amount; and

(2) with respect to coupons, the purpose of issue and date of the bonds to which the coupons appertain, the maturity date of the coupons, and, as to each maturity date, the denomination, quantity and total amount of coupons.

After recording the specified information, the treasurer shall have the canceled bonds and coupons destroyed either by burning or shredding, in the presence of an employee of the treasurer and an employee of the legislative auditor, each of whom shall certify that he saw the canceled bonds and coupons destroyed. Such certificates shall be made a part of the permanent record. Canceled bonds or coupons shall not be destroyed until after one year from the date of payment.

Method II — The treasurer may contract with any bank or trust company acting as paying agent or copaying agent for a bond issue of the State for the destruction of bonds and interest coupons which have been canceled by the paying agent. The contract shall require that the paying agent give the treasurer a written certificate containing the same information required by Method I. Such certificate shall include a sworn statement that the described bonds or coupons have been destroyed. The certificate shall be made a part of the treasurer's permanent record.

Each contract shall also require that the paying agent be responsible for proper payment and disposition of all bonds and coupons, and for any duplicate payments to unauthorized persons and nonpayment to authorized persons occurring as a result of destruction of bonds or coupons under this section. In addition, the treasurer may require the paying agent to submit an indemnity bond, in an amount to be determined by the treasurer, to assure performance of the duties specified in this section. Canceled bonds or coupons may not be destroyed until one year from the date of payment.

For purposes of this section, the term "bonds" shall include interim certificates.

Citation: WVC 57-1-7b

☞ **§ 57-1-7b. Same — Business and public records; destruction of originals.**

If any business, institution, member of a profession or calling, or any officer of a local governmental agency, including county officers, county boards of education and municipalities, in the regular course of business or activity has kept or recorded any memorandum, writing, entry, print, representation or combination thereof, of any act, transaction, occurrence or event, and in the regular course of business has caused any or all of the same to be recorded, copied or reproduced by any photographic, photostatic, microfilm, micro-card, miniature photographic, or other process which accurately reproduces or forms a durable medium for so reproducing the original, the original may be destroyed in the regular course of business unless held in a custodial or fiduciary capacity or unless its preservation is required by law: Provided, however, that destruction of records of local governmental agencies shall also be contingent upon the approval by those agencies of such disposition. Such reproduction, when satisfactorily identified, is as admissible in evidence as the original itself in any judicial or administrative proceeding whether the original is in existence or not, and an enlargement or facsimile of such reproduction is likewise admissible in evidence if the original reproduction is in existence and available for inspection under direction of court. The introduction of a reproduced record, enlargement or facsimile, does not preclude admission of the original.

Citation: **WVC 57-1-7c**

☞ ✪ **§ 57-1-7c. Use of microfilm and microcards to reproduce and preserve records; destruction or transfer of originals to archivist.**

The clerk of any court of record of the state may, with the approval of the court for which he or she is clerk, cause any or all records, papers, plats, or other documents kept by him or her to be reproduced on photographic microfilm or microcards and may, with the approval of the court for which he or she is clerk, record, keep and preserve any and all records, papers, plats, or other documents required by the laws of this state to be recorded or kept by said clerk or court exclusively upon photographic microfilm or microcards instead of in well-bound books or instead of by any other method heretofore prescribed by law.

Such photographic microfilm and microcards shall be of durable material and possess good, archival qualities. The device used to reproduce such records on such film and cards shall be one which accurately reproduces the original thereto in all details.

Such photographic microfilm and microcards shall be deemed to be an original record for all purposes, including introduction into evidence in all courts or administrative agencies. A transcript, exemplification, or photographic reproduction thereof shall, when properly authenticated by the clerk of such court, be deemed for all purposes to be a transcript, exemplification, or certified copy of the original.

Such photographic microfilm and microcards shall be put in convenient, accessible fireproof files and adequate provision shall be made for preserving, examining and using the same.

Any such records, papers, plats, or other documents not held for others by said clerk or court or required by law to be delivered to some other person, court, corporation or agency, may with the approval of the court keeping such records, papers, plats, or other documents be destroyed; but before any such records, papers, plats or other documents are authorized to be destroyed the court keeping them or the clerk thereof shall obtain the advice and counsel of the state historian or archivist, or his designated representatives, as to the desirability of placing the said records, papers, plats, or other documents in the department of archives and history. However, prior to destroying or otherwise disposing of the same, the court or clerk therof shall give written notice of the intention to do so to the director of the section of archives and history of the division of culture and history. Upon the written request of the director, given to the court or clerk therof within ten days of receipt of said notice, the court or clerk thereof shall retain the original record for a period of thirty days. In the event the director fails to retrieve the original document from the court or clerk therof within the thirty day period, the court or clerk therof may destroy or otherwise dispose of the original without further notice to the director.

Citation: **WVC 57-1-7d.**

☞ ✪ **§ 57-1-7d. Records provided on computer or optical disc.**

Not withstanding any other provision of this code to the contrary, where any provision of this code requires that a copy of any record of any branch of the government of this state be provided or delivered, the custodian of said record is authorized to comply with the requirement by providing or delivering a true copy in the form of a computer or optical disc which is not subject to alteration, is formatted to write once read many, and is attested by the custodian thereof to be a true, accurate and complete copy of the record required to be provided or delivered.

Article 5. Miscellaneous Provisions.

Citation: **WVC 57-5-12**

☞ **§ 57-5-12. Certain documents deemed duplicates.**

A reproduction of a document acquired from the employment of a system or microphotography, optical discs or computerized techniques which system does not permit additions, deletions or changes to the record of the original document contained within the system shall be deemed to be a duplicate for purposes of admission into evidence in the courts of this state.

A reproduction deemed a duplicate pursuant to the provisions of this section shall be authenticated by competent testimony or by an attestation which shall recite the type of recording system employed, that such system does not permit additions, deletions or changes to the record and that the attestation has actual knowledge of the aforementioned facts.

The provisions of this section shall be construed to provide an additional method of qualifying original writing or recordings and duplicates thereof as admissible in evidence, and shall not replace or derogate any other methods set forth elsewhere in this code or provided for in the West Virginia rules of evidence as adopted by the supreme court of appeals.

Source: **West Virginia Rules of Evidence**

ARTICLE X. CONTENTS OF WRITINGS, RECORDINGS, AND PHOTOGRAPHS.

☞ **Rule 1001. Definitions**

For purposes of this article the following definitions are applicable:

(1) *Writings and recordings.* — "Writings" and "recordings" consist of letters, words, or numbers, or their equivalent, set down by handwriting, typewriting, printing, photostating, photographing, magnetic impulse, mechanical or electronic recording, or other form of data compilation.

(2) *Photographs.* — "Photographs" include still photographs, X-ray films, video tapes, and motion pictures.

(3) *Original.* — An "original" of a writing or recording is the writing or recording itself or any counterpart intended to have the same effect by a person executing or issuing it. An "original" of a photograph includes the negative or any print therefrom. If data are stored in a computer or similar device, any printout or other output readable by sight, shown to reflect the data accurately, is an "original".

(4) *Duplicate.* — A "duplicate" is a counterpart produced by the same impression as the original, or from the same matrix, or by means of photography, including enlargements and miniatures, or by mechanical or electronic re-recording, or by

chemical reproduction, or by other equivalent techniques which accurately reproduces the original.

☞ Rule 1003. Admissibility of Duplicates.

A duplicate is admissible to the same extent as an original unless (1) a genuine question is raised as to the authenticity or continuing effectiveness of the original or (2) in the circumstances it would be unfair to admit the duplicate in lieu of the original.

[See Appendix A. Uniform Rules of Evidence for additional provisions.]

State: **Wisconsin**
Source: **Wisconsin Statutes Annotated**

CHAPTER 16. DEPARTMENT OF ADMINISTRATION

Citation: **WS 16.61**

✪ § 16.61. Records of state offices and other public records.

* * * * *

(6) *Procedure for microfilm reproduction of public records.* Any state agency desiring to microfilm public records shall submit a request to the board for the microfilm reproduction of each records series to be reproduced together with any information the board requires. In granting or denying approval, the board shall consider factors such as the long-term value of the public records, the cost-effectiveness of microfilm reproduction compared with other records management techniques and the technology appropriate for the specific application. Upon receiving written approval from the board, any state agency may cause any public record to be microfilmed in compliance with this section and rules adopted pursuant thereto.

(7) *When copy deemed original record.* (a) Any microfilm reproduction of an original record, or a copy generated from an original record stored in optical disk format, is deemed an original record if all of the following conditions are met:

1. Any device used to reproduce the record on film or to transfer the record to optical disk and generate a copy of the record from optical disk format accurately reproduces the content of the original.

2. The reproduction is on film which complies with the minimum standards of quality for microfilm reproductions, as established by rule of the board, or the optical disk copy and the copy generated from optical disk format comply with the minimum standards of quality for such copies, as established by rule of the department under § 16.611

3. The film is processed and developed in accordance with the minimum standards established by the board.

4. The record is arranged, identified and indexed so that any individual document or component of the record can be located.

5. The state agency records and forms officer or other person designated by the head of the state agency executes a statement of intent and purpose describing the record to be reproduced, the disposition of the original record, the disposal authorization number assigned by the board for state records, the enabling ordinance or resolution for cities, towns, villages or school districts, or the resolution which authorizes the reproduction for counties when required, and a certificate that the record was received or created and microfilmed in the normal course of business, and that the statement of intent and purpose is properly recorded as directed by the board.

(b) The statement of intent and purpose executed under par. (a)5 is presumptive evidence of compliance with all conditions and standards prescribed by this subsection.

(c) Any microfilm reproduction of an original record which was made prior to April 18, 1986, in accordance with the standards in effect under the applicable laws and rules for authenticating the record at the time the reproduction was made is deemed an original record.

(8) *Admissible in evidence.* (a) Any microfilm reproduction of a public record meeting the requirements of subsection (7) or copy of a public record generated from an original record stored in optical disk or electronic format in compliance with this section shall be taken as, stand in lieu of and have all the effect of the original document and shall be admissible in evidence in all courts and all other tribunals or agencies, administrative or otherwise, in all cases where the original document is admissible.

(b) Any enlarged copy of a microfilm reproduction of a public record made as provided by this section or any enlarged copy of a public record generated from an original record stored in optical disk or electronic format in compliance with this section that is certified by the custodian as provided in § 889.08 shall have the same force as an actual-size copy.

(9) *Preservation of reproductions.* Provisions shall be made for the preservation of any microfilm reproductions of public records and of any public records stored in optical disk or electronic format in conveniently accessible files in the agency of origin or its successor or in the state archives.

Contracts for microfilm reproduction. Contracts for microfilm reproduction of records to be made as provided in this section shall be made by the secretary provided in § § 16.70 to 16.77 and the cost of making such microfilm reproduction shall be paid out of the appropriation of the state agency having the reproduction made.

(10) *Contracts for copying.* Contracts for microfilm reproduction, optical imaging or electronic storage of public records to be performed as provided in this section shall be made by the secretary as provided in § § 16.70 to 16.77 and the cost of making such reproductions or optical disks or of electronic storage shall be paid out of the appropriation of the state agency having the reproduction made or the storage performed.

(11) *Authority to reproduce records.* Nothing in this section shall be construed to prohibit the responsible office of any state agency from reproducing any document by any method when it is necessary to do so in the course of carrying out duties and functions in any case other than where the original document is to be destroyed; but the original public record may be destroyed after microfilming or optical imaging without the approval of the board unless authorized under sub. (4) or (5).

(12) *Access to microfilm reproductions.* All persons may examine and use the microfilm reproductions of public records and copies of public records generated from optical disk storage subject to such reasonable rules as may be made by the responsible officer of the state agency having custody of the same.

* * * * *

Citation: **WS 16.62**

✪ § 16.62. Records management service.

(1) The department shall establish and maintain a records management service:

(a) To advise and assist state agencies and the University of Wisconsin Hospitals and Clinics Authority in the establishment and operation of records management programs through the issuance of standards and procedures and provision of technical and management consulting services.

(b) To operate a state records center and a central microfilm facility for state agencies and the University of Wisconsin Hospitals and Clinics Authority and to promulgate rules necessary for efficient operation of the facilities.

(bm) To operate a storage facility for storage of public records and records of the University of Wisconsin Hospitals and Clinics Authority in optical disk or electronic format in accordance with rules, promulgated by the department under § 16.611, governing operation of the facility.

(c) To periodically audit the records management programs of state agencies and the University of Wisconsin Hospitals and Clinics Authority and recommend improvements in records management practices.

* * * * *

CHAPTER 59. COUNTIES.

SUBCHAPTER 4. COUNTY OFFICERS

Citation: WS 59.40

✪ **§ 59.40. Clerk of court.**

* * * * *

(2)The clerk of circuit court shall:

(a) File and keep all papers properly deposited with him or her in every action or proceeding unless required to transmit the papers. The papers may be microfilmed or microphotographed, or transferred to optical disks or electronic format if authorized under § 59.52(14), and the originals may thereafter be destroyed upon compliance with SCR chapter 72.[former § 59.39 was amended and renumbered as above § 59.40(2).]

* * * * *

SUBCHAPTER 5. POWERS AND DUTIES OF COUNTIES.

Citation: WS 59.52

✪ **§ 59.52. County administration.**

* * * * *

(3) *Records where kept, public examination; rebinding; transcribing.* (a) The books, records, papers and accounts of the board shall be deposited with the respective county clerks and shall be open without any charge to the examination of all persons.

(b) When any book, public record or the record of any city, village or town plat in any county office shall, from any cause, become unfit for use in whole or in part, the board shall order that the book, record or plat be rebound or transcribed. If the order is to rebind such book, record or plat, the rebinding must be done under the direction of the officer in charge of the book, record or plat, and in that officer's office. If the order is to transcribe such book, record or plat, the officer having charge of the same shall provide a suitable book for that purpose; and thereupon such officer shall transcribe the same in the book so provided and carefully compare the transcript with the originals, and make the same a correct copy thereof, and shall attach to the transcript a certificate over that officer's official signature that that officer has carefully compared the matter therein contained with, and that the same is a correct and literal copy of the book, record or plat from which the same was transcribed, naming such book. Such copy of book, record or plat, so certified, shall have the same effect in all respects as the original, and such original book, record or plat shall be deposited with the treasurer and carefully preserved except in counties having a population of 500,000 or more where a book containing a tract index is rewritten or transcribed, the original book may be destroyed. The order of the board directing the transcribing of any book, record or plat duly certified by the clerk shall, with such certificate, be recorded in each copy of book, record or plat transcribed. The fee of the officer for such service shall be fixed by the board, not exceeding 10 cents per folio, or if such books or any part thereof consist of printed forms, not to exceed 5 cents per folio for such books or records, to be paid by the county.

(4) *Destruction, transfer of obsolete records.* (a)Destruction of obsolete county records.

Whenever necessary to gain needed vault and filing space, county or court officers and the custodian of the records of all courts of record in the state in the state may, subject to pars. (b) and (c), destroy obsolete records in their custody as follows:

(18) Case records and other record material of all public assistance that are kept as required under ch. 49, if no payments have been made for at least 3 years and if a face sheet or similar record of each case and financial record of all payments for each aid account are preserved in accordance with rules adopted by the department of health and family services. If the department of health and family services has preserved such case records and other record material on computer disc or tape or similar device, a county may destroy the original records and record material under rules adopted by the department.

(19) Marriage license applications and records and papers pertaining to the applications, including antenuptial physical examinations and test certificates, consents of parent or guardian for marriage and orders of the court waiving the waiting period, after 10 years.

(20) Books in the office of the register of deeds in counties with a population of 500,000 or more containing copies of deeds, mortgages, other miscellaneous documents and military discharges that are authorized by law to be recorded in the office if the records first shall be photographed or microphotographed and preserved in accordance with ch. 228.

(21) Case record and other record material of all public assistance kept as required under ch. 49, if no payments have been made for at least 3 years and if a face sheet or similar record of each case and a financial record of all payment for each aid account are preserved in accordance with rules adopted by the department of health and social services. If the department of health and social services has preserved such case records and other record material on computer disc or tape or similar device, a county may destroy the original records and record material under rules adopted by the department.

* * * * *

CHAPTER 77. TAXATION OF CROPLANDS; REAL ESTATE TRANSFER FEES; SALES AND USE TAXES; COUNTY AND SPECIAL DISTRICT SALES AND USE TAXES; MANAGED FOREST LAND; TEMPORARY RECYCLING SURCHARGE; LOCAL FOOD AND BEVERAGE TAX; LOCAL CAR RENTAL TAX.

SUBCHAPTER III. GENERAL SALES AND USE TAX.

Citation: WS 77.61

✍ **§ 77.61 Administrative provisions.**

* * * * *

(4)(a) Every seller and retailer and every person storing, using or otherwise consuming in this state tangible personal property or taxable services purchased from a retailer shall keep such records, receipts, invoices and other pertinent papers and records including machine-readable records in such form as the department requires. The department may, after giving notice, require any person to keep whatever records are needed for the department to compute the sales or use taxes the person should pay. Thereafter, the department shall add to any taxes assessed on the basis of information not contained in the records required a penalty of 25% of the amount of the tax so assessed in addition to all other penalties under this chapter.

* * * * *

CHAPTER 228. RECORDING AND COPYING OF PUBLIC RECORDS IN POPULOUS COUNTIES.

Citation: WS 228.01

✪ § 228.01. Recording of documents and public records by mechanical process authorized.

Whenever any officer of any county having a population of 500,000 or more is required or authorized by law to file, record, copy, recopy or replace any document, court order, plat, paper, written instrument, writings, record or book of record, on file or of record in his or her office, notwithstanding any other provisions in the statutes, the officer may do so by photostatic, photographic, microphotographic, microfilm, optical imaging, electronic formatting or other mechanical process which produces a clear, accurate and permanent copy or reproduction of the original document, court order, plat, paper, written instrument, writings, record or book of record in accordance with the standards specified under § § 16.61(7) and 16.612. Any such officer may also reproduce by such processes or transfer from optical disk or electronic storage any document, court order, plat, paper, written instrument, writings, record or book of record which has previously been filed, recorded, copied or recopied. Optical imaging or electronic formatting of any document is sugject ot authorization under § 59.52(14)(a).

Citation: WS 228.03

☞ ✪ § 228.03. Copy to be deemed to be original record.

(1) A photographic reproduction of an original document, court order, plat, paper, written instrument, writing, record, book of record, file or other material, or a copy of material generated from optical disk storage of the original material, bearing upon or pertinent to the activities and functions of any county office, department, agency, board, commission, court or institution, in counties having a population of 500,000 or more, is deemed to be an original for all purposes, if it meets the applicable standards established in § § 16.61 and 16.612.

(2) Any photographic reproduction of an original record meeting the standards prescribed in s.16.61(7) or copy of a record generated from an original record stored in optical disk or electronic format in compliance with § § 16.61 and 16.612 shall be taken as and stand in lieu of and have all of the effect of the original record and shall be admissible in evidence in all courts and all other tribunals or agencies, administrative or otherwise, in all cases where the original document is admissible. A transcript, exemplification or certified copy of such a reproduction of an original record, or certified copy of a record generated from an original record stored in optical disk or electronic format, for the purposes specified in this subsection, is deemed to be a transcript, exemplification or certified copy of the original. The custodian of a photographic reproduction shall place the reproduction or optical disk in conveniently accessible storage and shall make provision for preserving, examining and using the reproduction of the record or generating a copy of the record from optical disk or electronic storage. An enlarged copy of photographic reproduction of a record made in accordance with the standards specified in § 16.61(7) or an enlarged copy of a record generated from an original record stored in optical disk or electronic format in compliance with § § 16.61 and 16.612 that is certified by the custodian as provided in § 889.18(2) has the same effect as an actual-size copy.

Citation: WS 228.04

✪ § 228.04. Inspection of records and copies of records.

Every custodian of public records in counties having a population of 500,000 or more shall keep them in such arrangement and condition as to make them easily accessible for convenient use. Photographic, photostatic, microphotographic, microfilm or other mechanical process of reproduction of public records or optical imaging or electronic formatting of public records shall be considered as accessible for convenient use, provided that a suitable means for public inspection of the records is provided by the custodian. Except as otherwise expressly provided by law, the custodian shall permit all public records in his or her custody to be inspected, examined, abstracted or copied at reasonable times and under his or her supervision and regulation by any person; and the custodian shall, upon the demand of any person furnish certifeid copies thereof on payment in advance of fees not to exceed the fees prescribed by law.

Citation: WS 228.05

✪ § 228.05. Marginal references.

The register of deeds of any county having a population of 500,000 or more who has copied a document by microphotography, microfilm, optical imaging or electronic formatting that is accepted by him or her for recording or filing shall also, as a substitute for marginal references required, prepare an index for documents of ancillary nature for which marginal references are required. Such index for ancillary documents shall be prepared and maintained to show the document number or volume and page of the orignal recording or filing plus a record of any recordings or filings affecting or pertinent to such original recording or filing requiring marginal references subsequent to the date on which the county begins such recording or recopying by microphotography, microfilm, optical imaging or electroinic formatting.

CHAPTER 889. DOCUMENTARY AND RECORD EVIDENCE.

Citation: WS 889.29

☞ ✍ § 889.29. Photographic copies of business records as evidence.

(1) If any business, institution or member of a profession or calling, in the regular course of business or activity has kept or recorded any memorandum, writing, entry, print, representation or combination thereof, of any act, transaction, occurrence or event, and in the regular course of business has caused any or all of the same to be recorded, copied or reproduced by any photographic, photostatic, microfilm, micro-card, miniature photographic, or other process which accurately reproduces or forms a durable medium for so reproducing the original, or to be

recorded on an optical disk, the original may be destroyed in the regular course of business, unless its preservation is required by law. Such reproduction or optical disk record, when reduced to comprehensible format and when satisfactorily identified, is as admissible in evidence as the original itself in any judicial or administrative proceeding whether the original is in existence or not and an enlargement or facsimile of such reproduction of a record or an enlarged copy of a record generated from an original record stored in optical disk format is likewise admissible in evidence if the original reproduction is in existence and available for inspection under direction of court. The introduction of a reproduced record, enlargement or facsimile, does not preclude admission of the original.

(2) This section does not apply to public records.

(3) This section shall be so interpreted and construed as to effectuate it general purpose of making uniform the law of those states which enact it.

Source: **Wisconsin Rules of Evidence.**

CHAPTER 908. HEARSAY.

☞ **§ 908.03. Hearsay Exceptions; Availability of declarant immaterial.**

The following are not excluded by the hearsay rule, even though the declarant is available as a witness:

* * * * *

(6) *Records of regularly conducted business activity.* A memorandum, report, record, or data compilation, in any form, of acts, events, conditions, opinions, or diagnoses, made at or near the time by, or from information transmitted by, a person with knowledge, all in the course of a regularly conducted business activity, as shown by the testimony of the custodian or other qualified witness, unless the sources of information or other circumstances indicate lack of trustworthiness.

(6m) *Health care provider records.* (a) *Definition.* In this subsection, "health care provider" means a chiropractor licensed under ch. 446, a dentist licensed under ch. 447, a physician assistant certified under ch. 448 or a health care provider as defined in § 655.001(8).

(7) *Absence of entry in records of regularly conducted activity.* Evidence that a matter is not included in the memoranda, reports, records, or data compilations, in any form, of a regularly conducted activity, to prove the nonoccurrence or nonexistence of the matter, if the matter was of a kind of which a memorandum, report, record, or data compilation was regularly made and preserved, unless the sources of information or other circumstances indicate lack of trustworthiness.

* * * * *

CHAPTER 910. CONTENTS OF WRITINGS, RECORDINGS, AND PHOTOGRAPHS.

☞ **§ 910.01. Definitions**

For purposes of this article the following definitions are applicable:

(1) *Writings and recordings.* — "Writings" and "recordings" consist of letters, words, or numbers, or their equivalent, set down by handwriting, typewriting, printing, photostating, photographing, magnetic impulse, mechanical or electronic recording, or other form of data compilation.

(2) *Photographs.* — "Photographs" include still photographs, X-ray films, video tapes, and motion pictures.

(3) *Original.* — An "original" of a writing or recording is the writing or recording itself or any counterpart intended to have the same effect by a person executing or issuing it. An "original" of a photograph includes the negative or any print therefrom. If data are stored in a computer or similar device, any printout or other output readable by sight, shown to reflect the data accurately, is an "original".

(4) *Duplicate.* — A "duplicate" is a counterpart produced by the same impression as the original, or from the same matrix, or by means of photography, including enlargements and miniatures, or by mechanical or electronic re-recording, or by chemical reproduction, or by other equivalent techniques which accurately reproduces the original.

☞ **§ 910.03. Admissibility of duplicates.**

A duplicate is admissible to the same extent as an original unless (1) a genuine question is raised as to the authenticity of the original or (2) in the circumstances it would be unfair to admit the duplicate in lieu of the original.

Source: **SUPREME COURT RULES**

CHAPTER 72. RETENTION OF COURT RECORDS.

✪ **§ SCR 72.03. Destruction of original court record after microfilming or electronically or optically storing.**

(1) In this rule, "suitably microfilmed or microphotographed" means being microfilmed or microphotographed, to the extent practicable, in accordance with the minimum standards for microfilming and microphotographing as established by the American National Standards Institute.

(2) Notwithstanding the provisions of SCR 72.01, any record of a court that has been suitably microfilmed or microphotographed may be destroyed in accordance with SCR 72.02(1) or (2) 2 years after entry of final order in the action for which the record is maintained or 2 years after filing for records not specifically related to court actions.

(3) Any record of a court that has been electronically or optically stored and preserved in accordance with SCR 72.05 may be destroyed in accordance with SCR 72.02(1) or (2) one year after entry of a final order in the action for which the record is maintained or one year after filing for records not specifically related to court actions.

Source: **Wisconsin Administrative Code**

CHAPTER 11. SALES TAX.

Citation: **WAC TAX 11.92**

✍ **§ Tax 11.92. Records and record keeping.**

(1) *General.* All persons selling, leasing or renting tangible personal property or taxable services and every person storing, using or otherwise consuming in Wisconsin tangible personal property or taxable services shall keep adequate and complete records so that they may prepare complete and accurate tax returns. These records shall include the normal books of account ordinarily maintained by a prudent business person, together with all supporting information such as beginning and ending inventories, records of purchases and sales, canceled checks, bills, receipts, invoices which shall contain a posting reference, cash register tapes, credit memoranda which shall a carry

reference to the document evidencing the original transaction or other documents of original entry which are the basis for the entries in the books of account, and schedules used in connection with the preparation of tax returns. These records shall show:

(a) The gross receipts from sales of tangible personal property or taxable services, or rentals or leases of tangible personal property, including any services that are a part of the sale or lease, made within Wisconsin even if the seller or lessor regards the receipts as taxable or nontaxable.

(b) The basis for all deductions claimed in filing returns, including resale and exemption certificates obtained from customers. Exempt sales to governmental units and public schools need not be supported by exemption certificates, if the supplier retains a copy of the exempt entity's purchase order and the supplier's invoice or billing document. Sales to organizations holding a certificate of exempt status, CES, including religious or charitable organizations, can be shown to be exempt by recording the CES number on the seller's copy of the bill of sale. All other exempt sales must be supported by an exemption certificate signed by the purchaser and retained by the seller, unless the merchandise sold is specifically exempted by statute regardless of use (such as groceries). Documents necessary to support claimed exemptions from tax liability, such as bills of lading and purchase orders, must be maintained in a manner in which they readily can be related to the transactions for which exemption is sought.

(c) Total purchase price of all tangible personal property or taxable services purchased for sale or consumption or lease in Wisconsin.

(d) Every person subject to the county sales and use tax shall keep a record of sales the person completes in each county enacting an ordinance under § 77.70, Stats., imposing a county tax, separately from sales made elsewhere in the state. Every person shall also keep a record of the sales price of items on which the person is subject to county use or excise tax in each enacting county.

(2) *Microfilm records.* Microfilm (including microfiche) reproductions of general books of account (such as cash books, journals, voucher registers and ledgers) and supporting records of detail shall be acceptable if the following conditions are met:

(a) Appropriate facilities are provided for preservation of the films for periods required.

(b) Microfilm rolls are indexed, cross referenced, labeled to show beginning and ending numbers or beginning and ending alphabetical listing of documents included and are systematically filed.

(c) Transcriptions are provided for any information contained on microfilm which may be required for purposes of verification of tax liability.

(d) Proper facilities are provided for the ready inspection and location of the particular records, including adequate projectors for viewing and copying the records.

(3) *Records prepared by automated data processing (ADP) systems.* An automatic data processing (ADP) tax accounting system shall have the capability of producing visible and legible records which will provide the necessary information for verification of the taxpayer's tax liability.

(a) *Recorded or reconstructible data.* ADP records shall provide an opportunity to trace any transaction back to the original source or forward to a final total. If detailed printouts are not made of transactions at the time they are processed, then the system must have the ability to readily reconstruct these transactions.

(b) *General and subsidiary books of account.* A general ledger, with source references, shall be written out to coincide with financial reports for tax reporting periods. Where subsidiary ledgers are used to support the general ledger accounts, the subsidiary ledger shall also be written out periodically.

(c) *Audit trail and supporting documents.* The audit trail shall be designed so that the details underlying the summary accounting data may be identified and made available to the department upon request. The record keeping system should be so designed that supporting documents (such as sales invoices, purchase invoices, exemption certificates, credit memoranda) shall be readily available.

(d) *Program documentation.* A written description of the ADP portion of the accounting system shall be available. Important changes, together with their effective dates, shall be noted in order to preserve an accurate chronological record. The statements and illustrations as to the scope of operations shall be sufficiently detailed to indicate:

1. The application being performed.
2. The procedures employed in each application.
3. The controls used to ensure accurate and reliable processing.

(4) *Records retention.* The records shall be preserved and retained for the 4-year period open to audit under § 77.59(3), Stats. If any agreement is entered into to extend the 4-year audit period, the records shall be preserved for that extended period. If a notice of tax determination has been issued to the taxpayer by the department and if the taxpayer files a petition for redetermination, the records for the period covered by the notice of the tax determination shall be preserved and retained until such tax redetermination has been finally resolved.

(5) *Examination of records.* All records described in this section shall be made available for examination by the department at its request.

(6) *Failure to maintain records.* In the absence of suitable and adequate records, the department may determine the amount of tax due by using any information available, whether obtained from the taxpayer's records or from any other source. Failure to maintain and keep complete and accurate records may result in penalties or other appropriate action provided by law.

(7) *Penalties.* If the department has given notice to a person to keep certain sales and use tax records, and thereafter additional sales or use taxes are assessed on the basis of information not contained in the records, the department shall impose a penalty equal to 25% of the amount of sales or use tax assessed. This is in addition to all other penalties provided by law.

Agency: Department of Industry, Labor and Human Relations

CHAPTER IND 200. RECORDING AND REPORTING—OCCUPATIONAL INJURIES AND ILLNESSES.

✍ § Ind 200.03. Log of occupational injuries and illnesses.

(1) Each employer shall maintain in each establishment a log of all recordable occupational injuries and illnesses for that establishment, except that under the circumstances described in subsection (2) of this section an employer may maintain the log of occupational injuries and illnesses at a place other than the establishment. Each employer shall enter each recordable occupational injury and illness on the log as early as practicable but no later than 6 working days after receiving information that a recordable case has occurred. For this purpose, Occupational Safety and Health Administration Form OSHA No. 100 or any private equivalent may be used. OSHA No. 100 or its equivalent shall be completed in the detail provided in the form and the instruction contained therein. If an equivalent to OSHA No. 100 is used, such as a printout from data processing equipment, the information shall be as

readable and comprehensible to a person not familiar with the data processing equipment as the OSHA No. 100 itself.

(2) Any employer may maintain the log of occupational injuries and illnesses at a place other than the establishment or by means of data processing equipment, or both, under the following circumstances:

(a) There is available at the place where the log is maintained sufficient information to complete the log to a date within 6 working days after receiving information that a recordable case has occurred, as required by subsection (1) of this section.

(b) At each of the employer's establishments, there is available a copy of the log which reflects separately the injury and illness experience of that establishment complete and current to a date within 45 calendar days.

Source: **Attorney General Opinion**

✪ You have asked my opinion whether "Optical Imaging" conforms with the specifications of section 16.61(7), Stats., for use as a primary form of recordkeeping in accordance with chapter 228. I conclude that it does not.

Your letter and accompanying enclosure indicates that "Optical Imaging" is a technique for storing documents in a compact fashion through a combination of computer and laser technologies. The document is scanned by a machine which digitizes the information contained therein in much the same way that modern photocopying and facsimile (FAX) machines do. Instead of transferring the image to another sheet of paper, however, the machines use a laser to inscribe the digitized information onto a rotating write-once-read-many (WORM) optical disk, which is similar to the "CDs" used by today's music industry. This technology is touted to result in permanent storage and efficient retrieval and reproduction of document images.

Chapter 228 authorizes certain counties to record documents and public records by using approved mechanical processes. These approved processes include "photostatic, photographic, microphotographic, microfilm, or other mechanical process which produces a clear, accurate and permanent copy or reproduction of the original document, court order, plat, paper, written instrument, writings, record or book of record in accordance with the standards specified in s. 16.61(7)." Sec. 228.01, Stats. The statute thus allows alternative mechanical recordkeeping, but requires the official record to be a permanent, clear and accurate reproduction of the original and refers to certain standards to clarify these requirements.

Although Optical Imaging might be a mechanical process which produces a permanent record, the resulting record is not a copy or reproduction in the sense those terms are used in the statute. First, the stored documents are not, themselves, clear and accurate reproductions of the originals. According to Webster's Third New International Dictionary 1928 (4th ed. 1976), "reproduction" is defined as "something reproduced as . . . an exact copy: replica." However, documents stored on WORM disks are merely strings of digital data which must be translated by a computer in order to be viewed in a format which could be considered to be a copy or reproduction. Whereas the statute requires each record to be stored as a reproduction of the original document, Optical Imaging with WORM disks stores each record as a string of binary numbers which becomes a reproduction of the original document only after a computer translates the string of data into an image displayed on a screen or printed on a sheet of fanfold paper.

Second, documents recorded by Optical Imaging are not stored on film. As you noted in your letter to me, section 228.01 refers to standards set forth in section 16.61(7) to clarify the requirements for recording documents by mechanical processes, of which four out of five refer to using film as the storage medium:

[A reproduced] record is deemed an original record if all of the following conditions are met:

1. The device used to reproduce the record on film is one which accurately reproduces the content of the original.

2. The reproduction is on film which complies with the minimum standards of quality for microfilm reproductions, as established by the board.

3. The film is processed and developed in accordance with the minimum standards established by the board.

4. The record is arranged, identified and indexed so that any individual document or component of the record can be located.

5. The state agency records and forms officer or other person designated by the head of the state agency executes a statement of intent and purpose describing the record to be reproduced, the disposition of the original record, the disposal authorization number assigned by the board for state records, the enabling ordinance or resolution for cities, towns, villages or school districts, or the resolution which authorizes the reproduction for counties when required, and a certificate that the record was received or created and microfilmed in the normal course of business, and that the statement of intent and purpose is properly recorded as directed by the board.

Sec. 16.61(7)(a), Stats. Even if this statute could somehow be read to not require storage of the records on film, the storage medium must at least have the qualities of film. In other words, in addition to being permanent, the records must be capable of being read with the use of nothing more than light and magnification. Optical Imaging with WORM disks does use light, but instead of using light to transfer the image to the eye, it uses light to transfer digital data from the storage medium to a sophisticated translation device which converts the data to a recognizable image.

It might very well be the case that Optical Imaging with WORM disks is a superior means of recording public documents. However, the statutes do not currently authorize its use. Thus, until the Legislature chooses to amend the statutes, public documents such as deeds should not be recorded on WORM disks.

Donald J. Hanaway
Attorney General

State: **Wyoming**
Source: **Wyoming Statutes**

TITLE 9. ADMINISTRATION OF GOVERNMENT

CHAPTER 2. AGENCIES, BOARDS, COMMISSIONS AND DEPARTMENTS, GENERALLY

Article 4. State Archives, Museums, and Historical Department

Citation: **WS 9-2-406**

✪ **§ 9-2-406. Director; management of public records.**

(a) The director shall properly manage and safely keep all public records in his custody, and administer the state archives. He shall:

* * * * *

(vii) Establish and operate a central microfilm division in which all memoranda, writing, entry, print, representation or combination thereof, of any act, transaction, occurrence or event, may be microfilmed. The division shall microfilm public records approved for filming by the head of the office or original and by the director, and shall establish standards for microfilming. All state departments, agencies and subdivisions of the state government and all counties, municipalities and political subdivisions thereof shall consent with the director prior to microfilming within the departments, agencies or political subdivisions and shall comply with the standards for all microfilming established by the central microfilm division. The central microfilm division may microfilm records which are required to be kept a specified length of time or permanently, or to be destroyed by specific methods or under specific supervision. When records are microfilmed, the microfilm may be substituted for the original documents and retained in lieu of the original documents and the original documents may be destroyed;

* * * * *

Citation: **WS 9-2-413**

✪ § 9-2-413. Reproduction of public records of all political subdivisions.

(a) Subject to this section and with the approval of the governing body of the political subdivision, any department, agency, board or individual of any political subdivision may record or copy by any microfilming, microphotographic, photographic, photostatic or other permanent reproductive device any public record which the department, agency, board or individual of the political subdivision records, keeps, retains, or is by law, rule or regulation required to record, keep or retain for a period of years or permanently. The microfilm, microphotograph, photograph, photostat or other permanent reproduction is deemed the original or official copy of the public record so reproduced for all purposes. If any department, agency, board or individual of any political subdivision is required to record any writing or document in books or on other forms, recording done directly onto microfilm, microphotograph or other permanent storage medium in lieu of the other required form of recordation constitutes compliance with the requirement. A master negative of microfilm or microphotographs shall be made whenever any process is used to reproduce public records with the intent of disposing of the original or copies of the original. The master negative shall be sent to the director. One (1) copy of all master negative shall be retained by the governmental entity or officer having custody of the writings or papers thus recorded or copied as the official copy.

(b) If any document is presented for recording or notation in public records the document shall, after recording, be returned to the party from whom it was received. If the party cannot be located or refuses to accept it, the document shall be disposed of in accordance with W.S. 9-2-411.

(c) Prior to adopting any microfilming, microphotograhic, photographic, photostatic or other reproductive process, the governing body of a political subdivision shall consult with the director. If any of the public records which are reproduced pursuant to this section are permanent records or, under the laws, rules or regulations in effect at the time of reproduction, are required to be transferred at a later date to any agency or department of the state, the particular microfilming, microphotographic, photographic, photostatic or other reproductive process shall be approved by the director as one which clearly and accurately makes copies that will last the time they are to be kept or can be subsequently reproduced without distortions that substantially affect their legibility.

(d) If the original documents are disposed of as allowed by law, the set of official microfilm retained by the local governmental entity or official shall be stored in a safe place and protected from destruction. The official microfilm shall be available to the public for inspection in the same manner as the original documents would have been, and sufficient microfilm and microphotographic readers or other suitable devices shall be available to the public to permit inspection.

(e) The clerk of district court shall not microfilm, microphotograph, photograph, Photostat or otherwise reproduce, for official record purposes, the files of any action or proceeding kept in his office until two (2) years have lapsed since the initial filing in the action or proceeding. The clerk of district court shall make certified or other copies of documents in his office for individuals or officials.

(f) In recording, reproducing or copying any public records as authorized by this section and in disposing of the originals or copies, no restrictions or provisions of law regarding recording, reproducing or copying, or the disposition of originals or copies inconsistent with this section apply to the governmental entity or its officers, agents and employees.

Source: **Wyoming Rules of Evidence**

ARTICLE 10. CONTENTS OF WRITINGS, RECORDINGS, AND PHOTOGRAPHS.

☞ Rule 1001. Definitions

For purposes of this article the following definitions are applicable:

(1) *Writings and recordings.* — "Writings" and "recordings" consist of letters, words, or numbers, or their equivalent, set down by handwriting, typewriting, printing, photostating, photographing, magnetic impulse, mechanical or electronic recording, or other form of data compilation.

(2) *Photographs.* — "Photographs" include still photographs, X-ray films, video tapes, and motion pictures.

(3) *Original.* — An "original" of a writing or recording is the writing or recording itself or any counterpart intended to have the same effect by a person executing or issuing it. An "original" of a photograph includes the negative or any print therefrom. If data are stored in a computer or similar device, any printout or other output readable by sight, shown to reflect the data accurately, is an "original".

(4) *Duplicate.* — A "duplicate" is a counterpart produced by the same impression as the original, or from the same matrix, or by means of photography, including enlargements and miniatures, or by mechanical or electronic re-recording, or by chemical reproduction, or by other equivalent techniques which accurately reproduces the original.

☞ Rule 1003. Admissibility of duplicates.

A duplicate is admissible under this rule or as may be otherwise provided by statute to the same extent as an original unless (1) a genuine question is raised as to the authenticity or continuing effectiveness of the original or (2) in the circumstances it would be unfair to admit the duplicate in lieu of the original.

[See Appendix A. Uniform Rules of Evidence for additional provisions.]

Source: Digital Image System Standards and Guidelines

✪ **Published by the Governor's Committee for Policies, Standards and Guidelines for Electronic Imaging Systems**

[The commentary for the following standards and guidelines have been omitted.]

II. MANAGEMENT ISSUES

The adoption of optical media technology by a government agency is a major decision that carries with it responsibilities that extend well beyond the acquisition of the original hardware and software.

A. DOCUMENT PROCESSING AND WORKFLOW

GUIDELINE:

Manager, in consultation with qualified records manager, should analyze the existing records systems, practices, workflow, and indexes, and correct any deficiencies before implementing an imaging system.

B. INTEGRATION WITH EXISTING AND OTHER INFORMATION SYSTEMS

GUIDELINE:

An imaging system should be able to be integrated with existing information systems and be able to adapt, grow, change and cooperate with other systems and technologies. Refer to Technical Issues, "Imaging Environment" section.

C. SYSTEM MIGRATION

(1) Vendor Stability

GUIDELINE:

Assess carefully the viability of vendors when acquiring imaging systems that are heavily vendor-dependent. Consider imaging systems built from hardware and software that conform to non-proprietary standards or generally accepted standards within the industry.

When using vendor dependent proprietary hardware and/or software, strongly consider requiring the vendor to deposit a copy of the computer software source code with a bank or some other mutually accepted escrow agent. Software upgrades should also be deposited with the same escrow agent.

(2) System Obsolescence

STANDARD:

Agencies must require vendors to provide a bridge to imaging systems with non-proprietary configurations.

GUIDELINE:

Agencies shall minimize the obsolescence of imaging systems by:

Acquiring in imaging system that is backward compatible.

Require the vendor to guarantee the conversion of 100 percent of the stored images and index data in lieu of having the capability to use hardware.

(3) Media Longevity

(4) Migration Strategies

STANDARD:

Strategies must be developed by the users of optical disk systems to migrate existing data into new systems or configurations.

As applications migrate to new systems, existing security copies of the data must be duplicated as necessary to ensure that they may be accessible within the operating parameters of upgraded or successive systems.

GUIDELINE:

Budget annually between five and ten percent of the original system costs for maintenance.

Test and evaluate the condition of storage of storage media and system functionality on a regular basis.

D. **Conversion**

(1) Conversion Thoughput Rates

GUIDELINE:

Each agency needs to look at their individual needs and select the options that best fit their application.

(2) In-house Conversion

GUIDELINE:

Conversion processing must be performed in accordance with standards and procedures set forth in this document for normal production operations.

(3) Service Bureau/Imaging Contracted Services Conversion

GUIDELINE:

Work done by a service bureau, or a contracted imaging service vendor, must meet all the same standards and procedures as an in-house conversion as specified by contract.

E. **Scanner**

GUIDELINE:

Each agency needs to look at their individual needs and select the options that best fit their application. See also Technical Issues.

F. Indexing

(1) Index Location

GUIDELINE:

At retirement of an optical disk, the index information should be written to multiple locations on the disk that is being retired. Space must be saved to the disk to accommodate the index. See also Technical Issues, "Images, Indexes and Data" section.

(2) Indexing Parameters

GUIDELINE:

Each agency should perform careful analysis of data access points to determine appropriate indexes.

Each agency should create standardized naming conventions for all data values . . . .

(3) Index Data Entry

STANDARD:

Regardless of the data entry method chosen, index entry verification must be performed to ensure the accuracy of index information and to prevent rendering an image unretrievable due to a mis-entered character. See also Technical Issues, "Images, Indexes and Data" section.

G. **Storage**

(1) Recording Permanence

STANDARD:

Digital imaging may be used for the daily management of long-term public records, and the paper records may be authorized for destruction by the State Records Committee.

Digital imaging may be used for the daily management of permanent public records, provided the original paper records, or archival quality of microforms of the records, are maintained.

Digital imaging may be used for the daily management and replacement of short and medium term records and those records with a retention period of ten years or less may be authorized for destruction or other disposition without maintaining a copy in another medium.

STANDARD:

WORM technology should be utilized for records of legal or long-term value.

Records of legal or long-term value should be recorded on at least two separate optical disks or redundant magnetic tape backups, and stored in separate locations.

Recycled optical media should not be used for the storage of legal, long-term, or required records.

GUIDELINE:

The use of high-quality optical media that comply with ANSI/ISO standards, procured from known manufacturers, is preferred when possible.

(2) Storage Environment

STANDARD:

Optical disks used for legal and long-term storage should be inspected at least annually. This should include a visual examination of the medium and its housing and retrieval or playback of recorded information.

GUIDELINE:

Avoid storing optical disks in direct sunlight or near any intense heat source, including leaving disks on top of disk drives.

Storage and work areas must be cleaned regularly and manufacturer's cleaning kits should be used to clean disk drives and media.

Never touch the recording surface of optical disks; handle disks gently and by the edges.

Eating, drinking and smoking must be prohibited in areas where optical disks are used or stored.

Store optical disks in an upright, vertical position; do not stack horizontally. Do not place books or other heavy objects on top of optical disks.

Permanent magnets and other objects which generate magnetic fields must be prohibited in areas where magneto-optical disks are stored.

Never place labels directly on optical media.

H. **RETENTION SCHEDULES**

STANDARD:

All public records to be put on an imaging system must have retention schedules approved by the State Records Committee, either adopted or revised prior to the planning stage. All electronic records must also have retention schedules approved by the State Records Committee.

I. **PUBLIC ACCESS AND PRIVACY**

(1) Segregating Exempt and Non-Exempt Information

STANDARD:

Whatever solution is used to provide public access to records while preserving privacy must maintain the integrity of the record as well as ensure that material exempted from disclosure is not accidentally made available to the general public.

(2) Access Through Time

GUIDELINE:

Records custodians/managers should ensure that all records and information are transferred timely to new systems whenever the hardware, software, or storage medium is changed/upgraded.

(3) Ability to Make Copies

GUIDELINE:

Records custodians/managers should ensure that copies of records and information on optical media are available to all public requestors on a fair, equitable, and cost effective basis. Copies of records should be made available to individuals regardless of their technological know-how or whether they possess the latest technology. Public access of records should be considered when planning an imaging system.

J. **PUBLIC ACCESS TO IMAGE INFORMATION**

GUIDELINE:

Records custodian/managers must ensure that copies of records and information on optical media are available to all public requestors on a fair, equitable and cost effective basis.

Copies of records should be made available to individuals regardless of their technological know-how or whether they possess the latest technology. Public access of records must be considered when planning an imaging system.

K. **DISASTER RECOVERY**

STANDARD:

A disaster recovery procedure shall be prepared by the agency in cooperation with ARMM and CTD analysts, prior to the production of an imaging system.

L. **LEGAL CONSIDERATIONS**

REQUIREMENTS:

The media and system combined must be able to show, to the court's satisfaction, that the documents, records or information:

Has relevancy (pertinent to the matter before the court).

Is authentic (is a true and accurate copy of the original).

Was made near to the time of the event in question.

Input procedures used to create this information are documented and defined and must be able to verify the accuracy by proven tests.

The following elements define ways of accomplishing these requirements:

(1) Evidence and Authenticity Requirements

(a) Policy Statement

STANDARD:

Each agency shall adopt a written policy statement.

System Administrator

STANDARD:

Any agency implementing an optical image system involving document retention on optical media should assign an optical disk system administrator.

M. **QUALITY CONTROL**

GUIDELINE:

Require periodic maintenance of digital imaging and optical media storage system.

Recalibrate optical drives in accordance with manufacturer specifications.

Evaluate scanner quality based on standard procedures.

Perform visual quality control evaluation of each scanned image and related index data.

Write scanned image data to optical media only after quality control evaluation.

Establish a consensus on what constitutes the "best" image for different types of source documents. Periodically validate the scanning density selected by testing documents.

N. **TECHNICAL DOCUMENTATION**

STANDARD:

Each agency shall maintain adequate systems documentation.

O. **OPERATIONAL DOCUMENTATION**

STANDARD:

Each agency shall document its operating procedures.

GUIDELINE:

Agencies whose records are likely to be used in legal matters are highly encouraged to use identification certificates.

P. **SECURITY DOCUMENTATION**

STANDARD:

Each agency shall implement security provisions.

GUIDELINE:

An agency security strategy should generally include the following:

Control of data and information resources (including access and handling of sensitive information, audit trails and incident reporting).

Physical security and access to data processing facilities (including environmental controls, fire and water damage prevention and protection).

Logical and data access controls (including personal identification and access, password controls, access to software and data, security at the application, data and file encryption and network encryption).

Network security (including security at network entry and host entry, dial-up access).

Backup and recovery (including contingency planning).

Security awareness.

User lists and access privileges should be internally reviewed regularly.

Passwords should be changed regularly.

Q. **SECURITY**
(1) Media Selection
STANDARD:
WORM optical disks should be utilized especially for records of legal or long-term value.
If an agency uses rewritable optical disks, read/write privileges must be carefully controlled and each edit or alteration must be auditable to protect against tampering or accidental loss of data.
(2) Backup
GUIDELINE:
Records of legal or long-term value stored on optical disk should have security copies made periodically on fresh media to guard against image loss due to media instability. A schedule for regular duplication should be adhered to based on the life expectancy of the storage media. Off-site storage of media should also be considered in a long-term backup plan
(3) Access Restrictions
STANDARD:
Imaging systems must include access restriction procedures and software controls to prevent the retrieval of images or modification of index information by unauthorized personnel
GUIDELINE:
Access control procedures should be fully documented.
III. TECHNICAL ISSUES
A. **STORAGE**
(1) Disk Data Storage Capacity
STANDARD:
Select systems that utilize 12 inch or smaller optical disks unless specific programmatic needs require larger capacity disks.
(2) Image Storage Software
STANDARD:
Must support the storage of images on intermediate storage devices (electronic media - DASD) and optical storage devices while providing backup/recovery/restart capabilities consistent with a production class DBMS for both images and the index.
(3) Recording Permanence
STANDARD:
WORM technology for records of long-term and/or legal value should be utilized. Each agency should ensure that read/write privileges are carefully controlled and that an audit trail of rewrites is maintained when rewritable technology is used.
(4) Jukebox or Disk Changer Systems
GUIDELINE:
Select a jukebox or disk changer storage system by considering overall access needs and physical control requirements.
(5) Storage Environment
GUIDELINE:
Store optical media in areas with environmental conditions (temperature, humidity, etc.) that comply with manufacturers guidelines. Generally, stable room temperatures (65 to 75 degrees Fahrenheit) and relative humidity between 30 and 50 percent are acceptable.
An electrostatic copier or other electronic device may cause electrical interference, thus a digital imaging system should be located in an appropriate area.
Periodically clean optical media and equipment, according to the manufacturer's recommended guidelines, to remove dust and other particulates.
(6) Optical Platters Substrate
GUIDELINE:
Either polycarbonate or tempered glass substrate will be acceptable.
(7) Disk Durability
GUIDELINE:
Select optical disks with a pre-write shelf life of at least 5 (five) years and a post-write life of at least 20 (twenty) years.

B. **COMPRESSION AND DECOMPRESSION**
(1) Compressions
STANDARD:
Digital imaging systems must support the CCITT Group 3 and/or Group 4 standards with no proprietary alterations to the algorithm.
(2) Decompression
STANDARD:
Software used for decompression must be 100% compatible with hardware used for decompression.
C. **SCANNING**
(1) Scanning Density
STANDARD:
Select a scanning density of at least 200 dots per inch (dpi) for office documents.
GUIDELINE:
Select a higher scanning density of between 300 and 600 dpi, as needed, for engineering drawings, maps, and documents with background detail. See also "Scanner" in Management Issues section.
Validate the selected scanning density with test on actual documents.
(2) Scanner Color Spectrum
GUIDELINE:
Select a scanning density that has been validated by testing actual documents.
(3) Gray Scale
GUIDELINE:
As a general rule, use of gray scale should be restricted to continuous tone photographs.
(4) Image Enhancement
GUIDELINE:
Get the "best" image whenever possible. Where legal issues do not exist, enhancement of the image is acceptable, however, always consider the record type when capturing the "best" image. See also "Legal Considerations" in the Management Issues Section.
D. **IMAGING ENVIRONMENT**
(1) Planning Computer Product Acquisition
GUIDELINE:
Determine what products will enhance productivity.
1.) Interview users and document the daily tasks.
2.) Identify and discard any current inefficiencies.
3.) Determine what products will facilitate these tasks.
4.) Verify product compatibility with State environment.
5.) Write a specification on how the products will be used.
6.) Verify the specification with the users.
if verified acquisition may begin
if not verified start again at step 3.
GUIDELINE:
Operating System Selection
1.) Open System
2.) Window based OS or OS with Window Based Enhancement
3.) Multi Tasking or Task Switching.
STANDARD:
Computer Requirements
1.) Perform tasks within reasonable time.
2.) Display information efficiently.
3.) Contain enough memory to support OS and applications.
4.) Provide storage for OS, applications, and documents.
5.) Connectable to current state computers.
6.) Efficient access to current media.
E. **IMAGES, INDEXES, AND DATA**
(1) Image Distribution

STANDARD:
Must be able to distribute images in one of the following formats, at the option of the sender:
CCITT Group 3 or Group 4 FAX (recognizing Group 3 destination).
Bit mapped.
(2) Image Annotation and Modification
GUIDELINE:
Must support the ability to annotate an image without physically modifying the image.
(3) File Headers
STANDARD:
Must use non-proprietary file header formats to label digital images. Tagged Image File Format (TIFF) has been adopted as a de facto standard for file header information. However, there are several different implementations of TIFF so selecting TIFF does not automatically guarantee there will be no problems in transferring images from one system to another. Therefore, require the system developer to supply a detailed definition of the image file header label structure. Note: A TIFF file header standards has been developed by the CCITT group.
(4) Image Folder Management
GUIDELINE:
Image folder management software (if required within the system design) must support the combining of images into a single folder and must allow access to a single image in a folder.
(5) Image Indexing
STANDARD:
Image indexing must be done using an American National Standards Institute (ANSI) Standard Query Language (SQL) Data Base Management System (DBMS) which can reside remote from the image storage location. The index must be accessible and manipulatable through user written standards application development languages, subject to the appropriate security considerations.
(6) Image Entry
GUIDELINE:
Must provide automatic indexing at entry from bar codes, Optical Character Recognition (OCR), Intelligent Character Recognition (ICR), and/or operator entry. As technologies evolve (OCR and ICR), use industry standards wherever possible and avoid proprietary equipment.
(7) Redundant Index
GUIDELINE:
The index data for the contents for a specific disk should be written at multiple locations on the disk. Also, one should note "when" the index is actually written to disk. Software should rewrite the index every time the disk is unloaded.

Source:	**Executive Department**
Citation:	**EXECUTIVE ORDER 1993-2**

✪ Executive Order 1993-2

WHEREAS optical disk storage and electronic document image systems technologies are still relatively new and are advancing very rapidly; and

WHEREAS no industry wide standards has been established for a single file format and indexing scheme that would be required for disk compatibility between image hardware and software vendors; and

WHEREAS state agencies are not likely to wait for the industry to achieve full systems compatibility before using the business benefits offered by electronic image systems; and

WHEREAS, as Governor, I have authorized a committee consisting of representatives from the Departments of Revenue, Administration and Information, Commerce, and Employment to study and recommend policies, guidelines and standards for electronic imaging systems which recognize existing industry standards and policies; and

WHEREAS the Committee identified the following objective to support the need for standards and guidelines:

A. Allow documents and records to be accessioned into electronic imaging systems and stored on optical disks or digital tape.

B. Implement safeguards to assure that agencies utilizing optical disk storage have applied appropriate document management techniques in their system design.

C. Begin now to provide a platform for future image and data compatibility between systems installed by various agencies without mandating a particular vendor for hardware and software.

D. Provide bench marks for electronic image processing systems to assure a minimum image quality and storage life.

E. Minimize risks for legal admissibility in evidence of optically stored document by suggesting implementing and operational guidelines for electronic image systems; and

WHEREAS this order is intended to address the planning and implementation of electronic document imaging systems with emphasis on the following benefits:

A. To the extent possible, systems acquired should meet certain technical bench marks. This will ensure that there are means within each system to "port" images in a generic fashion to another system, even if the two systems utilize different internal techniques for image creation and management. This will also allow each agency to carefully choose the appropriate system to meets its business needs, so long as the system will meet the minimum requirements specified.

B. Establishing internal procedures now which emphasize planning and coordination will ease the technical transition and minimize legal and practical risks associated with each new system; and

WHEREAS the following definitions assist in understanding this order:

ARMM - Archives, Records Management and Micrographics Section, Parks and Cultural Resources Division Department of Commerce

CTD - Computer Technology Division, Department of Administration and Information

NOW THEREFORE, I, Mike Sullivan, Governor of the State of Wyoming, by virtue of the powers vested by the Constitution and the laws of the State of Wyoming, DO HEREBY ORDER THAT:

1. Electronic Image Standards and Guideline Committee made up of representatives from the Departments of Revenue, Administration and Information, Commerce, and Employment be established. This Committee will publish the Digital Image System Standards and Guidelines and review same on an annual basis.

2. Each agency, prior to implementing an image system, will develop a plan for electronic document image management in conjunction with Department of Commerce, Archives, Records Management and Micrographics Section (ARMM), and Department of Administration and Information, Computer Technology Division (CTD).

a) detailed procedures for paper flow

b) image indexation and media transmittal procedures

c) detailed business recovery procedures which outline processes for generating, transmitting and accessing the back up medium stored at the off-site security storage facility

d) a completed retention schedule analysis of paper records being scanned into the electronic image system.

3. Each agency shall comply with the published Digital Image System Standards and Guidelines manual. This manual

will be made available on request from ARMM and/or CTD libraries.

4. Records scheduled for permanent retention may be entered into digital imaging systems for more effective daily management, but the original paper records, or archival quality microforms of the records, must be maintained permanently by the agency of the State Archives.

5. Each agency shall understand that until approved by the State Records Committee, no agency shall destroy paper records which have been converted to an electronic image system.

6. Each agency shall understand that agency directors may authorize immediate destruction of non-permanent paper records after a test period successfully demonstrates the system to be reliable and procedures are implemented to assure image quality and accessibility.

7. Each agency shall understand that ARMM and CTD will:

a) review and approve any proposed system design prior to releasing a Request for Proposal or bid specifications for adherence to the standards.

b) review and approve the agency's selected vendor proposal.

c) test the system for compliance with these standards and guidelines prior to the system being placed into production.

8. Each agency director, upon implementation of an electronic image system, shall issue a written policy statement formalizing the recording of digitized image of public records on optical disks as part of the agency's regular business activities.

9. Each agency director upon implementation of an electronic image system will assure that characteristics of the electronic image system are fully documented as outlined in Digital Image Standards and Guidelines.

10. Each agency implementing an electronic image system will designate a minimum of one employee as the system administrator for the life of the electronic image system and understand that responsibilities of the system administrators should include adherence to the standards and guidelines published in Digital Image System Standards and Guidelines as well as:

a) establish and obtain approval from ARMM and CTD of all procedures for the electronic image system operation.

b) establish security measures to be undertaken during capture, storage, retrieval, manipulation and reproduction of documents, including passwords for and functional usage restrictions of certain users of the system.

c) control all file maintenance actions on 1) the optical disk media, 2) the documents residing on the media and 3) the index data base.

d) regularly perform the approved procedures to generate and submit backup optical media to ARMM.

e) maintain the business recovery plan as business functions or technical platforms are revised.

f) establishment of security restrictions and procedures for accessing backed-up data

Given under my hand and the Executive Seal of the State of Wyoming this 19th day of June 1993.

Mike Sullivan

Governor of Wyoming

Agency: **Wyoming Archives, Records Management and Micrographics Services Section (ARMM)**

Source: **ARMM BULLETIN NO. 1, FEBRUARY 8, 1994**

Citation: **ARMM BULLETIN NO. 1**

✪ TO: Officials and records personnel of all local government and all offices of political subdivisions.

SUBJECT: Use of electronic document image systems, and optical disks to store permanent government public records and temporary government public records in conformance with W.S. 9-2-413(c).

PURPOSE: This memorandum clarifies the State Archives policy regarding the use of electronic image and optical disk technology for the storage of permanent records that are scheduled for preservation as part of the archives of Wyoming. The same policy applies to unscheduled records that may be appraised as permanent. It also clarifies that policy regarding non-permanent/temporary records.

SCOPE: The policy stated in this memorandum applies to all offices of county and municipal governments, and to all political subdivisions and special districts, including school districts, fire districts, irrigation districts, water and sewer districts, weed and pest districts, and public hospitals.

EFFECTIVE: This policy is effective as of the above date, and will remain in effect until rescinded.

BASIS: Some local governments and offices of political subdivisions have begun using electronic document image systems and optical disks to store records. There have been several inquiries about current policy on the use of optical disks in records management wanting to know if regulations permit the use of optical disks for storing records and if the State Archives will accession optical disks containing permanent information.

RESPONSE: (a) Because of the lack of permanency standards for optical disks, and because of the hardware and software dependence of current optical disk systems and the absence of standards ensuring the portability of data from one system to another, ARMM cannot accession permanent records stored on optical disks at this time. Until the development of optical disk permanency standards and data portability standards, permanent records must be transferred to the Archives on paper or microforms. Microforms must conform to the requirements of W.S. 9-2-406 and the Micrographic Standards published by ARMM.

(b) Reminding local governments and offices of the political subdivisions of the requirements for transferring permanent records to the State Archives is not intended to discourage the use of electronic document image and optical disk technology for storing and retrieving large quantities of information. The technology is also usable for the enhancement of poor quality originals.

(c) Governments and offices may use optical disk systems for the storage and retrieval of permanent records while the records remain in their legal custody. However, no permanent records may be destroyed after scanning to an optical disk without the State Records Committee's approval, as required in W.S. 9-2-410. Normally, after permanent records have been scanned to an optical disk, the records should be transferred to the State Archives.

(d) Records appraised as temporary by ARMM, and approved by the State Records Committee, may be stored on any medium, including optical disks, that ensures the maintenance of the information until its authorized disposal. Consequently, the conversion of temporary records to optical disks, and disposal of the original paper or other media, does not require ARMM's approval.

(e) All local governments and offices of political subdivisions, planning to implement electronic imaging and optical disk technology are urged to obtain up-to-date and accurate records retention schedules. This is critical because the retention schedules contribute to the development of image systems during design phases. It is possible that new analysis of records series may make it practical to schedule some records series for long term retention, rather than for permanent retention as currently scheduled, thus allowing the records series to be electronically scanned into an image system and the paper destroyed.

Change:Industry standards for optical disks and data portability among optical disk systems are now under development which may enable ARMM to accession optical disks containing records scheduled for permanent retention. ARMM will continue to monitor developments in electronic imaging and optical disk technology that may permit a modification of the policy, regarding accessioning of optical disks, established by this bulletin. Local government entities are discouraged to inform ARMM of proposed uses of electronic document image and optical disk technology. In June 1993, the Governor's Committee for Policies, Standards and Guidelines for electronic imaging systems published the "State of Wyoming, Digital Image System Standards and Guidelines." Although the standards established in this manual are not mandatory for local governments and offices as they are for state government agencies, adhering to the standards and following the guidelines can contribute to ensuring that electronic image systems purchased and installed meet established needs and requirements. The manual is available from ARMM upon request.

Questions:Questions concerning this policy may be directed to the Archives, Records Management and Micrographics Services Section, Parks and Cultural Resources Division, Department of Commerce, Barrett Building, Cheyenne, Wyoming 82002; phone 777-7826.

Jim Donahue
ARMM Administrator

Source: **ARMM BULLETIN NO. 2 DATED MARCH 30, 1995**

Citation: **ARMM BULLETIN NO. 2**

✪

TO: Officials and records personnel of all local governments and all offices of Wyoming political subdivisions.

SUBJECT: Use of Compact Disk-Read Only Memory (CD-ROM) medium to store public records scheduled for permanent retention, and transfer records stored on CD-ROM to the State Archives.

PURPOSE: This bulletin announces that ARMM authorizes the limited use of the CD-ROM medium for the storage of permanent records, and the transfer of permanent records stored on CD-ROM Disks to the State Archives, provided the specific requirements, stated below, are met.

Scope:The policy stated in this bulletin applies to all offices of county and municipal governments, and to all political subdivisions and special districts, including school districts, fire districts, irrigation, drainage and conservation districts, water and sewer districts, weed and pest districts, and public hospitals.

Effective:The policy is effective as of the above date, and will remain in effect until rescinded.

BASIS: In July 1994, the National Archives and Records Administration (NARA) announced the acceptance, with certain requirements, of the use of CD-ROM medium for permanent records. Recognizing the interest of some local governments to use imaging systems for management of their record, including records scheduled for permanent retention, ARMM has reviewed NARA's requirements and has concluded that with adherence to similar requirements, the CD-ROM medium is suitable for the storage of Wyoming permanent records and the transfer of the permanent records on CD-ROM to the State Archives.

In no way does this conclusion, or policy statement concerning CD-ROM, apply to optical disk technology. The policy stated in ARMM BULLETIN NO. 1, February 8, 1994, concerning the use of optical disk systems for permanent records, as well as for temporary records, remains in effect. Copies will be provided upon request.

REQUIREMENTS:

a. Local governments and offices of political subdivisions may store permanent records, which included fielded data files or text files, on CD-ROM medium, and transfer permanent records stored on CD-ROM medium to the State Archives that are:

(1) in conformance to the International Organization for Standardization's ISO 9660 Standards, available from the American National Standards Institute (ANSI);

(2) in compliance with the American Standards Code for Informational Exchange (ASCII) standard as defined in the Federal Information Processing Standard 1-2 (11/14/84);

(3) not dependent on control character or codes which are not defined in the ASCII character set;

(4) not compressed unless the software to decompress the files is provided ARMM when the electronic records are transferred to the State Archives;

(5) individually addressable; and

(6) in compliance with the requirements of W.S. 9-2-413.

b. Local governments and offices should consult with and obtain approval of their legal counsel (county or municipal attorney) before storing permanent records on CD-ROM.

c. Local governments and offices of the political subdivisions must transfer CD-ROM glass master disks with necessary system documentation for those files that are to be accessioned into the State Archives.

d. Local governments and offices must maintain complete operational documentation of their CD-ROM systems if the records are to have evidential value in the courts.

e. Local governments and offices may use CD-ROM Disk systems for the storage and retrieval of permanent records while the records remain in their legal custody. However, no permanent records may be destroyed after scanning to a CD-ROM Disk without the State Records Committee's approval, as required by W.S. 9-2-410. Normally, after permanent records have been scanned to a CD-ROM Disk, the records should be transferred to the State Archives.

f. Records appraised as temporary by ARMM, and with a non-permanent records retention schedule approved by the State Records Committee, may be stored on any medium, including CD-ROM Disks, that ensures the maintenance of the information until its authorized disposal. Consequently, the conversion of non-permanent records to CD-ROM Disks, and disposal of the original paper or other media, does not require approval by the State Records Committee.

g. Local governments and offices storing permanent records on CD-ROM Disks must review their disks every ten years, and if there is any indication of deterioration of the data, the data must be transferred to a new CD-ROM Disk.

ARMM Action:

a. For those file on CD-ROM which meet the criteria in REQUIREMENTS in item a., ARMM will assume responsibility for their preservation, when the CD-ROM glass master disk is transferred to the State Archives.

b. Upon request and subject to legal restrictions, ARMM will provide access to any CD-ROM records transferred to and preserved in the State Archives, and will replicate on any medium offered to ARMM.

c. ARMM will continue to evaluate criteria for storing

permanent records on CD-ROM and transferring permanent records stored on CD-ROM to the State Archives.

RECOMMENDATIONS:

a. Adopt an open systems architecture or require a "bridge" to systems with non-proprietary configurations when establishing a CD-ROM system.

b. Recognize that long term accessibility of permanent records stored on CD-ROM can only be assured through migration to future technology generations, approximately every five years. ARMM should be notified when permanent records are migrated to upgraded CD-ROM technology, including both hardware and software.

c. CD-ROM systems established by local governments and offices of political subdivisions should have built-in data migration paths that have backward compatibility if long term accessibility is to be ensured.

d. Index systems design and capability decisions should be based on a thorough analysis of office operations and user needs.

e. CD-ROM systems should have a scanning resolution of at least 300 dpi for office documents, and a higher scanning resolution (between 300 and 600 dpi or higher) for engineering drawings, maps, and documents containing significant fine line and background information.

f. Permanently write the information on CD-ROM only after conducting a thorough quality inspection of the scanned images and index data.

QUESTIONS:Questions concerning this policy may be directed to the Archives, Records Management and Micrographics Services Section, Cultural Resources Division, Department of Commerce, Barrett Building, Cheyenne, Wyoming 82002; phone 777-7826

Jim Donahue

State Archivist

Adopted by the Wyoming State Record Committee, 3/31/95

[Editor's Note: The Wyoming Archives, Records Management and Micrographics Services Division has informally construed paragraph 7 of Bulletin No. 2 as follows:

Bulletin 1 refers to other types of optical imaging technology that do not conform to the CD-ROM format. Bulletin No. 2 specifically relates to CD-ROM format.]

Appendix D International Requirements

Country: Argentina

COMMERCIAL COMPANIES ACT OF 1972

CHAPTER 1. — GENERAL PROVISIONS.

✍ Section 9. — Documenting and Accounting.

Art. 61. The fulfillment of the formalities provided by Art. 53 of the Commercial Code can be prescinded by keeping books in the manner that the controlling authority of the Pubic Commercial Registry shall authorize, substituting them by controllers, mechanical, magnetic or other means, save those concerning balance sheets and inventory.

The petition must include an adequate discussion of the system with a technical report or history of its utilization, which, once authorized, must be recorded in the inventory book and balance sheet.

Authorization petitions shall be considered automatically approved within 30 days of their effectiveness, if they do not require prior observation or if their rejection is well-founded.

The Day book (Journal) may be kept with global entries that shall not cover periods of more than one month.

The accounting system must allow the itemization of negotiations, corresponding debit and credit accounts, and their later verification, with reference to Art. 43 of the Commercial Code.

Art. 63. Commercial books kept according to the prescribed form and requirements shall be admitted in Court as evidence between merchants on a fact of their commerce, in the way and in the cases expressed in this Code.

As against the merchants to whom the books belong and their successors, the entries shall be evidence, although they are not in form, without admitting evidence to disprove them. But the opposite party cannot accept the favorable entries and disprove those which prejudice him, but having adopted this means of proof he shall be bound by the combined entries relevant to the point in dispute.

Commercial books shall also be evidence in favor of their owners when the opposite party does not produce entries to the contrary made in the books lawfully kept or some other full and conclusive evidence.

Nevertheless, in that case the Judge has power to weight the evidence, and not to require supplementary evidence if the thinks is necessary.

Finally, when there is a contradiction between the books of the litigants and all are kept with the necessary formalities and without and defect, the Tribunal shall put aside this means of proof, and shall proceed according to the value of other evidence which is produced, weighing it in accordance with the provisions of this Code.

Art. 64. Commercial books will afford only a ground of proof, when non-commercial acts are written in question.

Art. 65. Books not required by the law are not evidence in favor of a merchant in the absence of those which the law declares indispensable, unless the latter had been lost without his fault.

Art. 66. Commercial books, to be admitted in an action must be kept in the language of this county. If they are in a different language through belonging to foreign men of business, they shall be previously translated, so far as is material, by an interpreter officially appointed.

Art. 67. Merchants are bound to preserve their commercial books for the space of 10 years, counted from the cessation of their business or commerce.

The heirs of a merchant are presumed to have the books of their ancestor and are bound to produce them as and when the person from whom they have inherited would have been so bound.

Country: Australia

THE CORPORATIONS LAW OF 1989 (AS AMENDED BY ACT 110 OF 1990, 110 OF 1991, 201 OF 1991, AND 27 OF 1992)

CHAPTER 1. — INTRODUCTORY.

DIVISION 8. — MISCELLANEOUS INTERPRETATION RULES.

☞§ 109S. Production of Records Kept in Computers, etc. (Added by Act 110 of 1990).

Where a person who keeps a record of information by means of a mechanical, electronic or other device is required by or under this law:

(a) to produce the information or a document containing the information to a court, tribunal or person; or

(b) to make a document containing the information available for inspection by a court, tribunal or person;

then, unless the court, tribunal or person otherwise directs:

(c) the requirement is taken to oblige the person to produce or make available for inspection, as the case may be, a writing that reproduces the information in a form capable of being understood by the court, tribunal or person; and

(d) the production of such a writing to the court, tribunal or person constitutes compliance with the requirement.

CHAPTER 9. — MISCELLANEOUS.

PART 9.3. — BOOKS.

✍§ 1300. Inspection of books.

(1) A books that is by this Law required to be available for inspection shall, subject to and in accordance with this Law, be available for inspection at the place where, in accordance with this Law, it is kept and at all times when the registered office in Australia of the body corporate concerned is required to be open.

(2) If any register kept by a company or a foreign company for the purposes of this Law is kept at a place other than the registered office of the company or foreign company, that place shall be open to permit the register to be inspected during the same hours as those during which the registered office of the company or foreign company is required to be open.

(3) A person permitted by this Law to inspect a book may make copies of, or take extracts from, the books and any person who refuses or fails to allow a person so permitted to make a copy of, or take an extract from the book is guilty of an offence.

✍§ 1301. Location of Books Kept on Computers, etc.

(1) This section has effect where a corporation records otherwise than in written form the matters required to be contained in a book and means are provided by which those matters are made available for inspection in written form at a place (in this section referred to as the "place of inspection") other than the place (in this section referred to as the "place of storage") where the material constituting the record is kept.

(2) If the place of inspection in respect of a books is at a place where, apart from this section, the books would be required to be kept, the corporation shall be deemed to have complied with the requirements of this Law as to the location of the book.

(3) Subsection (2) applies only if the corporation:

(a) has lodged a notice stating that is desires to avail itself of this section in respect of a specified book and specifying the situation of the place of inspection and the place of storage in respect of that book; and

(b) where such a situation is changed, has within 14 days after the change lodged notice of the change.

✍ § 1303. Court May Compel Compliance.

If any person in contravention of this Law refuses to permit the inspection of any book or to supply a copy of any book, the Court may by order compel an immediate inspection of the book or order the copy to be supplied.

☞§ 1305. Admissibility of Books in Evidence. (Amended by Act. No. 110 of 1991).

(1) A book:

(a) kept by a body corporate under a requirements of this Law; or

(b) kept by a corporation under a requirement of a previous law corresponding to a provision of this Law;

is admissible in evidence in any proceeding and is prima facie evidence of any matter stated or recorded in the book.

(2) A document purporting to be kept by a body corporate shall, unless the contrary is proved, be deemed to be a book kept as mentioned in subsection (1).

✍§ 1306. Form and Evidentiary Value of Books.

(1) A book that is required by this law to be kept or prepared may be kept or prepared:

(a) by making entries on a bound or looseleaf book;

(b) by recording or storing the matters concerning by means of mechanical electronic or other device; or

(c) in any other manner approved by the Commission.

(2) Subsection (1) does not authorize a book to be kept or prepared by a mechanical, electronic or other device unless:

(a) the matters recorded or stored will be capable at any time of being reproduced in a written form; or

(b) a reproduction of those matters is kept in a written form approved by the Commission.

(3) A corporation shall take all reasonable precautions, including such precautions (if any) as are prescribed for guarding against damage to, destruction of or falsification of work in, and for discovery of falsification of or in, any book or part of a book required by this Law to be kept or prepared by the corporation.

(4) Where a corporation records or stores any matters by means of a mechanical, electronic or other device, any duty imposed by this Law to make a book containing those matters available for inspection or to provide copies of the whole or a part of a book containing those matters shall be construed as a duty to make the matters available for inspection in written form or to provide a document containing a clear reproduction in writing of the whole or part of the, as the case may be.

(5) Where:

(a) by virtue of this Law a book that is required by this Law to be kept or prepared is prima facie evidence of any matters; and

(b) the book is kept or prepared by recording or storing the matters concerned by means of a mechanical, electronic or other device;

any writing that reproduces matters so recorded or stored is prima facie evidence of those matters.

(6) A writing that purports to reproduce matters recorded or stored by means of a mechanical, electronic or other device shall, unless the contrary is established, be deemed to be a reproduction of those matters.

✍ § 1307. Falsification of Books.

(1) An officer, former officer member or former member of a company who conceals, destroys, mutilates or falsifies any securities of or belonging to the company or any books affecting or relating to affairs of the company is guilty of an offence.

(2) Where matter that is used or intended to be used in connection with the keeping of any books affecting or relating to affairs of a company is recorded or stored in an illegible form by means of a mechanical device, and electronic device or any other device, a person who:

(a) records or stores by means of that device matter that the person knows to be false or misleading in a material particular;

(b) destroys, removes or falsifies matte that is recorded or stored by means of that device, or has been prepared for the purpose of being recorded or stored, or for use in compiling or recovering other matter to be recorded or stored by means of that device; or

(c) having a duty to record or store matter by means of that device, fails to record or store the matter by means of that device:

(i) with intent to falsify any entry made or intended to be complied, whole or in part, from matter so recorded or stored; or

(ii) knowing that the failure so to record or store the matter will render false or misleading in a material particular other matter so recorded or stored;

contravenes this subsection.

(3) It is a defence to a charge arising under subsection (1) or (2) of the defendant proves that he, she or it acted honestly and that in all the circumstances the act or omission constituting the offence should be excused.

(4) In this section, "officer" in relation to a company, includes a receiver of property of the company who is not also a manager.

EVIDENCE ACT 1905-1973

☞ PART 3. — PROOF OF CERTAIN INSTRUMENTS.

* * * * *

6. Whenever any book or document of the Commonwealth is of such a public nature as to be admissible in evidence on its mere production from the proper custody, any copy thereof or xtract therefrom shall be admissible in evidence in all Courts if —

(a) it is proved to be an examined copy or extract; or

(b) it purports to be signed and certified as a true copy or extract by the officer whose custody the original is entrusted.

7. (1) All documents purporting to be copies of the Votes and Proceedings or Journals or Minutes of either House of the Parliament, or of papers presented to either House of the Parliament, if purporting to be printed by the Government Printer, shall on their mere production be admitted as evidence thereof in all Courts.

(2) A document that purports —

(a) to be a copy of a motion, resolution or proposed law moved in, agreed to by or introduced in a House of the Parliament, or a particular committee of a House of the Parliament, on a date specified in the document; and

(b) to be printed by the Government Printer,

is admissible in all Courts as evidence that a motion, resolution or proposed law in the terms set out in the document was moved in, agreed to by or introduced in that House, or that committee of that House, as the case may be, and that it was moved, agreed to or introduced on the date specified in the document.

EVIDENCE AMENDMENT ACT OF 1978

☞ PART 3A. — ADMISSIBILITY OF BUSINESS RECORDS.

7A. (1) In this Part, unless the contrary intention appears —

"business" includes —

(a) any business, profession, occupation, calling, trade or undertaking whether or not engaged in or carried on for profit and whether engaged in or carried on in Australia or elsewhere, including any business, profession, occupation, calling, trade or undertaking engaged in or carried on by the Crown in right of the Commonwealth or of a State; and

(b) the administration of the government of the Commonwealth, of a State, of a Territory or of another country, whether carried on in Australia or elsewhere;

* * * * *

"document" includes —

(a) a book, plan, paper, parchment, film or other material on which there is writing or printing, or on which there are marks, symbols or perforations having a meaning for persons qualified to interpret them;

(b) a disc, tape, paper, film or other device from which sounds or images are capable of being reproduced; and

(c) any other record of information;

* * * * *

(2) For the purposes of this Part, a statement in a document shall be taken to be made by a person if —

(a) it is written, made, dictated or otherwise produced by him; or

(b) it is recognised by him as his statement by signing, initialing or otherwise.

* * * * *

7B. (1) Subject to this Part, where, in any proceeding, evidence of a fact is admissible, a statement of the fact in a document is admissible as evidence of the fact if —

(a) the document containing the statement forms part of a record of a business, whether or not the business is in existence at the time when the question of admissibility arises;

(b) the statement was made in the course of, or for the purposes of, the business; and

(c) the statement was made by a qualified person or reproduces, or was derived from, either or both of the following descriptions of information:

(i) information in one or more statements, each made by a qualified person in the course of, or for the purposes of, the business;

(ii) information from one or more devices designed for, and used for the purposes of the business in or for, recording, measuring, counting or identifying information, not being information based on information supplied by any person.

(2) This section makes a statement admissible notwithstanding —

(a) the rules against hearsay;

(b) the rules against secondary evidence of the contents of a document;

(c) that any person concerned in the making of the statement is a witness in the proceeding, whether or not he gives testimony consistent or inconsistent with the statement; or

(d) that the statement is in such a form that it would not be admissible if given as oral testimony, but does not make admissible a statement that is otherwise inadmissible.

* * * * *

7E. (1) Where, in any proceeding —

(a) the happening of an event of any description is in question; and

(b) in the course of a business, a system has been followed to make and keep a record of the happening of all events of that description, oral or other evidence to establish that there is no record of the happening of the event in question is admissible to prove that the event did not happen.

(2) Where evidence is, or is proposed to be, tendered under this section, the court may —

(a) require that the whole or a part of the record concerned be produced; and

(b) if the whole or a part of the record required to be produced is not produced — reject the evidence or, if it has been received, exclude it.

7F. (1) In estimating the weight (if any) to be attached to a statement tendered for admission or admitted under section 7B, regard shall be had to all the circumstances from which an inference can reasonably be drawn as to the accuracy or otherwise of the statement, including —

(a) in the case of a statement made by a person or a statement wholly or in part reproducing or derived from a statement made by a person —

(i) the recency or otherwise at the time when the person made his statement of any relevant matter dealt with in his statement; and

(ii) the presence and nature, or the absence, of any incentive for him to conceal or misrepresent any relevant matter in his statement;

(b) in the case of a statement wholly or in part reproducing or derived from information from one or more devices — the reliability of the device or devices; and

(c) in the case of a statement reproducing or derived from any information — the reliability of the means of reproduction or of derivation.

(2) In estimating the weight (if any) to be attached to evidence admissible under section 7E, regard shall be had to all the circumstances from which an inference can reasonably be drawn as to the accuracy or otherwise of the evidence, including whether any person concerned with the system had any incentive to omit recording the happening of the event concerned and, if so, the nature of that incentive.

* * * * *

7H. A court may, for the purpose of deciding questions of admissibility under this Part, draw inferences from the form or content of the document in which the statement is contained as well as from other matters from which inferences may lawfully be drawn.

7J. (1) Evidence relevant to the matters mentioned in section 7B, 7D or 7E may, if given by a person who had, at the relevant time or afterwards, a responsible position in relation to the making or keeping of the records concerned, be given on information and belief.

(2) Evidence given under sub-section (1) may include evidence of the contents of a document notwithstanding that the document is not produced and that its non-production is not accounted for.

7K. (1) For the purposes of section 7B —

(a) a statement in the document may, as prescribed or by leave of the court, be proved by the production of a copy of the document, or of the material part of the document;

(b) a statement in a document that is designed to be used to reproduce the statement in the form of a visible display or of sound may be proved by reproducing the statement in that form in the presence of the court; and

(c) a statement in the record of information made by the use of a computer may be proved by the production of a document produced by the use of a computer containing the statement in a form that can be understood by sight.

(2) For the purposes of section 7E, the absence of a record of the happening of an event in the record of information made by the use of a computer may be proved by the production of a document produced by the use of a computer containing a statement based on the absence of such a record.

(3) Where a person proposes to prove, or proves, a statement in a document otherwise than by producing the document, the court may require that the document be produced or be made available to the court or to other parties for examination or testing and, if the document is not so produced or made available, may reject the statement or, if it is in evidence, exclude it.

(4) Where a person proposes to prove, or proves, a statement by reproducing the statement in the form of a visible display or of sound, the court may direct a record of the statement to be produced and, if the record is not produced, may reject the statement or, if it is in evidence, exclude it.

(5) For the purposes of this section, "computer" means any device for storing or processing information.

7L. For the purposes of this Part, a document, a copy of a document or a copy of part of a document may be authenticated in such manner as is prescribed or the court approves.

* * * * *

✍ AUDIT AMENDMENT ACT OF 1979

* * * * *

3. Section 2 of the Principal Act is amended —

* * * * *

"information storage device" means —

(a) a computer;

(b) papers or other materials on which there are marks, symbols, perforations or other indicators having a meaning for persons qualified to interpret them;

(c) a disc, tape or other device on which information may be stored; or

(d) a device, whether electronic or otherwise, capable of storing information;

* * * * *

(6) For the purposes of this Act —

* * * * *

(c) a requirement under this Act to produce accounts or records to the Auditor-General or to another person shall be taken to include a requirement to produce, in a case where the accounts or records are kept by means of an information storage device, the information contained in the accounts or records, or in such extracts from the accounts or records as the Auditor-General or other person requests —

(i) in a form directed by the Auditor-General or other person; or

(ii) if the Auditor-General or other person has not given a direction for the purposes of subparagraph (i) — in a form that can be understood by sight;

* * * * *

ARCHIVES ACT 1983

AN ACT RELATING TO THE PRESERVATION AND USE OF ARCHIVAL RESOURCES, AND FOR RELATED PURPOSES

PART I. — PRELIMINARY.

* * * * *

✪ Interpretation

3.(1) In this Act, unless the contrary intention appears —

* * * * *

"record" means a document (including any written or printed material) or object (including a sound recording, coded storage device, magnetic tape or disc, microform, photograph, film, map, plan or model or a painting or other pictorial or graphic work) that is, or has been, kept by reason of any information or matter that it contains or can be obtained from it or by reason of its connection with any event, person, circumstance or thing;

* * * * *

PART V. — COMMONWEALTH RECORDS.

Division 2. — Dealings with Commonwealth Records.

✪ Disposal and destruction of Commonwealth records

24. (1) Subject to this Part, a person shall not —
(a) destroy or otherwise dispose of;
(b) transfer, or be a party to arrangements for the transfer of, the custody of;
(c) transfer, or be a party to arrangements for the transfer of, the ownership of; or
(d) damage or alter,
a Commonwealth record.
Penalty: $2,000.
(2) Subsection (1) does not apply to anything done —
(a) as required by any law;
(b) with the permission of the Archives or in accordance with a practice or procedure approved by the Archives;
(c) in accordance with a normal administrative practice, other than a practice of a Department or authority of the Commonwealth of which the Archives has notified the Department or authority that it disapproves; or
(d) for the purpose of placing Commonwealth records that are not in the custody of the Commonwealth or of a Commonwealth institution in the custody of the Commonwealth or of a Commonwealth institution that is entitled to custody of the records.

* * * * *

(5) For the purposes of the application of subsection (1) to a record of a kind used by means of any mechanical or electronic device or equipment, including a computer, any treatment or modification of the record that would prevent the obtaining from the record of information or matter that could previously have been obtained from the record shall be deemed to be destruction of the record.

Country: Bahama Islands

✍ TITLE 6. — DECLARATORY.

1. This Act may be cited as the Declaratory Act.

Common law of England, with certain exceptions, declared in force.

2. The Common Law of England, in all cases where the same hath not been altered by any of the Acts or Statutes enumerated in the Schedule to this Act or by any Act (except so much thereof as hath relation to the ancient feudal tenures, to outlawries in civil suits, to the wager of law or of batail, appeals of felony, writs of attaint and ecclesiastic matters), is, and of right ought to be, in full force within the Colony, as the same now is in that part of Great Britain called England.

3. The Acts and Statutes enumerated in the first part of the Schedule to this Act are, and of right ought to be, in full force and virtue within and throughout the Colony, as the same would be if the Bahama Islands were therein expressly named, or as if the aforesaid Acts and Statutes had been made and enacted by the legislature.

* * * * *

Country: Barbados

COMPANIES ACT.

DIVISION H. — CORPORATE RECORDS.

✍ FORM OF RECORDS

Article 173. All records required by this Act to be prepared and maintained
(a) may be in a bound or loose-leaf form or in a photographic film form, or
(b) may be entered or recorded
(i) by any system of the mechanical or electronic data processing, or
(ii) by any other information storage device
that is capable of reproducing any required information in intelligible written form within a reasonable time.

✍ CARE OF RECORDS

Article 174. A company and its agents shall take reasonable precautions
(a) to prevent loss or destruction of
(b) to prevent falsification of entries in, and
(c) to facilitate detection and correction of inaccuracies in,
the records required by this Act to be prepared and maintained in respect of the company.

Country: Belgium

PART 2. COMMERCIAL CODE

SECTION 4. CORPORATIONS

✍ STATEMENTS TO BE INCLUDED IN CORPORATE ACTS

Article 81. All acts, invoices, notices, publications and other documents issued by corporations must include the name of the corporation, immediately before or after which must appear the following text legibly written in full; Corporation (societe anonyme), with the full address of the statutory seat.

If the documents indicated above include a statement with respect to the corporate capital, this capital must be that which results from the last balance sheet.

Any change in the statutory seat must be published in the annexes of the Belgian State Gazette under the supervision of the directors.

✍ BUSINESS RECORDS

The Commercial Code requires that the following books and records are kept: (1) Inventory Book; (2) Official Journal.

These books must be legalized by a judge, i.e. the court's seal must be affixed to the books before any inscriptions are made. The books must be rubricated, that is, in bound form and with each page numbered and stamped by the Commercial Court Judge.

If corrections are needed in the books, new entries must be made as no erasures are permitted.

Copies of all correspondence must be retained.

All books and correspondence must be kept for 10 years.

In addition to the above books other government bodies and laws require books.

For Sales or Turnover Tax purposes (1) approves Sales and Purchase Journals must be kept.

For Income Tax purposes (1) books of account such as the general ledger, (grande livre) cost of sales records, expense analysis and cash books (livre de caisse) must be kept.

The Labor Laws require that corporation retain complete personnel records.

A share register must also be kept listing owners, etc., of all nominative shares.

Country: Bermuda

The Companies Act of 1981 (As amended and consolidated through Act No. 21 of 1996; effective as from July 24, 1996.)

✍ **PART 1. — INTERPRETATION AND APPLICATION. (Companies Act)**

* * * * *

2. Interpretation[2]

* * * * *

"Book and paper" includes minutes, financial statements, accounts, deeds, writings and documents;

* * * * *

Part 15. General.

273. Form of registers, etc. (1) Any book or paper required by this or any other Act, whether public or private, to be kept by the Registrar or a company may be kept by recording the matters in question in bound books or in any other permanent manner including a form otherwise than legible.

(2) Where any such book or paper is not kept in a bound book adequate precautions shall be taken for guarding against falsification and facilitating its discovery and where the book or paper is kept in a form otherwise than legible it shall be capable of being reproduced on a legible form.

(3) Where in this or any other Act, whether public or private, provision is made for the inspection or reproduction of any book or paper than it shall be treated as a provision to allow inspection or reproduction in a legible form.

(4) Copies of minutes referred to in section 81 and financial statements referred to in section 84 shall be preserved in the registered office of the company for a period of six years from the date when they were first required.

(5) Where any company fails to comply with any provision of this section, the company and any officer responsible for the default shall be liable to a fine of one thousand dollars.

274. Certain officers to be exempted from company fees and charges. The Accountant General, the Registrar, the Official Receiver and any person acting on their behalf shall be exempt from the payment of any fee or charges for inspecting or copying the register or any books or papers of a company when lawfully entitled so to do.

Footnote 2 - Amended by the Companies Amendment Act 1994 (No. 22).

Country: Bolivia

COMMERCIAL CODE

GENERAL PROVISIONS

BOOK 1. MERCHANTS AND THEIR OBLIGATIONS.

TITLE 1. — MERCHANTS.

✍ **CHAPTER 4. — ACCOUNTING.**
☞

Article 36. Obligation to keep accounts.

All merchants are obligated to keep an accounting adequate to the nature, importance and organization of the enterprise, on a uniform base permitting a demonstration of the situation of its negotiations and a clear justification of all and each act and operation subject to accounting; they must also keep in good state books, documents and correspondence relating.

Article 37. Books.

The merchant must obligatorily keep the following books: Journal, Ledger, Inventories and Balance Sheets, unless other books are specifically required by law.

He may also keep such books and record as he esteems convenient for greater order and clarity and to obtain information and exercise control. Such books are auxiliary books and are not subject to the provision in Article 40, even though those considered necessary may be legalized in order to serve as evidence along with the obligatory books.

Article 38. Small Merchants.

Individual merchants who carry on small business, whose volume of operations and capital employed in their commercial activities do not meet the minimum required by legal provisions on that matter, shall comply with the obligation imposed by the preceding article by daily registering a resume of purchases and sales on the accounts, and by a list of credit transactions including collections and payments realized for that purpose.

Article 39. Persons authorized to keep books.

The accounts shall be kept by legally authorized accountants who are regulated by rules on liability, system of procedure, remuneration, and guarding of accounting secrets, without prejudice to the liability of merchants to whom they render their services.

Article 40. Manner of presentation of the books.

Merchants shall present the books they are obligated to keep, bound and numbered by a Notary Public before they use them, including on the first page of each one what the books shall be used for, the name of the person to whom it belongs and the number of pages that it contains, dated and signed by the Notary, stamped also on all the leaves must be the stamp of the notary who authorize it a complies with the established fiscal requirements.

The entries and notations affected by any kind of mechanical or electronic method on removable leaves or cards are also valid, so long as they are bound correlatively afterwards into the obligatory books which must be legalized, provided that they facilitate the operations and shall serve as clear, complete and faithful evidence.

The authorization for their use shall be granted by the Commercial Register upon request of the interested party, requiring a resolution founded on the basis of opinion of experts, which may be dispensed with in the case of existing antecedents of use with respect to the proposed procedure.

In the case of stock corporations, the authorization shall be granted upon a favorable opinion of the respective administrative organization of control.

* * * * *

Article 51. Correspondence File.

The merchant must keep a file copy of correspondence relating to business negotiations by whatever means will assure the exactitude and durability of the copy. Also, he shall keep the correspondence he receives relative to his commercial activities, with notation of the date of receipt, reply or note of not having answered.

Also, he shall keep files of documents establishing entries in his accounting books, in a form which would facilitate their verification at any time.

If the books are made up of removable pages or cards, they must be numbered and kept in files for later binding.

Article 52. Conversation of books and commercial papers.

Books and papers to which the preceding article refers must be kept for at least 5 years from their closure or from the date of the last entry or proving document, unless special provisions establish another period for certain types of documents. After this period destroyed, provided the legal norms are complied with.

Article 53. Obligation to keep books and papers even in the case of ceasing of activities or the death of the merchant.

The cession of commercial activities does not exempt the merchant from the obligation referred to in the preceding article, and if he should die, the obligation falls upon his heirs. In the case of winding up of a company, the liquidators are obligated to comply with the preceding provision.

* * * * *

Article 56. Prohibition of investigations.

Official investigations of books and accounting registers are prohibited, except when carried out by provisions of judicial authority.

The provision of this article shall not restrict the right of inspection of the books, correspondence and documents or commercial companies that the law grants to partners, neither does it restrict their right to control, receivership or audit of them.

Article 57. De Officio inspection of books and papers.

The judicial or administrative authorities may only order de officio inspection of books, correspondence and documents of merchants in the following cases:

(1) To define amounts of taxes owed in cases of controversy;

(2) To exercise vigilance and control of stock corporations, banks, financial entities and other credit institutions, as well as insurance companies;

(3) In the investigation of felonies, in accordance with the provisions of Penal Procedure.

Article 58. Cases in which the books and other documents shall be investigated, exhibited or surrendered.

The investigation, exhibition or surrender of books, correspondence and other documents of merchants, may only be ordered de officio or at the request of a party in cases of secession, suspension of payments, bankruptcies and liquidation.

Article 59. Exhibition by request of party.

In the cases set forth in the preceding article, the exhibition of the books, correspondence, and documents of merchants may only be ordered by request of a party when the person has a legitimate interest or liability in the matter for which the exhibition is requested.

The examination shall be limited exclusively to the matters relative to the request.

Article 60. Place of exhibition.

In all cases, the exhibition shall be made in the establishment of the merchant or in the place where the books, correspondence and documents are kept, in the presence of the merchant or of the person he has commissioned for that purpose, without power to demand their transference.

Article 61. Refusal to exhibit.

If the merchant does not present books, correspondence and documents whose exhibition has been legally ordered, or if he should hide any of them or impede their examination, proceedings shall be ordered for their collection.

Article 62. Evidence among merchants.

Commercial books and papers kept with all the requirements demanded by this chapter shall constitute plenary evidence in mercantile controversies, whether judicial or extra-judicial.

If in a litigation, one of the parties presents books kept as required by Law, and the other party does not, the litigation shall be resolved in favor of the party who has kept the books properly, unless plenary evidence is presented which should destroy or discredit the contents of such books.

If the books of both parties are not subject to legal prescriptions, such books shall be totally rescinded, and only other evidence shall be taken into account for the litigation.

Article 63. Evidence with non-merchants.

In a litigation between a merchant and private parties who are not merchants, the books shall only constitute a rule of evidence which must necessarily be complemented with other legal evidence.

* * * * *

Article 65. Filing and reproduction of documents.

Merchants may keep their documents and correspondence in general by means of systems of micro-filming, photographic copies, photostats and other similar systems, in compliance with the legal requirements demanded for this purpose.

Country: Botswana

✍ **Companies Proclamation of 1959**[1]

PART 3. MANAGEMENT AND ADMINISTRATION.

Meetings and Proceedings

111. (1) The books or copies of the books certified by a director or secretary containing the minutes of proceedings of any general meeting of a company held after the commencement of this Proclamation shall be kept at the registered office of the company, and shall during business hours (subject to such reasonable restrictions as the company may by its articles or in general meeting impose, so that not less than two hours in each day be allowed for inspection) be open to the inspection of any member without charge.

* * * * *

Accounts and Audit

112. Keeping of books of account. (1) Every company shall cause to be kept in the English language proper books of account with respect to —

(a) all sums of money received and expended by the company and the matters in respect of which the receipt and expenditure takes place;

(b) all sales and purchases of goods by the company;

(c) the assets and liabilities of the company.

(2) For the purposes of sub-section (1) of this section, proper books of account shall not be deemed to be kept with respect to the matters aforesaid if there are not kept such books as are necessary to give a true and fair view of the state of the company's affairs and to explain its transactions.

(3) The books of account shall be kept at the registered office of the company or at such other place as the directors think fit, and shall at all times be open to inspection by the directors:

Provided that if books of account are kept at a place outside the Territory there shall be sent, and kept at a place in the Territory, and be at all times open to inspection by the directors such accounts and returns with respect to the business dealt with in the books of account so kept as will disclose with reasonable accuracy the financial position of that business at intervals not exceeding twelve months and will enable the company's balance to be prepared in accordance with this Proclamation.

* * * * *

PART 7. — GENERAL.

Form of Registers, Books: Inspection and Production

Form of Registers and Other Documents

293. (1) Any register, index, minute book or book of account required by this Proclamation to be kept by a company or external company may be kept either by making entries in bound books or by recording the matters in question in any other manner.

(2) Where any such register, index, minute book or book of account is not kept by making entries in a bound book, but by some other means, adequate precautions shall be taken for guarding against falsification and for facilitating its discovery.

(3) Any such register, index, minute book or book of account and every other book or document required by this Proclamation to be kept by a company or external company and every document required by this Proclamation or by a company's memorandum or articles to be issued or circulated by a company or external company shall be legibly printed in the English language.

(4) Where default is made in complying with sub-section (2) or (3) of this section the company or external company and every officer of the company or external company who is in default shall be guilty of an offence and liable to a fine not exceeding one hundred pounds and to a further fine not exceeding five pounds for every day during which the offence continues.

Production and Inspection of Books Where Offence Suspected

294. If on an application by the Resident Commissioner or by the Attorney-General, as the case may be, to a Judge of the High Court in respect of a company or external company there is shown to be reasonable cause to believe that any person has, while an officer of a company or external company, committed an offence in connection with the management of the affairs of the company or external company and that the evidence of the commissioner of the offence is to be found in any books or papers of or under the control of the company or external company, an order may be made —

(a) authorising any person named therein to inspect the said books or papers or any of them for the purpose of investigating and obtaining evidence of the offence; or

(b) requiring the secretary of the company or external company or such other office thereof as may be named in the order to produce the said books or papers or any of them to a person named in the order at a place so named.

---

[1] As amended by the Companies Amendment Law, 1961, GN of 51 of 1964, Act 8 of 1966, Act 84 of 1966, Act 7 of 1968, Act 38 of 1968 and Act 63 of 1970.

Country: Brazil

THE CIVIL CODE OF BRAZIL

PART III. THE CORPORATION LAW.

CHAPTER IX. CORPORATE BOOKS.

✍ **RECORDS OF COMPANIES.**

Art. 100. In addition to the books required of all commercial firms and subjet to the same legal formalities, a company shall keep the following:

I. a Nominative Shares Register book and a Ensorsable Shares Register book for recording annotation or registration of:

(a) sharholders names and the number of their shares;

(b) down-payments or installments towards payment of paid-in capital;

(c) conversions of shares from one form, type or class to another;

(d) redemptions, refunds and amortizations of shares, or their acquisition by the company;

(e) changes resulting from the alienation or transfer of shares;

(f) pledges, usufructs, trusts, fiduciary alienations in guarantee, or any onus whatsoever creating a charge on the shares or preventing the same from being traded.

II - A Transfers of Nominative Shares book for recording transfers, which must be signed by the assignor and the assignee, or their authorized representatives;

III - A Nominative Founders' Shares Register book and a Nominative Founders' Shares Transfers book, should such have been issued, subject, in both cases, as far as applicable, to the provisions of items I and II of the Article;

IV - Endorsable Founders' Shares Register, Endorsable Debentures Register and Endorsable Subscription Bonus Register books, should such have been issued by the company, subject, wherever application, to the provisions of the Endorsable Shares Register book;

V - A minutes of General Meetings book;

VI - A Record of Shareholders Attendance book;

VII - A Minutes of Meetings of the Administrative Council book, if any, and a Minutes of Meetings of the Board of Directors book;

VIII - A Minutes and Reports of the Fiscal Council book.

§ 1. Any individual may obtain certified copies of entries in the books mentioned in items I through IV of this Article, and the company may charge a reasonable fee to cover the cost of the same.

§ 2. In open companies, books referred to in items I through IV of this Article may be substituted for mechanized or electronic records, subject to rules issued by the Securities and Exchange Commission.

☞ **CHAPTER 4. — OF THE FORM OF JUDICIAL ACTS AND THEIR PROOF.**

Art. 136. Juridical acts, for which a special form is not required, may be proven by means of:

* * * * *

III. Public or private documents.

* * * * *

Art. 137. Textual certified copies of any judicial record (*peça*), of the record (*protocollo*) of hearings (*audiencias*), or of (*extrahidas*) by him or under his superintendence, and subscribed by him, as well as the copies of court record (*traslados de autos*), when compared by another clerk, shall be evidence the same as the originals.

Art. 138. The same probative force is had by the copies (*traslados*) and certified copies (*certidões*), made by a public official, of instruments or documents entered (*lançedos*) in their records (*notas*).

Art. 139. Copies (*traslados*) though not yet compared, and certified copies (*certidões*), shall be considered public instruments, if their originals have been produced in suit as proof of any act.

Country: British Virgin Islands

THE INTERNATIONAL BUSINESS COMPANIES ORDINANCE, 1984

PART 3. — CAPITAL AND DIVIDENDS (INTERNATIONAL BUSINESS COMPANIES).

✍ **28. Share register (International Business Companies).**

(1) A company incorporated under this Ordinance shall cause to be kept one or more registers to be known as share registers containing

(a) the names and addresses of the persons who hold registered shares in the company;

(b) the number of each class and series of registered shares held by each person;

(c) the date on which the name of each person was entered in the share register;

(d) the date on which any person ceased to be a member;

(e) in the case of shares issued to bearer, the total number of each class and series of shares issued to bearer; and

(f) with respect to each certificate for shares issued to bearer,

(i) the identifying number of the certificate;

(ii) the number of each class or series of shares issued to bearer specified therein; and

(iii) the date of issue of the certificate;

but the company may delete from the register information relating to persons who are no longer members or information relating to shares issued to bearer that have been canceled.

(2) The share register may in an any such form as the director may approve but if it is in magnetic, electronic or other data storage form, the company must be able to produce legible evidence of its contents.

* * * * *

✍ **32A. Optional register of directors (Added by Act No. 10 of 1990)**

(1) A company incorporated under this Act may keep a register to be known as a register of directors containing

(a) the names and addresses of the persons who are directors of the company;

(b) the date on which each person whose name is entered in the register was appointed as a director of the company; and

(c) the date on which each person named as a director ceased to be a director of the company.

(2) The register of directors may be in such form as the directors approve, but if it is in magnetic, electronic or other data storage form, the company must be able to produce legible evidence of its contents.

(3) A copy of the register of directors, commencing from the date of the registration of the company, shall be kept at the registered office of the company referred to in section 38.

(4) The register of directors is *prima facie* evidence of any matters directed or authorized by the Act to be contained therein.

✍ ☞ **115. Inspection of documents (International Business Companies).**

(1) Except as provided in subsection (2) of section 85, a person may

(a) inspect the documents kept by the Registrar pursuant to this Ordinance; and

(b) require a certificate of incorporation, merger, consolidation, arrangement, continuation, dissolution or good standing of a company incorporated under this Ordinance, or a copy of an extract of any document or any part of a document of which he has custody, to be certified by the Registrar; and a certificate of incorporation, merger, consolidation, arrangement continuation, dissolution or good standing or a certified copy or extract is prima facie evidence of the matters contained therein.

(2) A document or a copy or an extract of any document or an part of a document certified by the Registrar under subsection (1) is admissible in evidence in any proceedings as if it were the original document.

Country: Canada

CHAPTER 1. — NATIONAL ARCHIVES OF CANADA

✪ **INTERPRETATION**

2. In this Act,

* * * * *

"record" includes any correspondence, memorandum, book, plan, map, drawing, diagram, pictorial or graphic work, photograph, film, microform, sound recording, videotape, machine readable record, and any other documentary material, regardless of physical form or characteristics, and any copy thereof.

* * * * *

✪ **RECORDS OF GOVERNMENT INSTITUTIONS AND MINISTERIAL RECORDS**

5. (1) No record under the control of a government institution and no ministerial record, whether or not it is surplus property of a government institution, shall be destroyed or disposed of without the consent of the Archivist.

* * * * *

CHAPTER 20. — CANADA AGRICULTURAL PRODUCTS.

✍ **INSPECTION**

21. * * *

(2) In carrying out an inspection under this section, an inspector may

(*a*) use or cause to be used any data processing system at the place to examine any data contained in or available to the data processing system;

(*b*) reproduce any record or cause it to be reproduced from the data in the form of a printout or other intelligible output and take the printout or other output for examination or copying; and (*c*) use or cause to be used any copying equipment at the place to make copies of any record or other document.

* * * * *

CHAPTER B-1. — BANK.

✍ **Division F. — Records.**

155. (1) A bank shall preserve and maintain, at its head office or at any other place in Canada designated by the directors, records containing

(*a*) particulars of any restrictions and conditions established by the Governor in Council pursuant to section 28 or 114 that are from time to time applicable to the bank;

(*b*) in the case of a foreign bank subsidiary, the license issued to the bank pursuant to section 28 and particulars of renewals thereof and of any restrictions and conditions relating thereto;

(*c*) particulars of exceptions granted by the Governor in Council pursuant to section 269 that are from time to time applicable to the bank;

(*d*) particulars from Schedule I or II that are applicable to the bank as they are from time to time amended and published in the *Canada Gazette*;

(*e*) all by-laws of the bank that are in effect on December 1, 1980 and that are continued in effect by subsection 45(8) and all by-laws and amendments thereto made under this Act;

(*f*) all orders in council approving special resolutions of shareholders of the bank and changes in by-laws of the bank;

(*g*) minutes of meetings and resolutions of shareholders;

(*h*) copies of all returns and notices required by section 228; and

(*i*) a central securities register that complies with section 77.

(2) In addition to the records described in subsection (1), a bank shall prepare and maintain adequate corporate accounting records and records containing minutes of meetings and resolutions of the directors and any committee thereof.

* * * * *

157. (1) All registers and other records required or authorized by this Act to be prepared and maintained by a bank including any entries, books, vouchers, paid instruments, signature cards, signing authorities, and other documents and papers in the possession of the bank may be in a bound or loose- leaf form or in photographic film form, and may be entered or recorded by any system of mechanical or electronic data processing or any other information storage device that is capable of reproducing any required information in intelligible written form with a reasonable time and registers and records maintained in any form may be converted to any other form.

(2) Notwithstanding section 159, a bank may destroy any registers or other records that have been created and maintained at any time after those registers or other records have been converted to another form referred to in subsection (1).

* * * * *

(5) Subject to subsections (6) and (7), a bank may maintain copies of or take extracts from any records and registers referred to in subsection (4) and may further process information or data relating to such copies or extracts inside or outside Canada.

(6) Where a bank, in accordance with subsection (5), maintains copies of extracts of any records or registers referred to in subsection (4) or further processes information or data relating to such copies or extracts outside Canada, the bank shall so inform the Inspector and provide him with a description and the nature of those copies or extracts maintained outside Canada and a description of further processing of information or data relating to such copies or extracts outside Canada and such other information as the Inspector may require from time to time.

(7) In the event that an Inspector is at any time of the opinion that further processing outside Canada of information or data relating to any copies or extracts referred to in subsection (6) is incompatible with the fulfillment of his responsibilities under this Act or he is advised by the Minister that, in the opinion of the Minister, such further processing is not in the national interest, he shall direct the bank to further process information or data relating to such copies or extracts in Canada and the bank shall forthwith comply with such direction.

* * * * *

159. (1) Except as provided in subsection 209(4), a bank may destroy any record, other than the corporate records described in subsection 155(1) and the records referred to in subsection 155(2) containing minutes of meetings and resolutions of the directors and any committee thereof, required or authorized by this Act to be maintained and any other document, voucher, paid instrument or other paper in its possession that was dated or in existence or that contained entries or writings all of which were made more than ten years prior to the destruction.

(2) Except as provided in subsection (3), in any action or proceeding, the liability of a bank shall be determined by reference only to evidence of matters that have arisen or things that have occurred, including records or the portions thereof, and documents, vouchers, paid instruments and papers that are dated or came into existence, or that contain entries or writings made, during the period of ten years immediately preceding the commencement of the action or proceeding.

(3) In any action or proceeding to establish the ownership of shares of a bank, the ownership shall be determined by reference only to evidence of matters that have arisen or things that have occurred, including records, or the portions thereof, and documents, vouchers, paid instruments and papers that are dated or came into existence, or that contain entries or writings made, during the period of ten years immediately preceding the commencement of the action or proceedings, but this subsection does not apply in relation to the securities register of a bank.

(4) Nothing in subsection (1), (2) or (3) affects the operation of any statute of limitation or prescription or the right of a bank to destroy any records, documents, vouchers, paid instruments or papers not specified in subsection 209(4) or relieves the bank from any liability to the Bank of Canada in respect of any debt or instrument to which subsection 209(1) applies.

238. (1) A bank shall prepare and maintain records containing

(*a*) its incorporating instrument and the by-laws of the bank and all amendments thereto;

(*b*) minutes of meetings and resolutions of shareholders;

(*c*) the information referred to in paragraphs 527(1)(*a*), (*c*), and (*e*) to (*h*) contained in all returns provided to the Superintendent pursuant to § 527;

(*d*) particulars of any authorizations, conditions and limitations established by the Superintendent pursuant to § 53 or subsection 54(1) that are from time to time applicable to the bank;

(*e*) particulars of exceptions granted by the Governor in Council pursuant to section 39, 55 or 231 that are from time to time applicable to the bank; and

(*f*) particulars from Schedule I or II that are applicable to the bank as they are from time to time amended and published in the *Canada Gazette*.

(2) In addition to the records described in subsection (1), a bank shall prepare and maintain adequate

(*a*) corporate accounting records;

(*b*) records containing minutes of meetings and resolutions of the directors and any committee thereof; and

(*c*) records showing, for each customer of the bank, on a daily basis, particulars of the transactions between the bank and that customer and the balance owing to or by the bank in respect of that customer.

(3) For the purposes of paragraph (1)(*b*) and subsection (2),

(*a*) in the case of a body corporate continued as a bank under this Act, "records" includes similar records required by law to be maintained by the body corporate before it was so continued; and

(*b*) in the case of a body corporate amalgamated and continued as a bank under this Act, "records" includes similar records required by law to be maintained by the body corporate before it was so amalgamated.

243. (1) A register or other record required or authorized by this Act to be prepared and maintained by a bank

(*a*) may be in bound or loose-leaf form or in a photographic film form; or

(*b*) may be entered or recorded by any system of mechanical or electronic data processing or any other information storage device that is capable of reproducing any required information in intelligible written form within a reasonable time.

(2) Registers and records maintained in one form may be converted to any other form.

(3) Notwithstanding § 246, a bank may destroy any register or other record referred to in subsection (1) at any time after the register or other record has been converted to another form.

246. (1) A bank shall retain

(*a*) the records of the bank referred to in subsection 238(1);

(*b*) any record of the bank referred to in paragraph 238(2)(*a*) or (*b*); and

(*c*) the central securities register referred to in subsection 248(1).

(2) A bank shall retain all signature cards and signing authorities or copies thereof relating to any deposit or instrument in respect of which the bank has paid an amount to the Bank of Canada pursuant to § 438 until the Bank of Canada notifies the bank that they need no longer be retained.

(3) Copies of the signature cards and signing authorities referred to in subsection (2) may be kept in any manner or form referred to in paragraphs 243(*a*) and (*b*) and any such copies, or prints therefrom, are admissible in evidence in the same manner and to the same extent as the original signature cards and signing authorities.

(4) Nothing in this section affects the operation of any statute of limitations or prescription or relieves the bank from any obligation to the Bank of Canada in respect of any deposit or instrument in respect of which § 438 applies.

248. (1) A register or other record required or authorized by this Act to be prepared and maintained by a company

(*a*) may be in a bound or loose-leaf form or in a photographic film form; or

(*b*) may be entered or recorded by any system of mechanical or electronic data processing or any other information storage device that is capable of reproducing any required information in intelligible written form within a reasonable time.

(2) Registers and records maintained in one form may be converted to any other form.

(3) Notwithstanding § 251, a company may destroy any register or other record referred to in subsection (1) at any time after the register or other record has been converted to another form.

251. (1) The company shall retain

* * * * *

(3) Copies of the signature cards and signing authorities referred to in subsection (2) may be kept in any manner or form referred to in paragraphs 248(*a*) and (*b*) and any such copies, or prints therefrom, are admissible in evidence in the same manner and to the same extent as the original signature card and signing authorities.

* * * * *

CHAPTER C-5. — CANADA EVIDENCE.

☞ Documentary Evidence

23. (1) Evidence of any proceeding or record whatever of, in or before any court in Great Britain, the Supreme Court or Federal Court of Canada, any court in any province, any court in any British colony or possession or any court of record in the United States, of any state of the United States or of any other foreign country, or before any justice of the peace or coroner in any province, may be given in any action or proceeding by an exemplification or certified copy thereof, purporting to be under the seal of the court or under the hand or seal of the justice or coroner, as the case may be, without any proof of the authenticity of the seal or of the signature of the justice or coroner or other proof whatever.

* * * * *

24. In every case in which the original record could be admitted in evidence,

(*a*) a copy of any official of public document of Canada or of any province, purporting to be certified under the hand of the proper officer or person in whose custody the official or public document is placed, or

(*b*) a copy of a document, by-law, regulation or proceeding, or a copy of any entry in any register or other book of any municipal or other corporation, created by charter or Act of Parliament or the legislature of any province, purporting to be certified under the seal of the corporation, and the hand of the presiding officer clerk or secretary thereof, is admissible in evidence without proof of the seal of the corporation, or of the signature or official character of the person or persons appearing to have signed it, and without further proof thereof.

25. Where a book or other document is of so public a nature as to be admissible in evidence on its mere production from the proper custody, and no other Act exists that renders its contents provable by means of a copy, a copy thereof or extract therefrom is admissible in evidence in any court of justice or before a person having, by law or by consent of parties, authority to hear, receive and examine evidence, if it is proved that it is a copy or extract purporting to be certified to be true by the officer to whose custody the original has been entrusted.

26. (1) A copy of any entry in any book kept in any office or department of the Government of Canada, or in any commission, board, or other branch of the public service of Canada, shall be admitted as evidence of that entry, and of the matters, transactions and accounts therein recorded, if it is proved by the oath or affidavit of an officer of the office or department, commission, board or other branch of the public service of Canada that the book was, at the time of making of the entry, one of the ordinary books kept in the office, department, commission, board or other branch of the public service of Canada, that the entry was made in the usual and ordinary course of business of the office, department, commission, board or other branch of the public service of Canada and that the copy is a true copy thereof.

* * * * *

30. (1) Where oral evidence in respect of a matter would be admissible in a legal proceeding, a record made in the usual and ordinary course of business that contains information in respect of that matter is admissible in evidence under this section in the legal proceeding on production of the record.

(2) Where a record made in the usual course of business does not contain information in respect of a matter the occurrence or existence of which might reasonably be expected to be recorded in that record, the court may on production of the record admit the record for the purpose of establishing that fact and may draw the inference that the matter did not occur or exist.

(3) Where it is not possible or reasonably practicable to produce any record described in subsection (1) or (2), a copy of the record accompanied by an affidavit setting out the reasons why it is not possible or reasonably practicable to produce the record and an affidavit of the person who made the copy setting out the source from which the copy was made and attesting to its authenticity, each affidavit having been sworn before a commissioner or other person authorized to take affidavits, is admissible in evidence under this section in the same manner as if it were the original of the record.

(4) Where production of any record or of a copy of any record described in subsection (1) or (2) would not convey to the court the information contained in the record by reason of its having been kept in a form that requires explanation, a transcript of the explanation of the record or copy prepared by a person qualified to make the explanation, accompanied by an affidavit of that person setting out his qualifications to make the explanation, attesting to the accuracy of the explanation and sworn before any commissioner or other person authorized to take affidavits, is admissible in evidence under this section in the same manner as if it were the original of the record.

(5) Where part only of a record is produced under this section by any party, the court may examine any other part of the record and direct that, together with the part of the record previously so produced, the whole or any part of the other part thereof be produced by that party as the record produced by him.

(6) For the purpose of examining whether any provision of this section applies, or for the purpose of determining the probative value, if any, to be given to information contained in any record admitted in evidence under this section, the court may, on production of any record, admit any evidence in respect thereof given orally or by affidavit including evidence as to the circumstances in which the information contained in the record was written, recorded, stored or reproduced, and draw any reasonable inference from the form or content of the record.

* * * * *

(12) In this section,

"business" means any business, profession, trade, calling, manufacture or undertaking of any kind carried on in Canada or elsewhere whether for profit or otherwise, including any activity or operation carried on or performed in Canada or elsewhere by any government, by any department, branch, board, commission or agency of any government, by any court or other tribunal or by any other body or authority performing a function of government;

"copy", in relation to any record, includes a print, whether enlarged or not, from a photographic film of the record, and "photographic film" includes a photographic plate, microphotographic film or photostatic negative;

"court" means the court, judge, arbitrator or person before whom a legal proceeding is held or taken;

"legal proceeding" means any civil or criminal proceeding or inquiry in which evidence is or may be given, and includes an arbitration;

"record" includes the whole or any part of any book, document, paper, card, tape or other thing on or in which information is written, recorded, stored or reproduced, and, except for the purposes of subsections (3) and (4), any copy of transcript admitted in evidence under this section pursuant to subsection (3) or (4). R.S., c. E-10, s. 30.

31. (1) In this section,

* * * * *

"photographic film" includes any photographic plate, microphotographic film and photostatic negative.

(2) A print, whether enlarged or not, from any photographic film of

(*a*) an entry in any book or record kept by any government or corporation and destroyed, lost or delivered to a customer after the film was taken,

(*b*) any bill of exchange, promissory note, cheque, receipt, instrument or document held by any government or corporation and destroyed, lost or delivered to a customer after the film was taken, or

(*c*) any record, document, plan, book or paper belonging to or deposited with any government or corporation

is admissible in evidence in all cases in which and for all purposes for which the object photographed would have been admitted on proof that

(*d*) while the book, record, bill of exchange, promissory note, cheque, receipt, instrument or document, plan, book or paper was in the custody or control of the government or corporation, the photographic film was taken thereof in order to keep a permanent record thereof, and

(*e*) the object photographed was subsequently destroyed by or in the presence of one or more of the employees of the government or corporation, or was lost or was delivered to a customer.

(3) Evidence of compliance with the conditions prescribed by this section may be given by any one or more of the employees of the government or corporation, having knowledge of the taking of the photographic film, of the destruction, loss or delivery to a customer, or of the making of the print, as the case may be, either orally or by affidavit sworn in any part of Canada before any notary public or commissioner for oaths.

* * * * *

✍ CHAPTER C-44. — CANADA BUSINESS CORPORATIONS ACT.

22. (1) All registers and other records required by this Act to be prepared and maintained may be in a bound or looseleaf form or in a photographic film form, or may be entered or recorded by any system of mechanical or electronic data processing or any other information storage device that is capable of reproducing any required information in intelligible written form within a reasonable time.

* * * * *

✍ CHAPTER F-11. — FINANCIAL ADMINISTRATION.

60. (1) The Governor in Council may make such regulation as he deems necessary to provide for the management of the public debt of Canada and the payment of interest thereon and, without limiting the generality of the foregoing, may make regulations

(*a*) for the inscription or registration of securities and prescribing the effect of the inscriptions and registration;

(*b*) for the transfer, transmission, exchange, redemption, cancellation and destruction of any securities, and, without limiting the generality of the foregoing,

(i) for the transmission, transfer or redemption of securities pursuant to a judgment or as the result of the death, dissolution or bankruptcy of the registered owner of the securities, and

(ii) prescribing the conditions on which the transfer, transmission, exchange and redemption of securities registered in the names of infants, minors or other persons not in full capacity to enter into ordinary contracts may be made;

(*c*) for the issue of securities or making of payments in respect of damaged, lost, stolen or destroyed securities or interest coupons, and of the cheques pertaining thereto and prescribing conditions to the issue or payment.

(*d*) requiring guarantees to be given to the registrar in such manner and by such persons as the regulations may prescribe, before the registrar is authorized to make any entry in the register;

(*e*) authorizing the correction by the registrar, in such circumstances as may be prescribed by the regulations, of errors in the register and otherwise authorizing rectification of the register; and

(*f*) providing for the payment of losses out of the Investors' Indemnity Account.

(2) The register maintained pursuant to subsection (1) may be in a bound or looseleaf form or in a photographic film form or may be maintained by any system of mechanical or electronic data processing or any other information storage device that is capable of reproducing any required information in intelligible written form within a reasonable time.

(3) The register maintained pursuant to subsection (1) is deemed to be a record for the employee of the Bank of Canada who supervises the inscription or registration of securities in the register is deemed to be a manager of the Bank of Canada for the purposes of that Act.

✍ CHAPTER F-29. — FOREIGN EXTRATERRITORIAL MEASURES.

1. This Act may be cited as the *Foreign Extraterritorial Measures Act. 1984.*

2. In this Act,

* * * * *

"record" includes any correspondence, memorandum, book, plan, map, drawing, diagram, pictorial or graphic work, photograph, film, microform, sound recording, videotape, machine readable record, and any other documentary material, regardless of physical form or characteristics, and any copy thereof.

* * * * *

Country: Canada — Alberta

☞ CHAPTER A-21. — ALBERTA EVIDENCE ACT.

36(1) A copy of an entry in any book of account kept in any department, commission, board, or other branch of the Government of Canada or of Alberta is admissible in evidence as prima facie proof of the entry, and of the matters, transactions and accounts therein recorded, if it is proved by the oath or affidavit of an officer of the branched concerned that

(a) the book was, at the time of the making of the entry, one of the ordinary books kept in the branch,

(b) the entry was apparently, and as the deponent believes, made in the usual and ordinary course of business of the branch, and

(c) the copy is a true copy of the entry.

* * * * *

41(1) (1) In this section

(a) "person" includes

(i) The Government of Canada and of any province of Canada and any department, commission, board or branch of any such government,

(ii) a corporation, and

(iii) the heirs, executors, administrators or other legal representatives of a person;

(b) "photographic film" includes any photographic plate, microphotographic film and photostatic negative and "photograph" has a corresponding meaning.

(2) When a bill of exchange, promissory note, cheque, receipt, instrument, agreement, document, plan or a record or book, or entry therein kept or held by a person

(a) is photographed in the course of an established practice of that person for photographing objects of the same or a similar class in order to keep a permanent record thereof, and

(b) is destroyed by or in the presence of the person or of one or more of his employees or delivered to another person in the ordinary course of business or is lost,

a print from the photographic film is admissible in evidence in all cases and for all purposes for the object photographed would have been admissible.

(3) When a bill of exchange, promissory note, cheque, receipt, instrument, agreement or other executed or signed document was so destroyed before the expiration of 6 years

(a) from the date when in the ordinary course of business either the object or the matter to which it related ceased to be treated as current by the person having custody or control of the object, or

(b) from the date of receipt by the person having custody or control of the object, of notice in writing of any claim in respect of the object or matter prior to the destruction of the object,

whichever is the later date, the court may refuse to admit in evidence under this section a print from a photographic film of the object.

(4) Subsection (3) does not apply in any case where a photographic print is tendered by

(a) a government;

(b) the Bank of Canada;

(c) a municipal corporation;

(d) a board of a school district or school division under the *School Act*;

(e) a board of a hospital district under the *Hospitals Act*.

* * * * *

42(1) In this section,

(a) "bank" means a bank to which the *Bank Act* (Canada) applies, and includes a branch, agency or office of any such bank;

(b) "court" means the court, judge or arbitrator under the *Arbitration Act* or person before whom a legal proceeding is held or taken for the purposes of which the proceeding it is required to inspect or take copies of entries in the books or records of a bank;

(c) "legal proceeding" means any civil proceeding or inquiry in which evidence is or may be given, and includes and arbitration.

(2) Subject to this section, a copy of an entry in any book or record kept in any bank shall in all legal proceedings be received in evidence as prima facie proof of the entry and of the matters, transactions and accounts therein recorded.

(3) A copy of an entry in a book or record shall not be received in evidence under this section unless it is first proved

(a) that the book or record was at the time of the making of the entry one of the ordinary books or records of the bank,

(b) that the entry was made in the usual and ordinary course of

business,
(c) that the book or record is in the custody or control of the bank, and
(d) that the copy is a true copy thereof.
(4) Evidence to prove the matters required by subsection (3) to be proved may be given by the manager or accountant of the bank and may be given orally or by affidavit sworn before a commissioner for taking affidavits or other competent authority of the like nature.
(5) A bank or officer of a bank is not compellable in a legal proceeding to which the bank is not a party
(a) to produce a book or record, the contents of which can be proved under this section, or
(b) to appear as a witness to prove the matters, transactions and accounts therein recorded,
unless so ordered by an order of the court made for special cause.

* * * * *

☞ Copies of Instruments

54(1) A copy of a document certified to be a true copy under the hand and seal of office of the Registrar or Deputy Registrar under the *Land Titles Act*, in whose office the document is deposited, filed, kept or registered, is prima facie proof of the original except in the cases provided for in section 55.
(2) An abstract of title or a general certificate under seal furnished by a registrar in Alberta is prima facie proof of the contents thereof.
56(1) A party intending to prove the original of a telegram, letter, shipping bill, bill of lading, delivery order, receipt, account or other written instrument used in business or other transactions
(a) may give notice to the opposing party 10 days at least before the trial or other proceeding in which the proof is intended to be adduced that he intends to give in evidence as proof of the contents a writing purporting to be a copy of the document, and
(b) in the notice shall name some convenient time and place for the inspection thereof.
(2) The copy may then be inspected by the opposing party and without further proof is sufficient evidence to prove the contents of the original document and shall be accepted and taken instead of the original unless the party receiving the notice within 4 days after the time mentioned for the inspection gives notice that he intends to dispute the correctness or genuineness of the copy at the trail or proceeding, and to require proof of the original.
(3) The costs attending any production or proof of the original documents are in the discretion of the court.

✪ CHAPTER L-5. — LAND TITLES ACT.

20(1) The Registrar shall microphotograph
(a) every certificate of title when it is removed from the register,
(b) every new certificate of title when it is issued,
(c) every certificate of title mentioned in clause (a) or (b) immediately after a memorandum is endorsed thereon, and
(d) every
(i) caveat, and
(ii) instrument, other than a plan of survey,
accepted for filing or registration, after the memorandum of the filing or registration has been entered on the title and signed by the Registrar.
(2) The microphotographic films may be kept at a place or places that my be designated by the Attorney General.
21(1) When the Registrar is satisfied that a certificate of title has been destroyed or lost or cannot be found he may, if the certificate of title has been microphotographed, refer to the microphotographic film thereof or to a print therefrom and to the other records of the Land Title Office and then issue a new certificate of title based thereon which shall be marked "Substitute Certificate of Title".
(2) Notwithstanding anything in this Act or any other statute, a new certificate of title issued under subsection (1) shall for all purposes be the certificate of title to the land therein described, and has the same force and effect as the original certificate of title.
(3) When the Registrar is satisfied that any instrument filed or registered in the Land Titles Office, other than a certificate of title or duplicate certificate of title, has been destroyed or lost or mislaid he may, if the instrument has been microphotographed, certify that an enlarged print from the microphotographic film of the instrument is a copy thereof, and thereupon the print, without further proof, has the same force and effect as the original instrument.
22 When the Registrar is required to produce an instrument and is unable to do so by reason of its having been lost, mislaid or destroyed and not having been microphotographed, he shall furnish to the court or person requiring production of the instrument his certificate under seal stating that the instrument has been lost, mislaid or destroyed, as the case may be, and has not been microphotographed, and thereupon any memorandum, entry or record produced by him shall be the extent that it purports to show the nature and contents of the instrument that has been lost, mislaid or destroyed be received as evidence of the nature and contents thereof.

✪ ☞ **193** A photostatic copy of an instrument or caveat or a print, whether enlarged or not, from a photographic film of an instrument or caveat, if the photostatic copy or photographed print is attested under the signature of the Registrar who has the instrument or caveat in his possession, is admissible in evidence in all cases in which and for all purposes for which the instrument or caveat copied or photographed would have been received.

CHAPTER M-22. — MOTOR VEHICLE ADMINISTRATION ACT.

✍ Administration
✪
☞ **3**(1) The Minister may, on any terms or conditions he directs, authorize the Registrar to cause any item, including a document, class of document, a copy of a document or a document recorded on a photographic medium, computer tape or other similar device, that is filed or maintained in his office under this Act to be reproduced on a photographic medium, computer tape or similar device.
(2) A reproduction of an item referred to in subsection (1) certified by the Registrar
(a) stands in the place of the original item,
(b) shall be treated as the original item for all purposes under this Act, and
(c) is admissible in evidence in any court of law in the same manner and for all purposes as if it were the original item.
(3) When the Minister is of the opinion that an item or a reproduction of an item referred to in subsection (1) is no longer required he may, on any terms or conditions he directs, authorize the Registrar, subject to subsection (4), to destroy or dispose of the item or its reproduction, as the case may be.

(4) The destruction or disposal of any item or its reproduction under this section shall be carried out subject to the regulations made under section 21 of the *Department of Public Works, Supply and Services Act.*

3 The Minister may authorize the Registrar

(a) to cause any document, class of documents or copies of documents, filed in his office under this Act to be photographed on microfilm, and

(b) thereafter to destroy the document or documents or copies or dispose of them in accordance with his direction,

and the microfilm for the purposes of this Act shall be the original documents or copies and is admissible in evidence in any court of law in the like manner and for all purposes as are the documents so photographed.

Country: Canada — British Columbia

CHAPTER 59. — COMPANY.

Part 5.

Division (1)

Form of records

✍ Records office documents

187. (1) Every company shall keep at its records office

(a) its certificate of incorporation;

(b) a copy of its memorandum, including every amendment of it;

(c) a copy of its articles, including every amendment of it;

(d) its register of members, except as provided by section 69;

(e) its register of transfers, unless the register of members is kept elsewhere as provided by section 69;

(f) its register of directors;

(g) its register of debenture holders, except as provided by section 88 or 89;

(h) its register of debentures;

(i) its register of indebtedness;

(j) its register of allotments, unless the register of members is kept elsewhere as provided by section 69;

(k) the minutes of every general meeting and class meeting of the company'

(l) the minutes of every meeting of its directors;

(m) a copy of every document filed with the registrar;

(n) a copy of every certificate issued to it by the registrar;

(o) a copy of every order of the minister or the registrar relating to the company;

(p) a copy of every written contract under which the company has allotted any shares for a consideration other than cash;

(q) a copy of every other document and instrument approved in the preceding 10 years by the directors;

(r) a copy of every mortgage created or assumed by the company, whether or not required to be registered;

(s) a copy of every audited financial statement of the company and its subsidiaries, whether or not consolidated with the financial statement of the company, including the auditor's reports;

(t) where the company is an amalgamated company,

(i) every record, document or instrument described in paragraphs (a) to (i), (m) to (p) and (u) to (w);

(ii) every record, document or instrument described in paragraphs (l), (q) and (r); and

(iii) every record, document or instrument described in paragraphs (k) and (s); of each of the amalgamating companies;

(u) where the company is being wound up, the minutes of every meeting of its creditors;

(v) a copy of every prospectus and takeover bid circular issued in the preceding 10 years by the company or any subsidiary;

(w) a copy of every information circular issued in the preceding 10 years by the company or any subsidiary;

(x) a copy of the instrument of continuation under section 36 is any; and

(y) where a receiver or receiver-manager is appointed under an instrument registered in the office of the registrar, the name and address of the receive or receiver-manager, and date of the appointment of the receiver or receiver-manager and either the date he ceases to act or the date of the completion of his duties.

* * * * *

194. (1) Registers that are required by this Act to be prepared and maintained by or on behalf of a company may be in a bound or looseleaf form, or entered or recorded by any system of mechanical or electronic data processing, or by any other information storage device from which the company is capable of reproducing, in a reasonable time, any required information in intelligible form.

(2) Minutes that are required by this Act to be kept by a company shall be kept in a bound or looseleaf book.

(3) A company and its agents shall take adequate precautions with respect to the records and registers required by this Act to be prepared and maintained so as to

(a) avoid loss, mutilation or destruction;

(b) avoid falsification of entries; and

(c) provide simple, reliable and prompt access.

(4) Every person who contravenes this section commits an offense.

✪ Microfilm, Etc.

353.1 Where a document is registered in the office of the registrar, the registrar may have the document photocopied or otherwise reproduced and the reproduction is for all purposes deemed to be the document photographed or reproduced.

INTERPRETATION ACT

CHAPTER 206.

✪ Interpretation

1. In this Act, or in an enactment,

* * * * *

"record" includes books, documents, maps, drawings, photographs, letters, vouchers, papers and any other thing on which information is recorded or stored by any means whether graphic, electronic, mechanical or otherwise;

* * * * *

DOCUMENT DISPOSAL ACT

✪ CHAPTER 95.

1. In this Act,

"document" includes a record as defined in the *Interpretation Act;*

* * * * *

Approvals required

3. (1) No document shall be destroyed except on the written recommendation of a committee to be known as the Public Documents Committee, which consists of the Provincial Archivist, the Comptroller General, and 3 other persons to be named by the Lieutenant Governor in Council.

(2) No document shall be destroyed before the expiration of 7 years from the date on which it was created unless

(a) 2 years have expired from the date on which it was created and there is available to the officer who would, but for the destruction, have charge or custody of the document a microfilm copy of it;

(b) a recommendation under subsection (1) has been approved by the Legislative Assembly on the recommendation of the Select Standing Committee of the Legislative Assembly on Public Accounts and Economic Affairs; or

(c) it is

(i) listed in the records schedule approved by the Select Standing Committee of the Legislative Assembly on Public Accounts and Economic affairs, and

(ii) destroyed in accordance with the instructions in the records schedule.

(3) Subject to subsections (1) and (2), the Lieutenant Governor in Council may, on the recommendation of the minister having jurisdiction over the ministry concerned, order

(a) that any public document or any class or series of documents then in charge of the ministry be transferred to the archives or Provincial Library immediately on the expiration of the periods after the dates at which they were created as are specified in the order; and

(b) that any public document or class or series of documents then in the charge of the ministry be destroyed immediately on the expiration of the periods after the dates at which they were created as are specified in the order.

(4) No document deposited in a record office shall be destroyed without the approval of the Attorney General, and, in the case of an office of the Court of Appeal, without the further approval of the Chief Justice of British Columbia, and, in the case of an office of the Supreme Court, without the further approval of the Chief Justice of the Supreme Court.

(5) Every approval under subsection (4) shall be in writing, and shall designate the document to be disposed of, and shall be kept on file in the ministerial office, or record office to which it relates.

✪ **Certified copy evidence**
✍

5. A copy of photographic reproduction of any document in the archives certified under the hand of the Provincial Archivist to be a true copy shall be evidence of the authenticity and correctness of the copy or reproduction without proof of the appointment or signature of the Provincial Archivist.

☞ **CHAPTER 116. — EVIDENCE.**

Evidence of documents and proceedings of corporations

31. In every case in which the original record could be received in evidence, a copy of a document, bylaw, rule, regulation or proceeding, or a copy of any entry in any register or other book of any municipal or other corporation created by charter or by or under any statute of Canada or a province, purporting to be certified under the seal of the corporation, and the hand of the presiding officer, clerk or secretary of it, is receivable in evidence without proof of the seal of the corporation, or of the signature or of the official character of the person appearing to have signed the same, and without further proof of it.

Evidence of public books and documents

32. (1) Where a book or other document is of so public a nature as to be admissible in evidence on its mere production from the proper custody, and no other statute exists which renders its contents provable by means of a copy, a copy of it or extract from it is admissible in evidence in any court, or before a person having, by law or by consent of the parties, authority to hear, receive and examine evidence, if it is proved that it is a copy or extract purporting to be certified to be true by the officer to whose custody the original has been entrusted.

(2) The officer shall furnish the certified copy or extract to any person applying for it at a reasonable time, on paying for it a sum not exceeding 10 cents for every folio of 100 words.

Financial institution records

38. (1) Subject to this section, a copy of an entry in a book or record kept in a financial institution, in all legal proceedings to which the financial institution is not a party, shall be received in evidence of the entry, and of the matters, transactions and accounts recorded in it.

(2) A copy of an entry in that book or record shall not be received in evidence under this section unless it is first proved that

(a) the book or record was, at the time of the making of the entry, one of the ordinary books or records of the financial institution;

(b) the entry was made in the usual and ordinary course of business;

(c) the book or record is in the custody or control of the financial institution or its successor; and

(d) the copy is a true copy.

The proof may be given by the manager or accountant or a former manager or accountant of the financial institution or its successor, and may be given orally or by affidavit.

* * * * *

Interpretation of s. 40

39. In section 40 "person" includes

(a) the government of Canada and of a province of Canada, and a ministry or department, commission, board or branch of that government;

(b) a corporation; and

(c) the heirs, executors, administrators or other legal representatives of a person;

"photograph" includes photographic film, prints, reductions and enlargements, microphotographic film and photocopies.

Admissibility of photographic film

40. (1) Where a bill of exchange, promissory note, cheque, receipt, instrument, agreement, document, plan or a record or book or entry in it kept or held by a person is photographed in the course of an established practice in order to keep a permanent record, a photograph is admissible in evidence in all cases and for all purposes for which the object photographed would have been admissible.

(2) Where the court is of the opinion that it is in the interests of justice, it may refuse to admit a photograph in evidence under this section.

* * * * *

Interpretation of s. 48

47. In section 48
"business" includes every kind of business, profession, occupation, calling, operation or activity, whether carried on for profit or otherwise;
"document" includes any device by means of which information is recorded or stored;
"statement" includes any representation of fact, whether made in words or otherwise.

Admissibility of business records.

48. (1) In proceedings where direct oral evidence of a fact would be admissible, a statement of the fact in a document is admissible as evidence of the fact if the document was made or kept in the usual and ordinary course of business and if it was in the usual and ordinary course of business to record in that document a statement of the fact at the time it occurred or within a reasonable time after that.

(2) Subject to subsection (3), the circumstances of the making of the statement, including lack of personal knowledge by the maker, may be shown to affect its weight, but the circumstances do not affect its admissibility.

(3) Nothing in this section makes admissible as evidence a statement made by a person interested at a time when proceedings were pending or anticipated involving a dispute as to a fact which the statement might tend to establish.

(4) For the purpose of any rule of law or practice requiring evidence to be corroborated or regulating the manner in which uncorroborated evidenced is to be treated, a statement rendered admissible by this section shall not be treated as corroboration or evidence given by the maker of the statement.

Country: Canada — Manitoba

✪ ☞ **CHAPTER 33. — AN ACT TO AMEND THE REAL PROPERTY ACT.**

Certified copy of document as evidence of original document.

20(1) The original of any instrument, a certified copy of the original certified as previously having been registered at another land titles office, a certified copy of any record, document, plan, book or paper issued by a department of either the Federal or provincial governments or the Yukon Territory or Northwest Territories, a copy certified to the satisfaction of the registrar, or certified copy by a notary public to be a true copy where the original is also presented for comparison, is registerable as an instrument or as evidence and proof of the original record, document, plan, book or paper that is purports to be.

Microfilming of registered documents.

22(3) The district registrar may cause an instrument that is registered under this Act to be photographed on microfilm.

Certified copy as proof.

22(3.1) Where an instrument has been microfilmed under subsection (3), a printed reproduction from the microfilm certified by the district registrar as a true copy of the instrument is prima facie proof of the instrument and its contents for all purposes.

Destruction of instruments.

22(3.2) Where an instrument has been microfilmed under subsection (3), the district registrar may destroy the instrument or cause it to be destroyed forthwith, and upon destruction of the instrument the microfilm record of the instrument stands in place of the instrument for all purposes.

Transferring and copying uncancelled certificates of title.

56(1). The Registrar-General may order the certificates of title in a register in a land titles office that remain uncancelled,

(a) to be transferred to; or

(b) to be copied into; or

(c) in certain cases to be transferred to, and in other cases to be copied into;

a new register; and the district registrar shall attach to the new register

(d) the order; and

(e) his affidavit or declaration, or the affidavit or declaration of any person appointed by him for the purpose to the effect that the new register has been constituted in accordance with the order of the Registrar-General, and that the copies are true copies of the original certificates of which they purport to be copies;

and the copies shall, for all purposes, be accepted and received as original certificates and as evidence of the contents thereof.

Print-out of entry as evidence.

43.(3.1) A copy or print-out of an electronic entry made in accordance with subsection (1) or (2) and accepted and certified by the registrar to be a true copy of the original electronic entry or recording shall for all purposes be received and admitted in evidence as prima facie proof that the copy or print-out is a complete and accurate copy of the original electronic entry or recording.

Copies of instruments to be evidence.

165(1) Every copy of a certificate of title issued under this Act, and every copy of an instrument deposited, filed, or registered, in a land titles office, together with all memoranda and endorsements thereon, certified as such under the hand and seal of the district registrar, shall be received as evidence in any court in the province, in the same manner and with the same effect as if the original were produced, and is admissible in evidence as prima facie proof of the due execution of the original by all persons by whom it purports to have been executed, and whose execution has been verified by an affidavit of execution, endorsed upon or annexed to the original.

✪ ☞ **CHAPTER 50. — REGISTRY.**

Books becoming obliterated, etc., how dealt with.

43(1) Where, in any registry office or land titles office, any book, from age or use, is becoming obliterated or unfit for future use, the Registrar-General appointed under the Real Property Act may order the book to be recopied so far as it can be deciphered by examination thereof and of the original memorials relating thereto.

Copy as evidence.

43(2) The copy made as provided in subsection (1), and having attached thereto the direction of the Registrar-General to have the book recopied and the affidavit or declaration of the registrar or his deputy to the effect that the book so copied is a true copy of the original book of which it purports to be a copy, shall be to all intents and purposes accepted, received, and admitted in evidence as the original book, and as prima facie proof, that the copy is a true copy of the original book.

Destruction of instruments after microfilming.

43.1(3) Where an instrument has been microfilmed under subsection (1), the Registrar may destroy the instrument or cause it to be destroyed forthwith.

Registration of certified copies.

64 Copies of instrument registered in any land titles office, certified under the hand of the district registrar, may be registered under this Act in any registry office or land titles office in so far as those instruments affect land not under The Real Property Act, and when so registered have the same effect as if the original had been duly registered under this Act, if the original instrument of which the certified copy purports to be a copy is one that could have been registered in the land mentioned registry office or land titles office.

CHAPTER E150. — AN ACT RESPECTING WITNESSES AND EVIDENCE.

Part 1. — Respecting Evidence Generally.

Application of Part

☞ **CORPORATION DOCUMENTS**

Proof of official or public documents.

41. A copy of any entry, or statement of the absence of any entry, in any register or other book of any corporation, created by charter or statute of Canada or of the province, or of any other province of Canada, purporting to be certified under the seal of the corporation and the hand of the presiding officer, clerk, or secretary thereof, is receivable as evidence of the entry or the absence thereof.

Copy of bank books, etc., as evidence.

50(1) Subject to this section, a copy of any entry in a book or record kept in a bank shall, in all legal proceedings, be received in evidence as prima facie proof of the entry and of the matters, transactions, and accounts, therein recorded.

50(2) A copy of an entry in such a book or record shall not be received in evidence under this section unless it is first proved that

(a) the book or record was, at the time of the making of the entry, one of the ordinary books or records of the bank;

(b) the entry was made in the usual and ordinary course of business;

(c) the book or record is in the custody or control or the bank; and

(d) the copy is a true copy of the entry.

Admissibility in evidence of photographic print.

51(2) Where a bill of exchange, promissory note, cheque, receipt, instrument, agreement, document, plan, or record or book or entry therein, kept or held by any person,

(a) is photographed in the course of an established practice of that person of photographing objects of the same or a similar class in order to keep a permanent record thereof; and

(b) is destroyed by, or in the presence of, the person or of one or more of his employees, or delivered to another person in the ordinary course of business, or lost;

a print from the photographic film is admissible in evidence in all cases and for all purposes for which the object photographed would have been admissible.

Refusal to admit by court.

51(3) Where a bill of exchange, promissory note, cheque, receipt, instrument, agreement, or other executed or signed document, was so destroyed before the expiration of six years from,

(a) the date when in the ordinary course of business either the object or the matter to which it related ceased to be treated as current by the person having custody or control of the object; or

(b) the date of receipt by the person having custody or control of the object of notice in writing of any claim in respect of the object or matter prior to the destruction of the object;

whichever is the later date, the court may refuse to admit in evidence under this section a print from a photographic film of the object.

Country: Canada — New Brunswick

☞ **CHAPTER E-II. — EVIDENCE ACT.**

45(1) If a party desires to give in evidence a telegraph message or despatch sent to the opposite party, or shown to be in his possession, and notice to produce the same has been given as in ordinary cases, and the same is not produced under the notice, such party may give secondary evidence thereof; and if such message or dispatch is produced under the notice, if shall, if otherwise admissible, be received in evidence the same as an original document.

(2) Evidence that any such message or despatch was delivered at a telegraph office, and received thereat for transmission shall be *prima facie* evidence that the same was transmitted in due course, and received by the person to whom it was addressed.

(3) When a telegraph message or despatch is signed, addressed or written, or appears on its face to have been signed or addressed or written in whole or in part in figures or any number, word, name, phrase or sentence agreed upon or recognized by the sender and receiver of such message or despatch as meaning between them some other word, number, name, phrase or sentence, or as having any other than the ordinary or apparent meaning of such figure, number or word, such signature, address or writing shall, for the purposes of this and the last preceding two sections, be taken to be the word, number, name, phrase or sentence so agreed upon and recognized between the sender and receiver as a aforesaid, and such message or despatch shall for all purposes be treated as though the same had been written, addressed and signed in full, according to the meaning agreed upon or recognized as aforesaid and so transmitted.

✍ BANKER'S BOOKS

46(1). Subject to provisions of this section a copy of an entry in any book or record kept in a bank shall in all actions be received as *prima facie* evidence of such entry and of the matters, transactions and accounts therein recorded.

(2) A copy of a entry in such book or record shall not be received in evidence under this section unless it is proved that the book or record was at the time of the making of the entry one of the ordinary books or records of the bank and that the entry was made in the usual and ordinary course of business, and that the book or record is in the custody or control of the bank and that such copy is a true copy thereof, which proof may be given by the manager or accountant of the bank and may be given orally or by affidavit.

* * * * *

☞ MICROFILMS

47 (1) In this section

(a) "person" includes

(i) The government of Canada and of any province of Canada and any department, commission, board or branch of any such government,

(ii) a corporation, and

(iii) the heirs, executors, administrators or other legal representatives of a person;

(b) "photographic film" includes any photographic plate, microphotographic film and photostatic negative and "photograph" shall have a corresponding meaning.

(2) Where a bill of exchange, promissory note, cheque, receipt, instrument, agreement, document, plan or a record or book or entry therein kept or held by any person is photographed in the course of an established practice of such person of photographing objects of the same or a similar class in order to keep a permanent record of it, a print from the photographic film is admissible in evidence in all cases and for all purposes for which the object photographed would have been admissible.

(3) Where a bill of exchange, promissory note, cheque, receipt, instrument, agreement or other executed or signed document was so destroyed before the expiration of six years from

(a) the date when in the ordinary course of business either the object or the matter to which it related ceased to be treated as current by the person having custody or control of the object; or

(b) the date or receipt by the person having custody or control of the object of notice in writing of any claim in respect of the object or matter prior to the destruction of the object;

whichever is the later date, the court may refuse to admit in evidence under this section a print from a photographic film of the object.

(4) Where the photographic print is tendered by the Government of Canada or of any other province of Canada or any department, commission, board or branch of any such Government or of the Bank of Canada, subsection (3) shall not apply.

(5) Proof of compliance with the conditions prescribed by this section may be given by any person having knowledge of the facts either orally or by affidavit sworn before a notary public or a commissioner for oaths and unless the court otherwise orders, a notarial copy of any such affidavit is admissible in evidence in lieu of the original affidavit.

Country: Canada — Newfoundland

☞ CHAPTER 115. — AN ACT RESPECTING EVIDENCE.

18. Every document which is by any law now in force or hereafter to be in force, is or shall be admissible in evidence of any particular in any British Court of Justice without proof of the seal or stamp, or signature authenticating the same, or of the judicial or official character of the person appearing to have signed the same, shall be admitted in evidence to the same extent and for the same purposes, in any court of justice in this province, or before any person having by law or by consent of parties authority to hear, receive and examine evidence, without proof of the seal or stamp or signature authenticating the same, or of the judicial or official character of the person appearing to have signed the same.

19. Every register of a vessel kept under any of the acts relating to the registry of British vessels may be proved in any court of justice, or before any person having, by law or by consent of parties, authority to hear, receive and examine evidence, either by the production of the original or by an examined copy thereof, or by a copy thereof purporting to be certified under the hand of the person having charge of the original, and which person is hereby required to furnish such certified copy to any person applying at a reasonable time for the same, upon the payment of the sum of twenty-five cents; and such register and such copy of a register, and also every certificate of a registry granted under any of the acts relating to the registry of British vessels, and purporting to be signed as required by law, shall be received in evidence in any court of justice, or before any person having, by law or by consent of parties, authority to hear, receive, and examine evidence, as *prima facie* proof of all matters contained and recited in such register, when the register or such copy thereof as aforesaid is produced and of all matters contained or recited in or endorsed on such certificate of registry when the certificate is produced.

20. Whenever any book, or other document is of such a public nature as to be admissible in evidence on its mere production from the proper custody, and no statute exists which renders its contents provable by means of a copy, any copy thereof or extract therefrom shall be admissible in evidence in any court in this province or before any person having by law or by consent of parties authority to hear, receive and examine evidence: Provided it be proved to be an examined copy or extract or if it purport to be signed and certified as a true copy or extract, by the officer to whose custody the original is entrusted; and which officer is hereby required to furnish a certified copy or extract to any person applying at a reasonable time for the same, upon payment of a reasonable sum for the same, not exceeding sixteen cents for every folio of ninety words.

21. A document that is admissible in evidence of a matter in any British court of justice without proof of the seal or stamp, or signature authenticating it, or of the judicial or official character of the person appearing to have signed it, shall be admitted in evidence to the same extent and for the same purposes, in a court of justice in this province, or before a person having by law or by consent of parties authority to hear, receive and examine evidence, without proof of the seal or stamp or signature authenticating the same, or of the judicial or official character of the person appearing to have signed it.

22.(1) Every register of a vessel kept under an act relating to the registry of British vessels may be proved in any court of justice, or before a person having, by law or by consent of parties, authority to hear, receive and examine evidence, either by the production of the original or by an examined copy of the original, or by a copy purporting to be certified by the person having charge of the original.

(2) A person who has responsibility for an original under subsection (1) shall furnish a certified copy to a person applying for it.

(3) A register and a copy of a register, and also every certificate of a registry granted under an act relating to the registry of British vessels, and purporting to be signed as required by law, shall be received in evidence in any court of justice, or before a person having, by law or by consent of parties, authority to hear, receive, and examine evidence as, in the absence of evidence to the contrary, proof of all matters contained in that register, when the register or a copy of the register is produced and of all matters contained in or endorsed on that certificate of registry when the certificate is produced.

23. (1) Where a book or other document is of such a public nature as to be admissible in evidence on its mere production from the proper custody, and no Act exists which permits its contents to be provable by means of a copy, a copy or extract from that book or other document is admissible in evidence in a court of justice, or before a person now or in the future having by law or consent of parties authority to hear, receive and examine evidence

(2) A copy referred to in subsection (1) shall be certified as a copy by the person who has custody of the original.

27. (1) In this section,

(a) "person" includes

(i) The Government of Canada and of a province of Canada and a department, commission, board or branch of that government,

(ii) a corporation, its successors and assigns, and

(iii) the heirs, executors, administrators or other legal representatives of a person; and

(b) "photographic film" includes a photographic plate, microphotographic film and photostatic negative and "photograph" has a corresponding meaning.

(2) Where a bill of exchange, promissory note, cheque, receipt, instrument, agreement, document, plan or a record or book or entry in a plan or record or book kept or held by a person

(a) is photographed in the course of an established practice of such person of photographing objects of the same or a similar class in order to keep a permanent record thereof; and

(b) is destroyed by or in the presence of 1 person or more of his or her employees or delivered to another person in the ordinary course of business or lost,

a print from the photographic film is admissible in evidence in all cases and for all purposes for the object photographed would have been admissible.

(3) Where a bill of exchange, promissory note, cheque, receipt, instrument, agreement or other executed or signed document was destroyed before the expiration of 6 years from

(a) the date when in the ordinary course of business either the object or the matter to which it related ceased to be treated as current by the person having custody or control of the object; or

(b) the date of receipt by the person having custody, or control of the object of notice in writing of any claim in respect of the object or matter prior to the destruction of the object,

whichever is the later date, the court may refuse to admit in evidence under this section a print from a photographic file of the object.

(4) Where the photographic print is tendered by the Government of Canada or of another province of Canada or a department, commission, board or branch of that government or of the Bank of Canada, subsection (3) does not apply.

(5) Proof of compliance with the conditions prescribed by this section may be given by a person having knowledge of the facts either orally or by affidavit sworn before a notary public and unless the court otherwise orders, a notarial copy of that affidavit shall be admissible in evidence instead of the original affidavit.

☞ OF PHOTOGRAPHIC PRINTS

24. (1) In this section,

(*a*) "person" includes

(i) The government of Canada or of any province and any department, commission, board or branch of any such government,

(ii) a corporation, its successors and assigns, and

(iii) the heirs, executors, administrators or other legal representatives of a person; and

(*b*) "photographic film" includes any photographic plate, microphotographic film and photostatic negative and "photograph" shall have a corresponding meaning.

(2) Where a bill of exchange, promissory note, cheque, receipt, instrument, agreement, document, plan or a record or book, or entry therein kept or held by any person

(a) is photographed in the course of an established practice of such person of photographing objects of the same or a similar class in order to keep a permanent record thereof; and

(b) is destroyed by or in the presence of the person or of one or more of his employees or delivered to another person in the ordinary course of business or lost

a print from the photographic film is admissible in evidence in all cases and for all purposes for the object photographed would have been admissible.

(3) Where a bill of exchange, promissory note, cheque, receipt, instrument, agreement or other executed or signed document was so destroyed before the expiration of six years from

(a) the date when in the ordinary course of business either the object or the matter to which it related ceased to be treated as current by the person having custody or control of the object; or

(b) the date or receipt by the person having custody or control of the object of notice in writing of any claim in respect of the object or matter prior to the destruction of the object

whichever is the later date, the court may refuse to admit in evidence under this section a print from a photographic film of the object.

(4) Where the photographic print is tendered by the Government of Canada or of any other province of Canada or any department, commission, board or branch of any such Government or of the Bank of Canada, subsection (3) shall not apply.

(5) Proof of compliance with the conditions prescribed by this section may be given by any person having knowledge of the facts either orally or by affidavit sworn before a notary public or a commissioner for oaths and unless the court otherwise orders, a notarial copy of any such affidavit is admissible in evidence in lieu of the original affidavit.

26. A copy of any entry in any book in any Department of the Government shall be received as evidence of such entry and of the matters, transactions and accounts therein recorded, if it is proved by the oath or affidavit of any officer of such department that such book was, at the time of the making of the of the entry, one of the ordinary books kept in such department, that the entry was made in the usual and ordinary course of business of such department, and that such copy is a true copy thereof.

Country: Canada — Northwest Territories

CHAPTER E-4. — AN ORDINANCE RESPECTING WITNESSES AND EVIDENCE.

☞ Evidence of Other Pubic and Corporation Documents

31. Where a book or other document is of so public a nature as to be admissible in evidence on its mere production from the proper custody, and no other Ordinance exists that renders its contents provable by means of a copy, a copy thereof or extract therefrom is admissible in evidence, if it is proved that it is a copy or extract or if it purports to be certified to be a true copy by the officer to whose custody the original has been entrusted, without any proof of the signature or of the official character of the person appearing to have signed the same and without further proof thereof.

32. Where an original document, by-law, rule, regulation or proceeding, or an entry in any register or other book of any corporation created by charger or by or under any statute or ordinance of Canada or of any province is of so public a nature as to be admissible in evidence a copy of the document, by-law, rule, regulation or proceeding or of the entry purporting to be certified under the seal of the corporation, and the hand of the presiding officer, clerk, or secretary thereof, is admissible in evidence without proof of the seal of the corporation or of the signature or of the official character of the person appearing to have signed the same, and without further proof thereof.

36. A copy of an entry, or a statement of the absence thereof in any document belonging to or deposited or kept in any office or department of the Government of Canada or of a province or in the office of any commission, board or other branch of the public service of Canada or of a province is admissible as evidence of the entry, and of the matters, transactions and accounts therein recorded, or of the absence thereof respectively, if it is proved by the oath or an affidavit of an officer of the office or department or of the commission, board or other branch of any such public service that

(*a*) the document was at the time of the making of the entry, or during the time covered by the statement, one of the ordinary documents kept in such office or department, commission, board or other branch of any such public service;

(*b*) the entry was made, or in the case of its absence would have been made, in the usual and ordinary course of business of such office or department, commission, board or branch; and

(*c*) such copy is a true copy thereof or that such statement of absence is a true statement.

37. Where a document is in the official possession, custody or power of a member of the Executive Council of a province or of the Commissioner or of the head of a department of the public service of Canada or of a province, if the deputy head or other officer of the department or an officer in the public service of Canada or the province has the record, document, plan, book or paper in his personal possession, and is called as a witness, he is entitled, acting herein by the direction and on behalf of the member of the Executive Council, the Commissioner or head of the department, to object to produce the record, document, plan, book or paper on the ground that it is privileged; and the objection may be taken by him in the same manner, and shall have the same effect, as if the member of the Executive Council, the Commissioner or head of the department were personally present and made the objection.

38. (1) In this section, "business" includes every kind of business, profession, occupation or calling, whether carried on for profit or not.

(2) A record in any business of an act, condition or event, is, insofar as relevant, admissible in evidence, if the custodian of the record or other qualified person testifies to its identity and the mode of its preparation, and to its having been made in the usual and ordinary course of business, at or near the time of the act, condition or event, and if, in the opinion of the court, the source of information, method and time of preparation were such as to justify its admission.

39. (1) In this section

(*a*) "person" includes

(i) The government of Canada or of any province and any department, commission, board or branch of any such government,

(ii) a corporation, and

(iii) the heirs, executors, administrators or other legal representatives of a person; and

(*b*) "photographic film" includes any photographic plate, microphotographic film and photostatic negative and "photograph" shall have a corresponding meaning.

(2) Where a bill of exchange, promissory note, cheque, receipt, instrument, agreement, document, plan or a record or book, or entry therein kept or held by any person,

(*a*) is photographed in the course of an established practice of such person of photographing objects of the same or a similar class in order to keep a permanent record thereof and,

(*b*) is destroyed by or in the presence of the person or of one or more of his employees or delivered to another person in the ordinary course of business or lost,

a print from the photographic film is admissible in evidence in all cases and for all purposes for the object photographed would have been admissible.

(3) Where a bill of exchange, promissory note, cheque, receipt, instrument, agreement or other executed or signed document was so destroyed before the expiration of six years from

(*a*) the date when in the ordinary course of business either the object or the matter to which it related ceased to be treated as current by the person having custody or control of the object, or

(*b*) the date or receipt by the person having custody or control of the object of notice in writing of any claim in respect of the object or matter prior to the destruction of the object,

whichever is the later date, the court may refuse to admit in evidence under this section a print from a photographic film of the object.

(4) Where the photographic print is tendered by a government or the Bank of Canada, subsection (3) does not apply.

(5) Proof of compliance with the conditions prescribed by this section may be given by any person having knowledge of the facts either orally or by affidavit sworn before a notary public or a commissioner for oaths and unless the court otherwise orders, a notarial copy of any such affidavit is admissible in evidence in lieu of the original affidavit.

☞ Bank Books

42. (1) Subject to the provisions of this section, a copy of an entry in any book or record kept in a bank shall in all actions to which the bank is not a party be *prima facie* evidence of such entry, and of the matters, transactions, and accounts therein recorded.

(2) A copy of a entry in such book or record shall not be received in evidence under this section unless it is proved that the book or record was at the time of the making of the entry one of the ordinary books or records of the bank and that the entry was made in the usual and ordinary course of business, and that the book or record is in the custody or control of the bank and that such copy is a true copy thereof, which proof may be given

by the manager or accountant of the bank and may be given orally or by affidavit.

(3) A bank or officer of a bank shall not, in any action to which the bank is not a party, be compelled to produce any book or record the contents of which can be proved under this section, or to appear as a witness to prove the matters, transaction, and the accounts therein recorded, unless by order of the Court made for special cause.

* * * * *

Country:	**Canada — Nova Scotia**

☞ CHAPTER 94. — EVIDENCE.

21 (1) In this Section,

(*a*) "person" includes

(i) The government of Canada or of any province and any department, commission, board or branch of any such government,

(ii) a corporation, and

(iii) the heirs, executors, administrators or other legal representatives of a person;

(*b*) "photographic film" includes any photographic plate, microphotographic film and photostatic negative and "photograph" shall have a corresponding meaning.

(2) Where a bill of exchange, promissory note, cheque, receipt, instrument, agreement, document, plan or a record or book, or entry therein kept or held by any person

(a) is photographed in the course of an established practice of such person of photographing objects of the same or a similar class in order to keep a permanent record thereof; and

(b) is destroyed by or in the presence of the person or of one or more of his employees or delivered to another person in the ordinary course of business or lost,

a print from the photographic film is admissible in evidence in all cases and for all purposes for the object photographed would have been admissible.

(3) Where a bill of exchange, promissory note, cheque, receipt, instrument, agreement or other executed or signed document was so destroyed before the expiration of six years from

(a) the date when in the ordinary course of business either the object or the matter to which it related ceased to be treated as current by the person having custody or control of the object; or

(b) the date or receipt by the person having custody or control of the object of notice in writing of any claim in respect of the object or matter prior to the destruction of the object;

whichever is the later date, the court may refuse to admit in evidence under this section a print from a photographic film of the object.

(4) Where the photographic print is tendered by a government or the Bank of Canada, subsection (3) does not apply.

(5) Proof of compliance with the conditions prescribed by this section may be given by any person having knowledge of the facts either orally or by affidavit sworn before a notary public or a commissioner for oaths and unless the court otherwise orders, a notarial copy of any such affidavit is admissible in evidence in lieu of the original affidavit.

22 (1) In this section,

(a) "business" includes every kind of business, profession, occupation, calling, operation of institution, and any and every kind of regular organized activity, whether carried on for profit or not;

(b) "record" includes any information that is recorded or stored by means of any device.

(2) Any writing or record made of any act, transaction, occurrence or event is admissible as evidence of such act, transaction, occurrence or event if made in the usual ordinary course of any business and if it was in the usual and ordinary course of such business to make such writing and record at the time of such act, transaction, occurrence or event or within a reasonable time thereafter.

(3) Evidence to the effect that the records of a business do not contain any record of an alleged act, condition or event shall be competent to prove the non-occurrence of the act or event or the non-existence of the condition in that business if the judge finds that it was the regular course of that business to make such records of all such acts, conditions or events at the time or within reasonable time thereafter and to retain them.

(4) The circumstances of the keeping of any records, including the lack of personal knowledge of the witness testifying as to such records, may be shown to affect the weight of any evidence tendered pursuant to this Section; but such circumstances do not affect is admissibility.

(5) Nothing in this section affects the admissibility of any evidence that would be admissible apart from this Section or makes admissible any writing or record that is privileged.

☞ SHIPS TITLES

23 (1) Every register of, or declaration made in respect to, any British ship, in pursuance of any of the Acts relating to the registry of British ships, may be proved in any court, either by the production of the original, or by a copy thereof, purporting to be certified under the hand of the person having the custody of the original.

(2) Every register, or copy of register, and every certificate of registry granted under any of the Acts relating to the registry of British vessels, and purporting to be signed as required by law, shall be received in evidence in any court as presumptive proof of all the matters contained or recited in such register, then the register, or such copy thereof as aforesaid, is produced, and of all the matters contained or recited in, or endorsed upon, such certificate of registry when such certificate is produced.

☞ DOCUMENT ADMISSIBLE IN ENGLAND

24 Every document which is admissible in evidence of any particular in any court of justice in England, or Ireland, without proof of the seal, or stamp, or signature, authenticating the same, or of the judicial or official character of the person appearing to have signed the same, shall be received in evidence to the same extent, and for the same purposes, in any court without proof of the seal, or stamp, or signature authenticating the same, or of the judicial or official character of the person appearing to have signed the same.

☞ DEEDS, WILLS AND OTHER DOCUMENTS

27 A copy of any deed, or any document from the books of registry, certified under the hand of the registrar of deeds, or proved to be a true copy taken therefrom, shall be taken as evidence in the place of the original, if it is made to appear to the court, by the affidavit of the party, his agent, or solicitor, that such original is not in the possession or under the control of the party, and that he has been unable to procure the same.

27A (1) All records and copies of records that are required by law to be kept or held by a Registrar of Land Titles or Registrar General of Land Titles, and accurate reproductions of such records or copies, shall in any court be admissible in evidence as proof of the contents therein if certified as correct by the

Registrar or Registrar General.

(2) In this Section "records" means any information set down by handwriting, drawing, typewriting, printing, photostating, photographing, magnetic impulse, mechanical or electronic recording, or other manner of setting down information for the purpose of data compilation and storage and includes a printout from a computer or similar device in a form which may be understood whether the printout is the result of a process of data retrieval or a replica of data stored.

30 Every bill of sale or other document, filed in any registry of deeds, may be proved in any court by the production of a copy thereof, certified under the hand of the registrar of deeds.

31 (1) The registration of any deed or document registered in the registry of deeds may be proved in any court by the production of the certificate of registry, signed by the registrar, endorsed on such deed or document, or upon any such certified copy of such deed or document.

(2) No writ of subpoena, no summons and no other process shall be issued or sued out requiring a registrar of deeds to bring or produce before any court, judge or officer any books of registry or any other records pertaining to the office of registrar of deeds except upon an order of the court, judge or officer having jurisdiction in the cause or matter in respect of which the books of registry or records are required to be brought or produced.

33 (1) A copy of a notarial act, or instrument in writing, made in Quebec before a notary, filed, enrolled, or registered by such notary, and certified by a notary or prothonotary to be a true copy of the original thereby certified to be in his possession, as such notary or prothonotary shall be received in evidence in any court in the place of the original and shall have the same force and effect as the original would have it produced and proved.

36 In any section or other proceeding where a party intends to prove the sending and contents of a telegraphic message, he may give notice to the opposite party, at least ten days before the trial or other proceeding, that he intends, at such trial or proceeding, to give in evidence as proof of the contents of the telegraphic message alleged to have been sent, the message received by him from the telegraph office, and such message, so received, shall be received as evidence in any court, provided the party so receiving the same proves that it was received at the telegraph office of the place to which it purports to be addressed. The judge may dispose with such notice if he is satisfied that no injustice has been done by the want thereof.

Country: Canada — Ontario

✍ CHAPTER 4. — AN ACT TO REVISE THE BUSINESS CORPORATIONS ACT.

139. (1) Where this Act requires a record to be kept by a corporation, it may be kept in a bound or looseleaf book or may be entered or recorded by any system of mechanical or electronic data processing or any other information storage device.

(2) The corporation shall,

(*a*) take adequate precautions, appropriate to the means used, for guarding against the risk of falsifying the information recorded; and

(*b*) provide means for making the information available in an accurate and intelligible form within a reasonable time to any person lawfully entitled to examine the records.

(3) The bound or looseleaf book or, where the record is not kept in a bound or looseleaf book, the information in the form in which it is made available under clause (2)(*b*) is admissible in evidence as *prima facie* proof, before and after dissolution of the corporation, of all facts stated therein.

(4) No person shall remove, withhold or destroy information required by this Act or the regulations to be recorded, or,

(*a*) record or assist in recording any information in a record; or

(*b*) make information purporting to be accurate available in a form referred to in clause (2)(*b*), knowing it to be untrue.

140. (1) A corporation shall prepare and maintain, at its registered office or at such other place in Ontario designated by the directors,

(*a*) the articles and the by-laws and all amendments thereto, and a copy of any unanimous shareholder agreement known to the directors;

(*b*) minutes of meetings and resolutions of shareholders;

(*c*) a register of directors in which are set out the names and residence addresses, while directors, including the street and number, if any, of all persons who are or have been directors of the corporation with the several dates on which each became or cased to be a director;

(*d*) a securities register complying with section 141.

(2) In addition to the records described in subsection (1), a corporation shall prepare and maintain,

(*a*) adequate accounting records; and

(*b*) records containing minutes of meetings and resolutions of the directors and any committee thereof, but, provided the retention requirements of any taxing authority of Ontario, the government of Canada or any other jurisdiction to which the corporation is subject have been satisfied, the accounting records mentioned in clause (*a*) need only be retained by the corporation for six years from the end of the last fiscal period to which they relate.

(3) For the purposes of clause (1)(*b*) and subsection (2), where a body corporate is continued under this Act, "records" includes similar records required by law to be maintained by the body corporate before it was so continued.

CHAPTER 33. — AN ACT TO REVISE THE LOAN AND TRUST CORPORATION ACT.

✍ Part 8. — Books, Records and Returns.

125. (1) Where this Act requires a record to be kept by a corporation, it may be kept in a bound or looseleaf book or may be entered or recorded by any photographic system, any system of mechanical or electronic data processing or any other information storage system and it shall be kept for such period as may be prescribed.

(2) A corporation shall,

(a) take adequate precautions, appropriate to the means used, for guarding against the risk of falsifying the information recorded in its records; and

(b) provide means for making the information recorded in its records available in an accurate and intelligible form within a reasonable time to any person lawfully entitled to examine the records.

(3) The bound or looseleaf book referred to in subsection (1) or, where the record is not kept in a book, the information in the form in which it is made available under clause (2)(b) is admissible in evidence as *prima facie* proof, before and after dissolution of the corporation, of all facts stated therein.

(4) No person shall remove, withhold or destroy information required by this Act or the regulation to be recorded, or knowing any information to be untrue, shall record or assist in recording it is a record.

☞ CHAPTER 39. — EVIDENCE ACT.

32. (1) Where a book or other document is so public a nature as to be admissible in evidence on its mere production from the proper custody, a copy thereof or extract therefrom is admissible in evidence if it is proved that it is an examined copy or extract, or that it purports to be signed and certified as a true copy or extract by the officer to whose custody the original was entrusted.

33. (1) In this section, "bank" means a bank to which the *Bank Act* (Canada) applies or the Province of Ontario Savings Office, and includes a branch, agency or office of any of them.

(2) Subject to this section, a copy of an entry in a book or record kept in a bank is in any action to which the bank is not a party evidence of such entry and of the matters, transactions and accounts therein recorded.

(3) A copy of an entry in such book or record shall not be received in evidence under this section unless it is first proved that the book or record was at the time of making the entry one of the ordinary books or records of the bank, that the entry was made in the usual and ordinary course of business, that the book or record is in the custody or control of the bank, or its successor, and that such copy is a true copy thereof, and such proof may be given by the manager or accountant, or a former manager of the bank or its successor, and may be given orally or by affidavit.

(4) A bank or officer of a bank is not, in an action to which the bank is not a party, compellable to produce any book or record the contents of which can be proved under this section, or to appear as a witness to prove the matters, transactions and accounts therein recorded, unless by order of the court or a judge made for special cause.

* * * * *

34. — (1) In this section,

(a) "person" includes,

(i) the Government of Canada and of a province of Canada, and a department, commission, board or branch of any such government,

(ii) a corporation, its successors and assigns, and

(iii) the heirs, executors, administrators or other legal representatives of a person;

(b) "photographic film" includes any photographic plate, microphotographic film and photostatic negative, and "photograph" has a corresponding meaning.

(2) Where a bill of exchange, promissory note, cheque, receipt, instrument, agreement, document, plan or a record or book or entry therein kept or held by a person,

(a) is photographed in the course of an established practice of such person of photographing objects of the same or a similar class in order to keep a permanent record thereof; and

(b) is destroyed or in the presence of such person or of one or more of the person's employees or delivered to another person in the ordinary course of business or lost,

a print from the photographic film is admissible in evidence in all cases and for all purposes for which the object photographed would have been admissible.

(3) Where a bill of exchange, promissory note, cheque, receipt, instrument, agreement or other executed or signed document was so destroyed before the expiration of six years from,

(a) the date when in the ordinary course of business either the object or the matter to which it related ceased to be treated as current by the person having custody or control of the object; or

(b) the date of receipt by the person having custody or control of the object of notice in writing of a claim in respect of the object or matter prior to the destruction of the object,

whichever is the later date, the court may refuse to admit in evidence under this section a print from a photographic film of the object.

(4) Where the photographic print is tendered by a government or the Bank of Canada, or a municipality as defined in subsection 31(1), subsection (3) does not apply.

(5) Proof of compliance with the conditions prescribed by this section may be given by any person having knowledge of the facts either orally or by affidavit sworn or affirmed before a notary public, and, unless the court otherwise orders, a notarial copy of any such affidavit is admissible in evidence in lieu of the original affidavit.

35. — (1) In this section,

(a) "business" includes every kind of business, profession, occupation, calling, operation or activity, whether carried on for profit or otherwise;

(b) "record" includes any information that is recorded or stored by means of any device.

(2) Any writing or record made of any act, transaction, occurrence or event is admissible as evidence of such act, transaction, occurrence or event if made in the usual and ordinary course of any business and if it was in the usual and ordinary course of such business to make such writing or record at the time of such act, transaction, occurrence or event or within a reasonable time thereafter.

(3) Subsection (2) does not apply unless the party tendering the writing or record has given at least seven days notice of the party's intention to all other parties in the action, and any party to the action is entitled to obtain from the person who has possession thereof production for inspection of the writing or record within five days after giving notice to produce the same.

(4) The circumstances of the making of such a writing or record, including lack of personal knowledge by the maker, may be shown to affect its weight, but such circumstances do not affect its admissibility.

(5) Nothing in this section affects the admissibility of any evidence that would be admissible apart from this section or makes admissible any writing or record that is privileged.

39. — (1) A copy of a notarial act or instrument in writing made in Quebec before a notary and filed, enrolled or prothonotary to be a true copy of the original thereby certified to be in his possession as such notary or prothonotary, is receivable in evidence in the place and stead of the original, and has the same force and effect as the original would have if produced and proved.

* * * * *

55. (1) A party intending to prove the original of a telegram, letter, shipping bill, bill of lading, delivery order, receipt, account or other written instrument used in business or other transactions, may give notice to the opposite party, ten days at least before the trial or other proceeding in which the proof is intended to be adduced, that the party intends to give in evidence as proof of the contents in writing purporting to be a copy of the documents, and in the notice shall name some convenient time and place for the inspection thereof.

(2) Such copy may then be inspected by the opposite party, and is without further proof sufficient evidence of the contents of the original document, and shall be accepted and taken in lieu of the original, unless the party receiving the notice within four days after the time mentioned for such inspection gives notice that he intends to dispute the correctness or genuineness of the copy at the trial or proceeding, and to require proof of the original, and the costs attending any production or proof of the original document are in the discretion of the court.

✪ CHAPTER 445. — REGISTRY ACT.

15. (1) Upon receipt of a request in writing and the prescribed fees, a land registrar,

(a) shall produce for inspection in his or her office during office hours any instrument registered in the land registrar's office or any book of the office relating to any such instrument; and

(b) shall supply a copy of the whole or a part of any instrument registered in his or her office.

(2) Where a land registrar is unable to produce an instrument or book that is copied or microfilmed, he or she shall produce the microfilm copy for inspection.

16. (1) Where a registered instrument, a document deposited under Part II a written record of a land registry office is recorded electronically or on a magnetic medium, any writing that,

(a) represents the instrument, document, or record;

(b) is generated by or produced from the electronic record or magnetic medium; and

(c) is in a readily understandable form,

is admissible in evidence to the same extent as the original instrument, document or record.

(2) Where a record of a land registry office is recorded electronically or on a magnetic medium and there is no original written record that corresponds to the record, any writing that,

(a) represents the record;

(b) is generated by or produced from the electronic record or magnetic medium; and

(c) is in a readily understandable form,

is admissible in evidence to the same extent as the record would be if it were an original written record.

19. (1) It is the duty of every land registrar to preserve the abstract index books and other records of his or her office in good repair.

(2) A land registrar may, when he or she considers it necessary, and shall, when so directed by the Director, cause,

(a) any book that is becoming obliterated or unfit for further use to be copied or reproduced and, where portions of the entries in the book are missing, obliterated or cannot be deciphered, the missing details to be obtained, so far as possible, by examination of the instruments relating thereto and incorporated in the copy;

(b) plans and maps to be copied, repaired, restored, mounted, bound or otherwise preserved; and

(c) any book to be repaired,

in a manner approved by the Director.

(3) Where a book is copied or reproduced under clause (2)(a), the land registrar shall certify the correctness of the copy.

(4) The certificate of a land registrar under subsection (3) is, to be extent specified in the certificate, proof, in the absence of evidence to the contrary, that the copy is a true copy of the original book, and such certified copy shall be accepted and received as the original, but the land registrar shall nevertheless carefully preserve the original book and produce it upon demand.

(5) The Director may order as many counterparts or copies of any abstract index book to be made as he or she considers necessary for the public convenience, and may order new abstract indexes to be made when the indexes in use have become complicated or otherwise inconvenient.

(6) Where an abstract index is copied, every instrument, except an instrument to which section 62 applies, shall be copied, and the land registrar shall carefully preserve the original abstract index and produce it upon demand.

(7) Where a plan is copied under subsection (2), and the copy is certified by an examiner of surveys as a true copy of the plan, or a part thereof, as the case may be, the copy so made and certified has all the force and effect of the plan or of that part of the plan of which it is a copy.

Country: Canada — Prince Edward Island

☞ CHAPTER E-11. — EVIDENCE.
✪

26. Every register of or declaration made in respect of any British ship in pursuance of any of the Acts relating to the registry of British ships may be proved in any court in this province, or before any person having by law or by consent of parties authority to hear, receive and examine evidence either by production of the original or by an examined copy thereof purporting to be certified under the hand of the person having the charge of the original, and every register or copy of register, and also every certificate of registry granted under any of the Acts relating to the registry of British vessels, and purporting to be signed as required by law shall be received in evidence in any court in this province, or before any person having by law or by consent of parties authority to hear, receive and examine evidence, as *prima facie* proof of all the matters contained or recited on the register, when the register or a copy thereof as aforesaid, is produced, and of all the matters contained or recited in or endorsed on the certificate of registry when the said certificate is produced.

27. Whenever any book or other document is of such a public nature as to be admissible in evidence on its mere production from the proper custody, and no statute exists which renders its contents provable by means of a copy, any copy thereof or extract therefrom shall be admissible in evidence in any court in this province or before any person having by law or by consent of parties authority to hear, receive and examine evidence, if it is proven to be an examined copy or extract or if it purports to be signed and certified as a true copy or extract by the officer to whose custody the original is entrusted without any proof of the signature or of the official character of the person appearing to have signed the same and without further proof thereof, and the officer is hereby required to furnish such certified copy or extract to any person applying at a reasonable time for the same, upon payment of a reasonable sum for the same, not exceeding sixteen cents for every folio of ninety words.

29. Where documents are in the official possession, custody or power of a member of the Executive Council, or the head of a department of the civil service of this province, if the deputy head or other officer of the department has the documents in his personal possession and is called as a witness he shall be entitled, acting herein by the direction and on behalf of the member of the Executive Council or head of the department, to object to produce the document on the ground that they are privileged, and such objection must be taken by him in the same manner, and shall have the same effect as if such member of the Executive Council or head of the department were personally present and made the objection.

30. (1) In this section

(a) "bank" includes any branch, agency or office of the bank;

(b) "court" means the court, judge, arbitrator or person before whom a legal proceeding is held or taken;

(c) "legal proceeding" means any civil proceeding or inquiry in which evidence is or may be given and includes and arbitration.

(2) Subject to this section, a copy of an entry in any book or record kept in any bank, shall, in all legal proceedings, be received as *prima facie* evidence of such entry and of the matters, transactions and accounts therein recorded.

(3) A copy of an entry in a book or record referred to in subsection (1) shall not be received in evidence under this section

unless it is first proved that the book or record was at the time of the making of the entry, one of the ordinary books or records of the bank, and that the entry was made in the usual and ordinary course of business, and that the book or record is in the custody or control of the bank, and that such copy is a true copy thereof; the proof may be given by the manager or accountant of the bank and may be given orally or by affidavit.

31. (1) In this section

(a) "person" includes

(i) The government of Canada or of any province and any department, commission, board or branch of any such government,

(ii) a corporation, and

(iii) the heirs, executors, administrators or other legal representatives of a person; and

(b) "photographic film" includes any photographic plate, microphotographic film and photostatic negative and "photograph" shall have a corresponding meaning.

(2) Where a bill of exchange, promissory note, cheque, receipt, instrument, agreement, document, plan or a record or book, or entry therein kept or held by any person,

(a) is photographed in the course of an established practice of such person of photographing objects of the same or a similar class in order to keep a permanent record thereof; and

(b) is destroyed by or in the presence of the person or of one or more of his employees or delivered to another person in the ordinary course of business or lost;

a print from the photographic film is admissible in evidence in all cases and for all purposes for the object photographed would have been admissible.

(3) Where a bill of exchange, promissory note, cheque, receipt, instrument, agreement or other executed or signed document was so destroyed before the expiration of six years from

(a) the date when in the ordinary course of business either the object or the matter to which it related ceased to be treated as current by the person having custody or control of the object; or

(b) the date or receipt by the person having custody or control of the object of notice in writing of any claim in respect of the object or matter prior to the destruction of the object

whichever is the later date, the court may refuse to admit in evidence under this section a print from a photographic film of the object.

(4) Where the photographic print is tendered by a government or the Bank of Canada, subsection (3) does not apply.

(5) Proof of compliance with the conditions prescribed by this section may be given by any person having knowledge of the facts either orally or by affidavit sworn before a notary public or a commissioner for oaths and unless the court otherwise orders, a notarial copy of any such affidavit is admissible in evidence in lieu of the original affidavit.

32. (1) In this section,

(a) "business" includes every kind of business, profession, occupation, calling, operation of institution, and any and every kind of regular organized activity, whether carried on for profit or otherwise, including any activity carried on by any government, board, commission or agency of any government;

(b) "record" includes any information that is recorded or stored by means of any device.

(2) Any writing or record made of any act, transaction, occurrence or event is admissible as evidence of that act, transaction, occurrence or event if made in the usual and ordinary course of any business.

(3) Subsection (2) does not apply unless the party tendering the writing or record has given at least seven days notice of his intention to all other parties in the proceeding, and any party to the proceeding is entitled to obtain from the person who has possession thereof production for inspection of the writing or record within five days after giving notice to produce the same.

(4) The circumstances of the making of such a writing or record, including lack of personal knowledge by the maker, may be shown to affect the weight, but do not affect is admissibility.

(5) Nothing in this section affects the admissibility of any evidence that would be admissible apart from this section or makes admissible any writing or record that is privileged.

Country: **Canada — Quebec**

EVIDENCE ACT OF 1986.

☞ **CHAPTER 57.**

30. (1) Where a book or other document is of so public a nature as to be admissible in evidence on its mere production from the proper custody, and no other Ordinance exists that renders its contents provable by means of a copy, a copy thereof or extract therefrom is admissible in evidence, if it is proved that it is a copy or extract or if it purports to be certified to be a true copy by the officer to whose custody the original has been entrusted, without any proof of the signature or of the official character of the person appearing to have signed the same and without further proof thereof.

31. (1) Where an original document, by-law, rule, regulation or proceeding, or an entry in any register or other book of any corporation created by charter or by or under any statute or ordinance of Canada or of any province is of so public a nature as to be admissible in evidence a copy of the document, by-law, rule, regulation or proceeding or of the entry purporting to be certified under the seal of the corporation, and the hand of the presiding officer, clerk or secretary thereof, is admissible in evidence without proof of the seal of the corporation or of the signature or of the official character of the person appearing to have signed the same, and without further proof thereof.

35. (1) A copy of an entry, or a statement of the absence thereof in any document belonging to or deposited or kept in any office or department of the Government of Canada or of a province or in the office of any commission, board or other branch of the public service of Canada or of a province is admissible as evidence of the entry, and of the matters, transactions and accounts therein recorded, or of the absence thereof respectively, if it is proved by the oath or an affidavit of an officer of the office or department or of the commission, board or other branch of any such public service that

(*a*) the document was at the time of the making of the entry, or during the time covered by the statement, one of the ordinary documents kept in such office or department, commission, board or other branch of any such public service;

(*b*) the entry was made, or in the case of its absence would have been made, in the usual and ordinary course of business of such office or department, commission, board or branch; and

(*c*) such copy is a true copy thereof or that such statement of absence is a true statement.

37. (1) In this section, "business" includes every kind of business, profession, occupation or calling, whether carried on for profit or not.

(2) A record in any business of an act, condition or event, is, insofar as relevant, admissible in evidence, if the custodian of the record or other qualified person testifies to its identity and the mode of its preparation, and to its having been made in the usual and ordinary course of business, at or near the time of the act, condition or event, and if, in the opinion of the court, the

source of information, method and time of preparation were such as to justify its admission.

"books" includes any account, deed, writing or document and any other record of information however compiled, recorded or stored whether in written or printed form or microfilm by electronic process or otherwise;

☞ PART 2. — ADMINISTRATION OF ACT.

Section 8C. Copies or extracts of books to be admitted in evidence.

(1) Subject to this section, in any legal proceedings, whether proceedings under this Act or otherwise, a copy of or extract from a book relating to affairs of a corporation is admissible in evidence as if it were the original book or the relevant part of the original book.

(2) A copy of or extract from a book is not admissible in evidence under subsection (1) unless it is proved that the copy or extract is a true copy of the book or of the relevant part of the book.

(3) For the purposes of subsection (2), evidence that a copy of or extract from a book is a true copy of the book or part of the book may be given by a person who has compared the copy or extract with the book or the relevant part of the book and may b given either orally or by an affidavit sworn, or by a declaration made, before a person authorized to take affidavits, before a person authorized to take affidavits or statutory declarations.

Country: Canada — Saskatchewan

BUSINESS CORPORATIONS

PART 1. — PROVINCIAL BUSINESS CORPORATIONS.

✍ Division 4. — Registered Office and Records.

20. (1) A corporation shall prepare and maintain, at its registered office or at any other place in Saskatchewan designated by the directors, records containing:

(*a*) the articles and the bylaws, and all amendments thereto, and a copy of any unanimous shareholder agreements;

(*b*) minutes of meetings and resolutions of shareholders;

(*c*) copies of all notices required by section 101 to 108; and

(*d*) a securities register complying with section 46.

(2) In addition to the records described in subsection (1), a corporation shall

(a) prepare adequate accounting records and maintain them for at least six years after

(b) prepare and maintain records containing minutes of meetings and resolutions of the director and any committee of directors.

* * * * *

22. (1) All registers and other records required by this Act to be prepared and maintained may be in a bound or looseleaf form or in a photographic film form, or may be entered or recorded by any system of mechanical or electronic data processing or any other information storage device that is capable of producing any required information in intelligible written form within a reasonable time.

* * * * *

✪ CHAPTER A-26. — ARCHIVES.

7. All public documents shall be preserved by the department to whose business they belong until their transfer to The Saskatchewan Archives Board pursuant to this Act or their destruction if ordered by the Lieutenant Governor in Council pursuant to this Act or until their destruction is approved by the Legislative Assembly pursuant to this Act.

* * * * *

(3) No public document shall be destroyed before the expiration of ten years from the date at which it was or is created unless a recommendation by the Public Documents Committee has been approved by the Legislative Assembly upon the recommendation of the Select Standing Committee of the Legislative Assembly on Library.

* * * * *

16. A copy or photographic reproduction of any document in the archives, certified under the hand of the Provincial Archivist to be a true copy, shall be *prima facie* evidence of the authenticity and correctness of the copy or reproduction, without proof of the appointment or signature of the archivist.

☞ CHAPTER S-16. — WITNESSES AND EVIDENCE.

28. (1) In this section:

(*a*) bank" means a bank to which the *Bank Act* (Canada) applies or a credit union or caisse populaire incorporated under *The Credit Union Act* or any former *Credit Union Act*, and includes a branch, agency or office of a bank, credit union or caisse populaire;

(*b*) "court" means the court, judge, arbitrator, person or persons before whom a legal proceeding is held or taken;

(*c*) "legal proceeding" means any civil proceeding or inquiry in which evidence is or may be given, and includes an arbitration.

(2) Subject to the provisions of this section, a copy of an entry in a book or record kept in a bank shall in all legal proceedings be received as *prima facie* evidence of the entry, and of the matters, transactions and accounts therein recorded.

(3) A copy of an entry in such book or record shall not be received in evidence under this section unless it is first proved that the book or record was, at the time of the making of the entry, one of the ordinary books or records of the bank, that the entry was made in the usual and ordinary course of business, that the book or record is in the custody or control of the bank or its successor, and that the copy is a true copy. Such proof may be given by the manager or accountant of the bank and may be given orally or by affidavit sworn before any commissioner for oaths and to take and receive affidavits, declarations and affirmations within Saskatchewan.

(4) A bank or officer of a bank shall not, in a legal proceeding to which the bank is not a party, be compelled to produce a book or record the contents of which can be proved under this section, or to appear as a witness to prove the matters, transactions and accounts therein recorded, unless by order of the court of a judge made for special cause.

* * * * *

✍ TELEGRAPH MESSAGES AND MERCANTILE DOCUMENTS

30. (1) In an action, suit or proceeding in the case of telegraphic messages, letters, shipping bills, bills of lading, delivery orders, receipts, accounts, and other written instruments used in business and other transactions where, according to the existing rules of law exclusive of the provisions contained in this Act, it would be necessary to produce and prove the original document, the party intending to establish in proof the contents of the original document may give notice to the opposite party, ten days at least before the trial or other proceeding in which the said proof is intended to be adduced, that he intends at the said trial or other proceeding to give in evidence as proof of such contents an instrument purporting to be a copy of such document.

(2) Such copy may then be inspected by the opposite party at some convenient time and place; and in every such case the copy shall, without further proof, be sufficient evidence of the contents of the original document and be accepted and taken in lieu of the original unless the party receiving the notice, within four days after the time mentioned therein for inspection, gives notice that he intends to dispute the correctness or genuineness of the copy at the trial or proceeding and to require proof of the original; and the court or judge before whom such question is raised may direct by which of the parties the costs that may thereupon attend any production of proof of the original document according to the rules of evidence heretofore existing shall be paid.

31. (1) In this section:

(*a*) "business" includes every kind of business, profession, occupation, calling, operation, activity or government activity, whether carried on for profit or otherwise;

(*b*) "court" means the court, judge, arbitrator or person before whom a legal proceeding is held or taken;

(*c*) "legal proceeding" means any civil proceeding or inquiry, including an arbitration, in which evidence is or may be given;

(*d*) "record" includes any information that is recorded or stored by means of any device, including a computer.

(2) Any writing or record made of any act, transaction, occurrence, or event is admissible in any legal proceeding as evidence of the act, transaction, occurrence or event if:

(*a*) it is made in the usual and ordinary course of any business; and

(*b*) it was in the usual and ordinary course of such business to make the writing or record at the time of the act, transaction, occurrence or event or within a reasonable time thereafter.

(3) The circumstances of the making of a writing or record mentioned in subsection (2), including lack of personal knowledge by the maker, may be shown to affect its weight, but such circumstances do not affect its admissibility.

(4) Nothing in this section affects the admissibility of any evidence that would be admissible apart from this section or makes admissible any writing or record that is privileged.

Country: Canada — Yukon

STATUTES OF THE YUKON TERRITORY 1983

(1) This Act may be cited as the *Business Corporations Act*

✍ PART 1. — INTERPRETATION AND APPLICATION.

✪

22. (1) All registers and other records required by this Act to be prepared and maintained may be in a bound or looseleaf form or in a photographic film form, or may be entered or recorded by any system of mechanical or electronic data processing or any other information storage device that is capable of reproducing any required in formation in legible written form within a reasonable time.

38. (1) In this section

"person" includes

(a) The government of Canada or of any province and any department, commission, board or branch of any such government,

(b) a corporation, and

(c) the heirs, executors, administrators or other legal representatives of a person; and

"photographic film" includes any photographic plate, microphotographic film and photostatic negative and "photograph" shall have a corresponding meaning.

(2) Where a bill of exchange, promissory note, cheque, receipt, instrument, agreement, document, plan or a record or book, or entry therein kept or held by any person,

(a) is photographed in the course of an established practice of such person of photographing objects of the same or a similar class in order to keep a permanent record thereof; and

(b) is destroyed by or in the presence of the person or of one or more of his employees or delivered to another person in the ordinary course of business or lost;

a print from the photographic film is admissible in evidence in all cases and for all purposes for the object photographed would have been admissible.

(3) Where a bill of exchange, promissory note, cheque, receipt, instrument, agreement or other executed or signed document was so destroyed before the expiration of six years from

(a) the date when in the ordinary course of business either the object or the matter to which it related ceased to be treated as current by the person having custody or control of the object; or

(b) the date or receipt by the person having custody or control of the object of notice in writing of any claim in respect of the object or matter prior to the destruction of the object; whichever is the later date, the court may refuse to admit in evidence under this section a print from a photographic film of the object.

(4) Where the photographic print is tendered by a government or the Bank of Canada, subsection (3) does not apply.

(5) Proof of compliance with the conditions prescribed by this section may be given by any person having knowledge of the facts either orally or by affidavit sworn before a notary public or a commissioner for oaths and unless the court otherwise orders, a notarial copy of any such affidavit is admissible in evidence in lieu of the original affidavit.

CHAPTER E-6. — EVIDENCE ORDINANCE.

☞ Evidence of Other Public and Corporation Documents

✪

31. (1) Where a book or other document is of so public a nature as to be admissible in evidence on its mere production from the proper custody, and no other Ordinance exists that renders its contents provable by means of a copy, a copy thereof or extract therefrom is admissible in evidence, if it is proved that it is a copy or extract or if it purports to be certified to be a true copy by the officer to whose custody the original has been entrusted, without any proof of the signature or of the official character of the person appearing to have signed the same and without further proof thereof.

32. (1) Where an original document, by-law, rule, regulation or proceeding, or an entry in any register or other book of any corporation created by charger or by or under any statute or ordinance of Canada or of any province is of so public a nature as to be admissible in evidence a copy of the document, by-law, rule, regulation or proceeding or of the entry purporting to be certified under the seal of the corporation, and the hand of the presiding officer, clerk or secretary thereof, is admissible in evidence without proof of the seal of the corporation or of the signature or of the official character of the person appearing to have signed the same, and without further proof thereof.

36. (1) A copy of an entry, or a statement of the absence thereof in any document belonging to or deposited or kept in any office or department of the Government of Canada or of a province or in the office of any commission, board or other branch of the public service of Canada or of a province is admissible as evidence of the entry, and of the matters, transactions and accounts therein recorded, or of the absence thereof respectively, if it is proved by the oath or an affidavit of an officer of the office or department or of the commission, board or other branch of any such public service that

(*a*) the document was at the time of the making of the entry, or during the time covered by the statement, one of the ordinary documents kept in such office or department, commission, board or other branch of any such public service;

(*b*) the entry was made, or in the case of its absence would have been made, in the usual and ordinary course of business of such office or department, commission, board or branch; and

(*c*) such copy is a true copy thereof or that such statement of absence is a true statement.

38. (1) In this section, "business" includes every kind of business, profession, occupation or calling, whether carried on for profit or not.

(2) A record in any business of an act, condition or event, is, insofar as relevant, admissible in evidence, if the custodian of the record or other qualified person testifies to its identity and the mode of its preparation, and to its having been made in the usual and ordinary course of business, at or near the time of the act, condition or event, and if, in the opinion of the court, the source of information, method and time of preparation were such as to justify its admission.

39. (1) In this section

(*a*) "person" includes

(i) The government of Canada or of any province and any department, commission, board or branch of any such government,

(ii) a corporation, and

(iii) the heirs, executors, administrators or other legal representatives of a person; and

(*b*) "photographic film" includes any photographic plate, microphotographic film and photostatic negative and "photograph" shall have a corresponding meaning.

(2) Where a bill of exchange, promissory note, cheque, receipt, instrument, agreement, document, plan or a record or book, or entry therein kept or held by any person,

(*a*) is photographed in the course of an established practice of such person of photographing objects of the same or a similar class in order to keep a permanent record thereof; and

(*b*) is destroyed by or in the presence of the person or of one or more of his employees or delivered to another person in the ordinary course of business or lost;

a print from the photographic film is admissible in evidence in all cases and for all purposes for the object photographed would have been admissible.

(3) Where a bill of exchange, promissory note, cheque, receipt, instrument, agreement or other executed or signed document was so destroyed before the expiration of six years from

(*a*) the date when in the ordinary course of business either the object or the matter to which it related ceased to be treated as current by the person having custody or control of the object; or

(*b*) the date or receipt by the person having custody or control of the object of notice in writing of any claim in respect of the object or matter prior to the destruction of the object; whichever is the later date, the court may refuse to admit in evidence under this section a print from a photographic film of the object.

(4) Where the photographic print is tendered by a government or the Bank of Canada, subsection (3) does not apply.

(5) Proof of compliance with the conditions prescribed by this section may be given by any person having knowledge of the facts either orally or by affidavit sworn before a notary public or a commissioner for oaths and unless the court otherwise orders, a notarial copy of any such affidavit is admissible in evidence in lieu of the original affidavit.

Country: China

LAWS AND REGULATIONS OF THE PEOPLES REPUBLIC OF CHINA

THE ACCOUNTING REGULATIONS OF THE PEOPLE'S REPUBLIC OF CHINA FOR JOINT VENTURES USING CHINESE AND FOREIGN INVESTMENT

Promulgated on March 4, 1985 by the Ministry of Finance of the People's Republic of China

✍ CHAPTER 13. — ACCOUNTING DOCUMENTS AND ACCOUNTING BOOKS.

Article 67. A joint venture must acquire or fill out original documents for every transaction occurring. All the original documents must carry faithful contents, evidence of all the required procedures and accurate figures. Original documents from an outside unit must be signed and sealed by the unit. The original documents shall be verified and signed by the head of the department and the person responsible for handling the transaction.

A joint venture shall check and inspect the original documents seriously. Any falsified or altered original document, or any fraudulent application or request or other similar event must be rejected and reported to the relevant party. The original documents with incomplete contents, insufficient evidence of required procedures or inaccurate figures shall be returned, amended or refilled. Only the original documents examined and proved correct can be taken as the basis for preparing accounting vouchers.

Article 68. The accounting vouchers of a joint venture include receiving vouchers, disbursement vouchers, and journal vouchers. All vouchers must be filled out with the required contents and can be taken as the basis in bookkeeping only after being signed by the preparer, the designated verifier and chief officer of the financial and accounting department. A receiving or disbursement voucher shall also be signed by the cashier.

Each kind of accounting voucher shall be filed according to its sequential number and bound into books monthly together with the original documents attached thereto, and shall be kept in safety without any loss or damage. For important documents concerning claims and debts that need separate safekeeping, cross reference shall be made on the original documents of the transaction and on the related vouchers.

Article 69. A joint venture shall number sequentially all documents issued to the outside, and retain its duplicate copy (or copies) or the stub. An original of such documents with clerical errors or withdrawn for cancellation shall be kept together with the duplicate or stub of the same sequential number. If the original copy is missing or unable to be recovered, the reason shall be noted on the duplicate or stub.

Article 70. All the blank forms of important documents, such as cheque books, cash receipts, delivery orders, etc. shall be registered in a special registration book by the financial and accounting department. Requisition of those blank forms shall be approved by the chief officer or a designated person of the financial and accounting department, and the person making the requisition shall sign the registration book for receiving the forms.

Article 71. A joint venture shall set up three kinds of primary accounting books, namely, journals, general ledgers and subsidiary ledgers, as well as appropriate supplementary memorandum books.

All the books shall be kept with complete records, accurate figures, clear descriptions and prompt registration, on the basis of the examined original documents and vouchers or summary of vouchers that are proved correct.

No record in the books of a joint venture shall be destroyed, amended, altered or eliminated by correction fluid. When errors are made, they shall be amended by crossing off the error or by preparing additional vouchers according to the nature and circumstances of the error. When the crossing method of amendment is used, the person making the correction shall sign on the place of amendment.

Article 72. A joint venture keeping its accounts by electronic computer shall maintain properly its accounting records stored in or printed out by the computer and shall regard such records as accounting books. The tapes, discs, etc. shall be kept and no deletion shall be allowed unless the records in them are printed out in visible form.

Article 76. The accounting files of a joint venture, including accounting documents, accounting books, accounting statements, etc. must be appropriately kept with the territory of the People's Republic of China. No loss or spoilage shall be allowed.

Article 77. The annual accounting statements and all other important accounting files relevant to the rights and interests of all the participants of a joint venture, such as joint venture agreements, joint venture contracts, articles of association of the joint venture, resolutions of the board of directors, investment appraisal lists, certificates on capital validation, auditing reports of the Certified Public Accountants, long term economic contracts, etc. must be kept permanently. General accounting documents, accounting books and monthly and quarterly accounting statements shall be kept for at least 15 years.

Article 78. If the accounting files need to be destroyed after the expiration of the retention period, an itemized list of the files to be destroyed shall be prepared and reported to the board of directors, business regulatory department and tax authority for approval. No files can be destroyed unless such a list is approved. The list of destroyed accounting files must be kept permanently.

Country: Colombia

TITLE 4. — COMMERCIAL RECORDS.

CHAPTER 1.

✍ Books and Records of Merchants

Article 48. Every general merchant shall from his accounting system, books, accounting records, inventories and financial statements in general, to the provisions of this Code and all other stipulations covering the subject. These rulings may authorize the use of systems such as microfilming, which facilitate keeping of filing records and correspondence. Authorization is also granted for the use of other procedures with an acknowledged technical accounting value, in order to enter his operations, provided that they allow for easy access and evidence of a clear, complete and accurate history of individual entries and the general condition of the business.

Article 49. For all legal purposes, when reference is made to books of commerce, they will be assumed to be the books stipulated by the Law as compulsory and the auxiliary books necessary for the complete understanding of the former.

Article 50. Accounting may only be carried in the Spanish language, by the system of double entry, in registered books, in such a manner that they provide a clear, complete and accurate history of the business of the merchant, subject to the regulations issued by the Government.

Article 51. All the vouchers backing the entries in the books shall be an integral part of the accounting system, as well as correspondence directly relating to the business.

Article 52. At the beginning of his commercial activities, and at least once a year, every merchant shall prepare and inventory a general balance sheet that allow a clear and complete picture of the state of his patrimony.

Article 53. All the commercial operations and those reflecting on the patrimony of the merchant shall be entered in the books in a chronological order, and have accounting vouchers that support them.

The accounting voucher is the documents that must be prepared prior to the registry of entry of every operation and shall indicate the number, date, origin, description and amount of the operation, as well as the accounts affected by the entry. Each voucher shall be accompanied by the backing documents.

Article 54. The merchant shall keep a true copy of the correspondence addressed in relation to the business, using any procedure that will ensure the accuracy and duration of the copy. Likewise, he shall keep the correspondence he may receive in connection with his trading activities, with indication of the date of reply or a note to the effect that no reply was given.

* * * * *

Article 56. The books may be the loose-leaf type or be made up by series of cards, provided that all of them are numbered, may be orderly filed and are authenticated in accordance with the Government's provisions on the subject.

Article 57. In the commercial books it is prohibited:

1. To alter in the entries the order or date of the operations referred therein;
2. To leave empty spaces that facilitate intercalations or additions in the text of the entries or below them;
3. To include notes between lines, blotting out or corrections in the entries. Any error or omission shall be compensated by means of a new entry on the date it is found;
4. To erase or cross out all or part of the entries; and
5. To tear out sheets, alter the order thereof or mutilate the books.

* * * * *

Article 59. The entries in the books and the vouchers of the accounts, should agree, otherwise they will not have value as evidence in favor of the merchant.

CHAPTER 3.

☞ Value of Evidence of Commercial Books and Records

Article 68. The commercial books and records shall represent full evidence on commercial matters which tradesmen may debate among themselves, either through judicial or extrajudicial channels.

On civil matters, even among merchants, such books and records will have an evidence value against their owner, insofar as the aspects stated therein in a clear and complete manner, provided that the counterpart rejects them with regard to unfavorable aspects on him.

Article 69. Regarding commercial matters with a person who is not a merchant, the books shall only represent a principle of evidence in favor of the merchant, which will have to be complemented with additional legal advice.

Article 70. Regarding the differences arising among merchants, the evidence value of their books and records shall be determined according to the following rules:

1. If the books and records of both parties conform to the legal provisions and agree with each other, the decision shall be arrived, taking into account the content of their entries;
2. If the books of both parties conform to the law but their entries do not agree with each other, the decision will be reached taking into account that the commercial books and papers represent a confession;
3. If the books of either party are not carried in accordance with legal provisions, the decision will be reached in accordance with the party who carried them according to the law, if the former does not submit full evidence that invalidated the content of such books;
4. If the books of both parties do not conform to the legal provisions, they will be completely discarded and only the other evidence submitted in court shall be taken into consideration; and
5. If one of the parties carried books that conform to the law and the counterpart does not carry accounting records or fails to submit them, the decisions shall be reached taking into account the books of the former, without accepting evidence to the contrary.

Article 71. If one of the parties proposes to abide by the contents of the other party's books and records, it will be decided in line with the latter.

Article 72. The responsibility for keeping the books cannot be divided. Consequently, the party who accepts the favorable items in the books of the other party, must accept all the prejudicial statements contained therein, if they abide by the legal provisions and no fraud is proven.

Article 73. If the tradesmen to whose books and records the decision is referred, does not have books, or secrets them or keeps them in an irregular manner, the decision will be reached in accordance with the foregoing provisions.

Article 74. If a tradesman has a double set of books or engages in any other fraud of this kind, his books and records shall only have value of evidence against himself.

It is assumed that there is double accounting when a tradesman carries one or more identical books in which he enters the same operations in different ways, or when he keeps different vouchers covering the same facts.

Country: Costa Rica

THE COMMERCIAL CODE

BOOK 1.

TITLE 2.

✍ ☞ CHAPTER V. — ACCOUNTING AND CORRESPONDENCE.

Article 251. Without prejudice to the books required by the Income Tax Law to be kept by all individual and juridical persons, merchants must keep other books legalized by the Direct Tax Office, in which are recorded in an easy, clear and precise manner their commercial operations and financial situation. For this purpose, the following are indispensable: an Inventories and Balance Record Book, Journal and Ledger, bound with numbered pages. They may also keep columnar sheets and auxiliary books or records. These auxiliary books or records are not required to be legalized. The merchant may keep a Cash Book which shall not be subject to the prescriptions of this Chapter.

Article 252. Corporations and Limited Liability Companies must keep a Minute Book of acts of meetings of members.

* * * * *

Article 254. The books must be written in Spanish, with clarity, in chronological order without blank spaces, erasures, or interlineations. Any equivocation or omission may be corrected by means of a new entry on the date on which the error was found, and also may be put in the margin at the appropriate place, in a different color of ink, a note indicating that this was an error, and the page where the respective correction will be found.

Article 255. The Inventories Record Book shall open with an exact detailed description of the money, securities, credits, merchandise, movable goods and real property and other asset items as of the date of initiation of the operations, the liabilities, and details of the resulting net capital. The new inventory resulting at the closing of the fiscal year shall be recorded in the same book at the end of each fiscal year. This inventory must coincide with the balance taken in the Balance Record Book.

Article 256. The first entry in the Journal shall be the result of the inventory mentioned in the preceding article.

Article 257. In the Ledger, kept by a debit and credit system, shall be posted, in their order, the entries of the Journal or Auxiliary Books.

Article 258. In the Balance Book there shall be entered, as the first entry, the general balance sheet of the business or enterprise at the beginning of operations. At the close of operations, each fiscal year, there shall be entered the following statements:

(a) Trial balance, prior to the closing of the Ledger entries;
(b) Profit and Loss Statement;
(c) General Balance Sheet, after the said closing;
(d) Surplus statement or surplus distribution, in the case of a company.

These balances and statements shall be signed by the owner of the business or economic activity. In the case of a general partnership, they shall be signed by the partners, in a limited partnership, by the general partners in a corporation or limited liability company, by the accountant in charge.

Article 259. In the Minutes Book, which shall be bound and each page thereof numbered, there shall be entered the detailed minutes of each ordinary or extra-ordinary meeting of shareholders, and it shall include the following information:

(a) Place and date of the meeting;
(b) Number of shares or quotas of capital represented at the meeting;
(c) Computation of votes;
(d) Decisions made, showing the certified votes issued.

* * * * *

Article 262. The use of loose-leaf sheets shall be authorized for some books in accordance with the provisions of this Chapter. These sheets must be numbered consecutively and contain the name of the person or company to which they belong with other pertinent details.

Article 263. The company books must be presented before they are begun to the general office of Direct Taxation for legalization in a special register.

Article 264. It is absolutely prohibited to tear out pages or to alter the binding or numbering of the books to which this Chapter refers.

* * * * *

Article 267. The books constitute evidence against their owner, but the plaintiff may not accept some matters and reject others; only the result jointly shown by the books. If the books kept by the parties do not agree with each other, and if one party has kept his books correctly, and the other has not, the books correctly kept shall serve as evidence against the ones incorrectly kept, if there is no other admissible evidence to the contrary. Should one of the parties fail to present his books or state that he does not have them, the plaintiff's books shall constitute evidence against him if correctly kept and if he does not prove that the lack of such books is due to force majeure or a fortuitous event, except in the case of valid evidence against the entries which have been exhibited. If the books of both parties are equally correct and are still contradictory, the court shall resolve according to other evidence.

Article 268. Correspondence received must be carefully retained in the files. A copy of all correspondence mailed must be retained in the files.

Article 269. In the case of a sale of the establishment or enterprise to a new proprietor who also acquires the accounting books, he may use the same books if he has not decided to start a new accounting system. If he does decide to continue the old books, he shall present them to the Tax Office in order that it might attest the transfer to the new proprietor of the business or enterprise. If he decides to open new books he must also present the old books kept up to the moment of the transfer to the Direct Tax Office or its delegate, giving the reason for closing them and opening new ones in accordance with the law.

Article 270. When an individual or juridical person, having been obliged to keep books, closes his business, liquidating it, he is obligated to retain the books and correspondence for at least four years from the date the liquidation is accomplished. But, if he has judgment pending before the courts, and this continues for more than four years, he shall be obligated to retain them for the entire duration of the suit.

In the case of transfer of an enterprise to a third party, if the former owner should not have, for such reason, the books and correspondence and is confronting a judicial situation, the new owner is under the obligation to permit the judicial authorities to obtain copies or certifications that may be required. The non-compliance with this obligation shall make the holder of the books liable for resulting damages and losses.

Article 271. In case of decease of the merchant or entrepreneur, it shall be presumed that the books, records, and correspondence are in the power of the heirs. In case of liquidation, the liquidators must retain them for the indicated period of four years; and, in the case of bankruptcy, the respective court shall retain them. In any case, the holders of the books and records are obligated to exhibit them in the same form as kept by the original owner, under penalty of compensating for damages and losses, if they refuse to do so.

Country: Dominican Republic

PART 1. COMMERCIAL CODE.

BOOK 1.

✍ Title 2. — Commercial Books.

Art. 8. Any merchants shall be obliged to keep a Daily Transaction Book that presents, day by day, his business transactions, or that summarizes, at least monthly, the totals of his transactions provided that he shall keep in each case, all documents that would permit verification of those transactions day by day.

Art. 9. Any Merchant is obligated to make an annual inventory of the assets and liabilities of his business and to close all accounts for the purpose of establishing his balance and the profit and loss statement.

The balance and profit and loss statement shall be copied in the inventory book. (Libro de Inventorio)

Art. 10. The Daily Book and the Inventory Book shall be kept chronologically, in the Spanish language, without blanks or alterations of any kind. All books must be kept on special ruvricated paper and are inspected and stamped by judicial officials once a year.

Art. 11. The Daily Book and the Inventory Book shall be numbered, stamped with official approval, and certified once a year by the Judge of the Civil and Commercial Courts or by the Justice of the Peace or his deputy, in the ordinary form.

The books and documents indicated in Arts. 8 and 9 must be kept for a period of 10 years.

Correspondence received and copies of letters sent must be classified and kept for the same period.

Art. 12. Commercial books, kept with regularity, may be admitted by the court as evidence between merchants, in commercial cases.

Art. 13. If books which should be kept by persons engaging in commerce are not kept in the manner prescribed, they shall neither be presented nor have validity in Court against those who have kept proper books, without prejudice to that which is established in the book of Winding Up and Bankruptcy.

Art. 14. Books and inventories may not be ordered in court in cases of succession, joint assets, liquidation of companies and in cases of bankruptcy.

Art. 15. In the course of a litigation the court may also order, de officio, the exhibition of the books for the purpose of establishing a point in litigation.

Art. 16. In the case when books whose exhibition has been offered, solicited or ordered, are located in places distant from the court which is handling the matter, the jurors may issue letters requisitorial to the court of commerce of the respective place, or commission a Justice of the Peace to examine, get a legal copy of their contents and to send to the court that which is necessary in the case.

Art. 17. If the party, whose books were offered to give validity and credit, refuses to present them, the court may administer the oath to the other party.

Country: Ecuador

GENERAL PROVISIONS

BOOK 1. MERCHANTS AND COMMERCIAL AGENTS

TITLE 1. MERCHANTS.

Section 2. Obligations of Merchants.

✍ Subsection 3. Commercial Accounting.

Article 37. Every commercial operator or industrialist whose capital amount to ten thousand sucres is required to keep books. If his capital is less than fifty thousand sucres, he may keep his books personally or with an assistant or through a public accountant registered with the Registrar of Accountants. If his capital is fifty thousand sucres, he must use the services of a certified public account, entered in the Registry of Accountants, who will be in charge of and responsible for the accounting of the concern.

* * * * *

Article 39. Accounting of a wholesale merchant must be kept in not less than four bound books, complete and numbered consecutively, namely:

1. Journal;
2. Ledger;
3. Inventory; and
4. Cash.

These books will be kept in Spanish.

Article 40. In the Daily Journal, will be entered, day by day, and in Chronological order, all transactions effected by the merchants with indication of the nature and circumstances of each operation and the result ensuing, either to credit or debit, so that each item shows who is creditor or who debtor in the transaction in question.

General expenses of the establishment and the personal expenses of the merchant may be entered in summary form at the end of each month, but in separate accounts.

* * * * *

Country: France

COMMERCIAL CODE

BOOK 1.

✍ TITLE 2. ACCOUNTING.

Art. 16. Accounting documents are established in francs and in the French language.

The accounting documents and the justifying vouchers shall be kept for a period of ten years.

The accounting documents relative to the registration of transactions and the detailed balance sheet kept without blanks or erasures or other alterations of any kind, under the conditions established by decree in *Conseil d' Etat (Council of State).*

Art. 17. Regularly kept accounts may be admitted in court for evidence of acts or trade among merchants.

If such accounts show irregularities, they may not be invoked by their maker to his profit. The communication of the accounting documents may only be ordered in ocurt in matters of succession, community property, division of a company and, in case of judicial rule, liquidation of assets and provisory suspension of pursuits.

NEW CODE OF CIVIL PROCEDURE

BOOK 1. PROVISIONS COMMON TO ALL COURTS.

TITLE 7. — THE JUDICIAL ADMINISTRATION OF PROOF.

SUBTITLE 1. — WRITTEN EVIDENCE

☞ CHAPTER 1. — COMMUNICATION OF WRITTEN EVIDENCE BETWEEN THE PARTIES.

Art. 132. A party who relies upon (*Fait état*) written evidence must communicate it to the other party to the proceeding.

The communication of written evidence must be spontaneous.

On appeal, a new communication of the written evidence already admitted during the trial at first instance is not required. Nevertheless, any party may request it.

Art. 133. If the communication of written evidence is not made, the judge may be requested informally to order such communication.

Art. 134. The judge, if necessary on pain of *astreinte*, fixes the time-limit and, where appropriate, the method of communication of the written evidence.

Art. 135. The judge may exclude (*écarter du débat*) such written evidence as has not been duly communicated.

Art. 136. A party who fails to return the written evidence communicated by him may be compelled to do so, if necessary by *astreinte*.

Art. 137. The *astreinte* may be liquidated by the judge who has ordered it.

Country: Germany

COMMERCIAL CODE OF MAY 10TH, 1897 (AS AMENDED)

✍ BOOK 1. COMMERCIAL ENTITIES

PART 4. COMMERCIAL RECORDS

§ 43. Method of bookkeeping.

(1) In keeping his books and other required records, the merchant must employ a language in modern use. Where abbreviations, numerals, letters and symbols are utilized, the meaning must be clearly determinable in the individual case.

(2) The entries in books and the other required records must be complete, correct, timely and in proper order.

(3) An entry or recording may not be altered in any manner such that the original meaning is no longer ascertainable. Alternations also may not be made where it remains uncertain as to when they were made, i.e., either originally or at a later date.

(4) Commercial books and the requisite records can also consist of the filing in order of original records or be kept on other data storage records in so far as these accounting methods including the procedures used, comply with generally accepted accounting principles. In keeping commercial books and the records otherwise required on data storage records there must be assurance that the data is able to be retrieved during the period of storage and can be made legible at any time within a reasonable period of time. Paragraphs (1) through (3) apply analogously.

§ 44. Document storage; storage period.

(1) Every merchant is obligated to store the following documents in order:

(1) commercial business records, inventories, balance sheets as well as the instructions and other organizational documents necessary for interpreting such documents,

(2) incoming business correspondence,

(3) copies of outgoing business correspondence,

(4) the original records on the basis of which entries were made in the books to be kept by him pursuant to § 38 subsection (1).

(2) Business correspondence comprises only such records which pertain to a commercial transaction.

(3) With the exception of the balance sheet, the documents listed in subsection (1) can also be stored on film or on other data storage records, if this complies with generally accepted accounting principles and it is assured that the reproductions or data

(1) facsimilate the incoming business correspondence and original records and concur with the other documents with regard to content when they are made legible

(2) are available during the period of storage and can be made legible at any time within a reasonable period of time.

Where records were produced in a data storage record form by reason of § 43 subsection (4) sentence 1, the data can also be stored in a printout form instead of the data storage materials.

The printed records can also be stored pursuant to sentence 1.

(4) The records listed in subsection (1) number 1 are to be stored for ten years, the other records listed in subsection (1) for six years.

(5) The period of storage begins with the close of the calendar year in which the last entry in the commercial record is made, the inventory prepared, the balance sheet approved, the business correspondence is received or sent or the original record has come into existence.

☞ § 45. Production of records during the course of litigation.

(1) During the course of litigation the court can, on application or sua sponte, order the production of the commercial records of a party.

(2) The provisions of the Civil Procedure Code with respect to the duty of the adverse party to produce documents remain unaffected.

☞ § 46. Extract of material to be produced during litigation.

If commercial records are produced during litigation, they shall be inspected with the parties present in so far as it concerns the issue in contention; in appropriate cases an extract shall be made. The remaining content of the books must be revealed to the court to the extent necessary to ascertain that the books were properly kept.

* * * * *

☞ § 47a. The production of documents from film or data storage material.

One who can only produce stored documents in the form of a film or other data storage copy, is obligated at his own expense to make available the devices necessary to make the documents legible; in so far as necessary he must, at his own expense, print the records or furnish reproductions which can be read without auxiliary devices.

* * * * *

PART 8. COMMERCIAL BROKER.

✍ § 100. Brokers transaction book.

(1) The commercial broker is obligated to maintain a transaction book and enter each day into such book all transactions concluded. Entries are to be made chronologically: They have to include the information set forth in § 94 subsection (1).The entry is to be signed on a daily basis by the commercial broker.

(2) The provision of § § 43 and 44 concerning the establishment and storage of commercial records are applicable to the commercial broker's transaction book.

BOOK THREE. COMMERCIAL RECORDS.

PART ONE. REGULATIONS FOR ALL MERCHANTS.

First Subpart. Bookeeping; Inventory.

✍ ☞ § 238. Bookkeeping duty.

(1) Every merchant is obligated to keep books and to show clearly in them his commercial transactions and his financial position pursuant to generally accepted accounting principles. The bookeeping must be maintained in such a way that an outside expert can derive from it within a reasonable time an overview of the business operations and the position of the firm. The business operations must be comprehensible from their origins through their winding up.

(2) The merchant is obligated to retain copies of all mailed business correspondence that conform to the original (facsimile reprint, transcript or other reproduction of the contents on a written, photographic or other data storage medium) identical with the original document of dispatched business letters.

✍ ☞ § 239. Method of commercial bookkeeping.

(1) In the keeping of business books and other required records, the merchant must employ language in common use. If abbreviations, codes, characters or symbols are used, their meaning must in every case be clearly explained.

(2) The entries in books and other required records must be complete, accurate, up-to-date and presented in an orderly fashion.

(3) An entry or a record may note be altered in such a way that the original content can no longer be determined. In addition, changes should not be made in such a way that from their nature it is unclear whether they are original or were added later.

(4) The books and other required records of a business can consist in the regular filing of documents or can be maintained on data storage devices insofar as this form of bookkeeping, including the procedure used, corresponds to the principles of orderly accounting for the maintenance on data storage devices of books and other required records; it must be ensured, in particular, that the data are accessible throughout the duration of the period of preservation and can at any time be retrieved within a reasonable time. Subparagraphs (1) to (3) apply mutatis mutandis.

✍ ☞ § 257. Storage of records; time period of storage.

(1) Every merchant is obligated to store the following documents in an orderly fashion;

1. Commercial business records, inventories, opening balance sheets, annual balance sheets, situation reports, closing accounts of a concern, situation reports of a concern as well as the operational instructions and other organizational documents necessary to understand them.
2. Business letters received.
3. Copies of business letters sent.
4. the original records underlying the entries made in the books to be kept by him pursuant to § 238, paragraph 1 (accountinging records).

(2) Business correspondence comprises only such documents that pertain to a commercial transaction.

(3) Except for the opening balance sheets, annual financial statements and consolidated financial statements, the documents listed in paragraph 1 may also be stored as a reproduction on film or other data storage devices if this complies with generally accepted accounting principles and it is assured that the reproduction or data:

1. provides a picture-perfect duplicate of the incoming business correspondence and accounting records and exactly reproduces the content of the other documents whenever they are put into a legible form, and
2. is accessible during the period of storage and can be put into a legible form at any time within a reasonable period.

If records are placed in a data storage device on the basis of § 239, paragraph 4, sentence 1, the data may also be stored in print-out form instead of in the data storage device. The printed records may also be stored pursuant to sentence 1.

(4) The records listed in paragraph number 1 shall be stored for ten years and the other records listed in paragraph 1 for six years.

(5) The period of storage begins upon the close of the calendar year in which the last entry in the commercial record was made, the inventory prepared, the opening balance sheet or the annual financial statement determined, the consolidated financial statement prepared, the business correspondence received or mailed out or the accounting records originated.

☞ § 258. Production of records for litigation.

(1) In the course of litigation, the court may order on application or *sua sponte* the production of the commercial records of one of the parties.

(2) The provisions of the Code of Civil Procedure with respect to the duty of the adverse party to produce documents remain unaffected.

☞ § 259. Extract of material to be produced during litigation.

If commercial records are produced during litigation, their content shall be inspected to the extent that it concerns the issue in contention with the parties present. In appropriate cases, an extract shall be made. The remaining content of the books shall be revealed to the court to the extent necessary to determine that the books were properly kept.

☞ § 260. Production of documents for distribution of assets.

In the event of disputes relating to the distribution of assets, especially in probate, common property and partnership distribution matters, the court can order the production of commercial records in order to take notice of their entire content.

☞ § 261. Production of documents from film or data storage devices.

One who can produce stored documents only in the form of a reproduction from film or other data storage device is obligated to make available at his own expense the devices necessary to put the documents into a legible form. To the extent necessary, he must, at this own expense, print out the records or furnish reproductions which can be read without auxiliary devices.

Country: Ghana

CHAPTER 2. PROVISIONS APPLICABLE TO ALL COMPANIES

COMMERCIAL LAWS OF GHANA

Part N. — Accounts and Audit.

✍ *123.* (1) Every company shall cause to be kept proper books of account with respect to its financial position and changes therein, and with respect to the control of and accounting for all property acquired whether for resale or for use in the company's business, and, in particular with respect to:

(1)(a) all sums of money received and expended by or on behalf of the company and the matters in respect of which the receipt and expenditure takes place;

(b) all sales and purchases by the company of property, goods and services;

(c) the assets and liabilities of the company and the interests of the members therein.

(2) Proper books of account shall not be deemed to be kept if there are not kept such books as are necessary to give a true and fair view of the state of the company's affairs and to prepare proper profit and loss accounts and balance sheets in accordance with section 125 to 131 of this Code.

(3) The books of account may be kept either by making entries in bound volumes, or, subject to compliance with subsections (2) and (3) or section 264 of this Code, by a system of mechanical recording, or otherwise.

(4) The books of account shall be kept at the registered office of the company or at such other place as the directors shall think fit, and shall at all times be open to inspection by the directors, secretary and auditors of the company.

Country: Guatemala

COMMERCIAL CODE

BOOK 2. — PROFESSIONAL OBLIGATIONS OF MERCHANTS.

TITLE 3. — MERCANTILE ACCOUNTING AND CORRESPONDENCE.

✍ CHAPTER 1. — ACCOUNTING.

Article 368. Accounting and Indispensable Registers.

Merchants are obligated to keep their accounts in proper form in accordance with the system of double entry, bookkeeping and using generally acceptable accounting principles.

For this purpose, they must keep at least the following books or registers:

1. Inventories
2. Journal
3. Ledger
4. Financial Statements

Also any others that he esteems necessary may be used for accounting, exigencies, or for administrative purposes, or in virtue, of other special laws.

They may also keep their accounts by means of mechanized procedures, in looseleaf books, microfiche or by any other system, provided that it permits analysis and control.

Merchants whose total assets do not exceed 2,000 quetzals may omit the aforesaid books or registers with the exception of the register or book of inventories that, show financial statements and those which they are obliged to keep in virtue of special laws.

Article 369. Spanish Idiom and National Money.

The books and registers must be kept in Spanish and the accounts must be in the national money.

Branches and agencies of companies situated abroad may keep a duplicate in the language and money desired, with a column showing the conversion into the national money, upon previous advice from the mercantile registrar.

* * * * *

Article 375. Prohibition of Keeping More Than One Set of Books.

It is prohibited for the same enterprise to keep more than one set of books.

Article 376. Conservation of Books and Registers.

Merchants, their heirs or successors, shall keep the books and registers of the enterprise for all the time of its duration up to the liquidation of all its negotiations and mercantile dependencies.

Article 377. Financial Statements.

The book or register of financial statements shall contain:
1. The general balance sheet upon opening and the ordinary and extraordinary procedures practiced,
2. The profit and loss statements which correspond to the general balance sheets.
3. Any other statements judged necessary by the merchant for clarification of his financial situation.

Article 378. Auxiliary Registers.

The merchant may keep any auxiliary books and registers he esteems necessary.

Article 379. Exhibition of the Financial Situation.

The general balance sheet must express with veracity and in reasonable form the financial situation of the merchant and the results of his operations up to the date of its preparation.

Article 380. Publication of Balance Sheets.

Any mercantile company and foreign companies authorized to operate in the Republic must publish their balance sheets in the Diario Oficial at the closing of the operations of each accounting year, fulfilling for the purpose the requirements established in other laws.

Country: Hong Kong

PART 13. MISCELLANEOUS

PROVISIONS RELATING TO DOCUMENTS AND DISPOSAL THEREOF.

✪ **§ 347. Power of Registrar to Accept Information on Microfilm, etc. (Replaced by Ordinance No. 6 of 1984.)**

(1) The Registrar may, if he thinks fit, accept under any provision of this Ordinance requiring a document to be delivered to him any material other than a document which contains the information in question and is of a kind approved by him.
(2) The delivery to the Registrar of material accepted by him as aforesaid shall be a sufficient compliance with the provision in question.
(3) Section 305 shall have effect as if any material so accepted were a document kept by the Registrar.
(4) In this section any reference to delivering a document shall be construed as including a reference to sending, forwarding, producing or (in the case of a notice) giving it.

Country: Iraq

CODE OF COMMERCE

✍ **CHAPTER 3. — THE KEEPING OF COMMERCIAL BOOKS FOR THE PURPOSES OF INCOME TAX.**

Commercial books and registers shall be kept by all merchants.

Merchants are defined by the Commercial Code of March 15, 1984 (Law No. 30) as every natural or juristic person carrying out, regularly, commercial activity in his name and for his account. Merchants must be Iraqis who are deemed legally competent.
Non-Iraqis may carry on commercial activities in accordance with the necessities of the national development plan and the authorization of the competent authority.
The competent minister may determine the nature and the field of commercial activity which can be conducted by a merchant to guarantee the execution of the national development plan.
The following acts shall be considered as commercial activities if they are conducted with intention of profit. This intention shall be presumed unless the contrary is proved:
1) Purchase and letting of assets, whether movable or immovable, for the purpose of resale or letting.
2) Supply of goods and services.
3) Import and export of goods and the activity of import and export offices.
4) Industry and raw materials extraction.
5) Publishing, printing, photography and advertising.
6) Contracting relating to construction, repair demolition and maintenance.
7) Services of tourism offices, hotels, restaurants, cinemas, playgrounds and other exhibition halls.
8) Sale in public auction places.
9) Transport of persons and goods.
10) Freight, unloading and removal of goods.
11) Storage of goods in public warehouses.
12) Contracting in social events.
13) Banking operations.
14) Insurance.
15) Transaction in corporate stocks and bonds.
16) Commercial commission and transport agencies and other commercial brokerage activity.
The capital of a merchant must not be less than 30,000 and he must keep the books necessary for his commerce in order to show his financial position.
In all cases he must keep the following two books:
1. Journal.
2. Ledger.
A merchant may replace the books provided for above by using modern machines and techniques to establish his accounts and show his financial position.

Country: Italy

THE ITALIAN CIVIL CODE

BOOK 5. LABOR.

TITLE 2. LABOR IN THE ENTERPRISE.

CHAPTER 3. BUSINESS ENTERPRISES AND OTHER ENTERPRISES SUBJECT TO REGISTRATION

Section 3. Special Provisions for Business Enterprises

✍ **Article 2214. Mandatory books and other commercial books.**

The enterpriser who exercises a business activity shall keep a journal and an inventory book.
He shall, moreover, keep other accounting records required by the nature and size of the enterprise, and preserve in an orderly manner for each transaction the originals of the letters,

telegrams, and invoices received as well as copies of the letters, telegrams, and invoices sent out.

The provisions of this paragraph do not apply to small enterprises (2083).

Article 2215. Journal and inventory book.

The journal and the inventory book, before being put to use, shall be progressively numbered on each page and stamped on each sheet by the office of the register of enterprises (2188) or by a notary in accordance with the provisions of special laws.

The office of the register or the notary shall state on the last page of the books the number of sheets of which they are comprised.

Article 2216. Contents and certification of journal.

The journal shall show day by day the transactions relating to the exercise of the enterprise (2188) and shall be certified annually by the office of the register of enterprises or by a notary.

TITLE 5. — COMPANIES.

CHAPTER 5. JOINT STOCK COMPANIES.

✍ Section 8. — Company Books.

Article 2421. Mandatory Books.

In addition to books and other accounting documents prescribed in Article 2214 the company must keep:

1. A book for members in which must be entered the number of shares, the family name and given name of the holders of nominative shares, the transfers and liens relative thereto, and the payments made.
2. The book for obligations (debentures) (Article 2410) which will indicate the amount of obligations issued and amount of those paid off, the family name and given name of the title holders of nominative obligations and the transfer and liens relative thereto.
3. The book with the accounts of meetings (Article 2363), resolutions of the shareholders' meeting where there will be entered the minutes drawn up by public deed (Articles 2375, 2699).
4. The minutes books for meetings and resolutions of the Board of Directors. (Article 2380).
5. Minutes book for recording the meetings and resolutions of the auditors' collegium. (Article 2397).
6. Minutes book for meetings and resolutions of the executive committee, if there is one. (Article 2381).
7. Minutes book of meetings of the holders of obligations if certificates for obligations have been issued. (Article 2415).

The records books in numbers 1, 2, 3 and 4 are kept by the directors, the book referred to in No. 5 by the auditing collegium, the book indicated by No. 6 by the executive committee, and the book indicated under No. 7 by the joint representative of the holders of obligations (Article 2417).

The above record books, prior to use, must be numbered in sequence on each page, stamped on each folio and be approved once a year according to Articles 2215 and 2216.

BOOK 6. PROTECTION OF RIGHTS.

TITLE 2. — EVIDENCE.

CHAPTER 2. — DOCUMENTARY EVIDENCE.

☞ Section 2. — Private Writing.

Article 2702. Effects of private writings.

Subject to an action to establish falsity, a private writing constitutes full proof of the origin of the declaration set forth therein in the person who signed such writing. If the person against whom it is asserted recognizes the signature, or if the signature is legally deemed to have been recognized (Article 2703).

Article 2703. Authenticated signature.

A signature that has been authenticated by a notary or by another authorized public official is treated as having been recognized.

The authentication consists of a certification by the public official that the signature was written in his presence. The public official must previously verify the identity of the person who makes the signature.

Article 2704. Date of private writing as to third persons.

The date of a private writing in which the signature has not been authenticated (Article 2703) is not certain and cannot be asserted against third persons, except from the day on which the writing was registered or from the date of death or supervening physical incapacity to sign of the person or persons who signed it, or from the date on which the contents of such writing are reproduced in public acts (Article 2699), or from the date on which other circumstances occur which establish with equal certainty that the writing was drawn up previously.

The date of a private writing containing unilateral declarations which are not directed to any specified person can be ascertained through any kind of evidence.

The court, according to the circumstances of the case, can allow the introduction of any kind of evidence to ascertain the date of release of a debt (Article 1199).

Article 2705. Telegrams.

Telegrams have the same evidentiary value as a private writing (Article 2702), if the original delivered to the transmitting office has been signed by the sender, or if the sender himself delivered to or caused it to be delivered, even without signing it.

The signature can be authenticated by a notary (Article 2703).

If the identify of the person who signed the original of the telegram was verified in the manner provided for by applicable regulations, proof to the contrary is permitted.

The sender can also cause the telegram to indicate whether the original was signed with or without authentication.

Article 2706. Conformity of original to delivered text of telegram.

The text of a telegram delivered to the address is presumed to conform to the original, until proof to the contrary is offered.

If the sender caused the copy to be examined in comparison with the original, in accordance with the provisions of the applicable regulations, he is presumed not to be responsible for any difference between the original and the copy.

Article 2707. Household papers and books of account.

Household papers and books of account constitute evidence against those who write them in the following cases:
1) when they expressly recite a payment received;
2) when they expressly mention that the entry was made in substitution for a missing instrument of debt, in favor of the person who is indicated as being the creditor.

Article 2708. Notation at foot, on margin, or on back of document.

A notation made by a creditor at the foot, on the margin, or on the back of a document left in his possession has evidentiary value, if it tends to show release of the debtor, even if the notation is not signed by such creditor.

A notation made by a creditor at the foot, on the margin, or on the back of a release (Article 1199) or of a copy of the instrument of debt, held by the debtor, has the same effect.

☞ Section 3. — Accounting Records of Enterprises Subject to Registration.

Article 2709. Evidentiary value against enterpriser.

The books and other accounting records (Articles 2214, 2421, 2490) of enterprises subject to registration (Article 2195) constitute evidence against the enterpriser. One who tends to avail himself of them cannot, however select their contents.

Article 2710. Evidentiary effect between enterprises.

Books stamped and certified according to law (Article 2215) can constitute evidence between enterprisers, with respect to relationships connected with the exercise of the enterprises.

Article 2711. Surrendering and submitting books and other accounts.

The deposit for inspection of all books, accounting records, and correspondence can be ordered by the judge only in litigation concerning dissolution of a company, or common ownership (Article 1100 *ff*), or succession at death (Article 456 *ff*).

In all other cases the judge, can even *ex officio*, order that the books be submitted in order to select from the entries relating to the controversy at issue. He can also order that individual accounting records, letters, telegrams or invoices relating to such controversy be submitted.

☞ Section 4. — Mechanical Reproductions.

Article 2712. Mechanical reproductions.

Photographic or cinematographic reproductions, phonographic recordings and, in general, all other mechanical representations of facts or things, constitute full evidence of the facts or things represented, if the persons against whom they are offered do not deny their correspondence to the actual facts or things concerned.

☞ Section 5. — Tallies.

Article 2713. Tallies.

Tallies constitute full evidence among those who customarily account in such a way to prove the supply of goods furnished or received on a retail basis.

☞ Section 6. — Copies of Instruments.

Article 2715. Copies of deposited original private writings.

Copies of private writings deposited in public offices, when issued by authorized public depositaries, have the same value (Article 2714) as the original writing from which they originate.

Article 2716. Lack of original instrument or of deposited copy. Lacking the original of a public act (Article 2699) or a copy thereof deposited in the care of a public depositary, full evidentiary value is given to copies drawn up in accordance with Article 2714; but if such copies, or even the copy existing in the care of a public depositary when the original is lacking, show any deletions, erasures, insertions, or other visible defects, it is up to the judge to appraise their evidentiary value.

Lacking the original of a private writing (Article 2702), a copy thereof, issued in accordance with Article 2715, is given the same evidentiary value, but if such copy shows any deletions, erasures, insertions, or other visible defects, it is likewise up to the court to appraise its evidentiary value. In any case, questions concerning the authenticity of the missing original are unaffected.

Article 2717. Evidentiary value of other copies.

Copies issued by public officials in cases not contemplated in the preceding articles have the value of *prima facie* written evidence (Article 2724).

Article 2718. Evidentiary value of partial copies.

Partial copies, or reproductions of excerpts, issued with the required formalities by duly authorized public officials who are the depositaries of them, have full evidentiary value only in that part of the original which such copies literally reproduce.

Article 2719. Photographic copies of writings.

Photographic copies of writings have the same effect as authenticated copies, if their correspondence with the original is certified by a duly authorized public official or is not expressly denied.

Country: Jamaica

COMPANIES ACT

PART 12. — MISCELLANEOUS.

✍ Form of Registers, etc.

364. (1) Any register, index, minute book or book of account required by this Act to be kept by a company may be kept either by making entries in bound books or by recording the matters in question in any other manner.

(2) Where any such register, index, minute book or book of account is not kept by making entries in a bound book, but by some other means, adequate precautions shall be taken for guarding against falsification and facilitating its discovery, and where default is made in complying with this subsection the company and every officer of the company who is in default shall be liable to a fine not exceeding one hundred dollars and further shall be liable to a default fine.

Country: Japan

THE CODE OF CIVIL PROCEDURE

BOOK 2. PROCEEDINGS IN THE FIRST INSTANCE.

CHAPTER 3. EVIDENCE.

☞ **SECTION 4. — DOCUMENTARY EVIDENCE.**

Method of Production of Document

Article 322. Production or transmission of a document shall be made by that of the original, an exemplification or an authenticated transcript.

2. The court may order the production or forwarding of the original regardless of the provisions of the preceding paragraph.

3. The court may have a party produce an exemplification or an excerpt of a document which he has referred to.

Presumption of Authenticity of an Official Document

Article 323. A document shall, in the event that it is to be deemed to have been drawn by a government official or any other public official in the course of the exercise of his duties in view of the form and purport of the document, be deemed to be authentic.

2. If there is any doubt as to the authenticity of an official document, the court may inquire the government agency or the public office concerned upon its own authority.

Official Document of a Foreign Country

Article 324. The provisions of the preceding paragraph shall apply mutatis mutandis to such document as being deemed to be drawn by a foreign government agency or a public office.

Checking of Private Document

Article 325. Authenticity of a private document shall be proved.

Authenticity Presumed on a Private Document

Article 326. A private document shall be deemed to be authentic if it bears the signature or seal of the principal or his representative.

Checking of Writing or Impression of Seal

Article 327. The authenticity of a document may also be proved by comparing writings or seal impressions.

Production Procedure of Documents for Comparison

Article 328. The provisions of Article 311, Articles 314 to 317 inclusive, Articles 319 to 321 inclusive shall apply mutatis mutandis to the production or forwarding of a document or any other article having writings or a seal impression to be used for comparison.

2. The court shall, in case a third person does not comply with an order of production under the provisions of the preceding paragraph without justifiable reasons, punish him by a penalty of non-penal fine not exceeding a hundred thousand yen. An immediate Kokoku-appeal may be made against the foregoing ruling.

Article 331. In the event that a party or his representative disputes the authenticity of a document contrary to the truth intentionally or by gross negligences, the court shall punish him by a penalty of non-penal fine not exceeding a hundred thousand yen. An immediate Kokoku-appeal may be made against the foregoing ruling.

2. In the event that the party or his representative disputing the authenticity of the document recognizes its authenticity during the pendency of the litigation in such cases as mentioned in the preceding paragraph, the court may revoke the ruling as mentioned in the preceding paragraph according to the circumstances.

THE COMMERCIAL CODE OF JAPAN

BOOK 1. GENERAL PROVISIONS.

✍ **CHAPTER 5. — BOOKS OF ACCOUNT.**

Journal

Article 32. Every trader shall prepare accounting books and balance sheets for making clear the conditions of business properties and profit and loss.

2. In construing the provisions concerning preparation of the books of account, authentic accounting practices shall be taken into consideration.

Statement in Journal

Article 33. The following matters shall systematically and clearly be stated in the accounting books:

(1) Business properties and values thereof at the commencement of business and once in each year at a fixed time, as for a company, business properties and values thereof at the time of incorporation and at each settlement of accounts.

(2) Transactions, and other matters which give influence to business properties.

2. A balance sheet shall be prepared based on accounting books at the time of commencement of business and once in each year at a fixed time; and a company shall prepare it based thereon at the time of incorporation and at each settlement of accounts.

3. A balance sheet shall be compiled and bound together, or shall be entered in a book specially kept for that purpose.

4. A balance sheet shall contain the signature of the person who prepared it.

Preservation of Books of Accounts, Etc.

Article 36. Every trader shall preserve his books of account, and all important documents relating to his business for a period of ten years.

2. The period as mentioned in the preceding paragraph shall be computed in the case of a book of account as from the time at which the book has been closed.

Country: Jersey

JERSEY COMPANIES LAW OF 1991

✍ **PART 16. — ACCOUNTS AND AUDIT.**

Article 102. Accounting records.

Every company shall keep accounting records which are sufficient to show and explain its transactions and are such as to —

(a) disclose with reasonable accuracy, at any time, the

financial position of the company at that time; and

(b) enable the directors to ensure that any accounts prepared by the company under this Part comply with the requirements of this Law.

Article 103. Retention of records.

(1) A company's accounting records shall be kept at such place as the directors think fit and shall at all times be open to inspection by the company's officers and the secretary.

(2) If accounting records of a public company are kept at a place outside the Island, returns with respect to the business dealt within in the accounting records so kept shall be sent to, and kept in, the Island, shall at all times be open to such inspection, and shall be such as to —

(a) disclose with reasonable accuracy the financial position of the business in question at intervals of not more than six months; and

(b) enable the directors to ensure that any accounts prepared by the company under this Part comply with the requirements of this Law.

(3) Subject to Article 194, accounting records which a company is required by Article 102 to keep shall be preserved by it for 10 years from the date on which they are made.

✍ PART 24. — MISCELLANEOUS AND FINAL PROVISIONS.

Article 206. Form of company's records.

(1) The records, which a company is required by this Law to keep, may be kept n the form of a bound or loose-leaf book, or photographic film, or may be entered or recorded by a system of mechanical or electronic data processing or any other information storage device that is capable of reproducing any required information in intelligible written form within a reasonable time.

(2) A company shall take reasonable precautions —

(a) to prevent loss or destruction of;

(b) to prevent falsification of entries in; and

(c) to facilitate detection and correction of inaccuracies in,

the records required by this law to be kept, and a company which fails to comply with the provisions of this paragraph is guilty of an offence.

Article 207. Examination of records and admissibility of evidence.

(1) If any record referred to in paragraph (1) of Article 206 is kept otherwise than in intelligible written form, any duty imposed on the company by this Law to allow examination of or to furnish extracts from, such record shall be treated as a duty to allow examination of, or to furnish a copy of the extract from, the record in intelligible written form.

(2) The records kept by a company with this Law shall be admissible in the form in which they are made intelligible under paragraph (1) as *prima facie* evidence, before and after the dissolution of the company, of all facts stated therein.

Article 208. Production and inspection of records where offence suspected.

(1) If, in an application by the Attorney-General, there is shown to be reasonable cause to believe that a person has, while an officer of a company, committed an offence in connection with the management of the company's affairs and that evidence of the commission of the offence is to be found in any records of or under the control of the company, the court may make an order —

(a) authorizing a person named in it to inspect the records in question, or any of them, for the purpose of investigating and obtaining evidence of the offence; or

(b) requiring the secretary of the company or an officer of it named in the order to produce and make available the records (of any of them) to a person named in the order at a place so named.

(2) Paragraph (1) applies also in relation to records of a person carrying on the business of banking so far as they relate to the company's affairs, as it applies to records of or under the control of the company, except that no order referred to in sub-paragraph (b) of paragraph (1) shall be made by virtue of this paragraph.

(3) The decision of the court on an application of this Article is not appealable.

Country: Korea (Republic Of)

LAWS OF THE REPUBLIC OF KOREA

THE CODE OF CIVIL PROCEDURE

CHAPTER 3. — EVIDENCE.

☞ Section 4. — Documentary Evidence.

Article 315. How to apply for Production of Documentary Evidence.

Application for production of documentary evidence must be tendered by producing the document, or by applying for an order for production addressed to the person in whose possession it is.

Article 316. Duty to produce Document.

The holder of a document may not refuse to produce it in the following cases:

1. If a party himself holds the document which he has cited in the action;
2. If an applicant for the production of documentary evidence is entitled to demand that the holder deliver the document to him or permit him to peruse it;
3. If the document has been made out for the benefit of the applicant, or concerning a legal relation between the applicant and the holder of the document.

Article 317. How to apply for an Order for the Production of Document.

The following points must be made clear in an application for an order for the production of a document:

1. A designation of the document;
2. The purport of the document;
3. The holder of the document;
4. The fact to be proven;
5. The ground of the duty to produce the document;

Article 321. Effect of Hindering the Use of a Document by a Party.

Should a party, with the object of preventing the use by the other party, of a document which he is ordered to produce, destroy the same or otherwise render it unfit for use, the court may deem that the allegations of the other party relating to such document are true.

Article 325. Taking Evidence by a Commissioned or Requisitioned Judge.

(1) Where a commissioned judge or a requisitioned judge is required to take evidence in regard to a document in accordance with the provisions of Article 265, the court may decide what particulars are to be entered in the protocol (of the commissioned or requisitioned judge).

(2) A copy of, or an extract from the document must be annexed to the protocol referred to in the foregoing paragraph.

Article 326. How to Produce or Forward Document.

(1) A document must be produced or forwarded in the form of the original, an exemplification or a certified copy.

(2) The court may, if it deems necessary, order the original to be produced or order forward it.

(3) Where a party has cited a document, the court may require him to produce a copy, or an extract from the same.

PART 1. COMMERCIAL CODE

BOOK 1. GENERAL PROVISIONS.

✍ **CHAPTER 5. — TRADE BOOKS.**
☞

Article 29. Day Book.

(1) Every trade shall keep books and shall enter therein in a clear manner his daily transactions and other matters which may tend to affect his property. However, in regard to household expenses, it shall be sufficient to enter their total monthly amount.

(2) In regard to a small sum of transaction, only the total amount of every day's proceeds need be entered, separating cash sales from credit sales.

Article 30. Inventory of Property and Balance Sheet.

(1) At the time of commencement of business and once a year at a fixed time, every trader shall prepare an inventory of movables, immovables, claims and obligation, and of every other property, and a balance sheet.

(2) A company shall prepare the documents mentioned in the preceding paragraphs at the time of its formation and at the end of each term for the settlement of accounts.

(3) An inventory and a balance sheet shall contain the signatures and seals of the persons who prepared them, and these documents shall be entered in a book especially kept for that purpose or shall be compiled and bound together.

Article 32. Production of Trade Books.

The court may, on application or of its own motion, order a party to an action to produce his trade books or any part thereof.

Article 33. Preservation of Trade Books.

(1) Every trader shall preserve his trade books, and all important documents relating to his business for a period of ten years.

(2) The period mentioned in the preceding paragraph shall be computed in the case of a trade book as from the time at which the book has been closed.

Country: Lebanon

CODE OF COMMERCE

BOOK 1. — COMMERCE IN GENERAL.

PART 3. — TRADERS

✍ **CHAPTER 2. — BOOKS OF COMMERCE.**

Art. 16. Footnote 1,2,3 Every natural or juristic person having the capacity of merchant shall keep a journal book in which shall be entered day by day all operations relating in any way to the commercial enterprise or, when this is not made possible by the nature of work in the enterprise, in which shall at least be entered monthly the results of said operations, provided that, in this latter case, such person shall keep all documents permitting the verification of such operations day by day, during the whole period provided in Article 19 of the Code of Commerce.

Such person shall also draw up an annual inventory of all the elements of the enterprise and close all accounts for the purpose of drawing up a balance sheet, a profit and loss account, and enter at least the balance sheet and the profit and loss account in the inventory elements, documents relating to the inventory shall be prepared and kept during the whole period provided in Article 19 of the Code of Commerce.

Footnote 1 - (1) Article 2 of Decree No. 9800 of May 4, 1968 states: "In the second case relating to the journal book and inventory book provided in the first and second paragraphs of the Article 16 of the Code of Commerce, and contrarily to the provisions of Article 16 of the Court Fees Law, the fee of registration of such book is fixed at a flat rate of LL. 100 per annum, payable within the first three months of every year."

Article 3 of Decree No. 9800 of May 4, 1968 states: "Contrarily to the provisions of Article 30 of Legislative Decree No. 144 of June 12, 1959, the Minister of Finance may, in respect of the contraventions to the obligation of keeping the legal books having occurred between the date of the said legislative decree No. 144 and the date of enforcement of the present Law, and after taking the opinion of the Department concerned, make a settlement in respect of the fines imposed, whether such have been paid or not, or which are imposable, or dispense the merchant from paying the same provided that the latter proves his good faith and that his non-compliance with the provisions Article 16 is due to the kind and methods of work of the enterprise."

(2) The following is the text of Circular issued by the Minister of Finance, No. 386/S 2-5/1842 of March 27, 1972, setting up procedure of keeping the journal book and the inventory book: "In order to remove any ambiguity in respect of keeping these commercial books, we find it necessary to clarify the procedure to be applied in keeping the journal book and the inventory book as follows:

First - Journal Book

a) The journal book must be registered at the competent commercial court, kept in chronological order, and free from unused or blank spaces, marginal writings, insertions between lines and erasures.

The merchant (who is taxable on real profit) must enter in the journal book, day by day, all operations relating in any way to his commercial enterprise, using liquid or dry ink.

The term "all operations" means, for example, purchases, sales in cash an on credit, various expenses, all other income appertaining to the commercial enterprise, current account, special withdrawals and all debts, etc.

It shall be sufficient for a person subject to tax on lump-sum profit to record all his income (including sales) and all his expenses (including purchases).

b) When the nature of the work in the commercial enterprises does not make it possible to enter all commercial operations day by day, the merchant can record, monthly, the results of said operations, provided that, in this case only, he keeps all documents permitting the verification of such operations day by day for a period of ten years. In this latter case, the merchant must register the journal book at the competent commercial court and pay the fixed fee of LL. 100, within the first three months of each year.

It is to be noted that the merchant who desires his entries in the journal book, monthly, due to the nature of work in his enterprise, must obtain prior approval of the competent finance department (Revenue Department).

Second - Inventory Book

a) The inventory book must be registered at the competent commercial court, kept in chronological order, and free from unused or blank spaces, marginal writings, insertions between lines and erasures.

At the end of the financial year, the merchant must record the following in the inventory book, using liquid or dry ink:

1. Detailed inventory elements of goods.
2. Elements of fixed assets (non-negotiable and negotiable funds, whether movable or immovable, in detail.
3. Debts due to and by the enterprise.
4. Balance sheet.
5. Profit and loss account.
6. Statement of depreciation.
7. Reserves of all forms.

b) When the nature of work in the enterprise does not make it possible to enter the detailed inventory, the merchant must prepare documents relating to the detailed elements of inventory permitting the verification of details of inventory and must keep such documents for a period of ten years.

In this latter case, the merchant must register the inventory book at the competent commercial court, after obtaining prior approval of the competent finance department (Revenue Department), and pay the fixed fee of LL. 100, within the first three months of each year.

The procedure explained herein and in Circular No. 1464/A1, of June 25, 1971, shall be applicable with effect from the beginning of 1972 (year of assessment 1973), and for this purpose, the last paragraph of the said circular shall be canceled."

(3) There is no legal provision to exempt banks from keeping the letter book as well as the inventory and balance sheet book prescribed in Article 16 of the Code of Commerce. There is no way to show tolerance in the application of both the said Article and Article 460 of the same Code without explicit will of the legislator. It should be observed that the legislator has not allowed the judge the right to use his power of appreciation in this respect, contrarily to the latitude allowed the judge by the French legislator in the matter of judicial liquidation. (Court of First Instance in Beirut, Judgment No. 549 of Jan. 4, 1967)

Art. 17. The prescribed commercial books above must be kept in chronological order, without blank space, marginal entries, interlines or obliterations.

Art. 18. The books must be serially numbered, stamped and initialed by the president of the tribunal of first instance in the towns where such tribunal sits, or by a magistrate.

Art. 19. The books must be maintained by the trader for the period of ten years following the date on which they are closed.

Art. 20. Subject to their being regularly held, the books may be produced at court as evidence in favor of the trader in the case of trading conflicts arising between himself and another trader in respect of an act of commerce.[1]

In all cases they are considered as evidence against the trader who holds them.[2] Should the trader refuse to produce them, the court may bestow upon the other party the right to take the oath.[3]

---

[1] In conformity with article 20 of the Code of Commerce, the trader's books of account entries, if properly kept, shall serve as proof in his favor when produced in his favor, when produced in evidence against a trader provided they relate to a business act. The text of this article is so wide as to include all entries appearing in the trader's books, even those pertaining to the accounts of a third party provided they are relevant to the disputed transaction. (First Court Civil of Cassation, Decision 129 of Nov. 29, 1960)

[2] COMPANY BOOKS AND MANAGEMENT. The proper organization of company books is no hindrance to attack certain entries under article 170 (Civil Procedure) but to the lawfulness thereof. Although the partnership deed and articles 884, 887 and 888 (Obligations) vest upon the managing partner of the partnership the right to carry on, regardless of the other partners' opposition, all administrative works even disposing activities falling within the scope of the objects of the partnership, the general principles as well as the provisions of article 884 stipulate that there should be no cheating or fraud as these render everything null. (Civil Court of Appeal Beirut, Decision No. 1543)

[3] If documents bear in themselves strength of evidence, commercial books draw such evidential strength from the provisions of Art. 20 of the Code of Commerce. The commercial book serves as a documentary evidence against its owner, the same as the document itself; and there is no legal impediment to disproving a document by means of entries that have been made in commercial books by their owner. The oath provided for in Art. 20 of the Code of Commerce may not be administered by the Judge incidentally, as such an oath is complementary and not binding to the Judge. (Decision No. 33 of March 10, 1964)

THE LEBANESE LEGAL SYSTEM

CIVIL PROCEDURES

D. — OTHER DOCUMENTS.

☞ 1. Commercial Records.

The Code admits all kinds of evidence in commercial matters. The judge is not required to consider evidence of commercial data when other evidence inferred from documents, witnesses or presumptions suggests that the original data is incorrect.

The judge also has discretionary power to admit or reject evidence relevant to commercial litigation. This applies to evidence allegedly obtained either from nonbinding commercial books, binding commercial books or from binding commercial books irregularly kept.

Finally, when there is conflicting evidence from the commercial books of two opposing litigants (provided the books are regularly kept), the judge may consider all the circumstances in deciding whether the two books invalidate each other, or whether one must prevail.

Country: Lesotho

COMPANIES ACT

PART 7. — GENERAL.

✍ Forms of Registers, Books: Inspection and production.

Article 293. (1) Any register, index, minute book or book of account required by this Act to be kept by a company or external company may be kept either by making entries in books or by recording the matters in question in any other manner.

(2) Where any such register, index, minute book or book of account is not kept by making entries in a bound book, but by some other means, adequate precautions shall be taken for guarding against falsification and for facilitating its discovery.

(3) Any such register, index, minute book or account and every other book or document required by this Act to be kept by a company or external company and every document required by this Act or by a company's memorandum or articles to be issued or circulated by a company or external company shall be

legibly printed in English or the Sesotho language.

(4) Where default is made in complying with sub-section (2) or (3) of this section the company or external company and every officer of the company or external company who is in default shall be guilty of an offence and liable to a fine not exceeding two hundred rand and to a further fine not exceeding ten rand for every day during which the offence continues.

Country: Libya

ASSOCIATIONS LAW

CHAPTER 8. — CORPORATE RECORDS AND REPORTS.

✍ **S8.1. Requirements for keeping books of account, minutes and records of shareholders.**

1. *Books of account and minutes.* Every domestic corporation shall keep correct and complete books and records of account and shall keep minutes of all meetings of shareholders, of actions taken on consent by shareholders, of all meetings of the board of directors, of actions taken on consent by directors and of meetings of the executive committee, if any. A resident domestic corporation shall keep such books and records in Liberia.

2. *Records of shareholders.* Every domestic corporation shall keep a record containing the names and address of all registered shareholders, the number and class of shares held by each and the dates when they respectively became the owners of record thereof. In addition, any such corporation which issues bearer shares shall maintain a record of all certificates issued in bearer form, including the number, class and dates of issuance of such certificates. A resident domestic corporation shall keep the records required to be maintained by this paragraph at the office of the corporation in Liberia or at the office of its transfer agent or registrar in Liberia.

2. *Form of records.* Any of the foregoing books, minutes or records may be in written form or in any other form capable of being converted into written form within a reasonable time.

PART 8. — COMMERCIAL CODE RULES ON BOOKS OF ACCOUNT AND BALANCE SHEETS.

✍ **Journal**

The Libyan Commercial Code stipulates that every business must keep at least a journal where all daily operations relating to the business are entered and a book recording inventories and balances.

☞ **Court Authorization:**

Before use, these journals and books must be certified and stamped by the Court of First Instance, which numbers the pages of each book or folio, dates them, and indicates their use. All other invoices and correspondence related to the transaction of business are required to be kept in an orderly manner, prepared for inspection by duly authorized officials at any time. Records are to be retained for five years.

☞ **Books To Be Kept By Corporations:**

In addition to journal and inventory books, corporations are obliged to maintain the following:

(1) Shareholders books, in which are recorded all transactions and payments related to shares;

(2) Bond (obligation) books, showing the amount of bonds issued, those expired, and giving the names of bondholders, as well as all other information related to issuance and redemption of bonds;

(3) Record books of the meetings and deliberations of the administrative or management council, the auditing board, the executive committee (if such exists), and assemblies of bondholders, if bonds have been issued, and assemblies of shareholders.

Country: Luxembourg

PART 1. LAW OF COMMERCIAL COMPANIES.

JOINT STOCK CORPORATIONS

✍ **Business Records.**

The Commercial Code requires that the following books and records are kept:

(1) Inventory Book;

(2) official Journal; and

(3) copies of all correspondence.

If correction are needed in the books, new entries must be made as no erasures are permitted.

All books and correspondence must be kept for ten years.

Country: Malaysia

COMPANIES ACT, 1965

PART VI. — ACCOUNTS AND AUDIT.

Division 1. — Accounts (Companies Act).

✍ **s167. Accounts to be Kept** (1) Every company and the directors and managers thereof shall cause to be kept such accounting and other records as will sufficiently explain the transactions and financial position of the company and enable true and fair profit and loss accounts and balance-sheets and any documents required to be attached thereto to be prepared from time to time, and shall cause those records to be kept in such manner as to enable them to be conveniently and properly audited.

(1A) Every company and the directors and managers thereof shall cause appropriate entries to be made in the accounting and other records within sixty days of the completion of the transactions to which they relate.

(2) The company shall retain the records referred to in subsection (1) for seven years after the completions of the transactions or operations to which they respectively relate.

(3) The records referred to in subsection (1) shall be kept at the registered office of the company or at such other place in Malaysia as the directors think fit and shall at all times be open to inspection by the directors.

(4) Notwithstanding the provisons in subsection (3), the accounting and other records of operations outside Malaysia may be kept by the company at a place outside Malaysia and there shall be sent to and kept at a place in Malaysia and be at all times open to inspection by the directors, such statements and returns with respect to the business dealt with in the records so kept as will enable to be prepared true and fair profit and loss accounts and balance sheets and any documents required to be attached thereto.

(5) If any accounting and other records are kept at a place outside Malaysia pursuant to subsection (4), the company shall, if required by the Registrar to produce those records at a place in Malaysia, comply with the requirements.

(6) The Court may in any particular case order that the

accounting and other records of a company be open to inspection by an approved company auditor acting for a director, but only upon an undertaking in writing given to the Court that information acquired by the auditor during his inspection shall not be disclosed by him except to that director.

(7) If default is made in complying with this section the company and every officer of the company who is in default shall be guilty of an offence against this Act.

Penalty: Imprisonment for six months or 5,000 ringgit or both.

Country: Mexico

COMMERCIAL CODE

BOOK 1. COMMERCIAL CODE

✍ CHAPTER 3. — MERCANTILE BOOKKEEPING.

Article 33. (1) A merchant is obliged to take and maintain an adequate system of accounting. This system may be kept by means of instruments, resources and entry systems and processing which best accommodates the particular characteristics of the business, but in every case if must satisfy the following requirements:

A) It shall permit identification of individual transactions and their characteristics, as well as connect such individual transactions with their original substantiating documents.

B) It shall permit an audit of the progression from individual transactions to their aggregation resulting in the final accounting figures, and vice- versa.

C) It shall permit the preparation of statements which shall be included in the financial information of the business.

D) It shall permit the connection and audit between the figures of such statements, aggregations of the accounts and the individual transactions.

E) It shall include the systems of internal control and verification necessary for impeding the omission of the recording of the transactions, for assuring the correction of the accounting records and for assuring the correction of the resulting figures.

Article 34. Whatever the bookkeeping system employed, the books must be duly bound, lined and the pages of the ledger numbered and, in the case of legal entities, the book or books of minutes must be kept. The binding of these books may be done later, within the three months following the close of the fiscal year; without prejudice to the special requirements the fiscal laws and regulations establish for records and documents relating to the fiscal obligations of the merchant.

Article 35. The names or designations of the accounts, their balance at the end of the immediately preceding recording period, the total flow of charge or credit on each account in the period and their fiscal balance must be recorded in the ledger as a minimum, and at least once a month. More particulars may be kept for offices, segments of activity or any other classification, but in all cases a general ledger must exist in which all the transactions of the entity are recorded.

Article 36. In the book or books of minutes all the resolutions relative to the progress of the business made by the assemblies or meetings of members, partners or shareholders, and as the case may be, of boards of directors, shall be recorded.

Article 37. All the records to which this chapter refers must be kept in Spanish, even if the merchant is a foreigner. If the merchant does not comply with this requirement, he will incur a fine of not less than 25,000.00 pesos, which shall not exceed 5% of his capital, and the corresponding authorities may order that he translate them into Spanish by means of a duly recognized expert translator, charging all the costs of such translation to the merchant's account.

Article 38. A merchant must keep the original vouchers of his transactions, duly filed in the manner in which they may be related to such transactions and with the record which has been made of them, and they must be kept for a minimum period of 10 years.

Article 41. The following shall be expressed in the Minute Book to be kept by each company for General Meetings: the date, the people present at the meeting, the number of shares which each one represents, the number of votes which he may make use of and the resolutions passed, which must be recorded verbatim; when the voting is not by ayes and nays, the votes cast, care being taken to record everything which may conduce to a complete understanding of what was resolved. In the case of Minutes of Meetings of the Board of Directors, the following particulars only shall be entered: the date, names of the people present, and an account of the resolutions passed. These shall be evidenced by the signatures of the persons to whom the By-Laws give this power.

☞ CHAPTER 14. — INSTRUMENTS AND DOCUMENTS.

Article 1237. Public instruments are those reputed to be such by civil law and the records of mercantile contracts entered into with the intervention of a broker and legalized by him, in accordance with the provisions of this Code.

Article 1238. Private document is any other document under the provisions of the preceding article.

Article 1239. Whenever one of the litigants desires an ordinary or official copy of a part of a document or paper which is found in the public archives or in the records of brokers, the opposing party has the right to secure the addition of any part of said document at his own expense.

Article 1240. The production of documents existing in any other District than that in which the proceedings are held shall be compelled by letters rogatory addressed by the judge taking cognizance of the case to the place where the documents are located.

Article 1241. The private documents and correspondence proceeding from one of the interested parties, filed in a suit as evidence and not objected to by the opposing party, shall be considered as admitted and shall be effective as if they were expressly recognized. The express recognition may be demanded if the person who files them so requests it; for this purpose the originals shall be manifested to whoever must inspect them and the latter shall be allowed to see the entire document, not only the signature.

Article 1242. Private documents shall be filed in their originals, and when they are part of a book, file or dossier, the part that the interested parties stipulate shall be exhibited collated.

Article 1243. If the document is found in the books or papers of a commercial or industrial establishment, the party who requests the document or the voucher, must establish precisely which it is, and the certified copy shall be taken in the office of the establishment, provided that the directors thereof are not obligated to take the accounting books to the court, but only to present the portions or documents designated.

Article 1244. The provisions of Articles 1217 to 1219, 1221 to 1287 (items I and II) shall be observed in the acknowledgment proceedings.

Article 1245. A private document can only be acknowledged by the person who signed it or who mandated its formulation, or their legitimate representative holding a special power-of-attorney or power-of-attorney containing a special clause.

Article 1246. Authentic instruments issued by the Federal Authorities shall constitute evidence all over the Republic of Mexico without the need of legalization.

☞ CHAPTER 20. — VALUE OF EVIDENCE.

Article 1295. In order to estimate the force of the merchants' books as evidence, the following rules shall be observed:

I. Merchants' books shall constitute evidence against them, no proof being admitted to the contrary; but the opposing party cannot accept the entries which are favorable and reject those which are unfavorable to him, for, having accepted this means of evidence, he shall be subject to the result arrived at from the whole, equal consideration being given to all the entries relating to the question in litigation.

II. If the entries in the books kept by two merchants disagree, and one of them has kept his books with all the formalities required by this Code while the books of the other have some defect or lack some of the requisites specified in this same Code, the entries in the books properly kept shall prevail against those in the defective books, unless the contrary is demonstrated by other proof admissible in law.

III. If one of the merchants does not present his books or states that he has none, those of the other party, kept with all the legal formalities, shall be accepted as evidence against him, unless he proves that the lack of such books is due to force majeure, and always provided that evidence against the entries produced may be given by other methods admissible in law.

IV. If the merchants' books fulfill all the legal requisites but conflict with one another, the judge or the tribunal shall decide on the remaining evidence, estimating them according to the general rules of law.

* * * * *

Country: New Zealand

THE STATUTES OF NEW ZEALAND

THE COMPANIES ACT, 1993

PART 16. MISCELLANEOUS

✍ Forms of Registers, Books, Minutes, etc.

459. Form of registers, minute books, etc. —

(1) Any register, index, minute book, or accounting records required by this Act to be kept by a company may be kept either by making entries in bound books or by recording the matters in question in any other manner.

(2) Where any such register, index, minute book, or accounting records is not kept by making entries in a bound book, but by some other means, adequate precautions shall be taken for guarding against falsification and facilitating its discovery, and where default if made in complying with this subsection, the company and every officer of the company who is in default shall be liable to a fine not exceeding $100 and further shall be liable to a default fine.

THE EVIDENCE ACT OF 1908

☞ Documentary Evidence

Interpretation and savings

2.(1)In this Part of this Act —

"Document" includes books, maps, plans, drawings, and photographs:

"Statement" includes any representation of fact, whether made in words or otherwise:

"Proceedings" includes arbitrations and references and "Court" shall be construed accordingly.

(2) Nothing in this Part of this Act shall —

(a) Prejudice the admissibility of any evidence which would, apart from the provisions of this Part, be admissible; or

(b) Enable documentary evidence to be given as to any declaration relating to a matter of pedigree, if that declaration would not have been admissible as evidence if this Part had not been passed.

Admissibility of documentary evidence as to facts in issue

3.(1) In any civil proceeding where direct oral evidence of a fact would be admissible, any statement made by a person in a document and tending to establish that fact shall, on production of the original document, be admissible as evidence of that fact if the following conditions are satisfied, that is to say —

(a) If the maker of the statement either —

(i) Had personal knowledge of the matters dealt with by the statement; or

(ii) Where the document in question is or forms part of a record purporting to be a continuous record, made the statement (in so far as the matters dealt with thereby are not within his personal knowledge) in the performance of a duty to record information supplied to him by a person who had, or might reasonably be supposed to have, personal knowledge of those matters; and

(b) If the maker of the statement is called as a witness in the proceedings:

Provided that the condition that the maker of the statement shall be called as a witness need not be satisfied if he is dead, or unfit by reason of his bodily or mental condition to attend as a witness, or if he is beyond the seas and it is not reasonably practicable to secure his attendance, or if all reasonable efforts to find him have been made without success.

(2) In any civil proceedings the Court may at any stage of the proceedings, if, having regard to all the circumstances of the case, it is satisfied that undue delay or expense would otherwise be caused, order that such a statement as is mentioned in subsection one of this section shall be admissible as evidence, or may, without any such order having been made, admit such a statement in evidence —

(a) Notwithstanding that the maker of the statement is available but is not called as a witness:

(b) Notwithstanding that the original document is not produced, if in lieu thereof there is produced a copy of the original document or of the material part thereof certified to be a true copy in such manner as may be specified in the order or as the Court may approve, as the case may be.

(3) Nothing in this section shall render admissible as evidence any statement made by a person interested at a time when proceedings were pending or anticipated involving a dispute as to any fact which the statement might tend to establish.

(4) For the purposes of this section a statement in a document shall not be deemed to have been made by a person unless the document or the material part thereof was written, made, or produced by him with his own hand, or was signed or initialed by him or otherwise recognised by him in writing as one for the accuracy of which he is responsible.

(5) For the purpose of deciding whether or not a statement is admissible as evidence by virtue of the foregoing provisions, the Court may draw any reasonable inference from the form or contents of the document in which the statement is contained, or from any other circumstances, and may, in deciding whether or not a person is fit to attend as a witness, act on a certificate purporting to be the certificate of a registered medical practitioner, and where the proceedings are with a jury, the Court may in its discretion reject the statement, notwithstanding that the

requirements of this section are satisfied with respect thereto, if for any reason it appears to it to be inexpedient in the interests of justice that the statement should be admitted.

☞ Verification of Documents

Verification of documents executed out of New Zealand

6.(1) Every document of any kind duly executed out of New Zealand (whether before or after the commencement of this Act) shall, so far as regards the execution thereof, be admissible in evidence in any Court and before any person acting judicially if the execution is verified in any of the following ways, that is to say:

(a) Where the document is executed in any foreign country, then —

(i) If it purports to be executed before a Commonwealth representative exercising his functions in that country and to be sealed with his seal of office (if any), or if there is endorsed thereon or annexed thereto a declaration of the due execution thereof purporting to be made by an attesting witness thereto before any such Commonwealth representative as aforesaid, and to be sealed as aforesaid; or

(ii) By or before a notary public exercising his office in that country; or

(iii) In any case where the provisions of section nine of the Evidence Amendment Act 1945 apply, in the manner provided in that section:

(b) Where the document is executed in any Commonwealth country, then —

(i) If a manner prescribed by paragraph (a) of this subsection for documents executed in a foreign country; or

(ii) In the manner (if any) prescribed by the law of that country for the verification of documents to be used abroad.

(2) It shall be presumed that any seal or signature impressed, affixed, appended, or subscribed on or to any document tendered in evidence under this section is genuine, and that the person appearing to have signed or attested any such document had in fact authority to sign or attest it, and that any such document was in fact made in accordance with the law under which it purports to have been made, unless the party objecting to the admission of the document proves the contrary.

* * * * *

☞ Photographic Copies

Interpretation

3. For the purposes of the next two succeeding sections, unless the context otherwise requires, —

"Authorised person" means a bank carrying on business in New Zealand, or a company authorised by any Act to administer the estates of deceased persons or other trust estates; and includes such public bodies, local authorities, companies, and persons as are from time to time declared by the Governor-General by Order in Council to be authorised persons for the purposes of the principal Act:

"Document" includes any register, book, map, plan, drawing, or photograph; and also includes any part of a document:

"Film" includes any photographic plate, microfilm, or photostatic negative:

"Government" means the Government of New Zealand; and includes the Public Trustee, the Maori Trustee, and every other Department or instrument of the Executive Government of New Zealand:

"Public record" means any document of such a public nature as to be admissible in evidence on its mere production from the proper custody.

Photographic copies of public records to be evidence

4. A print, whether enlarged or not, from a film of any public record produced or certified by the officer to whose custody the film is entrusted shall be admissible in evidence in all cases in which and for all purposes for which the public record would have been admissible.

Proof of photographic copies of documents of Government and authorised persons

5.(1) A print, whether enlarged or not, from a film of any document kept or held by the Government or by any authorised person shall be admissible in evidence in all cases in which and for all purposes for which the document would have been admissible, upon proof that —

(a) While the document was in the custody or control of the Government or authorised person the film was taken in order to keep a permanent record thereof; and

(b) The document photographed was subsequently destroyed, whether deliberately or otherwise, or was so damaged as to be wholly or partly indecipherable, or was lost, or passed out of the custody or control of the Government or authorised person.

(2) Proof of compliance with the conditions prescribed by this section may be given in respect of any document or group of documents by any one or more of the employees of the Government or authorised person either orally or by affidavit or by statutory declaration.

(3) The death of any person by whom an affidavit or statutory declaration has been made for the purposes of this section shall not affect the admissibility of the affidavit or declaration.

(4) Unless the Court otherwise orders, a notarial copy of any affidavit or statutory declaration made for the purposes of this section shall be admissible in evidence in place of the original affidavit or declaration.

(5) The Governor-General may from time to time, by Order in Council, declare any public body, local authority, company, or person to be an authorised person, or any class of public bodies, local authorities, companies or persons to be authorised persons, for the purposes of the principal Act.

Country: Paraguay

TITLE 3. — BOOKS AND COMMERCIAL DOCUMENTATION.

✍ CHAPTER 1. — GENERAL PROVISIONS.

Article 74. Any merchant whose capital exceeds the amount corresponding to one thousand times the minimum daily wage established for miscellaneous unspecified activities in the Capital, shall be obligated to register, in such books as considered necessary to the professional accountant, an ordered regular accounting system, adequate to the characteristics and nature of his activities, which shall permit the determination of his patrimonial situation and the results of his activity. He must also keep his business correspondence and the accounting documentation which the nature of his commercial affairs demand.

Article 75. The number of books and the accounting system shall be left to the judgment of the merchant, duly keeping at least a Day-book (Journal) and an inventory, without prejudice to other books required for any certain class of activities.

Article 76. Judicial authorization shall be required for the use of mechanical methods or other modern systems of accounting, unless there is a provision to the contrary by special laws. Such judicial authorization shall be given by an established resolution, after receiving the opinion of the competent controller in authority, The court may also resort to antecedents used in analogous cases, or to the opinion of an expert designated de officio. The resolution shall be recorded in the Public Registry of Commerce.

The journal must be kept with global entries which shall not include periods greater than one month. The accounting method must permit the individualization of the operations, as well as their corresponding debit and credit accounts and their subsequent verification.

Article 78. Before books of commerce can be used, they must be presented to the Public Register of Commerce numbered on all their pages, in order that they shall be rubricated or stamped, and the number of books contained therein shall be recorded in a dated not on their first page.

The pages or microfiches of other accounting systems authorized shall comply with the same requirement. The Register shall close used books with an indication of the date and the number of books used on the last page.

Article 79. Accounting books shall be kept in the official language, the transactions being entered chronologically without interlineations, marginal markings or blank spaces. Neither erasures nor any other alteration can be made in them, and if any correction might be necessary, it must be made by means of a corresponding counter-entry. It is prohibited to mutilate any part of any book, whether obligatory or auxiliary, to put out or not use any pages, as well as alter the binding and pagination.

Article 80. Daily transactions of the merchant shall be entered in the Journal in detail in accordance with the order in which they were affected, so that each item shall result in the credit and debit in the negotiation carried out.

Article 81. If the merchant keeps a Cash book it shall be unnecessary that he enter the payments which he effects or receives in cash into the Journal. In this case, the Cash book shall be considered as an integral part of the Journal.

Article 82. The following shall be recorded in the inventory book:

a) the patrimonial situation at the beginning of operations, with an indication and valuation of the assets and liabilities; and,

b) the patrimonial situation and the results corresponding to the finalization of each fiscal year, showing the profits and losses.

In this book the list of the inventory must be consigned when the same is not listed in other registers; likewise, complementary accounting statements may be included.

Article 83. Every merchant must compound, within the first three months of each year, the general balance sheet of his operations, which shall contain a precise report of his assets, credits and stocks, as well as his pending obligations on the date of the compilement.

Article 84. The duration of each fiscal period may not exceed one year.

Article 85. The accounting books and records must be kept for five years as from the date of the last entry made in them. During this same time, the vouchers shall be kept in an ordered form, in a mode in which their verification shall be possible; this period shall be computed from the date on which the vouchers were handed over.

CHAPTER 2. — BOOKS OF COMPANIES.

Article 86. Every company shall be obligated to keep the books, records and documentation to which articles 74 and 75 refer, as well as those required by its nature.

Article 87. Stock corporation must also keep the following:

a) the Book of Stock Records which shall contain:

1) the name and surname of the subscribers, the number and the series of stocks subscribed and the payments made;

2) the transfer of registered shares, the date on which such transfer was verified and the obligations belonging to them;

3) specification of stocks which shall be converted into bearer shares and of the securities which shall be issued in exchange for them;

4) the number of shares given in guarantee of good performance of the administrators of the company, if the by-laws so require.

b) the Book of Bonds Records, in which shall be entered the amount of those issued and of those paid off, and name and surname of the bond-holders with registered titles, their transfer and data relative to it, and the payment of interest.

c) the Book of Attendance at the meetings;

d) the Book of Acts of the general meetings and of the meetings of the board of directors or governing board. Unless there exists a contrary provision in the by-laws, the acts of the general meetings shall be signed by the president and at least two members designated for the purpose. That of the sessions of the board of directors shall be signed by all those who attend.

Article 88. Copies of the balance sheet with the profit and loss statement must be deposited at company headquarters at the disposal of the members no less than 15 days in advance of their consideration at the general meeting. Also, copies of the minutes of the board of directors and of the auditor's report shall be kept at the disposal of the members.

☞ CHAPTER 3. — EXHIBITION OF THE BOOKS AND THE RESULTING EVIDENCE.

Article 95. Except for special provisions of public law, the general exhibition of books, records and vouchers of merchants may only be decreed at the request of one party, in estate proceedings, community property, or company administration or mercantile management for the account of another and in some cases of liquidation.

In the cases of a convocation of a creditors' meeting and bankruptcy, the provisions of the respective law shall rule.

Article 96. Outside of the cases specified in the preceding article, partial exhibition of the commercial books may only be judicially provided at the request of one party or de officio against the will of their owners, and then only to the extent that the items are related to the point or question dealt with.

In this case, the recognition of the books exhibited shall be verified by the presence of their owner or of the person representing him.

Article 97. The exhibition of the books may only be decreed when their owner is a party in a lawsuit, but the opposition to their exhibition may only be made by him, and not by the other parties. Nevertheless, the exhibition of the books of brokers and auctioneers may proceed, even if they are not parties in a lawsuit, provided that they have intervened in the operation in question.

Article 98. When a merchant keeps auxiliary books with the formality established for principals, the exhibition of them shall be subject to the rules established in the three preceding articles.

Article 99. The obligation to exhibit the accounting books shall include not only the heirs of merchants, but also the successor to a singular title, and to whoever the assets and liabilities of the merchant shall have been transferred.

Article 100. The books, records and vouchers shall be admitted in court as a means of proof of method, under the conditions which shall be established in the following articles of this section.

Article 101. The entries of the books or records and their vouchers shall be evidence against the merchants to whom they belong or their successors; but the adversary may not accept the entries and vouchers which are favorable to him and discard those which prejudice him.

Article 102. Among merchants and in acts proper to their business, the entries of the books and records kept in proper form shall be evidence in their favor or their successors, when their adversary does not present entries to the contrary kept in due form or other full and conclusive evidence, duly taking into account for this purpose, the nature of the litigation and the other evidence produced.

Article 103. When the entries of the books, records and their vouchers, kept in proper form, are contradictory, this method of evidence shall be rescinded and other means will be produced.

Article 104. In the case of non-commercial acts or those completed between a merchant and one who is not a merchant, the commercial books and records shall only be considered as the beginning of evidence.

Country: Portugal

✍ TITLE 4. — ACCOUNTING.

Article 29. Function of commercial books.

Every merchant is obligated to keep books on his commercial operations and capital in a recognizable, clear and precise manner.

Article 30. Method of accounting and its limits.

The number and kinds of books of each merchant and their arrangement shall remain entirely at his discretion, except for those books which the law specifies as indispensable.

Article 31. Obligatory books.

The following books are indispensable and every merchant must keep them:

Inventory and financial statement book;
Daily Journal;
Ledger;
Correspondence book.

Sole Paragraph: Companies must also keep books of minutes of meetings and other special records.

Article 32. Formalities provided for the inventory and daily journal.

The inventory and the daily journal must be previously legalized by the presiding judge of the commercial court of the jurisdiction, who shall number and sign all pages, as well as certify the first and last pages of the identification of the merchant and the number of pages contained.

1. In the judicial districts of Lisbon and Porto the commission for numbering and signing may be given to any notary public.

2. If after the numbering and signing is begun, the judge or person delegated by him to do so, cannot finish it, a person who has been legally substituted or who has the new commission shall continue it, and the document shall mention that circumstances on its last page.

Article 33. Function of the inventory and financial statement book.

The inventory and financial statement book must contain a description of all the assets and liabilities of the merchant, at the beginning of and throughout his commercial activity, as well as his balance sheets.

Article 34. Function and arrangement of the daily journal.

In the daily journal merchants shall register, day by day, in chronological order and separately, each of their transactions.

1. If entries for certain accounts are in great number, or when the transactions to be recorded are not performed at the main offices, subsidiary books may be kept, and their totals recorded, weekly, fortnightly or monthly in the daily journal. If auxiliary books are kept, they must be kept regularly, clearly and chronologically.

2. Retail merchants are not obligated to keep their sales individually in the daily journals; it is sufficient that the total amount of the transactions be recorded each day.

Article 35. Function and form of the ledger.

The ledger shall record the movement of all the operations of the day, organized by debit and credit, in relation to each one of the respective accounts, in order to know at any moment the exact position of any of them, without the necessity of examining and separating all the entries chronologically registered in the daily journal.

Article 36. Function of the correspondence book.

The correspondence book contains in chronological order the complete text, of every letter or telegram, either copied or in the original, sent by the merchant in connection with his activity.

Article 37. Minute books of companies.

Minute books of companies record the minutes of meetings held by partners, interested persons or administrators, one book for each type of meeting and stating the date of and the reason for the meeting, the names of assistants, votes issued, decisions made and any other related information. They must be undersigned by those attending.

Article 38. Bookkeeper.

Every merchant may either keep his own mercantile accounting or authorize another person to do so.

Sole Paragraph. If the merchant does not keep his own books, it shall be presumed that he has authorized another person to do so.

Article 39. Formal accounting requirements.

Entries in commercial accounting books shall be made without blanks, erasures or figures in the margins.

Sole Paragraph. If there is an error or omission in any entry, it shall be corrected by means of authorization.

Article 40. Obligation to keep correspondence books and documents.

Every merchant is obligated to file the correspondence and telegrams he receives, documents which are receipts for payments made, and books of mercantile documentation for a period of 10 years.

Article 41. Prohibition of search and other examinations.

No authority, court or tribunal may make or order a search or any investigation to examine whether or not the merchant is duly keeping his mercantile documentation books.

Article 42. A judicial exhibition of the complete set of books.

A judicial exhibition of the commercial documentation books in their entirety, and of documents relative to them, may be ordered in favor of interested parties in questions of universal succession, community property or partnership, and in the case of bankruptcy.

Article 43. Examination of books and documents.

In the cases provided in the preceding article the merchant's books and documents may be examined upon petition of the party or de officio, when the person to whom they belong has an interest or liability in the question.

Sole Paragraph: The examination of the merchant's books and documents shall take place in his presence, and shall be limited to verifying and extracting specific points relative to the question.

Article 44. Force of evidence of commercial documentary books.

Commercial documentary books may be admitted in court as evidence between merchants in commercial actions, in the following terms:

1. The items entered into the commercial books, even when not regularly arranged, shall prove against the merchants to whom they belong; the plaintiffs, however, who use such items,

must also equally accept those which are prejudicial to them;

2. Items entered into commercial books which are regularly arranged, shall be evidence in favor of their respective proprietors, insofar as the other litigant does not present contrary items in books arranged on the same terms or evidence to the contrary;

3. When the combination of mercantile books of one or the other litigant, regularly arranged, results in contradictory evidence, the court shall decide the question by the merit of any other evidence of process;

4. If there is a discrepancy between the items of the books or one or the other merchant, those which are regularly arranged shall be accepted and other should not be accepted, unless there is a demonstration of the contrary by means of other directly admissible evidence.

Sole Paragraph: If a merchant does not keep books, or refuses to present them, those of the other litigant shall be admitted as evidence against him, as long as they are duly arranged, unless his failure to present them is due to a case of force majeure, and provided that other evidence admissible in court does not refute the entries exhibited.

Country: Russia

SOVIET CIVIL LAW

PRIVATE RIGHTS AND THEIR BACKGROUND UNDER THE SOVIET REGIME

CODE OF CIVIL PROCEDURE OF THE RUSSIAN SOCIALIST FEDERATED SOVIET REPUBLIC, AS AMENDED TO JULY 1, 1947

PART 1.

CHAPTER 15. PARTICULAR FORMS OF EVIDENCE.

☞ **2. Written Evidence.**

140. Written evidence, such as all written instruments, documents, and correspondence of a business or private character shall be presented to the court by the parties themselves, or they may be procured by request of the court.

141. The party requesting, through the court, that the other party, or persons who are not parties in the case, submit certain documents must describe the required documents in detail, indicating the reason for his belief that the document is in the possession of the adverse party, or in that of other persons, and the circumstances which may be substantiated by said documents.

142. Documents requested by the court from government institutions and private persons shall be delivered directly to the court. The court may issue a certificate to the parties authorizing them to obtain documents, copies, and all kinds of information from government institutions and private persons for the purpose of submission to the court.

143. Institutions and persons described in the preceding section who are unable to submit to the court, within the specified period, the document requested must give notice thereof to the court, indicating the reason. Where the reason is not justifiable, or in case of failure so to notify the court, the court may impose a fine in accordance with Section 52 of the present Code.

144. If submission of documents to the court is difficult, for example, by reason of their large number, or because only some of them are relevant, the court may demand the submission of duly certified excerpts of have the documents examined on the premises.

145. Documents submitted in a language other than that in which the proceedings are conducted shall be accompanied by proper translations.

146. Written evidence may be contested except in cases especially provided for by law.

147. [Repealed]

148. If the adverse party alleges that a document filed in the case is a forgery, the party filing it may waive use of the document as evidence in the case and may move the court that the trial of the case be continued on the basis of other evidence.

149. If, at the request of the party who submitted the suspected document (Section 148), the document remains in the file as evidence, the party who alleges forgery must submit proof of the allegation within a period fixed by the court.

150. If an allegation concerning the forgery of a document is made in a court trying a civil case, the court shall verify the genuineness of the document by one of the following methods:

(a) By examining the document and comparing it with other documents;

(b) By examination of witnesses specified in the document, of those upon whom the parties rely, as well as those called by the court on its own motion;

(c) By comparing the writing and signatures on the suspected document with the signature of the same person on other undisputed documents;

(d) By means of expert testimony.

151. If the court becomes convinced that the document is a forgery, the court shall cause the removal of the document from the file of evidence submitted and shall cause the institution of a criminal prosecution.

Country: Singapore

COMPANIES ACT

PART 2. ADMINISTRATION OF ACT.

✪ **Section 12. Registers.** The Registrar shall, subject to this Act, keep such registers as he considers necessary in such form as he thinks fit.

* * * * *

✪ **Section 12A. Electronic filing service.**

(1) (Amended by 22/93) Where the Registry of Companies provides a service, whether before or after 15 May 1987, for the use of subscribers, whereby documents required under this Act may be filed electronically with the Registry, neither the Government nor any of its employees no any authorized agents shall be liable for any loss or damage, suffered by any person by reason of any errors or omissions, of whatever nature or however caused, appearing in any document obtained by any person under the service if such errors or omissions are made in good faith and in the ordinary course of the discharge of the duties of these employees or authorized agents or have occurred or arisen as a result of any defect or breakdown in the service or in any of the equipment used for the service.

(2) *Evidentiary value of copies of electronically filed documents certified by the Registrar.* A copy of or extract from any document electronically filed with the registry of Companies under subsection (1) supplied or issued by the registrar and certified to be a true copy or extract thereof under the hand and seal of the registrar shall in any proceedings be admissible in evidence as of equal validity with the original document.

(3) *Certificate in respect of documents filed electronically.* The Registrar may require a certificate, in respect of any document to

be filed electronically, from the party filing the document certifying to the effect that any stamp fee payable for the document has been duly paid and that he has witnessed the signing and execution of the document or that the document has been duly signed and executed by the person concerned and that such signing or execution has been duly witnessed by a notary public or a solicitor or approved company auditor or a person with such other qualifications as may be prescribed for the purposes of this section. The Registrar may require the production of any document that has been signed and executed under this subsection.

PART 6. ACCOUNTS AND AUDIT.

Division 1. — Accounts.

✍ **§ 199. Accounting records and systems of control.** (1) Every company and the directors and managers thereof shall cause to be kept such accounting and other records as will sufficiently explain the transactions and financial position of the company and enable true and fair profit and loss accounts and balance sheets and any documents required to be attached thereto to be prepared from time to time, and shall cause those records to be kept in such manner as to enable them to be conveniently and properly audited.

(2) The company shall retain the records referred to in subsection (1) for 7 years after the completion of the transactions or operations to which they respectively relate.

(2A) Every public company and every subsidiary of a public company shall devise and maintain a system of internal accounting controls sufficient to provide a reasonable assurance that —

(a) assets are safeguarded against loss from unauthorized use or disposition; and

(b) transactions are properly authorized and that they are recorded as necessary to permit the preparation of true and fair profit and loss accounts and balance sheets and to maintain accountability of assets.

(3) The records referred to in subsection (1) shall be kept at the registered office of the company or at such other place as the directors think fit and shall at all times be open to inspection by the directors.

(4) If accounting and other records are kept by the company at a place outside Singapore there shall be sent to and kept at a place in Singapore and be at all times open to inspection by the directors such statements and returns with respect to the business dealt with in the records so kept as will enable to be prepared true and fair profit and loss accounts and balance sheets and any documents required to be attached thereto.

(5) The Court may in any particular case order that the accounting and other records of a company be open to inspection by an approved company auditor acting for a director, but only upon an undertaking in writing given to the Court that information required by the auditor during his inspection shall not be disclosed by him except to that director.

(6) If default is made in complying with this section, the company and every officer of the company who is in default shall be guilty of an offence and shall be liable on conviction to a fine not exceeding $2,000 or to imprisonment for a term not exceeding 3 months and also to a default penalty.

SINGAPORE CIVIL CODE

✍ **§ 1.2(C)(1). Section 5 of the Civil Law Act.**

5(1) Subject to the provisions of this section, in all questions or issues which arise or which have to be decided in Singapore with respect to the law of partnerships, corporations, banks and banking, principals and agents, carriers by air, land and sea, marine insurance, average, life and fire insurance, and with respect to mercantile law generally, the law with respect to those matters to be administered shall be the same as would be administered in England in the like case, at the corresponding period, if such question or issue had arisen or had to be decided in England, unless in any case other provision is or shall be made by any law having force in Singapore.

* * * * *

PART 12. — GENERAL DIVISION ENFORCEMENT OF ACT.

✍ **§ 395. Form of registers, etc.**

(1) For the purpose of this Act, any register, index, minute book or books of account may be kept either by making entries in a bound books or by recording the matters in question in any other permanent manner.

(2) Where any register, index, minute book or book of account required by this Act to be kept is not kept by making entries in a bound book, but by some other means —

(a) reasonable precautions shall be taken for guarding against falsification and for facilitating the discover of any falsification; and

(b) proper facilities shall be provided to enable the register, index, minute book or book of account to be inspected,

and, where default is made in complying with the subsection, the company and every officer of the company who is in default shall be guilty of an offence and shall be liable on conviction to a fine not exceeding $1,000 and also to a default penalty.

Country: South Africa

CHAPTER 11. ACCOUNTING AND DISCLOSURE

ACCOUNTING RECORDS

✍ **§ 284. Duty of Company to keep Accounting Records.**

(1) Every company shall keep in one of the official languages of the Republic such accounting records as are necessary fairly to present the state of affairs and business of the company and to explain the transactions and financial position of the trade or business of the company, including —

(a) records showing the assets and liabilities of the company;

(b) a register of fixed assets showing the respective dates of acquisition and the cost thereof, depreciation, if any, the respective dates of any disposals and the consideration received in respect thereof: Provided that in respect of fixed assets acquired before the commencement of this Act, a company may, as at the end of its first financial year after the said commencement, take an inventory of all fixed assets and make a realistic allocation of the total value of fixed assets as shown in the financial statements as at that date over the inventory of assets;

(c) records containing entries from day to day in sufficient detail of all cash received and paid out and of the matters in respect of which receipts and payments take place;

(d) where the trade or business of the company has involved dealings in goods, records of all goods sold and purchased and (except in the case of ordinary retail trade) records showing the goods and the buyers and the sellers thereof in sufficient detail to enable the nature of those goods and those buyers and sellers to be identified; and

(e) statements of the annual stocktaking.

(2) The accounting records referred to in subsection (1) may be kept either by making entries in bound books or by recording the matters in question in any other manner, and where such records are not kept by making entries in bound books, adequate precautions shall be taken for guarding against falsification and facilitating its discovery.

* * * * *

Country: Spain

REGULATIONS RELATIVE TO THE COMMERCIAL CODE

BOOK 1. COMMERCIAL ENTERPRISES AND COMMERCE IN GENERAL

✍ TITLE 3. — BOOKKEEPING AND ACCOUNTS IN COMMERCE.

33. Every merchant must keep orderly accounting records which are adequate for their mercantile activity and must necessarily keep an inventory book and balance and other Journals, without prejudice to that which is provided in special laws or provisions.

Mercantile companies shall also keep a book or books of transactions, in which they shall spread upon the record all the decisions made by the General Meetings and other collective organs of the company.

34. Merchants may also keep such books, registers and documentation which they esteem convenient, in accordance with the accounting system which they adopt.

Those books shall not be subject to the provisions in article 36, even if those which might be considered opportune are legalized.

36. Merchants shall present the books which they are compelled to keep, stamped and page-numbered, to the organs of the Municipal Justice Department of the place where their mercantile establishment is located in order that, before they use the first page of each of them, a formality shall be signed by those who had taken the book. The stamp of the Judge who authorizes them shall also be stamped on all the pages of each book.

Nevertheless, the writing of entries and annotations by any qualified procedure on pages which shall have been stamped afterwards correlatively in order to form the obligatory books, shall be validated before the end of the four months following the date of the close of the fiscal year, except the book of inventories and balances which shall be validated within the month following each one of the transcriptions ordered by Article 37.

A merchant may demand that those validations performed by the organs of the Municipal Justice should take place in his own establishment.

The formation of books and the validation to which the preceding paragraphs refer shall be effected in the manner and with the guarantees which shall be determined by regulations, the successive numbering of the books being mandatory in any case.

Country: Sri Lanka

COMPANIES ACT OF 1982

✍ PART 4. MANAGEMENT AND ADMINISTRATION.

106. Form of registers, etc. (1) Any register, index or book of account required by this Act to be kept by a company may be kept either by making entries in bound books, or by recording the matter in question in any other manner.

(2) Regulations may be made in respect of the application of the provisions of subsection (1) to any minute book required by this Act to be kept by a company. In the absence of any such regulations, such minute book shall be kept by making entries in a bound book, and where it is not so kept, the company and every officer of the company who is in default shall be guilty of an offence and shall be liable to a fine not exceeding five hundred rupees and also to a default fine.

(3) Where any such register, index or other book to which the provisions of subsection (1) apply is not kept by making entries in a bound book, but by some other means, adequate precautions shall be taken for guarding against falsification and facilitating its discovery, and where default is made in complying with the provisions of this subsection, the company and every officer of the company who is in default shall be guilty of an offence and shall be liable to a fine not exceeding five hundred rupees and also to a default fine.

Country: Syria

✍ PART ONE. — COMMERCIAL CODE.

Article 16. Every trader shall keep the following three books at least:

(a) The journal in which shall be entered, day by day, all the transactions relating to the business, and, month by month, the expenses which the trader spends on himself and his family.

(b) The correspondence book, in which shall be copied the correspondence and cables sent by the trader.

(c) The stocktaking and balance sheet book, which shall be drawn once at least in every year.

The trader is also required to keep and arrange all the correspondence and cables he receives.

These are the obligatory books which every trader is supposed to keep. He may keep any other books which he considers necessary for his trade or business. If these books are regularly kept they may be received in evidence.

The above books must have their folio numbered, marked and signed by the Civil Court of First Instance or by the magistrate in towns where there is no Court of First Instance. The above books must be written in the Arabic language, with power given to the Minister of National Economy to fix transitory periods for compliance with the new provisions.

* * * * *

Article 19. Companies are not bound to preserve these books more than ten years.

Country: Turkey

BOOK 1. COMMERCIAL UNDERTAKING.

CHAPTER 5. ACCOUNTING BOOKS.

A) Obligations to Keep Accounting Books.

✍ I. Extent.

Section 66. Every merchant shall keep the books required by character and the importance of his undertaking, with a view to establish the economic and financial situation of his commercial undertaking, the relations of debts due from or owing to him and the results obtained in the course of each year, and particularly the following books, in the Turkish language, subject to the provisions of other laws:

1. If the merchant is a legal entity: the journal, the ledger, the balance- sheet book and the book of resolutions.

2. Commercial undertakings which have no corporate existence and are founded by public law corporations such as the State, provincial governments, municipalities, in order to be managed in accordance with the provisions of public law or to be commercially operated, commercial undertakings founded by associations and other similar commercial organizations which have no corporate existence: the books indicated in the foregoing paragraphs with the exception of the books of resolutions;

3. If the merchant is a real person; the books indicated in the first paragraph with the exception of the book of resolutions or only the exploitation book, according to the character and the importance of his undertaking.

Merchants shall keep regularly, in the form of files, the documents and papers such as letters, notes, telegrams, invoices, statements, bills received in connection with affairs concerning the undertaking, vouchers, indicating payments, copies of letters, notes and telegrams sent, contracts and instruments such as letters of engagement and of guarantee and other deeds of guarantee and judgments of courts.

✍ II — Responsibility.

Section 67. Entries made in these books by the person authorized by the merchant with a view to fulfill his obligations on keeping accounting books are as effective as if they had been made by the merchant.

Responsibility resulting through the total or partial non-existence of books or through their not being kept in accordance with the law or through books and records the conservation whereof is compulsory not being duly preserved, shall lie directly with the owner of the undertaking and, in the case of legal entities, with the members of the administrative organ or with the persons empowered to deal with administrative work and, in the case of organizations and undertaking who have no corporate existence, with the persons authorized to manage the same. These persons may not avoid responsibility by laying the blame on their employees.

Anyone who does not comply with or in pursuance of all the laws with the obligation of keeping the books enumerated in sub-paragraphs 1 to 3 of the first paragraph of Section 66 and is responsible under the second paragraph, shall be liable to a heavy fine of 100 to 1,000 liras. Where the books are not kept in conformity with the law, the persons in charge of keeping the same shall also be liable to the like penalty. Provided that the penal provisions of other laws are reserved.

When magistrates, notaries, registrars and other officials come to know, in connection with official formalities, that a merchant has not complied with the obligations of accounting books, they shall inform thereof the public prosecutor.

✍ III. — Period of Preservation.

Section 68. Anyone who is obliged to keep accounting books and his heirs who continue the undertaking shall preserve the books for a period of ten years after the date of the last entry and the other accounts and vouchers for a period of ten years after the date they carry.

In the event of death of the merchant who is a real person, his heirs and, if he closes his business, himself, shall preserve the books and documents according to the first paragraph. In case, however, of official winding up of the estate, the books and records shall be preserved by the court of peace during the period specified in the first paragraph.

In the event of dissolution, in any manner whatsoever, of general and special partnerships, their books and records shall be handed over by the responsible court of the locality where the head office of the partnership is situate, to one of the partners or to the notary, to be preserved in accordance with the first paragraph, and in the event of dissolution of other partnerships, they will be handed over to the notary. The charges and fees of the notary shall be paid out of the assets of the partnership.

When the books and records which a merchant is obliged to preserve are lost through a disaster such as fire, flood or earthquake and within the legal term the merchant may ask the responsible court of the locality where his undertaking is situate to give him a certificate, within fifteen days after he has come to know of the loss. The court may also other the gathering of such evidence that it will deem necessary. The merchant who has not obtained such a certificate shall be deemed to have refrained from producing his books.

✍ IV. — Obligations of certification and of handling a Declaration.

Section 69. The books indicated under Paragraphs 1 to 3 of Section 66 shall, before being used, be presented in a bounded form, to the notary of the locality where the commercial undertaking is situate. The notary shall ask the merchant to produce the certificate of the trade register, number each page of these books with indelible ink by setting his seal on each page, by indicating the number of pages contained in the book on the first and last pages, and by setting his official seal and signature. After having completed this work he shall communicate directly and immediately to the trade register where the merchant is registered the kind and number of books and the name of the person to whom they belong.

Every merchant shall hand to the registrar a declaration in duplicate stating the nature and kind and number of pages of each of the other books he is obliged to keep and of the books which he wishes to keep, before commencing to use the same. The registrar shall certify one of the copies and return it to the merchant. If the merchant does not comply with this obligation at all or in a manner inconsistent with the law, these books cannot serve a proof in his favour.

B) Various books.

✍ I. Journal.

Section 70. The journal is a book in which are entered the transactions to be passed in the accounts by taking them out of the documents by order of date and arranging them in the form of articles.

The articles of the Journal shall contain at least the following information:

1. The serial no. of the Article (this is not compulsory when using accounting machines);

2. The date;

3. The debtor account; (where collective accounts are used, the name of the final auxiliary account shall be indicated);

4. The creditor account (where collective accounts are used, the name of the final auxiliary account shall be indicated);

5. The amount (those apportioned between the auxiliary accounts shall be indicated in the column concerning remarks);

6. The kind and (if any) the date and No. of the documents on which is based each entry.

The journal shall be bound and its pages numbered consecutively.

Should however, the use of a loose-leaf journal be permitted by fiscal laws, these books may also be used provided they are in conformity with fiscal laws.

Entries to be made in the journal may not be delayed for more than ten days, without any cogent ground.

The Journal shall be presented to the notary at the latest up to the end of January of the new year and certified by him with the mention "seen" written at the end of the last entry, his seal and his signature.

✍ **II. — Ledger.**

Section 71. The Ledger is the book in which are gathered the transactions passed in the Journal, distributed regularly among the various accounts and grouped in the accounts in a classified form.

The entries in the ledger shall contain at least the following data:

1. The date;
2. the No. of the article of the Journal;
3. the amount;
4. in collective accounts, the name of the final auxiliary account.

The provision of the last paragraph of the foregoing section applies also to the Ledger.

✍ **III. — Balance-sheet Book.**

1. In General.

Section 72. The balance-sheet and inventories established at the opening of the undertaking and subsequently at the end of each year are passed in the balance-sheet book.

The data at which the inventory and the balance-sheet are drawn up is called the balance-sheet day".

The financial year may not be less than six months nor more than twelve months. Except as provided to the contrary in the law, the inventory and the balance-sheet to be drawn up for the end of the financial year shall be completed in the course of the first three months of the following financial year.

The inventory and the balance-sheet entered in the balance-sheet book shall be signed by the merchant, in general and special partnerships by all the active partners, in associations of shipowners and in the other partnerships and companies having the capacity of merchant by the persons charged with the administrative affairs and they will be presented to the notary. The last paragraph of Section 70 applies to the formality to be carried out by the notary. The provisions regarding the advertisement of the signed inventory and balance-sheet and their delivery to the authorities are reserved.

The balance-sheet book shall be bound and its pages numbered consecutively.

Country: United Kingdom

HALSBURY'S LAWS OF ENGLAND

COMPANIES ACT OF 1985

✍ **§ 63. Microfilm, etc.**

If he thinks fit, the registrar of companies may accept under any provision of the Companies Acts requiring a document to be delivered to him any material other than a document which contains the information in question and is of a kind approved by him. The delivery to him of material so accepted is sufficient compliance with the provision in question.

VOLUME 7(1). — COMPANIES REGULATED BY THE COMPANIES ACT 1985.

(iv) Commencement of Business and Company Records

✍ **682. Form of company records.**

Any register index, minute book or accounting records required by the Companies Act to be kept by a company may be kept either by making entries in bound books or by recording the matters in question in any other manner. Where any such register, index, minute book or accounting record is not kept by making entries in a bound book, but by some other means, adequate precautions must be taken for guarding against falsification and facilitating its discovery. If default is made in complying with this last requirement, the company and every officer of it who is in default is liable on summary conviction after continued contravention, to a daily default fine not exceeding one-fiftieth of the statutory maximum.

✍ **683. Use of computers for company records.**

The power conferred on a company to keep a register or other record by recording the matters in question otherwise than by making entries in bound books includes power to keep the register or other record by recording those matters otherwise than in a legible form, so long as the recording is capable of being reproduced in legible form. Any provision of an instrument made by a company before 12 February 1979 which requires a register of holders of the company's debentures to be kept in a legible form is to be read as requiring the register to be kept in a legible or nonlegible form.

If any such register or other record of a company, or a register of holders of a company's debentures, is kept by the company by recording the matters in question otherwise than in a legible form, any duty imposed on the company by the Companies Act of 1985 to allow inspection of, or to furnish a copy of, the register or other record or any part of it is to be treated as a duty to allow inspection of, or to furnish, a reproduction of the recording or of the relevant part of it in a legible form. The Secretary of State may by regulation in a statutory instrument make such additional provision as he considers appropriate in connection with such registers or other records as are mentioned above, and are kept as so mentioned; and the regulations may make modifications of provisions of the Companies Act of 1985 relating to such registers or other records.

✍ **§ 706. Delivery to the registrar of documents in legible form.**

(1) This section applies to the delivery to the registrar under any provision of the Companies Acts of documents in legible form.

(2) The documents must —

(*a*) state in a prominent position the registered number of the company to which it relates,

(*b*) satisfy any requirements prescribed by regulations for the purposes of this section, and

(*c*) conform to such requirements as the registrar may specify for the purpose of enabling him to copy the document.

(3) If a document is delivered to the registrar which does not comply with the requirements of this section, he may serve on the person by whom the document was delivered (or, if there are two or more such persons, on any of them) a notice indicating the respect in which the document does not comply.

Where the registrar serves such a notice, then, unless a replacement document —

(*a*) is delivered to him within 14 days after the service of the notice, and

(*b*) complies with the requirements of this section (or section 707) or is not rejected by him for failure to comply with those requirements.

the original document shall be deemed not to have been delivered to him.

But for the purposes of any enactment imposing a penalty for failure to deliver, so far as it imposes a penalty for continued contravention, no account shall be taken of the period between the delivery of the original document and the end of the period of 14 days after service of the registrar's notice.

(5) Regulations made for the purposes of this section may make different provision with respect to different descriptions of the document.

✍ § 707. Delivery to the registrar of documents otherwise than in legible form.

(1) This section applies to the delivery to the registrar under any provision of the Companies Acts of documents otherwise than in legible form.

(2) Any requirement to deliver a document to the registrar, or to deliver a document in the prescribed form, is satisfied by the communication to the registrar of the requisite information in any non-legible form prescribed for the purposes of this section by regulations or approved by the registrar.

(3) Where the document is required to be signed or sealed, it shall instead by authenticated in such manner as may be prescribed by regulations or approved by the registrar.

(4) The document must —

(*a*) contain in a prominent position the registered number of the company to which it relates,

(*b*) satisfy any requirements prescribed by regulations for the purposes of this section, and

(*c*) be furnished in such manner, and conform to such requirements, as the registrar may specify for the purpose of enabling him to read and copy the document.

(5) If a document is delivered to the registrar which does not comply with the requirements of this section, he may serve on the person by whom the document was delivered (or, if there are two or more such persons, on any of them) a notice indicating the respect in which the document does not comply.

(6) Where the registrar serves such a notice, then, unless a replacement document —

(*a*) is delivered to him within 14 days after the service of the notice, and

(*b*) complies with the requirements of this section (or section 706) or is not rejected by him for failure to comply with those requirements,

the original document shall be deemed not to have been delivered to him.

But for the purposes of any enactment imposing a penalty for failure to deliver, so far as it imposes a penalty for continued contravention, no account shall be taken of the period between the delivery of the original document and the end of the period of 14 days after service of the registrar's notice.

(7) The Secretary of State may by regulations make further provision with respect to the application of this section in relation to instantaneous forms of communication.

(8) Regulations made for the purposes of this section may make different provision with respect to different descriptions of document and different forms of communication, and as respects delivery to the registrar for England and Wales and delivery to the registrar for Scotland.

✍ § 722. Form of company registers, etc.

(1) Any register, index, minute book or accounting records required by the Companies Act to be kept by a company may be kept either by making entries in bound books or by recording the matters in question in any other manner.

(2) Where any such register, index, minute book or accounting record of not kept by making entries in a bound book, but by some other means, adequate precautions shall be taken for guarding against falsification and facilitating its discovery.

(3) If default is made in complying with subsection (2), the company and every officer of it who is in default is liable to a fine and, for continued contravention, to a daily default fine.

✍ § 723. Use of computers for company records.

(1) The power conferred on a company in § 722(1) to keep a register or other record by recording the matters in question otherwise than by making entries in bound books includes power to keep the register or other record by recording those matters otherwise than in a legible form, so long as the recording is capable of being produced in a legible form.

(2) Any provision of an instrument made by a company before 12th February 1979 which requires a register of holders of the company's debentures to be kept in a legible form is to be read as requiring the register to be kept in a legible or non-legible form.

(3) If any such register or other record of a company as is mentioned in § 722(1), or a register of holders of a company's debentures, is kept by the company by recording the matters in question otherwise than in a legible form, any duty imposed on the company by this Act to allow inspection of, or to furnish a copy of, the register or other record of any part of it is to be treated as a duty to allow inspection of, or to furnish, a reproduction of the recording or of the relevant part of it in a legible form.

(4) The Secretary of State may by regulations in a statutory instrument make such provision in addition to subsection (3) as he considers appropriate in connection with such registers or other records as are mentioned in that subsection, and are kept as so mentioned; and the regulations may make modifications of provisions of this Act relating to such registers or other records.

(5) A statutory instrument under subsection (4) is subject to annulment in pursuance of a resolution of either House of Parliament.

(i) Accounting Records

✍ 789. Accounting records.

Every company must cause accounting records to be kept in accordance with the following provisions. They must be sufficient to show and explain the company's transactions, and must be such as to (1) disclose with reasonable accuracy, at any time, the financial position of the company at that time, and (2) enable the directors to ensure that any balance sheet and profit and loss account prepared under the relevant provisions of the Companies Act 1985, comply therewith as to the form and content of company accounts and otherwise.

In particular the accounting records must contain entries from day to day of all sums of money received and expended by the company, and the matters in respect of which the receipt and expenditure takes place, and a record of the assets and liabilities of the company.

If the company's business involves dealing in goods, the accounting records must contain (a) statements of stock held by the company at the end of each financial year of the company,

(b) all statements of stocktaking from which any such statement of stock as is mentioned in head (a) above has been or is to be prepared, and (c) except in the case of goods would by way of ordinary retail trade, statements of all goods sold and purchased showing the goods and the buyers and sellers in sufficient detail to enable all these to be identified.

If a company fails to comply with any of the above requirements, every officer of the company who is in default is guilty of an offence unless he shows that he acted honestly and that in the circumstances in which the company's business was carried on the default was excusable. Otherwise he is liable on conviction on indictment to imprisonment for a term not exceeding two years or a fine, or both, or on summary conviction to imprisonment for a term not exceeding six months or a fine not exceeding the statutory maximum, or both.

✍ 790. Location and preservation of accounting records.

Subject to the following provisions, a company's accounting records must be kept at its registered office, or such other placed as the directors think fit, and must at all times be open to inspection by the company's officers.

* * * * *

Accounting records which a company is required so to keep must be preserved by it (1) in the case of a private company, for three years from the date on which they are made, and (2) in the case of a public company, for six years from that date.

* * * * *

VOLUME 17. — EVIDENCE.

PART VII. — DOCUMENTARY EVIDENCE IN CRIMINAL PROCEEDINGS

☞ § 69. Evidence from computer records.

(1) In any proceedings, a statement in a document produced by a computer shall not be admissible as evidence of any fact stated therein unless it is shown —

(a) that there are no reasonable grounds for believing that the statement is inaccurate because of improper use of the computer;

(b) that at all material times the computer was operating properly, or if not, that any respect in which it was not operating proper or was out of operation was not such as to affect the production of the document or the accuracy of its contents; and

(c) that any relevant condition specified in rules of court under subsection (2) below are satisfied.

(2) Provison may be made by rules of court requiring that in any proceedings where it is desired to give a statement in evidence by virtue of this section such information concerning the statement as may be required by the rules shall be provided in such form and at such time as may be so required.

☞ PROVISIONS SUPPLEMENTARY TO SECTION 69

8. In any proceedings where it is desired to give a statement in evidence in accordance with section 69 above, a certificate —

(a) identifying the document containing the statement and describing the manner in which it was produced

(b) giving such particulars of any device involved in the production of that document as may be appropriate for the purpose of showing that the document was produced by a computer;

(c) dealing with any of the matters mentioned in subsection (1) of section 69 above; and

(d) purporting to be signed by a person occupying a responsible position in relation to the operation of the computer,

shall be evidence of anything stated in it; and for the purpose of this paragraph it shall be sufficient for a matter to be stated to the best of the knowledge and belief of the person stating it.

4. — DOCUMENTARY EVIDENCE.

PROOF OF CONTENTS

(i) Primary Evidence

☞ 136. Production of documents at trial.

When the authenticity of a document which is in the possession of one of the parties is not in dispute, it is usual to take steps to secure the production and admission of it, or evidence of its contents, at the trial by means of notices to admit or produce, followed after inspection by an agreement between the parties to admit the originals or copies for the purposes of the trial or by an application for such writ of subpoena or order as may be necessary to secure the production of the document. Correspondence is frequently agreed between the parties.

☞ 137. Proof of authenticity.

Where a document is not in the possession of either of the parties, or because its authenticity is in dispute or for some other reason it is not possible to secure the admission of it or of an agreed copy of it at the trial, it may become necessary not only to secure its production, but also to give evidence that it is what it purports to be, or is tendered as being. The methods by which such evidence may in general be given have already been considered, but in respect of some classes of documents these methods may be replaced by some other method which, on grounds of public policy, is established either as the best and therefore the only method, or as an alternative method, of proving the contents.

(4) BOOKS OF BANKS, COMPANIES AND CORPORATIONS.

☞ 204. Examined copies of entries in bankers' books.

As a general rule a bank cannot be compelled to produce its books without an order of the court in any case to which it is not a party, but may instead allow examined copies of entries in those books to be made.

The admissibility of statements contained in documents produced by a computer is the subject of particular statutory provisions.

☞ 205. Books of companies and corporations.

The official books of a corporation are admissible to prove the public acts of a corporation, provided that they were kept publicly as the corporation books, and that the entries were made by the proper officer.

Particular statutes provide for the admissibility in evidence of the books of companies, the minutes of meetings of local authorities, extracts from the minutes of meeting of the managers or governors of certain schools, and documents issued by local education authorities.

POLICE AND CRIMINAL EVIDENCE ACT 1984

☞ **§ 71. Microfilm copies.**

In any proceedings the contents of a document may (whether or not the document is still in existence) be proved by the production of an enlargement of a microfilm copy of that document or of the material part of it, authenticated in such manner as the court may approve.

CIVIL EVIDENCE ACT 1968

☞ **5. Admissibility of statement produced by computers.**

(1) In any civil proceedings a statement contained in a document produced by a computer shall, subject to rules of court, be admissible as evidence of any fact stated therein of which direct oral evidence would be admissible, if it is shown that the conditions mentioned in subsection (2) below are satisfied in relation to the statement and computer in question.

(2) The said conditions are —

(a) That the document containing the statement was produced by the computer during a period over which the computer was used regularly to store or process information for the purposes of any activities regularly carried on over that period, whether for profit or not, by any body, whether corporate or not or by any individual;

(b) that over that period there was regularly supplied to the computer in the ordinary course of those activities any information of the kind contained in the statement or of the kind from which the information so contained is derived;

(c) that throughout the material part of that period the computer was operating properly or, if not, that any respect in which it was not operating properly or was out of operation during that part of that period was not such as to affect the production of the document or the accuracy of its contents; and

(d) that the information contained in the statement produces or is derived from information supplied to the computer in the ordinary course of those activities.

(3) Where over a period the function of storing or processing information for the purposes of any activities regularly carried on over that period as mentioned in subsection (2)(a) above was regularly performed by computers, whether —

(a) by a combination of computers operating over that period; or

(b) by different computers operating in succession over that period; or

(c) by different combinations of computers operating in succession over that period; or

(d) in any other manner involving the successive operation over that period, in whatever order, of one or more computers and one or more combinations of computers,

all the computers used for that purpose during that period shall be treated for the purposes of the Part of this Act as constituting a single computer; and references in this Part of this Act to a computer shall be construed accordingly.

(4) In any civil proceedings where it is desired to give a statement in evidence by virtue of this section, a certificate doing any of the following things, that is to say —

(a) identifying the document containing the statement and describing the manner in which it was produced;

(b) giving such particulars of any device involved in the production of that document as may be appropriate for the purpose of showing that the document was produced by a computer;

(c) dealing with any of the matters to which the conditions mentioned in subsection (2) above relate,

and purporting to be signed by a person occupying a responsible position in relation to the operation of the relevant device or the management of the relevant activities (whichever is appropriate) shall be evidence of any matter stated in the certificate; and for the purposes of this subsection it shall be sufficient for a matter to be stated to the best of the knowledge and belief of the person stating it.

(5) For the purposes of this Part of this Act —

(a) information shall be taken to be supplied to a computer if it is supplied thereto in any appropriate form and whether it is so supplied directly or (with or without human intervention) by means of any appropriate equipment;

(b) where, in the course of activities carried on by any individual or body, information is supplied with a view to its being stored or processed for the purposes of those activities by a computer operated otherwise than in the course of those activities, that information, if duly supplied to that computer, shall be taken to be supplied to it in the course of those activities;

(c) a document shall be taken to have been produced by a computer whether it was produced by it directly or (with or without human intervention) by means of any appropriate equipment.

(6) Subject to subsection (3) above, in this Part of this Act "computer" means any device for storing and processing information, and any reference to information being derived from other information is a reference to its being derived therefrom by calculation, comparison or any other process.

☞ **Provisions supplementary to ss 2 and 5.**

* * * * *

(3) In estimating the weight, if any, to be attached to a statement admissible in evidence by virtue of section 2, 3, 4, or 5 of this Act regard shall be had to all the circumstances from which any inference can reasonably be drawn as to the accuracy or otherwise of the statement and, in particular —

* * * * *

(c) in the case of a statement falling within section 5(1) of this Act, to the question whether or not the information which the information contained in the statement reproduces or is derived from was supplied to the relevant computer, or recorded for the purposes of being supplied thereto, contemporaneously with the occurrence or existence of the facts dealt with in that the supply of information to that computer, or with the operation of that computer or any equipment by means of which the document containing the statement was produced by it, had any incentive to conceal or misrepresent the facts.

* * * * *

CRIMINAL LAW, EVIDENCE AND PROCEDURE

☞ **§ 1158. Evidence from computer records.**

In any proceedings, a statement in a document produced by a computer is not admissible as evidence of any fact stated in it unless it is shown:

(1) that there are no reasonable grounds for believing that the statement is inaccurate because of improper use of the computer;

(2) that at all material times the computer was operating properly, or if not, that any respect in which it was not operating properly or was out of operation was not such as to affect the production of the document or the accuracy of its contents; and

(3) that any relevant conditions specified in rules of court are

satisfied.

In any proceedings where it is desired to give a statement in evidence in accordance with the above provisions, a certificate:

(a) identifying the document containing the statement and describing the manner in which it was produced;

(b) giving such particulars of any device involved in the production of that document as may be appropriate for the purposes of showing that the document was produced by a computer;

(c) dealing with any of the matters in heads (1) to (3) above; and

(d) purporting to be signed by a person occupying a responsible position in relation to the operation of the computer,

in evidence of anything stated in it.

However, a court may require oral evidence to be given of anything which evidence could be given by such a certificate.

In estimating the weight, if any, to be attached to a statement, regard must be had to all the circumstances from which any inference can reasonably be drawn as to the accuracy or otherwise of the statement; and in particular:

(i) to the question or not the information which the information contained in the statement reproduces or is derived from was supplied to the relevant computer, or recorded for the purpose of being supplied to it, contemporaneously with the occurrence or existence of the facts dealt with in that information;

(ii) to the question whether or not any person concerned with the supply of information to that computer, or with the operation of that computer or any equipment by means of which the document containing the statement was produced by it, had any incentive to conceal or misrepresent the facts.

PRACTICE AND PROCEDURE

☞ § 459. Classes of admissible hearsay evidence.

The following classes of statements are admissible as hearsay evidence, provided the conditions for their admissibility are complied with:

(1) statements made out of court, whether orally or in writing, and whether the person making the statement is or is not called as a witness;

(2) statements contained in certain records, namely in the document which is or forms part of a record compiled by a person acting under a duty to do so;

(3) statements produced by computer;

(4) statemnts made in previous legal proceedings;

(5) inconsistent, contradictory or rebutting statements made by a person not called as a witness;

(6) statements affecting the credibility of the matter of an out-of-court statement;

(7) statements of opinion; and

(8) statements, whether oral or in writing, agreed to be admitted by the parties.

In addition, certain classes of hearsay evidence which formerly would have been admissible at common law are now admissible by statute.

For the purpose of deciding whether or not a statement made out of court contained in certain records or produced by computer is admissible in evidence, the court may draw any reasonable inference from the circumstances in which the statement was made or otherwise came into being or from any other circumstance, including, in the case of a statement contained in a document, the form and contents of that statement.

ARMY ACT 1955

☞ § 198A. Evidence derived from the computer records.

(1) In any proceeding under this Act, a statement contained in a document produced by a computer shall be admissible as evidence of any fact stated therein of which direct oral evidence would be admissible, if it is shown that the conditions mentioned in subsection (2) below are satisfied in relation to the statement and computer in question.

(2) The said conditions are —

(*a*) that the document containing the statement was produced by the computer during a period over which the computer was used regularly to store or process information for the purposes of any activities regularly carried on over that period by any body or by any individual;

(*b*) that over that period there was regularly supplied to the computer in the ordinary course of those activities information of the kind contained in the statement or of the kind from which information so contained is derived;

(*c*) that throughout the material part of that period the computer was operating properly or, if not, that any respect in which it was not operating properly or was out of operation during that part of that period was not such as to affect the production of the document or the accuracy of its contents; and

(*d*) that the information contained in the statement reproduces or is derived from information supplied to the computer in the ordinary course of those activities.

(3) Where over a period the function of storing or processing information for the purposes of any activities regularly carried on over that period as mentioned in subsection (2)(*a*) above was regularly performed by computers or —

(*a*) by a combination of computers operating over that period; or

(*b*) by different computers operating in succession over that period; or

(*c*) by different combinations of computers operating in succession over that period; or

(*d*) in any other manner involving the successive operation over that period, in whatever order, of one or more computers and one or more combinations of computers,

all the computers used for that purpose during that period shall be treated for the purposes of this section as constituting a single computer.

(4) In any proceedings where it is desired to give a statement in evidence by virtue of this section, a certificate doing any of the following things, that is to say —

(*a*) identifying the documents containing the statement and describing the manner in which it was produced;

(*b*) giving such particulars of any device involved in the production of that document as may be appropriate for the purpose of showing that the document was produced by a computer;

(*c*) dealing with any of the matters to which the conditions mentioned in subsection (2) above relate,

and purporting to be signed by a person occupying a responsible position in relation to the operation of the relevant device or the management of the relevant activities (whichever is appropriate) shall be evidence of any matter sated in the certificate; and for the purposes of this subsection it shall be sufficient for a matter to be stated to the best of the knowledge and belief of the person stating it.

(5) For the purposes of this section —

(*a*) information shall be taken to be supplied to a computer if it is supplied thereto in any appropriate form and whether it is so supplied directly or (with or without human intervention) by means of any appropriate equipment;

(*b*) where, in the course of activities carried on by any

individual or body, information is supplied with a view to its being stored or processed for the purposes of those activities by a computer operated otherwise than in the course of those activities, that information, if duly supplied to that computer, shall be taken to be supplied to it in the course of those activities;

(*c*) a document shall be taken to have been produced by a computer whether it was produced by it directly or (with or without human intervention) by means of any; appropriate equipment.

(6) Subject to subsection (3) above, in this section "computer" means any device for storing and processing information, and any reference to information being derived from other information is a reference to its being derived therefrom by calculation, comparison or any other process.

(7) Subsection (9) of section 198 of this Act shall apply for the purposes of this section as it applies for the purposes of that section.

☞ § 198B. Supplementary provisions as to evidence derived from computer records.

(1) Where in any proceedings a statement contained in a document is admissible in evidence by virtue of section 198A of this Act, it may be proved by the production of that document or (whether or not that document is still in existence) by the production of a copy of that document, or of the material part thereof, authenticated by the person who would be authorised by section 198A(4) of this Act to sign a certificate identifying the original document.

(2) For the purpose of deciding whether or not a statement is admissible in evidence by virtue of the said section 198A, the court may draw any reasonable inference from the circumstances in which the statement was made or otherwise came into being or from any other circumstances, including, in the case of a statement contained in a document, the form and contents of that document.

(3) In estimating the weight, if any, to be attached to a statement admissible in evidence by virtue of the said section 198A regard shall be had to all the circumstances from which any inference can reasonably be drawn as to the accuracy or otherwise of the statement and, in particular —

(*a*) to the question whether or not the information which the information contained in the statement reproduces or is derived from was supplied to the relevant computer, or recorded for the purpose of being supplied thereto, contemporaneously with the occurrence or existence of the facts dealt with in that information; and

(*b*) to the question whether or not any person concerned with the supply of information to that computer, or with the operation of that computer or any equipment by means of which the document containing the statement was produced by it, had any incentive to conceal or misrepresent the facts.

(4) In section 198A of this Act and this section —

"document" includes, in addition to a document in writing —

(*a*) any map, plan, graph or drawing;

(*b*) any photograph;

(*c*) any disc, tape, sound-track or other device in which sounds or other data (not being visual images) are imbodied so as to be capable (with or without the aid of some other equipment) of being reproduced therefrom; and

(*d*) any film, negative, tape or other device in which one or more visual images are embodied so as to be capable (as aforesaid) of being reproduced therefrom;

"film" includes a microfilm; and

"statement" includes any representation of fact, whether made in words or otherwise.

(5) In section 198A of this Act and this section any reference to a copy of a document includes —

(*a*) in the case of a document falling within paragraph (*c*) but not (*d*) of the definition "document" in subsection (4) above, a transcript of the sound or other data embodied therein;

(*b*) in the case of a document falling within paragraph (*d*) but not (*c*) of that definition, a reproduction or still reproduction of the image or images embodied therein, whether enlarged or not;

(*c*) in the case of a document falling within both those paragraphs, such a transcript together with such a still reproduction; and

(*d*) in the case of a document not falling within the said paragraph (*d*) of which a visual image is imbodied in a document falling within that paragraph, a reproduction of that image, whether enlarged or not;

and any reference to a copy of the material part of a document shall be construed accordingly.

(6) If any person in a certificate tendered in evidence in proceedings by virtue of section 198A(4) of this Act intentionally makes a statement material in those proceedings which he knows to be false or does not believe to be true, he shall be liable on conviction on indictment to imprisonment for a term not exceeding two years or a fine or both.

STOCK EXCHANGE

✍ § 232. Retention and rights to inspection of records.

The holder of a principal's licence must retain for a period of not less than seven years originals or copies of all books, accounts and other documents required to be kept, as well as of every contract note issued or received by him, every investment management contract entered into by him and every written notice or confirmation given by him. He must also supply on demand to any person with whom or on whose behalf he or any representative on his behalf has carried out a transaction copies of all entries in his books relating to that transaction. Any requirement to keep books, accounts and other documents for a particular purpose and containing particular items of information is taken to be satisfied by recording the matters in question otherwise than in a legible form so long as the recording is capable of being reproduced without delay in a legible form sufficient for that purpose and containing that information.

BANKING

2. STATUTORY REGULATION OF BANKING.

✍ 38. Conduct of business.

* * * An institution is not, however, to be regarded as conducting its business in a prudent manner unless * * * (4) it maintains or, as the case may be, will maintain adequate accounting and other records of its business and adequate systems of control of its business and records; but those records and systems are not to be regarded as adequate unless they are such as to enable the business of the institution to be prudently managed and the institution to comply with the duties imposed on it by or under the Banking Act 1987 and, in determining whether those systems are adequate, the Bank must have regard to the functions and responsibilities in respect of them or any directors of the institution.

✍ 98. Obstruction of investigations.

A person who knows or suspects that an investigation is being or is likely to be carried out is guilty of an offence if he falsifies, conceals, destroys or otherwise disposes of, documents which he knows or suspects are or would be relevant to such an investigation unless he proves that he had no intention of concealing facts disclosed by the documents from persons carrying out such an investigation. A person guilty of such an offence is liable on conviction or indictment to imprisonment for a term not exceeding two years or a fine, or to both, or on summary convictions to imprisonment for a term not exceeding six months or a fine not exceeding the statutory maximum, or to both.

(8) BANKERS' BOOKS; PRODUCTION IN EVIDENCE, INSPECTION ETC.

☞ 238. Copies of entries as evidence.

In all legal proceedings, a copy of any entry in a banker's books, that is to say, in the ledgers, day books, cash books, account books and other records used in the ordinary business of a bank, whether those records are in written form or are kept in microfilm, magnetic tape or any other form of mechanical or electronic data retrieval mechanism, is to be received as prima facie evidence unless it is first proved that the book was at the time of the making of the entry one of the ordinary books of the bank, that the entry was made in the usual and ordinary course of business, and that the book is in the custody or control of the bank, or of the successors to the bank in whose custody or control it was when the entry was made, and such proof may be given by a partner or officer of the bank, and may be given orally or by an affidavit sworn before any commissioner or person authorised to take affidavits. It must also be proved that the copy has been examined with the original entry and is correct; and such proof must be given by some person who has examined the copy with the original entry and may likewise be given either orally or by an affidavit.

Although cheques and paying-in slips constitute part of a bank's records used in the ordinary course of its business, the adding of an individual cheque or paying-in slip to a bundle of cheques or paying-in slips does not constitute the making of an entry in those records. A microfilm recording the payment of cheques by photographing the name of the payee appears to be an entry in a banker's books within the meaning of the Bankers' Books Evidence Act 1879.

A letter from a banker to his customer is not a banker's book.

☞ 239. Production of originals.

No banker or officer of a bank, in any legal proceeding to which the bank is not a party, may be compelled to produce any banker's book the contents of which can be proved, or to appear as a witness to prove the matters, transactions and accounts therein recorded, unless by order of a judge made for special cause.

However, to obtain the benefit of this relief from attendance and production, the banker or officer must have furnished, or have been willing to furnish, verified copies of the required entries; and, if he has not done so, the books may still be obtained by subpoena duces tecum.

A back which is a party to litigation is under the ordinary duty to give discovery of relevant documents and to allow inspection.

PERSONAL PENSION SCHEMES (RELIEF AT SOURCE) REGULATIONS 1988.

✍ Section 15. Inspection of Records.

DATE-IN-FORCE: 1 JULY 1988

* * * * *

(2) Where records are maintained by computer the scheme administrator shall provide the person making the inspection with all facilities necessary to obtain information from them.

(3) Subject to paragraph (4), all books, documents and records referred to in paragraph (1), shall be preserved by the scheme administrator so as to be available for inspection under this regulation for a period of six years following the termination of the scheme, or of arrangements made in accordance with it, to which they relate.

(4) All particulars, certificates and declarations furnished under regulations 5 to 7 shall be so preserved for a period of six years following the date on which the individual to whom they relate ceased to make net contributions.

"Records" include documents, copies of documents and information stored in a computer or produced from a computer.

OCCUPATIONAL PENSION SCHEMES (ADDITIONAL VOLUNTARY CONTRIBUTIONS) REGULATIONS 1987

AUTHORITY: FINANCE ACT 1970

✍ Section 13. Inspection of Records.

* * * * *

(2) Where the records are maintained by computer the scheme administrator shall provide the person making the inspection with all facilities necessary to obtain information from them.

(3) Subject to paragraph (4) all books, documents and records referred to in paragraph (1), shall be preserved by the scheme administrator in such manner as may be approved by the Board so as to be available for inspection under this regulation for a period of three years following the termination of the scheme to which they relate.

(4) All particulars [declarations and undertakings] furnished under regulation 5 shall be so preserved for a period of [six years] following the date on which the scheme member to whom they relate ceased to [pay contributions to a scheme].

STAMP DUTY RESERVE TAX REGULATIONS 1986

AUTHORITY: FINANCE ACT 1986, s 98

✍ Section 15. Inspection of Records.

(1) Every accountable person shall, whenever required to do so, make available for inspection by an officer of the board authorised for that purpose all books, documents and other records in his possession or under his control containing information relating to any relevant transaction to which he was a party or in connection with which he acted.

* * * * *

(2) Where records are maintained by computer the person required to make them available for inspection shall provide the officer making the inspection with all facilities necessary for obtaining information from them.

✍ INCOME TAX (INTEREST RELIEF) REGULATIONS 1982

(1) Every person to whom payments of interest are made in respect of which a repayment claim is made by a lender under these Regulations shall, whenever required to do so, make available for inspection by an officer of the Board authorised for that purpose all such books, documents and other records in his possession or under his control containing information relating to:

(a) such interest and the terms of the loans (including relevant contracts or deeds) under which such interest is paid or,

(2) Where records are maintained by computer the person required to make them available for inspection shall provide the officer making the inspection with all facilities necessary for obtaining information from them.

(3)(a) Every notice given to it by the borrower under paragraph 7(1)(a) of Schedule 7 shall be preserved by the lender to whom it is given and in such manner as may be approved by the Board, so as to be available for inspection under this Regulation, until two years after the termination of the loan or, if earlier, from the date from which the interest ceases to be relevant loan interest;

(b) a copy of the notice shall on its written request be made available to the Board.

INCOME TAX (LIFE ASSURANCE PREMIUM RELIEF) REGULATIONS 1978

AUTHORITY: FINANCE ACT 1976, SCHEDULE 4, PARAGRAPH 16

✍ Section 12. Inspection of Records.

(1) Every person to whom premiums are paid in respect of which a claim is made under these Regulations shall, whenever required to do so, make available for inspection by an authorised officer of the Board all such books, documents and other records in his possession or his control containing information relating to —

(a) such premiums and the policies or contracts under which such premiums are paid, or

(b) the persons holding such policies or contracts or paying such premiums, as may reasonably be required for determining whether the deficiency for which any claim is made under these Regulations is properly recoverable.

(2) Where records are maintained by computer the person required to make them available for inspection shall provide the officer making the inspection with all facilities necessary for obtaining information from them.

(3) Every statement under Regulation 3 above shall be preserved by the life office to which it is made (or which is the insurer for the time being), in such manner as may be approved by the Board so as to be available for inspection under this Regulation, until three years after the termination of the insurance or contract to which it relates.

GREATER LONDON COUNCIL (GENERAL POWERS) ACT OF 1969

CROSS-HEADING: PART 5. DOCUMENTS AND EQUIPMENT

✪ Section 37. Microfilming of Documents.

(1) The Council may make and retain microfilm recordings of documents of the Council.

(2) Notwithstanding anything contained in the last foregoing section or in any other enactment, the Council may destroy any documents of the Council of which they have made and retained microfilm recordings:

Provided that —

(a) the Council shall not under this section destroy records deposited with them under the Public Records Act 1958 or acquired or accepted by them under section 2 of the Local Government (Records) Act 1962, as amended by the Act of 1963; and

(b) the Council shall afford a right of access for the public to a microfilm recording of a document which has been destroyed in pursuance of this section equal to the right of access, if any, of the public in the document so destroyed.

(3) An enlargement of a microfilm recording of a document of the Council shall be deemed for all purposes to be a copy of that document.

(4) Notwithstanding anything contained in any enactment or any rule of law, an enlargement of a microfilm recording of a document of the Council which has been destroyed shall be receivable in evidence for any purpose for which the document would have been receivable in any proceeding in any court in England or Wales if an officer of the Council designated by them for the purpose of this subsection certifies that —

(a) the document has been destroyed; and

(b) a microfilm recording of the document has been made; and

(c) the enlargement is an enlargement of a microfilm recording of the document.

(5) The Council and any association which appears to the Council to be representative of the borough councils, in consultation with such persons as appear to the Council and the said association to be the appropriate persons to consult with on matters relating to the destruction or retention of documents, may jointly prepare and agree a code of practice containing guidance and recommendations as to the principles which should, in their opinion, govern the exercise by any person of the powers to destroy documents conferred by subsection (2) of this section, including guidance and recommendations as to the considerations which should govern the retention of certain documents or classes or examples of documents on the grounds of the value which the documents have, or may reasonably be expected to have in the future, for administrative or historical purposes or for the purposes of sociological or other research.

✪ Section 38. Electronic, Mechanical or Other Equipment, Etc.

(1) The Council may, by agreement with any person, for that person's purposes, use or permit the use of any electronic, mechanical or other equipment for accounting, analytical, statistical or other purposes or for the printing or reproduction of documents (including equipment for microfilm recording) which the Council have provided for the purposes of all or any of their work, and may provide any facilities and services ancillary to, or necessary or convenient for, the use of the said equipment and make such charges as may be agreed for the use of such equipment and the provision of such facilities or services.

✪ Section 39. Application and Interpretation of Part 5.

(1) The provisions of this Part of this Act shall extend and apply to a borough council and the Common Council as if for any references therein to the Council (except in subsection (5) of section 37 (Microfilming of documents) thereof there were substituted a reference to the borough council or the Common Council (as the case may be):

Provided that the provisions of section 36 (Destruction of documents connected with applications) and section 37 (Microfilming of documents) of this Act shall not apply to the council of the borough of Hounslow, and the provisions of section 38 (Electronic, mechanical or other equipment, etc.) of this Act shall apply to that council only in so far as those provisions relate to the use of equipment for the printing or reproduction of documents (including equipment for microfilm recording).

(2) In this Part of this Act —

"document" includes the whole or part of a register, book, record, letter, map, plan, drawing, photograph or other document, and any notice, license, certificate, scheme or order made, passed or granted by the Council, and references to documents of the Council are references to documents belonging to or permanently in the possession of the Council;

"enlargement" means an enlarged reproduction of a microfilm recording which is legible with the naked eye;

"microfilm recording" means a reproduction of a document on film or other material which is a product of photography or any similar process and is in general beyond legibility with the naked eye, and any reference to a microfilm recording of a document shall be deemed to include a reference to any copy subsequently made of such microfilm recording.

BANKERS' BOOKS EVIDENCE ACT 1879

✍ Section 9. Interpretation of "bank," "banker," and bankers' books".

* * * * *

(2) Expressions in this Act relating to "bankers' books" include ledgers, day books, cash books, account books and other records used in the ordinary business of the bank, whether those records are in written form or are kept on microfilm, magnetic tape or any other form of mechanical or electronic data retrieval mechanism.

LICENSED DEALERS (CONDUCT OF BUSINESS) RULES 1983

CROSS-HEADING: PART 3 BOOKS, ACCOUNTS AND DOCUMENTS TO BE KEPT BY THE HOLDER OF A PRINCIPAL'S LICENSE IN RELATION TO ANY DEALING IN SECURITIES

✍ Section 26. Computer, etc. records; confidentiality of records.

(1) Any requirements in rules 20 to 24 for a holder of a principal's license to keep books, accounts and other documents for a particular purpose and containing particular items of information shall be taken to be satisfied by recording the matters in question otherwise than in a legible form so long as the recording is capable of being reproduced without delay in a legible form sufficient for that purpose and containing that information.

(2) The requirement in rule 24 for a holder of a principal's license to retain originals or copies of certain books, accounts and other documents for a specified period of time shall be taken to be satisfied by the retention of microfilm copies of those books, accounts or documents, so long as adequate arrangements are available for the inspection and supply, without delay, of full-size reproductions of those microfilm copies.

(3) The requirement of rule 25 for a holder of a principal's license to supply on demand copies of entries in his book relating to a transaction shall be taken to be satisfied —

(a) where the matters in question are recorded otherwise than in a legible form by the supply of a reproduction of the recording or of the relevant part of it in a legible form; and

(b) where microfilm copies of those books are retained, by the supply of a full-size reproduction of the microfilm copy or of the relevant part of it.

(4) The entitlement in Rule 25 of certain persons to inspect contract notes and vouchers relating to certain transactions shall be taken to be satisfied where microfilm copies of those contract notes or vouchers are maintained, by the inspection of full-size reproductions of those microfilm copies or of the relevant parts of them.

(5) Where a holder of a principal's license wishes to ensure that, on any inspection of his books by one person, information in those books concerning other persons remains confidential, that holder may, notwithstanding any other requirement of these rules, but subject to the requirements of any other enactment, maintain his books in such a manner that persons are identified in one part of them only by a number or symbol, so long as he maintains in another part of those books in the same building a separate record of the person to whom each such number or symbol relates and on request supplies a copy of every entry therein relating to a number or symbol used in recording a transaction in his books to any person entitled to copies of entries in his books relating to that transaction.

FINANCE ACT 1988

✍ Section 127. Production of computer records, etc.

(1) Any provision made by or under the Taxes Acts which requires a person —

(a) to produce, furnish or deliver any document or cause any document to be produced, furnished or delivered; or

(b) to permit the Board, or an inspector or other officer of the Board —

(i) to inspect any document, or

(ii) to make or take extracts from or copies of or remove any document,

shall have effect as if any reference in that provision to a document were a reference to the document within the meaning of Part 1 of the Civil Evidence Act 1968; and, accordingly, any reference in such a provision to a copy of a document shall be construed in accordance with section 10(2) of that Act.

(2) In connection with tax, a person authorized by the Board to exercise the powers conferred by this subsection —

(a) shall be entitled at any reasonable time to have access to, and inspect and check the operation of, any computer and any associated apparatus or material which is or has been in use in connection with any document to which this subsection applies; and

(b) may require —

(i) the person by whom or on whose behalf the computer is or has been so used, or

(ii) any person having charge of, or otherwise concerned with the operation of, the computer, apparatus, or material,

to afford him such reasonable assistance as he may require for the purposes of paragraph (a) above.

(3) Subsection (2) above applies to any document, within the meaning of Part 1 of the Civil Evidence Act 1968, which a person is or may be required by or under any provision of the Taxes Acts —

(a) to produce, furnish or deliver, or cause to be produced, furnished or delivered; or

(b) to permit the Board, or an inspector or other officer of the Board, to inspect, make or take extracts from or copies of or remove.

(4) Any person who —

(a) obstructs a person authorised under subsection (2) above in the exercise of his powers under paragraph (a) of that subsection, or

(b) fails to comply within a reasonable time with a requirement under paragraph (b) of that subsection,

shall be liable to a penalty not exceeding L500.

(5) In the application of this section to Scotland and Northern Ireland, references in this section to Part 1 of the Civil Evidence Act 1968 and section 10(2) of that Act shall be construed —

(a) in the case of Scotland, as references to Part 3 of the Law Reform (Miscellaneous Provisions) (Scotland) Act 1968 and section 17(4) of that Act respectively, and

* * * * *

CIVIL EVIDENCE ACT 1968

CROSS-HEADING: PART 1. — HEARSAY EVIDENCE.

☞ Section 6. Provisions supplementary to ss 2 to 5.

(1) Where in any civil proceeding a statement contained in a document is proposed to be given in evidence by virtue of section 2, 4 or 5 of this Act it may, subject to any rules of court, be proved by the production of that document or (whether or not that document is still in existence) by the production of a copy of that document, or of the material part thereof, authenticated in such manner as the court may approve.

(2) For the purpose of deciding whether or not a statement is admissible in evidence by virtue of section 2, 4 or 5 of this Act, the court may draw any reasonable inference from the circumstances in which the statement was made or otherwise came into being or from any other circumstances, including, in the case of a statement contained in a document, the form and contents of that document.

(3) In estimating the weight, if any, to be attached to a statement admissible in evidence by virtue of section 2, 3, 4, or 5 of this Act regard shall be had to all the circumstances from which any inference can reasonably be drawn as to the accuracy or otherwise of the statement and, in particular —

(a) in the case of a statement falling within section 2(1) or 3(1) or (2) of this Act, to the question whether or not the statement was made contemporaneously with the occurrence of existence of the facts stated, and to the question whether or not the maker of the statement had any incentive to conceal or misrepresent the facts;

(b) in the case of a statement falling within section 4(1) of this Act, to the question whether or not the person who originally supplied the information from which the record containing the statement was compiled did so contemporaneously with the occurrence or existence of the facts dealt with in that information, and to the question whether or not that person, or any person concerned with compiling or keeping the record containing the statement, had any incentive to conceal or misrepresent the facts; and

(c) in the case of a statement falling within section 5(1) of this Act, to the question whether or not the information which the information contained in the statement reproduces or is derived from was supplied to the relevant computer, or recorded for the purpose of being supplied thereto, contemporaneously with the occurrence or existence of the facts dealt with in that information, and to the question whether or not any person concerned with the supply of information to that computer, or with the operation of that computer or any equipment by means of which the document containing the statement was produced by it, had any incentive to conceal or misrepresent the facts.

* * * * *

OCCUPATIONAL PENSION SCHEMES (ADDITIONAL VOLUNTARY CONTRIBUTIONS) REGULATIONS 1987

✍ Section 13. Inspection of records.

* * * * *

(2) Where records are maintained by computer the scheme administrator shall provide the person making the inspection with all facilities necessary to obtain information from them.

(3) Subject to paragraph (4) all books, documents and records referred to in paragraph (1), shall be preserved by the scheme administrator in such manner as may be approved by the Board so as to be available for inspection under this regulation for a period of three years following the termination of the scheme to which they relate.

(4) All particulars [declarations and undertakings] furnished under regulation 5 shall be so preserved for a period of [six years] following the date on which the scheme member to whom they relate ceased to [pay contributions to a scheme].

EXCISE DUTIES (DEFERRED PAYMENT) REGULATIONS 1983

CROSS-HEADING: PART 1 PRELIMINARY.

✍ Section 2. Interpretation.

In these regulations —

* * * * *

"document", "copy" and "computer" have the same meanings respectively as they have in section 16 of the Finance Act 1980;

* * * * *

"records" include documents, copies of documents and information stored in, or produced from, a computer;

* * * * *

INCOME TAX (INTEREST RELIEF) REGULATIONS 1982

✍ Section 16. Inspection of records.

(1) Every person to whom payments of interest are made in respect of which a repayment claim is made by a lender under these Regulations shall, whenever required to do so, make available for inspection by an officer of the Board authorised for that purpose all such books, documents and other records in his possession or under his control containing information relating to —

(a) such interest and the terms of the loans (including relevant contracts or deeds) under which such interest is paid or,

(b) the persons holding such contracts or deeds or paying such interest as may reasonably be required for determining whether the amount for which any such claim is made is properly recoverable.

(2) Where records are maintained by computer the person required to make them available for inspection shall provide the officer making the inspection with all facilities necessary for obtaining information from them.

(3)(a) Every notice given to it by the borrower under paragraph 7(1)(a) of Schedule 7 shall be preserved by the lender to whom it is given and in such manner as may be approved by the Board, so as to be available for inspection under this Regulation, until two years after the termination of the loan or, if earlier, the date from which the interest ceases to be relevant loan interest.

* * * * *

POLICE AND CRIMINAL EVIDENCE ACT 1984

☞ Section 71. Microfilm copies.

In any proceedings the contents of a document may (whether or not the document is still in existence) be proved by the production of an enlargement of a microfilm copy of that document or of the material part of it, authenticated in such manner as the court may approve.

PUBLIC RECORDS ACT 1958

✪ **Section 6. Destruction of public records in Public Record Office or other place of deposit.**

If as respects any public records in the Public Storage Office or any place of deposit appointed under this Act it appears to the Keeper of Public Records that they are duplicated by other public records which have been selected for permanent preservation or that there is some other special reason why they should not be permanently preserved, he may, with the approval of the Lord Chancellor and of the Minister or other person, if any, who appears to the Lord Chancellor to be primarily concerned with public records of the class in question, authorise the destruction of those records or, with that approval, their disposal in any other way.

Country: Uruguay

TITLE 2. COMMON OBLIGATIONS

✍ **CHAPTER 3. — COMMERCIAL BOOKS.**

Article 54. Every merchant is bound to keep books of account and of his mercantile correspondence.

The number and form of those books are entirely at the discretion of the merchant, provided that his is regular and that he keeps the books which the law designates as indispensable.

Article 55. The books which a merchant is bound to keep are the following:

1. Daybook;
2. Stock-book;
3. Copies of correspondence.

Article 56. In the daybook shall be entered day by day, and according to the order in which they are effectuated, all the transitions by the merchant, bills of exchange and all other documents of credit (Papeles de credito) which he may give, receive, guarantee or endorse; and generally, whatever he may receive or deliver on his own account or that of another, by whatever title, so that each entry may show who is the creditor and who is the debtor in the transaction to which it refers.

It is sufficient to enter domestic expenses in a lump on the date on which they leave the cashier's office.

Article 57. If the merchant keeps a cash-book, it is not necessary that he enter in the day book the payments made. In that case the cash-book is considered an integral part of the daybook.

Article 58. Retail dealers (Art. 3) must enter day by day in the daybook the sum total of the cash sales, and, separately, the sum total of the sales on credit.

Article 59. The stock-book shall commence with an exact account of the money, movable and immovable property, credits and every other kind of asset which forms the capital of the merchant at the time of beginning of his business.

Afterwards, every merchant shall draw up within the first three months of each year, and shall write out in the same book, a general balance sheet of his business, comprising therein all his property, credits and shares, as well as all his outstanding debts and liabilities at the date of the balance, without any concealment or omission whatever.

The stock-books and general balance sheets shall be signed by all interested in the establishment who are present at the time of their being drawn up.

Article 60. If the private fortune of a merchant is distinct from the capital of his business or the funds devoted to his undertakings, then the latter only are to be entered in the inventory book.

Article 61. It will be sufficient to enter in the stock-books and general balance sheets of companies, the assets and liabilities common to the net worth, without including the separate property and liabilities of each partner.

Article 63. In the copy book merchants must copy unaltered and literally all letters written relating to their business.

They are similarly required to preserve in dockets and in proper order all letters received in connection with their business, noting on the back the date of answering them or plainly indicating in the same way that they have not answered them.

Article 64. Letter copies must be kept by order of date in the language of the original. Postscripts and addition after they have been registered shall be inserted as a continuation in the last copied letter of the respective reference.

Article 65. The three books which are declared indispensable shall be bound and paged, in which form each merchant of the department of the capital shall produce them to the Commercial Court so that the judge and clerk of the said Court may sign all the pages and place in the first page a note dated and signed by both of the number of leaves which the book contains.

In the other departments these formalities are fulfilled by the Ordinary Judge acting with the clerk, or failing him with two witnesses.

In neither case can fees or any other perquisites be demanded.

Article 66. In keeping both the books prescribed by Art. 55 and the extra books not required by the law, it is forbidden:

1. To alter in the entries the consecutive order of dates and transactions which must be entered according to the provisions of Art. 56;
2. To leave blanks or spaces, as all the entries must be successive, without there being between them any spaces for intercalations or additions;
3. To make interlineations, erasures or corrections; but all mistakes and omissions which may be made must be corrected by any fresh entry, made on the date on which the omission or mistake is noticed;
4. To spoil any entry;
5. To mutilate any part of the book, to tear out a leaf or alter the binding and paging.

Article 67. Mercantile books which lack any of the formalities prescribed in Art. 65 or have any of the defects or imperfections noted in the preceding article, have no value in an action in favor of the merchant to whom they belong.

Article 68. A merchant who omits any of the account books which are declared indispensable by Art. 55, or who conceals them when ordered to produce the same, shall be judged by the entries in the books of his adversary, both in the action which gave rise to the order for production and any; other action which he may have pending.

Article 69. In case of bankruptcy the merchant who has not kept his books in the form and with the requirements prescribed in the preceding articles shall be held culpable in accordance with the terms of the title "Of classification of bankruptcies".

The books of bankrupts, although duly kept always admit proof to the contrary (Art. 76).

Article 70. No authority, Judge or Tribunal may under any pretext make an official inquiry to ascertain whether merchants keep regular books or not.

Article 71. General production of the books of merchants may only be ordered at the instance of a party in suits relating to succession community of property or partnership, mercantile management or agency on another's account and in case of bankruptcy.

Article 72. In cases not within those specified in the preceding article, production of merchants' books against their will can only be ordered at the instance of a party or de officio to the extent that is relevant to the point or question in dispute.

In that case, the examination of the books which are produced shall take place in the presence of their owner or of his representative, and shall be confined exclusively to the entries which are relevant to the question in dispute.

Article 73. If the books are away from the place where the Court which ordered their production sits, this shall take place where the said books are, and in no case shall it be ordered that they be brought to the place of hearing.

Article 74. When a merchant has kept extra books (Art. 54), their production may be ordered in the same way and in the same cases as prescribed in the three preceding articles.

Article 75. Every merchant can keep his books or sign the documents of his business by himself or by another; but in the latter case he is obliged to give to the person he employs a special authority in writing.

Article 76. Commercial books kept according to the prescribed form and requirements shall be admitted in Court as evidence between merchants on a fact of their commerce, in the way and in the cases expressed in this Code.

As against the merchants to whom the books belong and their successors, the entities shall be evidence, with the exception of the case of Art. 69, paragraph 2. But the opposite party cannot accept the favorable entries and disprove those which prejudice him, but having adopted this means of proof he shall be bound by the combined result of the entries relevant to the point in dispute.

Commercial books shall also be evidence in favor of their owners when the opposite party does not produce entries to the contrary made in books lawfully kept or some other full and conclusive evidence.

Nevertheless, in that case the Judge has power to weigh that evidence, and to require supplementary evidence if he thinks it necessary.

Finally, when there is a contradiction between the books of the litigants and all are kept with the necessary formalities and without any defect, the Tribunal shall put aside this means of proof, and shall proceed according to the value of other evidence which is produced, weighing it in accordance with the provisions of this Code.

Article 77. Commercial books will afford only a ground of proof, when non-commercial acts are in question.

Article 78. Books not required by the law are not evidence in favor of a merchant in the absence of those which the law declares indispensable, unless the latter have been lost without his fault.

Article 79. The business books, to be admitted in Court, must comply with Art. 44, para. 2.

Article 80. Merchants are bound to preserve their commercial books for the space of 20 years, counted from the cessation of their business or commerce.

The heirs of a merchant are presumed to have the books of the ancestor and are bound to produce them as and when the person from whom they have inherited would be so bound.

Country: Venezuela

THE COMMERCIAL CODE OF VENEZUELA

BOOK 1

Title 1. — Capacity to Deal in Commerce.

✍ MERCANTILE BOOKS

Article 32. Merchants must keep their accounting records in the Spanish language. These records must be comprised of at least a journal, a ledger and an inventory book. The merchant may keep, in addition, all necessary auxiliary books that he deems advisable to clarify his operations.

Article 33. The Journal and Inventory Book — These books cannot be used, until they have been previously presented to the Tribunal or Mercantile Registrar, if there is such a Registrar in the community in which a merchant is located. If there is not such Registrar in the community where the merchant is located, then the books must be presented to the Judge of the highest category in the locality.

[COMMENT: It should be noted here that the Journal is also called the Day Book. These books must be bound, rubricated and numbered so that they may be numbered by a Judge of Commerce or his secretary or by the Mercantile Registrar. The first page of each book is signed by the Judge with the date and the seal of his office is stamped on all other pages of each book. The old Commercial Code states that only four bolivares can be collected as a fee for stamping each book.]

Article 34. Mercantile operations must be entered in the journal or day book each day. Each entry must clearly state who is the creditor and who is the debtor, in every transaction covered. A monthly summary of the total of all transactions and operations must also be provided.

Retail merchants, however, who habitually sell only by retail directly to the consumer, shall comply with the obligations imposed in this Article by merely writing a summary each day of the purchases and sales made for cash, but the retail merchant must enter in detail all sales made on credits and the payments and collections arising from sales on credits.

Article 36. Merchants are forbidden:

(1) to alter, in the entries, the order and date of the operations described;

(2) to leave blank spaces in the body of the entries or in continuation thereof;

(3) to make entries on the margin and to make interlineations, erasures or corrections;

(4) to erase entries or parts thereof;

(5) to take out leaves, alter the binding or numbering and to mutilate any part of the books.

Article 37. The errors and omissions that are committed in forming the entry shall be corrected by writing another entry, on the date on which the error is noted.

Article 38. Books kept pursuant to the foregoing Articles may serve as proof among merchants for acts of commerce. With respect to another person who is not a merchant, the entries in the books shall serve as proof only against their owner; but the other party cannot accept it as proof without also admitting any adverse proof which the books may contain.

Article 39. In order that all auxiliary books of account kept by merchants may be used by them in litigation, they must meet all the requirements that are prescribed with respect to the necessary books described herein.

Article 44. The books and their vouchers must be preserved for a period of ten years, counting from the last entry of each book. Incoming correspondence and copies of outlying matters shall be classified and preserved for a period of ten years. It should be mentioned here that the old Code provided that books had to be maintained for ten years after dissolution of the business. This latter requirement also included business correspondence.

Article 45. No investigation can be made officially by the Tribunal or any authority to inquire whether or not merchants kept books, or whether the latter are or are not kept in accordance with the regulations of this Code.

Appendix E Standards and Guidelines

Association:	**Association for Information and Image Management**
Source:	**Performance Guidline for the Legal Acceptance of Records Produced by Information Technology Systems (ANSI/AIIM TR-31)** **Part I: Performance Guideline for the Admissibility of Records Produced by Information Technology Systems as Evidence**

1 Scope and purpose

1.1 Scope

Admissibility into evidence of records produced by information technology systems employing media such as microfilm, magnetic tape or magnetic disk (and, by implication optical disk) has been addressed at the federal level by statutory laws and by special rules prescribed by the Supreme Court that accommodate such records. Of particular note are the Federal Rules of Evidence. (Agency administrative hearings are not bound by the Federal Rules of Evidence. As a consequence, the Administrative Law Judge has wide discretion with admitting records into evidence regardless of how they were produced.)

Reported decisions indicate that the courts are quite lenient in interpreting these laws and rules as applicable to records produced by information technology systems (analog or digital). However, problems arise if appropriate procedures are not followed in creating and maintaining such records, making it difficult to lay a proper foundation for admissibility. The court must be convinced that the process or system used is trustworthy in producing accurate records, i.e., the records reflect the source data used to create them. (Whether the source data are correct is another matter.)

Each state has adopted laws or rules related to records as evidence. Most have either adopted the *Uniform Photographic Copies of Business and Public Records As Evidence Act* or the *Uniform Rule of Evidence* (which are similar to the *Federal Rules of Evidence*). Although the wording between these two uniform laws vary, they exhibit similar phraseology and purpose. Some states have adopted unique verbiage related to reproductions that only permit technologies such as microfilm, miniature photographic or photostatic reproductions (where the latter could include paper prints produced from optical disk records).

1.2 Purpose

Laws of reproduction related to government produced or maintained records often reflect the concerns of government archivists. The laws might specify a particular technology that meets longevity and retrieval or copying requirements. Some government requirements severely restrict the use of technology other than microfilm, while a few states, such as California, have enacted legislation to enable government agencies to use optical disk technology.

As with federal records, there is generally no absolute bar to admissibility of records produced by analog or digital information technology systems in any state, providing a proper foundation is laid. However, there are both federal and state laws, regulations, or rules that specifically require the maintenance and production of original documents for certain purposes.

2 Evidence law: definitions and doctrines

The federal government and the states have enacted statutes and set forth rules pertaining to evidence that are similar in purpose and intent. Nevertheless, there is some disparity among the states in phraseology or terms used to describe or list technology devices, systems or processes that are covered by a particular statute or rule.

The performance guideline for admissibility into evidence of records produced by information technology systems must conform to the law of evidence of the jurisdiction in which judicial proceedings are brought. Therefore, it is important to have a basic understanding of definitions and doctrines embodied in this area of law.

The following definitions and doctrines are based in large part on federal evidence law set forth by particular statutes and by special rules prescribed by the Supreme Court, and on interpretations of this law by federal courts. (Much of the following is excerpted or paraphrased from *Admissibility of Electronically Filed Federal Records as Evidence: A Guideline for Federal Managers and Counsel,* a publication of the U.S. Department of Justice.)

In both federal and state courts, admissibility of photocopies and microfilm is well settled based on their acceptance as duplicates produced by techniques which by their nature accurately reproduce the original. Such duplicates are generally admissible to the same extent as an original. In contrast, given the ease with which computer records can be purposely or inadvertently altered, a printout of data stored in a computer or similar device is admissible only if it is shown to reflect the data accurately.

Admissibility of printouts of optical disk files is yet to be widely tested, but it is expected that they will be treated no differently than printouts from magnetic disk or tape files, i.e., accepted as originals if it is shown that they reflect the data accurately.

Although the cases cited in the following discussions deal primarily with computer records stored on magnetic tape or disk, the doctrines apply to information technology systems in general.

2.1 Discovery

Litigation involving evidence in the form of records produced by information technology systems often requires more than just a copy of the records. For example, if the records are produced with a computer-based process, the opposing party is entitled to test and examine the input, computer programs and output involved in the process.

Rules of civil and criminal procedure prescribed by the highest court in a given jurisdiction provide for pretrial disclosure of evidence in the form of documents and tangible objects, commonly referred to as discovery. (For example, discovery in a federal court is provided by Civ. Rule of Proc. 34 and Crim. Rule of Proc. 16.)

Case law makes it clear that computer programs and data compilations maintained in information technology systems are discoverable under both of these rules. In a civil case, any party may serve a discovery request on any other party to the suit at specified times, whereas in a federal criminal case, the government has a reciprocal right of pretrial discovery, which "arises only after the defendant has successfully sought discovery" under the rules. *United States v. Nobles*, 422 U.S. 225, 95 S.Ct. 2160 (1975).

The courts have long encouraged pretrial discovery of computer programs and related materials, recognizing that the use of "computerized data" can impede affective cross-examination "because of the difficulty of knowing the precise methods employed in programming the computer as well as the inability to determine the effectiveness of the persons responsible for feeding data into the computer." *United States v. Cepeda Penes*, 577 F.2d 754, 760-61 (1st Cir. 1978), citing *United States v. Dioguardi*, 428 F.2d 1033, 1038 (2d Cir. 1970), *cert. denied*, 400 U.S. 825, 91 S.Ct. 50 (1970). See also *United States v. Russo*, 480 F.2d 1228, at 1241, 1243 (6th Cir. 1973).

Ordinarily, the trial preparation work-products of an attorney such as correspondence, memoranda and trial briefs are not discoverable. However, it should be noted that information produced in the ordinary course of government business does not automatically transform into non-discoverable attorney work-product when subjected to analysis by specially designed computer programs during an investigation. In *State of Colo. v. Schmidt Tiago Const. Co.*, 108 F.R.D. 731 (D.Colo. 1985) the state's computer printouts were deemed undiscoverable because the information was "simply computerized for easier reading and evaluation." *Id.*, at 734.-35.

A motion for discovery of information technology materials can be quite technical, requiring the assistance of a professional who understands the technology for proper descriptive language. The importance of this assistance is that the opposing party will likely produce only what is asked for and no more.

2.2 Admissibility

Admissibility of electronically filed records stored in media such as magnetic disks or tapes as evidence has been challenged often in federal courts. Although such files are considered "writings or recordings." Fed. Rule of Evid. 1001(1), considering the ease of altering codes or patterns represented by electronic impulses or magnetic fields, admissibility of these files (or printouts thereof) can present special problems in establishing their genuineness or trustworthiness. Following is a discussion of these problems and how they have been treated by the courts.

2.2.1 The Best Evidence Rule Before the courts, an "original" of a record is the record itself. The "best evidence rule" generally states that only the best form of the evidence is admissible. Rigidly applied in the absence of a qualifying rule or statute, the rule precludes admissibility of anything but the original record to prove its content. However, modern courts interpret the rule as allowing admission of secondary evidence (e.g., a duplicate) if it is shown that the original was lost or destroyed, or is beyond the jurisdiction of the court without fault of the offering party. Modern rules of evidence go even further by allowing admission of duplicates to the same extent as originals, provided they meet specified conditions.

Recognizing the impracticality of the best evidence rule when applied to computer files, many states and the federal government have adopted definitions that consider computer printouts as originals, provided they have been shown to accurately reflect the information in the computer files. Fed. Rule of Evid. 1001(3). Absent such a provision, at least one court has taken the view that printouts of records stored in magnetic media are admissible because they are "unavailable and useless except by means of the printout sheets." *King v. State ex. rel. Murdock Acceptance Corp.*, 222 So.2d 393, 398 (Miss. 1969).

With regard to duplicates and public or official records, the federal rules state in pertinent part:

> A "duplicate" is a counterpart produced by the same impression as the original, . . . or by mechanical or electronic re-recording, . . . or by other equivalent techniques which accurately reproduce the original. [Emphasis added.] Fed. Rule of Evid. 1001(4).
>
> A duplicate is admissible to the same extent as an original unless (1) a genuine question is raised as to the authenticity of the original or (2) in the circumstances it would be unfair to admit the duplicate in lieu of the original. Fed. Rule of Evid. 1003.
>
> The contents of an official record, or of a document authorized to be filed and actually recorded or filed, including *data compilations in any form,* if otherwise admissible, may be proved by copy, certified by a witness who has compared it with the original. If a copy which complies with the foregoing cannot be obtained by the exercise of reasonable diligence, then other evidence of the contents may be given. [Emphasis added.] Fed. Rule of Evid. 1005.

These rules would seem to consider as duplicates, or copies of official records, additional printouts of the same information contained in a magnetic file produced at different times (as well as carbon, photostatic or xerographic copies).

It should be noted that the courts have long recognized admissibility of computer printouts as probative evidence, subject to the same scrutiny for trustworthiness as business records. In other words, the printout themselves and not their contents are used to prove the trust of a matter asserted. See *United States v. Liebert*, 519 F.2d 542, at 548, citing *United States v. De Georgia,* 420 F.2d 889 (9th Cir. 1969), where the court referred to computer printouts as a "major 'witness' confronting the defendant) . . . indicating that the IRS has not record of having receiving his returns."

Modern rules of evidence and court decisions appear to have rendered the basic legal principle found in the best evidence rule as essentially outmoded regarding records produced by information technology systems. Much of the need for evidence rules equating products of specified technologies to originals can be eliminated by focusing instead on the reliability and accuracy of the process or system used to produce the records in question. The rationale for this is discussed at length in section 3.

2.2.2 Authentication Anything offered as evidence is subject to challenge regarding its genuineness or authenticity. Computer-produced evidence is no exception.

Fed. Rule of Evid. 901(b) lists examples of authentication requirements. Of particular note regarding computer evidence is example (9):

> Evidence describing a *process or system* used to produce a result showing that the process or system produces an accurate result. [Emphasis added.]

This would seem to particularly include evidence describing a computer "process" or "system" to show that a computer printout is accurate.

In *United States v. Vella,* 673 F.2d 86, 90 (5th Cir. 1982), the defendant attacked admissibility of telephone bills prepared with computers, arguing that failure to establish that the computers were in proper working order denied him of confrontation rights. The court held that "computer evidence is not intrinsically unreliable," citing *United States v. Fendly,* 522 F.2d 181, 187 (5th Cir. 1975), *Olympic Insurance Co. v. H. D. Harrison, Inc.*, 418 F.2d 669, 670 (5th Cir. 1969), and that "failure to certify the brand or proper operating condition of the machinery involved does not betray a circumstance of preparation indicating any lack of trustworthiness." (See also *United States v. Croft*, 750 F.2d 1353, 1364 (7th Cir. 1984).)

The *Vella* analysis clearly distinguishes between authenticity or genuineness of computer printouts (based on the accuracy of the process that produces them), and the trustworthiness of the information fed into the computer, a distinction that is explicitly supported by the following statement in *United States v. Downing,* 753 F.2d 1224 (3rd Cir. 1985):

> . . . The question whether a particular machine works as intended is a question distinct from one directed toward the authentication of a process generally. Saltzburg & Redden, Federal Rules of Evidence Manual 702 (3d ed. 1982). Rule 901(b)(9) speaks only to the former question. See McCormick on Evidence 885 n. 6 (3d ed. 1984) ("The emphasis of Rule 901 is upon showing that the offered item (e.g., computer printout) is what it is claimed to be, i.e., that it is genuine . . . rather than that what is in the (computer) is correct.").

(In both *Vella* and *Croft*, a proper foundation was laid for introduction of the printouts, i.e., appropriate witnesses described the process or system in question sufficiently to satisfy the court as to its reliability and accuracy.)

As with other kinds of evidence, admissibility by the court of computer-produced evidence is not tantamount to a mandatory presumption of trustworthiness. In other words, the evidence is allowed to be introduced but its trustworthiness remains subject to challenge or rebuttal. See *United States v. Goichman*, 547 F.2d 778, 784 (3rd Cir. 1976), where admissibility required only a prima facie showing that a document offered into evidence is what its proponent claims, whereupon the burden of going forward with respect to authentication shifts.

2.2.3 Hearsay Fed. Rule of Evid. 801(c) defines hearsay as "a statement, including a written assertion, other than one made by a witness testifying at a trial or hearing, offered in evidence to prove the truth of the matter asserted." Hearsay is not admissible except as provided by statute of rule of evidence through specified exceptions to the hearsay rule.

As was pointed out earlier, a computer printout (or output readable by sight) is regarded as an original writing or recording. In any case, it is an out-of-court "statement" and if offered to prove the truth of its contents, it is considered hearsay and treated accordingly regarding its admissibility.

As with other "writings" or "records," computer printouts not offered to prove the truth of their contents are not hearsay. (For example, if offered to support testimony that incomplete information was knowingly submitted for computer processing, *United States v. Evans*, 572 F.2d 455 (5th Cir. 1978), *cert. denied*, 439 U.S. 870, 99 S.Ct. 100 (1978).)

Among the exceptions enumerated in Fed. Rule of Evid. 803(6) regarding records of a regularly conducted activity is particularly relevant to computer printouts given the common practice of maintaining business records on computers. (This rule and the related Business Records Act are discussed in the following section.) The other exceptions have no special significance regarding computer-produced evidence.

2.2.4 Business or regularly conducted activity records *The Business Records Act*, U.S.C. Sec. 1732, provides for admission of records produced in the regular course of business. (All states have a similar law.) The Act specifically provides for admissibility of such records that are "recorded, copied, or reproduced by any process which accurately reproduces or forms a durable medium for so reproducing the original," and allows the destruction of the original in the regular course of business "unless its preservation is required by law."

It should be noted that "[t]he best evidence rule has repeatedly been held inapplicable to records admitted under the Business Records Act." *United States v. Miller*, 500 E.2d 751 (5th Cir. 1974), citing *United States v. Anderson*, 447 E.2d 883, 839 (8th Cir. 1971), *United States v. Vandersee*, 279 F.2d 176, 180 (3rd Cir. 1960), *United States v. Kimmel*, 274 F.2d 54, 57 (2d Cir. 1960).

Fed. Rule of Evid. 803(6) provides in pertinent part:

> The following are not excluded by the hearsay rule, even though the declarant is available as a witness:
>
> (6) Records of regularly conducted activity. A memorandum, report, record, or *data compilation*, in any form, of acts, events, conditions, opinions, or diagnoses, made at or near the time by, or from information transmitted by, a person with knowledge, if kept in the course of a regularly conducted business activity, and if it was the regular practice of that business activity to make the memorandum, report, record, or data compilation, all as shown by the testimony of the custodian or other qualified witness unless the source of information or the method or circumstances of preparation indicate lack of trustworthiness. . . . [Emphasis added.]

As with the *Business Records Act*, "computer data compilations may constitute business records for purposes of Fed.R.Evid. 803(6) and may be admitted at trial if a proper foundation is established." *United States v. Croft*, 750 F.2d, *supra*, at 1364; *United States v. Catraban*, 836 F.2d 453, 457 (9th Cir. 1988). The common standard for determining admissibility of computer records under Rule 803(6) follows: "Computer business records are admissible if (1) they are kept pursuant to a routine procedure designed to ensure their accuracy, (2) they are created for motives that tend to assure accuracy (e.g., not including those prepared for litigation), (3) they are not themselves mere accumulations of hearsay, " *United States v. Sanders* 749 F.2d 195, 198 (5th Cir. 1984). (It is noteworthy that in *United States v. Scholle*, 553 F.2d 1109, 1124 (8th Cir. 1977), the court used the specific inclusions of "data compilations in Rule 803(6) to support the contention that computer printouts are covered under the *Federal Business Records Act.*)

In rejecting the defendant's argument that the computer printouts in question were records prepared for litigation (hence not business records), the *Sanders* court pointed out that although the printouts themselves may have been made in preparation for litigation, the data contained in the printouts were the results of business transactions that were neither added to nor modified after the transactions took place. The court concluded that "[i]t is not necessary that the printout itself be ordered in the ordinary course of business, at least when the program that calls forth the data *only orders* it rather than sorting, compiling or summarizing the information." [Emphasis added.] *United States v. Sanders*, supra, at 198.

The courts have recognized the irrationality of requiring that computer printouts must be made "at or near the time" the business record input is transmitted by a person with knowledge. See *United States v. Hutson*, 821 F.2d 1015, 1240; *United States v. Sanders, supra,* at 198, *citing United States v. Russo.*

2.3 Laying a proper foundation

Laying a foundation is "the practice or requirement of introducing evidence of things necessary to make further evidence relevant, material or component. . . ." Black's Law Dictionary.

Evidence is considered competent if it is legally qualified as sufficiently trustworthy as proof of the truth of a matter asserted.

Heretofore, discussions centered on admissibility of computer-produced evidence in terms of the intrinsic nature or character of the evidence. Laying a foundation that will qualify the evidence as being what it is purported to be can be an even greater burden to overcome.

Business records exceptions notwithstanding, laying a foundation for computer-produced records can be particularly difficult:

> Even where the procedure and motive for keeping business records provide a check on their trustworthiness . . ., the complex nature of computer storage calls for a more comprehensive foundation. Assuming properly functioning equipment is used, there must be not only a showing that the requirements of the Federal Business Records Act have been satisfied, but in addition the original source of the computer program must be delineated, and procedures for input control including tests used to assure accuracy and reliability must be presented.
>
> [*United States v. Scholle, supra,* at 1125.]

However, a more recent decision downplays the difference between computer records and other records, which probably reflects the increased use of computers in creating and maintaining business records:

> While the suggestion has been made that there are unique foundation requirements for the admission of computerized business records under 803(6), see generally *United States v. Scholle* . . . this court has previously held that "computer data compilations . . . should be treated as any other record of regularly conducted activity."
>
> [*United States v. Vella, supra,* at 90, citing *Rosenburg v. Collins*, 624 F.2d 659, 665 (5th Cir. 1989).]

Russo summarizes what is required in laying a proper foundation for computer-produced business records:

> . . . [T]he foundation for admission of (computerized records) consists of showing the input procedures used, the tests for accuracy and reliability and the fact that an established business relies on the computerized records in the ordinary course of carrying on its activities. The (opposing) party then has the opportunity to cross-examine concerning company practices with respect to the input and as to the accuracy of the computer as a memory bank and retriever of information. . . . [T]he court (must) "be satisfied with all reasonable certainty that both the machine and those who supply its information have performed their functions with utmost accuracy." . . . [T]he trustworthiness of the particular records should be ascertained before they are admitted and . . . the burden of presenting an adequate foundation for receiving the evidence should be on the parties seeking to introduce it rather than upon the party opposing its introduction. . . .
>
> [*United States v. Russo, supra,* at 1241, citing *De Georgia, supra.* See also, *United States v. Weatherspoon,* 581 F.2d 595, 598 (7th Cir. 1978).]

Care must be taken to select a witness "competent" to testify in laying the foundation for admissibility of computer-produced evidence. The court in *Fendley* emphasized that the "the preparer" of a record is not required to establish its authenticity:

> . . . A witness laying the foundation for admissibility of a document as a business record need not have been the preparer of the document. *United States v. Gremillion*, 464 F.2d 901, 906 (5th Cir. 1972) — for indeed this Court stated that:
>
> "Section 1732 was adopted in part to eliminate the requirement that the entrant appeared to authenticate the record." *United States v. Miller, supra,* 500 F.2d at 754. "[T]he person who actually keeps the books and records and makes the entries need not testify if a person does testify who is in a position to attest to the authenticity of the records." *United States v. Dawson*, 400 F.2d 194, 199 (2d Cir. 1968). . . . [N]othing in the Business Records Act requires either that the foundation witness be able to personally attest to the accuracy contained in the document, or that he have personally prepared the document. In fact, (this) requirement (has) been frequently held to have been specifically eliminated by 28 U.S.C. Sec. 1732.
>
> [*United States v. Fendley, supra,* at 185. See also *United States v. Briscoe,* 896 F.2d 1476 (7th Cir. 1990). (For examples of proper witnesses, see

United States v. Croft, supra, at 1363-65; *United States v. Russo, supra,* at 1233-34, 124]; and *United States v. Weatherspoon, supra,* at 598.)]

Crimes involving computers invariably require the seizing of materials difficult to describe to persons unfamiliar with computer terminology and with the particular processes that produced the materials. Hence, special care must be exercised by investigators or prosecutors in preserving the chain of custody, which requires that the object offered as evidence must be supported by testimony that the object is the one involved in the incident, and that its condition is substantially unchanged.

In seizing records contained on information technology storage devices such as computer tapes or disks, printouts of the records must be verified by a computer expert as representing the contents of the seized tapes or disks. This can be done by having a computer expert testify that he or she produced or witnessed the production of the printouts from the seized tapes or disks.

2.4 Conclusion

Modern rules of evidence and court decisions appear to have come to terms with the realities of business and professional practices, i.e., the ever-growing dependency on digital and analog information technology systems for records production and maintenance. Traditional legal principles regarding admissibility of records have been accommodated by the artifice of equating records produced by specified technologies to originals or to reproductions of originals.

Much of the need for this artifice can be eliminated by focusing on the reliability and accuracy of the process or system used to produce the records in question rather than on whether they are originals. The rationale for this is discussed at length in section 3.

Fostering rules of evidence that accommodate emerging technologies is the principal purposes of the guideline.

Nevertheless, such rules do not diminish avenues open for challenging the trustworthiness of these technologies in producing accurate records.

Common assaults on the integrity of computer-based technologies include challenges to:

a. the source of the input data and the process for transcribing it to machine-readable form;

b. the process that creates, edits and updates the files;

c. the process that produces the output or retrieves the records; and

d. the reliability of the equipment and vendor supplied software that systematically manages the internal system processes.

Of particular importance in fending off these assaults is to assure the existence of up-to-date documentation that fully and accurately describes the procedural controls employed in producing the records. Additionally, records managers or custodians must be prepared to describe these controls in laymen's terms, showing how they account for every link involved in producing the records.

3 Performance guideline - evidence

3.1 Background

3.1.1 Traditional rules of evidence

3.1.1.1 Hearsay Courts have traditionally classified records as "hearsay" — written evidence of a statement made out of court offered to show the truth of the matter asserted, where the person who made the statement is not in court for cross-examination. Such records were initially excluded from evidence because they depended upon the veracity and competence of the out-of-court asserter. Later, courts admitted these records into evidence, through exceptions to the hearsay rule, if the records met established criteria for admissibility allowed for the presumption that the records reflected accurate information produced by trustworthy procedures.

These exceptions were at first restricted to original "writings" but were later modified to accommodate impact printing and other duplication technologies (e.g., micrographics and photocopying machines) as they became common business tools.

3.1.1.2 The best evidence rule The courts also developed the "best evidence rule." The rule generally states that only the best form of the evidence is admissible. Initially, only original documents were admissible. As the rule evolved, the courts allowed secondary evidence if it was shown that the original was unavailable without fault of the offering party. Early duplicate records were probably not admissible since they were made using the transcription process — the copying of records by hand involving human intervention. Due to the high likelihood of error, transcription could not produce trustworthy results.

Over time, courts allowed true duplicate records — dupliates produced by a mechanical or other non-human process — to be admitted into evidence in limited circumstances when the originals were not available because: 1) they were public records; 2) the originals had been destroyed; 3) the originals were in the possession of an adverse party who refused to cooperate; or 4) the originals simply could not be found with reasonable effort. Once these situations were adequately proven to the court, reproductions could then be admitted.

Besides the historical basis for the best evidence rule, the preference for original records serves to reduce forgeries or other fraud in duplicates. Alterations can readily be detected in original documents while similar detection is difficult if not impossible in duplicates. Handwriting analysts can more accurately analyze signatures from original records than from duplicates.

3.1.2 Modern rules of evidence Modern rules of evidence are based on statutes and special rules prescribed by the courts, rather than on individual court decisions. The federal government follows the Federal Rules of Evidence while most states have adopted one or more uniform laws that establish the admissibility of records in evidence such as the *Uniform Business Records Act*, the *Uniform Photographic Copies of Business and Public Records As Evidence Act*, and the *Uniform Rules of Evidence*. Some states have adopted their own unique language to accomplish a similar result.

Now, rules of evidence permit original and duplicate records to be admitted into evidence provided that a proper foundation is laid. For example, visible records produced with a computer in the form of computer printouts or computer output microfilm (COM) are considered originals if an appropriate witness convinces the court that they accurately reflect the information in the computer files. Information processing methods commonly employed in the business world are readily accepted as reliable, while new information system technologies are subject to greater scrutiny.

3.1.3 Problems with rules of evidence Based upon the traditional position of courts and regulatory agencies, original, paper records are the best evidence and duplicate records are considered secondary evidence. Modern rules of evidence perpetuate this concept but provide exceptions for properly made duplicate records.

The basic legal principle found in the Best Evidence Rule has been essentially outmoded in the world of information technology. Paper records systems can be inferior to automated systems in terms of preserving evidence for the following reasons:

> *Paper records systems generally result in the preparation of one copy of the record.* In case of fire, flood or other natural disaster, the single version of the records will be destroyed and no longer available for any evidence, regulatory or other purpose.
>
> *Documents can be removed from paper records systems without detection.* While erasures can be detected on originals, most other forms of fraud cannot. For example, when

records are subpoenaed by the court or requested by government agencies, certain documents can be provided while others destroyed or hidden. The fraud resulting from the selective withholding of records can rarely be detected.

Alternatively, original paper records can inappropriately be destroyed. These records may then be unavailable for any purpose including evidence and regulation. Unless the fraud related to the destruction is detected, the omission as well as the content of the records will effectively be excluded from consideration.

Original paper records may not have a very long life expectancy. This is especially true today because original paper records are often produced using poor quality paper, poor quality ink, lift-off typewriter ribbons, or other inexpensive, short-term methods. Even records properly organized and stored may not be usable by the time they are needed for a court proceeding.

Paper records are rarely created as part of a rigorous process or system. Many (if not most) organizations do not even have a records management program. Even those that do, rarely establish rigorous procedures related to records creation, maintenance and disposition. Many records created in each organization reflect individual whims rather than systematic policy. The accuracy of records will therefore vary based upon the integrity, accuracy and capabilities of the individuals involved.

Paper records are rarely audited for accuracy. Few organizations audit paper records systems to determine the accuracy of the information recorded.

Paper records are rarely subjected to adequate security. Any individual including the janitor may get access to paper records. The types of fraud discussed above can be accomplished without detection.

Modern information technology systems often differ from paper-based systems through the establishment of processes or systems that reliably produce accurate results. Modern reproduction systems such as microfilm or optical disk, and even data processing systems, offer the following characteristics that generally provide for more accurate and trustworthy records than possible with paper records systems:

Modern information technology systems by their nature produce records are part of a process or system that requires a disciplined operation based on standard procedures, written documentation, adequate training, and thoroughly tested equipment and software components.

Modern information technology systems can provide an audit trail that identifies not only what actions were taken related to records but also the individuals involved.

Modern information technology systems can prohibit or detect alterations and attempted alterations to records. Most optical disk systems, for example, inherently preclude alteration of images. Bypass of alteration safeguards can be very difficult, requiring special knowledge and technical capabilities.

Modern information technology systems can provide for routine security background for records produced. Typically, microfilm, magnetic tape or disk, and optical disk systems will produce backup records at appropriate intervals as required. These records are generally stored in properly maintained remote locations where they can be retrieved if the original information is damaged or destroyed.

In sum, properly designed, implemented and maintained information technology systems are capable of producing records that are more reliable and accurate than paper-based systems.

It should be noted, however, that although paper-based systems are more susceptible to irretrievable loss or destruction of records and undetectable omission, without the safeguards stated above, disasters and fraud can be much more costly and damaging to an organization dependent on an information technology system.

3.1.4 Future challenges With the safeguards that can be built into today's modern information technology systems, the best evidence of a record should not be dependent on a specifically sanctioned technology, but on a showing that the record was the result of a process or system that accurately produced it.

Rule 901(b) of the *Uniform Rules of Evidence* lists examples that conform with the requirement of authentication or identification as a condition precedent to admissibility of evidence, i.e., "evidence to support a finding that the matter in question is what its proponents claim." Example (9) reflects what should be the criteria for introducing records produced by information technology systems into evidence in all jurisdictions.

Example (9) provides for authentication or identification by "evidence describing a process or system used to produce a result and showing that the process or system produces an accurate result." This example was designed for evidence such as X-rays and computer printouts where accuracy of the evidence is dependent upon the process or system that produces it.

When applied to records produced by information technology systems, this provision is literally independent of a bias towards originals, duplicates, or any particular technology. The accuracy of the process or system used to produce the result will determine the authenticity or identification, and hence the admissibility, of the evidence.

As new information technologies evolve, such as electronic imaging and optical disk systems, some jurisdictions feel compelled to modify existing laws to establish additional criteria for legal acceptance in evidence. If left to their own resources, some jurisdictions will continue to develop complex and sometimes conflicting requirements. New statutes or regulations may thwart the potential benefits and advancements of merging information technology.

The performance guideline represents reasonable criteria to enable courts to evaluate the accuracy, reliability, and ultimately, the trustworthiness of information technology used to produce records introduced into evidence. Once implemented, the guideline can apply to future technologies.

The guideline relates to the functional or performance criteria for the system used to produce the records rather than to the media or specific technology involved. Only the trustworthiness of the process or system determines the legal admissibility of records in evidence, not the type of media or technology utilized.

3.2 Reference

3.2.1 Uniform laws Uniform laws are typically developed by the National Conference of Commissioners on Uniform State Laws. The philosophy behind uniform laws is to "promote uniformity in state laws where uniformity is deemed desirable and practicable." (See Jacobstein and Mersky, *Fundamentals of Legal Research*, p. 352, 1977.) The process has also promoted uniformity between state and federal law.

Once the conference approves a uniform law, the law must then be approved by a state before it is binding in that state. Because each state may accept, reject or accept with modification the uniform law, the goal of true uniformity is rarely achieved. Some states have some or all of these uniform laws, others have none. The publication *Uniform Laws Annotated* (West Publishing Company) publishes the names of states that have adopted each uniform law.

Three major uniform laws establish the basic requirements for admissibility of records in evidence and relate to this guideline. (See annex B for the text of each law.) These uniform laws plus the background evidence law from section 2, establish the legal basis for the performance guideline.

3.2.1.1 Uniform Business Records Act This law provides for the admissibility of records "if, in the opinion of the court, the sources of information, method and time of preparation were such as to justify its admission." The term "records" appears to include both original and duplicate records, although the law includes no definitions.

3.2.1.2 Uniform Rules of Evidence This law provides for the admissibility in evidence of both original and duplicate records. Records will be admissible contingent on " . . . evidence sufficient to support a finding that the matter in question is what its proponents claim . . . " such as by " . . . evidence describing a process or system used to produce a result and showing that the process or system produces an accurate result . . . ."

Original records include " . . . letters, words, sounds, or numbers, or their equivalent, set down by handwriting, typewriting, printing, photostating, photographing, magnetic impulse, mechanical or electronic recording, or other form of data compilation . . . " as well as " . . . any printout or other output readable by sight, shown to reflect the data accurately . . . " from a computer or similar device.

Duplicate records include counterparts "produced by the same impression as the original, or from the same matrix, or by means of . . . (several enumerated technologies) . . . or by other equivalent techniques which accurately reproduce the original." Duplicate records are " . . . admissible to the same extent . . . " as the original records.

3.2.1.3 Uniform Photographic Copies of Business and Public Records as Evidence Act This law addresses duplicate records produced in the regular course of business through the use of several enumerated technologies or " . . . other process which accurately reproduces or forms a durable medium for so reproducing the original." In essence, the law covers duplicate records produced by any technology that accurately reproduces the original.

Once the legal standard is met, the original records may be destroyed in the regular course of business provided that the originals are not required by law (statute or regulation) such as the following circumstances:

> *If a law specifically requires the preservation of the original records.* Only a few laws actually require original records. Normally, when the law requires records to be maintained, any form of the records may be used.
>
> *If a law specifies additional requirements for duplicate records before the originals can be destroyed.* Some regulatory agencies have specified additional requirements, others have not. Courts do not specify additional requirements not included in the uniform law except that judges tend to require paper prints of microfilm or other duplicate records not in paper form.
>
> *If the original records are held in a custodial or fiduciary capacity.* Original records that "belong to another" cannot be destroyed, even after reproduction, without the permission of the owner. Although the duplicate records would contain the same information as the original records, the physical, original records still belong to the owner.

The duplicate records may then be used "in any judicial or administrative proceeding." Most analysts also believe that this law permits duplicate records to be used for all regulatory purposes (including administrative proceedings) unless the regulatory agency requires the original to be kept or has established restrictions on the duplicate records.

3.2.2 Related articles and publications See annex D for detailed selected readings.

3.3 Definitions

The following definitions apply to the process or system assessment criteria set forth below:

3.3.1 Record: Information preserved by any technique in any medium, now known, or later developed, that can be recognized by ordinary human sensory capabilities either directly or with the aid of technology.

3.3.2 Original record: A record prepared in the first instance or any counterpart intended to have the same effect by a person executing or issuing it. If data are stored in a computer or similar device, any printout or other output readable by sight shown to reflect the data accurately is an "original."

3.3.3 Duplicate record: A record that is produced by the same impression as the original, or from the same matrix, or by any other technique that accurately reproduces the original.

3.3.4 Information technology system: Any process or system that employs a mechanical, photo-optical, magnetic, electronic or other technological device for producing or reproducing records.

3.4 Applicability

The guideline applies to records produced by information technology systems regardless of the physical characteristics of the record media or technology employed. This includes records produced by any technique employing an information technology system as defined above.

3.5 Information technology system assessment criteria

Following are criteria for assessing an information technology system in determining admissibility of records into evidence.

3.5.1 Quality Quality relates to ability of the information technology systems to reliably produce and preserve records so that they can be used or recognized by the intended audience.

3.5.1.1 General requirements The following should appear with sufficient clarity so that each can be recognized:

Individual letters, numbers and symbols

Combinations of letters, number and symbols forming words or sentences

Graphics such as signatures, logos, pictures, etc.

Sound

Other features of records such as color, shape, texture, etc., that relate to the content of the information

3.5.1.2 Original records Original records preserve information over time in the identical or functionally equivalent for to the original information.

Original records may present information in a form different from the original information without affecting its quality. For example, information preserved in digital format may be printed on paper using different print fonts at different times.

3.5.1.3 Duplicate records Duplicate records accurately reproduce original records. Information that is readable or recognizable on originals should be readable or recognizable on duplicates. Similarly, information that is readable or recognizable on duplicates must be readable or recognizable on originals, except that duplicates may contain production, control, indexing, certification or other data not related to informational content of the records.

The exception allows additional data to be included on duplicates for administration of the reproduction process if it does not adversely affect the informational content of the record. For example, control and indexing data stored with digital images may be necessary to retrieve the images, but does not affect the content of the records themselves.

Image enhancement techniques may be used provided that they do not change the information content of the records.

When duplication processes change informational content of the records, the results records will be new originals.

3.5.2 Records retention versus life expectancy of data on media Records should be retained, regardless of media, for the period required by the organization's records retention program for any legal, user, historical or other purpose. The life expectancy of the media per se has no bearing on the admissibility of the records.

The information maintained on the media and the ability of the system to produce records from the information must achieve the required retention period. This means that for some technologies it may be necessary to periodically convert, regenerate, copy or transfer the information from one medium or technology to another to preserve the information for the required period.

Regardless of the retention period or life expectancy of the media, records must continue to exist when litigation, government investigation or audit is pending, imminent or, in some cases, merely foreseeable. In some instances, a court order will issue prohibiting specified records from being destroyed or otherwise rendered unavailable.

Procedures followed to convert records from one medium or technology to another should be carefully documented. Conversion of the records should not affect their legal status provided that quality and accuracy does not functionally change during conversion.

3.5.3 Form of evidence Records produced by any technique may be introduced into evidence provided that they meet the requirements of this guideline.

Records should be presented in a readable or recognizable form acceptable to the court. For written records, the records may be readable without any equipment or readable using equipment available to the court. The court may also accept records in other forms when equipment for their retrieval and use is also provided.

The form of records acceptable in evidence will vary based upon the nature of the information. For example, digitized voice information must be presented in an audible, understandable form while digitized video information must be presented in a readable or recognizable form. Records that contain information that relates to multiple human senses such as video records that must be both seen and heard to be complete must be presented in a form that provides all the necessary sensory information to the court.

3.5.4 Process or system used to produce records

3.5.4.1 Characteristics Characteristics of the process or systems used to produce the information facilitate the accuracy of the information. A description of these characteristics in simple terms facilitates the showing that the process or system is reliable and accurate, hence capable of producing trustworthy records.

(a) Records produced as part of a regularly conducted activity

Records produced a start of a regularly conducted activity such as those produced in the regular course of business are admissible subject to s showing that the process or system used to produce them is reliable and accurate. A regularly conducted activity may include a regular pattern of activity to produce the records on a daily, weekly, monthly, yearly or other cyclical schedule.

A regularly conducted activity may also include records created as part of a regular program of the organization, but at irregular times. For example, when a planned program results in the reproduction of records created prior to a specific year, this will be viewed as a program proceeding in the regular course of business, even though it only occurred once.

(b) Accuracy

Records produced by methods to ensure or enhance accuracy will be more readily admissible in evidence. This may include systematic quality control and audit procedures, as well as operational oversight by somebody with detailed knowledge of the process or system used to produce the records.

(c) Timeliness

Records produced within a short period after the even or activity occurs tend to be more readily acceptable as accurate than records produced long after the event or activity. However, a challenge to admissibility of a later-produced record can be overcome by a showing that the time lapse had no effect on the record's content. For example, a computer printout of a statistical report produced annually in the regular course of business can be shown to accurately consolidate data compiled over the course of a year.

3.5.4.2 Components The process or system components determine how well the preparation of records are controlled. The admissibility of records can successfully be defended from challenge to the trustworthiness if the program includes adequate procedures, training programs, audit trails and audits.

(a) Procedures

Procedures reflect the detailed steps to be followed when creating, modifying, duplicating, destroying or otherwise managing records. They provide for consistent quality control, problem resolution and other activities that might otherwise be subject to inconsistent action, multiple interpretation or misinterpretation.

Established procedures demonstrate what an organization plans to do in managing and controlling the process or system — as opposed to what it actually does. The trustworthiness of an organization's records offered in evidence might well be judged by the established procedures and how closely they are followed. Deviations can be expected to be closely scrutinized, especially if the deviations are from legally required procedures.

(b) Training programs

Formal training programs for staff on details of the system procedures raise a strong presumption that the procedures were correctly followed. If an organization can show the court that staff knew what procedures they were supposed to follow, it can also show that there is a high likelihood that the procedures were in fact followed.

(c) Audit trails

Audit trails document who used the system, when they used it, what they did while using the system, and what were the results. Properly implemented audit trails can automatically detect who had access to the system, whether staff followed standards procedures or whether fraud or other unauthorized acts occurred or might be suspected. They provide independent confirmation that proper procedures were in fact followed.

(d) Audit

Audits performed periodically confirm that the process or system produces accurate results. Audits should compare the procedures stated in the procedure's documentation with procedures they actually followed. They confirm that the process or system adheres to this guideline.

The term "audits" as used in this section is different than quality control specified in most system procedures. Quality control can be performed by individuals creating the records to verify the accuracy at the time of creation. This ensures the accuracy of the system for operational purposes.

Audits confirm the accuracy of the results for purposes of admissibility of records in evidence. For purposes of establishing the credibility of the records for evidence, audits should be performed by an independent source (i.e., persons other than those who created the records of persons without an interest in the content of the records). As a minimum, an audit should be performed by an individual other than those involved in creating or duplicating the records (e.g., trained auditor having organization-wide audit responsibilities).

No particular method of auditing is required. For purposes of original records, audits should focus on whether the records incorporate the information of the acts, events, or activities leading to the record.

For duplicates, audits should confirm that the duplicates accurately reproduce the originals. This normally involves comparing statistically valid sampling of originals to their corresponding reproductions prior to destruction of the originals.

3.5.4.3 Documentation Documentation of the process or system provides an ensuring verification of the process or system followed to produce the records. Without documentation, witnesses must rely solely on memory — a form of evidence that, over times, becomes less trustworthy and susceptible to contradiction. Documentation preserves the information about the process or system independent of the individuals involved and can be used to prepare exhibits to guide witness testimony. The documentation, along with the exhibits, can be introduced into evidence for the jury to scrutinize during their deliberations.

(a) Content

A knowledgeable person should prepare and maintain documentation for the process or system used to produce the records. Documentation should be complete and up-to-date. This enables staff to be aware of and follow the most current procedures. It also ensure that reliable systems documentation is immediately available if needed for court proceedings.

No particular form or level of detail is required to describing the process or system to the court, although visual aids outlining the documentation can be helpful. Typically, documentation should be sufficient to demonstrate the steps required to get from the beginning to the end of the process. In some proceedings, only a general, non-technical description of the process or system will be required, including verification that any equipment or software involved operated properly at the time the records were produced. It might be appropriate to prepare documentation with different levels of detail and complexity to meet anticipated future needs.

Training documentation could include documentation of distribution of the written procedures, course materials, attendance of individuals at training sessions, remedial or refresher training programs, certifications of training completion and other relevant information.

The actual audit trail records will demonstrate what activities actually took place as part of the process or system. The actual audit reports indicate whether the statistically valid sampling of records produced accurate results and what remedial procedures were followed if the expected level of accuracy was not achieved.

For purposes of laying a foundation for admissibility of records in evidence, actual system procedures followed during the period the records in question were produced should be maintained in sufficient detail to enable a qualified witness (e.g., the records custodian) to rely on the documentation in describing the process or system to the court. The documentation should explain what should have been done and what was actually done, and explain any deviations from standard procedures. The training, audit trail and audit documentation should also be presented to confirm the accuracy of the process or system.

(b) Retention

At least one set of documentation should be maintained during the period for which the records produced by the process or system could likely be subject to court review. When the documentation changes, the old versions should continue to be maintained for the requisite period. As indicated earlier, the court will determine the admissibility of the records in evidence based on the accuracy of the process or system in effect at the time the records were produced.

3.5.5 Availability of process or system for outside inspection The courts encourage pretrail discovery of computer programs and related materials, recognizing that the use of computer-produced data as evidence can otherwise impede effective cross-examination. The guideline applies this principle to records produced by any information systems technology, as follows.

The process or system used to produce records introduced into evidence is subject to outside inspection by opposing parties and the court. Outside inspection may include review of procedures documentation, review of system operation, independent inspection and quality control tests, independent audit, testing of process or system operation, review of equipment design and software documentation, review of training program or any other matter related to the operation of the process or system.

If the records were produced on the current or substantially similar system, access to the system may be required to be provided to outside parties upon request to process their own test data. If the system used to produce the records no longer exists, any existing documentation described above must be made available. Failure to produce pertinent documentation because it no longer exists may jeopardize admissibility of the records if their trustworthiness cannot otherwise be established.

In sum, any relevant step of the process or system can be reviewed by the outside party.

3.5.6 Legal status of records offered as evidence

When determining the admissibility of records into evidence, the court will consider the reliability and accuracy of the process or system used to produce the records. The particular form or format of the records shall have no bearing on their legal status regarding admissibility. Likewise, the destruction of original records after reproduction shall not affect the legal status of duplicate records regarding their admissibility.

All that is required for records to be deemed admissible in a *prima facie* showing that the process or system is trustworthy in terms of producing an accurate result. Once the records are admitted, the trustworthiness of their content will remain subject to challenge. (For example, a computer printout of a record is admissible if it is shown to be an accurate reflection of the source data used to create the record, but this does not mean the source data is necessarily correct.)

Source: **Performance Guideline for the Legal Acceptance of Records Produced by Information Technology Systems (ANSI/AIIM TR-31)**
Part II: Performance Guideline for the Acceptance by Government Agencies of Records Produced by Information Technology Systems

---

1 Scope and purpose

1.1 Scope

State and federal legislative bodies enact statutes that establish the law in specified areas. Statutes often authorize government regulatory agencies to promulgate detailed rules and regulations to implement the statutes. Together, the statutes and regulations constitute laws that affect the public.

Disputes arising from these laws are decided by the courts. The courts will interpret the laws in terms of the issues raised in the dispute and, sometimes, determine the laws to be unenforceable (e.g., void for vagueness) or unconstitutional.

This part of the guideline addresses laws enacted by government that affect personal or business recordkeeping practices. In particular, it addresses laws containing recordkeeping provisions that require records to be kept available for government audit, require records to be submitted to government, or establish the form of records. Organizations that fail to comply with these laws are subject to fines, penalties and loss of rights. It does not address laws related to evidence (see Part One) or government internal activities (other than those regulations that apply similarly to private and government activities such as health and safety, employment, etc.)

Laws often require that organizations submit information to a government agency, maintain records to confirm compliance or, otherwise, assist government agencies to fulfill their regulatory responsibilities.

Some laws address the creation, maintenance, retention, form, availability, standards or other issues affecting an organization's records and information. Others merely state that certain information must be created, maintained or reported without specifying the form of the record — paper, microfilm, computer, optical disk, or other media.

Only a few, limited laws explicitly require maintenance of paper records. Other laws permit the records to be maintained in computer or microfilm form provided that stated requirements have been followed.

A majority of jurisdictions have adopted either the *Uniform Photographic Copies of Business and Public Records as Evidence Act* or the *Uniform Preservation of Private Business Records Act.* Both uniform laws establish the statutory basis for reproducing records required to be kept by law and using the reproduction for legal compliance purpose. Other, non-uniform laws that address reproductions specify unique requirements or verbiage.

1.2 Purpose

Legislators and regulators have a legitimate interest to ensure that organizations maintain required information to enable government to perform its legally-authorized purpose. By requiring the public to submit information and maintain records, government can determine the impact of the laws and verify compliance. But the degree of burden placed on the public through recordkeeping laws should be balanced against the relative costs and benefits to society of the entire legislative and regulatory scheme.

When laws establish unique requirements for records and information management systems, a significant and sometimes onerous burden may be placed on the public. Organizations that conduct business in numerous jurisdictions and are therefore subject to numerous laws, face an even greater burden in the identification, comprehension and implementation of the multitude of complex and even contradictory requirements.

Records and information system managers need to develop systems that comply with the law and best meet the needs of the organization. New advances continue to be made in information technology that can assist organizations to become more efficient, effective and profitable. These advances may be thwarted, or even precluded, due to inconsistencies in laws and the slow pace lawmakers follow to recognize new technologies.

This part of the performance guideline establishes criteria for legislators to incorporate into statutes that affect recordkeeping and guidelines to appropriate restrict the scope and content of regulations. Regulators can use this guideline in drafting regulations to specify performance requirements for records and information systems developed by the public. Systems designers can also use this guideline to develop systems and procedures that increase the likelihood of legal compliance even before a national consensus is reached relating to legal acceptance of records produced by information technology systems.

2 Background

2.1 Purpose of laws addressing recordkeeping requirements

Lawmakers create laws addressing recordkeeping requirements to achieve a number of purposes.

2.1.1 Information gathering Lawmakers review the activities of organizations to uncover problems for which laws may offer resolutions. By requiring an organization to maintain or report information, government is relieved of the enormous burden of gathering the information using its own resources. From the information received, lawmakers can prepare regulations that respond to the problems and conditions that exist in the"real world".

2.1.2 Rulemaking Rules are the likely result of information gathered from regulated organizations. The impact of existing and proposed laws can be determined based upon the information received. The information can also lead to the repeal of irrelevant or inappropriate laws, or confirmation that existing laws have achieved their goals.

2.1.3 Compliance monitoring The information received through reporting or that which is obtained during government investigations helps the regulatory agency determine whether all or most organizations are complying with the law. The information will often help detect those organizations that may not be in compliance. Without this type of information, if is difficult to determine compliance by monitoring activities alone. Records provide on-going documentation from which government can reach reasonable conclusions.

2.1.4 Auditing Government will periodically audit or investigate an organization on-site to determine compliance. This provides confirmation of the accuracy of information previously provided to government. Auditing also serves as a coercive measure that encourages organizations to comply so they will not be fined or penalized as a result of an adverse audit.

2.1.5 Enforcement When an organization fails to comply with the law, government may impose fines and other penalties to punish the offenders, coerce compliance and warn other organizations about the consequences of non-compliance. Records also enable government to determine the effect of a particular fine or penalty placed on an organization for non-compliance. Records also indicate who may be affected by the violation of the laws, such as in a product recall, so that the offending party can be forced to take remedial steps.

2.1.6 Education Records laws often provide useful information to organizations on how to comply or how to develop and operate effective systems. Government sometimes identifies model systems during its information gathering and auditing, and describes a key feature of a good system in the law. Some regulated organization welcome legal requirements for systems, both as a blueprint of how to develop a legal system and as a coercive reason for developing improved systems in their organization.

2.1.7 Notice Published records-related laws inform regulated organizations of standards that must be met to avoid fines, penalties or other punishment. When a law is vague, government may be barred from enforcing it, since the organization may claim that they were never placed on "notice" of what government expected from them to do.

2.1.8 Standardization Records-related regulations occasionally force regulated organizations to adopt a single standard that promotes the public interest. Additionally, it also forces organizations to follow comparable practices. Therefore, government auditors can monitor standard industry practices more efficiently and effectively.

2.2 Laws affecting record media

Laws may specify the form for maintaining records, such as microfilm, computer, optical disk or other designated form. Only a few limited laws require that records be kept in paper form.

Many states have adopted uniform laws that establish specific and uniform legal requirements for records. Other jurisdictions have developed unique laws that may contain different or even contradictory provisions.

The following sections summarize many of the laws that have resulted in some standards requirements for recordkeeping in the United States. These laws are either uniform laws or federal laws that have led to uniform practices. Section 3 provides the performance guideline based on the prevailing position already taken in these laws.

2.2.1 Uniform laws Uniform laws are typically developed by the National Conference of Commissioners on Uniform State Laws to, "promote uniformity in state laws where uniformity is deemed desirable and practicable." (See Jacobstein and Mersky, *Fundamentals of Legal Research*, p. 352 (1977.) The process has also promoted uniformity between state and federal law.

Once the Conference approves a uniform law, the law is then approved by Congress or individual states before it is binding in the jurisdiction. Because each state may accept or reject the uniform law or, accept it with modifications, the goal of true uniformity is rarely achieved. Some states have some or all of these uniform laws, others have none. The publication *Uniform Laws Annotated* (West Publishing Company) lists the names of jurisdictions that have adopted each uniform law.

Two uniform laws establish the basic requirements for information technology systems for regulatory purposes. One also addresses the admissibility of records in evidence as well. (See Annex A for the text of each law.)

2.2.1.1 Uniform Photographic Copies of Business and Public Records as Evidence Act This law addresses duplicate records produced in the regular course of business through the use of several enumerated technologies or, "... other processes which accurately reproduce or form a durable medium for so reproducing the original." In essence, the law permits an organization to duplicate records in the regular course of business using any technology that accurately reproduces the original.

Once the legal standard is met, the original records may be destroyed in the regular course of business, except as follows:

1) *The law specifically requires the preservation of the original records.* Only a few laws actually require original records. Normally, when the law requires records to be maintained, any form of the records may be used.

2) *The law specifies additional requirements for duplicate records before the originals can be destroyed.* Some regulatory agencies have specified additional requirements, others have not. These additional requirements have the power of law and must be met before the originals can be legally destroyed.

3) *The original records are held in a custodial or fiduciary capacity.* Original records that "belong to another" cannot be destroyed, even after reproduction, without the permission of the owner. Although the duplicate records would contain the same information as the original records, the physical, original records will belong to the owner.

Duplicate records produced under this uniform law may then be used "in any judicial or administrative proceeding." Most analysts also believe that this law permits duplicate records to be used for all regulatory purposes (including administrative proceedings) unless another specific law requires the original be kept or establishes restrictions on the duplicate records.

2.2.1.2 The Uniform Preservation of Private Business Records Act This law has been adopted by the states of Colorado, Georgia, Illinois, Maryland, New Hampshire, Oklahoma and Texas in either the language specified in the Uniform Law or in a slightly modified version referred to as the "Uniform Records Retention Act". This law establishes when records must be legally kept under state law, but the law does not establish a records retention period. The records can be destroyed "after the expiration of 3 years from the making of such records without constituting an offense under such law".

All jurisdictions that have adopted this law, however, have also included an additional paragraph found in the original uniform law related to reproductions. The paragraph states:

> If in the regular course of business a person makes reproductions of original business records, the preservation of such reproductions constitutes compliance with any laws of this state requiring that business records be kept or preserved.

Since the *Uniform Preservation of Private Business Records Act* has been adopted in these seven states as a statute, this provision will prevail over any state regulation adopted by organization from using reproduced records. The definition of "reproduction" provided in this law is almost identical to the language of the *Uniform Photographic Copies of Business and Public Records as Evidence Act — a reproduction can be made through the use of several enumerated technologies or by "other means which accurately reproduces or forms a durable medium for so reproducing the original."*

2.2.2 Federal laws

2.2.2.1 Federal Paperwork Reduction Act The *Federal Paperwork Reduction Act* (Title 44, United States Code, Chapter 35) controls the paperwork burdens that the United States federal agencies may place on the public. The Act strives to "minimize and control burdens associates with the collection of information by federal agencies from individuals, businesses, and other private institutions, and state and local government". The Act also establishes the basis for coordinating information policy within the federal government.

The Federal Paperwork Reduction Act authorizes the Office of Management and Budget (OMB) to promulgate regulations to implement the Act. In Title 5, Code of Federal Regulations, Part 1320, OMB lists the situations when it will require an agency to justify placing recordkeeping burdens:

> **§ 1320.6 General information collection guidelines**
>
> Unless the agency is able to demonstrate that such a collection of information is necessary to satisfy statutory requirements or other substantial needs, OMB will not approve a collection of information:
>
> * * * * *
>
> (f) Requiring respondents to retain records, other than health, medical, or tax records for more than three years:
>
> * * * * *
>
> (j) Requiring respondents to maintain and provide information in a format other than that which the information is customarily maintained.

In essence, no federal agency can require the public to collect or maintain information (including records) in any form unless that collection has been reviewed and approved by the Office of Management and Budget. This law also prohibits federal agencies from issuing their own regulations that require records to be kept in unusual or extraordinary forms. Since no interpretation of the phrase "customarily maintained" is provided, it is difficult to determine whether certain requirements that an agency believes appropriate would result in OMB rejection of the proposed regulation.

The public is entitled to comment on paperwork burdens for proposed new federal regulations by either writing the sponsoring regulatory agency or contacting OMB directly. OMB determines whether the regulations complies with the *Federal Paperwork Reduction Act* by determining the burden being placed on the public. For definitional purposes, "burden" is defined as follows:

> **§ 1320.7 Definitions.**
>
> (b) "Burden" means the total time, effort, or financial resources required to respond to a collection of information, including that to read or hear instructions; to develop, modify, construct, or assemble any materials or equipment; conducts tests, inspections, polls, observations, or the like necessary to obtain information, to organize the information in the requested format; to review its accuracy and the appropriateness of its manner of presentation; and to maintain, disclose or report the information.
>
> (1) The time and financial resources necessary to comply with the collection of information that would be incurred by persons in the normal course of their activities (e.g., in compiling, maintaining business records), will be excluded from the "burden" if the agency demonstrates that the reporting and recordkeeping activities needed to comply are usual and customary.
>
> * * * * *
>
> (c) "Collection of information" means the obtaining or soliciting of information by the agency from ten or more persons by means of identical questions, whether such a collection of information is mandatory or voluntary or required to obtain a benefit. For purposes of this definition, the "obtaining or soliciting of information" includes any requirements or request for persons to obtain, maintain, retain, report, or publicly disclose information.

2.2.2.2 Internal Revenue Service: Revenue Procedures The Internal Revenue Service (IRS) has published Revenue Procedure 81-46, describing procedures for taxpayers that maintain records for tax purposes on microfilm, and Revenue Procedure 91-59, describing procedures for computer records. These procedures establish specific system details for taxpayers that are acceptable to the Internal Revenue Service.

Internal Revenue Service regulations, 26 CFR 1.6001-1 states the Internal Revenue Service's basic recordkeeping requirements as follows:

> . . . any person required to file a return of information with respect to income, shall keep such permanent books of account or records, including inventories, as are sufficient to establish the amount of gross income, deductions, credits, or other matters required to be shown by such person in any return of such tax or information . . . . The books or records required by this section shall be kept at all times available for inspection by authorized internal revenue officers or employees, and shall be retained so long as the contents thereof may become material in the administration of any internal revenue law.

The regulation establishes the principle that a taxpayer must maintain records sufficient to support a return and to provide access to those records in case of an audit. The revenue procedures specify a "safe harbor" or IRS-approved methods for using microfilm and computer technology. Other forms of records may also be maintained by a taxpayer provided that the legal requirements are met — adequate records are maintained to support the return and access to information is provided when requested by IRS agents.

Since tax records constitute a large portion of records maintained by the private sector, the IRS regulations and procedures in these areas establish a de facto standard for recordkeeping in other areas of an organization. For example, the computer systems used for tax purposes generally are used by various people in the organization to perform their operational tasks. The procedures established, including documentation standards, security, etc., for tax purposes, also affect the procedures followed for other organizational purposes.

2.2.2.3 Federal Acquisition Regulations The *Federal Acquisition Regulations* (48 CFR Part 4) establish requirements for recordkeeping by contractors doing business with the federal government. These regulations may also affect other recordkeeping functions due to the volume of business conducted by a large number or organizations with the federal government. Title 48 CFR 4.706 provides the requirements for microfilm systems. After records have adequately been microfilmed, the regulation permits the destruction of the original records when "(1) all claims under the contract are settled; (2) eighteen months has passed since final payment; or (3) the time the original records are required to be kept by other laws or regulations has elapsed".

The *Federal Acquisition Regulation* itself establishes specific retention periods for records ranging from two to four years for many records, and three years after final payment under the contract for others.

2.2.3 State laws Besides the uniform laws discussed above, state laws tend to be unique except for certain tax regulations. When the Internal Revenue Service adopted revenue procedures affecting microfilm and computer records in the 1970's, several state revenue departments adopted the same or similar language for regulations affecting state taxes, other than income tax. Income tax regulations were generally precluded in deference to the specific requirements and enforcement powers of the Internal Revenue Service. Even after the Internal Revenue Service modified its regulations in the 1980's, these state revenue agencies maintained the old language in their regulations.

The state tax regulations typically recognize computer and microfilm records and provide certain requirements that taxpayers must follows.

2.2.4 Absence of laws Even with the existing laws stated above, many organizations remain in a "legal quandary". While the law may not prohibit or regulate certain records technologies such as electronic imaging systems, the law may not explicitly permit them either.

In industries that require licensing or other forms of prior approval before certain activities can be undertaken, the legal departments or business managers may not feel confident recommending new technologies or approaches that have not yet been endorsed by the government entities that regulate them. Some may believe that it is not prudent to proceed with new system development because the risk is too great. What if the regulatory agency rejects the license application because it is not "confortable" with the new records technology (even though it never prohibited or regulated the technology)? What would the cost of delays in the approval process or protracted litigation?

Clearly, the uniform laws and general principles of American law grant "implicit" permission to use any records technology. But, these organizations would prefer "explicit" permission from the law before proceeding. Many wait for definitive court decisions before embarking on development of systems using new technology.

Some organizations prefer this legal quandary because of the opportunities offered. Realistically, without specific prohibitions and regulations, any technology system would arguably comply with the law, provided that the basic requirements for recordkeeping are met. These organizations would prefer that government refrain from enacting new laws that may restrict their options.

2.2.5 Court decisions The courts have already ruled on legal issues related to paper, microfilm, computer, facsimile copies, photocopies and other forms of records and information technology systems that produce original and duplicate records. The basic principles related to the legal admissibility of records as evidence and the legal acceptance of records under statutes and regulations have been established.

Some technologies, however, have not specifically been addressed. For example, through 1992, the courts have not considered legal issues related to records produced by electronic imaging technology. Does that mean that such records are not legally acceptable? Some believe that no form of evidence is legally acceptable until it is confirmed by the courts. Others believe any form is acceptable unless proven otherwise.

Realistically, the courts cannot and will not rule anew on every issue. The courts and legal system utilize precedent (previous court decisions) to determine the law in new areas. When an issue has already been resolved by previous court decisions, it would be fruitless and wasteful to appeal the case to a higher court, absent a compelling reason to revisit the issue.

The courts have already determined that records produced in any form are legally acceptable, based on its previous acceptance of records in a large variety of forms — provided they are shown to be accurate and reliable.

A regulatory agency may object when a regulated organization uses a records technology that is neither prohibited nor regulated. The organization affected could still reproduce the records in a form that meets the needs of the agency (e.g., paper prints). If the agency still deems the records unacceptable, the organization can take the matter through the administrative law process for resolution. If that fails, the organization can litigate the matter in court. It is inconceivable that a court would rule adversely against an organization that used a records technology that was neither permitted nor prohibited, provided that the information required by law was maintained or submitted to government in an appropriate form (e.g., paper).

If the law did not prohibit or regulate the offending records technology, the court will determine whether or not the organization was "placed on notice" that it was violating the laws. Under administrative law principles, a regulatory agency could not impose fines and penalties on an organization without notice (a law stating that the conduct is not permitted). Additionally, the court could also point to all the implicit legal support for any records technology, such as the uniform laws. For either reason, the organization could prevail. (The test is whether the agency was acting in an "arbitrary and capricious" manner.)

If the records technology system is upheld at trial, the agency could appeal the decision to a higher court. Realistically, the appeal court should uphold the lower court's decision, unless it is "clearly erroneous". Since the lower court decision to accept the system is supported by precedent, administrative law principles and implicit laws, it seems inconceivable that the lower court decision could be overturned.

For these reasons, the AIIM committee does not expect appeals related to the legal acceptance of records produced by a particular technology system. Instead, appeals are more likely related to specific practices or procedures that a trial court finds do not result in accurate records, or records that do not meet requirements established by law, independent of the technology used to produce them.

However, the judicial process does not always proceed as expected. You always take some risk when operating in a "legal quandary".

2.3 Problems with existing laws

The courts and regulatory agencies have traditionally viewed the original, paper records as the best evidence and duplicate records as inferior evidence. Modern rules of evidence still recognize this concept but provide exceptions for properly made duplicate records.

The basic legal principle found in the Best Evidence Rule has been negated by advances in information technology. Paper records can sometimes be inferior to duplicate records or automated systems in terms of preserving evidence for the following reasons:

1) *Paper records systems generally result in the preparation of one copy of the record.* In case of fire, flood or other natural disaster, the single version of the record may be destroyed and no longer available for any evidentiary, regulatory or other purposes.

2) *Documents can be removed from paper records systems without detection.* While erasures can be detected on originals, most other forms of fraud cannot. For example, when records are subpoenaed by the court or requested by government agencies, certain documents can be provided while others can be destroyed or hidden. The fraud resulting from the selected withholding of records can rarely be detected.

Alternatively, original paper records can inappropriately be destroyed without detection. These records may then be unavailable for any purpose including evidence and regulation. Unless the fraud related to the destruction is detected, the content of the records will effectively be excluded from consideration.

3) *Paper records may not have a very long life expectancy.* This is especially true today because original paper records are often produced using poor quality paper, poor quality ink, life-off typewriter ribbons, or other inexpensive, short-term methods. Even records properly organized and stored may not be usable by the time they are needed for a court proceeding.

4) *Paper records are rarely created as part of a rigorous process or system.* Many (if not most) organizations do not even have a records management program. Even those that do rarely establish rigorous procedures related to records creation, maintenance and disposition. Many records created in each organization reflect individual whims rather than systematic policy. The accuracy of records therefore varies based upon the integrity, accuracy and capabilities of the individuals involved.

5) *Paper records are rarely audited for accuracy.* Few organizations audit paper records systems to determine the accuracy of the information recorded.

6) *Paper records are rarely subjected to adequate security.* Any individual in an organization may get access to paper records. The types of fraud discussed above can be accomplished without detection.

Even laws that prefer or require paper records can prove to be harmful to the public interest.

1) *Laws preferring or requiring paper records discourage the reproduction of records.* Complex and contradictory regulations discourage organizations from using modern technology systems. Many fear that technology systems that have not yet been approved by an organization may result in adverse consequences during an audit or government investigation.

When laws discourage the use of modern technology systems, especially reproduction systems, users tend to maintain only one version of the record — the paper version. In case of disaster, the organization's records may be destroyed or damaged to the point that a regulatory agency cannot adequately perform its function. If, alternatively, laws encourage the use of information technology systems, especially those that result in reproductions or a backup of the systems, the records will still be available even in case of natural disaster. Additionally, fraud is much more difficult to perpetrate when records have been reproduced or backed up and maintained at different locations.

2) *Laws that prefer paper records result in cumbersome and conflicting legal requirements for other forms of records among multiple jurisdictions and create a harsh burden for businesses operating in interstate commerce.* An organization that does business in a number of states, plus the federal jurisdictions, must comply with all applicable state and federal laws. Inconsistent and complex records-related laws can crate a severe burden for those who design and operation information systems. The system developer should understand the laws and develop a system that meets the requirements of them all. It is not realistic to expect that multiple systems should be developed to meet multiple legal requirements.

Modern information technology systems often differ from paper-based systems because they establish processes or systems that reliably reproduce accurate results. Modern reproduction systems, such as microfilm, optical disk, and even data processing systems, offer the following characteristics that generally provide for more accurate and trustworthy records than are possible with paper records systems:

1) *Modern information technology systems, by their nature, produce records as part of a process or system that requires a disciplined operation based on standard procedures, written documentation, adequate training, and thoroughly tested equipment and software components.*

2) *Modern information technology systems can provide an audit trail that identifies not only what actions were taken related to records, but also the individuals involved.*

3) *Modern information technology systems can prohibit or detect alterations and attempted alterations to records.* Most optical disk systems, for example, inherently preclude the alteration of images. Bypassing alteration safeguards an be very difficult, requiring special knowledge and technical capabilities.

4) *Modern information technology systems can provide for routine security backup and reproductions of records produced.* Typically, microfilm, magnetic tape or disk, and optical disk systems will produce backup records at appropriate intervals as required. These backup records are generally stored in properly maintained remote locations where they can be retrieved if the original information is damaged or destroyed.

In reality, fraud can be committed in any type of information system. But, properly designed, implemented and maintained information technology systems — including systems based on paper, computer, microfilm or other records media — are all capable of producing records that are reliable and accurate. Following the procedures determines the reliability and accuracy of the records, not the specific technology.

[It should be noted, however, that although paper-based systems are more susceptible to irretrieval loss or destruction of records and detectable omissions, without the safeguards stated above, disasters and fraud can be much more costly and damaging to an organization that is dependent on an information technology system.]

2.4 Factors affecting the burdens imposed by law

Lawmakers generally attempt to refrain from developing laws that conflict with other laws in the same jurisdiction or laws that fail to protect the public interest. But lawmakers in other jurisdictions operate under different laws or they may interpret the public interest differently.

Rules and regulations developed by regulatory agencies cannot explicitly violate a statue or constitutional provision. A regulatory agency is free, however, to regulate in areas authorized by the granting statute that is not prohibited by these types of other legal constraints.

Lawmakers consider a variety of legal approaches to achieve the regulatory purpose. Many factors are weighed to determine the scope and degree of regulation in the final law. Significant consideration should be given to the burden that the regulation places on the public versus the benefits recognized by the public for full compliance.

The federal government has enacted the *Federal Paperwork Reduction Act* (see previous discussion) to establish a formal process to identify the burdens placed on the public by recordkeeping provisions and determine the level of recordkeeping that establishes the minimum burden on the public while fulfilling the regulatory purpose. The states and territories have not established a comparable, formal procedure to achieve this goal.

An overly burdensome regulation may also create significant harm to the public. For example, when a regulated organization is required to keep large quantities of records that would otherwise not be needed by the organization to conduct its daily business, the organization incurs significant costs (e.g., staff, space, equipment, etc.) to keep the records. These costs are reflected as expenses to the organization. They also result in legitimate tax deductions on the organization's tax return, thus reducing the organization's taxable income. As a result of the excessive burden placed on such a regulation, the organization would pay less taxes than it would with a less burdensome regulation. If a large number of organizations are affected by the regulation, the net loss in tax revenues to the various jurisdictions could result in harm to the public that far exceeds the benefit gained by compliance with the regulation.

For these reasons, laws should only establish the minimum level of burden on regulated organizations necessary to achieve the regulatory purpose. Complex, inconsistent and expensive requirements may negate the benefits expected by lawmakers.

2.5 Regulatory strategies

Laws specifying recordkeeping requirements should reflect the concerns stated in Section 2.0. When new laws conform to the following criteria, users of information system technology should be in full compliance by following the positions presented in Section 3.0.

2.5.1 Laws should reflect the regulatory need, not technical system details As stated above, laws are developed to meet a variety of different government needs. New laws that address information technology systems should focus on those needs rather than the details of the specific technology. Clearly, technology will change over time, rendering laws obsolete when specific technologies have been enumerated. Legislators and regulators should identify the functional capabilities of the systems (stated in Section 3.0 below) rather than their preferences for specific technologies.

2.5.2 Laws should permit organizations to establish information technology systems that best meet their needs The public interest is best served when organizations develop systems that best meet their needs at the lowest possible cost. Effective systems should also meet government needs at the lowest possible cost to taxpayers.

2.5.3 Laws should not discourage the reproduction of records and the destruction of the original records, except when a compelling need for the original records exists Laws that discourage the reproduction of records violate the public interest. When government establishes cumbersome and burdensome requirements before the introduction of appropriate modern information technology systems, many potential users may be discouraged or dissuaded from adopting those systems. As a result, they may rely exclusively on the paper records system.

Modern reproduction systems offer the opportunity to reproduce records and store them in multiple locations. In case of disaster or even attempted fraud, at least one set of records will probably remain available to government to perform its regulatory function.

In a few instances, such as negotiable instruments, original records may be necessary to prevent fraud or abuse. But, few other records are needed in original form.

2.5.4 Laws should not discourage information technology systems that provide sophisticated security for information Modern technology systems provide a series of passwords, audit trails, physical security and other methods for protecting the security of information. These measures help ensure the reliability of information and help detect or prevent potential fraud. Paper record systems, on the other hand, rarely include any measure of security and are susceptible to fraud by even unsophisticated users.

2.6 References

See Annex B for selected readings.

3 Performance guideline

3.1 Definitions

The following definitions apply to the process or system assessment criteria set forth below:

3.1.1 Record Information preserved by any technique in any medium, now known, or later developed, that can be recognized by ordinary human sensory capabilities either directly or with the aid of technology.

3.1.2 Original record A record prepared in the first instance or any counterpart intended to have the same effect by a person executing or issuing it. If data are stored in a computer or similar device, any printout or other output readable by sight shown to reflect the data accurately is an "original."

3.1.3 Duplicate record A record that is produced by the same impression as the original, or from the same matrix, or by any other technique that accurately reproduced the original.

3.1.4 Information technology system Any process or system that employs a mechanical, photo-optical, magnetic, electronic or other technological device for producing or reproducing records.

3.2 Applicability

This part of the guideline applies to records produced by information technology systems regardless of the physical characteristics of the record media or technology employed. This includes records produced by any technique employing an information technology system as described above.

3.3 Information assessment

Information technology systems developed to provide required information to government or maintain required records should ensure that the information fulfills statutory and regulatory requirements.

3.3.1 Content The records and information must provide government with the substance and detail required by law.

3.3.2 Completeness The records and information must be sufficiently complete to fulfill the intent of the law and the need of government for that information as stated in the law.

3.3.3 Accuracy The records and information must attain a sufficient level of accuracy to ensure the utility of the information for the intended legal purpose.

3.3.4 Accessibility The records and information must be made accessible to government in a standard form of communication within the statutorily required time, if provided, or within reasonable time, following any government request for records and information.

3.3.5 Retention Records and information must be retained for the period of time required by statute regulation, other government published guidance, users' needs, precedent or other sources. In the absence of a specific or derivable retention period for required records, the records and information should be kept for at least a reasonable period of time, such as three years.

3.4 Information technology system assessment

3.4.1 Quality Quality refers to the ability of the information technology system to reliably produce and preserve records so that they can be used or recognized by the intended audience.

3.4.1.1 General requirements The following should appear with sufficient clarity so that each can be recognized:

1) Individual letters, number and symbols

2) Combinations of letters, number and symbols forming words or sentences

3) Graphics such as signatures, logos, pictures, etc.

4) Sounds

5) Other features of records such as color, shape, texture, etc., that relate to the content of the information

3.4.1.2 Original records Original records preserve information over time in the identical or functionally equivalent form to the original information.

Original records may preserve information in a form different than the original information without affecting its quality. For example, information preserved in digital format may be printed on paper using different print fonts at different times.

3.4.1.3 Duplicate records Duplicate records accurately reproduce original records. Information that is readable or recognizable on originals should be readable or recognizable on duplicates.

Similarly, information that is readable or recognizable on duplicates must be readable or recognizable on originals, except that duplicates may contain production, control, indexing, certification or other data not related to the informational content of the records.

The exception allows additional data to be included on duplicates for administration of the reproduction process if it does not adversely affect the informational content of the record. For example, control and indexing data stored with digital images may be necessary to retrieve the images, but does not affect the content of the records themselves.

Image enhancement techniques may be used provided that they do not change the informational content of the records.

When duplication processes change the informational content of records, the resulting records are considered new originals.

3.4.2 Form of information Records may be produced by any technique and maintained in any form, provided that they meet the requirements of this guideline.

When government requests submission or review of records, the record should be presented in a readable or recognizable form acceptable to government. For written records, the records may be provided in paper form or another form that is readable using equipment available to government. Government representatives may also review records at the system site, using system equipment. Government may also accept record in other forms when the equipment for their retrieval and use is provided by the organization.

The form of records provided to government varies based upon the nature of the information. For example, digitized voice information may be presented in an audible, understandable form while digitized image information must be presented in readable or recognizable form. Records that contain information relating to multiple human sensory capabilities, such as video recordings that must be both seen and heard to be complete, must be presented in a form that provides all the necessary human sensory information to government.

3.4.3 System components The process or system components determine how well the preparation of records are controlled. The legal acceptance of records can successfully be defended from challenge to trustworthiness if the program include adequate procedures, training programs, audit trails and audits. This formula was taken from the *Uniform Rules of Evidence* that establishes the basis for the legal admissibility of records in evidence.

3.4.3.1 Procedures Procedures reflect the detailed steps to be followed when creating, modifying, duplicating, destroying or otherwise managing records. They provide for consistent quality control, problem resolution and other activities that might otherwise be subject to inconsistent action, multiple interpretation or misinterpretation.

Established procedures demonstrate what an organization plans to do in managing and controlling the process or system — as opposed to what it actually does.

Records produced as part of regularly conducted activity, such as those produced in the regular course of business, demonstrate that the process or system used to produce them is reliable and accurate. A regularly conducted activity may include a regular pattern of activity to produce the records on a daily, weekly, monthly, yearly or other schedule.

A regularly conducted activity may also include records created as part of a regular program of the organization, but at irregular times. For example, when a planned program results in the reproduction of records created prior to a specific year, this will be viewed as a program proceeding in the regular course of business, even though it only occurred once.

3.4.3.2 Training Formal training programs for staff on details of the system procedures raise a strong presumption that the procedures were correctly followed. If an organization can show the court that the staff knew what procedures they were supposed to follow, it can also show that there is a high likelihood that the procedures were, in fact, followed.

3.4.3.3 Audit trails. Audit trails document who used the system, when they used it, and what they did while using the system. Properly implemented audit trails can automatically detect who had access to the system, whether staff followed standards procedures, or whether fraud or other unauthorized acts occurred or might be suspected. They provide independent confirmation that proper procedures were followed.

3.4.3.4 Audit Audits performed periodically confirm that the process or system produces accurate results. Audits should compare the procedures stated in the procedure's documentation with procedures actually followed. They confirm that the process or system adheres to this guideline.

The term "audit" as used in this section is different than quality control specified in most system procedures. Quality control is performed while creating the records to verify their accuracy at the time of creation. This ensures the accuracy of the system for operational purposes.

Audits confirm the accuracy of the results for purposes of legal acceptance by government. Audits should be performed by an independent source (i.e., persons other than those who created the records or persons without an interest in the content of the records). As a minimum, an audit should be performed by an individual other than those involved in creating or duplicating the records (e.g., an experienced auditor having organization-wide audit responsibilities).

No particular method of auditing is required. For purposes of original records, audits should focus on whether the records incorporate the information of the acts, events, or activities leading to the record.

For duplicates, audits should confirm that the duplicates are accurate reproductions or the originals. This normally involves comparing statistically valid samplings of the originals to their corresponding reproductions, prior to destruction of the originals.

3.4.4. Documentation Documentation of the process or system provides an enduring verification of the process or system followed to produce the records. Without documentation, witnesses in court or administrative proceedings must rely solely on memory — a form of evidence that, over time, becomes less trustworthy and susceptible to contradiction. Documentation preserves the information about the process or system independent of the individuals involved and can be used to prepare exhibits to guide witness testimony. If necessary, the documentation, along with the exhibits, can be introduced into evidence for the jury to scrutinize during their deliberations.

3.4.4.1 Content A knowledgeable person should prepare and maintain documentation for the process or system used to produce the records. Documentation should be complete and up-to-date. This enables staff to be aware of and follow the most current procedures. It also ensures that reliable system documentation is immediately available if needed for court proceedings.

No particular form or level of detail is required for describing the process or system to the court, although visual aids outlining the documentation can be helpful. Typically, documentation should be sufficient to demonstrate the steps required to get from the beginning to the end of the process. In some proceedings, only a general, non-technical description of the process or system will suffice. In others, more detailed documentation will be required, including verification that any equipment or software involved operated properly at the time the records were produced. It might be appropriate to prepare documentation with different levels of detail and complexity to meet anticipated future needs.

Documentation developed for training could include guidance for the distribution of the written procedures, course materials, attendance of individuals at training sessions, remedial or refresher training programs, certifications of training completion and other relevant information.

The actual audit trail records will demonstrate what activities actually took place as part of the process or system. The actual audit reports indicate first, whether the statistically valid sampling of records produced accurate results, what remedial procedures were followed, if the expected level of accuracy was not achieved.

For purposes of establishing the accuracy of the records, the actual system procedures followed during the period the records in question were produced, should be maintained in sufficient detail to enable a qualified witness (e.g., the records custodian) to rely on the documentation in describing the process or system to the court or government agency. The documentation should explain what should have been done and what was actually done, and explain any deviations from standards procedures. The training, audit trail and audit documentation should also be presented to confirm the accuracy of the process or system.

3.4.4.2 Retention At least one set of documentation should be maintained during the period for which the records produced by the process or system could likely be subject to court or government review. When the documentation changes, the old versions should continue to be maintained for the requisite period. The accuracy of the records is based on the accuracy of the process or system in effect *at the time the records were produced.*

3.5 Access and availability of records and systems

3.5.1 Availability of records Records must be available for inspection and audit by a government representative for the full period required by law. The life expectancy of the media, per se, has no bearing on the legal status or legal acceptance of the records. The information maintained on the media and the system used to produce the records must achieve the required retention period. This means that for some technologies, it may be necessary to periodically convert, regenerate, copy of transfer the information from one medium or technology to another to preserve the information for the required period.

Regardless of the retention period or life expectancy of the media, records must continue to exist when litigation, government investigation or audit is pending, imminent, or in some cases, foreseeable. In some instances, a court order may prohibit specified records from being destroyed or otherwise rendered unavailable.

Procedures followed to convert records from one medium or technology to another should be carefully developed, documented and implemented. Conversion of records should not affect their legal status provided that the quality and accuracy does not functionally change during the conversion.

An organization that fails to retain adequate records for the required period may be subject to fines and other penalties. System failures, errors in conversion, technical obsolescence, accidental erasure and inability to read record media does not relieve an organization of its obligation to preserve records. Problems that occur due to abnormal or unexpected natural causes — e.g., hurricane, earthquake, flooding, etc. — may mitigate the level of penalties, but does not relieve an organization of its responsibility to maintain records. A vital records or disaster recovery program should be provided as part of all information technology systems to ensure the continued operation of the organization and the continued availability of required records.

3.5.2 Access to records Authorized government representatives should be given access to records produced by the information technology system when it is requested. In order to facilitate the review, readers, printers or other equipment for system access must be made available at a work station for the representative. Training and simplified procedures manuals should also be made available to facilitate access and use of the system.

When the scope of government review has been defined or narrowed in advance, the organization can select those records covered by the scope and provide them for immediate access to the representative. This will reduce the time necessary for the representative to review the appropriate records and also restrict the representative from reviewing records outside the scope of authority. At the representative's request, the organization shall demonstrate that the selected records provided for review represent the complete response to the request for information or, alternatively, it shall provide the representative with access to the entire system to independently determine the completeness of the records.

3.5.3 Access to the system Government representatives shall be provided access to the system to determine whether the procedures stated by the organization are actually being followed. Authorized representatives may review the procedures documentation, review system operation, perform independent inspection and quality control tests, perform an independent audit, test the process or system operation, review equipment design and software documentation, review training programs or any other matter related to the operation of the process or system.

If the records were produced on the current or a very similar system, access to the system by government representatives must be provided to enable them to process independent test data and review the hardware, software and data. If the system used to produce the records no longer exists, existing documentation describing the above operations must be made available. Failure to produce pertinent documentation may jeopardize the acceptance of the records if their trustworthiness can not otherwise be established.

3.6 Legal status of records

When determining the acceptance of records, government will consider the reliability and accuracy of the process or system used to produce the records. The particular format of the records shall have no bearing on their legal status. Likewise, destruction of original records after reproduction shall have no effect on the legal status of the duplicate records.

The acceptance of records by government does not ensure that the substantive information in the records fulfills the legal requirements established by law. Records produced by any information system technology under this guideline should be presumed to meet the substantive requirements of the law. Government retains the right to request additional information, require modification to the system to meet the requirements of the law, and impose penalties for the failure to comply with the requirements of the law.

Source: **Performance Guideline for the Legal Acceptance of Records Produced by Information Technology Systems (ANSI/AIIM TR-31-1994)**
Part III: Implementation of the Performance Guideline for the Legal Acceptance of Records Produced by Information Technology Systems

1 Scope and purpose

1.1 Scope

Every organization should be cognizant of state and federal laws that affect its recordkeeping practices. In particular, an organization should be aware of how to avoid problems whenever its records happen to be scrutinized in litigation or in an administrative action by a government agency.

The *Performance Guideline* developed by the AIIM task force makes recommendations to government agencies. These recommendations are designed to ease the burdens on organizations regarding acceptance of records for regulatory compliance purposes, while providing to both government and private industry guidance in good recordkeeping practices.

This report presents a method for organizations to conduct a self-assessment of their recordkeeping practices, applying the recommendations in the *Performance Guideline*. It also suggests ways for industry groups, professional associations, and government agencies to encourage incorporation of the model act and rule's principles in new ore revised statutes and regulations governing the keeping of records.

Purpose

For purposes of the *Performance Guidelines*, an information technology system is any process or system that employs mechanical, photo-optical, magnetic electronic, or other technological devices for producing or reproducing records. Widespread use of these systems for recordkeeping "in the ordinary course of business" has resulted in rules and regulations that specify particular requirements for acceptance by government agencies, or admission into evidence by courts, of records produced by technological devices.

This report provides a systematic approach for implementing recommended recordkeeping practices that meet legal acceptance criteria set forth in Parts I, II, and IV of the *Performance Guideline*. Adherence to the guideline facilitates legal acceptance of records produced by information technology systems. Acceptance of the model act and rule promotes uniform treatment of records across jurisdictions and reduces barriers to the beneficial use of information technology. This report also includes a strategy for professional associations, industry groups, and others to promote the adoption of the model act and rule presented in Part IV of the guideline, that establishes requirements consistent with the recommended practices.

The self-assessment process will help an organization determine if it has established and is following recordkeeping practices that will minimize problems with legal acceptance requirements. Promotion of the model act and rule is intended to bring about uniformity in laws and policies affecting the use of information technology systems for recordkeeping, and to minimize restrictions that unnecessarily discourage or hamper the use of such systems.

2 Background

The primary purpose of laws and regulations concerned with recordkeeping is to prescribe acceptable recordkeeping practices and requirements for meeting the needs of government. These practices and requirements address such government activities as information gathering, rule-making, compliance monitoring, auditing, enforcement, education, notice, and standardization. (See TR31-1993, Part II for elaboration.)

Advances in recordkeeping technology have made it increasingly difficult for lawmakers to reconcile traditional legal acceptance requirements based on records produced by original human-readable physical impressions such as handwritten or typed records with records produced as printouts or displays by devices that translate machine-readable codes or patterns to human-readable form, such as computer and optical disk systems. Too often, this reconciliation has resulted in poorly drafted statutes or regulations with confusing or outdated requirements, which are compounded by a lack of uniformity among the states. The *Performance Guideline* is intended to minimize these discrepancies and to promote uniformity in laws and regulations regarding use of various information technology systems for the creation and maintenance of records.

Some uniformity has been achieved through the adoption by seven states of the *Uniform Preservation of Private Business Records Act*, or the *Uniform Records Retention Act*, and through adoption by most states of the *Uniform Photographic Copies of Business and Public Records as Evidence Act*, or the *Uniform Rules of Evidence* (modeled after the *Federal Rules of Evidence*). Part IV of the *Performance Guideline* presents a model act that is a modified version of the *Uniform Preservation of Private Business Records Act* and the *Uniform Records Retention Act*, and also a model rule, both of which express policies and requirements consideration in drafting status, rules, or regulations regarding acceptance of records. The model act or rule more clearly accommodate evolving information technology systems as well as those that are in common use by government and industry. Their adoption by all states will tend to minimize restrictions in government regulations that unnecessarily discourage or hamper the use of information technology systems, and will tend to reduce or eliminate burdensome requirements imposed by government agencies regarding acceptance of records produced by such systems.

Organizations involved in the development and implementation of information technology systems for production of records need to have knowledge of laws and policies affecting their activities, and a method for assuring that recordkeeping practices are being followed that will avoid problems in meeting requirements of these laws and policies. In addition, these organizations should actively seek changes in laws that impose unnecessary burdens on their operations. To these ends, this report offers guidance in implementing appropriate recordkeeping practices and a strategy for promoting the model law and rule.

3 Self-assessment procedure

In determining whether good recordkeeping practices are being followed that will avoid problems regarding acceptance of records by government agencies, or as evidence in the event of litigation, an organization should periodically assess its practices and procedures. When an organization commits to such a self-assessment, it should also be prepared to make needed changes. (Note: Results of such self-assessment may be discoverable in legal or regulatory proceedings.) After-the-fact realization that records are unacceptable by a government agency or inadmissible during litigation can be very costly.

The *Performance Guideline* includes recommendations — in the form of assessment criteria — that specifically address requirements for legal acceptance of records produced by information technology systems. Assessment results of systems that have been carefully developed to account for recordkeeping legal requirements will likely be in conformance with most, if not all, legal acceptance criteria presented in the *Performance Guideline*. However, system designers and managers too often are only concerned with developing a recordkeeping system that meets the organization's primary business objective, paying little attention to laws that assure acceptance of the records by government agencies or by the courts, where admissibility of these records may be crucial to the organization's case.

A reliable self-assessment requires a comprehensive review of every aspect of an information system, from input sources to final production and distribution of records. It should be accomplished by consulting individuals with up-to-date detailed knowledge of system operations and procedures involved in the total recordkeeping process. Outside consultants and third parties can assist, but assessment documentation must represent factual information provided by individuals involved in day-to-day operations.

3.1 Assessment strategy, organization, and resources

Organizations typically have many kinds of records kept many different ways, in many different places, by many different people. When should your organization begin a self-assessment and how much should be spent? Clearly, the first steps must be to formulate a strategy, consistent with the resources that the organization is willing to allocate to the effort, and to create norms for the assessment documentation, along with some expectation of how many discovered deficiencies will be remedied.

The first task is to determine if the organization knows what records it keeps, where they are, and who is responsible for their content and condition. A basic question to ask is whether the organization has a recordkeeping counterpart to the account "chart of accounts."

Assuming that the organization has something akin to a structure for its records, and an inventory to indicate what the records are, where they are, and who is responsible for them, an *assessment priority* might be developed. The highest priority for assessment might be given to those records that the organization is required to maintain by some statute or governmental regulation.

Following is an example of categories of record sources (listed alphabetically) where self-assessment of their respective recordkeeping processes may warrant a prioritized schedule:

- accounting and budgeting activities;
- business transactions with customers and suppliers;
- decision making regarding products and services;
- decision making regarding materials and wastes;
- financing decisions and activities;
- management-employee-union relations, personnel decisions;
- real estate and site decisions and activities;
- research and development decisions and activities.

Self-assessment can be done by employees of the organization. Third parties such as consultants and auditors can be involved in the process. A prioritized schedule might be established to assess a portion of the organization's records each year, particularly if such assessment were to be coupled with the annual independent auditing.

3.2 Description of the system environment and functions

An initial task in a self-assessment procedure is to update or verify the accuracy of existing documentation that describes the system environment in terms of the organizational structure, functions and responsibilities, and system processes. Updated documentation should include descriptions of the elements listed.

Beyond their need in the self-assessment procedure, valid documentation of these descriptions are invaluable in supporting system integrity in the event of a government audit. They are also useful for preparing a witness to testify as to the accuracy and reliability of the system or process in laying a foundation for admissibility as evidence in litigation.

3.2.1 Organizational responsibilities

Organizational responsibility needs to be very specific, i.e., more than the usual organizational chart, particularly for large organizations with decentralized system processes. Each unit involved in the recordkeeping process should be identified and its pertinent functions described in detail, including interfaces with other units. Key individuals should be identified, such as the records custodian and supervisors of such critical functions as source data capture and quality control. Position titles alone should not be depended upon to identify functions and responsibilities of these individuals. Position descriptions, functions, and duties are also needed.

3.2.2 Information flows and handling

The description of the information technology system should focus on the flow of data and information and its manipulation and transformations, together with the hardware and software components that are involved. This description need not be highly technical. For example, the function of an optical scanning device can be described as a hardware/software component that transcribes specific data from certain source documents into a properly encoded form for storage on an optical disk, from which the data is retrieved for subsequent printing or display. Similarly, a Computer Output Microfilm (COM) program may be described as software used for producing records in a form for automatic conversion to microfilm. The function of common utility software such as sort/merge or statistical calculation subroutines need not be described. Note: The important point to bear in mind is to document the information flows, with all changes, and the role played by each component of technology.

3.3 Description of the records produced.

The description of records produced by the recordkeeping system should include identification of each informational element contained in the records (e.g., in a personnel record, this might include starting date, job title, salary, etc.), the purpose of the records, the form in which they are stored (e.g., magnetic disk), their classification in terms of security or privacy constraints, their custodianship, and their management accountability.

In current information technology systems, many records are not "produced" on individual forms or paper like birth certificates and deeds. Rather, electronic records may reside in host computers, decentralized servers, and even desktop computers — sometimes simultaneously. In this environment, records may include data and information stored in different locations, paper printouts, backups, electronic communications, etc.

3.4 Disposition of the records

Records can be "disposed" in many ways, including destruction, storage in a long-term repository, or transfer to a third party. Additionally, in data base and document management system environments, "records" may be updated dynamically, with only a journal recording or timed back-up to show the replacement of old data with new. However the records or information are disposed, the process must, be consistent, thoroughly documented, and in compliance with all applicable statutes and governmental regulations and established records retention schedules.

3.5 Description of the system processes

Of primary importance in a self-assurance procedure is a description of each activity performed on information, its contents or forms, or both. Of course, before the steps can be described, they must be identified. Existing system documentation (including flowcharts depicting the system process) explained by knowledgeable system designers or analysts would be a good starting point. Accuracy of the documentation would then be verified by interviews with individuals directly responsible for accomplishing each step. During these interviews, descriptions of the steps should be based on explanations of actual procedures.

3.6 Laws and regulations governing the system recordkeeping

With the aid of the organization's legal counsel, the pertinent recordkeeping statutes, regulations, rules, and policies with which the organization must comply should be identified, compiled, and included with the system documentation. (Note: Regulations and rules also have the force of law.) A review of these laws and policies should be conducted and a determination made as to which organizational unit is responsible for assuring compliance with their various provisions. The assessment criteria discussed below will aid in determining how to address elements of the recordkeeping process found to be in noncompliance.

4 Assessment criteria

The *Performance Guideline* lists assessment criteria that should be considered in drafting laws and policies prescribing requirements for acceptance of records produced by information technology systems. Key criteria from this list are presented below. Upon completion of the previously identified self-assessment tasks, the findings should be assessed against these criteria, taking into account the requirements of pertinent laws and regulations.

The legal acceptance criteria listed apply to both acceptance of records by government agencies and to determining admissibility of records as evidence in litigation. Some of the criteria reflect definitions of terms commonly found in federal and state rules of evidence. (Note: Some of the criteria elements have been augmented with additional information not found in the guideline.)

The following ten assessment criteria for the legal acceptance of records produced by information technology systems are the primary factors on which to focus the information technology assessment. The goal is to explain that the organization followed generally accepted guidelines.

4.1 Quality

Definition: Quality relates to the ability of the information technology system to reliably produce and preserve records so that they can be used or recognized by the intended audience. It also relates to the quality of information in terms of its accuracy and reliability.

Discussion. Quality assurance requires routine checking of a statistically valid sampling of records, a function usually performed by a quality control specialist using statistical sampling techniques.

Assessment action: The review should look at samples of products produced by the system and ascertain use and adherence to appropriate standards and technical reports such as *ANSI/AIIM MS23-1991, Practice for Operational Procedures/Inspection and Quality Control of First-Generation, Silver Microfilm of Documents.*

4.2 Original records

Definition: A record produced from the data stored in an information technology system is considered an original record if a printout or other output readable by sight is shown to reflect the data accurately.

Discussion: Original records may present information in a form different from the source information without affecting its quality. For example, information preserved in digital format may be printed on paper using different print fonts at different times. (Note: for some legal purposes, original documents such as deeds and wills may have different legal significance than duplicates. Other originals, such as promissory notes and laboratory notebooks, may be required by law.)

Modern rules of evidence equate records produced by specified technologies as either originals or reproductions of originals, thus accommodating records produced by information technology systems regarding their admissibility.

Assessment Action: The assessment should identify original records as opposed to copies or duplicates.

4.3 Duplicate records

Definition: Duplicate records accurately reproduce original records.

Discussion: Duplicate records accurately reproduced by an information technology system are treated as originals. Information that is readable or recognizable on originals will be readable or recognizable on duplicates. Similarly, information that is readable or recognizable on duplicates must be readable or recognizable on originals, except that duplicates may contain production, control, indexing, certification, or other data not related to the information content of the records.

Image enhancement techniques may be used provided that they improve readability of information contained on the records, rather than change the information content of the records. When conversion processes change the information content of records, the resulting records will be new originals or different records.

Assessment Action: The assessment should distinguish characteristics of duplicate records in the information technology system being reviewed.

4.4 Records retention, versus life expectancy of data on media

Definition: Records must be retained, regardless of media, for the period required by the organization's records retention program for any legal, user, historical, or other purpose.

Discussion: The life expectancy of the media per se has no bearing on the retention requirements of the records. The information maintained on the media and the ability of the system to produce records from the information must meet the required retention period. This means that for some technologies it may be necessary to periodically convert, regenerate, copy, or transfer the information from one medium or technology to another to preserve the information for the required period.

Regardless of the retention period or life expectancy of the media, records must continue to exist when litigation, government investigation, or audit is pending, imminent or, in some cases, merely foreseeable. In some instances, a court order will impose a restraint from causing specified records to be destroyed or made otherwise available.

Assessment Action: The assessment should determine if records fall under approved records retention schedules. If yes, are the schedules being adhered to? If not, what general retention guidelines or procedures are followed? Procedures followed to convert records from one medium or technology to another should be carefully documented. Conversion of the records will not affect their acceptance provided that quality and accuracy does not functionally change during conversion. Also the reviewer should determine if there is any pending litigation involving the organization and which records might be affected.

4.5 Trustworthiness and admissibility of records

Definition: Admissibility of records as evidence is dependent on a showing that the process or system that produced them is trustworthy.

Discussion: As part of maintaining the integrity of recordkeeping operations, reasonable measures should be taken to assure that records offered for acceptance are trustworthy in terms of either unintentional or purposeful alteration. Records custodians and other appropriate witnesses must be prepared to meet foundational requirements for admission of records into evidence in an administrative or judicial proceeding. These requirements place the burden on the proponent to demonstrate that the records production process is accurate and reliable in that it produces results that accurately reflect the input or source information.

Records produced by any technique may be offered as evidence; however, their admissibility will be greatly enhanced if they meet the requirements set forth in the *Performance Guideline*. Rules of evidence specifically provide for admissibility of records accurately produced in the regular course of business or in the course of a regularly conducted activity, permitting the routine destruction of originals. Courts attach a (rebuttable) presumption of trustworthiness to such records.

Assessment Action: The assessment report should list specific individuals who would be the best witnesses to describe various aspects of the technology information system and attest to its trustworthiness.

4.6 Information clarity

Definition: All elements of information produced by an information technology system must be clear and readily recognizable.

Discussion: The following record elements must be considered, as appropriate:

- individual letters, numbers, and symbols;
- combinations of letters, numbers, and symbols forming words or sentences;
- graphics such as signatures, logos, pictures, etc.;
- sounds;
- other features of records such as color, shape, texture, etc., that relate to the content of the information.

With multimedia systems there may be several elements to consider in the same system.

Assessment Action: The evaluation process should assess which elements exist in the system being reviewed and determine clarity by sampling.

4.7 Process or system characteristics

Definition: Accuracy and timeliness are the primary process or system characteristics that determine reliability and trustworthiness.

Discussion: The operational characteristics of the recordkeeping process or system used to produce records will determine the accuracy of the records. A description of these characteristics in non-technical language facilitates the showing that the process or system is reliable and accurate, hence intrinsically capable of producing trustworthy records. Two primary characteristics that attest to good recordkeeping practices are accuracy and timeliness.

1) Accuracy

Records produced by methods shown to ensure or enhance accuracy will be more readily accepted as being in compliance with regulatory requirements and more easily admissible in evidence.

Such methods may include systematic quality control and audit procedures, as well as operational oversight by an official who has a thorough knowledge of the system or process used to produce the records.

2) Timeliness

Records produced within a short period of time after an event tend to be more readily accepted as accurate than records produced much later. However, a challenge to acceptance of a later-produced record can be overcome by a showing that the time lapse had no effect on the record's contents. For example, a computer printout of a statistical report produced annually in the regular course of business can be shown to be simply a consolidation of data compiled throughout the year as the events occurred.

Assessment Action: The assessment should describe in layman's terms measures taken to ensure accuracy and timeliness of records produced on the system being reviewed. If deficiencies are discovered, the assessment should describe the recommended remedial actions that should be taken.

4.8 Process or system components

Definition: Procedures, training, audit, and documentation are critical components in al technology information systems.

Discussion: Process or system components determine how well the production of records is controlled. This, in turn, will determine whether a challenge to the trustworthiness of the records based on inadequate procedures or inefficient operation can be overcome.

1) Procedures

Effective system procedures reflect the detailed steps to be followed when creating, modifying, duplicating, destroying, or otherwise managing records. They provide for consistent quality control activities, problem resolution approaches and other functions that might otherwise be subject to inconsistent action, multiple interpretation, or misinterpretation.

Established procedures demonstrate what an organization plans to do in managing and controlling the process or system — which can be considerably different from what it actually does. The trustworthiness of an organization's records offered in evidence might well be judged by the established system procedures and how closely they are followed. Deviations and the reasons therefor can be expected to be closely scrutinized, especially if they are legally required procedures.

System procedures documentation should be a regular assignment of a person who has detailed knowledge of the process or system *in terms of the flow of information* and operational activities involved. (Note: The fact that the process or system is computer-based does not mean a computer programmer is required to document system procedures; however, a complex system might require someone trained as a systems analyst.)

A typical documentation tool employed is a flowchart depicting all operations and decisions made in the process or system — from the collection of input data to the production of output. The flowchart should relate clearly to the operational responsibilities of individuals directly involved in the process or system.

Documentation should be regularly updated to reflect any changes. This provides new employees with a credible reference for understanding the system, isolating and solving problems, and recording subsequent modifications. However, documentation is also important if the documented procedure is ever questioned in court.

For purposes of laying a foundation for the admissibility of records in evidence, *actual* system procedures followed during the period the records in question were produced should be documented in sufficient detail to allow a qualified witness (e.g., the records custodian) to depend on the documentation in describing the process or system to the court. The documentation should include an explanation of deviations from established procedures.

2) Training

A formal program for training staff on details of system procedures along with documented training sessions raises a strong presumption that the procedures were correctly followed. Training documentation could include distribution of written procedures, course materials used, attendance of individuals in training sessions, remedial or refresher sessions, certifications of completed training, and other relevant information.

3) Audit

Audit consists of two components: 1) an audit trail that documents the procedures followed; and 2) results of periodic audits of the process or system to confirm that records produced are accurate.

Audit Trail. An audit trail documents who used the system, when they used it, what they did while using the system, and what the results were. An audit trail can detect who had access to the system, whether staff followed standard procedures, or whether fraud or other unauthorized acts occurred.

Audit of System or Process. The process or system should be audited periodically to confirm the accuracy of results. An audit should compare procedures stated in the procedures documentation with procedures actually followed. An audit confirms that the process or system adheres to the precepts of this guideline.

The audit can be performed by individuals creating the records to verify the accuracy at time of creation. However, to enhance the credibility of the records, audits should be conducted by an independent external source (i.e., persons other than those who created the records or persons without an interest in the content of the records). At a minimum, such audits should be performed by individuals in the organization other than those involved in creating or duplicating the record (e.g., trained auditors having organization-wide audit responsibilities).

No particular method of auditing is required. For original records, an audit should focus on whether the record incorporates the information of the acts, events, or activities leading to the record. For duplicates, an audit should confirm that the duplicates accurately reproduce the originals. A statistically valid sampling of originals should be compared to the related reproductions prior to destruction of the originals. The audit confirms the accuracy of your system. (Note: One hundred percent perfect quality cannot ordinarily be achieved.) The statistically valid level of quality should be based on sampling techniques accepted industry-wide, qualified by costs and the importance of the records.

4) Documentation

Documentation relating to the process or system provides an enduring verification of the process or system followed to produce the records. Without documentation, the court must rely on witness memories which tend to become less trustworthy over time. Documentation preserves the information about the process or system independent of the individuals involved and can itself be submitted as evidence or as an exhibit.

A knowledgeable person, i.e., someone very familiar with the process or system, should prepare and maintain the documentation. Documentation should be complete and up-to-date. This enable staff to be aware of an to follow the most current procedures. It also ensures that reliable system documentation is immediately available if needed for administrative or judicial proceedings. Typically, documentation should be sufficient to demonstrate the steps required to get from the beginning to the end of the records production process and the activities involved in records maintenance.

Assessment Action: The assessment should review procedures, training, audit, and documentation in accordance with the previous discussion on system components.

4.9 Availability of process or system for outside inspection

Definition: Pretrial discovery in litigation subjects and information technology system to inspection by the opposing party.

Discussion: The courts have long encouraged pretrial discovery of computer programs and related materials, recognizing that the use of computer-produced data as evidence can otherwise impede effective cross-examination. Hence, the process or system used to produce the records introduced into evidence is subject to outside inspection by opposing parties and the court. Outside inspection may include review of documentation, system operation, independent inspection and quality control tests, independent audit, testing of process or system operation, review of equipment design and software documentation, review of training programs, or any other matter related to the operation of the process or system.

If the records were produced on the current or a substantially similar system, access to the system must be provided to outside parties, upon request, to process their own test data. If the system used to produce the records no longer exists, any existing documentation must be made available. Failure to produce pertinent documentation because the system no longer exists may jeopardize admissibility of the records if their trustworthiness cannot otherwise be established.

In sum, any relevant step or the process or system can be reviewed by the outside party.

Assessment Action: The reviewer should develop scenarios for outside inspection and assess the feasibility of such actions if the organization is called upon to make the system available to outsiders.

4.10 Legal status of records offered as evidence

Definition: The legal status of records offered as evidence in litigation or for acceptance by a government agency is not affect by their form or format, or by the fact that they are duplicates rather than originals.

Discussion: When determining the admissibility of records into evidence, the court will consider the reliability and accuracy of the process or system used to produce the records. The particular form or format of the records will have no bearing on their legal status regarding admissibility. Likewise, the routine destruction of original records after reproduction in the ordinary course of business will not affect the legal status of duplicate records regarding their admissibility. If the process or system is deemed to be trustworthy, the records will ordinarily be deemed admissible, but their contents will continue to be subject to challenge.

Assessment Action: In this final part of the review, questions should be raised regarding difficulties the organization may have concerning records that might be offered as evidence or to prove actions which have been taken by the organization.

5 Self-assessment documentation

The self-assessment should be documented and treated as an important component of the organization's operational files. The written assessment should identify the areas of the recordkeeping process that need attention based on results of the self-assessment, and corrective action should be taken as soon as possible lest the self-assessment become outdated in critical areas.

The documentation components should be developed as part of each assessment task and accomplished by individuals performing the particular task. The components should be edited and consolidated by individuals familiar with the overall recordkeeping process. (Note: The documentation should be the result of a cooperative effort of professional staff involved in accomplishing the assessment tasks.)

6 Management review

The self-assessment should be documented and presented formally to management, including supervisors of the recordkeeping process and legal staff. Management should be apprised of the risks and possible consequences of various alternatives. Recommended actions and associated costs should be presented for management approval.

7 Reflections on the model act and rule

The model act and rule presented in Part IV of the *Performance Guideline* reflect the recordkeeping practices recommended in the guideline. The act is a modified version of the *Uniform Preservation of Private Business Records Act* and the *Uniform Records Retention Act* which have been adopted by a number of states. The rule was developed in recognition of the long time usually needed for adoption of a law. By comparison, a rule can be promulgated and implemented by a government agency rather quickly (although adoption of the rule does not preclude the need for adoption of the act).

Statutes and regulations affecting acceptance of records produced by information technology systems should be media-neutral and uniform throughout the nation. That is, they should not list specific technologies as "acceptable." This will minimize inconsistent policies and rules (which encourage "forum shopping") and the need for revising laws to accommodate new technologies. Experience has shown that statutes or rule that enumerate specific "acceptable" technologies often deter use of an unlisted new technology, albeit unintentionally.

The model act and rule provide a basis for establishing durable legal requirements for acceptance of records produced by information technology systems that use advanced as well as existing technologies.

8 Promoting a uniform policy

As our nation enters an era of multi-state and multi-national organizations and activities, and the pervasive use of electronics in the conduct of all kinds of business, it must shed outmoded and inconsistent restraints. One such restraint is recordkeeping laws and rules that force organizations to delay or even forego the use of new technologies.

The model law and rule proposed in these guidelines is not a complete break with the past. It preserves the established legal principles and traditions and will bring about uniformity that is essential to multi-state enterprises and activities. The challenge is to convey this message to the lawmakers and government rulemakers.

The recommendations need to be brought to the attention of government agency, legislative and judicial management and staff personnel involved in creating and revising statutes, regulations or rules dealing with recordkeeping. Professional associations and industry groups can use their collective influence with elected and appointed officials and their staffs to revise the laws to conform with provisions of the model act and rule. This process has begun in a few jurisdictions. There have already been some instances of changed laws governing recordkeeping processes to incorporate the principles and recommendations set forth in the guideline; the most notable is a recent rule promulgated in the state of New Mexico (See Annex B).

To obtain uniformity nationally, the best approach is through the National Conference of Commissioners on Uniform State Laws, which reviews proposed uniform laws that have been submitted for its consideration. Once the Conference approves a uniform law, the law must then be adopted formally by a state before it is binding in that state. Experience has shown that because each state may accept, reject, or accept with modification a uniform law, the goal of absolute uniformity is rarely achieved.

Considering the current conditions of inconsistency and uncertainty, great improvements can be made even if absolute uniformity is not achieved. But those improvements will not happen without active involvement by those committed to the principles of the model act and rule. Recordkeeping is not the highest priority on lawmakers' or rulemakers' agendas; but recordkeeping has a significant impact on the bottom-line of businesses and organizations. The recognition of that cost is the best reason for action.

[Note: The Annex has not been reproduced. See the full publication for details.]

Source: **Performance Guideline for the Legal Acceptance of Records Produced by Information Technology Systems (ANSI/AIIM TR-31-1994) Part IV: Model Act and Rule**

1 Scope and purpose

1.1 Scope

Seven states have either adopted the *Uniform Preservation of Private Business Records Ac*t (UPPBRA) or the *Uniform Records Retention Act* (URRA). (Copies of these acts are included as Annexes A and B.) The model act presented is a modified version of these uniform acts, incorporating recommendations of the AIIM task force. States are encouraged to consider adopting the model act in preference to the UPPBRA and URRA because the model act tends to more clearly accommodate evolving information technology systems as well as those that are currently in common use by government and industry.

Rules and regulations are statements of general or particular applicability promulgated by agencies to "implement, interpret, or prescribe law or policy," and have the same force and effect as statutes. Therefore, adoption of the rule presented will provide a state agency a statement of particular applicability to records produced by an information technology system, interpreting or prescribing requirements of related regulations or statues such as the model act.

The model act sets forth policies and requirements for consideration by government agencies, legislators and the judiciary when drafting statutes, rules or regulations regarding acceptance of records. It was developed within the following framework or rationale:

- The rule is guided by good recordkeeping practices and incorporates recommendations made in the AIIM performance guideline.
- The task force is cognizant of the fact that regulations or rules are often criticized for being too constraining in defining key terms, leaving little room for variance in complying with requirements of regulatory agencies. Hence, definition of terms is kept to a minimum, leaving the need for additional definitions to the legislative body or agency adopting the model rule. (Terms alluded to appear without definition in existing laws — based on the premise that they are not likely to be misinterpreted in the context of their use. Examples are the terms "accurately" and "trustworthiness.")
- The task force agreed that the *Federal Rules of Evidence* and the *Uniform Rules of Evidence* do an adequate job in providing for admissibility of records produced by an information technology system. (Note: Although existing rules are adequate, the performance guideline recommends changes in phraseology and emphasis to more clearly accommodate new or emerging information technology systems.) Trustworthiness and admissibility of records are addressed in the model rule to provide guidance in recognition of that fact that acceptance of records by an agency subjects it to being the custodian of records produced by an external organization. Hence, if these records are involved in litigation and offered as evidence by the agency, the burden is on the agency as the proponent to show that the system that produced them is accurate and reliable.
- The rule recognizes that records must be preserved for a period of time for a variety of reasons (e.g., legal, business, back-up, audits, possible litigation and to meet government archival requirements). The rule addresses terms like "quality," "original records," and "duplicate records."
- Issues such as the application of copyright laws to "imaged" records and the life expectancy of records on particular media are beyond the scope of both the guideline and the rule, as is the legal efficacy and acceptability of electronic signatures.

In the course of its deliberations, the task force determined that it was appropriate to make recommendations related to the *Federal Paperwork Reduction Act.* Annex E contains the recommendations developed, which embody the principles of the model act and model rule.

1.2 Purpose

The model act and rule are designed to encourage good recordkeeping practices by providing direction to legislators and government agencies in the establishment of requirements for acceptance of records produced by information technology systems. The model act, as proposed, will have precedent over other contradictory laws and restrict the content of regulations in the recordkeeping area. The task force also developed a model rule, since it takes a considerable amount of time to have a uniform law enacted, whereas, a rule can be implemented by government agencies in a relatively short period of time.

An underlying purpose of the model act and rule is to encourage use of information technology systems in the production of records. To this end, a delineation of benefits of such systems (as opposed to paper-based systems) is included.

The model rule can be adopted independent of the model act, so long as it is properly promulgated, i.e., it is not arbitrary or capricious or does not violate the dictates of a law. However, adoption of both is encouraged.

2 Proposed Uniform Records Act: A revision of the Uniform Preservation of Private Business Records Act

2.1 Proposed uniform law: The Uniform Records Act

§ 1. Definitions

The following definitions are used in this Act:

Record Information preserved by any technique in any media, now known or later developed.

Original records A record prepared in the first instance; a record derived from other records or any counterpart intended to have the same effect. If data are stored on a computer or similar device, any printout or other output readable by sight shown to reflect the data accurately is an "original."

Duplicate record A record that accurately reproduced the original.

Information technology system Any process or system that employs a mechanical, photo-photo-optical, magnetic, electronic, or other technological device for producing or reproducing records.

§ 2. Records retention period

Records required to be created or kept by the laws of this state may be destroyed after three years from the time of creation unless the law establishes a specific different retention period or a specific procedure to be followed prior to destruction that results in a different retention period.

§ 3. Form of record

Original and duplicate records may be produced by any process or system, including any information technology system, regardless of the physical characteristics of the record media or technology employed. Retention of duplicate records produced under the laws of this state constitutes compliance 'with any laws of this state requiring that records be created or kept.

§ 4. Records requirements specified by law

No law in this state requiring records to be created or kept may specify that records be kept longer than three years, restrict the media used to maintain records, restrict the information technology system used to create or duplicate records, or require the maintenance of original records unless express, documented findings conclude that the law is necessary to satisfy specific statutory requirements or to meet other compelling needs of the government or the public. Laws may specify the data or information to be maintained, the form and content of information to be submitted to government, the requirement that records be available for inspection and audit by government, and other requirements necessary to facilitate law enforcement and government operation.

§ 5. Scope

This Act shall apply to records prepared by private individuals, partnerships, corporations or any other associations, whether carried on for profit or not, and to any government entity operating under the laws of this state.

§ 6. Uniformity of interpretation

This Act shall be so interpreted and construed as to effectuate its general purpose to make uniform the law of those states which enact it.

§ 7. Short title.

This Act will be cited as the *Uniform Records Act.*

§ 8. Effective date

This act shall become effective on (insert date) and shall apply to all records created before and after that date.

2.2 Background

The *Uniform Records Act* was taken, with modifications, from the *Uniform Preservation of Private Business Records Act* (Annex A), developed by the National Conference of Commissioners and Uniform Acts in 1951, and the *Uniform Records Retention Act* (Annex B), developed by the Association for Records Managers and Administrators in 1987.

The Uniform Records Act differs from previous uniform laws in the areas described in 2.2.1 through 2.2.5.

2.2.1 Definition differences

The definitions were modified significantly to more closely reflect definitions prepared by the Association for Information and Image Management in ANSI/AIIM TR31, Parts I and II referred to as the "*Performance Guideline.*"

In some cases, the definitions were further simplified from the *Performance Guideline* to better reflect more modern word usage. The intent of these revised definitions is to better describe the process or system used to prepare records so that the definitions remain effective into the foreseeable future, without need for modification when new technologies emerge. The following describes changes in the definitions:

The definition for "record" eliminated the phrase found in the *Performance Guideline*" — "that can be recognized by ordinary human sensory capabilities, either directly or with the aid of technology." The committee felt that final definition provided a clear and complete definition without the phrase.

The definition for "original record" contains the phrase "a record derived from other records" to also define an original record as one that incorporates components from other original or duplicate records. Information from two or more records that is momentarily brought together, but never *preserved*, does not constitute a "record."

The definition for "duplicate record" eliminates the phrase essentially taken from the *Uniform Rules of Evidence* — "is produced by the same impression as the original, or from the same matrix, or by any other technique." Instead, it focuses the key legal criteria — a duplication is a record that accurately reproduces the original — rather than the technique used to produce the duplicate.

The term "information technology system" includes such common concepts as "information system," "information processing system," and "date processing system." The word "technology" is used to highlight the reality that existing laws focus on technology, rather than on the entire process or system. The *Uniform Records Act*" addresses legal issues totally independent of technology.

2.2.2 Records kept in any form

Section 3 of the *Uniform Records Act* specifies that records, including original records, may be kept in any form. Existing versions of the uniform law only permitted maintenance of reproductions of records to constitute compliance. The purpose of this paragraph is to reflect today's reality that the distinction between originals and duplicates has been bridged by modern information technology systems. The legal standard for record should be based on the accuracy of the process or system used to produce the records, and not whether the records are originals or duplicates.

2.2.3 Restriction of other laws

Section 4 was added to restrict other laws intended to dictate form, media or technology used to produce records. Regulatory agencies may still override this position if "express, documented findings conclude that the law is necessary to satisfy specific statutory requirements or to meet other compelling needs of government and the public." Those states that closely monitor regulations or have implemented programs like the *Federal Paperwork Reduction Act* could require these "express, documented findings" to be reviewed and approved.

The second sentence clarifies that traditional requirements for maintaining records, submitting records and providing records for government audit are not modified by this law.

2.2.4 Records prepared by government

Section 5 includes the provision first found in the *Uniform Records Retention Act* that includes records prepared and maintained by government.

2.2.5 Uniform guidance

This proposed new legislation clarifies the requirements for records produced by information technology systems and records retention, and provides uniform guidance throughout the United States. The net results of its wide-spread adoption would be:

- lower costs to the public,
- lower costs to the government,
- increased profits to the private sector,
- greater revenue in the form of taxes to the government,
- continued flow of necessary information to government entities.

2.3 Research and analysis

The justification for the proposed *Uniform Records Act* is documented in depth in ANSI/AIIM TR31 Part I and summarized in the following sentences:

- Laws should reflect the regulatory needs for information, not technical system requirements.
- Laws should permit organizations to establish information technology systems that best meet their needs.
- Laws should not discourage the reproduction of records and the destruction of original records, except when a compelling need for the original record exists.
- Laws should not discourage information technology systems that provide sophisticated security for information.

The background section of *Performance Guideline: Part II* provides extensive information regarding existing laws and the problems faced by both the private and government sectors. The *Uniform Records Act* offers a solution to the burden that now exists while still providing government with information necessary to fulfill its legal responsibility and assure courts of the reliability of records submitted in evidence. Without uniformity, organizations face a costly and difficult burden to comply with competing sets of requirements and, yet, potentially are restricted by law from developing the systems which best enable them to meet these requirements.

The following section from the *Performance Guideline: Part II* summarizes the impact of this burden:

> **2.4 Factors affecting the burdens imposed by law**
>
> Lawmakers generally attempt to refrain from developing laws that conflict with other laws in the same jurisdiction or laws that fail to protect the pubic interest. But lawmakers in other jurisdictions operate under difficult laws, or they may interpret the public interest differently.
>
> Rules and regulations developed by regulatory agencies cannot explicitly violate a statute or constitutional provisions. A regulatory agency is free, however, to regulate in areas authorized by the granting statute that is not prohibited by these types of other legal constraints.
>
> Lawmakers consider a variety of legal approaches to achieve the regulatory purpose. Many factors are weighed to determine the scope and degree of regulation in the final law. Significant consideration should be given to the burden that the regulation places on the public versus the benefits recognized by the public for full compliance.
>
> The federal government has enacted the *Federal Paperwork Reduction Act* to establish a formal process to identify the burdens placed on the public by recordkeeping provisions and determine the level of recordkeeping that establishes the minimum burden on the public while fulfilling the regulatory purpose. The states and territories have not established a comparable, formal procedure to achieve this goal.
>
> An overly burdensome regulation may also create significant harm to the public. For example, when a regulated organization is required to keep large quantities of records that would otherwise not be needed by the organization to conducts its daily business, the organization incurs significant costs (e.g., staff, space, equipment, etc.) to keep the records. These costs are reflected as expenses to the organization. They also result in legitimate tax deductions on the organization's tax return, this reducing the organization's taxable income. As a result of the excessive burden placed on such a regulation, the organization would pay less taxes than it would with a less burdensome regulation. If a large number of organizations are affected by the regulation, the net loss in tax revenues to the various jurisdictions could result in harm to the public that far exceeds the benefit gained by compliance with the regulation.
>
> For these reasons, law should only establish the minimum level of burden on regulated organizations necessary to achieve the regulatory purpose. Complex, inconsistent and expensive requirements may negate the benefits expected by lawmakers.

2.4 Similar legislation already in effect

To date, seven states have adopted either the *Uniform Preservation of Private Business Records Act* or the *Uniform Records Retention Act*: Colorado, Georgia, Illinois, Maryland, New Hampshire, Oklahoma, Texas. In essence, much of the *Uniform Records Act* is already in effect in those states (see Annex B).

The federal government of the United States has not adopted the *Uniform Preservation of Private Business Records Act.* A similar goal was stated in the *Federal Paperwork Reduction Act* of 1980 (4 USC Chapter 35) in Section 3501:

> The purpose of this chapter . . .[i]s —
>
> 1) to minimize the federal paperwork burden for individuals, small businesses, state and local government and other persons;
>
> 2) to minimize the costs of the federal government collecting, maintaining, using, and disseminating information;...

This legislative goal was reflected in the implementing regulations prepared by the Office of Management and Budget (5 CFR 1320) effective March 1983:

> **§ 1320.6 General information collection guidelines**
>
> Unless the agency is able to demonstrate that such collection of information is necessary to satisfy statutory requirements or other substantial need, OMB will not approve a collection of information: . . .
>
> (f) requiring respondents to retain records, other than health, medical, or tax records, for more than three years; . . .

While this regulation and the *Federal Paperwork Reduction*

Act do not specify that records required to be created or kept can be destroyed after three years, the OMB regulation does imply that only OMB can grant permission to an agency to require records to be kept longer than the three year period. If the law does not specify a specific retention period, clearly OMB did not provide specific permission to that agency to require that those records be kept longer than three years.

It is recognized that this argument only represents a presumption based upon the wording in the law. A new law, such as the proposed *Uniform Records Act*, would clarify the issue substantially on the federal level.

Regardless, as a result of the *Federal Paperwork Reduction Act*, the vast majority of new regulations being promulgated by the federal agencies do in fact have a records retention period of three years or less. A review of all legal requirements related to recordkeeping prepared by the United States federal government as published in *Legal Requirements for Business Records* indicated that 60.3% of all federal recordkeeping requirements have a records retention period of three years or less. If all recordkeeping requirements that do not specify a retention period are presumed to require a 3-year retention, the average retention period for all federal laws is 3.21 years (compared to 3.66 years if those laws not specifying a retention period are considered).

Approximately 30 states and the federal government have adopted the *Uniform Photographic Copies of Business and Public Records as Evidence Act* which permits an organization to reproduce records in the regular course of business using "any process which accurately reproduces . . . the original." The original records may then be destroyed "unless held in a custodial or fiduciary capacity or unless its preservation is required by law."

The *Uniform Rules of Evidence* has been adopted by approximately 32 states and the federal government. The *Rules* permit "a memorandum, report, card, or data compilation, in any form" and duplicates produced by specified technologies and "other equivalent techniques which accurately reproduce the original" to be admitted into evidence.

2.5 Background information regarding the Uniform Records Retention Act

The *Uniform Records Retention Act* was initially prepared in 1987 by the United States Legislative and Regulatory Affairs Committee, ARMA International. The *Uniform Records Retention Act* drew heavily on the wording of the *Uniform Preservation of Private Business Records Act*, but differed in that the *Uniform Records Retention Act*:

- provided revised definitions that reflected definitions already found in the *Uniform Rules of Evidence*,
- included government entities within the scope of the law,
- simplified and clarified the language to facilitate comprehension and enactment.

Additional commentary originally prepared in conjunction with the *Uniform Records Retention Act* has been included in Annex D.

3 Proposed model rule for acceptance of records

3.1 Proposed model rule for acceptance by government agencies of records produced by information technology systems

§ 1. Purpose and objectives

It is in the public interest to minimize the administrative burden and cost of submitting information to a government agency. Therefore, when the use of information technology systems offers administrative or economic benefits, the laws and policies of government regarding acceptance of records produced by such systems should not obstruct or detract from those benefits. To this end, these laws and policies should be uniform among the states and the federal government and written, to the extent practicable, so as to be media neutral — thus minimizing the need to modify them to accommodate new or evolving information technology systems.

The purpose of this rule is to encourage the use of information technology systems in recordkeeping by providing direction to government agencies in establishment of requirements for acceptance of records produced by such systems.

The specific objectives of the rule are as follows:

- to minimize restrictions in government regulations that unnecessarily discourage or hamper the use of information technology systems for the production of recorded information in both the public and private sectors;
- to reduce or eliminate burdensome requirements imposed by government agencies regarding acceptance of records from private sector organizations produced by information technology systems;
- to harmonize the interests of information preservation and the desire to obtain maximum benefits from developments in information technology systems.

The policies and requirements apply to records produced by information technology systems regardless of the physical characteristics of the record media or technology employed. This includes records produced by any technique employing an information technology system as defined below.

§ 2. Definitions

The following definitions apply to purposes of this rule:

Government agency Any organizational entity empowered to administer and enforce the functions of government.

Record Information preserved by any technique in any medium, now known or later developed.

Original record A record prepared in the first instance, a record derived from other records, or any counterpart intended to have the same effect. If data are stored in a computer or similar device, any printout or other output readable by sight shown to reflect the data accurately is an "original."

Duplicate record A record that accurately reproduces the original.

Information technology system Any process or system that employers a mechanical, photo-optical, magnetic, electronic or other technological device for producing or reproducing records.

§ 3 Creation and storage of records

1) Records submission requirements of government agencies shall not prescribe or restrict the information technology systems used by others to create or store records. However, they may, within the scope of agency authority, prescribe or restrict information content of records and the length of time that records must be maintained.

2) Government agencies, within the scope of their authority may issue requirements for the identification , validation, verification, protection, integrity and inspection of records, provided that such requirements do not, without justification, have the practical effect of preventing or limiting use of an information technology system that would otherwise meet the reasonable needs of the organizations or enterprises effected.

§ 4. Acceptance of records

1) Records produced by an information technology system submitted or made available to a government agency shall be in a form, or forms, prescribed by that agency, unless specifically accepted.

2) Submissions prescriptions shall endeavor to accommodate both the present records handling or processing capability of the agency and the records production and reproduction capabilities of organizations subject to the prescriptions.

3) Submission prescriptions shall endeavor to accommodate organizations that product their records through both commonly used and new or evolving information technology systems or processes.

§ 5. Records retention

1) Records retention or archival requirements shall endeavor to accommodate for long-term storage whatever technologies are used in the creation of records or their subsequent processing, provided that the technologies can meet the length of time and retrieval capability requirements without loss of information content.

2) When a technology cannot meet retention or archival requirements, or the technology, as a practical matter, cannot be accommodated, the records to be retained or archived may be printed on paper or copied to another technology that meets the requirements.

§ 6. Criteria for determining acceptance of records

Laws and policies prescribing requirements for acceptance of records produced by information technology systems shall consider the following criteria, as applicable:

1) Quality

Quality relates to ability of the information technology system to reliably produce and preserve records so that they can be used or recognized by the intended audience.

2) Original records

A record produced from data stored in an information technology system shall be considered an original record if a printout or other output readable by sight is shown to reflect the data accurately.

Original records may present information in a form different from the source information without affecting its quality. For example, information preserved in digital format may be printed on paper using different print fonts at different times.

3) Duplicate records

Duplicate records accurately reproduce original records. Duplicate records accurately produced by an information technology system shall be considered originals.

Information that is readable or recognizable on originals shall be readable or recognizable on duplicates. Similarly, information that is readable or recognizable on duplicates must be readable or recognizable to the same extent as on originals, except that duplicates may contain production, control, indexing, certification or other data not related to informational content of the records.

Image enhancement techniques may be used provided that they improve readability of information contained on the records rather than change the information content of the records.

When duplication processes change informational content of the records, the resulting records will be new originals of different records.

4) Records retention versus life expectancy of data on media

Records shall be retained, regardless of media, for the period required by the organization's records retention program for any legal, user, historical or other purpose. The life expectancy of the media per se has not bearing on the retention requirements of the records.

The information maintained on the media and the ability of the system to produce records from the information must achieve the required retention period. This means that for some technologies it may be necessary to periodically convert, regenerate, copy or transfer the information from one medium or technology to another to preserve the information for the required period.

Regardless of the retention period or life expectancy of the media, records must continue to exist when litigation, government investigation or audit is pending, imminent or, in some cases, merely foreseeable. In some instances, a court order will impose a restraint from causing specified records to be destroyed or made otherwise unavailable.

Procedures followed to convert records from one medium or technology to another shall be carefully documented. Conversion of the records shall not affect their acceptance provided that quality and accuracy does not change during conversion.

5) Trustworthiness and admissibility of records

As part of maintaining integrity of agency operations, agencies shall take reasonable measures to assure that accepted records are trustworthy in terms of either unintentional or purposeful alteration of information.

As custodians of accepted records, agencies shall be prepared to meet foundational requirements for admission of such records as evidence in an administrative or judicial proceeding.

These requirements place the burden on the proponent to demonstrate that the records production process or system is accurate and reliable in that it produces results that accurately reflect the input or source information.

6) General requirements

The following shall appear with sufficient clarity so that each can be recognized:

- individual letters, numbers and symbols;
- combinations of letters, numbers, and symbols forming words or sentences;
- graphics such as signatures, logos, pictures, etc.;
- sounds;
- other features of records such as color, shape, texture, etc., that relate to the content of the information.

3.2 Background

The model rule is based on recommendations made in the *Performance Guideline for the Legal Acceptance of Records Produced by Information Technology Systems* developed by the AIIM C22 NHPRC Task Force. It represents a statement of particular applicability for implementation of a statute or regulation that prescribes recordkeeping practices similar to those specified in the model act Section 3.1.1 provides additional guidance in interpreting provisions of the rule.

3.2.1 Trustworthiness of records

Following are factors to be considered by an agency when determining trustworthiness of records produced by an information technology system:

1. Process or system characteristics

Characteristics of the process or system used to produce records determine the accuracy of the records. A description of these characteristics in layman's terms facilitate the showing that the process or system is reliable and accurate, hence intrinsically capable of producing trustworthy records.

a. Records produced as part of a regularly conducted activity

Records produced as part of a regularly conducted activity, such as those produced in the regular course of business, are presumed to accurately reflect the source information subject to a showing that the process or system used to produce them is reliable and accurate. A regularly conducted activity may include a regular pattern of activity to produce records on a daily, weekly, monthly, yearly or other cyclical schedule.

A regularly conducted activity may also include records created as part of a regular program of the organization, but at irregular times. For example, when a planned program of a business results in the production of records originally created prior to a specific year, this will be viewed as a program proceeding in the regular course of business even though it only occurred once.

b. Accuracy

Records produced by methods shown to ensure or enhance accuracy will be more readily acceptable. This may include systematic quality control and audit procedures, as well as operational oversight by somebody with detailed knowledge of the system or process used to produce the records.

c. Timeliness

Records produced within a short period of time after the recorded even or activity occurs tend to be more readily accepted as accurate than record produced long after the event or activity. However, later-produced records are acceptable if it is shown that the time lapse had no effect on the records' contents. For example, a computer printout of a statistical report produced annually in the regular course of business can be shown to be simply a consolidation of data compiled on a computer disk over the year as events occurred.

2. Process or system components

Process or system components are determinative of how well the production of records is controlled. This, in turn, will determine whether trustworthiness of the records will be suspect based on inadequate procedures or inefficient operation.

a. System procedures

Effective system procedures reflect the detailed steps to be followed when creating, modifying, duplicating, destroying or otherwise managing records. Such procedures provide for consistent quality control activities, problem resolution approaches and other functions that might otherwise be subject to inconsistent action, multiple interpretation or misinterpretation.

Established procedures demonstrate what an organization plans to do in managing and controlling the process or system — which can be considerably different than what it actually does. The trustworthiness of an organization's records might well be judged by the established system procedures and how closely they are followed. Deviations and the reasons therefor can be expected to be closely scrutinized, especially if they are legally required procedures.

b. Documentation of system procedures

System procedures documentation shall be a regular assignment of a person who has detailed knowledge of the process or system in terms of the flow of information and operational activities involved. (The fact that the process or system is computer-based does not mean a computer programmer is required to document system procedures; however, a complex system might require someone trained as a systems analyst.)

Documentation shall be regularly updated to reflect any changes.

c. Training

A formal program for training staff on details of system procedures along with documented training sessions raises a strong presumption that the procedures were correctly followed.

d. Audit of system or process

The process or system shall be audited periodically to confirm the accuracy of results. An audit shall compare procedures stated in the procedures documentation with procedures actually followed.

3.2.2 Admissibility of records as evidence

Following is a summary of what is determinative of admitting records produced by information technology systems.

1. Form of records offered as evidence

Records produced by any technique may be introduced into evidence provided that they meet certain requirements. Records introduced to show that their literal or numerical contents prove the truth of the matter asserted should be presented in a readable or recognizable form acceptable to the court. (Records can also be used as probative evidence, e.g., to show that a file has missing records.) For written or printed records, the records may be readable without any equipment or readable using technology available to the court. The court may also accept records in other forms when adequate equipment for their readability is also provided.

The form of records admissible in evidence will vary based upon the nature of the information. For example, digitized voice information must be presented in an audible understandable form while digitized video information must be presented in a readable or recognizable form. Records that contain information that relates to multiple human senses such as video records that must be both seen and heard to be complete must be presented in a form that provides all the necessary information to the court.

2. Accuracy and reliability

With the safeguards that can be built into today's modern information technology systems, the best evidence of a record should not be dependent on a specifically sanctioned technology (as suggested by some rules of evidence), but on a showing that the records was the result of a process or system that accurately produced it. Once admitted into evidence, records are deemed authentic products of the process or system used to create them. (However, the truthfulness of their content remains subject to challenge.)

3. Laying a proper foundation

Laying a foundation for admissibility requires witnesses that will qualify the records as being what they are purported to be, i.e., authentic products of the system used to create them. Care must be taken to select witnesses competent to testify as to the accuracy and reliability of the system. (NOTE: A witness need not be able to personally attest to the correctness of information contained in the records.)

3.2.3 Benefits of information technology systems

Modern information technology systems often differ from paper-based systems through the establishment of processes or systems that reliably produce accurate results. Modern reproduction systems such as microfilm or optical disk,, and even data processing systems, offer the following characteristics that generally provide for more accurate and trustworthy records than possible with paper records systems:

- Modern information technology systems by their nature produce records as part of a process or system that requires a disciplined operation based on standards procedures, written documentation, adequate training and thoroughly tested equipment and software components.
- Modern information technology systems can provide an

audit trail that identifies not only what actions were taken related to records but also the individuals involved.

- Modern information technology systems can prohibit or detect alterations and attempted alterations to records. Most optical disk systems, for example, inherently preclude alteration of images. Bypass of alteration safeguards can be very difficult, requiring special knowledge and technical capabilities.
- Modern information technology systems can provide for routine security backup for records produced. Typically, microfilm, magnetic tape or disk, and optical disk systems will produce backup records at appropriate intervals as required. These records are generally stored in properly maintained remote locations where they can be retrieved if the original information is damaged or destroyed.

In sum, properly designed, implemented and maintained information technology systems are capable of producing records that are more reliable and accurate than paper-based systems.

It should be noted, however, that although paper-based systems are more susceptible to irretrievable loss or destruction of records and undetectable omissions, without the safeguards stated above, disasters and fraud can be much more costly and damaging to an organization dependent on an information technology system.

[Note: Only Annex E is reproduced below. See the full publication for Annex A-D.]

ANNEX E

Recommended Change to OMB Regulations Implementing The Federal Paperwork Reduction Act

The task force recommends that the regulations prepared by the Office of Management and Budget to implement the Federal Paperwork Reduction Act, Title 5, Code of Federal Regulations, § 1320.6(j)) be revised as follows:

> **Part 1320 Controlling Paperwork Burdens on the Public**
>
> **§ 1320.6 General Information Collection and Guidelines.**
>
> Unless the agency is able to demonstrate that such collection of information is necessary to satisfy statutory requirements or other substantial need, OMB will not approve a collection of information:
>
> * * * * *
>
> (j) *Prohibiting or restricting the form, format, media or system used by respondents to maintain information and* requiring respondents to provide information in a format other than that in which the information is customarily maintained. (New section in italics.)

This change permits the public to maintain the information in any form and, yet, ensures that an agency can obtain and review required information in a customary form. The reason for this change is fully documented in TR31-1993, Part II. In short, this change will eliminate potentially costly, inconsistent and burdensome restrictions on the public's use of information technology systems. By allowing the public to use systems that best meets its needs, the public reduces its costs and increases profits (taxable income).

Agencies may still regulate in all the areas of importance to them:

- Type of information maintained
- Retention period
- Form of information submitted to agency (any customary form)
- Access to information by auditors

The previous paragraph (j) read as follows:

(j) Requiring respondents to maintain or provide information in a format other than that in which the information is customarily maintained.

Association: American Bar Association
Source: House of Delegates, Resolution Number 115

The American Bar Association supports action by federal and state governments, international organizations, and private entities to:

a) facilitate and promote the orderly development of legal standards to encourage the use of information in electronic form, including appropriate legal and professional education;

b) encourage the use of appropriate and properly implemented security techniques, procedures and practices to assure the authenticity and integrity of information in electronic form; and

c) recognize that information in electronic form, where appropriate, may be considered to satisfy legal requirements regarding a writing or signature to the same extent as information on paper or in other conventional forms, when appropriate security techniques, practices, and procedures have been adopted.

Index

Other Publications and Services . . .

Recordkeeping Requirements

Legally, how long must you keep tax returns? How soon can you destroy old employment records? How many hours would it take you to track down the hundreds of applicable federal and state laws? How many documents are needlessly, expensively stored because no one knows the answers?

Recordkeeping Requirements gives the answers, saves time, and frees up valuable space by identifying in clear, simple language, what the laws say and how to comply. The only book of its kind, *Recordkeeping Requirements* is a guide to what you have to keep and what you can — and perhaps should — destroy.

- *Provides quick answers:* What are your legal responsibilities? What laws affect your records, and how do you apply them?

- *Provides detailed analysis:* How to analyze the six types of records retention laws that affect your records. How to apply the laws to your records.

- *Avoids confusing legal jargon:* Written in straightforward and non-technical style for those with little or no recordkeeping experience (yet is sufficiently detailed for those who need in-depth, accurate information).

- *Provides exact language of the most needed laws:* Includes state and federal laws for tax, employment, contracts, etc.

Records Retention Procedures

Your old, valueless records cost you space, time and money. Yet, you may suffer fines, penalties or other legal consequences if you do not keep your records long enough or you destroy them improperly. If you keep them too long, adverse parties may also subpoena your records during litigation — records that could and should have been destroyed legally in the regular course of business — to help them win *their* case against you!

Realistically, you have to make a decision. You can no longer decide *whether or not* to destroy records . . . only *when* to destroy them! Keeping records for too short a time may cause you problems! Keeping them too long could even be worse!

Records Retention Procedures gives you the solution! We show you how to establish a records retention program for destroying records at the right time. We show you the step-by-step *Skupsky Retention Method* — proven in actual use:

- Step 1. The Preliminary Procedures
- Step 2. The Legal Research
- Step 3. The Legal Research Index
- Step 4. The Legal Group File
- Step 5. The Records Retention Schedule
- Step 6. The Records with Retention Periods
- Step 7. The Concluding Procedures

Take the mystery out of records retention. The records nightmare can become a thing of the past! Clean old records out of your valuable storage areas.

Law, Records and Information Management: The Court Cases

Compliance with statutes and regulations is not enough. The courts interpret these laws and expect you to have a system in place to identify and retrieve records when presented with a subpoena in litigation.

This 600-page book provides you:

- Selected text from over 200 court cases.
- Detailed legal analysis of the important cases.
- Indexes, table and cross reference to help you find relevant information.
- Practical, procedureal recommendations.
- Annual supplements to keep you informed.

Legal Requirements for Business Records

For those who need all the information regarding legal requirements for your records. Legal Requirements for Business Records contains over 8,500 state and federal laws affecting recordkeeping. Our annual update helps you comply with the new laws. (Call for pricing.)

RETENTIONMANAGER™

Our new software package gives you *The Skupsky Retention Method* in computer form. We also provide you with the basic data to help you develop a records retention schedule quickly and accurately, plus the text of the records retention laws in computer-readable form taken from *Legal Requirements for Business Records*. (Call for pricing.)

Order Form

Please complete and send to:

Information Requirements Clearinghouse
5600 South Quebec Street, Suite 250C
Englewood, Colorado 80111
(303) 721-7500 , FAX (303) 721-8849

Please complete this form to order additional books or request information.

Name ______________________________ Title ____________________
Company ____
Address ____
(Street Address Only. No P.O. Box Numbers.)
City ______________________________ State _____ Zip Code _________
Phone (   ) ________________________

Number	Description	Price	Total
	Law, Records and Information Management: The Court Cases	$ 95.00	
	Legal Requirements for Information Technology Systems	$ 85.00	
	Records Retention Procedures	$ 39.00	
	Recordkeeping Requirements	$ 35.00	
	Subtotal		
	Tax (Colorado residents add sales tax)		
	*Shipping and Handling: $8.00 for first book, plus $3.00 for each additional book		$ 8.00 $
	Total		

☐ Enclosed is $ ___________ check or money order for payment in full.

☐ Charge to: ___ MasterCard ___ Visa   Date card expires: ____________________

Credit Card Number: ☐☐☐☐☐☐☐☐☐☐☐☐☐☐☐☐

Signature of card holder ____

☐ Send me information about your records retention software, **RETENTIONMANAGER™.**

☐ Send me information about your seminars and consulting services.

*Special Orders

Alaska/Hawaii: Add $15.00 additional shipping and handing.
Canada: Add $15.00 additional shipping and handing.
Other International: Add $35.00 additional shipping and handling.
Overnight: Add $30.00 additional handing and provide your Fed-X number.

GUARANTEE: If you are dissatisfied with our publication for any reason, please return it in resalable condition with proof of purchase within 30 days of receipt. Information Requirements Clearinghouse will promptly refund your purchase price.

Prices valid through June 30, 1998.